D0754677

THE INTERNATIONAL ENCYCLOPEDIA
OF
TEACHING AND TEACHER EDUCATION

THE INTERNATIONAL ENCYCLOPEDIA

OF

TEACHING AND TEACHER EDUCATION

Edited by

MICHAEL J. DUNKIN
The University of Sydney, Australia

PERGAMON PRESS

OXFORD · NEW YORK · BEIJING · FRANKFURT
SÃO PAULO · SYDNEY · TOKYO · TORONTO

U.K.	Pergamon Press, Headington Hill Hall, Oxford OX3 0BW, England
U.S.A.	Pergamon Press, Maxwell House, Fairview Park, Elmsford, New York 10523, U.S.A.
PEOPLE'S REPUBLIC OF CHINA	Pergamon Press, Qianmen Hotel, Beijing, People's Republic of China
FEDERAL REPUBLIC OF GERMANY	Pergamon Press, Hammerweg 6, D-6242 Kronberg, Federal Republic of Germany
BRAZIL	Pergamon Editora, Rua Eça de Queiros, 346, CEP 04011, São Paulo, Brazil
AUSTRALIA	Pergamon Press Australia, P.O. Box 544, Potts Point, N.S.W. 2011, Australia
JAPAN	Pergamon Press, 8th Floor, Matsuoka Central Building, 1-7-1 Nishishinjuku, Shinjuku-ku, Tokyo 160, Japan
CANADA	Pergamon Press Canada, Suite 104, 150 Consumers Road, Willowdale, Ontario M2J 1P9, Canada

First edition 1987

Library of Congress Cataloging-in-Publication Data

The International encyclopedia of teaching and teacher education.
1. Teaching—Handbooks, manuals, etc. 2. Teachers—Handbooks, manuals, etc. 3. Teachers—Training of—Handbooks, manuals, etc. I. Dunkin, Michael J.
LB17.I56   1986   371.1'002'02   86-9325

British Library Cataloguing in Publication Data

The International encyclopedia of teaching and teacher education.
1. Teaching
I. Dunkin, Michael J.
371.1'02   LB1025.2

ISBN 0-08-030852-X

Computer data file designed and computer typeset by Page Bros (Norwich) Ltd.

Printed in Great Britain by A. Wheaton & Co. Ltd., Exeter

CONTENTS

SECTION 2—METHODS AND PARADIGMS FOR RESEARCH

SECTION 3—TEACHING METHODS AND TECHNIQUES

SECTION 4—CLASSROOM PROCESSES

SECTION 5—CONTEXTUAL FACTORS

Contents

SECTION 6—TEACHER EDUCATION

PREFACE

Developments in the study of teaching and teacher education have reached a stage where this Encyclopedia is warranted. In 1985 the growth towards maturity in these two crucial areas of educational knowledge was evidenced by three particularly significant occurrences. One was the creation of a special Division of Teaching and Teacher Education within the American Educational Research Association, the largest such organization in the world. Another was the formation of the European Association for Research on Learning and Instruction, the first such association on that continent. A third was the appearance of an *avowedly* international journal in the field, *Teaching and Teacher Education: An International Journal of Research and Studies*. Evidence of the interest in studying these processes and of the productivity of the research is also to be found in the large number of articles about them published in nonspecialist national or regional education journals and in the number of books of readings that appear year after year through attempts to bring the best of the research efforts before students of the teaching process.

Access to the major concepts that have occupied the minds of students of teaching and teacher education has not been easy. Textbooks there are aplenty in the more general areas of educational psychology, educational philosophy, and educational sociology, to mention but a few, but these are quite limited resources for anyone wishing to pursue concepts involving teaching and teacher education in some depth. Apart from occasional articles in the few review journals and in the even fewer encyclopedias of education in general, there have, of course, been the admirable *Handbooks of Research on Teaching* sponsored by the American Educational Research Association. The latter, however, have been national rather than international, and have been organized differently from the present work.

This Encyclopedia is designed to enable readers to learn about key concepts from scholarly, comprehensive, and systematic expositions brought together within an organizing framework that facilitates integration and permits easy cross-referencing. Its entries were written by leading scholars from many countries. The authors were invited initially to contribute to *The International Encyclopedia of Education: Research and Studies* whose entries in the areas of teaching and teacher education have been brought together in this volume. The authors were selected on the basis of their demonstrated expertise in relation to particular topics. The topics themselves were identified partly on the basis of the amount and quality of scholarship invested in exploration of them and the knowledge thus yielded. Just as importantly, however, the topics were delineated according to a conceptual framework mapping the major developments of thought and research about teaching and teacher education. An initial list of topics and potential authors was discussed by members of the Editorial Board of the parent Encyclopedia at a meeting in March 1981. In the light of that discussion a final list was prepared and soon after the process of inviting authors commenced. For this present volume, authors were invited to update the bibliographies included in their original articles.

Some limitations had to be placed on the size, and therefore the scope, of this volume. For example, there are no articles on the teaching of specific curriculum areas, such as Mathematics or Music, here. Readers are advised, therefore, to consult the parent Encyclopedia for information of that kind.

This Encyclopedia is also organized differently from the parent Encyclopedia. The latter presented its entries in strict alphabetical order. Thus, an entry drawn from the realm of economics of education might follow an entry from research methods in education and precede one from teaching and teacher education. Here, however, the entries are grouped together on the basis of broad themes rather than alphabetical order. The rationale for the grouping of the articles is outlined below.

1. Conceptual Framework of the Encyclopedia

This Encyclopedia is an expression of a view of knowledge about teaching and teacher education in the 1980s. In its contents and organization it contains assumptions and beliefs about the nature of knowledge in the area of teaching and teacher education at that time. An attempt is made here to make explicit the main assumptions that have guided the development of the Encyclopedia.

It is assumed that there are two main levels of knowledge about teaching and teacher education. For want of better terms, these levels are labelled "meta-knowledge" and "substantive knowledge". "Meta-knowledge" refers to attempts to classify and analyse conceptual and theoretical positions about the nature and proper functioning of, and methods of obtaining empirical evidence about, teaching and teacher education. Knowledge that there are humanistic, behavioural, and information-processing models of teaching is an example of meta-knowledge about theory. Knowledge of issues raised in debates about different methods of observing in classrooms, and of statistically manipulating data thus obtained, are examples of meta-knowledge about methodology.

In summary, meta-knowledge is the result of studying attempts to answer the central questions: what is the most valuable knowledge to have, and what are the best ways of obtaining it? The first two sections of this Encyclopedia are presented as belonging to the meta-knowledge of teaching and teacher education. The first section reflects assumptions about the meta-knowledge of concepts and theoretical models. The second section is based upon assumptions about the meta-knowledge of research methods and paradigms. These two, the theoretical and the methodological, are assumed to interact so that theory determines method and method affects the quality of evidence required to validate theory.

"Substantive knowledge" as used here refers to information about teaching and teacher education obtained as a result of attempts to test hypotheses and answer questions about those two processes, their relationships with each other, and with other phenomena. Knowledge about teaching methods and other classroom occurrences is the core of this Encyclopedia. From it arises other knowledge emerging from the realization that teaching occurs in contexts which vary according to physical and social psychological environments, characteristics of students and teachers, and features of the occupation of teaching. These contextual factors impinge upon classrooms and have the potential to influence events occurring in them, if only by setting boundaries. In the longer term, however, and sometimes indirectly, teaching has the potential to affect the contextual factors.

Teacher education exists for the purpose of influencing teaching. In turn, it also is affected by conditions in schools and classrooms which it serves and which serve it. Like the teaching it seeks to enhance, teacher education is subject to the potential effects of contextual factors and has itself the capacity to exert reciprocal effects upon them.

Substantive knowledge about teaching and teacher education is presented in four sections of the Encyclopedia. One is devoted to Teaching Methods and Techniques (Sect. 3), the second is concerned with Classroom Processes (Sect. 4), the next contains articles on Contextual Factors (Sect. 5), and the last is on Teacher Education (Sect. 6).

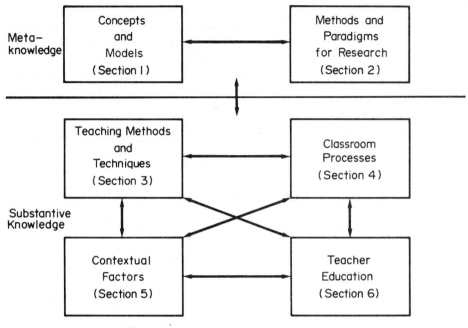

Figure 1
Schematic representation of the Encyclopedia

This conceptual framework for the Encyclopedia is represented in Fig. 1. It is a two-level, six-block framework as outlined above. The two levels are portrayed as interacting, so that as knowledge about teaching is synthesized and accommodated within conceptual and theoretical structures, it thereby changes them. Similarly, new knowledge is generated through the application of research paradigms and methods, but the quality of knowledge thus yielded leads to refinement and sometimes wholesale change in those very paradigms and methods. The contents of the Encyclopedia, as outlined in the following section, consist of articles on topics belonging to the six blocks contained in Fig. 1. Each is portrayed as interacting with the others, with Teaching Methods and Techniques and Classroom Processes occupying the central panel. Thus, teaching processes are seen to be the subject of concepts and theoretical models of teaching and of research on teaching. Teaching processes are also seen to be influenced by and to influence their contexts and the process of teacher education.

2. Contents

The contents of the Encyclopedia are organized on the basis of the conceptual framework described above. The first section is *Concepts and Models*. In it are found entries dealing with the major conceptual orientations that have appeared in relation to the study of, first, teaching and, second, teacher education. The section begins with a consideration of definitional issues surrounding the concept of teaching itself, such as whether learning must eventuate for an activity to be regarded as teaching. Subtle ways in which biases can be built into definitions of teaching are important here as are distinctions among types of interpersonal influence associated with teaching, such as indoctrination and brainwashing. Teaching is a coat of many colours and so it is not surprising that there are several different orientations in thought and investigation about it. To some, teaching is best characterized as a predominantly linguistic activity whose central process is communication. To others, teaching is seen to rely for its effectiveness principally on the ways in which stimulus, response, and reinforcement are scheduled.

Teaching is undeniably an occasion for the processing of ideas and information. Its intellectual challenges are to many its foremost properties, while to others teaching needs to be more concerned with its potential to encourage inquiry and discovery in learners rather than the mere passing on of information already possessed by someone else. Finally, in this section, the crucial elements of teaching are the opportunities it provides to learn through the management of time and learners' attention. The nature and organization of learning tasks and individualization in terms of learner characteristics and other contextual features, including levels of mastery, become critical in these approaches to the practice and study of teaching.

All of the above orientations have been applied to that particular aspect of teaching that involves the teaching of teachers. While there is a wide range of conceptual stances adopted with respect to teacher education, two stand out so far. One emphasizes humanistic imperatives in the development of teacher sensitivities and attitudes to learners. The other is more oriented to the acquisition of pedagogical skills and competencies through the careful analysis and synthesis of observable teaching behaviours and through repeated practice in real and simulated teaching situations.

The second section of this Encyclopedia is devoted to *Methods and Paradigms for Research*. The ways in which teaching is researched necessarily reflect the ways in which teaching is conceptualized. With few exceptions, research on teaching up until the 1950s was appropriately described as following a "black box" paradigm in which the data gathered concerned inputs and outputs with only second-hand information, if any, about actual classroom processes and events. Much of the latter was evaluative rather than descriptive and so its contribution to the knowledge and understanding of teaching itself was severely limited. The study of the development of approaches and techniques of research in classrooms is illuminating and essential for a proper realization of how much progress was made in subsequent decades. This is not to say that solutions were always there for the seeking or that progress was achieved without controversy. Indeed, immersion in the literature of debate about paradigms, measurement, criteria of evaluation, research roles, units of analysis, and ways in which research results might be synthesized to arrive at "state-of-the-art" conclusions, leads sometimes to frustration but always to an awareness that this is a fully alive research enterprise. No one can now be excused for naive expectations of success in discovering laws connecting teaching and learning. Simple causal connections simply do not exist, so that progress often takes the form of identifying even more difficult problems to solve and more vexing issues to resolve. Probably the most prominent set of problems and issues to emerge during the 1970s and 1980s concerned deep-seated assumptions constituting epistemologies of teaching. Thus, to some the very notion of cause and effect in human affairs, the idea of analysing and quantifying small categories of classroom behaviour, of nonparticipant observation, and noninvolvement of teachers in the research other than as subjects have been anathema. In reaction, paradigms have been expanded, methodologies have been broadened, and teacher participation has increased.

Regardless of results of research on teaching, the most common concept of what teachers do in classrooms is the concept of *Teaching Methods* which are the subject of the third section. It has been said that the wheel has been rediscovered in education more often than in any other domain of human activity, but whether or not this claim is validated when the history of teaching methods is systematically pursued remains to be seen. The third section of the Encyclopedia contains a large selection of entries on teaching methods. In the past, students of teaching methods experienced frustration by virtue of two main problems. First, teaching methods tended to be quite vaguely defined, so that it was very often difficult to discern the essential ingredients of each and to distinguish one from another. Second, teaching methods were almost always prescriptive, often to the extent that teachers should feel guilty if they were not using them, and yet rarely was even remotely scientific evidence in their support available. In some cases where methods were researched, it seemed doubtful that anything homogeneous enough to be called a method existed, or if it did that there was any reason for using it instead of an alternative. Fortunately, things are different nowadays and there are teaching methods, such as the Keller Plan, for which there are large research bases that can inform decisions to adopt or reject. The concept of teaching method itself remains a difficult one, however. Sometimes what is advocated seems more a philosophy of education than a mere teaching method. In other cases, the method seems to involve the cessation of teaching rather than an alternative way of practising it. Many methods have central notions involving the teacher's withdrawal from centre stage, but those grand examples of teacher dominance, such as lecturing, remain. One important lesson which has emerged from research on teaching methods is that it is often inappropriate to pit one against another in a competition to find *the best method* and that it might be more fruitful to detect and evaluate within-method variations. For example, it is probably better to learn how to lecture well than to discard lecturing as a method altogether.

The fourth section of this Encyclopedia is about more specific *Classroom Processes* than teaching methods. Within any one teaching method there are likely to appear many different types of classroom processes. This section is concerned with them. Some of the classroom processes that have been defined and researched are associated with more prescriptive approaches to the study of teaching. On the other hand, many of them have been derived from objective attempts to describe what actually happens. The more observable classroom processes are the overt behaviours of teachers and students. Several facets of these have attracted researchers in the twentieth century. First, there is what has been named the *socioemotional facet* involving such behaviours as praising, criticizing, accepting, encouraging, rejecting, and reprimanding. From these more specific instances have been constructed larger notions of warmth, nurturance, autocracy, democracy, and the like. Constructs of classroom climate, teacher flexibility in influence patterns, competition, cooperation, and reinforcement appear in relation to the socioemotional facet in this section.

Traditionally, classroom teaching and learning occur most explicitly in relation to subject matter thought to be important to learn. It is not surprising, therefore, that one facet to have been explored in research on classroom processes is the *substantive facet*, together with the type of *logical* processes carried on in association with it. Substantively and logically, behaviour in classrooms varies according to its level of abstraction, the complexity of the intellectual operations performed, the vagueness or clarity of communications, the types and amounts of content covered, the extent to which students are engaged, and the ways in which time is allocated and used.

Looked at in another way, classrooms are milieux in which pedagogical roles are performed. Most simply, it seems, the roles enacted by teachers and students may be compared in terms of the sharing of four predominantly verbal activities: structuring, soliciting, responding, and reacting. The teaching role in more formal classroom environments is one that relies heavily upon structuring, soliciting, and reacting. The student role is the reciprocal of the teaching role in that, while students enjoy a smaller slice of structuring, soliciting, and reacting, they emit a very large proportion of the responding that occurs. Furthermore, sequential patterns that are discernible over time in the occurrence of these activities are stable, predictable, and seemingly consistent from one culture to another. This so-called *pedagogical facet* of classroom behaviour has provided a rewarding and insightful body of research on teaching and learning.

Schools and the classrooms within them are complex social environments that depend for a considerable measure of their viability and success upon the maintenance of order. This is not meant to imply that teachers should be sergeant majors or police but simply that whatever the preferred social–psychological environment, desired learning is minimized by chaos. It just so happens that teachers are especially responsible for the establishment and maintenance of order in classrooms and that the study of strategies adopted to secure it will focus upon the teacher as manager. Some of the research into classroom management has concentrated on the types of deviant behaviour that occur and the ways in which teachers react to it. Others take the view that the establishment of a favourable atmosphere is a preventive measure which obviates disruption and deviance. In either case, the *management facet* of teaching is a rewarding subject of study.

The most difficult types of classroom processes to research are obviously those that are most difficult to observe. Even the most sophisticated observational procedures have been incapable of finding direct access to the thoughts of the participants as they occur. In research on teaching, as in any other field of empirical inquiry, one must make do with the data that can be obtained. In some of the research that has been referred to above, observational data about overt classroom behaviour was used as a basis for inference about covert intellectual processes. However, research identified with teachers' thinking is more commonly research that has relied on the subjective reporting by teachers of what was exercising their minds at particular times during lessons. The classroom processes section of the Encyclopedia concludes with a series of entries on the major areas of research on *cognition in classrooms*. These include articles on teachers' thinking, teachers' epistemologies, the theories they entertain about teaching and learning, the number and types of decisions they make during face-to-face teaching, as well as the occasions for such decision making, and their thinking in the course of planning for teaching. Finally, and perhaps most importantly, there is an article on students' thought processes.

The fifth section of the Encyclopedia is devoted to *Contextual Factors*. In the traditional school of box-like classrooms it might seem that teachers and students interact in splendid isolation from the rest of the world. The environment does intrude, however, and there is a growing literature of research on the contexts within which teaching is practised. There are, indeed, architectural variations, largely associated with the development of "open plan" schools. There are variations in the types and amounts of materials and equipment that teachers and students have at their disposal, in the size of the class, and in the seating arrangements for the students within it. Indeed, the investment of money, time, and energy in the building and maintenance of these physical features of school and classroom environments leads to the expectation that their influence upon what happens in classrooms is great and that they are important determinants of success at school. Physical influences are accompanied by psychological factors such that being a participant in a class where the general atmosphere is one of nurturance and challenge is bound to be very different from membership of a class surrounded by threat and boredom. Not all of these conditions depend upon the class teacher, for the climate of the institution as a whole no doubt permeates its parts. Similarly, curricula and syllabi are often determined by a central authority and can, along with other systemic features, frame what goes on in classrooms with such strong effect as to coerce and inhibit.

The characteristics that students bring with them into the teaching–learning situation are surely among the most important determinants of what occurs there. These have been thoroughly researched over many decades as influences upon learning in the sense of products of classrooms. It has only been in quite recent decades, however, that they have been investigated systematically in relation to teaching methods and other classroom processes. The literature of education is replete with value statements and prescriptions concerning fitting learning tasks, curricula, and materials to the student. Whole programmes of schooling have been tailored to accommodate the handicapped, the disadvantaged, and the talented, but just how individual and group differences in these regards make a difference to life in classrooms needs much more documentation. This Encyclopedia includes entries on five main types of student characteristics. They are affective and cognitive attributes, ethnicity, sex, and social background.

Teachers' characteristics occupy an important place in the history of research on teacher effectiveness but have been much less commonly represented in research on teaching behaviour. Presumably, the ways in which teachers relate to students are associated to some degree with teachers' expectations of student behaviour and learning, and other educational activities. Teachers' attitudes, values, and beliefs, not to mention their physical traits, have sometimes been used as criteria for admission to the profession of teaching on the assumption that they are vital influences upon their behaviour and upon students' reactions. There is also evidence of systematic processes resulting in greater representation of teachers from certain levels of socioeconomic background than others within the teaching profession. Do these differences really affect the ways in which teachers and students behave in classrooms?

Questions concerning teacher supply and demand, selection, and recruitment become especially important in the light of the above. So too do issues involving the ways in which new members become socialized into the profession. These topics are treated in a series of entries which conclude the fifth section of the Encyclopedia.

The final section of the Encyclopedia focuses upon *Teacher Education*. Teaching and teacher education are not such separate processes that matters affecting the latter do not appear in the earlier sections of the Encyclopedia. Indeed, they do, and not least by implication from the great body of research on teaching that is represented in the first five sections. In this sixth section, however, the focus is decidedly upon the formal procedures that have been developed and studied concerning the acquisition of teaching competence, not just in preservice programmes but also for already practising teachers.

Included in this section are entries on the more traditional elements of teacher education programmes. These elements include laboratory schools, practice teaching, and the supervision associated with the latter. Less traditional are procedures such as the systematic analysis of protocols of lessons in the form of transcripts and audio- and video-recordings presented for the purpose of stimulating the development of concepts of teaching and to promote discussion and theorizing about classroom occurrences deemed to be significant. Closely related to the analysis of lesson protocols are attempts to identify and define specific, technical skills of teaching which might be incorporated in training programmes. One of the most influential innovations in teacher education in the 1960s and 1970s was microteaching, which employs lesson analysis and sets of technical skills of teaching in carefully designed and presented scaled-down teaching situations. Research on microteaching and its associated components of modelling and feedback, together with evidence relating to its effectiveness in inculcating teaching skills are presented in a set of entries in this section. While microteaching was developed primarily for use in preservice teacher education, its basic principles were accepted in the development of techniques for individualized application by inservice teachers. These adaptations became known as minicourses. Inservice teacher education has involved much more than training in specific teaching skills, however. Its beginnings consist of the induction of new teachers and the continuing support of them through facilities such as teachers' centres. Associated with these developments of provision for inservice teacher education is the concept of teacher *recyclage* used in French speaking countries.

Finally the Encyclopedia contains entries on the education of teachers for educational contexts other than normal primary and secondary schooling. These are adult education, early childhood education, higher education, special education, and vocational and industrial education. All of these are areas in which there has been a great increase in activity in recent decades. While many of the practices discussed in relation to teacher education for regular school contexts are used in the education of teachers in these special contexts, their methods of recruitment and the distinctive characteristics of their student clientele warrant their being treated in special articles grouped together in the Encyclopedia.

It would be almost miraculous if there were no serious omissions from the Encyclopedia. New concepts, new orientations, new methods, and certainly, new research appear daily in the literature on teaching and teacher education. It is to be hoped that such omissions are few and that the inclusions are of such durability as to make the Encyclopedia useful for years to come before it is relegated to the status of an historical document.

3. How to Use the Encyclopedia

The Encyclopedia is designed to serve two main purposes. Its first purpose is to enable readers to obtain authoritative statements concerning specific topics in teaching and teacher education. Each entry concludes with a list of references which the reader will find useful in locating further reading on that topic.

The second purpose of the Encyclopedia is to enable readers to obtain comprehensive and systematic knowledge of the whole area of teaching and teacher education or perhaps important large areas of knowledge that form parts of the whole. For this purpose the reader might begin with the sections of this Preface concerned with the Conceptual Framework of the Encyclopedia and its Contents. Then the Table of Contents might be consulted in order to see the titles of individual articles and where they fit into the general framework. Next each section of the Encyclopedia begins with a figure illustrating which part of the conceptual framework is focused upon and an overview of the articles within it. These overviews include summaries of the articles and indicate associations between individual articles and others, both in the same section and in other sections. Again, readers will find helpful reference lists at the end of each article.

Should the reader discover that there is no special article on a particular topic, the Subject Index at the back of this volume should be consulted. Authors were asked to identify key words or phrases in their articles which constitute cornerstones in the structure of information they wished to convey. These terms formed the basis of the Subject Index. In addition, the Author Index also provides a useful entry point.

Also included is a full list of contributors and their affiliations, indicating which articles they have written.

4. Acknowledgments

Many people from several continents and many countries rendered invaluable assistance and encouragement in the production of this volume. Robert Maxwell conceived the idea for the parent Encyclopedia and invited me to undertake the editorship of this one. For that I am grateful. Torsten Husén and Neville Postlethwaite, the Editors-in-Chief of the parent Encyclopedia, first suggested the possibility of this Encyclopedia to me and continued to provide advice and encouragement throughout its development. Gilbert De Landsheere, my Co-Editor of the Section on Teaching and Teacher Education in the parent Encyclopedia, gave indispensable and expert help in the overall design of the entries, and particularly those concerned with the Francophone world. Other Section Editors of the parent Encyclopedia assisted in the selection of topics for entries and suggested authors for them. Some of them carried out the initial editing of articles included here. The Authors, without whose expertise, commitment, and forbearance the Encyclopedia would never have existed, responded magnificently to the challenge. It is from them that those who use the Encyclopedia will learn. Barbara Barrett, Managing Editor, Priscilla Chambers, Publishing Manager, and Clare Watkins, Editorial Assistant, all at Pergamon Press, were models of efficiency, skill, tolerance, and genuine friendship throughout. Many others from Pergamon Press also contributed importantly. My most sincere thanks are extended to all the above.

I especially appreciate the help I received from my secretary at The University of Sydney, Alwyne Morgan, who spent countless hours facilitating this enterprise. She unselfishly contributed support of the highest quality.

Finally, I should like to thank The University of Sydney for its support and especially for granting me several periods of leave from my normal duties so that I might complete this task on time.

December 1986

MICHAEL J. DUNKIN
Sydney, Australia

SECTION 1
Concepts and Models

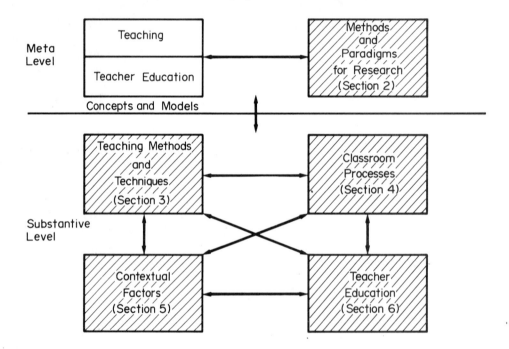

Schematic representation of Section 1 in relation to other Sections

SECTION 1

Concepts and Models

INTRODUCTION
TO SECTION 1

What is teaching? Is it different from other human activities and, if so, how? How shall teaching be understood and improved? These are representative of the questions discussed in the articles in this first section of this Encyclopedia. At first they are pursued with respect to teaching itself and then in relation to teacher education. Ideas about the nature of teaching guide the ways in which it is practised, thought about, and researched. The reader should expect, therefore, that the articles which follow in this first section will be linked to the articles that appear about more specific topics in later sections.

1. Teaching

Definitions of teaching are verbal expressions of concepts of teaching. In the first article in this section Smith establishes the importance of different notions of "teaching" and delineates four developed definitions and a fifth which he regards as emerging. The first four he terms "descriptive", "success", "intentional", and "normative" while the fifth is a "scientific" definition. Smith explains that a *descriptive definition* of teaching expresses the conventional meaning of the word. He notes changes in the conventional meaning by tracing the etymology of the word "teaching" and discusses the problems of ambiguity that arise in conventional definitions such as the following: "teaching is imparting knowledge or skill".

The association between "teaching" and "learning" becomes crucial in the discussion of the *success notion* of teaching. Here, there can be no teaching unless learning results, as though teaching and learning are analogous to selling and buying. Distinctions between "task" verbs and "achievement" verbs enter into this discussion, so that while it might be acceptable to say that "teaching" was unsuccessful it might not be acceptable to say that "learning" was unsuccessful. One difficulty of the success definition of teaching is that it is not possible to tell whether an activity is teaching until outcomes in the learner are available for analysis. In practical terms, Smith notes that teaching is normally expected to lead to learning but that it would be unreasonable to hold teachers fully responsible for their students' learning since they do not have control over all the variables that affect learning.

To see teaching as an *intentional* activity is to recognize the importance of teachers' goals, thoughts, and beliefs as determinants of their performance. Smith argues that if teachers' beliefs are important influences then the contexts in which those beliefs are developed are significant considerations for teacher education. If first-hand experiences in schools are more powerful in shaping beliefs about teaching than experiences had in colleges or universities, then school-based teacher education programmes would seem more appropriate than others.

Definitions of teaching that are based on ethical principles are *normative* definitions. The issues raised by Smith in relation to this approach are elaborated upon by Robertson in the second entry in this section and so are reviewed below in association with her article.

Smith concludes his article by outlining the form that a *scientific* definition of teaching might take. Such a definition, he writes, would be devoid of imprecision and ambiguity. Its terms would be adopted on the basis of universal agreement on their usage and would consist of sentences denoting teaching behaviours whose effect had been fully verified empirically. One consequence of the development of pedagogical science writes Smith, might be that "teaching" as a concept might become no more important than "doctoring" is to medicine, or "engineering" is to engineering science.

In the second entry in this section, Robertson continues the consideration of concepts of teaching and discusses a set of conditions that might be required before an activity would be classified as teaching. She offers the "intent" definition as the generic meaning of teaching and considers whether the following conditions are necessary: that there be an encounter between the teacher and the learner; that at the beginning of the encounter the teacher knows more than the learner about the content of instruction; that the teacher intends to enhance the student's learning through that content; that the teacher's actions be "reasonably conducive" to the student's learning the content; that those actions be such as to reveal to the student the content to be learnt; and that the teacher be successful at least in inducing the student to try to learn the content. These stipulations are sometimes regarded as necessary in order to distinguish teaching from other activities that might result in others' learning, such as throwing Johnny into the water until he learns to swim, or engaging in activities which others imitate although the imitated had no intention of influencing others in that way.

Robertson then concentrates upon normative approaches to the definition of teaching and, in particular, treats training, conditioning, and indoctrination as they relate to "educative teaching"—that which "engages the rational faculties of students and respects them as independent centres of thought and action". The discussion of conditioning provides a useful background for the consideration of the entry on *Behavioral Models* that appears later in this section.

In the third entry in this section a return is made to considering the possibility of a scientific definition of teaching. The debate presented in this article by Dunkin concerns whether teaching is best regarded as an art or a science and the implications of both viewpoints for the practice and understanding of teaching. This debate ranges from the position that scientific methods threaten to destroy teaching, to the position that scientific methods are the best hope for improvements in teaching. The controversy approaches resolution, it seems, when there is acceptance that teaching undoubtedly contains much scope for artistic elements but stands to gain through the development of a scientific basis in the manner of medicine and engineering.

At this point the entries in this section become more concerned with models of teaching than with concepts of teaching. Models of teaching vary according to whether they are primarily concerned with the way teaching is or with the way teaching ought to be. The former models, the *descriptive* ones, are models in the sense of being attempts to portray the nature of teaching so that it might be better understood. They are representations of reality often highlighting some parts rather than others and offering particular perspectives that are abstracted from the whole. No one of them gives the complete picture but together they provide a comprehensive view. The other types of models, the *prescriptive* ones, are models in a different sense. They are there to be modelled, for teachers to model their teaching on, as prescriptions to be implemented. Sometimes they have been devised with a particular type of educational objective in mind, such as discovery learning. Sometimes they are applications to teaching of principles arising from a particular theory of learning, such as reinforcement theory.

The first models discussed are the human interaction models in general. In this article Flanders explores the meaning of the phrase "model of teaching" and discusses characteristics of models, illustrating how the one set of classroom events can have different meanings depending upon the perspectives provided by different models. He presents an overview of developments in recent decades and shows strengths and weaknesses in some of them. In this he focuses upon process–product models and implications of research for the practice of teaching and teacher education, mentioning innovations such as microteaching described more fully in Sect. 6 of this Encyclopedia. Flanders also introduces more specific models of teaching, including the Carroll model and the mastery learning model which are the subjects of articles appearing later in this section.

The second approach discussed in this section is the aptitude–treatment interaction (ATI) model which Snow describes as designed to take account of individual differences among learners in their readiness to profit from instruction. This type of model involves matching instructional programmes with learner aptitudes in recognition of the fact that some teaching methods are more suitable for some students than for others. Aptitudes, however, are not seen as fixed and unamenable to instruction, so that part of an ATI model might well be the development of the learner's aptitude in preparation for later instruction. Snow argues that no single theoretical framework provides an adequate basis for ATI instructional models, since there are many different types of aptitudes, treatments, and outcomes possible of conception and measurement. Furthermore, the unsystematic character of research on ATI makes it as yet an unpromising basis for the design of teaching programmes. For the present, therefore, it seems that the concrete realities of the local context have to be the bases for determining proper aptitude–instruction combinations.

The third model of teaching presented in this section is the behavioural model, which is based on reinforcement theory. Bushell and Dorsey describe ancient applications of reinforcement principles in the inducement of Jewish boys to love the Talmud and medieval knights to strike accurately with their lances. The authors then state five basic principles of behavioural models and discuss eight questions that act as decision points in the application of the models.

Those eight questions are:

(a) What is the final form of the behaviour to be acquired?

(b) What are the components and prerequisites of the final behaviour?

(c) What behaviour is already available?

(d) Are there sufficient opportunities to respond?

(e) What reinforcers are readily available?

(f) How can reinforcement be scheduled?

(g) What are the natural contingencies of reinforcement?

(h) Are the first seven answers socially acceptable?

Indeed, write Bushell and Dorsey, the last question is of such significance that it modifies the others so that social acceptability becomes a criterion in attempts to answer the whole set of questions.

While the attributes of the learner play a key role in ATI models of teaching, and reinforcement has special status within behavioural models, in the fourth model in this section, time is of the essence. The Carroll model of school learning is based on the idea that learning at a desired level will occur provided that the learner spends the required amount of time at the learning task. The concept of a discrete learning task is an important ingredient in the Carroll model, as Clark writes in his article in this section, but the elaboration of the concept of time in learning is especially valuable and involves concepts of "opportunity"—the time allowed, "perseverance"—the time the learner is willing to spend, and "aptitude"—the amount of time needed under ideal conditions modified by the quality of teaching and the learner's ability to understand the teaching. Although the model is one of learning, it is clear that teaching occupies an important place, especially in so far as the quality of teaching is seen to affect the amount of time needed for learning, and also because the time allowed and student motivation to persevere are influenced by teachers.

Clark provides an interesting application of the Carroll model by showing how it might be used as a basis for inquiring into the decline in Scholastic Aptitude Test performances of American secondary-school students between 1967 and 1981. He demonstrates the model's value "as a powerful heuristic device for generating questions and hypotheses about issues that did not even exist at the time the model was first presented".

Information processing models of teaching include those which focus on teacher thinking, student thinking, and interaction between the two. They are distinguishable from behavioural models of instruction in that, unlike the latter, they assume that the mental processes of teachers and students influence events in the classroom. Furthermore, they offer scope for explaining variations in learning which do not seem to conform to behavioural models.

Teacher focused models are represented in this article by Corno and Edelstein by models of teachers' interactive decision making, teachers' judgments, the "advance organizer" model of teaching, and inquiry teaching. Student focused models considered in this article are a model of tutoring, computer-assisted instruction, a concept attainment model of instruction, and a model of learning from text. The two interactive models discussed are one devised to enhance learning from lectures and another concerned with the cognitive organizing practised by teachers and students in the classroom as they sort the relevant from the irrelevant, integrate, analyse, and otherwise transform information.

Corno and Edelstein conclude their article with a useful discussion of points of debate between adherents to behavioural models and adherents to cognitivist models. Issues referred to here include how it is that students profit from instruction, the role of environmental conditioning in the development of introspection, and whether knowledge is internally constructed.

Linguistic models of teaching are based upon the realization that verbal communication is the most noticeable feature of classroom interaction. Young and his colleagues distinguish between two main types of students of language used in the classroom—the categorizers and the interpreters. The former are described as those who employ a "logical–empirical" approach typical of the behavioural sciences, and apply objective categories to the counting of instances of verbal behaviour. According to the authors, this research tradition produced a "mechanistic and oversimplified view of communication in education". The interpreters, on the other hand, "concentrated instead on semantics and pragmatics, on the full meaning of what was said, on the way language is used by participants to act on each other". The authors show a preference for the interpretative approach and after discussing the suitability of nonparticipant and ethnographic methods in the observation of classrooms, conclude that collaboration between logical–empirical and interpretative approaches is possible.

While linguistic models of teaching are predominantly descriptive, mastery models are predominantly prescriptive. Anderson and Block state that there are two basic characteristics of mastery approaches. One is a philosophical assertion that any teacher can help all students to learn "excellently, quickly, and self-confidently". The other is a set of ideas and procedures achieving that desired outcome—either through a "group-based, teacher-paced" approach or through an "individual-based and learner-paced" approach. After describing ways in which individualization under the mastery models differs from other types of individualization, Anderson and Block provide a brief history of the model and elaborate on the basic tasks facing developers of mastery programmes. These are defining mastery, planning for mastery, teaching for mastery, and grading for mastery. Research on the mastery approach has enabled three major generalizations to be derived:

(a) Mastery learning is "effective".

(b) The key to its effectiveness lies within the feedback/corrective mechanism.

(c) Mastery learning is differentially effective for different types of students, with lower ability and older students benefiting more than others.

The authors predict that the use of mastery-based programmes will increase and that the model's potential as a preventative rather than as a remedial measure will be explored. Finally, Anderson and Block see the need for more research into the conditions under which mastery approaches succeed and fail and into the limits of student learning possible under mastery programmes.

In the final entry on models of teaching, Wittrock discusses approaches to heuristic teaching, that is, teaching designed to enhance problem solving and learners' ability to learn. Wittrock finds examples of concern with these matters as early as in Plato's writings and traces developments through the ages in the work of Aristotle, Cicero, Quintilian, and Aquinas. Modern approaches are to be seen in the cognitive models of instruction of Judd, Montessori, Piaget, Bruner, Ausubel, Galperin, Feuerstein, Wittrock, and Rogers. After describing several applications to teaching, Wittrock summarizes several characteristics of the successful teaching of heuristics as supported by early research and concludes that the research evidences positive effects of the approach on learning, retention, and comprehension, and that the process of learning facts and concepts is not incompatible with the learning of strategies and heuristics.

2. *Teacher Education*

Teacher education is one context in which teaching occurs. It is an especially interesting context because teaching is the basis of the *objectives* guiding teacher education programmes, as well as a *process* by which those objectives are attained, and the main *outcome* by which the success of the programmes is judged. To a large extent, therefore, the concepts and models of teaching discussed in the first 11 articles in this section apply to teacher education as well as to teaching. The next three articles differ from the first 11, however, in that they are directed specifically to teacher education.

There must have been a very different idea of teacher education underlying the eighteenth- and nineteenth-century "normal schools" from that underlying the late twentieth-century four- or five-year degree programmes in universities. According to De Landsheere, in the earlier times a teacher's certificate was of about the same status as a lower secondary school certificate and did not even gain its holder admission to colleges or universities. De Landsheere's overview of the history of teacher education in Western Europe leads him to a discussion of principles underlying modern teacher education. He introduces notions concerning the professionalization of teachers, of the balance between general and vocational education, of teacher credentials, and of initial and further teacher education. These and related matters are then taken up in a discussion of the curriculum for teacher education. The place of general education, specific subject mastery, the study of psychology and education, the problem of integrating those elements, and the form of practical or applied experiences in schools and classrooms are presented. Finally De Landsheere takes up two topics that are elaborated upon in articles appearing later in this Encyclopedia. They are competency-based teacher education and inservice teacher education.

Two main models of teacher education are represented by the two remaining articles in this section. The first article by Lorin Anderson and Min Ching presents the affective model in which emphasis is placed upon development of teachers' feelings and self-awareness, together with interpersonal and human relations skills. The authors explain that the affective model is based upon the perceived neglect of the attitudinal and emotional domains of human development in other approaches, such as the performance-based or competency-based model. They also cite research findings that observers commonly employ affective criteria in distinguishing between "more effective" and "less effective" teachers. Several applications of the principles of the affective model are described before the authors consider the issue of the effectiveness of such programmes. Here it is argued that two questions are important: "to what extent do teachers acquire appropriate feelings and interpersonal skills as a result of participating in these programmes?" and "to what extent are teachers who participate in such programmes more effective in their classrooms than teachers who do not participate in these programmes?" The authors report the conclusions of two reviews of research indicating that positive effects on teachers' levels of interpersonal functioning can be expected and that experienced teachers master affective skills better than student or new teachers. Furthermore, research was found in support of the hypothesis that teachers in possession of higher levels of interpersonal skills are more effective teachers. Lacking, however, is evidence that the above questions can be answered positively with respect to teachers' feelings and self-awareness.

Anderson and Min Ching conclude their article by discussing the future of the affective model of teacher education. They perceive a need for a reconciliation between affective and cognitive approaches and emphasize the contribution by adherents to the affective model in correcting the historical predominance of cognitively based teacher education.

If teachers' feelings, emotions, self-awareness, and interpersonal skills are accepted as competencies which enhance teacher effectiveness then they are eligible for inclusion in competency-based teacher education (CBTE) or performance-based teacher education (PBTE) programmes, so that there is no necessary incompatibility between the objectives of affective models and competency models of teacher education. In the final article in this first section Houston discusses the CBTE model. There is much in this article that relates to earlier articles in this section. Thus the "success" notion of teaching discussed in the first article by Smith appears, and origins of CBTE in mastery models and in the Carroll model are traced, along with links to behavioural models. Historical antecedents of CBTE are presented and the concept of CBTE clarified mainly through the specification of four central and 12 implied or related characteristics. The four central ones are:

(a) "Program requirements are deduced from, and based on, the practice of effective teachers".

(b) "Requirements are stated as competencies".

(c) "Instruction and assessment are specifically related to competencies".

(d) "Learner progress is determined by demonstration of competencies".

Houston proceeds to explain why the body of research available on CBTE is so small but points out that what there is tends to support the model. Criticisms of the fragmentation of the teaching act into many small components, and of the apparent anti-intellectualism together with the lack of a research base for underlying assumptions are presented. Nevertheless, surveys indicate widespread adoption of the model during the 1970s. The article contains a clear and very useful report of a case study of the implementation of a CBTE programme and concludes with a discussion of the future of CBTE. He concludes that "years of research and development are necessary" and that "without the philosophical, pedagogical, and psychological analyses that are the essence of CBTE, teacher education will flounder with global goals and complex unanalysed variables".

There are many examples within and across the articles in this Encyclopedia of the ways in which attempts to solve educational problems are dependent upon concepts and models of teaching and learning. The recurrence of issues involving individual differences among students, the accountability of teachers for student success and failure; the acceptability of proposed solutions to educational problems; the standards of student achievement demanded; the ways in which time is allocated; the scheduling, supervision, and evaluation of teacher practice in teacher education programmes; and definitions of teaching skills all depend heavily upon these basic notions. These examples are found in the subsequent sections of the Encyclopedia.

Teaching

Definitions of Teaching

B. O. Smith

Efforts to define "teaching" have centered on explorations of various facets of the concept of teaching rather than on the formulation of explicit definitions. Altogether there have been four attempts to define "teaching," but none has resulted in an explicit definition. One takes its substance from precedent, two pursue the task through the techniques of linguistic analysis, and the remaining one is controlled by ideological considerations. A fifth definition, a scientific one, is beginning to take shape and in all probability will supersede the others. These five definitions are: teaching in the conventional sense, or the descriptive definition; teaching as success; teaching as an intended activity; teaching as a normative activity; and the emerging scientific notion of teaching. The characteristics of each of these will be treated.

1. Descriptive Definition of Teaching

Words have a history. They develop crescively from primitive observations and experiences over long periods of time, taking on a multiplicity of meanings—denotations, connotations, nuances, and emotional tinges—so that it becomes next to impossible for anyone to encompass the full range of experiences and observations evoked by a single word. This is why ordinary language is a poor vehicle for precise thought and expression and why no reader of literature ever exhausts its subject matter.

In ordinary language words are typically used before they are defined. They designate objects or events with reasonable specificity, depending on the context, and they rule out, or do not apply to, certain others. Between these lie a multitude of phenomena for which it is difficult, if not impossible, to decide whether the word applies. Sometimes it is desirable that the conventional usage of a term be stated and an attempt made to decide the limits of what the term denotes. A statement of the conventional meaning together with an explanation of what the term covers is referred to as a descriptive definition (Scheffler 1960 pp. 15–22). Now, a descriptive definition expresses the predefinitional

uses of a word. It must be faithful to prior uses. If the term has been used to denote certain objects or events, the definition must cover these uses.

The word "teach" has a long history and its uses have varied from one period to another. From early times it has been associated with "learn." In Shakespeare's *The Tempest*, Caliban exclaims: "You taught me language; and my profit on't is, I know how to curse; the red plague rids you, for learning me your language." Both "learn" and "teach" are used by Caliban to mean the same thing.

Brief recourse to the history of these words will help to reveal their kinship. "Learn" comes from middle English *lernen*, meaning to learn or teach. *Lernen* is derived from Anglo-Saxon *Leᵒrnian*, the base of which is *lar*, the root of *lore*. *Lore* originally meant learning or teaching, but is now used to mean that which is taught, especially traditional facts and beliefs. Thus the words "learn" and "teach" are derived from the same source (Oxford Universal Dictionary 1955). Archaically, "I will learn you typewriting" is correct English. In this derivation "learn" is associated with the content of instruction.

The word "teach" also has another derivation. It comes from Old English *taecan* that is in turn derived from the Old Teutonic *taikjan*, the root of which is *teik*, meaning to show, and is traceable to Sanskrit *dic* through pre-Teutonic *deik*. The term "teach" is also related to "token"—a sign or symbol. "Token" comes from the Old Teutonic word *taiknom*, a cognitive with *taikjan*, Old English *taecan*, meaning to teach. So, "token" and "teach" are historically related. To teach, according to this derivation, means to show someone something through signs or symbols; to use signs or symbols to evoke responses about events, persons, observations, findings, and so forth. In this derivation, "teach" is associated with the medium in which teaching is carried on.

A descriptive definition of "teaching" in the 1500s would have been somewhat different from that of today. A descriptive definition then would have been formulated from such notions as to teach is to give information; to show a person how to do something; to give lessons in a subject. The conventional sense of teaching nowadays is not entirely different. A descriptive definition of teaching can be stated as follows: teaching is imparting knowledge or skill.

The purpose of such a definition may be to point out the reference of the term, or to show how instances covered by the term differ from others with which it can be confused. Terms such as "imparting," "knowledge," and "skills" are often ambiguous. A descriptive definition will remove, as much as possible, this indefiniteness by resorting to contextual usage. For example, in one context "imparting" means to share, as when someone says to teach is to share experiences. In another context "imparting" signifies the communicating of information by lecture. But even when ambiguities are eliminated by resorting to context, so that the term clearly denotes certain objects and just as clearly rules out others, there will be cases to which the term might or might not apply. Is the spreading of propaganda to be counted as teaching? Some persons will say yes and others no, depending upon their concept of propaganda and how it fits their notion of what it means to be educated. The descriptive definition of teaching as imparting knowledge allows the matter to be settled either way.

A descriptive definition can focus thinking upon a particular course of development (Scheffler 1960 pp. 19–28). It is then said to shade off into a programmatic definition. For example, if "imparting information" is taken to mean that lecturing is the imparting mode, those who advocate inquiry as the mode of teaching will be quick to oppose the descriptive definition. They may admit the accuracy of the historical definition of "teaching," but still turn to their own programmatic definition of "teaching" as inquiry. Thus pedagogical discourse is often fraught with semantic issues.

2. Teaching as Success

"Teaching," as success, signifies the idea that learning is implicated in teaching. This implication is suggested by the hyphenated expression "teaching–learning" found in much pedagogical literature, signifying that teaching and learning are inextricably intertwined.

The brief reference above to the early history of "teach" and "learn" hints at a kinship between the two that foreshadows the practice of some authorities today of using them as if they were inextricably related. "I will learn you typewriting" weakly implies that you will know how to typewrite if I teach you. This is the point of the success concept of teaching—that teaching entails learning. According to this view, teaching can be defined as an activity such that X learns what Y teaches. If X does not learn, Y has not taught. This concept of teaching is succinctly stated by Dewey in the equation: Teaching is to Learning as Selling is to Buying (Dewey 1934 p. 35). This statement is generally taken to mean that since there is no selling when no-one buys, there is

no teaching when no-one learns. "Teach" means not merely that some interaction is taking place, but also that the learner is acquiring what is being taught.

One objection to this notion of teaching is grounded in Ryle's distinction between task verbs and achievement verbs (Ryle 1950 p. 149). Words such as "racing," "treating" (as in medical care), "traveling," and "search" are task words. They signify some sort of performance. "Win," "cure," "arrive," and "find" are corresponding achievement verbs. They signify occurrences, ends, terminals. "Teaching" is said to be a task verb and "learn" the corresponding achievement verb.

Of course, "learn" has two meanings. It can signify an outcome or a process, depending upon the context. The statement "Jane has learned how to solve quadratic equations" expresses an outcome. "Learn" is used here as an achievement verb. It implies that Jane can now solve problems involving such equations time after time under normal circumstances. The statement "Jane is learning how to solve quadratic equations" implies that she is studying, working on problems involving these equations, or paying attention as someone shows how to solve these problems. This use of "learn" signifies activities.

Achievement verbs cannot be qualified in certain ways. It is not possible to say that a student has learned the multiplication tables unsuccessfully, or solved a problem incorrectly, or created something unsuccessfully. To do so would be logically contradictory. It should be noted, however, that a student can try to learn the multiplication tables. It can be said that the trying is in vain, but not that he or she has learned the multiplication tables in vain.

Task verbs indicate activities or actions that do not signify successful performance. They indicate actions or activities of which it can be said that they are done skillfully or unskillfully, successfully or unsuccessfully. It can be said that the physician was amiss in diagnosing and treating the patient, but it is not possible to speak of the cure as being amiss. The teacher and pupils can search for a solution to a problem unsuccessfully, but it would be contradictory to say they found it unsuccessfully. Likewise the teacher can teach spelling effectively or ineffectively, but it would be odd to say that the students learned spelling ineffectively.

To return again to the selling–buying analog, "sell" and "buy" are both achievement verbs. To sell is to exchange, to give up something for a return. To buy is to get something by exchange or by paying money. These are transactions and as such are completions. It is logically contradictory to say that one buys incompletely or unsuccessfully or sells unsuccessfully. No-one can sell unless someone buys, and one cannot buy unless someone sells. Selling thus implicates buying. Not so, say the critics, with the relation between "teaching" and "learning" (Smith and Ennis 1961 pp. 97–101). An individual can teach how to spell a list of words without success, but a student cannot learn the words unsuccessfully. A student can learn without being taught, and a teacher can teach even though the student does not learn.

Moreover, the success concept of teaching makes it difficult to answer the question: Is what Brown is now doing an instance of teaching? It is not possible, by the success concept, to tell whether what he is doing can be counted as teaching by observing his performance. Instead, it is necessary to find out whether the student has learned from Brown's performance before the question can be answered. Those who oppose the success notion of teaching hold that at any moment it is possible to tell by observation whether or not someone is teaching, regardless of knowledge about the student's learning.

Perhaps the most significant reply to critics of the success concept of teaching emphasizes contextual rather than logical implications. One statement implicates another statement if the rules of ordinary language entitle us to infer the second statement from the first in the context in which the statements are made (Nowell-Smith 1954 p. 80). To have written a letter is to have done more than occupy oneself in an activity. It is also to have succeeded. In the same sense, for Brown to have taught John the multiplication tables is more than simply to have been engaged in certain activities; it is to have succeeded (Scheffler 1960 p. 41). While contextual implications do not follow logically, they are often strong enough to warrant the inferences they suggest.

The practical import of the success concept is that teaching is normally expected to result in learning. If it does not do so, an explanation is called for. Nevertheless, it is questionable that evaluation of teachers should be based upon the achievement of their students, for teachers, like other professionals, do not have control over all the variables that affect the outcome.

3. Teaching as Intentional Activity

While teaching may not logically implicate learning, it can be anticipated that it will result in learning. A teacher may not succeed, but he or she is expected to try to teach successfully. To try to teach is not just to engage in activities, but to pay attention to what is going on, to make diagnoses and to change one's behavior. Furthermore, to try to do something is partly to intend to do it. If Brown says he is trying to teach John how to spell a list of words, by the rules of ordering language it would be legitimate to infer that he intends to do so. It would be unusual for Brown to say I am trying to teach John a list of words, but that is not my intention. Of course, an actor can mimic the discourse of a teacher, saying the same words and making the same gestures, and if abstracted from the context of a play, the performance would appear to be teaching. But the intention of the actor would be to portray a pedagogue, not to induce learning. In normal circumstances, however, if someone is engaged in teaching students a list of words, it is understood that he or she is trying to get the students

to know how to spell each word. Teaching is then intended behavior for which the aim is to induce learning (Scheffler 1960 pp. 60–75).

Intentions are associated with what is deemed to be important; they are goal oriented. And what is perceived as important at any given time is dependent upon the situation and one's beliefs. If a student disrupts classroom activities, the teacher will think it important to restore order. But what the teacher does to restore order depends upon the teacher's system of beliefs. A teacher whose beliefs lead to the thought that the disruptive child is either fatigued or seeking attention will act differently from a teacher who believes that disruptive conduct flows from an evil disposition.

The intentional concept of teaching gives support to researchers who study the ways teachers think. The performance of teachers is considered as guided by their intentions, grounded in the teacher's belief system and modes of thinking (Fenstermacher 1980 pp. 35–49). If it is to be understood why teachers do what they do, it is necessary to understand their thought processes and what they believe and how they come to believe it.

The work place and programs of preparation are taken to be primary sources of beliefs. One of the tasks of research is to ascertain the relative effects of these two influences. If the work place is the most potent determiner of teachers' beliefs and hence their intentions, as some thinkers suggest, teachers might then be trained as apprentices. On the other hand, if discipline in the concepts and principles of pedagogical science results, as in the mastery of other sciences, in shaping beliefs, then university preparation in pedagogy is indicated.

Intentional uses of "teaching" rule out purely behavioristic accounts of teaching. It is possible, of course, to ascertain the effects of teaching in behavioral terms. But just because behavioral evidence is used to show that teaching is or is not effective, it does not follow that teaching can be characterized in advance, that one can say what pattern of behavior constitutes a sufficient condition for teacher success. In short, successful teaching cannot be reduced to a set of general rules, or a prescribed pattern of behavior, any more than the sufficient conditions of problem solving or creativity can be specified.

4. Teaching as Normative Behavior

The normative concept of teaching requires that the activities of teaching conform to certain ethical conditions. Of course, all concepts of teaching are by the nature of definition specified by rules. This is but another way of saying that a definition, being the verbal counterpart of a concept, specifies criteria for exclusion and inclusion of instances. These criteria are sometimes tinged with preferences. For example, the intentional definition of "teaching," exemplified in teaching a single lesson, emphasizes a person in a particular context intellectually trying to get someone to learn something. It rules out techniques of strict behaviorism and pre-scribed patterns of behavior. The normative concept thus shades over into other concepts of teaching, the chief differences among them being the objective character of criteria, and the degree of explicitness of criteria, by which certain types of activities are excluded.

In the normative concept, "teaching" is a generic term. It designates a family of activities: training and instructing are primary members and indoctrinating and conditioning are near relatives while propagandizing and intimidation are not family members at all (Green 1968 pp. 28–62). By what rules are these distinctions made? They have to do with what is to be learned and how it is to be learned. Training and conditioning consist of activities that shape skills and other behavior while instruction and indoctrination are made up of activities by which knowledge and belief are induced.

All can agree that training and instructing comprise what is called teaching, but people will differ in their opinions about whether conditioning and indoctrinating should count as teaching. The distinction ultimately go back to the amount of intelligence—use of factual evidence and reasons—in the activities by which teach-ing is carried on. Conditioning relies on neither evidence nor reasons and is deemed to be only remotely related to teaching. Training may and often does involve instruction—giving information in the form of direc-tions, reasons, and evidence—and is thereby a form of teaching.

Both instruction and indoctrination are used to induce belief just as training and conditioning are used to shape behavior. Beliefs are held in various ways. Some things are believed because they can be logically derived from other propositions believed to be true, and other things can be believed because of factual evidence. Some things are held to be true even though there is no factual evidence and no valid reasons to support that confidence. False beliefs as well as true ones may be held with or without evidence. Nevertheless, instruction attempts to induce beliefs by reason and factual evidence, by welcoming objections and criticisms, and by the persuasive power of logic. The further instruction drifts away from these criteria, the more it approaches indoctrination and ultimately sheer propagandizing beyond which lies plain lying.

A concept that identifies teaching with instruction and training and less so with conditioning and indoc-trinating, places a heavy burden upon the teacher, both pedagogically and ethically. There are many situations where the teacher may not have access to all the facts, or where his or her own perspective is less than catholic. For example, in teaching history it is not easy for a teacher to be objective about international events in which his or her own country was involved. His or her national culture often narrows perspective, and the available instructional materials are typically written from a provincial rather than a world view. Perhaps the best the teacher can do is to become ever more aware of what class discussion and text materials assume and subject it to scrutiny.

5. Toward a Scientific Definition of Teaching

The forgoing definitions of teaching are rooted in the ordinary language and while they clarify to some extent the various senses in which the word "teaching" is used in pedagogical discourse, they are not precise enough for everyone to agree on their application. For the study of an occupation to become scientific, it is necessary to some extent to abandon lexical definitions even though terms of the ordinary language are retained. Every field of scientific endeavor has its beginnings in primitive observations and experiences and goes forward, at least initially, with words adapted from everyday language. "Work," "force," and "horsepower" have precise mean-ings in mechanics, but each one had a history of use before it was defined in mechanics in ways not derivable from its daily uses.

While "teach" is found in everyday language, it is retained in pedagogical science where it is defined by empirically confirmed statements of the effects of teacher performance. For example, if a teacher gives a definitional rule and positive and negative instances in teaching a concrete concept, the probability that the student will master the concept is increased; or if a teacher gives corrective feedback to a pupil who makes a mistake, the chances that the student will learn are enhanced. Of course, in the research literature, these propositions are stated in technical terms and with far more care than can be given here. Now, a technical definition of teaching will consist of a set of such sen-tences connected by the words "and," "or," "implies." This form of definition is called, by Reichenbach, a definition by coordination of propositions, and has the general form $a = df[b, c, \ldots]$ where a indicates the sentence "Teaching is effective," and "$[b, c, \ldots]$" stands for a combination of sentences such as "The teacher gives feedback," "The teacher states the defin-ing rule and gives positive and negative instances;" and where "$= df$" stands between sentences instead of words or phrases."

In this form of definition "teaching" is not explicitly defined, but its meaning is implicated in the sentences where it occurs. This mode of defining brings our think-ing closer to the observable and manipulative level of experience than is possible by the classical form of definition where one abstract term is defined by ref-erence to other abstract terms. To know the sentences that make up this definition is to know what is known empirically about teaching.

The coordinated sentences represent teacher per-formance, the effects of which have been confirmed. This mode of definition allows us to define certain other terms used in discussions of teaching. These are "competency," "competence," "performance," and "effective." "Competency" signifies that a teacher knows what a single sentence says and can do what it specifies; "competence" signifies that a teacher knows what all the sentences say and can act in conformity with them. A teacher is then said to be competent. "Performance" designates the behavior of a teacher in the classroom (Medley 1981 p. 3). If the behavior conforms to the definition of "effective teaching," the teacher is acting as a professional. However, the teacher's students may not learn up to par even though the teacher's performance squares with the definition of "effective teaching." This can be the case because of conditions over which the teacher has no control although they affect student achievement (Gustafasson 1977, Lundgren 1972).

As the science of pedagogy continues to develop, its language will more and more consist of terms on whose use there will be universal agreement. Dependable inferences are possible only when precise and unambiguous terms are used. And this is what the science of pedagogy requires, not only for the advancement of its knowledge base, but also for the development of an effective system of practice. The present tendency to argue whether a particular term applies to a given object or whether "this is an *x*" will be abandoned. Somewhere along the line, "teaching" may become no more significant in pedagogical discourse than "doctoring" or "engineering" now enjoy in the discourse of the medical and engineering sciences.

See also: Teaching and Related Activities; Teaching: Art or Science?

Bibliography

Dewey J 1934 *How We Think*. Heath, Boston, Massachusetts
Fenstermacher G D 1980 What needs to be known about what teachers need to know? In: *Exploring Issues in Teacher Education: Questions for Future Research*. Research and Development Center for Teacher Education, University of Texas, Austin, Texas
Green T F 1968 A topology of the teaching concept. In: MacMilland C J B, Nelson T W (eds.) 1968 *Concepts of Teaching: Philosophical Essays*. Rand McNally, Chicago, Illinois
Gustafasson C 1977 *Model of Teaching 1*. Stockholm Institute of Education, Department of Educational Research, Stockholm
Lundgren U P 1972 *Frame Factors and the Teaching Process: A Contribution to Curriculum Theory and Theory on Teaching*. Almqvist and Wiksell, Stockholm
Medley D M 1981 *The Role of Teacher Educators in Teacher Competency Assessment*. University of Virginia Press, Charlottesville, Virginia
Nowell-Smith P H 1954 *Ethics*. Penguin, London
Peters R S 1963 *Authority, Responsibility, and Education*, rev. edn. George Allen and Unwin, London
Reichenbach H 1947 *Elements of Symbolic Logic*. Macmillan, New York
Ryle G 1950 *The Concept of Mind*. Hutchinson's University Library, London
Scheffler I 1960 *The Language of Education*. Thomas, Springfield, Illinois
Smith B O, Ennis R H (eds.) 1961 *Language and Concepts in Education*. Rand McNally, Chicago, Illinois [*Lengua y Conceptos en la Educación*. Libreria "El Anteneo", Buenos Aires]

Teaching and Related Activities

E. Robertson

When one person imparts information or skill to another, it is common to describe the action as teaching. But not every way of bringing about learning in another counts as teaching, and not every act of teaching has a place within a program of education. Philosophers of education have analyzed the concept of teaching in its generic sense and have attempted to distinguish educative teaching from related concepts such as training, conditioning, and indoctrination. A central theme of these efforts has been to show that these related activities result in a defective form of learning because they fail to engage adequately the rational powers of students.

1. The Generic Concept of Teaching

In its generic sense, "teaching" denotes action undertaken with the intention of bringing about learning in another. In this way, teaching is different from mere telling or showing how. No doubt, in order to qualify as teaching, the activities engaged in must meet some additional criteria, although exactly what these are is open to dispute. Given two persons T and S and the content of instruction X, major candidates for necessary conditions for the truth of the teaching claim, "T is teaching X to S," are:

(a) There is some encounter (normally face-to-face) between T and S.

(b) At the beginning of the encounter, T knows X and S does not know X.

(c) T intends what he or she does to contribute to S's learning X.

(d) T's actions are reasonably conducive to bringing about S's learning X.

(e) T's actions are such as to reveal to S the X he or she is supposed to learn. (This means that normally teaching acts fall within a range of activities that includes explaining, describing, demonstrating, exemplifying, guiding, etc.)

(f) T's actions succeed at least to the extent that S *tries* to learn X as a result of T's actions.

Each of these conditions is intended to rule out as teaching encounters relationships between T and S in which S might learn X as a result of something T did, but it would still not be plausible to describe T's actions as teaching X to S. For example, S might learn philosophy of education from reading Dewey's books, but it seems inappropriate to say that Dewey taught S philosophy of education [Conditions (a) and (c) disqualify this case.] Or again, suppose that T is so uninformed about the capacities of the young that T tries to teach calculus to average 5-year-olds. Then T may intend that they learn, but T's actions probably are better described as trying to teach, rather than as teaching. [Condition (d) rules out this situation.] The intent of condition (e) is difficult to capture. It is supposed to eliminate situations in which T's actions are calculated to cause S to learn X, but the interaction between T and S does not appear to be of a type which is appropriately classified as instruction. Simply throwing Johnny into the water, for example, is not a way of teaching him to swim even if in his panic he discovers how. The intent condition [condition (c)] rules out cases where S learns X by imitating T but T has no pedagogic intentions. For example, students may acquire the mannerisms of their teachers, but it would be misleading to say that their teachers taught them to behave in that way. Finally, exactly how strong condition (f) should be is in dispute. Sometimes a teaching claim seems to imply that the student actually learned (as in "I taught her to ride a bicycle" where surely one would have a legitimate complaint against the speaker if the student could not in fact ride). But "I taught him algebra last year" could be true, it seems, even if the student never learned algebra. There are various ways of trying to account for these differences. One might say that "teaching" has both effort and success uses. Or one might hold that, when learning fails to appear, one can with equal propriety say either "T taught unsuccessfully" or "T tried to teach but failed." As stated, condition (f) formulates a minimal success claim. It suggests merely that, however eloquent the lecture, teaching is not going on if all the students are listening to their radios instead of the instructor.

Most of these proposed conditions have been challenged. Some say condition (a) runs afoul of televised instruction. Condition (b)—that T knows X prior to the teaching encounter—might not hold true of advanced graduate seminars where teacher and student are jointly trying to discover the truth. Some find it natural to say "Smith taught me how not to teach, although, of course, that wasn't her intention." This claim, if correct, is a counterexample to condition (c). Others argue that learning is not the only goal of teaching because specific teaching acts can have nonlearning objectives such as

"grasping the point" or "following the proof." So-called "inductive teaching" where students are led to discover things for themselves is sometimes held to be a counterexample to condition (e). Some would eliminate the success condition altogether while others would require that it be stronger.

Defenders of the original conditions have their rejoinders, of course. But settling these issues is perhaps of less importance than seeing what is at stake in the debate, and that does not become clear until the discussion turns to a more specific conception of teaching. About "teaching" in its most general use little more can be said. "Teaching" is a term which lacks well-defined boundaries. Teaching aims at learning and hence at knowledge, although, as all know, falsehoods can be taught and learned. Classifying an action as teaching implies no judgments about the moral or educational worth of the content or about the methods employed [except possibly as suggested in condition (e) above]. People can be taught to kill as well as to save lives, and to play tiddledywinks as well as chess, and they may be taught through the use of threats and intimidation as well as by kindness.

However, the term "teaching" is sometimes used in ways which suggest that a contrast is being drawn between teaching and other ways of bringing about learning. In this more distinctive sense, "teaching" is used to denote effort directed towards bringing about learning of a certain kind or quality—typically learning which is part of a program of education. By "education" in this context is meant a special transformation of thought, feeling, and action distinct from mere socialization. Often education in this sense is understood as a process whose goal is the development of critical, reflective agents. It is in this context that teaching is commonly distinguished from related activities such as training, conditioning, and indoctrination. These activities may also involve the intent to bring about learning, but of a kind or quality which is judged to be defective on a range of criteria from the standpoint of shared educational ideals. The ways in which these activities are taken to miss the educational mark reveals the contours of a central normative conception of educative teaching.

2. Training

"Training" is used in a pejorative way less frequently than either "conditioning" or "indoctrination" and, accordingly, has a more substantial area of overlap with "educative teaching." In many contexts, "teaching" can be substituted for "training" without a change in meaning. The focus of training is on the development of skills, on knowing-how rather than knowing-that (although, of course, a person may need to acquire a lot of propositional knowledge in the course of learning a complex skill). Sometimes "training" is reserved for use in the context of the teaching of routine tasks which allow total mastery, but this is by no means always the case. One can speak of the trained judgment of historians as well as of training a dog to jump through a hoop. When "training" does have a negative connotation by contrast with "educative teaching" (e.g., "He's been merely trained rather than taught to think for himself"), the focus is on learning which is narrow, inflexible, and uninformed by the point of the activity undertaken. (Sometimes "drill" is used as the negative term and "train" as the positive one.) Teaching someone a skill, on the other hand, requires developing the learner's capacity to respond to the unexpected, to understand what he or she is doing and why, to be intelligent and reflective in the exercise of his or her skill. Such teaching therefore involves the giving of reasons rather than (or in addition to) drill.

3. Conditioning

When conditioning is compared with teaching, normally it is operant conditioning, not classical conditioning, which is thought of as a possible cousin. Pavlov's dogs came to salivate at the sound of a bell, but Pavlov did not teach them to do that and some think it doubtful whether they learned to do it. Operant conditioning, however, may seem to be simply a systematic form of training and hence teaching. Common school practices such as giving rewards for good behavior can be described as setting up a situation in which a reinforcer depends upon the occurrence of a response and that is the procedure for operant conditioning. Conditioning, in this sense, will have taken place if the probability of the desired response in the particular circumstances (the stimulus conditions) increases because of its association in the experience of the child with the positive reinforcer. This description of the situation implies nothing about how the stimulus brings about the response or why the frequency of the child's behavior increases (except that it was reinforced). It seems possible that a child's behavior could be altered through conditioning without the child's being consciously aware of the change or having any notion of why behaving in this way might be appropriate in the particular circumstances. Such persons act because of their conditioning, not because of any judgments they have made about what they ought to do. Processes which by-pass human rationality in this way are generally held to be unacceptable in a program of education. Such processes seem less like a form of teaching and more like something resorted to when normal instruction fails (as a way of dealing with phobias, for example). On the other hand, it has been held that such rational processes as a person's learning some fact by reading or hearing statements in its favor and evaluating the evidence can be described appropriately as a process of operant conditioning. If this is so, then educative teaching would not be incompatible with conditioning students but only with some ways of doing so.

4. Indoctrination

Most dictionaries list a meaning for "indoctrination" in which it is synonymous with "teaching" in its generic sense. But there is also a notion of indoctrination in which it is thought of as a form of miseducation. This section is concerned with the pejorative sense of the term.

The concept of indoctrination has received extensive treatment by philosophers of education. Perhaps this is because indoctrination is sometimes mistaken for genuine education and also because, while some have thought that indoctrination is always to be avoided, others have held that its use is inevitable (even if lamentable) with young children. Thus the place of indoctrination in a genuine program of education is in doubt.

Although there has been much disagreement about the essential features of indoctrination, most of the proposals fall into one of the following categories (or some combination of them).

4.1 Content

Etymology would seem to suggest that indoctrination is connected with the teaching of doctrines. But what is a doctrine? The answer to this question is by no means clear, but some central features have been identified. A doctrine is a system of beliefs that provides an explanation or interpretation of the world and indicates how humans ought morally to act in light of the general features of existence that the system has identified. A doctrine differs from a scientific theory in containing assertions which are, in principle, not open to empirical investigation; not only are these assertions not known to be true, but it would be difficult to say what states of affairs would count for and against their truth.

Some have argued that "indoctrination" applies only when the content of instruction is a doctrine in this sense. Isolated factual claims could, according to this view, never be indoctrinated. For, though "indoctrinate" takes as its object beliefs, not actions, still characteristically it is beliefs, which have intimate connections to action, which form the content of indoctrination. Further, some have thought that *any* attempt to teach a doctrine (except in the sense of teaching a student what statements form part of the doctrine) is necessarily indoctrination. Others, however, have left open the possibility that the content of a doctrine could be either educatively taught or indoctrinated depending upon the methods the instructor uses.

4.2 Method

Sometimes indoctrinators are thought of as permitting no questions or expressions of doubt from the students, but a skillful indoctrinator need not shy away from all such confrontations. The crucial issue is whether the instructor makes clear to the students the epistemic status of the claims that form the content of instruction. One who is educatively teaching tries to engage the reason of students, to encourage them to hold their beliefs on the basis of the available evidence, to subject their beliefs to appropriate tests, and to stand ready to revise their beliefs in light of new discoveries. In areas in which there are alternative points of view equally supported by the evidence, the teacher must make this known. The indoctrinator, by contrast, must be prepared to use methods which go beyond rational appeal, if necessary, and to misrepresent the weight of the evidence which is available.

Some argue that when systematic distortion and irrational persuasion of this sort are in evidence, indoctrination is taking place regardless of the intention of the instructor. Others have claimed that, however miseducative these methods are, the result is not indoctrination unless the instructor has certain special intentions.

4.3 Intention

Self-conscious indoctrinators, it is generally agreed, aim at implanting beliefs within their students in such a way that the beliefs are immune to change. They are interested in fixity of belief because of the connection the beliefs they are inculcating have with actions they are endeavoring to promote. Because the world at large may be hostile to their programs, they must prepare their students to deal with questions without their beliefs being genuinely open to criticism and refutation.

Some have held, however, that instructors need not have such explicit intentions for a charge of indoctrination to stick. For suppose that the worldview which forms the content of instruction is the predominant ideology of the society of which the school is a part. Then teachers, along with other members of the society, may have uncritically taken on these socially dominant beliefs and be transmitting them to students (either consciously or unconsciously) in good faith. Still one might ask whether teachers as educators should not be held responsible for holding these societal beliefs up for scrutiny. And the failure to do so, some have argued, is appropriately labelled indoctrination. Indeed, some hold that it is in this case that the need to distinguish genuinely educative teaching from indoctrination is greatest. For the socially dominant world-view will likely have shaped the institutional structure of the school and its ethos as well as the formal and informal curriculum. Hence it is here that the self-awareness and independence of thought and action that education aims at is most crucial.

5. Educative Teaching

What has the discussion of training, conditioning, and indoctrination shown about how educative teaching should be conducted? Clearly the literature reveals an emphasis upon educative teaching as a practice which engages the rational faculties of students and respects them as independent centers of thought and action. Such teaching aims not only at encouraging beliefs which are supported by the evidence, but also at developing the power of students to gather the evidence and

assess its adequacy for themselves. This means that a program of education must include the acquisition of the most reliable methods humans have developed for discovering the truth about themselves and the world. When teaching skills, the educator makes the students aware of the reasons for what they are doing and encourages them to be intelligent and reflective in the exercise of their skills. And though the environment (and schools and teachers are part of that environment) may shape the behavior of students through operant conditioning, educative teachers desire students to act because of their perceptions of what they ought to do rather than merely because of their history of reinforcements.

Is this *an* educational ideal, *one* understanding of the appropriate relationship between teacher and student in an educational encounter, or is it *the* educational ideal? However that question should be answered, plainly there is a fit between this educational ideal and certain assumptions about modern life in a democratic, culturally plural, liberal state. When many doubt that the good life can be objectively specified in any substantial way, then the appropriate educational response seems to be to prepare students to develop their own rational life plans and act upon them. Hence preparation for life in such a society requires developing the capacity for intelligent freedom of choice rather than simply acquiring the patterns of thought, feeling, and action possessed by the elders. Yet even in a society in which there is consensus about the nature of the good life, educative teachers might well desire that students come to act as the elders do, not simply because they do it, but rather because reason supports such actions.

See also: Definitions of Teaching; Behavioral Models

Bibliography

Crittenden B S 1973 *Education and Social Ideals: A Study in Philosophy of Education.* Longman Canada, Don Mills, Ontario

Dearden R F, Hirst P H, Peters R S (eds.) 1972 *Education and the Development of Reason.* Routledge and Kegan Paul, London

Dietl P 1973 Teaching, learning, and knowing. *Educ. Philos. Theory* 5: 1–25

Green T F 1971 *The Activity of Teaching.* McGraw-Hill, New York

Lehman H 1974 Conditioning and learning. *Educ. Theory* 24: 161–69

McClellan J E 1976 *Philosophy of Education.* Prentice-Hall, Englewood Cliffs, New Jersey

Macmillan C J B, Nelson T W (eds.) 1968 *Concepts of Teaching: Philosophical Essays.* Rand McNally, Chicago, Illinois

Passmore J 1980 *The Philosophy of Teaching.* Harvard University Press, Cambridge, Massachusetts

Peters R S 1964 *Education as Initiation: An Inaugural Lecture Delivered at the University of London Institute of Education, 9 December 1963.* Evans, London

Scheffler I 1960 *The Language of Education.* Thomas, Springfield, Illinois

Snook I A (ed.) 1972 *Concepts of Indoctrination: Philosophical Essays.* Routledge and Kegan Paul, London

Teaching: Art or Science?

M. J. Dunkin

In ordinary conversation it is not uncommon for teaching to be referred to as either an art or a science. In most cases the speaker has no strong commitment to one view or the other and so the distinction is not important. Sometimes the distinction is made after considerable thought and reflects a carefully developed concept of teaching. The latter in turn affects attitudes to such issues as whether teaching should, or can, be researched empirically and whether teachers can be trained scientifically.

The leading protagonists in the debate about teaching as an art or a science have been Highet (1954) and Gage (1964, 1978), both of whom made the distinction an important aspect of the titles and themes of whole books. According to Highet, teaching is an art, not a science, principally because it involves human beings, their emotions and their values, which he regarded as "quite outside the grasp of science" (1954 p. viii) and even threatened by attempts to apply scientific aims and methods. To Gage, the issue became not so much whether teaching is an art or a science as whether scientific methods can be employed in understanding more about teaching. He argued that artistic activities have inherent order and lawfulness that make them quite suitable for scientific analysis. Moreover, he could see little danger to art itself in the scientific study of it. "The artist whose lawfulnesses are revealed does not become an automaton; ample scope remains for his subtlety and individuality" (1964 p. 270).

Gallagher (1970) had no doubt that teaching is an art, but thought that it could benefit by being less of one. He compared teaching with surgery and noted that many people used to die because surgery was too much of an art and not enough of a science. Gallagher also made valuable comments about what is meant by classifying something as an art. He saw two implications of calling something an art—only a few people possess the skills required to be called "artists", and even the artists find it difficult to describe their artistry and pass it on only by acting as models to imitate. To Gallagher, the improvement of teaching and education involved removing some of the mystery of teaching by the application of systematic study of it.

In Gage's later comment on the subject, he agreed that teaching is an art, but saw it as "a useful, or practical, art rather than one dedicated to the creation of beauty and the evocation of aesthetic pleasure as ends in themselves" (Gage 1978 p. 15). In relation to decisions made concerning materials, pacing, and especially in face-to-face interactions with students, Gage saw much scope for intuition, expressiveness, improvisation and creativity, which are commonly accepted ingredients of artistry.

While there has been much debate about the application of scientific methods to the study of teaching, there has been very little discussion about the application of "artistic" methods for that purpose. According to Eisner (1977), the distinctive methodology for "artistic" evaluation is "connoisseurship" as applied in appreciation in the visual arts, music, and literature. According to Gage (1978), when applied to teaching, connoisseurship would probably be more concerned with high, rather than low, inference variables, such as warmth.

Given, then, that teaching is an art, the real issue seems to be whether or not it is amenable to understanding through the application of scientific methods. To Gage the problem is to establish for teaching a scientific basis. This is different from making teaching a science, which implies rigorous laws and high predictability and control. Even medicine and engineering are not sciences, according to Gage. They have strong scientific bases but artistry is required to apply the scientific bases to achieve practical ends. Although teaching lacks the highly developed scientific bases underlying medicine and engineering, it is analogous to them in its artistic elements and in its scope for development of a scientific basis.

The nature of the scientific basis, says Gage, will be "established relationships between variables in teaching and learning" (1978 p. 22). Some of these relationships might merely allow predictions to be made from one variable to another. The more the relationships are causal, as established through experimental rather than correlational research, the stronger the scientific basis. The stronger the latter is, the better will be opportunities to improve teaching.

Bibliography

Eisner E W 1977 On the uses of educational connoisseurship and criticism for evaluating classroom life. *Teach. Coll. Rec.* 78: 345–58

Gage N L 1964 Theories of teaching. In: Hilgard E R (ed.) 1964 *Theories of Learning and Instruction.* National Society for the Study of Education Yearbook No. 63, Part 1. University of Chicago Press, Chicago, Illinois

Gage N L 1978 *The Scientific Basis of the Art of Teaching.* Teachers College Press, New York

Gallagher J J 1970 Three studies of the classroom. In: Gallagher J J, Nuthall G A, Rosenshine B (eds.) 1970 *Classroom Observation.* American Educational Research Association Monograph Series on Curriculum Evaluation, No. 6. Rand McNally, Chicago, Illinois, pp. 74–108

Highet G 1954 *The Art of Teaching.* Vintage Books, New York

Human Interaction Models

N. A. Flanders

The human interaction models of teaching discussed in this article are limited to situations in which a teacher interacts with students in a classroom using instructional materials so the students can learn selected educational outcomes consisting of knowledge, attitudes, and skills. To be concerned with interaction is to focus on the continuous stream of behavior which occurs in the classroom as a series of individual acts. An act might consist of a teacher contacting the class or a single student, a student contacting a teacher, a student contacting another student, or a student acting upon an object (after Piaget) in order to reformulate knowledge. A model of teaching is merely a tool for thinking about classroom teaching; it is a set of concepts carefully arranged to explain what teachers and students do in a classroom, how they interact, how they use instructional materials, and how these activities affect what students learn. Each model imposes a point of view that transforms the behavior to be analyzed just like new tinted glasses can modify the view of familiar objects by altering color and contrast. This transformation is due, in part, to the concepts chosen, but a model also sets priorities among conceptual relationships, it suggests what things go together, what should be considered first, second, third, and so on, what is to be in the foreground, and what is to be relegated to the background.

The use of the word human in the phrase "human interaction model" is a reminder that any model of teaching is concerned with rich human experience and it should have the capacity to synthesize the affective and cognitive in a way that would please John Dewey or Sören Kierkegaard were they alive today.

Interaction models of teaching are needed today for the same reasons they were needed in the past. They have helped and will continue to help in understanding instruction and to a limited extent in explaining why certain patterns of classroom interaction are associated with desired educational outcomes. In turn, this influences subsequent research on teaching, programs of teacher education, and ultimately the conduct of classroom teaching itself, but at each step, progress has not been easy. Initially researchers were more concerned with acts than models. Morsh and Wilder (1954 p. 4) summarized early efforts as follows, "No single, specific, observable act has yet been found whose frequency or percent of occurrence is invariably (and) significantly correlated with student achievement." Since then more than a dozen reviews have nominated patterns of teacher acts that are associated with student learning (Fenstermacher 1979 p. 160), but the adaptation of knowledge about instruction to programs of teacher education and to classroom practice itself has been slow and the subject of considerable criticism (Gage 1978 p. 42). Because of these difficulties, this article contains, wherever possible, a selection and discussion of models of teaching that have been used not only to guide research, but also to guide teacher education programs.

Readers interested in a general review of research on teaching effectiveness should turn to other entries (see *Evolution of Research on Teaching*). No distinction is made here between the following words: "models," "theories," and "paradigms" and, instead, they are used as synonyms. Readers interested in such distinctions should consult Gage (1963), Brodbeck (1963), Lundgren (1972), and Nuthall and Snook (1973).

1. The Characteristics of Models of Teaching

Most models of teaching serve as simplifying metaphors to reduce the fantastic complexity of human interaction as it occurs in the classroom. A model provides the answer to four questions. What do you want to know? How will you describe what you see? How often will you look? How many variables will you use at the same time? The answer to the first question sets the scope of the model—is everything in the classroom to be explained, or just a few things? The second answer indicates whether your descriptions will be general or specific, broad or detailed. The third answer indicates the frequency of observation. Will there be several in one second or just one during the year? The fourth answer is a little more difficult. The human mind can juggle about half a dozen variables at once. With this limitation, there has to be a balance between scope, specificity, and the number of variables. If the scope is modest and the variables specific enough to be recognized, then a classroom teacher may be able to use them.

These choices in the analysis of human behavior are analogous to making a motion picture film: one can choose a telephoto lens that magnifies tiny details but excludes most of the scene with its narrow field of vision, or one can choose a wide-angle lens to identify only the most prominent features in the scene at the cost of less detail. With regard to the time dimension, a camera operator can increase the number of pictures per second to several hundred or choose slower speeds. To really slow things down, one could take a picture every two minutes, as in time-lapse photography, producing 30 relatively disconnected *tableaux vivants* to summarize one hour of classroom instruction. These choices about scope, specificity, time periods, and the number of variables are determined by the purposes of the investigator. A good model is one that accomplishes its purposes with the fewest limitations. It specifies what is to be identified in the continuing flow of behavior, it predicts how these things probably are related, and its most important function is to show how all these separate things can be put back together. The end product is not intended to reproduce human interaction, it is intended to show relationships among selected abstract features of human interaction and to trace these over time. Perhaps an example will help.

Imagine a classroom—a teacher asks a question, a student answers, and the teacher commends the student. The interpretation could be quite different depending upon the model chosen and the decisions made when constructing the model. If a person said, "There are three events, a stimulus, a response, and a contiguous reinforcement," it might be guessed that the model was based upon behavior modification (Nuthall and Snook 1973 p. 49). A second person might say, "The teacher is taking the initiative, focusing the attention of the student with a narrow question, thereby making the student more dependent." This inference is likely to be made by a person using the ten-category system by Flanders (1970). A third person might see three acts as a single event and say, "The teacher is building a body of facts. Later the students will discuss them, decide which go together, and then arrange them into groups." This model might be based on an inductive–discovery lesson following the work of Taba (1966). Notice how different these interpretations are, how the model predisposes a person to reach particular conclusions, and how much information about the behavior must have been ignored or discarded.

Not very much has been written about how to make choices that determine the specificity of concepts, frequency of assessment, and the complexity of a model, but these choices will be greatly influenced once the researcher defines a unit of behavior. Since this choice is critical an interested reader can turn to Barker and Wright (1955) who chose to have research observers follow children all day and write down everything that happened. They discussed in considerable detail how they chose a unit of behavior and Dickman (1963) has added his ideas to theirs.

2. Past and Current Trends in Models of Instruction

Mitzel (1960) was the first to suggest that research on teaching involved presage, process, and product variables. When Dunkin and Biddle (1974 p. 38) reviewed the same field of research almost 15 years later, they needed an additional class of variables called context variables which included, in their case, characteristics of the pupils, the classroom, the textbooks, the school, and the community. The main purpose of this model was to help organize a review of research and discuss the findings, but it also may have served to set higher standards of research. During the 1960s and 1970s many researchers underestimated the importance of controlling context variables and this model probably reminded researchers that context should be considered.

While the Dunkin and Biddle review included context variables which permitted them to interpret process–product relationships, Gage (1978 p. 26) criticized their procedures because he thought they led to conclusions that were unneccesarily equivocal. Rosenshine (1971) and Gage (1978) chose to focus on process–product relationships, in their reviews of research on teaching, using student achievement as the only outcome variable. They grouped studies with the same process variables in their search for predictors of achievement. Gage sought a "scientific basis for the art of teaching" by summarizing simple bivariate relationships, "If X, then Y," where Y was student achievement. By identifying different "X's" that were significantly correlated with achievement, science would provide clues to reveal what makes a difference in teaching. Gage recognizes the limitations of bivariate relationships (1978 p. 18):

> In practical affairs, the laws and trends relating any two variables are subject to modification by the influence of a third variable and many more variables . . . . When any additional variable [influences] the relationship between two variables, we are unwise to follow [its] implications.

Further limitations of bivariate relationships are discussed later in this article, at this point note that simple process–product relationships provide teachers and teacher educators with meagre clues and very little dynamic explanation. Perhaps the role of scientists, in an immature field, is to identify promising process–product relationships and nominate them as building blocks for models.

This discussion might lead some readers to conclude that because "the process–product model" has severe theoretical limitations, all models with two or three kinds of variables have very little value. Such judgments may be misleading. For example, Carroll chose to explain "degree of learning" as a function of the "time actually spent" in proportion to the "time needed," a deceptively simple model. This model influenced Bloom's ideas about mastery learning and more recent research on "academic learning time," both to be discussed later as examples of models that result in practical applications. The scope is narrow when Carroll focuses on what a single student does to complete a short learning task. The implications of the model are also fascinating since it suggests a student can learn anything if given enough time and individual effort.

Turning to more complex models, Smith and Geoffrey (1968) studied one classroom for six months and drew the diagrams for 36 models involving several hundreds of variables on topics as diverse as "How Irma got caught in a vicious circle," to a flow chart of "textbook teaching." It is little wonder that their book was entitled *The Complexities of an Urban Classroom*. The model about Irma (p. 81) is a diagram showing features of her personality, her behavior, and the reactions of other students to explain how, over a period of six weeks, Irma became isolated. Most of the concepts in the 36 models refer to specific observable behaviors or characteristics. Some of the models are indeed complicated, but they are the product of discussions between an observer–theoretician and a classroom teacher. Each model had to pass two tests: does it "feel" intuitively right to the teacher and make sense; and does it fit the carefully recorded notes of the observer? The authors argue that an extended ethnographic observation tends to produce models that focus on practical problems and reflect what really goes on in the classroom.

The phrase "models of teaching" has, for some time, been associated with Bruce Joyce and his colleagues. The second edition of *Models of Teaching* (Joyce and Weil 1980) and a new book on flexibility in teaching (Joyce and Hodges 1981) add fresh ideas and new research evidence to support their point of view. Their approach to models of instruction and their use is really quite different to that of other educators. Most model builders create one model which embodies their unique point of view, Smith and Geoffrey being exceptions, and then advocate its use to analyze teaching or teacher education. The eclecticism of Joyce et al. raises new and interesting issues about the characteristics of models. First, Joyce et al. are interested in models that can be used to make decisions. This means the model and its concepts cannot be too vague and general or too microscopic and lost in detail. They want to look at behaviors classroom teachers can recognize. Second, the time frame of a model cannot be too long or too short. Models concerned with single events or even a single teaching skill cover too short a time span and a curriculum guide is always available to present the long-range point of view. Thus models should encompass strategies that occur in a single lesson or perhaps a unit of study. Third, models should not be too complex or overly simple. Complexity is a combination of the number of different concepts in the model and the range of behaviors the model takes into consideration. If the task of helping a teacher improve instruction is very, very complex and if the models teachers can use have the forgoing limitations, then it follows that no one model will be satisfactory. Instead, different models will have to be used for different purposes. Later, when the practical application of models is discussed, the use of multiple models will reappear as a viable option.

3. Moving Beyond Process–Product Research

In the summer of 1974 the United States National Institute of Education convened an international conference on studies in teaching. Its purpose was to criticize research on teaching and to recommend new directions. The task of Panel 2 was to consider the research which conceived of teaching as a form of human interaction rather than skill performance, linguistic process, or similar topics assigned to the nine other panels. In the final report of Panel 2 (Flanders 1974), research on teacher education received special emphasis. Apparently the Panel members, all recognized for their accomplishments in research on teaching, decided it was time to find out how their own research could be utilized to improve instruction. They recommended programs

of research to investigate how teachers made use of knowledge of pedagogy and discussed related ideas some of which appear below.

3.1 The Limitations of Process–Product Research

The results of process–product research, like those summarized by Rosenshine and Furst (1973), Dunkin and Biddle (1974), and reanalyzed by Gage (1978), represent a prodigious research effort and constitute the most objective evidence there is about teaching, but this knowledge has had limited value for the improvement of classroom instruction. As mentioned earlier, process–product research produces knowledge in the form of a conditional generalization, "If X, then Y." If a teacher praises a student, he or she works harder. Suppose a teacher were to follow a generalization of this kind on 100 separate occasions while teaching, the generalization would be valid more often than not, but in some instances it would be invalid. Thus, a teacher uses a generalization of this kind tentatively and must be prepared to use other options if necessary.

(a) The correlation between an "X" and a "Y" in most cases is nonlinear. This means there is some intermediate level of "X" which produces a maximum "Y," but too little or too much "X" will reduce "Y." As an example, the relationship between teacher indirectness and pupil achievement (Gage 1978 p. 102) can be chosen which has been replicated in more than 20 independent studies. The presence of an optimum level has been presented by Soar and independently discovered by Coats (see Flanders 1970 p. 403). If one could design the research properly, it seems likely that all nine variables cited by Rosenshine and Furst (1973 p. 156) such as clarity variability, enthusiasm, businesslikeness, criticism, and so on would have an optimum level. In the classroom, a teacher must decide how much praise (or anything else) is too much and too little.

(b) Nearly all generalizations about teaching must be qualified by the phrase—"all other things being equal." But every classroom teacher knows "other things" are never equal and one situation is always different, in some way, from another. In a classroom, a teacher may decide to praise a pupil in order to encourage more work, but this may result in overlearning a misconception. Given present knowledge, there will always be limitations when one attempts to predict human behavior. This is what Brodbeck (1963 p. 75) meant when she wrote that knowledge of pedagogy derived from research is often imperfect.

(c) The most serious limitation of process–product research on teaching does not depend on the flaws to be found in one study or another. It is the tendency of process–product research to be atheoretical, if not antitheoretical. The bivariate model operates as if an understanding of classroom interaction depended only on quantity, on how many acts of a particular kind did or did not occur, and to ignore changes in the situational context, the instructional purposes, and the sequence of teaching acts. This issue has been discussed at length by Gage (1978 p. 69f), and was expressed as follows by Dunkin and Biddle (1974 p. 353):

> . . . the greatest single flaw in much of the research we have reviewed is the persistent assumption . . . that teaching can somehow be reduced to a scalar value that can be indicated by the frequency of occurrence for some teaching behavior. We suspect, with Taba, that this simply is not true.

To assert, for example, that the total number of questions asked over a six-month learning period is associated with a desirable outcome, is to assume that each question and the context in which it was asked are roughly equivalent, one question compared with another, that with respect to question asking, the six-month period is reasonably homogeneous. This assumption is faulty, because it ignores the flexible use of different kinds of questions. By correlating question frequency with outcome in this fashion, the dynamic explanation of how questions facilitate learning is locked up, as in a "black box," and ignored.

3.2 Flexibility in Patterns of Instruction

The need to take theorizing more seriously and build models that help explain instruction becomes more evident when such features of teaching as flexibility are considered. Flexibility in teaching is the ability to change patterns of interaction according to the exigencies of the moment as well as to plan and carry out quite different teaching functions during different phases of the same lesson or a longer unit of study.

The notion that the most effective teachers are more flexible prompted Flanders (1960a pp. 95–109) to look for evidence of it in his initial seventh- and eighth-grade samples (ages 12–14). The more effective teachers, those whose pupils learned more and liked learning better, did indeed alter their interaction patterns in a flexible manner in ways significantly different than less effective teachers. Furthermore, some of the variations of flexible teachers appeared to be lawful. This led to a tentative theory (Flanders 1960b) to explain these variations in terms of instructional goals and classroom structure. This theory was elaborated 10 years later (Flanders 1970 pp. 308–35), but much more work will be required to build models of flexibility.

There is a long history of research to investigate how teachers adapt their behavior to the cognitive requirements of classroom interaction. Chapter 10 in Dunkin and Biddle (1974) reviews the contributions of Smith and Meux, Nuthall and Lawrence, Bellack, and Taba, among others. Since the work of these early pioneers, researchers interested in the developmental psychology of Piaget have been very active, but the impact of this point of view on teacher flexibility can be seen most clearly when Piaget emphasizes how students must interact with ideas and objects in order to reformulate physical knowledge. In their teaching model on how to improve thinking, based on Piaget's ideas, Joyce and Weil (1980 p. 105) show how special learning environments need to be created for different kinds of knowledge and how the teacher must be flexible and responsive to encourage self-discovery learning.

Brophy and Good (1974) emphasize the need for teachers to react to individual students in ways that expand learning opportunities in spite of the teacher's perception of the student's ability. They also discuss how to help teachers change this aspect of their teaching.

Studies of flexibility show that creative and artistic teachers are sensitive to cues students provide and adapt their behavior to the cognitive, emotional, and social needs of each student and to different classes. These teachers also plan flexible class formations that require different patterns of communication and make use of them as the class progresses from one instructional purpose to the next.

3.3 The Transition From Research to Practice

This article began with a description of models of instruction and some of the choices to be made when they are designed. One model, involving presage, process, and product variables, has had a prominent position in the more important reviews of research on teaching ever since it was first used in 1960. During the decade of the 1970s the reviews of Rosenshine and Furst (1973), Dunkin and Biddle (1974), and Gage (1978) helped to make the phrase "process–product" research a popular label when referring to knowledge of more effective and less effective teaching. In all three of these reviews it was made very clear that teaching is more complicated than simple process–product relationships. Although many models of teaching have been proposed to explain its more complicated features, the tendency to report research in terms of simple bivariate relationships still predominates. It is quite clear (Rist 1977) that some scholars became interested in ethnographic research methods because they were dissatisfied with what they called "quantitative scientific methods" primarily because the latter were insensitive to the richness of human behavior in the classroom and therefore were unlikely to produce theories and models which reflected this richness. It has also been suggested that process–product research has had a limited impact on programs of teacher education.

In the remaining sections of this article, programs which have had some success in teacher education are described. All of these programs make use of the results of research on teaching. Thus, models are involved in the original research as well as in the design of the teacher education activities. The next section describes programs that were based on process–product research. The last section turns to more complicated models of teaching and learning.

4. Models for Applying Results from Process–Product Research

The research-based education programs discussed in this section and the next were arbitrarily chosen to illustrate problems in translating research into practice—they are not necessarily representative of programs currently in use.

4.1 Microteaching, Interaction Analysis, and Modeling

These three techniques have been used to help teachers identify different teaching skills, to practice these skills, and to understand their purpose (Peck and Tucker 1973). Their use in teacher education materials has been carefully developed by Borg and his co-workers (Borg et al. 1970 p. 29). His model is arranged as a series of training activities, one following another. First, a teacher reads about a particular skill (e.g. "redirecting questions," "because extensions," "wait time," etc.): how is it defined; how can it be recognized; and how, why, and when is it used? Second, a teacher views an instructional film or a model film: the main purpose is to review the theory of the first step and to see the skill demonstrated in a practical classroom situation. Third, the teacher plans a lesson for the purpose of practicing the skill which requires the trainee to apply what was learned in steps one and two. Fourth, the teacher teaches the lesson and records it. Fifth, the teacher analyzes the playback of the recording making use of a simple checklist or a more elaborate system of interaction analysis. Sixth, the analysis is discussed with peers or a supervisor to clarify how the skills can best be used and whether further practice is appropriate.

This model of a minicourse, as the package was named at the Far West Laboratory in San Francisco, combines the techniques of microteaching, interaction analysis, and modeling. Each minicourse released by the Far West Laboratory successfully completed a main field test which produced evidence that the intended changes in teacher behavior could be achieved in a field setting, by an average group of teachers, at a reasonable level of performance. Several minicourses have been redesigned, produced, and evaluated in different countries including the United Kingdom, the Netherlands, Sweden, the Federal Republic of Germany, and Israel.

One of these translation projects was carried out by Klinzing-Eurich and Klinzing (1981) at the University of Tubingen, in the Federal Republic of Germany, at a center directed by Professor W. Zifreund. They redesigned Minicourse 4, Interaction Analysis, and spent more than four years evaluating their product with preservice and inservice adult students. The minicourse is a self-instructional training package divided into five lessons. Lesson one is training in Flanders Interaction Analysis. Lessons two to four involve learning particular teaching skills in a microteaching format. Lesson five involves trying to apply what was learned to one's own classroom. For the full course, about 50 to 70 hours are required.

What are the major conclusions? The field tests of the German translation produced results which replicated the original field tests at the Far West Laboratory (Lai et al. 1973). Teacher interaction skills can be improved (or created) with carefully designed and field-tested self-instructional materials based on the Borg model. The Tubingen field studies attempted to find out how each of the five different lessons contributed to the expected changes of teacher behavior. It was found that the entire package produced change, but separate lessons did not. This suggests that as a trainee works through several cycles of Borg's model, the probability of change in teaching behavior increases. Perhaps some kind of momentum develops whereby several successful training cycles help to install a skill in the trainee's repertoire and stopping too soon may jeopardize skill acquisition.

Minicourses in the United States and other countries have demonstrated that most inservice and preservice teachers can learn new teaching skills consistent with the course objectives. As a research and development contribution in the field of teacher education, the Borg model emphasizes the need to provide time, space, resource materials, and feedback technology in quantities sufficient for the needs of the trainee.

Since their release in about 1970, minicourses have had an insignificant influence on teacher education in the United States, have not been sold and distributed as well as expected, and are no longer in production. Other countries such as England, Israel, and the Federal Republic of Germany have shown a somewhat higher interest, but it is too early to predict how effective this form of teacher education will be.

4.2 Time-on-task

Time-on-task is a process–product research variable that has been found to be related to learning outcomes and to vary widely in the classroom. For example, the magnitude of variation among pupils in the same class, between classes of the same subject and grade level in the same school district can be a factor as high as three or four, which is quite a contrast (Borg 1980 p. 43). Researchers have investigated allocated time, engaged time, and that portion of engaged time during which the pupil has a reasonably high success rate. Each of these qualifications of time-on-task produces, in the order listed, higher correlations with pupil achievement. Two teacher education programs are related to this research: the first is mastery learning associated with Bloom (1976) and Block and Burns (1977) which has spread across the United States and to other countries since 1970; the second is the work of Stallings (1982) with a small staff south of San Francisco.

(a) Mastery learning began with Carroll's model as did research on time-on-task. Mastery learning seeks, by a variety of methods, to have each pupil exposed to the following model which presents a cycle of steps to be followed in sequence: (i) diagnose present performance, (ii) prescribe appropriate learning activities based on diagnosis, (iii) encourage learning activities and provide appropriate feedback, (iv) assess progress frequently and adjust learning activities if necessary, (v) assign a grade in terms of final test score, and (vi) after mastery go to enrichment activities, to the next unit of study, or to help another pupil by tutoring. The program requires genuine curriculum revision since objectives must be clearly stated, tests and quizzes designed and produced as well as certain kinds of optional self-instructional materials. A staff must decide which of several operating programs it intends to follow. For example, Individually Prescribed Instruction (Glaser and Rosner 1975) uses "packages", Project PLAN (Flanagan et al. 1975) employs a learning guide, Individually Guided Education (Klausmeier 1975) uses small-group teaching, and the Annehurst Curriculum Classification System (Frymier 1977) aims toward the complete classification of most if not all of the instructional materials in the school according to a typology of learner characteristics (to match materials with the learner) with the hope of computer storage, retrieval, and record keeping. Mastery learning masquerades as an innovation that does not require new teaching skills, but identifying and sequencing instructional objectives, developing evaluation measures, identifying learning difficulties, prescribing instruction, and measuring outcomes are in mastery learning teacher training modules (Block and Burns 1977 p. 36).

(b) The Stallings Teaching and Learning Institute (STALI) conducts inservice teacher education programs designed to improve classroom time-on-task and to improve remedial reading instruction. The staff uses the following model: (i) observe and assess teachers, start where they are; (ii) use assessment to link theory to practice; (iii) set a few self-development goals so as not to overwhelm trainees, provide feedback and encouragement; and (iv) use post-training observation opportunities for teachers to discuss their successes or failures and set goals for the next cycle of evaluation. Teachers attend about six weekly seminars conducted by the STALI staff, but local supervisory personnel are brought in as staff associates since an important goal of the program is to train local persons to conduct their own staff development programs.

The STALI programs to improve reading (Stallings and Mohlman 1982) began with research, then shifted to teacher education. The research provided a list of more effective and less effective teaching practices for teachers of reading in the secondary-level schools. The teacher education, following the same model (see above), guided the teachers through the steps of research.

The Borg model made use of observation of interaction as feedback in training, but in the STALI programs progress in student achievement is also used for feedback. In mastery learning programs, student progress is constantly monitored, and the teacher uses the information in selecting instructional materials.

5. The Utilization of More Elaborate Models

Two approaches to teacher education are described in this section. The first is almost a perfect case study of how research and models of instruction can be used in a successful field application. The second approach makes use of multiple models.

5.1 Teacher Expectations and Student Achievement

Interest in teacher expectations began with an experiment by Rosenthal and Jacobson (1968) which they described in the book *Pygmalion in the Classroom*. They reported that when teachers were given false information about student ability, they treated students differently, and this affected student achievement. The national controversy that followed stimulated extensive research which has been reviewed by Brophy and Good (1974) who also conducted their own research on this problem. Two models were involved: one explains how the teacher's expectations affect student achievement and the other is concerned with how a teacher's contacts with students can be modified.

(a) A model to explain the effects of teacher expectations has been developed by Brophy and Good (1974 p. 39) after extensive classroom observation and interviews with teachers. (i) Early in the year teachers form expectations about each student's academic potential and personality. Some of these are inaccurate. (ii) The teachers contact students in ways consistent with their expectations and students react in a complementary fashion. If the expectations are low, inaccurate, and rigidly held, the student's achievement and class participation suffers. (iii) If these patterns continue for a school year, student achievement may be higher or lower than expected, depending on whether the inaccurate, rigidly held, expectation was too high or too low.

(b) The following model of teacher education is a synthesis of the work of Brophy and Good (1974) and Kerman et al. (1980). Kerman's inservice teacher education program started in about 1970. It is based on the model below set in a context of good human relations training. Currently, the team in Los Angeles conducts workshops throughout the United States to train supervisors and teachers who, in turn, train others.

(i) The teacher-trainee's classroom interaction is observed to record the frequency and qualities of teacher contacts with all students, in addition, high- and low-achieving students are identified.

(ii) Teachers study the research evidence about teacher expectations, student achievement, and teacher contacts with high- and low-achieving students and discuss the implications.

(iii) Particular skills for contacting below-average students are identified (e.g., proximity, courtesy, listening, delving, reasons for praise, building on ideas, etc.) and arranged into a training schedule. If possible, paired colleagues take turns observing and teaching as they follow the schedule. Problems with special students are discussed.

(iv) Several cycles, each two to four weeks long, start with the study of new skills, and continue with special practice periods twice a week in which a teacher trainee practices new ways of contacting students. After each practice session the trainee and colleague–observer discuss what happened with the help of the observation data. These experiences are shared with other trainees at the next workshop session.

There are some consistent developments now beginning to appear as the work of Borg, the Tubingen team, mastery learning, Stallings, Brophy and Good, and Kerman et al. is considered. One trend is toward practice with colleague support and feedback as new behaviors are transferred to one's own classroom.

5.2 Multiple Models of Teaching

Joyce and Weil (1980) are primarily concerned with teacher education. It occurred to them that learning one teaching skill at a time may be difficult because it is much too small a part of the process of teaching. Rather than learn this skill or that skill, why not present a set of interrelated skills in the form of a coherent model? They searched the literature for models and found more than 100. Their revised book presents about 25 models, divided into four "families" because each family looks at the classroom from a different point of view. These are models that emphasize social interaction, information processing, personal development, and behavior modification/cybernetics. This division is somewhat similar to Nuthall and Snook (1973).

Joyce and Hodges (1981 p. 48) "see the need for teachers who have great flexibility, . . . who do not have a single fixed style of teaching, but exhibit a variety of styles." Joyce et al. (1981) believe teachers can learn one or two models in each family to build the repertoire required for flexible teaching. Joyce and Showers (1981) completed a two-year examination of the ability of teachers to acquire new skills. They report that most teachers can "fine tune" existing skills and can even master new models, although the latter is more ambitious, but the conditions required to help teachers change their teaching have been consistently underestimated by those who direct inservice and preservice teacher education. By isolating studies in which there is clear evidence that teaching behavior has changed, the following components are seen as requirements for successful teacher education programs:

(a) A presentation of theory through readings, lectures, films, and discussions provides a rationale. The level of impact must be high enough so a trainee knows, in terms of theory, when, how, and why an instructional strategy is used.

(b) Demonstrations and modeling help to translate theoretical images into a practical classroom setting. When films or video recording are used, there are often too few examples. Many demonstrations may be required to help a teacher locate situations in

which a model is inappropriate and to learn how a model can be adapted. The level of impact should include several practical examples for each concept in the model and to imagine adaptations and modifications of the model.

(c) Practice under simulated conditions facilitates learning a skill or model because the teacher is less distracted by the complex responsibilities of a normal classroom. Practice is essential and closely related to the next three components.

(d) Structured feedback means being systematic, learning a system of interaction analysis, or using a checklist to analyze one's own teaching. A cycle of teach–analyze–reteach can be repeated as often as necessary.

(e) Unstructured feedback consists of informal discussion with a colleague which, of course, may be limited in terms of that person's ability. Informal discussion helps to create awareness of a problem, may be good for brain storming, and may give the trainee courage to continue.

(f) Coaching is to have the assistance of a colleague or supervisor when the teacher trainee adapts a skill or model to the full-size classroom. Adapting and adjusting patterns of teaching is much easier as a two-headed task, especially when the new model is quite different than one's natural style.

The idea of having a coach act as the midwife of a teaching innovation is unique and interesting. The role would be much more active than serving as a partner for an informal discussion. It would take joint planning and smooth cooperation.

6. Guided Inquiry into Teaching

What is to be learned from these successful teacher education programs? Borg's model for minicourses emphasizes two things: first, repeated feedback from cycles of microteaching and the need for modeling teaching, and second, careful field testing during the development of instructional materials for teachers. The Tubingen field studies suggest the use of entire minicourses. Mastery learning, Stallings, and programs on teacher expectations all show how teacher education can be tied to student learning. Joyce brings to our attention the need for teacher flexibility which requires a repertoire and this requires several models of teaching, not one. Stallings, Kerman and Brophy, and Good start where the teacher is because they all start with an analysis of current class interaction. This is closer to what Joyce would call a personal exploration of one's own teaching.

6.1 A Model for Guided Inquiry into Teaching

Figure 1 is an attempt to synthesize these contributions into a single model. Boxes A through E, above the

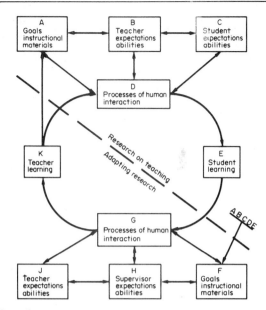

Figure 1
A model for teacher inquiry

diagonal line, represent the activities of students as they learn with the assistance of a teacher. Box D is the point of contact, the interaction of students with materials and objects, with each other, and with the teacher. Remember, the important features of boxes A, B, and C can be inferred from box D. That is, the reality of teacher and student expectations and abilities and the impact of the purposes that guide learning should become apparent during an analysis of the classroom interaction in box D.

Boxes F through K, below the diagonal line, represent the activities of a teacher learning more about teaching in general and his/her own teaching in particular. Box G is the point of contact where a teacher interacts with classroom data, with video or tape recordings, and confers with a supervisor, colleague, or coach regarding teaching skills, strategies, and models. The short arrows from A B C D E to box F have special importance, suggesting that a teacher's curriculum of self-development is the thoughtful analysis of classroom interaction—D, its consequences—E, and the contextual effects of teacher—B, students—C and task—A.

Notice the dynamics of improving instruction through the use of process–product research are illustrated by the inner ring of boxes D, E, G, and K. Start with teacher events in D that correlate with learning—E, such as more, or fewer, teacher questions, teacher praise, or teacher criticism. These patterns are to be learned through activities in box G, but if they remain separate skills, they may reach the classroom directly (G, K, D), but still separate. How are separate teaching skills to be synthesized and integrated into a coherent

teaching style? The burden is on the teacher to find a route like G K A B C to D. The latter is more like what Joyce would call a model of teaching.

6.2 *The Current State of the Art*

Each of these studies reviewed illustrates an innovation in the improvement of instruction. In each case teachers are encouraged to see their own class interaction as an object of inquiry, to step outside of their own skins and see themselves teaching "from the outside." Kerman was able to do this by starting with teacher expectations. Stallings did this, starting with the problems of students learning to read. Together, these innovations represent the current state of the art in teacher education and the improvement of instruction.

See also: Evolution of Research on Teaching; Paradigms for Research; Flexibility; Time; Teachers' Expectations; Mastery Learning Models; Linguistic Models; Minicourses; Micro-teaching: Conceptual and Theoretical Bases

Bibliography

Barker R G, Wright H F 1955 *Midwest and its Children: The Psychological Ecology of an American Town.* Harper, New York

Block J H, Burns R B 1977 Mastery learning. In: Schulman L S (ed.) 1977 *Review of Research in Education*, Vol. 4. Peacock, Itasca, Illinois

Bloom B S 1976 *Human Characteristics and School Learning.* McGraw-Hill, New York

Borg W R 1980 Time and school learning. In: Denham C, Lieberman A (eds.) 1980 *Time to Learn.* United States Department of Education, National Institute of Education, Washington, DC

Borg W R, Kelley M L, Langer P, Gall M 1970 *The Minicourse: A Microteaching Approach to Teacher Education.* Macmillan Educational, Beverly Hills, California

Brodbeck M 1963 Logic and scientific method in research on teaching. In: Gage N L (ed.) 1963

Brophy J E, Good T L 1974 *Teacher–Student Relationships: Causes and Consequences.* Holt, Rinehart and Winston, New York

Dickman H R 1963 The perception of behavior units. In: Barker R G (ed.) *The Stream of Behavior: Exploration of its Structure and Content.* Appleton-Century-Crofts, New York

Dunkin M J, Biddle B J 1974 *The Study of Teaching.* Holt, Rinehart and Winston, New York

Fenstermacher G D 1979 A philosophical consideration of recent research on teacher effectiveness. In: Schulman L S (ed.) 1979 *Review of Research Education*, Vol. 6. Peacock, Itasca, Illinois

Flanagan J C, Shanner W M, Brodner H J, Marker R W 1975 An individualized instructional system: PLAN. In: Talmage H (ed.) 1975 *Systems of Individualized Education.* McCutchan, Berkeley, California

Flanders N A 1960a *Teacher Influence, Pupil Attitudes, and Achievement.* Final report, Cooperative Research Project No. 397. University of Minnesota, Minneapolis, Minnesota

Flanders N A 1960b Diagnosing and utilizing social structures in classroom learning. In: Henry N B (ed.) 1960 *National*

Society for the Study of Education, 59th Yearbook, Part 2: *The Dynamics of Instructional Groups*. University of Chicago Press, Chicago, Illinois

Flanders N A 1970 *Analyzing Teaching Behavior*. Addison-Wesley, Reading, Massachusetts

Flanders N A 1974 Panel 2, teaching as human interaction. In: Gage N L, Viehoever K (eds.) 1974 NIE *National Conference on Studies in Teaching*. National Institute of Education, Washington, DC

Frymier J R 1977 *Annehurst Curriculum Classification Systems: A Practical Way to Individualize Instruction*. Kappa Delta Pi, West Lafayette, Indiana

Gage N L *Handbook of Research on Teaching: A Project of the American Educational Research Association*. Rand McNally, Chicago, Illinois

Gage N L 1978 *The Scientific Basis of the Art of Teaching*. Teachers College Press, Columbia University, New York

Glaser R, Rosner J 1975 Adaptive environments for learning: Curriculum aspects. In: Talmage H (ed.) 1975 *Systems of Individualized Education*. McCutchan, Berkeley, California

Joyce B R, Hodges R E 1981 Flexibility as repertoire. In: Joyce B R, Brown C C, Peck L (eds.) 1981

Joyce B R, Showers B 1981 Improving inservice training. In: Joyce B R, Brown C C, Peck L (eds.) 1981

Joyce B R, Weil M 1980 *Models of Teaching*. Prentice-Hall, Englewood Cliffs, New Jersey

Joyce B R, Brown C C, Peck L (eds.) 1981 *Flexibility in Teaching*. Longman, New York

Joyce B R, Weil M, Wald R 1981 A structure for pluralism in teacher education. In: Joyce B R, Brown C C, Peck L (eds.) 1981

Kerman S, Kimball T, Martin M 1980 *Teacher Expectations and Student Achievement* (Coordinators Manual) Phi Delta Kappa, Bloomington, Indiana

Klausmeier H J 1975 IGE: An alternative form of schooling. In: Talmage H (ed.) 1975 *Systems of Individualized Education*. McCutchan, Berkeley, California

Klinzing-Eurich G, Klinzing G 1981 *Lehrfertigkeiten und Ihr Training*. Neue Lernverfahren-6. Lexika-Verlag, Weil der Stadt, Baden-Wurttemburg

Lai M K, Elder R A, Newman J, Gall M D 1973 *Main Field Test Report: Interaction Analysis*. Report A73-12. Far West Laboratory for Educational Research and Development, San Francisco, California

Lundgren U P 1972 *Frame Factors and the Teaching Process: A Contribution to Curriculum Theory and Theory on Teaching*. Almqvist and Wiksell, Stockholm

Mitzel H E 1960 Teacher effectiveness. In: Harris C W (ed.) 1960 *Encyclopedia of Educational Research*, 3rd edn. Macmillan, New York

Morsh J E, Wilder E W 1954 *Identifying the Effective Instructor: A Review of the Quantitative Studies*, 1900–1952. Air Force Personnel and Training Center, Lackland Airforce Base, Research Bulletin No. AFPTRC-TR-54-44

Nuthall G, Snook I 1973 Contemporary models of teaching. In: Travers R M W (ed.) 1973 *Second Handbook of Research on Teaching: A Project of the American Educational Research Association*. Rand McNally, Chicago, Illinois

Peck R F, Tucker J A 1973 Research on teacher education. In: Travers R M W (ed.) 1973 *Second Handbook of Research on Teaching: A Project of the American Educational Research Association*. Rand McNally, Chicago, Illinois

Rist R C 1977 On the relations among educational research paradigms: From disdain to detente. *Anthrop. Educ. Q.* 8: 42–49

Rosenshine B 1971 *Teaching Behaviors and Student Achievement*. National Foundation for Educational Research, Slough

Rosenshine B, Furst N 1973 The use of direct observation to study teaching. In: Travers R M W (ed.) 1973 *Second Handbook of Research on Teaching: A Project of the American Educational Research Association*. Rand McNally, Chicago, Illinois

Rosenthal R, Jacobson L 1968 *Pygmalion in the Classroom: Teacher Expectation and Pupil's Intellectual Development*. Holt, Rinehart and Winston, New York

Smith L M, Geoffrey W 1968 *The Complexities of an Urban Classroom: An Analysis Toward a General Theory of Teaching*. Holt, Rinehart and Winston, New York

Stallings J A 1982 *What is Effective Staff Development?* Stallings Teaching and Learning Institute, Palo Alto, California

Stallings J A, Mohlman G G 1982 *Effective Use of Time in Secondary Reading Classrooms*. Stallings Teaching and Learning Institute, Palo Alto, California

Taba H 1966 *Teaching Strategies and Cognitive Functioning in Elementary School Children*. United States Office of Education (USOE) Cooperative Research Project No. 2404. San Francisco State College, San Francisco, California

Aptitude–Treatment Interaction Models

R. E. Snow

Aptitude–treatment interaction refers to the fact that characteristics of persons sometimes moderate the effects on those persons of instructional conditions administered to them. In turn, the importance of some personal characteristic with respect to some valued educational outcome often depends on what instructional conditions are administered. The study of aptitude–treatment interactions in education aims at understanding when, how, and why different persons benefit from different kinds of instruction, so that educational conditions can be improved by adapting them to the needs and characteristics of each kind of person. An adaptive instructional system is the goal.

Aptitude–treatment interaction research is a special case of the scientific study of person–environment interaction. The possibility of interactions has long been routinely acknowledged in the physical scientist's qualifier "other things being equal. . ." and in the social scientist's question "Can we generalize to other groups (communities, cultures, etc.)?" Evolutionary biology is also basically interactionist. And such interactions have been put to practical use in medicine; the physician's choice of antibiotic depends on the patient's answer to the test question: "Have you ever had an allergic reaction to penicillin?," for example. Cronbach (1957, 1975) first realized that person–environment interaction was both a fundamental concept and a fundamental problem for psychology. Interactional research has now accumulated in a variety of fields of psychology (Endler and Magnusson 1976, Pervin and Lewis 1978). While signs of interactional thinking appear in educational philosophies as old as the Haggadah of Passover or the writings of Quintilian (Snow 1982a), the full implications of aptitude–treatment interaction for education have been systematically addressed only recently (Cronbach and Snow 1977).

1. Substantive Definition and Implications for Education

In education, many kinds of individual differences among learners can be observed and measured. When such measures predict individual differences in learning from instruction, they are interpreted as indicators of aptitude, that is, individual readiness to profit from instruction. When aptitude measures provide differential predictions for learning under different instructional conditions, a conclusion of aptitude–treatment interaction (ATI) is justified. Many kinds of aptitude measures have been studied, including general and special cognitive abilities, personality and motivational attributes, and cognitive styles. Many kinds of instructional treatment comparisons have also been studied. Since ATI findings have often been obtained, there is no doubt that ATI exists in education (Cronbach and Snow 1977, Snow 1977a). But theoretical and practical understanding of the ATI phenomenon has not yet advanced to the point where routine use of ATI in educational planning or instructional design is possible. It is already clear, however, that routine use is both possible and required in educational evaluation. ATI methodology is a requisite part of any evaluation study aimed at comparing alternative educational methods or environments because the evaluation question is never simply: which treatment is best on average? It is always: which treatment is best for each of the individual learners to be served?

Aptitude–treatment interactions are of interest theoretically because they demonstrate construct validity for aptitude and learning measures in a new way: they show how aptitude–learning relations can be experimentally manipulated and thus understood in a causal rather than only a correlational framework. This suggests that neither aptitude constructs nor educational learning processes can be fully understood without reference to one another, and raises the important possibility that common psychological processes underlie both aptitude and learning differences.

Practical interest stems from the possibility that such interactions can be used to adapt instruction to fit different learners optimally (see *Individualizing Teaching*). Many previous attempts at individualizing instruction have failed to eliminate individual differences in learning outcome because they were adapted to individuals only (or mainly) by allowing differences in pace. The hope is that research on ATI can provide decision rules that indicate how to vary instructional conditions in other ways that mesh with particular learner strengths while avoiding particular learner weaknesses. A related hope is that such research will indicate how best to develop aptitudes directly for persons with different initial aptitude profiles (Snow 1982b). Again, the general question for research, and for evaluation studies, is: which of the available or conceivable teaching methods, media, or environments is most likely to provide equality of educational opportunity to each individual learner, for aptitude development and for educational achievement, despite the diversity of initial aptitudes in any group of persons to be served? The commitment to optimal diversity of educational opportunity, for example, to truly adaptive education as defined by Glaser (1977), demands that educational environments be chosen or invented and evaluated within an ATI perspective.

However, ATI research has shown that interactions are complex in education. No simple or general principles for matching students and teachers, teaching methods, or school environments have emerged. This may be in part because investigators are only now learning how to conduct this new kind of study. But it appears due also to the multidimensional, dynamic, often local, and often even transient character of the person–environment interface. Results to date suggest that work toward instructional theories that seek to optimize instruction for individuals in real school settings will need to be built up from continuous local diagnosis, description, and evaluation activities; local instructional models rather than general educational theory seem to be the only realizable goal (Snow 1977b).

2. Statistical Definition and Methodology

An ATI is a statistical interaction—the multiplicative combination of at least one person variable and at least one treatment variable in affecting at least one dependent or instructional outcome variable. ATI exists whenever the regression of outcome from one treatment upon some kind of information about pretreatment personal characteristics differs in slope from the regression of outcome from another treatment on the same information.

Figure 1 gives the basic patterns of possible relationships. Each graph assumes that student aptitude scores taken before instruction and student outcome scores taken after instruction have been plotted, on the abscissa and ordinate respectively, to form a bivariate distribution for each treatment under investigation. Linear regression slopes have been fitted to each such distribution and treatment average effects have been identified (the heavy centered dots). In Fig. 1(a),

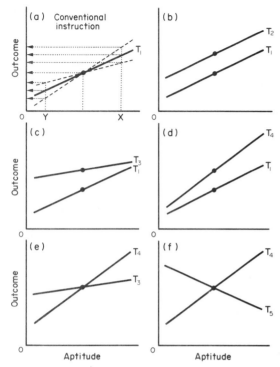

Figure 1
Possible effects of alternative instructional treatments (T)
on outcome averages and outcome-on-aptitude regressions.
See text for discussion

labeled "conventional instruction," the solid slope (T_1) depicts an aptitude–outcome relationship corresponding to a correlation coefficient of 0.50; the dashed slopes depict variation in this relationship between coefficients of 0.30 and 0.70. These data approximate what has often been found in United States public schools, using general intelligence or prior achievement tests as aptitude measures and cognitive achievement measures to reflect instructional outcomes. Note that a student with aptitude score at X is predicted (dotted arrows) to obtain outcome scores in the upper range above the mean while a student with aptitude score at Y is predicted to obtain outcome scores well below the mean.

An important aim of educational research is to improve upon this state of affairs by finding or devising instructional treatments such as T_2 [in Fig. 1(b)] that raise the average outcome for everyone over that expected from T_1. When such regression slopes are parallel, as shown here, there is no ATI; T_2 is the better treatment for all students regardless of aptitude. Unfortunately, many educational studies have looked only for such average treatment differences, assuming that aptitude slopes were parallel without investigating them. The pattern in Fig. 1(c) schematizes the goal of special education and of much research on individualized instruction, where it is hoped that a treatment

T_3 can be found to improve achievement for lower aptitude students such as Y while maintaining the high achievements of higher aptitude students such as X. However, in searching for generally improved treatments the result shown in Fig. 1(d) can also be obtained; treatments such as T_4 turn out to be most beneficial for the higher aptitude students rather than for the lower aptitude students. One can think of T_4 as the goal of special programs for the gifted. The reader can trace the dotted projections for Students X and Y onto these and other graphs to see the differences in predicted outcomes for the different educational treatments.

The T_3 result has at times been obtained for programmed instruction in comparison to conventional instruction T_1, while the T_4 result has sometimes been obtained in studies of discovery or inductive teaching. This leads to the possibility of combined results such as those shown in Fig. 1(e). Here, alternative treatments produce improvements for different kinds of students; it is apparent that T_4 should be given to students such as X, and T_3 should be given to students such as Y. In the extreme, if optimal instructional treatments could be found or devised for students like X and Y, the result depicted in Fig. 1(f) might be expected. Negative slopes approximating T_5 do occur at times using cognitive measures, but are more likely when personality or attitudinal characteristics rather than cognitive abilities are used as aptitudes.

Aptitude–treatment interaction research seeks to detect nonparallel regression slopes of the sorts shown in Fig. 1 and to understand how instructional treatments can be designed to produce such effects. To the extent that stable interactions like those of Fig. 1(e) and 1(f) can be established, they can be used as suggested above to form decision rules for the assignment of students to optimally different treatments. The regression slopes cross to define the point on the aptitude continuum where persons should be divided to achieve optimal outcome in different instructional treatments. The same regression slope expectations apply to compensatory education programs or to other attempts to develop aptitude directly (see Snow 1982b). And, the same patterns can be used to interpret evaluation studies not aimed directly at adapting instruction to individual differences.

Beyond the simplest cases shown in Fig. 1, there are many technical complications involved in particular study designs and data analyses. Aptitude, treatment, and outcome variables can be multiple, and regressions can be nonlinear. Special problems in ATI research attach to the disattenuation of measurements, the evaluation of power of statistical inferences, and the disentangling of regression effects at different levels of aggregation (e.g., individual student, classroom, and school). Since an adaptive instructional system based on ATI would presumably involve periodic aptitude monitoring and reclassification of students, there are also technical issues involved in the sequential assessment of aptitudes and outcomes, and the evaluation of utilities in placement decisions. Further readings and references on these and related topics are available from Cronbach (1982), Cronbach and Gleser (1965), Cronbach and Snow (1977), and Rogosa (1980).

3. Examples of Instructional Models

An instructional model based on ATI can be exemplified using the outline of an adaptive instructional system provided by Glaser (1977) and the results of ATI research reported by Snow (1977a). In Glaser's view (see also Snow 1982a), an adaptive instructional system would contain at least two, and often three or more, alternative instructional routes to successful attainment of some criterion achievement level. Which route or treatment is taken by each learner would depend on an initial diagnosis of aptitude, defined using one or more prior cognitive measures as indices of aptitude or learning readiness. Also available in such a system would be at least one form of compensatory, direct training of aptitude for learners diagnosed as unready for any of the available instructional treatments.

A variety of alternative instructional treatments have been evaluated using measures of prior scholastic ability and generalized achievement as aptitude. From a summary of that research (Snow 1977a), it appears that instructional treatments differ in the information processing burdens they place on, or remove from, the responsibility of the learner, and the regressions of achievement outcome on scholastic ability become steeper or shallower, respectively, as a result. As learners are required to puzzle things out for themselves, to organize their own study, and to build their own comprehension, more able learners do well—they can capitalize on their strengths profitably—while less able learners do poorly. However, as instructional treatments relieve learners from difficult reading and inferencing or analyzing of complex concepts on their own, the more such treatments seem to compensate for or circumvent less able learners' weaknesses. Unfortunately, the structured and simplified treatments that seem to be improved for less able learners are suboptimal for able learners, relative to the more burdensome treatments where they excel. The ATI results from a variety of studies of this hypothesis often approximate the pattern shown in Fig. 1(e), and occasionally that in Fig. 1(f).

For some course of instruction, then, alternative treatment T_4 might be designed to provide relatively unstructured and minimal guidance and to encourage learner self-direction in a discovery-oriented approach. The teacher might guide the inductive process but instruction would clearly be student centered. In contrast, T_3 might be designed to break down the learning task to give clear step-by-step guidance, feedback, and correction through a series of small units, with frequent summary and review, and simplified demonstrations of the use of the concepts to be learned. Students would be assigned to either T_3 or T_4 on the basis of prior scholastic ability scores taken at the start of instruction. Periodic aptitude and achievement assessments would show the degree to which outcome criterion levels were being achieved for each learner in the particular treatment assigned.

For those students with the very lowest prior ability scores, who might not be expected to profit from either alternative, compensatory aptitude training might be assigned. This might consist of directed work on academic learning or reading skills, study habits, self-management skills, and so on. The aim of this direct training would be to develop readiness for entry into treatment T_3 as soon as possible.

As another, related example, student anxiety might also be considered as an aptitude in this adaptive instructional system. It has often been found that more anxious students do relatively poorly under unstructured or student-centered forms of instruction, as compared to teacher-structured conditions. In contrast, less anxious students often appear not to need teacher structure. Furthermore, ability and anxiety appear to combine in higher order interaction in relation to this treatment contrast.

The initial placement decision in the instructional system would thus depend on both prior ability and anxiety indices. Able learners showing little anxiety would be assigned to treatment T_4. The more anxious, able learner and the less able, less anxious learners would receive treatment T_3. The least able and the most anxious students might be given compensatory training adapted to their particular needs—cognitive skills training focused on ability deficits and therapeutic interventions designed to alleviate the effects of anxiety. Periodic monitoring would need to be designed to indicate when particular learners should be switched to alternative treatment assignments.

While these examples provide a simple demonstration here, no such system can be properly designed in the abstract. Local instructional and populational conditions must be considered, aptitude measures and alternative treatment designs must be adjusted to these conditions, and periodic local evaluation must be relied upon to realize an effective system (see Snow 1977b).

4. Prospects for Research and Development

Instructional models based on ATI must be developed locally, and these may be based in turn on a variety of theoretical frameworks involving many different kinds of aptitude constructs and measures, instructional treatments, and outcome criteria. Furthermore, practical improvements in local instructional systems require programmatic research and development; such improvements cannot be derived from the hundreds of isolated studies that have been reported. A few such programmatic lines of research and development have been operating in several places around the world in recent years. One program of work in Ontario, Canada, derives from Hunt and Sullivan (1974). It focuses on teaching adaptations designed to match student cognitive styles. Another, conducted by Gustafsson and Härnqvist (1977) in Göteborg, Sweden, focuses on verbal and spatial abilities in relation to the cognitive demands of different kinds of illustrations in text materials. Still another, directed by Peterson (1977, 1979) in the United States has pursued hypotheses about ability–personality–motivational combinations in relation to alternative styles of teacher and student structuring and participation.

Beyond these programmatic efforts, the ATI approach has opened up important new directions for theory-oriented research. From past studies it has become evident that the aptitude constructs and measures themselves have not been adequately understood. Several lines of cognitive information processing research are now providing analyses of cognitive ability constructs, identifying the underlying component processes and strategies on which individuals may differ (Sternberg 1977, Snow et al. 1980, Underwood 1978). Another approach has been to trace through the individual differences in learning strategies and learning activities engaged in during instruction that appear to mediate aptitude–outcome relations (see Snow 1982a, 1982b). Task analyses of instructional conditions also suggest mediational differences among alternative treatments that may control aptitude–outcome relations (Resnick 1981). Finally, more intensive analysis of outcome measures has led to faceted tests that help diagnose in detail the particular kinds of cognitive effects that derive from particular aptitude–treatment combinations. Future research on all these fronts in instructional psychology can be expected to link up together within the ATI framework.

Bibliography

Cronbach L J 1957 The two disciplines of scientific psychology. *Am. Psychol.* 12: 671–84
Cronbach L J 1975 Beyond the two disciplines of scientific psychology. *Am. Psychol.* 30: 116–27
Cronbach L J 1982 *Designing Evaluations of Educational and Social Programs*. Jossey-Bass, San Francisco, California
Cronbach L J, Gleser G C 1965 *Psychological Tests and Personnel Decisions*, 2nd edn. University of Illinois Press, Urbana, Illinois
Cronbach L J, Snow R E 1977 *Aptitudes and Instructional Methods: A Handbook for Research on Interactions*. Irvington, New York
Endler N S, Magnusson D (eds.) 1976 *Interactional Psychology and Personality*. Hemisphere, Washington, DC
Glaser R 1977 *Adaptive Education: Individual Diversity and Learning*. Holt, Rinehart and Winston, New York
Gustafsson J-E, Härnqvist K 1977 *Begavningstyper och Undervisnings-metoder*. Skolöverstyrelsen, Liberläromedel, Stockholm
Hunt D E, Sullivan E V 1974 *Between Psychology and Education*. Dryden, Hinsdale, Illinois
Pervin L A, Lewis M 1978 *Perspectives in Interactional Psychology*. Plenum, New York
Peterson P L 1977 Interactive effects on student anxiety, achievement orientation and teacher behavior on student achievement and attitude. *J. Educ. Psychol.* 69: 779–92
Peterson P L 1979 Aptitude × treatment interaction effects of teacher structuring and student participation in college instruction. *J. Educ. Psychol.* 71: 521–33
Resnick L B 1981 Instructional psychology. *Annu. Rev. Psychol.* 32: 659–704
Rogosa D 1980 Comparing nonparallel regression lines. *Psychol. Bull.* 88: 307–21
Snow R E 1977a Research on aptitudes: A progress report. In: Shulman L S (ed.) 1977 *Review of Research in Education*, Vol. 4. Peacock, Itasca, Illinois
Snow R E 1977b Individual differences and instructional theory. *Educ. Res. AERA* 6: 11–15
Snow R E 1982a Education and intelligence. In: Sternberg R J (ed.) 1982 *Handbook of Human Intelligence*. Cambridge University Press, New York
Snow R E 1982b The training of intellectual aptitude. In: Detterman D K, Sternberg R J (eds.) 1982 *How and How Much Can Intelligence Be Increased?* Ablex, Norwood, New Jersey
Snow R E, Federico P-A, Montague W E 1980 *Aptitude, Learning, and Instruction*, Vol. 1: *Cognitive Process Analyses of Aptitude*. Vol 2: *Cognitive Process Analyses of Learning and Problem Solving*. Erlbaum, Hillsdale, New Jersey
Sternberg R J 1977 *Intelligence, Information Processing, and Analogical Reasoning: The Componential Analysis of Human Abilities*. Erlbaum, Hillsdale, New Jersey
Underwood G 1978 *Strategies of Information Processing*. Academic Press, London

Behavioral Models

D. Bushell Jr; D. Dorsey

Behavioral models of instruction are systems for arranging the relationships among three variables: prompts, behavior, and consequences. Skinner described these relationships as the "contingencies of reinforcement under which learning takes place" (Skinner 1968 p. 4). Thus, in behavioral models, teaching is the practice of changing the form or occasion of a behavior by deliberately arranging the contingencies of reinforcement. The effects of different contingency arrangements have been clearly described by the laboratory science called the experimental analysis of behavior, which is an outgrowth of Skinner's early work (Skinner 1938). The principles of behavior and learning revealed by experimental analyses specify a great deal about how to form, maintain, change, and eliminate behavior in laboratory settings. The relevance of these principles to human learning in natural social settings began to emerge in the field of applied behavior analysis. The prototype of behavioral models of instruction appeared in the 1950s when Skinner applied the principles of behavior to design the technology of teaching known as programmed instruction (Skinner 1954).

Pieces of the model have been evident at least since Jewish teachers put honey on the pages of scripture they were teaching to boys in the hope that when the young scholars kissed the pages, love of honey would encourage a love of Talmud and love of learning. Medieval knights learned to use a lance by tilting at a device called a quintain. Struck properly in the center, the quintain toppled; improperly, it swung around and knocked the knight from his horse (a rude consequence for an off-center strike). Both examples illustrate arrangements of contingencies of reinforcement, but neither provides a coherent model of instruction. The necessary levels of detail have been specified by the experimental analysis of behavior, and reified by applied behavior analysts, who have used a small number of principles to develop a large number of procedures that arrange prompts and consequences in ways that predictably change behavior.

1. A Few Basic Principles

In the years since Skinner provided the first paradigm for applied behavioral instruction by inventing programmed instruction, new research journals have been created to describe the expanding range of successful social applications. *Behaviour Research and Therapy* was first published in England in 1963, the *Journal of Applied Behavior Analysis* began in the United States in 1968, and they have been joined by scores of others. In all cases, however, the contingencies of reinforcement described in these journals are witness to the same few principles illustrated by the examples of Talmudic scholarship, the blunt persuasiveness of the quintain, and all behavioral models of instruction.

1.1 Behavior is a Function of its Consequences

This simply stated proposition is the keystone of all behavioral models. Behaviors are not acquired or developed by simple repetition; they are strengthened and altered—learned—because of their consequences. Consequences are classified only according to their effects on behavior. Those that strengthen a behavior are classified as reinforcers; those that weaken or reduce responding are classified as punishers.

1.2 Behavior Must Occur Before it Can be Reinforced

Hence, the potential effectiveness of any instructional situation is proportional to the rate at which it provides opportunities to make appropriate responses, and the frequency and magnitude of the reinforcers it can provide for those behaviors.

1.3 Consequences that are Most Immediate are Most Effective

Good instructional contingencies provide frequent on-the-spot consequences for ongoing behavior. Because this presents practical problems in most group instruction settings, behavioral models include procedures for bridging unavoidable gaps between desirable behaviors and their reinforcing consequences.

1.4 Reinforcement Builds New Reinforcers

Events that consistently and repeatedly lead to reinforcement become reinforcing in their own right. If what a student does in a particular classroom is consistently reinforced, the behavior of going to that classroom is likely to become reinforcing. Even the behavior of getting ready to go to that classroom can become reinforcing. The permutations are endless.

1.5 Complex Behaviors—Skills—Develop Gradually

Any behavior that is repeated has slight variations in its form from occurrence to occurrence. By reinforcing only those variations that are closer approximations to the final form of the behavior, a new distribution of variations is developed. The better variation that was previously infrequent (weak) is strengthened, as are the variations close around it. The process is called shaping. The essential procedure is to provide more, or faster, reinforcement for each successive behavior that comes closer to the final form of the behavior.

Even these few basic principles, however, do not constitute a model. Behavioral models of instruction share the characteristic of asking eight questions that arise from these principles. They are questions that call for analyses of the relationships between the learner's behavior and the learner's environment. Because they are common to all behavior analysis programs, these questions, together with the current means for answering them, constitute a behavioral model of instruction. It is a model for planning behavioral change, or teaching.

2. A Model in Eight Questions

Each of the following questions poses both a procedural and a measurement problem. Behavioral models are characterized by the repeated measurement of the behavior of the learner, of the teacher, and of the settings where they occur. Where responding is free and unrestrained (as in an experimental laboratory), the preferred measure is the rate at which a behavior occurs. Where a particular response is appropriate only on certain occasions (as in a classroom where teachers and books ask questions and give instructions), the necessary measures describe the frequency of those occasions, the proportion of those occasions on which the appropriate response was made, and (ideally) the promptness of the response on those occasions. These measures, repeatedly made prior to instruction (the baseline), are not merely compared to the posttreatment scores. Rather, they are repeated continuously to provide a running account of the behavior of interest, the strength of the reinforcement procedures, and the appropriateness of the setting arrangements. It is these repeated measures that govern decisions about what to do next.

2.1 What is the Final Form of the Behavior?

Before any measure can influence practice, the final form of the behavior to be taught must be described. For the student who is currently working with difficulty (at a low rate) in the first chapter of a well-designed arithmetic book, the instructional goal might be to complete the midbook test accurately by the end of the first term, and the last test in the book before the last week of school. As an answer to the question about the final form of the behavior to be taught, the statement is admirable for its simplicity, clarity, and utility. Some detail can be added about accuracy and rate criteria, but the objective is clear enough that a teacher can recognize the presence or absence of day-to-day progress and make decisions about what to do next. Performance goals dealing with social poise, conversation skills, courtesy, and cooperation involve behaviors that do not leave results on paper (permanent products). In these cases, reliable observational records permit informed decisions. The form is different, but the function is exactly the same.

2.2 What are the Components and Prerequisites of the Final Behavior?

Specifying the final form of a behavior describes the top of a hierarchy of skills. Reaching the top requires mastering, each in its turn, the sequence of prerequisite skills in that hierarchy. The process of specifying all the prerequisites of the components of the final performance is called task analysis. The resulting description of the sequence is a curriculum. Consequently, a behavioral curriculum is a sequence of learning objectives in which mastery of lower, simpler skills facilitates learning higher, more complex skills; and the ability to perform more complex skills predicts the ability to perform simpler skills.

The initial pattern for a curriculum is created by a logical analysis of the components of the final behavior—and the prerequisites of those components. From that initial pattern, a behavioral curriculum is built, one student at a time. The problems, slowdowns, and errors of the first student through the sequence point to probable errors or omissions in the task analysis. Those problems indicate the student's lack of some (previously unanalyzed) skill that is needed for continued progress. The curriculum is refined to teach that missing skill. As the errors and problems of successive individual students identify more of the necessary prerequisites, successive refinements produce a curriculum that incorporates all of the skills in the hierarchy topped by the final form of the behavior.

Only a few of the many goals assumed by, or imposed on, schools are supported by curricula that completely identify and teach their component and prerequisite parts. Until recently, the most effective curricula have been the product of creative and artistic teachers and authors. The infrequent product of great artistry is becoming more frequent as behavioral curricula appear in the form of programmed instruction, personalized systems of instruction (PSI), and direct instruction (see *Keller Plan: A Personalized System of Instruction*; *Direct Instruction*).

2.3 What Behavior is Available?

Theoretically, some aspect of the final form of any behavior is always available. The vocal babble of an infant is the seed of oration. Practically, teachers encounter entry behaviors of a limited range. Within that range, different students enter any curriculum with different skills. To avoid subjecting individuals to unnecessary instruction in skills they already have, checkpoints are embedded in the curriculum to assess current ability. A criterion performance at one checkpoint moves the student ahead to the next checkpoint. Poor performance indicates that the student needs to learn the skill taught in the next segment. Checkpoint performance can be observed on formal placement tests, or, for some curricula, in informal conversation with a new student. Once identified, the entering skill marks the beginning point in the instructional sequence leading to the final form of the behavior.

2.4 Are there Sufficient Opportunities to Respond?

Because effective instruction requires frequent responding by the learner, behavioral models arrange lots of opportunities to respond. The time allotted to various activities, the materials provided, the physical arrangement of furniture and supplies, the instructions of teachers, and the examples of peers are all designed to set the occasion for (to prompt) responding—responding that can produce improved approximations and reinforcement. Programmed instruction exemplifies how materials can be designed to increase student responding. The use of paraprofessional teaching aides and peer tutoring procedures, even teaching students to talk to themselves and record their own progress, all illustrate behavioral models' preoccupation with designing techniques for expanding the learners' opportunity to respond with yet another approximation.

2.5 What Reinforcers are Readily Available?

The most attention getting, and most frequently misunderstood, feature of behavioral models of instruction is their deliberate use of contrived reinforcers. It would be ideal if all the responses students are asked to make in school were intrinsically reinforcing. There is, however, little intrinsic reinforcement in the first awkward attempts at any skill. Initial attempts to distinguish letters, read Shakespeare, conjugate a verb, play a piano scale, or tie a shoe are unreinforcing to the point of unpleasant. Neither do they automatically lead to consequences that are naturally reinforcing. Once developed, however, the use of a skill is often reinforced by the natural consequences of reading, the content of the play, or by the effects of persuasive speech, skilled piano performance, or a secure shoe.

To speed progress from unpleasant awkwardness to dexterity, behavioral models use a variety of contrived reinforcers. Whatever their form, they permit the teacher to deliver relatively immediate reinforcement to early approximations of a skill. These teacher-managed reinforcers are delivered less quickly and less often as skill improves. Thus, while the teacher's rate of delivering reinforcers may appear to be uniform, the contingency is constantly changing as successively better approximations are reinforced; or as one skill is turned over to natural reinforcers and yet another becomes the object of temporary contrived support.

Contrived reinforcers must be easy to deliver to an individual quickly and frequently without interrupting ongoing behavior. The many reinforcement systems devised by behavioral programs fall into two categories: those that provide attention and approval contingent on appropriate or improved responding, and those that provide contingent access to preferred activities.

Some of the earliest experimental classroom applications of contingencies of reinforcement demonstrated, in the opening years of the 1960s, that the behaviors of preschool children that were immediately followed by a teacher's attention rapidly rose to a high rate, and fell to a low rate when that attention was withdrawn or shifted. Since the 1960s, the reinforcing function of contingent social attention has been reconfirmed countless times and extended to include the attention of school principals, older students, and age mates. Teacher attention is a powerful reinforcer, but it can be difficult to manage well. The danger of accidental attention to inappropriate behavior is chronic; and the attention of some people is inherently more reinforcing than that of others. These problems may be reduced by new procedures being developed to teach children to observe their own behavior and accurately distinguish when it is good.

Contingent access to preferred activities is a different, but complementary system that takes many forms. In every case, however, the learner provides some amount of necessary behavior (teacher requested), in exchange for the opportunity to engage in some amount of reinforcing activity (student selected). Providing free time contingent on accurate assignment completion is an easy and frequent application of this technique. Some teachers have negotiated formal performance contracts with students. The principle is the same when classroom token systems award a token, along with praise, to the learner's good performance or improved response. Numbers of accumulated tokens can later be exchanged for the opportunity to engage in a favorite activity. It is a system that depends on the teacher's ability to arrange an array of reinforcing activities from which students may select, according to their preferences and the number of tokens they have accumulated. All the versions of this system take advantage of the fact that the opportunity to choose is a reinforcer; and they make allowance for the fact that what is preferred differs from child to child and from time to time (see *Reinforcement*).

2.6 How can Reinforcement be Scheduled?

As initial responses occur, the more desirable variations are reinforced more enthusiastically. Shaping is a gradual process that treats yesterday's new accomplishments as today's beginning point. It is more an art than it is the application of a formula. Reinforcement must be held contingent on improvement, but not require too much improvement. If it is withheld pending an improvement beyond current ability, reinforcement stops, and so does responding. When this happens the sequence is restarted by dropping back to an earlier, readily available approximation and restoring the former vigor of the behavior.

Just as problems are created by progressing too rapidly, too much reinforcement for a single variation will reduce the variability needed for further progress. Thus, the criterion must be raised just far enough, but not too far, to generate successively better performance. A few textbooks, well-built programmed instructional materials, and carefully designed PSI courses are constructed to call progressively for more sophisticated responding. Although such materials reduce the artistry required of the teacher, effective shaping continues to be a product of teacher vigilance and judgment.

Because any event, including a behavior, that consistently leads to reinforcement is likely to become reinforcing itself, engaging in the behavior being shaped often becomes reinforcing. As it does, there is progressively less need for the consistent and immediate delivery of the teacher's contrived reinforcers. Their delivery is delayed, made more intermittent, and less predictable. Progressively, more of the immediate contingencies are contained within the activity itself. The form of the resulting behavior has been called good motivation, self-control, and maturity. Whatever it is called, it is the product of carefully arranged contingencies of reinforcement. It is taught.

2.7 What are the Natural Contingencies of Reinforcement?

Much of the literature describing classroom applications of behavior analysis has resulted from teachers' requests for help in dealing with the disruptive and undesirable behavior of uncooperative students. Published accounts describing the correction of these problems early established the existence of a large collection of techniques that allowed teachers to manage their classrooms better (see *Classroom Management*). The procedures of classroom management are those of any behavioral model of instruction with one important exception. Classroom management procedures teach students how to behave in a particular teacher's classroom. That specific form of conduct is determined by the personal style and tolerance levels of an individual teacher, not necessarily teachers in general. The behavior taught is appropriate to the setting in which it is taught. That is the exception.

The term instruction, as opposed to management, implies that the behaviors taught have value outside the instructional setting. Behavioral models of instruction seek to teach skills that will make contact with, and be sustained by, natural contingencies of reinforcement outside the training setting. Natural contingencies are not very good teachers, but they provide precise, dependable, and durable reinforcers for established skills. The world outside the classroom may not teach reading, but it provides many reinforcers for skillful reading. Identifying the natural contingencies available to support a particular skill is fundamental to constructing the instructional sequence so it will put *that* skill in contact with *those* contingencies.

2.8 Are the First Seven Answers Socially Acceptable?

The ingredients of all behavioral models of instruction can be simply described because they are coherently related to each other and to a few basic principles. They embrace a range of practical techniques that can be used by anyone in the role of teacher to improve the skills of students. Because of their effectiveness, behavioral models have been applied to a variety of student populations and instructional problems around the world. The rate at which this growth in application will continue depends on the social approval accorded each program identified as behavioral.

Wolf (1978) has made a persuasive case that a behavioral program, or any program, is socially valued to the extent that all of its consumers endorse its goals, approve its procedures, and appreciate its results. For programs, as for individuals, performances that are reinforced by social approval will grow and multiply. If social approval is withheld, that form of program will weaken and finally disappear. It is the natural process that Skinner (1981) calls "selection by consequences."

Consequently, the final question amends the prior questions in one specific way, so they now read: (a) What is the final form of the socially valued behavior to be taught? (b) What are the components and prerequisites of that final behavior? (c) What behavior is available? (d) Are there sufficient opportunities to respond in socially acceptable ways? (e) What socially acceptable reinforcers are readily available? (f) How can reinforcement be scheduled to develop the behavior in the most effective and socially acceptable way? and (g) How can the behavior be sustained by naturally occurring, socially approved, contingencies of reinforcement outside the teaching situation?

Behavioral models of instruction that incorporate Wolf's lesson by devising techniques for staying in touch with, and being responsive to, the fundamental issue of consumer satisfaction will find support from the natural contingencies of reinforcement provided by an appreciative and approving society. It is the ultimate reassurance that only the best among the many behavioral models of instruction will survive to reproduce their own kind.

See also: Classroom Management; Direct Instruction; Reinforcement

Bibliography

Becker W C, Engelmann S, Thomas D R 1975 *Teaching*, Vol. 1: *Classroom Management*. Science Research Associates, Palo Alto, California

Bijou S W, Baer D M 1961 *Child Development*, Vol. 1: *A Systematic and Empirical Theory*. Appleton–Century–Crofts, New York

Brigham T A, Hawkins R, Scott J W, McLaughlin T F 1976 *Behavior Analysis In Education: Self-Control and Reading*. 5th Conference on behavior analysis in education, Kansas City 1974. Kendall/Hunt, Dubuque, Iowa

Catania A C, Brigham T A 1978 *Handbook of Applied Behavior Analysis: Social and Instructional Processes*. Irvington, New York

Skinner B F 1938 *The Behavior of Organisms: An Experimental Analysis*. Appleton–Century–Crofts, New York

Skinner B F 1953 *Science and Human Behavior*. Macmillan, New York

Skinner B F 1954 The science of learning and the art of teaching. *Harvard Educ. Rev.* 24: 86–97

Skinner B F 1968 *The Technology of Teaching*. Appleton–Century–Crofts, New York

Skinner B F 1981 Selection by consequences. *Science* 213: 501–04

Wolf M M 1978 Social validity: The case for subjective measurement or how applied behavior analysis is finding its heart. *J. Appl. Behav. Anal.* 11: 203–14

The Carroll Model

C. M. Clark

In 1963 John B. Carroll published a paper entitled "A Model of School Learning" in which he proposed the then novel idea that all of the variables that directly influence the learning of children in school could be defined in terms of time. As Carroll began to define his model, he briefly and clearly stated the essential idea expressed in the model: ". . . the learner will succeed in learning a given task to the extent that he spends the amount of time that he needs to learn the task" (Carroll 1963 p. 725). This simple idea was then elaborated by defining the factors that influence the amounts of time needed by individual learners and the time actually spent engaged in trying to learn. The reason that Carroll gave for expressing the components of his model in terms of time was "to capitalize on the advantages of a scale with a meaningful zero point and equal units of measurement" (Carroll 1963 p. 724).

1. Why Model School Learning?

Carroll's paper is addressed directly to his fellow educational psychologists. He defines the job of the educational psychologist as "to develop and apply knowledge about why pupils succeed or fail in their learning at school, and to assist in the prevention and remediation of learning difficulties" (Carroll 1963 p. 723). His focus is directly on learning, not teaching. It is clear that he believed that learning is the central purpose of schooling, at least as far as educational psychologists are concerned. His statement of the problem is that, while the field of educational psychology has produced a great deal of knowledge relevant to learning and behavior, these concepts and findings are "difficult to build . . . into an integrated account of the process of school learning" (Carroll 1963 p. 723). Carroll goes on to say that what he has to offer is a "schematic design or conceptual model of factors affecting school learning and of the way they interact" (Carroll 1963 p. 723). His hope is that his model will accomplish three things: (a) suggest new research questions; (b) aid in the solution of practical educational problems; and (c) help to reconcile the often conflicting results of different research studies.

2. Assumptions of the Model

Before Carroll defined the elements of his model, he specified a crucially important set of three simplifying assumptions. First, the model assumes that the work of the school can be broken down into a series of discrete learning tasks. Task can be defined broadly or narrowly, but Carroll's use of the term requires that "the task can be unequivocally described and that means can be found for making a valid judgment as to when the learner has accomplished the learning task—that is, has achieved the learning goal which has been set for him" (Carroll 1963 p. 724). Second, Carroll points out that the model applies to only one learning task at a time, but that it should be possible to describe a student's success in learning a series of tasks (e.g., all the work of a certain school year) by summating the results of applying the model to each component task. The third simplifying assumption of the model is that it is not intended to apply to goals of the school that have to do with attitudes and dispositions (what would today be called social and emotional goals of schooling). While Carroll acknowledges that learning tasks may play a role in support of attitude development, "the acquisition of attitudes is postulated to follow a different paradigm from that involved in learning tasks" (Carroll 1963 p. 724).

One final caveat that Carroll makes about his model is a disclaimer that it should not be confused with what is ordinarily called "learning theory." His model is intended as a "description of the 'economics' of the school learning process" (Carroll 1963 p. 725) rather than as an exact scientific analysis of the essential conditions for and process of learning itself. Carroll's use of the expression "economics of school learning" is telling, for it suggests that behind his model lies a metaphor of the school or classroom as an economic entity—a factory producing learning in task units, with teachers acting as supervisors and managers, and with children as the laborers working on an individual piece work basis.

At this point it is useful to summarize what Carroll intended to offer his readers in 1963. In order to use the model it is necessary to accept the assumption that school learning (or an important part of it) can be validly described as a series of discrete learning tasks that can be combined in a simple additive fashion. Furthermore, the model applies to only one particular learner at a time. In short, one has the promise of a model of the factors influencing individuals learning cognitive tasks that take place in schools, expressed in terms of time.

3. Components of the Model

For a particular learner attempting a particular learning task, the Carroll Model states that the degree of learning will be a function of the amount of time the learner actually spends on the learning task to the total amount needed. Carroll expresses this symbolically as:

$$\text{Degree of learning} = f\left(\frac{\text{time actually spent}}{\text{time needed}}\right)$$

Time actually spent on the learning task is defined as being equal to the smallest of three variables:

(a) Opportunity—the time allowed for learning.

(b) Perseverance—the time the learner is willing to engage actively in learning.

(c) Aptitude—the amount of time needed to master the task under ideal conditions, increased by whatever amount necessary in view of poor quality of instruction and lack of ability to understand less than optimal instruction (Carroll 1963 p. 730).

Therefore, the numerator of this ratio can be established by a teacher (allocating little or no time for a learning task), by the student (who may be unwilling to spend any time attempting the task), or by interaction of student aptitude and student ability to understand instruction with the quality of instruction. The denominator of the fraction is aptitude—time needed to learn after adjustment for quality of instruction and ability to understand instruction. (Note that aptitude is also one of the three possible values of the numerator.)

Both teacher and student can influence the size of the denominator.

The model uses only five variables to explain degree of student learning of particular tasks: aptitude, ability to understand instruction, quality of instruction, opportunity to learn, and perseverance. The first three of these determine time needed to learn a task and the last two determine time actually spent in learning. Let us take a closer look at how Carroll defined each of these three variables.

3.1 Aptitude

Perhaps the most novel feature of the Carroll model of school learning is its definition of learning aptitude as the time required to master a particular learning task under ideal conditions. Carroll moved away from the concept of aptitude as a relatively fixed and generic ability to perform various kinds of learning tasks, and substituted learning rate as the operational definition of aptitude. In so defining aptitude, Carroll acknowledged that many factors may influence a student's learning rate, including task-specific prior experience (learning history) and genetically or environmentally determined traits and predispositions. However, the model was not intended as an explanation of the genesis and development of learning aptitudes. Rather, Carroll simply used the empirical observation of variation in individuals' rates of learning task completion as the definition of the most important of his three student individual difference variables.

3.2 Ability to Understand Instruction

This variable is distinct from student aptitude and has two components: (a) general intelligence, and (b) verbal ability. Carroll's reasoning is that, in tasks in which the burden of making inferences, conclusion, and deductions falls heavily on the learner, general intelligence would be an important moderator of learning rate. In tasks in which the language of instruction is complex or unfamiliar, the verbal ability of the student would moderate learning rate.

3.3 Quality of Instruction

Carroll describes high quality instruction as consisting of specification of learning objectives, communication of these objectives and learning procedures to students, optimal sequencing of learning activities, clarity of teacher language, and appropriate accommodation of the process of instruction to special needs and characteristics of the learner. When these stringent conditions are met, the learner can master the task as efficiently and rapidly as his or her aptitude permits. But teaching seldom meets this standard of perfection. When quality of instruction is less than optimal, the learner may be able to compensate somewhat through exercise of superior ability to understand instruction. The model predicts that less than perfectly organized and delivered instruction will increase the time required for mastery of a learning task (see *Mastery Learning Models*).

3.4 Opportunity to Learn

An important function of teacher planning is allocating instructional time to particular learning tasks. In an ideal situation, every topic in the curriculum would be allocated exactly the amount of time that each learner needs to master it. But time is limited in schools, and individual differences in learning rate are often large. Teachers typically must compromise by allocating a "reasonable" amount of time for each learning task and by adjusting the pace of instruction so that most students succeed. In Carroll's model, opportunity to learn refers to the maximum amount of time that a learner actually could have spent attempting to master a school learning task. Insufficient opportunity to learn will, of course, lower the probability of task mastery. Excessive opportunity to learn may also have deleterious effects on the motivation of fast learners.

3.5 Perseverance

Perseverance is defined as the amount of time that a student is willing to spend learning. Carroll postulates that the concept of motivation for learning plays a large part in determining how long a student will persist at a learning task. Motivation, in turn, may be influenced by interest in the subject matter, intrinsic and extrinsic rewards, tolerance of uncertainty or frustration, and other factors. Like aptitude, perseverance is a task-specific individual difference variable. Like opportunity to learn, insufficient perseverance in attempting to learn a given task will limit mastery of the task.

4. An Example of the Carroll Model in Action

John B. Carroll offered his model as a useful tool in framing research questions for educational researchers. To illustrate the ways in which his model may be used, an example of a current puzzle in American education can be considered: the decline in test scores of secondary-school students. From 1967 until 1981, the average scores achieved by high-school students on the Scholastic Aptitude Test (SAT), an instrument widely used in university admission decisions, were declining. The size of the decline was significant, amounting to about 70 points on a scale of 200–800 during the intervening 14 years. To date, no satisfactory explanation has been discovered, although the second component of the Carroll model (see below) may account for part; that is, there was an increase in the proportion of low-ability students taking the exams.

How would the Carroll model of school learning guide researchers in an attempt to solve the test score decline puzzle? They would consider each of the five components of the model and generate hypotheses about how changes in each of these components might contribute to test score decline. Then they would create a test of each of these hypotheses and proceed to determine whether each hypothesis is supported. The parsimony of having only five major variables to explain school learning makes the model very attractive as an organizer for inquiry.

Before each part of the model is examined in relation to the test score decline issue, two assumptions must be specified. First, it must be assumed that the Scholastic Aptitude Test is measuring performance that is directly related to school learning (a question of test validity). To the extent that this assumption is valid, Carroll's model of school learning should help in understanding the reasons for the test score decline and perhaps suggest ways to continue the reversal of the trend. Second, it must be assumed that the test score decline is not an artifact of changes in the form, content, or method of scoring of the test.

Each of the five elements of the Carroll model will be considered in turn. First, there is aptitude. Remembering the unique way in which Carroll defines aptitude, it is necessary to ask what might have contributed to slowing down the rate of learning and performance of secondary-school students, beginning in 1967. The vast majority of students who take the Scholastic Aptitude Test are juniors and seniors in high school (age 16 to 18). If indeed their rate of learning and performance slowed down, it could have been due to factors present during the high-school years, or to influences that acted during the elementary-school years or before, but were not appreciated until the students sat for the examination. A further puzzle here is that the test score decline, once begun, became larger each year until a halt in 1981. This suggests that the cause of the change was not a one-time perturbation of learning or performance, but rather a cumulative influence, affecting each succeeding cohort of students more severely.

The second component of the Carroll model is ability to understand instruction. What factors could have affected one or both of the elements of ability to understand instruction: general intelligence and verbal ability? Have average scores on general intelligence and verbal ability tests declined in parallel with the decline in SAT scores? Did a different population with lower general intelligence and verbal ability begin to take the SAT in 1967?

Third, the quality of instruction must be considered. Have teachers and the way that they teach changed significantly and in a cumulatively negative way since the early 1960s? In attempting to answer this question the changing demographics of the teaching profession, the effects of unionization and collective bargaining, changes in teacher education, changes in the average intelligence and academic performance of undergraduate education majors, and changes in the ways that instruction is actually organized and delivered in the classroom could be examined.

Opportunity to learn is the fourth variable in the Carroll model. In considering the possible influence of change in opportunity to learn on SAT performance decline, both the information and skills needed by a student to answer test questions correctly and also the familiarity of students with testing situations of the sort experienced in the SAT must be considered. The first consideration leads directly to an examination of the curriculum of elementary and secondary schools. What changes have taken place in what is taught in schools and in the amount of time devoted to these topics in the years that led up to the beginning of the test score decline? Has the curriculum or the content of the test changed in such a way that they overlap less than was formerly the case? Has the school curriculum become so crowded with electives and new topics that less time is available to learn and practice those subject matters sampled on the SAT? Have school absenteeism, truancy, and the transience of the North American family resulted in fewer hours or days of school per year for the average child? Have school districts shortened the number of hours of actual instruction for economic or other reasons? Are students less familiar with taking standardized tests under rigidly enforced testing conditions?

Finally, the possible contributions of a change in student perseverance to the test score decline will be considered. What pedagogical or social changes might have operated to decrease student motivation to perform well on the test in question? What could have reduced student motivation to learn the information and skills measured by such tests? Have the relatively relaxed admissions policies of many colleges and universities eroded the significance of SAT scores as a determiner of admission to higher education? Has the alleged increase of permissiveness in schools influenced students to try less hard to learn or to perform well on tests? Is there any evidence in the test data themselves that suggests that students are completing fewer items, spending less time per item, or giving up on challenging test items?

The purpose of this example has been to illustrate how the Carroll model of school learning could be used to organize inquiry into an educational issue. As has been seen, the model can serve as a powerful heuristic device for generating questions and hypotheses about issues that did not even exist at the time that the model was first presented. This alone is a significant contribution to educational research and practice. But beyond this, the Carroll model of school learning has been used to generate research and development as diverse as mastery learning (Block 1971, Bloom 1974) (see *Mastery Learning Models*), the Keller Plan (see *Keller Plan: A Personalized System of Instruction*) for individualized instruction (Keller 1968), policy research on length of the school day and school year (Wiley and Harnischfeger 1974), classroom research on time and learning (Berliner 1979) (see *Time*), curriculum research in international education (Carroll 1975), and econometric analyses of classroom instruction (Brown and Saks 1981). It can even be argued that the recent focus of educational research on classroom management (see *Classroom Management*) was influenced by Carroll's implied metaphor of the school as a production system and the derivative role of the teacher as a manager. The Carroll model of school learning has stood the test of time as a powerful tool for conceptualizing educational issues and organizing systematic research to explore them.

See also: Time; Opportunity to Learn

Bibliography

Berliner D 1979 Tempus Educare. In: Peterson P L, Walberg H J (eds.) 1979 *Research on Teaching*. McCutchan, Berkeley, California

Block J H (ed.) 1971 *Mastery Learning: Theory and Practice*. Holt, Rinehart and Winston, New York

Bloom B S 1974 Time and learning. *Am. Psychol.* 29:, 682–88

Brown B, Saks D 1981 The microeconomics of schooling. In: Berliner D (ed.) 1981 *Review of Research in Education*, Vol. 9. American Educational Research Association, Washington, DC, pp. 217–54

Carroll J B 1963 A model of school learning. *Teach. Coll. Rec.* 64: 723–33

Carroll J B 1975 *Teaching French as a Foreign Language in Eight Countries*. International Studies in Evaluation, Vol. 5. Almqvist and Wiksell, Stockholm

Keller F S 1968 "Good-bye, Teacher . . ." *J. Appl. Behav. Anal.* 1: 79–89

Wiley D E, Harnischfeger A 1974 Explosion of a myth: Quantity of schooling and exposure to instruction, major educational vehicles. *Educ. Res. AERA*. 3(4): 7–12

Information Processing Models

L. Corno; M. Edelstein

The manner in which diverse information can be processed—that is, integrated, reduced to categories, symbolically transformed, stored, and subsequently retrieved—has long been the focus of artificial intelligence research. As a model of the human mind, the computer has been used to interpret perceptual displays, solve problems, play strategy games, and teach subject matter, among other things. Such analyses have helped explicate the processes and knowledge that underlie cognitive endeavor, so improvements may be made. They have also added an important dimension to the understanding and potential improvement of teaching and instruction.

The first generation of instructional research was dominated by behavioral research models and B. F. Skinner's operant learning paradigm. Studies representative of this generation investigated the influence of instructional variations such as feedback and reinforcement, systematic practice, and pacing on student response. Knowledge was gained from such studies about how learning may be maximized under a variety of instructional conditions. But the effectiveness of different instructional manipulations was found to vary across studies, particularly as experimental conditions became more representative of real-world instruction (as in classrooms, for example). This generation of research was not able to explain the practice of teaching and instruction under less optimal conditions, where critical environmental variables are uncontrolled and subjects are heterogeneous. Here student responses are seen to depend on a variety of factors that interact—or occur in combination—with the nature of instruction. Student aptitude, teacher characteristics, and structural features of the subject matter are examples. The advent of cognitive psychology has given instructional researchers a way to refine the meaning of terms like student "aptitude," teacher "characteristics," and "structural" features of subject matter. Such refinement has opened the door to investigations of the mental processes underlying and resulting from oral and written instruction.

Information-processing models of instruction are many and varied. Some models are representations of teacher thinking during classroom instruction (instruction where teachers and students communicate verbally). This family of models includes models of teacher "decision making," of how teachers cope with the information "overloads" in classrooms, of how they consciously structure and direct the flow of classroom information, and of how they analyze and use pedagogical theories in practice. In other models the focus is on students and how their mental processes direct the flow of instruction. Models of tutoring (see *Tutoring*), of computer-assisted instruction, of concept attainment, and of learning from text fall into this family. And finally, there are information-processing models that highlight the interaction among the thinking of instructors and students as they address subject matter—models of instruction in the broader sense.

Walter Doyle (1977) has termed the study of mental processes that occur during instruction the "mediating process" research paradigm. In contrast to the operant learning paradigm, here mental processes of teachers and learners are presumed to alter the influence teacher and learner behavior and curricula might have on student outcomes during instruction. Below are described representative examples from each of the three above-defined families of models—where the teacher, the student, or the teacher–student interaction is focal, respectively. While these families are not totally distinct (some models might reasonably fit into one or the other category), the separation is useful for discussion purposes.

Another distinction that bears definition has been made between "stable" and "unstable" instructional systems. A system of instruction is considered stable if the available instructional cues are known. Written instruction of all forms is thus a stable instructional system, but its stability may be compromised if unpredicted events are permitted to alter the flow of instruction. Interactive instruction, such as computer-assisted instruction (CAI) and programmed material, is potentially more stable than noninteractive written instruction such as textbooks, since it attempts to control the student's attention in specific ways. Classroom teaching (when not controlled by research design) is of course an unstable instructional system. Interruptions inevitably compromise the flow of classroom teaching and various instructional cues are not known in advance. Like the distinction among families of models, the stable–unstable distinction is useful for categorizing the information-processing models. In less stable instructional systems it is generally more important to consider the thought processes of persons other than or in addition to the student (like thought processes of the teacher), so that the interaction among teachers and students becomes more focal.

Following descriptions of the various models is a discussion of major difficulties inherent to all information-processing models. Perceived advantages ought to be balanced by appropriate concerns. The final section also describes general instructional processes that are common to the models outlined.

1. Teacher-focused Models

The teacher-focused models described range from (a) the pioneering and more recent models of interactive teacher decision making and judgments, which have spawned theoretically based research on classroom information processing, to (b) selected information processing, "models of teaching" developed by Joyce and Weil (1978, 1980) as vehicles for training teachers in classroom applications of information processing concepts and techniques. An effort has been made to draw into the discussions of these models, implications for classroom teaching and teacher training or recent theory and research as appropriate.

1.1 A Model of Teacher Classroom Decision Making

There are a number of models of teacher decision making (see *Interactive Decision Making*). These may be distinguished according to the context in which decisions are made. For example, Shulman and Elstein (1975) describe a model of clinical decision making where teachers process information similar to the way in which physicians plan, anticipate, judge, diagnose, prescribe, and solve problems. In this model the decision-making context is assumed to be different for different individual students (who will have different diagnosed needs). Another decision-making context is preactive planning (see *Planning*)—teachers make decisions about topics and teaching strategies, for example, before they enter the classroom. Clark and Yinger (1977) present a model of teacher planning in which planning is "the progressive elaboration of a major idea, in contrast to the development of a number

of alternatives and selection of the optimum alternative from this set" (p. 300). In the context of the classroom itself, preactive decisions interact with on-the-spot decisions made with less regard for individual students than for the average level of the classroom group on factors important to learning. Shavelson (1976) has described a five-featured model which is perhaps the most comprehensive of the classroom context models.

According to Shavelson, teachers analyze aspects of five features to decide how they will behave in the classroom. The five features include goals or objectives for student learning and behavior, "states of nature," alternative teaching acts, in-progress student outcomes, and the utility of those outcomes for the teacher. Teachers confront these five features in both the planning and interactive phases of instruction.

For example, when teachers confront the issue of what is expected of students, they are seen in this model to assign priority to alternative behavioral, socio-emotional, and cognitive goals. Assigned priorities typically reflect a combination of the teacher's personal preferences and skills and the curriculum foci of the school and community. Whatever instructional goals are selected affect the teacher's focus and behavior in the classroom.

"States of nature" are also seen as subjectively deduced by teachers, again before and during instruction. These include estimates of students' relative standing on cognitive and socioemotional variables, and characteristics of the school environment, such as the attitudes of school administrators and classroom activity levels. The model holds that teachers estimate states of nature by comparing current situations to past situations whose details they know, by matching their perceptions to their existing knowledge of student behavior patterns, and by adjusting their deduction as they gain new information about the current situation.

The features of student outcomes and utilities are combined in this model, with the rationale that the utility or payoff for a course of action (given a specific state of nature) is largely determined by its outcome (positive or negative; meeting or missing an initial objective). Utility occurs when positive outcomes follow from appropriately selected teaching acts. For example, a positive student outcome—that learning occurred following a certain teaching act and state of nature estimate—has high utility for future teacher decisions. A negative student outcome following a similar pattern of activity has low future utility. Teachers make decisions about what to continue teaching, and how to continue teaching it, on the basis of such utility estimates made during teaching.

The model specifies that teachers weigh each of these five features rationally, using what is assessed as the most probable interpretation of each factor, to make decisions. Teachers fix on a curriculum objective or goal—be it specific and behavioral or general and more philosophical—in either the planning or interactive stages of teaching. They also make some estimate of the states of nature that prevail based on what they perceive as the likely probabilities of such states. For instance, at the beginning of a lesson a teacher may use lower order questions because the estimate is that the class's knowledge of the lecture topic (state of nature) at that particular moment is low. Later in the lesson the teacher may use higher order questions because the state of nature estimate has changed. The teacher adjusts, choosing from among what Shavelson calls "alternative courses of action," according to that change. As teaching acts begin to demonstrate high payoff, or utility, they are added to the teacher's repertoire of frequently used techniques.

Rational views of teacher decision making are fallible to the extent that the "real" manner in which instructional decisions are made can be shown to be nonrational or otherwise biased. Shavelson (1978) has used psychological research on biases in human judgment and decision making to outline several potential sources of teacher decision bias as a focus for further research. As studies indicate the extent to which teachers' instructional decisions are more or less rational, Shavelson's model will be adapted and revised.

1.2 A Model of Teacher Perceptual Judgments

Following this line of research on teacher decision making, Marland (1979) developed a "customized response" model of teacher perceptual judgments (see *Teachers' Judgments*) using a research technique known as "stimulated recall." Stimulated recall involves having teachers view videotapes of their teaching to identify and discuss instructional decision points. Marland's model describes a particular thought sequence that teachers he observed characteristically followed as they considered instructional tactics to use in the classroom. The three ideational units, and the chief junctions in the preparation of those classroom tactics, are "perception," "interpretation," and "prospective tactical deliberation."

The sequence begins with a perception, which Marland argues, tends to be limited to more obvious classroom stimuli, such as student noise, inattention, or movement, rather than more subtle stimuli, such as facial expressions. The teacher assigns a meaning to the perception according to his or her existing mental representations or schemata. If no meaning is available in long-term memory, the teacher attempts to construct meaning from environmental cues and existing related information.

Once a meaning is established, an interpretation is made. Consistent with Shavelson's "estimates of student states," Marland's interpretations include inferences about student's emotions, and their cognitive states. Marland's teachers also attributed to students certain motives for their behavior. An important finding from Marland's research was that the teachers did not check their interpretations in any consistent way—they tended to assume their interpretations of students were accurate, even though they might not have been.

Once the interpretation was made, Marland's teachers searched their memories for a suitable instructional tactic. If none was uncovered, the teacher mentally planned new and appropriate tactics. Marland was concerned that teachers sometimes planned tactics without considering the alternatives, or considered too few alternatives, when they did use a rational approach. The teachers in this study typically generated only two alternative instructional approaches at decision points rather than examining a range of possible tactics and weighing which might be best. Most importantly, perhaps, Marland perceived his teachers as underconcerned with the quality of improvement of generated alternatives. Alternatives teachers mentioned seemed to arise almost spontaneously with less deliberate analysis than Marland expected to observe.

The possibility that teachers perceive their role as more intuitive than reflective is supported by additional findings from Marland's study. First, when there were "flurries of activity" in the classroom, teachers appeared to make fewer decisions. Marland speculated that their attention may have been diverted from contemplative internal decision making and monopolized by the perceptual demands of classroom events. Alternatively, teachers' decisions may have been so rapid-fire in these situations that they remained at a preconscious level (and this did not get reported). Second, the "cognitive overload" of such activity flurries somehow may obscure teachers' confidence in their teaching ability. In dealing with a high level of classroom activity teachers may lose perspective on their own roles and their effects on students. Marland did find his model used less often by the middle-school teachers than by elementary teachers. He suggests this difference may be due to the fact that middle-school teachers have less activity flurry to monitor, increasing their ability to employ deliberate tactics.

This research and the revised teacher judgment model it supports have implications for teacher preparation programs supported also by other research on teacher thinking (e.g., Clark and Yinger 1977). First, teacher preparation programs might profitably address ways to help teachers focus their perceptions during instructional activity flurries so they can maintain a rational demeanor. And second training might also instruct teachers in ways to use environmental cues to make unbiased interpretations and in the dangers of letting personal stereotypes or beliefs interfere with the unbiased evidence.

1.3 An Advanced Organizer Model of Teaching

A number of "information processing models of teaching" were developed by Joyce and Weil (1978, 1980) from an analysis of psychological learning theories. Among these is the "advance organizer model" derived from Ausubel's theory of how learning can be improved by using the propositional structure of subject matter to anchor information in memory. An advance organizer is defined by Ausubel as introductory information presented at a higher level of abstraction or generality. Joyce and Weil designed their teaching model for use in lecture-format classrooms, where the amount of information conveyed has priority over the means of processing.

By Joyce and Weil's analysis, teachers intending to use advance organizers in lectures will need a strong grasp of their subject matter, including an understanding of its propositional structure—which concepts are most abstract and which are instantiations, for example. An understanding of this structure will permit the teacher to devise alternative advance organizers, which may then be used in the lecture as "scaffolding" upon which students can be led to build up subject matter knowledge. A sentence like the following was described by Bruner as an advance organizer for learning sentence grammar: "The man ate his lunch." The sentence contains the critical parts of all sentences, which the skillful teacher can identify as higher order categories, and use to promote student-generated sentences that exemplify the categories (e.g., "A boy stole a bike.").

> . . . There are five places and you can put lots of things in each place. But which kinds of words will fit into each column? Type and token begin to emerge as ideas. Now we reach a very critical point. Ask, for example, whether they (students) can make up some more columns. (Bruner 1966 p. 106)

A critical aspect of the model is that the organizer is actually used by students during the lesson to build up knowledge of the subject. The teacher makes the presence of the advance organizer known, then gives examples from the subject that make the relationship between the advance organizer and the subject clear. For an organizer that concerns the representation of cultural trends in art, a teacher would think of how certain artwork demonstrates this and use such examples in the lecture. The subject here is art, but the organizer—art's cultural meaning—sets the subject in a context that makes it more memorable for students. To draw out this context, the teacher has to consider alternative advance organizers and their probable effects on the way students perceive and process the subject matter. He or she must also estimate the possible effects of such alternative organizers and select one that will be likely to accomplish the planned objective.

Ausubel identified three activities that distinguish lecturing based on this model from traditional lecturing. The advance organizer promotes "integrative reconciliation" by focusing students on the relationships (a) among parts of an idea, and (b) between the idea's parts and its whole. It also aids "active reception learning" by taking into account the student's frame of reference in the presentation of new material and by having students take on alternative points of view. A third distinguishing aspect of advance organizer lecturing is that it is necessarily structured around the principles that define a discipline. There are principles of art, for example, which set it apart or define it as a discipline

(e.g., that it is expressive of culture). When students are given such information to use as they investigate artwork they have broader categories within which they can view specific representations, and their experience, as a consequence, should be enriched.

1.4 A Model of Inquiry Teaching

A second information-processing model of teaching developed by Joyce and Weil (1978, 1980) is the "inquiry training model," based on the work of Richard Suchman. Inquiry training is defined as a "process for investigating and explaining unusual phenomena" (Joyce and Weil 1980, p. 62). Suchman's theory assumes students will acquire a firm grasp of subject matter by learning that all knowledge is tentative and that, as tentative knowledge is disconfirmed, it may be replaced with new knowledge. The essence of Joyce and Weil's training model is for students to learn through teacher modeling the nature of scientific inquiry.

A typical classroom instance of inquiry teaching involves the presentation of a puzzling situation—"Why is a once inhabited area of the world no longer inhabited?" Teacher and students then engage in a Socratic-type dialogue in which together they derive a list of potentially relevant causal influences, analyze alternative hypotheses concerning the proposed influences, and pare the set down to a reasoned subset. During this process students learn existing rules and theories *and* generate new rules and theories.

Collins and Stevens (1981) have outlined the inquiry processes teachers use in more detail. With protocols in a wide range of subjects and a variety of grade levels, these authors used the instruction of teachers considered masters of inquiry teaching to formulate a process model of inquiry teaching. Their analysis resulted in a three-part framework consistent with general theories of problem solving. That is, master teachers have a set of instructional goals they hope to obtain during instruction. They use a variety of specific strategies to realize goals. And they implement an elaborate control or verification structure for selecting and monitoring goal accomplishments during instruction.

In general, teachers' goals in inquiry lessons alternate between efforts to teach existing rules and theories, and to press students to develop new rules or theories. When the focus is teaching existing rules, instructional strategies involve (a) selecting case examples in some "optimal" order—an order that enables teachers to help students distinguish between correct and incorrect influences on the outcome in question, and (b) helping students see sources of their reasoning errors by using relevant counterexamples, cases, and "entrapment" strategies (trapping students into making incorrect predictions about the outcome or incorrect rule formation). When the focus is developing new rules, teachers tend to use slightly different strategies. They ask probing questions and use entrapment strategies to (a) prompt students to generate predictions, form rules, and identify relevant causal influences, and (b) encourage student evaluation of their own predictions, rules, and influences.

The empirically derived control structure teachers use to steer classroom dialogues consists of three features. The agenda of goals and subgoals is adapted as the dialogue proceeds according to some definable "rules." For example, errors are discussed before omissions of information; easy errors are corrected before difficult errors; and the most important factors in theories are discussed first. Second, teachers similarly appear to follow rules for selecting case examples. Selected cases are most often familiar to students; they permit the group to highlight most important influences in the system early-on, and they can be grouped with other cases to force an important deduction. Finally, teachers constantly monitor and verify the flow of discussion using judgments of student performances to guide case selection, questions, and remarks to individuals concerning errors. They avoid topics that seem obvious or beyond students' judged capabilities; they use questions as informal assessments of student knowledge; and they are able to spot and redirect errors and misleading dialogue when they occur.

Collins and Stevens' judged advantages of this model are consistent with those outlined by Joyce and Weil. Not only does the model teach inquiry strategies, it also permits the teacher to model "the values and attitudes essential to an inquiring mind" (Joyce and Weil 1980 p. 72). Among these values are causal reasoning skills (observing, collecting, and organizing data; identifying and controlling variables, formulating and testing hypotheses), learning autonomy, verbal expressiveness, tolerance for ambiguity, and persistence. Collins and Stevens call for increased teacher training in inquiry teaching as they have defined it, pointing out that the method does entail a model of cognitive activity teachers are not generally trained to engage in with students. The Joyce–Weil and Collins–Stevens models might profit by systematic integration of the parallel ideas.

2. Student-focused Models

Each student-focused model selected involves a different mode of instruction—tutoring, computer-assisted instruction, classroom teaching, and textbook instruction. The aim was to discern different student processes that operate across instructional modes. Like the teacher-focused models described, these models are "generic" with regard to subject matter. They are seen to apply to a range of subject areas, rather than one subject in particular. In each case, however, the model makes clear the importance of considering different structural features of subjects and how these might influence the proposed cognitive processes.

2.1 A Model of Tutoring

Stevens et al. (1979) have used extensive tutoring protocols to construct a model of tutorial dialogue. The model describes how tutors use two information sources

to engender student learning—(a) the structure of the subject being taught (structure refers to the hierarchy and causal ordering among the concepts and processes of a subject), and (b) the student's knowledge of functional relationships between subject attributes—the key concepts in the subject and results of processes the subject describes. For example, the structure of the subject of physics includes the process of rainfall. To explain this process it is necessary to define concepts such as "body of water" and "air mass." Together with the factor of "temperature" these concepts can be used to explain the subprocess within rainfall of "evaporation." The explanation is typically given by tutors in some temporal or sequential order, but it may be presented spatially or metaphorically. Generally, examples (rainfall in Ireland) then follow.

This inherent hierarchy and sequence of subject matter is what the tutor uses to sequence major topics and present information. But the tutor also extracts information from the student during the dialogue to assess understanding. The extraction process revolves around the interplay between the student's existing knowledge of related physical principles, his or her growing knowledge of the subject, and an ability to see functional relationships among important concepts, or reason about the subject. The tutor probes the student's understanding to suggest possible sources of error. Such probes typically center on relationships among concepts and processes: "How is the moisture content of the air related to heavy rainfall?"; "What causes evaporation?" (p. 152).

This kind of information-processing analysis led Stevens et al. to speculate about ways to improve tutorial dialogues and create more effective tutors:

> We believe that much of the teacher's skill as a debugger depends on knowledge about the types of conceptual bugs students are likely to have, the manifestations of these bugs, and methods for correcting them. It is thus clear that an important component of any teaching system is a method of representing, diagnosing, and correcting bugs. (p. 152)

One method for representing common student errors or "bugs" is to extensively examine student errors in specific subject domains. Another method is to conduct interviews with subject matter experts and practiced tutors. Such efforts will be important to improving tutoring in specific subjects. The general tutoring principles that characterize the Stevens et al. model, however—that topic sequences and examples follow the structure of the subject, that dialogue probes revolve around student reasoning about key relationships, and that together these features emphasize the necessity for a thorough understanding of the subject and fluency with diagnostic questioning—may serve as guidelines for tutors in any subject area.

2.2 A Model of Computer-assisted Instruction

Computer-assisted instruction (CAI) is a form of individualized instruction where a student works at his or her own pace through written material displayed visually on the computer terminal. Written material used on the computer is sequenced logically according to the structure of the subject. Some advantages to this form of instruction are that it permits several paths to be taken through the same course of information (this is called "branching," and is also a feature of programmed texts), it provides immediate feedback for diagnostic questions asked during instruction, it may be programmed to handle specific student errors in certain ways and as a "teacher," the computer has unlimited patience.

It has taken time for computers to become cost-effective for most instructional situations. Only recently with the breakthroughs in microelectronics have the costs of CAI systems been reduced enough for schools and homes to take advantage of this instructional opportunity. Also, personal computers have made it possible for students to learn programming by doing it instead of simply accessing existing CAI programs and letting the computer "program" the student through drill and practice.

One advanced model of CAI builds on the student's thought processes to assist in learning without performing drill and practice. The model, known as "computer coaching," was developed by Goldstein (1980) for use in a variety of problem-solving tasks. The computer serves as a counselor to the student, helping him or her make "better" decisions. The counselor monitors the student's performance and at important decision points interjects advice about improvements. Forms of computer coaching are available for task domains as diverse as medical diagnosis, strategy games, and electronic troubleshooting.

The instructional model is based on a core set of problem-solving rules specific to the task domain. In addition to these core rules the model contains a representation for a subject matter "expert," who uses the core rules along with the student's moves to recommend alternative moves, which may be better. The expert is assisted by two additional counselors—a "psychologist" and a "tutor." The psychologist's role is to compare the student's performance to the advice of the expert, and determine if the student is improving. In instances where the psychologist determines the student has made a poor move or a critical error, the tutor is accessed for remediation. The tutor's programming, of course, contains an appropriate set of instructional strategies and debugging advice for each possible incorrect move.

Like all CAI models, this system is hampered by its programming limits; the psychologist, for example, cannot make leaps to the unconscious. Also, development of such systems still takes considerable time. As advances in software writing techniques continue, as more technicians are trained to write software, and as personal computers become widespread, the utility of such CAI models should increase. A major strength is the attempt to use student responses and multiple "counselors" together in one system.

2.3 A Concept Attainment Model of Instruction

Instructional models of concept attainment are based on early studies by Bruner et al. (1967) describing the processes by which people discriminate essential features of events or things, and group them into cohesive categories. Weil and Joyce (1978) outline a model of teaching for concept attainment, in which new concepts are taught by presenting sequences of examples and nonexamples, analyzing the attributes of the examples and nonexamples, and generating hypotheses about what the concept is. In this "receptive" process the teacher presents information initially, but later retreats and encourages students to reflect on the responses they generate on their own. A variation on this procedure is to have students determine, through questioning the teacher, which examples are positive or negative instances of concepts, instead of having the teacher present this information initially. The variant is closer to discovery, or "inquiry" teaching as previously described.

Other researchers have refined concept attainment instruction through experimental studies. Tennyson and Park (1980) reviewed research in this area and outlined an "optimal" sequence of empirically based instruction. A major point these authors make is that concept attainment must be considered a "response-sensitive" approach to instruction (the instruction will change, depending on student responses). If students are confusing concepts or are having trouble acquiring abstract concepts, the instructor's charge is to adapt the presentation of information accordingly. Abstract concepts may, for example, be better taught by stories than by definitions and examples.

A second variation Tennyson and Park emphasize is that the surrounding structure of a concept is important. These authors stress—consistent with Bruner and his colleagues' work—that concepts exist in context, as part of larger networks of concepts. The concept of "mammal" is superordinate to the concept of "cat." The concepts of "tiger" and "leopard" are coordinate (or lateral) on this hierarchical network. The research on concept attainment indicates such networks can be used to instructional advantage—as a way of tying down new concepts to things students already know, and as a way of providing transfer from knowledge about concepts in one category to knowledge about concepts in other categories. When students understand the general principle that concepts exist in networks they will seek to establish or extend such networking as they learn new concepts.

The Tennyson–Park empirically based model of instruction consists of four steps: (a) the instructor analyzes the conceptual network involved (and determines the network location of the particular concept to be taught). This step entails determining the critical and variable attributes of the concept (a critical attribute of the concept, "population," is that it consists of the same kind of living things; a variable attribute of this concept is the geographical location of the group of things). (b)

The instructor defines the concept and presents a pool of examples and nonexamples. (c) Instructor and students engage in a matching exercise whereby they determine which examples in the pool are actually examples of the concept, using the criteria of critical and variable attributes (nonexamples should vary on critical attributes; examples should vary on variable attributes). During this phase the goal is to eliminate errors of overgeneralization, undergeneralization, and misconception. Finally, (d) the instructor presents a new set of examples according to students' increased levels of knowledge about the concept.

While this model has demonstrated effectiveness for concept attainment in the subject groups with which it was tested (across a range of ages and academic content areas, but only within the American culture), it is not a model of concept formation or retention. Moreover, its purported adaptivity to learner individual differences and stylistic preferences of instructors (e.g., towards more experimental learning) has been less carefully documented to date.

2.4 A Model of Learning from Text

Written instruction has long been considered an archetype for other stable instructional systems. Perhaps more research exists on written instruction than on instruction of any other form (e.g., McConkie 1977). Since the instruction remains stable throughout the learning process, effectiveness depends largely on what the student *does* mentally with the text. A model of how students typically learn from written instruction can be derived by integrating various reviews of this research, but a basic model was outlined on a 1977 research-training audiotape-lecture prepared for the American Educational Research Association by Ernst Rothkopf.

Studies of how students acquire information from text show that students frequently infer information beyond that given. They acquire information while reading that is not explicitly included in the text but which is thematically related. This result highlights the complex interactive character of text learning. Rothkopf called the text the "nominal" stimulus, because it contains potentially instructive features (organization, questions, a variety of propositional networks, etc.), which are not effective on their own. The content of the inference the student makes (the information that is added by the student to what is explicit in the text) is influenced by knowledge structures regarding the subject that already exist in the student's head. Such knowledge structures are termed by Rothkopf the "effective" stimuli (the actual representations in the student's memory). Other writers have called such memory representations instantiations of a text, script, frames, and, more commonly, schemata.

The instructional model derived holds that these two characteristic features of learning from text are reciprocally related. More processing activity (encoding, inferencing, elaborating, etc.) is required when the student

has a more limited level of prior, related knowledge; but the amount and manner of processing can enrich the knowledge base as well.

In general, a student approaches the text with a "top-down" processing strategy. That is, he or she uses the nominal stimulus to decide what schemata are most appropriately brought to bear and then uses those selected memory representations to "interrogate" the text. The interrogation process also fills gaps in the student's schemata (builds knowledge structures in memory). Cognitive psychology supports this general model, but adds also that the cognitive system must be able to discard or replace accessed schema that turn out to be inappropriate to the text. The student monitors information processing from the "bottom-up," and is thus able to modify ineffective processing.

When the student's knowledge base is underdeveloped and/or the monitor system is not fully operative, processing information from text can be burdensome. Research also shows that students who must spend extensive time encoding information from text have less time to spent elaborating, or constructively extending, that information. Such results imply that effective written instruction will be different for low and high ability students. Low ability students should benefit from instruction that either encodes for the student or models the encoding process; such instruction will help "compensate" the student for a lack of knowledge and processing ability (Salomon 1979). Potentially instructive text features for such students include "advance organizers," questions in text, multiple examples, and so on. The research has indicated, however, that such features are not necessarily instructive for high ability students. They may interfere with the effective processing and accessing of knowledge structures these students automatically carry out.

Thus a model of learning from text—like the other student-focused models of instruction—has interesting implications for those who actually develop written instruction. A general principle that evolves is that no instructional model is complete without considering the full range of complexity that exists among the instructional features and processes used, the structure of the subject matter, and what the student brings to the instructional situation. While this article was constrained by space limitations to descriptions of generic models (models that do not apply to any particular subject and are assumed to hold across subjects), there are many subject-specific information-processing models of instruction which are in some cases more refined embodiments of this principle than the models described.

3. Models that Focus on the Interaction Between Teacher and Student Information Processing

Representative of this final category are two models that highlight the interaction between teachers and students as they process information during instruction.

The first model was developed by Winne and Marx (1977) to guide a research program in instructional psychology. The model is generic, with three categories of events seen to occur before, during, and after instruction. Teacher planning, for example, is one pre-instructional event in the model. A teacher's planning for instruction is expected to influence how the teacher processes information during instruction, which in turn affects student information processing and classroom behavior.

Results of two experiments showed that training which required students to use the proposed lecture learning strategy during class had a less favorable influence on student learning than training which simply made students aware of specific behaviors teachers were using to aid learning. The evidence suggested that these adult students had already acquired their own effective "learning from lectures schemata," which tended to interfere with the strategy they were being asked to use in the study. When students were made aware of teacher learning cues, but not forced to process information in a particular way, learning improved.

These results do not falsify Winne and Marx's model; rather, they suggest that the authors' operationalization of the lecture learning strategy was faulty *within* the context of the proposed model. College students do not appear to learn from lectures in the precise manner Winne and Marx proposed, but they do have cognitive mechanisms for learning from lectures which they call upon during instruction (and after instruction takes place, when reviewing their notes). The combination of having these cognitive schemata and of perceiving what the teacher is doing in the way of learning guidance does engender learning. As the authors point out, further research in this arena should attempt to examine the cognitive schemata such students have for learning from lectures, how these schemata and other lecture scripts are intertwined by students during instruction, and what discrete learning processes occur as a result. Again it may be driven home that even within narrowly defined content areas and teaching methods, and with relatively homogeneous subject pools, instruction is an exceedingly complex enterprise within which information processing plays a critical role.

A second model that highlights the interaction between teacher and student information processing during instruction was developed by one of the present writers (Corno 1981). Like the Winne–Marx model, this "model of cognitive organizing in classrooms" was derived from existing models to guide a cognitively based research program in instruction. The focal information processing variable, cognitive organizing, refers to parallel efforts by teachers and students to filter and transform mentally a variety of classroom information. "Classroom information" has been shown to consist of a multiplicity of academic and nonacademic (social or procedural) content. Student learning is clearly not limited to only the former body of information. While the academic information base of a classroom may well

influence student academic competence, so may the social–procedural information base influence student self-views and social competence.

The model proposes that differing levels (quantities) and forms (qualities) of teacher and student cognitive organizing are important to promoting these alternative student outcomes in classrooms. That is, given that academic content or subject matter has a structure, and that teachers plan logical ways to present such information to students, an important determinant of academic achievement during classroom instruction should be how extensively academic information is analyzed and integrated by students (information transformation). When the focal student outcome is not academic achievement, but rather, social judgments, the picture changes somewhat. The information base used to form a judgment is generally scattered and non-systematic—cues leap from academic lessons as well as during social interactions. Students attempting to form judgments about themselves as students, for example, would be weighing together information from teacher evaluations, peer reactions, and test scores, at least. For the self-judgment to be unbiased the student must carefully filter out relevant from irrelevant information, and apply to that some logical structure. Thus student judgments should be at least as dependent on the organizing process of selectivity (separating critical from irrelevant information) as on transformation. Different levels and forms of cognitive organizing are important for accomplishing different instructional objectives, but cognitive organizing in the broader sense is viewed as critical to both academic and social objectives.

The model describes parallel processing activities for teachers and students that come together when teachers and students interact. Teachers must discern critical from irrelevant academic information as they plan instruction; they must manage instruction so students focus, appropriately in turn, on academic information and social events. Also during instruction, teachers should carry out more or less information integration and elaboration (i.e., noticing patterns and viewing old information in new ways, extending information given to other pertinent areas, etc.), depending on their level of planning at the start of a lesson, and on the cognitive abilities of the students being taught. Students would be expected to engage in parallel cognitive organizing at a somewhat lower level than the teacher's to the extent that (a) the information presented is not organized for them, (b) the teacher demands such processing, or (c) the student is actively accessing his or her own cognitive schemata to help learn the information presented, rather than accepting the categories and examples provided by the teacher.

In this model there is a major emphasis placed on the interface between what the teacher and the instructional materials used are accomplishing *for* students in the way of cognitive organizing, and on the cognitive organizing students must be made to carry out on their own. As some research has shown, a major function of much written and oral instruction is to systematically sift relevant from irrelevant information, and diagram, integrate, and repeat what is critical to learn. The relative influence such "short-circuiting" of students' own cognitive organizing has on instructional outcomes is an important question that has been studied to some extent (e.g., Salomon 1979, Wittrock 1978). Yet, "When is it important for teachers and texts to organize and when for students?" and "How ought switches in control of organizing to take place in classrooms?" are among the important unanswered research questions that follow from the present model.

4. Discussion: Cautions and Conclusions

Despite the clear explanatory appeal of information processing models, the measurement of internal processes is a difficult undertaking. Verbal reports of cognitive processes, though easy to obtain, can be misleading. Apart from bias generated when subjects attempt to respond in "socially desirable" ways (e.g., "I always pay attention when my teacher talks"), self-statements are often based on information salience (Nisbett and Wilson 1977). In making cognitive judgments, individuals reduce a wide range of information to that which is readily available in memory. When information is reduced in a biased manner, even if unintentionally, judgments can be erroneous. Researchers who use stimulated recall, for example, must become skilled at drawing out from subjects information that typically occurs in a few seconds of thought. The video cues assist subjects to focus on important environmental factors but the process still requires retrospective thinking in which some information is inevitably lost.

Avoiding socially desirable cognitive questions, cueing subjects when recall is necessary, and training researchers in techniques for promoting unbiased introspection can help overcome measurement difficulties. But verbal reports of mental processes should also be augmented by and verified against appropriate behavioral measures. The careful measurement of classroom language and certain nonverbal behavior such as student eye movements during seatwork, the contents of note taking during lectures, and error patterns on tests may be used to support verbal reports obtained in instructional research. Beyond this, what has been termed the "black box" of the human mind will likely continue to elude total illumination.

Perhaps the most outspoken opponent of mental process models is B. F. Skinner (1974). As is widely known, Skinner's thesis is that students profit from instruction because they have previously learned that certain academic behaviors produce learning outcomes (e.g., effective problem solving). These behaviors are routinely called into play in new academic situations with similar environmental contingencies. They are not "constructed" as from an environmental vacuum through thought alone.

Skinner further contends that the very capacity for

introspection is the result of environmental conditioning. A student is *able* to think through what should be learned during instruction because past performance history includes internal thoughts and external learning events (e.g., knowledge of correct answers and teacher probing), which occur concurrently. Skinner believes that internal operations or introspections are symptoms, rather than causes, of behavior. Thus information-processing models are of little use because environmental contingencies and not self-awareness are the direct explanations for human behavior. Skinner's arguments have been used to resolve the measurement problem in mental process research by avoiding it altogether. If, as Skinner believes, mental activities can be acquired and taught in overt forms (where they are readily observable), there is no need to examine how they might be carried out at a covert (and, by definition, less reliable) level.

There is of course literature aimed at refuting the Skinnerian position. This literature questions the influence of environmental factors, and argues that knowledge is internally constructed (e.g. Piaget 1970 after Kant). These internal constructions of knowledge permit human beings to create or invent academic learning and other knowledge processes they have not observed (Chomsky 1968).

The models described herein depict, for education, the benefits of a more balanced view—a view that emphasizes the interplay between internal and external influences on students and how together these influences may be used to expand and enrich what the student currently offers the instructional situation. Three cognitive processes that dominate and unite the variety of models described support this position. Both teachers and students have been shown to begin the instructional process with some sequence of active interrogation. Classroom environment, teacher, and text are all scanned for learning cues. When such cues are absent—when the data are not there—the learning experience is less vibrant. Second, teachers and students both use existing knowledge or cognitive schemata to assist in this active interrogation; existing knowledge provides a sorting key for separating relevant from irrelevant information, for setting priorities and goals. Again, the smaller the accessible knowledge store, the less comparison and elaboration are possible. And finally, the scene is monitored throughout instruction. Moves are followed; hunches are verified; problems are anticipated; and errors are corrected. A halting monitor or a failure to monitor entirely, further compromise the learning of students and teachers alike.

Ultimately, experience may prove models of external influence to be more useful than internal processing models when the objective is the improvement of student learning. Clearly, however, such models must be informed by knowledge of internal influences and by information on where in given instructional situations the two sets of influences are most likely to become entangled.

See also: Tutoring; Models of Heuristic Teaching; Written Instruction; Students' Cognitive Processing

Bibliography

Bruner J S 1966 Some elements of discovery. In Shulman L S, Keisler E R (eds.) 1966 *Learning by Discovery: A Critical Appraisal.* Rand McNally, Chicago, Illinois

Bruner J, Goodnow J J, Austin G A 1967 *A Study of Thinking.* Science Editions, New York

Chomsky N 1968 *Language and Mind.* Harcourt, Brace and World, New York

Clark C M, Yinger R J 1977 Research on teacher thinking. *Curric. Inq.* 7: 279–304

Collins A, Stevens A L 1981 A cognitive theory of interactive teaching. In: Reigeluth C M (ed.) 1981 *Instructional Design Theories and Models: An Overview.* Academic Press, New York

Corno L 1981 Cognitive organizing in classrooms. *Curric. Inq.* 11: 359–77

Doyle W 1977 Learning the classroom environment: An ecological analysis. *J. Teach. Educ.* 28: 15–55

Goldstein I 1980 Developing a computational representation for problem-solving skills. In: Tuma D T, Reif F (eds.) 1980 *Problem Solving and Education: Issues in Teaching and Research.* Erlbaum, Hillsdale, New Jersey

Joyce B R, Weil M 1980 *Models of Teaching*, 2nd edn. Prentice-Hall, Englewood Cliffs, New Jersey

McConkie G W 1977 Learning from text. In: Shulman L S (ed.) 1978 *Review of Research in Education*, Vol 5. Peacock, Itasca, Illinois, pp. 3–48

Marland P V 1979 A study of teachers' interactive information processing. Paper presented at the annual meeting of the Australian Association for Research in Education, Melbourne

Nisbett R E, Wilson T D 1977 Telling more than we can know: Verbal reports on mental processes. *Psychol. Rev.* 84: 231–59

Piaget J 1970 *Science of Education and Psychology of the Child.* Orion, New York

Rothkopf E Z 1977 *Ten Years of Prose Learning Research.* AERA research training audio cassette

Salomon G 1979 *Interaction of Media, Cognition, and Learning.* Jossey-Bass, San Francisco, California

Shavelson R J 1976 Teachers' decision making. In: Gage N L (ed.) 1976 *The Psychology of Teaching Methods*, 75th yearbook of the National Society for the Study of Education (NSSE), Pt 1. University of Chicago Press, Chicago, Illinois, pp. 372–414

Shavelson R J 1978 Teachers' estimates of student 'states of mind' and behavior. *J. Teach. Educ.* 29: 37–41

Shulman L S, Elstein A S 1975 Studies of problem solving, judgment and decision making: Implications for educational research. In Kerlinger F W (ed.) *Review of Research in Education*, Vol. 3. Peacock, Itasca, Illinois

Skinner B F 1974 *About Behaviorism.* Vintage, New York

Stevens A, Collins A, Goldin S E 1979 Misconceptions in student's understanding. *Int. J. Man–Machine Studies* 11: 145–56

Tennyson R D, Park O-C 1980 The teaching of concepts: A review of instructional design research literature. *Rev. Educ. Res.* 50: 55–70

Weil M, Joyce B R 1978 *Information Processing Models of Teaching: Expanding your Repertoire.* Prentice-Hall, Englewood Cliffs, New Jersey

Winne P H, Marx R W 1977 Reconceptualizing research on teaching. *J. Educ. Psychol.* 69: 668–78

Wittrock M C 1978 The cognitive movement in instruction. *Educ. Psychol.* 13: 15–31

Linguistic Models

R. E. Young; R. Arnold; K. Watson

When researchers look inside classrooms they find that teachers and learners are usually talking to one another. If they are not talking, they are reading or writing about something before later talking about it. Although language involves the use of sign systems other than language (e.g., posture, gesture, facial expression, physical positioning of speakers, cadence, tone of voice), it appears to provide the single, richest channel of classroom communication. And while teaching and learning may involve many other important nonverbal experiences (e.g., working with materials, vicariously experiencing the feelings of a character in a play, doing mathematics), the most significant parts of the learning process are usually the subject of discussion, verbal explanation and formulation, prior to a verbal summing up, usually by the teacher (see *Nonverbal Communication*).

The study of language in schooling contexts is many-sided. A further narrowing of the present focus is upon ways in which language throws light on teaching and learning rather than upon the study of language for its own sake. Thus general linguistics, psycholinguistics (the study of the mental process of language acquisition, production, and interpretation), and sociolinguistics (the study of language behaviour in the light of the social circumstances of language use), provide a resource for this study but do not, of themselves constitute it.

The study of teaching and learning from the standpoint of language involves a "double" perspective. Language is both an educational medium and a competence for the learner which is itself one of the goals of education. In both perspectives, language is not seen as static but as a form of action which is capable of engendering changes in other people, in conjunction with their cooperative activity. In the case of education, the changes which it might be desirable to call "educational" will depend upon a person's philosophy of education. In any case, these changes will not be confined to changes in the information in a hearer's mind brought about by the production, transmission, and reception of knowledge or even to changes in a hearer's beliefs, although a lot of educational talk and writing consists of what might be called "factual" or referential language. Language can also be used to maintain *or* change relationships between people, and to express and affect feelings, especially the way a person feels about the content of what is being said and the people they are speaking to.

The study of language in education is also the study of "language roles", of the structure of talk over time, of who says what, when, and why, who gets to raise doubts, make statements, evaluate other people's talk, and who does not. It is easy to understand that language can embody the views of reality which belong to particular social groups, but it is a bit more difficult to realize that communication structures can also do this. A particular set of language roles (or norms) can be a medium for the imposition of a particular view of reality on people or it can be an avenue for a process of inquiry and exploration which might eventually change people's views of reality. For example, if a teacher consistently evaluates a pupil's language in terms of its correctness according to a particular view of correct language which the pupils do not necessarily share, many pupils may experience a sense of cultural rejection or stigmatization.

In this sense, language in education is in tension between the preservation of existing cultures, social relationships, and acceptable ways of feeling, and the development of a dialogue between teachers and learners which has the potential to change these things.

1. Two Methods of Studying Educational Language

Before discussing the findings of linguistic research on teaching and learning it is necessary to realize that historically there have been two quite different approaches to this field of study. These might be called, very broadly, the logical–empirical and the interpretive. To some extent these two traditions have been associated with two different styles of research. The first of these drew its methods from the behavioural sciences and attempted to apply objective categories to counting instances of behaviour. The interpretive method applied a more intuitive approach aimed at understanding the meaning of language. Later work in both traditions exhibited a degree of convergence, with the logical–empirical approach paying more attention to meaning and the interpretive approach, informed by sociolinguistics, developing more rigorous methods.

The logical–empirical approach was characterized in its early stages by a tendency to employ broad research categories (questions, answers, expression of feeling, initiation of inquiry) rather than a detailed study of actual texts and the meanings of what was said by participants. In addition, the educational effects of language were theorized in terms of the supposed effects of variation in the frequency or order of incidence of the categorized behaviours rather than in terms of a study of the way language works (as a sign system) and the relation between this and the way it functions as a form of human action. There was a tendency to see language either as a medium for conveying information in which case the logical and propositional content of language was analysed, or as a form of affective action, which was analysed in terms of broad categories of feeling and action (expresses negative affect, issues directions) rather than in terms of the details of the way specific linguistic features of utterances do such affective work. When the logical and informational features of talk were emphasized, its functions as a form of interpersonal action (persuasion, warning, apologizing) were largely ignored. But it is not the simple fact of information being transmitted which is of interest to educators. It is also necessary to ask questions about the way information is used, about who is making what statements to whom at what time and to what purpose. Speakers do not simply "transmit" information—they seek to persuade, warn, question, or doubt. Thus, work in this tradition tended to produce a mechanistic and oversimplified view of communication in education, rather than one based on an analysis of the way languages work as meaning systems, and the way humans create and interpret speech and writing, intend to affect others and are themselves affected, in turn, in interpersonal communicative relationships.

The interpretive approach concentrated instead on semantics and pragmatics, on the full meaning of what was said, and on the way language is used by participants to act on each other. Its analyses were often quite deep, revealing hidden nuances of language meaning and use, but they were often confined to a few cases rather than large samples of data, thus providing only limited evidence for the generalizability of their findings. The view of language and its role in teaching and learning produced by this tradition is complex and rich, but not readily reducible to practical implications of the kind that can be widely and routinely applied.

The first tradition may be exemplified by the work of Romiett Stevens (1912) and later work by Flanders (1970), Bellack (1966), Smith and Meux (1962) in the United States, and Sinclair and Coulthard (1975) in the United Kingdom. Work in this tradition gradually became more sophisticated and complex, absorbing in recent years, ideas from functional linguistics and from the interpretive tradition. The second approach may be exemplified by the early work of Barnes et al. (1969) in the United Kingdom, and more recently, by the more systematic work of Hugh Mehan and his colleagues in the United States.

The first tradition began by asking educational questions although some later developments, influenced by new developments in linguistics, limited themselves to providing systems for categorizing classroom language by function, making the application of educational analysis to the functional patterns so observed a separate step (e.g., Sinclair and Coulthard 1975); other later workers attempted to build educational questions into their categories (Smith and Meux 1962).

Stevens (1912), whose work may be seen as a forerunner of the first tradition, attempted to analyse certain of the cognitive aspects of the teacher/learner relationship. To do this she employed commonsense language categories such as "question" and "answer". She was concerned mainly with changing teacher questions so that they "made children think" and in opening up opportunities for children to use language more in their learning. She worked theoretically with a simple model of classroom communication based on counting instances of questions and answers of different "educational" kinds and producing aggregate percentages of teacher questions versus pupil questions, and so on.

Later work, such as that of Bellack et al. (1966) and Smith and Meux (1962), involved the creation of more comprehensive records of classroom communication by the use of audiotapes and videotapes, making transcripts of talk from them, and further analyses of these through more and more elaborate category systems, particularly those which identify specific language forms with specific language and/or educational functions. A parallel approach (e.g., Flanders) involved by-passing the step of making transcripts by the development of methods of direct observation and counting of instances of interaction based on communication (e.g., asks for information, gives direction). This approach involves analysing utterances on the basis of their presumed interactional function rather than more detailed features of the actual form of words used—the language form.

Developments in this tradition, which included new methods of time sampling of language, produced a deeper and more generalized understanding of the dominant and variant communication patterns in contemporary classrooms. They enabled relatively large samples of data to be collected, particularly in the case of the more economical methods such as Flanders', and so enabled general comparative studies to be undertaken. More elaborate category systems such as Sinclair and Coulthard's require rather more time and effort to achieve samples of the same size but were able to reveal more of the detail of classroom life. Even so, work in this tradition has been unable to shake off the basic weaknesses of Steven's first study: such studies are only as good as the theory associating particular utterance forms (and language structures) with eductional functions permits them to be, and, as shall be seen below, the fact that language form and language functions do not completely coincide means that studies of this kind have a basic and inbuilt limitation.

The interpretive approach adopted by Barnes, based on a broad "humanism", an eclectically grounded sensitivity to the varieties of language, informed by the study of rhetoric and literature, as well as more recently by functional linguistics, was open to insights about the educational uses of language that the more systematically empirical tradition was not. A similar richness and openness of approach was exhibited by the "symbolic interactionist" analyses of classroom talk carried out by ethnomethodologists and others on both sides of the Atlantic. In recent years, approaches in this tradition have become more exhaustive and systematic, although they still have some problems when it comes to making generalizations and extending the analysis from one classroom to others.

The essential difference between the two traditions centres as much around the problem of generalization in the study of human action as around different views of explaining it. In recent years, workers in both traditions have, perhaps, become more receptive to the possibilities inherent in the views of the other. Both those who have attempted to develop exhaustive, logically noncontradictory category systems and clearcut relationships between these and educational implications, and proponents of more open, ideographic methods of analysis, have come to agree on the value of attending to both "meaning" and "function" in language rather than simply to surface form. That is, few workers today would want to treat language interaction in terms of broad behavioural categories. Both agree that the total social context of talk influences meaning and function, but they part company when it comes to method. The "categorizers" concern themselves with that which is to be gained by applying the same category system to a sample of texts, uniquely and reliably assigning each utterance with a particular linguistic form to a single category. The "noncategorizers" use categories more tentatively and provisionally, alert to the fact that the match between form and function is sometimes sensitive to slight contextual differences.

The latter view is almost certainly correct in that it has not yet been possible to produce a scheme for the completely valid and reliable coding of utterances by meaning and function. While it may be possible to produce lists of the functions of utterances in abstraction from actual examples of language use, and to discuss meanings in a similar way, the interpretation of historically located utterances is dependent on an inferential process employed by participants, a process which is not yet fully understood. The more information that is available about participants and the context (including the history of the interaction), the more plausible certain interpretations may become, but plausibility does not necessarily amount to completely valid and reliable categorization. An attempt to precode meaning and function by identification of syntactical/grammatical form is dependent for its usefulness on the degree to which the domain of application of the code (e.g., the sample of utterances, situations) is uniform in respect to the range of forms employed by participants to communicate particular meanings and perform particular functions. But the theoretical aim of the analyses carried out on the basis of such coded data is often to establish the degree of uniformity of a domain or the nature of systematic variation in it. And variation in social relationships across a sample of situations (e.g., classrooms) will always be accompanied by variation in the forms, meanings, and functions of the language which mediates the relationships. Accordingly, precoded methods of analysis are blunt instruments for the detection of variation, particularly if it occurs as a rare (but theoretically significant) departure from a near-ubiquitous pattern. Similarly, such methods may tend to overestimate uniformity. They appear better adapted to the study of the transmission of an agreed text in socially and culturally homogenous samples than to identifying rare but potentially educationally worthwhile forms of language use.

While such coding schemes are essential if large samples of data are to be processed economically, they also remain relatively insensitive to more subtle variations (e.g., of style) which may be of considerable social and emotional significance. More open approaches such as that of Barnes, while they run the risk of overgeneralizing from a few cases, or of adopting anecdotal rather than exhaustive procedures, are fully able to take into account the fact that, dependent upon context, a single utterance may perform several different functions simultaneously, just as the same functions may be performed by several alternative utterances. To sum up, it would appear that the two traditions of research are capable of complementing each other.

2. The Categorizers

Romiett Stevens recorded talk in American classrooms by shorthand, over a period of four years. She found that on average 64 percent of class time was taken up with teacher talk. She found little difference between the amount of talking done by teachers at different grade levels or in different subjects. Most significantly, about 80 percent of the classroom talk was devoted to asking, answering, or reacting to questions. Teachers asked questions at a rate ranging from one to four questions per minute, with the average being about two per minute (see *Soliciting*).

Stevens made detailed criticisms of the practices she observed:

> The fact that one teacher has the ability to quiz his pupils at the rate of two or three questions in a minute is a matter of comparatively slight importance; the fact that one hundred different classrooms reveal the same methods in vogue is quite another matter. (Stevens 1912 p. 16)

Stevens was critical of the question/answer method for a number of reasons: it generated nervous tension in the classroom; the teachers were doing most of the work, rather than the pupils; verbal memory and superficial judgment were stressed above all else; and little attention was given to the needs of individuals or their development as self-reliant, independent thinkers.

It is tempting to think that Steven's results are an

historical phenomenon relevant only to the early years of this century. But subsequent studies from 1922 to 1966, and beyond, confirmed the continuation of patterns of talk closely related to that identified by Stevens, while filling out the details of the picture of them (e.g., Bellack et al. 1966). Similar results have been obtained quite recently in studies carried out in other developed countries such as Sweden, the United Kingdom, the Federal Republic of Germany, and Australia; the Stevens pattern was identified in many developing countries too. While some variation exists from subject to subject and grade level to grade level, the Stevens pattern is so widespread that it can truly be said that in most schools, teaching means asking questions (and assigning readings or texts), and learning means answering teacher questions (often questions about assigned texts).

Bellack et al. summed up the classroom "language game" in terms of the rules which teachers and pupils appeared to be using in their talk. The following set of rules is inspired by Bellack et al. but incorporates additional information from other studies (see also Hoetker and Ahlbrand 1969:

(a) The ratio of teacher talk to pupil talk is about 75 percent to 25 percent. This means that if pupil talk were evenly distributed (which it is not), each pupil in a class of more than 25 gets less than 1 percent of the opportunity to use talk, even to answer teacher questions, let alone to ask questions of their own.

(b) Teachers ask qbout 90 percent of questions, pupils about 10 percent between them and most of the pupils' questions have to do with details of class routine, layout of notebooks, and so on, rather than the subject matter of the lesson. The main classroom task of pupils is to answer teachers' questions. In a school year, most teachers ask as many as 50,000 questions while pupils ask 10 each or less. Pupils do more than 80 percent of answering of questions in classrooms and question answering constitutes about 75 percent to 80 percent of pupil (official) talk in classrooms. More than 80 percent of teacher questions typically require only a rote or memory response rather than a reasoning process.

(c) In addition to asking questions, which constitute about 35 percent of teacher talk, teachers structure the lesson and organize and control pupils (about 20 percent of teacher talk) and react to or comment on pupil answers to teacher questions (about 40 percent of teacher talk). Teachers display fairly constant or stable proportions of different types of talk over different class sessions and variation across samples of teachers is not wide.

(d) Asking questions, pupil answers, and teacher reaction to pupil answers in all constitute about 60 percent of all public, official talk in classrooms. Questions are asked at the rate of about two per minute, on average. Little time is given for the production of answers and teachers move on to another pupil if a pupil delays answering for even a few seconds. One study suggests that there is little difference in the questioning behaviour of teachers, even when specially selected groups of "good" and "bad" teachers (from the principal's viewpoint) are chosen.

The approach adopted by Flanders (1970) differed from the research mentioned above since it treated a wide range of communications including nonverbal communication and communication in the affective as well as the cognitive area (e.g., accepts pupils' feelings, praises, or encourages). However, results of Flanders-type studies are comparable with research of the kind just discussed at a number of points, and where such comparisons can be made (e.g., proportion of teacher talk versus pupil talk) have generally confirmed the domination of the Stevens pattern. Indeed, the Stevens pattern is implicit in the restricted range of categories provided by Flanders for coding instances of pupil and teacher talk. Teacher talk:

(a) accepts feeling

(b) praises or encourages

(c) accepts or uses ideas of pupils

(d) asks questions

(e) lecturing

(f) giving directions

(g) criticizing or justifying authority

Pupil talk:

(a) response—pupil to teacher

(b) initiation—pupil to teacher initiation

Both the earlier research and Flander's approach tend to assume that interpretation of the communication functions and educational functions of talk can be readily routinized and as readily understood. Much of the educational discussion about the style and dominance of teacher questioning was carried out in the absence of any research evidence about the effects of different kinds and quantities of teacher questions and different logical structures in teacher/pupil exchanges. Research of that kind came much later (mainly from the 1960s on) and, at the time of writing, has not been entirely decisive as to the educational value or lack of it which (in some given conception of education) might be attributed to the dominant pattern of teaching through questions or to the logical structures of classroom talk. Similarly, it is reasonable to assume that teachers may "praise or encourage" in qualitatively quite different ways with, for instance, quite different effects on the pupil–teacher relationship. While the broad categories used by Flanders established useful generalizations about broad and ubiquitous features of the pattern of classroom talk, and no doubt will continue to have their uses in comparative studies of such features, the attention of many researchers was directed instead to more complex and detailed studies of classroom talk and to features of the educational process which required a finer analytical mesh.

Research on the pattern of classroom talk turned in two directions. Sociological research addressed itself to the reasons for the universality and persistence of the Stevens pattern, to a fuller understanding of the teacher and pupil "roles" embodied in this pattern. Other researchers turned to a more detailed analysis of the logical structure of talk in classrooms and, in particular, to the logical limitations of the dominant pattern and its implications for cognitive learning outcomes. Research of the first kind tended to the conclusion that the pattern was the outcome of "outside" pressures on teachers to cover a set curriculum in a given time ensuring at least an elementary mastery of the more routine and factual material in it by most pupils, while maintaining control over a relatively large group of pupils proceeding through the curriculum in concert (e.g., Smith and Geoffrey 1968). Research of the second kind, employing coding systems based on the logically relevant features of the grammar of classroom language, among other things, explored the way in which describing or explaining were carried out in classrooms. In agreement with earlier research it was found that classrooms were dominated by describing rather than explaining (Smith and Meux 1962). The theory of teaching derived from the work on logic in classroom discourse tended to be a refinement and an updating of the "neosocratic" assumptions inherent in Stevens' 1912 study. However, despite further developments in the study of logical features of classroom talk, a full understanding of the way logical aspects of classroom life connect up with the affective side of classroom life and with the political and organizational constraints on classrooms remains to be developed.

The category systems developed in the study of the logic of teaching in classrooms, and in associated refinements in the study of classroom language, were more sophisticated than previous systems. In part this was because they drew on linguistics, but the linguistics they drew on were what might be called the linguistics of structure, of grammar, and of syntax, rather than the more recent functional linguistics exemplified by the work of Halliday (1973). Modern functional linguistics appear to provide a better, more general theory of the way talk works, and their application to the study of educational talk was attempted by Sinclair and Coulthard (1975) who produced what is probably still among the most comprehensive and detailed categorization procedures for the study of classroom talk.

Sinclair and Coulthard's system of analysis is closely modelled on Halliday's *Categories of a Theory of Grammar* (1961). The terms used—structure, system, rank, level, delicacy, realization, marked, unmarked—are Halliday's, as they acknowledge (p. 24). In a hierarchical system, working downwards, ranks include elements of structure. The link between one rank and the next below is through classes. Ranks include lessons, transactions, exchange (boundary), exchange (teaching), moves (opening, answering, follow-up, framing, focusing).

Sinclair and Coulthard classified five classes of moves between teacher and pupils which realize two classes of exchange—boundary and teaching. Framing and focusing moves realize boundary exchanges and opening, answering, and follow-up moves realize teaching exchanges. Each move has a different function and as it is usually the teacher who controls the moves and the pupils who respond (or not), there is a high degree of predictability in much classroom discourse.

This system of analysis, with all its hierarchical subcategories and its close relationship to functional grammar, systematically, but not exhaustively, analyses distinctive features of classroom discourse. In part, its shortcomings are characteristic of single function classificatory systems. That is, an observer has to assign discourse elements to a rank or class as if these elements had a single unambiguous function.

However, as argued above, many functions can be subsumed within a single discourse exchange. For example, an apparently ritualistic "good morning" could frame the opening of a lesson, or provide a reminder to the pupils that the teacher usually initiates classroom exchanges, or signal the degree of formality appropriate to the lesson, particularly if the teacher usually says "Hi!". (Of course, only an observer who has been present over a sufficient length of time would be in a position to have access to meanings which are dependent on changes from expected and habitual speech patterns).

Classroom discourse systems which focus primarily on the spoken language content of lessons tend to ignore much of the less obvious but equally significant affective elements of exchanges. While these might be less apparent than question–answer routines, or teacher narratives, they are an influential motivating element for pupil learning partly because they are most often carried in the nonverbal parts of classroom communication.

As a system of analysis it also shares the weakness of all attempts to devise universally applicable systems of categorizing talk, in that it fails to account for atypical relationships between form and function, (and as mentioned above, for multifunctionality) and for the historical development of particular meanings and routines over time in a group—the development of the group's own "private" meanings and rituals.

Sinclair and Coulthard appear to recognize these limitations (e.g., p. 123) and, in addition, are well-aware that an educational analysis of classroom talk involves the employment of further analysis to the functional patterns identified by applying this category system. In this way, analyses of the social influences on

the communication roles of participants, of the logic of classroom talk, and of other aspects of teaching and learning may be built on the base provided by the functional analysis of talk.

Perhaps some conclusions which all of the studies so far mentioned have in common, either explicitly or implicitly, are that the observational study of classrooms reveals teaching and learning to be mediated primarily by language, and that the success of learning is dependent in some way on the active, interpretive participation of students just as much, if not more, than upon the messages emitted by teachers. That is, teaching is not a technology but a two-sided process of communication. The alternative tradition which began with this very insight but with little in the way of publicly agreed systematic evidence to demonstrate its utility will now be examined.

3. The Interpreters

Investigations of classroom language that are confined to describing pedagogical moves or plotting linguistic sequences do not, of themselves, illuminate all of the problems faced by teachers. They are concerned very much with the surface features of language; they do not, in general, attempt to grapple with its semantic qualities or gauge the influence of sociocultural factors on the shaping of meaning. Until recently they have not paid much attention to the development of discourse structures over the duration of lessons, to issues of "talk strategy". Further, since they offer data gathered, in almost all cases, from one type of classroom, the "chalk-and-talk" classroom where the teacher clearly "owns the interaction", they offer little guidance to the teacher in a less formal setting, where for example, turn-taking (who speaks and in what order) may involve a greater degree of negotiation between teacher and pupils, or where the pupils are working in groups only occasionally monitored by the teacher. It is not surprising, therefore, that since the late 1960s there has been a movement away from investigations which attempt to categorize classroom language according to some analytical system in favour of an anthropological or ethnographic approach which attempts to encompass the many kinds and levels of meaning making in the classroom.

In a seminal study of the language interaction in 12 lessons in classes in their first term in secondary school, Barnes et al. (1969) showed that real barriers to learning can be created by the teacher's reliance on the specialist language of his or her subject, or simply by use of a register ("vocabulary and way of talking") peculiar to secondary education. A powerful example of the gulf between teacher and taught is provided by this excerpt from Barnes's research, taken from a science lesson where the teacher is explaining that milk is an example of suspension of solids in a liquid:

T   You get the white . . . what we call casein . . . that's . . . er . . . protein . . . which is good for you . . . it'll help to build bones . . . and the white is mainly the casein and so it's not actually a solution . . . it's a suspension of very fine particles together with water and various other things which are dissolved in water . . .

P1 Sir, at my old school I shook my bottle of milk up and when I looked at it again all the side was covered with . . . it . . . like particles and . . . er . . . could they be the white particles in the milk . . .?

P2 Yes, and gradually they would sediment out, wouldn't they, to the bottom . . .?

P3 When milk goes very sour though it smells like cheese, doesn't it?

P4 Well, it is cheese, isn't it, if you leave it long enough? Anyway can we get on? We'll have a few questions for later. (Barnes 1969 p. 28)

Barnes's explication of what is happening here deserves quoting:

> The teacher talks about milk, using his specialist language to help him perceive it as an exemplar of the category "suspension", and to free him from all other contexts and categories it might appear in. But for his pupils "milk" collocates not with "suspension" but with "cheese", "school", "shook", "bottle"; they perceive it in that context and his use of "casein" and "fine particles" signals to only two of them that some different response is expected. (Barnes 1969 pp. 28–29)

Barnes's study also revealed that the establishment of a relationship between teacher and pupils is evident more in instructional sequences than in those sequences solely concerned with social control. Further, he was able to demonstrate that while language was seen as an instrument of teaching, it was seldom functioning as an instrument of learning. ". . . in these lessons the failure to demand active involvement of the pupils *has gone hand in hand with a failure to demand that they verbalise their learning*, that is, that they use language as an active instrument for reorganising their perceptions" (Barnes 1969 p. 66). Barnes's conviction that verbalization helps children to solve problems was based on the evidence of studies in the logical–empirical tradition, but in his investigation of communications and learning in small groups (see below) he himself was later to provide further evidence in support of the view that students learn by using language.

Another interesting finding of Barnes's 1969 research related to the kinds of questions asked. Barnes found that in the "arts subjects lessons" observed—English, history, and religious education—there was a predominance of factual over reasoning questions. "This . . . suggests that the three arts teachers were teaching as though their tasks were more concerned with information than thought" (Barnes 1969 p. 22). This finding is supported by other studies of teachers' questioning behaviour.

While teachers' questioning has been subjected to a good deal of attention, their reception of pupils' responses has seldom been the object of study. This is the more surprising since in traditionally organized classrooms it is in the reactions of the teacher to pupil responses that crucial pedagogical work is carried out. If teaching involves a transformation process in which pupil consciousness is "changed", then in such classrooms the public manifestation of this is the work of transformation that teachers do on pupil responses. The typical structure of teachers' reactions to pupil answers is evaluation followed by reformulation, and then a short additional statement or the next question. Evaluations can be overt ("O.K.", "Right", "Good girl!") or nonverbal (nods, accepting noises, i.e. " . . . mmm").

So far, one of the few studies of teacher reformulations of pupil responses appears to be that of Watson and Young (1980). Working with transcripts of lessons in secondary classrooms, Watson and Young identified a range of functions in teacher reformulations, ranging from repeating a pupil's response so that everyone may hear, repeating it with positive approval because it is what the teacher wants, partial repetition of those parts the teacher wants to make a resource for further development, to a series of transformations which may complete, generalize, draw inferences from, replace terminology in, or otherwise transform the pupil utterance. Reformulations may function primarily to "check back" or "display understanding" or to provide an intersubjective frame of reference for the talk, or they may go beyond that to various degrees of replacement of pupil discourse by teacher discourse. Quite frequently, it seems that pupil responses are being treated as deficient in some way—as incomplete, ungeneral, incorrectly worded, and so on:

T: How would they react to him? (i.e., to the way he speaks).

P: They would start being more posh.

T: They might think some of his language was inaccurate or bad.

Watson and Young concluded that teacher reformulations often function to stigmatize and replace student discourse, and that too much of the semantic work of inference, generalization, implication, and so on is being done by the teacher rather than the pupils. The picture that emerges from investigations of traditional classrooms has been described by Edwards and Furlong (1978 p. 101) as a working out of the teacher's authority:

> The teacher provides a framework into which pupil talk is fitted, and that talk is assessed according to the closeness of fit. Brief pupil contributions are taken as being representative of the group, and the interaction then proceeds *as though* the other pupils either knew already, or shared the same and now *corrected* inadequacies as those who spoke. In its orderliness, and in the shaping of meanings, the interaction can be seen as the managed product of one of the participants.

And even in their investigation of a school committed to resource-based learning and making extensive use of structured course materials designed to foster independent learning, Edwards and Furlong found that " . . . pupils still have to suspend their own meanings and generate new ones in line with those implied by the teacher" (Edwards and Furlong 1978 p. 107). An alternative pattern is possible, but it is empirically quite rare. In this pattern there are fewer evaluations of pupil talk, reformulations are aimed more at clarification than correction, and a new teacher move makes its appearance. This move, called an "ownership marker", occurs in a process of "checking back", for example "Let me see if I have understood you correctly, you are saying x . . . is that right?" A move of this kind acknowledges that learners *own* knowledge too, and it invites learners to avail themselves of a "second chance" to refine their thoughts. The appearance of this move in transcripts is usually accompanied by other empirically rare features, such as the presence of a considerable number of departures from the dominant teacher–pupil 1–teacher–pupil 2–teacher sequence of turn taking (e.g., teacher–pupil 1–pupil 2–pupil 3–teacher–pupil 2). Obviously the attitude educators adopt towards findings of this kind will depend upon the value placed upon the development of intellectual independence and the capacity for critique in their philosophy of education. It should be noted, however, that the above discussion has focused almost exclusively on public teacher/pupil talk; the researchers did not see whether the pupils engaged in exploratory talk amongst themselves in order to help them to come to terms with new experiences.

It is in this connection that the later work of Barnes (Barnes and Todd 1977) is of particular significance. Studying the communication and learning of 13-year-olds working in small groups without a teacher present, Barnes and Todd demonstrated the value of giving the learner control over his/her language strategies. The children in these groups used dialogue as a mode of learning: freed from the need to give responses that meet with the teacher's approval, they felt able to raise questions, formulate hypotheses, think aloud. The quality of the children's discussion generally far exceeded the calibre of their contributions when the teacher was present.

3.1 The Search for an Appropriate Methodology

The approach to the classroom research of Barnes and Todd, and of Watson and Young, may be termed non-participant observation. Unlike, say, Flanders, they have not entered the classroom equipped with some observation instrument designed to standardize their collection of data; this has made them open to aspects of classroom life and language other than those being coded, and has also meant that the language, since it is generally recorded rather than coded on the spot, is open for reanalysis by others. But the complexity of classroom communication is such that the outside observer can miss a great deal, because he or she does not share assumptions peculiar to that class group and teacher which have been built up over time.

This consideration has led some classroom researchers to emulate more closely the methods of the anthropologist and adopt the role of participant observer, involving themselves in the teaching and describing of all aspects of the classroom situation over an extended period of time. Approaches of this kind also appear necessary if a clear idea is to be had of the constraints which give classroom discourse the dominant pattern noted earlier.

Field studies of this type have, however, been criticized by Mehan (1978 p. 35) as tending " . . . to have an anecdotal quality. Researchers cull a few exemplary instances of behaviour from field notes, but they seldom provide the criteria used to include certain instances and not others. As a result, it is difficult to determine the representativeness of the events described . . .". Mehan has therefore proposed a somewhat different approach which he calls constitutive ethnography. Constitutive ethnography stresses the importance of retrievable data, in addition to longer term ethnography. Data of this kind allow researchers to "examine interactions extensively and repeatedly, often frame by frame" (Mehan 1978 p. 36). Exhaustive treatment of all the data is a necessary part of the methodology, a check against the tendency of researchers to see only what they want to see. Further, constitutive ethnography includes what Mehan calls, (not to be confused with Flanders' terminology) "interactional analysis", by which he means an attempt to ground any social structural or educational abstractions on a clear foundation of those communicative events which concretely constitute the reality of social life in classrooms. Finally, " . . . constitutive ethnographers seek to ensure that the structure they see in events is the same as the structure that orients the participants in those events" (Mehan 1978 p. 37). That is, they seek to uncover the mental or cultural life of participants through the observation of the public dimension of talk and its structure. Further, they seek to bring the scientific process of generalization (e.g., about classrooms), into a relationship with "lay" generalization. That is, they bring the process whereby scientists attempt to treat essentially unique or different events (no two lessons are exactly the same) as if for certain purposes they were the same, into a relationship with the process whereby participants treat essentially different events as the same (e.g., classroom lessons). In this endeavour one of the main purposes is to discover how, by regarding separate events as being "the same", participants make it so.

In many ways, Mehan's view permits a reconciliation with some of the concerns which characterize the most recent research in the logical–empirical tradition. Mehan's insistence on exhaustive analysis of whole data records, on the construction of plausible interpretations of utterances given an ethnographic analysis of context, and his openness to reconstructing the way in which similarities across settings (e.g., from one classroom to another) may not only be necessary scientific constructs, but also perceptions constructed by participants who thereby form predictable and classifiable events in their own lives, brings together a concern for a sufficiently deep and rich interpretation of language with a classical logical–empirical concern for generalization.

Work of this kind suggests the possibility of collaborative methods which attempt to identify, through large-sample designs, the general incidence (and level of association with other factors) of qualitative elements of discourse which are originally selected for the key or paradigmatic role they may play in particular complexes of meaning revealed ethnographically.

4. Educational Implications

The educational implications of the study of teaching and learning through language are only now beginning to be understood. Three main groups of implications appear to emerge. First, teaching and learning are communicative activities which, for success at any level, require the linguistic and interpretive cooperation of the learner. Metaphors and models of teaching which treat ideas as packages, susceptible to some form of transportation from one mind to another, neglect the active linguistic, cognitive, and affective role of the listener (you can lead a horse to water but you cannot make it drink). Second, approaches to teaching and learning which fail to take full advantage of the active communicative role of the learner, in particular the possibility of learners using language in an active way to develop and fine tune their own understanding, may also be failing to take full advantage of an essential resource for effective learning. Third, unreflexive views of teaching and learning fail to recognize that communicative competence is an essential prerequisite of effective learning in the wide variety of learning contexts in later life, particularly those outside formal schooling situations. The development of this competence is not independent of the opportunities for its development and exercise provided in the communication structure of school classrooms themselves.

In short, the quality of education is affected by the cognitive and affective quality of the communicative relationship or dialogue which is, concretely, the major medium of schooling. Relationships with significant adults and the tasks which are defined as important within these relationships are the milieus in which children (and adults) acquire language competence and other developmental competence throughout their schooling. Ultimately it is necessary to be committed to an holistic understanding of classroom life in which the interactional processes mediated by language are seen as the emotional motor of development. In turn, the structure of the curriculum tasks given importance through their place in interaction must be seen as a major source of opportunities for cognitive and communicative development. A view of this kind permits significant questions to be asked about the relationship between competing definitions of the goals of education and the communicative roles of teachers and learners which are best adapted to each.

Readers will have noticed that little has been said about written communication, early language development, or the problems of teaching in classrooms where the language of instruction is not the first language of many pupils. Written language plays an important role in schools. If a survey were done of all the kinds of written communication in schools it would reveal a great deal of diversity: notes to parents, school reports, notes from the administration to staff, notices on notice boards, written work done in class in various parts of the curriculum, written comments by teachers on students' work, and so on. The language of textbooks and of examination papers is also worthy of attention. The variation in language from discipline to discipline is another area of interest.

Teachers (and pupils) may gain a better understanding of the many-sided role of language in schools, if some systematic collection of different examples of language is made. Tape recorders provide a convenient way of doing this for spoken language, photocopying for written language. Since teachers and pupils are themselves already highly skilled producers, users and interpreters of language, it is possible for them to produce useful and insightful analyses of language and to explore communication structures from an educational point of view.

Simple questions often yield penetrating answers: who said or wrote this, to whom, with what audience or distribution, and what were they trying to achieve with this language, and so on? Were they trying to change people's conduct or relationships with them or each other? Were they trying to deceive someone (and if so why)? Were they trying to change someone's opinion, attitudes, feelings? To what purpose? Was the purpose of this educational or the pursuit of some other value? Was the main purpose examination-oriented learning?

It is also possible to question the form of communication, given some sort of answer to the above questions. Is this way of speaking or writing, or this kind of audience or way of distributing the message best calculated to achieve the purpose in mind? Does the structure of communication (who is permitted to say what, who has access to what audiences or modes of distribution) help or hinder the achievement of educational goals? Is the structure of turn taking flexible or does the person in authority dominate it by having almost every second turn? Do different social categories of participants (e.g., teachers, pupils, principals) have an equal chance to make various kinds of moves when their turn comes, or does one category of person ask all the questions, evaluate all the answers, or criticize other speakers?

Teachers and pupils can become their own researchers and in sensitive exploration of the functioning of language around them explore ways of creating a better, more educational communication pattern in their schools.

See also: Evolution of Research on Teaching; Logical Operations; Teaching Cycles and Strategies

Bibliography

Barnes D, Todd F 1977 *Communication and Learning in Small Groups*. Routledge and Kegan Paul, London

Barnes D R, Britton J, Rosen H 1969 *Language, The Learner and the School*. Penguin, Harmondsworth

Bellack A A, Kliebard H M, Hyman R T, Smith F L 1966 *The Language of the Classroom*. Teachers College Press, New York

Edwards A D, Furlong V J 1978 *The Language of Teaching: Meaning in Classroom Interaction*. Heinemann, London

Flanders N A 1970 *Analyzing Teaching Behavior*. Addison-Wesley, Reading, Massachusetts

Halliday M A K 1961 Categories of the theory of grammar. *Word* 17: 241–92

Halliday M A K 1973 *Explorations in the Functions of Language*. Arnold, London

Hoetker J, Ahlbrand W 1969 The persistence of the recitation. *Am. Educ. Res. J.* 6(2): 145–67

Mehan H 1978 Structuring school structure. *Harvard Educ. Rev.* 48: 32–64

Sinclair J M, Coulthard R M 1975 *Towards an Analysis of Discourse: The English Used by Teachers and Pupils*. Oxford University Press, London

Smith B O, Meux M O 1962 *A Study of the Logic of Teaching*. University of Illinois, Urbana-Champaign, Illinois

Smith L M, Geoffrey W 1968 *The Complexities of an Urban Classroom*. Holt, Rinehart and Winston, New York

Stevens R 1912 *The Question as a Measure of Efficiency in Instruction: A Cultural Study of Classroom Practice*. Teachers College, Columbia University, New York

Watson K, Young R E 1980 Teacher reformulations of pupil discourse. *Aust. Rev. of Appl. Ling.* 3(2): 37–47

Mastery Learning Models

L. W. Anderson; J. H. Block

A prominent feature of contemporary educational thinking in both developed and developing countries has been a growing concern about the effectiveness and efficiency of schools. Whether educational policy makers have looked locally, regionally, nationally, or internationally, they have found that few schools seem to be promoting quite the degree of learning excellence of which they are capable and/or is expected of them. As a consequence, an increasing number of policy makers are searching for ways to reduce the gap between the existing and desired quality of school learning, not only within their respective countries, but across countries as well.

This article describes one approach for improving the quality of school learning that currently is being examined and evaluated by policy makers worldwide. This approach, called mastery learning, was introduced into the professional literature in the late 1960s (Bloom 1968). Since that time a great deal has been learned about mastery learning: what it is and isn't, how it works, and how well it works. The purpose of this section is to discuss what is currently known about mastery learning as well as what remains to be known.

The section begins with a definition of the model of teaching and learning called mastery learning. Subsequent subsections detail the historical development of mastery learning, the basic tasks facing educators desiring to use mastery learning as a vehicle for improving teaching and learning, the effectiveness of such programs in producing desired learner outcomes, and the future of mastery learning as a model of school teaching and learning. An extensive bibliography on mastery learning is available from Dr. Glenn Hymel, Clearinghouse on Mastery Learning, Loyola Center for Educational Improvement, Loyola University.

1. A Definition of Mastery Learning

What is mastery learning? Basically, it is two things. First, mastery learning is an old, optimistic philosophy about teaching and learning. Essentially this philosophy asserts that any teacher can help virtually all students to learn excellently, quickly, and self-confidently; the teacher can help "dumb," "slow," and "unmotivated" students to learn like "smart," "fast," and "motivated" students. Such learning, the philosophy contends, not only improves many students' chances for long-term social and personal prosperity, but many teachers' chances as well. In particular, the students acquire those basic personal competencies which ensure that they can and want to undertake lifelong learning, and the teachers acquire some basic professional competencies which ensure that they can and want to keep teaching.

Second, mastery learning is a set of old and new individualized instructional ideas and practices that consistently help most students to learn excellently, quickly, and self-confidently. These ideas and practices produce instruction that is systematic, provides help to students when and where they have learning difficulties, provides sufficient time for students to achieve mastery, and provides a clear criterion of what constitutes mastery (Bloom 1974 p. 6).

Two genotypic approaches to the use of these ideas and practices currently exist. The first is a group-based, teacher-paced approach. Students learn cooperatively with their classmates and the teacher controls the delivery and flow of instruction. The prototype for this approach is Bloom's Learning for Mastery (see, for example, Block and Anderson 1975). This approach has evolved from within the field of education and has had a major impact at the elementary and secondary levels of schooling.

The second approach is individual based and learner paced. Students learn independently of their classmates and each student controls the delivery and flow of instruction. Ideas and practices related to this latter approach lie at the heart of Keller's Personalized System of Instruction (PSI) (see *Keller Plan: A Personalized System of Instruction*) and Postlethwait's Audio-tutorial Instruction (see Postlethwait et al. 1964). This second approach evolved from the fields of psychology and biology and has had its major impact at the college and university levels.

Both of these mastery learning approaches are similar to, yet different from, other individualized instructional approaches such as Individually Prescribed Instruction, Individually Guided Education, Program for Learning According to Needs, and the matching of learning styles with teaching styles. The major similarity lies in their attempts to provide instructional settings that will accommodate a diversity of students. They all attempt to modify the instructional setting so that students possessing a variety of entering abilities, skills, knowledge, attitudes, and values can succeed.

The major differences reside in the type and timing of the individualization. Four types of individualization exist: (a) matching learner aptitudes or learning styles with appropriate instructional settings and/or teaching strategies; (b) placing learners at appropriate points in a relatively fixed sequence of instructional units or objectives, and permitting them to progress at their own rates; (c) providing a variety of materials and activities related to particular goals or objectives and allowing the learner (often with teacher guidance) to select from among them; and (d) providing supplementary, alternative instruction so as to correct learner errors identified by short formative tests. The mastery learning model of school teaching and learning relies almost exclusively on the final two types of individualization. Quite typically the variety of materials and activities is introduced after the formative tests have been administered.

In addition to differing in the type of individualization, individualized instructional programs also differ in the timing of the individualization. Most approaches to individualized instruction (including the individual-based, student-paced approach to mastery learning—see Block and Burns 1976) provide individualized instruction all the time; that is, to the extent possible the instruction is responsive to the needs of individual learners. Put simply, the use of group-based, teacher-paced mastery learning implies that instruction will be individualized as needed; that is, when it becomes evident that certain students are experiencing difficulty in benefiting from the group-based, teacher-paced practices. After the individualization has occurred, however, the students are placed back into the more traditional group-based, teacher-paced practices.

The emphasis on individualized corrective instruction is a key element of mastery learning and is based on the following assumption. No matter how good the match is between learner and learning environment, no matter how exact the sequence of objectives might be, and no matter how large the variety of materials and activities that exist for each objective, it is likely that some learner errors and misunderstandings will occur. As a consequence, the provision of extra time and help to some learners so that errors and misunderstandings will be corrected before they accumulate and interfere with future learning seems necessary to ensure the success of any form that individualized instruction may take.

One final distinction between mastery learning and other individualized instructional approaches is worth noting. Unlike other individualized approaches, mastery learning approaches are designed for use in the typical classroom situation where teachers already possess curricula they must "cover" or complete in a fixed period of calendar time, where inordinate amounts of instructional time cannot be spent on testing, and where student learning must be evaluated and grades or marks must be assigned periodically. Moreover, mastery learning approaches rely primarily on human beings for their success rather than on machines and other technological devices. Teachers and students are responsible for ensuring that time is used productively and that available techniques and materials are employed as needed.

2. A Historical Perspective on Mastery Learning

While future historians of education may say otherwise, the evolution of mastery learning as a model of school teaching and learning seems to fall into two distinct periods. The first period, dominated by the writings of Bloom at the University of Chicago (hereafter called the Bloom period), spanned the years from 1968 to 1971. The second period, dominated by the writings of Bloom's students and colleagues (hereafter called the post-Bloom period), spanned the time from 1971 to the present. Each of these periods will be described briefly.

2.1 The Bloom Period

As noted briefly at the outset of this article, mastery learning as an idea—a belief system—is old. But as the idea was periodically introduced in schools over the centuries, it constantly floundered due to the lack of a practical sustaining technology (Block 1971). It was Bloom who first provided the theoretical and practical basis for such a technology.

Bloom's theoretical contribution to the evolution of mastery learning was to transform the conceptual model of school learning developed by Carroll into a working model for mastery learning. Central to Carroll's model were three propositions.

(a) A student's aptitude for a given subject could be defined in terms of the amount of time he or she needs to learn the subject to a given level, rather than the level to which the subject would be learned in a given amount of time. That is, aptitude could be viewed as an index of learning rate, rather than learning level.

(b) The degree of learning for any student in a school setting is a simple function of the time he or she actually spends in learning relative to the time he or she needs to spend. Thus, to the extent that each student is allowed sufficient time to learn a given subject to some prespecified level, and he or she spends the time needed to learn, the student will likely learn the subject to the specified level.

(c) In a school learning situation, the time a student actually spends learning a subject as well as the time he or she needs to spend will be determined by certain instructional and personal characteristics. The two major instructional characteristics are the student's opportunity to learn (that is, the amount of classroom time allocated to learning the subject) (see *Time*), and the quality of instruction (that is, the degree to which the presentation, explanation, and ordering of the elements of the subject are optimal for the student). In addition to aptitude, the relevant personal characteristics are the student's ability to understand instruction and his or her perseverance.

Bloom synthesized these three propositions as follows. If aptitude is predictive of the rate at which, rather than the level to which, a student could learn, it should be possible to fix the degree of learning expected of students at some mastery level and to systematically manipulate the relevant instructional variables in Carroll's model such that all or almost all students attained mastery. Bloom argued that if students were normally distributed with respect to their aptitude for a subject and were provided uniform instruction in terms of both quality and time, then their achievement at the subject's completion would be normally distributed. Furthermore, the relationship between aptitude and achievement would be high (see Fig. 1).

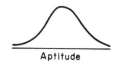 

Figure 1
Uniform instruction per learner

If, however, students were normally distributed on aptitude but each received optimal quality of instruction and adequate learning time, then a vast majority of students could be expected to attain mastery. In addition, there would be little or no relationship between aptitude and achievement (see Fig. 2).

Bloom's practical contribution to the evolution of the mastery learning approach to instruction was to outline a classroom teaching strategy that would systematically vary, as necessary, how and how long each student was taught. For this purpose, he returned to the earlier

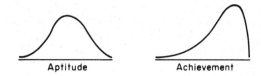

Figure 2
Optimal instruction per learner

approach of Washburne (1922) called the "Winnetka Plan" (see *The Winnetka Scheme*) and especially to the approach of Morrison (1926) at the University of Chicago's Laboratory School. And out of the similarities of these two approaches, he culled the basic elements of his own approach. Some of these elements have been summarized by McNeil (1969 p. 308).

(a) The learner must understand the nature of the task to be learned and the procedure to be followed in learning it.

(b) The specific instructional objectives relating to the learning task must be formulated.

(c) It is useful to break a course or subject into small units of learning and to test at the end of each unit.

(d) The teacher should provide feedback as to the learner's particular errors and difficulties after each test.

(e) The teacher must find ways to alter the time some individuals have available to learn.

(f) It may be profitable to provide alternative learning opportunities.

(g) Student effort is increased when small groups of two or three students meet regularly for as long as an hour to review their test results and to help one another overcome the difficulties identified by means of the test.

2.2 Post-Bloom Period

Some educators immediately viewed both Bloom's theoretical and practical ideas as being a great boondoggle while other educators viewed them as being a great boon. Most practitioners, however, stood on the sidelines of the boon–boondoggle debate until they better understood the theory and, in particular, the practice of mastery learning. While Bloom turned his attention to developing the theory (for example, Bloom 1976), a number of Bloom's students and their colleagues devoted their attention to developing the practice.

At first, the efforts of some of these individuals were concentrated on applying the theory and related practices to the improvement of classroom and then school-wide practices. Soon it became apparent that interest in the evolving mastery learning approach had spread far beyond the classroom and school level. Entire local, regional, and even national school systems desired to plumb the potential of the evolving mastery learning approach for their particular problems (Block 1979). As a consequence the efforts of many individuals shifted to the improvement of systemwide practices. Since systemwide applications of mastery learning practices require the cooperative efforts of many individuals at many levels (e.g., university, faculty, school administrators, classroom teacher) a network of mastery learning practitioners was formed in the United States. This network, known as the Network of Outcome-based Schools, is affiliated with the American Association of School Administrators (Arlington, Virginia). Its primary purpose is to encourage the discussion, summarization, and dissemination of mastery-related strategies, practices, and materials. Through the network practitioners are spared the grief of rediscovering the wheel and instead can profit from the attempts and mistakes of others.

Also, since the mid-1970s, mastery learning has been applied to an ever-increasing variety of subject areas (many technical in nature) and extended beyond the secondary-school level. Subjects such as geography, biology, psychology, sociology, music, public speaking, allied health, nursing, pharmacy, and veterinary pathology have experienced the intrusion of mastery learning. Mastery learning programs have been implemented in community colleges as well as four-year colleges.

3. Basic Tasks Facing Developers of Mastery Learning Programs

Educators desiring to plan and implement mastery learning programs in their schools and classrooms must accomplish four major tasks. These tasks are (a) defining mastery, (b) planning for mastery, (c) teaching for mastery, and (d) grading for mastery. Each of these major tasks can be divided into several subtasks, the accomplishment of which is related to the accomplishment of the overall task.

Before moving to a discussion of the tasks and subtasks, two additional points must be made. First, if mastery learning programs are to be as successful as they might be, *all* of the tasks and related subtasks must be accomplished. That is, one cannot have a mastery learning program if one stops after defining mastery, for example.

Second, and somewhat related to the first point, *how* these tasks and subtasks are accomplished is less important than that they *are*, in fact, accomplished. Each of the tasks and related subtasks serves an important function within the context of mastery learning (Anderson and Anderson 1982). These functions should be understood by developers of mastery learning programs.

In light of the previous discussion the next four subsections will focus on the nature and function of the tasks and subtasks involved in the development of a successful mastery learning program. The majority of examples and illustrations will reflect the group-based, teacher-paced approach since this approach is the easiest and least costly to implement. The function of each major task will be presented at the beginning of each section. Following the presentation of the function of the task a sequence of subtasks will be described. Where appropriate the functions served by particular subtasks will be included in the discussion of the subtasks.

The focus on the nature and function of the tasks and subtasks at the expense of a discussion of the methods and techniques available for accomplishing these tasks is not meant to minimize the importance or availability of such methods or techniques. Indeed a vast, ever-improving technology has developed around many of the critical subtasks. A large number of papers and articles have been written on the topic of mastery testing, for example. Rather a focus on the nature and significance of the tasks and subtasks seems more appropriate for fostering a general understanding of mastery learning as a model of school teaching and learning.

3.1 Defining Mastery

As has been mentioned earlier, mastery learning programs are outcome based. Thus, the first task facing educators who want to employ mastery learning ideas and strategies is to define precisely what is meant by mastery. Such a definition includes the specification of long-term and short-term outcomes, and a specification of abstract outcomes (i.e., goals) and concrete representations of these abstract outcomes (i.e., tests and acceptable levels of performance on the tests). The major function of defining mastery by clearly specifying the goals, tests, and performance standards at both the course (long-term) and unit (short-term) level is the communication of learner and learning expectations to students, teachers, administrators, and parents.

The initial subtask related to defining mastery is the identification of the most essential, critical course outcomes or objectives. One of the major trade-offs involved in mastery learning is the substitution of excellent learning of a limited number of highly desirable objectives (which is called a "mastery" emphasis) for the mediocre learning of virtually all conceivable objectives with a course (which is called a "coverage" emphasis). If this trade-off is to be worthwhile, however, the objectives selected must be those with the greatest potential for transfer or applicability to future learning.

Once the objectives have been identified, a final, summative test is prepared. The functions of this test are to (a) assess the degree of student learning over the entire course, and (b) evaluate (i.e., grade) the overall quality of student learning.

Based on an examination of the objectives and related test items a standard of performance for the summative test is set that, when achieved, will be accepted as mastery of the course. Thus mastery can be defined as the answer to the question "What test evidence will be accepted that the desired type and degree of excellent learning has occurred?'' Pragmatically, a standard is set which corresponds to the score typically attained or surpassed by the best students taught by traditional or nonmastery methods.

Next, the entire course is divided into a series of smaller learning units. A set of objectives for each unit, based on identified or hypothesized interrelationships, is delineated. Each unit is long enough to allow sufficient time for students to learn an interrelated set of facts, concepts, principles, skills, and appreciations. At the same time, however, the units are short enough to permit the close monitoring of each student's learning as the units and course unfold. The function of such units is to facilitate the teaching and learning of new objectives in a context (rather than in isolation).

Once the units have been formed they are sequenced or ordered so that the facts, concepts, principles, skills, and appreciations acquired in one unit are used over and over again in subsequent units. This approach to sequencing helps ensure that the things learned in one unit will not be forgotten by the students and, hence, will be available for later use. A second function of sequencing or order is to increase the likelihood that subsequent objectives will be at an appropriate level of difficulty for students who have mastered the objectives of the previous unit(s).

The final subtask of defining mastery involves deciding what will constitute mastery of each learning unit. Tests appropriate for the assessment of student learning vis à vis the unit objectives are designed. These tests, called formative tests, are intended to help teachers identify student errors and misunderstandings. Such information is to be used to improve student learning rather than to evaluate the quality of that learning. Once again, as in the case of the summative test, performance standards are set for each formative test. These mastery performance standards will aid the teacher in the determination of those students who have successfully mastered the unit and those who will require additional time and help if mastery is to be attained.

3.2 Planning for Mastery

Once mastery has been defined, the next task is to plan for mastery. Plans for helping students acquire the objectives of each unit are designed. These plans must be consistent with the way in which mastery has been defined. Specifically, the plans must include activities and materials related to the unit objectives and must include additional, supplementary activities and materials for those students failing to attain the performance standard on the unit formative test.

The function of planning for mastery is to permit teachers to be proactive in their classroom teaching. Rather than having to react to situations as they arise and having to manufacture solutions on the spot, proactive teachers are ready for such situations. They can anticipate likely problems and respond in one of a variety of appropriate, preplanned ways (see *Proactive Teaching*; *Reactive Teaching*).

In essence, planning enables teachers to monitor student learning on a unit by unit basis. If the evidence gathered from the formative tests (and other sources such as homework) suggests that the learning is not proceeding as well as expected and/or desired, then steps can be taken to intervene so that, ultimately, the desired degree of learning is attained. If steps are not taken to overcome the errors and misunderstandings identified by the tests, then these errors and misunderstandings will probably accumulate and interfere with future learning.

The first subtask of planning for mastery is to design a general plan for helping all students master the unit objectives. Initial concerns for the development of such a plan focus on two important aspects of high quality instruction. First, the material relating to each objective should be presented in a way that is appropriate for the vast majority of students in the classroom. Second, the activities in which the relevant material is embedded should involve or engage the vast majority of students in the process of learning. This general plan is often referred to as the "original instructional plan" (Block and Anderson 1975).

The second subtask involves the preparation of methods for interpreting and using the information gathered from the formative tests. Quite typically, a set of alternative instructional materials and learning activities keyed to each objective on the unit's formative test is developed. These correctives, as they are called, are designed so as to reteach each unit's objectives, but to do so in ways that differ from the original instruction. Small-group study sessions, peer or cross-age tutoring, or alternative learning aids such as different textbooks, workbooks, and audiovisual materials are often used in this regard (Block and Anderson 1975).

If the correctives are to be used during regular class time, then plans for those students initially achieving mastery on the formative tests must be designed. Anderson and Jones (1981) suggest several options for use with these students. The options tend to develop, in the order to be presented, over the duration of a mastery learning program.

Option 1 involves using the initial "masters" as tutors for the "nonmasters." For this option to be entirely successful, however, the students must be willing to serve as tutors, they should have specific tutorial materials available, and they must be trained as tutors. Option 2 requires that the initial "masters" be permitted to complete work in other subject areas or engage in nonacademic work, such as recreational reading. Option 3 requires that the initial "masters" engage in structured independent study. Students specify (a) what they are to learn, (b) how they will learn, and (c) how they are to demonstrate they have learned. In many ways, such independent study reinforces the basics of mastery learning. Finally, option 4 allows the students to engage in "vertical enrichment." In one sense, student pacing permits "faster" students to engage in "horizontal enrichment." That is, students progress from unit to unit acquiring an increasing number of concepts, facts, and skills. In contrast with horizontal enrichment, vertical enrichment consists of materials and activities that allow students to probe more deeply into the content and ideas included in a learning unit by examining the relationships among the content and ideas within or across units. Examples of vertical enrichment are provided in Anderson and Jones (1981).

One aspect of planning which is often overlooked is the planning of time. Approximate amounts of time must be allocated to the original instruction, corrective instruction, and testing. Such time planning serves three functions. First, it provides the opportunity for realistic estimates of the amount of material and objectives that can be included in a course. Second, it increases the quantity of time that each student spends in learning. Essentially, each student is constrained to spend as much time as necessary to master the objectives of one unit before moving to another unit. Such constraints are the core of the Carroll model (see Sect. 3). Third, time planning helps to increase the quality of the time that each student spends in learning. This increase in quality stems from two sources. Students increasingly possess the knowledge and skills necessary to profit from each subsequent unit's instruction. In addition, students are exposed to several ways of presenting the material and involving them in learning. At least one of these ways is likely to be effective for virtually every student.

3.3 Teaching for Mastery

Following defining and planning, the next task is teaching. The focus when teaching for mastery is on managing learning rather than managing learners. Inside the classroom "the function of the teacher to specify what is to be learned, to motivate pupils to learn it, to provide them with instructional materials, to administer these materials at a rate suitable for each pupil, to monitor students' progress, to diagnose difficulties and provide proper remediation for them, to give praise and encouragement for good performance, and to give review and practice that will maintain pupils' learning over long periods of time" (Carroll 1971 pp. 29–30).

Since many students are not accustomed to learning for mastery or the possibility that they all might earn A's, the first subtask of teaching for mastery is the orientation of students. Students are informed of what they are expected to learn, how they will learn it, how they are expected to demonstrate their learning, and how the adequacy of their learning will be judged. They are told about the grading system (emphasizing that their learning will be graded relative to a predetermined performance standard, not relative to the learning of their classmates). Finally, they are told that they will receive extra time and help as needed in order to ensure their learning.

A series of subtasks occur in fairly rapid succession following this initial orientation of students. The second subtask involves teaching each learning unit in sequence using the original instructional plan. After the initial instruction has been completed, and before moving to the next unit, the next subtask, the administration of the unit's formative test, is performed. Based on the formative test results, those students who have achieved the performance standard are certified and those who have not are identified. Next, students initially classified as masters are free to engage in enrichment activities and/or to serve as tutors for their "slower" classmates; the nonmasters move to the corrective stage of the mastery learning instructional model. The day on which initial instruction relative to the next unit will begin is announced. If teachers desire to postpone the start of the next unit students are given in-class as well as out-of-class time to complete their assigned or selected corrective activities and materials. If not, out-of-class time must be used.

Since formative tests provide information about the adequacy of instruction as well as learning, two phases of corrective instruction can be visualized. The first phase provides corrective instruction for those objectives not mastered by a substantial number of students. In all likelihood such massive nonmastery indicates an instructional problem. As a consequence, additional class time can be taken to provide whole-class or large-group corrective instruction relating to such objectives.

The second phase provides alternative activities and materials which are keyed to each objective and which can be used for corrective instruction. A sheet of paper identifying each objective, appropriate test items, and recommended activities and materials can be presented to each student. The objectives not mastered can be designated in some manner. Such a sheet becomes a "feedback/corrective" vehicle. Students are expected to explore these alternative ways of learning, to select, often with teacher guidance, those best suited to their individual needs and interests, and to spend sufficient time engaged in this relearning.

This cycle of original instruction, formative testing, and certification or correction is repeated, unit by unit, until all units have been completed. This cycle is paced by the teacher so that about as much material and as many objectives are covered as would be covered in the time available had traditional methods of instruction been used. Such pacing helps to ensure that all students, the "faster" as well as the "slower," are exposed to as much course material and as many course objectives as they would ordinarily encounter.

The teacher has two pacing options. If all the time for correctives and enrichment is available outside of the regular class period, then the pacing of the instruction proceeds as usual. If some part or all of the time for correctives (and enrichment) is available during the regular class period, the teacher can adjust the pace of the instruction. Such an adjustment can be made by allowing more time for the earlier units and less time for the later ones. Essentially, time that would ordinarily be spent on later units is "borrowed" and spent on the earlier units. The assumption underlying this borrowing is that the additional time spent early will yield great time benefits later. Students who learn for mastery at the onset of a course or program should learn more effectively and efficiently as the course proceeds than they would were they learning under more traditional methods.

3.4 Grading for Mastery

The final major task facing developers of mastery learning programs is grading for mastery. The function of grading in mastery learning programs is to reward students for the acquisition of the essential, critical course objectives. Thus grades are assigned to students based on their performance on the summative test relative to the predetermined performance standard, not based on their performance relative to the performance of other students.

Such mastery grading is designed to engage students in what White (1959) has called "competence motivation," that is, the desire to compete against oneself and the objectives to be learned, and to disengage students from what Block (1977) has termed "competition motivation," that is, the desire to compete against others. From the standpoint of developing the talents of all students, rather than the talents of a select few, competence motivation is preferable to competition motivation.

The first subtask of grading for mastery is the administration of the summative test. All students whose scores are at or above the mastery performance standard earn grades of "A" or equivalent. At least two options are available for the grading of students who score below the performance standard. The choice of an option constitutes the second subtask. A first option, one most consistent with the philosophy of mastery learning, is to assign grades of "incompletes" (or equivalent) to these students. From a mastery learning perspective these students have not yet spent sufficient time and/or received sufficient help. If this option is selected a so-called "open transcript" is required. An open transcript is one that allows students to demonstrate and receive credit for improved levels of performance at any time.

A second option is to assign the remainder of the traditional grades (that is, "B," "C," "D," and "F") to scores at various gradations below the mastery performance standard. If this option is selected the grades assigned to these students should reflect the number of objectives acquired as evidenced by their performance on the summative test. Even a grade of "F" should indicate the acquisition of some number of objectives.

One issue related to grading for mastery must be raised. First, some teachers prefer to, or are required to, assign grades based on the results of several summative tests. The preference for this practice stems from the belief that sound evaluation of student learning is enhanced by multiple pieces of information, each test viewed as one piece of information. The necessity for

this practice is based on the multiple marking periods which exist in many schools. To the extent that the length of a course is one academic year and that academic year is divided into, say, four marking periods, then a minimum of one summative test per marking period would be required for grades to be assigned each marking period. Course grades would be some composite of these four grades.

Some educators have expressed the desire to use formative test results as part of the grading process, rather than increasing the number of summative tests. Such a use of formative tests is contrary to their function. From a functional perspective, formative tests are intended to provide evidence that can be used to monitor (rather than evaluate) student learning so that quality of instruction decisions (not quality of learning decisions) can be made. As has been mentioned, summative tests are intended to gather cumulative information for use in grading students. In view of the different functions of the two tests the use of only summative tests for grading purposes is highly recommended. If this recommendation is followed, then multiple summative tests must be prepared when defining mastery. The preparation of such tests should be consistent with their intended functions as described in Sect. 3.1.

4. Research on Mastery Learning

Research on the mastery learning model of teaching and learning is abundant. Comprehensive reviews of the research have been conducted by Block and Burns (1976), Bloom (1976), Dolan (1977–78), Burns (1979), and Guskey and Gates (1985). The purpose of this section is to present what we consider the three major generalizations that can be derived from this research.

4.1 Mastery Learning is Effective

This generalization is evident to anyone who performs even a cursory examination of the research literature. Beginning with the early studies which were small-scale, used laboratory-like learning tasks, and occurred in rather contrived classroom settings (for example, programmed instruction) and continuing to the present studies which are large-scale (often involving entire school districts in the United States, or entire countries, such as the Republic of Korea and Indonesia), use school-related learning tasks, and take place in naturally occurring classroom settings, the effectiveness of mastery learning programs has been demonstrated repeatedly (about 90 percent of the time, in fact).

Recent reviews have begun to quantify this effectiveness. Burns (1979), for example, has estimated the average "effective size" of mastery learning programs compared to nonmastery programs. Based on this estimate, the research suggests that the average student enrolled in mastery learning classes would achieve better than 80 to 85 percent of the students in nonmastery classes.

Research on the effectiveness of mastery learning

programs is not limited to studies of immediate achievement. Although not as numerous as those focusing on immediate achievement, several studies have examined the effectiveness of mastery learning programs in terms of students' retention and rate of learning, as well as students' attitudes and self-perceptions. In the vast majority of these studies students enrolled in mastery learning classes outperformed their nonmastery counterparts. That is, students learning under mastery-based conditions (a) retained a greater portion of what they learned, (b) learned to learn more efficiently, (c) were more positive in their attitudes toward the subject being learned, and (d) developed greater self-confidence in their ability to learn.

4.2 The Key to Effectiveness Lies Within the Feedback/ Corrective Mechanism

At least two aspects of this generalization are worth noting and describing. The first is the level at which the mastery performance standard is set; the second is the provision and utilization of corrective instruction.

The level at which the performance standard is set is critical to the success of mastery learning programs. Block (1972) was the first to pursue the issue of the setting of mastery performance standards. Block examined the teaching of matrix arithmetic to eighth graders (13-year-olds). Based on his results, Block concluded that a mastery performance standard set at 95 percent correct produced maximal cognitive learning. Unfortunately, this 95 percent standard had somewhat negative effects on students' attitudes and interests. Setting the standard at 85 percent correct, however, produced maximal interests and attitudes and somewhat reduced, but acceptable, levels of cognitive achievement.

In a more recent study Chan (1981), using a mastery learning approach to the teaching of reading comprehension to third-grade students, partially replicated Block's findings concerning cognitive learning. Once again, the 95 percent correct mastery performance standard yielded maximal learning. Students required to attain a lesser standard (i.e., 75 percent correct) achieved no better than did students learning under the nonmastery approach. Unfortunately, Chan did not include a standard of 85 percent correct in her study.

The results of the research on standard setting suggest the standard must be set sufficiently high so as to ensure that the desired learning has occurred. Capricious standard setting may result in no real, functional standards at all. The research suggests that standards somewhere between 85 and 95 percent are most appropriate.

As indicated earlier, the provision and utilization of corrective instruction is a second key to the effectiveness of mastery learning. The importance of corrective instruction was first hinted at in a study by Collins (1970) and established by Block (1970). A more recent study by Nordin (1980), however, provides greater details of the role that corrective instruction plays in the overall effectiveness of mastery learning. Nordin focused on three of the major components of Bloom's (1976) conceptualization of quality of instruction: cues (or the clarity of presentation of the material to the students), participation (or the extent to which students were actively engaged in the learning process), and feedback/correctives. Nordin formed five groups of Malaysian sixth-grade students. He provided enhanced cues to one group, enhanced participation to a second, enhanced cues and participation to a third, feedback and correctives to a fourth, and conventional group instruction to a fifth. In terms of both cognitive achievement and learning rate, the students in the feedback/corrective group outperformed the students in the other four groups. And, in terms of student interest, students in the feedback/corrective group were more positive than the students in three of the other four groups. The exception was the enhanced cues group whose students had levels of interest similar to the students in the feedback/corrective group.

Vivid graphical evidence of the improvement in student performance following the use of correctives is displayed in Soemarso et al. (1980). Furthermore, the importance of utilization (as opposed to mere provision) of correctives is shown in Jones et al. (1975).

The importance of the corrective instruction component of mastery learning can be attributed largely to the increase in time available for learning. Quite clearly, corrective instruction increases the amount of time available for learning. And there is some evidence to suggest that, following corrective instruction, students spend an increasing proportion of the available time involved in learning or on-task (Anderson 1976).

4.3 Mastery Learning is Differentially Effective for Different Types of Students

This generalization is derived from research on two student characteristics: ability and age.

(a) *Ability*. One of the questions posed to proponents of mastery learning is whether students at all ability levels benefit equally well from mastery learning or whether the increased learning of the lower ability students is purchased at the cost of decreased learning of high-ability students. The results from several studies have shed some light on this question.

Kim (1969) stratified his sample according to the students' general ability. Two strata of ability, above average and below average, were formed. Students were assigned to either a mastery learning or nonmastery class. Following completion of the study Kim examined the results of the summative test separately by ability stratum. Using 80 percent correct as the summative mastery performance standard, Kim found for the low-ability students that 50 percent of those in the mastery learning class as compared with only 8 percent in the nonmastery class achieved mastery. For the high-ability students 95 percent of the mastery learning students and 64 percent of the nonmastery students achieved mastery.

Detheux et al. (1974) used socioeconomic status as a proxy for entering ability level. Three levels of socioeconomic status were formed: underprivileged (60 percent), average (30 percent), and privileged (10 percent). The results of the Detheux et al. study suggested that while the mastery learning program was especially beneficial for the underprivileged students, all three groups benefitted from the program. The Detheux et al. study is important since a more elite group of high-ability students (10 percent) was included than in the Kim study (50 percent).

The results of studies which have examined students of different ability levels indicate that the lower ability students, do, in fact, benefit more from mastery learning than the high-ability students. At the same time, however, the high-ability students do not suffer. Either they also benefit somewhat from the mastery learning program or, at the very least, do not do any worse than their high-ability counterparts in nonmastery programs (Anderson and Reynolds 1979).

Some may attribute the comparable results of high-ability students in mastery learning and nonmastery classes to the ceiling effect of the test. A recent study (Chan 1981) tends to dispute this attribution. Chan devised three sets of reading comprehension items. The first set was targeted for grade 3, the second set for grade 4, and the third set for grade 5. These sets of items were "linked" together using techniques underlying the Rasch psychometric model. Since the students were enrolled in grade 3, the summative test was virtually "ceilingless." Chan found that the high-ability students in the mastery learning groups achieved at virtually the same level as their nonmastery counterparts.

(b) *Age*. Recent school-based evaluations of mastery learning programs have begun to examine the impact of these programs at different grade levels (Abrams 1981, Cohen 1981). Most frequently these programs have been implemented over a period of several years, typically in grades 1 through 8. A time-series design has been used to evaluate program effectiveness. The results suggest that mastery learning programs have their greatest impact on students in grades 5 through 8. Relatively little impact has been seen at grades 1 through 4.

These results are somewhat surprising given the assertion of both some proponents and critics of mastery learning that mastery learning is especially effective when (a) it is introduced very early in the schooling process and (b) it is employed in the teaching of simple, "closed" subjects rather than more complex, "open" subjects. Quite clearly subject matters become increasingly "open" and complex as students progress through the grades (Block and Burns 1976).

Taken as a whole, the research evidence suggests that the mastery learning model of school teaching and learning represents one of those major breakthroughs to the improvement of student learning and school teaching for which both the educational practitioner community and the educational research, development, and dissemination community have been searching. Indeed, this growing body of research strongly suggests that mastery learning strategies usually have met, wholly

or in part, general research criteria usually unmet by most other innovative approaches to the improvement of school teaching and learning. Mastery learning strategies can be taught to teachers, are being used, and are effective for large numbers of students.

5. The Future of Mastery Learning Practice and Research

Having lasted for 15 years the mastery learning model of instruction can no longer be considered a fad or passing fancy. Rather it must be viewed as a legitimate attempt to improve the quality of teaching and learning in the schools. What does the future hold for mastery learning? This article concludes with several speculations.

5.1 Speculation 1

The number and variety of schools employing some type of mastery learning program will continue to increase. This increase will be greater in countries whose philosophy of education and/or societal needs are congruent with mastery learning as a philosophy and instructional strategy; countries in which the prevalent belief system is that virtually all students can learn and/or there is a societal need for an increase in the number of competent individuals.

However, two issues must be attended to if mastery learning programs are to expand and improve. First, key elements of the mastery learning model of teaching and learning should be included in the curriculum materials. Objectives should be clearly stated in meaningful (not necessarily behavioral) terms. Tests relating to each objective should be available and the relationship between test items and objectives clearly specified. Meaningful performance standards should be recommended. Such performance standards should be set on the basis of the application of some systematic procedure. The curriculum should be organized into learning units not book chapters. Criteria should be established for the development of such learning units. Multiple sets of teaching–learning activities and related materials should be available for each objective. These sets will be used to provide the initial and corrective instruction relative to the objectives. If possible, the types of students for which the different sets are likely to be particularly effective should be described. Finally, supplemental booklets of secure, summative tests should be included. The inclusion of these key elements will reduce the amount of time and effort needed by school personnel to define and plan for mastery. In essence, the first two major tasks described previously will have been accomplished.

Second, a strong staff development program needs to be prepared in order to teach teachers to teach for mastery. Many teachers must develop the skills needed to properly implement mastery learning programs. Specific teaching skills related to clarity of presentation, involving students in the learning process, providing knowledge of results, providing encouragement, using test results to make instructional decisions, prescribing appropriate corrective instruction, and monitoring student learning processes and outcomes are critical to the success of mastery learning programs.

To date attempts at large-scale implementation of mastery learning programs have tended to either (a) embed key elements into the curriculum and curricular materials, *or* (b) develop a strong staff development program. These two approaches have been identified and labeled as the curriculum/materials approach and the staff development approach. For mastery learning to be successful over the long haul, both the curriculum/materials approach *and* the staff development approach must be employed.

5.2 Speculation 2

Educators will begin to explore the preventative power of mastery learning. To date the major use of mastery learning has been remedial rather than preventative. It is not uncommon in the United States, for example, to find mastery learning programs used in grades 11 and 12 to undo the learning problems accumulated by many students over the previous 10 or 11 years. Quite clearly, certain subjects, classes, teachers, and schools throughout the world already have many students, especially older ones, who have already failed to learn excellently, and educators must use approaches such as mastery learning in an attempt to discontinue this negative trend. At the same time, however, it may be possible to introduce mastery learning early in the grades to immunize students from future problems and failure. If such an immunization occurs it may be possible to eliminate mastery learning at the later grades because mastery learners have been produced.

6. Needed Research

Several areas of research require future attention if the full potential of mastery learning is to be realized and if a better understanding of mastery learning is to be gained. Additional studies of the overall effectiveness of mastery learning are simply not needed. Such studies already abound. Rather, it would be more profitable to turn attention to two related areas of research: (a) research which examines the conditions under which mastery learning is more and less effective, and (b) research which examines the limits of student learning that are possible to achieve using the mastery learning approach to school teaching and learning. Each area will be considered briefly.

Are there conditions which are more and less conducive to the effective use of mastery learning programs? If so, do these conditions involve conditions of classrooms, teachers, administrators, and/or students? These two questions form the basis for this entire area of needed research. Replications of the research on student ability level and student age/grade level are needed. Research on the level or type of administrative

support necessary for successful implementation of mastery learning programs would be useful. There is a need for research on the effectiveness of mastery learning programs in the hands of preservice and inservice teachers. Research focusing on the extent to which the effectiveness of mastery learning programs depends on classroom contextual characteristics such as the ability distribution of the students (homogeneous versus heterogeneous), classroom organization (open versus traditional), or class size seems important.

Finally, can empirically verified estimates of the limits of student learning be obtained under mastery learning conditions? Bloom (1968, 1976) has provided a theoretical estimate. He contends that approximately 95 percent of students can learn well what is taught in schools. Yet only a few studies have supported this theoretical estimate. These studies have been what Bloom (1976) labeled microlevel studies; that is, studies of relatively short duration, focusing on clearly defined learning tasks, and under relatively tight experimental control. The question remains: to what extent is it possible, under normal schooling conditions, to replicate the results of the microlevel studies and, as a consequence, to provide empirical support for Bloom's theoretical limits. If ways can be found to approach these theoretical limits the future of mastery learning is bright indeed. The only question remaining to be answered by educators is whether it is truly desirable to approach these limits.

See also: The Carroll Model; Individualizing Teaching

Bibliography

Abrams J D 1981 Precise teaching is more effective teaching. *Educ. Leadership* 39: 138–39
Anderson L W 1976 An empirical investigation of individual differences in time to learn. *J. Educ. Psychol.* 68(2): 226–33
Anderson L W, Anderson J C 1982 A functional approach to the definition of mastery learning. Paper presented at the Annual Meeting of the American Educational Research Association, New York
Anderson L W, Jones B F 1981 Designing instructional strategies which facilitate learning for mastery. *Educ. Psychol.* 16(3): 121–38
Anderson L W, Reynolds A 1979 The effect of mastery learning on the achievement of high ability students and the academic self-concept of low achieving students. Paper presented at the Annual Meeting of the American Educational Research Association, San Francisco, California
Block J H 1970 The effects of various levels of performance on selected cognitive, affective, and time variables. (Unpublished Ph.D. Dissertation, University of Chicago)
Block J H 1971 Introduction to mastery learning: Theory and practice. In: Block J H (ed.) 1971 *Mastery Learning: Theory and Practice.* Holt, Rinehart and Winston, New York, pp. 2–12
Block J H 1972 Student learning and the setting of mastery performance standards. *Educ. Horizons* 50: 183–91
Block J H 1977 Individualized instruction: A mastery learning perspective. *Educ. Leadership* 34: 337–41

Block J H 1979 Mastery learning: The current state of the craft. *Educ. Leadership* 37: 114–17

Block J H, Anderson L W 1975 *Mastery Learning in Classroom Instruction.* Macmillan, New York

Block J H, Burns R B 1976 Mastery learning. In: Shulman L S (ed.) 1976 *Review of Research in Education*, Vol. 4. Peacock, Itasca, Illinois

Bloom B S 1968 Learning for mastery. UCLA-CSEIP *Eval. Comment.* 1(2)

Bloom B S 1974 An introduction to mastery learning theory. In: Block J H (ed.) 1974 *Schools, Society, and Mastery Learning.* Holt, Rinehart and Winston, New York

Bloom B S 1976 *Human Characteristics and School Learning.* McGraw-Hill, New York

Burns R B 1979 Mastery learning: Does it work? *Educ. Leadership* 37: 110–13

Carroll J B 1971 Problems of measurement related to the concept of learning for mastery. In: Block J H (ed.) 1971 *Mastery Learning: Theory and Practice.* Holt, Rinehart and Winston, New York, pp. 29–48

Chan K S 1981 The interaction of aptitude with mastery versus non-mastery instruction: Effects on reading comprehension of grade three students. (Unpublished Ph.D. Dissertation, University of Western Australia)

Cohen S A 1981 Dilemmas in the use of learner responsive delivery systems. Paper presented at the annual meeting of the American Educational Research Association, Los Angeles, California

Collins K M 1970 A strategy for mastery learning in modern mathematics (Unpublished study, Purdue University, Division of Mathematical Sciences)

Detheux M, Leclerq E, Paquay J, Thirion A M 1974 From compensatory education to mastery learning. *London Educ. Rev.* 3(3): 41–50

Dolan L 1977–78 The status of mastery learning research and practice. *Administrator's Notebook.* 26(3): 1–4

Guskey T R, Gates S L 1985 A synthesis of research on group-based mastery learning programs. Paper presented at the annual meeting of the American Educational Research Association, Chicago, Illinois

Jones E L et al. 1975 *Mastery Learning: A Strategy for Academic Success in a Community College (Topical Paper No. 53).* ERIC Clearinghouse for Junior College Information, University of California, Los Angeles. ERIC Document No. ED 115 315

Kim H et al. 1969 *A Study of the Bloom Strategies for Mastery Learning.* Korean Institute for Research in the Behavioral Sciences, Seoul

McNeil J D 1969 Forces influencing curriculum. *Rev. Educ. Res.* 39: 293–318

Morrison H C 1926 *The Practice of Teaching in the Secondary School.* University of Chicago Press, Chicago, Illinois

Nordin A B 1980 Improving learning: An experiment in rural primary schools in Malaysia. *Eval. Educ.* 4: 143–263

Postlethwait S N, Novak J D, Murray H 1964 *An Integrated Experience Approach to Learning with an Emphasis on Independent Study.* Burgess, Minneapolis, Minnesota

Soemarso, Suharaini Arikunto, Moh. Said, Muhain Lubis 1980 *Dalam Bidang Studi: 1) Mathematika Kelas IV, 2) Bahasa Indonesia Kelas IV, 3) Ilma Pengetahuan Alam Kelas VI.* Departemen Pendidikan dan Kebudayan, Jakarta

Washburne C W 1922 Educational measurement as a key to individualizing instruction and promotion. *J. Educ. Res.* 5: 195–206

White R W 1959 Motivation reconsidered: The concept of competence. *Psychol. Rev.* 66: 297–333

Models of Heuristic Teaching

M. C. Wittrock

Since ancient times, people have tried to understand and improve instruction and teaching. From their thoughts, studies, research, and trial and error experience with learners they have built models of instruction. These models organize and convey to others their authors' conceptions of the essentials of instruction and its facilitation.

The following article discusses the group of these models that pertains to the teaching of heuristics. It begins by briefly discussing historical approaches to heuristic instruction. It then turns to modern conceptions developed in different parts of the world.

Models of heuristic instruction present their authors' conceptions of the teaching of methods of problem solving and learning strategies, including methods of learning and remembering information. These models elucidate some of the multiple effects of teaching that go beyond the learning of facts and answers to include learning how to learn, how to solve problems, and how to develop and use strategies and plans. In the eyes of many of the authors of models of heuristic instruction, the learning of these useful and transferable methods, such as the scientific method or an effective learning strategy, is a centrally important educational objective. The attainment of this objective implies that instruction should be designed to accomplish multiple purposes at several levels simultaneously, such as learning to solve problems while also learning facts and answers to specific questions.

1. Historical Approaches

The perennial quest for effective methods to teach heuristics in the process of presenting subject matter dates to antiquity, to ancient Greece and Rome. Plato's *Meno* exemplifies the ancient debate about these teaching problems.

In the *Meno*, Socrates taught the pythagorean theorem to a slave boy. But the context of the discussion between Socrates and Meno indicates that the teaching of the theorem was not the only or even the central issue of the work. Socrates was interested in whether it was possible to teach virtue, and even to inquire of its meaning. Because Plato believed that the basic forms of knowledge were innate in all people he argued that a lowly slave could, with proper teaching, learn to recall a mathematical theorem.

In the process of developing his arguments, Plato teaches not only mathematics, but the nature of virtue, the role of heredity and memory in teaching, and some heuristics of logic and argumentation. He teaches methods of inquiry as well as the following substantive ideas about teaching. He implies that even the lowly slave boy in the *Meno* could learn the pythagorean theorem if he had a skillful teacher who would help him recall it from memory. He maintains that an instructor does not teach a student, in the usual sense of the word. Instead, through skillful questioning a teacher helps learners to recall inherited concepts which they have stored in memory, but do not recollect.

The Socratic technique of teaching, which is widespread in use today, for example in many law schools, derives in large part from Plato's beliefs about heuristic instruction and its relation to learners' memories. In this conception of instruction, as in modern day cognitive and information processing models, the learners' thought processes and memories are critical in the design of teaching. The learner is active, and the teacher functions by stimulating the learner to recall concepts and to construct solutions to problems, rather than by teaching answers to questions.

In several sources, such as his short work entitled *Memory and Recollection*, Aristotle discusses his thoughts about memory and learning, which influenced teaching in ancient times and in the middle ages, and which still influence modern ideas about instruction. Aristotle believed that experiences determine what is learnt and remembered. One remembers experiences by actively creating and storing images in memory. One recollects or retrieves these stored memories for use later by associating them with one another in order, according to the principles of similarity, contrast, and contiguity. Learning is in large part the process of actively constructing a strategy for storing images in a readily retrievable, ordered sequence. Teaching is, again in part, the process of facilitating the learners' construction and use of a strategy for forming images, associating them with one another in order, and retrieving them from memory.

Aristotle's model of memory and recollection has also influenced instruction. Along with pedagogical systems for teaching people to form images and to store them in order, which are described in Cicero's *De Oratore*, Quintilian's *Institution Oratoria*, and the anonymously authored *Rhetorica Ad Herennium*, Aristotle's model comprised half of the ancient Art of Memory. This ancient art was regularly taught in Greek and Roman higher education as part of rhetoric, which in those days was the art of public speaking. Teachers, students, scholars, statesmen, actors, and politicians were taught heuristic imagery systems, such as the loci method, which enabled them to remember long lists of ordered points and arguments for use during lectures, examinations, court cases, plays, and speeches.

These beliefs about imagery training systems were also taught to clergymen during the middle ages. Saint Thomas Aquinas and Albertus Magnus taught the ancient art of memory to monks. The art of memory may also have influenced the widespread use of elaborate and beautiful statues, paintings, frescos, friezes, and tapestries that adorned religious and public buildings in the middle ages. These colorful and decorative works of art also had instructional purposes. They provided memorable, concrete representations of important abstractions, such as love and bravery, and of important religious and secular historical events. In these ways the ancient art of memory influenced teaching in the middle ages. The art of using imagery to remember abstract ideas or important events was useful for teaching millions of people, many of whom could not read or write.

The pedagogical use of imagery to teach ideas and events waned in many parts of the world during modern times. However, recent interest in instructional media — including television, movies, and computerized graphic displays — leads to renewed interest in images, in their role in facilitating memorable learning, and in methods of teaching learners how to construct them. As a result, the ancient heuristic systems for facilitating memory and retrieval through learner-constructed images survive today in most of the commonly taught mnemonic systems used to enhance recall of names, facts, and concepts. These systems all depend upon the learners' construction of relations between familiar concepts and new or unfamiliar concepts or facts to be remembered. This sound principle of learning is an important part of many current models of heuristic instruction.

The other principles of learning and memory Plato and Aristotle discussed, including similarity, contrast, and contiguity, the role of organized memory in learning new information, the development of interactive relations in images and in verbal propositions, the active generation of mental representations for information to be learned, and the teachers' roles in facilitating these learning processes, have also contributed to modern-day models of heuristic instruction. Those models will be discussed next.

2. Modern Approaches

Current models of heuristic instruction derive largely from behavioristic, cognitive, and humanistic psychological perspectives. These three perspectives differ from one another in their focus on the importance of heuristics, and in their methods of studying heuristic instruction.

Behavioristic models, as different from cognitive

models, relate characteristics of environments directly to learned behavior. The people who develop behavioristic models believe that it is more productive to study how environments and their characteristics, such as reinforcers, teacher characteristics, teaching materials, classroom conditions, and teacher classroom behaviors directly influence learners' behavior. The teaching of heuristics is not especially emphasized or studied in these models.

On the contrary, people who develop cognitive models of instruction believe that it is more scientifically productive to study how environmental variables, including teacher classroom behaviors, influence learners' mental processes, such as thinking, problem solving, and heuristics, which in turn influence learning, knowledge acquisition, attitude formation, beliefs, and actions. Both behaviorists and cognitivists share interest in behavior, its prediction, and its understanding. However, they differ on the better way to attain these scientific ends, and in their interest in the study of heuristics of learning, strategies, and problem-solving methods.

Humanistic psychologists also study thought processes, learning strategies, and affective processes, such as feelings and attitudes. However, they focus their attention on the individuality and uniqueness of learners and their developing self-concepts. They tend to view the individual learners as people who should be helped to actualize their potentialities through making choices and decisions for which they are held responsible. In the following paragraphs, models of instruction derived from these perspectives that have influenced the teaching of heuristics will be discussed.

Behavioristic approaches to instruction have implications for research on teaching, but have not often focused on the teaching of heuristics. Instead, these approaches imply that researchers should look for direct relations between environmental variables, such as teacher classroom behaviors, and student achievement. The so-called "process–product" research on teaching examines correlations between teacher activities or characteristics, as stimuli for the learner, and student achievement, as the learners' responses. The goal of this research is to predict teacher effectiveness. Any of a large number of teacher activities or characteristics can be correlated with a wide variety of student behaviors as measures of achievement. This method of research implicitly assumes that the teacher's characteristics and behaviors cause student learning and achievement, not only predict it. From this line of inquiry, teacher enthusiasm, clarity of presentation, and direct instruction seem to predict student achievement in a variety of contexts. One of the limitations of this approach is that it does not lead to explanations about how teacher enthusiasm or clarity influence student achievement. Nor does the approach help one to select one over another characteristic of a teacher to observe or to study as a possible cause or predictor of achievement. What does enthusiasm by the teacher cause the learner to do? Pay atten-

tion? Relax? Construct a strategy? Rehearse information better? At a deeper level, this approach assumes that useful relations exist and are to be found between teacher or environmental variables and achievement, rather than between learners mediating processes—their strategies and plans—and achievement, or between teacher and other environmental variables and learners' mediating processes. With these limitations in mind, one still finds that the model has utility for educational research, including the design of programmed materials to teach problem solving using principles of reinforcement and practice (see *Paradigms for Research*).

Reminiscent of ancient writings about imagery and verbal thought processes, modern cognitive models for teaching heuristics emphasize the importance of the learners' cognitive and affective processes in mediating the effects of instructional environments upon student achievement. From this perspective, instruction, differently for different people, induces learners to use their thought processes and memories to generate strategies, plans, and mental representations of ideas, facts, and concepts. Learning involves an interaction between the students' knowledge and memories and the information to be learned. Instruction is the process of inducing the learners to construct these interactions. Although reinforced practice is compatible with this perspective, it emphasizes instructional procedures, such as modeling, observational learning, discussions, and the learner construction of images, analogies, inferences, strategies, and plans.

In these models, the learners' perceptions, strategies, plans, and interpretations are critical to learning. Teaching produces its effects upon learning only by influencing the learners' thought processes, not by automatically enhancing learning as a function of reinforced practice.

These cognitive models of instruction date to antiquity, including the writings of Aristotle and Plato. They have again become prevalent around the world during the twentieth century. Recently, they have enjoyed a resurgence of interest in the study of heuristics and learning strategies. Several of these models chosen to reflect problems of heuristic instruction and to represent work from different parts of the world will be examined, beginning with models developed by Judd, Montessori, and Piaget, then turning to recent work by Brunner, Ausubel, Galperin, Feuerstein, Wittrock, and Rogers (see *Information Processing Models*).

2.1 Charles Judd's Transfer Model

Charles Judd (1980) contrasts his approach to that of Thorndike in a simple experiment he and Scholckow conducted with fifth and sixth grade pupils (ages 10–12). One group of boys in the study was asked to throw darts to hit a target submerged under 12 inches of water. This group of boys was taught the principle of refraction, that is, how light rays bend when they pass from water to air. The second group of boys was given the same task but no instruction in refraction. When the depth of the water over the target was changed from 12 to 4 inches, the boys given the instruction in the theory of refraction quickly learned to hit the target in shallower water, while the boys not taught the theory were confused by the change. The practice with the water 12 inches deep did not profit the boys who learned without the theory of refraction. More than reinforced practice was involved in this task. Understanding the principle of refraction was important for developing a strategy relevant to performing in a new situation. In Judd's model, being active means thinking, relating thoughts to action, principles to dart throwing, and developing a transferable strategy.

2.2 Jean Piaget's Model of Knowledge Acquisition

Jean Piaget wrote extensively about children's cognition, including intellectual development, imagery, perception, mathematics learning, science learning, and language development. He also wrote about education, teaching, instruction, and how knowledge is acquired (1970, 1973). In these two sources, he repeatedly states (e.g. 1970 pp. 71–72) that activity means internal manipulations of objects, and that meanings come from the actions the child performs on these objects, rather than from these objects themselves. He develops the theme of construction learning in a book appropriately titled *To Understand is to Invent* (1973 pp. 15, 20, and 34). Genuine activity, he writes, requires the students to reconstruct or to rediscover facts they are trying to learn. For the teaching of arts and sciences he advocates: (a) active learners, in the sense just described, and (b) learner experience with the experimental method, including testing one's hypotheses as explanations of historical events or physical phenomena. In his model, productive learning, understanding, and creativity are highly valued. Student discovery, or rediscovery of concepts and principles through active experimentation, juxtaposing principles and data, is a primary method of instruction. Direct instruction, or direct imparting of concepts and principles, is not advocated. Piaget's model of constructive learning, which he describes often with examples from science learning, shares principles with John Dewey's model of problem solving and the scientific method as a foundation for designing instruction.

As Judd, Piaget, and Dewey wrote, instruction involves more than teaching learners to make specific responses at the right times and in the right places. It involves learning problem-solving strategies, heuristics, and learning strategies. Instruction involves teaching principles and abstractions by having the learners reconstruct them in carefully designed educational settings involving experiments and problems. According to Piaget, one accommodates cognitive structures to encompass new experience, or one assimilates the new experience into previously formed cognitive structures. This juxtaposition of organized knowledge structures, events, and experience is the essential intellectual process involved in learning from instruction. Teaching

requires the learner to be mentally active in transforming objects by relating schemata or knowledge structures to them. Knowledge acquisition consists of the rediscoveries that this interactive process entails, not in the learning of objects or events in themselves.

2.3 Maria Montessori's Method and Materials

From quite a different perspective, Maria Montessori (reprinted twice in 1965) designed carefully structured didactic materials to teach motor skills, to train the senses, and to provide discovery learning experiences to underprivileged children in Rome. She began with Edward Seguin's educational methods designed for use with children who were deaf, paralyzed, or suffering from other physical or mental diseases or injuries. From these methods, she designed materials that she used to teach mentally retarded children in Rome's Orthophrenic School. The materials and methods she developed are now used in many parts of the world to teach children of all levels of intellectual ability.

The first level of the Montessori curriculum, called "preparatory experiences," is for children aged $2\frac{1}{2}$ to 4 years. The prepared environment scales the learning materials, furniture, and equipment in the classroom to the child's physical and mental ability. Motor education tasks and materials teach the children to walk, sit, and carry, for example. Sensory education materials train the senses of smell, hearing, touch, and so forth. Increasingly fine sensory discriminations are taught using materials that the children manipulate to learn to discriminate or to match sounds, smells, shapes, textures, and temperatures. Language education focuses upon naming qualities of objects, recognizing the objects, and pronouncing their names.

Academic learning begins at age 4 and emphasizes writing, reading, and arithmetic. The teaching of writing precedes the teaching of reading. Arithmetic concepts, such as number concepts, are represented and learned perceptually before they are taught symbolically, using materials such as beads and rods. Learning by discovery within a carefully structured physical environment, replete with educationally important materials, is the method of instruction employed in Montessori schools. The method is designed to develop cognitive and heuristic skills, sensory discriminations, and symbolic and perceptual abilities, rather than specific behaviors in association with specific stimuli. The Montessori materials and methods show how a structured classroom and inductive procedures can be used to try to teach cognitions, general skills, and abilities.

2.4 Jerome Bruner's Model of Discovery Learning and Instruction

In a number of writings about education (1960, 1966) Bruner describes his model of instruction, which emphasizes learning by discovery. The first of four main features of the model is the predispositions of the learners, the cultural experiences in children's background needed to encourage children to learn and to want to learn.

The second part of the model is the structure and form of knowledge to be presented to the learner, including its mode of representation. Bruner maintains that any domain of knowledge can be represented to learners: (a) enactively, that is, by a set of actions, (b) iconically, that is by images or graphics, and (c) symbolically, that is, by verbal symbols or by logical propositions. The problem of $2 + 2 = ?$ can be represented enactively with groups of two objects, such as apples, which the child manipulates, iconically by pictures of two groups of two apples, and symbolically in a word problem that asks how many total apples one has if one has two groups of two apples.

The sequence of instruction is the third part of Bruner's model. The normal sequence of instruction for most learners is from enactive through iconic to symbolic representation (1966 p. 49). However, some learners can skip the first or second representations, if they have the appropriate background of experience.

The fourth and last part of the model is the form and pacing of reinforcement. Hypothesis testing, using a test–operate–test–exit (TOTE) heuristic procedure, is the heuristic used by people to learn and to solve problems, he maintains. They proceed in a hierarchical manner, eliminating unknowns and incorrect hypotheses, using knowledge of results, and reinforcement to evaluate their hypotheses. In Bruner's model, reinforcement functions as any other form of knowledge, not as an automatic process to facilitate forming bonds or associations. The learner increasingly becomes independent of the teacher's supply of reinforcers and information by learning to discover concepts and answers through the heuristic of testing hypotheses and revising them based on feedback. In this model, an emphasis is found upon teaching students several thought processes, such as hypothesis testing or a scientific method, as well as teaching them facts, concepts, and answers. As in the other cognitive models discussed, the learners' cognitions and thoughts are important, both as a way to learn facts and concepts and as a procedure for solving problems and creative thinking. Practice at the process of solving problems and creating new schemata is the heuristic called discovery learning, which results in meaningful learning.

2.5 David Ausubel's Model of Meaningful Verbal Learning

Ausubel (1963) distinguishes between discovery learning, in which the essence of the learning is not given but must be derived by the learner, and reception learning, in which the essentials to be learned are given or are taught directly to the learner. Ausubel maintains that either of these types of learning, including verbal reception learning, can be meaningful or rote. He states that one need not discover information, concepts, or rules to achieve meaningful learning. On this issue, he differs

from some cognitive instructional theorists who imply or state openly that discovery learning is necessary to produce meaningful learning and retention. In his model, meaningful learning results, whether discovered or not, when the new information is related to relevant and inclusive concepts in one's cognitive structure. Information which cannot or is not related to more inclusive cognitive structures is rotely learned. Forgetting of meaningful material occurs because it is increasingly incorporated into the general inclusive anchors or subsuming categories. It is subsumed.

In Ausubel's model, for information to be learned meaningfully, it must first be logically, rather than arbitrarily, relatable to relevant concepts in the learner's cognitive structure. Second, the material must be relatable to the particular cognitive structure of an individual learner. That is, the learner must have the appropriate background. If the material meets these conditions, then meaningful learning occurs provided the learners have a set or expectation to relate the new material to their cognitive structure. It follows then that reception learning can also be meaningful, when these conditions are met. It follows also that learners should be taught the heuristics of relating new material to their cognitive structure. Learners might also be given these relationships, for example in advanced organizers.

Ausubel has conducted a lengthy series of studies on instruction. Many of these studies test the effect of advance organizers upon meaningful learning. They often indicate that enhancing the relation between relevant cognitive structure and new material facilitates learning.

2.6 P. Y. Galperin's Model of the Stages of Mental Operations

The close relationship between intellectual development and instruction has been studied by a number of people in the Soviet Union, including Lev Vygotsky and his students, colleagues, and successors, such as Leontiev and Davydov. This school of thought emphasizes how instruction influences and changes the mental activity of the child. Instruction influences and even precedes development. The teaching of mental acts and heuristics, not behavior, is the core of instruction.

Galperin (1957, 1969) presents his model of mental actions in instruction. Instruction in this model involves the successive internalization of the control over a learner's actions or activities. During instruction, an action or mental activity develops along four dimensions: (a) its level of mastery, (b) its generalization to other situations, (c) its completeness, and (d) its degree of mastery, or its familiarity.

The first dimension, level of mastery, has been explored in several studies of instruction. Five stages of instruction have been identified along this dimension of level of mastery. They represent progressive steps toward the internal control of behavior. The initial stage is one where the child cannot act. This one is not considered a stage in the instruction. The first instructional stage is called "creating a preliminary conception of the task". In this stage, the teacher demonstrates the task and the children become familiar with it. This orienting period draws the learners' attention to the task and motivates them to learn. The task might be to count the items in a set. The second stage of mastery is called "mastery of the action using objects". In this stage, the learners go beyond observational learning to perform an externally controlled, teacher-directed action. The learners use concrete materials or objects. A child might count buttons, moving them from one pile to another.

In the third stage, called "mastering the action on the plane of audible speech", the children learn to perform the activity without physical objects. They could, for example, count aloud without buttons. This stage represents the transition from concrete to conceptual and verbal control of activity or learning. The fourth stage is called "transferring the action to the mental plane". Now the children are asked not to speak aloud, but to whisper and then to "speak" silently to themselves, using language or imagery. The children might count the buttons silently, for example. The transfer to control by thought is practiced until it becomes automatic.

Last, the fifth stage of mastery, called "consolidating the mental action", involves abbreviating the mental action, and "short-circuiting" it so that the desired behavior is performed quickly and well, when the appropriate problem occurs. The counting might occur silently in units larger than one, or perhaps instantly without enumeration of the items in a small set. The teaching of a mental action, then, proceeds through these five steps, increasing the internal, largely verbal control, as well as bringing the action under conceptual control, generalizing it, and abbreviating it.

Recently, De Corte (De Corte and Verschaffel 1981) used Galperin's model to teach elementary-school children heuristics to solve arithmetic problems involving understanding the concepts of equals and part-whole relations. Compared with a standard textbook instruction, the experimental teaching program enhanced learning, retention, and transfer.

2.7 Reuven Feuerstein's Model of Instrumental Enrichment

Feuerstein (1980) presents a model of instruction in which learning strategies determine the behavior of retarded learners. Through direct exposure to the environment and through culturally mediated experiences (that is, through the people who guide children's learning) cognitions and heuristics grow and develop, and cognitive structure is modified. With retarded learners, Feuerstein maintains that mediated learning experiences need to be improved or changed to enable the children to become modified through direct exposure to stimuli and to extract meaning from experi-

ence. Feuerstein presents exercises and instructional materials to train deficient cognitive strategies in the input phase, the elaboration phase, and the output phase, as well as to train affective and motivation processes. These interventions are aimed directly at changing the cognitive processes of the learners, not their environmental learning or living conditions, including poverty or discrimination. According to this model, impoverished environmental conditions *may* reduce mediated learning. But the best of materially rich environments and high socioeconomic status *may* also reduce mediated learning. Meaningful learning depends upon more than its environment. It depends upon the learners' strategies and problem-solving methods and their engagement in culturally mediated experiences. Feuerstein's instrumental enrichment program aims at correcting learners' deficient cognitive functions, teaching basic heuristics, developing intrinsic motivation for learning and for performing specific tasks, learning reflective thinking, and acquiring autonomous cognitive behavior (1980, Chap. 6). Through training in these functions, Feuerstein intends to improve the learners, rather than the environments, and thus to initiate self-regulated and lasting remediation of deficient learning in schools resulting in successful adaptation to the demanding conditions of modern technological societies.

2.8 M. C. Wittrock's Model of Generative Learning and Teaching

Wittrock (1974, 1981) described a cognitive model of learning and instruction in which the generations the learners performed on information influenced their learning and comprehension of it. As different from elaborations, which are comments and explanations given by teachers, generations are mental activities performed by learners, usually upon request by the teacher. Generations include summaries, pictures, headings, inferences, evaluations, underlinings, metaphors, analogies, diagrams, and discussions. As in the other cognitive models of instruction discussed, generative instruction predicts learning as a function of the learners' mental activities during teaching.

In several studies generative instruction has consistently enhanced reading comprehension and retention among elementary-school, high-school, and college students. In these studies the learners are asked to generate headings or summaries of paragraphs they read (Doctorow et al. 1978), to develop verbal and spatial analogies and relations between new information and experience (Linden and Wittrock 1981), or to use familiar themes to generate meaning for unfamiliar words (Wittrock et al. 1975). The learners actively generate relations between their experience and the text they read or among the different parts of the text (Wittrock and Carter 1975). The heuristic of generating one's own interpretation or representation facilitates memory and comprehension.

2.9 Carl Rogers' Model of Experiential Learning and Instruction

Rogers (1967, 1969) contrasts associative learning, which he maintains does not change individuals, with experiential learning, which changes people. Experiential learning has the following characteristics. It involves the whole person, both cognitively and affectively. It is self-initiated by the learner, even when an external impetus may be involved. It is pervasive, in that it is important to the learners' behaviors, attitudes, and sometimes to their personalities. It is evaluated by the learner. Last of all, its essence is meaning.

For Rogers, instruction should not aim to transmit knowledge, which is quickly outmoded. Instead, instruction should aim at teaching the heuristics of discovery, by which knowledge is acquired. Learning how to learn and how to change are primarily goals of education for Rogers.

Rogers makes several assumptions about learners, from which he derives conditions of instruction that will facilitate the learning he values. Briefly summarized, these assumptions include the beliefs that people have a natural potential to learn by discovery, and that learning is significant when it is perceived by the learners as relevant to their purposes. He also believes that instruction should often allow the learners to learn by doing—by solving problems. He further believes that learners should participate responsibly in learning, including making choices about resources and problems, and living with the consequences of those choices. Teaching that involves the learners' feelings and cognitions produces the most lasting and valued learning, according to Rogers. Teaching that involves learner self-evaluation as primary feedback, and evaluation by others, as secondary feedback, best facilitates creativity. Last of all, he feels that society needs people who have acquired an openness to experience and who have learned how to change.

Rogers (1967) lists Richard Suchman's (1961) inquiry training program, a science teaching program that emphasizes student generation of hypotheses from data, as an example of instruction that stimulates experiential, self-directed learning. He also maintains that classroom simulation of historical events or of social conflicts is another way of obtaining significant learning through instruction. Short programs of instruction, in books or in teaching machines, can also enable learners to acquire knowledge that they need to solve significant problems, according to Rogers.

These comments conclude the discussion of models of instruction relevant to the teaching of heuristics. The next section discusses teaching applications of these models of heuristic instruction.

3. Teaching Applications

In recent years several research studies designed to teach heuristics have been conducted. These studies build upon the principles of learning and models of instruction discussed earlier.

The Productive Thinking Program (Covington et al. 1972) teaches elementary-school children a heuristic for solving problems. The program includes a set of stories, with pictures, in which mysteries are presented to two youngsters, a boy and a girl, and their uncle. These three characters provide models for the readers to emulate as they read the program and try to solve each problem. For example, the uncle demonstrates the importance of collecting facts and evidence, developing hypotheses consistent with the observations, and testing the adequacy of the hypothesized explanations to account for the data. In this system the authors use the principles of modeling, practice, and reinforcement to teach a problem-solving heuristic.

From a cognitive perspective, Suchman's (1961) inquiry training program presents filmed physics problems to elementary-school children. For example, one problem shows that a tiny floating sailboat moves across water when a small motor-driven fan situated on the side of the tub blows air into its sail. However, when the same functioning and portable fan and its electric motor are mounted on the boat, it no longer moves across the water; even though its sail is filled with air from the revolving fan. The inquiry training program, unlike the Productive Teaching Program, uses discovery learning. Children are taught the heuristic of gathering data first, by asking questions, followed by actively developing a hypothesis that explains the event they have observed.

Pólya (1975) in his book *How to Solve It* presents a four-part heuristic for solving problems. The first part involves understanding the problem by isolating its parts, unknown quantities, and conditions. The second step is devising a plan, which includes perceiving relations between the problem and earlier experience, or among the parts of the problem. The third step is carrying out the plan and checking each step. The fourth part is *looking back*, including checking the answer and generalizing the technique to related problems. Pólya's problem-solving heuristic has not been developed into a teaching program.

However, independently from Pólya's work, and in a different area of study, a similar four-part teaching program has been developed to teach impulsive and aggressive elementary-school boys a strategy for controlling their attention. Using principles of cognition developed by Donald Meichenbaum and his colleagues, Camp (1980) teaches these boys to ask themselves four questions: (a) What is my problem?; (b) How shall I do it?; (c) Am I following my plan?; and (d) How did I do? Her data indicate that after 30 training sessions, impulsive elementary-school age boys showed gains in the control of attention and in IQ, reading, and teacher ratings of interpersonal behavior.

In research on the acquisition of knowledge, heuristics have also been successfully taught to students to help them learn, remember, and comprehend information.

Teaching children to draw pictures as they read (Bull and Wittrock 1973) or to construct mental images of the sentences they read (Pressley 1976, Linden and Wittrock 1981) enhanced their learning and their retention of the text. Constructing relations among words (Wittrock and Carter 1975), or among sentences, by writing summaries of each paragraph one reads (Doctorow et al. 1978) also facilitated memory and comprehension, sometimes doubling it.

Imaginary mnemonics, such as modern-day applications of the ancient loci method, sizably enhanced the memory of foreign-language vocabulary words (Atkinson and Raugh 1975). In research on knowledge acquisition and retention, both verbal methods and imaginary techniques seem to facilitate learning or memory.

In research on creativity, a large number of training programs, including synectics and brainstorming, have been developed for use in industry and in schools. In their book *Creative Learning and Teaching*, Torrance and Myers elaborate their model and discuss teaching materials designed to teach creativity in elementary schools. Their model consists of five steps: (a) sensing problems and challenges; (b) recognizing the real problem; (c) producing alternative solutions; (d) evaluating ideas; and (e) preparing to put ideas into use (Torrance and Myers 1970 pp. 78–82). Their teaching materials apply this heuristic to the problem of teaching subjects in elementary school. In brief, in several areas of research, models of heuristic instruction have been applied to some practical problems of enhancing learning, memory, comprehension, and creativity.

4. Summary

The teaching of problem-solving strategies, learning strategies, heuristics of discovery, and memory mnemonics is an ancient, often neglected topic that has recently become a center of research interest in the study of teaching. In diverse areas, such as the study of creativity, knowledge acquisition, attention, learning disabilities, science teaching, and mathematics, recently developed models and empirical findings, indicate that strategies, heuristics, and mnemonics can often be successfully taught to students who can and do transfer these general cognitive skills to the problems of learning, remembering, and comprehending information taught in schools.

Most recently, educational researchers have begun to study methods of teaching these strategies and heuristics that will enhance their continued effective use of schools after the training in the heuristic has been completed. This research is just beginning, and it is too early to make any definite comments about its findings. However, from the data available, it seems that several characteristics are important in the teaching of transferable and lasting, useful heuristics. First, learner awareness or knowledge about the strategy, often called metacognition, increases its lasting utility. Second, learner monitoring of one's own use of heuristics seems

likely to enhance their continued use. Third, learner generation of specific applications of practical strategies also seems important to sustaining and transfering their use. Generation of summaries, questions, analogies, pictures, and inferences in a variety of learning contexts seems likely to enhance transfer, retention, and comprehension in a variety of subjects taught in school.

In sum, recent empirical research on the teaching of heuristics has shown sizable gains in learning, retention, and comprehension attributable to the use of strategies and problem-solving methods. Equally importantly, these research studies indicate that in the process of learning facts and concepts people also learn strategies and heuristics. Learner awareness of the significance of the strategies, monitoring of their use, and generation of specific applications of them in the classroom promise to increase further their widespread and effective use.

See also: History of Teaching Methods

Bibliography

Atkinson R C, Raugh M R 1975 An application of the mnemonic keyword method to the acquisition of a Russian vocabulary. *J. Exp. Psychol. Hum. Learn. Memory* 104: 126–33

Ausubel D P 1963 *The Psychology of Meaningful Verbal Learning: An Introduction to School Learning.* Grune and Stratton, New York

Bruner J S 1960 *The Process of Education.* Harvard University Press, Cambridge, Massachusetts

Bruner J S 1966 *Toward a Theory of Instruction.* Harvard University Press, Cambridge, Massachusetts

Bull B L, Wittrock M C 1973 Imagery in the learning of verbal definitions. *Br. J. Educ. Psychol.* 43: 289–93

Camp B W 1980 Two psychoeducational treatment programs for young aggressive boys. In: Whalen C K, Henker B (eds.) 1980 *Hyperactive Children: the Social Ecology of Identification and Treatment.* Academic Press, New York, pp. 191–219

Covington M V, Crutchfield R S, Davies L, Olton R M 1972 *The Productive Thinking Program: A Course in Learning to Think.* Merrill, Columbus, Ohio

De Corte E, Verschaffel L 1981 Children's solution in elementary arithmetic problems: analysis and improvement. *J. Educ. Psychol.* 73: 765–79

Doctorow M J, Wittrock M C, Marks C B 1978 Generative processes in reading comprehension. *J. Educ. Psychol.* 70: 109–18

Feuerstein R 1980 *Instrumental Enrichment: An Intervention Program for Cognitive Modifiability.* University Park Press, Baltimore, Maryland

Galperin P Y 1957 An experimental study in the formation of mental actions. In: Simon B (ed.) 1957 *Psychology in the Soviet Union.* Routledge and Kegan Paul, London pp 213–25

Galperin P Y 1969 Stages in the development of mental acts. In Cole M, Maltzman I (eds.) 1969 *A Handbook of Contemporary Soviet Psychology.* Basic Books, New York

Judd C H 1980 The relation of special training to general intelligence. *Educ. Rev.* 36: 28–42

Linden M, Wittrock M C 1981 The teaching of reading comprehension according to the model of generative learning. *Read. Res. Q.* 17: 44–57

Montessori M 1964a *The Montessori Elementary Material.* Bentley, Cambridge, Massachusetts (originally published in 1917 by Stokes, New York)

Montessori M 1964b *The Montessori Method: Pedagogy as Applied to Child Education in the Children's Houses.* Bentley, Cambridge, Massachusetts (originally published by 1912 by Stokes, New York)

Piaget J 1970 *Science of Education and the Psychology of the Child.* Orion Press, New York

Piaget J 1973 *To Understand is to Invent: The Future of Education.* Grossman, New York

Pólya G 1975 *How to Solve It*, 2nd edn. Princeton University Press, Princeton, New Jersey

Pressley G M 1976 Mental imagery helps eight-year-olds remember what they read. *J. Educ. Psychol.* 68: 355–59

Rogers C R 1967 The facilitation of significant learning. In: Siegel L (ed.) 1967 *Instruction: Some Contemporary Viewpoints.* Chandler, San Francisco, California

Rogers C R 1969 *Freedom to Learn: A View of What Education Might Become.* Merrill, Columbus, Ohio

Suchman J R 1961 Inquiry training: Building skills for autonomous discovery. *Merrill-Palmer Q.* 7: 147–69

Torrance E P, Myers R E 1970 *Creative Learning and Teaching.* Dodd, Mead, New York

Wittrock M C 1974 Learning as a generative process. *Educ. Psychol.* 11: 87–95

Wittrock M C 1981 Reading comprehension. In: Pirozzolo F T, Wittrock M C (eds.) 1981 *Neuropsychological and Cognitive Processes in Reading.* Academic Press, New York

Wittrock M C, Carter J 1975 Generative processing of hierarchically organized words. *Am. J. Psychol.* 88: 489–501

Wittrock M C, Marks C B, Doctorow M J 1975 Reading as a generative process. *J. Educ. Psychol.* 67: 484–89

Teacher Education

Concepts of Teacher Education

G. De Landsheere

Teacher education or teacher development can be considered in three phases: preservice, induction, and inservice. The three phases are now considered as parts of a continuous process (see *Induction of Beginning Teachers*; *Inservice Teacher Education*).

While the education of professionals like medical doctors, engineers, and agronomists, is to a great extent basically similar all over the world, the nature of teacher education, often limited to teacher training, is strongly dependent on the level of economic development and the social context. Furthermore, it is deeply influenced by the local culture and history. That is why one can find in the contemporary world the full range of institutionalized teacher-education schemes or programs that developed throughout the history of humankind, from no specific preparation at all to sophisticated university education.

This is a nearly perfect instance of a situation that cannot be understood and interpreted without some historical background.

1. Historical Perspective

While compulsory schooling is a twentieth century phenomenon, generalized school education mainly goes back to the nineteenth century in the West. In the past, instruction was linked with socioeconomic status (SES), the majority of peasants, artisans, and other "small people" learned their skills on the job, while the educated minority in power was privately instructed in the line of its social function. Religious education, certainly the most widespread, was again limited for the majority to inculcation of beliefs and rules. With the joint philosophical influence of eighteenth century Enlightenment (to know has a moral value) and the growing pressure of the emerging Industrial Revolution (to know has an economic value), this situation changed.

During the nineteenth century, the structure of our modern school systems developed, strictly parallel to the social order of the time. Primary schools were mainly for the lower-class and for lower-middle-class children; they were schools for the "people" and their teachers were also of lower social origin. The lower-secondary schools (middle schools) educated future middle-class members who needed knowledge and skills for civil servant service, clerical jobs, and commerce. Hence the practical orientation of these schools was entrusted to non-university-trained teachers (mostly coming from the middle class). At the beginning of the twentieth century, vocational schools, of very low status too, were strictly separated from general education. Finally, grammar schools—called "learned schools" (*Gelehrtenschule*) in Germany because they prepared for university education—were entrusted to university-trained teachers.

The future kindergarten or nursery school appeared in the nineteenth century first under the name of asylum—that is, a place where poor preschool children found shelter while the mother was at work. (The Italian cradle school is still called *asilo nido* today.) For several decades, the women in charge of an "asylum" had no specific education and often lacked any basic instruction. Their qualification was about the same as today's car park attendants and their job was somehow similar: they watched parked children.

The evolution of primary-school teacher training is also striking. Until the beginning of the nineteenth century, education could be provided in elementary schools by anyone who had a certain command of reading, writing and arithmetic (the so-called three R's). Similar situations could still be observed in some parts of the world not so long ago. Soon after 1800, however, specific training institutions appeared. They were based on the eighteenth century Austrian *Normalschule* and the German *Lehrerseminar*. The *Normalschule* was not an independent institution, but consisted of a short course of a few weeks or months for teachers or aspirant teachers, given in a model elementary school (De Vroede 1981 p. 7), and called *Normalschule* because of the pedagogical courses given there. The eighteenth century German *Lehrerseminar* was not an independent institution either, and the curriculum of the "seminars" varied a great deal from place to place. It was, however, the model of the *Schullehrerseminar* that became normative in the nineteenth century and its parallel was surprisingly to be called "normal school" in many Western countries (*école normale, escuela normal, scuola normale, normal-skolan*).

It must be emphasized that the eighteenth century "normal schools" were essentially training in teaching methods: experienced primary-school teachers showed how they taught; something akin to recipes were given which were then tried and imitated on the job.

At the beginning of the nineteenth century, especially under the influence of Francke and Niemeyer (*Waisenhaus* in Halle, Germany), the model of the autonomous seminar appeared and spread first over Prussia, to be soon imitated in the whole Western world.

Typically, a *Lehrerseminar* or "normal school" was open to pupils having completed primary school: it had a three-year theoretical and practical curriculum, a boarding school system, and its own practice school (De Vroede 1981 p. 7). The basic components of the curriculum were: religious and moral education, content and skills to be taught later on, and teaching practice. Any "learned" instruction—be it philosophic or scientific—was avoided and even forbidden (Minister von Raumer's order, Berlin, 1856). Primary-school teachers were lower-class members who had to educate lower-class children in the respect of religion and social order and equip them with the three R's needed for work. Hard fights were fought by progressive educators like Diesterweg to obtain a significant enrichment of the general education curriculum (De Landsheere 1967) and, even later, the study of psychology and theoretical pedagogy.

From an administrative point of view, the typical normal school was part of the primary-school system; it had the status of a lower-vocational school. A teacher certificate was practically equivalent to a lower-secondary school certificate; consequently it did not give access to college or university. This situation was still common in many countries in the middle of the twentieth century.

There were of course some exceptions to this pattern. For instance, in about 1840, a rich curriculum including Latin and high-level general education were adopted by some English and Welsh training colleges (Alexander 1979) but were soon pushed down to elementary level.

Some nineteenth-century United States normal schools were of the German type (Massachusetts), while in Wisconsin, they were conceived as "multipurpose" educational institutions and were in fact the original public secondary schools (Herbst 1979).

The situation was totally different for grammar-school teachers or the equivalent: they would have a full college education in a field of specialization and some, mostly philosophically oriented, introduction to psychology and pedagogy. Teaching skills and methods occupied little place, if any, in their preparation. Again, this situation can still be found in many countries today.

As for university professors, they would have resented as a sort of insult any obligation to study educational theory and practice. A reaction that has far from completely disappeared yet.

This background information should help clarify why giving paradigmatic value to teacher education systems as they exist in England and Wales, in the United States, and in some other countries would be misleading. In these countries, teacher education is of college level and all primary- or secondary-school teachers have at least bachelor degrees. Even then, there are still doubts and debate about the optimal solution: autonomous teachers colleges, or university-integrated teacher education, or—as in some cases in England and Wales—close cooperation between teacher colleges and university. As for internship or its equivalent, there is also much discussion about its length, its nature, and its best time within the training process.

But before these questions are discussed further, the dimensions of the teacher education problem must be remembered. Wherever—that is nearly everywhere now—generalized schooling exists, many thousands of teachers are immediately needed. This is the quantitative dimension. Furthermore, how can most developing countries afford to college-train enough teachers while most of them cannot afford the few dozens or hundreds of university-trained professionals they need in medicine, engineering, agriculture, finance, administration, and so on?

2. Normative View

How can teacher education be conceived in the light of the present advancement of social sciences? (see *Definitions of Teaching*).

A first distinction must be made between initial and further training. A second distinction is between teachers who choose this vocation as their first and only career, and others who either acquire a rich experience in a craft or a profession before turning to the teaching profession. It is obvious that educating a college-aged future teacher or a mature adult already possessing much experience will call for different approaches.

While, in many countries, putting kindergarten, elementary–secondary, and vocational-school teachers on the same footing would have been considered as sheer utopia a few years ago, a trend towards unification of the status of all members of the teaching profession can now be observed. The perspective generally adopted by the Organisation for Economic Co-operation and Development (OECD) is typical in this regard: "All structural differences between teacher categories must be abolished. Most teacher unions or associations want, for all teachers, an initial education of the same duration (at least four years at postsecondary level)" (Enderwitz 1974).

2.1 Principles

The trend is universal: in future, all teachers will enjoy higher education. This is implied by another trend: in all developed countries, basic or fundamental education for all tends to include completion of high school. This extension of general education and the retardation of a vocational specialization are needed in a very rapidly changing culture.

For psychological, educational, socioeconomic, and strategic reasons, all teachers of the future should have university status. The psychological and educational justifications of this principle will be analyzed with the presentation of the curriculum. Socioeconomic and strategic reasons only are discussed here.

In many countries, only the senior-high-school teachers hold a full university degree and are paid accordingly. As a consequence, and especially where provision is made to help access for the gifted to higher education, only the less gifted choose the preprimary- or primary-school career. This situation differs radically from the past when the summit of ambition for most bright lower-class children was becoming a primary-school teacher. This explains why Western Europe primary schools for about a century (roughly 1840 to 1940) were staffed by elite teachers.

Today, while the crucial impact of the first years of schooling is acknowledged, the qualification of the teachers responsible for the lower-school levels is rather low in many countries. There are, of course, some individual or local exceptions, but this phenomenon definitely exists. Even when equal basic salary is granted to all teachers, a difference of prestige—and consequently of attraction—remains between training in colleges and universities. Research shows that the schools of education are far from being the first choice of high-achieving secondary-school students. As a conclusion, real professionalization of the teacher is not only a qualification need (as will be discussed later) but also a necessary recruitment strategy.

The foundation of university education is also general education. The faster knowledge advances, the less valid is a narrowly conceived initial education. That is why at university level also, initial teacher education should be primarily focused on laws, basic principles, understanding of processes, skill learning, as well as research methods and techniques in the field of study and in the related fields. More specialized knowledge would be gained as a sort of illustration of more universal approaches and as something needed for practice. The place of field work and internship should be more important than in the past.

This does not mean that specialized knowledge can be superficial; on the contrary, to make general and high-level specialized education possible, curriculum reform will be needed in many universities where advanced and encyclopedic education still remain synonymous.

Teacher education should normally comprise general education, specific subject mastery, strong psychological background (including educational psychology), and good command of instructional methods and techniques in the broad sense of these terms. Not only are all those components rapidly advancing, but they

also represent such a learning load that a four- or five-year university curriculum cannot suffice. This is why initial teacher education must now be conceived in direct relation to further education.

The model (Frey 1971) portrayed in Fig. 1 illustrates the way teacher education as a whole can be conceived. Frey's model shows how, after completion of two year's full-time university theoretical studies, teaching practice begins and gradually increases, from 10 percent to 90 percent of the working time. During the remainder of a teacher's career, 10 percent of the time is devoted to further education. Another main characteristic of this model is the continuity between initial and further education.

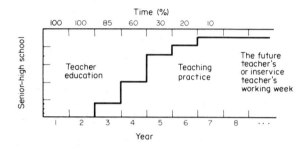

Figure 1
Teacher education model[a]

a Source: Frey (1971)

2.2 The Curriculum

Any teacher education should always come back to four basic questions and should offer opportunities to pose them in a great variety of educational situations: What are the objectives of education? How do the objectives vary from individual to individual? How can the objectives be achieved? How does one know that they are achieved?

All the components of teacher education should help in answering these questions and are thus to be learned in an integrated, interdisciplinary curriculum, building upon life experience. It must be stressed that future teachers will be able to make their pupils independent in learning and in everyday life only if they too enjoy the same independence during their training. Lasting learning only occurs if the learner solves meaningful problems and to that purpose feels the need to appropriate the curriculum content. As long as content learning is an objective in itself, it does not influence field behavior. That is why psychological and educational theory learned by the students just to pass their examinations have so little influence on actual teaching practice.

The components of teacher education can be categorized under the headings of general education, specific subject mastery for preprimary-, primary-, and secondary-school teachers, psychology, and educational theory and practice.

(a) *General education.* This is understood as the set of knowledge, skills, and affective and psychomotor behaviors learned to contribute to a harmonious development of an individual in a given environment. The individual must learn to understand his or her environment, to modify it, to analyze it critically, and this not only to his or her benefit, but also to the benefit of society.

In this perspective, it is hardly thinkable that the level of general education should vary among teachers according to the school levels. For instance, what could justify a poorer command of the mother tongue by preprimary teachers than by high-school teachers? If a difference were acceptable, and considering the critical influence of preschool development, the strong side should benefit the younger pupils.

General education is no formalistic encyclopedism but a critical discovery and acquisition of meaningful factual knowledge, of principles and methods in the domains of health, science, literature, aesthetics, philosophy, politics, and ethics. It includes the development of higher cognitive skills, of ability to communicate, to obtain information, to work independently and in groups, to socialize, and so on.

It is also knowledge and understanding of the way of life of others. Teachers have to educate children coming from different social backgrounds and even from foreign cultures. Unfortunately, many teachers have never really left the school environment: as soon as they ceased to be students, they became educators. Except for their own family background, they have, as a consequence, no experience of life in a factory, in business, of social contexts differing much from their own.

Of course, general education must continue after university graduation and cannot and should not be standardized. But its level should be high for all.

(b) *Specific subject mastery.* In the nineteenth century, full university specialized education was deemed necessary for grammar-school teachers, while content learning could be limited for primary-school teachers to what they had to teach.

As Woodring (1957 p. 71) puts it, the ideal teacher for a self-contained classroom of elementary-school children "would be possessed of an impossible combination of virtues": masterly understanding of the learning process; ability to arouse and sustain the interest of children from a wide variety of social, economic, and intellectual backgrounds; capability of effective communication with children of IQ's ranging from 50 to 150 or higher; scholarly knowledge of varied school subjects; warm, sympathetic personality; mastery of clinical psychologist skills; ability to establish cordial working relations with colleagues; and an ability to cooperate effectively with parents. Of course, few people can play so many roles effectively. Teams of professionals helped by aides and technicians are needed.

Specific aspects of preprimary-, primary-, and secondary-school teacher education will now be examined; also the case of individuals coming to teaching after practicing another vocation.

Considering the critical importance of the early development, it can be said that the most decisive battle for equality of opportunities and democratization of education is to be won at preschool level. Some of the main tasks of the preprimary teacher are:

(i)   to create an affective climate providing security;

(ii)   to create favorable situations for cognitive, affective (including aesthetic), and psychomotor development;

(iii)   to enrich the social experience of the child;

(iv)   to enrich the cultural background of the child;

(v)   to promote language development;

(vi)   to help in acquiring the basic concepts of time, space, and quantity;

(vii)   to foster readiness for primary instruction;

(viii) to help the family in its educational task.

That is why the study at university level of developmental and clinical psychology can be considered as a prerequisite. Special room must also be made for the study of psycholinguistics, and of the foundations of mathematics.

As for primary teachers, it seems that two types of primary teachers should be distinguished: for the age group 5 to 8 and for the group beyond age 8. The first group is at the transition of preprimary and primary education, and for that reason should be nongraded. The teachers should have practically the same preparation as the preprimary teachers plus a high-level training in the teaching of reading and writing, in oral communication, mathematics instruction, and in diagnostic and remedial techniques (see *Teacher Education for Early Childhood Education*).

The education of teachers for the age group 8 to 12 or 8 to 15 or 16 should be conceived in a team perspective. This is justified by the fact that, contrary to old beliefs, high-quality teaching of elements requires advanced knowledge of the subject. For instance, before teaching arithmetic basic skills, the teacher must be aware of the nature and content of more advanced mathematics to prepare for its acquisition. Similarly, it is not acceptable that early foreign language teaching could be the duty of teachers with superficial, or even incorrect command of the language. That is why future teachers for this age group should major in one of the following: (a) mother tongue and history; (b) mathematics (including computer technology) and physics; (c) natural sciences and geography; (d) art; or (e) one of the following: foreign language, music, physical education.

The case of high-school teachers can now easily be dealt with. While the preparation of junior-high-school teachers has been sketched above, senior-high-school teachers would major in one subject and have a much stronger training in psychology and education than they have had so far.

How can education be conceived for people who become full- or part-time teachers after several years of practice of teaching in another field, or other jobs or professions? There is no reason why their teacher education should be poorer than the education of "first career teachers." But it is also obvious that the members of the first category are more mature people, and have, in many cases, a rich social experience on which it is possible to capitalize. In this case, a tailor-made teacher education program should be defined in close cooperation with the "student." The credit system common in Anglo-Saxon countries appears here as the most satisfying and efficient solution. The individualized curriculum to be mastered within certain time limits, but at individual pace, would normally include wherever needed: (i) general education; (ii) development of the expression and communication skills; (iii) psychology and educational theory and practice; (iv) eventually more advanced subject matter study in an instructional perspective.

(c) *Psychology and education study.* Knowledge of the laws of behavior, of learning processes, of development, and of the ways of guiding it, is a prerequisite of education. Furthermore, an active introduction to experimental psychology should help understanding of learning processes and prepare teachers to be critical consumers of psychological research data.

Ethological and participant observation is the key: using tests and other evaluation techniques, it will continuously swing between qualitative and quantitative analysis. Cultural anthropology will help in interpreting socially bound behavior. Introduction to group dynamics should also be a part of the teacher training. It must be emphasized that the study of psychology will influence and enlighten teaching behavior only if it is grounded in personal experience, and in participation in situations in which the individual is involved and in which he or she feels concerned.

The main psychological aspects of the teacher's intervention are:

(i) Self-expression—to avoid censorship of expression of feelings sometimes creating earnest internal tension, the learner must be able to express problems and feelings, and become tolerant to the feelings of others.

(ii) Empathy—to learn to understand the others, to accept them as they are.

(iii) Positive perception of others while developing positive self-image.

(iv) Feedback—informing others of the reactions of self to their behavior.

(v) Autonomy, including tolerance of, and positive reaction to, aggression and negative evaluation from others.

Like medicine, teaching is an art and a science (see *Teaching: Art or Science?*). Pedagogy is the set of theories and rules governing teaching practice. With the quick development of educational theory in the twentieth century a growing number of specific disciplines have emerged and piled up instead of integrating functionally: philosophy of education, educational foundations, history of education, teaching methods comparative education, educational psychology, sociology of education, technology of education, measurement and evaluation, educational planning, and so on. Studying all these (important) subjects in a sort of encyclopedic mosaic has had little impact on teaching theory and practice. There is a growing tendency to stress the total structure. To that effect, the training strategy is the thematic approach or the educational project method.

In this integrated perspective, the field of education can be structured in three domains: (i) foundations of education, integrating philosophy, history, sociology, and comparative education; (ii) empirical research and development—research methods, measurement, evaluation; (iii) applied education—teaching methods, technology, and internship.

Before possibly modifying it, education is first the expression of a society trying to conserve, and to reproduce itself. The ends and aims of education that are the keystone of the whole educational system are primarily the expression of the dominant ideology and values. Understanding why some values dominate in other times or in other places helps understanding of the present situation. Showing the necessary coherence between aims and educational practice should be the main role of the study of educational foundations.

There is today a growing consensus on the need for teachers to be regular innovative agents and thus regular consumers of research and development products, and also to be themselves associates or agents of research and development.

It is now more and more clearly recognized that the only efficient way to educate the future consumer of research and development data is by the introduction actively, in a nonsuperficial way, to research and development methods and techniques, including the necessary statistical concepts. It seems that an efficient way to do this is to offer a minimum research framework and then have the future or inservice teachers participate in a modest but genuine research project: from the formulation of the rationale and the definition of the problem and formulation of the hypothesis to the conclusion, through the choice of a research design, the choice or the construction of the necessary instruments, the field work, the data analysis, and interpretation (see *Teachers as Researchers*).

Opportunity should also be given to contrast this nomothetic approach with the anthropological approach and discover how both supplement each other.

3. Applied Education

Applied education is understood as the set of studies and actions developed for instruction and independent learning.

After philosophizing and researching, the problem is now to run school on a day-to-day basis, that is, making decisions and fostering the development of the many pupils and students in the school system. This is the purpose of teaching methods founded on human experience and intuition, if scientific knowledge is not available to solve problems arising here and now.

Curriculum development and evaluation are also part of applied education and teachers should be trained to prepare the instructional activities along the stages of curriculum development, that is: defining objectives, selecting content of learning experiences, choosing the appropriate method and classroom organization, gathering or developing the necessary material, and making decisions about formative and summative evaluation.

Practice in laboratory schools and internship play a very important role in teacher education. In this regard, many systems exist: they go from gradual familiarization with the school context and increasing instructional practice, to systems where future teachers are first immersed into schools for several weeks or months before being given any specific training.

There is no clear evidence of the superiority of any system. The most important thing is that educational theory relies on field observation and teaching practice, and that observation and practice are analyzed in the light of theory.

It is now generally accepted that microteaching is an efficient training technique. It should develop in three stages:

(a) analytical instructional training—small group animation, practice of specific skills, critical observation of teaching behavior;

(b) self-evaluation of teaching session;

(c) initiating microsituations of problem solving and cooperative research in the classroom (see *Microteaching: Conceptual and Theoretical Bases*).

The Frey model introduced above shows how teaching practice takes a growing part in teacher education.

An often neglected aspect of practice and internship is the school level at which it is to take place. Of course, the choice of the level or type of school for which the future teacher specially prepares must be made. It

seems, however, that some teaching practice or, at least, observation at other levels fosters a better understanding of the teacher role and of the corresponding curriculum development.

4. General Versus Competency-based Teacher Education

The type of teacher education described so far is general or empirical; this commonsense or idealistic curriculum seems to work. However, in most instances, a direct relationship between that sort of knowledge and teacher effectiveness is difficult, if not impossible to demonstrate.

Competency-based teacher education is a reaction against this vagueness. Such a program specifies the competencies to be demonstrated by the student, and makes explicit the criteria to be applied in assessing the student's competencies. The word competency is here taken in the broad sense of knowledge, attitudes, skills, and "behaviors that facilitate intellectual, social, emotional, and physical growth in children" (Weber 1972). At the conclusion of such a program, the critical success criterion is not the achievement on essay or oral examination, but mainly the student's ability to do the job for which he or she is preparing.

Definite advantages of this approach are: functional learning, clarity of objectives, easiness of modular individualized instruction, and a more objective evaluation. The danger of this system is that it can be rather mechanistic, that its content and construct validity is not easy to establish; furthermore, it can be feared that in a rapidly changing culture, the teacher could lack flexibility and transfer ability in new unexpected educational situations.

There is so far no clear answer to this debate. Since "competency" can also be flexibility, creativity, critical spirit, the difficulty just mentioned could be overcome. However, it is hard to imagine that, for instance, flexibility could be developed in one or a few learning units; it should rather be fostered in all, as one of the components also including creativity, critical thinking, and so on (which could bring us back to the general approach) (see *Competency-based Teacher Education*).

5. Inservice Education

The need for further education during a teacher's entire career has been recognized. For teachers who have enjoyed an education of good quality, further education can be limited to reading the disseminated information, to periodical seminars, short refresher courses and, of course, postgraduate study (see *Inservice Teacher Education*).

There are cases, however, where the teacher's education has become obsolete (at least to a significant extent) or has practically never existed in certain aspects deemed important for their job. Examples of such situations are the introduction of a "new mathematics" curriculum when teachers have never studied it themselves, or the introduction of teachers to educational research methods and techniques when they had no place in the initial training program. In such a case, further teacher training is often called "recycling " (see *Teacher Recyclage*).

6. Conclusion

Enjoying the same social status and prestige as all those who eminently serve society, today's or tomorrow's teacher must be a professional, whose educational program and level should be more and more comparable with the physician's education. The teaching profession must unify: we would not dream of less education or less pay for pediatricians than for doctors who look after adults.

The teaching profession has and will keep having its "generalists" and its "specialists." Most "generalists" will probably be entrusted the education of younger pupils; with time, their role may appear so crucial for the future of humanity and society that they may become the most distinguished members of the profession.

See also: Inservice Teacher Education; Microteaching: Conceptual and Theoretical Bases; Competency-based Teacher Education

Bibliography

Alexander J L 1979 *The Early Evolution of the Curriculum of Elementary Teacher Training in England.* International Standing Conference on the History of Education, Louvain

De Landsheere G 1967 Les idées politiques et sociales de F A Diesterweg. *Paedag. Hist.* 7(1): 50–76

De Landsheere G 1976 *La Formation des enseignants demain.* Casterman, Paris

De Vroede M 1981 The history of teacher training. *Hist. Educ.* 10(1): 1–8

Enderwitz H 1974 *La Rénovation des profils de carrière et le développement de la mobilité professionnelle des enseignants.* Document no. SME/ET/74.90, Organisation for Economic Co-operation and Development, Paris, p. 44

Frey K 1971 Das Lehrerinformations—und Lernsystem. *Schulblatt des Kantons Zürich* 86: 10

Herbst J 1979 *Nineteenth Century Normal School in the United States: A Fresh Look.* International Standing Conference on the History of Education, Louvain

Turney C (ed.) 1981 *Anatomy of Teaching.* Novak, Sydney

Weber W A 1972 Competency-based teacher education. In: Houston W R (ed.) 1972 *Strategies and Resources for Developing a Competency-based Teacher Education.* New York State Education Department, New York

Woodring P 1957 *New Directions in Teacher Education: An Interim Report of the Work of the Fund for the Advancement of Education in the Areas of Teacher Education and Recruitment.* Fund for the Advancement of Education, New York, pp. 71–72

Affective Teacher Education

L. W. Anderson; Min Ching

In planning a teacher education program, the goals of such a program must be considered. These goals can be categorized in many ways. Quite frequently three classifications of goals are suggested: teacher knowledge, teaching skills (both pedagogical and interpersonal), and teacher feelings and self-awareness. Affective teacher education programs focus primarily on teacher feelings and self-awareness. More recently, however, these programs have begun to address interpersonal and human relations skills. In Carkhuff's (1982) words, affective teacher education programs initially "emphasized the development of intrapersonal values and attitudes. Increasingly, they [have] emphasized the development of interpersonal feelings and skills" (p. 485). The purposes of this article are (a) to indicate the need and rationale for affective teacher education; (b) to discuss the nature of affective teacher education programs; (c) to present data relating to the effectiveness of such programs; and (d) to speculate on the future of affective teacher education.

1. Need and Rationale for Affective Teacher Education

Proponents of affective teacher education suggest that the vast majority of teacher education programs focus solely on the development of teacher knowledge, teaching skills, or both. The traditional undergraduate teacher education programs, replete with an emphasis on knowledge about educational psychology, school and the social order, and methods and materials are frequently given as examples of the exclusive focus on teacher knowledge. Similarly, the recent emphasis on performance-based and competency-based teacher education programs is cited as support for the exclusive focus on teaching skills (see *Competency-based Teacher Education*). All of these programs are believed to neglect completely the area of teacher feelings and self-awareness. Mehnert (1979), for example, suggests that current teacher education programs neglect (a) the teacher's awareness of the emotional reactions of students; (b) the teacher's empathy to respond to these emotions; and (c) the ability to organize teaching strategies which consider the emotional needs of the students. Similarly, Murray (1972) contends that "teachers who make the most significance must be more than competent technicians; they must also be people who know something about themselves and others, who possess interpersonal competencies as well as pedagogical skills" (p. 387). Finally, Myrow (1978) states that "teachers . . . are, first and foremost, evolving, maturing persons whose feelings and beliefs about themselves and others color their work with students and school personnel" (p. 49).

There is some evidence that practicing teachers themselves perceive a need for affective teacher education. In an early study, 229 graduate education students were surveyed. The results suggested that over one-third of them felt they "needed outside help in dealing with such significant personal concerns as hostility, sexual conflicts, and feelings of hopelessness" (Jersild 1955 cited in Myrow 1978 p. 49).

Similarly there is some evidence that the affective characteristics of teachers (rather than the cognitive characteristics of teachers) best permit the differentiation of "more-effective" and "less-effective" teachers (Berliner and Tikunoff 1976). Specifically, Berliner and Tikunoff found that of 52 teacher characteristics or qualities used by observers and raters to distinguish more and less effective teachers, 38 (almost 75 percent) were affective in nature. Only 14 referred to aspects of teacher knowledge or particular teaching skills. Examples of such affective characteristics or qualities included "belittling," "encouraging," "flexibility," "job satisfaction," "optimism," and "recognition seeking" (i.e., teacher calls attention to self for no apparent reason).

In summary, then, the affective component of teacher education is typically neglected. Furthermore, this neglect has been apparent to theoreticians, researchers, and practitioners alike.

2. Nature of Affective Teacher Education Programs

From an affective perspective the "act of teaching has to be seen as an interaction between two selves, teacher and learner, neither superior or inferior, in which the more experienced serves as the gentlest sort of guide" (Joyce 1975 p. 131). As a consequence, two fairly general goals form the basis of affective teacher education programs: increased awareness of oneself and others, and improved skills in human and interpersonal relations. Depending on the specific program, these two goals may be specified in different ways. Myrow (1978), for example, describes the objectives of the Transactional Analysis and Personal Development Program in the following manner. The program was designed to "help teachers . . . increase their understanding of the process of human development, understand how they influence their interactions with others, and help them

become more facile in dealing with students and colleagues" (p. 49). Similarly, Brown (1975) describes the objectives of the Affective Education Program as follows. "The program focuses on helping teachers become more aware of . . . students' concerns, identifying how concerns appear in the classroom context, providing teachers with a variety of strategies to deal with these concerns, and producing models of the curriculum which make connections between the concerns of the students and academic subject matter" (p. 193).

Affective teacher educators use a variety of approaches in an attempt to achieve these objectives. In addition to the Transactional Analysis and Personal Development Program and the Affective Education Development Program mentioned above, many other models and programs are available. The Teacher Effectiveness Training Program (Gordon 1974), the Human Resource Development Model (Aspy and Roebuck 1982), and the Communication Network Training Program (Newberg and Loue 1982) are three such programs. Approaches within these programs range from behavioristic (Egan 1975) to humanistic (Brown 1975). Finally, because the approaches vary, the specific techniques used also vary. Among the more common techniques are role playing, guided imagination experience, games and simulations, joint decision making, conflict resolution, T-groups, and psychotherapy.

3. Effectiveness of Teacher Education Programs

Two questions can be raised concerning the effectiveness of affective teacher education programs. First, to what extent do teachers acquire the appropriate feelings and interpersonal skills as a result of participating in these programs? Second, to what extent are teachers who participate in such programs more effective in their classrooms than teachers who do not participate in these programs?

Concerning the first question, Aspy and Roebuck (1982) suggest that one major conclusion can be drawn from a survey of the available research. Specifically, "teachers can learn to enhance their levels of interpersonal functioning" when enrolled in training programs lasting approximately 18 hours (p. 489). In addition, Brown cites research which suggests that "experienced classroom teachers master affective skills during training more successfully than student teachers or new teachers" (p. 194).

Concerning the second question, several studies have examined the impact of affective teacher education programs on several school and student variables. Reporting on the evaluation of the Affective Education Programs, Brown (1975) states that "students with an affectively trained team improved significantly over a comparison group in reading as measured by a silent reading comprehension test; that in a four-month period students in the affective group were absent from school nearly half as often and tardy less than one-third as comparison group students; and that parents were enthusiastic about the effects of the program on their children" (p. 146). Similarly, Aspy and Roebuck (1979) found that "students of teachers with higher-level (interpersonal) skills generated significantly fewer disruptive incidents and significantly less severe problems. The strength of the relationship indicated that about one-third of all disruptive behavior in classrooms can be accounted for by the variance in teacher levels of interpersonal skills" (p. 490).

In addressing this same question Carkhuff (1982) states that "perhaps the largest reservoir of research data is presented for the HRD (Human Resource Development) affective–interpersonal skills" (p. 486). In a summary of 28 studies involving more than 1,000 teachers and 30,000 students, "teachers with high levels of affective–interpersonal skills are more effective in teaching learners a variety of cognitive skills, including those addressed by traditional achievement measures" (p. 486). Similar results have been reported for the Communication Network Training Program (Newberg and Loue 1982). The impact of affective teacher education programs in terms of students is perhaps best summarized by Aspy and Roebuck (1982). "The levels of the teacher's interpersonal functioning are related directly to pupil achievement, attendance, self-concept, attitudes toward school, and behavior in school" (p. 489).

In summary, then, the results of a variety of research studies suggest that interpersonal skills can be transmitted to teachers both economically and efficiently. Furthermore, teachers who possess these skills are more effective in their classrooms in terms of students' behavior, attitudes, and achievement. Whether teachers' feelings or self-awareness can be altered is not at all clear from the available research. Similarly, few if any studies suggest a clear relationship between teacher feelings and self-awareness and student behavior, attitudes, or achievement. In essence, then, the two goals of affective teacher education programs mentioned earlier appear to be differentially attainable. Furthermore, only the relationship between teacher interpersonal skills and student development has been empirically supported.

4. The Future of Affective Teacher Education

Two issues must be resolved if affective teacher education is to emerge as a critical aspect in the future of teacher education. The first issue concerns the relation between the two major goals of affective teacher education: (a) increased self-awareness, and (b) improved interpersonal skills. The second concerns the relation between affective teacher education and, for the lack of a better phrase, cognitive teacher education.

Most affective teacher educators tend to consider awareness as a precondition for interpersonal skills. Pine and Boy (1979), for example, contend "it is easier for the teachers who respect their own intrinsic values to have deep respect for learners. To value learners,

teachers must first value themselves. The teacher who does not have self-esteem cannot view others as having esteem. To the degree that a person believes in his or her own dignity will the person believe in the dignity of another" (p. 146). Despite the passionate rhetoric, this sequential relationship between feelings and actions has not to date been empirically validated. In fact, the bulk of the research evidence has been directed toward interpersonal skills. Research on teacher feelings, emotions, and self-awareness is scant. Future research studies should focus on testing the hypothesis that teacher affect is a necessary but not sufficient condition for teacher behavior. The importance of the distinction between teacher education and teacher training rests in the balance.

The relationship between affective teacher education and cognitive teacher education also needs to be clarified. In the mid-1970s, Brown (1975) coined the phrase "confluent education" to indicate a merger between affective and cognitive education. More recently Gideonse (1982) clarified this relationship. In Gideonse's words "teaching is an intellectual activity with intellectual ends. . . . But teaching is also a profoundly moral activity. It involves value choices that adults make for individual children and society on an ongoing basis, in a particular culture, at a given moment in time" (p. 15). Of the 10 goals Gideonse sets out for his "revolution in teacher education," four fall squarely in the affective realm. The four are the knowledge of "small-group processes; professional responsibilities and obligations; . . . parent/professional relations (including community relations); . . . self-awareness, or the ability to be in touch with oneself" (p. 16). Three of his goals are clearly cognitive in nature. These include the knowledge of "different instructional approaches, including use of existing and emerging media; . . . curriculum models and theories, especially in subjects for which a given teacher will be responsible; . . . a capacity for inquiry and design to meet the specific needs of individual learners, including diagnosis, instructional and curricular design, and evaluation skills" (p. 16). The remaining three goals represent some combination of cognitive and affective. These three goals are a knowledge of "the relationship between diverse characteristics of learners and instructional strategies; . . . consultation skills to work with other professionals, including knowledge of their roles and of the organization and administration of schools; . . . classroom and behavior management" (p. 16). This list of goals illustrates the necessity of considering an integration of affective teacher education with cognitive teacher education. Given the predominance of cognitively based teacher education both historically and presently such an integration not only places affective teacher education in its proper perspective but also ensures the future of affective teacher education as a key component of an integrated, comprehensive teacher education program.

See also: Affective Characteristics of Student Teachers; Students' Cognitive Processing

Bibliography

Aspy D N, Roebuck F N 1979 *The National Consortium for Humanizing Education: An Update of Research Results.* Paper presented at the annual meeting of the American Educational Research Association, San Francisco, California

Aspy D N, Roebuck F N 1982 Affective education: Sound investment. *Educ. Leadership* 39: 489–93

Berliner D C, Tikunoff W J 1976 The California beginning teacher evaluation study: Overview of the ethnographic study. *J. Tech. Educ.* 27: 24–30

Brown G I 1975 The training of teachers for affective roles. In: Ryan K (ed.) 1975 *Teacher Education.* Seventy-fourth Yearbook of the National Society for the Study of Education, Part 2. University of Chicago Press, Chicago, Illinois

Carkhuff R R 1982 Affective education in the age of productivity. *Educ. Leadership* 39: 484–87

Egan G 1975 *The Skilled Helper: A Model for Systematic Helping and Interpersonal Relating.* Brooks/Cole, Monterey, California

Gideonse H D 1982 The necessary revolution in teacher education. *Phi Delta Kappan* 64: 15–18

Gordon I 1974 *TET: Teacher Effectiveness Training.* Wyden, New York

Joyce B 1975 Conceptions of man and their implications for teacher education. In: Ryan K (ed.) 1975 *Teacher Education.* Seventy-fourth Yearbook of the National Society for the Study of Education, Part 2. University of Chicago Press, Chicago, Illinois

Mehnert W 1979 The affective aspect of adult education. *Lifelong Learning: The Adult Years* 2(5): 38–29

Murray E 1972 Students' perceptions of self-actualizing and non-self-actualizing teachers. *J. Teach. Educ.* 23: 383–87

Myrow D L 1978 Personal development: The missing link in teacher evolution. *J. Teach. Educ.* 29(5): 49–52

Newberg N A, Loue W E 1982 Affective education addresses the basics. *Educ. Leadership* 39: 498–500

Pine G J, Boy G V 1979 The humanist as teacher. *The Humanist Educator* 17(4): 146–52

Competency-based Teacher Education

W. R. Houston

Highly visible and hotly debated during the decade of the 1970s, competency-based teacher education (CBTE) reflected general cultural trends in the United States as well as specific educational goals. The CBTE movement, also referred to as performance-based teacher education (PBTE), was spawned in the late 1960s, supported by grants from federal, private, and state sources, lauded as the most effective process to prepare teachers, damned as a mechanistic approach, and employed nominally for several years by over 400 institutions. By the end of the decade, the term itself was less frequently used in teacher education, but the concept pervaded practice.

The CBTE movement is analyzed in the following sections. After a brief historical perspective, the concept and rationale of CBTE are delineated. Descriptions of the application of CBTE in teacher education and in other fields are followed by a case study of one CBTE program. Program development reflecting the CBTE concept is discussed. Finally, the concerns of implementors and critics, issues derived from the movement, and future directions are discussed.

1. Concept of CBTE

The appeal of CBTE is in its emphasis on pragmatism in determining the content of teacher-education programs, its potential for improvement through research, and its systematic approach to preparing teachers. The basic concepts are simple and straightforward.

1.1 Program Requirements are derived from, and Based on, the Practice of Effective Teachers

This contrasts sharply with approaches where the content of the behavioral sciences, such as psychology, and the structure of academic disciplines, such as mathematics, are used to determine content and organization of teacher education. Rather than systematically studying disciplines such as psychology and mathematics, CBTE is based on, and organized around, conceptualizations of effective teacher practice. CBTE programs consider what teachers should know, be able to do and to accomplish, with graduation requirements based on such outcomes.

1.2 Requirements are Stated as Competencies

Requirements describe what the student must demonstrate for successful completion of the program. Such requirements employ observable verbs (using objectives such as "use," "organize," "sequence learning"), while avoiding nonobservable verbs such as "understand" and "perceive."

Five classes of competencies have been defined. The first—cognitive-based competencies—define knowledge and intellectual skills and abilities that are expected of the learner (for example, "the prospective teacher can list and illustrate five levels of questions"). Secondly, for performance-based competencies, the learner demonstrates that he or she can *do* something rather than simply *know* something. While contingent upon knowledge, performance-based competencies define skills and overt actions ("the prospective teacher leads a class discussion in which at least 50 percent of the students participate orally"). The third class is referred to as consequence-based competencies. To demonstrate competence, the person is required to bring about change in others. Thus, the criterion of success is not what one knows or does, but what one can accomplish. A teacher's competence, for example, is assessed by examining the achievements of pupils being taught.

In CBTE, greater emphasis is placed on performance-based and consequence-based competencies than on cognitive-based objectives. What teachers know about teaching seems less important than their ability to teach and to bring about change in their pupils. The fourth type of competency is affective. These affective competencies, which define expected attitudes and values, tend to resist the specificity and are more difficult to assess than the first three types (the prospective teacher values the contribution of all students in a class discussion). They are typically embedded in other competency statements. The fifth type, exploratory competencies, does not fit well with the four other types in the CBTE classification system, since the definition of desired learner outcomes is defaulted. Instead, activities that promise significant learnings are specified. CBTE programs may require the learner to work 30 hours in a community center, discuss schooling with three parents, or act as a teacher aide for four weeks. Such activities are exploratory; they provide opportunities for students to learn about teaching, but the specific nature of such learning is not defined. The idiosyncratic dispositions and experiences of the learner and the particular set of experiences in the activity largely influence the outcomes. Exploratory competencies have also been referred to by educators as experience objectives or expressive objectives. CBTE programs do not depend on exploratory competencies, but do employ them when precise outcomes have yet to be explicated.

1.3 Instruction and Assessment are Specifically Related to Competencies

Competencies are defined prior to program implementation and are made known to learners. The major criterion for including content and activities in a specific instructional program is, "To what extent will this contribute to the demonstration of program competencies?" Instruction not directly linked to competencies is eliminated from the program. Instructional experiences are integrated across the total program as they are related to previously completed objectives rather than, as in conventional programs, the completion of a collection of often unrelated and seldom sequenced courses.

Assessment of student teachers is also based exclusively on program competencies. Student teachers are not expected to complete requirements other than those specified as competencies. In theory and in a few instances, competency statements include a criterion level so that assessment determines whether or not the learner has demonstrated a competency to the degree previously established. The answer becomes either "yes" or "not yet" rather than simply pass or fail. Because of the emphasis on performance and consequence competencies in CBTE, traditional written tests are less important than performance measures.

1.4 Learner Progress is Determined by Demonstration of Competencies

Length of time in a program is not the primary variable in learner progress; it is demonstration of competence in the various areas and to the specific levels identified for a program. In traditional courses, a student who excels in one phase of the course can compensate for weaknesses in other phases, ultimately earning a passing grade. In CBTE, students are expected to meet at least the minimum standards for each and every competency required in the program.

This approach brings about one other major shift from traditional programs: it shifts the emphasis in evaluation from how well a learner does in comparison to other learners, to how well a student does in demonstrating specified outcomes. In traditional programs a student may be graded "B" on a course. This is often based on the normal curve so that some students receive As, some Bs, some Cs, and some lower grades. Requirements are based on what previous or current students have accomplished in the course, and students tend to be compared on the basis of achievement in one or a series of courses ("fourth in her class," "81st percentile," etc.). CBTE, on the other hand, relates achievement to preset objectives, and a grading system includes lists of such objectives with a place to mark whether each has been passed or not. In traditional programs, students graduate when they have completed all courses with an average grade that is prespecified (2.5 grade point average required), whereas in CBTE, each of the competencies must be passed.

1.5 Implied and Related Characteristics

In 1971, a committee of the American Association of Colleges for Teacher Education (AACTE) sponsored a conference to analyze CBTE/PBTE. Stanley Elam (1972) prepared a perceptive report of their deliberations, which suggested that in addition to the essential elements of CBTE previously discussed, there were implied characteristics and related or desirable elements. The implied characteristics often found in CBTE programs were: (a) instruction is individualized and personalized; (b) the learning experience of student is guided by feedback; (c) the program as a whole is systematic; (d) the emphasis is on exit, not on entrance requirements; and (e) instruction is modularized.

Less central to the specific conceptualization of CBTE were several related characteristics, including (a) the program is field centered; (b) the base for program decision making is broad, including college/university faculty, students, and public-school personnel; (c) materials and experiences focus on concepts, skills, and knowledges which can be learned in a specific instructional setting; (d) both teachers and students are designers of the instructional system; (e) the program includes research and is open and regenerative; (f) preparation is career continuous; and (g) role integration takes place as the prospective teacher gains an increasingly comprehensive perception of teaching problems.

These implied and related characteristics, while idealistic, describe the operational elements of CBTE programs. While some could also be used as descriptions of other types of programs, the combination uniquely applies to CBTE.

2. Conceptual Clarity

Educational terms often have multiple meanings; different terms may refer to the same concept and the same term may refer to different concepts. Some terms are appropriately used when dictionary definitions are considered. So it is with CBTE. In this section the dictionary definition of CBTE will be considered, then the relation of CBTE and PBTE, CBTE and competency-based education (CBE), and finally CBTE and the competency-based assessment movement.

"Competence" ordinarily is defined as "adequate for the purpose; suitable, sufficient", or as "legally qualified, admissible", or as "capable." In a sense it refers to adequate preparation to begin a professional career, and has a direct linkage to certification requirements. Standard dictionaries provide no definition of "competency-based." This is a coined term used to describe a movement.

In addition to CBTE, the term performance-based teacher education (PBTE) has been used to identify the same movement. Advocates of performance-based terminology refer to the way in which teachers demonstrate teaching knowledge and skills. This demonstration is observable and overt action or performance is important.

Competency-based teacher education emphasizes a minimum standard; it adds criterion levels, value orientations, and quality to the definition of the movement. Competency-based teacher education advocates pressing for consequence competencies as the most important measures of teacher effectiveness. They rely on the ultimate purpose of schools (pupil learning) as the major rationale for their position. They would hold teachers accountable for pupil achievement, but would permit a wide range of teacher actions and teaching strategies.

Performance advocates point out that there are many intervening variables affecting pupil learning in addition to the competence of the teacher. Because teachers have little control over many intervening variables (home environment, community life, motivation), they cannot be held responsible for controlling or overcoming them.

For PBTE advocates, the behavior or performance of the teacher with respect to previously established standards is the major basis for determining competence.

Some PBTE advocates press for criteria based on the decision-making process undergirding performance. For a physician, as an example, competence would not be defined in terms of whether the patient lived or died, but in terms of the adequacy of the decision-making process as the physician diagnosed and prescribed treatment. Teachers, too, would be expected to demonstrate behaviors known to generally bring about pupil learning, but would not be held accountable for pupil achievement.

The terms CBTE and PBTE emphasize important elements of the movement—one focusing on objectives, the other on criteria. Both are useful, not conflicting, and both refer to the same movement. In practice, most programs use both performance and consequence competencies, thus not entering the conceptual debate about appropriate terminology.

The acronym, CBTE, applies competency-based education (CBE) principles to teachers. Likewise, CBE has been used in preparing professionals such as dentists (CBDE), physicians, nurses, engineers, attorneys, and school administrators. It has been used to train karate experts, oil field workers, and restaurant managers. It has been used in teaching social sciences, natural sciences, and humanities at the British Open University, Alverno College in Milwaukee, Wisconsin, and many community colleges in the United States. CBE has been used as a generic term describing the application of competency-based training strategies to a wide range of fields.

The term CBE also has been used to describe the competency-testing movement. It is important, however, to distinguish the two meanings. During the 1970s, front-page headlines throughout the United States charged that teachers did not have adequate knowledge of the content they taught. Legislatures in several states required minimum scores on "competency" tests as a prerequisite to initial certification. Such examinations tested knowledge of basic skills of English usage and mathematics, general liberal arts education, and specific subjects for which certification was being sought. Several urban school districts required applicants to pass local tests of achievement prior to being considered for employment. As used in these circumstances, CBE relied on written cognitive tests rather than performance-based measures. The purpose of such paper-and-pencil assessments was to test basic knowledge rather than professional performance and the consequences of these tests were to screen out prospective teachers, rather than to provide a basis for improved practice.

These distinctions between the two uses of the term CBE are so basic that they actually refer to two different movements in education. The first, used with prospective teachers in CBTE, was to enhance learning, while the second was to screen out incapable persons.

3. Historical Antecedents

The roots for improved practice in teacher education extend hundreds of years in history to the emphasis on performance by Greek educators of the third century BC and European educators of the eighteenth century. A growing demand during the 1950s and 1960s for greater relevance in educational practice, a stronger research base, and explicit conceptualizations of teacher roles led the United States Office of Education (USOE) in 1967 to request proposals for model elementary-teacher-education programs. What was requested were detailed educational specifications that could be used as guides in developing sound teacher-education programs.

Nine sets of specifications were developed during 1968. The following year, eight institutions (including seven of the original eight) conducted feasibility studies. While each project had unique educational assumptions upon which its program was based, clearly definable trends permeated all of them. Each program included objectives, instructional components to meet the objectives, assessment procedures, a design for program management, an opportunity for cooperative interaction between universities and schools, and a systematic approach to comprehensive teacher-education programs. Each relied heavily on feedback from research for improving the program.

Copies of the models were distributed widely and the project directors were commissioned to work with institutions interested in testing the concepts in practice. The third phase of the effort, implementation by the designing institutions, was never supported because of leadership changes in USOE and a shortage of funds. Between 1967 and 1973, however, over 12 million US dollars were expended in conceptualizing the models, analyzing them, and disseminating information about them. While the general nature of the movement was present prior to the elementary models program, CBTE took form and substance out of these many activities.

Two forces permeating American society had supported the development of the movement. The first was the press for accountability that was derived from the commercial and industrial sector of society. With increasing budgets and restricted funds, it was charged that educators should more appropriately use resources (funds, personnel, buildings) to improve student achievement—and that educators should be accountable for such outcomes.

The second force that shaped education was the need for personalization. Rapid changes in society and technology, combined with an increasingly urban population and more sharply defined vocational specializations, had led to a depersonalized society. CBTE was developed as a viable response to these two societal forces. With explicit goals and assessment systems that were linked to outcomes in schools, it offered accountability. With options for participants, prior knowledge of require-ments, and alternative instructional programs, CBTE offered both individualization and personalization.

4. Rationale Supporting CBTE

The basis for CBTE is in its reliance on objectives specified in advance and known to the learner. It assumes that humans are goal oriented and that they are more likely to achieve such goals and objectives when overt actions are taken to achieve them. Advocates point out the research basis for this position in psychology through incidental/intentional learning studies, in experiments in mastery learning by Benjamin Bloom, John Carroll, and their associates, and in the studies of behaviorally stated objectives (see *Mastery Learning Models*). The basic concept has been used extensively in behavioral psychology, particularly in industrial and military training programs. Keller's Personalized System of Instruction (PSI) (see *Keller Plan: A Personalized System of Instruction*) relied on precise objectives and standards for university science courses. In this setting, research conclusions did not always substantiate the rationale upon which CBTE was based. However, the preponderance of studies tended to support the CBTE hypothesis: students who know in advance the specific objectives of instruction achieve more than those unaware of the objectives.

As CBTE applied this approach to professional training of teachers, two important notions were added. First, objectives were based on the role requirements of teachers, and second, performance rather than knowledge alone was required for program completion. This extension of the concept was made to insure the validity of objectives that were selected for the preparation program of teachers. Graduates of teacher-education programs and critics of educational practice such as James R. Conant and James D. Koerner had questioned the validity and the usefulness of preparation programs. By basing program requirements and standards on the behavior of effective teachers, teacher educators could most closely attune programs to valid bases.

5. Effectiveness of CBTE

Despite the extensive rhetoric, publications, and discussions related to CBTE, almost no basic definitive research was conducted to prove or disprove its effectiveness. Hundreds of publications recommended ways to design CBTE programs, described what institutions were planning to do, outlined lists of competencies, and included instructional units referred to as modules. Few reported research on the CBTE concept, competency validation, or program effectiveness. Carefully controlled experimental studies were seldom conducted. No developmental sequence of studies in a comprehensive research program was undertaken. Few studies reported conditions, procedures, and tests adequately to replicate the research. Many conclusions were based on the feelings or perceptions of faculty or students.

This criticism is not unique to CBTE. In no area of

teacher education has there been adequate research. Such a continuing practice has severely limited the improvement of preparation programs. What makes this shortcoming so apparent in CBTE is the expressed need for research by those supporting the movement. The future of CBTE was inextricably tied to an empirical base for teacher education. Critical in this process was the identification of valid competencies of effective teachers. Second, CBTE implied the determination of appropriate teacher-education curricula and methods that would modify behaviors of trainees so that they would demonstrate such competencies. Third, it implied that adequate assessment procedures were available or could be constructed to measure sensitively the changes in behavior. Finally, it assumed that institutions would devote the needed resources to research and refine competencies, programs. assessments, and research.

In its search for ideal preparation for ideal teachers, CBTE assumed that, though recognized, these limitations could be surmounted by concerted national efforts. The findings of one researcher or institution would be shared with others in a growing body of research evidence. For two reasons, this was not the case. First, the variants among CBTE programs were too great; each program proliferated its own set of competency statements and devised its own instructional program and assessment procedures. Comparison among programs was difficult. Second, no national or international communication network emerged to share results of those studies that were conducted.

Typical of these studies was one completed by Enos at San Diego State University. Enos compared elementary education graduates of a CBTE curriculum track with those of the traditional track, basing his study on the set of objectives the university had certified to the State of California as the basis for their program. He found that CBTE students had significantly greater knowledge about teaching and learning, significantly better verbal interaction with children, significantly greater use of individualized instruction, and significantly higher ratings of their performance by children they taught. In dozens of comparisons, CBTE-trained teachers outperformed graduates of the traditional program.

Positive findings favoring CBTE were reported at the University of Nebraska, University of Houston, Weber State University, Oregon College of Education, and University of Toledo while negative findings were reported at Illinois State University. Such studies generally concluded that CBTE students felt more confident as they completed the program, were evaluated more highly by their supervisors and by employing principals on their first job, had a wider repertoire of teaching skills, and believed their preparation program was better than that of other prospective teachers.

6. Concerns of Critics

Humanistic educators attacked CBTE for its prespecified objectives. Their argument pivoted on whether the learner controlled his own learning or was controlled by some external system. Their view of education as developing free, self-determining, self-renewing, self-actualized persons was antithetical to the basic CBTE conceptualization.

Others charged CBTE with being anti-intellectual. With the emphasis in CBTE on performance, they noted that a naive actor could fulfill requirements without the undergirding knowledge base. They distinguished the performer from the professional who performs, noting that a good actor could receive passing marks simply by mimicking the actions of an effective teacher; that is, by following the script.

The specification of competencies was criticized because such lists atomized the teaching process. Teachers do not teach using independent competencies, but in context and using in an integrated fashion a number of skills and knowledges. The value of dissecting general competence into a number of specific and autonomous objectives was questioned. Further, limiting objectives to those leading to observable action or results appeared to stifle the development of professionals whose personal characteristics might lead to a wide range of successful teaching practices.

Finally, since each competency was to be measured, the use of a single-variable procedure was considered inadequate. These critics opted for multivariate measures of the total integrated teaching process of a teacher. In his early document on CBTE, Elam (1972 p. 21) stated that: "The overriding problem before which the others pale to insignificance is that of the adequacy of measurement instruments and procedures." Although hundreds of instruments have been developed and several conferences held on the topic, assessment persists as the major problem in CBTE as in all of teacher education.

Use of teacher assessment through pupil achievement as a measure of teacher competence (e.g., consequence competencies) was challenged because of lack of research which linked teacher knowledge or actions with pupil outcomes. That research which had been conducted was based primarily on nonexperimental studies where teacher behaviors were observed in natural settings, change in pupil achievement measured, and the results of the two analyzed for relationships. Whenever researchers found a relationship between teacher behavior and pupil achievement, even when the correlations were very low, the conclusion was reached that such behaviors were characteristic of effective teachers. Critics charged that this relationship was too simplistic to reflect the realities of human action and interaction; that it assumed too great an influence by the teacher on pupil learning; that pupil learning was multidimensional; that some teacher behaviors, while enhancing certain pupil outcomes, may diminish others; and that the overall effect should not become the basis for certification.

The lack of carefully controlled and constructed research on the effectiveness of CBTE and of specific competencies is a major weakness in development of the movement. The tragedy of the decade of the 1970s was the lack of research in a program that required and espoused research.

While not explicit, the CBTE movement to reform teacher education pitted those in universities who traditionally had controlled teacher education against increasingly militant teachers and others who called for its reform. In such an atmosphere, it was not likely that logic, research, or persuasive arguments would have much effect on the outcome. As with many issues, the ultimate positions of individuals and institutions were taken on political rather than educational grounds.

7. Extensiveness of Implementation

The decade of the 1970s marked the growth spurt of CBTE. Four national surveys traced this development. Their results are summarized in Table 1.

Throughout the decade, the number of institutions operating full-scale CBTE programs increased. By 1980, 80 institutions (13 percent) reported full-scale CBTE programs while 284 institutions were operating small-scale programs. The percent of institutions with small-scale programs remained relatively constant (44 percent in 1975, 49 percent in 1977, and 46 percent in 1980). More institutions were not involved in 1980 (41 percent) than in 1977 (29 percent) or in 1975 (17 percent). Further, fewer institutions were exploring CBTE in 1980 (14 percent) than in 1977 (26 percent) or 1975 (47 percent).

The number of documents on CBTE has increased rapidly since the early 1970s. In 1971, Allen Schmieder listed 22 items in his first bibliography on CBTE and 800 items two years later. In 1976, Cappuzzello and his associates identified over 6,000 items. The number of publications on CBTE continued at a steady pace through the early 1980s. The quality and freshness of their content reflected few new ideas, little research, and no major breakthroughs in problem areas, however.

The United States federal government supported numerous projects encouraging CBTE principles. Among them were programs in vocational–technical education, special education, community education, Teacher Corps, Teacher Centers, and the elementary teacher education models. In every state,

the education agency studied and made recommendations, prior to 1975, concerning CBTE. Every major professional education association in the United States was involved during the 1970s through task forces, position papers, and/or conference speeches and papers.

Educators from all parts of the world have been involved in CBTE programs. A special one-week training program was sponsored by UNESCO in Paris for its chief technical advisors from 60 developing countries. CBTE programs have been reported in Australia, Brazil, Indonesia, Israel, Japan, Nigeria, Taiwan, and the Federal Republic of Germany.

8. Case Study

The development and implementation of CBTE at the University of Houston is typical of those institutions which fully implemented competency-based principles in their undergraduate teacher education programs. Beginning in 1970, a team of about 20 faculty began exploring a new approach to their undergraduate program. After nearly a year of design and development activities, the program was piloted with 64 students who entered the two-year sequence. A year later, 125 additional students entered a second pilot test. In the spring of 1973 just as the first group was finishing the pilot test and the second was halfway through, the faculty voted to implement the program fully for about 1,100 students per year, beginning in the fall of 1974.

While the mechanics of an individualized program for so many students was a real problem for the first two years of full implementation, the content and approach were virtually the same seven years later.

In the original program, 16 competency statements were hammered out by faculty. The prospective teacher (a) diagnoses the learner's emotional, social, physical, and intellectual needs; (b) identifies and/or specifies instructional goals and objectives based on learner needs; (c) designs instruction appropriate to goals and objectives; (d) implements instruction that is consistent with plan; and (e) designs and implements evaluation procedures which focus on learner achievement and instructional effectiveness. Other competencies were related to cultural awareness, demonstration of a repertoire of instructional skills, classroom communication,

Table 1
Extensiveness of CBTE implementation

| Involvement | Percentage of colleges responding[a] | | | |
	1973 (n = 783)	1975 (n = 570)	1977 (n = 686)	1980 (n = 624)
Operating full-scale CBTE program	1	8	9	13
Operating limited CBTE program	15	44	49	46
Exploring or developing CBTE program	54	47	26	14
Not involved	29	17	29	41

a Column totals may not total 100 percent due to overlap in categories of involvement adequate knowledge of subject matter, and analysis of one's own professional effectiveness.

These competencies were based on a number of assumptions that guided program development. Teachers are more effective when they are liberally educated, when they are students of human behavior, when they make decisions on rational bases, and when their preparation includes a wide range of active school-based experiences.

Three other competencies have been added since 1975 in response to new state requirements. These competencies related to mainstreaming students, teaching reading in content areas, and making career decisions. Each competency is stated briefly (as in the first five, listed above), then described more fully as a paragraph, then expanded as instructional objectives which are in turn rearranged and integrated. The statement of the 19 competencies is a logical exposition of program requirements; the hundreds of instructional objectives are grouped psychologically for developmental and instructional purposes.

Upon entering the program, the prospective teacher receives a module or booklet that specifies program requirements and includes basic directions for completing each phase of the two-year program. Each section in the module includes objectives, rationale, instructional activities, needed resources and their location, and a description of the assessment used to determine completion of that phase of the program.

Some activities occur in groups: 40 students listen to a lecture on Piaget or 6 students interview 30 children using Piagetian methods and draw tentative conclusions about child development from their own study before considering the broader scope of Piaget's developmental conclusions. Some activities are completed individually. On the third floor of the College of Education building, the Learning Resources Center (LRC) contains dozens of individual carrels and hundreds of slide-tapes, videotapes, instructional resources, and other materials for student use. Each resource is keyed directly to a section in the module; prospective teachers study them at their pace rather than on a scheduled basis. Some activities require work in schools. In mathematics, for example, students tutor one or two pupils—diagnosing, prescribing instruction, teaching using a variety of instructional aids, and evaluating the achievement gain of pupils over several weeks. In science, students demonstrate use of an inquiry approach to teaching while in social science they demonstrate ability to lead class discussions. Some school-based lessons are videotaped and later analyzed in the LRC by students and university professors. Portable videotape equipment is always available for student checkout and use.

In the final three months of the program, prospective teachers are expected to demonstrate in classroom settings an integrated use of appropriate teaching strategies. They are observed by school and university personnel and judged on the extent to which they have mastered and demonstrated each competency.

Thus, a set of broad competencies for the program were agreed to by the university faculty; a set of specific objectives were drawn from these competencies and instruction and assessment related to objectives during the program; finally, assessment of program completion was tied directly to demonstration of competencies in actual school settings. While some time limitations are imposed, in general students progress at their own rate, based on demonstration of objectives.

9. Developmental Progress

This case study illustrates a developmental process implied in CBTE. Competency-based teacher education assumes that the instructional program is based on a set of defined competencies, therefore the specification of, and agreement on, competencies occurs first, then instruction is designed which logically and directly relates to learner achievement and demonstration of those competencies. Finally, assessments are designed to relate to the competencies.

Specifying competencies is a major factor in program design. Seven approaches have been used by CBTE developers. The most often used approach is professional perception. A group of teachers, school administrators and/or college faculty list the behaviors they believe characterize effective teachers. These are refined by combining similar behaviors, editing statements, and selecting only those rated highest by some relevant group.

A second approach is based on a conceptual model. Some programs were based on a single model: the University of Toledo designed its program for teachers in Individually Guided Education (IGE) schools; Missouri around a conceptual role model; and Michigan State University around the notion of the teacher as a practicing behavioral scientist.

Bruce Joyce and Marsha Weil described 16 models of teaching that are used. Preparation programs could select from these models those believed to be most important, and hold their students accountable for demonstrating them. In the social inquiry model, the teacher acts as a sharpener, focuser, and counsellor as students are encouraged to focus on social issues, develop hypothetical solutions, explore solutions, and gather facts to support or negate the solutions.

Competencies for the social inquiry model differ from those, for example, of the advance organizer model. The latter assumes that each discipline includes a set of basic concepts and principles. The teacher first focuses student attention on these key ideas, then relates cognitive information to the lesson organizers. With the first model, need is defined in terms of social problems and issues; for the second, need is based on the logical sequence of the content of a discipline. The purpose of the first model is understanding social change; the purpose of the second is to increase the efficiency of information processing by structuring the flow of cognitive knowledge.

Each conceptual model has its own integrity—its own set of assumptions, values, parameters, and operating procedures. Teachers demonstrate different sets of competencies with each model.

The third approach to specifying competencies is based on task analysis. Either teachers are asked to log their activities or trained observers outline all the activities in which teachers engage. These are listed, rated in terms of how often a behavior is exhibited and how crucial it is in teaching, then refined into a set of competencies.

The fourth approach is based on research. Developers review the research literature for cues to effective practice, then base program requirements on those that seem most promising.

Course translation, the fifth approach, involves simple reformulation of the requirements of current courses into competency statements without reconceptualizing the program or the relevancy of content to the roles of teachers.

Needs of school learners is a sixth basis for specifying competencies. In this approach, the needs and goals for pupils in schools (Kindergarten–secondary school) are first identified, then the school organization and curriculum developed to achieve these goals, and finally the competencies needed by teachers in such a school are specified.

The last approach, needs assessment, is similar to number six but it begins by assessing the needs of society and of a particular community before speculation on pupil needs and values, thus it adds a basic step prior to completing the process in number six.

Most CBTE developers relied on more than one of these approaches in designing their programs. The University of Houston, considered in the case study of a CBTE program, used task analysis (20 teachers maintained logs for six weeks); perception of College of Education faculty, school pupils, and teachers; and the conceptual model based on work at Michigan State University and the various models of teaching delineated by Joyce and Weil as the basis for using appropriate teaching strategies (listed as competency number four).

Such a systematic process requires a complete overhaul of existing programs. Instructors cannot simply revamp their current courses. Neither can they simply list objectives for currently taught content. An examination of the final dimensions and specifications for student competence is necessary before any of the parts can be logically developed.

A few institutions undertook this task during the 1970s. Others took a part of their program and used CBTE principles in redesigning that part, while other institutions implemented a total program for a small number of students. The question posed earlier about the extensiveness of CBTE implementation cannot be answered adequately until not only the quantity of institutions undertaking full and partial implementation is studied, but also the quality of their developmental processes and program congruence to CBTE principles.

10. Concerns of Implementors

How do those who have devoted time since the early 1970s to implementing CBTE feel about the process? What are their concerns as expressed in written documents?

Time and energy were most often mentioned. Developing a new approach, new materials, selling it to those in decision-making positions, all require considerable time. It is not surprising, then, that burnout occurred after two to five years of concentrated effort by an individual. It is also not surprising that when a new group continued that effort, they often began again as they reconceptualized the program.

CBTE programs are more difficult to develop because they are integrated and linked to final student outcomes. Because they are considered a system, any changes in one subsystem tend to affect all subsystems. In the more traditional organization of programs, each course could be modified with relative ease since it was relatively independent. Not so with CBTE where courses, modules, units, or experiences are intertwined. This changes the process of decision making. The group as a group rather than individuals determines content, approach, and balance in each phase of the program. The process is therefore more time-consuming and energy-draining.

The emphasis in CBTE on performance leads to greater interaction with schools and their personnel—the superintendent, principals, teachers. They too join the consortia that becomes the CBTE program, and they too add to the mix of professionals developing and implementing the program. Problems of interinstitutional missions, policies, organizations, and communication patterns exasperate the situation.

What to include in the program and whether to base content on research, practice, or professional judgments was an early problem for most. The level of specificity of objectives and competencies was a related concern. Should there be a few broad competencies or dozens of very specific ones? Identifying and achieving agreement on a set of competencies and their precise wording was a time-consuming task.

A related problem was implementing relevant instruction. Modules were conceived of as flexible, relatively small instructional delivery systems that could be related directly to objectives. Often in practice they became fairly rigid booklets, made up of pre- and post-tests and instructional guidelines that were completed independently by students who often criticized them for lack of human interaction.

Assessment was considered a problem in most programs. Finding or designing appropriate and sensitive measurement instruments and determining realistic cut-off scores for passing each competency required more advanced and sophisticated assessment skills than were available in education.

The traditional institutional system is not geared for CBTE. It is prepared for letter grades (A, B, C, D, F), not "Pass–Fail" or "Pass–Not Yet." When letter grades are used in CBTE, the grade most often given for successful completion of work was "A." Administrators charged that CBTE instructors were giving too many high grades, and thus were destroying the integrity of the normal curve used in university grading systems.

Traditional institutions are organized around semesters or quarters, and students are expected to begin courses at the beginning of each semester or quarter and finish them during that period. CBTE's emphasis on individual progress leads to continuous initiation and completion of instructional units; tying this to time-bound semesters requires developers to group experiences and to give Incomplete (I) grades to those students not completing the entire group of experiences within a semester or quarter. CBTE programs are likely to have a greater proportion of "I" grades, leading to yet other conflicts with the institution. Because CBTE students are often enrolled also in traditional courses, coordinating instructional experiences requires articulation and accommodation with the system.

Finally, the development phase in CBTE programs never seems to end. Competency statements, instructional units, and assessment systems all require revisions as they are used. Faculty need to be trained, and new faculty integrated into the system. Changes in leadership of schools require careful attention. The never-ending tasks of development drain the energy of those implementing the programs.

For CBTE developers, the problems and concerns are similar to those of anyone initiating new processes within an established system. Accommodating to that system while modifying it requires resources and energy. When the program is no longer considered special, as is the case with many CBTE programs today, the period of infusion has passed—and perhaps the period of greatest effectiveness and growth.

11. Present Challenges and Future Directions

With all the activity related to CBTE since the early 1970s, a number of issues have surfaced. These are listed below as a basis for probing deeper into the movement and proposing unique and important contributions. What constitutes evidence that a specific competency or cluster of competencies are related to effective teaching? Can the competency-based approach be used in training teachers for nonobjective-based instructional systems? Should it be? Does CBTE preserve humanistic values? Does CBTE limit academic freedom? To what extent is the knowledge base in professional education adequate to base certification of teachers on demonstrated competence? Does CBTE lead to atomistic learning? Do minimum acceptable levels become maximum levels of achievement for teachers? Does the CBTE emphasis on exit requirements imply open admissions? Is this desirable in terms of resource allocations? Who should make the decisions about which competencies are to be required? Should competency specifications be standardized on a statewide basis because of certification, on a local basis—either for a specific school district or a specific teacher education institution, on an individual student basis, or not at all? Are there generic competencies?

Amid the worldwide actions in CBTE, it must be remembered that, while the concept is sound and fundamental, the implementation is still primitive in terms of its inherent promise. Years of research and development are necessary for adequate testing of the concept. The temptation to continue with current programs and not experiment with new approaches must be dissuaded. Without the philosophical, pedagogical, and psychological analyses that are the essence of CBTE, teacher education will flounder with global goals and complex unanalyzed variables. Only in continual, databased, thoughtful change will teacher preparation programs improve. The CBTE approach provides the conceptual frame to make that possible.

See also: Mastery Learning Models; Keller Plan: A Personalized System of Instruction; Effects of Teaching

Bibliography

Elam S 1972 *Performance-based Teacher Education: What is the State of the Art?* American Association of Colleges for Teacher Education, Washington, DC

Enos D F 1976 A cost-effectiveness analysis of competency-based and non-competency based teacher education at San Diego State University (Unpublished doctoral dissertation, University of Texas, Austin)

Grant G (ed.) 1979 *On Competence: A Critical Analysis of Competence–based Reforms in Higher Education.* Jossey-Bass, San Francisco, California

Hall G E, Jones H L 1976 *Competency-based Education: A Process for the Improvement of Education.* Prentice-Hall, Englewood Cliffs, New Jersey

Houston W R 1974 *Exploring Competency-based Education.* McCutchan, Berkeley, California

Medley D M 1977 *Teacher Competence and Teacher Effectiveness: A Review of Process-Product Research.* American Association of Colleges for Teacher Education, Washington, DC

Sandefur W S, Nicklas W L 1981 Competency-based teacher education in AACTE institutions: An update. *Phi Delta Kappan* 62: 747–48

Spady W G 1977 Competency-based education: A bandwagon in search of a definition. *Educ. Res.* AERA 6(6): 9–14

SECTION 2
Methods and Paradigms for Research

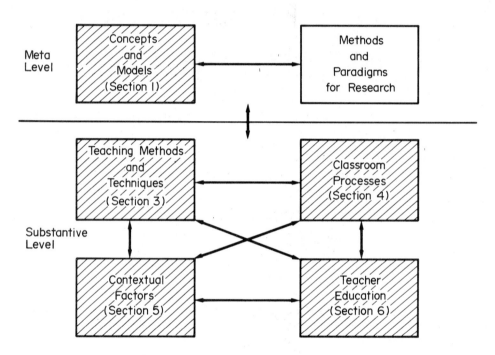

Schematic representation of Section 2 in relation to other Sections.

SECTION 2

Methods and Paradigms for Research

INTRODUCTION
TO SECTION 2

Some of the concepts of teaching presented in Sect. 1 are more compatible with classroom research than others. For example, "success" notions of teaching seem to obviate research on teaching effectiveness because effectiveness has to be present for teaching to exist. "Intent" notions of teaching do not obviate the need for research on teaching effectiveness but they make research on teaching difficult since it is necessary to know what teachers' intentions are before it is possible to say that teaching is in progress. The researcher's solution to this problem is sometimes to make inferences about the teacher's intent on the basis of other information. This section is about researchers' attempts to solve problems that face them when they try to gather evidence about teaching.

In the first article Medley traces the evolution of quantitative research on teaching which has been concerned with teaching effectiveness. Not all research on teaching seeks knowledge about the connections between the activities of teaching and the attainment of the objectives of education. Some research on teaching seeks merely to describe teaching without regard to its relationship with anything else. Still other research on teaching explores relationships between characteristics of teachers, such as their sex or age, and the ways in which they behave towards students. And yet another type seeks evidence of the links between teaching variables and contexts within which teaching occurs, such as the type of school or curriculum. Medley's article is not concerned with these latter types of research on teaching. Neither is it concerned with nonquantitative types of research or with research that has not involved practising teachers as subjects. The types of research he regards as nonquantitative are explained in later articles in this section.

Medley delineates six main categories and four subsidiary categories of variables employed in quantitative research on teaching effectiveness. The first six types comprise learning outcomes in students; student classroom activities; teacher classroom behaviours; "preactive" teacher behaviours, such as planning and preparing materials; teacher competencies in the form of knowledge, skills, and values needed for effective functioning; and pre-existing teacher characteristics that make up aptitudes for teaching. The subsidiary types of variables consist of individual student characteristics such as abilities that determine individual learning outcomes, student characteristics that affect students' responses to teacher behaviour, external contextual variables including materials, administration, community features and so on, and teacher-training experiences that affect teacher competencies. According to Medley, only research that involves one or more of the first six types of variables can be described as research on teaching.

The evolution of research on teaching must also be seen in the light of four elements of a strategy for explaining why the quality of teaching varies. These four elements are: conceptualization, instrumentation, design, and statistical analysis. To a very large extent the whole of this section of the Encyclopedia is concerned with those four elements delineated by Medley. The rest of Medley's article is an explanation of the ways in which the 10 types of variables and the four types of elements have appeared in research on teaching since its beginnings. He describes major elements and trends in the evolution, and rounds off his article with a set of specifications for the conceptualization, instrumentation, design, and analysis elements for research in the future. Medley concludes by comparing the stage reached in scientific knowledge about teaching with that of medicine at the beginning of the twentieth century. He writes:

> Research on teaching has begun to yield results which suggest that much of the lore of the profession may be as worthless as those leeches, purges, and other procedures that made up the lore of nineteenth century medicine. . . . For the first time in its history, research on teaching shows some promise of beginning . . . to transform the practice of teaching in the way that the practice of medicine has been and continues to be transformed by medical research. 'Tis a consummation devoutly to be wished.

In the second article in this section, Doyle covers some of the same ground covered by Medley but while Medley emphasizes advances made by the adoption of the "process–product" paradigm for research on teaching, Doyle expresses dissatisfaction with that paradigm for its incapacity to *explain* how teaching behaviour influences student learning. Doyle advocates an elaboration of the process–product paradigm by the inclusion within research studies of attention to "processes that intervene between what teachers do and what students learn". Doyle mentions several examples of research adopting this "mediating process" paradigm and variables such as student engagement and academic learning time about which there are articles in later sections of this Encyclopedia.

Doyle also observes a shift from quantitative observational techniques to narrative records, qualitative analyses, sociolinguistic studies with an "anthropological flavor", research on classroom structures and on teachers' and students' thinking, but considers that the diversity of these approaches in terms of the types of questions asked and interpretative framework adopted, together with their more theoretical and descriptive orientations, makes them unlikely to be adopted as paradigms for research on teaching unless closer links with practice are forged. Several of these approaches are the subjects of articles appearing later in this Encyclopedia. Doyle's comments should be seen in the light of those made by the other authors.

In the third article in this section Biddle and Dunkin are careful to distinguish between research on teaching effectiveness and research on teaching effects, arguing that the former is a narrower enterprise than the latter. Teaching effectiveness, they state, is a matter of the teacher's success in facilitating the attainment of accepted educational objectives, whereas the effects of teaching can include unplanned, and even undesirable, outcomes. Biddle and Dunkin also caution against the sometimes naive causal reasoning that is conducted in relation to the effects of teaching. After elaborating upon teaching as an independent variable and the almost endless list of variables that might be dependent variables, the authors discuss the design requirements for establishing causality. Here they rely on John Stuart Mill's three requirements:

(a) variation in the presumed cause must be associated with variation in the effect;

(b) the causative event must precede the effect in time; and

(c) conditions that might account for the relationship between the two events must be controlled for.

In their elaboration on the third requirement Biddle and Dunkin discuss designs in research on teaching and their strengths and shortcomings. In reviewing the findings of these endeavours the authors explain the difficulties, if not impossibility, of obtaining incontrovertible evidence of causal effects in the complex social contexts of teaching, but express optimism in view of the conceptual and theoretical developments accompanying such research. They conclude their article by calling for more comparative and more longitudinal research, and more research into aptitude–treatment interactions.

In their discussion of the findings of research on the effects of teaching, Biddle and Dunkin mention approaches to the reviewing of research findings and make particular mention of the technique known as meta-analysis. In the fourth article in this section Giaconia and Hedges write about several traditional methods for synthesizing research evidence and elaborate in detail about meta-analysis. They state that reviewers of research pursue three goals: to summarize findings across different studies; to detect the consistency with which findings have been obtained; and to resolve contradictions among the findings of different investigations. The tasks of the synthesizer are six in number:

(a) selecting questions or hypotheses;

(b) sampling studies to be synthesized;

(c) representing characteristics of the studies;

(d) analysing the studies;

(e) interpreting the results;

(f) reporting the synthesis.

There have been four main methods of performing them: "narrative approaches", "vote counting methods", "combined significance test methods", and "effect magnitude methods", each of which the authors fully describe and evaluate in terms of its success in achieving the summarizing, consistency-checking, and contradiction-resolving goals of the reviews.

Giaconia and Hedges conclude their article with a section devoted to the question: "Do different research synthesis methods produce substantially different conclusions?"

and answer, "Often, yes". They justify this conclusion by showing that different approaches to synthesizing findings concerning the relationship between teacher indirectness and student achievement, and between teachers' questions and student achievement have produced different conclusions. Finally, the reader is directed to the article by Giaconia entitled *Open Versus Formal Methods* in Sect. 3 of this Encyclopedia as another example of different conclusions being reached depending upon the synthesizing procedures adopted.

The first four articles in this section are general in the sense that they deal with the broader issues of the evolution, orientation, design, and reviewing of research on teaching. The next four articles focus on more specific issues associated with methods of obtaining data about teaching variables themselves through observing in classrooms. The first of these articles, *Structured Observation*, is about methods more often associated with quantitative methods while the following two, *Naturalistic Inquiry* and *Ethnographic Methods*, are usually seen to be more suited to qualitative approaches. In a sense this distinction between quantitative and qualitative is misleading for it suggests that the former is unconcerned with qualitative differences in teaching variables. In fact, the categories of behaviour which are counted or rated in the so-called quantitative observational methods are formulated and defined on the basis of qualitative differences in the behaviours that occur. It is the often rigorous and arduous work that has gone into the defining of these categories that allows them to be reliably identified and counted.

Galton's article on *Structured Observation* outlines the beginnings of the approach and describes its characteristics. Galton distinguishes between low- and high-inference techniques, between category and sign systems, and describes data collection on the basis of live observation and from the analysis of recordings of classroom events. He explains the importance of using trained observers to apply these systems and discusses the issues and methods associated with their reliability and validity. The complexities of applying structured observational systems emerge clearly from the author's explication of the coding and analysis tasks involved, and of decisions to be made about units of analyses and behaviour sampling methods. Galton concludes by presenting some of the evidence of teaching effectiveness, and some of the gaps, that have emerged from the application of structured observational techniques.

In the sixth article in this section, Guba and Lincoln distinguish between "naturalistic" and "rationalistic" or "scientific" approaches to enquiry. They reject the terms "qualitative" and "case study" when applied to the former because those terms suggest that the distinctive features of it are its format, methods, or setting. Rather, they argue, the differences are matters of interpretation based on basic axioms or assumptions concerning the nature of reality, the relationship between the enquirer and the object of enquiry, the nature of truth statements, causality and the place of values in enquiry. For example, the authors claim that while rationalists assume a single tangible reality fragmentable into independent variables, naturalists assume multiple realities existing in the minds of people which can be studied only in holistic and idiosyncratic fashion.

As well as these differences regarding basic axioms, the authors present a set of postural differences which they regard not as logically necessary for either approach but which characterize the "style" of each. These differences apply to preferred methods (and it is here that the authors use the terms "quantitative" and "qualitative"), to sources of theory, knowledge types, instruments, designs, and settings in which studies are conducted. In their systematic contrasts between the two positions regarding the above, the authors list differences in the place of nonhuman devices, laboratory settings, preordinate designs, and a priori hypotheses in research.

In their treatment of the issue of the "trustworthiness" of naturalistic research, the authors suggest ways in which credibility might be enhanced and argue that, given time, the naturalistic paradigm will prove to be as useful as the rationalistic paradigm. Guba and Lincoln conclude with the advice that choice between the two paradigms should "revolve about the assessment of fit to the area under study, rather than to any intrinsic advantages or disadvantages of either".

Taft, in his article on *Ethnographic Methods* which is the next to appear in this section, raises the important distinction between participant and nonparticipant observation and includes case studies within the concept of ethnographic research. He also discusses the important issues of subjectivity, reliability, and validity of observations and considers the role of theory, hypotheses, and generalizations in ethnographic research. With particular reference to ethnography as a case study method, Taft writes: "an ethnographic account of a school . . . derives its value largely from the fact that the investigator—and also the readers—are familiar with other schools and with schools in general", but he subsequently issues the caution that "in ethnographic studies no generalization can be treated as final, only as a working hypothesis for further studies". He concludes his article by writing that the ethnographic method "can make its own legitimate independent contribution at any stage of a research including the confirmation of hypotheses that have emerged out of other sources provided that the basic principles on which its credibility rests are observed".

The next article to appear is especially relevant to researchers who are sophisticated with regard to statistical methods of treating quantitative data, but the more general problems of selecting units of analysis are relevant to any approach to empirical research. Burstein defines "units of analysis" as "those entities or objects whose behaviour one is trying to understand or describe; they are the explanatory focus of an investigation". Burstein explains that typical units of analysis in educational research are teachers, students, classrooms, schools and so on. Units of analysis vary in level from scores for individuals (lower level) to aggregations for groups (higher level) so that it often happens that multilevel analyses are found in educational research. The existence of these possible variations in level of analysis creates problems in choosing the appropriate units of analysis.

Burstein discusses these issues as they are affected by research design, conceptual considerations and technical considerations, especially those that are statistical. He points out that while most process–product research on teaching uses the class or teacher as the unit of analysis, research on aptitude–treatment interactions typically uses the individual student as the unit. Burstein sees good sense in allowing the purpose of the investigation to determine the unit of analysis. He also sees advantages in a multilevel perspective and, after discussing measurement and analysis issues associated with such a perspective, concludes that its adoption will accelerate progress in understanding educational phenomena.

The next two articles in this section are related to one another because they are both concerned with the roles and rights of people who are often the subjects in research on teaching. In the article on *Teachers as Researchers*, Elliott is particularly interested in the role of teachers in curriculum change. He traces the involvement of teachers in data collection and hypothesis construction and testing in the British Schools Council's Humanities Project (1967–72) and states that the idea of teachers as researchers emerged as one solution to the problems of curriculum implementation and as a concomitant of a process model of curriculum within which curriculum and teacher development were seen as one and the same activity. Elliott writes that the teachers as researchers "movement" regards theorizing, researching, decision making, and implementing to be integral parts of professional practice. Furthermore, the movement necessitates that external change agents adopt facilitative rather than controlling roles, for example, by assisting teachers to learn research techniques.

Examples of implementation of these principles are provided in the Ford Teaching Project and in the Schools Council's TIQI project and some of the major problems of facilitating teachers' research efforts are presented. Elliott concludes by claiming that the type of research which he refers to as "educational action research" is "not only practical but emancipatory".

Dockrell's article on *Ethical Considerations* presents principles involving relationships between researchers and their subjects, their customers, their colleagues, and the community. Concerning researcher–subject relations, he says that the research "must not minimize or indeed exaggerate the demands that are to be made in terms of time, effort, or stress on subjects". It is the researcher's duty to ensure that subjects are informed about and agree upon the information to be disclosed about them. This principle, he says, requires that subjects be able to read reports before they are published.

Another principle is that the researcher must specify "what return there will be to the subjects and not mislead them about the benefits of the investigation to themselves". As part of this, Dockrell sees that it is incumbent on researchers not to make demands on subjects that cannot be offset by the potential benefits of the research.

The researcher's obligations to the customer, that is, someone who commissions research, are mainly to do with communication about the limits of the research and the conclusions generated from it. It is incumbent on the researcher to ensure that the customer understands the problems of generalizability, precision, significance, and so on, and that interpretations and extrapolations be distinguishable from findings.

In relation to their colleagues, writes Dockrell, researchers have two obligations: "to ensure that they can make the fullest use of their research" and "that what they say does not detract from the status of the [research] community". With respect to the wider community, researchers need to communicate implications for policy of their research and exercise good judgment about when it is appropriate and when it is not, to raise certain issues for investigation.

The last two articles in this section are about the evaluation of teaching. Issues involved in coming to a judgment about the worth of teaching are germane to research on teacher effectiveness. The alternatives for adoption as criteria for the evaluation of teaching are several and range from the most immediate or proximal to the longer term or ultimate. After defining "criterion", "teaching", and "evaluation" for the purposes of this article, Medley delineates three main tasks in the evaluation of teaching. These are eliciting an appropriate sample of teaching behaviour, establishing a basis for scoring records of the behaviour, and ensuring equivalence of tasks allocated to different teachers. He discusses these three tasks in the light of three criteria for the evaluation of teaching: learning outcomes in students; teaching behaviour; and student behaviour.

Medley considers that the major problem in using learning outcomes as a criterion is isolating and assessing that share of student learning that is attributable to the teaching being evaluated. His explication of this problem and of attempts to solve it by using raw gain scores, residual gain scores, and so on, is enlightening.

The main problem in using teaching behaviour as a criterion of teaching effectiveness is lack of knowledge of what constitutes effective teaching. Nevertheless, rating scales and systematic observation are often used to gather data about teaching behaviour for evaluative purposes. In discussing these approaches Medley provides a brief history of the use of rating scales for this purpose, and makes an important distinction between ratings of teachers' personality characteristics, and ratings of classroom behaviours, concluding that the rating scale should be abandoned in favour of systematic observation. He then elaborates upon observational schedules, distinguishing among sign, category, and muitiple coding systems and advising on ways in which they might be developed and used. He finds cause for optimism regarding the choice of an observation instrument based on a set of teaching behaviours known to comprise teaching effectiveness.

As an example of the type of student behaviour that might be used as a criterion for evaluating teaching, Medley suggests academic learning time which is a measure of student engagement or involvement in learning tasks and which is discussed more fully in Sect. 4. Medley argues that the types of student behaviours involved do not necessarily have to be ones known to be associated with learning outcomes, for there are some behaviours that are valued for other reasons. These would include expressions of satisfaction or enjoyment which might be independent of subject-matter learning and the like.

Medley concludes his article by writing about the obligations of the evaluator, thus supporting some of the ethical principles discussed in the previous article by Dockrell. He writes that the evaluator should make explicit assumptions about the relationships between teaching behaviours and student outcomes and the evidence available concerning the validity of those assumptions. Furthermore, the evaluator should constantly monitor research literature in order to test and review the assumptions and evaluation procedures.

In the final article in this section, Marsh writes about students as evaluators of teaching. He points out that most of the research and practice on this topic has occurred in higher education institutions, and in North America. His article explores six key issues: dimensions of student ratings; their reliability, stability, and generalizability; their validity; potential biases in student ratings; the Dr Fox effect; and the utility of student ratings. He concludes that student ratings are multidimensional, that their reliability is comparable to that of the best objective tests, that they are stable over time, that ratings of the same instructor are generalizable across different courses, that they correlate significantly with student achievement and instructor self-evaluations, and that they are relatively free of bias. Marsh's conclusion concerning the Dr Fox hypothesis that students are more influenced by instructor expressiveness than by content coverage, is that such a hypothesis ignores the multidimensional nature of student ratings.

When considering the utility of student ratings, Marsh refers to evidence that instructors given feedback on student evaluations halfway through a course tend to receive higher ratings at the end of the course than their colleagues who received no feedback. While there is evidence of increasing use of student evaluations in relation to tenure and promotion decisions there is apparently little evidence that the latter are enhanced by them. Finally, there is a small amount of evidence suggesting that students find reports on their peers' ratings of instruction helpful in choosing courses.

Evolution of Research on Teaching

D. M. Medley

It would be impossible within the scope of this article to provide a detailed treatment of the history of research into the nature of the teaching process, and no attempt will be made to do so. An effort will be made, instead, to provide an overview for the reader not particularly familiar with the subject. An understanding of the present state of the art of research in teaching depends on awareness of the principal issues which have arisen in its progress to its present state, and of the likely direction of further developments. This is what the article will seek to provide.

In scope the article will be limited to studies which have applied quantitative methods of analysis to the behaviors of practicing teachers in an effort to advance knowledge about the nature of effective teaching.

1. The Variables of Research on Teaching

Such research reduces to the assessment of relevant variables and analysis of relationships among them. The principal variables with which research in teaching is concerned may be classified into 10 major categories, six of which are "online" variables, ones which lie along a direct line of influence of the teacher on pupil learning; and four of which are "offline" variables, ones which affect pupil learning but are not under the direct control of the teacher.

The six online categories are as follows:

Type A—Learning outcomes are changes in pupils measured after the teaching is over. The production of learning outcomes is generally agreed to represent the ultimate purpose of teaching and the final criterion on which any assessment of teaching must be based. "Good" teaching generally means teaching which produces maximum pupil learning outcomes, that is, maximum progress toward the goals of education.

Type B—Pupil learning activities occur in the classroom. The principal means by which teaching can affect learning outcomes is through its influence on pupil behaviors in the classroom. The function of teaching is to provide pupils with experiences that will result in desired outcomes. It is axiomatic that all learning depends on the activity of the learner.

Type C—Interactive teacher behaviors are the behaviors usually referred to when someone speaks of teaching—the behaviors of the teacher while in the presence of the pupils. Interactive teaching is the process of teaching, the means by which a teacher affects pupil learning activities and, through them, learning outcomes. It is the point of contact between the child and the entire educational enterprise.

Type D—Preactive teacher behaviors include such activities as planning, evaluation, and other out-of-class activities of teaching, the things a teacher does to promote pupil learning while no pupils are present. They are the principal means by which the teacher exercises control of teaching, the main means by which a teacher's professional knowledge affects the process of teaching, and therefore, how well the teacher performs the central function of teaching and how successfully the teacher accomplishes the purpose of teaching.

Type E—Teacher competencies are the knowledges, skills, and values which a teacher possesses: they are the tools of teaching. Only the teacher who possesses all the skills, knowledge, and values needed to function effectively in a teaching situation is competent to teach in that situation.

Type F—Pre-existing teacher characteristics include those abilities, knowledges, and attitudes that a candidate for admission to teacher preparation possesses on entry; they make up a candidate's aptitude for teaching. Part of it consists of the characteristics a teacher needs in order to acquire those competencies that training and experience can provide; part of it consists of those competencies that a teacher must possess on entry.

These are the six types of online variables. In addition, research in teaching must also be concerned with variables that are offline, variables which affect the relationships among online variables even though they are not under the teacher's control and are not viewed as any part of teaching itself.

Type G—Individual pupil characteristics are abilities and other personal qualities of a pupil which finally determine the outcomes of any specific learning experience that pupil has. Even if two pupils have identical learning experiences, they do not show identical outcomes because of differences in these characteristics. Type G variables attenuate relationships between A and B variables.

Type H—Internal context variables are characteristics of pupils and groups of pupils which affect their responses to teacher behavior. The fact that pupils whose teachers behave identically would not have identical learning experiences reflects the influence of differences in internal context variables. Type H variables attenuate relationships between B and C variables.

Type I—External context variables reflect the support system in which the teacher practices: the materials, the facilities, the supervision and administrative support provided by the school, community support, and so on. Teachers with equal, even identical, sets of competencies will behave differently in similar classes if the support systems differ. Type I variables attenuate relationships between D and E variables.

Type J—Teacher training variables are experiences designed to increase the teacher's repertoire of competencies. Two candidates with identical preexisting characteristics may differ in the competencies they bring to the job situation because of differences in the amount and type of training they have had. Type J variables are of intrinsic interest for the impact they have on Type E variables.

Ten types of variables have been identified; within each type there are many individual variables, of course; they are grouped into these 10 types because relationships between variables of different types are of greater interest than relationships between variables of the same type (as a rule). Research in teaching usually involves the measurement of two or more variables of different types and the study of the relationships between them. Only those studies in which one or both of the variables studied lies on the line between pre-existing teacher characteristics and pupil learning outcomes can be described as research on teaching.

2. Some Methodological Issues

Research on teaching is research based on the assumption that the quality of teaching that goes on in today's schools varies widely; and the overall strategy of the research is to try to find out why—to find differences in other teacher characteristics that account for this variation. Implementation of this strategy requires first of all a conception of what good teaching is; next it requires a valid instrument or device which will distinguish good and poor teaching as conceptualized, and instrumentation for measuring the "explaining" variables validly and reliably is also essential. Third, there must be a design or plan for collecting accurate and valid data about these variables; and finally, an analytic procedure is needed for extracting from the data all of the information about the relationships that they contain.

These four elements—conceptualization, instrumentation, design, and statistical analysis—give rise to four continuing methodological issues which each investigator confronts and must resolve in planning and executing a study. The evolution of research on teaching has been made possible by advances made in the ways in which each of them has been dealt with.

The conceptualization of a study has to do with the identification and definition of the variables chosen for study. One example is "good teaching," a concept which runs through all of the research on teaching. Each study must implicitly or explicitly define "good" teaching or the "good" teacher. Even when the value connotations of the word "good" are set aside, the meaning attached to the term in any one study is often unclear. How does the investigator identify good teaching, or distinguish it from mediocre or poor teaching? To which category does the variable of teaching quality, as defined in the study, belong? Is the best teacher the one whose pupils learn the most (Type A)? The teacher whose pupils have the best learning experiences in school (Type B)? The teacher whose classroom behavior conforms most closely to some conception of "best" practice (Type C)? The one who diagnoses pupil difficulties and prescribes remedies for them most accurately (Type D)? The teacher who has the largest repertoire of professional knowledges and skills (Type E)? Or the teacher who has a set of personal characteristics closest to those of the ideal teacher (Type F)? All of these definitions—and others as well—have had their advocates in the past. It will be assumed in this review that good teaching is a Type A variable by its very nature and that the validity of a definition in any lesser category must be measured against a criterion based on pupil learning outcomes (Type A).

The nature of a study of teaching, the interpretation of its findings, and the criteria for evaluating the study: all of these depend very much on what the investigator's concept of good teaching is. This aspect of the study—how it defines good teaching—is what is meant by its conceptual base.

The instrumentation used in a study is often the best and only clue to the nature of the variables studied, including but not restricted to the variable called "good teaching." The earliest studies of teaching were done before the first instruments designed to measure any of the six categories of variables were developed; these studies, of course, did not use any formal measuring instruments. As will become apparent, one important component in the evolution of research in teaching from that day to this has been a steady refinement and improvement of the instrumentation used.

Design considerations refer to the decisions about the procedures used in collecting data that must be made before the data are collected. The principles of research design—and especially those of experimental design—can, if properly exploited, greatly increase the validity, the sensitivity, and the efficiency of an investigation without increasing its size or cost. Many researchers who have studied teaching in the past seem to have been unaware of these matters, and have collected their data in designs that reflect no consideration of the use to be made of them. Progress in the design of research on teaching has been slow and uncertain.

Statistical analysis refers to the means used to extract information from the data of a study once they have been collected. When research on teaching began, available statistical methodology was primitive indeed. The elaborate and powerful analytical techniques that are commonplace today were little used in those days, partly because they were unknown to the researchers, and partly because the clerical labor involved in their use made them impractical. As computer technology has grown, neither is a factor any longer; the popular computer packages have made even the most elaborate techniques accessible to the most naive researchers.

3. The Beginnings: The Consensual Approach

As might be expected, the earliest studies of teaching dealt with the four methodological issues in only the most primitive fashion (Medley 1972). These first studies conceived of the quality of teaching as determined by personal characteristics of teachers as individuals; they defined good teaching in terms of variables of Types C, E, and F, depending heavily upon an assumption which is still widely held; indeed, one which seems to qualify as one of the universal beliefs of humankind. This is the belief that anyone can recognize good teaching when it occurs. To test this assumption it is necessary only to ask any adult (or almost any child) to think of the best teacher he or she knows. The reply will be prompt and confident. And the reply to the follow-up question, "Why was this teacher the best?" is equally quick and confident. The same result is obtained whether the expert educator is asked or whether the least educated layperson is approached. All of them seem to know what good teaching is, and what makes it good.

It is not surprising, then, that the first study of teaching was one in which a large number of school children were asked to do just this: to think of the best teacher they knew and then to write a paragraph describing what made that teacher so good (see *Student Evaluations of Teaching*). The idea was so obvious that the only question is why no-one had done such a study before. Certainly it was logical. No need to specify what good teaching is since everyone knew already. Certainly the pupils had ample opportunity to observe the teachers to be able to describe—in simple language, of course—the visible personal characteristics which are the mark of a good teacher. No need for instrumentation to identify good teachers for the same reason. The design of the investigations was perfectly straightforward: the only procedure then known for ensuring the validity of data was to use a large sample, and this was done. The statistical procedure used was to compile frequencies of mention of various characteristics of good teachers, to calculate percents, and to look for large percents as evidence of a consensus as to which traits characterize good teachers.

Primitive though this design may be, it has proven particularly robust. For a number of years it was the preferred method and many large-scale studies in the same design were done in the next few decades, studies which laid the basis for a concept of the effective teacher that is still held by many professional educators. It reached its apotheosis in the Commonwealth Teacher Training Study (Charters and Waples 1929), a very large and important study which modified the original design only slightly. This time the people who described the effective teacher were experts, professional educators who had studied the research on teaching done up to that time.

In recent years this ancient design has been reincarnated and used in what is called "consensual validation" of competency lists. During the brief vogue of competency-based teacher education (see *Competency-based Teacher Education*), the compilation of a list of competencies (Type E variables) to be used as a specification of the objectives of teacher education program was an important step in program development. The question whether a list of competencies was valid, whether it constituted an accurate list of the competencies necessary to effective teaching (Type A variables) was answered by asking experts for their opinions of the validity (in this sense) of each competency. The same approach has also been used to "validate" the competencies candidates for certification must demonstrate in order to be certified in what is called "competency-based teacher certification."

This method of validation is particularly satisfying to the researcher, because the competencies or other characteristics that the researcher believes to be related to teacher effectiveness are the ones that turn out to be "valid" almost every time.

4. The Age of the Teacher Rating Scale

The first major innovation in research on teaching had to do with instrumentation; it was the introduction of the teacher rating scale. Although this popular device seems to have been in use for some years already, it apparently became widely known mainly through the publication of the *Fourteenth Yearbook of the National Society for the Study of Education* (Boyce 1915). The rating scale was used in this study, and in many others as well, in two ways. It was used to obtain information about how effective a teacher was, sometimes as a Type A variable, sometimes as a Type C variable. It was also used to obtain information about why the teacher was effective (Type E and F variables).

The study introduced a 45-item rating scale with items divided into five categories. Twelve items dealt with "personal equipment" (Type F variables). Twelve dealt with "social and professional equipment" or teacher competencies (Type E variables). Four were "school management" and 10 were "techniques of teaching" items (Type C and D variables for the most part). And five items dealt with "outcomes" (Types A and B). Thus the rater was asked to judge variables along the entire line of influence from learning outcomes to pre-existing teacher characteristics. The existence and importance of all six types was recognized by that time; but there was little awareness of how difficult it was to measure some of them.

The main function that the rating scale could serve would be to assist judges of teacher characteristics (including how good they were) in quantifying their observations and impressions and, as a result, to increase the accuracy of their judgements. It was a genuine forward step; and it was widely adopted not only as a research tool but as an instrument for evaluating teachers. To this day it is by far the most widely used device for this latter purpose.

The study reported in the yearbook used a design often repeated since. Ratings on the last item, which asked for the rater's overall judgement of how good the teacher was, were used as the criterion or dependent variable with which all of the other items were correlated to find out which of the characteristics rated discriminated good teachers from poor ones.

This study also introduced the correlation coefficient as a technique for the statistical analysis of this kind of data. Correlational analysis became just as popular as a statistical technique as the rating scale was as an instrument. A great many studies have appeared in following years which, like this one, intercorrelated ratings of individual characteristics of teachers with overall ratings of teaching quality made by the same raters.

Neither the studies described in the preceding section nor those using rating scales made any lasting contribution to scientific knowledge of the nature of effective teaching, however. Nowhere in the cycle were actual measures of pupil learning outcomes (bona fide Type A variables) included; no evidence was produced that teachers rated high overall were really any more effective than teachers rated low. At best these studies could only clarify the components of expert judgments, that is, indicate which teacher characteristics seemed to earn high overall ratings, seemed to impress raters most favourably. The contamination of both variables which results from having them rated at the same time on the same instrument by the same rater makes it difficult to draw valid conclusions even about this matter. Although overall ratings purported to measure teacher effectiveness (Type A) they seem to reflect interactive teacher behaviors (Type C) at best; or, at worst, preexisting teacher characteristics (Type F).

There were some half-dozen studies published in those days which attempted to establish the validity of overall ratings by correlating them with actual measurements of outcomes (Type A). They were unanimous in concluding that the two were uncorrelated—that is, that pupils learn as much on average from teachers with low overall ratings as they do from teachers with high overall ratings (Gage 1963 pp. 257–58). Such evidence as exists consistently indicates that overall ratings of teacher quality are invalid when teacher quality is defined in terms of learning outcomes.

The melancholy fact is that neither of these two approaches to research on teaching thus far described produced any valid information about differences between effective and ineffective teaching because no measures of teacher effectiveness were used in any of them. Because practically all research on teaching published in the first half of this century used one or the other of these two designs, no scientific basis for the practice of teaching existed at midcentury. The only basis for the practice of teaching was the lore of the profession, which was based almost entirely on the personal experiences of teachers.

5. Process–Product Research

One other obstacle to progress in research on teaching which characterized research in those days was conceptual, the persistent belief that the key to the understanding of effective teaching lay in the study of characteristics of teachers as individuals (Type E and F variables). As a result, many attempts were made to explain the differences in the quality of teaching in different classrooms in terms of personality and interest tests, tests of intelligence or more specialized aptitudes, grades in teacher education courses, and so on (Barr 1948).

Some time in the 1950s interest in the study of the teaching process itself, of the behavior of teachers and pupils in the classroom while the teaching was going on (Type B and C) began to grow. This point of view was clearly enunciated in a paradigm advanced by Mitzel (Gage 1963 pp. 118–21). In essence, Mitzel distinguished four classes of variables which have come to be referred to as presage, process, product, and context variables. Presage variables include pre-existing teacher characteristics (F), teacher competencies (E), and training variables (J); process variables include interactive teacher behaviors (C) and pupil behaviors (B); product variables correspond to learning outcomes (A); and context variables include variables of Types G, H, and I.

The important conceptual advance was the proposal that instead of intercorrelating presage and product variables, it would be more productive to intercorrelate presage and process variables and also to intercorrelate process and product variables. The presage–product correlations research had sought up to that time were almost certain to be small because intervening variations in classroom processes act as errors of estimation and attenuate them. This phenomenon might well account for the fact that such correlations are invariably small. And it seemed much more reasonable to expect substantial correlations between presage variables (such as teacher skills and attitudes) and process variables (such as teacher behavior) and between teacher behaviors in the classroom and product variables (that is, pupil learning gains) because in each case the two types of variables are closer to each other than presage and product variables are.

At about this same time there began a general move to abandon the use of teacher ratings in research either as criteria of teaching quality or as measures of classroom process. Two timely publications pointed toward alternatives to each. The evolution of criteria based on pupils' learning gains up to that point was sketched by Mitzel and Gross (1958); it pointed to a better way of measuring product variables. A chapter reviewing the development of systematic observation systems in the *Handbook of Research on Teaching* (Gage 1963 pp. 247–328) provided a viable alternative to ratings for measuring process variables.

Two other developments greatly facilitated the emergence of process–product research. One was the rapidly increasing availability of digital computers which removed all practical barriers to the use of complex and powerful analytical procedures; and the other was a dramatic increase in financial support for educational research due to new legislation on the part of the government of the United States. Process–product research is relatively expensive to do; and it yields masses of data too great to be analyzable without the use of a computer.

Research on teaching was revolutionized by simultaneous major advances on four fronts: in the conceptualization of the research, in its instrumentation, in the designs used, and in the available analytical tools. The time was ripe for the first advance in the scientific basis for the practice of teaching to occur, and studies in the process–product model began to appear almost everywhere, it seemed.

5. The Knowledge Base of the Practice of Teaching

The first attempt to synthesize and assess the substantive findings of these new process–product studies was so prompt as to be almost premature. In 1971, when Rosenshine's first review appeared, the scientific study of teaching was still in its infancy. Rosenshine's 142-item bibliography contains references to fewer than half that many actual studies; and not all of these were of a quality sufficient to justify any confidence in their findings. This does not, of course, in any way lessen the value of the review; nor has it prevented it from having an important and, on balance, beneficial impact on the profession. For the first time it demonstrated that research on teaching can and does have something important and useful to say to the practitioner.

Three years later, another precedent was set with the appearance of a textbook for teacher-education students that was clearly and explicitly based on research on teaching (Dunkin and Biddle 1974). The 356-item bibliography appended to this book listed more than twice as many original studies as Rosenshine's. On this basis it would appear that at least as many studies appeared in the three years between the two publications as had appeared in all of the years preceding that period. Unlike the earlier volume, this one summarized not only the process–product studies but also the presage-process, context–process, and process–process studies.

A third volume appeared two years later which was designed to communicate the findings of process–product research directly to the practitioner (Brophy and Evertson 1976). Unlike the other two, this volume was primarily based on research conducted by its authors, and cites other research only for corroboration. As might be expected, the presentation is quite different—more synthetic than Dunkin and Biddle and less analytical than Rosenshine—and the picture of the effective teacher presented is more coherent and better integrated, if less firmly based.

In recent years there have been a small number of large-scale, heavily funded projects which have increased both the knowledge base and the dependability of the evidence that supports it. One of them was a large-scale study of Follow Through Programs throughout the United States; it emphasized "planned variation" by seeking out and concentrating on sites committed to a wide variety of different models for effective instruction. Another was a study of beginning teachers (see *Induction of Beginning Teachers*) in the state of California. A third was a large-scale experiment in the teaching of beginning reading which, unlike most experiments, incorporated measures of classroom processes in its design. A fourth was the Texas teacher effectiveness study upon which Brophy and Evertson's book was based. These studies generated a large number of process–product correlations which have been reviewed and synthesized in a number of recent reviews. One such was done by Rosenshine (Peterson and Walberg 1979 pp. 28–56); another by Medley (1972 pp. 430–39).

The last-named review was the only one to apply strict quality criteria to the research studies and to interpret only what were called the "dependable" findings. The criteria of quality used had to do with the conceptualization of teaching quality in the study, the instrumentation and the design used, and the significance of the findings. One criterion was that the measure of learning outcomes used be based on long-term progress of pupils toward recognized goals of education; another was that the process measures used had to be both objective and descriptive; a third criterion required that the design incorporate an error estimate that would justify generalization of findings to a population of teachers larger than the sample used in the study; and the fourth required that the results obtained should be practically as well as statistically significant. The basic bibliography contained 289 empirical studies. Fourteen met all four quality criteria. This suggests one of the reasons why research has had so little impact on practice in the past: its findings have been either contradictory or insignificant in so many instances that the practitioners have despaired of making sense of them and have based practice, instead, on personal experiences.

What were the findings of this research? The reader should consult the reviews themselves for a full understanding, and will find some differences in detail in the several interpretations, but essential agreement on the main conclusions.

Medley's reading will be summarized here, because it was based on a relatively small number of studies and limited to replicated findings. It should be noted that most of the reliable findings (of all reviews) were obtained in classes of pupils who were in their first three years of school, most of whom came from homes classified as low in socioeconomic status. The findings may be classified under three major headings: classroom environment, use of pupil time, and conduct of class discussions.

With respect to the classroom environment, the research indicates that effective teachers' classrooms are orderly places, and that this order is maintained by the teacher with little visible effort, with positive motivation, and with a minimum amount of negative affect.

Pupil time is tightly structured in effective teachers' classrooms; more than the average amount of time is devoted to academic matters with the pupils organized in one large group led by the teacher. Pupils spend less time working in small groups or on individual tasks than in the average class.

Class discussions are also closely controlled by effective teachers. The teacher asks more "low-level" questions and fewer "high-level" questions than the average. Pupils ask relatively few questions, and when they answer teacher questions they are less likely to get feedback and the effective teacher is less likely to discuss or amplify their answers than the average teacher is. When the pupils work independently they are more closely supervised.

On the whole, this image of the effective teacher differs in important respects from the image projected by many teacher educators. Where is the individualization, the democracy, the higher order questions, the use of pupil answers that so many preservice teachers are trained to demonstrate?

Rosenshine has developed a teaching model from this research which he calls direct instruction (Peterson and Walberg 1979 pp. 28–56). The model has five characteristics: (a) a strong academic focus, (b) strong direction by the teacher, (c) large groups with the teacher, (d) frequent factual lessons, and (e) few high-order questions (see *Direct Instruction*).

Fisher and others have concluded from their work in the concluding phases of the Beginning Teacher Evaluation Study (Fisher et al. 1980) that a Type B variable they call ALT (Academic Learning Time) is the key factor in determining teacher effectiveness, that how much a pupil learns is closely related to how much ALT he gets in school. ALT is time during which the student is engaged in learning tasks of appropriate difficulty (defined in terms of success rate). Presumably the teacher behaviors identified by Medley and Rosenshine are effective because they maximize ALT in the classrooms where they are most frequent (see *Time*).

In addition to being inconsistent in many respects

with the conventional wisdom of the profession about the nature of effective teaching, the results so briefly summarized here will seem to many inadequate to account fully for the range of quality of teaching that exists in the schools today, much less to define a level of quality which could be set up as an ideal which teachers might seek to approach. There must be a better way than that, one says. If this is all there is, who would want to be a teacher?

7. Future Evolution of Research on Teaching

The future evolution of research on teaching will be discussed in terms of the same four areas of concern that were used in reviewing the past: conceptualization of the problem, instrumentation, design, and analysis.

7.1 Conceptualization of the Problem

Future evolution will be most rapid if certain oversimplifications in the process–product model are abandoned and all six online variables are clearly recognized and incorporated into research designs. The gains made by process–product research just presented were in part due to a belated recognition of the fact that process variables intervene to attenuate correlations between presage and product variables. The principle that applies may be stated as follows: only variables adjacent to one another along the line of influence should be intercorrelated. Future research must develop the relationships along the line of influence from pre-existing teacher characteristics (F) to learning outcomes (A) a step at a time. Five types of research are needed.

(a) Type BA research relates learning outcomes to pupil learning experiences. It has been identified as research in classroom learning. Knowledge of these relationships is essential to preactive teaching for planning the learning experience pupils should have in order to maximize learning outcomes.

(b) Type CB research relates interactive teacher behavior to pupil learning activities. It is properly called research in classroom teaching. Research designed to test the various "models of teaching" receiving so much attention today (Joyce et al. 1981), for example, will be more productive if it addresses the question whether the implementation of a model succeeds in providing pupils with the learning experiences they need than if it attempts to relate model implementation to learning outcomes directly.

(c) Type DC research relates preactive teacher behavior to interactive teacher behavior. It falls under the heading of research in teacher decision making. How teachers relate the problems they encounter in the practice of teaching to professional knowledge in deploying the resources available to them (including their own abilities) is clearly a major determinant of the quality of their teaching (Peterson and Walberg 1979 pp. 136–60, 231–63, Joyce et al. 1981 pp. 227–299).

d) Type ED research deals with the problem of deciding which competencies a teacher needs, a problem that has concerned teacher educators for many years. This is the kind of research that may be called research in teacher competence. Such research is important.

e) Type FE research is the proper research to provide support for selective admission to teacher preparation, and may be called research in teacher selection. What characteristics of entering students identify teachers who will acquire the competencies they need as a result of training?

Research designed to correlate nonadjacent points is not worth doing. The complex factors which determine which individuals become effective teachers can be understood only if they are studied one by one. The chances of detecting a significant correlation between, say, some characteristic of a teacher measured before the teacher enters into professional training and how much pupils will learn in that teacher's class a few years later are so small that it is hard to believe anyone would ever try to do so; but not a few researchers have (Barr 1948). The fact that process–product studies, which correlate C and A variables and so violate this rule, have produced meaningful results is a fluke which should not mislead future researchers. And more attention needs to be paid to contextual variables (Types G, H, and I) and to training variables (Type J) which distort the relationships which are the focus of research on teaching.

7.2 Instrumentation

Better procedures must be developed for measuring all of these variables, particularly those near the center (Types B, C, D, and E). The problem is most severe in regard to pupil behaviors (Type B) and preactive teaching (Type D), which are coming under close scrutiny for the first time. Means currently used to measure these variables are much too subjective; but as the variables become better understood it is to be expected that more objective techniques will be developed and used.

There is no reason to doubt that the dramatic increases in the objectivity and validity of measures of interactive teacher behavior (Type C) that have taken place since the late 1960s will continue at very nearly the same rate for some time to come. As the distinctions between all six types of variables become better understood, similar advances should occur all along the line.

The spectacular growth of knowledge of the physical universe that has come about during the last few centuries was made possible by advances in instrumentation. Research on teaching awaits inventions like the telescope and microscope; perhaps one is close at hand.

Maybe such a breakthrough will never come; if not, then the future evolution of research on teaching will advance slowly; but advance it will.

There is little doubt that the rapid advances in computer technology that have characterized the brief history of this device will continue for some time to come; and these developments have important implications for research on teaching. The increasing availability of such devices has removed the practical limits which the massive amounts of data such studies yield once imposed on this kind of research. A typical study of 30 teachers yields multiple measures on 1,000 pupils which may contain as many as 1,000,000 or more items of information, in addition to voluminous data about the behavior of the teachers. But these devices have other exciting uses.

Already available is a computer no larger than a pocket calculator which can be carried into the classroom by an observer who can then key in a running record of a classroom interaction. The full sequence of events during a class period can be stored in the computer memory. The record can be stored by the computer and/or stored on cassette tape for later retrieval and analysis. A small printer is also available which can print hard copies of the record and the scores, if desired.

A conventional microprocessor has been programmed to simulate the behavior of a class of pupils, all of whom behave like different individuals. A teacher in training can interact orally with such a class, and particularly objective and accurate measurements can be made of certain interactive competencies under carefully controlled conditions, conditions which can be duplicated exactly to obtain comparable measurements of as many teachers as desired.

These are only examples of what might be expected in the future in the way of advances in instrumentation for research on teaching.

7.3 Design

During most of past history of research on teaching, research training was largely concerned with developing the basic analytical skills which the researcher needed, and relatively slight attention was paid to the topic of research design—that is, to a study of methods a researcher can use to increase the precision, the validity, and the sensitivity of a study without increasing its size. Advances in computer packages have made most of the skill training obsolete; at the same time, it has made training in research design more important. Training has not yet caught up with these advances, but it will in the future; and when it does it may be expected that the designs used in research on teaching will improve. Such improvements may be expected greatly to increase the productivity of the research.

Too many investigators have assumed in the past that, because it is now possible to analyze any data set however incomplete and imperfect, design considerations do not matter. This has been accompanied by a tendency to regress to the belief common in the beginning of the century that defects in the quality can be corrected by increasing the amount of data collected. Nothing could be farther from the truth. A well-designed study, one in which replication, randomization, and local control are wisely applied, will yield far more information (even when the sample is small), than a much larger study in which data are haphazardly obtained; more important, the information will be more valid and interpretable. Unless future research uses better designs than have been typical this far, the future evolution will continue to be slowed down by conflicting findings, false conclusions, and inefficient use of resources. But as better designs come into use, these problems will be minimized and progress will be steady and inevitable.

7.4 Analysis

Trying to predict future advances in statistical methodology is like trying to predict the spin of a roulette wheel a week in advance. But there are some advances in the application of available techniques which may be anticipated. One example has to do with the level at which data are aggregated for analysis. The relevance of this issue to research on teaching was pointed out many years ago (Gage 1963 pp. 321–26). When variables measured at the classroom level are intercorrelated in a sample of teachers drawn from different schools, the coefficients of correlation may be estimated either from variation within schools, from variations between schools (aggregated at the school level), or from total variation, mixing the two levels indiscriminately. Estimates of correlations between the same two variables are often very different when calculated between schools than when calculated within schools; as a result, a coefficient estimated from a mixture of both is meaningless and (not surprisingly) usually nonsignificant. And yet virtually every process–product correlation reported in the literature (before or since) has been estimated from data mixed in this way. Modern statistical packages make it particularly simple to avoid this egregious error; future research will certainly avoid it. The importance of facet analysis in establishing the reliability of Type C variables in particular (or their generalizability, as it has come to be called) was pointed out in the same source; it is also coming into general use, which augurs well for the future.

The problem of deriving an unbiased measure of teacher effectiveness from pre- and posttest data on pupils, one which yields an estimate of the teacher's contribution to pupil learning that is independent of those pre-existing differences between classes that can be measured is another whose solution is at hand. Raw gains, residual gains, and adjusted mean gains all tend to favor teachers whose classes are easier to teach. (Mitzel and Gross 1958). The posttest score that a pupil with a specified pretest score (such as the "average" pupil in a grade or subject) would get in any class can be predicted on the basis of the regression of postscores on prescores within that class. In this way it might be

estimated that a child whose pretest score was, say, 5 (the mean for the grade), would gain 5 points in class A, 8 in class B, and 12 in class C.

To isolate the contribution of the teaching to them these estimated gains should in turn be regressed on class pretest means and residual gains calculated around this between-class regression line. If the three residual were 6, 4, and 3, for example, it would be estimated that if the average pupil were assigned to the average class, that pupil would gain 6 points if teacher A taught the class, 4 if teacher B taught it, and 3 if teacher C taught it. These numbers are measures of teacher effectiveness which are unaffected by class ability and are based on comparable pupils.

A final development that an optimist might expect to see in future research on teaching is more study of the structure of teacher behavior along the lines of the work described by Soar and Soar in the area of classroom climate and control (Peterson and Walberg 1979 pp. 97–119).

8. Concluding Remarks

An instructive parallel can be drawn between the evolution of research on teaching (designed to lay a scientific base for the practice of teaching) and the evolution of medical research (designed to lay a scientific base for the practice of medicine) as reported by Lewis Thomas, a leading medical researcher, in *Science*.

At the beginning of the twentieth century the practice of medicine had no scientific basis. Physicians had at their disposal a vast collection of methods for curing every known disease, almost entirely based on personal experiences of practitioners (which they liked to call clinical research). Virtually all of these methods were worthless; what kept the practice going, and what created the illusion that these treatments were effective, was the tendency of many patients to recover spontaneously, regardless of treatment.

Medical research established these facts and they were reluctantly accepted by the profession; for a number of years there was a period of "therapeutic nihilism" in which the curricula of the better medical schools emphasized prognosis rather than treatment. This ended with the discovery of potent new treatments and drugs such as penicillin: and now physicians are again being trained to cure diseases.

The current state of the scientific base for the practice of teaching resembles that of medicine at the beginning of the century: it does not exist. Current practice of teaching is based on personal experiences rather than rigorous research. A large proportion of school children learn spontaneously, regardless of how they are taught, but the teacher attributes these outcomes to the method of instruction used.

Research on teaching has begun to yield results which suggest that much of the lore of the profession may be as worthless as those leeches, purges, and other procedures that made up the lore of nineteenth-century medicine. Does the teaching profession face a period of instructional nihilism to be endured while research on teaching struggles to lay a scientific basis for future practice?

Someone has said that the function of research is to separate the part of common knowledge that is true from the part that is false. For the first time in its history, research on teaching shows some promise of beginning to perform this function and to transform the practice of teaching in the way that the practice of medicine has been and continues to be transformed by medical research.

See also: Criteria for Evaluating Teaching; Competency-based Teacher Education; Direct Instruction; Paradigms for Research; Teaching: Art or Science?; Synthesizing Research Evidence; Effects of Teaching

Bibliography

Barr A S 1948 The measurement and prediction of teaching efficiency: A summary of investigations. *J. Exp. Educ.* 16: 203–83
Boyce A C 1915 *Methods for Measuring Teachers' Efficiency. 14th Yearbook of the National Society for the Study of Education,* Pt. 2. Public School Publishing, Bloomington, Illinois
Brophy J E, Evertson C M 1976 *Learning from Teaching: A Developmental Perspective.* Allyn and Bacon, Boston, Massachusetts
Charters W W, Waples D 1929 *The Commonwealth Teacher Training Study.* University of Chicago Press, Chicago, Illinois
Dunkin M J, Biddle B J 1974 *The Study of Teaching.* Holt, Rinehart and Winston, New York
Fisher C W et al. 1980 Teaching behaviors, academic learning time, and student achievement. In: Denham E, Lieberman L (eds.) 1980 *Time to Learn.* National Institute of Education, Washington, DC, pp. 7–32
Gage N L (ed.) 1963 *Handbook of Research on Teaching: A Project of the American Educational Research Association.* Rand McNally, Chicago, Illinois
Joyce B R, Brown C C, Peck L (eds.) 1981 *Flexibility in Teaching: An Excursion into the Nature of Teaching and Training.* Longman, New York
Medley D M 1972 Early history of research on teacher behavior. *Int. Rev. of Educ.* 18: 430–39
Mitzel H E, Gross C F 1958 The Development of pupil-growth criteria in studies of teacher effectiveness. *Educ. Res. Bull.* 37: 178–87, 205–15
Peterson P L, Walberg H J (eds.) 1979 *Research on Teaching: Concepts, Findings, and Implications.* McCutchan, Berkeley, California
Rosenshine B 1971 *Teaching Behaviors and Student Achievement.* National Foundation for Educational Research, Slough

Paradigms for Research

W. Doyle

An analysis of paradigms focuses on the subjective aspects of research, on the shared perceptions of adequacy that operate, often informally and tacitly, among investigators interested in a common problem or an approach to a problem (Kuhn 1970, Phillips 1981). Paradigms form around questions, such as what are the characteristics of effective teachers or which instructional methods are most appropriate for particular types of learners? Over time, the core concepts that define a question, the methods for conducting studies, and implicit assumptions about cause–effect relationships are partially standardized and taken for granted by investigators. These loosely defined concepts and rules play an important role in designing studies and interpreting results. They also provide stability for a research program in the face of anomalies which naturally occur in data, and criticisms which arise as part of the dynamics of research funding and publication.

During the 1970s there was a notable self-consciousness about paradigms for research on teaching (Doyle 1977, Gage 1978). Much of the analytical work on paradigms was directed to teaching effectiveness research and in particular to studies which attempt to relate measures of teacher behavior to student attitudes and achievement. This concern for paradigms signaled certain fundamental shifts in concepts and methods for research on teaching, shifts which continue to radiate throughout the field.

This article provides a survey of major features of paradigms for research on teaching and an introduction to some emerging issues and directions for inquiry.

1. Traditional Approaches to Research on Teaching

As an applied area, research on teaching is dominated by the question of effectiveness, and much of the work culminates in a set of prescriptions for improving teaching practice. In turn, the study of teaching is shaped by issues of policy, control, and direct applicability, that is, by the perspective of users of research findings. Because teaching is a pervasive experience in most societies, occurring in a wide range of formal and informal contexts from the family to the university, there is a large and diverse body of common understandings and assumptions about how to teach. Thus, those who conduct research and those who use it have a rich store of implicit beliefs about the nature of teaching and teaching effectiveness. Such beliefs are fully represented in the paradigms which guide systematic inquiry into teaching.

Traditionally there have been three major approaches to answering the effectiveness question: (a) research on teachers' characteristics; (b) methods research; and (c) teacher behavior research.

1.1 Research on Teachers' Characteristics

Research on teachers' characteristics focuses on personal qualities, such as intelligence, experience, personality (see *Teachers' Personality*), attitudes, expectations (see *Teachers' Expectations*), knowledge, or beliefs, as predictors of effectiveness (Getzels and Jackson 1963). To conduct such a study, scores on paper-and-pencil measures of teachers' attributes are correlated with measures of effectiveness such as student achievement or, more commonly, ratings by supervisors or trained observers. The products of such investigations are useful primarily for devising criteria to select teachers who are likely to be successful. For those attributes subject to modification by experience (such as knowledge, attitudes, expectations, and perhaps some aspects of personality), the findings of research on teachers' characteristics are potentially useful for teacher education.

The fundamental assumption of this type of research on teaching is that the qualities of teachers as persons account for their differential effectiveness. With the exception of research on teacher expectations, few attempts have been made to explain precisely how the personal qualities of teachers affect students' learning. The most plausible explanation is motivation: teachers with certain "positive" qualities are presumably able to motivate students better.

1.2 Methods Research

A second approach to answering the effectiveness question focuses on teaching methods, that is, plans or blueprints for conducting teaching episodes (Wallen and Travers 1963). In this domain, the unit of analysis is not the individual teacher's personal qualities but rather a program for selecting content and objectives, arranging space and materials, and interacting with students. Research on methods follows an "experimental" format (although the degree of experimental control is often low) in which two or more methods are compared in terms of their effectiveness in producing student learning or attitudes. Typical comparisons include lecture versus discussion, open versus closed or traditional classrooms (see *Open Versus Formal Methods*), discovery versus expository or prescriptive teaching, phonics versus whole-word methods, and cooperative versus individualistic learning. This comparative approach also characterizes studies of instructional media in which the effects of programmed instruction, television, films, and computer-assisted instruction are compared with each other or with "traditional" teaching. One variation on the comparative model is research on attribute-by-treatment interactions (ATIs) which focuses on interactions between conditions of instruction and attributes of learners rather than on simple main effects. The ATI paradigm provides one means of bringing individual differences among students into research on teaching.

Research on methods is closely allied with curriculum research and is a common form of research on teaching within subject matter areas such as science, mathematics, or history. The findings of methods research are potentially useful to curriculum developers and textbook writers as well as to teachers and teacher educators.

Methods are constructed from a variety of sources, including academic disciplines such as philosophy, psychology, or social psychology (Nuthall and Snook 1973), and commonsense notions about ideally educative experiences. In other words, basic claims to efficacy as well as notions about how or why a method works are extrapolated from inquiry outside the field of research on teaching. Although there is a rich array of constructs used to justify the various approaches, the concepts of structure, motivation, and engagement are useful in differentiating between two broad classes of methods. On the one hand there are methods which emphasize personal freedom and choice (e.g., the open classroom) or self-directed inquiry (e.g., the discovery method). To accomplish this end, the visible structure of the learning environment is generally low or at least not intrusive or constraining. Such methods presumably motivate students to engage in learning by appealing to their natural desires to express themselves and to understand and resolve puzzles. Advocates often claim that these unstructured methods foster higher level cognitive abilities as well as self-insight and social interaction skills. On the other hand there are methods which emphasize directed practice accompanied by substantial prompting and guidance from a teacher or an instructional program (e.g., mastery learning or programmed instruction). Objectives are well-defined and explicitly stated, and the program is carefully structured to lead the student through a graduated sequence of exercises with feedback to correct mistakes early. Motivation to engage in learning is managed by manipulating external rewards, giving knowledge of results, and adapting learning tasks to fit the abilities of individual students. These structured methods are usually associated with teaching basic skills in such areas as reading and mathematics.

1.3 Teacher Behavior Research

For many people, the study of teacher behaviors is synonymous with research on teaching effectiveness. In this tradition, inquiry is focused on aspects of teacher actions during teaching episodes using either (a) low-inference coding systems which record the frequency of specific teacher behaviors, such as types of questions or feedback; or (b) high-inference rating sheets which capture more qualitative features of teaching such as enthusiasm or clarity. Some of this work is primarily descriptive in intent, that is, directed to explicating the underlined structure of teaching events. For the most part, however, the emphasis is on establishing prescriptions for teachers by relating behavior measures to some criterion of effectiveness such as supervisor ratings or gains in student achievement.

The findings of teacher behavior research are considered by most researchers to be applicable to defining the content of teacher education programs (Gage 1978). In some cases, the instruments used to record teacher behaviors have also been used widely to provide feedback to teachers. Such feedback is intended to increase teachers' awareness and help them change their behavior toward presumably more effective practices. The field has also been traditionally tied to teacher evaluation, and some practitioners (but fewer researchers) envision that research findings can be used to define criteria for judging directly the quality of teaching.

Since the 1960s, teacher behavior research has been dominated by a process–product paradigm (Gage 1978, Rosenshine and Furst 1973). According to this paradigm, statements about effective teaching take the form of empirically established connections between teaching behaviors (processes) and gains in student achievement (products). The intent here is to rule out claims to effectiveness based on either the inherent properties of certain behaviors (such as higher order questions) or judgments by supervisors and other "experts." The initial phase of the process–product research program is correlational. Observations are made of naturally occurring teaching behaviors in a sample of classrooms. Variables extracted from these observational records are then correlated with mean gains in achievement for the classes. This correlational phase is designed to sort out those variables which are most likely to be connected to achievement. The second phase of the research program involves experimental studies to test whether the variables identified in the correlational phase are causally related to outcomes.

In contrast to methods research, there is little explicit concern for theoretical models in process–product research. For the most part, coding systems have provided the language for describing teaching within this paradigm, and the categories which are included in coding systems have often reflected the preferences and ingenuity of their creators rather than an integrated conceptual framework (Rosenshine and Furst 1973). The criterion for the "significance" of a given variable is a correlation coefficient rather than a theory. As a result, any variable can be incorporated into an observation scheme and entered into an analysis. Whether a variable is eventually considered important depends upon the magnitude of its correlation with mean class achievement.

In the absence of an integrated conceptual framework, attention in process–product research is centered on single variables. Any aggregation of discrete teaching variables is done by statistical procedures (e.g., factor analysis) or by informal post hoc interpretations of statistically significant correlations. In either case, findings are typically explained by reference to motivation and practice as key mechanisms by which teaching effects are produced.

Issues of aggregation from single-variable correlations with achievement became important as investigators moved toward experimental studies in the 1970s. Early experimenters maintained the single-variable character of the paradigm by attempting to isolate the effects of discrete teaching variables in controlled laboratory experiments. In later field experiments, investigators constructed "models" for teaching by combining results of correlational analyses and adding recommendations from other sources to produce integrated plans for instruction or classroom management (Emmer et al. 1981). These plans were then taught to teachers in the experimental groups, and investigators attempted to determine whether the plans were followed and whether mean scores on achievement for experimental classes were higher than those for control classes. At this level, process–product research is strikingly similar to methods research in format and even substance. For instance, the direct instruction or active teaching model which has emerged from process–product research corresponds in many ways to the structured methods which emphasize explicit objectives and guided practice.

Despite the lack of theoretical self-consciousness among process–product investigators, there are several implicit assumptions which grow out of the methods and the practical orientation of research within this paradigm. A preference for low-inference coding systems, for instance, has directed attention to frequency as a key dimension of teacher behavior. Comparatively less attention has been given to such dimensions as timing or appropriateness, in part because of the difficulties of recording these dimensions at a low-inference level.

Along similar lines, there has often been an emphasis on observing public contacts between teachers and students during whole-class events rather than private contacts during seatwork or other activities. Such an emphasis implies that teaching happens primarily in the public arena of a classroom and that participation in whole-class episodes is synonymous with engagement in learning tasks.

Finally, there has been a traditional focus on the teacher and a presumption of a teacher-to-student direction of causality in process–product research. Less attention has been given to students either as joint participants in constructing social events in classrooms or as active thinkers who selectively attend to and process information from multiple sources. The search for teacher effects has also tended to limit the amount of attention process–product investigators have given to specific aspects of content or instructional materials.

In sum, process–product research has generally focused on teachers and given less explicit attention to instructional resources in classrooms or to processes that intervene between what teachers do and what students learn. As a result, several factors operating to affect student outcomes have slipped through the empirical net of this paradigm.

2. Emerging Questions and Paradigms

During the 1970s, major studies in the process–product tradition were conducted, and the general view of the productivity for such research changed from pessimistic to optimistic. At the same time, some clear shifts occurred within the paradigm. Observations focused more explicitly on student behaviors in classrooms. More attention was also given to content and instructional materials and to classroom management in contrast to the previous emphasis on teacher "motivators" such as praise and encouragement. In addition, some rumbling was heard in the background which threatened to rock the paradigm at deeper levels. All of these developments have given rise to possibilities of new paradigms for research on teaching. A brief review of these possibilities will give some sense to the controversy and vigor in the field.

2.1 The Treatment Mechanism in Teaching

A nagging question in any consideration of teaching is how teacher moves or attempts to influence students get translated into learning outcomes. What, in other words, are the mechanisms by which teaching affects learning? In process–product research these connecting processes are not studied directly. More explicit attention is given to such treatment processes in methods research, but little attempt is made to ascertain whether the hypothesized mechanisms used to design the method actually operate in the prescribed manner in the classrooms. Moreover, there has been a growing sense in recent years that laboratory-based conceptions are less than adequate to account for learning under the complex conditions that exist in classroom environments.

A concern for mechanisms which connect teacher behaviors to outcomes has become apparent in the move within process–product research toward a mediating process paradigm (Doyle 1977). At a conceptual level, investigators have begun to argue that teachers do not cause achievement but rather cause students to engage in behaviors which produce learning. At the level of data gathering, investigators began to record student attention and engagement as well as various indices of opportunity to learn, such as time allocations, content covered, and the pacing of the curriculum. The most comprehensive construct for this set of variables is academic learning time (ALT) which is a measure of the time students spend engaged in working successfully with content covered on the criterion test (see *Time*).

For process–product research, this shift toward students and a mediating process paradigm has certainly broadened the concepts of how classroom conditions affect outcomes. The previous emphasis on teacher-pupil exchanges has now been augmented by information about content and about the way teachers manage classroom events (such as whole class presentations and seatwork) in order to elicit and sustain engagement.

Interest in students and mediating processes has also stimulated some broader scale investigations into students in classrooms. Within process–product research, the central student variable is engagement, which is typically viewed as either an intervening variable or a short-term effect of teaching practices. Some investigators are attempting, however, to look beneath this global indicator to disentangle the processes that operate when students learn in classrooms. The focus, in other words, is on what students do when they engage in academic tasks. At the present time, this work is following the lines of research on students' perceptions and cognitive processes.

2.2 The Nature of Classrooms

In conventional process–product research, few questions were asked about how the conditions recorded on coding sheets were established in the first place or how they might fluctuate over the course of a term or a year. An impression was sometimes given that creating conditions of effective teaching is a relatively simple process of doing what has been shown to be best and that "ineffective" teaching occurs because some teachers are poorly trained or not motivated to try harder. Descriptive studies, in contrast, portrayed classrooms as complex settings in which teachers are required to face a large number of contingencies and adjust activities to meet immediate demands and changing circumstances. This picture of daily life in classrooms has given rise to a number of questions about how students affect teachers, how teachers manage classroom groups and implement complicated teaching strategies, how teachers make decisions, and how students navigate the demands of classroom settings (Shavelson and Stern 1981).

Interest in these questions of management and decision making has created a push toward more descriptive studies which attempt to model the event structure and the processes of classrooms. Even if one is using stimulated recall, think aloud, or other interview approaches to the study of thinking, it is helpful to know what teachers and students are required to think about in classroom environments. Traditional approaches in research on teaching, oriented primarily toward improvement, have not been as especially useful in describing existing classroom structures and processes. Models used to design teaching methods provide a blueprint for how teachers should behave but do not model how teachers actually perform in classrooms or what tasks they are required to accomplish. Classroom descriptions based on process–product studies are also limited by the presuppositions built into observation instruments and by their static quality. The isolation of single variables from the flow of events and the aggregation of codes across several observations are practices which tend to freeze the action of classrooms. In the end, such analyses produce a list of characteristics of processes rather than a direct description of the processes themselves. Finally, ratings fail to provide adequate descriptions because a record of actual behavior upon which a rating was made is not preserved. To interpret ratings it is necessary to imagine what processes occurred to elicit a particular judgment from an observer.

Attempts to capture classroom processes has led to a shift in observational method from a traditional measurement emphasis on scores that can be used in statistical analyses to qualitative analyses of long-term narrative records similar to those used for participant observation and ethnographic studies. A shift from scores to narratives is fundamental in research on teaching. Narrative records do not lend themselves directly to correlational analyses and thus are not particularly useful in answering effectiveness questions formulated in process–product terms. Reducing narratives to scores by counting or rating methods seems, from a process–product perspective, especially cumbersome because such scores can be obtained directly during observations. In turn, from a participant observation or ethnographic viewpoint, simply transforming narratives into scores for predetermined categories wastes a large amount of information about processes that a qualitative analysis of these records might produce. It is at such junctures that paradigm shifts become especially apparent. A change in method often changes the questions that can be answered.

In addition to providing an alternative for observing in classrooms, the use of long-term narrative records and qualitative analyses has brought a variety of new conceptions into research on teaching, including phenomenological and neo-Marxist critiques of educational thought and school practice (Hurn 1978, Woods 1980). At one level these perspectives emphasize the subjective character of knowledge, including scientific knowledge, and the extent to which "objective" categories reflect particular ways of interpreting the world. In addition to raising questions about the intellectual foundations of research on teaching, this subjective emphasis has underscored the need to understand how teachers and students make sense of classroom events and has challenged the conventional use of presumably neutral coding systems which may or may not reflect the use of participants. At another level, schools are portrayed as instruments of cultural reproduction which serve the interests of the power elite by sustaining existing social-class inequalities and teaching attitudes and forms of knowledge which preserve the status quo. Within this economic and political framework,

classrooms are the arena in which cultural reproduction occurs and attention is focused on the mechanisms by which this effect is achieved and on the ways in which classroom processes are constrained by factors operating at school and societal levels (Lundgren 1977, Woods 1980).

As contributions to classroom research, sociolinguistic studies are especially prominent (Green and Wallat 1981). Conceptually, these studies focus on the rules which define competence in interactions and on the ways in which social events are jointly constituted by participants. Emphasis is placed on the participation structures of classroom lessons (i.e., the rules which govern speaking, listening, and taking turns) and the communicative competence students need to interpret events in these contexts and contribute to the lessons. Given the anthropological flavor of much of this work, there has also been a concern for the discontinuities between the participation patterns of a student's native culture and the participation demands of the classroom system. Such discontinuities are seen as factors accounting for school failure.

From a broader perspective, an interest in structural models is characteristic of most research programs that focus on the nature of classrooms. Of particular importance are the models based on the concepts of task and activity (see Doyle 1979). These models, which are being derived from such disciplines as ecological psychology, sociology, and cognitive psychology, place central emphasis on how cognition and behavior are organized and directed toward goals in classroom environments.

Research on describing classroom structures and processes has had important implications for interpreting process–product findings and conceptualizing the relationship between research on teaching and classroom practice. From an interpretive perspective, such studies have sounded a note of caution in presuming a direction of causality in process–product findings. In some instances, it is possible that students who obtained high scores on achievement tests also behave in classrooms in ways that elicit enthusiasm and a task orientation from teachers. Low achieving students, on the other hand, may create classroom conditions which limit the amount of academic content that is covered and the amount of instructional guidance a teacher can provide. Thus, conditions associated with effectiveness may be shaped by students themselves. At the same time, descriptive research in classrooms has opened up avenues for understanding how teachers go about the task of creating classroom conditions and establishing practices which are likely to enhance achievement. Such insights have suggested new ways of thinking about how research on teaching can be considered practical. Traditionally, only statements of effectiveness have been considered to be useful knowledge for teacher education. Problems of how to go about using effective practices were seldom investigated directly. Yet from a teacher's or a teacher educator's perspective, information about implementing practices in classrooms and adjusting them to fit changing circumstances seems to be essential. It is here that research on classroom structures and on teachers' and students' thinking is potentially applicable.

3. The Status of Paradigms for Research on Teaching

As developed by Kuhn (1970), the concept of paradigm is associated with fundamental changes within a research community. It is natural, therefore, to raise questions about status and future directions in a discussion of paradigms for research on teaching. At the same time, answering such questions is a precarious business because neither the popularity of a given paradigm nor a shift of paradigms is necessarily logical or predictable.

In several respects, the traditional approaches to research on teaching are healthy and secure. The process–product paradigm continues to dominate research among investigators who do not identify with a particular curricular area, and methods research typifies inquiry within subject fields. The separation of these two approaches probably reflects basic differences in emphasis and historical origins. Process–product research reflects a focus on teachers and learning processes and has traditionally been directed to general indicators of teaching effectiveness. Methods research, on the other hand, reflects an interest in content and how it can be organized pedagogically. That is, the emphasis in methods research is more on curriculum than on teachers.

Two major factors probably contribute to the stability of these traditional approaches. First, they are specifically designed to address a problem of immediate practical significance, namely, teaching effectiveness. Unequivocal indicators of effectiveness would reduce substantially the uncertainty surrounding the decisions policy makers and administrators are required to make about the quality of teachers and educational programs. In addition, such indicators promise to supply a justification for curriculum decisions in teacher education. Second, both of these approaches have produced clearly defined methods which can be emulated by a large number of investigators, including graduate students. Thus, research within these two traditions is both useful and feasible, qualities which can easily attract disciples.

Research on teachers' characteristics provides an instructive case. Studies in this tradition are much less common now than in earlier decades, and interest in the personal qualities of teachers has moved toward models of teacher development which emphasize education and growth rather than selection, and toward studies of how teachers' knowledge and beliefs seem to influence decisions. On the criteria of the utility and feasibility, this decline and shift is difficult to explain. Measuring characteristics and relating them to effectiveness indicators seemingly produces practical information and is relatively easy to do. One might point

to the general inconclusiveness of studies of teachers' characteristics but process–product and methods research have a strong legacy of inconsistent findings. One possibility is that information about selection criteria is not particularly useful to the teacher education establishment because it does not necessarily define content that can be incorporated directly into programs for teachers. Moreover, there are inherent problems in using statistically derived indicators to make decisions about individuals. Thus, findings from this approach may not be useful.

Despite a general picture of health, there are signs of serious problems within traditional approaches to research on teaching, especially for process–product research. Phillips (1981) presents the view that notions of decline and growth are useful in assessing the strength (but not the "truth") of a research program. This argument calls attention to the ways in which investigators seek to protect the conceptual core of a paradigm and anticipate new findings. If seen from this perspective, process–product research appears in some ways to have reached a standstill. As results have converged on a common model of direct instruction or active teaching, the field seems to have answered some of the basic questions which activated research and there is a sense that further work in this tradition is not likely to produce any surprises. This effect is compounded by the fact that process–product studies perceived as "successful" have been very expensive field studies with large samples of classes and a large number of teaching variables. There is little motivation to launch such studies when the results are likely to be highly predictable. Moreover, studies of this magnitude are not feasible for researchers with limited funds and time. Such factors reduce the number of investigators interested in conducting studies within this paradigm.

In addition, process–product research has faced serious challenges to its conceptual core. An increased interest in students and classrooms has altered the two-factor structure of the paradigm to include processes that operate between teaching variables and outcomes as well as those which shape teacher behavior in classroom environments. There has also been a move toward content and materials as factors affecting student achievement and away from an exclusive focus on the teacher. Finally, questions have been raised about the misuse of process–product findings as absolute indicators of teaching quality, questions which have directed attention to new ways of thinking about the relationship of research on teaching to classroom practice. Whether such challenges can be accommodated by adjustments in the conceptual core or whether the boundaries of the paradigm itself have to be withdrawn remains to be seen.

Phillips (1981) has also pointed out that paradigms or research programs persist in the absence of a compelling alternative. It would seem that the emerging paradigms reviewed earlier have not yet provided such an alternative. Part of the problem is the diversity among these pproaches. Although there is a common interest in qualitative analyses, differences in types of questions and interpretive frameworks militate against the development of a coherent perspective or a common research program. In addition, the emerging paradigms tend to be theoretical and descriptive in their orientation and ess immediately focused on questions of effectiveness and practical applications. Unless more direct ties with practice are established, it is unlikely that any approach can become a paradigm for research on teaching, despite the fact that it may remain an area of interest in anthropology or sociology.

Among the emerging paradigms, the study of mediating processes would seem at its present stage, at least, to have limited utility for classroom teachers or teacher educators, although it probably will make important contributions to instructional design and methods. The work on classroom structures and on teachers' decisions, on the other hand, has a greater likelihood of becoming a resource for classroom practice as conceptions of what is practical broaden from indicators of effectiveness to include processes involved in using teaching practices in the classroom.

One obstacle remains for emerging paradigms. Many of the questions addressed in these paradigms present formidable methodological barriers. Moreover, the existing methods are not easily emulated.

On balance, conceptions of what constitutes research on teaching are broadening as definitions of practical knowledge expand to include statements of how conditions of effective teaching are established, maintained, and adjusted in classrooms. It is unlikely, however, that process–product or methods research will be replaced because these approaches provide ways of answering the effectiveness question, which in an applied area will always be the basic question. What seems to be evolving is an additional paradigm for research on teaching, one that does not answer the effectiveness question directly but points to ways in which such answers can be used.

See also: Evolution of Research on Teaching

Bibliography

Doyle W 1977 Paradigms for research on teacher effectiveness. In: Shulman L S (ed.) 1977 *Review of Research in Education*, Vol. 5. Peacock, Itasca, Illinois

Doyle W 1979 Making managerial decisions in classrooms. In: Duke D L (ed.) 1979 *Classroom Management*. 78th Yearbook of the National Society for the Study of Education, Part 2. University of Chicago Press, Chicago, Illinois

Emmer E T, Sanford J P, Evertson C M, Clements B S, Martin J 1981 *The Classroom Management Improvement Study: An Experiment in Elementary School Classrooms*. Report Number 6050. Research and Development Center for Teacher Education, The University of Texas, Austin, Texas

Gage N L 1978 *The Scientific Basis of the Art of Teaching*. Teachers College Press, New York

Getzels J, Jackson P 1963 The teachers' personality and characteristics. In: Gage N L (ed.) 1963 *Handbook of Research on Teaching: A Project of the American Educational Research Association*. Rand McNally, Chicago, Illinois

Green J L, Wallat C 1981 *Ethnography and Language in Educational Settings*. Ablex, Norwood, New Jersey

Hurn C J 1978 *The Limits and Possibilities of Schooling: An Introduction to the Sociology of Education*. Allyn and Bacon, Boston, Massachusetts

Kuhn T S 1970 *The Structure of Scientific Revolutions*, 2nd edn. University of Chicago Press, Chicago, Illinois

Lundgren U P 1977 *Model Analysis of Pedagogical Processes*. Liber Läromedel, Lund

Nuthall G, Snook I 1973 Contemporary models of teaching. In: Travers R M W (ed.) 1973 *Second Handbook of Research on Teaching: A Project of the American Educational Research Association*. Rand McNally, Chicago, Illinois, pp. 47–76

Phillips D C 1981 Post-Kuhnian reflections on educational research. In: Soltis J F (ed.) 1981 *Philosophy and Education*. 80th Yearbook of the National Society for the Study of Education, Part 1. University of Chicago Press, Chicago, Illinois

Rosenshine B, Furst N 1973 The use of direct observation to study teaching. In: Travers R M W (ed.) 1973 *Second Handbook of Research on Teaching: A Project of the American Educational Research Association*. Rand McNally, Chicago, Illinois, pp. 122–83

Shavelson R J, Stern P 1981 Research on teachers' pedagogical thoughts, judgments, decisions, and behavior. *Rev. Educ. Res.* 51: 455–98

Wallen N E, Travers R M W 1963 Analysis and investigation of teaching method. In: Gage N L (ed.) 1963 *Handbook of Research on Teaching: A Project of the American Educational Research Association*. Rand McNally, Chicago, Illinois

Woods P (ed.) 1980 *Teacher Strategies: Explorations in the Sociology of the School*. Croom Helm, London

Effects of Teaching

B. J. Biddle; M. J. Dunkin

The concept of teaching effects refers to conditions which come about because of teaching. The effects of teaching are the outcomes that are influenced by teaching activities. As such, teaching effects cover many types of phenomena, and a good deal of educational research may be said to concern them. Moreover, much of the literature written about and by educators focuses on the effects of teaching and their improvement. Despite this broad interest, confusion has appeared concerning the concept of teaching effects, methods for studying those effects, and the interpretation of findings concerning teaching and its outcomes. The purpose of this article is to discuss these issues briefly.

1. Effects and Effectiveness

Confusion has appeared concerning the related concepts of teaching effects and teacher effectiveness. As a rule, the latter concept deals with a narrower range of events. Whereas the effects of teaching include all outcomes that can be shown to be influenced by teaching, teacher effectiveness concerns only those outcomes that reflect the agency of the teacher and the objectives of education. To illustrate, a given teacher may be found both to instill love of mathematics in pupils and to annoy his or her colleagues because of sarcasm. Both outcomes qualify as effects of teaching, but only the former involves teacher effectiveness.

Since they focus on the objectives of education, studies of teacher effectiveness tend to have two limitations. On the one hand, their stress is on the accomplishment of explicit tasks. It is quite possible for teaching to contribute to implicit tasks, or for the effects of teaching to be undesired, but these latter are not often studied by those interested in teacher effectiveness. On the other hand, studies of teacher effectiveness focus largely on the direct effects of teaching, such as changes in pupil knowledge or attitudes. Teachers may have indirect effects on parents, political or economic processes in the community, or on other educators in the school system, but the latter are largely ignored in studies of effectiveness.

The reason why studies of teacher effectiveness have limited focus is that they usually have the goal of rating or evaluating the individual teacher. To illustrate, this goal underlies the long-standing tradition of research on the effectiveness of college instructors (Centra 1979). It is also explicit in research stimulated by recent efforts of state legislators in the United States to set standards for teacher competency. Research on the effects of teaching, in contrast, reflects a wider set of goals: curiosity, the desire to develop or improve curricula, an interest in educational media, a concern for the impact of school organization, and so forth.

2. Studying the Effects of Teaching

To conclude that a given outcome is affected by teaching requires that a cause–effect relationship be established between some aspect of teaching and the outcome in question. Establishing cause–effect relationships is always difficult in the social sciences, and confusion has also appeared concerning designs for research on the effects of teaching.

2.1 The Independent Variable

Teaching is the independent variable for studies of teaching effects, and in order to draw conclusions from such studies it is necessary to establish that variation

has appeared in the activities of instruction. Ideally this is accomplished through observation. (Various examples of teaching are observed, and some are found to score more highly than others on some activities.) Unfortunately, observing teaching is difficult and expensive, and many studies use substitute data which are supposed to represent teaching activities. Sometimes teachers, pupils, or others presumably familiar with the teaching context are asked to describe the activities they have observed. In other cases, proxy variables are used to represent variations in teaching, such as the noise level in the room, utilization of teaching resources or curricula, size or composition of the pupil group, or background characteristics of the teacher. Needless to say, studies that use substitute or proxy variables offer less persuasive evidence than those in which teaching activities are observed.

An even weaker case appears in some studies where no attempt is made to measure teaching at all, and the investigator merely argues that variation in the outcome indicates that teaching did, or did not, have an effect. Studies of this design are particularly likely to appear in effectiveness research where teachers may be rated differentially for their ability to "produce" pupil learning, regardless of how this was accomplished or whether, in fact, the teacher was responsible for that growth. Studies of this type have little to recommend them.

Most research on the effects of teaching is conducted in real-world contexts, and those contexts usually offer only a limited range of teaching activities. This means that the findings of even well-designed studies may or may not generalize to other contexts. This fact may be forgotten by some researchers or interpreters of research. To discover that a given type of teaching activity has effects for one type of teacher, school, or pupil population does not guarantee that it will have similar effects elsewhere. Moreover, the fact that variations in teaching are found to have minimal effects in one context does not mean that teaching is ineffective. Consider what might have been found had pupils who are taught in a conventional manner been contrasted with pupils who are not taught at all!

2.2 The Dependent Variable

Teaching can have many outcomes, and the list of variables that may be studied as effects of teaching is literally endless. Most studies of teaching effects concern pupils, but teaching also has an impact on others in the school, parents, members of the community or nation, and the teacher himself or herself. Effects may be conceptualized as applying to individuals, groups, institutions, or the entire society. They may also be conceived as changes in behavior or thought, as cognitive, affective, conative, or psychomotor events, as immediate or long-term, as incremental or cumulative. Moreover, variables that may be examined for teaching effects may be generated by various theories ranging from behaviorism to cognitive psychology, Marxism,

developmental psychology, role theory, symbolic inter-
actionism, ethnomethodology, psychoanalytic theory,
or concepts of leading educators.

Whatever variables are chosen to study as outcomes
of teaching, some means must be adopted for measuring
them. Some outcomes may be observed directly (such
as pupil behavior in the classroom), but most effect
variables require operations that are indirect. A standardized test for achievement, for example, presumably
represents only a portion of the material a pupil may
have learned from teaching. Controversy has arisen
over the validity of instruments used for measuring
some potential outcomes of teaching, such as the self-
concept, empathy, or anomie. Other outcome concepts,
such as "attitude" or "value," may be measured by
literally dozens of different methods in various studies,
and occasionally a given measuring technique (such as
the semantic differential) may be thought by different
authors to measure concepts ranging from "attitude,"
to "value," "motivation," or "modes of affective
response." These problems mean that one must carefully examine the methods used for measuring outcomes
before concluding anything from research on the effects
of teaching. Those unfamiliar with this problem are
sometimes tempted to read only the abstracts or textual
summaries of research findings. Unfortunately, findings
are always limited by the methods used by the
investigators.

Another problem concerns the measurement of
change. Most outcomes of teaching represent a change
in some variable that had a measurable state just before
teaching occurred. (To illustrate, pupils normally know
a few things about a given subject before being exposed
to teaching, although they often know a lot more afterwards.) Different strategies have appeared for dealing
with the issue of change in effects. Some studies ignore
the prior state of the outcome variable and base conclusions on postmeasures only. Some measure outcome
variables both before and after teaching and base conclusions on difference scores. And some use the pre-
measure as a covariate or as a predictor of the post-
measure in a multiple regression analysis. Each of these
strategies makes somewhat different assumptions, and
each may actually lead to different conclusions about
the data. Contemporary practice favors the regression
strategy because it allows comparison of the size of
effects of teaching with those of prior experience, but
readers of research on teaching effects should be aware
that many studies use other strategies for measuring
change.

These problems do not mean that measuring the
outcomes of teaching is impossible or hopelessly
chaotic. On the contrary, broad agreement has certainly
appeared on techniques for measuring such variables as
subject matter learning in pupils, but other outcome
variables have rarely, if ever, been studied. Occasionally
one reads that a given teaching strategy had "no effect"
when compared with other strategies. Such conclusions
should be taken with a grain of salt since they are

limited by the outcome variables conceptualized and the
techniques with which they were measured.

2.3 Causal Relationships

To conclude that teaching has an effect requires evidence demonstrating a causal relationship. John Stuart
Mill suggested that three conditions must be met in
order to establish causality. First, variation in the presumed cause must be associated with variation in the
effect. Second, the causative event must precede the
effect in time. Third, conditions that might account
for the relationship between the two events must be
controlled for. Most well-conducted studies of the
effects of teaching meet the first two of these criteria
easily. (Positive correlations are reported between the
activities of teaching and one or more subsequent, outcome variables.) Fulfilling Mill's third condition is more
difficult, however, and most studies of teaching effects
provide little evidence that the effect in question was
produced by teaching and not by some other, causative
factor.

To illustrate, consider a study in which some characteristic of teacher behavior, for example "warmth,"
is found associated with an outcome variable, pupil
"achievement." Most authors will interpret this evidence to indicate that warm behavior on the part of the
teacher will cause higher levels of achievement in pupils,
but is this interpretation justified? Unless other variables are controlled that might affect achievement, it
will be impossible to tell whether the interpretation is
or is not correct. It might be, for example, that the
teacher responds to brighter pupils with greater warmth,
in which case the "real" cause is pupil intelligence. Or
it might be that teachers who exhibit greater warmth
are also spending more time in classroom instruction,
and pupil achievement responds largely to time-on-
task. It is impossible to know whether these alternative
explanations, or others, are plausible unless evidence
has been examined pertaining to them.

Two strategies have appeared for meeting Mill's third
condition in research on teaching. One strategy is to
conduct experiments in which conditions leading to
teaching are manipulated by the investigator, and pupils
(or whoever is to be studied for effects) are assigned
to experimental conditions at random. Two types of
experiments have appeared in research on teaching
effects. One type attempts to control for all characteristics of teaching except the variable that is being
investigated (see, for example, Gall et al. 1978). The
other manipulates a set of teaching variables that are
known from field research to be jointly associated with
desired outcomes (an example appears in Good and
Grouws 1979). Whereas both types presumably meet
Mill's third condition, they may do so at the cost of
creating artificial teaching contexts that are not likely
to appear in the real world. In addition, although conditions that lead to teaching may certainly be manipulated, teaching itself is a form of social interaction and
cannot be completely controlled. Thus, any exper-

imental manipulation may lead to unanticipated conditions in teaching that can affect outcomes. These difficulties mean that experiments cannot provide definitive, causal information for research on the effects of teaching. They may suggest ways for improving those effects, however.

The second strategy is to conduct field research in which the influence of potential, confounding variables is controlled statistically. Two procedures have been employed by those who adopt this strategy for research on teaching effects: the matching of comparison groups, and the study of multiple variables. The former procedure is exemplified in research by Brophy and Evertson (1976) in which the investigators examined the impact of teaching strategies on matched groups of low-socioeconomic status (SES) and high-SES pupils. (Among other results, they found that teacher control over the details of instruction and a relaxed classroom atmosphere were more important for the achievements of low-SES than for high-SES pupils.) This procedure has the advantage of providing useful information about the potential, confounding variable examined. It does not tell us anything about other confounding variables not yet studied.

The latter procedure appears in studies where multiple teaching variables are examined for their impact on a given outcome, or several outcome variables are studied for their response to teaching conditions. To illustrate, Kounin (1970) examined the impact of 10 different teaching variables ("momentum," "withitness," "smoothness," etc.) on two outcome variables ("pupil work involvement" and "pupil deviancy"). Such a procedure has the advantage of allowing one to discriminate important from weak effects. It does not, however, provide definitive evidence of a cause–effect relationship.

Other and stronger procedures have appeared for the control of confounding variables in social science research, but to date these have rarely been applied to research on the effects of teaching. Procedures such as multistage regression analysis, the use of cross-lagged panel correlations, and causal modeling require a large sample, and most studies of teaching effects have used small samples. In sum, then, research on the effects of teaching does not generally provide evidence that the effects claimed are definitive. This does not mean that these claims are wrong. On the contrary, research on the effects of teaching has generated a host of new concepts, many empirical findings, and a number of empirically based theories of instruction. But it should be understood that the evidence for these contributions is often weak.

3. Findings of Research on Teaching

What is presently known about the effects of teaching? What may reasonably be expected as a conclusion from research on this topic, and has the extensive research on teaching effects been worth the effort?

Many persons concerned with social research presume that the primary purpose of conducting it is to establish "facts"—universal and definitive relationships between causes and effects. In the case of research on teaching this means that one should expect to learn that a given teaching strategy always has certain effects or that a given outcome is more likely to be produced by one type of teaching than by another. This expectation underlies many traditional reviews of research on the effects of teaching. It also stands behind much of the recent enthusiasm for the meta-analysis of teaching–effect studies.

In brief, traditional methods of reviewing research have used textual or tabular means for summarizing the conclusions of studies, whereas meta-analyses use inferential statistics for combining the findings of various studies that have presumably examined the same topic so that one can reach a single, best conclusion. (To illustrate, Glass et al. 1982, examined studies concerned with class size and pupil achievement and concluded that these variables were negatively related, "on average.") Meta-analyses make many questionable assumptions and should be used cautiously for research on the effects of teaching. However, traditional reviews may also presume that research will produce universal "facts" about teaching effects. How realistic is this expectation?

It probably is not very realistic. As many philosophers have stressed, research evidence can overturn a hypothesis unambiguously, but it cannot confirm that hypothesis for all occasions in the hereafter. This means that research conclusions are always subject to the limitations of the evidence so far collected and may be challenged by new evidence in the future. Although this argument also applies to the physical sciences, it is particularly true for the social sciences where behavior can be expected to change radically from context to context. This means that the effects of teaching are likely to differ: for pupils of differing interests and abilities, depending on grade level and subject matter of the lesson, in working-class and middle-class schools, or in classrooms conducted in American suburbs, Central American barrios, or in French Provinces. Indeed, one reviewer of teacher effects suggests that "there do not appear to be any universal teaching competencies . . . that are appropriate to all teaching circumstances" (Brophy 1979 p. 735).

Whether Brophy's conclusion is or is not correct cannot be judged at this time. It is certainly true, that few universal "facts" have yet appeared in research on teaching effects. This does not mean that the effort is useless. On the contrary, a number of contributions have clearly appeared in this research. One form of contribution is the development of insights about teaching—new concepts for describing teaching and its outcomes, and new propositions about the relationships between these two realms. Another concerns the development of evidence which is useful for testing theories and telling how teaching works in those contexts studied. Another concerns practical innovations such as new curricula, methods for teacher training, or techniques for measuring the outcomes of instruction. Yet another—perhaps the most important of all—is the stimulation of theory concerning teaching and its effects which has the capacity for affecting future generations of educators. These contributions are of great importance and make research on the effects of teaching a valuable enterprise. In fact, Gage (1978) suggests that future improvements in teaching will largely come about through this research.

4. Crucial Issues and Research Designs

Research on the effects of teaching may be said to have passed through its initial phase in which simple research designs were required and the major tasks were to establish that teaching, in fact, had effects, and to debunk simple but erroneous theories concerning their relationship. Research is now entering a new phase in which the task will be to examine relationships between teaching and outcomes in various contexts and among persons who vary in interests and abilities. This phase demands more complex research designs, and it is useful to review several of the latter.

4.1 Comparative Research

Studies that fall within the comparative research tradition are designed to contrast two or more samples of persons who represent contextual variation. To illustrate, a comparative study of teaching effects might examine teaching and its outcomes in classrooms that varied by grade level, subject matter, pupil ethnicity, type of school, or national context. Such studies allow investigators to see whether teaching has similar effects in various contexts or, if it does not, to examine how those effects vary depending on context characteristics. Such studies have both practical and theoretical goals. Among the former, if it can be discovered how teaching effects vary depending on context, there will be a better understanding of when a given teaching strategy should be successful and when it should be avoided. Among the latter, contextual variation in the effects of teaching may suggest reasons for explaining why a given teaching effect is obtained. Comparative research is difficult to manage, and those who fund research on the effects of teaching often do not understand the need for studies that use comparative research designs, but there should be a lot more such studies.

4.2 Aptitude–Treatment Interaction

Studies of aptitude–treatment interaction (ATI) focus on the ways in which different pupils in the classrooms react to variations in teaching (see *Aptitude—Treatment Interaction Models*). For example, a typical ATI study might examine the ways in which high- and low-ability pupils respond to teaching which is "flexible" versus that which is "rigid." Good ATI research is also difficult to manage, and results from studies that use ATI designs have often been disappointing (Good and Stipek 1983).

In addition, the practical implications of findings from ATI research are moot as long as teachers are to continue to teach in large classrooms wherein pupils vary in terms of interests and abilities. Nevertheless, pupils obviously differ in the ways in which they respond to teaching, and studying those differences enables insights to be gained about why the effects of teaching appear. Examination of ATI effects may be built into most studies of the effects of teaching, and there should be more of this type of research.

4.3 Longitudinal Research

Most research on the effects of teaching presumes a stable teaching environment and that effects will appear quickly. But the real world of teaching is far from stable, and teaching may have effects that cumulate or are delayed. Lessons have a sequential character, as does the school day, the term, and the school year. Moreover, pupils progress from grade to grade within the school, and the effects of teaching to which they are exposed presumably accumulate. Also, teaching is presumably conducted because of its positive, long-term effects on the lives of pupils. The best way to study the cumulative, sequential, or delayed effects of teaching is through longitudinal research in which pupils are followed over time. Examples of case studies that examined longitudinal effects may be cited (Smith and Geoffrey 1968, Rist 1973), but it is difficult to find good, longitudinal research on teaching effects that involves multiple teachers or classrooms. Subsequent pupil achievement, occupational choice, and status attainment are frequently cited as potential effects of teaching, but most longitudinal research on these topics simply does not provide measures of teaching, and attempts to interpret findings from this research as applying to the study of teaching effects is suspect. Longitudinal studies of teaching are also difficult to manage, and most designs for them require a wait of months or years to learn about the research, but the need for them is also great.

As the above paragraphs suggest, good research on the effects of teaching is complex and difficult to manage. It also requires a good deal of money and (particularly for longitudinal research) long-term funding. Most studies of the effects of teaching conducted to date were funded in the apparent hope of discovering universal "facts" that lead to improvement of instruction. That hope has not been realized, nor is it likely ever to be fulfilled. Instead, research on teaching effects has led to development of insights, innovations, theories, and information about the ways in which teaching works in various contexts. This information is invaluable, but to extend it will require support for more complex research designs in the future. Researchers and funding agencies should be prepared to understand both the need and the limited, though utterly necessary, contributions that research on the effects of teaching can provide to the understanding and improvement of education.

See also: Criteria for Evaluating Teaching; Evolution of Research on Teaching; Synthesizing Research Evidence

Bibliography

Biddle B J, Anderson D S 1984 Theory, knowledge, and methods of research on teaching. In: Wittrock M C (ed.) 1984 *Handbook of Research on Teaching*, 3rd edn. Macmillan, New York

Brophy J E 1979 Teacher behavior and its effects. *J. Educ. Psychol.* 71: 733–50

Brophy J E, Evertson C M 1976 *Learning from Teaching: A Developmental Perspective*. Allyn and Bacon, Boston, Massachusetts

Centra J A 1979 *Determining Faculty Effectiveness*. Jossey-Bass, San Francisco, California

Gage N L 1978 *The Scientific Basis of the Art of Teaching*. Teachers College Press, New York

Gall M D, Ward B A, Berliner D C, Cahen L S, Winne P H,

Elashoff J D, Stanton G C 1978 Effects of questioning techniques and recitation on student learning. *Am. Educ. Res. J.* 15: 175–99

Glass G V, Cahen L S, Smith M L, Filby N N 1982 *School Class Size: Research and Policy*. Sage, Beverly Hills, California

Good T L, Grouws D A 1979 The Missouri Mathematics Effectiveness Project: An experimental study in fourth-grade classrooms. *J. Educ. Psychol.* 71: 355–62

Good T L, Stipek D J 1983 Individual differences in the classroom: A psychological perspective. In: Fenstermacher G D, Goodlad J I (eds.) 1983 *1983 Yearbook of the National Society for the Study of Education*. Chicago, Illinois

Kounin J S 1970 *Discipline and Group Management in Classrooms*. Holt, Rinehart and Winston, New York

Rist R C 1973 *The Urban School: A Factory for Failure: A Study of Education in American Society*. MIT Press, Cambridge, Massachusetts

Smith L M, Geoffrey W 1968 *The Complexities of an Urban Classroom: Analysis Toward a General Theory of Teaching*. Holt, Rinehart and Winston, New York

Synthesizing Research Evidence

R. M. Giaconia; L. V. Hedges

Synthesizing research on teaching effectiveness means using the results of several empirical studies to derive generalizations about the theoretical relationship between variables. The aim of research synthesis is threefold: (a) to summarize findings across studies; (b) to assess the consistency of findings across studies; and (c) to resolve contradictory findings across studies.

Other articles in this Encyclopedia describe the variables, paradigms, and methods relevant to conducting individual studies on a particular topic on teaching effectiveness (see *Effects of Teaching*). This article discusses the tasks, issues, and methods relevant to integrating a series of studies on a particular topic on teaching effectiveness. The emphasis of this article is on the most recent quantitative research synthesis techniques. Some computational examples of these techniques are also given.

1. Importance of Research Synthesis

The synthesis of empirical research results is an essential activity in the social sciences. Its careful execution is important for both theoretical and practical reasons. First, research on teaching effectiveness, as a field of inquiry that purports to have a scientific basis, has as one of its aims the cumulation of knowledge. As such, the field should maintain the same degree of rigor in the methods used to synthesize research studies (cumulate knowledge about a topic) that are required in executing the primary research studies that are to be synthesized. Second, the practical uses made of research syntheses suggest the importance of maintaining high standards in their execution. For example, Light and Smith (1971)

described how public policy decisions, such as which preschool education programs should be funded, are often based on the findings reported in several empirical studies. Thus, valid ways of combining the evidence across research studies and resolving the often conflicting findings are important in helping public policy makers arrrive at the correct conclusions about the true effects of a treatment or the true degree of relationship between variables.

Similarly, the results of research synthesis are sometimes used to characterize (or mischaracterize) the methodological and substantive contributions of a whole field of inquiry. For example, Gage (1978) noted that many writers have given rather dismal assessments of the fruitfulness of the field of research on teaching effectiveness. He cited as an example Doyle (1978), who reported, "Reviewers have concluded, with remarkable regularity, that few consistent relationships between teacher variables and effectiveness criteria can be established" (p. 164). Gage argues that the dismal summations are due in large part to weaknesses inherent in the methods used to synthesize the research findings. He suggested that more valid ways of summarizing research on teaching effectiveness might lead to more positive conclusions and demonstrated this with studies of the effects of teacher indirectness. Gage's example, as well as others illustrating how different research synthesis methods lead to different conclusions, are described at the end of this article.

Thus, research synthesis is important both in itself as a scientific activity and also because of the practical uses made of the conclusions derived from research syntheses.

2. State of the Art of Research Synthesis

Research synthesis is currently a topic of widespread discussion and investigation. But this has not always been the case. It is only since the early 1970s or so that researchers have questioned the rather wide gap between the rigor applied to primary research and the rigor applied to methods that synthesize this primary research. Some writers (e.g., Cooper 1982, Glass 1978, Pillemer and Light 1980) have suggested that the relative inattention to standards for research synthesis may be due to the facts that: (a) it is only since the early 1960s or so that the empirical research base has expanded to such large proportions, and (b) synthesizing research has typically been a less valued activity than conducting primary research.

Light and Smith (1971) were among the first writers to question the prevalent practices of research synthesis (narrative and voting methods) and highlighted the inability of these practices to account for contradictory findings across studies.

Rosenthal (1978) characterized the situation as follows:

> It has become almost obligatory to end one's articles with a clarion call for further research. Yet, it seems fair to say that we are better at issuing such calls than at knowing what to do with the answers. There are many areas of the behavioral and social sciences for which we do in fact have available the results of many studies, all addressing essentially the same question. Our summaries of the results of these sets of studies, however, are not nearly as informative as they might be, either with respect to summarized significance levels or with respect to summarized effect sizes. Even the best reviews of research by the most sophisticated workers rarely tell us more about each of a set of studies than whether it did or did not reach a given p level and whether the direction of the relationship between the variables investigated was or was not in the predicted direction. (p. 185)

Similarly, Pillemer and Light (1980) noted that, ". . . pulling together existing evidence is not considered a truly scientific activity by some because it deals with old data. We disagree. Perhaps the key idea in all of this is 'discovery.' A systematic effort to draw conclusions from many existing studies can be every bit as likely to lead to a 'discovery' about, say, program effectiveness, as one new study" (p. 194).

And, Glass (1978) commented

> The fiction that science progresses along a string of dramatic, critical experiments dies hard. For educational research, the priorities need to be changed. The integration of research studies requires the best minds. It should be valued more highly than many forms of original research." (p. 353).

It was in the *Zeitgeist* characterized by the comments of these writers that the methodological, technical, and theoretical properties of research synthesis methods became an area of serious inquiry. Most of the work on research synthesis was aimed at the development of quantitative methods; that is, methods that summarized results in terms of numerical indices. Underlying this work was the assumption, expressed by Glass (1978) that "The accumulated findings of dozens or even hundreds of studies should be regarded as complex data points, no more comprehensible without the full use of statistical analyses than hundreds of data points in a single study could be so casually understood" (p. 352).

Some of the work on quantitative research synthesis methods proceeded independently (e.g., Rosenthal 1976, Glass 1976); other work built explicitly on that of previous researchers (e.g., Hedges 1981, 1982a, 1982b). Subsequent sections in this article describe and illustrate some of the most recent developments in research synthesis methods. It should be understood, however, that these methods are still evolving; the particular techniques described may eventually be supplanted as researchers continue to examine the statistical properties and practical utility of these methods. But it is probably safe to assume that research synthesis will continue to be studied extensively and will never again be treated as casually as it has been in the past.

3. Tasks Involved in Research Synthesis

In keeping with the notion that research synthesis should be a systematic scientific enterprise, Jackson (1980) proposed that many of the tasks involved in research synthesis parallel the tasks involved in conducting primary research studies. He identified these tasks as: (a) selecting the questions or hypotheses; (b) sampling the primary studies; (c) representing characteristics of the primary studies; (d) analyzing the primary studies; (e) interpreting the results; and (f) reporting the review. Cooper (1982) carried the parallels between research synthesis and primary research even farther, and suggested that many of the threats to the internal and external validity of primary research studies (Campbell and Stanley 1966, Bracht and Glass 1968) also applied to research synthesis. Following are descriptions of the six tasks involved in research synthesis, some of the current issues relevant to these tasks, and potential sources of invalidity in some of the tasks.

3.1 Selecting the Questions or Hypotheses

How broadly or narrowly the research question is framed (both conceptually and operationally) directly affects which studies will be included in the review and thus the results of the review. For example, a conceptually broad question such as "which variables affect outcome Y?," includes more studies than the question, "how does variable X affect outcome Y when condition Z is present?"

Similarly, how broadly the question is operationally stated influences the choice of studies and therefore results. A good example is provided by the empirical research on open versus traditional instruction (see *Open Versus Formal Methods*). Horwitz (1979) identified over 200 empirical studies comparing an open education program to a traditional education program and summarized results across all 200 studies without regard to how open education had been operationalized. A later review (Giaconia and Hedges 1982) showed that the variability in how open education was operationalized in these studies was extensive and that the effects of open education could be explained in part by variations in the operations used in implementing the open education program.

Cooper (1982) argued that the major threat to validity involved in this task is the use of operational and conceptual definitions that are narrow; broader definitions can potentially provide more robust conclusions. Jackson (1980) suggested that the research integrator should consult four sources when developing the review questions or hypotheses: available theory, prior reviews on the topic, the primary research targeted for review, and the integrator's intuition, insight, and ingenuity.

3.2 Sampling Studies to be Synthesized

The collection of studies reviewed by the research integrator is always a sample, even if the integrator has accumulated all the studies that currently exist on the topic. That is, the population of studies on a topic includes all studies past, present, and future. Thus, the task of the research integrator is to draw inferences about this larger population of studies on the basis of the sample of studies he or she is integrating, and the inferences are only as valid as the sample is adequate. Two recent issues related to the sampling of studies include: (a) Sources of studies: published versus unpublished? The use of only published studies (e.g., journal articles) and not unpublished studies (e.g., dissertations) would bias the results of the review, if there were systematic differences between the results that appear in published and unpublished studies. Glass et al. (1981) demonstrated that this is often the case. He compared the results in 10 reviews in which the treatment effects were reported separately for studies in journals, books, dissertations, and other unpublished sources. Results showed that the average treatment effects reported in published journal articles were about one-third standard deviation higher than in unpublished theses or dissertations. Thus using only published studies in the review could slightly bias the conclusions reached. (b) Good versus bad studies? Jackson (1980) noted that some reviewers eliminate all studies from the review which have methodological flaws and often end up with only one or two studies to be synthesized. He argued that there are at least three reasons for not routinely eliminating studies that have methodological flaws: firstly, almost all research studies have at least a few methodological inadequacies; secondly, methodological inadequacies do not always cause biased findings; and thirdly, it is difficult to determine when methodological weaknesses have caused biased findings and when they have not.

Other writers (Eysenck 1978) have argued that studies with methodological flaws should be excluded from reviews, that it makes no sense to expect that combining many weak studies can produce strong conclusions.

Glass et al. (1981) and Gage (1978) have claimed that many weak studies *can* indeed lead to valid conclusions, especially when the methodological flaws do not overlap. As Gage (1978) noted, "Thus the path to increasing certainty becomes not the single excellent study, which is nonetheless weak in one or more respects, but the convergence of findings from many studies, which are also weak but in many different ways. The dissimilar, or nonreplicated, weaknesses leave the replicated finding more secure. Where the studies do not overlap in their flaws, but do overlap in their implications, the research synthesizer can begin to build confidence in those implications" (p. 35).

Glass et al. (1981) also noted that whether good studies produce results different from bad studies is an empirical question and one which the research integrator should systematically analyze, that is, whether the effects reported in studies varies with ratings of the quality of the study. Glass et al. (1981) examined 12 research syntheses on a variety of research topics that reported effects separately for studies whose quality (internal validity) was coded as either: "high," "medium," or "low." They found that in some research syntheses, high quality studies produced treatment effects different from those in low quality studies; in other research syntheses, quality of the study was unrelated to treatment effects.

Thus, the research integrator should probably include in his or her sample of studies as many as possible from all sources (published and unpublished) and of all degress of quality.

3.3 Representing Characteristics of Primary Studies

This task is the "data collection" phase of research synthesis and involves the collection of two classes of information: (a) reported results about treatment effects or the relationship between variables; and (b) characteristics of the studies themselves. What is considered relevant for this first set of information (results) varies with the type of research synthesis method used. Some research synthesis methods (e.g., narrative and vote counting) extract only the direction and statistical significance of the reported results. Other methods (e.g., combined significance test methods) rely on the size of test statistics (e.g., t-ratio, chi-square) reported in the studies. Still other methods (effect magnitude procedures) extract means, standard deviations, sample sizes, sample correlation coefficients and ignore the reported statistical significance. How these four research synthesis methods summarize this information is described in greater detail in later sections in this article.

The second set of information (study characteristics) should be collected in order to help the research integrator identify variables that might plausibly explain inconsistent results across studies. For example, Giaconia and Hedges (1982) found that specific features of the treatment variable (an experimental design characteristic) were systematically related to treatment effects in studies of open versus formal instruction. Table 1 lists some of the study characteristics that have been used in research synthesis. A major weakness of some of the research synthesis methods described later is their failure to take into account in any systematic way the relation of study characteristics to results.

The main concern in executing this third task is the reliability with which information is extracted from the studies. The collection of some information is a straightforward clerical task, for example, recording *p*-values, means, and so on, but the collection of other information, such as quality of the study, involves a fair degree of judgment on the part of the research integrator. Stock et al. (1982) conducted two studies of intercoder reliability for 30 studies to be synthesized. They reported interrater agreement separately for several types of study information that required calculations (e.g., mean, age, sample size) and for information that required judgments (e.g., theoretical framework, quality of study). The interrater agreement rates exceeded 80 percent for about 88 percent of both calculations and judgment-types of information.

3.4 Analyzing the Primary Studies

This task entails the procedures used by the research integrator to combine the information in studies to arrive at generalizations about the theoretical relationship between the variables being studied. Section 4 describes in detail the procedures used in four of these research synthesis methods.

Table 1

Characteristics of studies coded in research syntheses

1. *Subject characteristics*
   (a) Grade level studied
   (b) Sex ratio of pupils
   (c) Ethnicity of pupils
   (d) Socioeconomic status of pupils

2. *Experimental design characteristics*
   (a) Type of design (random assignment experimental, quasiexperimental, mixed)
   (b) Duration of teaching
   (c) Number of schools, teachers, and pupils
   (d) Method of measuring the independent variable
   (e) Specific features of the treatment of independent variable
   (f) Control for pre-existing differences among pupils

3. *Experimenter characteristics*
   (a) Mandatory versus voluntary teacher participation
   (b) Commitment of the investigator (pro/neutral/against the treatment being studied)

4. *Experimental context characteristics*
   (a) Form of the publication (journal, dissertation, book, etc.)
   (b) Year of publication
   (c) Clarity and quality of the research report

3.5 Interpreting the Results

Confirming or disproving existing theory, suggesting new theory, stating recommendations for policy or educational practice, and suggesting directions for both future primary research and reviews are all relevant aspects of interpreting the results of a research synthesis. Jackson (1980) examined the extent to which each of these aspects of interpretation was found in 36 randomly selected research reviews found in social science journals. He reported that seven of the 36 reviews discussed results in terms of existing or new theory; six of the 36 stated recommendations for policy or practice; 28 of the 36 described directions for future primary research; and only three offered suggestions for future reviews.

Whichever of these aspects of interpretation the research integrator chooses to emphasize, the validity of these interpretations depends directly on the research synthesis method used. Section 12 describes two examples of how interpretations of essentially the same set of studies differed markedly when different research synthesis methods were applied.

3.6 Reporting the Review

Research integrators should adhere to the same standards for reporting their work that primary researchers do, but often they do not (Jackson 1980). That is, the reports of research syntheses should contain enough information about each of the five tasks (framing the question to interpreting the results) to allow the reader to critically appraise the validity of the conclusions presented in the review. Jackson (1980) examined 36 randomly selected reviews published in social science journals and concluded that most of these failed to report important methodological aspects of the review. For example, only one of the 36 reviews reported the information retrieval systems used to locate primary studies on the topic; only half of the reviews indicated the direction and magnitude of the findings of any of the primary studies; and very few reviews reported how study characteristics were related to results of the studies.

Thus, the research integrator should be concerned with not only the careful execution of tasks (a) through (e), but also the thorough reporting of the procedures used in completing each of these tasks.

4. Research Synthesis Methods

The aim of research synthesis was described in the introduction to this article as threefold: (a) to summarize findings across studies; (b) to assess the consistency of findings across studies; and (c) to resolve contradictory findings across studies. Research synthesis methods should provide mechanisms for dealing with all three of these aims; most do not. The following sections describe four methods of research synthesis and how each addresses the threefold aim. Table 2 also summarizes some of this information.

These four methods fall into two categories: those

Table 2
How each of the research synthesis methods addresses the threefold aim of research synthesis

Method	How results summarized	How consistency of results assessed	How conflicts in findings resolved
(a) Narrative	Verbal description of procedures used and statistical significance of reported results Overall conclusions based on reviewer's subjective weighting of studies	No systematic mechanism Verbal description of concurrence of statistical results	No systematic mechanism Verbal description of study characteristics that seem to mediate reported results
(b) Vote counting	Tabulation of direction and statistical significance of reported results: positively significant, negatively significant, no significant differences Category into which most studies fall is the effect or relationship between variables	No systematic mechanism Proportion of studies falling into each category	No systematic mechanism Tally studies separately for subsets of studies that differ on study characteristics
(c) Combined significance test	Combine p-values or size of test statistics (t-ratio, chi-square, z, etc.) and assess statistical significance of this overall index	No systematic mechanism	No systematic mechanism
(d) Effect magnitude	Average standardized indices of effect magnitude computed for each study	Plot distribution of effect magnitudes Statistical test of homogeneity of effect magnitude	Correlation of study characteristics with indices of effect magnitude Test homogeneity of effect magnitude separately for clusters of studies that differ on study characteristics

that rely on the statistical significance of results of individual studies (narrative and vote counting) and those that do not (combined significance test and effect magnitude procedures).

5. Narrative Approaches

Narrative approaches consist of a verbal description of the research studies and particular topic, usually chronologically arranged, in terms of what the investigators of each study did and the results they found. Glass (1978) suggested that strictly narrative approaches to the synthesis of educational research are probably more an historic fact than a present reality. That is, narrative approaches were most suitable when the number of studies on a topic was small, but were supplanted as the numbers increased.

The specific strengths of such narrative approaches include the following: (a) They can provide a richness of detail about study characteristics (such as those in Table 1) that methods that rely heavily on the reported results cannot; (b) The chronological arrangement of studies in the narrative approach allows the researcher to trace the evolution of thought, theory, and empirical evidence about a particular topic; that is, the method can provide historical perspective about an issue; and (c) Narrative approaches can be used to synthesize two or more very different lines of research that may bear only indirectly on each other.

5.1 Summarizing Results Across Studies

Most narrative approaches either implicitly or explicitly rely on the statistical significance of the results reported in the individual studies to arrive at overall conclusions about the true treatment effects or true relationship between variables. However, which statistical results the research integrator chooses to portray as representation of the overall results is a highly subjective matter. That is, if there are contradictory findings across studies, it is the subjective opinion of the research integrator about the credibility and validity of the studies that determines which statistical results are presented as *the* results. This subjectivity in summarizing findings inherent in narrative approaches can lead to different conclusions about treatment effects or relationships between variables. For example, Glass et al. (1981) described how three narrative reviews of research studies of whether the combination of verbal psychotherapy and doing therapy was superior to drug therapy alone produced very different conclusions. The three reviews were all conducted within about a five-year period and were based on essentially the same set of studies. Yet, one reviewer concluded that there was a striking advantage for the combined treatment, a second reviewer concluded there was little difference, and a third reviewer suggested that the results were inconclusive.

5.2 Assessing the Consistency of Results Across Studies

In narrative approaches, consistency of results is defined in terms of consistency of the statistical significance and direction of the results reported. Narrative approaches provide no specific mechanism for assessing consistency of results other than a verbal description such as, "Investigators X, Y, and Z found a statistically significant treatment effect, whereas investigators A and B did not."

5.3 Resolving Contradictory Findings Across Studies

Narrative approaches rely heavily on the study characteristics, especially design of the study, in resolving apparent contradictions in results across studies. Again, however, there is a great deal of subjectivity in which study characteristics a particular research integrator chooses to highlight (or downplay) in order to bolster (or debunk) the credibility the results reported. Thus, there are no systematic mechanisms for resolving contradictory findings.

Also, narrative approaches in their attempt to resolve contradictory findings and subjectively weighted studies are particularly susceptible to what Glass (1978) termed the confusion between research criticism and research integration. He noted: "The critic often reads a published study and second guesses the aspects of measurement and analysis that should have been anticipated by the researcher. If a study 'fails' on a sufficient number of these criteria—or if it fails to meet conditions of which the critic is particularly fond—the study is discounted or eliminated completely from consideration. Research design has a logic of its own, but it is not a logic appropriate to research integration" (p. 355).

6. Vote Counting Methods

Vote counting methods involve categorizing studies on the basis of the direction and statistical significance of the reported results. Many of the specific details of the studies are ignored; it is primarily the reported p value which is of interest to the research integrator. The "voting," "box score," or "vote counting" method is still the most commonly used method. It supplanted narrative approaches as the number of studies on a particular topic grew too large to be synthesized in a strictly narrative fashion. The method was characterized by Light and Smith (1971) as follows:

> All studies which have data on a dependent variable and a specific independent variable of interest are examined. Three possible outcomes are defined. The relationship between the independent variable and the dependent variable is either significantly positive, significantly negative, or there is no significant relationship in either direction. The number of studies falling into each of these three categories is then simply tallied. If a plurality of studies falls into any one of these three categories, with fewer falling into the other two, the modal category is declared the winner. This modal categorization is then assumed to give the best estimate of the direction of the true relationship between the independent and dependent variable. (p. 433)

The specific strengths of the vote counting method include the following: (a) once the relevant set of studies to be synthesized has been identified, the method can be executed fairly quickly; (b) results of vote counting methods (using the same set of studies) should be highly replicable; there is little of the subjectivity inherent in narrative approaches. That is, the reported results of a study can be classified fairly unambiguously and only gross clerical errors in tallying the number of studies in each category would lead to different conclusions across research integrators.

6.1 Summarizing Results Across Studies

Summarizing results across studies in vote counting methods is a straightforward process. The category (significantly positive results, significantly negative results, no significant results) into which the statistical results of most studies fall is described as the treatment effect or the relationship between variables.

6.2 Assessing the Consistency of Results Across Studies

In using the vote counting method, the research integrator might describe the proportion of studies falling into each category and in this way indicate the degree of consistency of results. But assessing the consistency of results is not of particular importance in the vote counting method. Indeed, the vote counting method assumes that there will be inconsistency in findings across studies and the object is to identify which statistical result among the set of inconsistent results is most prevalent. Thus, vote counting methods provide no systematic mechanism for assessing consistency of results.

6.3 Resolving Contradictory Findings Across Studies

In general, the vote counting method does not attempt to resolve contradictory findings across studies. Again, contradictory findings are assumed to exist (for whatever reasons) and the aim of the synthesis is to identify the most prevalent statistical finding.

Some research integrators who used the vote counting

method have, however, tallied studies separately on the basis of study characteristics. For example, Winne (1979), in his review of experiments of the effects of teachers' use of higher cognitive questions on pupil achievement, summarized the statistical significance of results across studies separately for "skills" and "training" studies, that is, on the basis of how the treatment variable was manipulated.

Similarly, other investigators have tallied the number of statistically significant results separately for studies deemed "sufficiently valid" and "insufficiently valid," that is, on the basis of the quality of the design of the study and its execution.

Tallying studies separately on the basis of study characteristics is one way to begin to resolve contradictory findings across studies, that is, if results vary systematically with study characteristics, then apparent contradictions actually become explainable. But research integrators who use the vote counting method have not applied such approaches to resolving contradictory findings in any consistent or systematic way.

7. Weaknesses of Narrative and Vote Counting Methods

Despite the simplicity and intuitive appeal of research synthesis methods that tabulate the number of statistically significant and nonsignificant findings, either informally (narrative) or formally (vote counting), these methods have serious problems as methods for making inferences about true treatment effects or the true relationship between variables. The problems with such vote counting methods stem from the fact that these methods combine the results of statistical decisions (hypothesis tests) rather than directly combining information about the treatment effect or degree of relationship between variables that is contained in the individual studies. Each statistical decision is fallible, and the naive combination of these fallible decisions implicit in vote counting methods compounds this tendency to err. More precisely, the usual narrative and vote counting methods provide neither: (a) a reliable method of summarizing research results; nor (b) an adequate method of drawing valid inferences about the magnitude of treatment effects or extent of relationship between variables; nor (c) a systematic method of assessing the consistency of findings and resolving contradictory findings.

7.1 Summarizing Research Outcomes

A pervasive fallacy in statistical thinking is that if two studies addressing the same research question reach the same statistical decision (to reject or not to reject the null hypothesis), then the finding is "replicated" and the state of the underlying parameters (effects) is said to correspond to the result of the statistical decision. For example, suppose that two identical studies are conducted to test the efficacy of an educational treatment. Table 3 illustrates the four possible configurations

Table 3

Possible outcomes configurations of two studies addressing the same research question

	Results of hypothesis test	
Configuration	Study 1	Study 2
A	Significant	Significant
B	Not significant	Not significant
C	Significant	Not significant
D	Not significant	Significant

of outcomes of the two studies. Many researchers would agree that configurations A and B represent cases of "consistent" results or replication of a finding. Most would say that configuration A provides clear evidence of the consistent effectiveness of the treatment whereas configuration B provides clear evidence of the consistent ineffectiveness of the treatment. Configurations C and D, conventional logic would imply, show evidence of failure to replicate and inconsistency in the effect of the treatment. Two examples show that the conventional logic is incorrect.

Suppose that each of two experiments use two equal-sized groups (control and treatment) of 32 students each, for a total n of 64 in each study. Suppose also that the treatment produces a true (population) mean difference of one-half standard deviation (a "moderate" effect). If statistical hypothesis tests are conducted on the outcome measures at the usual $\alpha = 0.05$ significance level, then each of the four configurations of outcomes is equally likely! That is, despite the fact that the treatment produces a consistent and moderately large population effect in both studies, there is only a 25 percent chance that the outcomes of the studies would appear to support a consistent positive treatment effect. It is equally likely that the outcomes would appear to favor consistently no effect of the treatment.

Suppose that two other experiments are performed, and that the treatment again produces a true (population) mean difference of one-half standard deviation (moderate effect for the treatment). But suppose that the two experiments now use a sample size of only 20 students in each group, for a total n of 40 for each experiment. Under these conditions, configuration A has only an 11 percent chance of occurring. Configuration B has a 45 percent chance of occurring, and each of configurations C and D will happen 22 percent of the time. Thus, although there *is* a consistent and moderately large positive effect of the treatment, the least likely outcome of the two studies is configuration A which appears to support the consistent effectiveness of the treatment. Configuration B of results, which appears to support the ineffectiveness of the treatment is more than four times as likely to occur as the configuration of results (A) that appears to support the correct conclusion!

The source of the problem in these two examples is the probabilistic nature of the statistical tests of significance. Sometimes statistical tests reach the correct conclusion about the effectiveness of a treatment, but sometimes they do not. When studies have sample sizes that are small to moderate and the true effect of the treatment is small to moderate, statistical tests are likely to have low power, that is a small chance of correctly detecting a real treatment effect. In research on teaching effectiveness, small sample sizes are the rule when classrooms or schools are used as the unit of analysis. And, the treatment effects of interest are also likely to be small. For example, Gage (1978) noted that the teaching–learning process is so complex that it would be unlikely that any single dimension of teacher behavior would be highly related to (or produce large effects in) pupil achievement or attitude. Yet such small effects are nonetheless of interest and practical importance.

Thus, the power of statistical tests in research on teaching effectiveness is typically very low. This implies that the pervasive error of statistical inference in such research is the failure to correctly detect a true effect of a treatment or a relationship among variables.

When many different studies all use statistical tests with low statistical power, relatively few of these studies should be expected to produce significant results even when the treatment *is* effective. Table 4 illustrates the percentage of studies that should be expected to yield significant results when the studies have the sample sizes shown. Examination of the table shows that unless sample sizes or treatment effect magnitudes are quite large, the expected proportion of significant results is not large. In most cases less than half the studies would be expected to yield significant results assuming that the treatment is effective or a relationship between variables actually exists.

A theoretical analysis of the performance of vote counting as a statistical decision method was conducted by Hedges and Olkin (1980). They assessed the performance of decision methods that conclude that a treatment is effective (or that variables are related) if the proportion of significant results exceeds some fixed

proportion. They showed that such vote counting methods tend to err frequently. Moreover, for sample sizes and effect magnitude that are typical of research on teaching effectiveness, as the number of studies to be combined increases, the probability that vote counting methods will detect a true treatment effect approaches zero!

7.2 Determining the Magnitude of Treatment Effects

A second general weakness of narrative and vote counting methods is their failure to provide any indication of the magnitude of a treatment effect or the strength of relationship between variables. As Glass (1978) characterized this deficiency: "To know that televised instruction beats traditional classroom instruction in 25 of 30 studies—if, in fact, it does—is not to know whether TV wins by a nose or in a walkaway" (p. 359). That is, the formal or informal tabulation of the numbers of statistically significant and nonsignificant results does not reveal the strength or importance of a treatment or relationship between variables.

7.3 Assessing the Consistency of Results and Resolving Contradictory Findings

A third weakness of narrative and vote counting methods is their failure to provide systematic mechanisms for assessing the consistency of results across studies and resolving contradictory findings. Inconsistency in findings is almost inevitable in any series of studies of research on teaching effectiveness. Indeed, were this not the case, the task of the research integrator would be much simplified since all the studies would produce the same results. Part of the inconsistency in findings is clearly attributable to chance, and a research synthesis method should provide some means of assessing whether the observed inconsistency in results across studies can be explained solely by chance or whether there are systematic factors (such as study characteristics) that explain this inconsistency. Narrative and vote counting methods do not provide such mechanisms.

Table 4
Percentage of studies expected to yield significant ($p < 0.05$) results for various sample sizes and effect magnitudes

Total sample size	Effect magnitude					
	$\rho^a = 0.1$ (small)	$\rho = 0.3$ (moderate)	$\rho = 0.5$ (large)	$\delta^b = 0.2$ (small)	$\delta = 0.5$ (moderate)	$\delta = 0.8$ (large)
10	6	13	33	6	11	20
20	7	25	64	7	18	39
30	8	37	83	8	26	56
40	9	48	92	9	33	69
50	11	57	97	11	41	79

a ρ is the population correlation   b δ is the population mean difference in standard deviation units

7.4 Overcoming the Weaknesses of Narrative and Vote Counting Methods

Light and Smith (1971) were among the first researchers to expose the weaknesses of the vote counting methods. They further noted that the apparent contradictions in research results that the research integrator finds by merely sorting studies on the basis of statistical significance might often be explained by identifiable differences in the research studies. They suggested a clustering procedure designed to help reviewers identify differences among studies, aggregate results within similar clusters, and thus resolve apparent contradictions. Unfortunately, their approach requires access to the original data of the study, a requirement that makes the method unfeasible for most research reviews.

Two other approaches that attempt to overcome the weaknesses of the narrative and vote counting methods are described next (see Sects. 8, 9, 10, and 11): combined significance test methods and effect magnitude procedures.

8. Combined Significance Test Methods

Combined significance test methods of research synthesis involve combining either the probabilities (*p*-values) or common test of significance statistics (*t*-ratio, chi-square, *z*-scores, etc.) across several studies addressing the same research question and assessing the statistical significance of this overall value. Some of these combined significance test methods have existed since the early 1930s; others are recent developments. It was an increasing emphasis on the weaknesses of vote counting methods that sparked new interest in these methods. Rosenthal (1978) provided an excellent description of the procedures, advantages, limitations, and applicability of nine combined significance test methods: (a) adding logs; (b) adding *p*'s; (c) adding *t*'s; (d) adding *Z*'s; (e) adding weighted *Z*'s; (f) testing mean *p*; (g) testing mean *Z*; (h) counting; and (i) blocking. He also gave several computational examples of how to use these methods.

The specific strength of combined significance test methods is that they help eliminate the problem of low

power to detect treatment effects inherent in the vote counting method. Small sample sizes result in low power, but these combined significance test methods effectively increase sample size (by pooling *n*'s across studies) and thereby increase the probability that a true treatment effect will be detected.

8.1 Summarizing Results Across Studies

Summarizing results across studies in combined significance test methods is a fairly straightforward process; the probability associated with the combined index across studies is described as the treatment effect or the relationship between variables. The information contained in Table 5 can be used to illustrate three of the nine methods described by Rosenthal (1978). The table contains data from six hypothetical two-group (experimental versus control) experiments in which the researcher performed a *t*-test. The *t*-ratio and degrees of freedom (*df*) for each of the six experiments are given. The one-tailed *p*-value (probability) for each of the given *t*-ratios and associated *df* were taken from a table (found in most statistics textbooks) showing the *p*-values for various values of *t*. The *Z*'s in Table 5 were taken from the standard normal ("normal curve") table found in most statistics texts. That is, for each *p*-value in Table 5, the corresponding *z*-score was recorded.

(a) *Method of adding t's.* The formula for adding *t*'s is given by:

$$Z = \frac{\Sigma t}{\sqrt{\Sigma[df/(df-2)]}} \tag{1}$$

In this example,

$$Z = \frac{13.45}{\sqrt{(30/28 + 25/23 + 20/18 + 25/23 + 40/38 + 15/13)}}$$
$$= 5.25 \tag{2}$$

Using the values in the standard normal table, it can be seen that the *p*-value associated with this value of *Z* is 0.0001. That is, although the *p*-values associated with two of the six studies were not signifi-

Table 5
Data from six hypothetical studies used to illustrate combined significance test methods[a]

Study	*t*-ratio	*df*	*p*	*Z*
1	2.46	30	0.01	2.326
2	1.32	25	0.10	1.282
3	0.68	20	0.25	0.674
4	1.71	25	0.05	1.645
5	5.13	40	0.001	3.090
6	2.15	15	0.025	1.96
	$\Sigma t = 13.45$	$\Sigma df = 155$	$\Sigma p = 0.436$	$\Sigma z = 10.98$
	Mean = 2.24	Mean = 25.83	Mean = 0.073	Mean = 1.83

a Source: Rosenthal (1978)

cant ($p = 0.10, 0.25$), the combined results across studies is highly statistically significant.

(b) *Method of testing the mean p.* The formula for testing the significance of the average p-value across studies is given by:

$$Z = (0.50 - \bar{p})(\sqrt{12N}) \tag{3}$$

where $\bar{p}$ = average p across studies and N = number of studies.

In this example,

$$Z = (0.50 - 0.073)[\sqrt{(12)(6)}] = 3.62 \tag{4}$$

The values in the standard normal table show that a Z of 3.62 has a probability value of 0.001. Again, the combined results across studies suggests that there is a highly statistically significant treatment effect.

(c) *Method of adding Z's (unweighted).* The formula for testing the significance of combining Z's is given by:

$$Z = \frac{\Sigma Z}{\sqrt{N}} \tag{5}$$

where N = number of studies.

In this example, $Z = 10.98/2.45 = 4.48$. The p-value associated with this Z is 0.0001.

Thus, the three methods of combined significance testing show that across studies there is a highly significant treatment effect, even though the results of two of the six individual studies were not statistically significant. The reader should consult Rosenthal (1978) for a description of all nine methods and when it is most appropriate to use each.

8.2 Assessing the Consistency of Results Across Studies

Combined significance test methods of research synthesis provide no systematic mechanism for assessing the degree of consistency of results across studies. Indeed, the process of pooling probabilities across studies tends to mask any inconsistencies in findings. For example, the overall indices computed for the data in Table 5 were statistically significant, but one-third of the studies actually showed no statistically significant results. Yet these methods provided no means for addressing this inconsistency.

8.3 Resolving Contradictory Findings Across Studies

The explanation of contradictory findings across studies is not central to most combined significance test methods. Again, the process of pooling probabilities across studies tends to obfuscate conflicting findings and there is no systematic method of resolving such conflicting results. Rosenthal (1978) did, however, describe a blocking procedure that allows the research integrator to search for moderator variables.

9. Weaknesses of Combined Significance Test Methods

The major weaknesses of combined significance test methods are: (a) their failure to provide any indication of the magnitude of a treatment effect or degree of relationship between variables, and (b) their inability to provide mechanisms for explaining variability of results across studies in terms of study characteristics.

Thus, combined significance test methods improve on the first weakness of narrative and vote counting methods (low power), but not on the second and third weaknesses (not providing index of effect magnitude and not assessing consistency/resolving conflicting findings).

10. Effect Magnitude Methods

Glass (1976) coined the term "meta-analysis" to refer to methods of research synthesis that are quantitative and statistical in nature. At the heart of the techniques proposed by Glass is the concept of "effect magnitude," that is, a standardized numerical index of the strength of the treatment effect or degree of relationship between variables that can be derived for individual studies or independent findings within studies. These standardized indices of effect magnitude can then be combined across studies to produce an overall index of treatment effect. Much recent work on research synthesis (e.g., Hedges 1981, 1982a, 1982b) has been aimed at the development of statistical theory for indices of effect magnitude, ways of optimally combining effect magnitude indices, and methods for determining the consistency of effect magnitude indices across studies. The specific strength of effect magnitude procedures (as they are currently evolving and not as they have been used in the recent past) is that they provide mechanisms for dealing with all three of the aims of research synthesis.

10.1 Indices of Effect Magnitude

Indices of effect magnitude used in research synthesis should satisfy two conditions. First, the value of the index should depend only on the properties of the constructs or variables that are being investigated, not on properties of the studies (such as sample size) used to investigate those constructs. This requirement effectively eliminates p-values and test statistics that depend on sample size. A second consideration in the selection of indices of effect magnitude is that the value of the index should not depend on the particular test or procedures used to measure underlying constructs in a study. That is, the value of the index of effect magnitude should be unaffected if the scores on a particular test were replaced by scores on an equivalent (perfectly correlated) test. Therefore indices such as raw regression coefficients, or raw mean differences are unacceptable as indices of effect magnitude because regression coefficients and mean differences depend on the variance of the particular test or other measurement used as the dependent variable.

Two indices of effect magnitude that satisfy these conditions have been found to be useful in research synthesis: (a) In studies where the independent and dependent variables are measured continuously (e.g., correlational studies), the index of effect magnitude is the population value of the correlation coefficient (ρ). The following guidelines (Cohen 1969) are often used in assessing the magnitude of the effect represented by the population value of the correlation coefficient.

small effect: $\rho = 0.1$
moderate effect: $\rho = 0.3$
large effect: $\rho = 0.5$

(b) In studies that use a two-group design (experimental/control), the index of effect magnitude is the population value of the standardized mean difference or effect size. If the population mean of the scores in the experimental and control groups of the ith study are μ_i^E and μ_i^C, respectively, and σ_i is the population standard deviation of the scores within the groups of the ith experiment, then the effect size δ_i is defined as

$$\delta_i = \frac{\mu_i^E - \mu_i^C}{\sigma_i} \tag{6}$$

A positive value of the effect size means that the performance of subjects in the experimental group exceeded that of subjects in the control group; a negative value of the effect size indicates that, on the average, the control group outperformed the experimental group. Effect sizes can be interpreted as the z-score for the average person in the experimental group relative to the average performance of persons in the control group. Thus (because z-scores have a mean of 0, and a standard deviation of 1.0), a positive effect size of 0.50 indicates that the average score of a person in the experimental group is one-half a standard deviation higher than that of the average student in the control group. Alternatively, because z-scores can be translated into percentile ranks, an effect size can be interpreted as the percentile rank of the performance of the average person in the experimental group relative to the average control subject's performance. For example, an effect size of 0.50 indicates that if the performance of the average person in the control group is considered to be at the 50th percentile, the performance of the average person in the experimental group is at the 69th percentile. A more complete discussion of the interpretation of effect sizes is available in Glass (1978).

The following guidelines (Cohen 1969) are sometimes used in assessing the magnitude of effect sizes from two-group experiments.

small effect: $\delta = 0.2$
moderate effect: $\delta = 0.5$
large effect: $\delta = 0.8$

It is important to note that the two indices of effect magnitude just described (population correlation coefficient and effect size) are population parameters. That

is, they are the "true" values that would be obtained if the information was available for all subjects in the population of interest. Research synthesis always deals with samples, the subjects within individual studies are a sample of a larger population and the collection of studies is itself only a sample of all possible studies. Thus, quantitative methods of research synthesis use data contained in research reports to draw inferences about (estimate) the population effect magnitudes.

10.2 Estimating Effect Magnitude from a Single Study

Methods for estimating effect magnitude from a collection of studies involve combining the estimates of effect magnitude obtained from each of the studies. Thus, one of the first steps in these research synthesis methods is to calculate an unbiased estimate of the population effect magnitude for the results reported in each study. Two sample estimates of effect magnitude correspond to the two population indices of effect magnitude just described.

(a) The best estimate of a population correlation (ρ) is the sample correlation *(r)*. Thus the estimate of effect magnitude from a correlational study is just the sample correlation coefficient (*r* value) reported in the study. Sometimes researchers do not report the results of a correlational study as an *r* value (Pearson product moment correlation coefficient), but rather as summary statistics such as point-biserial correlations, Mann–Whitney *U*, chi-square, contingency coefficient, and so on. Because effect magnitude methods of research synthesis involve combining similar standardized indices of effect magnitude, it is important to convert these various statistics to *r* values before they can be combined. Glass (1978) has provided simplified guidelines for converting a variety of summary statistics into *r* values. Table 6 shows hypothetical *r* values from six correlational studies of the same research problem. The other information in Table 6 will be used to illustrate subsequent discussions about combining *r* values across a collection of studies.

(b) The best estimate of an effect size δ is slightly more complicated than the estimate of the population correlation. The obvious estimate of the population effect size for a study is the sample effect size defined by

$$\frac{\overline{X}^E - \overline{X}^C}{S} \tag{7}$$

where $\overline{X}^E$ and $\overline{X}^C$ are the experimental and control group sample means, respectively, and S is the pooled within-group standard deviation. But Hedges (1981) has shown that the estimate Eqn. 7 of the effect size is biased and requires a slight downward correction. Thus the best estimate of the effect size from a single study is

$$g = c\frac{\overline{X}^E - \overline{X}^C}{S} \tag{8}$$

Table 6
Data from six hypothetical correlational studies used to illustrate effect magnitude procedures

| Study | Study characteristics | | | r_i | z_i | n_i | $n_i - 3$ | $(n_i - 3)z_i$ | $(n_i - 3)z_i^2$ |
	A	B	C						
1	Yes	Yes	Yes	0.54	0.604	45	42	25.368	15.322
2	Yes	No	Yes	0.28	0.288	35	32	9.216	2.654
3	Yes	Yes	No	0.46	0.497	40	37	18.389	9.139
4	No	No	No	0.12	0.121	50	47	5.687	0.688
5	No	Yes	Yes	−0.15	−0.151	45	42	−6.342	0.958
6	No	No	Yes	0.34	0.354	30	27	9.558	3.383
							$\Sigma(n_i - 3) = 227$	$\Sigma(n_i - 3)z_i = 61.876$	$\Sigma(n_i - 3)z_i^2 = 32.144$

r_i is the correlation coefficient for study i
z_i is the Fisher z-transform of correlation r_i for study i
n_i is the sample size for study i

where c (the correction factor) is given by

$$c = 1 - \frac{3}{4n^E + 4n^C - 9} \tag{9}$$

and n^E and n^C are the experimental and control group sample sizes respectively. Note that the value of the correction factor c depends on the sample size, and the value of this correction factor will change from study to study.

Computing an unbiased sample estimate of an effect size can be illustrated with the information shown in Table 7. Table 7 contains hypothetical summary data from six two-group experiments on the same research question. The c_is (correction factors) shown in the table were computed very simply using the n^E and n^C and the formula given in Eqn. (9). For example, for study 1,

$$c_1 = 1 - \frac{3}{4(40) + 4(40) - 9} = 0.990 \tag{10}$$

The effect size (g_1) for study 1 would be computed as follows:

$$g_1 = (0.990)\frac{(10.935 - 8.648)}{7.889} = 0.287 \tag{11}$$

Unfortunately, researchers sometimes fail to report one or more of the pieces of information needed to compute an unbiased estimate of effect size (means, pooled standard deviation, n's). For example, a researcher might report only the t value from a t-test, the n's, and the significance level. Glass et al. (1981), however, have given a number of formulas for obtaining an uncorrected estimate of effect size from various test statistics that may be reported.

10.3 Summarizing Results Across Studies

Once the research integrator has computed an index of effect magnitude for each study (or independent finding within a study), he or she is faced with the task of optimally combining indices of effect magnitude across

studies to produce the best estimate of the population values of effect magnitude. Some research integrators have reported simple averages of indices of effect magnitude across studies (e.g., Peterson 1979, Kulik et al. 1980); other research integrators have calculated averages weighted by the sample size used in each study (e.g., Redfield and Rousseau 1981). Intuitively, it seems that studies with larger sample sizes should provide more accurate information about effect size than studies with smaller sample sizes and should therefore be weighted more heavily in overall estimates of effect magnitude across studies. Hedges (1981) demonstrated that this intuition is correct, and that the best estimate of effect magnitude across studies is always a weighted average of the estimates of effect magnitude from each of the studies. The optimal weighted estimators of the population correlation and the population effect size are slightly different.

(a) *Weighted estimates of the population correlation.* Let $r_1, r_2, \ldots, r_k$ denote the correlation coefficients from k studies with sample sizes $n_1, n_2, \ldots, n_k$. The first step is to obtain the Fisher z-transforms of each of the correlations (since r values should never be directly averaged). The Fisher z-transform for r values is given by

$$z_i = \frac{1}{2}\log\left(\frac{1 + r_i}{1 - r_i}\right) \tag{12}$$

Many statistics textbooks contain a table showing the Fisher z-transforms for values of r, so these need not be directly calculated.

If the correlations across studies are homogeneous, the best estimate of the population correlation corresponds to the z value (i.e., is the r that gives a z value) of

$$z. = \frac{\displaystyle\sum_{i=1}^{k}(n_i - 3)z_i}{\displaystyle\sum_{i=1}^{k}(n_i - 3)} \tag{13}$$

Table 7
Data from six hypothetical two-group experimental studies used to illustrate effect magnitude procedures

Study	Study characteristics A	B	C	$\bar{X}_i^E$	$\bar{X}_i^C$	$n^E = n^C$	S_i	c_i	g_i	v_i	$v_i g_i$	$v_i g_i^2$
1	Yes	Yes	Yes	10.935	8.648	40	7.889	0.990	0.287	19.796	5.681	1.631
2	Yes	No	Yes	15.213	13.984	60	2.283	0.994	0.535	28.964	15.496	8.290
3	Yes	Yes	Yes	7.889	6.039	30	2.403	0.987	0.760	13.990	10.632	8.081
4	No	No	Yes	11.910	9.105	50	6.170	0.992	0.451	24.380	10.995	4.959
5	No	Yes	Yes	5.417	3.065	30	3.364	0.987	0.690	14.157	9.769	6.740
6	No	No	No	16.216	16.973	60	5.375	0.994	-0.140	29.927	-4.190	0.586
										$\Sigma v_i = 131.214$	$\Sigma v_i g_i = 48.383$	$\Sigma v_i g_i^2 = 30.287$

$\bar{X}_i^E$ is the mean performance of the experimental group in study i
$\bar{X}_i^C$ is the mean performance of the control group in study i
n^E, n^C are the sample sizes for the experimental and control groups in study i
S_i is the pooled within group standard deviation in study i
c_i is the correction factor for study i
g_i is the effect size estimate for study i

The information contained in Table 6 can be used to illustrate how the overall $z.$ is computed. First, each of the r values for the six studies were converted to $z_i s$, using a Fisher z-transform table in a statistics textbook. For example, in study 1 the r of 0.54 corresponds to a z of 0.604. Next, the value $(n_i - 3)$ was computed for each study. This was simply the total sample size for that study minus 3. Then, the value $(n_i - 3) z_i$ was calculated for each study. This value weights each z_i by the study's sample size and is simply the $(n_i - 3)$ for each study multiplied by the z_i for each study. For example, in study 2, the z_i of 0.288 multiplied by the $(n_i - 3)$ of 32 equals 9.216, the $(n_i - 3) z_i$ value for that study.

Finally, the overall $z.$ was computed by adding together the $(n_i - 3) z_i$ values for the six studies and dividing by the sum of the $(n_i - 3)$ values for the six studies, so that $z. = 61.876 \div 227 = 0.27$.

Converting this $z.$ back to an r value (again using the Fisher z-transform tables), shows that the estimate of the average population correlation for these six studies is 0.265. This would be described as a small to moderate effect (Cohen 1969). However, this average correlation should be interpreted cautiously until it has been established that the correlations from each study that entered the average are homogeneous.

Once the research integrator has calculated an overall estimate of the population correlation across studies, he or she may want to either: (i) calculate a confidence interval for ρ or (ii) test the specific hypothesis that the overall population correlation is different from zero.

(i) If the correlations across studies are homogeneous, a $100(1 - \alpha)$ percent confidence interval for z_ρ, the z-transformed value of the population correlation ρ' is given by

$$z. - c_{\alpha/2}\sigma_z \le z_\rho \le z. + c_{\alpha/2}\sigma_z \tag{14}$$

where $c_{\alpha/2}$ is the $100(1 - \alpha/2)$ percent critical value from the standard normal table and

$$\sigma_z^2 = \frac{1}{\sum_{i=1}^{k}(n_i - 3)} \tag{15}$$

The confidence interval establishes the range of values that would contain the true population correlation with a given probability. For example, a 95 percent confidence interval for the z_ρ calculated from the data in Table 6 would be computed as follows. The value $c_{\alpha/2}$ is taken from the standard normal table found in most statistics books. A 95 percent confidence interval corresponds to $\alpha = 0.05$, so $\alpha/2 = 0.025$ and therefore $c_{\alpha/2} = 1.96$. (A 99 percent confidence interval corresponds to $\alpha = 0.01$, so $\alpha/2 = 0.005$ and $c_{\alpha/2} = 2.58$.)

The value $\sigma_z = 0.66$, which is simply the square root of 1 divided by the sum of the $(n_i - 3)$ for the six studies. Thus, a 95 percent confidence interval for $z. = 0.27$

is given by:

$$0.27 - (1.96)(0.066) \le z_\rho \le 0.27$$
$$+ (1.96)(0.066)$$
$$0.141 \le z_\rho \le 0.399 \tag{16}$$

(ii) A test statistic for testing the hypothesis that the common correlation is different from zero is

$$T_z = z./\sigma_z \tag{17}$$

If $|T_z|$ exceeds the $100(1 - \alpha/2)$ percent critical value of the standard normal distribution the hypothesis that the common correlation, ρ, is equal to zero is rejected at the 100α percent significance level.

For example, using the data in Table 6, $T_z = 0.27/0.066 = 4.09$. The critical value from the standard normal table for $\alpha = 0.05$ ($\alpha/2 = 0.025$) is 1.96. Therefore, since the value of T_z is greater than this critical value, the hypothesis that the population correlation is equal to zero is rejected. The combined results of the six studies support the conclusion that there is a relationship between the variables in question.

(b) *Weighted estimates of the population effect size.* The logic described for combining and testing estimates of the population correlation applies also to combining estimates of the population effect size, but the procedures are different. Let $g_1, g_2. . ., g_k$ be the estimates of effect size based on k studies and let n_i^E and n_i^C be the experimental and control group sample sizes in the ith experiment. If the effect sizes are homogeneous, the best estimate of the common effect size δ from k studies is

$$g. = \frac{\sum_{i=1}^{k} v_i g_i}{\sum_{i=1}^{k} v_i} \tag{18}$$

where the v_i are defined by

$$v_i = \frac{2n_i^E n_i^C(n_i^E + n_i^C)}{2(n_i^E + n_i^C)^2 + g_i^2 n_i^E n_i^C} \tag{19}$$

The information contained in Table 7 can be used to illustrate how the overall $g.$ is computed. The v_i for each study shown in the Table were computed simply by manipulating the experimental and control group sample sizes (n^E and n^C) and the effect size (g_i) for that study. For example, for study 1,

$$v_1 = \frac{(2)(40)(40)(40 + 40)}{2(40 + 40)^2 + (0.287)^2(40)(40)}$$
$$= 19.796 \tag{20}$$

The $v_i g_i$ for each study were simply the v_i value for that study multiplied by the g_i value for that study. For example, for study 1,

$$v_i g_i = (19.796)(0.287)$$
$$= 5.681 \tag{21}$$

137

The overall $g.$ across studies was computed by adding the $v_i g_i$ for the six studies and dividing by the sum of the v_i for the studies. Thus, $g. = 48.383/131.214 = 0.37$. This $g.$ could be described as a small to moderate treatment effect (Cohen 1969). Again, this average effect size should be interpreted cautiously until it has been established that the effect sizes from each study that entered that average are homogeneous.

The logic of calculating a confidence interval for the population effect size and testing the hypothesis that the population effect size is different from zero is the same as that for population correlations described earlier, but the procedures are different.

(i) If the effect sizes are homogeneous, a $100(1 - \alpha)$ percent confidence interval for the common effect size δ is given by

$$g. - c_{\alpha/2} \sigma_g \leq \delta \leq g. + c_{\alpha/2} \sigma_g \qquad (22)$$

where $c_{\alpha/2}$ is the $100(1 - \alpha/2)$ percent critical value from the standard normal distribution and σ_g^2 is given by

$$\sigma_g^2 = \frac{1}{\sum\limits_{i=1}^{k} v_i} \qquad (23)$$

For example, using the information in Table 7, the $g.$ previously calculated, and the value of $c_{\alpha/2}$ reported in the standard normal table, a 95 percent confidence interval for δ is given by:

$$0.37 - (1.96)(0.087) \leq \delta \leq 0.37$$
$$+ (1.96)(0.087)$$
$$0.195 \leq \delta \leq 0.545 \qquad (24)$$

(ii) A statistic for testing the hypothesis that the common effect size is different from zero is

$$T_g = g./\sigma_g \qquad (25)$$

If $|T_g|$ exceeds the $100(1 - \alpha/2)$ percent critical value of the standard normal distribution, the hypothesis that the common effect size, δ, is equal to zero is rejected at the 100α percent significance level.

For example, for the studies in Table 7, $T_g = 0.37/0.087 = 4.25$. The critical value from the standard normal table for $\delta = 0.05$ ($\delta/2 = 0.025$) is 1.96. Therefore, since the value of T_g is greater than the critical value, the hypothesis that the population treatment effect is equal to zero is rejected. The combined results of the six studies support the conclusion that there *is* a significant treatment effect.

10.4 Assessing the Consistency (Homogeneity) of Effect Magnitude Across Studies

Indices of effect magnitude inevitably vary in size across studies; some are large and positive, others are near zero, some are negative. Before averaging these indices of effect magnitude across studies, the research integrator should assess whether an average effect mag-

nitude is a good representation of a common underlying effect magnitude, that is, whether the observed variability in indices of effect magnitude can be explained solely by chance variation.

Until recently, the research integrator had no systematic statistical means of assessing the consistency or homogeneity of effect magnitude indices across studies. Some earlier research syntheses (Kulik et al. 1980, Cohen 1981) plotted the distribution of effect magnitude indices, as an informal way of pictorially assessing the variability in these effect magnitude indices. Hedges (1982a, 1982b) recently developed systematic statistical tests of the homogeneity of effect magnitude. A statistical test for homogeneity of effect magnitude should always be used before describing the average effect magnitude as the effect of a teaching variable. Two tests of the homogeneity of effect magnitude correspond to the two indices of effect magnitude (population correlation and population effect size).

(a) The statistic for testing homogeneity of correlations is given by

$$H_z = \sum_{i=1}^{k} (n_i - 3)(z_i - z.)^2 \qquad (26)$$

where $z.$ is given by equation (13).

The formula above illustrates that H_z is essentially a weighted sum of squared deviations of the z_i from the weighted mean $z.$. Although equation (26) is useful in showing the intuitive nature of the statistic, H_z is easier to calculate using the computational formula

$$H_z = \sum_{i=1}^{k} (n_i - 3) z_i^2 -$$
$$\left(\sum_{i=1}^{k} (n_i - 3) z_i \right)^2 \Big/ \left(\sum_{i=1}^{k} (n_i - 3) \right) \qquad (27)$$

The statistic H_z has the chi-square distribution with $(k - 1)$ degrees of freedom when the k correlations are homogeneous. Thus if the value of H_z exceeds the $100(1 - \alpha)$ percent critical value of the chi-square distribution with $(k - 1)$ degrees of freedom, the homogeneity of the correlations is rejected at the 100α percent significance level.

Using the data in Table 6, $H_z = 32.144 - [(61.876)^2/227] = 15.278$.

The critical value to which the value $H_z = 15.278$ was to be compared to determine if it was large enough to reject the hypothesis that the correlations were homogeneous was taken from the chi-square distribution table (found in most statistics texts) for $\alpha = 0.01$ and degrees of freedom (df) equal to the number of studies minus one, in this case, five. The critical value in this example was 15.10. Because H_z exceeded this critical value, the hypothesis of homogeneity must be rejected for these six correlations. If homogeneity of the correlations is rejected, then it does not make sense to speak of a common underlying correlation or to pool the correlations across studies to obtain an estimate of the single (nonexistent) underlying effect magnitude. Thus the average z of 0.27 ($r_z = 0.265$) that was computed earlier for the six studies in Table 6 cannot be accepted as *the* one true population correlation for the variables in question. In this case the research integrator must search for characteristics that differentiate studies and look for clusters of studies that do have homogeneous correlations. The test of homogeneity of correlations provides one test for establishing homogeneity of correlations for these clusters of studies. Other techniques used by research integrators to resolve such conflicting findings across studies are described in a subsequent section of this article.

(b) The statistic for testing homogeneity of independent effect sizes is given by

$$H_g = \sum_{i=1}^{i} v_i (g_i - g_\cdot)^2 \qquad (28)$$

where $g_\cdot$ is defined by equation (18).

The formula above illustrates that H_g is a weighted sum of squared deviations of the g_i from the weighted mean $g_\cdot$. Equation (28) makes the intuitive nature of H_g clear, but it is easier to compute the value of H_g using the computational formula

$$H_g = \sum_{i=1}^{k} v_i g_i^2 - \left(\sum_{i=1}^{k} v_i g_i \right)^2 \bigg/ \left(\sum_{i=1}^{k} v_i \right) \qquad (29)$$

The statistic H_g has the chi-square distribution with $(k-1)$ degrees of freedom when the k effect sizes are homogeneous. Thus if the value of H_g exceeds the $100(1-\alpha)$ percent critical value of the chi-square distribution with $(k-1)$ degrees of freedom, homogeneity of the effect sizes is rejected at the 100α percent significance level.

Using the data in Table 7, $H_g = 30.287 - [(48.383)^2/131.214] = 12.446$.

The critical value to which the value of H_g was to be compared to determine if it was large enough to reject the hypothesis that the effect sizes were homogeneous was taken from the chi-square distribution table for $\alpha = 0.05$ and degrees of freedom (*df*) equal to the number of studies (*k*) minus one, in this case, five. The critical value in this example was 11.10. Because H_g exceeded this critical value, the hypothesis of homogeneity must be rejected for these six effect sizes.

If homogeneity of the effect sizes is rejected, it does not make sense to speak of a common underlying effect size or to pool effect size estimates to obtain an estimate of the single (nonexistent) underlying effect size. Thus the average effect size, $g_\cdot = 0.37$ that was computed earlier for the six studies in Table 7 cannot be accepted as the one true population treatment effect for the variables in question. In this case the research integrator must search for characteristics that differentiate the studies and lead to clusters of studies that do have homogeneous effect sizes. The next section describes ways to resolve such conflicting findings across studies.

10.5 Resolving Contradictory Findings Across Studies with Effect Magnitude Procedures

Two major approaches have been used by research integrators who use effect magnitude procedures to resolve conflicting findings across studies (or explain widely variable indices of effect magnitude). The first step in both these approaches is to identify characteristics of studies that might plausibly be systematically related to treatment effects. Table 1 described earlier lists the types of study characteristics often used.

(a) *Correlational approaches.* Some research integrators have used correlation or regression techniques to compute a summary index of the extent to which study characteristics are related to indices of effect magnitude. For example, Kulik et al. (1980), in their research synthesis of studies of the effects of computer-based college teaching, found small to near zero correlations between study characteristics such as duration of the treatment, year the study was published, course level, random assignment of comparison groups, and so on and effect sizes for achievement.

(b) *Cluster approaches.* Other research integrators have computed average indices of effect magnitude separately for clusters of studies defined by a study characteristic. For example, Redfield and Rousseau (1981), in their research synthesis of studies of the effects of cognitive level of teacher questioning on pupil achievement, computed average effect sizes separately for studies classified as either "sufficiently valid" or "insufficiently valid" on the basis of the design of the study. They also calculated average effect sizes separately for training studies and skills studies, on the basis of how the independent variable was manipulated.

The two tests of homogeneity of effect magnitude described earlier can provide a basis for establishing homogeneity of effect magnitude for these separate clusters of studies. The research integrator may then conclude that a treatment produces a consistent effect or there is consistent relationship between variables for studies with given characteristics, but that the effect is different for other studies. For example the research integrator might find that studies which are randomized experiments yield a consistent effect of a treatment on achievement, while the nonrandomized quasi-experiments do not yield consistent effects for the treatment. Such results were obtained in a synthesis of the effects of open education on self-concept (Hedges et al. 1981).

The data contained in Tables 6 and 7 can be used to illustrate this use of the homogeneity tests. Table 6 includes information on three characteristics (A, B, and C) of the six hypothetical correlational studies. These characteristics might be any of those given in Table 1. Each of these hypothetical characteristics of the studies is coded using a yes/no dichotomy, that is, the characteristic was or was not present in each study. Because the overall homogeneity statistics, H_z, that was calculated earlier indicated that the correlations from the six studies were not homogeneous, the research integrator should test for homogeneous subsets or clusters of the six studies.

Examination of the correlations with respect to the study characteristics suggests that studies with characteristic A have much higher correlations than studies that do not have characteristic A. Thus it might be asked whether the correlations are homogeneous among the studies that have characteristic A. The entries in the last three columns of Table 6 can be used to calculate · the value of the homogeneity statistics H_{z1} for the studies that have characteristic A, and the value of the homogeneity statistic H_{z2} for studies that do not have characteristic A, using the formula given in (27). The values obtained are $H_{z1} = 1.834$ and $H_{z2} = 4.346$.

Comparing these values with the 95 percent critical value of the chi-square distribution with 2 degrees of freedom, it can be seen that the correlations *may* be considered to be homogeneous within the two groups of studies. Thus it makes sense to calculate an average estimate of the correlation within the two groups of studies separately. For the studies that have characteristic A, the average estimate of $z_{\rho1}$ is 0.477 using equation (13), and 95 percent confidence interval for $z_{\rho1}$ using equation (14) is $0.291 \leqslant z_{\rho1} < 0.663$. For the studies that do not have characteristic A, the pooled estimate of $z_{\rho2}$ is 0.077, and 95 percent confidence interval is $-0.105 \leqslant z_{\rho2} \leqslant 0.259$.

Thus, the research integrator could conclude that when characteristic A is present, the overall relationships between variables is moderate to large. When characteristic A is not present, the relationship is small to near zero.

Table 7 includes a yes/no dichotomous coding of three characteristics (A, B, and C) that the six hypothetical experimental studies might have. Because the overall homogeneity statistic, H_g that was computed earlier indicated that the effect sizes from the six experimental studies were not homogeneous, the research integrator should test for homogeneous clusters of the six studies. Examination of the effect size estimates from each study suggests that studies one through five have similar effect sizes while the effect size for study six appears to be different. Furthermore, study six is the only study that does not have characteristic C. Therefore an attempt may be made to estimate the effect size for studies one to five, that is, for studies with characteristic C. The value of the homogeneity statistic for the first five studies, using equation (29), is $H_g = 2.413$. Comparing this value with the 95 percent critical value of the chi-square distribution with four degrees of freedom, it can be seen that the homogeneity of effect sizes in the first five studies cannot be rejected, that is, the five effect sizes are homogeneous. Thus the average effect size for these five studies using equation (18) can be calculated to obtain $g. = 0.519$. A 95 percent confidence interval for δ based on the first five studies, using equation (22) is $0.324 \leqslant \delta \leqslant 0.714$. The research integrator might therefore conclude that when characteristic C is present, there is a moderate treatment effect.

11. General Weaknesses of Effect Magnitude Procedures

The research synthesis methods that rely on indices of effect magnitude have been portrayed in this article as superior to narrative, vote counting, and even combined significance test methods. Yet, these effect magnitude methods have not been received wholly uncritically by the research community. Jackson (1980) highlighted some of the criticisms of such methods. Glass et al. (1981) provided an excellent review of some of the criticisms of quantitative research synthesis methods and gave counterarguments (some supported with data) to those criticisms.

Many of the criticisms aimed at quantitative research synthesis methods are equally applicable to other research synthesis methods. For example, effect magnitude procedures are often challenged for combining the results of high quality and low quality studies. But, as was discussed earlier in describing the six tasks involved in research synthesis, whether "good" studies produce different results to "bad" studies is an empirical question. Similarly, Jackson (1980) noted that valid and reliable coding of the characteristics of the primary studies may be problematic for quantitative research synthesis methods. But *any* research synthesis method that examines study characteristics faces this problem. And, more importantly, failure to consider study characteristics at all (e.g., in some narrative and vote counting methods) is probably more a threat to the validity of conclusions than some degree of unreliability in coding study characteristics. Also, the study described earlier by Stock et al. (1982) showed that a high degree of interrater reliability in coding study characteristics *can* be achieved.

12. Do Different Research Synthesis Methods Produce Substantially Different Conclusions?

Four research synthesis methods were described in this article: narrative approaches, vote counting, combined significance test methods, and effect magnitude procedures. It was argued that combined significance test methods were superior to narrative and vote counting approaches and effect magnitude methods were superior to combined significance test approaches. Yet, the two quantitative synthesis methods involve many statistical computations and can be quite time-consuming relative to the other two approaches. The research integrator faced with many studies to be synthesized and few resources might reasonably ask, "Even if quantitative research synthesis methods are more theoretically justifiable than narrative and vote counting approaches, do they provide conclusions that are really any different to those provided by the simpler research synthesis methods?" The answer, based on some recent reviews, is: "Often, yes." Two examples will illustrate this.

2.1 Reviews of the Relation of Teacher Indirectness to Pupil Achievement

Dunkin and Biddle (1974) used a procedure that involved clinical judgment, but was based primarily on the statistical significance of reported results, to summarize the results of studies on the relation of teacher indirectness to pupil achievement, that is, they used a review approach that was a combination of narrative and vote counting. Their summaries suggested that the majority of studies (15) showed no significant relationship between teacher indirectness and pupil achievement, but also that a large number of studies (10) did show a significant relationship.

Gage (1978) applied a combined significance test procedure to 19 of the studies of teacher indirectness reviewed by Dunkin and Biddle and arrived at a very different conclusion. He converted the *p*-value reported for each study to a value of chi-square, then summed the chi-squares across studies, and determined the *p*-value associated with the overall chi-square. Results of his combined significance test showed that across studies there *was* a statistically significant relationship ($p < 0.001$) between teacher indirectness and pupil achievement.

Glass et al. (1977) applied effect magnitude procedures to the same 19 studies on teacher indirectness reviewed by Gage. He converted the results of each of the studies to an *r*-value, and averaged these effect magnitude indices separately for two groups of studies: those in which the students were in grades kindergarten to 6 and those in which students were in grades 7 to 12. Results showed that the average relationship between teacher indirectness and pupil achievement was higher for pupils in grades 7 to 12 ($r = 0.30$, "moderate" effect) than in grades kindergarten to 6 ($r = 0.16$, "small" effect).

Thus these three reviews of the relation of teacher indirectness to pupil achievement all provided different answers. Dunkin and Biddle showed that the majority of studies favored no relationship between the variables, but that results were highly inconclusive. Gage demonstrated that the relationship between variables was highly statistically significant, when combined significance test procedures were used. And Glass showed that the relationship between the variables depended on study characteristics; the effect magnitude was moderate for one subset of studies and small for another. The procedures used by Glass are probably the most informative of the three: they provide an index of effect magnitude, as well as relate study characteristics to effect magnitude.

12.2 Reviews of the Effects of Cognitive Level of Teachers' Questions on Pupil Achievement

Winne (1979) used a combination of narrative and vote counting approaches to synthesize the results of experiments of the effects of cognitive level of teachers' questions on pupil achievement. He sorted comparisons within studies into one of three categories, based on the direction and statistical significance of the results: (a) significantly favors higher cognitive questions; (b) significantly favors fact questions; or (c) no statistically significant difference. Winne reported that 15 percent of the results for all studies favored higher cognitive questions, 25 percent favored fact questions, and 60 percent favored neither. He concluded, ". . . there is no sturdy conclusion which can be offered here about the relative effectiveness of teachers' use of higher cognitive questions for enhancing student achievement" (p. 46).

Redfield and Rousseau (1981) used an effect magnitude procedure to summarize the results of 13 of the 18 studies reviewed by Winne. They computed an effect for each dependent variable for each study. They then computed average effect sizes both weighted and unweighted for the number of students studied for various groupings of studies, for example, all studies, sufficiently valid studies, and studies with a control group design. The average weighted effect size for all studies was 0.73 (moderate to large advantage for higher order questions). They concluded that there *is* a positive overall effect for predominant use of higher cognitive questions in the classroom.

A third example of how different research synthesis methods lead to different conclusions can be found in the reviews of open versus traditional instruction (see *Open Versus Formal Methods*).

See also: Ethnographic Methods

Bibliography

Bracht G, Glass G V 1968 The external validity of experiments. *Am. Educ. Res. J.* 5: 437–74

Campbell D T, Stanley J C 1966 *Experimental and Quasi-experimental Designs for Research.* Rand McNally, Chicago, Illinois

Cohen J 1969 *Statistical Power Analysis for the Behavioral Sciences.* Academic Press, New York

Cohen P A 1981 Student ratings of instruction and student achievement: A meta-analysis of multisection validity studies. *Rev. Educ. Res* 51: 281–309

Cooper H M 1982 Scientific guidelines for conducting integrative research reviews. *Rev. Educ. Res.* 52: 291–302

Cooper H M 1984 *The Integrative Literature Review: A Systematic Approach.* Sage, Beverly Hills, California

Doyle W 1978 Paradigms for research teacher effectiveness. In: Shulman L S (ed.) 1978 *Review of Research in Education.* Vol. 5. Peacock, Itasca, Illinois

Dunkin M J, Biddle B J 1974 *The Study of Teaching.* Holt, Rinehart and Winston, New York

Eysenck H J 1978 An exercise in mega-silliness. *Am. Psychol.* 33: 517

Gage N L 1978 *The Scientific Basis of the Art of Teaching.* Teachers College Press, New York

Giaconia R M, Hedges L V 1982 Identifying features of effective open education. *Rev. Educ. Res.* 52: 579–602

Glass G V 1976 Primary, secondary, and meta-analysis of research. *Educ. Res.* AERA 5: 3–8

Glass G V 1978 Integrating findings: The meta-analysis of research. In: Shulman L S (ed.) 1978 *Review of Research in Education*, Vol. 5. Peacock, Itasca, Illinois

Glass G V, Coulter D, Hartley S, Hearold S, Kahl S, Kalk J, Sherretz L 1977 Teacher "indirectness" and pupil achievement: An integration of findings. Unpublished manuscript, University of Colorado, Boulder, Colorado

Glass G V, McGaw B, Smith M L 1981 *Meta-analysis in Social Research*. Sage, Beverly Hills, California

Hedges L V 1981 Distribution theory for Glass's estimator of effect size and related estimators. *J. Educ. Stat.* 6: 107–28

Hedges L V 1982a Estimation of effect size from a series of independent experiments. *Psychol. Bull.* 92: 490–99

Hedges L V 1982b Fitting categorical models to effect sizes from a series of experiments. *J. Educ. Stat.* 7: 119–37

Hedges L V, Giaconia R M, Gage N L 1981 *Meta-analysis of the Effects of Open and Traditional Instruction*, Vol. 2. Stanford University Program on Teacher Effectiveness Meta-analysis Project, Final Report. Stanford, California

Hedges L V, Olkin I 1980 Vote-counting methods in research synthesis. *Psychol. Bull.* 88: 359–69

Hedges L V, Olkin I 1985 *Statistical Methods for Meta-academic*. Academic Press, New York

Horwitz R A 1979 Psychological effects of the "open classroom." *Rev. Educ. Res.* 49: 71–85

Jackson G B 1980 Methods for integrative reviews. *Rev. Educ. Res.* 50: 438–60

Kulik J A, Kulik C C, Cohen P A 1980 Effectiveness of computer-based college teaching: A meta-analysis of findings. *Rev. Educ. Res.* 50: 525–44

Light R J, Pillemer D B 1984 *Summing Up: The Science o Reviewing Research*. Harvard University Press, Cambridge Massachusetts

Light R J, Smith P V 1971 Accumulating evidence; Procedure for resolving contradictions among different researc studies. *Harvard Educ. Rev.* 41: 429–71

Peterson P L 1979 Direct instruction reconsidered. In: Peterso P L, Walberg H J (eds.) 1979 *Research on Teaching Concepts, Findings and Implications*. McCutchan, Berkeley California

Pillemer D B, Light R J 1980 Synthesizing outcomes: How t use research evidence from many studies. *Harvard Educ Rev.* 50: 176–95

Redfield D L, Rousseau E W 1981 A meta-analysis of exper imental research on teacher questioning behavior. *Rev Educ. Res.* 51: 237–45

Rosenthal R 1976 *Experimenter Effects in Behavior Research*. Irvington, New York

Rosenthal R 1978 Combining results of independent studies *Psychol. Bull.* 85: 185–93

Rosenthal R 1984 *Meta-analytic Procedures for Social Scienc Research*. Sage, Beverly Hills, California

Stock W A, Okum M A, Haring M J, Miller W, Kinney C Ceurvorst R W 1982 Rigor in data synthesis: A case stud of reliability in meta-analysis. *Educ. Res.* AERA 11(6): 10 14

Winne P H 1979 Experiments relating teachers' use of highe cognitive questions to student achievement. *Rev. Educ. Res* 49: 13–50

Structured Observation

M. Galton

Structured observation, as used to monitor classroom events, requires an observer to assign such events into previously defined categories. These events may be either recorded by mechanical means such as film, audiotape, or videotape and subsequently coded, or the observer can record and code the events simultaneously while present in the classroom. The three stages of the process therefore involve (a) the recording of events in a systematic manner as they happen, (b) the coding of these events into prespecified categories, and (c) subsequent analysis of the events to give descriptions of teacher–pupil interaction. Structured observation is also referred to as systematic observation or more particularly as interaction analysis, although the latter term is more usually applied to observation systems derived from the Flanders (1964) Interaction Analysis Category System (FIAC). According to Flanders, interaction analysis is a "specialized research procedure that provides information about only a few of the many aspects of teaching and which analyzes the content-free characteristics of verbal communication" (Flanders 1964 p. 198). Structured observation techniques have, however, also been used to monitor nonverbal behaviours so that

Flanders' definition of the methodology is now seen to be too restrictive.

1. The Origins of Structured Observation

The origin of these observational techniques arose, in part, from the creation of the committee of child development by the American National Research Council at the beginning of the 1920s. This committee sponsored research into teaching methods at nursery and kindergarten stages and the researchers found it necessary to observe these infants and record their behaviour "as it happened". The first attempts to do this consisted of diaries or narrative logs of the activities observed but the sheer volume of descriptive material collected made the task a very arduous one. Olson (1929) introduced the notion of time sampling whereby certain categories of behaviours were recorded at specified fixed intervals of time. Although other approaches existed (Barr 1935), an essential distinction used to classify behaviours by workers in the child development movement was that between direct teaching where pupils were told what to do and indirect teaching where pupils were consulted nd decisions reached by means of discussion and consensus. By the early 1970s, an anthology of American observation systems listed 92 instruments (Simon and Boyer 1970) of which the majority appear to be derived from FIAC (Rosenshine and Furst 1973). This system of 'Flanders' has been widely criticized, however, for its limited applicability in that it was originally designed for relatively static classrooms where teachers stood in front of pupils who were arranged before them in rows while working on the same subject matter (Silberman 1970, Hamilton and Delamont 1974). More recently, with the increase of "open" or informal approaches to classroom organization, a greater variety of observational methods have been developed. In the United Kingdom, for example, a review of observation studies (Galton 1979) identified only two systems derived from FIAC and showed that most of the research has been carried out at the primary stage of schooling where informal approaches are more likely to be found.

2. Characteristics of Structured Observation

Structured observation involves low-inference measurement (Rosenshine 1970). This requires the development of unambiguous criteria for assigning the various events into categories. Provided that the criteria are sufficiently explicit to be shared by different people, then different observers should arrive at identical descriptions of the same events. Thus an important requirement of a successful systematic observation system is high inter-observer agreement. Although the choice of categories and the definition of the criteria may be highly subjective, reflecting the values of those who construct the system, the technique is objective in the sense that the criteria used to describe classroom life are clearly defined so that when the system is used correctly it is unaffected by the personal biases of individual observers. This is in sharp contrast to ethnographic methods where the researcher, although sometimes claiming to take a total view of the classroom before gradually focusing on the more meaningful features (Hamilton and Delamont 1974), in practice, can only offer a partial view in which the criteria governing the selection are rarely available for consideration by others (see *Ethnographic Methods*).

Low-inference measurement may be contrasted with high-inference measurement where the criteria are less specific. Rating systems are the most common example of high inference measures, where an observer has to integrate his or her impressions into some global assessment of a teacher's or a pupil's performance on such dimensions as warmth, application, or sociability. Such rating systems do not give a direct record of classroom events so that no analysis of teacher and pupil behaviour is possible.

Low-inference observation schedules may be described as either category or sign systems. An observer, using a sign system of observation, is provided with a list of specific behaviours and records the occurrence of these behaviours during a given time period. Certain events are therefore ignored. The alternative approach is to use a category system of observation where the observer is provided with a list of more generalized categories and within a given unit of time classifies every behaviour which occurs into the category that is best thought to represent that behaviour. An early example of a sign system was the OSCAR observation system (Medley and Mitzel 1958) while Flanders' FIAC is an example of a category one. In practice, most modern observation schedules are combinations of category and sign systems. For example, the Pupil Record (Boydell 1975) uses a category system to code the pupils' activities but a sign system to code teacher–pupil and pupil–pupil interactions. The selection of behaviours for use in a sign system is dependent upon those which are thought to be most useful for the particular research purpose. In classroom research, such variables are selected because they are thought to be related to learning outcomes or to systematic differences between teachers and their pupils.

3. Data Collection

At first sight, the use of mechanical means of recording classroom behaviour would appear to have several advantages over the use of an observer recording and coding events as they happen. When the observer carries out direct observation in the classroom there is no permanent record of the interaction available for re-examination. Mechanical recording, using either audiotape or videotape, allows for repeated observation thereby increasing the likelihood of interobserver agreement. However, the observer in the classroom enjoys certain advantages when attempting to code more complex behaviours. After a certain amount of time the observer will come to appreciate something of the shared meanings which exist between pupils and the teacher and so will be able to interpret certain behaviours in the light of this experience. Permanent records also tend to be highly selective, focusing on the pupil or the teacher so that the listener or viewer does not know what is going on in the remainder of the classroom. A category such as "target pupil is interested in another pupil's work" might not be coded from videotape because the camera focuses directly on the target pupil and a viewer is uncertain whether the target is looking at someone elsewhere in the classroom or simply staring into space. To try to overcome this latter difficulty, two cameras are used, one focused on the teacher and one providing a general view of the classroom. Another method of producing visual cues is the use of stop-frame photography with synchronized sound (Adelman and Walker 1974). The flexibility of such systems has been greatly increased by the development of hand-held television cameras and by the use of radio microphones which, because they do not have leads, allow the teacher to move freely around the classroom and lessen the problem of background noise.

The process of transcribing the permanent record from a recording is however very tedious and time consuming. It is estimated that to transcribe one hour's audiotape takes nearly a week of an efficient typist's time. Research involving a large number of teachers will therefore tend to favour direct observation methods because of the costs involved in transcribing and processing the data. In practice, studies which seek to examine the nature of the language used by teachers and pupils tend to require a permanent record, while researchers who investigate such matters as teacher-pupil contacts, the nature of the pupil's task, and the proportion of time that is spent on it favour direct observation.

4. Training Observers

According to Flanders, one of the main problems of training observers in the use of systematic observation is "converting men into machines" (Flanders 1967 p. 158). The usual training technique is to concentrate on a few categories at a time using a teach–test and feedback–reteach cycle. Usually audiotape and videotape recording are used to introduce the observer to the problems of classifying particular categories and at the end of a training session another tape can be used to test if the observers can achieve acceptable levels of agreement. It is important to provide simple examples initially with the guarantee that most observers will obtain total mastery. Observers who fail to identify behaviours correctly during training can often develop hostile reactions to the observation instrument. It is also useful to provide observers with experience of coding under classroom conditions as soon as possible. As stated earlier, it is often difficult to identify the context in which a behaviour takes place on videotape which in turn means that the decision about the use of a particular category is not as clear cut as the trainer might wish. Once the initial training has been completed, it is important to build into any observation study refresher periods in which the observers go over the categories and check on their reliability. This is to protect against what is termed "observer drift" where observers who have come to accept criteria which do not conform to their own view of a particular behaviour gradually modify the category definitions over time to fit in with their own view.

5. Reliability and Validity

Reliability serves to indicate how free a particular measurement is of error. Two major potential sources of error in the classroom concern the extent to which two or more observers can agree in their coding of the same event—the interobserver agreement coefficient, and the degree to which the observed variation in classroom behaviour is consistent from occasion to

occasion—the teacher stability coefficient. Since the total amount of time spent observing is usually only a small fraction of the total time spent teaching, it is important to be able to demonstrate that the sample of teacher and pupil behaviour is representative.

Most studies, however, record only the observer agreement reliability. The simplest measure is the percentage of occasions on which a pair of observers agree but this does not allow for the fact that even two observers who were coding categories at random would still code the same categories on certain occasions by chance. The Scott (1955) coefficient corrects for this chance effect and is a more rigorous test of reliability. A weakness of this method, however, is that it does not permit study of observer agreement using a number of teachers. Medley and Mitzel (1963) offer a number of designs, based upon analysis of variance in which each teacher is visited on one occasion by a pair of observers such that different observers are paired on each visit. Such a design also allows the teacher stability coefficient to be estimated.

If an observation instrument is to be used by researchers other than the authors then the question of interinvestigator agreement arises, since each group may achieve high levels of observer agreement but interpret the categories differently (Rosenshine and Furst 1973). Some authors of observation systems therefore provide videotape examples already coded so that new users can check their degree of agreement with the authors on a trial tape (Eggleston et al. 1975).

Most researchers concern themselves only with the face validity of the observation instrument, assuming that the definition of the categories is so clear cut that validity may be assumed, providing observer agreement is high. The more complex the observation instrument however, the less advisable it is to take this face validity for granted. A number of alternative procedures then suggest themselves. Where cluster analysis is used to create a typology of teaching styles or pupil types then observers can be asked to write descriptive accounts (mini case studies) of the teachers and the appropriate pupils. These accounts can then be cross-referenced with the descriptions derived from the clusters. Such descriptions can also be fed back to the observed teachers who can be asked to identify their own particular style or recognize particular types of pupil present in their class. Where two different observation systems exist having a similar focus then they can be used in the same classroom to compare and contrast results. This type of cross-validation is recommended by Rosenshine and Furst (1973) but few studies have attempted this task. In the ORACLE study, however, both the teacher and the pupils were observed using two instruments and the asymmetry of classroom behaviour from both the teachers' and the pupils' perspective was contrasted (Galton et al. 1980). The same study also made it possible to compare and contrast the "real curriculum" as perceived through both the teachers' and the pupils' activity.

6. Coding and Analysis

In any observation system, discrete analytic units must be used in order to code the behaviours. The simplest division is based on some form of time sampling where the time unit may vary from three seconds, as used by Flanders, to five minutes as used in Medley and Mitzel's OSCAR schedule. Every system has its own ground rules which differentiate between the beginning and the end of successive time units and which deal with the problem of behaviours which overlap from one unit to the next. It is important to choose time units so that observed behaviours do not regularly overlap into the next unit since when this happens it is found that the degree of agreement between observers decreases rapidly. Observer agreement is also improved when a steady rhythm of recording can be maintained

Researchers using time sampling methods tend to proceed in one of two ways. Some use point sampling whereby behaviours occurring at regular time intervals are recorded. The extent to which the sample of behaviour recorded is representative of the total behaviour during the lesson is clearly dependent on the length of the interval between recordings. If the period is too short, the observers are likely to make mistakes while if the time interval is too long it may record the behaviour accurately but underestimate its overall frequency.

When difficult and complex decisions have to be made by the observer, many researchers prefer a one–zero time sampling procedure. Here the observer is required to record a behaviour only once when it occurs within a given time unit. As the time interval of a one–zero time sampling method decreases it begins to approximate to a continuous recording of classroom activity. With longer time intervals—and some researchers have used five minute units (Eggleston et al. 1975)—then only the minimum frequency of occurrence is recorded and the data cannot be used to estimate the overall occurrence of individual categories within the classroom.

The above sampling methods are generally used with sign systems. Where time sampling is used with a category system it is usual to employ a ground rule where only one category is recorded, either because it is the dominant one occurring or because it is infrequently used. If the time interval is very short, then the observer is in effect recording a change of category rather than sampling behaviour within a defined period. Recording a new behaviour every time a different category is used employs the use of what are termed naturalistic units. The problem for the researcher is to define a set of rules which will identify the unit of classroom transaction which will then be coded under a particular category. Smith and Meux (1962) defined these natural units as episodes and monologues where an episode involved more than one speaker and a monologue identified a solo performance. The ground rules for identifying the nature of the transaction, however, make it difficult, if not impossible, for an observer to use such a system live in a classroom. For this reason the use of naturalistic units is most frequently used for analysis based upon transcribed recordings. Observers can play and replay recordings until general agreement is obtained on the classification of the transaction.

When naturalistic units are used, the total number of episodes represents the total recorded behaviour, since one tally only is made for each episode. In such a case, some record of the sequence of events can be obtained but the most usual practice is to sum the number of recorded tallies for each category and to divide this sum by the total number of analytic units observed. With naturalistic units, this ratio closely represents the proportion of the total behaviour occurring in a particular category. With longer time units, when a point-time sampling procedure is used, the ratio of the sum of tallies in a particular category compared to the total number of tallies recorded can again be interpreted as a proportion of total behaviour. One–zero time sampling methods in which frequently occurring events may only be coded once during a time unit can give no absolute value for the frequency of the particular behaviour. Instead, an estimate of the minimum frequency of occurrence is obtained by dividing the total number of tallies obtained for a category by the total number of observation units.

Much criticism has recently been directed at the use of one–zero time sampling procedures and it is claimed that they seriously underestimate the total frequency by as much as 85 percent (Dunkerton 1981). Properly used, however, such systems fulfil an important function. Their main purpose is not to chart the frequency with which particular behaviours occur but to discriminate between different teachers according to their use of certain categories of behaviour. Behaviours which serve to discriminate between teachers are usually the very infrequent ones. For example, in the analysis of the Science Teacher Observation Schedule (Eggleston et al. 1976), the schedule clearly underestimates the degree to which teachers made statements of fact but even with a five-minute time sampling interval it was rare for a teacher to make problem-solving statements, to hypothesize, or to make statements concerned with the design of experimental procedure. Yet it was the latter categories which served to discriminate most sharply between teachers. Categories involving more common behaviours such as making factual statements, were retained in the schedule because they helped observer reliability. It was found that unless observers were able to code continuously they tended to become anxious and their concentration and reliability decreased. The advantage of a one–zero time sampling procedure was that the observers quickly coded the more frequently occurring categories and were then able to concentrate on the more difficult ones. Systems using this procedure are therefore able to include a greater variety of behaviours in the observation instrument because they give the observer time to reach decisions in the more difficult coding areas.

In theory, time sampling systems where the recorded

behaviours provide a representative sample of the overall pattern of classroom interaction can be used to determine the sequence of events. Most attempts to do this have used probabilistic models based on Markov chains. A one-stage model tries to predict the behaviour at $T + X$ seconds given a knowledge of the behaviour at T seconds where X is the length of time unit. A two-stage model will attempt to predict the behaviour at $T + X$ seconds from a knowledge of the behaviours at both T and $T - X$ seconds respectively. In theory, higher order models can also be developed. In practice, however, a two-stage model involving upwards of a dozen categories of behaviour offers so many different combinations of possible behaviours that the total number of observations recorded would need to be impossibly high to test the model.

With transcribed accounts of lessons, either from videotape or audiotape, greater attention can be paid to the sequential character of exchanges between teachers and pupils. Once suitable units of transcript have been identified, then different patterns in the sequence of these units can be identified. Unfortunately, successive researchers have tended to use different units for analysis. Thus the episode developed by Smith and Meux (1962) became the incident in Nuthall and Lawrence's (1965) study. Others have defined pedagogical moves (Bellack et al. 1966) and thought units within teaching modules (Taba 1966). Comparison between different studies is therefore difficult and although it is attractive to believe that effective teaching will eventually be explained in terms of sequential behaviour rather than simple frequency units, there has been little progress in this direction since the early 1970s.

7. General Conclusions

In spite of these difficulties, there remains a continued interest in the collection of systematic data. Recent reviews of research on teaching in the United States list a large number of studies which have been carried out since the publication of Rosenshine's review (Rosenshine and Furst 1973). According to Brophy (1979), studies since the early 1970s have provided firm evidence to suggest what teachers should do in order to improve their pupils' performance on basic skills. Central to these ideas is the provision of warm, highly structured teaching designed to ensure that pupils remain actively engaged on their task and are provided with the maximum amount of feedback. However, some recent studies have suggested that such conditions apply only in the case of fairly low-level cognitive outcomes (Galton and Willcocks 1982) and more emphasis should be placed on increasing the degree of teacher–pupil interaction both in individual and group settings. There is also a conspicuous lack of evidence about the nature of the learning strategies adopted by children. It may be expected that the next generation of classroom studies will turn its attention to these key issues.

See also: Naturalistic Inquiry; Synthesizing Research Evidence; Psychological Environment

Bibliography

Adelman C, Walker R 1974 Stop-frame cinematography with synchronized sound: A technique for recording in school classrooms. *J. Soc. Motion and Picture and Television Engineers* 83: 189–91

Barr A S 1935 The validity of certain instruments employed in the measurement of teaching ability. In: Walker H (ed.) 1935 *The Measurement of Teaching Efficiency.* Macmillan, New York, pp. 73–141

Bellack A A, Hyman R T, Smith F L, Kliebard H M 1966 *The Language of the Classroom.* Teachers College Press, Columbia University, New York

Boydell D 1975 Pupil behaviour in junior classrooms. *Br. J. Educ. Psychol.* 45: 122–29

Brophy J E 1979 Teacher behaviour and its effects. *J. Educ. Psychol.* 71: 733–50

Dunkerton J 1981 Should classroom observation be quantitative? *Educ. Res.* 23: 144–51

Eggleston J F, Galton M J, Jones M E 1975 *A Science Teaching Observation Schedule.* Macmillan, London

Eggleston J F, Galton M J, Jones M E 1976 *Processes and Products of Science Teaching.* Macmillan, London

Flanders N A 1964 Some relationships among teacher influence, pupil atttitudes and achievement. In: Biddle B J, Ellena W J (eds.) 1964 *Contemporary Research on Teacher Effectiveness.* Holt, Rinehart and Winston, New York, pp. 196–231

Flanders N A 1967 Problems of observer training and reliability. In: Amidon E J, Hough J B (eds.) 1967 *Interaction Analysis: Theory, Research, and Applications.* Addison-Wesley, Reading, Massachusetts, pp. 158–66

Galton M 1979 Systematic classroom observation: British research. *Educ. Res.* 21: 109–15

Galton M, Simon B, Croll P 1980 *Inside the Primary Classroom.* Routledge and Kegan Paul, London

Galton M J, Willcocks J 1982 *Moving from the Primary Classroom.* Routledge and Kegan Paul, London

Hamilton D, Delamont S 1974 Classroom research: A cautionary tale. *Res. Educ.* 11: 1–15

Medley D M, Mitzel H E 1958 A technique for measuring classroom behaviour. *J. Educ. Psychol.* 49: 86–93

Medley D M, Mitzel H E 1963 Measuring classroom behavior by systematic observation. In: Gage N L (ed.) 1963 *Handbook of Research on Research on Teaching: A Project of the American Educational Research Association.* Rand McNally, Chicago, Illinois, pp. 247–328

Nuthall G A, Lawrence P J 1965 *Thinking in the Classroom: The Development of a Method of Analysis.* New Zealand Council for Educational Research, Wellington

Olson W C 1929 *The Measurement of Nervous Habits in Normal Children.* University of Minnesota Press, Minneapolis, Minnesota

Rosenshine B 1970 Evaluation of classroom instruction. *Rev. Educ. Res.* 40: 279–300

Rosenshine B, Furst N 1973 The use of direct observation to study teaching. In: Travers R M W (ed.) 1973 *Second Handbook of Research on Teaching: A Project of the American Educational Research Association.* Rand McNally, Chicago, Illinois, pp. 122–83

Scott W A 1955 Reliability of content analysis: The case of nominal coding. *Public Opinion Q.* 19: 321–25

Silberman C E 1970 *Crisis in the Classroom: The Remaking of American Education.* Random House, New York

Simon A, Boyer E G (eds.) 1970 *Mirrors for Behavior: An Anthology of Classroom Observation Instruments.* Research for Better Schools, Philadelphia, Pennsylvania

Smith B O, Meux M 1962 *A Study of the Logic of Teaching.* Bureau of Educational Research, University of Illinois, Urbana, Illinois

Taba H 1966 *Teaching Strategies and Cognitive Functioning in Elementary School Children.* San Francisco State College, San Francisco, California

Naturalistic Inquiry

E. G. Guba; Y. S. Lincoln

Persons concerned with disciplined inquiry have tended to use what is commonly called the scientific paradigm—that is, model or pattern—of inquiry. A second paradigm, also aimed at disciplined inquiry, is currently emerging; this paradigm is commonly known as the naturalistic paradigm, although it is often referred to (mistakenly) as the case study or qualitative paradigm. Its distinguishing features are not, however, its format or methods, or even, as its title might suggest, the fact that it is usually carried out in natural settings. What differentiates the naturalistic from the scientific (or, as it is sometimes referred to, the positivistic paradigm) approach is, at bottom, the different interpretations placed on certain basic axioms or assumptions. In addition, the two approaches characteristically take different postures on certain issues which, while not as basic as axiomatic propositions, are nevertheless fundamental to an understanding of how the naturalistic inquirer operates.

1. Axiomatic Differences Between the Naturalistic and Positivistic Paradigms

Axioms may be defined as the set of undemonstrated (and undemonstratable) propositions accepted by convention or established by practice as the basic building blocks of some conceptual or theoretical structure or system. As such they are arbitrary and certainly not "self-evidently true." Different axiom systems have different utilities depending on the phenomenon to which they are applied; so, for example, Euclidean geometry as an axiomatic system has good fit to terrestrial phenomena but Lobachevskian geometry (a non-Euclidean form) has better fit to interstellar phenomena. A decision about which of several axiom systems to employ for a given purpose is a matter of the relative "fit" between the axiom sets and the characteristics of the application area. It is the general contention of naturalists that the axioms of naturalistic inquiry provide a better fit to most social/behavioral phenomena than do the positivistic axioms.

1.1 Axiom 1: The Nature of Reality

Positivists assume that there exists a single, tangible reality fragmentable into independent variables and processes, any of which can be studied independently of the others; inquiry can be caused to converge onto this single reality until, finally, it is explained. Naturalists assume that there exist multiple realities which are, in the main, constructions existing in the minds of people; they are therefore intangible and can be studied only in holistic, and idiosyncratic, fashion. Inquiry into these multiple realities will inevitably diverge (the scope of the inquiry will enlarge) as more and more realities must be considered. Naturalists argue that while the positivist assumptions undoubtedly have validity in the hard and life sciences, naturalist assumptions are more meaningful in studying human behavior. Naturalists do not deny the reality of the objects, events, or processes with which people interact, but suggest that it is the meanings given to or interpretations made of these objects, events, or processes that constitute the arena of interest to investigators of social/behavioral phenomena. Note that these constructions are not perceptions of the objects, events, or processes but of meaning and interpretation.

1.2 Axiom 2: The Inquirer–Respondent Relationship

The positivist assumes that the inquirer is able to maintain a discrete and inviolable distance from the "object" of inquiry, but concedes that when the object is a human being, special methodological safeguards must be taken to prevent reactivity, that is, a reaction of the object to the conditions of the inquiry that will influence the outcome in undesirable ways. The naturalist assumes that the inquirer and the respondent in any human inquiry inevitably interact to influence one another. While safeguards need to be mounted in both directions, the interaction need not be eliminated (it is impossible to do that anyway) but should be exploited for the sake of the inquiry.

Naturalists point out that the proposition of subject–object independence is dubious even in areas like particle physics, as exemplified in the Heisenberg Uncertainty Principle. The effect is certainly more noticeable in dealing with people, they assert. Nor should it be supposed that the interpolation of a layer of apparently objective instrumentation (paper and pencil or brass) solves the problem. Inquirers react to the mental images they have of respondents in developing the instrumentation; respondents answer or act in terms of what they perceive to be expectations held for their behavior as they interpret the meaning of the items or tasks put before them; inquirers deal with responses in terms of their interpretation of response meaning and intent, and so on. Nor, say the naturalists, is interactivity a generally undesirable characteristic; indeed, if interactivity could be eliminated by some methodological tour de force, the trade-off would not be worthwhile, because it is precisely the interactivity that makes it possible for the human instrument to achieve maximum responsiveness, adaptability, and insight.

1.3 Axiom 3: The Nature of Truth Statements

Positivists assert that the aim of inquiry is to develop a nomothetic body of knowledge; this knowledge is best encapsulated in generalizations which are truth statements of enduring value that are context free. The stuff of which generalizations are made is the similarity among units; differences are set aside as intrinsically uninteresting. Naturalists assert that the aim of inquiry is to develop an idiographic body of knowledge; this knowledge is best encapsulated in a series of "working hypotheses" that describe the individual case. Generalizations are not possible since human behavior is never time or context free. Nevertheless, some transferability of working hypotheses from context to context may be possible depending on the similarity of the contexts (an empirical matter). Differences are as inherently important as (and at times more important than) the similarities. Naturalists well-understand the utility of generalizations such as $f = ma$ or $e = mc^2$ in physics, although even in the hard or life sciences, as Cronbach (1975) has pointed out, generalizations are much like radioactive materials, in that they decay and have a half-life. Surely it is unreasonable to suppose that analogous tendencies do not exist in the social and behavioral sciences.

1.4 Axiom 4: Causality

For the positivist, the determination of cause–effect relationships is of the highest importance. For each effect, it is believed, there is a cause which can be detected by sufficiently sophisticated means: controlled experiments. Naturalists on the other hand assert that the determination of cause–effect is a search for the Holy Grail. Human relationships are so caught up in interacting factors, events, and processes that the hope that *the* cause–effect chain can be sorted out is vain. All of these factors, events, and processes are constantly exerting influences on one another, mutually impinging, changing, and being changed simultaneously. Naturalists point out that there has been a variety of causation theories proposed, including constant conjunction and regularity theory, "law" theories, formulations about "necessary and sufficient" conditions, and more recently, various attributional and semantic theories. All have flaws, in the opinion of epistemologists. Naturalists argue that at best *only plausible inferences that depend on the purpose of the inquirer* are possible. Thus, whether the cause of malaria is taken to be the mosquito

or the interaction of a certain type of plasmodium with the corpuscles of the blood is likely to depend on whether the inquirer is an ecologist or a hematologist. The naturalist replaces the concept of cause with the parallel concept of *mutual simultaneous shaping*, arguing that any particular inference about the nature of that shaping is purpose dependent and time and context bound.

1.5 Axiom 5: Relation to Values

Positivists assume that inquiry is value free and can be guaranteed to be so by virtue of the "objective" methodology which the positivist employs. The naturalist asserts that values impinge upon an inquiry in at least five ways, in terms of: the selection made by the investigator from among possible problems, theories, instruments, and data analysis modes; the assumptions underlying the substantive theory that guides the inquiry (for example, a theory of reading or an organizational theory); the assumptions underlying the methodological paradigm (as outlined in the preceding section on axioms); the values that characterize the respondents, the community, and the culture in which the inquiry is carried out (contextual values); and, finally, the possible interactions among any two or more of the preceding, which may be value consonant or value dissonant. Of particular interest is the possibility of resonance or dissonance between the substantive and methodological assumptions which can produce quite misleading results. Naturalists in particular take the position that many of the ambiguities and other irresolutions that tend to characterize social and behavioral research can be traced to such dissonances. So long as methodologies are assumed to be value free, naturalists assert, the problem of dissonance will not be recognized, since by definition it cannot exist. But once the role that values play in shaping enquiry is recognized, the problem becomes very real.

2. Methodological Differences Between the Naturalistic and Positivistic Paradigms

Contrary to the position taken by Miles and Huberman (1984a, 1984b) and others that methods of inquiry are independent of paradigms, the naturalist argues that methodology—if not methods themselves—is very much determined by the paradigm implicitly or explicitly followed by the inquirer. How a building tradesperson uses a hammer, saw, or wrench does not depend on the nature of hammers, saws, and wrenches; but what is accomplished with those tools very much depends on whether that tradesperson sees himself or herself as, say, a carpenter, electrician, or plumber. Naturalism implies a very particular methodology (Guba and Lincoln in press a), of which the following are some of the more important but not the sole elements. As will be seen, these elements do not constitute a random selection from among a variety of choices, but represent a synergistic set that can be rationalized in terms of the basic axioms.

2.1 Preferred Methods

Positivists tend to prefer quantitative methods, probably because of their apparently greater precision and objectivity and because of the enormous advantage of being mathematically manipulable. Naturalists prefer qualitative methods, probably because they appear to promise the most holistic products and they seem more appropriate to the use of a human as the prime data collection instrument. The distinction between quantitative and qualitative methods is often mistakenly taken to be the chief mark of distinction between the paradigms. Either methodology is appropriate to either paradigm, even though in practice there is a high correlation between quantitative and positivistic, on the one hand, and qualitative and naturalistic on the other.

2.2 Source of Theory

Positivists insist on a priori formulations of theory; indeed, they are likely to assert that inquiry without a priori theory to guide it is mindless. The naturalist believes that it is not theory but the inquiry problem itself that guides and bounds the inquiry; that a priori theory constrains the inquiry to those elements recognized by the investigator as important, and may introduce biases (believing is seeing). In all events, theory is more powerful when it arises from the data rather than being imposed on them. The naturalist does not, of course, insist on grounding theory afresh in each and every inquiry; what the naturalist does insist on is that the theory to be used shall have been grounded at some time in experience.

2.3 Knowledge Types Used

Positivists constrain the type of knowledge admissible in an inquiry to propositional knowledge; that is, knowledge that can be stated in language form. In view of their commitment to a priori theory and their interest in shaping inquiry preordinately about particular questions and hypotheses, this is not surprising. The naturalist, often intent on the use of the human-as-instrument, also admits tacit knowledge—insights, intuitions, apprehensions that cannot be stated in language form but which are nevertheless "known" to the inquirer. Of course naturalists seek to recast their tacit knowledge into propositional form as quickly as possible. It is equally clear that positivists depend upon tacit knowledge at least as much as do their naturalist counterparts; however, the reconstructed logic of positivism militates against exposing this dependency.

2.4 Instruments

The positivist prefers nonhuman devices for data collection purposes, perhaps because they appear to be more cost efficient, have a patina of objectivity, and can be systematically aggregated. The naturalist prefers humans as instruments, for reasons such as their greater insightfulness, flexibility, and responsiveness, the fact that they are able to take a holistic view, are able to utilize their tacit knowledge, and are able simultaneously to acquire and process information.

2.5 Design

The positivist insists on a preordinate design; indeed, it is sometimes asserted that a "good" design makes it possible for the inquirer to specify in dummy form the very tables he or she will produce. The naturalist, entering the field without a priori theory, hypotheses, or questions (mostly), is unable to specify a design (except in the broadest process sense) in advance. Instead, he or she anticipates that the design will emerge (unfold, roll, cascade) as the inquiry proceeds, with each step heavily dependent on all preceding steps. Clearly, the naturalist is well-advised to specify as much in advance as possible, while the positivist should seek to keep as many options open as possible.

2.6 Setting

The positivist prefers to conduct studies under laboratory conditions, probably because the laboratory represents the epitome of control. The naturalist prefers natural settings (it is this propensity that has lent its name to the paradigm), arguing that only in nature can it be discovered what does happen rather than what can happen. Moreover, studies in nature can be transferred to other, similar contexts, whereas laboratory studies can be generalized only to other laboratories.

Some writers have pointed out that the different methodological positions preferred by advocates of each paradigm may be thought of as complementary, leading to the possibility of an accommodation—a kind of conceptual ecumenicism. Thus, it is argued, there is no reason not to use both qualitative *and* quantitative methods, to permit the use of tacit knowledge during discovery while reverting to propositional knowledge during verification, to use both human instruments as well as "more objective" types, and so on. Acceptance of this line of argument would lead both naturalists and positivists to attempt "mix and match" strategies, using a more positivistic approach here and a more naturalistic one there, as occasion seemed to demand. But despite good intentions, neither group has been able to follow this well-meant advice, giving rise to the suspicion that, unless one wishes to write off inquirers of both camps as deliberately obstinate or intransigent, there must be some more fundamental barrier to such ready compromise.

This reason, simply stated, is that there exists a synergism among methodological elements such that commitment to one paradigm's preference *on any one* methodological element requires, if one is to be true to the axiomatic system, commitment to counterpart positions on the others as well. Consider positivists, for example. Begin with any methodological element, say their preference for *a priori* theory. Positivists do not exhibit this preference by accident. In part they prefer a priori theory because they deal in propositional language, and theory is the best means for formulating and clarifying their propositional statements. The hypotheses or questions are propositional deductions from theory. Because of the precision of these hypotheses or questions it is possible to imagine a design for testing them, and to devise appropriate instruments. Having such instruments makes it unnecessary to interpolate a "subjective" human between data and respondents. Moreover, these instruments can best be used in the highly controlled environment of the laboratory. And precise instruments yield data that can conveniently be expressed in quantitative form, a marked advantage since numbers can be easily manipulated statistically. Hence quantitative methods. And of course numbers can be aggregated and summarized, yielding apparent generalizations, expressions of causality, and so on. The sum exhibits a synergism such that each posture depends on every other one.

Similar observations can be made about the naturalists' preference. Naturalists are forced into a natural setting because they cannot tell, having no a priori theory or hypotheses, what is important to control, or even to study. They could not set up a contrived experiment because they do not know what to contrive. If theory is to emerge from the data, the data must first be gathered. Since the nature of those data is unknown, an adaptive instrument is needed to locate and make sense of them—the "smart" human. Humans find certain data-collection means more congenial than others; hence they tend toward the use of qualitative methods such as observation, interview, reading documents, and the like, which come "naturally" to the human. These methods result in insights and information about the specific instance being studied but make it difficult to produce aggregations, generalizations, or cause–effect statements. Again, the naturalists' behavior demonstrates a kind of synergism among postures which is understandable and defensible only in terms of the totality of positions.

3. Rigor, Trustworthiness, and Authenticity

In view of its unusual axioms and the apparent "softness" of its methodological choices, naturalistic inquiry is sometimes attacked as not rigorous, in contrast to positivistic inquiry, which has a well-developed standard of *rigor*. But what counts as a standard of rigor is itself determined by the axiomatic system underlying the paradigm being followed, as Morgan (1983) has cogently argued. Accordingly the usual criteria of scientific rigor—internal and external validity, reliability and objectivity—are of dubious applicability.

Naturalists have taken two approaches to this problem. On the one hand they have devised a set of criteria, *parallel* to the usual criteria of rigor but redefined to take account of naturalistic axioms; these are commonly called criteria of *trustworthiness* to dis-

tinguish them from their positivistic counterparts. Thus it has been proposed to replace internal validity with *credibility*, external validity with *transferability*, reliability with *dependability*, and objectivity with *confirmability* (Guba 1981, Lincoln and Guba 1985). Particular techniques have been proposed both to assist in establishing conditions essential for meeting the criteria as well as providing evidence that they have been met in the concrete case, including most notably prolonged engagement, persistent observation, peer debriefing, triangulation, negative case analysis, member checking, thick description, and auditing (Lincoln and Guba 1985).

A second approach has been the development of what might be called indigenous or intrinsic criteria, those generated by the naturalistic axioms themselves without reference to other paradigmatic systems. While not well-developed in 1986, these *authenticity* criteria (so-called to distinguish them from the scientific criteria of rigor and the parallel criteria of trustworthiness), give promise of opening new lines of thought on the question of how inquiries are to be judged. For example, one such criterion is *fairness*: if reality is multiple, what steps does the inquirer take to give a fair and impartial hearing—and an equal chance at inclusion—to each of the several constructions that might be formulated in a given situation? Another such criterion is *ontological authenticity*: what evidence exists that an inquiry has succeeded in raising *everyone's* construction of reality to more informed and sophisticated levels? Initial attempts at formulating such authenticity criteria may be found in Guba and Lincoln (in press a) and Lincoln and Guba (1986).

It is premature to expect that adherents of the naturalistic paradigm would have evolved as sophisticated an approach to issues of trustworthiness and authenticity as have positivists, who have had several centuries to shape and refine their standards on issues of rigor. While naturalist standards may not at this time prove compelling, there can be little doubt, however, that they can contribute greatly to persuading a consumer of an inquiry of its meaningfulness.

4. Summary

Naturalistic inquiry is one of two paradigms currently being used by investigators within the framework of disciplined research. While this paradigm has distinguished antecedents in anthropology and ethnography, it is nevertheless relatively emergent and not as much is known about its properties as might be desired (see *Ethnographic Methods*).

Naturalistic inquiry differs from positivistic inquiry in terms of interpretations based on five basic axioms: reality, inquirer–object relationship, generalizability, causality, and value freedom. In addition, a number of salient methodological elements also play important roles: methods, sources of theory, knowledge types used, instruments, design, and setting.

As a relatively new paradigm, naturalism suffers in not having yet devised as solid an approach to trustworthiness as has its positivistic counterpart. Nevertheless important strides are being made. It seems likely that, given several decades in which to develop, the naturalistic paradigm will prove to be as useful as the positivistic paradigm has been historically. The major decisions to be made between the two paradigms revolve about the assessment of fit to the area under study, rather than to any intrinsic advantages or disadvantages of either.

See also: Ethnographic Methods

Bibliography

Cook T D, Campbell D T 1979 *Quasi-experimentation: Design and Analysis Issues for Field Settings.* Rand McNally, Chicago, Illinois

Cook T D, Reichardt C S 1979 *Qualitative and Quantitative Methods in Evaluation Research.* Sage, Beverly Hills, California

Cronbach L J 1975 Beyond the two disciplines of scientific psychology. *Am. Psychol.* 30: 116–27

Cronbach L J, Suppes P (eds.) 1969 *Research for Tomorrow's Schools: Disciplined Inquiry for Education.* Macmillan, New York

Filstead W J (ed.) 1970 *Qualitative Methodology: Firsthand Involvement with the Social World.* Rand McNally, Chicago, Illinois

Glaser B G, Strauss A L 1967 *The Discovery of Grounded Theory: Strategies for Qualitative Research.* Aldine, Chicago, Illinois

Guba E G 1978 *Toward a Methodology of Naturalistic Inquiry in Educational Evaluation.* Center for the Study of Evaluation, University of California, Los Angeles, California

Guba E G 1981 Criteria for assessing the trustworthiness of naturalistic inquiries. *Educ. Comm. Tech. J.* 29(2): 75–92

Guba E G, Lincoln Y S 1982 *Effective Evaluation.* Jossey-Bass, San Francisco, California

Guba E G, Lincoln Y S in press a Do inquiry paradigms imply inquiry methodologies? In: Fetterman D L (ed.) *A Silent Paradigm Revolution.* Sage, Beverly Hills, California

Guba E G, Lincoln Y S in press b The countenances of fourth generation evaluation: description, judgment and negotiation. In: Palumbo D J (ed.) *The Politics of Program Evaluation.* Sage, Beverly Hills, California (A briefer version appears in: Lipsey M, Cordray D (eds.) 1986 *Evaluation Studies Review Annual—1986.* Sage, Beverley Hills, California)

Kaplan A 1964 *The Conduct of Inquiry: Methodology for Behavioral Science.* Chandler, San Francisco, California

Lincoln Y S, Guba E G 1985 *Naturalistic Inquiry.* Sage, Beverly Hills, California

Lincoln Y S, Guba E G 1986 But is it rigorous? Trustworthiness and authenticity in naturalistic evaluation. In: Williams D (ed.) 1986 *Naturalistic Evaluation, New Directions in Program Evaluation,* No. 30. Jossey-Bass, San Francisco, California, pp. 73–84

Miles M B, Huberman A M 1984a Drawing valid meaning from qualitative data: Toward a shared craft. *Educ. Researcher* 13: 20–30

Miles M B, Huberman A M 1984b *Qualitative Data Analysis: A Sourcebook of New Methods.* Sage, Beverly Hills, California.

Morgan G 1983 *Beyond Method.* Sage, Beverly Hills, California.

Polanyi M 1966 *The Tacit Dimension.* Doubleday, Garden City, New York

Scriven M 1971 Objectivity and subjectivity in educational research. In: Thomas L G (ed.) 1971 *Philosophical Redirection of Educational Research.* University of Chicago Press, Chicago, Illinois

Ethnographic Methods

R. Taft

Some educational researchers have recently advocated the adoption of the ethnographic methods employed by cultural and social anthropologists in their field studies of social groups and communities. These methods are considered to be particularly appropriate for empirical research on the relatively bounded system of a school or classroom but they also have their place in the study of the role of the family, social organizations, or ethnic communities in education. Ethnographic research consists essentially of a description of events that occur within the life of a group, with special regard to the social structures and the behaviour of the individuals with respect to their group membership, and an interpretation of the meaning of these for the culture of the group. Thus ethnography is used both to record primary data and to interpret its meaning. It is naturalistic inquiry as opposed to controlled, and a qualitative, as opposed to quantitative, method. In ethnography the researcher participates in some part of the normal life of the group and uses what he or she learns from that participation to produce the research findings. It is consequently often treated as being equivalent to participant observation, in contrast with nonparticipant observation in which the observer as an outsider records the overt behaviour of the subjects, but it involves more than that. Participation in a group provides investigators with an understanding of the culture and the interactions between the members that is different from that which can be obtained from merely observing or conducting a questionnaire survey or an analysis of documents. The investigators' involvement in the normal activities of the group may be treated as a case of partial acculturation in which they acquire an insider's knowledge of the group through their direct experience with it. These experiences provide them with tacit knowledge which helps them to understand the significance to the group members of their own behaviour and that of others and enables them to integrate their observations about that behaviour with information obtained from other sources such as interviews with informants and documentary material.

1. The Development of Ethnographic Methods

Field research was employed by anthropologists and sociologists in the nineteenth and early twentieth centuries, but the first to stress the need for a systematic approach to its conduct was the Polish–British scholar Malinowski, who emphasized the need for ethnographers to employ controls in their assembly of data in a manner that he described as analogous, although by no means similar, to those of the natural scientists. Malinowski laid down the requirement that observers should tabulate the data on which their conclusions are based, including verbatim statements, and should indicate whether they are derived from direct or indirect sources, a method that he called "concrete statistical documentation" (see the introductory chapter on methodology in Malinowski 1922). He stressed the need for the investigator to establish "trustworthiness" in respect of the study. Malinowski described the goal of ethnographic studies as "to grasp the native's point of view, his relation to life, to realise his view of his world" (p. 25). In order to achieve this, the investigator should learn the language of the community being studied—preferably out of contact with "white" people, and use both observation and informed interviews with selected informants from within the community as sources of data.

The field methods laid down by Malinowski have, to a greater or lesser degree, been adapted for studies of segments of modern, urbanized societies which have provided a model for the application of the methods to educational research. For example, studies have been carried out of the unemployed in Austria, industrial organizations (Tavistock Institute), urban areas in the United States (Middletown, Yankee City), hobos, gangs, and dance musicians, to name just a few. These studies each raised their own peculiar problems of research strategy, but what they all have in common is their method of research in which the investigator becomes closely involved over a prolonged period in the everyday life of the members of a designated group or community in order to understand its culture. This contact enables the researchers not only to obtain an intimate and a broad knowledge of the group but also to test and refine hypotheses about the phenomena being studied.

Ethnographic methods of research came to education fairly late. The team of sociologists from the University of Chicago who studied medical students (Becker et al. 1961) were probably the pioneers in the field of education, while Smith and Geoffrey (1968) were the first to base a study of classroom processes on anthropological field studies using a method which they described as microethnography. They stated that their "primary intent was to describe the silent language of a culture, a classroom in a slum school, so that those who have not lived in it will appreciate its subtleties and complexities" (p. 2). Smith observed the classroom every day for one semester and kept copious field notes, which he used as a basis for his daily discussions with the class teacher, Geoffrey, with the purpose of clarifying the intentions and motives behind the teacher's behaviour in order to move towards a conceptualization in abstract terms of the teaching process. Both of the investigators were participants in the classroom, although one was more of an observer and the other more of an initiator and an informant.

A word should be added about the terms used in describing ethnographic studies in education. Smith and Geoffrey seem to have simply meant an intensive field study by their term microethnography, while Erickson (1975) confines it more narrowly to studies that use extensive observation and recording to establish the interactional structures in the classroom, a usage which Mehan (1978) prefers to call constitutive ethnography. For the purposes of this present article, the term ethnography is interpreted liberally to include case studies, the concept preferred by the ethnographers in the United Kingdom. The intensive study of a bounded community is a clear example of a simple case study, even though there are many individuals who make up that community.

2. The Scientific Status of the Ethnographic Method

The use of ethnographic methods involves some important questions relating to the tactics, ethics, and validity of the study.

2.1 The Social Role of the Investigator

The description of the investigator as a participant in the life of the group implies that he or she has some role in it which is recognized by the group. Sometimes this role is simply that of participant observer, a role which does not usually exist in most formal group structures, but one which does have a meaning in many classrooms where outsiders come to observe the class on occasions for one purpose or another. Thus, Louis Smith was introduced to both the children and the teachers as someone from the university who was interested in children's learning, a role which is understood and accepted in modern classrooms. In other cases the investigator fills a normal role in the group other than that of a researcher. For example, a study of an orthodox Jewish school was conducted while the researcher concerned was a regular classroom teacher in the school, a situation that represents participant observation in the fullest sense of the word. Another example would be a student who studies his or her college or professors on the basis of his or her normal personal experience with them. The role of participant observer has some advantages as a viewing point over that of the participant who plays the additional role of observer. The former is expected by the group to share, probe, ask questions, take notes, and so on because this is consistent with his or her role as an observer whereas the latter has tactical and ethical problems in doing so because of his or her obligations as a participant. On the other hand there is a danger that a participant observer can become so much absorbed into the group after a time that his or her status as an observer may be compromised.

The group member who also acts as an investigator may do so overtly or covertly, or as a mixture of both where it is known to some members of the group that he or she is observing for research purposes but not to others. Covert observation raises serious ethical issues as does semicovert, but, on the other hand, overt observation by a person who has another role in the group can place him or her in an anomalous position with regard to the carrying out of a normal group role. Furthermore, colleagues are likely to respond to him or her as an observer in a biased fashion because of their other involvement with him or her. A distinction is often made between obtrusive and unobtrusive methods of research according to whether the subjects of the research are aware that they are being studied. A participant observer, by definition, plays an obtrusive role and this fact may influence the behaviour of the group whereas the observer participant may or may not be obtrusive as a researcher.

2.2 The Inside–Outside View

One of the main advantages of the ethnographic method is that, in the course of becoming involved in the group, the investigator becomes acculturated to it. This means that he or she develops personal knowledge about the rules of the group and begins to perceive the same meanings in events as do the members of the group. The investigator learns what behaviour is expected when, where, and in response to what situations. This process of acculturation is sometimes described as transition from the status of a "stranger" to that of "a friend", that is, a person who knows the "silent language" of the group and is in intimate communication with its members. It is, however, significant that a scholar who is studying the subculture of a school in his or her own society is unlikely to be as complete a stranger at the beginning as an anthropologist studying a traditional society.

Nevertheless, being an insider has its drawbacks as a method of studying a group. First, as already indicated, there are constraints imposed by propriety and ethics on an insider revealing to others the secrets of the group (see *Ethical Considerations*). There may, of course, be the same constraints on an outsider but, at least, the group can usually control his or her access to information by barring entry.

Second, the insider may not always have even as much access to information as an outsider. He or she may have personal knowledge of only a segment of the group's life, sometimes without being aware of the limitation. He or she may even be denied access to the other segments: for example, a teacher may not be permitted to study the classroom of a colleague. In contrast, a stranger who is accepted as an observer may be deliberately informed and invited to observe just because he or she is a stranger. Futhermore, an outsider is more likely to be able to take steps to obtain a representative sampling of people, occasions, and settings in the group and thus can help to offset the suspicion of biased observation. A third drawback that may arise as a result of being an insider is that highly salient data may be overlooked just because it is so familiar. Strangers will notice events that stand out as a result of their contrast with the expectations that they have brought with them from their own cultural background and may therefore be better placed to infer their meaning and significance for other events in the group. Some element of surprise aids awareness. A further problem is the one mentioned earlier of the subjects' reactivity to being studied, particularly when the observer is a full participant in the group. Whether or not the observation is obtrusive, it is reactive observation; that is, the observer affects the behaviour of the people being studied and consequently will have to take into account his or her own influence when assessing the group. As Everhart puts it "the fieldworker, rather than appearing to be one of many in the audience observing the drama on stage, is himself on stage, interacting with the other actors in 'his' setting and playing a role in the resolution of the production" (1977 p. 14). In order to take into account their own contributions and to assess what the situation would be if it were not for the fact that their presence is influencing the group, investigators need a great deal of self-awareness and a thorough understanding of the group processes. This necessity for playing the dual roles of participant and detached observer can impose a severe strain on the ethnographic investigator and calls for continual monitoring of the effect the investigator has on others.

2.3 Subjectivity, Reliability, and Validity

The fact that investigators have a role in the group not only requires them to be aware of their own influence but also may give them an emotional stake in a particular research outcome. For example, if the observer is also a teacher, there may be a tendency for observation to be slanted towards a justification of the style of teaching normally used. Since ethnographic researchers use themselves as the instrument through which they observe the group, the method lends itself to extreme subjectivity; that is, the interpretation may be idiosyncratic to the observer with all of the associated limitations, eccentricities, and biases and is not matched by the interpretation of other observers. This raises questions concerning the reliability of the observations and the validity of the conclusions. The difficulty is that the observations are not easily subject to public scrutiny. Observations and interpretations are by their very nature subjective but they still can be made susceptible to reliability checks and it is still possible for the investigation to follow rules that can increase the validity of the conclusions.

Reliability, that is accuracy, of the observations can be enhanced by following the prescription laid down by Malinowski of recording wherever possible the concrete data in the form of a "synoptic chart" on which the inferences are to be based, including verbatim utterances and opinions. Modern audiovisual methods of recording events so that they can be examined at leisure offer ethnographers unprecedented possibilities today of attaining accuracy, but there are still sampling problems in the selection of the data and limitations to accuracy due to bias and lack of opportunity, as well as tactical and ethical considerations in making the recordings.

The reliability of the observations is assisted by the long period of exposure to the data in ethnographic research which provides opportunities for investigators to cross check their observations over time and to reconcile inconsistencies. Cross checks may also be made by triangulation, a procedure in 'which multiple sources are used to obtain evidence on the same phenomenon. Thus, the observations may be supplemented by interviews, feedback to the members of the group for their comment, and documentary evidence such as school notices, correspondence, minutes, and other archives. An additional source of reliability is to have more than one observer as, for example, in the study by Smith and Geoffrey (1968), a situation which is relatively rare in traditional anthropological studies. In the typical case, the multiple observers may be members of a team who are exposed to the same events and are then able to cross check each other's data.

Validity is a quality of the conclusions and the processes through which these were reached, but its exact meaning is dependent on the particular criterion of truth that is adopted. In ethnographic research the most appropriate criterion is credibility although even that term is subject to fuzziness in meaning. Here the concern will be only with the steps that ethnographic research workers can take to improve the credibility of their analyses. Credibility is dependent on the apparent accuracy of the data and all the steps described above that are intended to increase reliability are relevant. Much depends on the way in which the study is communicated to the scientific audience. A report in which the investigator describes the precautions that have been taken to ensure the accuracy of the observations has more credibility than one in which the reader is merely asked to take the data and findings "on faith". The report should contain indications that the investigator is aware of the need to convince the audience of the validity of the study. The interpretations made from

the data are more credible when the researcher describes the evidence on which they are based and also any efforts made to test for evidence that would tend to disconfirm any tentative conclusions. One of the procedures that is often followed in ethnographic studies to confirm the validity of interpretations is to feed them back for comment to selected members of the group or to other persons who know the group. In the case of literate participants such as are found in educational research, the research workers may submit to the members drafts of sections of their reports as well as oral accounts of their impressions. If necessary, the interpretations can be "negotiated" with the participants so that the final product is more likely to represent the situation as they see it, but there is always a danger in this procedure that the participants may exercise distortion and cover-up for their own reasons or that the researcher finds it impossible to obtain consensus. Different members of the group may hold different perceptions of the events, for example, teachers and students, or boys and girls. Some researchers have attempted to overcome these problems by setting up small groups of about four participants to engage in discussions towards establishing their shared meanings by acting as "checks, balances, and prompts" for each other, but in practice there are distinct limitations to the possible application of this procedure.

2.4 The Role of Theory, Hypotheses, and Generalizations

Malinowski specifically recommends that a field worker should commence with "foreshadowed problems" arising from his or her knowledge of theory, but should not have "preconceived ideas" in which he or she aims to prove certain hypotheses. The ethnographic method is qualitative and holistic, making use of the investigator's intuition, empathy, and general ability to learn another culture. The investigator is more concerned with discovery than with verification and this requires preparedness to formulate, test, and, if necessary, discard a series of hunches. As investigators develop hypotheses in the course of pursuing a foreshadowed problem they should be alert for data which refute, support, or cast doubts on their hypotheses and should be prepared to alter them in accordance with increased acquaintance with the phenomena. Research workers as they puzzle over the meaning of the behaviour of the group, and perhaps seek help from informants, are likely to obtain illumination through a sudden shaft of understanding. Thus there is a continual dialogue between an orientation towards discovery and one towards verification. Gradually a theoretical basis for the understanding of the group processes may emerge through the process often described as grounded theory, that is, grounded in the research process itself. Theory that emerges from exposure to the data is more likely to fit the requirements than theory that is preconceived on an abstract basis. Also the actual data are more likely to produce categories that are appropriate for describing the particular case. The main problem that arises from grounded theory derived from a case study is that of making generalizations beyond the particular case viewed at a particular time. A straight out description of concrete happenings has some value as an addition to the corpus of information that is available to the investigator and to other interested people—including members of the group itself. However, its value is greatly enhanced when the case can be "located as an instance of a more general class of events" (Smith 1978 p. 335). To achieve this, the investigator treats the case in point as either a representative of, or a departure from, a particular type. Sometimes the actual group or groups that are studied have been chosen initially as representatives of a designated type of case and this facilitates generalizations based on it but they should still be treated with reserve.

2.5 Ethnography as a Case Study Method

The problem of the relationship between the One and the Many, a perennial one in philosophy, arises in different guises in the social sciences—idiographic versus nomothetic treatments of data, -emic versus -etic approaches to comparative studies, and the case study versus the sample survey research design. In order to generalize from an individual case study of behaviour in one group to behaviour in others it is necessary to reach sufficient understanding about the significance of the events in relation to the context in which they occur in order to extend interpretations to other contexts and other groups. In the process of generalizing it is necessary to violate somewhat the full integrity of any one group by describing events in some language that extends beyond the bounds of the culture of that group. The ethnographers are partially acculturated to the group that they are studying, but they are also familiar with other groups with which they compare their experience of the group. To maintain the analogy, an ethnographer is multicultural with respect to the object of study. When an investigator attempts to understand one group, he or she is aided by knowledge of other ones and his or her impressions are partially consolidated with the others. Thus, generalizations are built up through the investigator being able to mediate between one group and others; an ethnographic account of a school, then, derives its value largely from the fact that the investigator—and also the readers—are familiar with other schools, and with schools in general. Diesing refers to this as "pluralism" which he describes as

follows: "one might say the method is relativistic in its treatment of individual cases and becomes gradually absolutistic as it moves toward broader generalizations" (1971 pp. 297–98).

In ethnographic studies no generalization can be treated as final, only as a working hypothesis for further studies which may again be ethnographic, or may consist of a survey by means of interviews, questionnaires, or tests. The ethnographic method gains credibility when it combines both subjective and objective methods but it need not be regarded as deriving its value only as a preliminary and exploratory procedure prior to the use of more conventional semiobjective techniques. It can make its own legitimate independent contribution at any stage of a research including the confirmation of hypotheses that have emerged out of other sources provided that the basic principles on which its credibility rests are observed.

See also: Naturalistic Inquiry

Bibliography

Becker G S, Geer B, Hughes E, Strauss A 1961 *Boys in White: Student Culture in Medical School.* University of Chicago Press, Chicago, Illinois

Diesing P 1971 *Patterns of Discovery in the Social Sciences.* Aldine-Atherton, Chicago, Illinois

Erickson F 1975 Gatekeeping and the melting pot: Interaction in counseling encounters. *Harvard Educ. Rev.* 45: 44–70

Everhart R B 1977 Between stranger and friend: Some consequences of "long term" fieldwork in schools. *Am. Educ. Res. J.* 14: 1–15

Malinowski B 1922 *Argonauts of the Western Pacific: An Account of Native Enterprise and Adventure in the Archipelagoes of Melanesian New Guinea.* Routledge, London

Mehan H 1978 Structuring school structure. *Harvard Educ. Rev.* 48: 32–64

Roberts J I, Akinsanya S K (eds.) 1976 *Educational Patterns and Cultural Configuration: The Anthropology of Education.* McKay, New York

Smith L M 1978 An evolving logic of participant observation, educational ethnography, and other case studies. In: Shulman L S (ed.) 1978 *Review of Research in Education*, Vol. 6. Peacock, Ithaca, Illinois, pp. 316–77

Smith L M, Geoffrey W 1968 *The Complexities of an Urban Classroom: An Analysis Toward a General Theory of Teaching.* Holt, Rinehart and Winston, New York

Spradley J P, McCurdy D W 1972 *The Cultural Experience: Ethnography in Complex Society.* SRA, Chicago, Illinois

Wilson S 1977 The use of ethnographic techniques in educational research. *Rev. Educ. Res.* 47: 245–65

Units of Analysis

L. Burstein

"Units of analysis" are those entities or objects whose behavior one is trying to understand or describe; they are the explanatory focus of an investigation (Burstein 1980a, 1980b, Cronbach 1976, Haney 1980, Wiley 1970). The typical units of analysis in educational investigations are students, classrooms, teachers, schools, and so on, which are the entities from the various levels of the multilevel educational hierarchy. A pupil's test score, the size of the class, the teacher's chosen instructional method, and the availability of a school library are examples of measured variables based directly on units at a given level. The units for other measured variables, for example, teacher–student interaction, are less obvious since they can characterize behavior at more than one level.

Data collected on units at a lower level (students) can be aggregated to yield a characteristic of a unit at a higher level (e.g., class average, class standard deviation, school average). This characteristic may take on special meaning at the higher level or simply be indicative of aggregated lower level properties. While a student test score is an individual (student) characteristic, the average test score for students in a given class is a class characteristic.

A variable measured strictly at a higher level such as the class or school (e.g., teacher's previous years of experience) cannot be disaggregated to yield a student characteristic. Such variables are often called global properties of groups as opposed to aggregated properties like average test scores. Though they cannot be disaggregated, global properties do represent a particular kind of variable, the context, associated with lower levels. Thus students are said to be learning in a "high inquiry" context if their teachers use instructional methods that emphasize inquiry.

Aggregated characteristics can also represent the context of lower level units. Thus, a student in a class with a high mean pretest score can be said to be in a "high ability" context. Similarly, when the performance of students within the same class varies substantially, the student is in a "heterogeneous ability" context.

The hierarchical structure of educational data results in yet another class of measures, relative standing or status, that are properties of lower level units. That is, the deviation of a student's score from the class average is a student-level measure of relative or comparative ability. Similarly, the deviation of the teacher's years of experience from the school average is a teacher or class measure (relative experience of the teacher). These characteristics are typically labeled within-group or pooled within-group measures.

While the literature is somewhat confusing on this point, the "level of analysis" is typically defined in terms of the units of the dependent variable or outcome in a study. Thus if posttest scores of students are the data used as outcomes, the analysis is said to be conducted at the student level; on the other hand, analyses with the class mean posttest scores as dependent variables are class-level analyses.

In many educational investigations, there is interest in explaining the behavior of units from more than one level. For example, the investigator may wish to estimate the relationship between students' entering ability relative to their classmates and their relative posttest performance and may also want to estimate the

effects of teacher's time allotments for a given topic to the average posttest performance of the class. Separate analyses conducted at two or more levels are termed multilevel analyses.

A much broader category of multilevel analyses, encompassing much of the literature on school and educational effects, employs a set of explanatory variables that are characteristics from two or more levels. For example, the regression of students' posttest scores on their own pretest scores, the average pretest scores for the class, and the teachers' reports of emphasis on whole-class instruction is a multilevel analysis because explanatory variables from multiple levels are included.

The apparent ease with which units and levels of analysis were defined above masks the often difficult task of selecting the appropriate units and levels in a given context. Educational researchers typically assume that only one unit is appropriate. They then attempt to justify their choice of unit and thereby the level at which the analysis should be conducted.

The desire to determine a single "correct" unit is perhaps a natural reaction to the results from various empirical studies involving multilevel educational data. In particular, attempts at cross-level inference, that is, using group-level data to infer about individual behavior and vice versa, are likely to be futile. Analyses of educational effects at different levels consistently reveal different results across levels (Burstein 1980a, Cronbach 1976). While the treatment of such differences as evidence of aggregation bias or cross-level bias has subsided in recent years, there are lingering doubts about the wisdom of mechanically choosing the units that serve as outcomes. The conduct of routine analyses at any level without concern for the general investigative intent and for possibly confounding technical considerations is also beginning to disappear.

The remainder of the discussion of unit and levels of analysis focuses on the kinds of issues that arise in selecting units, on an alternative perspective (which is termed multilevel) regarding unit and level considerations, and on major measurement and analysis issues that can be examined once this alternative perspective is adopted. Readings which provide more comprehensive discussions of these topics include Burstein (1980a, 1980b), Cronbach (1976), Haney (1980), Roberts and Burstein (1980), Treiber (1980), and Wiley (1970).

1. Issues in Selecting Units

Traditionally, a variety of conceptual and technical arguments have been cited as justification of the choice of either students or groups (classes, schools, etc.) as the appropriate units of analysis. There are several extensive discussions of units of analysis issues. The major conceptual and technical issues are highlighted below.

1.1 Research and Decision Contexts

Clearly, the results of an educational study are more salient and supportable when substantive questions of interest guide the investigation. The specific research paradigm employed can, however, complicate the selection of units by constraining the type of information collected and the manner of collection. That is, whether specific conceptual or technical considerations are pertinent in selecting a unit of analysis is dependent, in part, on the type of study being conducted and the types of outcomes and processes of interest.

For the purposes of this article, the types of studies that warrant consideration are empirical investigations involving units from multiple levels where quantifiable data are collected about specific outcomes (test scores, attitudes, occupational or educational attainments, etc.), specific educational processes and practices (instructional characteristics, educational treatments, structural characteristics of schooling context, etc.), and perhaps about specific background or entry characteristics (home circumstances, entering abilities, community circumstances, etc.). The units under investigation may be either a random, stratified random, purposive, or nonrandom sample from some population of units (students, classrooms, teachers, schools, etc.) or they may be the entire population of possible units (e.g., all schools in a given state). To further complicate matters, the sampling units may be the units of interest or perhaps a higher level unit.

The contrast of a well-defined and implemented treatment randomly assigned to units with a loosely defined and implemented treatment or with naturally occurring educational "treatments" is also relevant in understanding the salience of various unit selection criteria. In an experimental context where units are assigned at random to different treatment conditions, the choice of a unit would appear to be straightforward. Unless, however, the units assigned to treatments are also the focus of the investigation, in which case the decision is no longer clear cut. For example, assigning intact classrooms or schools to treatments when the intent is to investigate individual student behavior can introduce statistical and substantive dependencies among the observations on individual students that cause many investigators to shift to a higher level for analysis. Even under random assignment conditions, the nature of the treatment contrasts (e.g., individualized instruction versus whole-group lecture) and the possibility of interactions among student attributes and treatments may point toward students as units despite the assignment of intact classes to treatments. The differential implementation of treatments in an experiment can also have a bearing on which units are considered appropriate.

The above concerns multiply in the quasiexperimental and nonexperimental investigations that dominate large-scale empirical inquiry in education. The heart of the matter is that investigators typically are studying the educative process within the context of the sociopolitical multilevel organizational settings. Neither the context nor the levels can be ignored without risk of misinterpretation.

Two other generic study attributes condition the choice of units in nonexperimental contexts. First, the type of data collection concerning educational processes impacts on the choice. Survey data gathered from school principals and teachers represent a different depth of description than an observational study of classroom practices (e.g., teacher–student and student–student interactions). Even when the variables of interest are the same, collection by one method (questionnaire, interview, observation) as opposed to another and/or from one source (student, teacher, principal) as opposed to another introduce different amounts of surplus meaning and analytical complexity. A student's report of his or her own opportunities to learn a specific topic involves different kinds of information than would a teacher's or observer's report of the individual's learning opportunities. Decisions about units of analysis and interpretations of results are obviously influenced by these distinctions.

The second consideration is the purpose of the investigation. The distinction between research and evaluation is relevant here. In research contexts—that is, research on school effects, educational effects, teacher effectiveness, classroom instruction, student learning, process–product relationships, educational production functions, contextual effects, aptitude–treatment interactions, and so forth—the intent is to clarify the linkages among the various attributes of the educational system and the behavior of the entities (students, teachers, classrooms, principals, schools, administrators) within the system. The products of such investigations are presumably a better understanding and further explanations about how the system and its elements work.

In contrast, there may be little concern for explaining how things work in many evaluations. The emphasis is upon generating information that contributes to some decision (e.g., Should handicapped children be mainstreamed? Does the scope and sequence for middle schools need revision? What happens to instructional programs when schools are allocated more or less funds? Will instructional decision making improve if criterion-referenced testing systems are substituted for norm-referenced systems?). Arguments can be made that the salience of information for a particular decision is affected by the closeness of the units from which it was collected (or the level at which it was analyzed) to the organizational level at which the decision is to be made. Yet these units may be either the same or different from those required to provide a valid explanation of why a particular program works the way it does.

The points emphasized in this discussion of research and decision contexts barely mention, much less elucidate, the specific conceptual and technical considerations that an investigator can expect to encounter in selecting units of analysis. Nonetheless, they presumably caution the reader against assuming that the discussion of conceptual and technical considerations represents general as opposed to context-specific aspects of the decision process regarding units and levels of analysis. Moreover, it foreshadows a later argument for an altered approach to decisions about units.

1.2 Conceptual Considerations

Conceptual considerations pertain to the purpose of an investigation. As such, they incorporate the first stage of empirical inquiry—question identification and formulation and theory specification—in other words, what is to be examined and how it fits within the broader scheme of things. These considerations are fundamental in determining units of analysis. Indeed, Haney (1980) and others view the purpose of the investigation as the preeminent consideration.

In investigations involving multilevel data, the alignment of the purpose with a single unit is seldom clear cut. While at times a particular analyst may consider a given unit as central, another analyst approaching the same empirical situation from a somewhat different perspective might find a different unit better serves his or her purpose.

There are several ways to better delineate this dilemma. A comparison of the primary units in various lines of empirical inquiry highlights historical disciplinary alignments with choice of focus. For example, schools and even school districts were typically the primary units for the economists and sociologists conducting large-scale school effects and educational production function research during the 1960s and early 1970s. In some cases they were guided by data availability considerations; many used district-reported school-level outcome (e.g., mean test scores) and schooling characteristics (availability of libraries, average teacher salary, experience, or education, pupil–teacher ratios, etc.). Others believed that the manipulable elements of educational programs were those factors controllable at the school or district level; that is, it is possible to "buy" better educated or more experienced teachers, smaller class sizes, and more science equipment.

Much of the process–product research on teaching from the 1970s, on the other hand, employed either classes or students as their units of analysis (Burstein 1980a). These studies typically involved observations of teacher behavior and teacher–student and student–student interactions. Thus activities in the classroom—what the teacher does and how it affects student behavior—were central. While not always clearly stated, the choice between classes and students as units in such studies typically depended on whether the investigator was more interested in teaching behaviors or student learning. For instance, when there was interest in possible aptitude–treatment interactions, students were typically the units of analysis.

In much of the large-scale program evaluation activities, the determination of a specific unit is more complicated. As Haney (1980) points out, "social interventions have complex goals aimed at different levels of social life" (p. 3). In his examination of units of analysis issues in Project Follow Through (FT)), Haney explains why different choices are possible. Even though "the ultimate goal of FT was to develop educational processes and environments that would enable children to develop to their full potential . . . intermediate goals were . . . the promotion of changes in individual students, teachers, and educational institutions" (Haney 1980 pp. 3–4). Clearly the student is a fundamental unit in such circumstances. But questions about the ability of teachers to implement a specific curriculum faithfully and the school to target and administer program resources appropriately identify classes and schools as relevant foci for the evaluation. These same concerns were implicit in the earlier units of analysis debate generated by Wiley's (1970) presentation at a 1967 conference on evaluation of instruction sponsored by the Center for the Study of Evaluation (see Wittrock and Wiley 1970 for a detailed and illuminating account of the conference).

To further document the dilemma implied above, a subset of the appealing but competing conceptual perspectives in support of either students or groups as units can be paraphrased:

(a) Since the ultimate aim is to determine the effects on pupil outcomes of the educational resources that an individual pupil receives, his or her background, and the influence of his or her community setting and peers, pupils are the units for which questions must be finally addressed.

(b) Pupils react as individuals, and the effects on them should be the focus (Bloom in Wittrock and Wiley 1970).

(c) Effects in classrooms (schools) are esentially the effects of environmental arrangements on individuals (Wittrock and Wiley 1970).

(d) In classroom interaction research, teacher behavior is typically directed at individual students rather than at the whole class and student individual differences affect such teacher behavior.

(e) The effects of a treatment on a classroom (school) are fundamentally different from the effects of the treatment on the individuals within it. Thus the appropriate unit of study is the collective—class or school—rather than the individual (Wiley 1970).

(f) The utility of evaluation data depends on the number of organizational levels between the action the data describes and the decision processes they are intended to influence. Each decision maker should choose analysis units at his or her organizational level or at immediately adjacent levels.

The points cited are generally compelling and disagreements are unresolvable if a choice of a single unit is required.

1.3 Technical Consideration

While resolution of conceptual complexities is a necessary condition for appropriate selection of units, it is not necessarily sufficient in the presence of complicating technical considerations. Haney (1980) cites three types of technical considerations—evaluation (research) design, statistical considerations, and practical considerations—that also arise in unit selection decisions.

Evaluation or research design considerations encompass issues of units of treatment and independence of units, among others. The concerns about units of treatment are derived from the classical conception of experimental units as the smallest units (lowest level) which can receive different treatments or different replications of the same treatment. For example, if the teacher or the specific program of study implemented by the teacher were considered to be the "treatment" in a given investigation, then the classroom would be judged the appropriate unit of analysis (Wittrock and Wiley 1970). Likewise, if the program were instituted schoolwide (e.g., a violence prevention program in secondary schools), schools would be the units. But if the program were so organized that each student received a distinct replication of the treatment, as might be possible in a laboratory study or in a highly individualized learning setting, then the pupil might qualify as the unit under this criterion.

The independence of unit issue is closely related to the units of treatment concern but focuses on the independence of the response rather than on the treatment per se. Experimental canons caution that "experimental units should respond independently of one another . . . [there should be] no way in which the treatment applied to one unit can affect the observation obtained from another unit" (Cox 1958). Dependencies among units of the type described confound treatment effects and complicate the estimation of the within-treatment error.

Obviously, both types of design concerns are likely to arise in the typical nonexperimental investigation. In fact, literal adherence to classical experimental canons can virtually paralyze many educational studies since the presumably statistically required unit (because of dependency problems) might be very different from units associated with the research purpose (Hopkins 1982).

While the consequences of dependencies among observations and contaminated treatments are certainly real, their role in educational research and thus the means of handling them are best understood by a specification of their statistical and substantive manifestations. For example, the statistical consequences of dependency have to do primarily with complications in specifying the correlation structure among disturbances (errors) which in turn yield spuriously liberal tests of treatment effects in many instances (Burstein 1980a).

Yet the most direct way to resolve this problem is to devote more attention to specifying an appropriate error structure and adjusting the analysis accordingly. The substantive manifestation is that dependencies among observations within groups (classes, schools, etc.) are a function of the treatment or processes under investigation as well as the manner in which groups are formed and their composition. Thus within-group dependency is information about substantive educational processes and should be examined accordingly (Bidwell and Kasarda 1980, Webb 1980).

The statistical considerations cited by Haney (1980) include measurement reliability, degrees of freedom, and analysis considerations. Conventional wisdom is that aggregation to higher levels produces more reliable measures but reduces degrees of freedom for analysis. The analysis considerations focus on the unreliability problem as it affects estimation of treatment effects in the analysis of covariance. But these concerns are often erroneously applied, especially on the degree of freedom question, and are certainly peripheral to more immediate questions about the substantive focus of the investigation. Moreover, there is a clear tradeoff between reliable measurement of the wrong variable and less reliable measurement of the right one. Similarly, practical considerations such as missing data problems and the change in setting in multiple-year investigations are nuisances rather than central elements in unit selection, albeit highly visible ones. Haney's conclusion that the purpose of the investigation should guide choice rather than these other technical matters is eminently sensible.

2. A Multilevel Perspective

An alternative perspective on the selection of units is that the attention given to the selection of the unit of analysis is misdirected (Burstein 1980a, 1980b, Barr and Dreeben 1977, Rogosa 1978). As Rogosa (1978) points out, "no level is uniquely responsible for the delivery of and response to educational programs . . . confining substantive questions to any one level of analysis is unlikely to be a productive research strategy" (p. 83). Similarly, Barr and Dreeben (1977) contend that "school events should be observed where they occur; school, track, classroom, or whichever. . . . A full range of organizational levels and their interconnections" (pp. 101–02).

A multilevel perspective shifts the investigative focus toward the development of adequate theories of educational processes and analytical strategies for assessing their effects. The multilevel structure of the data is not merely a nuisance; it reflects reality. What is needed is an appropriate model of the educational phenomena of interest and analytical strategies that disentangle effects from a variety of sources so that the interface of the individuals and the "groups" to which they belong and the implications of this interface for educational effects can be examined.

The shift to a multilevel perspective offers the possibility of important benefits by focusing attention on key measurement and analytical issues that naturally arise in investigating data on individuals in social structures. Certain of these issues are discussed below.

2.1 Measurement Issues

The measurement issues most salient from a multilevel perspective are those associated with the possibility of change in the meaning of variables across levels and with indices of group-level performance. The former conveys more than the fact that relationships among variables may be specific to particular levels of aggregation. More importantly, the relationship between a theoretical construct and its measurable indicator may also be level specific; the aggregation of the manifest variable will not always lead to an aggregate indicator of the original construct operationalized by the disaggregated measure.

The principle that the same observable variable can measure different constructs at different levels of aggregation is well-established (Burstein 1980a, 1980b, Burstein et al. 1980, Cronbach 1976, Sirotnik 1980, Sirotnik and Burstein 1985). A few examples serve to emphasize its ubiquity in educational research. Take, for instance, the standard measures of socioeconomic background typically found in school effects research. At the individual level, they may properly convey the parental investment in the individual child's learning. Once aggregated to the school level, social background measures also reflect the community context (e.g., wealth, urbanism, commitment to quality education) which in many countries determines the resource allocations to schools. Within an educational level, relative social background positions students within a potential status hierarchy (e.g., a big fish in a small pond) that can affect their experiences. All three measures of social background may be important in understanding the experiences and performances of students but they do represent distinctly different mechanisms.

In a reanalysis of data from an observational study of the factors influencing student learning, Burstein (1980a) demonstrated how the interpretation of a measure of the relative amounts of student learning tasks judged easy changed as the analysis shifted from the student to the class level. Students' success rates in learning tasks at the individual level captured proximal student ability and thus were positively related to student performance. At the class level, this same observational variable reflected teachers' policies with regard to task difficulty and in many instances exhibited negative relationships with student outcomes.

The problems of change in variable meaning across levels are particularly evident in the literature on organizational and educational climate (Sirotnik 1980, Sirotnik and Burstein 1985). The distinction between a specific student's perception of classroom climate, which reflects both absolute and comparative aspects of individual personality and perception, and the average perception of the class, a normative measure of the instructional environment, is an important one. Whether the "organizational" or the "psychological" aspect of the climate is most salient in a given context is unclear. For instance, aggregate responses of teachers within schools on scales purported to measure the degree of innovation and teacher influence have been construed as indicators of the atmosphere and organizational structure of the school program. In contrast, the individual teacher responses, relative to the responses of other teachers in the school, were interpreted as indicators of the teachers' sense of personal efficacy. That the effects of aggregated and individual measures on pupil outcomes were opposite in sign and consonant with expectations reinforces the need for a better understanding of how aggregation affects the measurement of program and process characteristics.

The other measurement issue, alternative indicators of group-level outcomes, reflects the concern that the decision to examine group-level phenomena leaves the question of relevant measures of group-level indices unresolved. The most typically investigated group-level index is the group (class, school) mean. While interest in overall level of performance, as captured by means or medians, is certainly reasonable in most contexts, means alone cannot capture the full detail that is contained in individual-level scores. Some of this additional detail may reflect student achievement differences that vary as a function of educational process variables. For example, in schools and classrooms with a high proportion of children with poor entering performance, say in the bottom quartile, an effective school or teacher might be one which manages to shift a significant proportion of the pupils above the bottom quartile when instructional outcomes are measured.

The main alternative to group means in the literature is measures of the distribution of performance within groups such as the within-group standard deviation. The "tastes" of the educational organization might cause schools or programs to reduce the spread of test performance rather than concentrate solely on shifting the overall level. Advocates of mastery learning and individualized instruction are often interested in such outcomes and their chosen indicators of group-level performance should be sensitive to the consequences of their programs (see *Mastery Learning Models*; *Individualizing Teaching*).

An analogous case has recently been made for treating within-group regressions of outcomes on inputs as measures of group-level performance (Burstein 1980a, Burstein et al. 1978).

The logic of within-group slopes as indicators is that they can potentially convey within-group processes in a group-level analysis. For a given distribution of entering student abilities, different teachers and different programs, through their choice of instructional processes, can relatively benefit either initially low-achieving or high-achieving students or provide equal benefits regardless of initial abilities. These differences across instructional settings can be reflected by variation in the within-group slopes. Whether the use of slopes as indicators of group-level outcomes is a fruitful investment of investigative resources remains a relatively unexplored question (Rachman-Moore and Wolfe 1984).

2.2 Analysis Issues

Once a multilevel perspective is adopted, a salient concern is how to conduct an analysis that considers effects at all pertinent levels. Multilevel analyses, that is, separate analyses at two or more levels or a combined analysis containing explanatory variables at two or more levels, are typically necessary. The central issues, then, focus on the development of strategies that combine the features of analyses at more than one level.

While earlier forays into estimating educational effects at multiple levels concentrated on the estimation of variance components or proportions of variation, current emphasis is on the decomposition of relationships (covariances, correlations, regression coefficients). Certain methods are basically direct extensions of widely used regression methods for handling multilevel data. Cronbach (1976), for example, decomposes the individual-level regression relationships into between-group and within-group components and recommends that between-group and pooled within-group regressions be separately estimated. On the other hand, there is the danger of the confounding of compositional effects (aggregated individual effects) with true group-level effects in the analysis of means when individuals are nonrandomly assigned to groups. Alternative analytical procedures which purportedly adjust estimates of group effects for within-group composition should be considered. Whether these adjustments are the proper ones is the subject of continuing debate, however.

A set of more elaborate multilevel estimation procedures have been proposed recently (Aitkin et al. 1981, Aitkin and Longford 1986, Erbring and Young 1979, Goldstein 1986, Mason et al. 1984, Rachman-Moore and Wolfe 1984, Raudenbush and Bryk 1986, Schneider and Treiber 1984). These methods are intended to model multilevel processes and outcomes more conscientiously and involved more powerful estimation procedures. To date, however, their application to actual educational data has been limited. Further conceptual, analytical, and empirical work on these methods is clearly warranted as they have yet to be subjected to the kinds of analytical and empirical tests that could identify their properties, much less their range of utility.

In summary, treating the analysis of multilevel data as simply a matter of selecting an appropriate unit and, thereby, level of analysis is too narrow a conception of the issues. Rather, the focus should be on the identification of the appropriate set of substantive research questions at and within various levels and the specification of appropriate models for analyzing multilevel data. Once this shift occurs, the measurement and ana-

lytical problems that typically arise in multilevel settings rightfully dominate the examination of interrelations among units at and within various levels of the educational system. As a consequence, progress in the understanding of educational phenomena will accelerate.

See also: Synthesizing Research Evidence

Bibliography

Aitkin M, Anderson D, Hinde J 1981 Statistical modeling of data on teaching styles. *J. R. Statist. Soc. A.* 144: 419–61

Aitkin M, Longford N 1986 Statistical modeling issues in school effectiveness studies. *J. R. Statist. Soc. A.* 149: 1–26

Barr R, Dreeben R 1977 Instruction in classrooms. In: Shulman L S (ed.) 1977 *Review of Research in Education*, Vol. 5. Peacock, Itasca, Illinois, pp. 89–162

Bidwell C E, Kasarda J D 1980 Conceptualizing and measuring the effects of school and schooling. *Am. J. Educ.* 88: 401–30

Burstein L 1980a Analysis of multilevel data in educational research and evaluation. In: Berliner D (ed.) 1980 *Review of Research in Education*, Vol. 8. American Educational Research Association, Washington, DC, pp. 158–233

Burstein L 1980b The role of levels of analysis in the specification of educational effects. In: Dreeben R, Thomas J A (eds.) 1980 *The Analysis of Educational Productivity*, Vol. 1: *Issues in Microanalysis*. Ballinger Press, Cambridge, Massachusetts, pp. 119–90

Burstein L, Fischer K, Miller M D 1980 The multilevel effects of background on science achievement: A cross-national comparison. *Sociol. Educ.* 53: 215–52

Burstein L, Linn R L, Capell F J 1978 Analyzing multilevel data in the presence of heterogeneous within-class regressions. *J. Educ. Statist.* 3: 347–83

Cox D R 1958 *Planning of Experiments*. Wiley, New York

Cronbach L J 1976 *Research on Classrooms and Schools: Formulation of Questions, Design, and Analysis*. Occasional Paper, Stanford Evaluation Consortium, Stanford, California

Erbring L, Young A A 1979 Individuals and social structure: Contextual effects as endogenous feedback. *Soc. Meth. Res.* 7: 396–430

Goldstein H 1986 Multilevel mixed model analysis using iterative generalized least squares. *Biometrika* 72

Haney W 1980 Units and levels of analysis in large-scale evaluation. In: Roberts K H, Burstein L (eds.) 1980

Hopkins K D 1982 The unit of analysis: Group means versus individual observations. *Am. Educ. Res. J.* 19: 5–18

Mason W M, Wong G Y, Entwisle B 1984 Contextual analysis through the multilevel linear model. In: *Sociological Methodology 1983/1984*. Jossey-Bass, San Francisco, California

Rachman-Moore D, Wolfe R G 1984 Robust analysis of a nonlinear model for multilevel educational survey data. *J. Educ. Statist.* 9: 277–93

Raudenbush S, Bryk A S 1986 A heirarchical model for studying school effects. *Soc. Educ.* 59

Roberts K, Burstein L (eds.) 1980 *New Directions in Methodology of Social and Behavioral Sciences*. Jossey-Bass, San Francisco, California

Rogosa D 1978 Politics, process, and pyramids. *J. Educ. Statistics* 3: 79–86

Schneider W, Treiber B 1984 Classroom differences in the determination of achievement changes. *Am. Educ. Res. J.* 21: 195–211

Sirotnik K A 1980 Psychometric implications of the unit-of-analysis problem (with examples from the measurement of organizational climate). *J. Educ. Meas.* 17: 245–81

Sirotnik K A, Burstein L 1985 Measurement and statistical issues in multilevel research on schooling. *Educ. Adm. Quart.* 21: 169–85

Treiber B 1980 Mehrebenenanalysen in der bildungsforschung.

Z. Entwicklungspsychol. Paedagog. Psychol. 12: 358–86

Webb N M 1980 Group process: The key to learning in groups. In: Roberts K H, Burstein L (eds.) 1980

Wiley D E 1970 Design and analysis of evaluation studies. In: Wittrock M C, Wiley D E (eds.) 1970 *The Evaluation of Instruction: Issues and Problems.* Holt, Rinehart and Winston, New York, pp. 259–88

Wittrock M C, Wiley D E (eds.) 1970 *The Evaluation of Instruction: Issues and Problems.* Holt, Rinehart and Winston, New York

Teachers as Researchers

J. Elliott

The idea of teachers as researchers is usually associated with Stenhouse, director of the Schools Council's Humanities Project (1967–72). Stenhouse integrated the idea into an imaginative conception of the curriculum project as a concrete expression of educational ideas for teachers to reflect upon as they attempted to implement it in practice. The "curriculum project" was conceived as a device for linking theory to practice, and holding theorists accountable to teachers. These ideas were elaborated as an alternative process model of curriculum development, to the objectives model (Stenhouse 1975).

The two models constituted different solutions to a dilemma centrally funded developers faced in the United Kingdom during the late 1960s and early 1970s. Their curricula were being misused by teachers, who adapted them to match their traditional pedagogy and the assumptions about knowledge and teaching which underpinned it. This problem was exacerbated by the prevailing ideology of teacher autonomy, which gave developers little control over the use of their products. All they could do was to market them with "suggestions". So the dilemma was how to effect change in classrooms while respecting teachers' autonomy of judgment.

The objectives model (Tyler 1949) was used to establish a rational foundation for the adoption of curriculum projects. Its emphasis on analysing broad curricular aims into quantifiable learning outcomes as a basis for developing and evaluating curriculum activities, opened the possibility of rationally demonstrating their effectiveness.

A major assumption underlying the use of the objectives model as a basis for securing "rational adoption" was that curricula, like washing machines, can be mass produced. The influence of contextual factors on the way curricula "shape up" in different settings was ignored. In spite of positive evaluation findings teachers continued to misuse innovations.

Stenhouse's solution to the dilemma was a highly original one. Rather than developing a curriculum which appealed to teachers as rational adopters the Humanities Project addressed them as pragmatic sceptics.

Instead of analysing the teaching aim of the project— "to develop an understanding of controversial value issues"—into behavioural objectives, Stenhouse claimed it could be logically analysed into the following procedural principles governing the way teachers handle controversial issues with students.

(a) Discussion rather than instruction should be the core activity in the classroom.

(b) Divergence of view should be protected.

(c) Procedural neutrality should be the criterion governing the teachers' role.

(d) Teachers have responsibility for quality and standards in learning, for example by representing criteria for understanding evidence about peoples' views.

These principles are not couched as precise technical rules governing exactly what teachers ought to do in classrooms. They constitute an operational philosophy mediating between a rather abstract ideal or aim and the practicalities of teaching. Stenhouse's logic provided an orientation for classroom practice but left questions about how it was to shape up in particular circumstances for teachers' own research. They were encouraged to tape or video record episodes of classroom interaction and elicit students' perceptions of the extent to which their teaching exemplified or negated the principles of procedure. Teachers were asked to use this data as a basis for formulating and testing hypotheses about strategies which either negated or enabled the realization of the principles. Since the work in schools involved groups, teachers were encouraged to share and discuss each others' data, and thereby generate hypotheses collaboratively.

The initiative for hypothesis generation came, at least initially, from central team members, who assisted the teacher groups to collect observational data and elicit feedback from students. At a midpoint in the trials the central team identified a number of hypotheses which might be generalizable to a variety of contexts, and teachers were asked to test them in the second half of the trials. At the end, a number of teachers produced detailed case studies of their work (Elliott and Mac-Donald 1975), and on the basis of these the author (a member of the Humanities Project from 1967–72) distilled a number of general hypotheses about the problems of implementing the project's logic of teaching in secondary schools. These not only referred to concrete teaching strategies, but also to factors in the institutional context which constrained and facilitated classroom implementation.

The Humanities Project has been emphasized in order to clarify certain features of the context in which the idea of teachers as researchers emerged.

First, it emerged as one solution to the problems of implementing curriculum innovations in classrooms. Secondly, it was linked with a process model of curriculum development, which posited curriculum and teacher development as one and the same enterprise. Within the terms of this model, teachers develop the curriculum and themselves through cycles of action research—of reflection upon action followed by action upon reflection. It is important to grasp the contrasting views of professional development implicit in the process and objectives models.

Aristotle long ago made a distinction in his "Ethics" (1955) between activities of doing and making. The latter involves the application of precise technical rules to the production of quantifiable results. Precise technical rules can be prescribed because the product can be clearly specified in advance. Therefore what constitutes competent performance can be discovered and prescribed independently of the performer, who can simply be trained to apply the rules correctly. Technical rules cannot be applied to activities of doing, Aristotle claimed, because ends here refer to abstract ethical ideals which constitute qualities to be realized in the activities themselves rather than quantities to be produced as a result of them. No perfect method of doing is possible. What constitutes the best method is always something of a shot in the dark, and therefore a subject for deliberative reflection and discussion by participants in the light of their particular circumstances. Although practical knowledge (wisdom) of what worked in the past is a resource for such deliberation it cannot determine its outcome. The context of practice is always changing and requires continuous innovation. Moreover, it is only through retrospective reflection about their strategic responses that participants develop their understanding of the ends-in-view. By identifying negative and positive instances of good practice, par-

ticipants clarify the ideals which constitute it. Thus the improvement of practice proceeds interactively with a developing understanding of the ideals which guide it; means and ends are joint objects of reflection. Practical deliberation integrates empirical with theoretical/philosophical inquiry.

Aristotle's idea of practical deliberation has inspired a tradition of curriculum theorizing in the United States and the United Kingdom (Schwab 1971, Reid 1978) which has only recently begun to link with the literature stemming from the classroom action-research movement. But the link is obvious.

Aristotle's distinction illuminates understanding of the different implications of objectives and process models of curriculum for teacher education. On the former model, curriculum development is a technology requiring an hierarchical system of specialized roles. Educational theorists clarify objectives; empirical researchers discover rules (or correlations) through process–product studies; developers translate rules into methods; and teacher technicians implement them correctly. The model provides another group of specialists, staff developers, with standardized criteria for identifying and rectifying deficiencies in performance. Construed as technicians, teachers become objects to be developed by experts.

When curriculum development is viewed as a doing activity it constitutes a professional practice guided by an ethic or logic. Here teachers develop themselves as a professional group through collegial deliberation about their curricular practices. This process assumes an absence of hierarchical control through a system of specialized roles. From the standpoint of the teachers as researchers movement theorizing about, researching into, deciding upon, and implementing the curriculum are integral components of professional practice.

The teachers as researchers movement entails a radically different role for external change agents; one of facilitation rather than control. Curriculum theorizing and research by external agents is a legitimate part of facilitation, providing it focuses on teachers' conceptions of ends and means and helps them to clarify and extend their ideas through dialogue. Facilitation also involves helping teachers learn techniques for collecting, sharing, and analysing data about their practical problems.

The Ford Teaching Project (Elliott 1976) provided ample illustrations of the facilitating role. Groups of teachers in the United Kingdom investigated the implementation of inquiry/discovery-based curricula. Working from tape-recorded discussions of classroom situations Adelman and Elliott identified a number of key concepts teachers employed. They then analysed the logical relationships between the teachers' concepts and the aim of inquiry/discovery teaching, which teachers defined as "enabling independent reasoning". This logic was specified as a set of pedagogic principles, and after discussion with teachers, used as a common framework for the study of classrooms.

Teachers were helped to use a triangulation procedure (Adelman 1980) for generating a database consisting of teachers', students', and observers' perceptions. The database was then subjected to collaborative analysis by all three parties, in dialogue—a process often extended to involve other project teachers and schools. This collaborative reflection led to further refinements of the initial logic and the generation of a commonly agreed set of hypotheses concerning implementation problems and strategies.

In generating a logic of teaching in dialogue with teachers, rather than specifying it in advance, the Ford Project anticipated the mid-1970s trend in the United Kingdom towards school-based curriculum development. This tendency to give teachers greater responsibility for theory generation was pushed even further in Elliott's work with Ebbutt on the Schools Council's TIQL Project (Elliott 1985).

During the latter half of the 1970s the teachers as researchers movement mushroomed with the growth of school-based curriculum development in the United Kingdom and Australia. As a result an international classroom action research network (CARN) was established to promote exchanges of ideas between teacher researchers and facilitators. It holds an annual conference and produces regular bulletins (Elliott and Whitehead 1980, 1982).

There exists an increasing amount of second-order action research into the problems of facilitating teachers' research (Brown et al. in Elliott and Whitehead 1982). Some of the major facilitation problems being addressed are:

(a) *Data analysis.* Winter (1982) claimed that although much has been written on data collection methods in action research, little has emerged on data analysis. His "dilemma analysis" focuses on the practitioner's experiences of conflicting action requirements in the classroom.

(b) *Producing written accounts.* Increasingly teachers' accounts of their research are being published (Nixon 1981). Many reflective teachers however, are reluctant to make their deliberations public, claiming that private reflection is sufficient as a basis for improvement. However, in as much as action research involves discussion with professional peers, it must be accountable to some degree, and should be differentiated from purely private self-evaluation activities.

(c) *Institutionalizing and utilizing teachers' research.* In order to reduce the dependence of teacher groups on external facilitators, attention is now being given to the institutionalization and utilization of action research in schools. Increasingly attempts are being made to give major facilitation responsibilities to school staff. The Schools Council TIQL Project was structured around school based coordinators who are both senior teachers and trained action researchers (Ebbutt 1982). Some have already begun to make major contributions to second-order educational action research (Holly and Wakeman in Elliott and Whitehead 1982).

As facilitators reflect upon their practices they are also beginning to refine the theory of educational action research. In Australia, Grundy and Kemmis (1981) have argued that action research must focus on the structural determinants of practice as well as on those elements which teachers can change. By entertaining critical theorems about "structures of domination" teachers can begin to collaboratively devise strategies for emancipating themselves from them. Educational action research is not only practical but emancipatory. As the educational context of the teachers as researchers movement becomes more bureaucratized and hierarchized, so action-research theory develops a political dimension.

See also: Ethical Considerations

Bibliography

Adelman C 1980 On first hearing. In: Adelman C (ed.) 1980 *Uttering, Muttering.* Grant McIntyre, London

Aristotle 1955 *The Ethics of Aristotle*, Book 6. Penguin, Harmondsworth

Ebbutt D 1982 *Teachers as Researchers: How Four Teachers Co-ordinate the Process of Research in Their Respective Schools.* Cambridge Institute of Education, Cambridge

Elliott J 1976 *Developing Hypotheses about Classrooms from Teachers' Practical Constructs.* North Dakota Group on Evaluation, University of North Dakota, North Dakota

Elliott J 1985 Facilitating action-research in schools: Some dilemmas. In: Burgess R E (ed.) 1985 *Field Methods in the Study of Education.* Falmer, London

Elliott J, MacDonald B (eds.) 1975 *People in Classrooms: Teacher Evaluations of the Humanities Curriculum Project.* Occasional Publications, No. 2. Centre for Applied Research in Education, University of East Anglia, Norwich

Elliott J, Whitehead D 1980 CARN Bulletin No. 4. Cambridge Institute of Education, Cambridge

Elliott J, Whitehead D 1982 CARN Bulletin No. 5. Cambridge Institute of Education, Cambridge

Grundy S, Kemmis S 1981 *Educational Action-research in Australia: The State of the Art.* Deakin University, Victoria

Nixon J (ed.) 1981 *A Teachers' Guide to Action Research.* Grant McIntyre, London

Reid W H 1978 *Thinking About the Curriculum: The Nature and Treatment of Curriculum Problems.* Routledge and Kegan Paul, London

Schwab J J 1971 The practical: A language for curriculum. In: Schwab J J 1971 *Science, Curriculum, and Liberal Education.* University of Chicago Press, Chicago, Illinois

Stenhouse L et al. 1970 *The Humanities Project: An Introduction.* Heinemann, London

Stenhouse L 1975 *An Introduction to Curriculum Research and Development.* Heinemann, London

Tyler R W 1949 *Basic Principles of Curriculum and Instruction.* University of Chicago Press, Chicago, Illinois

Winter D 1982 Dilemma analysis: A contribution to methodology for action research. *Camb. J. Educ.* 12(3): 161–74

Ethical Considerations
W. B. Dockrell

Concern with ethical considerations in educational research has grown in recent years, whereas in earlier years the emphasis was on technical standards. This concern can be viewed as relating to the subjects of study, to the customers for a particular investigation, to the scientific community, and finally to society in general. These sets of concerns are not independent but are interrelated, posing questions for researchers themselves and for all those concerned with research.

1. The Growth of Concern

Most books on educational research published in the 1970s (Butcher and Pont 1973, Kerlinger 1973, Taylor 1973), not only do not include a chapter or section on ethics but do not even include the term in their indexes. There is, however, a discussion of ethics as they apply to social research in general in a book published in 1979 (Barnes 1979), and a later book (Dockrell and Hamilton 1980) does have a chapter which includes ethics in its contents (Walker 1980), but even in this book the term does not appear in the index.

There has been, since the early 1970s, an increased awareness of ethical questions in research involving people. Earlier concern was with technical issues as manifested in such volumes as the *Technical Recommendations for Achievement Tests* (American Educational Research Association 1955) prepared by a committee of the American Educational Research Association and the National Council on Measurement Used in Education and a similar one, *Technical Recommendations for Psychological Tests and Diagnostic Techniques* prepared by a committee of the American Psychological Association (American Psychological Association 1954). These two volumes were replaced by one prepared by a committee representative of the three organizations, on standards for educational and psychological tests (American Psychological Association 1966). More recently the emphasis has shifted. In 1973, a book on ethical principles in research with human participants (American Psychological Association 1973) was published as well as a substantial volume on standards for evaluation of educational programmes (Joint Committee on Standards 1981). This latter report continued the concern with technical matters but also included a section on propriety standards, which was largely ethical.

Technical standards are an important aspect of ethics in educational research. Whatever procedures are used must be valid, that is, they must provide accurate information relevant to the purposes for which they are used. Accuracy is relative. In most measurements, physical as well as educational, there is some error. Precise accuracy is not possible. The scales used in a maternity hospital for weighing new-born infants need to be more accurate than those used for measuring overweight middle-aged adults in a gymnasium. Each needs to be accurate enough for its purpose. Much of the 1966 volume issued by the American Psychological Association is devoted to this question of the validity of instruments and the rest to other related matters like the reliability of instruments, scales and norms used, instructions for scoring, and the general adequacy of the manuals.

The 1981 report of the Joint Committee on Standards for Educational Evaluations goes beyond this even in technical matters. Additional questions are raised with ethical implications.

2. Ethics in Relation to Subjects

The focus of the manual on ethical principles (American Psychological Association 1973) is exclusively on the subjects of an experiment. This is a major area of concern, but not the only one. The first question for the researcher in relation to his or her subjects is, do they understand fully what is being asked of them? The researcher must not minimize or indeed exaggerate the demands that are to be made in terms of time, effort, or stress on subjects.

It is easiest to be clear about the amount of time that will be required. It is sometimes difficult for a researcher to appreciate the stress that may be induced, for example, in school pupils by a test which proves to be too difficult for them. School children do not always understand the distinction between data which are being gathered anonymously for research purposes and assessments which are being made of them personally.

It may be easier for teachers to make this distinction. However, at the beginning of a study of the effects of different teaching styles, the extent to which their actual classroom practices will be monitored by an outsider may not be clear to the teachers involved. Whatever disclaimers may be made, the observer may appear to be a figure of some authority or at least in close contact with people in authority. The presence of a student in the classroom for a prescribed period may be quite acceptable. The presence of a researcher over a considerable period of time may be a source of considerable stress.

The mere presence of a researcher in a classroom or indeed in a school studying the use of corporal punishment may be a source of stress both to those who would wish to use corporal punishment but are constrained from doing so and to those who wish to see it eliminated but fear their discipline may not be tight enough. The researcher cannot be expected to anticipate the amount of stress in each case but can reasonably be expected to make clear precisely what is being expected and to ensure as far as possible that there is no misunderstanding about what will be involved.

The second area in which the researcher has obligations concerning the subjects of the study is the confidentiality of the information obtained. It is up to the researcher to ensure that the subjects know and agree what will be disclosed about them. Many research organizations have rules about the identification of schools or school districts, teachers, or pupils in published reports (as does the Scottish Council for Research in Education, for example). The application of this principle is easier in the traditional survey-type studies where information is disclosed only about categories of schools, teachers, or pupils. It is only in those rare circumstances where there are only a few cases in any one category that it is possible to identify individuals. However, with case studies which rely on providing substantial information about a limited number of subjects it may not be possible to disguise the individuals concerned. The use of a fictional name as in Elmstown (Hollingshead 1949) or Hightown Grammar (Lacey 1970) may not be sufficient to disguise the source of the information. It may be necessary in those cases to do as Richardson did in her Nailsea study (Richardson 1973), that is, to negotiate with all concerned before the publication of a report.

Whether an attempt is made to disguise individual persons or institutions by the use of a fictional name, or a number, or a letter, or whether their identity is fully disclosed, all concerned must have a chance to read the material before it is published. Should they also have the right to require the removal of any material about themselves to which they object even if this were to weaken the report to the point of rendering it valueless? What is the balance between the rights of the subjects in the study and of the community for whose benefit the study was carried out?

With unpublished materials a similar problem may arise. Information about an individual, whether he or she is explicitly identified or not, may be used as a basis of discussion for clarification or for explanation with colleagues or superiors. The individuals clearly have a right to know beforehand that this may happen to them. Do they equally have a right to exclude from such discussion any material about themselves which they find unacceptable?

The first concern outlined above was about the effects on the subjects. A second concern is about the benefits of research to them. A researcher must specify what return there will be to the subjects and not mislead them about the benefits of the investigation to themselves. It is not unusual for researchers to offer to provide the results of tests to participants in a study. If the test scores are to be meaningful to the participants it may be necessary to provide an interpretation which is not required for research purposes. For example, a test of academic achievement may be administered which provides only raw scores for experimental purposes. That information might be all that the researcher needs.

Those scores, however, might be quite meaningless to teachers, pupils, or administrators unless they were related in some way to the objectives of the teaching or the performance of a reference group. If the subjects are to be offered benefits for themselves those benefits must be real.

A serious dilemma may arise when there is concern about the effect on subjects of knowledge of the object of the research. It may be important to know whether classrooms following a particular regime are more likely to induce persistence in their pupils than those adopting an alternative approach. It might be possible to devise an acceptable measure of persistence but what would the effect be on that measure of informing the children that this is what was being measured and not level of attainment? The same problem arises with classroom observation studies which are concerned with particular aspects of teacher behaviour. If teachers are told precisely what it is that the researchers are looking for, are they more likely to act in that way than if they were simply given general information? If the researcher believes that full disclosure would affect the behaviour of the subjects, under what circumstances is he or she free to withhold relevant information and by doing so mislead? Is it ever legitimate to make false statements in order to disguise the true objective of an investigation?

It is incumbent on the researcher to be explicit in the definition of the role of both sets of participants in a study, researchers and subjects. In some cases the responsibility of each is clear enough. In others, for example in action research, it is sometimes not clear what the subjects can expect of the researchers by way of support for their activities. By contrast there are some research designs which require the researcher to take an authoritarian role and to ensure that certain actions are carried out. It should be clear to all participants what they can expect of each other. This does not mean that they need to follow a rigidly predefined path. Flexibility may be essential for the progress of the research. What is required is that at each stage the mutual expectations be explicit.

A final consideration with respect to the subjects is general cost effectiveness. Is the value that is to be gained from the investigation commensurate with what is being asked of the subjects? It is very rarely that educational research would involve actual psychological harm to children. However, parents sometimes raise this question when a new curriculum is being tried out in the schools. They are concerned that their children may be put at a disadvantage in comparison with others. It is a question which arises with experimental studies rather than with observation of variation in current practice. If a researcher introduces a change in practice he or she is depriving children of something they would otherwise have had, and providing a substitute. In what circumstances is the informed consent of parents required for such an experiment? Does a school have to get consent before trying a new reading scheme, a new form of grouping, a new teaching method? The existence of laboratory schools which parents choose to send their children to, provides one answer. However, it is not an alternative that is universally available (see *Laboratory Schools*).

It is also important not to make an excessive demand on the time or resources of pupils or schools. Excessive in this context means not commensurate with any foreseeable benefit from the studies.

3. Ethics in Relation to Customers

A second set of concerns relates to the customers of research. In this context, customer refers to someone who has commissioned the research. At its simplest this can be summarized by saying that researchers should not promise more than they can deliver and that consequently they should deliver what they have promised. This principle applies whether the customer is looking for guidance about a specific course of action, or for better understanding of some theoretical issue. In this section the focus will be on customers whose interest is in research as a basis for action.

Ethical considerations in relation to customers refer primarily to communication. The first concern must be that the customer understand the limits of the information that will be made available. Research findings are rarely prescriptive. They never pre-empt careful consideration of the issues. It is unlikely that research will tell an administrator or teacher what to do. Usually it can only contribute to the examination of the options. The researcher therefore must be clear about what the data from a specific study can and cannot contribute to the thinking about a particular issue or set of issues.

The conclusions from research may range from a plausible hypothesis to a substantiated generalization. Whitehead's distinction in his paper on the rhythm of education (Whitehead 1932) may be applied to research (Dockrell and Hamilton 1980). He talks about the stage of romance which is when the researcher has an insight into the possible interpretation of a set of facts, the stage of precision where he or she attempts to specify the circumstances where the insight might apply, and finally the stage of generalization where the researcher can assert a particular principle or a particular set of relationships that will be of universal application. There is a risk that a research report which is at the stage of romance or indeed at the stage of attempted precision will be misconstrued as at the stage of generalization, even when the authors are careful to point out the limitations of their work as did Rutter and his colleagues (Rutter et al. 1979). The researchers must make clear to the customer what is the status of their conclusions.

It is in this area of relationships with customers that the traditional concern with technical questions is relevant. Researchers understand the meaning of statistical significance, that is, the probability of findings being other than accidental, but the customer may not. He or she may be presented with tables of relationships

between groups and assume that the sample findings can be safely generalized to the population. Professional journals would insist on the inclusion of probability levels. They may, however, be excluded from unpublished reports to customers. Even some published reports have presented results which were not statistically significant in a way that might mislead a reader.

One of the conventional distinctions in discussion of educational, research is between statistical significance and educational significance. Relationships which it is reasonable to assume actually exist in the population might be so small as to be irrelevant for practical purposes. A customer who is told that results are significant might assume that this means important and not merely probable. The importance of relationships is a matter of judgment and it is therefore the responsibility of the researcher to see that the customer understands the probable size of the differences as well as the likelihood of them being found in the parent population. A customer who thinks that a correlation of 0.5 is high might not do so if he or she appreciated the extent of the covariation that it indicated.

The measures used in research are frequently not direct measures of the variables which are of concern to the customers. Researchers might talk easily of achievement in mathematics or science, of intelligence or social class, always understanding that what is being referred to is a score on a particular measure. Whether that measure adequately represents what the customer means by the variable in his or her particular set of circumstances needs clarification. Scores on any test of attainment in, for example, physics, will cover only a sample of the skills and concepts which might legitimately be thought of as included in physics. As long as the sets used in the research coincide with those the customer had in mind for this purpose, no problems arise. It is up to the researcher to ensure that the customer understands the nature and content of the test and is consequently in a position to judge for himself or herself whether the measure is appropriate.

The problem is particularly acute in studies where surrogates are used. It is not easy, for example, to define social class and even where a definition is attempted it is the practice to use some surrogate like a scale of occupations. Surrogates may be satisfactory for research purposes but quite unsuitable for policy making. It is probably wisest to avoid using a general label like reading or physics or social class as far as possible and to be specific in saying what the scale assesses.

Where do the researchers' responsibilities end? Have they met their commitments when they present a set of results, or have they a responsibility to their customers to interpret their findings, to say what they mean in a particular context? The extent to which researchers can do this will vary from project to project, but it will be done by somebody and researchers do not absolve themselves from responsibility by saying that they have presented their results. Rather, their responsibility is to facilitate and participate in interpretation, ensuring that any conclusions are in accord with their understanding of the data.

If researchers do accept responsibility for interpreting and explaining their findings, they have the further responsibility of distinguishing between their findings and their extrapolations from them. It is legitimate to interpret results in the light of theory. It is important too to specify which of the researchers' opinions arise from the specific set of findings and which from theoretical or other considerations.

The researcher has a final responsibility to the customer, that is, to ensure that he or she is understood. Researchers frequently use terms which have limited or extended meaning. That may be a convenient form of communication for people who share a particular background. It may be misleading to a customer who does not share the researcher's knowledge or assumptions. Many research organizations employ editors whose job it is to translate research findings into the language of the customers. Where researchers do not have this professional service available to them, they should be particularly alert to the needs and problems of their readers.

4. Ethics in Relation to Colleagues

The researchers' obligations to their colleagues are twofold. One is to them as scientists to ensure that they can make the fullest use of their researches and second, as members of the research community to ensure that what they say does not detract from the status of the community.

Research data are not private property. They are an individual contribution to a common wealth of knowledge and understanding. The first set of responsibilities are those most frequently specified and indeed frequently enforced by colleagues through the medium of reviewing research proposals for funding, articles for publication, and books once they have been published.

In technical reports which are addressed to the research community, far more detail about the way the data have been gathered and how the analyses have been made is called for than in a report to customers so that an adequate professional evaluation of findings may be made. Some research institutions prepare several reports on the same study, designed for different audiences. The report to colleagues should be sufficiently detailed for them to understand the limitations in the data and their analysis. The kind of interpretation and perhaps simplification which is involved in a popular report can be avoided and replaced with specific detail.

One common way of dealing with the question of analysis is to make data available for reanalysis. Social science archives are one way of doing this, though it may be appropriate for some kinds of data to be held in confidence and only made available in carefully controlled circumstances. This does not of course answer all the questions. It only makes available the data on file. It does not answer questions about how the data

were gathered. It is important therefore to retain copies of tests, questionnaires, and other material.

In the case of ethnographic studies, the raw data may well be field notes including reports of interviews, descriptions of observations, and so on. In this case the raw data should be available for other scholars to read and interpret but so should a description of the circumstances in which the encounters took place.

Some researchers achieve fame or have it thrust upon them. It is in these circumstances that the researchers' responsibility to the research community is greatest. What is written will be seen as "research". When they are reported it will be "researcher says". They will be taken as representing the whole research community. The clearest responsibility is not to make statements which will bring research into disrepute. This does not mean that they must not participate or indeed provoke debate on important issues. If they do not make clear the significance of their findings for general issues who will? Researchers must not, however, overstate their cases—and must not assert the infallibility of research findings, particularly of their interpretation of their own findings.

5. Ethics in Relation to the Community

Finally, the researcher has responsibilities to the community as a whole. One of them is implicit in the last consideration of responsibility to colleagues. It may well be the responsibility of researchers to draw attention to the implications of their researches for policy. If they do not, they may be neglected or misinterpreted and the community as a whole may suffer. Important improvements that could have been made might not be made because of a researcher's reluctance to take part in social debate.

It is at this stage that researchers can be the voices of the voiceless. The customer in educational research is more likely to be an administrator with resources than teachers, parents, or pupils. The researcher can be the advocate of a different set of clients—the pupils who might suffer educationally from an apparently efficient set of arrangements or the teachers who might be forced into practices which have been evaluated from only one perspective and that one not their own.

There is a final consideration for the researchers. That is, whether it is appropriate to carry out a particular piece of research in specific social circumstances. A researcher like everyone else is responsible for the foreseeable consequences of his or her actions. In some societies simply to raise certain issues about racial or social differences might now or in the past have been a basis for the abridgement of human rights. The researcher has the obligation to ask questions fearlessly. He or she also has the obligation to be aware of the consequences of raising certain issues.

The relevance of a broad range of ethical questions to the conduct of research has been recognized in fields like medicine for many cultures. In physics, the development of nuclear weapons provided a jolt that led to soul searching and laid the old certainties open to question. As educational research has become less an academic pursuit and more directly a guide to educational practice, ethical issues have become more prominent and concern with them a topic of discussion among researchers.

See also: Teachers as Researchers

Bibliography

American Educational Research Association/National Council on Measurements Used in Education 1955 *Technical Recommendations for Achievement Tests*. National Educational Association, Washington, DC

American Psychological Association 1954 *Technical Recommendations for Psychological Tests and Diagnostic Techniques*. American Psychological Association, Washington, DC

American Psychological Association 1966 *Standards for Educational and Psychological Tests and Manuals*. American Psychological Association, Washington, DC

American Psychological Association 1973 *Ethical Principles in the Conduct of Research with Human Participants*. American Psychological Association, Washington, DC

Barnes J A 1979 *Who Should Know What? Social Science, Privacy and Ethics*. Penguin, Harmondsworth

Butcher H J, Pont H B (eds.) 1973 *Educational Research in Britain*, 3. University of London Press, London

Dockrell W B, Hamilton D (eds.) 1980 *Rethinking Educational Research*. Hodder and Stoughton, Dunton Green, Kent

Hollingshead A B 1949 *Elmstown's Youth: The Impact of Social Classes on Adolescents*. Wiley, New York

Joint Committee on Standards for Educational Evaluation 1981 *Standards for Evaluations of Educational Programmes, Projects, and Materials*. McGraw-Hill, New York

Kerlinger F N (ed.) 1973 *Review of Research in Education*, Vol. 3. Peacock, Itasca, Illinois

Lacey C 1970 *Hightown Grammar: The School as Social System*. Manchester University Press, Manchester

Richardson E 1973 *The Teacher, the School and the Task of Management*. Heinemann, London

Rutter M, Maughan B, Mortimore P, Ousten J, Smith A 1979 *Fifteen Thousand Hours: Secondary Schools and Their Effects on Children*. Open Books, London

Taylor W (ed.) 1973 *Research Perspectives in Education*. Routledge and Kegan Paul, London

Walker R 1980 The conduct of educational case studies: Ethics, theory and practice. In: Dockrell W B, Hamilton D (eds.) 1980, pp. 30–63

Whitehead A N 1932 *The Aims of Education, and Other Essays*. Williams and Norgate, London

Criteria for Evaluating Teaching

D. M. Medley

Efforts to improve the quality of teaching in the schools depend for their effectiveness on the availability of accurate, detailed, and objective evaluations of teaching. This article presents an overview of the state of the art of teacher evaluation in the early 1980s and is organized around three distinct criteria which may be used in such evaluations. It is addressed to professional educators and others concerned with the problem. No attempt is made to present both sides of controversial issues or to fully document every assertion made. The reader interested in these matters should consult some (or all) of the references listed.

The focus is on the evaluation of teaching rather than on the evaluation of teachers; more specifically, it is on interactive teaching, on what is called the teaching act itself. A discussion of teacher evaluation would need to address a broader range of problems which arise from the need to isolate the contribution of the teacher's abilities (and other characteristics) to the quality of the teaching from the many other factors that affect it.

1. Definitions

1.1 Criterion

The term "criterion" is used here in sharp distinction from the term "standard." A criterion is an aspect or dimension of the quality to be evaluated, which is to be assessed and then compared with an arbitrary standard or level of this quality as a basis for evaluating it. The concern of this article is with criteria rather than standards.

Evaluation of teaching may be based on one of three distinct types of criteria: (a) the outcomes of the teaching; (b) the learning behaviors or experiences of pupils that the teaching provides; and (c) the behavior of the teacher while teaching.

By far the largest part of all evaluation of teaching made by supervisors employs the third criterion, teacher behavior. Informal evaluations are based on impressions formed from casual observations of teacher behavior; formal evaluations are based on observations using some kind of a teacher rating scale. Teachers, on the other hand, tend to evaluate their own teaching on the basis of observations of how their pupils behave in class. The first type of criterion—outcomes—is the one favored by the public and its legislative and policy-making representatives, who seem to feel that it is reasonable to judge teaching by its results just as they do most other activities.

The purpose of teaching is, of course, to produce pupil learning; it seems perfectly logical, therefore, to evaluate teaching on the basis of outcomes. But since the function of the teacher in the production of learning is to provide pupils with experiences likely to result in learning, it also seems logical to evaluate teaching on the basis of the experiences it provides—that is, on the basis of pupil behavior in the classroom. And yet, since the means by which the teacher affects pupil behaviors and (through them) learning outcomes are the behaviors the teacher exhibits, it seems equally logical to base evaluations of teaching on teacher behavior.

1.2 Teaching

The formulation of an authoritative definition of teaching is much too large a task to be undertaken here. But it is necessary to formulate a working definition, one which can guide efforts to evaluate teaching. Depending on the type of criterion to be used, one of three approaches to this problem may be used (see *Definitions of Teaching*).

For present purposes a merely formal definition, one which specifies the types of tasks a teacher must perform, without saying how they are to be performed, will suffice. It is useful to think of teaching as involving the simultaneous performance of three tasks: (a) maintaining the classroom learning environment; (b) providing learning experiences appropriate to the changing needs of individual pupils; and (c) implementing those experiences in which the teacher is an active participant.

For convenience, performance of the first task is referred to as "environmental maintenance," the second as "managing learning," and the third as "instructing."

Performance of the first two tasks requires the teacher in the classroom to make hundreds of decisions each day; and each decision must be made almost instantaneously, because a failure to make a decision in time to implement it is in itself a decision—a decision not to make a decision. The quality of these decisions is, of course, the principal determiner of the quality of the teaching. The effects of all of the knowledge and skill a teacher possesses depend almost entirely on their being deployed appropriately, on their being used at the right time and with the right pupil; in short, on the interactive decisions the teacher makes.

However, it is unrealistic to expect a teacher to base interactive decisions directly on any knowledge of research, theory, subject matter, or anything else: there just isn't enough time to recall such knowledge. Effective teaching involves a two-stage decision process. In the pre-active phase of teaching the teacher must draw on his or her own knowledge base, knowledge of pedagogy and of subject matter, of the pupils and community, of the resources available, to decide upon a plan, strategy, or model of teaching to be followed during the interactive phase of teaching. Out of this must come a set of rules that will guide the teacher's interactive decisions. In the classroom the teacher must decide what to do next according to the strategy or model he or she has decided to follow, not by any direct appeal to the knowledge base. Because the knowledge base is used in choosing the strategy or model rather than in implementing it, the choice can be rational. Because it is made outside the classroom there is time

to reflect, to consult the literature, or even a colleague (see *Interactive Decision Making*; *Planning*).

1.3 Evaluation

The problem of defining evaluation is almost as large as that of defining teaching and, like it, lies outside the scope of this entry. But again it is necessary for present purposes to develop only a working definition of evaluation as it applies to human performance. Assessment of teaching, regardless of which type of criterion is being assessed, is but one instance of the assessment of human performance—that is, of the assessment of purposive human behavior in the execution of some task. Successful performance assessment involves three phases or steps, all of which are essential.

(a) *The standard task or set of tasks*. The first step in the assessment of human performance is the definition of the task or tasks the candidate for evaluation is to perform. The task must be specified in such a way that three requirements are met. First, the task must be of such a nature that the candidate has to demonstrate possession of the ability or the quality being evaluated in order to perform the task successfully. Second, the task must be specified so that it is possible to discriminate appropriate elements in a performance from inappropriate ones as a basis for scoring the performance. And, finally, the task or tasks set for all candidates must be either identical or equivalent, so that differences in the quality of performances will not arise because of differences in tasks.

(b) *The documentary record*. Those elements in the behavior or performance of a candidate on which the score will be based must be recorded in scorable and permanent form. Such a record is essential for objective and accurate scoring; it constitutes the only tangible basis for checking the scoring, for defending its fairness, objectivity, and validity. And how valid the score is depends almost entirely on how detailed, objective, and accurate the record is.

(c) *The scoring key*. Finally, there must be a procedure for deriving a criterion score from the record which will yield valid scores that are equal when based on records of equal quality, no matter who does the scoring.

Among these three critical phases or steps in performance assessment, the second—the documentary record—is the one most often neglected in the evaluation of teaching. This is probably due to the fact that most assessment theory is derived from experience with paper-and-pencil tests. When a candidate takes such a test, the record is automatically produced as the candidate answers the questions.

A well-constructed multiple-choice test represents the state of the art of performance assessment—or, more correctly, of its technology. In such a test the three steps are accomplished in the following manner:

(a) *The standard tasks*. The items on an objective test define the set tasks to be performed. The items are exactly the same for everyone who takes the same form of the test; they are equivalent for candidates who take alternative forms.

(b) *The documentary record.* The candidate records his own performance; as he or she answers the items and marks the answer sheet the candidate creates an accurate record of the outcomes of his or her peformance. The record is perfectly objective, since no other person is involved in its creation.

(c) *The scoring key.* The use of a machine-scorable answer sheet makes it possible for a machine to be programmed to recognize appropriate responses and so ensure that the same score is assigned to equivalent performances, without regard to other characteristics that may distinguish different candidates.

The validity and reliability of assessments based on objective test scores depend, then, on the nature of the tasks or problems presented and on the nature of the scoring key; neither is affected by the wisdom, skill, or sophistication of the scorer or of any other human being, once the instrument has been built.

When the focus of assessment is on the process used by the candidate rather than on the results obtained from its use, it is not usually possible for the candidate to create the record. Someone else must observe the performance and record the process used in a quantifiable form.

This person presents a grave threat to objectivity, one that is quite different from any threat to objectivity in a paper-and-pencil test: a threat to the objectivity (and accuracy) of the record itself rather than to the objectivity of the procedure used to score it. When different observers record the performance of different candidates, there may be differences between records of different candidates which have nothing to do with differences between their performances, but which reflect differences in the perceptions of the two observers instead. The validity of process assessments therefore depends at least as much on the accuracy and objectivity of the records as on those of the scoring key.

These definitions of criteria, teaching, and evaluation will provide the basis for the rest of this article. The next section will be devoted to a consideration of the first step in the process of teacher evaluation, that of defining the task to be set.

2. Defining Tasks for Evaluating Teaching

It might appear on first thought that the nature of the task defined for a teacher whose teaching is to be evaluated would depend on the nature of the criterion on which the evaluation is to be based. If the evaluation is to be based on certain behaviors of the teacher, such as explaining clearly or asking higher order questions, would it not be most efficient simply to ask the teacher to conduct a discussion and ask a number of higher

order questions during it? If the evaluation is to be based on the teacher's ability to provide certain pupil experiences, such as getting pupils to interact with one another during a class discussion, why not ask the teacher to demonstrate that he or she can do these things? Or if the evaluation is to be based on the ability to teach pupils new spelling words, why not ask the teacher to teach the words on a list?

The answer is, of course, that none of these tasks requires the teacher to *teach*. In the instance in which the task specified a teacher behavior, only the ability to exhibit that behavior on demand was required. In the instance in which the task specified pupil behaviors to be elicited, the same objection applies. At best, these tasks call for the use of certain skills which are used in the process of teaching but are by no means equivalent to it: they do not provide samples of teaching behavior on which an assessment of teaching can be based. The third example requires the teacher to achieve an outcome which falls far short of those a teacher must achieve.

2.1 Eliciting a Relevant Behavior Sample

In order to elicit a sample of teaching behavior, the task the candidate is to perform must be defined in terms of outcomes, not process; and the outcomes must be ones that teachers are expected to accomplish in the practice of their profession. Limited or artificial goals like the teaching of 10 spelling words may elicit instructional behavior, but they do not require the candidate to bear the full range of responsibilities or deal with the full complexities of teaching.

Nor can a true sample of teaching behavior be obtained by having the candidate "teach" a group of pupils especially assembled for the purpose. A teacher teaching his or her own class works toward a very different set of objectives than one "teaching" some other group of pupils for whom the teacher has no long-term responsibility. In the latter situation the teacher is responsible only for helping the pupils increase their score on whatever test the evaluator uses to assess the outcomes the teacher produces; in the former situation, the teacher is responsible for helping the pupils to grow toward all of the goals of education in that school system. What one gets in the artificial situation is a sample of coaching rather than of teaching behavior.

It seems clear, then, that the task specified must be the one the teacher performs every day.

2.2 Laying a Basis for Scoring

When the criterion used is based on outcomes, specifying the task in this way also ensures that the second requirement—that the specification provide a basis for scoring the records—is met. Changes in pupils toward the goals of the system are seen as indicators of good teaching; changes in the opposite direction, or absence of change, are seen as indicators of poor teaching.

When the criterion is based on in-class behaviors of teachers or pupils, the basis for scoring records is less obvious; but it rests ultimately upon knowledge of what the teacher is trying to accomplish, knowledge available when the task is specified in this way.

2.3 Defining Equivalent Tasks

The final requirement, ensuring equivalence of tasks assigned to different teachers, is by far the most difficult of the three requirements to satisfy, mainly because the characteristics of pupils as individuals and of classes as groups have so much to do with the nature of the task the teacher faces. No two classes are identical, even within the same school, subject, and grade; much less when they come from different schools and grades.

There is a theoretical solution to this problem: to assign pupils to classes by a random process. This would ensure that the classes differed only by chance; it would also provide a standard error to serve as a yardstick to use to detect nonrandom differences in the performances of different teachers.

But such randomization is, of course, impossible. Restricted randomization—randomization within schools, grades, and subjects is not impossible; but it is and will remain impractical unless and until the administrators responsible for assigning pupils to classes decide that valid assessments of teaching are worth the small extra effort such assignments would entail.

Creating a situation in which valid assessments of teaching based on outcomes criteria are feasible is, then, difficult if not impossible. The requirement that the task specification elicit genuine samples of teaching behavior can be met by basing the evaluation on the performance of a teacher with a class that he or she teaches regularly. The requirement that the task specification provide a valid basis for scoring can also be met in this way. But the problem of providing identical or equivalent tasks for different teachers has no practical solution. All that can be done is to make some sort of adjustment to compensate for this nonequivalence as part of the scoring procedure.

3. Assessing Teaching on the Basis of Learning Outcomes

When learning outcomes are to be used as the criterion of teaching quality, the elements on the documentary record take the form of scores earned by the teacher's pupils on measures of the knowledge, abilities, and other characteristics that pupils are supposed to acquire as the result of teaching; the major problem in scoring the record is that of isolating and assessing the parts of these measurements that are attributable to the teaching that is being evaluated (see *Effects of Teaching*).

3.1 Obtaining Records of Learning Outcomes

Because the records in this case consist of pupils' scores on tests and self-report questionnaires, there are no technical problems in obtaining them beyond those involved in any testing program. It will be presumed that any system that proposes to evaluate the teaching

in its schools will have in place a testing program designed to measure students' achievement of the major objectives of the system. If this is not so, then the setting up of such a program must be the first step in the assessment process.

This particular use of the systemwide testing program requires that the tests be administered at both the beginning and end of the school year in which the evaluation is to take place, so that changes during the year can be assessed. It is strongly recommended that such a program be supplemented by the administration of measures of other outcomes of teaching besides those adopted as school objectives, in order to detect any side effects or unintended outcomes. Sometimes goals identified as important are achieved at the expense of other equally important goals, especially when teachers know that their teaching is to be evaluated in terms of achievement of the former. Quality teaching cannot be assessed without some heed being paid to the full range of outcomes it produces. Failure to do so can reduce the quality of teaching instead of enhancing it.

3.2 Scoring Records of Learning Outcomes

There are two major problems which must be solved before a defensible criterion of the quality of teaching can be derived from a set of pretest and posttest scores of the pupils who have been taught. One is the problem of isolating the portion of changes in pupil scores that is attributable to the teaching from the portion that is not—the part that would have happened anyhow. The other problem is the problem of weighting the various kinds of changes shown in the record in arriving at a composite measure of outcomes that may be used as a criterion of the overall quality of teaching performance.

The second problem is not the sort of problem that can be dealt with in a methodological discussion; its solution depends on such value considerations as the philosophy of the school and of the community. It will therefore be assumed in the discussion to follow that this difficult problem has somehow been resolved so that there exists a single posttest score Y which measures the status of each pupil with respect to the goals of education in that school at the end of the period during which the teaching takes place. It is the problem of deriving from this score a measure of the effectiveness of the teaching that has occurred which will be dealt with here.

The problem may be restated as one of assessing the effect on Y of all factors other than the teaching, and then somehow adjusting the value of Y to remove these effects. These "contextual" factors manifest themselves at pretest time in two ways: in their effect upon the status of the individual pupil and in their effect on the status of the class as a group.

Suppose that the pretest battery is equivalent to the posttest battery and that the score it yields is X. Then it follows that all pre-existing factors of any kind that affect X will also affect Y in the same way. Thus a pupil's score on X will measure the past effects on that pupil of all such factors, known and unknown; and the mean score of the class on X will measure the past effects of such factors on the class as a group. If a value of Y differs significantly from the corresponding value of X, the difference will be attributed to the teaching that took place between X and Y.

In the past, a variety of different statistical procedures have been used to adjust the mean posttest score $\bar{Y}$ of a teacher's class to allow for the factors measured by the mean pretest $\bar{X}$. The earliest (and simplest) procedure was to use the "mean raw gain" $\bar{Y} - \bar{X}$ as a measure of the effects of teaching. Unfortunately, there is an artifactual negative correlation between this gain score and the pretest mean $\bar{X}$; this means that the lower the mean pretest score of the class, the less effective the teaching will appear. Since this is precisely the error which the adjustment is supposed to prevent, the adjustment fails in its purpose.

The use of mean raw gains was replaced by the use of "residual gains." In this procedure, class mean values $\bar{Y}$ were regressed on class mean values $\bar{X}$, and the regression line obtained was used to predict the value of $\bar{Y}$ that would be expected if there were no variations in the quality of teaching between classes. The difference between the actual mean value of $\bar{Y}$ in a class and its predicted value was taken as a measure of the quality of teaching in that class. Mitzel and Gross (1958) pointed out that the use of the between-class regression in this manner actually removes some of the differences between classes that the technique is supposed to measure, and recommended the use of the analysis of covariance to estimate the regression. The measure so obtained is called the "adjusted mean gain." But unless the pupils have been assigned to the classes at random, this procedure also tends to overcorrect. In other words, the effect of the teaching in a class which scores low on the pretest is underestimated while that in a class which scores high is overestimated (Campbell and Erlbacher 1970).

None of these procedures yields an unbiased estimate of the effects of teaching, then. Moreover, none of them estimates the effects of teaching on individual pupils. In each instance the effects measured are those on the class mean; what varies is the method used to compensate for differences in the means of different classes. None of the methods is successful.

There is an alternative procedure (which so far as is known has not been described in print before) that seems to be free from this defect. This procedure uses information that the other procedures ignore, information that is highly relevant to the quality of teaching. This information is contained in the correlation between pupils' pretest and posttest scores within the same class.

This information is used to set up a separate regression equation within each class for predicting a pupil's score at the end of the year from the pupil's score at the beginning. Outcomes of teaching in different classes can then be estimated, not just for the average pupil in each class but for a pupil with any specified pretest score in each class.

Suppose that the regression equations for the classes of three teachers are as follows:

Teacher A:	$Z = 16 + 0.8X$
Teacher B:	$Z = 20 + 0.7X$
Teacher C:	$Z = 26 + 0.6X$

Then the posttest score of a pupil whose pretest score is 35 would be expected to be 44 in class A, 44.5 in class B, or 47 in class C; such a pupil would learn most in class C. But the posttest score of a pupil whose pretest score is 65 would be expected to be 68 in class A, 65.5 in class B, or 65 in class C; such a pupil would do best in class A.

The value of Z for a pupil with a specified pretest score would seem to be a particulary simple and direct measure of the learning outcomes in that class; and so it is. However, it should not be interpreted as a measure of the quality of the teaching because there is a possibility that if the same teacher had taught in the same way in a different class, the results might have been different.

The correlation between the Z value in a class and $\bar{X}$, the mean pretest score of the class, provides a measure of the degree to which the average ability of a class is related to how much the specified pupil learns (regardless of who teaches the class). And the regression equation for predicting Z from $\bar{X}$ provides an estimate Z' of this quantity in any given class, such as class A. If Z, the pupil's posttest score when Teacher A teaches the class, is higher than Z', this indicates better than average teaching in that class. This difference is the measure of the learning outcomes attributable to the quality of teaching in that class.

There is no need to restrict the number of pretest scores used to one; characteristics of pupils or of classes that are not expected to change as the result of teaching, but which may affect pupil learning—such as socioeconomic status or sex—can be controlled in this way when randomization is not feasible.

This seems to be the only way, short of random assignment of pupils to classes, to ensure any kind of equivalence in the tasks performed by different teachers.

Unless there is good reason for using some other value it seems logical to assess teaching quality in terms of its effects on a pupil whose pretest score is equal to the mean in the grade and subject taught.

Some readers may conclude from this that the development of a criterion for evaluating teaching in terms of learning outcomes involves some rather elaborate statistical gymnastics. So it does. Most of them would be unnecessary if obtaining valid assessments of teaching were considered important enough to justify taking the trouble to assign pupils randomly to classes. It has been shown that these statistical manipulations do control those contextual factors that can be measured before the teaching begins; but there may be others, unknown to the evaluator. These remain uncontrolled.

4. Assessing Teaching on the Basis of Teaching Behavior

In practice, most of the evaluation of teaching that goes on in today's schools is process based, that is, based on the behavior of the teacher in the classroom. Process assessments use records of how the teacher teaches rather than of the effect that the teaching has on pupils.

There are two advantages in using teacher behavior as the criterion for evaluating teaching: the evaluations obtained are diagnostic and they are timely. If the quality of a teaching performance is low, it is possible to examine the record to ascertain what the teacher is doing—or failing to do—that makes his or her score so low. And this can be done promptly—as soon as the evaluation is complete. When pupil learning outcomes are used as the criterion for evaluating teaching, it is only some months after the teaching took place that the record on which the evaluation is based becomes available. And when the record does become available it contains no description of the teaching behavior being evaluated, no clue as to what the teacher should do differently in order to get a higher score the next time.

The principal drawback in process-based teacher evaluation is that the evaluations lack the validity intrinsic to outcomes-based evaluations. The validity of process assessments depends on the amount of reliable knowledge of the nature of effective teaching behavior available, on how accurately it is possible to distinguish in a record of teaching behaviors those which indicate competent effective teaching from those which do not. At present the amount that is known about the nature of effective teaching is woefully inadequate, and process records must be and are scored mainly to reflect someone's best judgment rather than verified research findings.

4.1 The Teacher Rating Scale

The device used in almost all formal evaluations of teaching since the early twentieth century has been the teacher rating scale. A teacher rating scale essentially consists of a list of dimensions or aspects of teacher behavior (or other teacher characteristics) to be assessed, and provision for recording the assessments, usually by entering a number or marking a point on a graphic scale (most commonly in a range from one to five or ten) for each item to be rated.

The person who makes the assessment is called the rater. The rater is instructed (a) to observe a sample of the teaching behavior of a candidate; (b) to form the best judgment he or she can of the degree to which the observed behavior exemplifies each characteristic on the list; (c) to record (or mark) the number (or point) on the scale which most accurately reflects that judgment; and (d) to form some sort of a composite of the ratings on all of the listed characteristics (usually a simple total or mean) which is used as an overall assessment of the quality of the teaching observed. The individual ratings remain as an aid to diagnosis.

Hundreds of such devices have been used since 1915, when the publication of a 45-item rating scale in an early yearbook of the National Society for the Study of Education gave this new procedure wide visibility (Boyce 1915). The quality of any one rating scale depends mainly on three characteristics: which aspects of teaching (or characteristics of teachers) it lists; how clearly each one is defined; and how accurate the raters' perceptions are of each of them (see *Evolution of Research on Teaching*).

Much thought and research has been devoted to the selection of the dimensions of teaching that should be included as items in a rating scale in order to maximize its validity. What indicators of the quality of teaching are visible in the behavior of teachers (and of their pupils) during the process of teaching? Since these instruments are designed primarily for use in evaluating teachers, they often include ratings of other characteristics (such as knowledge of subject matter) than ones that have to do with how the teacher performs in the classroom, as well as ratings based on behaviors of pupils (e.g., the level of pupil involvement or the amount of disorderly behavior).

Until around 1950, it was generally assumed that how well a teacher taught was mainly a matter of personality characteristics of the teacher. It was assumed that there were certain abilities and traits which characterized effective teachers; and teacher rating scales were intended to indicate which of these characteristics a teacher possessed, and to what degree, rather than to describe how the teacher behaved in the classroom while teaching.

During this period a considerable amount of research was conducted whose purpose was to identify the "characteristics of effective teachers" so that rating scales could be designed which would measure these characteristics (Charters and Waples 1929). The data on which this research was based consisted entirely of the opinions of teacher educators, school administrators, and others who might be expected to possess insight into the nature of effective teaching and the characteristics of effective teachers.

Early in this period an attempt was made by Barr to validate some of the rating scales then in use by comparing ratings of teachers with the outcomes they produced. As Barr pointed out, the ultimate criterion of the quality of teaching is its effect on pupils, not its effect on expert observers. The findings of the study were negative, indicating that the average correlation between the overall rating a teacher received and the amount of gains showed by that teacher's pupils was close to zero. Only three raters were involved in the study—not a large enough sample to produce definitive conclusions—but the results were suggestive and (as it turned out) prophetic.

During the next decade or two, at least six other

investigators tried to verify this finding in as many different studies. Their results were unanimous in reaching the same conclusion. In every instance, the correlation between supervisors' ratings of teacher effectiveness and measured pupil gains in their classrooms was near zero (Medley and Mitzel 1963 pp. 257–58). It is somewhat curious that so few researchers have attempted to look at this lack of correlation, or to explain it empirically. By default it appears necessary to conclude that, whatever the average rating scale measures, it does not measure how effective teaching is. If by the quality of teaching is meant how well it achieves its ultimate purpose of facilitating those changes in pupil achievement that schooling is supposed to produce, such evidence as exists unanimously concludes that rating scales do not measure the quality of teaching at all.

The lack of validity of these devices (designed to codify the judgments of the raters as to how closely the characteristics of the teacher rated corresponded to those that experts believed were associated with teaching quality) also suggests that these experts' idea of what an effective teacher is like were erroneous. Since different raters tended to agree rather well, they must have been agreeing about the wrong things.

Some time between 1950 and 1960 scholars interested in research in teacher effectiveness began to abandon the assumption that how well a teacher teaches depends on his or her personality, and to assume instead that it depends on how the teacher behaves while teaching. The first tangible outcome of this change in viewpoint was another rating scale, all 25 items on which were defined in terms of classroom behavior (Ryans 1960). This instrument was a kind of hybrid which purported to describe only teacher characteristics manifest in the classroom. Wisely enough, Ryans postponed doing any research to indicate which characteristics were related to teacher effectiveness, and how they might be weighted in achieving a composite measure of the quality of teaching, until some time that is still in the future.

A few years later, teacher educators became interested in an approach to the preparation of teachers called competency-based teacher education (see *Competency-based Teacher Education*), which assumed that the quality of teaching was mainly determined by the competencies the teacher possessed; and rating scales began to contain competencies rather than behaviors or other teacher characteristics.

The teacher rating scale has few or none of the properties essential for valid performance assessment. No standard task to be performed by the teacher is defined, no record of behavior is made, and the procedure used to assign numbers to the various elements of the performance rated is completely subjective. The observer is required to perform two difficult tasks simultaneously: to observe the performance in considerable detail while making the difficult discriminations needed to assess the contribution of each detail to one of 25 or more different dimensions of performance.

Raters are rarely given adequate training in performing these feats; nor are they selected with any particular care. Just about every supervisor and principal in any school uses one rating scale or another. It is possible that among all of these raters there are some who are naturally gifted with a knack for judging the quality of teaching; their ratings are probably valid enough. But no-one knows who they are; the ratings made by others who lack this talent are used interchangeably with ratings made by these few gifted raters. As has been noted, the average validity of all these ratings is near zero.

Factor analyses of ratings generally suggest the operation of what is called the "halo" effect. What most raters seem to do is to form a strong general impression of the competence of the teacher which has more to do with the rating of the teacher's performance on any given item than any specific behavior that the teacher may exhibit. If the general impression is related to the overall quality of the performance observed, then the composite rating of that sample of teaching is related to its quality and the rating has validity. Most of the time the impression is unrelated and the rating has no validity.

For reasons such as these it is strongly recommended that educators follow the example set by the process–product researchers and discard the teacher rating scale in favor of the systematic observation system.

4.2 The Systematic Observation System

The usefulness of the rating scale in the evaluation of teaching is limited primarily by the fact that it attempts to bypass entirely one of the three essential phases of the assessment process: the creation of the record of performance. Until fairly recently, no alternative procedure for assessing teacher performance was available; but this is no longer true. An alternative is the structured observation system, a form of instrument developed for use in process–product research. Process–product research is a form of research which seeks to establish correlations between measurements of classroom behavior (process) and measures of pupil learning (product) in the same classrooms, and to learn something about the nature of effective teaching from these correlations. A large number of different observation systems have been developed (including among many others *Flanders Interaction Analysis Categories* (FIAC), OSCAR *(Observation Schedule and Record)*, and the *Reciprocal Category System*, many of which have been collected and reprinted by Simon and Boyer (1967, 1969, 1970).

The observer using an instrument of this kind is expected to record classroom behavior in quantifiable form, but not to judge or evaluate it in any way. The observer's record is scored much as a paper-and-pencil test is; that is, by applying an objective scoring key to it, one which yields a weighted composite score based on the events in the record. The judgments of experts are incorporated into the scoring key rather than being applied to individual samples of behavior, as they are when ratings are obtained. The scoring of a record becomes a clerical task, one which can be performed by a computer.

Objectivity is, of course, a matter of degree, and records made by different observers using different observation schedules vary somewhat in objectivity. But even the least objective record yields a much more objective score than the most objective rating scale.

Observation systems tend to take one of three forms referred to as sign systems, category systems, or multiple-coding systems.

A sign system is the simplest to construct and to use. In form it is a list of discrete events, each one of which has been included because its occurrence in a classroom is believed to indicate either the presence or the absence of a competency, behavior dimension, or other element of teaching that the instrument is supposed to measure.

The time an observer using a sign system spends in a classroom is divided into several brief periods of equal length—usually between three and five minutes long. The observer's task is to record which of the signs in the system occur during these three to five minutes, but not how often. Any sign not recorded as having happened is assumed not to have happened. During a single visit to a classroom, the record may show that any given sign did not occur at all, that it occurred in every three-minute interval, or that it occurred in one, two, or more of them. Thus the approximate frequency of occurrence of the event is indicated.

The fact that the observer need not record each sign each time it occurs makes it possible to include many more items on the list than would otherwise be possible, without making the task so difficult that the reliability of the records would be reduced and the task of learning to use the system would become too difficult.

One of the advantages of the sign system is the ease with which it can be revised. Signs can be added or deleted without noticeable effect on other items. Signs related to a great variety of aspects of classroom behavior can be mixed together—verbal and nonverbal, pupil and teacher behaviors, or whatever.

A category system is quite different from a sign system in a number of ways. For one thing, it requires that every event in a specified domain of events be recorded each time it occurs. For another thing, only events in a single domain can be included. Most category systems deal with the domain of verbal interaction and require that each utterance made by the teacher or a pupil—and nothing else—must be recorded.

The observer's task is to record the frequency of occurrence of verbalizations in each of the set of categories which defines the system. The set of categories must be finite in number; the categories must be mutually exclusive, so that any one verbal event is classifiable in one and only one category. The categories must also be all-inclusive; that is, there must be a category into which any verbal event can be classified.

The most widely used of all existing category systems,

without a doubt, is that devised by Flanders, called the *Flanders Interaction Analysis Categories* (FIAC).

Instead of recording individual events, it requires the observer to code the interaction observed in each three-second interval during a visit. The system consists of just 10 categories, seven of which cover teacher utterances, two of which apply to pupil utterances, and one which covers silence or confusion. These 10 categories have been in continuous and extensive use since before the 1960s.

Most category systems are built around some set of assumptions about, or model of, teaching which determines how the domain of behaviors is subdivided into categories. This makes subdividing existing categories just about the only way in which a category system can be revised without destroying it.

However, it is often possible to devise scoring keys for an existing instrument that extract information about dimensions of teaching behavior other than the one the instrument was designed to measure, a possibility to be borne in mind during the search for an existing instrument which can be used to evaluate teaching.

A multiple coding system may be thought of as a scheme for coding classroom events on two or more different category systems simultaneously. Most multiple coding systems are time based; that is, call for a record of what happened during a brief interval or at a particular point in time, and disregard events that occur at other times. Thus only a sample of what occurs is recorded, but the loss of information incurred is offset by the greater detail recorded about events in the sample.

One of the most widely used multiple coding systems is the one developed by Jane Stallings at the Stanford Research Institute (Stallings 1977). Each interaction observed is coded on four sets of categories: *Who, To Whom, What,* and *How.* The *Who* categories have to do with who initiates the event; the *To Whom* with the passive participant; the *What* categories with the type of event (command, open-ended question, instruction, etc); and the *How* categories are descriptive (happy, touch, academic, etc.).

Because several categories are available on each of four separate dimensions, the number of possible combinations is very large. This means that a very large number of different events can be distinguished in a record. This richness of detail simulates what would be available in a detailed narrative record of what happened; but records made on this system are precoded so that a computer can easily be programmed to "read" a record to extract almost any data one might wish to see from it in the quantitative form.

The evaluator interested in using an observation system must either choose one (or more) of the systems already in existence or construct a new one. The former course will be preferred by many. Most of the systems that have received widespread use in research studies will be found to be the end products of several years of development and revision, as a consequence of which they tend to be substantially more reliable and (for the purposes for which they have been used) valid than any newly constructed device is likely to be.

The principal problem the evaluator will encounter in following this strategy arises from the fact that most existing systems were developed by research workers to measure variables they wished to study rather than to assess the quality of teaching. As a result, it becomes difficult to find one suitable for the present use. In examining one of these systems it is best to look not at the scores it yields or the dimensions it measures, but at the events that can be distinguished in the records from which the scores are derived.

It is useful to think of an observation system primarily as a device for obtaining an accurate record of a sample of classroom events. Once such a record has been obtained it may be scored in many different ways for many different purposes. The user need not be able to use the scoring keys developed by the originator of the system in order to capitalize on the intrinsic quality of the system: the application of a new scoring key to a record after it has been obtained does not affect the quality or accuracy of the record in any way. The decision whether to use a system or not should be based, then, on whether the record contains the information needed—on what events are recorded—not on whether useful scoring keys are available. A multiple coding system like that described by Stallings, for instance, yields records with much more information than Stallings and her associates were able to use. A careful study of the instrument will make it clear whether this information can be adapted to the evaluation of teaching.

If a decision is made to develop a new system, a valid and reliable homemade sign system can be developed far more easily and rapidly than any other kind. It is much easier to set down and compile a list of indicators of teaching quality than it is to construct a set of mutually exclusive, all-inclusive categories whose relative frequencies will indicate teaching quality. There are almost no restrictions on the type of indicators that can be included, and (as was noted earlier) it is much simpler to add or delete signs than to revise a set of categories in a trial-and-error process.

The first set of signs adopted should represent the best judgment of the constructors about how good teaching looks, about what behavioral cues are the most valid on which to judge teaching quality. The instrument should then be tried out and its effectiveness in discriminating good and poor teaching should be studied item by item. The results may call for a reappraisal of the original concept of good teaching and the deletion, addition, and redefinition of some of the signs on the list. A second version of the instrument should then be tried out and revised in the same way, and the process repeated as necessary until a satisfactory instrument is obtained.

This process forces one to define what good teaching is in behavioral terms specific enough so that observers can use them, and gives immediate—and merciless—feedback which provides an experience so valuable in itself as to almost justify the effort for what can be learned from it, without regard to the value of the instrument that is produced.

4.3 Obtaining the Records

Because the observer's function is merely to observe and code, not to evaluate, when a systematic observation system is used, it is not necessary—and probably not desirable—to use expert teachers or researchers or highly trained professionals as observers. When rating scales were used to evaluate teaching, the professional expertise of the rater was critically important, since the validity of the ratings depended on the quality of the rater's judgments. When a systematic observation system is used, however, how much professional expertise the observer possesses does not matter. The validity of the scores obtained is unaffected by any characteristic of the observer except skill in using the system.

It is recommended that only paraprofessional personnel be trained and used as observers—personnel who have no other responsibility in the institution that employs them than to make visits to classrooms and code behaviors. They do not need to know anything about how the codes they make are to be scored or used; indeed, the less they know, the more objective their codings are likely to be.

Professional personnel should be used as professionals: they should be expert not in obtaining but in interpreting behavior codings and scores derived from them.

When codings of teaching behavior are being collected for use in teacher evaluation, the most efficient strategy is (a) to make as many visits per classroom as possible, (b) to have only one observer code behavior in a classroom at any one time, and (c) to have a different observer code behavior on each visit to the same teacher.

Increasing the number of visits increases the reliability of the assessments much more rapidly than increasing the length of a visit or the number of coders per visit; using a different observer on each visit may lower the reliability of the measurements, but it will do so by reducing the effect of the biases that individual observers may develop. If the budget will cover only four visits per teacher, then four observers should be trained and each one should visit every teacher who is to be evaluated.

It has been suggested that instead of sending observers into the classroom, technicians or camera operators should be sent to record the behaviors on audiotapes, videotapes, or film which can then be evaluated more thoroughly and exhaustively than the transient behaviors in the classroom can. This strategy is relatively costly: even if an hour of videotape costs no more to obtain than an hour recorded on an observation system, the data collection costs would be equal in both cases. But the videotapes would still have to be viewed by trained observers and coded on the observation system before they could be scored. This would double the cost—unless the observers took advantage of the permanence of the videotapes to replay them one or more times to increase the accuracy of their coding, in which case the cost per hour of behavior coded could treble or quadruple.

For most categories of teaching behavior used in observational instruments, there is in reality no advantage to be gained from coding and recoding the behavior recorded on a single videotape until the record is as accurate as possible, or in having two or more observers visit a class together to insure the accuracy of the coding of that particular sample of behavior. The additional information gained about the behavior of the teacher is minuscule in either case, particularly when compared with the gain that would accrue if a different sample of the teacher's behavior had been coded each time. Moreover, since a visit from a camera operator is much more intrusive than one from a human observer, and since the observer can see much more of what is going on when he or she is physically present than when he or she watches a tape of it, the validity of codings made live is almost certainly greater, except in those cases where the complexity of the behavioral unit to be coded is so great that live coding is out of the question.

4.4 Scoring the Records

The central problem involved in scoring a record of teacher performance is that of assessing the appropriateness of the teacher behaviors that are observed and coded during the performance. The traditional approach to this problem has been to employ an observer who is an expert judge of teaching, one who is (presumably) able to decide what portion of the decisions the teacher makes are correct ones in the context in which they are made, as a basis for rating performance.

It seems clear that in order to be able to do this, the expert must have at least as full and complete an understanding of the context in which the teacher works as the teacher has (or should have). The rater must know as much as the teacher does about the pupils, about their personal characteristics, the interpersonal relationships among them, their previous experiences in this class and out of it; the rater must also know the teacher's intentions and the resources available for carrying them out, which include the teacher's own personal strengths and weaknesses as well as the materials, media, and so on available; and the rater must also understand any other factors that enter into, or should enter into, the teacher's decisions. All of this special knowledge is necessary in addition to the general knowledge of professional practice which the rater brings to the situation.

It is difficult to see how a rater who visits a teacher's class for less than an hour could possibly have all this knowledge; but without it, how is it possible for the rater to second-guess the teacher, to say that the teacher

should have done something else, that some other decision would have been better than the one the teacher made?

In the definition of teaching presented earlier in this article, a distinction was made between preactive and interactive decisions which is relevant here. What the classroom observer sees are, of course, the interactive decisions the teacher makes. So long as the assessment is based on them alone there is no adequate method by which the quality of the teacher's preactive decisions can be judged, because the data on which these decisions are based are not available to the observer. It might be possible to assess a teacher's preactive decisions by the use of some combination of questionnaires and interviews which make the bases of the teacher's decisions visible. (Much more needs to be done along this line than is done at present; but these are matters that fall outside the scope of this discussion.)

As the definition of teaching indicates, one product of preactive decision making is (or ought to be) a set of decision rules which the teacher plans to follow during the interactive phase of teaching. This set of rules, defined by the teacher, provides the best basis for deciding whether any given action of the teacher is appropriate or inappropriate. Effective teaching depends first on making correct decisions about what to do in the classroom; and, second, on implementing those decisions. It is the second aspect that the observations are designed to assess, not the first.

Without knowing what rules the teacher has decided to follow during the period of observation it would seem impossible for anyone, however expert, to discriminate appropriate actions from inappropriate ones. Even if the observer knew the rules, the task would be extremely difficult. But the observer need not know anything about these rules in order to make an accurate record of what happens. This knowledge becomes relevant later, when an attempt is made to score the record.

Use of structured observations (rather than ratings) requires unequivocal a priori decisions about the weight to be assigned to each item in a record. Keys can be (and should be) revised from time to time: but between times these weights constitute the definition of effective teaching with which the evaluator must live. Process–product researchers have faced this problem in their efforts to derive empirical weights for scoring performances; in doing so, they have evolved two strategies. One is direct, the other is indirect.

An example of the use of the direct strategy is provided by a precedent-setting experiment in helping teachers to become more effective teachers of reading in small groups (Anderson et al. 1979). These researchers correlated events in behavior records with outcomes one by one to identify those that were associated with greater learning gains, and translated the results into prescriptions for better teaching. The decision whether an event was appropriate (which would be part of the prescription) was made directly—on the basis of that item's correlation with outcomes.

The indirect strategy first groups items into separate clusters on scoring keys that are internally consistent and which measure different aspects or dimensions of teaching behavior, and then intercorrelates these clusters or dimensions with outcomes (Soar pp. 97–119 in Peterson and Walberg 1979). Individual events are selected on the basis of their relationship to the cluster rather than directly to outcomes.

The main advantage claimed for the indirect approach is that cluster scores are more reliable and interpretable than scores on single items, and that they provide a smaller number of variables to consider in specifying decision rules and in communicating diagnostic information to teachers. The direct approach may be defended as less susceptible to distortion by the biases and preconceptions of the evaluator.

Sets of decision rules defined by teachers have been referred to by terms such as "teaching strategies" and "models of teaching." The most elaborate development of this idea has been the work of Joyce and Weil (1980), who propose that teacher education be organized around the selection and implementation of a set of models, at least one of which is appropriate to any situation a teacher encounters. Evaluation of teachers trained in this way would require the use of a different scoring key (if not a different observation system) for each model; whenever a teacher's performance was to be evaluated the teacher would declare which model he or she would use so it could be evaluated properly.

Very few teachers are trained in this way at present, because the profession has not yet developed definitions of alternative models, strategies, or sets of decision rules which are generally accepted and which form part of the teacher education curriculum. Most present-day teachers have been trained to use a single, general purpose set of decision rules—often called a "teaching style"—and use this style with only minor changes (usually unplanned) in all teaching situations. They are better prepared for the task of maintaining the general learning environment than for the task of managing learning experiences.

This seems to work fairly well for the teachers; the best of them are adept at making those decisions that relate to maintaining the learning environment. Pupils learn to work within the limits that the teacher sets on their behavior more rapidly because the limits are stable and consistent. But managing learning activities is a different matter; it seems obvious that appropriate decisions in this area would lead the teacher to change the rules from time to time and from pupil to pupil. For some purposes it is best to praise pupils whenever they do well; for others, it may be best to withhold praise and provide neutral feedback only; for still others, it may be best to withhold feedback, too, and encourage pupils to evaluate their own performances.

The fact that such adaptations are relatively rare, that teachers today do not vary the models or strategies they use to any measurable degree, probably explains the recent emergence of a number of reliable findings from process–product research. Classroom observations made in such studies are made at random times, and variations in teacher behavior from visit to visit are treated as errors of measurement. And yet some highly stable differences in teacher behavior are found which correlate significantly with learning outcomes (Medley pp. 11–27 and Rosenshine pp. 28–56 in Peterson and Walberg 1979).

These findings support the notion that there exists a single general teaching style which is characteristic of the most effective teachers in the schools today. The teachers whose pupils are making the greatest gains in basic skills as measured on standardized achievement tests seem to behave in this way whenever they are observed, regardless of variations in the immediate goals set that day or hour. It makes sense, then, to seek an evaluation instrument which will measure how closely the behavior of a teacher conforms to this pattern, and in what ways it deviates from it. This pattern may provide the basis for choosing or constructing an observation instrument and developing a key for scoring it. But it is important to remember that this is only an interim solution.

5. Assessing Teaching on the Basis of Pupil Behavior

In many ways this is the most attractive of the three types of criteria available for evaluating teaching. By not basing the evaluation on how the teacher behaves it lessens the pressure on the teacher to display atypical behavior while being evaluated. By basing it on what happens while the teaching is in progress, it provides results promptly enough so that they can be used immediately. And its validity is much less dependent on the teacher's own decision rules.

In the past, pupil behavior has been used in teacher evaluation in combination with teacher behavior; most rating scales include ratings of pupil involvement and the like along with those of teacher characteristics; and so do many observation systems. But it seems worthwhile to separate pupil behaviors (which are outcomes) from teacher behaviors (which are means). It might appear logical to say that only those pupil behaviors which are known to relate positively (or negatively) to learning outcomes should be used in teacher evaluation; but most educators and parents as well have some definite and strong convictions about the kinds of experience pupils should have in school. It is widely agreed, for example, that pupils should enjoy school; and this has nothing to do with how much pupils learn. Children spend many hours in school, and society is reluctant to have them be miserable for so large a part of their lives.

One attempt to move toward this use of pupil behavior is the work done in the later phase of the Beginning Teacher Evaluation Study. This has defined a construct called academic learning time (ALT), and hypothesized that how much a pupil learns in school is a direct function of the amount of ALT the pupil gets in school (see *Time*). Academic learning time is "time a student spends engaged in an academic task that he/she can perform with success. The more ALT a student accumulates, the more the student is learning" (Fisher et al. 1980 p. 8). The proposal is that pupil behavior be substituted for learning outcomes as a criterion for evaluating teaching. More conservatively it may be regarded as a measure of how well the teaching is succeeding in providing pupils with experiences most likely to result in learning. The means used by these investigators to measure ALT may leave something to be desired, but they represent an important methodological innovation.

6. Concluding Remarks

It is not any part of the responsibility of the author of such a piece as this to tell those who happen to read it what to do. For this reason, no attempt has been made to define the criteria for evaluating teaching in a substantive way; no attempt has been made to say which teacher behaviors are appropriate or inappropriate, which learning outcomes are important and which are not, or what kinds of experiences pupils should be having. The group or individual concerned with evaluating teachers must define these things in accordance with the purposes of the evaluation. If research in teaching had established strong relationships between learning outcomes and pupil learning activities in the classroom, or between those learning activities and teaching behavior, then these definitions would need to be specified in terms of the relative importance of outcomes.

But these relationships have not yet been established; indeed, very little is known about them. This makes it necessary for the evaluator to define good teaching at whatever level he or she proposes to assess it: in terms of process (how the teacher behaves), of function (how the teacher gets pupils to behave), or of effectiveness (the changes the teacher brings about). Defining good teaching in terms of outcomes and then proceeding to evaluate it in terms of process makes no sense unless the evaluator is prepared to make some strong assumptions about the relationships between the two. And these assumptions should be explicit and visible. Certainly the evaluator has a right to his or her own opinions about these relationships—about how a teacher should act in order to be most effective, for example—and to base his or her evaluation procedures squarely upon these opinions.

But there is also an obligation to the pupils, the teacher, and society to make it clear how much or how little evidence there is that these assumptions are true, because if they are not true, the ministrations of the evaluator may be worthless. Worse yet, they may do harm: harm to the pupil who is deprived of the opportunity to learn which is his or her right; harm to the teacher whose effectiveness is eroded; harm to society by wasting some of its resources.

This obligation implies a second: the obligation constantly to review and test these assumptions not only against the literature on teaching but also by follow-up and evaluation of the evaluator's own efforts. A complete evaluation system must collect data of all three types, and must monitor the impact of one upon the other. If changes in teacher behaviors indicated by the evaluation are implemented but no change takes place in the experiences of pupils as a result, the definition of effective teacher behavior which led to the changes needs to be reexamined and revised. Evaluations based on pupil behaviors must also be tested against the outcomes that result from them. When such monitoring becomes a part of all of the teacher evaluation systems operating in the schools and in the teacher education colleges of the world, then progress will be steady and inevitable not just toward a solution of the problem of evaluating teaching, but toward the better teaching that the world so desperately needs.

See also: Affective Characteristics of Student Teachers; Technical Skills of Teaching

Bibliography

Anderson L M, Evertson C M, Brophy J E 1979 An experimental study of effective teaching in first grade reading groups. *Elem. Sch. J.* 79: 193–223

Borich G D, Fenton K S 1977 *The Appraisal of Teaching: Concepts and Processes.* Addison-Wesley, Reading, Massachusetts

Boyce A C 1915 *Methods of Measuring Teachers' Efficiency. Fourteenth Yearbook of the National Society for Study of Education*, Part 2. Public School Publishing, Bloomington, Illinois

Campbell D T, Erlbacher A 1970 How regression artifacts in quasi-experimental evaluations can mistakenly make compensatory education look harmful. In: Hellmuth J (ed.) 1970 *The Disadvantaged Child*, Vol. 3: *Compensatory Education: A National Debate.* Brunner/Mazel, New York

Charters W W, Waples D 1929 *The Commonwealth Teacher-training Study.* University of Chicago Press, Chicago, Illinois

Fisher C W, Berliner D C, Filby N N, Marliave R, Cahen L S, Dishaw M M 1980 Teaching behaviors, academic learning time, and student achievement: An overview. In: Denham C, Lieberman A (eds.) 1980 *Time to Learn.* National Institute of Education, Washington, DC

Gage N L (ed.) 1963 *Handbook of Research on Teaching: A Project of the American Educational Research Association.* Rand McNally, Chicago, Illinois

Joyce B, Weil M 1980 *Models of Teaching*, 2nd edn. Prentice-Hall, Englewood Cliffs, New Jersey

Medley D M, Mitzel H E 1963 Measuring classroom behavior by systematic observation. In: Gage N L (ed.) 1963

Mitzel H E, Gross C F 1958 The development of pupil growth criteria in studies of teacher effectiveness. *Educ. Res. Bull.* 37: 178–87, 205–15

Peterson P L, Walberg H J (eds.) 1979 *Research on Teaching: Concepts, Findings, and Implications.* McCutchan, Berkeley, California

Ryans D G 1960 *Characteristics of Teachers: Their Description, Comparison, and Appraisal: A Research Study.* American Council on Education, Washington, DC

Simon A, Boyer E G (eds.) 1967, 1969, 1970 *Mirrors for Behavior: An Anthology of Classroom Observation Instruments.* Research for Better Schools, Philadelphia, Pennsylvania

Stallings J A 1977 *Learning to Look: A Handbook on Classroom Observation and Teaching Models.* Wadsworth, Belmont, California

Travers R M W (ed.) 1973 *Second Handbook of Research on Teaching: A Project of the American Educational Research Association.* Rand McNally, Chicago, Illinois

Student Evaluations of Teaching

H. W. Marsh

Students' ratings of teaching effectiveness are commonly collected at United States and Canadian institutions of higher education, and are widely endorsed by students, faculty, and administrators (Leventhal et al. 1981, Centra 1979). The purposes of these evaluations are variously to provide: (a) a source of diagnostic feedback to faculty about the effectiveness of their teaching; (b) a measure of teaching effectiveness to be used in tenure/promotion decisions; and (c) a source of information for students to use in the selection of courses and instructors. While the first purpose is nearly universal, the second two are not. At some universities, student input is required before faculty are even considered for promotion, while at others the inclusion of students' evaluations is strictly optional. Similarly, the results of student ratings are published and sold in campus bookstores at some universities, while at others the results are considered to be strictly confidential.

The use of students' evaluations, especially for tenure/promotion decisions, has not been without opposition, and the investigation of different aspects of the ratings has stimulated considerable research. Particularly since the early 1970s this has become one of the most frequently studied areas in educational research in the United States and literally thousands of papers have been published on the topic. Nearly all this research focuses on evaluations of college/university teaching in the United States and Canada. A small amount of research has been conducted at the precollege level, and several instruments designed for this purpose are reviewed by Borich and Madden (1977). Research from other countries is described in the proceedings of the International Conferences on Improving University Teaching. Nevertheless, research into, and application of, students' evaluations of teaching effectiveness is a phenomenon limited largely to United States and Canadian colleges/universities, and this will be the focus of this article.

1. Dimensions of Student Ratings

The information from student ratings necessarily depends upon the content of the evaluation items. Poorly worded or inappropriate items will not provide useful information. Student ratings, as is the teaching that they represent, are unequivocally multidimensional (e.g., a teacher may be quite well-organized but lack enthusiasm). This contention is supported by common sense and a considerable body of empirical research. Unfortunately, most evaluation instruments do not provide measures of the separate components of teaching effectiveness. If a survey contains a heterogeneous mixture of different items and student ratings are summarized by an average of these items, then there is no basis for knowing what is being measured. If a survey contains separate groups of related items, and empirical procedures such as factor analysis demonstrate that these items do measure the same underlying trait, then it is easier to interpret what is being measured. Many of the ambiguous and contradictory findings in the student evaluation literature stem from ignoring the multidimensionality of student ratings and assuming that student ratings—no matter what items they are based upon—all measure the same thing.

Some researchers, while not denying the multidimensionality of student ratings, argue that a total rating or an overall instructor rating provides a more valid measure. However, this is not the case. First, there are many possible indicators of effective teaching and the component that is "most valid" will depend upon the criteria being considered (Marsh, 1982c). Second, reviews of different validity criteria show that specific components of the student ratings are more highly correlated with each criterion than an overall rating (student learning—Cohen 1981; effect of feedback—Cohen 1980; instructor self-evaluations—Marsh 1982b; Marsh et al. 1979).

The student-rating literature does contain several examples of instruments that have a well-defined factor structure and provide measures of distinct components of teaching effectiveness (e.g., Frey et al. 1975, Marsh 1982a, 1982b; Hildebrand et al. 1971).

These researchers and extensive literature reviews describing the components that have been found in other studies generally describe dimensions similar to those identified by Marsh in his SEEQ survey (see Fig. 1).

Particularly compelling evidence for the multi-

Figure 1
The SEEQ form used at the University of Southern California to evaluate teaching effectiveness

dimensionality of student ratings comes from the research conducted with the Students' Evaluation of Educational Quality (SEEQ) instrument (see Fig. 1 and Marsh 1982c for a review). Factor analysis has consistently demonstrated the same SEEQ factors in student ratings from different disciplines, different institutions, and even different countries. Factor analysis of faculty self-evaluations of their own teaching effectiveness, using SEEQ, also resulted in the same evaluation factors. Multitrait–multimethod analyses, looking at student–teacher agreement on the SEEQ factors and the consistency in the pattern of SEEQ factors in different courses taught by the same instructor, provide further evidence for the distinctiveness of the factors. The logical relation between SEEQ factors and a variety of other variables (e.g., class size is most highly correlated with group interaction) adds further support to this conclusion.

Items on standardized rating forms must be applicable to all instructional settings. Marsh (1982c) argues that this core of items *and* the provision for supplemental items, offers a good compromise between standard-

ization and flexibility. SEEQ (see Fig. 1) provides for responses to as many as 20 supplemental items that can be selected or written by the instructor. Responses to these items are summarized on the computerized report sent to each instructor. More elaborate schemes allow the instructor to have a "personalized" form of selected items printed for his or her class (Centra 1979). Little research has been done on the value of this added flexibility, but it appears to offer more specific information and greater flexibility than just the standardized items.

2. Reliability, Stability, and Generalizability of Student Ratings

2.1 Reliability

The reliability of student ratings is most appropriately estimated with coefficients of interrater agreement (agreement among different students rating the same course). The interrater reliability (Feldman 1977) depends primarily upon the number of students rating a class. Given a sufficient number of student responses (20 or more), the reliability of student ratings compares favourably with the best objective tests.

2.2 Long-term Stability

Critics suggest that students cannot recognize effective teaching until after being called upon to apply course materials in further coursework or after graduation. Cross-sectional studies (Centra 1979, Marsh 1977) have shown close agreement between the retrospective ratings of former students and those of currently enroled students. In a longitudinal study (Overall and Marsh 1980) the same students were asked to evaluate classes at the end of a course and again several years later, at least one year after graduation. End-of-class ratings in 100 courses correlated 0.83 with the retrospective ratings (a correlation approaching the reliability of the ratings), and the median rating at each time was nearly the same. Firth (1979) asked students to evaluate classes shortly before graduation (rather than at the end of each class) and one year after graduation, and he also found close agreement. These studies demonstrate that student ratings are quite stable over time, and suggest that added perspective does not systematically alter the ratings given at the end of classes.

2.3 Generalizability

Researchers have also asked how highly correlated are the ratings of the same instructor in different classes, or even the ratings of different instructors in the same class. This level of generality is greater than that tested by interrater reliabilities, and might be considered an indication of construct validity. Two related questions stem from this research. First, what is the relative importance of the particular instructor and the specific course in determining student ratings? Second, should ratings be averaged across different courses taught by the same instructor?

Marsh (1982a) arranged ratings of 1,364 classes into sets of four such that each set contained ratings of: (a) the same instructor teaching two offerings of the same course; (b) the same instructor teaching a different course; and (c) a different instructor teaching the same course. He demonstrated that the instructor is the most important determinant of student ratings and that the particular course being taught plays a small role.

Gilmore et al. (1978) reached similar conclusions with a different approach, and argued that ratings for a given instructor should be averaged across different classes to enhance generalizability. If it is likely that an instructor will teach many different classes, then personnel decisions should be based upon as many different courses as possible—Gilmore et al. suggest at least five. However, if it is likely that an instructor will continue to teach the same classes in which he or she has already been evaluated, then adequate results can be obtained from ratings of two offerings of each of these different courses. These recommendations suggest that a longitudinal archive of student ratings should be maintained and used for personnel decisions. The longitudinal data provide for more generalizable summaries, the assessment of changes over time, and the determination of which particular courses are best taught by a specific instructor.

3. Validity of Student Ratings

Student ratings, one measure of teaching effectiveness, are difficult to validate since there is no universal criterion of effective teaching. Researchers, using a construct validation approach, have attempted to demonstrate that student ratings are logically related to a variety of other indicators of effective teaching. Within this framework, evidence for the long-term stability and the generalizability of student ratings support their validity. The most commonly employed criterion is student learning, but others include changes in student behaviours, instructor self-evaluations, and the evaluations of colleagues who actually attend class sessions.

3.1 Multisection Validity Studies

Student learning, measured by objective examinations, cannot usually be compared in different classes. However, this is possible in large multisection courses. Ideally, (a) there are many sections of a large multisection course; (b) students are randomly assigned to sections; (c) each section is completely taught by a separate instructor; and (d) each section has the same course outline, textbooks, course objectives, and final examination.

Cohen (1981) conducted a meta-analysis of all known multisection validity studies and found student achievement was consistently correlated with ratings of skill (0.50), overall course (0.47), structure (0.47), student progress (0.47), and overall instructor (0.43). The correlations were higher when ratings were of full-time teachers, when students knew their final grade when

rating instructors, and when achievement tests were graded by an external evaluator. These findings provide good support for the validity of student ratings.

3.2 Instructor Self-evaluations

Instructor self-evaluations of their own teaching are not limited to special instructional settings, and provide a persuasive criterion for the validation of student ratings. Particularly if instructors evaluate their own teaching on the same form as used by their students, then both sets of responses can be factor analysed and multitrait–multimethod analyses can be applied. In two such studies (Marsh 1982b; Marsh et al. 1979), the correlations between student and instructor ratings averaged 0.50 and were statistically significant for every SEEQ factor. Separate factor analyses of student and instructor responses both identified the same SEEQ factors that had been found in previous studies. Furthermore, multitrait–multimethod analysis showed that student–teacher agreement on any one factor was distinct from agreement on other factors. Other researchers have also reported similar correlations between student ratings and instructor self-evaluations.

3.3 Peer/Colleague Ratings

Peer/colleague ratings, based upon actual classroom visitation are a possible indicator of effective teaching and another criterion for testing student ratings. At the precollege level, observational records compiled by specially trained observers are positively correlated with both student ratings and student achievement.

Studies at the postsecondary level are less encouraging. Centra (1979) reported a lack of agreement among different peers, visiting the same classroom ($r = 0.26$), thus precluding any good correspondence with student ratings ($r = 0.20$). Morsh et al. (1956) found that while student ratings correlated with achievement, thus supporting their validity, peer and supervisor ratings, though highly correlated with each other, were not related to either student ratings or achievement. Webb and Nolan (1955) reported good correspondence between student ratings and instructor self-evaluations, but neither of these indicators was positively correlated with supervisor ratings. Ward et al. (1981) suggest another problem with peer ratings—the presence of a colleague in the classroom apparently affects the classroom performance of an instructor. Reviews of the peer evaluation process (Centra 1979, French-Lasovik 1981) have also failed to provide adequate empirical support for the validity of peer ratings as an indicator of effective college teaching or as a criterion for student ratings.

4. Potential Biases to Student Ratings

The construct validity of student ratings requires that they be related to variables that are indicative of effective teaching, but unrelated to variables (i.e., potential biases) that are not. The search for potential biases is voluminous, confused, contradictory, misinterpreted, and methodologically flawed. Important and common methodological problems include:

(a) Using correlations to argue for causation—implying that some variable biases student ratings argues that causation has been demonstrated.

(b) The distinction between practical and statistical significance—all conclusions should be based on some index of "variance explained".

(c) The multivariate nature of both potential biases and the student ratings.

(d) Selection of the appropriate unit of analysis—the class-average response is nearly always appropriate and any finding based upon individual student

responses must also be demonstrated to operate at the class-average level.

(e) The nature of variables that influence student ratings—if a variable actually affects teaching effectiveness and this effect is accurately reflected in the student ratings, then the variable is not a bias.

Furthermore, many older studies have been inaccurately described, and researchers, apparently relying upon secondary sources, have perpetuated these inaccuracies. A series of excellent review articles by Feldman (1976a, 1976b, 1977, 1978, 1979), the older review by Costin et al. (1971), and Centra's (1979) book explore this area in detail.

Marsh (1980) examined the multivariate relationship between 16 "potential biases" (student/course/instructor background characteristics) and SEEQ ratings. Few

Table 1

Overview of relationships found between student ratings and background characteristics

	Background characteristics	Summary of findings
(a)	Prior subject interest	Classes with higher interest, rate classes more favourably, though it is not always clear if interest existed before start of course or was generated by course/instructor
(b)	Expected grade/actual grades	Classes expecting (or receiving) higher grades give somewhat higher ratings, though the interpretation depends on whether higher grades represent grading leniency or superior learning
(c)	Reason for taking a course	Elective courses and those with higher percentage taking course for general interest tend to be rated higher
(d)	Workload/difficulty	Harder, more difficult courses requiring more effort and time are rated somewhat more favourably
(e)	Class size	Mixed findings but most studies show smaller classes rated somewhat more favourably, though some find curvilinear relationships where large classes are also rated favourably
(f)	Level of course/year in school	Graduate level courses rated somewhat more favourably; weak, inconsistent findings suggesting upper division courses rated higher than lower division courses
(g)	Instructor rank	Mixed findings, but little or no effect
(h)	Sex of instructor and/or student	Mixed findings, but little or no effect
(i)	Academic discipline	Weak tendency for higher ratings in humanities and lower ratings in sciences, but too few studies to be clear
(j)	Purpose of ratings	Somewhat higher ratings if known to be used for tenure/promotion decisions
(k)	Administrative conditions	Somewhat higher if ratings not anonymous and instructor present when being completed
(l)	Student personality	Mixed findings, but apparently little effect, particularly since different "personality types" may appear in somewhat similar numbers in different classes

Note: For most of these characteristics, particularly the ones that have been more widely studied, some studies have found results opposite to those reported here while others have found no relationship at all. The size of the relationships often vary considerably—in some cases even the direction of the relationship—depending upon the particular component of student ratings that is being considered. Few studies have found any of these characteristics to be correlated more than 0.30 with class-average student ratings, and most reported relationships are much smaller of these background characteristics explained more than 5 percent of the variance in any one of the SEEQ factors and none did so for even half of the factors. The combined effect of the entire set of 16 characteristics explained 12–14 percent of the variance in the ratings. Four background characteristics were found to be most influential; more favourable ratings were associated with higher prior subject interest, higher expected grades, higher levels of workload/difficulty, and a higher percentage of students taking a course for general interest only. A path analysis demonstrated that prior subject interest had the strongest impact on ratings, and that this variable also accounted for much of the relationship between expected grades and student ratings.

Marsh, in this study and other investigations stemming from it, went on to argue that even the modest relationships that were found should not necessarily be interpreted as biases (see Marsh 1982c for an overview). The workload/difficulty relationship is in the opposite direction to that predicted by a bias hypothesis. The prior subject interest relationship occurs primarily with ratings of the overall course and learning value, and the same pattern of relationships exists with faculty self-evaluations of their own teaching. This suggests that prior subject interest actually affects teaching effectiveness in a way that is accurately reflected by the student ratings. Similarly, the class size relationship is limited primarily to ratings of group interaction and individual rapport, and this same pattern is evident in instructor self-evaluations. Part of the expected grade relationship is spurious, being eliminated by controlling for prior subject interest. Furthermore, the interpretation of this relationship depends upon whether higher expected grades represent grading leniency or superior student achievement. For example, Marsh has shown that when the same instructor teaches the same course on two occasions—presumably holding grading leniency constant—the class that expects to get the higher grades also evaluates teaching effectiveness more favourably.

A summary of "typical" relationships between background characteristics and student ratings is presented in Table 1. The summary is based upon the work of many different researchers and reviews of the literature. The observed relationships tend to be small, and often inconsistent. Furthermore, their interpretation as a bias may be unwarranted. Perhaps the best summary of this area is McKeachie's (1979) conclusion that a wide variety of variables that could potentially influence student ratings apparently have little affect.

5. "Dr. Fox Effect"

The Dr. Fox effect is defined as the overriding influence of instructor expressiveness on students' evaluation of college/university teaching. The results of the Dr. Fox studies have been interpreted to mean that an enthusiastic lecturer can entice favourable evaluations, even though the lecture may be devoid of meaningful content,

and have been cited as evidence of the invalidity of student ratings. In the standard Dr. Fox paradigm a series of six lectures, all presented by the same professional actor were videotaped. Each lecture represented one of the three levels of course content (the number of substantive teaching points covered) and one of the two levels of lecture expressiveness (the expressiveness with which the actor delivered the lecture). Students viewed one of the six lectures, evaluated teaching effectiveness, and completed an achievement test based upon all the teaching points in the high content examination. Ware and Williams who originated this paradigm, reviewed research in this area and concluded that differences in expressiveness consistently explained much more variance in-student ratings than did differences in content (Ware and Williams, 1980).

Marsh and Ware (1982) reanalysed data from the Ware and Williams' studies. A factor analysis of their rating instrument identified five evaluation factors which varied in the way they were affected by the experimental manipulations. Particularly in the condition most like the college classroom where students were given incentives to do well on the achievement test, the Dr. Fox Effect was *not* supported in that: (a) the instructor expressiveness manipulation only affected ratings of instructor enthusiasm—the factor most logically related to the manipulation; and (b) content coverage affected ratings of instructor knowledge—the factor most logically related to that manipulation. When students were not given incentives to perform well, instructor expressiveness had more impact on all five student rating factors than did content coverage, but it also had a larger impact on the achievement test scores (i.e., presentation style had more to do with how well students did on the examination than did the number of examination questions that were covered by the lecture). This reanalysis of the Dr. Fox studies points to the critical importance of considering the multidimensionality of student ratings and not assuming that any variable that affects ratings is necessarily a source of invalidity.

6. Utility of Student Ratings

6.1 Improvements of Instruction

The introduction of a broadly instituted, carefully planned programme of instructional evaluations is likely to lead to the improvement of teaching. Faculty will have to give serious consideration to their own teaching in order to evaluate the merits of the programme. The institution of a programme will serve notice that teaching effectiveness is being taken more seriously by the administrative hierarchy. The results of student ratings—as one indicator of teaching effectiveness—will provide a basis for informed administrative decisions and thereby increase the likelihood that quality teaching will be recognized and rewarded. The social reinforcement of getting favourable ratings will provide added incentive for the improvement of teaching, even at the tenured faculty level. Finally, faculty report that the feedback from student evaluations is useful to the improvement of teaching. None of these observations, however, provide an empirical demonstration of the improvement of teaching effectiveness that results from students' evaluations.

In most studies, classes are randomly assigned to one or more experimental condition, and a control group; students' evaluations are collected near the middle of the term; results are returned to teachers in the experimental group; and the various groups are compared at the end of the term on students' evaluations and other variables. SEEQ has been used in two such studies, using multiple sections of the same course. In the first study, results from an abbreviated form of the survey were simply returned to faculty, and the impact of the feedback was modest (Marsh et al. 1975). In the second study (Overall and Marsh 1979), researchers actually met with instructors in the feedback group to discuss the evaluations and possible strategies for improvement. In this study, students in the feedback group subsequently rated teaching effectiveness more favourably, performed better on a standardized final examination, and experienced more favourable affective outcomes (feelings of mastery, and plans to pursue and/or apply subject). These two studies suggest that feedback, coupled with a candid discussion with an external consultant, can be an effective intervention for the improvement of teaching effectiveness.

Cohen (1980) conducted a meta-analysis on all known feedback studies and found that instructors who received midterm feedback were subsequently rated about one-third of a standard deviation higher on the total rating (an overall rating or an average of multiple items), and even larger differences were observed for ratings of instructor skill, attitude toward subject, and feedback to students. Studies that augmented feedback with consultation produced bigger differences, but other methodological variations had no effect. Feedback from student's evaluations can lead to improvement in teaching effectiveness.

6.2 Usefulness in Tenure/Promotion Decisions

A variety of surveys conducted in universities in the United States demonstrate that the importance and use of student ratings have increased dramatically since the late 1950s (Centra 1979, Leventhal et al. 1981). Each survey found that classroom teaching was considered to be the most important criterion in evaluating total faculty performance, though research effectiveness may be more important at prestigious research universities. The earlier studies found that systematically collected student ratings were among the least commonly used methods of evaluating classroom teaching. In more recent surveys, they are among the most commonly used, and respondents indicate that they should be even more important.

6.3 Usefulness in Student Course Selection

Little empirical research has been conducted on the use of ratings by prospective students in the selection of courses. Students say that information about teaching effectiveness influences their selection and students who select a class on the basis of information about teaching effectiveness are more satisfied with the quality of teaching than students who indicate other reasons (Centra and Creech 1976). In an experimental field study, Coleman and McKeachie (1981) presented summaries of four comparable political science courses to randomly selected groups of students during preregistration meetings. One of the courses had received substantially higher ratings, and it was chosen more frequently by students in the experimental group than the control group. Based upon this limited information, it seems that student ratings are useful to students in the selection of instructors and courses.

See also: Synthesizing Research Evidence; Teaching: Art or Science?

Note:

For a more extensive version of this article see Marsh (1984). See also a forthcoming monograph by Marsh in *The International Journal of Educational Research*.

Bibliography

Borich G D, Madden S K 1977 *Evaluating Classroom Instruction: A Sourcebook of Instruments*. Addison-Wesley, Reading, Massachusetts

Centra J A 1979 *Determining Faculty Effectiveness: Assessing Teaching, Research and Service for Personnel Decisions and Improvement*. Jossey-Bass, San Francisco, California

Centra J A, Creech F R 1976 *The Relationship Between Student, Teachers, and Course Characteristics and Student Ratings of Teacher Effectiveness*. Project Report 76-1. Educational Testing Service, Princeton, New Jersey

Cohen P A 1980 Effectiveness of student-rating feedback for improving college instruction: A meta-analysis of findings. *Res. Higher Ed.* 13: 321–41

Cohen P A 1981 Student ratings of instruction and student achievement: A meta-analysis of multi-section validity studies. *Rev. Educ. Res.* 51: 281–309

Coleman J, McKeachie W J 1981 Effects of instructor/course evaluations on student course selection. *J. Educ. Psychol.* 73: 224–26

Costin F, Greenough W T, Menges R J 1971 Student ratings of college teaching: Reliability, validity, and usefulness. *Rev. Educ. Res.* 41: 511–35

Feldman K A 1976a Grades and college students' evaluations of their courses and teachers. *Res. Higher Educ.* 4: 69–111

Feldman K A 1976b The superior college teacher from the student's view. *Res. Higher Educ.* 5: 243–88

Feldman K A 1977 Consistency and variability among college students in rating their teachers and courses: A review and analysis. *Res. Higher Educ.* 6: 223–74

Feldman K A 1978 Course characteristics and college students' ratings of their teachers: What we know and what we don't. *Res. Higher Educ.* 9: 199–242

Feldman K A 1979 The significance of circumstances for college students' ratings of their teachers and courses. *Res. Higher Educ.* 10: 149–72

Firth M 1979 Impact of work experience on the validity of student evaluations of teaching effectiveness *J. Educ. Psychol.* 71: 726–30

French-Lazovik G 1981 Peer review: Documentary evidence in the evaluation of teaching. In: Millman J (ed.) 1981 *Handbook of Teacher Evaluation.* Sage, Beverly Hills, California

Frey P W, Leonard D W, Beatty W W 1975 Student ratings of instruction: Validation research. *Am. Educ. Res. J.* 12: 435–44

Gilmore G M, Kane M T, Naccarato R W 1978 The generalizability of student ratings of instruction: Estimates of teacher and course components. *J. Educ. Meas.* 15: 1–13

Hildebrand M, Wilson R C, Dienst E R 1971 *Evaluating University Teaching.* Center for Research and Development in Higher Education, University of California, Berkeley, California

Leventhal L, Perry R P, Abrami P C, Turcotte S J C, Kane B 1981 Experimental investigation of tenure/promotion in American and Canadian universities. Paper presented at the American Educational Research Association annual conference, Los Angeles, California

McKeachie W J 1979 Student ratings of faculty: A reprise. *Academe* 65: 384–97

Marsh H W 1977 The validity of students' evaluations: Classroom evaluations of instructors independently nominated as best and worst teachers by graduating seniors. *Am. Educ. Res. J.* 14: 441–47

Marsh H W 1980 The influence of student, course and instructor characteristics on evaluations of university teaching. *Am. Educ. Res. J.* 17: 219–37

Marsh H W 1982a The use of path analysis to estimate teacher and course effects in student ratings of instructional effectiveness. *Appl. Psychol. Meas.* 6: 47–59

Marsh H W 1982b Validity of students' evaluations of college teaching: A multitrait–multimethod analysis. *J. Educ. Psychol.* 74: 264–79

Marsh H W 1982c SEEQ: A reliable, valid, and useful instrument for collecting students' evaluations of university teaching. *Br. J. Educ. Psychol.* 52: 77–95

Marsh H W 1984 Students' evaluations of university teaching: Dimensionality, reliability, validity, potential biases and utility. *J. Educ. Psychol.* 76: 707–54

Marsh H W, Ware J E 1982 Effects of expressiveness, content coverage, and incentive on multidimensional student rating scales: New interpretations of the Dr. Fox Effect, *J. Educ. Psychol.* 74: 126–34

Marsh H W, Fleiner H, Thomas C S 1975 Validity and usefulness of student evaluations of instructional quality. *J. Educ. Psychol.* 67: 833–39

Marsh H W, Overall J U, Kesler S P 1979 Validity of student evaluations of instructional effectiveness: A comparison of faculty self-evaluations and evaluations by their students. *J. Educ. Psychol.* 71: 149–60

Morsh J E, Burgess G G, Smith P N 1956 Student achievement as a measure of instructional effectiveness. *J. Educ. Psychol.* 47: 79–88

Overall J U, Marsh H W 1979 Midterm feedback from students: Its relationship to instructional improvement and students' cognitive and affective outcomes. *J. Educ. Psychol.* 71: 856–65

Overall J U, Marsh H W 1980 Students' evaluations of instruction: A longitudinal study of their stability. *J. Educ. Psychol.* 72: 321–25

Ward M D, Clark D C, Harrison G V 1981 The observer effect in classroom visitation. Paper presented at the annual meeting of the American Educational Research Association, Los Angeles, California

Ware J E, Williams R G 1980 A reanalysis of the Doctor Fox experiments. *Instr. Evaluation* 4: 15–18

Webb W B, Nolan C Y 1955 Student, supervisor, and self-ratings of instructoral proficiency. *J. Educ. Psychol.* 46: 42–46

SECTION 3
Teaching Methods and Techniques

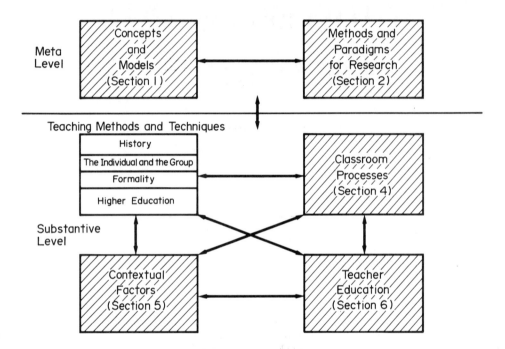

Schematic representation of Section 3 in relation to other Sections

SECTION 3

Teaching Methods and Techniques

INTRODUCTION
TO SECTION 3

The concept of teaching method is not a clear one. In some cases, what is termed a teaching method seems more like a whole theory of education or a way of organizing whole schools. In other cases the teaching method seems more like a learning method or a way of removing teaching altogether from learning experiences. Nevertheless, those theories, techniques, and curriculum strategies that are sometimes given the label "teaching methods" all have implications for the activity of teachers and so no attempt has been made to apply a rigorous definition in gathering together the articles presented in this section. Rather, an attempt has been made loosely to group the articles under headings that will hopefully communicate central themes they share. That there are overlaps among the categories is inevitable, indeed desirable, because it shows that the problems and successes experienced by educationists in trying to devise ways and means of achieving educative aims do not occur in isolation.

Four categories have been found useful for presenting the articles in this section. They are history, the individual and the group, formality, and higher education.

1. History

In the opening article of this section, Connell concludes his outline of the history of teaching methods by distinguishing between an instructional approach, in which the main concern is subject matter, and an educational approach, in which the main concern is the student. "The history of teaching methods", he writes, "might well be regarded as largely a study of various instructional patterns from which the teaching profession has had periodically to be rescued".

Connell writes about the early development and methods of literary education in Europe, with its concerns about grammar, style in expression, and eloquence, and points out that early Chinese literary education involved similar methods to Graeco–Roman practice. Memorization, textual analysis, oral and written composition, were predominant and apparently continued to be at least until the seventeenth and eighteenth centuries when there were the beginnings of a "science of teaching method" to be seen in the work of Comenius, Pestalozzi, Froebel, and Herbart. In Comenius, Connell sees the beginning of a developmental view of educational psychology with the suggestion that the curriculum might be fitted to the student's stage of intellectual development and that students be actively involved in learning tasks. Pestalozzi continued the concern with developmental stages of learners and gave emphasis to the structuring and integration of sensory perception, while Froebel gave further impetus to the concern for learner activity as well as broadening conceptions of learner development beyond the intellectual to include the emotional. The most influential, however, was Herbart who with his followers introduced the concept of interest into considerations about teaching methods and whose psychology of apperception led to the formulation of a series of five instructional steps most often appearing as preparation, presentation, association, assimilation, and application. The Herbartian steps, writes Connell, became so popular in teaching and teacher training that by the twentieth century they had supplanted the psychological advances behind them to form "a useful but somewhat barren technique of instruction and a refuge for conservative teachers seeking for a well-tried routine".

Among the "progressives" in Europe and America, those who expressed criticism of the formalized Herbartianism, Connell selects Dewey and Clapèrede as the best representatives. He writes that activity was the essential ingredient of progressivism. Activity methods emphasized needs and interest, functional knowledge through purposive work and problem solving, opportunity for creative expression, and participation in cooperative exercises.

Other twentieth-century matters discussed by Connell are innovations in literary education, including the French *Explication des Textes* and the English notion of *A Language for Life*, the impact of educational psychology, and teaching for a collective society in the Soviet Union and China.

In accounting for change in teaching methods, Connell sees evolutionary rather than revolutionary processes to have operated. He perceives four main times of change to be the early Italian Renaissance under humanistic influences; the seventeenth century, with the scientific movement; the late eighteenth and early nineteenth centuries with the psychological approaches of Pestalozzi, Herbart, and Froebel; and the early twentieth century with concerns about mass culture among the Progressives and educators in communist countries.

The next three articles in this section provide examples of the implementation of progressive educational ideas in the United States early in the twentieth century. In them, Lawry discusses *The Dalton Plan*, *The Winnetka Scheme*, and *The Project Method*. Under the Dalton Plan students were to be free to work at their own pace without interruption under a contract system involving monthly tasks. Individual and cooperative group work were parts of the plan within which student progress was charted and regularly reviewed. In the morning students pursued their learning contracts individually while afternoons were set aside for group work. Lawry writes that the Dalton Plan's potential for individualizing learning became limited by the demands of the contracted monthly assignments—especially for slow and reluctant students.

Similarly, the Winnetka Scheme was devised to strike a balance between individualization and cooperation. Students in it were also to pursue individual assignments at their own pace in the morning and group activities in the afternoons. Student progress was monitored with carefully prepared tests, and curriculum offerings were widened enormously. Apparently the Winnetka Scheme made use of self-instructional materials, scientific principles of curriculum construction, and techniques for group and creative activities in ways that surpassed the Dalton Plan.

Lawry writes that whereas the Project Method originated as a specific learning activity it became part of "a general method of education for the free society based on modern learning theory". He locates its intellectual origins in the child study and the scientific movements and in progressive education's stress on development of the whole person, relevance, and flexibility. It emerged as a challenge to formalism and had its beginnings in the Home Project of 1908 in Massachusetts, but is usually identified with W. H. Kilpatrick whose paper on the topic was published in 1908. Lawry outlines the main types of projects envisaged: practical tasks; aesthetic appreciation; problem solving; and mastery of a skill or knowledge, and the four main steps to be followed in problem solving. He notes the similarity of these to Dewey's main features of scientific method and distinguishes the project method from similar methods on the basis of students' freedom to select projects and methods for completing them. The article concludes with an account of the gradual incorporation of the Project Method into a general method of instruction associated with developments in philosophy, psychology, and metaphysics.

2. The Individual and the Group

After the previous four articles which are grouped as developments in approaches to teaching methods from an historical perspective, there follows a large group of articles representing contemporary methods that can be seen to have strong roots in history and which apply particularly to primary and secondary education contexts. Some of these methods pursue further the concern with striking an optimal balance between individualized and group learning.

In the first of these articles, Thomas writes about contemporary approaches to the individualization of teaching. Many of the concepts he introduces are revisited in later articles and some of them can be seen to have grown out of earlier concerns. Thomas discerns four main approaches to individualized instruction. The first is by way of arranging students into groups so that variability within those groups might be reduced. He sees the formation of homogeneous groups occurring at interschool, intraschool, and intraclassroom levels on the basis of physical characteristics, academic background or potential, religious affiliation, ethnic origin, or vocational interests. The main problem with grouping to produce homogeneity, writes Thomas, is that members of such groups are likely to be heterogeneous on other characteristics than the one on whose basis the group was formed. Not all grouping is done to produce homogeneity and in some cases heterogeneity might be the goal. Thomas goes on to outline other considerations involved in this approach to catering for individual differences in students.

A second way of attempting to individualize instruction is through the deployment of teachers and other school personnel. This can involve team teaching, teacher aides, parents, older students, student teachers, and members of the community.

Third, there are specially designed instructional materials and systems, for example, the Dalton Plan and the Winnetka Scheme, and finally there are ways in which individualization can be facilitated through the physical arrangement of the classroom to set up such resources as learning centres, exhibits, and media corners at which students might work individually.

While Thomas in his discussion of grouping is concerned mainly with acquainting the reader with the variety of ways in which grouping practices could be used to cater for individual differences, Calfee and Piontkowski concentrate on research on those practices. With respect to the assignment of students to particular types of schools or classes within them on the basis of measured ability, achievement, or teachers' judgments (a practice known as "tracking" or "streaming"), the authors cite research findings that while there is little apparent effect on high-ability students, low-ability students perform less well than in heterogeneous classes. Their discussion of these findings, however, suggests that there is scope for much more research on this practice, particularly research on what happens within the tracks or streams and how that affects outcomes.

In their review of research on grouping practices within classrooms, the authors conclude that it is the way in which teaching occurs within the groups, rather than the formulation of groups as such, that is important. They also make some timely and interesting observations about teachers' exertion of leadership or control in classrooms organized for whole class or smaller group instruction, and on student–student relationships according to grouping practices. Their comments about cooperation and competition establish connections with the articles by Slavin and Owens appearing later in this Encyclopedia (see *Small Group Methods*; *Cooperation*; *Competition*).

After discussion of the effects of such innovations as mastery learning, mainstreaming, and open-plan classrooms upon grouping practices, Calfee and Piontkowski conclude that the central issue in grouping students is often, "Who makes the decisions and on what grounds?" and suggest that "teachers and administrators could benefit from training in techniques for rational analysis of such problems". Moreover, they observe that grouping practices are often "all-or-none" when flexibility in this regard would be more effective.

The question of what happens in groups formed for instructional purposes is considered by Gall in his article on *Discussion Methods*. Small groups are sometimes used to promote discussion in the belief that verbal interaction through discussion is a particularly effective way of achieving certain types of learning including subject-matter mastery, attitude change, moral development, problem solving, and the acquisition of communication skills.

Gall considers the effectiveness of discussion in relation to each of those educational objectives. He also examines the influence of group size, composition, cohesiveness, communication patterns, leadership functions, and group norms upon group dynamics. Gall concludes his article with the observation that discussion methods are not often used in schools and suggests that this is because teachers find it especially difficult, it involves relinquishing teachers' authority and control, and class sizes are too large.

Slavin takes up the question of making small group instruction effective. He looks particularly at cooperative learning methods involving the division of the class into heterogeneous groups of four or five students who form learning teams. The methods he describes include the Student Teams Achievement Divisions (STAD), the Teams–Games–Tournament (TGT), Jigsaw and Jigsaw II, Team-Assisted Individualization (TAI), Learning Together, and Group Investigation. Slavin points out that group work in pursuit of a group goal is the characteristic common to all these methods, but that they vary in the degree of structure, the types of rewards, the curriculum area they are designed for, the use made of competition, and the types of skills aimed at.

In the second half of this article, Slavin reviews research on the effectiveness of cooperative learning techniques in relation to academic achievement, intergroup relations, mainstreaming, self-esteem, and other social and affective outcomes. He concludes that while there are still many unanswered questions, "these methods have proven their effectiveness on a wide range of outcomes".

The smallest possible instructional group is a group of two. In the next article in this section, Medway writes about teaching methods involving groups that are often no bigger than two. "Tutoring is a method of instruction in which a student or small group of students receives personalized and individualized education from a teacher", according to Medway. He writes that tutoring is usually a remedial or supplementary teaching method and that the tutor can be anyone from a student peer, to a parent, to a paid private teacher. He distinguishes between the method as applied to children and as applied to adults and traces its history back to first century AD Rome and through to the Bell–Lancaster monitorial systems of the nineteenth century. His discussion includes peer or cross-age tutoring, the Keller Plan's student proctoring, and even the use of computers. In his presentation of guidelines for tutors, he stresses the importance of positive attitudes by the tutor to the tutee, training of the tutor in basic instructional techniques, the desirable duration of tutorial sessions, and administrative support and appropriate evaluation.

3. Formality

Much of the debate about teaching methods during the 1960s and 1970s concerned the concept of open education in contrast with formal or traditional education. In the first article in this subsection, Giaconia writes about these concepts and discusses the great volume of research generated by the controversy involving them.

After discussing the many meanings of the term "open", Giaconia tries to distinguish it from "traditional" education as the two terms have been used in research. So various and vague have these usages been that she is left with a definition of "traditional education" which is merely "current educational practices in a particular region". The reviewer of this research, therefore, faces the particularly difficult task of synthesizing research findings about an innovation and the status quo without knowing clearly what those two really are and how they differ.

Giaconia compares the results of three attempts to review the research, one using what she calls the "box score" approach, which in her article with Hedges in the previous section of this Encyclopedia was called the "vote-counting" approach and the others using "meta-analysis" which in the earlier article was called the "effect magnitude method" (see *Synthesizing Research Evidence*). Giaconia writes that two major conclusions seem warranted on the basis of the three reviews:

> First, in general, open education is somewhat more effective than traditional education for nonachievement outcomes. Traditional education is only slightly more effective than open education for the traditional academic achievement measures. . . .

> Second, these general conclusions about the effectiveness of open education must be tempered by the fact that the variability of the effects of open education programs is often quite high.

The pursuit of elements of open education methods that distinguish more effective from less effective applications of that method led to the exploration of a set of seven features of open education. They were: open space; materials to manipulate; multiage grouping of students; individualized instruction; the role of the child in learning; team teaching; and diagnostic evaluation. In relation to nonachievement outcomes, the more effective open methods contained more of the seven elements than the less effective. However, the opposite was true in relation to achievement outcomes. Four of the seven features emerged as being particularly associated with nonachievement outcomes but only one of them was associated with achievement. Giaconia concludes that few general conclusions about open methods can be drawn from the research and suggests what type of further research is needed.

The problem of defining teaching methods is raised again in the next article, that on *Direct Instruction* by Rosenshine, who concludes that the term and its synonyms refer to "explicit, step-by-step instruction, in which there is an emphasis upon all students practicing successful responses and achieving academic success". "If you want students to learn something", writes Rosenshine, "teach it to them directly". He then overviews the behaviours of effective exponents of the method and elaborates on three key elements: demonstration, guided practice, and independent practice, making reference where appropriate to research supporting those elements. The second and third elements are elaborated upon with suggestions involving the frequency and type of teachers' questions, the percentage of correct student responses, teachers' checking for student understanding, calling on students, issuing feedback and correction, managing independent practice, and students helping students. Rosenshine concludes by acknowledging the method's historical roots but claims that what is new is the research support for it. The interested reader will find rewarding a comparison of the method with those described at various points in Connell's article in this section (see *History of Teaching Methods*).

The problems of defining and describing teaching methods, techniques, lessons, and other educational processes are highly relevant to the next article in this section. In it Dunkin reports on lesson formats and reviews several attempts to delineate significant dimensions of classrooms which might be useful for the purposes of describing variations within and between them. One system allowed for activities such as isolated seatwork, supervised study, and whole-class recitation to be identified, while another set proved useful in discovering similarities and differences in the lesson formats used by teachers from the United States, Australia, England and Wales, and New Zealand.

Posner's article on *Pacing and Sequencing* class activities includes reference to much that has preceded it in this Encyclopedia. He sees bases for his topic in the educational practices of the Hebrews, the Spartans, the American Indians, and others and makes connections with the Carroll model of school learning, the mastery learning model, and the behavioural model. He comments on the sequencing implicit in the Herbartian steps and presents an elaborate categorization scheme containing principles, key ideas, and examples relating to sequencing activities in the classroom.

Two entries follow that are about quite different topics but which share the attribute of being valuable for the potential they create for providing feedback on students' learning. The first is the article by Coulter about *Homework*, while the second is about *Thinking Aloud*, or in the French, *reflexion parlée*, and is written by Bonboir.

Coulter makes the interesting point that homework often takes the form of work unfinished during the school day so that it is done often by the slower students, left to work alone on tasks not fully understood or completed in class and, presumably, most in need of teachers' guidance. He also comments on the common exclusion of homework from paradigms for research on teaching and suggests that the extent of relevance of this form of individual private work might explain the generally low correlations found between teaching behaviour and student achievement. After critically reviewing the research on homework and school achievement, Coulter turns to research on the introduction and structuring of homework and reports interesting findings concerning the enormous variation in time spent by students on the same homework assignment. The need for instruction in independent study skills emerges and Coulter reports that when teachers planned, structured, explained, and used homework assignments for diagnosis and assessment students tended to participate more in the homework exercises.

Coulter's review of the effects of grading and feedback on homework upon subsequent student achievement failed to identify differences in effects. He found these results difficult to accept and attributed the null findings to deficiencies in the research. After presenting a model for future research on homework, Coulter concludes by advocating that homework be seen "as an aspect of overall time-on-task which, by the end of secondary school, apparently contributes as much to achievement in some subjects as the time allocated during regular school hours".

Bonboir traces the technique of thinking aloud to the belief that "in order to assist the learning subject, it is often more important to grasp the structure of the line of reasoning or behaviour than to measure its results", and describes its use both in research and in teaching. Students are induced to verbalize their thought processes as they work through a learning task or problem and this "thinking aloud" is monitored either by the researcher or the teacher, directly or from recordings made at the time. Unlike the Piagetian clinical interrogation, writes Bonboir, "thinking aloud is the study for the purpose of applying the results in practical teaching, of purposive processes which are intentionally directed towards certain objectives in the cognitive domain".

In the final article in this subsection, Richaudeau writes on *Written Instruction* with emphasis upon the words, sentences, and typography involved in the writing of educational texts. He considers the issue of readability, describes two procedures for introducing new words to young readers, and discusses the implications of psycholinguistic research. In his discussion of typology, Richaudeau considers the size of characters, and their design in terms of both execution and style, spaces between and breaks within words, and margins. He concludes the article with a discussion of the make-up of texts, presenting several principles involving contrast and variety, with reminders about the relative lack of expertise of the eye of the young reader and limitations in the latter's discriminatory memory.

4. Higher Education

Brown sees a threefold purpose of lectures: to convey information, to generate understanding, and to stimulate interest. The processes of lecturing are cognitive and affective and consist of structuring and conveying ideas, procedures, and facts as well as attitudes and values. The skills involved in lecturing are, therefore, interpersonal as well as intellectual.

After a brief historical sketch, Brown suggests that there are four key aspects of lecturing: intention, transmission, receipt, and output. He discusses each of these and then reviews research on lecturing focusing upon studies comparing lecturing with other methods, research on the views of students and lecturers regarding lecturing, and research on the four key aspects listed above. He advises caution in interpreting the results of comparisons with other methods, noting that lectures are rarely prepared as carefully as the alternatives and that they cost much less to produce than, for example, television productions. He reviews research reported by Land in Sect. 4 of this Encyclopedia (see

Vagueness and Clarity) concerning the importance of clarity in lecturing and refers to the content and expressiveness variables included in the Dr Fox studies reviewed by Marsh in Sect. 2 (see *Student Evaluations of Teaching*).

Brown sees implications for further research but writes that the quality of lectures and learning from them can already be improved by giving lecturers and students more information on structuring and presentation by training lecturers in specific lecturing skills and by training students in skills of listening, observing, and note taking.

Jaques's comprehensive discussion of *Group Teaching* explores issues similar to those discussed by Gall earlier in this section. He organized his article to give prominence to theory, research, and experience; characteristics of groups, such as time boundaries, physical environment, and group size; tutor's skills, particularly in asking questions; variety; social and educational contexts; and approaches to the evaluation of group teaching.

One of the main features of this article is the questions posed by Jaques in relation to many of the above topics. For example, in relation to time boundaries, two of the questions he raises are:

(a) "What do students need to know beforehand—place, time, aims, membership, roles, prior tasks?"

(b) "What are students expected to do after the meeting?"

And, concerning the physical environment:

(a) "What associations does the room have in the minds of students?"

(b) "Can everyone make eye contact with each other?"

In relation to group size he asks:

(a) "Is the group large enough to avoid total dominance by the tutor?"

Jaques also makes suggestions for promoting discussion by asking questions, for introducing variety, and for evaluating group teaching. Examples are as follows:

(a) "Try to ask questions which give informative answers. Not 'Did you calculate the mean?'; 'Did you subtract the mean from each reading?'. Rather ask: 'Tell me exactly what you did', followed by 'What about . . .', 'What else?', 'Uh-huh'."

(b) "If you fail to get the answer you want, consider the possibility that the answer a student gives may be the answer he or she wants, or that you have asked the wrong question."

Readers should find this article a rich source of ideas for their own practice.

Teaching in science laboratories is not confined to institutions of higher education so that the next article in this subsection, that by Hegarty-Hazel on *Science Laboratory Teaching*, is relevant also to schools. Hegarty-Hazel points out that laboratory teaching is an umbrella term that encompasses such different activities as demonstrations, audio-tutorials, computer-assisted laboratory instruction, case studies, projects, and research participation. She discusses the goals of laboratory teaching and sees them varying according to the types of programmes pursued by students, concluding that laboratory work is superior for inculcating manual skills involving scientific apparatus; in providing practice in the processes of scientific enquiry and some problem-solving skills; in developing appreciation of the scientific method, scientific attitudes, and resourcefulness; and in providing for individual differences. She then considers in greater detail the goals involving knowledge and comprehension, manual skills, and processes of scientific enquiry.

In the course of these discussions, Hegarty-Hazel presents many interesting and challenging research findings. Among them is evidence that university science students in the United Kingdom, the United States, Australia, and Israel show significantly less awareness of scientific enquiry than high school science students in the same countries. Her subsequent review of research on "life in laboratory classes" includes a suggestion by the authors of one study "that instructors were randomly reacting to situations as they arose in the laboratory and did not show evidence of systematic teaching and especially not of enquiry-oriented teaching". After discussing the effects of enquiry-oriented curriculum materials on behaviour in science laboratories, Hegarty-Hazel concludes:

> If the underlying assumptions are warranted, the data suggest that many science teachers have limited understanding of scientific enquiry or of the teaching skills likely to promote students' understanding of scientific enquiry in a laboratory classroom setting.

The next article, *Clinical Teaching* by Cranton is interesting because, as the author points out, it is about teaching in settings that are not designed primarily for instruction and that involve the presence of individuals who are neither the teacher nor the taught, but who are in a position to influence the instruction. Cranton discusses four main aspects of clinical teaching. They are objectives, sequencing instruction, teacher roles, techniques and teaching materials, and the evaluation of student performance. Cranton reports a lack of systematic studies of the effectiveness of the explicit statement and use of objectives in clinical teaching, and the effectiveness of implementing principles of sequencing different types of clinical learning experiences. However, she reports research in which she was involved and which found that the sequence of clinical rotations through different disciplines (such as surgery, paediatrics, and psychiatry) did influence student learning, particularly in the affective domain.

In relation to instructor roles and techniques, Cranton cites evidence that instructors saw themselves performing as role models much less often than their students did and that the frequent use of instructor demonstration was inconsistent with students' perceptions of effective teaching behaviours. After discussing a variety of approaches to the evaluation of student acquisition of clinical skills and desired affective qualities, Cranton concludes that there is a great need for research which takes account of the unique environment in which clinical teaching occurs.

The final article in this section is entitled *Keller Plan: A Personalized System of Instruction* and is written by Kulik. The Keller Plan or PSI as it is frequently referred to is one of the most frequently researched teaching methods in existence. In outlining its history and its relationship with the behavioural and mastery learning models of instruction (see Sect. 1), Kulik locates the method firmly within the domain of attempts to individualize instruction (see *Individualizing Teaching*). He lists the five distinguishing features of PSI courses as: mastery orientation; individual pacing; few lectures; printed study guides; and student proctors to evaluate quizzes. After describing what these involve for the student proceeding through a PSI course, Kulik summarizes the findings of a meta-analysis (see *Synthesizing Research Evidence*) conducted by him and his colleagues of research evaluating the Keller Plan and its components.

That meta-analysis synthesized findings using final examinations, follow-up examinations, and student attitudes as criterion outcomes of instruction. In relation to all three it was found that the Keller Plan courses were clearly superior to the alternatives with which they were compared. When the focus of the synthesis changed to evaluate the contributions of the various components of the Keller Plan, it was found that some components were more effective than others. Those apparently most responsible for the success of the method were the mastery requirement, the use of relatively small course units, immediate feedback on frequent quizzes, and the provision of review materials. The less effective components were tutorial help from proctors, self-pacing, and the occasional lectures.

After discussing the theoretical implications of these results and considering whether the success of the method is attributable to students' spending more time working than in conventional courses, Kulik concludes the article by exploring the issue of *what* is learned by students in PSI courses. He writes: "The result is that students in PSI classes learn very well those things that instructors consider important. On measures of incidental or irrelevant learning, PSI students may not do so well, but on tests that measure mastery of course essentials, PSI students show what they have learned".

History

History of Teaching Methods
W. F. Connell

Throughout most of the world's educational history the central feature of formal education has been the study of language. The methods of literary education were worked out in some detail in classical Greece and at about the same time in China. Their basic pattern with various modifications remained viable for much of the next 2,000 years in the Western world and in China. This article looks at the patterns of teaching in general education. It does not include vocational education or methods of teaching particular subjects. It traces the main changes in the literary tradition and the impact of social and cultural changes on methods of teaching up to the present time. The ideas and practices of the leading contributors during the Renaissance, the sixteenth-century revolution in scientific thinking, the romantic period of the early nineteenth century, and mass culture of the twentieth century are examined. Finally, there is a review of the contribution made by progressive educators, the development and impact of educational psychology, and the teaching methods used by communist educators to develop a collective society.

1. The Early Development and Methods of Literary Education

The most long-lived and widespread set of teaching methods are those associated with the study of language and literature. From about the fifth century BC until the early part of the twentieth century AD the civilized parts of Europe and China were nurtured on a literary education. In Europe its shape was set by the teachers of rhetoric in fourth-century Greece of whom the most notable was Isocrates and later, at Rome, in the first century BC by Cicero and in the first century AD by Quintilian. In China, the pattern had been emerging probably since the seventh century BC and was effectively developed probably during the Han period (204 BC–220 AD).

From Isocrates' time for the following 800 years to the end of the Roman empire, the general design of Western literary education remained stable and clear. It was designed on the premise that its eventual products would use their education in some form of public speaking. Within the European literary pattern of education there were three areas of study: grammar, style, and eloquence.

1.1 Grammar

The study of the structure of language and the usage of words began in fourth century Athens and reached a peak two centuries later in Alexandria. It was used as a basic introduction to the cultural heritage and became the foundation of primary education. In its more sophisticated form it was somewhat akin to the modern study of linguistics and was studied by advanced scholars.

Dionysius Thrax c.100 BC wrote the first comprehensive grammar of the Greek language. The word and paradigm framework initiated by him became the established approach to the study of grammar in the Western world and "remained a standard work for thirteen centuries" (Robins 1967 p. 31). It was expanded by later grammarians, such as Donatus and Priscian in the Latin language, and the general approach in it dominated the teaching of languages, especially classical and foreign languages, until modern times.

The two main elements in learning grammar were memorization and analogical reasoning. The various grammatical classifications of words, the paradigms for declension and conjugation, and the syntactic structures had to be learnt by heart. They provided a basis for the correct use of language by the pupil. The framework was reinforced and understanding of it deepened by exercises in finding similarities and patterns among words and in word usage. Pupils were led through it into the detailed textual study of good literature which formed part of the course in grammar.

1.2 Style in Expression

Grammar was also the basis of style. An important emphasis in a literary education was that of developing and appreciating written and oral expression. It involved the teacher in several processes.

A basic method, as in grammar, was that of memorization, often of long passages or even the complete speeches or works of celebrated orators and poets. A second basic exercise was that of textual analysis. This was a step beyond the kind of work done by grammarians. For teachers such as Isocrates and Quintilian it was a search for excellence in expression and a study of the way in which the intended effect was produced. It was the beginning, in the history of language teaching, of what was eventually developed in France during the twentieth century as *l'explication des textes*. Speeches of the great orators, notable passages from poets and prose writers, and models written by the master-teacher, Isocrates himself, provided pupils with all possible examples of rhetorical composition. The teacher would comment on these works and the pupils would analyse them carefully. They would look at the purpose of each composition, seek out the general structure of each passage, and study the manner in which various rhetorical effects were produced.

Excellence in style, however, was more than appositeness of purpose, articulation of structure, or originality of verbal usage. It was what the literary critic, Longinus, called "elevation". The author must seek not merely the applause of his contemporaries but the favourable judgment of "all men at all times" (Longinus 1935 p. 18). He must strive to write for all eternity. In addition, the author must be a person of high quality in mind and soul. Excellence, for Longinus, had the unmistakable ring of intellectual power and great character.

1.3 Eloquence

"Eloquence is the queen of the world", wrote Quintilian. Oratory in Greece and Rome was divided into three main types, display, deliberative, and forensic. Each, though based on common processes, had its own structure and special features. In the Roman imperial period oratory as an art simply for display became the most widespread and most sought after and rewarded accomplishment in rhetorical education. Many of the great rhetoricians then were also teachers, and found their profession more lucrative and generally attractive in that period than perhaps at any other time in the history of education.

The formal study of rhetoric involved five segments: training in the finding of suitable subject matter, arrangement, style, memorization, and delivery. Much of the training in each segment was done by exercises already mentioned. They were brought together in the rhetorical school in various approaches to the composition of orations. In preliminary exercises pupils constructed stories based on fables, wrote lives of famous men, compared good and bad characters, put together arguments for and against well-known decisions in history, and held carefully structured discussions of well-known sayings and debatable propositions. More advanced students were required to compose substantial orations on fictitious legal cases, or on abstract themes.

By a judicious choice of reading, their minds were to be stored with a knowledge of the great culture in which they lived, and their judgment sharpened by contemplation and serious intellectual discussion. But the great orator was to be a cultured man in a further sense. Quintilian's ideal was to produce "a good man skilled in speaking". A great talent for oratory carried with it a great responsibility that it would be used for good purposes. The teacher of rhetoric, therefore, had also to be a teacher of virtue. By precept, by discussion of moral ideas, by supervision and correction of behaviour, by insistence on sincerity in composition, and by encouragement to strive to express constantly in their speeches only what was honourable and good, the teacher of rhetoric hoped to produce persons of both fine character and fine speech.

The whole programme of rhetorical education was a nice balance of lecture, reading, and memorization on the one hand, and discussion, composition, and pupil performance on the other. Each side of the programme was related to the other in a well-graded sequence. Pupils were closely involved in active participation with the teacher and other pupils at all levels, culminating in the creative work of individual composition and the delivery of major orations in the later stages of education.

The methods used by the teachers do not seem to have varied greatly over the centuries. Standard expositions of them were written and widely used. Pupils and teachers had uniform expectations concerning the nature of teaching and the performance of the product, and the expectations appear largely to have been fulfilled.

2. Chinese Literary Education

Chinese experience in methods of teaching was reasonably similar to Graeco–Roman practice. Literary education started to become widespread and systematic probably during the Han dynasty in the second century BC. Like its European contemporary it was concerned with the cultivation of style and good character, and was partly vocational in intent. A public examination system was gradually built up for which teachers prepared their candidates, the degree of success in the various grades of the examinations largely determining the level of the position which scholars could subsequently occupy or aspire to. The virtues of loyalty, respect, and civic responsibility were taught by precept, example, continued inculcation, and a close study of various writings of Confucius.

Literary study was based on books designated as classics and its content and method of study varied little over the next 2,000 years (Galt 1951 p. 212). From time to time additional books and commentaries were added to the classics, but scholars of the Ching dynasty in the nineteenth century studied much the same literature as those of the Tang dynasty of the seventh century, who, in turn, had a prescribed syllabus not much different from that of their predecessors in the Han period.

Teachers encouraged their pupils to memorize and reproduce orally or in writing the great works of literature. They spent much time in explication, and required pupils to write compositions on historical and philosophical aspects of them. Understanding and analytical ability, and a grasp of moral principles were prized, but in the later dynasties style came to be especially valued. Fashions in style varied from time to time. For the most part, however, a composition in prose or a poem that was well-structured, subtly expressed, pure in language, and attractive in calligraphy was the goal at which teachers and pupils aimed (Biot 1969 pp. 125, 360, 445–46).

3. Survival of Western Literary Education

The work of the teachers of rhetoric in the West did not die out with the fall of the Roman Empire. It was maintained, for example, in Southern France, Northern Italy, Africa, and Spain for several centuries at a lower pitch by numerous scholars and teachers, and eventually passed into the keeping of the monastic and episcopal schools of the growing Christian system. With the general decline in learning, however, from about the fifth century on, it was the more elementary aspects of literary education that survived. Grammar, with its associated textual exposition, was the principal study. Donatus and Priscian determined the teaching methods rather than Isocrates and Quintilian.

In the eastern Mediterranean, the Byzantine continuation of the Roman Empire lasted, with many vicissitudes, until the fifteenth century and maintained various aspects of the culture out of which it had grown. Again, grammar predominated, but rhetoric survived in a somewhat uneasy alliance with the Orthodox Christian church. Lexicons and literary commentaries were compiled, and classical texts were indefatigably copied. In this way the written word of the Hellenic heritage was in great measure preserved. Literary education was focused on writing not speech.

At the end of the fourteenth century a gifted teacher, Michael Chrysoloras, became prominent. His methods were those of Quintilian though he was not directly acquainted with Quintilian's work. He emphasized wide reading, detailed analysis of the works read, use of a notebook to record interesting extracts, constant repetition and memorization of apt expressions and useful subject matter, and repetition by the student of his new knowledge at regular intervals to test his retention of it. This saturation was intended to create an intimate association between the student and the classical world.

Chrysoloras visited Italy in 1391. His arrival in Florence was greeted with great enthusiasm and stimulated the classical revival of the Italian Renaissance. Guarino da Verona, one of the early leaders of the Renaissance, and other scholars went back with him to Constantinople as his pupils. Subsequently Chrysoloras returned to Italy and taught there until his death in 1415.

4. Language Teaching in the Renaissance

The educators of the early Italian Renaissance of the fourteenth century had the talent to blend in an effective and lasting way three educational traditions to which they were the heirs: the Christian tradition which placed education at the service of religion and insisted on an integral association between religion and schooling, the later medieval education of courtesy which favoured an interest in cultural and physical accomplishments, and the literary tradition from Greece and Rome which was revived in the fourteenth century. The blending of these three strands produced a distinctly Renaissance pattern that modified the received literary tradition and gave a new and lasting direction to European education.

The methods that were developed throughout the Renaissance can be seen evolving progressively through the work of Vittorino de Feltre and Guarino da Verona during the initial period in the fifteenth century, in the contribution by Erasmus during the early sixteenth century in Northern Europe, and in the well-matured programmes of a number of notable secondary schools during the later years of the Renaissance and Reformation.

4.1 Guarino da Verona

Guarino's devotion to Greek learning led to his writing a Greek grammar based on one by Chrysoloras. He also became a keen student of Cicero, and, when Quintilian's *Institutio Oratoria* was rediscovered in 1416, he made it the guide for his educational methods. The foundation of education was to be laid in Latin grammar. By repetition, memorization, testing, and correction of oral and written exercises, pupils would learn basic accidence and syntax. The rules were to be worked at until they became ingrained. Pupils were then introduced to the poets and historians. Virgil was to be learned by heart, and pupils were taught to write Latin verse which "is one of the essential marks of an educated person". The programmes in Greek was similar, and was followed by exercises in translation from Latin into Greek, and Greek into Latin. The serious study of rhetoric was then begun by concentrating on Cicero's works on oratory, and on Quintilian. Guarino would frequently guide his pupils into a close textual analysis of chosen passages, lecturing on and discussing points of style, the use of words, and various literary allusions. Rhetoric for the Renaissance educators meant the study of style, in written as much as in oral expression. Exercise in written composition was therefore of great importance and occupied much of the pupil's time.

4.2 Vittorino da Feltre

Vittorino, a pupil of Guarino, established a school at Mantua which was attended by the aristocratic youth of northern Italy for almost a quarter of a century between 1423 and 1446. In his school, more than in any other institution of the time, was to be found the blending of traditional influences that set a pattern of future education. Its curriculum was a general all-round preparation for a life of distinction and civic responsibility: health, physical education, mathematics, drawing, music, and, above all, the study of Latin and Greek through which language, literature, history, morals, and philosophy were learnt.

Vittorino adopted towards the teaching of Greek and Latin the same approach as his master, Guarino. The success of his school and its wide reputation helped to confirm the direction toward which literary studies henceforth were to move. Morality, good taste, and style were the three chief concerns of the literary educators as they tried to reconcile their Christian responsibilities with their enthusiasm for their heritage from Greece and Rome. Of all the classical writers, Cicero, with his view of *humanitas*, came closest to the humanism of the educators of the Renaissance. His style, therefore, became the model of excellence, his philosophical writings a useful moral supplement to Christian teachings, and his judgments a guide to good taste.

4.3 Erasmus

Erasmus in the century following Vittorino, with the Renaissance in full-tide, described the object of the new synthesis in education as *pietas litterata*, a scholarly reverence. It was to be achieved through the kind of literary education that Guarino and Vittorino had outlined, but he argued for a sounder basis for the methods that might be employed. He suggested that the pupil's nature should be the starting point. Teaching and practice should follow "the path which Nature points out". The programme should therefore have three characteristics. It should be adjusted to the age, ability, and stage of learning of each pupil. It should be pleasurable and be seen by the pupil to contribute to his growth. And, as it went hand in hand with natural growth, it should take care to build the pupil's competence slowly and persistently, and to maintain his self-confidence in the face of the various linguistic difficulties he would encounter. Erasmus pointed the way to Comenius and Rousseau.

In keeping with his general view of teaching method, Erasmus took a situational approach to the teaching of grammar. Pupils should learn their grammar in the course of reading illustrative passages. They should try to work out the rules before committing them to memory. To assist this process he produced elementary phrase books, and a number of colloquies or dialogues written by him in good Latin style and dealing with commonplace activities. His colloquies provided vocabulary and constructions suitable for pupils to use in everyday speech and were so popular that they were still in use in the early part of the twentieth century.

4.4 Leading Secondary Schools of the Sixteenth Century

In the mid-sixteenth century the work of earlier Renaissance educators was consolidated in several countries into formal school patterns. The most prominent examples were Johann Sturm's *Gymnasium* at Strasbourg,

the *Collège de Guyenne* at Bordeaux, and the secondary schools of the Jesuits which spread through many of the catholic areas of Europe. Each made literary studies the central and most extensive part of the curriculum.

Their methods had three characteristics. First, as befitted establishments of the protestant and catholic reformation, they consolidated the synthesis between the classics and the Christian religion, the protestant Sturm, and the catholic Jesuits developing their respective programmes in almost identical ways.

Secondly, though Greek was taught, they emphasized the teaching of Latin. Senior pupils were taught in Latin and were required to speak Latin at all times even on their way to school. The Jesuits were noted for the Latin drama, expurgated classics or specially written pieces, that were acted by their pupils. At Sturm's school the pupils also frequently acted Latin plays in class, and arranged law courts in which people delivered Cicero's forensic speeches against the spirited defences of other pupils. Younger pupils would use Latin colloquies such as those of Erasmus or the equally popular Cordier who taught at the *Collège de Guyenne*. The general orientation was towards the development of excellence in style of writing and speaking Latin. This was what was then understood as rhetorical education. Beginning with the study of grammar it followed the well-established path through analytical textual study, intensive reading, memorization, reproduction, and graded composition, to the study of eloquence and style. Cicero was the model. To write in Ciceronian periods, with the vigour, rhythm, cadence, and polish of the master was the ideal of elegance towards which teachers and pupils in these schools directed their attention.

Thirdly, a characteristic of these schools of significance for the future development of teaching methods was an effort to consider the motivation of pupils. Vittorino, following Quintilian's lead, had tried to make the pupils' work more pleasurable by introducing some play activities. The later Renaissance educators were made of sterner stuff. They had much larger schools, sometimes of 1,000 pupils, whom they had begun to divide for the first time in educational history into a number of sequentially organized large classes. Their clientele was changing steadily as their pupils began to come increasingly from the growing, competitive, middle classes. Competition, usually called emulation, was deliberately developed as a useful and appropriate form of motivation by these educators. Sturm's pupils were graded and promoted by regular examinations, and, with the Jesuits, competition was vigorously encouraged and elaborately developed into contests between individuals within a class, between selected teams of pupils, and between classes.

The schools of the sixteenth century became the models on which the dominant schools of Europe, such as the German *Gymnasium*, the French *lycées*, and the English public schools, developed up until the twentieth century. In them, literary education remained predominant. Two significant and related cultural changes, however, had already begun and were eventually to have important effects on methods of teaching.

First, vernacular languages had begun to develop a significant literature, to command more scholarly interest, and to enter the school programme. By the eighteenth century the vernacular had become the language in which schooling was carried on and had emerged as a study in its own right, taught with methods taken from the classics but still lacking the prestige of the older languages.

Secondly, during the sixteenth century, there was a slow increase in the demand for elementary education and, in some Western countries, a rise in the number of elementary schools. It was a movement that steadily increased during the following centuries to become an explosion in the nineteenth century. It produced pupils with different backgrounds and expectations, increased interest in vernacular teaching, and eventually caused a change in the purpose and nature of secondary education.

5. The Beginning of a Science of Teaching Method: Comenius, Pestalozzi, Froebel, and the Herbartians

5.1 J. A. Comenius (1592–1670)

The seventeenth century in Europe was a period of cultural crisis. Intellectually, the impact of the Renaissance had been disturbing, and the revolution in scientific thinking that grew out of it had begun to have a fundamental effect on views of the nature of human behaviour and the ways of examining the human and physical world. Materially, it was a time of urban expansion, increase in commerce, growth in the power and importance of the middle class, immense religious dissention, and widespread and devastating war. Comenius, a Czech teacher and religious leader, lived through this period of disquieting change, suffered drastically throughout the Thirty Years War, and was deeply affected in his thought by the current disintegration of European culture. His life concern became the reestablishment of unity by building a brotherhood of mankind based on Christian principles and supported by common universal education.

Comenius set out in various publications his ideas on the kind of teaching methods that would be a central part of a necessary reform of education. They were processes that he had tested in many years of teaching. He incorporated them in a series of graded textbooks which he wrote for language teaching, and argued them persuasively in two major works, his *Great Didactic* (c. 1632), and his *Analytical Didactic* (1648).

He read and admired his older contemporary, Bacon, and felt himself to be part of the growing scientific movement. His was the first comprehensive attempt to construct teaching methods on scientific principles. In his approach there were five main elements.

(a) He accepted the prevailing Aristotelian–Baconian view on the importance of sense experience, stating in the idiom of the time, "There is nothing in the understanding that was not first in the senses" (Comenius 1953 p. 128). It was the world of sense experience not the word of a teacher or book that should be used as a starting point—hence Comenius's most widely known production, *Orbis Sensualium Pictus* (The World in Pictures), the first to use pictures deliberately and ingeniously as part of the method of teaching languages. By examining their experience and their relationship with the world of sense perception, pupils could move further into the cognitive process. The analysis of things and facts would develop reasoning and understanding on a sure basis.

(b) Comenius was interested in the contribution to educational method that "Nature" itself could make. Nature, in most of his writings, appears to have been equivalent to the phenomena of the biological and physical world. In the *Great Didactic* he developed a series of methodological principles and, in introducing them, would point out what Nature does, for example, "Nature observes a suitable time", then provide an example of Nature's behaviour, and explain how man imitates this practice, how teachers contravene it, and finally how school practice might be rectified.

(c) Comenius, in Piaget's view, "may undoubtedly be considered as one of the precursors of the genetic idea in developmental psychology" (Comenius 1957 p. 9). Comenius wrote "that nothing should be taught to the young, unless it is not only permitted but actually demanded by their age and mental strength" (Keatinge 1896 p. 290). Here is the beginning of a developmental view of educational psychology. Comenius criticized the teachers who imposed material on pupils before they were ready for it, and he came up with the interesting idea that has since become known as the spiral curriculum. It should be possible to teach the same things in a different manner at successive levels by utilizing a knowledge of the stage of intellectual development reached by the pupil in each case.

(d) Man, according to Comenius was a creature of action. Thinking was related to action as well as to sense impression, and out of the interrelationship of the three came learning. Action should be prior to skill training and theory. Let the pupil learn to write by writing, to forge metal by forging, to carve by carving. Activity and the learning that proceeds from it should be interesting, pleasant, and relevant. In Comenius's developmental and activity-type approach, the nature of the pupil, the relevance of the process to him, and his reaction to the teaching method were seen to be of considerable importance. It was the beginning of a move from instruction in which methods were primarily related to subject matter to an educational approach in which the viewpoint of the pupils was treated as a fundamental criterion to be used in designing teaching methods.

(e) Finally, it was part of Comenius's view of an educated human being that he did not accept truth merely on authority but examined and probed facts and ideas for himself. If the world was to be brought into harmony "all men should be educated fully to full humanity". It was a move away from the dependence on imitation, memorization, and observance of rules that characterized much of the practice of traditional literary education. It was an invitation for teachers to encourage pupils themselves to seek and discover by their own efforts.

5.2 J. H. Pestalozzi (1746–1827)

"I want to psychologize education", wrote Pestalozzi in 1800 in the opening sentence of a pamphlet issued "at the moment when the Method was created" (Green 1913 p. 291). Pestalozzi followed Comenius's lead, rediscovering and then developing and deepening much the same approach to teaching.

Meanwhile Rousseau in the middle of the eighteenth century had written *Emile* and *The Social Contract*, both published in 1762. He had an immense influence on educational thinking. He drew attention to the artificiality of contemporary education and argued strikingly for designing curricula and methods of teaching suited to the natural stages through which children developed. He regarded education as a positive instrument by which a corrupt and unequal society might be reconstructed. Pestalozzi read and was excited by Rousseau's ideas.

Pestalozzi was a Swiss schoolmaster who experimented for many years with agricultural, orphan, model, and training schools, slowly and painstakingly evolving his views on educational method. In 1781 he wrote one of the gems of educational literature, *Leonard and Gertrude*, a novel in which he told the story of the regenerative force of elementary education in the hands of a sympathetic, resourceful, and determined teacher who transformed a backward Swiss village into a flourishing, intellectually and morally reconstructed society. In his own schools, Pestalozzi developed a close teacher–pupil relationship and family atmosphere. In his last school at Yverdon he had a talented staff and attracted a stream of international visitors many of whom spread his ideas widely abroad.

By psychologizing education he meant two things: (a) to develop methods in line with the developmental pattern of children's growth; and (b) to make the process of perception the central element in his teaching method.

(a) Much of his teaching life was spent, as he put it, in tracking down Nature, in trying to discover the psychological unfolding of various human capacities. This was a concrete and persistent effort to make the intellectual development of children the starting point of the teaching process. In the past, much of the teaching method had been based on tradition modified by a teacher's practical experience; a significant innovation by Pestalozzi was that he did not merely rely on his ordinary teaching experience, he substituted deliberate experimentation for tradition or current practice, and he continued to innovate through experimentation over a period of several decades.

(b) Like Comenius he affirmed that sense perception was the beginning of all knowledge. But what should a teacher do with sense perceptions? He must follow, Pestalozzi decided, a process which would make initial sensory contact into clear and distinct ideas. This was the fundamental task of a teacher in the intellectual development of the pupil. A sense perception must be related to others already in the mind, the essentials of it distinguished from the unessentials, and it should be described and possibly classified, so that it became distinct and capable of use. All these activities must be in accord with the level of the pupil's intellectual development.

The principal tools in the process were language, form, and number. By associating language with sense impressions through the processes of analysis, description, and classification, he considered that ideas would be developed and clarified into thought patterns. Similarly, number and form were basic elements that teachers should use in the clarification and development of sense impressions into human thought. To facilitate the process, Pestalozzi developed object lessons which were to become something of a fetish with elementary-school teachers in the course of the nineteenth century. An object lesson, an elementary form of discovery learning, could involve the examination of a concrete object such as a piece of mineral, or the immediate environment such as the classroom, or a special environment, to which pupils have gone on an excusion, such as a forest or river valley. In each case the procedure was to use the sense perceptions of the object as the basis for examination, clarification, and development into ideas appropriate to the object.

Many of the leading educators of the nineteenth century studied Pestalozzi's ideas and observed his work. Two, in particular, Froebel and Herbart took their main inspiration from him and built extensively on his foundations.

5.3 F. Froebel (1782–1852)

Froebel's methods laid great emphasis on the study of the child, taking account of emotional as well as intellectual development. His starting point was not the pupils' sense impressions but the self-activity of the pupils. He found in them a quasireligious drive, a creative force which it was the teachers' job to encourage and guide into worthwhile activities. The individual was an active organism which operated as a unity. Because of this fundamental interrelatedness the teacher must be concerned with every facet of the child's growth. The interconnectedness was matched by an outerconnectedness which related all individuals to one another and to the world they live in. The teacher's task was to set the stage for and assist with his greater experience the self-activity of the pupils. Their self-activity, well-cultivated by their teachers, ensured that they became their own creative individual selves and at the same time a responsible and responsive part of humanity. Froebel's line of development led from Pestalozzi direct to the progressives of the twentieth century.

5.4 J. F. Herbart (1776–1841) and the Herbartians

Herbart, too, was innovative but the impact of the Herbartian method was considerably different. Herbart was a philosopher and psychologist who taught at the Universities of Königsberg and Göttingen and developed an educational psychology based on the association of ideas. After visiting Pestalozzi he wrote a series of essays analysing Pestalozzi's views of sense–perception. He made this work the starting point for a comprehensive study of perception and it became the basis for his proposals on educational method. It was an attempt to found "a scientific pedagogy, with psychology as its basis". (Compayré 1908 p. 7). His ideas were taken up enthusiastically in the second half of the nineteenth century by a succession of talented German educators. Towards the end of the century Herbartian ideas in curriculum and method dominated educational thinking in most Western countries. Herbartianism became the basic approach taken in many teachers' colleges and was so built into the thinking of young teachers in the growing educational systems of the early twentieth century that the impact of the Herbartian method long out-lasted the time when it was formally taught. It is safe to say that much of the teaching in elementary and secondary schools and many of the proposals on teaching method made by educational psychologists throughout the world at the present time have recognizably Herbartian features.

The contribution to teaching method made by Herbart and his followers was a threefold one. They produced a systematically worked out educational psychology as a basis on which to build a readily understandable and convincing method of teaching; they brought the concept of "interest" into a central place in the teaching process; and they demonstrated that education could be a carefully considered process of building the minds and characters of the pupils.

Herbart developed Pestalozzi's embryonic ideas into a substantial theory of cognition centring on the process of apperception. For the Herbartians a human mind consisted of ideas associated together in groups of related ideas. The first step in the process of learning was a contact with the outer world by sense–perception. This sensory impression was presented to ideas already within the mind and might be built into one of the existing groups. The process of fusing with an acceptable group and being related to the ideas within the group was called apperception. It was a vital part of the learning process not to be left to chance.

To guide the teachers in their efforts, the Herbartians devised a series of instructional steps that became the most widely used aspect of Herbartian teaching method. The sequence differed slightly in nomenclature from time to time; its most popular form was in five steps: (a) preparation; (b) presentation; (c) association; (d) assimilation; and (e) application.

The teacher's task was, first, in preparation, to stir up in the pupil's mind the ideas upon which he wished to graft the new material in his lesson. He then presented his material clearly, succinctly, and attractively, and proceeded to associate it with the ideas previously in the pupil's mind, knitting it skilfully into the existing pattern. The next step was to examine the fresh pattern formed out of the association of the new and old ideas. What was the meaning of the new apperception mass that had been formed? The final step was that of fixing the new material in the pupil's mind by applying it in a variety of ways, in tests, classroom exercises, and assignments for homework. This sequence became a standard approach in the twentieth century for many subjects of the curriculum in primary and secondary schools in many countries. It was systematic, suitable for many different kinds of material, and was based on an easily comprehended theory of learning. In the hands of a skilful teacher it could be both thorough and intellectually exciting.

The instructional sequence was associated with what the Herbartians referred to as the "doctrine of interest". The discovery and marketing of interest as a leading ingredient in teaching was an important Herbartian achievement. It had never before been an integral part of teaching method. Interest was associated with every step in the teaching process. The use of interest meant that each pupil should be motivated in a suitable way to attend to and to learn the material presented to him. The material must be within the pupils' range of apperception and adapted to the level of their interests. It meant also that there should be as much scope for self-activity as possible through the stimulation of curiosity, inquiry, imagination, and reflection. And it meant that there should be a constant drive towards the mastery and permanent acquisition of what was being learnt.

Interest had a further significance in the area of teaching method. The Herbartians, like most educators throughout history, were interested in moral as well as intellectual education. The five step process might be an admirable way of enabling pupils to acquire knowledge but could they learn virtue by the same method? A knowledgeable person is not necessarily a good person. The Herbartians contended that interest was the critical factor. To have an interest in an idea was to indicate that it was valued. There was no difficulty in teaching a pupil to know what was good. By interesting him in what was good he came to value it; once he valued the good he was inclined to act in accordance with it. Thus interest was the intermediary and the driving force throughout the process of converting knowledge into virtuous action.

The third contribution by the Herbartians was the powerful idea that teaching was a process of building a person's mind and character. The Herbartian teacher was a constructor consciously building up and expanding his pupils' apperception masses. By controlling the initial presentations, by stimulating this or that association, by promotiing certain interests, and carefully tending the whole apperception process and the actions which flowed from it, the Herbartian teacher was, in fact, making men. It was, as Dewey remarked, "the Schoolmaster come to his own" (Dewey 1916 p. 83).

6. Progressive Education

Herbartianism easily became formalized. When teaching became simply a matter of following the pattern of five formal steps with no concern for the psychological insight that had been put into the creation of them, or the interest and rich variation that a skilled Herbartian could develop in every aspect of them, they became a useful but somewhat barren technique of instruction and a refuge for conservative teachers seeking for a well-tried routine. Early in the twentieth century a number of educators became increasingly critical of current education including the widespread practice of Herbartianism.

It is difficult to categorize the methods of the educators who came to be known as Progressives. They emerged in several European countries and in the United States about the turn of the century and remained an important influence on educational theory and practice until about 1950. Thereafter their impact, though by no means extinguished, was in part absorbed into the mainstream, in part changed in character, and in part overlain by new and conservative influences.

Some idea of the range of ideas within the movement can be gained by studying the diversity of interests displayed by some of the more prominent members. They ranged from scientifically minded educators like Decroly in Belgium and Shatsky in the Soviet Union; creative teachers of art and literature like Cizek in Austria, Caldwell Cook in England, Mearns in the United States, and Dalcrose in Switzerland; educators interested in using the insights of psychoanalysis like Margaret Naumberg in the United States and A. S. Neill in England; champions of individual development like Montessori in Italy and Washburne in the United States; and advocates of community building like Kerschensteiner, Geheeb, and Petersen in Germany, Cousinet in France, and Rugg in the United States.

Two educators came closest to stating the essence within the variety of approaches of progressive education. John Dewey, an American philosopher and educator, wrote the basic philosophy for the movement,

Democracy and Education in 1916, and Edouard Claparède, a Swiss educator and psychologist, published series of perceptive essays in the 1920s and 1930s analysing its salient features.

The essential element in the methods of all progressive educators was activity. *L'école active* was the name used by Claparède for a progressive school. The heart of the matter was, in Dewey's phrase, the continuing reconstruction of the pupil's experience. Education was a process of living by developing and redeveloping one's needs, purposes, interests, ideas, and actions. Activity methods of teaching therefore tended to emphasize (a) the importance of pupils' needs and interests, (b) the acquisition of functional knowledge through purposive work and problem solving, (c) appropriate opportunity for expression, and (d) involvement in cooperative experiences.

(a) Interest was as important to the progressives as to the Herbartians. "Interest", wrote Decroly, "is the sluice gate. By means of it the reservoir of attention is opened and directed" (Hamaïde 1925 p. 32). It was an expression of a pupil's inner drive, an indication of the direction of his growth. It was, however, not the starting point in teaching method but a sign of the pupil's felt needs which were the true starting point. The concept of needs was never satisfactorily defined. Most Progressives took account of basic human needs, current social conditions, and aspirations, and the individual's own expectations, and, from them, made a judgment on what the individual's needs were and how they could be best catered for.

(b) Functional education was the kind of learning and teaching that could be seen by teachers and pupils to have a use and purpose which they could see and approve. The project method was originally designed to be an educational process of this kind (see *The Project Method*). It was purposive and it involved a process of discovery. One of the most useful ways of ensuring that education was functional was to adopt a problem-solving technique. Problem solving, through the influence of the progressives, began to become popular as a method of teaching a wide range of topics in the social sciences and languages as well as in the physical and biological sciences and mathematics. Dewey was its best exponent with his view that reflective thinking begins when a person finds himself in a situation of perplexity which must be resolved by tackling the problems that cause the perplexity. In *How We Think* published in 1910, he set out a pattern of investigatory thinking that many progressive educators accepted as a basis for much of the intellectual side of their teaching. It was an exercise in finding and defining problems as well as solving them. The actual process of problem solving involved practice in gathering and evaluating data, in putting forward and testing hypotheses, and in reaching appropriate conclusions and presenting them effectively. Problem solving was to be a method which would equip pupils to cope intelligently with, and take part effectively in, the changing life of the twentieth century.

(c) The Progressives took the view that expression was quite as important an activity as discovery. Isocrates and Quintilian would have agreed. Expression for the Progressives was more than excellence in speech and writing. It was the teacher's task to emphasize not elegance but sincerity, in essence to teach pupils to express their experience aptly and accurately in whatever was the appropriate and preferred medium. It could take form in one of the fine arts, drama, dance, and music, as well as speech and writing. Expression was regarded as an important means by which pupils could come to understand more fully their knowledge and experience.

(d) Discussion between teachers and pupils, and between pupils in small groups became a common technique among most progressive teachers. It was part of their wider interest in encouraging cooperation as a desirable practice in both the educational process and in the wider life of society. Activities were neither teacher nor pupil centred but were to develop out of cooperation between teacher and pupil in an effort to build up a sense of community throughout the school. For many Progressives the justification of this approach was in their profound belief in democracy, and their conviction that, as Dewey had expressed it, democracy "is the idea of community life itself" (Dewey 1927 p. 148). The Progressive teacher hoped to develop methods that would change the typically conservative attitude of school teachers into one concerned with developing a new culture for the twentieth century whose citizens were to be intellectually equipped to face up to rapid change and capable of cooperating effectively in building a democratic society (see *The Project Method*; *The Dalton Plan*; *The Winnetka Scheme*; *Teacher-centered and Learner-centered Teaching*).

7. The Literary Tradition and the Twentieth Century

Support for a classics-based literary education began to waver even in the sixteenth century but it was not seriously challenged until the mid-nineteenth century. Nor did the methods of its teachers change significantly during that period.

The principal innovations in literary education were in the methods of teaching the increasingly popular vernacular languages. Broadly speaking, up to the present time, two approaches emerged. One was an adaptation, in a highly skilled way, of the language teaching tradition bequeathed by the late Renaissance schools and exemplified at its finest in the early part of the twentieth century in France as *l'explication des textes*. The other, equally skilled and demanding, developed out of the progressive education movement of the twentieth century and was expounded in 1975 in *A Language for Life*, known also as the Bullock Report on the teaching of English.

7.1 Explication des Textes

In the latter part of the nineteenth century, vernacular literature began to assume importance as a vehicle of liberal education. From the beginning of the twentieth century, particularly in French secondary education, the teaching methods learnt on the classics were extended and refined into a powerful vehicle for making the examination and appreciation of vernacular literature into the foundation of general culture. Known as *l'explication des textes* this consolidation of teaching methods for the teaching of French became the centrepiece and distinctive mark of teaching in French schools (*Encyclopédie pratique de l'éducation en France* 1960 p. 620). It had several interesting features.

The teacher would usually select a poem or prose passage of good quality suitable for study in a particular age group and would proceed to examine it with the pupils. There was an insistence on a thorough knowledge of the meaning of every word and idiom and on a firm grasp of the general theme and its relationships with the minor ones. Thus the structure would be thoroughly explored, understood, criticized, and appreciated. The subject matter and mode of expression in the passage were then subjected to a similarly detailed and perceptive analysis. The pupils would be encouraged to comment on the balance and cadence developed throughout the poem or prose extract, they would contemplate the composition and pertinence of the imagery being used, and they would try to place the work in its contemporary social and moral environment. They would be expected to read the piece aloud expressively and with understanding, to write appropriate and reasoned analyses of its structure, theme, language, and style, and to discuss them in a fluent and intelligent manner with the teacher and fellow pupils. The total process was intended to be an exacting exercise in logical thinking, and a training in aesthetic perception (Connell 1980 p. 185).

It was the culmination of the long tradition of literary education. It demonstrated the intimate relationship between language and thought, and the close dependence of traditional European education on literary culture. Criticisms and problems, however, were not long in arising. Concerned with the maintenance of traditional good taste, it easily became conservative and oriented to the past. No sooner was the teaching method well-established than educational thinking became widely affected by the views and activities of progressive educators. There was a considerable debate about ways of adapting *l'explication française* to activity methods and to the demand for contemporary relevance, and, when secondary education became less selective, there was some questioning of the appropriateness of this highly intellectual exercise to the interests and capacities of the new and expanded generation of pupils. Literary education, thus, by the mid-twentieth century had developed into a highly sophisticated method of intellectual teaching only to find that it was being seriously challenged both in principle and in pedagogical detail.

7.2 A Language for Life

Early in the twentieth century in England the prevailing method of teaching English, which was also based on the teaching of the classics, was criticized for its inappropriateness to a modern language and for its suppression of personal expression and spontaneity. The Progressives argued for more activity and opportunity for individual expression in schools. Their views were taken up by several talented teachers and writers and applied to the teaching of English. O'Grady, for example, produced a fascinating textbook on composition which omitted grammar and encouraged pupils into the art of writing through experimentation with various styles. Caldwell Cook inspired his pupils with a play-way approach which stimulated their imagination and gave them constant practice in writing spontaneous compositions on activities in which they were interested. In the 1930s various linguists and psychologists linked emotional and intellectual growth with language development, and educators argued the value of English literature as a means of illuminating and raising the quality of life. In the post Second World War period these themes were taken up more widely. Current linguistic theory, too, supported the movement away from traditional methods by directing attention to language as it was currently used and by looking for a grammatical structure that fitted the usage of the living language.

The Bullock Report entitled *A Language for Life* written for the British government in 1975, helped to integrate a number of twentieth-century trends. Its problem, in respect to teaching method, was to retain something of the orderliness and quality of the traditional process while giving to language learning the thrust, relevance, and freedom of more recent approaches.

The attempt, traditionally, to draw up the boundaries of grammar, reading, dictation, composition, and literature, and to allot each its separate time and place, did not succeed. It was decided that knowledge of the grammatical structure of language should not be taught as a separate unrelated exercise but should arise as the pupils needed it in the course of their own speech and writing or observed it by studying how it worked in various literary situations. Pupils, it was suggested, learned language by using the four modes of talking, listening, writing, and reading in close relationship with one another. The teacher should maintain these relationships in such a way that the whole business of language learning was constantly enriched by the interplay of the various modes, and that each mode, too, was duly

benefitted by the interactive process. In writing, for example, "the first task for the teacher is one of encouraging vitality and fluency in the expressive writing that is nearest to speech. Children will move out into other modes in their own various ways and at various times that no one can predict in any detail. Their reading interests will be an influential factor, particularly in the early stages. To develop, they must take in written forms of the language and articulate these with their own general language resources, built up by years of listening and speaking. And they must do this in such a way that the whole corpus is within call when they sit down to write" (Bullock Report 1975). Fluency and intelligent speech were to be encouraged by classroom discussion which was not to be a debate in defence of established positions but an uncontrived mutual exploration of personal and literary experiences. Versatility and precision in written expression were to be encouraged by writing for various audiences.

The committee saw the teacher's task as that of extending, through language, the pupils' range of experience and understanding. The teacher was to create the conditions necessary for fluent expression, help the pupils develop technical control of the process of expression, and enable them to gain an understanding of a range of communication styles and increasing control over the quality of their own speech and writing. It was a process of discovery. But the pupils' discoveries were not random ones. They were controlled by the life which the pupils led and by the teachers' planning. The teacher must use knowledge and judgment to ensure that pupils could feel that their language experiences were purposefully related to their lives and to their own further intellectual, emotional, and linguistic development.

8. The Impact of Educational Psychology

The Herbartians had prided themselves that they were establishing a science of education. It was a science that was to be based on psychology. It was not Herbart's brand of psychology, however, that managed to continue the scientific tradition in the twentieth century but an empirical psychology from another German source, the Wundtian school, whose outstanding representative in education was E. L. Thorndike. Thorndike was, like Herbart, also an associationist but of a different kind. He was usually described as a connectionist, interested in the bonds or connections between sense impressions and impulses to action, and largely convinced that the establishment of these bonds owed little to ideas and could be made largely a mechanical matter of stimulus and response.

Thorndike made a massive contribution to the scientific movement in education by endeavouring to test empirically the outcomes of methods of teaching and learning and by formulating his theories and suggestions largely on the basis of verified data. His influence on teaching methods did not lead to the establishment of any systematic approach, and, in fact, tended to favour Herbartian methods. His work pointed to the importance of adequate motivation, and it reinforced much that the Herbartians had said and done. His research on transfer of training made teachers aware of the unlikelihood of an automatic transfer of learning from one situation to another, and suggested the desirability of taking specific steps to connect programmes together in some way if a transfer was desired between them. His study of the effect of practice indicated that repetition was of little importance as a teaching–learning device unless it was reinforced by reward or punishment, and that, of the incentives, rewards were the most powerful.

Thorndike and his successors strengthened the movement for the development of more adequate achievement and ability tests. In the course of the century a great variety of tests became available to teachers and became a regular part of teaching method. In some cases, testing took charge of normal teaching processes and dictated the teachers' style. The classic example was the introduction of a system of payment by results in England and Wales in the latter part of the nineteenth century. Elementary-school teachers were paid according to the success of their pupils in several basic subjects at annual examinations, and they adapted their teaching to ensure that pupils could reproduce at the appropriate time the minimum knowledge required. In the twentieth century, testing programmes were more flexible but they came to be of great importance. It was the teachers' expectation that tests would not change basic methods but would be an added technique providing a more objective measure of a pupil's level of ability or achievement. They were, however, also widely used to motivate pupils in their work, and were regularly employed as a basis for allotting rewards and punishments. A system of programmed learning became popular for a few years. It was arranged by combining teaching and testing in a series of small steps with limited behavioural goals so as to reward the successful learner and reteach the unsuccessful. This line of thinking tended to concern itself largely with the modification of overt and measurable behaviour in various ways to improve the pupil's performance.

Another line in educational psychology stemmed from the interest taken by Comenius and Rousseau in the nature of the child and the efforts of Pestalozzi and Froebel to make the study of child development one of the main bases of methods of teaching. The child study movement of the early twentieth century and a succession of notable psychologists, such as Hall, Binet, Terman, Stern, Vygotsky, Gesell and Piaget, produced systematic empirical material on children's intellectual, emotional, social, moral, and physical growth. By using a knowledge of the sequential stages of children's growth, teachers were able to adjust curricula and methods to make learning more relevant to the capacity and structure of their pupils' minds and to ensure their more efficient development into succeeding stages. This group of educational psychologists tended to support the methods of progressive educators. In particular, Piaget's insistence on a close link between action and cognition brought him out in favour of what his predecessor in Geneva, Claparède, had referred to as activity methods. Much of the research on the relationship of cognition and action, and its implications for methods of teaching was done in the Soviet Union where it fitted well with the existing educational tradition.

Parallel to the study of child development through the twentieth century, readiness became a significant part of teaching method. Teachers were counselled to be alert to teach material to pupils at the moment when they were intellectually ready for it. Many ideas and processes in the traditional school schedule, it was found, were better postponed to a later period when pupils were ready for them. One of the great virtues of the Winnetka Plan was the careful grade placement of items that resulted from observation and experimentation by teachers in the Winnetka schools (see *The Winnetka Scheme*).

In contrast to the educational psychologists who were interested in behaviour modification, Piaget and the cognitive psychologists such as Bruner and Gagné, in the 1960s and 1970s, were concerned with the cognitive constructs which pupils might make in the course of learning. This was another continuation of Herbart's approach in a different context. In place of an analysis of the way in which a teacher might help to build perceptions into apperception masses, Bruner wrote of the teacher's role in organizing knowledge into a structure suitable for the pupil to grasp, in presenting and sequencing concepts appropriately, and in encouraging the use of discovery learning. Gagné described the phases of learning and the sequence of processes associated with the teaching of them. Both were interested, like Herbart, in looking at teaching as a means of giving order to the pupil's existing knowledge, using it as a basis on which to investigate new skills and ideas, and building up meaningful new structures in the pupil's mind.

Teachers had also begun, by the 1950s, to study more closely how to use group techniques in their teaching. The work of Moreno, Lewin, and other field theorists prompted an interest in the pupils' social environment, school morale and school climate, the influence of peer groups, and the teaching potential of small group discussion. In consequence, methods of developing cohesiveness in small groups, of teaching role playing to improve the group's performance, and of devising ways of raising the productiveness of the group, became part of the training of many teachers, particularly in the social sciences. It was an aspect of teaching that had been experimented with and highly valued in the Soviet Union. An interest in group work became characteristic of teaching throughout the whole communist world and received its strongest emphasis probably in China during the Cultural Revolution of the 1960s and 1970s.

9. Teaching for a Collective Society

Progressive education flourished in the Soviet Union in the 1920s but did not wholly meet the requirements of the new and developing society. The educator who worked out in spirit and in detail the methods appropriate for education in the new collective society was A. S. Makarenko.

Makarenko (1888–1939) was an experienced teacher and attractive writer who worked throughout the 1920s and early 1930s in boarding schools for neglected and delinquent children. The colonies, as they were called, were developed with much skill and sensitivity into small collective societies. Out of this experience he wrote *The Road to Life* and a number of other books and articles explaining and analysing his activities and his views. From the 1940s on, his books became basic texts for teacher trainees, were widely read throughout the Soviet Union, and were generally regarded as the most effective expression of a teacher's role in the collective society.

"Our day", Makarenko wrote, "has seen the beginning of a new order in human relations, a new morality, a new law, the foundation of which is the victorious idea of human solidarity" (Makarenko 1937 p. 407). In support of the new order, education was to be, at the same time, intellectual, vocational, political, and moral. Makarenko demonstrated how to combine all four aspects of education in a way that would give pupils the kind of experience which would lead to the development of a collective society. It was an education that had a clearly political purpose. In making this plain, Makarenko demonstrated more clearly than most educators, the politicization of education that became a feature of education in various ways in all countries throughout the twentieth century (Connell 1980 p. 234). In his view, a good teacher was one who had two principal characteristics—a political conviction to collectivist society and a particular concern for human relations. In developing methods of teaching appropriate to these views he placed an emphasis on several significant features: style, pupil–teacher relationships, perspectives, sense of collectivity, and productive work.

(a) Of central importance to a teacher and a school was the development of style. It was behavioural not literary style. "Style and tone", he wrote, "have always been ignored in pedagogical theory" but they were of the greatest importance (Makarenko 1951 Vol. 3 p. 263). Style was the combination of outward form and inner feeling. Teachers should help to establish among pupils suitable and recognizable routines and habits of behaviour that they could welcome as a characteristic style for their group. But, more important, teachers should work to cultivate in their pupils an inner awareness of the responsibilities and opportunities of belonging to their group.

(b) A teacher's relationship with his or her pupils was a crucial matter. Makarenko oriented his teaching sensitivity to the pupils' interests, development, and future possibilities, and he imposed great trust in them, showing his confidence by making considerable demands on them. The better the pupil, the greater were Makarenko's expectations and the more severe were his demands. He described the relationship neatly as one of "exacting affection".

(c) Teachers, he thought, should be optimists, looking ahead with confidence and teaching pupils to develop a sense of continual progression and improvement. "A standstill", he wrote, "can never be allowed in the life of the collective" (Makarenko 1951 Vol. 2 p. 277). Teachers must therefore keep their pupils working at a series of activities with short-, medium-, and long-range perspectives, so that they can experience a sense of achievement and also have an incentive to move on to further accomplishments.

(d) The collective person was intellectually, politically, and also morally committed to his or her task. Teachers were to try to produce persons energetically devoted to the collective idea and "capable resolutely at all times of finding at every moment of their life the right standard for their personal actions, and of demanding at the same time the right conduct from others". Moral education might be taught by studying models of exemplary behaviour, by exhortation and the study of appropriate literature, by appeal to recently developed traditions, by following the customs and practices of collectively-minded peer groups, by discussion and intellectual conviction, and, above all, by saturation in collective experience.

(e) The most significant collective experience was productive work. At the largest of Makarenko's colonies, the pupils and teachers owned and ran two factories for making electric drills and producing cameras that had a wide market throughout the Soviet Union. One of the earliest educational reforms in the Soviet Union was the introduction of productive work into the general school curriculum. It was intended to provide for all pupils an opportunity to learn useful work skills, to gain some experience of proletarian habits and attitudes, and to realize the place of productive work in a communist society. To attain these objectives Makarenko insisted that work in his colonies should be both productive and collective. The pupils, consequently, had to plan and organize the production, establish and maintain standards of quality, market the products, and make decisions on expansion and new equipment. Productive work could involve teachers and pupils in intellectual, vocational, political, and moral education; and, not least, it could tie the pupils effectively into the pattern of interests, attitudes, and needs and into the tempo of the life of the wider collective society of the Soviet Union.

When China became a communist state in 1949 its teachers accepted much the same approach to education. In Mao Tse-tung, however, they had a teacher who added several distinctive characteristics to it. He saw teachers as a body of skilled and devoted persons who could help to ensure the continuation, maintenance, and deepening of the revolution. Teachers were to encourage pupils to look for problems and gather data by becoming involved in practical investigations. Solutions came from adopting the right political attitude and by resolving the contradictions in ideas that emerged in studying a problem. Intellectual and political education were closely related, and teachers had to "put proletarian politics in command" of their teaching. A teacher's task was to simplify his material, systematize it, apply it in practical ways, and saturate the learner with it. These were not four Herbartian-like steps but basic principles to be applied whenever possible in a problem-oriented, collective, and revolutionary society.

10. Overview

It will be apparent from this brief and selective sketch that many teaching methods have a long history. The main changes that have occurred have been rearrangements of existing patterns, the development of new emphases, or, as in more recent times, a more thorough psychological analysis of learning and teaching, and, as a result, a change in the nature and effect of some of the processes used by teachers.

Teaching methods are not random collections of techniques. They fit into a general framework which gives consistency to the teaching processes and provides a reasonable justification for them. The framework or general approach may be built from various elements. Commonly, there may be a theory of learning, a view of the nature of teaching, and a conviction about significant educational goals. In addition, there is inevitably a current mode or view of what is needed at the present time, a kind of educational *zeitgeist* that determines the flavour and thrust of the framework. For a variety of reasons, political, cultural, educational, or even idiosyncratic, an interest in methods may develop that favours a particular point of view at a particular time. It may be a conviction that children should be taught to think, or compose speeches, or drilled more thoroughly in basic skills, or taught discipline and obedience, or encouraged to express themselves more effectively, or any of several other considered judgments.

Most teachers throughout history have readily accepted and used the traditional methods by which they were themselves taught. They were habituated to them over the many years of their schooling, and their own scholastic achievements were evidence of the success of such methods. For them to change to a different pattern they must be convinced of the need to change and they must be provided with a feasible alternative or a means of developing one for themselves.

Change in methods of teaching has been an evolutionary movement with little that can be regarded as a substantial or drastic innovation. The more noticeable changes in teaching methods have usually been associated with wider social and cultural changes. Four obvious times of change and the educators associated with modifications in teaching methods have been those of the early Italian Renaissance in which the humanists Guarino and Vittorino played leading parts, the seventeenth-century scientific movement which exercised Comenius's mind, the romantic and reconstructive period of the late eighteenth and early nineteenth century which produced Pestalozzi, Herbart, and Froebel, and the initiation of mass culture in the early years of the twentieth century which stimulated the Progressives and the educators in communist countries.

Each of these persons and groups had perceptive and interesting minds and made significant contributions. Three, Pestalozzi, the Progressives, and the communist educators initiated ideas on method that had a pronounced and immediate effect on modern education. Pestalozzi introduced the notion that teaching methods should be based on a careful psychological analysis of human thinking and demonstrated in practice the kinds of methods that resulted from such an approach. He thereby provided a lead from which Herbart developed a powerful instructional technique and he opened the way for the considerable contribution that educational and cognitive psychologists were to make to the further refinement of teaching processes. The Progressive's innovatory contribution was twofold. They broke the traditional mould more drastically than had ever been done before, and thus made more feasible the development of new teaching methods suitable to the new societies of the twentieth century. They were also the first to use pupil activity as the central component in teaching and learning. Activity was expressed physically, emotionally, and intellectually. The Progressives, in exploring the connection between action and intellectual development, made wide use of teaching through problem solving, and encouraged creative kinds of expressive activities. They did, in fact, bring a new dimension into teaching. The communist educators concentrated on a particular kind of activity, productive work, and made it a fundamental part of education; but, more significantly, they worked out comprehensive and successful methods of teaching for a widespread new form of society, the collective.

Changes also appear to correspond to major shifts in the way in which teachers view their task. From time to time there is a swing between what might be called an instructional approach and an educational one. When teachers find their main interest to be in the subject matter which they teach, and conceive their task to be principally that of organizing the subject matter in ways by which they can most readily expound it and their pupils most easily assimilate it, they are adopting an instructional pattern. Its characteristics are formality, orderliness, and the transference of information from an authoritative source to a pupil. An educational approach makes its point of focus the learner rather than the content to be learned, and, although the teacher may be no less scholarly than his instructional counterpart, his educational priorities lie in understanding his pupils and fostering their development. Its characteristics are pupil initiative and involvement, and a care for a wide range of pupil growth. In this sense Vittorino, Erasmus, Comenius, Pestalozzi, Froebel, Makarenko, and the Progressives were the initiators of educational methods. In due course their methods were taken up by teachers in a changed context and were transformed and consolidated into new instructional patterns which tended to endure. The transition from Vittorino to Sturm, and from Pestalozzi to the Herbartians are two clear examples of the swing from educational to instructional processes. The conservatism of the teaching profession, its steady affection for routine, and the attraction of the seemingly greater efficiency of an instructional system have ensured a continuing popularity for instructional methods.

The history of teaching methods might well be regarded as largely a study of various instructional patterns from which the teaching profession has had periodically to be rescued.

Bibliography

Biot E C 1969 *Essai sur l'histoire de l'instruction publique en Chine, et de la Corporation des Lettrés, depuis les anciens temps jusqu'à nos jours.* Cheng Wen, Taipei
Bullock A 1975 *A Language for Life.* Report of the Committee of Enquiry Appointed by the Secretary of State for Education and Science. Her Majesty's Stationery Office, London
Comenius J A 1953 *The Analytical Didactic.* [Edited and translated by Jelinek V.] University of Chicago Press, Cambridge, Massachusetts
Comenius J A 1957 *Selections.* Introduction by Jean Piaget, UNESCO, Paris
Compayré G 1908 *Herbart and Education by Instruction.* Harrap, London
Connell W F 1980 *A History of Education in the Twentieth Century World.* Teachers College Press, Columbia University, New York
Dewey J 1916 *Democracy and Education: An Introduction to the Philosophy of Education.* Macmillan, New York
Dewey J 1927 *The Public and its Problems.* Holt, New York
Galt H S 1951 *A History of Chinese Educational Institutions.* Probsthain, London
Green J A 1913 *The Life and Work of Pestalozzi.* University Tutorial Press, London
Hamaïde A 1925 *The Decroly Class: A Contribution to Elementary Education.* [Translated by Hunt J L]. Dent, London
Keatinge M W 1896 *The Great Didactic of John Amos Comenius.* Black, London
L'Institut Pédagogique National, Ministère de l'Education Nationale 1960 *Encyclopédie practique de l'éducation en France.* Société d'Edition de Dictionnaires et Encyclopédies, Paris
Longinus C 1935 *Longinus On Elevation of Style.* [Translated by Tucker T G]. Melbourne University Press, Melbourne
Makarenko A S 1937 *A Book for Parents.* [Translated by Daglish R]. Foreign Language Publishing House, Moscow
Makarenko A S 1951 *The Road to Life: An Epic of Education.* [Translated by Litvinov I]. Foreign Language Publishing House, Moscow
Quintilian M F 1958–1961 *Institutio Oratoria.* [Translated by Butler H E]. Heinemann, London
Robins R H 1967 *A Short History of Linguistics.* Longman, London

The Dalton Plan

J. R. Lawry

The system of dividing the subjects of the curriculum into two parts and providing highly individualized contracts of work to students for the academic subjects, and class groups for the vocational, social, and physical activities developed by Helen Parkhurst was known as the "Dalton Plan". It was very popular and widely imitated throughout the United States, the Soviet Union, England and Wales, other English-speaking countries, and Europe from the early 1920s. Academic subjects were organized sequentially and students worked individually. The vocational subjects were grouped and students worked in classes in a nongraded way. The freedom allowed to individual children and the organization of teaching were said to increase the efficiency of schools when compared to the traditional forms of school organization and instruction, and to introduce into schools "community principles and practices". The Dalton plan offered procedures for organizing learning when changes were being contemplated, and appealed to the educational progressives' concern for freedom, individual expression, and social cooperation as an alternative to the formalism of the class lesson.

Helen Parkhurst developed the Dalton plan, known also as the "Dalton Laboratory Plan", to meet the criticisms of contemporary education and to provide a favourable environment in which children could prepare for life, freedom, and responsibility as "industrious, sincere, open-minded, and independent" individuals (Parkhurst 1923 p. 5). Learning had to be combined with experience to test character, to form judgment, and to develop self-discipline in social experience. She drew on her experience teaching in a rural school with 40 pupils over eight grades and in high school, primary school, normal training schools, and a training college. Her reading in 1908 of E. J. Swift's *Mind in the Making: A Study in Mental Development* (Scribners', New York) introduced the idea of an "educational laboratory" where student activity replaced the didactic method. A plan of work for children between 8 and 12 years of age which was finalized in 1913 "aimed at the entire reorganization of school life" (Parkhurst 1923 p. 11). Further work eliminated the restriction of the timetable through organizing pupils into groups with a free choice of the studies in laboratories with specialist instructors. Additional experience included working with Dr Maria Montessori in Italy and introducing the Montessori Method to California in 1915, undertaking a practical test of the laboratory plan through the help of Dr F. Burk, and more work on the laboratory plan in 1918 with the support of Dr M. V. O'Shea of Wisconsin University. In 1919 the laboratory plan was applied in the ungraded Berkshire Cripple School for boys, and, after attracting much interest, it was introduced on a larger scale in 1920 at the Dalton High School, Massachusetts. One early visitor to the school was Belle Rennie, an English pioneer of educational change, whose account of the Dalton laboratory plan in the *Times Educational Supplement* in May 1920 led to Helen Parkhurst visiting England in July 1921. Her ideas were received enthusiastically.

The Dalton plan called for the reorganization of the school so that it functioned as a community where the individual was free to develop in culture and experience and prepare for life. The school both provided freedom for the students to work without interruption and at their own pace, and required cooperation in the social experience of the school community. Character and knowledge were determined by the experience of living and working as a member of society rather than upon the subjects of the curriculum. The Dalton plan was not advanced as a panacea for academic ailments. Rather it provided "a way through which the teacher can get at the problem of child psychology and the pupil at the problem of learning". School situations were diagnosed "in terms of boys and girls. Subject difficulties concern students, not teachers. The curriculum is but our technique, a means to an end" (Parkhurst 1923 p. 23).

Teaching and learning were reconciled in the educational reorganization involved in implementing the Dalton plan. Once the curriculum was agreed to, students were assigned to a class. The work for 12 months was presented to all students at the beginning of the year. Students accepted the tasks assigned for each month as contracts to be signed and returned to the teacher when the tasks were completed. The curriculum was arranged for convenience into major and minor subjects. The major subjects were: mathematics, history, science, English, geography, foreign languages, and so on. The minor subjects were: music, art, handiwork, domestic science, manual training, gymnastics, and so on. Students progressed at their own rate, organizing their methods of working as they thought best. This arrangement secured the understanding of the work and gave students a sense of purpose and responsibility.

One laboratory for each subject of the curriculum with a specialist teacher in each was an essential feature of the Dalton plan. The laboratories were places where the students were free to work on their contract tasks without the distraction of shifts from one task to another determined by a time-table. Group work was encouraged by the requirement that all members of any class in any laboratory at one time should work together as a stimulus to discussion and as part of the exercise of social influences. The progress of students was recorded on graphs and reviewed regularly by the teacher and the students as a vital means of assessing progress and providing support.

Written assignments were central to the contract system. These set out the work to be covered in each subject in as much detail as determined by the specialist teachers bearing in mind the books, equipment, and other teaching materials available in the relevant laboratory. Typically the school day was divided into free time for work on contract assignments in the morning from 8.45 a.m. to 12 noon, followed by a pupil assembly and faculty conference until 12.30 p.m., and group conferences for reviewing progress until lunch at 1.00 p.m. The afternoon session was devoted to work in class groups on vocational or recreational activities.

The widespread popularity of the Dalton plan lay, in part, in the ease with which it could be varied and modified to suit particular circumstances such as limitations of space and the size of schools. Parkhurst encouraged this provided the spirit of the plan was preserved and schools for children under 9 years of age were excluded. Despite the emphasis on the suitability of the Dalton plan in catering for individual differences, the prescription of monthly work contracts in the case of slow or reluctant learners became a major limitation on the success of the plan as outlined by Parkhurst. It also lacked the detailed form and preoccupation with research and experimentation of the Winnetka scheme.

See also: The Winnetka Scheme; Individualizing Teaching; Keller Plan: A Personalized System of Instruction; History of Teaching Methods

Bibliography

Connell W F 1980 *A History of Education in the Twentieth Century World*. Curriculum Development Centre, Canberra

Dewey E 1922 *The Dalton Laboratory Plan*. Dent, London

Parkhurst H 1923 *Education and the Dalton Plan*. Bell, London

Selleck R J W 1972 *English Primary Education and the Progressives, 1914–1939*. Routledge and Kegan Paul, London

The Winnetka Scheme

J. R. Lawry

Action to improve the schools by the community and school board of Winnetka, Illinois, from 1912 led to the adoption of a scheme of individualized methods of instruction for tool subjects and group and creative activities for other areas of the curriculum, and the application of research and experimentation to the whole process of schooling (see *Individualizing Teaching*).

Carleton Washburne, superintendent of Winnetka schools from 1919 to 1943, and later professor of education at the Brooklyn College of the City University of New York, contributed to a method of curriculum organization which catered for the individual differences of students and to the scientific study of education. The approach, referred to by Washburne as the "Winnetka Plan", allowed students to progress individually in arithmetic, reading, and writing with self-paced individually assigned materials in the morning and to participate in group activities for social studies, creative arts, and physical education in the afternoon. It was adopted widely in elementary schools in the United States and was an influential pioneer in the self-correcting and programme instruction movement. Along with the Dalton Plan (see *The Dalton Plan*), the Winnetka Scheme made a significant contribution to the attempts to cater for individual differences in schools providing mass education for a heterogeneous population.

Washburne, a Stanford graduate in physiology and an untrained teacher in a two-room rural school, responded to differences in the children's readiness for learning by detailed planning of work, and by extensive use of groups for mutual help in coping with small classes in the main subjects. All the children were taught together for music, art, story-telling, and school organization. He then moved from the La Pirente District and gained experience with a special class in Tulare and in 1914 was appointed by Dr Frederic Burk to do research-based work in elementary science curricula at the San Francisco State Normal School. Burk had encouraged innovations in self-instructional materials and his work, *Remedy for Lock-step Schooling* distributed by the State of California Department of Education, was a well-reasoned attack on the traditional system of class instruction.

The Winnetka schools were to feel the impact of Washburne's early teaching experience and his research in science teaching, psychology, and the development of tests of children's achievement, and the work of Burk, who recommended his appointment. The Winnetka scheme developed quickly from 1920 onwards with group meetings of teachers, research to find the scientific answers to problems, the writing of self-instruction textbooks, and the preparation of diagnostic and review tests. The main object was "to stimulate and help every child to develop his own personal and social potentialities in accordance with his individual design of growth" (Washburne and Marland 1963 p. 22). The work in the schools led to the pursuit of key research questions such as "At what mental age can children most effectively learn each aspect of arithmetic and reading?" and to the publication of results by the Committee of Seven on arithmetic and by the American Library Association and the Carnegie Corporation on mental age, intelligence, phonics, and book selection for reading in *The Winnetka Graded Book List* in 1926.

The school curriculum was divided into two parts. The "tool subjects" of arithmetic and reading, and the language arts, which included penmanship, spelling, written English, and grammar, requiring the acquisition of a high degree of skill mastery. They were taught on an individual basis using the techniques of self-instruction, self-correction, and diagnostic testing, and individual rates of progress for each student. Washburne claimed the Winnetka schools were "the first progressive public schools to carry out systematic measurement of their results in comparison with more traditional ones" (Washburne 1953 p. 96). Standardized tests were used to check the efficiency of the programme. Other schools, including the Francis W. Parker School in Chicago under Flora J. Cooke, had developed methods which emphasized interest, social activity, and task-oriented learning but Washburne and his teachers developed the practice of setting minimum requirements in the basic or tool subjects and incorporating both individual and social work. The work in the tool subjects was analysed and set out in sequence. Texts and other materials were prepared for individual pupil use and progress was tested at set points to ensure mastery of skills and knowledge. Achievement and diagnostic testing were based on detailed research. In time, science and social sciences were included as tool subjects.

Knowledge, understanding, appreciation, desirable attitudes and interests, and the development of the personal and social potentialities of all students were part of the second and essential aspect of the programme. This consisted of the group and creative activities where "adaptation to individual differences of children takes on a different meaning and requires different techniques" (Washburne and Marland 1963 p. 87). Projects, agricultural and business ventures, art, musical performances, play productions, elective studies and clubs, school journalism, physical education and recreation activities, and school student government provided for the development of the potentialities of each child in the social group of the class. The Winnetka projects involved group activities lasting from a month to four or five months for two hours each school day. This group, but nevertheless "individualized", activity work was based on knowledge and experience with no subject matter boundaries being accepted. No attempt was made to teach specific skills or to learn particular facts as part of the group and creative activities. Creative activity and cooperation were emphasized and all aspects of school work were used. The individualization of the "tool subjects", which was directed at the mastery of skills at the appropriate stages of development (see *Mastery Learning Models*), and the efficiency of the methods of instruction allowed time to be devoted to the extensive group and creative activities.

Washburne claimed never to have used or liked the term "The Winnetka Plan". The essence of his scheme was the distinction between individual mastery of skills and group and creative activities "and the techniques for developing both *and* assuring their interaction" (Washburne and Marland 1963 p. 107). There was no fixed plan as there was continuous review and improvement of the work designed to provide "children with the best education that research and experimentation" could offer. This was in contrast to the Dalton Plan of which Washburne was critical, since it lacked the research work, the self-instruction materials, the scientifically constructed curriculum, and the techniques used in group and creative activities (Washburne and Marland 1963 p. 152). When the influence of Washburne's own dynamic spirit of change and discovery diminished the scheme tended to ossify. Some materials produced in the 1930s were still in use in 1956 and some Winnetka teachers were reluctant to accept any further change to the scheme or to engage in a revision of the materials.

Under Washburne's influence, Winnetka schools became a centre for educational ideas, practices, and research with an emphasis on freedom, creativity, purposiveness, and social responsibility. The content of the curriculum was arranged according to the best available knowledge about the mental age and the experiential background of each child. The self-instruction materials were influential in the development of programmed instruction. The scheme was developed with intense participation by teachers in the research and the preparation of teaching materials. Washburne did not try to set a pattern for all schools, but the Winnetka schools attracted visitors from around the world and contributed to the provision for individual differences, and to the systematic study of education.

See also: The Dalton Plan; Individualizing Teaching; History of Teaching Methods

Bibliography

Connell W F 1980 *A History of Education in the Twentieth Century World.* Curriculum Development Centre, Canberra

Washburne C W 1953 *Schools Aren't What They Were: A Book For Parents and Others.* Heinemann, London

Washburne C W, Marland S P 1963 *Winnetka: The History and Significance of an Educational Experiment.* Prentice-Hall, Englewood Cliffs, New Jersey

The Project Method

J. R. Lawry

Many innovative practices, including the "project method", were developed early in the twentieth century through a questioning of the personal, individual, and social purposes of education and the formalism of the traditional classroom, where the cultivation of knowledge and character took place by recitation and rote learning within a narrowly constrained curriculum.

The project method is generally associated with W. H. Kilpatrick's advocacy of purposeful activity, problem solving, and the needs and interests of the individual child in action, learning, and conduct. It was influenced in particular by Dewey's support for a problem method of teaching. It was absorbed later into the activity methods movement of the 1920s. What commenced as a specific activity became part of a general method of education for the free society based on modern learning theory. The programmes developed for primary and secondary schools did not draw directly on either the experience with projects in higher education, adult learning, research, and self-learning, or the literary models to be found, for example, Rousseau's *Emile*, Froebel's *The Education of Man*, Cobbett's *Advice to Young Men*, and Swift's *Gulliver's Travels*.

Its intellectual origins were associated with the child study and scientific movement and the educational progressives' stress on the development of the whole person, the relevance of the curriculum to social existence, and the need for flexibility in schools. The practical pressures came from achieving a degree of mass education through raising the level of school attendance. The project method acknowledged the increasingly diverse and heterogeneous student body, in part the result of compulsory school attendance, and as it developed it adopted the imprecise rhetoric of the child study movement to describe its main features.

It emerged as part of the challenge to formalism in the classroom and reflected the increasing freedom of intellectual and physical movement offered to students in socially approved practical activities. The ambiguities implicit in many of the phrases used to describe these activities—freedom and activity, building on the child's interests and experience, encouraging social contacts and desirable attitudes—suggest the variety of motives, programmes, and achievements of the promotors of the project method. At one extreme, the activities had economic and practical significance, and at the other they were part of a general method of instruction linking desirable social aims with practical efficiency so that every child could succeed at something worthwhile in preparation for democratic citizenship.

1. Home Project

The first formal project recognized as such was introduced in 1908 in the Massachusetts Vocational Agricultural High School. R. W. Stimson, an agent of the Massachusetts Board of Education, used the term "home project" to describe a plan of part-time work done away from school and only partially under school direction. Projects of this kind were specific instructional techniques which arose out of concrete and natural conditions—the growing of potatoes as a cash crop at home was based on material learned at school and the amount of money earned by each student was carefully recorded—and had specific practical and economic significance in an agricultural community.

2. The Project Method

When William Heard Kilpatrick of Columbia University published his paper on "The Project Method" in 1918 (Kilpatrick 1918), he provided not an exposition of a specific practical teaching technique but an account of the main features of a directly functional curriculum organization, based on an instrumental view of knowledge. The project method was related to what Dewey advanced as the problem method of teaching in his work on reflective thinking. This was based on the concept of the complete act of thought which proceeds from the initial effort of thought to the solution of a problem. The problem method and the project method were natural corollaries of the pragmatist philosophy which held that concepts are understood through observable consequences and that learning involved direct contact with things.

Kilpatrick defined the basic unit of classwork as "the hearty purposeful act" involving the factor of action, the laws of learning, and the ethical quality of conduct. There was a marked contribution to character building as "Education based on the purposeful act prepares best for life" (Kilpatrick 1918 p. 334). The project method offered an approach to education morally appropriate in a free society and technically consistent with modern learning theory.

Knowledge was applied instrumentally to assist in the completion of four main types of projects:

(a) Practical tasks such as the construction of a useful article—"to embody some idea or plan in external form".

(b) Appreciation of an aesthetic experience—"to enjoy some experience".

(c) Problem solving—"to solve some problem".

(d) Mastery of a skill or knowledge—"to obtain some action or degree of skill or knowledge".

The main steps in problem solving were "purposing, planning, executing, and judging" (Kilpatrick 1918 p. 333). These are similar to what Dewey had described as the main features of scientific method: adjustment, purpose, imagination, execution, assessment of worth, and evaluation of satisfaction. The general method of problem solving to be developed in school was applicable to many real-life situations.

The main feature distinguishing the project method from similar methods was the degree of freedom offered to students to select the project topic and the means of working through it. The project method was based also on the socially acceptable interests and needs of the individual child.

The project method gained widespread acceptance as an adjunct to the main curriculum, and was popular because of its emphasis on developing the whole person and not simply intellectual performance, and the importance it gave to education as a process of living in association with others. The practical details of the project method quickly became less important than its association with progressive education and the development of a general method of teaching. There was a blurring of the distinctions between the project method and the problem-solving method as both were identified with the activity movement as forms of "active learning" in which all students were involved.

Several attempts were made to preserve the distinctive qualities and the early practical emphasis of the project method. Monroe (1926) differentiated between the problem method where "the exercise is assigned" and the project method where "it is proposed by the pupil". He regarded the project method as incompatible with a fixed curriculum, especially as it made planning difficult when a teacher had to rely on the intentions of the students. Alberty (1927) stressed the practical, independent, real-life activity involving direct experience which had made it possible to judge objectively whether an activity was a project, and queried why Kilpatrick's subjectively defined "whole-hearted purposeful activity proceeding in a social environment" was ever called the project method. The association of the project method with "learning by doing" ignored the need to know about and understand the activity and diverted attention away from the learning it was expected to accomplish. Alberty sought to restore the practical meaning of the project method by a redefinition:

The project method in education . . . aims at securing learning (i.e., the acquisition of knowledge, habits, skills, ideals, etc.) *indirectly* by means of activities which have the following characteristics: 1. the goal which is supposed to dominate the pupil and lure him on to the accomplishment of the end, is not the *learning* sought by the teacher, but is some concrete result or accomplishment. 2. The learning essential to the satisfactory completion of the activity is always *instrumental* to this goal. That is, whatever learning is achieved is a by-product of the activity and is not directly arrived at by the pupil. (Alberty 1927 pp. 81–82 quoted Brauner 1964 p. 263)

By 1934, when the National Society for the Study of Education devoted a yearbook to the activity method, the identification of the project method with a general method of instruction was complete. From being essentially a practical learning technique it had become associated with the exploration of new features of philosophy and psychology and the metaphysics of experience.

Bibliography

Adderley K, Ashwin C, Bradbury P, Freeman J, Goodlad S, Greene J, Jenkins D, Rae J, Uren O 1975 *Project Methods in Higher Education*. Society for Research into Higher Education Working Party on Teaching Methods Techniques Group. Society for Research into Higher Education, Guildford

Alberty H B 1927 *A Study of the Project Method in Education*. Ohio State University Press, Columbus, Ohio

Brauner C J 1964 *American Education Theory*. Prentice-Hall, Englewood Cliffs, New Jersey

Connell W F 1980 *A History of Education in the Twentieth Century World*. Curriculum Development Centre, Canberra

Kilpatrick W H 1918 The project method. *Teach. Coll. Rec.* 19: 319–35

Knox H M 1961 *Introduction to Educational Method*. Oldbourne, London

Monroe W S 1926 Projects and the project method. *Univ. Illinois Bull.* 23(30)

The Individual and the Group

Individualizing Teaching

R. M. Thomas

One of the most active areas of educational innovation in recent decades has been that of individualized instruction. In educational settings throughout the world, an expanding variety of techniques for suiting individual differences among learners has been developed.

An important conclusion drawn from studies in this field is that no single technique for individualizing instruction is appropriate in all situations. Which technique will succeed best depends on the combination of variables affecting learning in that setting. Among the most influential variables are: the type of goals being pursued, the learners' levels of ability, the number of students being instructed by a single teacher, the type and amount of equipment available, the teacher's skills and personal style, and the breadth of individual differences among the learners in the group.

As a consequence, if educators are to select suitable methods of individualization for a given setting, they need to know a range of methods and the advantages and disadvantages of each. The purpose of the following review is to describe representative methods and conditions under which they are appropriate.

The intention of this article is not to describe in detail any particular way of individualizing instruction. Rather, it is to furnish an overview of diverse techniques of individualization, then to direct readers to other articles treating specific techniques in some detail.

Before surveying the methods, two often unstated principles can be noted that typically underlie modern-day proposals for individualizing instruction. They are the principles of mastery learning (see *Mastery Learning Models*) and of continuous progress.

The principle of mastery learning holds that each student deserves a fair chance to achieve the learning objectives, regardless of the ways the student differs from other learners. Techniques for implementing this mastery principle include allowing slower students more time to reach the goals, constantly evaluating students' progress to determine how well they are achieving the goals, providing alternative instructional routes to suit different learners' abilities and learning styles, and

offering remedial teaching to students who have not succeeded with the usual methods of instruction.

The principle of continuous progress holds that each student should continually be moving forward to new learning tasks in order to accomplish all that he or she is capable of achieving in the time available. No learners should waste time repeating tasks they have already mastered, nor should fast learners be expected to wait for slower ones to catch up before pursuing more advanced learning tasks. Techniques for implementing this continuous-progress principle include furnishing students with advanced self-instruction lessons they can complete at their own pace and offering them enrichment activities which broaden the scope of their studies beyond the areas covered by their slower classmates.

Some individualization techniques are better suited to carrying out the mastery-learning principle than to implementing the continuous-progress principle, and vice versa. Therefore, to achieve both principles, educators often employ a combination of several individualization methods rather than relying on a single approach.

The techniques surveyed below are described under four categories: grouping learners, assigning personnel, providing materials, and arranging classroom facilities.

1. Grouping Learners

One popular way of suiting teaching to individual differences has been to divide the learners into groups. In most cases the intention of grouping has been to reduce the variability among those learners who are to be taught together. The logic behind this practice is that students usually must be taught in groups, since society cannot furnish a separate teacher for each learner; so the most convenient way to suit teaching to the individual characteristics of students is to divide the learners into homogeneous groups with each group composed of learners who are alike.

1.1 Administrative Levels of Grouping

Homogeneous grouping appears at three administrative levels—interschool, intraschool, and intraclassroom. At the interschool level, separate institutions are established for students of different types. In some cases the basis for the selection of students is a physical characteristic, usually a handicapping situation, as in schools for the blind, the deaf, or the cerebral palsied. In other cases the criteria for admission to a school are aptitudes or abilities, as in institutions for the mentally retarded or the gifted, or in schools focusing on an academic or vocational speciality—college preparation, science, art, music, drama, business, home economics, industrial, technical. One of the oldest bases for interschool grouping is religious affiliation, with learners separated on the grounds of the type of religious studies their parents deem best—Buddhist, Hindu, Christian, Jewish, Moslem, or the like. Ethnic origin has also been a common basis for interschool grouping, with separate schools for different racial, ethnic, or tribal backgrounds.

Intraschool grouping is the type in which pupils within a school are divided into different classes or into different streams or tracks on the basis of their aptitudes and abilities, their interests, their future academic or vocational plans, or certain social characteristics. With a streaming or tracking system, students may be divided into three or four groups in which they remain throughout their years in the particular school. At the primary-grade level, the groups may be founded on children's apparent academic ability, with one group considered to be composed of the gifted or fast learners, another of the average learners, and still another of the slow learners. At the secondary-school level, there also may be tracks composed of students of different academic abilities, or else the tracks can bear labels indicating the students' academic or vocational future—a science and mathematics track, a languages track, a humanities track, a business track, an industrial arts track, or a homemaking track. Within a school there also can be separate tracks for the handicapped—for the sight-impaired or hearing-impaired learners or for pupils who display behavior problems or learning disorders.

Intraclassroom grouping consists of forming subgroups within the class. A rather common practice in some countries is for teachers to divide a class into three groups—fast, medium, and slow learners—and to teach each group separately. But perhaps more frequently, pupils are assigned to subgroups only for certain subject-matter areas and then are taught as a single unit for other areas. For example, children in a primary school may be divided into three or four groups for reading and mathematics, but then taught together as an entire class for social studies, science, art, music, health education, and physical activities.

All three levels of grouping—interschool, intraschool, and intraclassroom alike—have been accompanied by two interrelated sets of problems, one set technical and the other sociopolitical.

The technical problem is seated in the fact that when learners are grouped so they are alike or homogeneous on one characteristic, they are still very different on a range of other characteristics that are important for learning. Typically, when students are divided into groups on the basis of their similarities in reading skill, members of each group can still differ markedly from each other in mathematical ability, initiative, social adaptability, interest in science, and in many other ways. In recognition of this reality, educators have devised a variety of methods for achieving flexibility in their grouping systems. Some nations that traditionally have maintained separate schools for different types of students or curricula have converted secondary schools from specialized into comprehensive high schools, that is, into ones that provide several internal curricular tracks within the same school rather than maintaining separate schools. Then students are not rigidly assigned to a single track but are permitted to take classes in more than one track so as better to fit their individual abilities and interests (Petrequin 1968). Within classrooms teachers seek to conduct flexible groups that permit a child to move from one group into another as the child's progress and interest warrant (Murray and Wilhour 1971) (see *Flexibility*; *Activities: Structures and Functions*).

The sociopolitical problem accompanying grouping practices is that ethnic, socioeconomic, or religious factions within a society can feel they are discriminated against when learners are segregated into groups on the basis of their neighborhood or of a level of academic success that may be correlated with social class, ethnic, or religious status. Therefore, in many nations today, strong political forces press for the elimination of specialized schools (in favor of comprehensive schools) and of rigid tracks within a school as ways of accommodating for individual differences. As a consequence, when separate schools and ability tracking are diminished, the responsibility for adjusting learning tasks to individual differences falls increasingly on the classroom teacher.

1.2 Classroom Grouping Decisions

A variety of considerations can influence teachers' grouping practices within the classroom.

First is the question of what portion of the school day's program should involve a particular pattern of grouping. Should pupils be divided into fast, medium, and slow groups and remain in those same groups throughout the entire school day? Or should they be divided into such groups only for mathematics? Or for both mathematics and language study? Or for some other combination of subject-matter fields? As an aid in answering such questions, teachers can be guided by a principle founded on the technical problem noted above. The principle is: in general, the practice of making different combinations of membership for different subject-matter fields (one combination for mathematics, another for reading, another for physical education) will better suit individual students' needs than will the practice of maintaining a single pattern of membership throughout the entire school day.

Sometimes a teacher's purpose in forming classroom groups is not to achieve homogeneity but rather to ensure heterogeneity within each group. For example, a teacher wishes to encourage students to work efficiently with people who are from different social backgrounds and who have different levels of talent than their own. In this event, the teacher purposely mixes the membership of each group so as to achieve variety in the social characteristics and abilities of group members.

Another consideration in grouping centers on the number of different groups to be supervised and the size of each group. Should the groups all be the same size, or should they be uneven in size, with one perhaps containing 15 members, another 13, a third 6, and a fourth only 2? Should the class be divided into two groups, into four, into six? Answers for these questions can be guided by two interrelated common-sense principles. First, the number of different groups should not exceed the number the teacher can supervise without allowing students to waste time or to become confused and unruly. Second, the number of learners assigned to a given group should be the number who can most profit from the kind of activity that group is pursuing. In one case this number might be 20 students, in another only 5 or even 1. In effect, the answer depends upon a combination of (a) the diversity of pupil abilities and needs and (b) the supervisory skills of the teacher (see *Grouping for Teaching*; *Small Group Methods*).

A further consideration is whether the grouping should be visible or unobtrusive. Grouping is visible when the learners are clustered together physically. Grouping is unobtrusive when the learners are dispersed physically, and only in the teacher's mind—and in the individualized assignments given to them—are the learners grouped. Unobtrusive grouping is appropriate (a) when the teacher wishes to avoid emphasizing achievement differences among students by physically separating the more able from the less able learners and (b) when students' assignments are ones they can complete individually with little or no direct instruction from the teacher.

The type of grouping that will be most feasible in a classroom depends as well on the sorts of instructional personnel available, as the following discussion illustrates.

2. Personnel Assignments

In recent decades, educators have devised an increasingly varied array of ways of assigning personnel so as to care more adequately for students' individual differences.

One approach has been for two or more teachers to function as a team rather than as entirely separate individuals in charge of self-contained classrooms. Team teaching can assume numerous forms. For a given lesson, two teachers' total number of students may be regrouped so that one teacher instructs the more advanced half of the group and the other teacher instructs the less advanced. Or, in the study of science, one instructor may lecture to the majority while the other instructor directs the minority of the group in laboratory work or else offers them remedial aid in topics they have failed to master.

Not all team teaching serves to individualize instruction. Often it merely lightens a teacher's instructional burden. When two teachers combine their classes so that one teacher can lecture the combined group while the other is released to relax or prepare a future lesson, the students' chance of having instruction suited to their individual needs becomes even less than if the two classes had never been combined.

In many school systems individualization has been fostered by the addition of auxiliary personnel. The auxiliary staff members may be parents, older students, members of the community with special skills (a foreign language or a vocational skill), or teacher-training candidates. A variety of terms have been used to identify these subsidiary team members—paraprofessionals, teacher aides, teaching assistants, interns, and student teachers. When the aides are of the same age as the learners or only slightly older, they may be called peer teachers. These supplementary personnel usually perform under the guidance of a regular classroom teacher, who is then referred to as the master teacher or supervising teacher (see *Nonteachers and Teaching*; *Tutoring*).

Not only has the number of semitrained aides grown over the years, but the variety of specially trained experts has increased as well. The assignment of most specialists is to assist pupils who suffer learning difficulties because of impaired sight, hearing, speech, intellectual ability, perceptual–motor skills, or personality adjustment. Some specialists assist children who come from unfavorable home environments or schooling backgrounds.

Less frequently, specialists are provided to assist students with special talents, as in the arts or in such academic fields as mathematics and science.

Sometimes the specialists work directly with students. For example, a child with a disability in reading skill may be sent out of the regular classroom during certain periods of the day to receive remedial instruction from a reading expert. Other times the specialist enters the classroom to help children in that setting. Or a specialist may serve only as a consultant to the classroom teacher, suggesting ways the teacher can help the handicapped or the talented learners, but the specialist does not work directly with the students.

In sum, there are many ways that regular classroom teachers and auxiliary personnel can be combined to individualize instruction. In performing their jobs, they profit from using the growing variety of instructional materials and systems described in the following paragraphs.

3. Individualization Materials, Systems, and Packets

The word "materials" as used here means physical objects—such as books, filmstrips, games, tape recordings—employed to accommodate learners' individual differences. A system here means the series of steps that make up a particular process for individualizing instruction. A packet is a combination of both a system's series of steps and the physical objects needed for operating that system.

3.1 Materials for Individualizing Instruction

The past several decades have witnessed an accelerating growth in both the types of materials available and the numbers of items within each type (see *Equipment and Materials*).

Until well into the twentieth century, books and charts or drawings functioned as the only types of instructional materials for individualized teaching. Today the types have expanded to include such a diversity as textbooks, supplementary reading books, workbooks in which students write answers to problems, magazines, booklets, comics, programmed books, motion pictures, photographic slides, filmstrips, brief cassette films (film loops) to teach a single concept or skill, videotape cassettes and videodiscs to view on a television receiver, audio recordings on discs or tapes, charts, graphs, collections of photographs and drawings, simulation games, radio and television broadcasts, programs on electronic computers, and more.

Within each of these types a growing collection of materials is being produced to suit individual students' levels of achievement and learning styles. There is, however, a striking difference between nations in the types and amounts of materials available. Several socioeconomically advanced societies have a great host of media for meeting individual needs, while less developed societies have very few types of materials from which to choose. Regions in which minority-group languages are the media of instruction in the schools are particularly lacking in suitable teaching materials. As a consequence, the opportunity for students to have learning materials that match their individual differences is influenced to a great degree by the economic and educational affluence of the area in which they live.

3.2 Individualized Instruction Systems

A further advance in services to the individual learner has been the increase in instructional systems which delineate steps to be taken and materials to be used in accommodating for differences among learners. The notion of learning systems is not new. In early nineteenth-century Britain, the Lancaster–Bell system was devised for using bright students as peer tutors to teach small groups of students under the overall guidance of a classroom teacher who had 100 or more learners gathered in a large hall or auditorium. During the 1920s and 1930s such systems as the Dalton Plan (see *The Dalton Plan*) and the Winnetka Plan (see *The Winnetka Scheme*) in the United States and the Decroly Plan in Belgium were designed to suit instruction to individual needs by providing self-teaching study materials to students so they could progress at their individual speeds (Cubberley 1934 pp. 128–36, 528–30).

However, in recent times an array of more sophisticated systems has been created. One that has received much attention has been called "mastery learning"; it has been applied in several versions in such widely dispersed countries as the Republic of Korea, Indonesia, Brazil, the United States, Belgium, Australia, and Lebanon. The American psychologist, B. F. Skinner, devised a programmed-learning system by which students study small segments of information and then receive immediate appraisals of how well they have learned the segments before they move ahead to new information (Lange 1967). Another American, Fred S. Keller, created a Personalized System of Instruction known as the Keller Plan, which is based on operant conditioning principles like those underlying Skinner's programmed learning. Postlethwait developed an independent-study system using audiotapes and films (Postlethwait and Novak 1967) (see *Aptitude–Treatment Interaction Models*; *Keller Plan: A Personalized System of Instruction*; *Mastery Learning Models*).

The nature of steps that compose a system can be illustrated with the modular-teaching approach developed for experimental schools in Indonesia (Soedijarto 1976). As the first step, students are evaluated to determine their command of the skills underlying the content of the upcoming unit of study (with a unit lasting from two days to as long as two weeks of study). On the basis of this pretesting, students judged ready to begin the new unit will start studying the content, while students judged unready will be given remedial work in the underlying skills. When they have gained command of these skills, they, too, begin the unit. Throughout the course of the unit—which may involve individualized self-instruction as well as group activities and lectures—students continually assess their own progress and receive aid with aspects they do not understand. For faster learners who complete the unit before their classmates, enrichment activities are provided so the faster ones do not wait idly for the rest of the students to finish the unit. The enrichment experiences may involve individual or group projects that expand pupils' knowledge beyond that gained by the more average or slower class members. At the close of the unit, students' mastery of the unit objectives is evaluated, and remedial aid is given to class members who have fallen short of the desired mastery level, while those who have mastered the objectives are given enrichment activities until the remedial group has achieved the unit goals. Then the entire class begins a new unit of study.

For steps that compose other systems, see PLAN (Program for Learning in Accordance with Needs), IPI (Individually Prescribed Instruction), and UNIPAC (packaged units) in Weisgerber (1971). See also IGE (Individually Guided Education) in Holzman (1972).

Some systems care for individual differences mainly by providing remedial work for slower learners and enrichment activities for faster ones, as in the Indonesian modular system described above. Other systems depend on the principle of acceleration rather than remediation and enrichment. With acceleration, there is a single track of learning content that all students follow. However, the faster learners speed ahead of their average and slower classmates, so that before long nearly all of the students are at different points along the learning track, each progressing at his or her own speed. The advantage of acceleration over remediation/enrichment is that the teacher need provide only one set of learning materials. The disadvantages are: (a) students are at so many different points on the track that the teacher can never teach them as a single group or even as several small groups, (b) many pupils may need the teacher's aid at the same moment, but since the pupils are all facing different problems at that moment, they must often wait a long time to be helped individually, and (c) some students need different teaching media to suit their individual learning styles (some learn better by ear than by eye), and a single learning track does not usually accommodate as well to individual styles as does a remedial/enrichment approach.

3.3 Individualized Learning Packets

Some systems for individualization are simply descriptions of the steps that can be followed, and it becomes the task of the classroom teacher or a school's curriculum committee to find or create the learning materials that pupils will use—the booklets, worksheets, supplementary books, audio recordings, pictures, simulation games, and films. However, other systems provide all of these materials in the form of packets. The advantage of packets is that they relieve the teacher of the task of developing instructional materials. The disadvantages are that the packets are sometimes expensive and they may not fit the learning conditions in a particular school, that is, they may not be in the language of the region or may not refer to situations familiar in the daily lives of the learners. Increasingly, the packet consists of a set of small "floppy discs" used in a microcomputer.

One of the most popular fields for commercially published individualization packets has been that of the language arts. A typical example is the widely imitated Science Research Associates set of Reading Laboratories that provide children a graduated sequence of English-language reading passages accompanied by self-evaluation tests that keep pupils informed of their progress. Somewhat less common are packets in the areas of mathematics, science, and the social studies.

4. The Physical Arrangement of the Classroom

As more attention has been directed at ways of suiting instruction to individual needs, changes have been effected in the physical plan of classrooms. Classroom furniture no longer consists of benches or desks secured permanently to the floor in rows, but rather the furniture is movable so that small groupings of students can be formed (see *Seating Patterns*).

Particularly in primary and lower-secondary schools, classrooms may be organized in the form of learning centers, which are areas containing learning materials that can be used by from one to six or seven students at a time. Each center focuses on the development of particular skills or subject matter areas. One corner may contain instructional table games, another mathematics equipment, a third area may have science exhibits, and a fourth reading materials. In a secondary-school science classroom each of several learning centers may be dedicated to a different type of science experiment. Students are scheduled for the centers in a pattern that suits their individual learning speeds and interests.

In short, methods of meeting individual differences among students have called for increased flexibility and variety in classroom equipment (Bennie 1977, Murray and Wilhour 1971, Stephens 1974).

See also: Keller Plan: A Personalized System of Instruction

Bibliography

Bennie F 1977 *Learning Centers: Development and Operation*. Educational Technology Publications, Englewood Cliffs, New Jersey

Buffie E G, Jenkins J M (eds.) 1971 *Curriculum Development in Nongraded Schools: Bold New Venture*. Indiana University Press, Bloomington, Indiana

Charles C M 1980 *Individualizing Instruction*, 2nd edn. Mosby, St Louis, Missouri

Cubberley E P 1934 *Public Education in the United States*. Houghton Mifflin, Boston, Massachusetts

Dell H D 1972 *Individualizing Instruction: Materials and Classroom Procedures*. Science Research Associates, Chicago, Illinois

Holzman S 1972 *IGE: Individually Guided Education and the Multiunit School*. Education USA, Arlington, Virginia

Lange P C (ed.) 1967 *Programed Instruction*. University of Chicago Press, Chicago, Illinois

Murray E M, Wilhour J R 1971 *The Flexible Elementary School: Practical Guidelines for Developing a Nongraded Program*. Parker, West Nyack, New York

Musgrave G R 1975 *Individualized Instruction: Teaching Strategies Focusing on the Learner*. Allyn and Bacon, Boston, Massachusetts

Petrequin G 1968 *Individualizing Learning Through Modular-Flexible Programming*. McGraw-Hill, New York

Postlethwait S N, Novak J D 1967 The use of 8 mm loop films in individualized instruction. *Annals of the New York Academy of Science* 142: 464–70

Soedijarto 1976 *The Modular Instructional System as the Teaching–Learning Strategy in the Indonesian Development School*. UNESCO, Jakarta

Stephens L S 1974 *The Teacher's Guide to Open Education*. Holt, Rinehart and Winston, New York

Ward P S, Williams E C 1976 *Learning Packets: New Approach to Individualizing Instruction*. Parker, West Nyack, New York

Weisgerber R A (ed.) 1971 *Developmental Efforts in Individualized Learning*. Peacock, Itasca, Illinois

Grouping for Teaching

R. C. Calfee; D. C. Piontkowski

Research on grouping for instruction is motivated by the assumption that grouping practices influence students' academic and social learning. Most research has focused on the following questions:

(a) What decisions guide assignment of students to instructional groups?

(b) What are the structural and functional characteristics of groups?

This entry provides a review of research on questions of assignment decisions, group structure and function, and the effects of recent innovations on grouping practices. Throughout, the aim is for international coverage, although the weighting reflects the situation in the United States.

1. Assignment to Instructional Groups

Students are assigned to instructional groups at three levels: the school, the class and teacher, and the instructional group within the class. Assignment decisions by school administrators and classroom teachers at each level affect the character of instruction provided to students (Yates 1966). How are assignment decisions made at each level?

Assignment to school is often taken for granted rather than viewed as a decision. In the United States, parents usually follow school district guidelines when they enroll their children in public schools. District personnel assign students to a particular school on the basis of age and proximity to the students' homes. While the American comprehensive high school might seem to embody democratic assignment, the impact of neighborhood housing patterns is about the same as in elementary schools. In recent years racial integration practices have brought about some mix in assignments of students, but mainly to meet minimal legal requirements.

Current trends in the United States indicate that parents are seeking increased control over their children's assignment to a school. First, enrollment in private schools has increased in some regions. Second, there is serious discussion of a voucher system that would allow parents to enroll their children in the public school of their choice in exchange for a state-issued voucher.

Assignment to a class within a school is a significant grouping decision. Most often, age and academic ability are the criteria for class assignment. The notion is that teachers can carry out instruction more effectively when all students within a class share about the same ability level. Small differences between students can be ignored and the group taught as a unit with a common curriculum, standard pacing, and identical assessment. The success of this strategy rests on the assumptions that (a)

small differences in ability can be disregarded, and (b) differences other than ability are irrelevant for planning instruction and managing the class.

There are several reasons for questioning class assignment based on ability. First, it can be viewed as an elitist practice and contrary to democratic principles. Second, it may lead the teacher to ignore significant individual differences. Third, it is almost certainly unfair to those students who happen to be misassigned, especially for students put into the low-ability group who may remain fixed at that level. Finally, unless teacher assignment to class is carefully considered, homogeneous grouping decisions may actually maintain ability differences. For example, evidence from England and Wales showed that teachers of lower ability tracks were themselves less able (Jackson 1964). The rather ambiguous evidence from research in the United States (Weinstein 1976, Brophy and Good 1970) indicates little systematic attention to decision making on teacher assignments.

In a class with varied ability levels, on the other hand, children have opportunities to learn from and about one another, and it is easier for lower ability students to move forward. Some proponents claim that within-class diversity forces the teacher to attend to the needs of individual students, thereby improving the instruction given students in all ability levels.

Within the classroom, the teacher may instruct the class as a whole, may divide the class into smaller groups for instruction, or may set each student to work on an individual task. Whole-group instruction is characterized as a single teacher working with the entire class of students. The real "art" here is keeping all students actively engaged and on task (Rutter et al. 1979).

Division of the class into small groups usually has the aim of achieving instructional homogeneity, as in the case of ability grouping by class. Individualized instruction aims to meet students' needs by "treating each child as an individual" (see *Individualizing Teaching*).

The dilemma in grouping students is to balance orderliness and structure against human diversity and curriculum variety with the goal of optimizing student learning. Simple formulaic answers are not likely to work. Evidence is accumulating from a variety of studies that provides guidance in assigning students to instructional groups.

2. Research on Assignment to School and to Class

The effects of school assignment on students' achievement have been the focus of several large-scale studies. Earlier findings (Coleman 1966, Jencks 1972, Plowden 1967) led to interpretations of limited school effects; the important factors seemed to be family influence or "luck." More recently, measures of students' general ability have been replaced by tests that tap skills taught in schools. This has led to an increase in the estimated effects of the school, especially in schools with disproportionately large low-ability enrollment (Postlethwaite 1975, Madaus et al. 1976, Brimer et al. 1977, Rutter et al. 1979).

A common practice in many school systems is tracking, the assignment of students to schools or classes according to their ability as measured by a test, previous academic achievement, or the teacher's judgment. Coleman (1966) reported that about 40 percent of the elementary schools and 75 percent of the secondary schools in the United States followed some sort of tracking scheme. Tracking at the elementary levels may actually be greater than indicated by Coleman's survey. Elementary schools are smaller and draw their clients from fairly homogeneous neighborhoods, leading to de facto tracking by schools, based on housing patterns. To determine the extent of ability grouping by class in elementary schools requires a careful examination of the relation of within-class to between-class variance, information which appears not to be readily available in the literature.

Tracking has its main influence on the achievement of low-ability students. When a class is composed entirely of low-ability students, individual students perform less well than when they are placed in classes with a wider range of ability. High-ability students are often not influenced by the makeup of the class, though they sometimes benefit from assignment to homogeneous classes (Marascuilo and McSweeney 1972, Levy et al. 1969, Esposito 1973, Postlethwaite and Denton 1978, Rutter et al. 1979).

This pattern of findings conforms to what Cronbach and Snow (1977) have labeled an aptitude–treatment interaction (see *Aptitude—Treatment Interaction Models*). It may make little difference on the average whether a school decides on ability grouping or mixed classes. However, the decision will have differential impact on students of high- and low-ability levels. In the heterogeneous classroom, the high-ability student is less challenged than in a classroom consisting solely of high-ability peers. However, the positive influence of the heterogeneous classroom for the low-ability student is even more marked, or to put it in the negative, there is a substantial detriment from placing a low-ability student with low-ability peers. Much remains to be learned about the classroom processes which yield this pattern of performance, but there seems little doubt of the basic result.

A common practice in secondary schools is the assignment of high-ability students to college preparatory tracks and below-average students to vocational tracks. In some countries, this placement entails assignment to different schools; in countries with comprehensive high schools, the tracks take the form of assignment to different classes within the same school, with the possibility of intermingling of students in some subject matters (e.g., physical education).

Recent studies have tried to separate the effects on achievement of (a) the student variables which determine track assignment and (b) the impact of the curricula as such (Alexander et al. 1977, Goodlad et al. 1979, Oakes 1981a). The results indicate that placement in a track contributes to student achievement over and above the student characteristics used to make the placement.

The college preparatory and vocational tracks differ in a number of more or less obvious ways. Alexander et al. (1977) present alternative hypotheses about how these differences may influence student achievement. On the one hand, it may be that assignment to a track provides students with positive learning experiences that are relevant to students' functional skills and abilities. Or, the achievement of academic students may be improved while general and vocational track members are discouraged from competing with more able peers. This latter point of view is consistent with that of the "cultural reproduction" theorists (e.g., Bourdieu and Passeron 1977, Bowles and Gintis 1976, Bernstein 1977) who view the school as an institution designed to maintain present patterns of social and economic stratification, including any inequities that are part of the current social order.

In the research on tracking located, the emphasis has been on academic achievement and its correlates ("leadership," "attitude toward school," and the like). It seems plausible that the general and vocational tracks are associated with benefits that are unique to them, and that provide benefits to the students in them and to the society. Outcomes sensitive to these benefits may be hard to measure by standard tests, and may require a point of view and type of experience foreign to the academically inclined researchers who have been responsible for most investigations of tracking. There is a substantial literature on "applied performance" testing, and there might be great value in studying the effects of well-designed vocational programs on the development of vocational skills—it is essential, in evaluating educational programs, to ensure that the outcome measures are reasonably well-matched to the program goals.

3. Research on Assignment to Within-class Groups

What grouping arrangements are observed in classrooms? What is known about relations between grouping patterns and student performance? Some evidence is found in field studies and case histories on elementary reading and mathematics instruction.

3.1 Field Studies

The Follow Through study of elementary education in the United States provides information about grouping arrangements during reading and mathematics (Stallings 1975). Within the several instructional programs included in the study, some required that students work independently on a variety of materials. In other programs, students were taught in large groups, with considerable reliance on whole-class instruction and a fixed set of materials.

Stallings found a clear relation between grouping practices and students' work-study and academic behaviors. Students in programs that emphasized independent or small group patterns appeared able to decide quickly and freely on how to do their school work, but they were less persistent in completing these tasks than students in programs where work was assigned and monitored by the teacher. These students had a lower rate of absences, were more cooperative, and showed more initiative than students in programs where the teacher played a more directive role.

Reading and mathematics achievement was also related to grouping arrangements. In first grade (age 6) classrooms, reading level was higher when there was a great deal of small group (three to eight students) instruction; by third grade (age 8), achievement was higher in classrooms where the typical group was somewhat larger (nine or more students). Correlations between grouping practices and mathematics achievement were less clear-cut, though there is some indication that students did better when they received close supervision in large groups, rather than working on their own as individuals.

In a large field study in California, McDonald and Elias (1976) observed a clear relation between grouping practices and academic outcomes. Consistent with Stallings' findings, patterns varied from one grade to another, and from one subject matter to another. The strongest relations were found in second grade (age 7) reading: students who did well worked mainly in small groups, or individually but with supervisors. The teacher's role was to arrange for appropriate assignments, to provide a variety of instructional activities and materials, to monitor students' progress, and to give guidance and praise. A similar pattern occurred for second-grade mathematics—there was less variety in the material than in reading, with individualization provided by variation in pace, but the effective teacher was constantly on the move, supervising student work. Although profiles of the effective fifth-grade (age 10) teacher were less clear, the extent to which the class was taught as a whole was consistently related to lower achievement.

These two field studies both found that neither didactic whole-class teaching nor totally individualized instruction was effective for teaching elementary reading and mathematics. What seemed to work best was a well-managed program for individuals or for small groups, in which students received clear-cut assignments, and where continuous monitoring by teacher or by aide ensured that the student was making progress on assignments.

3.2 Case Studies

Barr (1975) observed 12 first-grade classrooms in four schools in the Midwestern United States. Three factors appeared to guide teachers' decisions on grouping students for reading instruction.

First, if materials were available, teachers planned grouping around workbooks. Otherwise, teachers tended to work with larger groups of students. Second, teachers grouped students for more intensive instruction in those areas of the curriculum that they thought were more important: teachers who emphasized reading for meaning and enjoyment grouped students for stories and recitation; those who focused on mastery of letter–sound correspondences divided their students for instruction on phonics. Third, all teachers started the school year with larger groups, dividing students into smaller groups as differences in learning rates emerged.

In the second case study, Piontkowski (1981) analyzed observational data from three first-grade classrooms in three schools. All classes operated on a split schedule—half the students came to class early in the morning for reading instruction; the remaining students arrived later in the morning and had reading instruction in the late afternoon.

Although all three teachers had about the same number of students available (12 to 15), they differed markedly in how they organized the youngsters for instruction. One teacher worked without an aide, instructing the group of 15 students as a whole. She combined direct instruction with assessment, and worked mostly on phonics drill and dictation. The six target students in this class performed above average on all reading measures, and could read independently by April.

The second teacher started each reading period by instructing all students. After about 15 minutes, she selected 5 or 6 students to stay working with her and dismissed the other students to seatwork, supervised by aides. The instructional program in this class combined a reading-for-meaning approach with some phonics drill. Measures of the target students' reading achievement indicated that the instructional program was successful for some students, but not for others.

The third teacher always divided students into two or three small groups, and followed the teacher's manual "to the letter." As the school year progressed, she assigned increasing numbers of students to aides, while she moved ahead through the basic program with fewer and fewer students. Only one target student learned to read during the school year, and all students tended to turn to any available adult to help them as they struggled with the text.

There are similar findings in the two case studies. First, availability of instructional materials increases the likelihood of multiple groups during reading instruction. If the instructional program includes student workbooks, teachers are likely to assign some students to seatwork and to instruct a subset of students. Second, grouping decisions also differ across the school year as teachers assign students to homogeneous instructional groups. In some cases, this works to students' advantage—in others, it may mean permanent assignment to an instructional aide.

3.3 Pooling the Evidence on Within-class Grouping

The evidence from the four studies on intraclass grouping provides some useful generalizations. Instructional decisions during reading are linked with grouping practices (Barr 1975, Piontkowski 1981, Stallings 1975). Direct instruction of the class leads to superior performance in reading and mathematics achievement, whether in the form of individualized (McDonald and Elias 1976) or group instruction (Piontkowski 1981, Stallings 1975). To be effective, individualized instruction must be arranged so that the teacher presents students with a limited set of choices, where they are not free to roam either physically or cognitively (see *Individualizing Teaching*). When effectively implemented, these programs of individual and small group work promote achievement as well as independence, cooperativeness, and initiative (Stallings 1975). However, some individualized and small group instructional programs provide a free-for-all atmosphere in which little learning occurs and dependency on the teacher is fostered (McDonald and Elias 1976, Piontkowski 1981).

4. The Structure and Function of Instructional Groups

Instructional grouping practices can be analyzed according to structure and function (Dunkin and Biddle 1974). Structure includes such facets as size, composition, purpose, leadership and membership patterns, and relationship to other groups. By function is meant such variables as the operational rules of the group, what the group is doing, and how the students within the group are carrying out instructional activities. Ideally, the function of a group should dictate its structure. Principals and teachers must frequently deal with formal constraints or with prevailing custom so that little thought is given to alternative schemes for organizing students.

5. Research on Group Structure and Function

The reviews by Henry (1960) and Schmuck and Schmuck (1975) of the literature on the structure and function of classroom groups are comprehensive and reasonably up-to-date. The following remarks are restricted to discussion of a case history and to some observations about the effects of grouping decisions on leadership, on norms, and on communication.

5.1 Leadership

Bossert's (1977) case study of within-class grouping practices and teachers' leadership styles illustrates the functional influences of class management (see *Classroom Management*) on the social climate of the classroom (see *Classroom Climate*). He classified instructional time into recitation and other whole-class tasks, small group and independent tasks, free time, and man-agement time. Two of the four teachers in the study relied on whole-class activities about 75 percent of total time; the other two teachers relied on whole-class activities only 50 percent of the time, placing much more emphasis on small group and independent work, and free time.

To investigate how teachers' authoritarian or democratic styles related to their grouping decisions, Bossert analyzed teachers' disciplinary actions following violation of rules by students. In all classrooms, teachers exerted considerably more control during whole-class activities than during small group work, which suggests that organizational structure determines the form of teacher control. Whole-group instruction leads to repressive actions. However, the two "authoritarian" teachers exerted more control than the two "democratic" teachers under all organizational conditions.

Bossert's study illustrates two other important points about intraclass grouping. Seldom is a class properly characterized in an all-or-none fashion—it is rare for a class to receive only whole-group instruction, only small-group instruction, or only independent work. The better question is the extent of reliance on various structural groupings, and the appropriate use of grouping for instructional purposes. Second, Bossert remarked on the influence of the "ripple" effect—the spread of misconduct from a few students to the entire group. In general, the more the class worked as a whole, the greater the ripple effect. When the class was divided into small groups, the teacher could handle misbehavior within the confines of each group, chastising or redirecting the individual student as appropriate within the group. When dealing with the class as a whole, equity in punishment and praise for all students was an implicit requirement. Under these circumstances, the teacher's options were sharply limited.

One has to examine the actual working of a class to understand the mechanisms of control. The teacher who shares leadership with students gives them opportunities to learn to handle responsibility. This sharing entails more than the teacher's giving up power; it requires a positive act of training students in self-direction and in the fine art of when and how to seek help. Under these conditions, as the teacher relaxes control, students become more autonomous and self-directed.

5.2 Social Norms and Diversity

Schooling can teach students how to handle themselves in a wide variety of social settings. In particular, schools have the potential to provide students with experiences in cultural and social diversity. The range of experiences in the school depends on the extent of heterogeneity within the school. If, on the other hand, social class or ethnicity serves as a basis for between- or within-school grouping, schooling may actually contribute to any separatism and inequality present in the society. Oakes (1981b) argues for a "neutral" school—one in which students with a variety of social backgrounds are distributed randomly among track levels. This practice would provide equal socialization of students and emphasize the importance of individual merit in scholastic progress.

Diversity in ability can also be used to modify status characteristics within groups. The student who does poorly in reading and mathematics may think of himself or herself as incompetent in *all* academic and social facets of schooling. Cohen and her colleagues (1979) have developed a program of directed group activities designed to equalize the status characteristics of students within the class. These activities are planned so that every student has a more or less equal chance of success; the hypothesis is that the successful accomplishments of the students who are otherwise "failures" will demonstrate to themselves and their classmates that they also possess skills and competence relevant to the classroom. The curriculum depends on group interaction—it cannot be individualized.

5.3 Communication

The teacher does most of the talking in the typical classroom—60 to 80 percent of the verbal interchanges (Dunkin and Biddle 1974, McDonald and Elias 1976). By talking less and relying on other formats, the teacher can enhance student communication. For example, students can be engaged in class meetings and small work groups (Glasser 1969). In forming within-class groups, the teacher makes decisions that strongly affect the communication patterns. The size of the group influences the opportunity for individual students to enter discussion. Diversity in the group makes it possible for some individuals to dominate the conversation, but also increases the variety of information available in the group. Unfortunately, as late as 1975, Schmuck and Schmuck could report only that "little direct research has been done on student–student communication patterns" (p. 31).

Dreeben (1968), in looking at cheating and cooperation, discusses interesting examples of using work groups to teach students task-appropriate behavior. The teacher can arrange a group structure which makes cheating a virtual impossibility, or can encourage the sort of small group collaboration that makes "cheating" a natural consequence. For the students, the key is to know (a) when they must perform work on their own and be held individually accountable, and (b) when it is proper to seek the assistance and knowledge of others.

The literature on small groups suggests that the successful functioning of a group depends on the leader's ability to organize and manage the group. In the classroom, group leadership is the teacher's responsibility, and it is up to the teacher to provide guidance in several critical areas. For instance, if the teacher's goal is to promote cooperative group activity, what grouping assignments facilitate cooperation and what specific conditions lead students to cooperate rather than compete? This question is far from trivial, especially if conditions emphasize efficient completion of the task, or if the cultural mode is rugged, competitive individualism.

Cooperative groups are not necessarily more effective in solving problems, and academic gains are not always greater for classrooms built upon a cooperative model. The research does show that experiences in cooperative groups do help students learn to cooperate, the students show more interest in cooperative classroom activities, and the general tone of the classroom is more positive and friendly (e.g., Slavin 1977).

6. *The Effects of Recent Innovations on Grouping Practices*

Several recent trends in educational programs have influenced grouping decisions. Some of these changes result from legislative mandates; others are fads; relatively few are supported by evidence of their effectiveness in achieving specific outcomes. Nonetheless, they warrant attention because they are likely to influence the educational community in future years. The following examines in turn (a) innovations in curricula, (b) changes in class assignment procedures, (c) new forms of school architecture, and (d) new patterns of school organization.

6.1 *Innovations in Curricula*

The popular trend toward individualization views the optimal instructional group as an "N of one." The aim is to alter the instructional pace and sequence in accord with each student's learning history and current performance. A number of individualized curricula have been developed, which rely on a relatively fixed test–instruct–retest approach to guide the student through a planned sequence of minitests, workbooks, and other materials (Klausmeier et al. 1977).

Individualization can place considerable strain on teachers' (and students') record-keeping and decision-making skills. It seems natural for proponents of individualized instruction to look toward the computer for assistance; whether this technology will provide the necessary support remains an open question.

Another popular curriculum innovation is mastery learning (Block 1974, Bloom 1976) (see *Mastery Learning Models*). The basic idea is that the student should not move on to advanced material until he or she can perform simpler tasks with accuracy and speed. Since some students take longer than others to master a task, fixed amounts of learning time mean that students become increasingly varied in their preparation for advanced tasks. The mastery learning approach, in contrast, allows each student the time he or she needs to master the task. Differences between students show up not as differences in competency, but as variations in pacing.

How is instruction managed under mastery learning? According to Block (1974), mastery learning allows the teacher to focus on the management of learning rather than on management of learners. Instruction starts with a relatively conventional small group approach. After the first instructional unit, students are tested to evaluate their mastery of skills included in the unit. Those students whose test performance identifies deficiencies are then required to complete additional modules before moving on to the next unit. Unfortunately, there is little or no advice about what to do with students who have achieved mastery while others are completing their learning. It is left to the creative teacher to find solutions to this problem.

6.2 Changes in Class Assignment Procedures

One of the most significant developments affecting the assignment of students to classes within schools in the United States is the legal mandate to "mainstream" handicapped students by assigning them to the "least restrictive environment." In the ideal case, mainstreaming entails regular classroom assignment for all handicapped students, whatever their physical, mental, educational, or emotional disabilities. The principle of least restrictive environment requires that these students must be placed in the regular classroom, or in an instructional environment as similar as possible to the one provided for nonhandicapped peers. These requirements increase the demands on the teacher's skills in management (Goodman and Miller 1980, Naor and Milgram 1980).

Another significant development in the assignment of students to classes in the United States is the adoption of minimum performance standards for grade advancement and graduation (*Phi Delta Kappan 1978*). Social promotion was the common practice in the United States—students were promoted on the basis of age and time in school rather than according to their demonstrated competence. This practice meant that the students within a given grade were fairly similar in age, size, and social maturity. With the institution of retention programs, teachers will have to deal with an increase in the number of relatively older students—this practice may also decrease the range of variation in ability within the classroom. Once again, the key to teachers' success in handling this situation will be their skills in classroom grouping practices. For instance, the assignment of low-ability students to a single reading group is likely to pose problems when some students are young or immature and others are old and repeating the grade. The issues here are closely related to the decisions about age of entry into school.

6.3 School Architecture and Reorganization

Architectural creativity seems limited when the challenge is to design the school to house teachers and classes in self-contained classrooms (Yates 1966). The decade of the 1960s, however, witnessed a major innovation in school architecture—the "open space" school (see *Open Versus Formal Methods*). The British primary schools had previously experimented with team teaching, in which groups of teachers worked as instructional colleagues. The fit of the team-teaching concept to open-space architecture was obvious, and in the United

States schools began to be built without walls (George 1975).

Open-space advocates probably imagined that the new architecture would be a boon to teaching staffs who were already using a team-teaching approach. It has often not worked that way. When a school faculty moves from self-contained classrooms into an open-space school, it is virtually forced to reorganize. There are new risks, new problems, and new patterns of communication and interaction. As Roper and Nolan (1976) have aptly put it, the problem is "How to survive in the open-space school." The key to survival is communication, especially about standards for student behavior, student movement patterns, scheduled activities, and arrangement of furniture, equipment, and supplies.

Teachers' (and sometimes students' and parents') opposition to open architectural designs has often led to little more than walling up the school (Truesdell and Newman 1975). On the other hand, studies of open space show that sometimes teachers experience positive changes in their roles—they interact with one another more frequently, engage in informal collegial evaluation, influence one another's teaching practices, and feel that principals spend more time with them and positively influence their teaching (Brunetti et al. 1972).

School reorganization, however, does not depend on new architecture alone. As noted above, the concept of team teaching preceded open-space schools and conventional school buildings can be adapted to the functional requirements of team teaching. Two plans for school reorganization that are independent of architecture are described below.

The Individually Guided Education (IGE) program of the Wisconsin Research and Development Center brings together several concepts for school reorganization, including principles for between- and within-class grouping. The philosophy of the program is that "children should participate in a variety of instructional groupings . . . [which range] from whole class . . . to individual" (Klausmeier et al. 1977 p. 118). Incorporated in the IGE program is a computer-management system which, among other things, provides regular recommendations for intraclass grouping to the teacher. The assignments, which are based on continuous student assessments, are based on the themes of common needs and preparation—the system follows a homogeneous grouping strategy.

Our second example is the Hawaii English program (Dykstra 1971). Though designed as an elementary language arts curriculum, it calls for novel styles of inter- and intra-class grouping. Central to the operation of the program are the Planning and Evaluation Circles in which each learner is an active partner with the teacher in planning and carrying out his or her course of study (Peters 1975). The program is designed as an integrated kindergarten to grade 6 package, so that the elementary school must agree as a whole on adoption of the program. More significantly, the program entails such a novel method of organization for instruction that the entire school must work together, or else it has to deal with the disruption that results when students trained to work independently in one grade are expected to stay in their seats in a later grade.

7. Conclusion

This article has covered various facets of instructional groups—the arrangement of students into work groups, the operation of these groups once formed, and the effects of various organizational schemes on student performance. Classroom management practices are critical for promoting student achievement and growth in social skills.

The central issue in grouping students often comes down to the question: who makes the decisions and on what grounds? One can focus on patterns of school and class grouping. Current practice is for administrators to make assignments early in the student's school career, after which the student is effectively "locked" in place. The student's background—race, sex, and socioeconomic status—affect the original placement.

Teachers also make grouping decisions. These may be based on prevailing custom in the school, on previous experience, on analysis of the situations, on intuition, or on "orders from above." But class-level decisions must be made. For example, should the teacher arrange the class into one, two, three, or many groups for reading? The "best" answer to this question depends on answers to several other questions: what is the range of ability and personality of the students assigned to the class? What resources are available for instruction? What is the relative importance of various outcomes?

It would seem desirable for the several actors in the decision-making process to be well-trained in their roles. Grouping decisions require the informed judgment of teacher, principal, counselor, parent, and perhaps the student. Influences from outside the school further complicate the process. For example, legislative and judicial mandates on tracking and school segregation in the United States clash with teachers' and principals' predilection for grouping in homogeneous ability groups. The advantages of homogeneous grouping for high-ability students can be apparent to their parents, who may be quite vocal. Heterogeneous, "integrated" grouping pays off for low-ability students, but at some cost to other parties. Teachers and administrators could benefit from training in techniques for rational analysis of such problems.

Discussions of grouping practices are often characterized by an all-or-none tone. The high school is tracked or not. The primary school is "nongraded" or self-contained. Special education students are mainstreamed or not. Gifted students are in a "pullout" program or given "enrichment" in the regular classroom.

The resolution of these conflicts, both for students and teachers, requires finding a middle road between these extremes. There are practical problems in carrying out programs that include variety and flexibility in grouping assignments—the routine of the same assignment from one day to the next may be broken, and nonstandard decisions may be required. The effects of the extra effort may be subtle, and may not lead to an immediate increase in average achievement. Nonetheless, it might be the only approach for handling the differences among individuals who make up "the group."

See also: Mastery Learning Models; Small Group Methods; Classroom Management; Individualizing Teaching; Classroom Climate

Bibliography

Alexander K L, Cook M, McDill E L 1977 Curriculum tracking and educational stratification: Some further evidence. Report No. 237. Johns Hopkins University, Baltimore, Maryland

Barr R C 1975 How children are taught to read: Grouping and pacing. *Sch. Rev.* 83: 478–98

Bernstein B B 1977 *Class, Codes, and Control*, 2nd edn. Vol. 3. Routledge and Kegan Paul, London

Block J H (ed.) 1974 *Schools, Society and Mastery Learning*. Holt, Rinehart and Winston, New York

Bloom B S 1976 *Human Characteristics and School Learning*. McGraw-Hill, New York

Bossert S T 1977 Tasks, group management, and teacher control behavior: A study of classroom organization and teacher style. *Sch. Rev.* 85: 552–65

Bourdieu P, Passeron J-C 1977 *Reproduction in Education, Society and Culture*. Sage, Beverly Hills, California

Bowles S, Gintis H 1976 *Schooling in Capitalist America: Educational Reform and the Contradictions of Economic Life*. Basic Books, New York

Brimer M A, Madaus G F, Chapman B, Kellaghan T, Wood R 1977 Sources of difference in school achievement. Report to the Carnegie Corporation, New York

Brophy J E, Good T L 1970 Teachers' communication of differential expectations for children's classroom performance: Some behavioral data. *J. Educ. Psychol.* 61: 365–74

Brunetti F A, Cohen E G, Meyer J W, Molnar S R F 1972 Studies of team teaching in the open-space school. *Interchange* 3(2–3): 85–101

Cohen E G 1979 Status equalization in the desegregated school. Paper presented at the Annual Meeting of the American Educational Research Association, San Francisco

Coleman J S 1966 *Equality of Educational Opportunity: Summary Report*. United States Department of Health, Education and Welfare, Office of Education, Washington, DC

Cronbach L J, Snow R E 1977 *Aptitudes and Instructional Methods: A Handbook for Research on Interactions*. Irvington, New York

Dreeben R 1968 *On What is Learned in School*. Addison-Wesley, Reading, Massachusetts

Dunkin M J, Biddle B J 1974 *The Study of Teaching*. Holt, Rinehart and Winston, New York

Dykstra G 1971 Hawaii English Project language skills manual, Vol. 2. University of Hawaii, Honolulu, Hawaii

Esposito D 1973 Homogeneous and heterogeneous ability grouping: Principal findings and implications for evaluating and designing more effective educational environments. *Rev. Educ. Res.* 43: 163–79

George P S 1975 *Ten Years of Open Space Schools: A Review of the Research*. Florida Educational Research and Development Council, Gainesville, Florida

Glasser W 1969 *Schools Without Failure*. Harper and Row, New York

Goodlad J I, Sirotnik K A, Overman B C 1979 A study of schooling: An overview. *Phi Delta Kappan* 61: 174–78

Goodman L, Miller H 1980 Mainstreaming: How teachers can make it work. *J. Res. Dev. Educ.* 13: 45–57

Henry N B (ed.) 1960 *The Dynamics of Instructional Groups: Sociopsychological Aspects of Teaching and Learning*. 59th yearbook of the National Society for the Study of Education, Pt. 2. National Society for the Study of Education, University of Chicago Press, Chicago, Illinois

Jackson B 1964 *Streaming: An Education System in Miniature*. Routledge and Kegan Paul, London

Jencks C 1972 *Inequality: A Reassessment of the Effect of Family and Schooling in America*. Basic Books, New York

Klausmeier H J, Rossmiller R A, Saily M 1977 *Individually Guided Elementary Education in Elementary and Middle Schools: A Handbook for Implementors and College Instructors*. Academic Press, New York

Levy P, Gooch S, Kellmer-Pringle M L 1969 A longitudinal study of the relationship between anxiety and streaming in a progressive and a traditional junior school. *Br. J. Educ. Psychol.* 39: 166–73

McDonald F J, Elias P 1976 *Beginning Teacher Evaluation Study: Phase II Final Report*, Vol. 1, Chap. 10. Educational Testing Service, Princeton, New Jersey

Madaus G F, Kellaghan T, Rokow E A 1976 School and class differences in performance on the leaving certificate examination. *Irish J. Educ.* 10: 41–50

Marascuilo L A, McSweeney M 1972 Tracking and minority student attitudes and performance. *Urban Educ.* 4: 303–19

Naor M, Milgram R M 1980 Two preservice strategies for preparing regular class teachers for mainstreaming. *Excep. Child.* 47: 126–29

Oakes J L 1981a The reproduction of inequity: The content of secondary school tracking. Unpublished manuscript. University of California at Los Angeles

Oakes J L 1981b Classroom social relationships: Exploring the Bowles and Gintis hypothesis. Unpublished manuscript. University of California at Los Angeles

Peters W G 1975 Evaluation and validation of an initial reading curriculum (Doctoral dissertation, Stanford University, 1975) *Dissertation Abstracts International* 1975 35: 7623A (University Microfilms No. 75-13, 576)

Phi Delta Kappan 1978 5 (complete volume)

Piontkowski D C 1981 A structural analysis of classroom processes in beginning reading instruction (Unpublished doctoral dissertation, Stanford University)

Plowden Report 1967 *Children and Their Primary Schools*. Her Majesty's Stationery Office, London

Postlethwaite K, Denton C 1978 *Streams for the Future? The Long-term Effects of Early Streaming and Non-streaming—The Final Report of the Banbury Enquiry*. Pubansco, Banbury

Postlethwaite T N 1975 The surveys of the International Association for Evaluation of Educational Achievement (IEA): Implications of the IEA surveys of achievement. In: Purvis A C, Levine D V (eds.) 1975 *Educational Policy and International Assessment: Implications of IEA Surveys of Achievement*. McCutchan, Berkeley, California

Roper S S, Nolan R R 1976 How to survive in the open-space school. Occasional paper No. 10. Stanford Center for Research and Development in Teaching, School of Education, Stanford University

Rutter M, Maughan B, Mortimore P, Ouston J 1979 *Fifteen Thousand Hours: Secondary Schools and Their Effects on Children*. Harvard University Press, Cambridge, Massachusetts

Schmuck R A, Schmuck P A 1975 *Group Processes in the Classroom*, 2nd edn. Brown, Dubuque, Iowa

Slavin R E 1977 Classroom reward structure: An analytical and practical review. *Rev. Educ. Res.* 47: 633–50

Stallings J 1975 Implementation and child effects of teaching practices in Follow Through classrooms. *Monogr. Soc. Res. Child Dev.* 40, Serial No. 163

Truesdell B., Newman J 1975 Can junior highs make it with the wide open spaces? *Learning* 4(3): 74–77

Weinstein R S 1976 Reading group membership in first grade: Teacher behaviors and pupil experience over time. *J. Educ. Psychol.* 68: 103–16

Yates A (ed.) 1966 *Grouping in Education: A Report Sponsored by the UNESCO Institute for Education, Hamburg*. Wiley, New York

Discussion Methods

M. D. Gall

The discussion method of teaching is a process in which a small group assembles to communicate with each other—using speaking, listening, and nonverbal processes—in order to achieve instructional objectives. The first part of this definition highlights the fact that discussion occurs in groups, usually involving six to ten persons (see *Small Group Methods*). The group members perform one of two roles: leader–moderator (typically, the teacher), and participant (typically, the students). Because group members have reciprocal influence over one another, the learning of each student in a discussion group is affected by the behavior of other students in the group. Other teaching methods, such as lecture and computer-assisted instruction, are much less dependent on reciprocal influence among students to facilitate learning.

A limitation of the discussion method is that it requires students and teacher to assemble at a designated time and place. If this requirement cannot be met, other methods (for example, independent study and televised instruction) need to be used.

Another distinguishing feature of discussion is that participants use the available time to communicate with each other. The person who has the floor addresses his or her remarks to the entire group, and each group member has the right to speak. Discussions in a classroom setting should have many sequences in which one student remark is followed by another. By contrast, the prevailing method of classroom discourse is the recitation, in which the predominant pattern of interaction is teacher question–student response–teacher feedback–new teacher question.

A discussion member communicates to others in the group by speaking (utterances and intonation of voice) and by nonverbal signs, such as facial expressions, hand gestures, and bodily movement (see *Nonverbal Communication*). The other participants receive these communications by listening and by visually attending to the nonverbal signs. These processes of speaking, listening, and observing are critical attributes of the discussion method. Bridges (1979) noted that discussion has the advantage of encouraging young children and illiterate people to express their ideas and to learn new ones, despite the fact that they cannot read and write. Furthermore, the exercise of the basic communication processes involved in discussion may facilitate development of more abstract learning processes, such as are involved in reading and writing.

Discussion can easily degenerate into a superficial, disconnected exchange of opinion, unless it stays focused on explicit instructional objectives. Because the elements of discussion are flexible, it has been adapted to achieve these broad instructional objectives: subject matter mastery, attitude change, moral development, problem solving, and acquisition of communication skills. Additionally, a good discussion motivates students to engage in further inquiry and provides the teacher with feedback on student progress.

1. Effectiveness of the Discussion Method

Much evidence on the effectiveness of the discussion method in promoting instructional objectives has accumulated. Most of this research has involved college students, workers in business and industry, and adult volunteers for psychological experiments. A relatively small amount of discussion research has been done with elementary and secondary students. The sources of the research evidence cited in the following sections are available in several literature reviews (Gall and Gall 1976; Gage and Berliner 1979).

1.1 Subject Matter Mastery

Hill (1977), and many other educators, advocate the use of discussion (supplemented by textbook study or related instructional activity) for promoting critical thinking and other cognitive objectives. In Hill's model of discussion, the discussion agenda includes a review of key concepts and topics, integration of the subject matter with other knowledge, application of the subject matter, and evaluation of the author's presentation. McKeachie and Kulik (1975) reviewed the many studies evaluating the effectiveness of discussion for promoting subject matter mastery at the college level. They concluded that lecture is more effective for promoting acquisition of information, whereas discussion is more effective for promoting retention of information and higher level thinking. Discussion was also found to be more effective for stimulating students to have positive attitudes and motivation.

Bridges (1979) claimed that discussion contributes to participants' understanding of subject matter by: (a) supplementing each participant's information on a subject with the information that other participants have; (b) stimulating different perspectives on the subject; (c) allowing participants to put forth conjectures about the subject; (d) providing opportunity for other participants to criticize and refute a conjecture; and (e) encouraging mutual adjustments among participants' opinions to produce a group decision or solution. These processes may not facilitate subject matter mastery for all students, though. Dowaliby and Schumer (1973) found that in a college discussion class, low-anxiety students did better than high-anxiety students on course examinations. In a college lecture class, however, the high-anxiety students outperformed the low-anxiety students. Since discussion is less structured and certain than lecture, it may provoke anxiety in predisposed students and thereby interfere with their learning.

1.2 Attitude Change

Discussion provides a good forum for the expression of students' attitudes toward a topic or issue. Attitudes can be expressed at three levels: beliefs, feelings, and dispositions to act on the basis of one's beliefs and feelings. Discussion can simply aim to help students become aware of their own attitudes and the attitudes of other group members. More ambitious objectives are to use discussion to critically evaluate and change group members' attitudes. Oliver and Shaver (1966) developed the jurisprudential model of instruction, which makes use of discussion to achieve this type of learning outcome.

There is ample research evidence that discussion is effective in changing attitudes. This research has included such groups as parents, industrial workers, and students at all levels. Discussion may produce this effect through confronting group members with new data or through group coercion. Concerning the latter, educators have expressed concern about coercive forces— including the tendency to press for group consensus— in discussion groups. In the Humanities Curriculum Project in England, for example, the project directors (Bridges 1979) found that pressure towards consensus inhibited open discussion among group members. Also, attitude change through discussion can fail if all the group members share a similar undesirable attitude, such as racial prejudice, at the outset.

1.3 Moral Development

Some educators advocate the use of discussion to advance students' capability for moral reasoning. This capability has been investigated using the six developmental stages of cognitive–moral reasoning identified by Lawrence Kohlberg and his colleagues. Reviewers of this line of research (Berkowitz 1981, Lockwood 1978) found that discussion generally develops students' moral reasoning by one-third to one full stage. Lockwood observed that discussion appears to be effective at moving students through the first three of Kohlberg's stages, but not through the next three stages.

Moral discussions focus on an issue with underlying value conflicts that the participants attempt to resolve. The most critical feature of a good moral discussion is the presence of arguments that exceed students' present moral reasoning stage. These arguments presumably create cognitive conflicts in students. In attempting to resolve the conflicts, students are stimulated to advance to the next stage of moral reasoning. Teachers can create such conflict by presenting advanced-stage arguments or by asking Socratic questions that note contradictions and problems in students' reasoning. Another approach is to form heterogeneous discussion groups that include students at different stages of cognitive–moral development.

The use of discussion to stimulate advances in cognitive–moral reasoning is still largely experimental. Procedures to be used by teachers in initiating and guiding discussions have been developed, but they have not been rigorously validated. Also, little is known about whether student gains in cognitive–moral reasoning are reflected in other important outcomes of education, such as good citizenship behavior.

1.4 Problem Solving

The discussion method is often advocated to help a group reach a solution to a problem. For example, brainstorming is a problem-solving procedure in which a discussion group first generates as many solutions as possible while withholding criticism (Osborn 1979). In the second stage the group critically discusses the solutions and converges on the one that best satisfies explicit criteria.

Researchers have found that problem-solving groups of a certain size are usually less effective than an equal number of individuals working alone. Maier (1967) suggested several explanations for this finding. Majority opinions in a discussion are more likely to be accepted than minority opinions, irrespective of their soundness. Also, once group consensus on a particular solution is reached, subsequent high-quality solutions tend to be rejected. Another adverse factor is that less capable individuals may dominate the discussion and thereby prevent more capable individuals from influencing the problem-solving process.

Despite the shortcomings of discussion group problem solving, it is probably more effective than individual effort in certain situations. For example, Maier (1967) suggested that when a solution will commit a group to a given course of action, the solution will be better accepted and implemented if it has been reached through the process of group discussion. Also, group discussion may be more effective than individual effort when working on problems that have multiple solutions or that require a variety of talents not likely to be present in a single individual.

1.5 Communication Skills

Discussion participants can choose to focus on their communication processes rather than on the outcomes of discussion described above. They might focus on such communication skills as: inviting silent group members to speak, avoiding monopolization of talk time, acknowledging and paraphrasing what other participants have said, and asking participants to clarify or elaborate on their remarks. Bridges (1979 pp. 29–32) classified these communication skills into three types: (a) intellectual rules of discourse (e.g., showing concern for reasons and evidence in one's remarks); (b) procedural rules and conventions (e.g., who speaks, when, in what order, and for how long); and (c) social conventions (e.g., whether the norm is to be abrasive or mild in criticizing another participant's ideas).

Systematic training has been demonstrated to improve these skills (Oliver and Shaver 1966, Gall et al. 1975). Few studies have been done, though, to determine whether training in communication skills improves the ability of group members to achieve the other outcomes of discussion—subject matter mastery, attitude change, moral development, and problem solving. Also, little is known about the effect of training in discussion communication skills on student's academic motivation.

2. Discussion Group Dynamics

How a teacher structures and leads a discussion will affect students' functioning within the group. The quality of group functioning in turn affects how much students learn from the discussion. Research on group dynamics has identified a number of structural and leadership factors that hinder or facilitate a discussion. Six of these factors are described below.

2.1 Group Size

Researchers have found consistently that small group size results in higher satisfaction, more participation from each discussion group member, and greater academic achievement. The optimal group size for discussion is between five and eight participants.

The reduced effectiveness of large discussion groups may be due to the fact that individual participants have less opportunity—given a constant amount of time—to contribute to the discussion. Another explanation is that more time in large discussion groups must be spent in regulating group processes, thus leaving less time for task-relevant talk.

2.2 Group Composition

Researchers have investigated the effects of discussion groups whose participants are similar (homogeneous) or diverse (heterogeneous) with respect to certain characteristics. The general finding of their research is that homogeneous groups are more cohesive than heterogeneous groups, but they are not always more effective in performance. In fact, under certain conditions discussion groups that are heterogeneous with respect to attitude or prior experience may be more effective than homogeneous groups. For example, Hoffman (1959) found that heterogeneous groups of college students showed superior performance on a problem that required multiple perceptions and cognitive reorganizations.

2.3 Group Cohesiveness

Discussion group cohesiveness is usually defined as the extent to which group members like each other. Research studies have demonstrated that high cohesiveness has several desirable effects on a group. Cohesiveness helps to maintain participants' membership in a group and leads to increased communication among participants. Members of a cohesive group also tend to experience heightened self-esteem and satisfaction with the group.

The effects of cohesiveness on group performance are less clear. A positive relationship between cohesiveness and group performance has been found in some research studies, but not in others. One explanation of these results is that group norms are more influential in high-cohesive groups than in low-cohesive groups. If norms in a high-cohesive group favor performance, its members will probably work harder than low-cohesive group members to achieve goals. If norms in a high-cohesive group denigrate such matters as academic learning or minority opinions, however, its members are likely to be less productive than members of a low-cohesive group.

2.4 Communication Patterns

Various aspects of communication in a discussion group affect its functioning and performance. One such aspect is the network of communication barriers and channels between the members of a discussion group. Decentralized communication networks, where communication channels between participants are open, have been compared with centralized networks, where messages must be channeled through a person who occupies a central position in the group. Student–student interaction is frequent in discussions with a decentralized network, whereas the teacher or a few assertive students control discussions with a centralized network. Researchers have found that participants in a decentralized communication network tend to be more satisfied with their groups, and they are likely to be more effective on complex tasks.

The spatial arrangement of participants in a discussion group has a pronounced effect on communication patterns. For example, researchers have confirmed the obvious principle that a group member is more likely to interact with other members if he or she can see as well as hear them. It is difficult to imagine, then, how discussion can occur in the usual classroom seating pattern, where students sit in rows facing the teacher. A circular seating pattern, such as may occur in a seminar, is preferable because all participants are in face-to-face contact.

2.5 Group Leadership

McKeachie (1978) identified six leadership functions in a discussion that a teacher should perform directly or should assign to students: (a) agenda setting; (b) calling the meeting to order and introducing the topic for discussion; (c) clarification of goals during the discussion; (d) summarization; (e) mediation and clarification of differences of opinion; and (f) evaluation of group progress.

Research on leadership styles suggests that these functions can be performed using an authoritarian, instructor-centered style or a democratic, student-centered style. Teachers characterized by the former style tend to determine all policies and procedures, to use personal praise and criticism, and to remain aloof. Democratic, student-centered teachers tend to submit policies and procedures for group discussion, to use objective praise and criticism, and to be involved in the group's work. Research findings generally favor a democratic, student-centered leadership style. The opposite leadership style may be more effective, though, if it is accepted or expected by group participants (see *Teacher-centered and Learner-centered Teaching*).

2.6 Group Norms

Students usually enter a discussion with a set of beliefs about the discussion process and about their fellow participants. As these beliefs become communicated (often, nonverbally), they form a set of group norms that determine discussion process and outcomes.

Bridges (1979 pp. 21–26) identified six group norms, which he calls "moral dispositions," that are necessary for good discussion: (a) willingness to be reasonable and to be influenced by others' evidence; (b) peaceableness and conformance to such rules as "only one person talks at a time"; (c) truthfulness in what one says; (d) giving each person the freedom to speak his or her mind; (e) the belief that participants are equal in that each one of them potentially has knowledge of relevance to the discussion; and (f) respect for all members of the discussion group. It is difficult to imagine that the objectives of discussion (e.g., subject matter mastery, moral development) can be achieved unless these norms are shared by all or most of the participants.

3. Educational Applications of the Discussion Method

The discussion method has been the subject of much experimental research, yet little is known about its prevalence and form under actual conditions of schooling. Discussion is probably rare at the precollege level, despite the fact that researchers have found it can be used to achieve instructional outcomes even with young children. Teachers may report that they use discussion when in fact they are using the recitation method, to which discussion is superficially similar. In a study of high-school discussion classes, Dillon (1981) found that teachers spoke at almost every turn of talk, for an average total time that was longer than the average talk time of all of the students.

Discussion may be used occasionally in college and university teaching, especially at the graduate level. University seminars, for example, are intended to promote discussion among participants. Discussion is probably more frequent in informal settings outside the classroom. Small groups of students can share perceptions about their coursework without worrying about the professor's reaction.

Discussion is included as a component of complex instructional methods, such as Herbert Thelen's group inquiry model and Oliver and Shaver's jurisprudential model. Because of the complexity of these methods and their radical departure from conventional instruction, it is unlikely that they are used with any frequency in teaching.

Discussion is generally considered most appropriate for instruction in the social sciences and the humanities, which are thought to be "low-consensus" fields (Gage and Berliner 1979 p. 479). Discussion is considered less appropriate for such "high-consensus" fields as mathematics, the physical sciences, and engineering. In fact, a careful analysis of most academic disciplines would reveal issues, problems, and subject matter that can be profitably approached through discussion. It is interesting to observe the absence of controversy in many textbooks, yet scholars and researchers in the disciplines represented by these textbooks find much to debate in their professional journals and conventions.

The explanation for the infrequent occurrence of classroom discussion is complex. Some teachers report that they do not use discussion because they tried it once and were discouraged by their lack of success. Because a good discussion requires highly skilled leadership, it is not surprising that teachers' initial experiences would be frustrating. For success to occur, both teachers and students need training in the rationale and techniques of discussion. Resources for such training range from brief textbooks (for example, Stanford and Stanford 1969) to extensive multimedia programs (for example, Gall et al. 1975).

Another reason why some teachers reject the discussion method is that it requires relinquishing part of their authority and control over the instructional process. Students can steer the discussion in directions unanticipated by the teacher, whereas other instructional methods (especially lecture) give the teacher continuous control of the pace and flow of instruction. Furthermore, teachers may be threatened by the occasional lack of control and discipline in discussion because they believe their effectiveness is judged by the ability to maintain quiet, orderly instruction.

A major use of discussion is to help students develop their attitudes and moral reasoning. Teachers, especially at the precollege level, may be reluctant to engage in this type of discussion because of concern about community reaction. Certain segments of the community are quite vocal in their belief that the school curriculum should not deal with issues, attitudes, and values.

Another obstacle to the use of discussion is that the school curriculum tends to emphasize acquisition of facts and skills. Discussion is less suited for these instructional objectives than such methods as lecture and mastery learning approaches.

Finally, teachers may avoid discussion because they feel their classes are too large to accommodate it. Groups of six to eight discussants are optimal, yet teachers usually have 20, 30, or more students in their classes. This problem can be solved by breaking a large class into small discussion groups, assigning a student leader for each group, and walking around to monitor each group's work. Another approach is to use the "fishbowl" technique in which the teacher and a small group conduct a discussion while the other students sit beyond the discussion circle. Following the small-group discussion, these other students may contribute additional ideas or complete a discussion-related assignment.

For the reasons described above, the discussion method is not easily incorporated into classroom instruction. Yet the classroom use of discussion should be promoted because of ample research evidence that it facilitates subject matter mastery, attitude change, moral development, problem solving, and communication skill. The discussion method is also important because it promotes the values and processes of democratic society.

See also: Grouping for Teaching; Group Teaching

Bibliography

Berkowitz M W 1981 A critical appraisal of the educational and psychological perspectives on moral discussion. *J. Educ. Thought* 15: 20–33

Bridges D 1979 *Education, Democracy and Discussion.* National Foundation for Educational Research, Slough

Dillon J T 1981 Duration of response to teacher questions and statements. *Contemp. Educ. Psychol.* 6: 1–11

Dowaliby F J, Schumer H 1973 Teacher-centered versus student-centered mode of college classroom instruction as related to manifest anxiety. *J. Educ. Psychol.* 64: 125–32

Gage N L, Berliner D C 1979 *Educational Psychology,* 2nd edn. Houghton Mifflin, Boston, Massachusetts

Gall M D, Gall J P 1976 The discussion method. In: Gage N L (ed.) 1976 *The Psychology of Teaching Methods.* 75th Yearbook of the National Society for the Study of

Education, Pt. 1. University of Chicago Press, Chicago, Illinois

Gall M D, Weathersby R, Elder R A, Lai M K 1975 *Discussing Controversial Issues.* Agency for Instructional Television, Bloomington, Indiana

Hill W F 1977 *Learning Thru Discussion: Guide for Leaders and Members of Discussion Groups.* Sage, Beverly Hills

Hoffman L R 1959 Homogeneity of member personality and its effect on group problem solving. *J. Abnorm. Soc. Psychol.* 59: 27–32

Lockwood A L 1978 The effects of value clarification and moral development curricula on school-age subjects: A critical review of recent research. *Rev. Educ. Res.* 48: 325–64

McKeachie W J 1978 *Teaching Tips: A Guidebook for the Beginning College Teacher,* 7th edn. Heath, Lexington, Massachusetts

McKeachie W J, Kulik J A 1975 Effective college teaching. In: Kerlinger F N (ed.) 1975 *Review of Research in Education*, Vol. 3. Peacock, Itasca, Illinois

Maier N R F 1967 Assets and liabilities in group problem solving: The need for an integrative function. *Psychol. Rev.* 74: 239–49

Oliver D W, Shaver J P 1966 *Teaching Public Issues in the High School.* Houghton Mifflin, Boston, Massachusetts

Osborn A F 1979 *Applied Imagination,* 3rd edn. Scribner, New York

Stanford G, Stanford B D 1969 *Learning Discussion Skills Through Games.* Citation Press, New York

Small Group Methods

R. E. Slavin

The reduction in sizes of groups involved in school learning has been advocated continuously for many decades with one goal or another in mind. Sometimes smaller groups are sought because they make the teacher's job less complex, enabling less time to be spent on management and more on instruction. Sometimes smaller groups are advocated because they are seen to allow for greater participation and involvement by the students. It has only been fairly recently, however, that the question of how the smaller groups might actually be managed in order to bring about the desired learning outcomes has been investigated.

These studies of small-group methods of teaching have given particular emphasis to cooperation as a social condition of learning. Thus, in the 1980s small-group methods of teaching are usually methods directed toward increasing cooperation in learning.

The term "cooperative learning" refers to instructional methods in which students work in small groups (usually four to six members) and are rewarded in some way for performance as a group. For example, a class of 32 students might be divided into eight groups of four, and members of these groups might study together and receive recognition based on the sum of their individual quiz scores.

The theory on which cooperative learning methods are based is quite old and well-established in social psychology. The kernel of this theory can be stated simply. When individuals work together toward a common goal, they are dependent on one another's efforts to achieve that goal. This interdependence motivates the individuals to: (a) encourage one another to do whatever helps the group to succeed; (b) help one another to do whatever helps the group to succeed; and (c) like one another, because individuals like others who help them achieve their goals and because cooperation typically increases positive contact among group members.

Principles of cooperation have been applied for many years in industry, in the military, in sports, and in other activities. They have also been used in education for a long time, but their use has tended to be occasional and informal. Systematic cooperative learning programs that could be used as the principal means of delivering instruction were developed in the early 1970s. The rationale for this new emphasis on cooperation in the classroom was a profound dissatisfaction with the traditional classroom system, in particular, traditional grading. It was felt that the competitive nature of grading was counterproductive, as it led students to discourage their classmates from doing well academically. Coleman (1961) contrasted adolescents' norms favoring academic success with their norms favoring sports success. In team sports, each individual's success helps the team and the school to succeed, and it is thus strongly supported by the peer group. On the other hand, academic success typically reduces others' chances to succeed (because there is a limited supply of good grades), and this leads students to oppose their classmates' academic efforts. Competitive grading was also seen as ineffective (as well as unfair) because most students have little chance of getting good grades, regardless of their efforts. Individual tasks have been criticized for isolating students and for being boring.

For these reasons and others, several independent groups of researchers developed programs designed to make the principles of cooperation applicable to the classroom setting. Most of the methods included features designed to correct many of the inherent problems of cooperation. For example, a danger of a cooperative arrangement is that one or two students will be able to do all of the work, as in laboratory groups that are asked to submit a single report. Also, students often do not naturally help one another, so means must be developed to make the contributions of low-achieving students important to the group. Finally, cooperative principles must be adapted to the real-life characteristics and problems of the classroom.

1. Cooperative Learning Methods

The only feature in common to all of the cooperative learning methods is the division of the class into learning groups of four to six members who are of all levels of ability. These groups also typically have a mix of boys and girls and students of different racial and ethnic backgrounds in about the same proportion they represent in the class as a whole.

1.1 Student Team Learning

The most extensively researched and widely used cooperative learning techniques are the student team learning methods developed by Robert Slavin, David DeVries, and Keith Edwards at Johns Hopkins University (Slavin 1980a). Three of the student team learning methods are now in widespread use. These are Student Teams-achievement Divisions (STAD), Teams–Games–Tournament (TGT), and Jigsaw II. A fourth technique, Team-assisted Individualization (TAI) has been developed and evaluated more recently. These methods are described below.

(a) *Student Teams-achievement Divisions* (STAD). In Student Teams-achievement Divisions, or STAD, students are assigned to four- or five-member learning teams. The teams are made up of high, average, and low performing students, boys and girls, and students of different racial or ethnic backgrounds, so that each team is like a microcosm of the entire class. Each week, the teacher introduces new material in a lecture or discussion. The team members then study worksheets on the material. They may work problems one at a time in pairs, or take turns quizzing each other, or discuss problems as a group, or use whatever means they wish to master the material. The students are given worksheet answer sheets, so it is clear to them that their task is to learn the concepts, not to simply fill out the worksheets. Team members are told that they are not finished studying until they and their team-mates are sure that they understand the material.

Following team practice, students take quizzes on the materials they have been studying. Team-mates may not help one another on the quizzes; at this point they are on their own. The quizzes are scored in class or soon after class. These scores are formed into team scores by the teacher.

The amount each student contributes to his or her team is determined by the amount the student's quiz score exceeds the student's own past quiz average. A base score is set five points below each student's average, and students earn points, up to a maximum of 10, for each point by which they exceed their base scores. Students with perfect papers always receive the 10-point maximum, regardless of their base scores. This individual improvement score system gives every student a good chance to contribute maximum points to

the team if (and only if) the student does his or her best and thereby shows substantial improvement or gets a perfect paper. This improvement point system has been shown to increase student academic performance even without teams (Slavin 1980b), but it is especially important as a component of STAD since it avoids the possibility that low-performing students will not be fully accepted as group members because they do not contribute many points. To illustrate this, think of a baseball team. A baseball team is a cooperative group, but it has one serious drawback; the "automatic strikeout," the team member who rarely hits the ball no matter how much he or she practices. In STAD, no-one is an automatic strikeout, and by the same token no-one is guaranteed success, because it is improvement that counts, and anyone is capable of improvement.

The teams with the highest scores are recognized in a weekly one-page class newsletter. The students who exceeded their own past records by the largest amounts or who got perfect papers are also recognized in the newsletter.

(b) *Teams–Games–Tournaments*. Teams–Games–Tournaments, or TGT (DeVries et al. 1980) uses the same teams, instructional format, and worksheets as STAD. However, in TGT, students play academic games to show their individual mastery of the subject matter. These games are played in weekly tournaments. Students compete in the tournaments with members of other teams who are comparable in past performance. The competition takes place at tournament tables of three students. While teams stay together for about six weeks, the tournament table assignments are changed every week according to a system that maintains the equality of the competition. This equal competition makes it possible for students of all levels of past performance to contribute maximum points to their teams if they do their best, in the same way as the individual improvement score system in STAD makes it possible for everyone to be successful.

After the tournament, team scores are figured, and a newsletter recognizes the highest scoring teams and tournament table winners. Thus, TGT uses the same pattern of teaching, team worksheet study, individual assessment, equal opportunities for success, and team recognition as that used in STAD, but uses academic games instead of quizzes.

(c) *Team-assisted Individualization*. Team-assisted Individualization (TAI) is the most recently developed of the Johns Hopkins student team learning methods (Slavin et al. 1984a). It is a combination of team learning and individualized instruction applied to the teaching of mathematics. In TAI, students are assigned to four- or five-member heterogeneous teams as in STAD and TGT. After being placed in the appropriate unit by means of a diagnostic test, each student works through a set of programmed mathematics units at his or her own pace. Students follow a regular sequence of activities, involving reading an instruction sheet, working on successive skillsheets that break the skill into fine subskills, aking a checkout to see if the skill has been mastered, nd finally taking a test. Team-mates work in pairs, xchanging answer sheets and checking each other's killsheets and checkouts. When a student has passed a heckout with a score of 80 percent or better, he or she akes a final test which is scored by a student monitor. students' test scores and the number of tests they can omplete in a week go into a team score, and team nembers receive certificates for exceeding preset team tandards. Because of this preset standard, any number f teams can receive certificates.

Because all skillsheets and checkouts are scored by eam-mates and all tests are scored by student monitors, he teacher is able to work with individuals and small roups on problems they are having or to prepare them or upcoming units.

Team-assisted Individualization is unique among all ooperative learning methods in its use of individualized nstead of class-paced instruction. It was developed to e used when a class is too heterogeneous to be taught he same material at the same rate, especially when here are mainstreamed children who need the positive ocial interaction that takes place in the teams but also eed to have material at their own level.

(d) *Jigsaw*. In Aronson's (1978) Jigsaw method, students are assigned to six-member teams. Academic naterial is broken down into five sections. For example, a biography might be broken into family history, early ife, first accomplishments, major setbacks, and later ife. Each team member reads his or her unique section, xcept for two students who share a section. Then, nembers of different teams who have studied the same ections meet in "expert groups" to discuss their ections. Then the students return to their teams and ake turns teaching their team-mates about their ections. Since the only way students can learn the ections other than their own is to listen carefully to heir team-mates, they are motivated to support and how interest in each other's work. Jigsaw does not ctually use a cooperative incentive structure. Following he team reports, students take individual quizzes covering all of the topics, and they receive individual grades on their quizzes. However, Jigsaw is classed as a cooperative learning method because it uses a cooperative ask structure that creates a great deal of interdependence among students.

A modification of Jigsaw was developed by Slavin (1980a) at Johns Hopkins University and then incorporated in the student team learning program. In this method, called Jigsaw II, students work in four- or five-member teams as in TGT and STAD. Instead of each student having a unique section, all students read a common narrative, such as a book chapter, a short story, or a biography. However, each student is given a topic on which to become an expert. The students who had the same topics meet in expert groups to discuss them, and then return to their teams to teach what they have learned to their teammates. Then, students take individual quizzes, which are formed into team scores

using the improvement score system of STAD, and the highest scoring teams and individuals are recognized in a class newsletter. Thus, Jigsaw II, unlike original Jigsaw, does use cooperative incentives as well as tasks.

1.2 Learning Together

The Learning Together model of cooperative learning (Johnson and Johnson 1976) was developed by David and Roger Johnson at the University of Minnesota. The cooperative methods they have researched involve students working in four- or five-member, heterogeneous groups on assignment sheets. The groups hand in a single sheet, and receive praise as a group based on how well they are working together and how they do on the group task. In one study of Learning Together, students received grades based on their group's average on individual achievement tests. It should be noted that the methods described by Johnson and Johnson (1976) include the appropriate use of competitive and individualistic methods, as well as many alternative means of using cooperation. However, the program referred to here as "Learning Together" is the cooperative method, described above, that was used in the research.

1.3 Group Investigation

Group Investigation (Sharan and Sharan 1976), developed by Shlomo Sharan at the University of Tel Aviv, is a general classroom organization plan in which students work in small groups using cooperative inquiry, group discussion, and cooperative planning and projects. In this method, students form their own two- to six-member groups. The groups choose subtopics from a unit being studied by the entire class, further break their subtopics into individual tasks, and carry out the activities necessary to prepare a group report. The group then makes a presentation or display to communicate its findings to the entire class.

1.4 Other Cooperative Learning Methods

The six techniques described above are by far the most extensively researched and widely used cooperative learning methods, but there have been a few interesting studies of other methods. Wheeler (1977) investigated a cooperative technique in which students were assigned specific roles (such as coordinator, analyzer, or recorder) within cooperative groups and worked on social studies inquiry activities to produce a single workbook. The group making the best workbook received a prize. Peterson et al. (1980) used a simple method in which students worked in four-member groups. Group members completed their own worksheets with help from their groupmates. No group rewards were given; students were simply expected to work together. Starr and Schuerman (1974) also used a relatively simple method in which groups of as many as eight students considered science questions and then reported back to the entire class. As in the Peterson studies, no group rewards were given. Weigel et al. (1975) used a combination of cooperative methods including group information gathering, discussion, and interpretations, with prizes given to groups with the best products.

Thus, the cooperative learning methods share the idea that students work in groups to accomplish a group goal, but in every other particular they are quite different from one another. Student Teams-achievement Divisions, TGT, and TAI are highly structured, with well-specified group tasks and group rewards (recognition in a newsletter or certificates), while Group Investigation and Learning Together give more autonomy to students and usually have less well-specified group rewards. Jigsaw and Group Investigation are used primarily in social studies, and TAI is designed only for mathematics, while STAD, TGT, and Learning Together are used in all subjects. The three original student team learning methods (STAD, TGT, and Jigsaw II) use competition between teams to motivate students to cooperate within their teams, while Group Investigation, Learning Together, TAI, and the original form of Jigsaw do not. Finally, STAD, TGT, and TAI are designed to help students learn a specific set of skills, such as adding fractions, putting commas in a series, reading charts and graphs, or understanding how chemical compounds are formed, while Group Investigation in particular is designed primarily to get students to think creatively about social studies concepts and learn group self-organizational skills.

2. Cooperative Learning: The Research

The effects of cooperative learning that have been studied most intensively fall into two categories: student achievement and student social relationships. Improved achievement was expected because in a cooperative group, students are likely to encourage and help one another to learn. Positive effects on social relationships were also expected, because cooperative learning is, after all, a social intervention; cooperation increases positive contact among individuals and puts them into a position of helping one another. The most important application of cooperative learning to problems of social relationships is the application to intergroup relations, where cooperative learning fulfills Allport's (1954) conditions for positive race relations: cooperative, non-superficial contact, sanctioned by institutional norms, between individuals of equal status (Slavin and Hansell 1983). The same principles have been applied to improve acceptance of mainstreamed, academically handicapped students (see Slavin 1983). A wide array of achievement as well as attitudinal outcomes have been studied in the course of the cooperative learning field research. This research has been recently reviewed by Slavin (1983), who emphasized methodologically rigorous studies in elementary and secondary schools that had durations of at least two weeks (but more typically 8–12 weeks). The major conclusions of this research are summarized below.

2.1 Academic Achievement

Anyone who has seen students working in cooperative groups can see that they enjoy doing so, that working cooperatively makes school work social and exciting. But what are the effects of working cooperatively on student achievement?

Thirty-three studies in regular elementary or secondary classrooms have investigated the effects of cooperative learning programs on student learning, comparing the cooperative programs to traditional control groups in experiments lasting at least two weeks. A significant positive effect on student achievement was found in 22 of these studies, no differences in 10, and in one study there was a significant difference favoring the control group. The most successful methods for improving student achievement appear to be the student team learning techniques; six of eight STAD studies, eight of nine TGT studies, both TAI studies, one Jigsaw II study and one study of a combination of TGT, STAD, and Jigsaw II all found significantly positive effects on student achievement (see Slavin 1983). Three of the 21 student team learning studies found no experimental-control differences in achievement.

One study of the original Jigsaw method found positive effects of this method on student achievement. A second study found no differences. One study of Group Investigation found positive effects of this method on what the authors call "high cognitive-level" skills, such as analysis, evaluation, and interpretation, but not on basic skills, while another found no differences (see Slavin 1983).

The pattern of results of the many cooperative learning studies indicates the importance of designing cooperative methods to resolve the problems inherent in cooperation. The Learning Together model is the closest of the cooperative learning models to "pure" cooperation; the students work in small groups to complete a single worksheet and receive praise for doing so. This method does not explicitly make it necessary for every group member to contribute to the group's work, and the use of an informal group reward does not give group members a clear reason to help one another or to encourage their group-mates to learn. This Learning Together model was found in one study to be equal to the control group in achievement effects and lower than the control group in another, the only negative finding for a cooperative learning method. However, a modification of the Learning Together method gave students grades based on the sum of their group-mates' individual quiz scores, as in STAD, TAI, and Jigsaw II. In this study, positive achievement effects were found. This striking difference in achievement outcomes between two studies, one which did not provide specific group rewards based on the group members' individual learning, and one which did provide such rewards, underlines the importance of making sure that group members' learning is the group's concern. Other studies of cooperative learning methods also bear this out.

The positive effects of cooperative learning methods on student achievement appear equally frequently in elementary and secondary schools, in urban, suburban, and rural schools, and in subjects as diverse as mathematics, language arts, social studies, and reading. There is a tendency for blacks to gain outstandingly in achievement as a result of working cooperatively, although whites also gain more in achievement as an outcome of cooperative learning. Most studies show high, average, and low achievers gaining equally from the cooperative experience. A few have shown somewhat greater gains for low achievers but a few others have shown the greatest gains for high achievers (see Slavin 1983). Peterson et al. (1980) found a curvilinear interaction, with high and low achievers doing best in cooperative groups while middle achievers learned best alone. However, most studies found no ability by treatment interactions, and this fact plus the inconsistent directions of the interactions when they are found, probably indicates that cooperative learning is generally equally effective for students at all achievement levels.

2.2 Intergroup Relations

The effect of cooperative learning strategies on relationships between black, white, and Hispanic students in desegregated schools is an outstanding case of social psychology in action. Studies of voluntary interracial interactions during lunch time (e.g., Schofield and Sagar 1977) indicate that although students of different ethnicities might attend the same schools, there is a long way to go before having them form friendships and interact on an equal and amicable basis. Numerous studies of friendship between students of different ethnic groups (e.g., Gerard and Miller 1976) have confirmed this observation; students make few friendship choices outside of their own racial or ethnic groups, and this situation does not improve over time of its own accord.

Cooperative learning techniques place students of different races or ethnicities into cooperative groups, where each group member is given an equal role in helping the group achieve its goals. These are the conditions of the most widely accepted theory of positive intergroup relations: Allport's (1954) contact theory of interracial relations. Allport's theory holds that if individuals of different races are to develop positive relationships, they must engage in frequent cooperative activity on an equal footing. Put another way, it seems logical that if we assign students to work together on a common task toward a common goal, where each individual can make a substantial contribution to the mutually desired goal, the students will learn to like and respect one another.

The results of the cooperative learning studies support this expectation. Most of the intergroup relations research has been done with the student team learning methods. Three studies of STAD, three of TGT and two of Jigsaw II (see Slavin 1983) all found positive effects of the student team learning methods on improving relationships between students of different ethnicities. In addition, Cooper et al. (1980) found that students in the Learning Together program made more cross-racial friendships than did students who were not allowed to interact, but not more than students who competed with each other in homogeneous "clusters."

Two of these studies included follow-ups of interethnic attitudes. Both found that several months after the students experienced student team learning, they still had significantly more friends outside of their own ethnic groups than did students who had been in traditional classes.

2.3 Mainstreaming

The barriers to friendship and positive interaction presented by ethnic differences are serious, but they are small compared to the gap between mainstreamed academically handicapped students and their nonmainstreamed classmates. However, this is another area in which cooperation may overcome substantial differences. Several researchers have found that cooperative learning improves relationships between mainstreamed and nonmainstreamed students. In a study of STAD, Madden and Slavin (1983) found that student team learning helped nonmainstreamed students accept their mainstreamed classmates while also improving the class's achievement and self-esteem. Similarly, a study of TAI (Slavin et al. 1984b) found that this method increased the acceptance of mainstreamed students by their classmates while also increasing all students' achievement, self-esteem, and positive behavior. Ballard et al. (1977) introduced cooperation between educable mentally retarded students and their nonretarded classmates, and found a marked increase in friendships toward EMR students. Armstrong et al. (1981) and Cooper et al. (1980) found positive effects of the Learning Together model on acceptance of mainstreamed learning disabled children.

2.4 Self-esteem

Several of the cooperative learning studies have included measures of student self-esteem. Self-esteem has been anticipated as an outcome of cooperative learning both because students in cooperative groups feel more liked by their classmates (which they usually are) and because they are likely to feel more successful academically (which they also usually are).

The technique whose structure is most directly targeted to improving student self-esteem is Jigsaw, in which students are each given special information that makes them indispensable to their groups. Positive effects on self-esteem have been found in two studies of Jigsaw, but not in a third (see Slavin 1983).

Teams–Games–Tournament and STAD have each documented effects on student self-esteem, as has TAI. Also, a study that combined the three student learning methods showed positive effects on self-esteem (see Slavin 1983).

2.5 Other Effects of Cooperative Learning

The outcomes discussed above—student learning, intergroup relations, mainstreaming, and self-esteem—have been studied most extensively in the cooperative learning research because they have so much importance as outcomes of schooling. However, there is a wide range of other outcomes that have also been studied in this research (see Slavin 1983).

Not surprisingly, most evaluations of cooperative learning have found that students who work together like school more than those who are not allowed to do so. They also like their fellow students more. Students who have worked cooperatively are more likely than other students to be altruistic and to believe that cooperation is good. They are also likely to say that they want their classmates to do well in school and that they feel that their classmates want them to do well. Finally, they are more likely than control students to believe that their success depends on their efforts, and they are more likely to be on-task during class time.

One study found that emotionally disturbed adolescents who experienced TGT were more likely than traditionally taught students to interact appropriately with other students, and this effect was maintained five months after the end of the project. Janke also found positive effects of TGT on the behavior and attendance of emotionally disturbed adolescents. Another study found that students who worked cooperatively were better able than other students to understand someone else's point of view (see Slavin 1983).

3. Use of Cooperative Learning

Actual application of cooperative learning methods in classrooms has increased dramatically since the late 1970s and continues to increase at a rapid rate. The most widely used methods are the student team learning methods, STAD, TGT, and Jigsaw II. As of the end of the 1983–84 school year, more than 20,000 teachers located throughout the United States were estimated to be using these methods and this number continues to grow. The Johnsons' Learning Together model and Jigsaw are also used in many schools, and Group Investigation is widely used in Israel.

4. Conclusions

There are still many unanswered questions in the research, but at this point it is possible to say that the principal cooperative learning methods have essentially proven their effectiveness on a wide range of outcomes. They have proven to be practical and widely acceptable to teachers. The research has clearly shown that changing from a traditional competitive classroom to a cooperative one does not diminish student achievement; most often it significantly improves achievement. When cooperative learning methods are used in which groups are rewarded based on their members' learning and students are individually accountable for their academic performance, positive effects on achievement are consistently found. The research overwhelmingly supports the usefulness of cooperative learning for improving self-esteem and for improving the social outcomes of schooling, such as intergroup relations, attitudes toward mainstreamed students, and general positive relations between students.

See also: Competition; Cooperation

Bibliography

Allport G W 1954 *The Nature of Prejudice*. Addison-Wesley, Cambridge, Massachusetts

Armstrong B, Johnson D W, Balow B 1981 Effects of cooperative vs. individualistic learning experiences on interpersonal attraction between learning-disabled and normal-progress elementary school students. *Contemp. Educ. Psychol.* 6: 102–09

Aronson E 1978 *The Jigsaw Classroom*. Sage, Beverly Hills, California

Ballard M, Corman L, Gottlieb J, Kaufman M J 1977 Improving the social status of mainstreamed retarded children. *J. Educ. Psychol.* 69: 605–11

Coleman J S 1961 *The Adolescent Society*. The Free Press of Glencoe, New York

Cooper L, Johnson D W, Johnson R, Wilderson F 1980 Effects of cooperative, competitive, and individualistic experiences on interpersonal attraction among heterogeneous peers. *J. Soc. Psychol.* 111: 243–52

DeVries D L, Slavin R E, Fennessey G M, Edwards K J, Lombardo M M 1980 *Teams–Games–Tournament: The Team Learning Approach*. Educational Technology Publications, Englewood Cliffs, New Jersey

Gerard H B, Miller N 1976 *School Desegregation: A Long-range Study*. Plenum, New York

Johnson D W, Johnson R T 1976 *Learning Together and Alone*. Prentice-Hall, Englewood Cliffs, New Jersey

Madden N A, Slavin R E 1983 Cooperative learning and social acceptance of mainstreamed academically handicapped students. *J. Spec. Educ.* 17: 171–82

Peterson P L, Janicki T, Swing S 1980 Individual characteristics and children's learning in large-group and small-group approaches: Study II. Wisconsin Research and Development Center for Individualized Schooling Report No. 561

Schofield J W, Sagar H A 1977 Peer interaction patterns in an integrated middle school. *Sociometry* 40: 130–38

Sharan S, Sharan Y 1976 *Small-group Teaching*. Educational Technology Publications, Englewood Cliffs, New Jersey

Slavin R E 1980a *Using Student Team Learning*, rev. edn. Center for Social Organization of Schools. The Johns Hopkins University, Baltimore, Maryland

Slavin R E 1980b Effects of individual learning expectations on student achievement. *J. Educ. Psychol.* 72: 520–24

Slavin R E 1983 *Cooperative Learning*. Longman, New York

Slavin R E, Hansell S 1983 Cooperative learning and intergroup relations: Contact theory in the classroom. In: Epstein J, Karweit N (eds.) 1983 *Friends in School*. Academic Press, New York

Slavin R E, Leavey M, Madden N A 1984a Combining cooperative learning and individualized instruction: Effects on student mathematics achievement, attitudes and behaviors. *Elem. Sch. J.* 84: 409–22

Slavin R E, Leavey M, Madden N A 1984b Effects of cooperative learning and individualization on mainstreamed students. *Except. Child.* 50: 434–43

Starr R, Schuerman C 1974 An experiment in small-group learning. *The American Biology Teacher.* pp. 173–75

Weigel R H, Wiser P L, Cook S W 1975 Impact of cooperative learning experiences on cross-ethnic relations and attitudes. *J. Soc. Issues* 31: 219–44

Wheeler R 1977 Predisposition toward cooperation and competition: Cooperative and competitive classroom effects. Paper presented at the Annual Convention of the American Psychological Association, San Francisco, California

Tutoring

F. J. Medway

Tutoring is a method of instruction in which a student or small group of students receives personalized and individualized education from a teacher. The teacher is called a tutor and the student is commonly referred to as a tutee. Tutoring is most often used to provide remedial or supplemental instruction to students who have difficulty learning by conventional methods or who have special needs that prevent them from participating in a regular instructional program. Tutoring is also used to relieve the teacher of instructional and non-instructional duties.

Tutoring is widely used as a teaching method for learners of all ages and all levels of ability. Tutorial learning is most often practiced in elementary and secondary schools; however, tutoring is also practiced in higher education, adult education, and vocational education. Tutoring is most often given during or after the regular school day by someone other than the student's regular teacher. The tutor may be a paid private instructor, a volunteer, a teacher's aide, the student's parent or guardian, another child, or even a machine; the tutor may or may not be like the student in terms of age, ability, background, or personal characteristics; the tutor may or may not be a trained educator; the tutor may focus on just one or several subjects; and the tutor may provide counseling and encouragement in addition to academic instruction. Another usage of the word tutor is as a college or university official who advises undergraduates, maintains discipline standards, and has teaching assignments, (for example, at many universities in the United Kingdom and at some American colleges).

1. Tutoring of Children

Tutoring of school-aged children is widespread. At home, parents frequently help their children with homework and other assignments. Although much of this help is not systematic, a great deal of recent attention has been focused on providing parents with training to help them modify their children's behavior and improve their children's learning through the use of behavior modification and communication procedures. Within the school the use of parents and retired persons as volunteer tutors is common. Programs have been developed that employ nonprofessional child-aides to work on a one-to-one basis with infants and children at risk for adjustment and learning problems.

Since the early 1970s, an impressive literature has developed describing different programs in which children teach other children (Allen 1976; Ehly and Larsen 1980; Gartner et al. 1971). This practice is called "peer tutoring" or "cross-age tutoring." Although, in a strict sense peer tutoring refers to children teaching others their age who are not functioning at an average level and cross-age tutoring refers to children teaching others younger than themselves, the terms are often used interchangeably with the term peer tutoring used most frequently. Cross-age tutoring is the more accurate term when the students are several years younger than the tutors; for example, when the students are of elementary age and the tutors are high-school students, college students, or occasionally, adult volunteers.

Paolitto (1976) traced the historical roots of peer tutoring back to first century AD when Quintilian noted the practice of having younger children taught by older children in his *Institutio Oratoria*. The method was subsequently employed on a limited basis in Germany and Spain in the sixteenth century. Establishment of peer tutoring on a formalized and widespread basis is generally credited to Andrew Bell, a Scotsman, who in the late eighteenth century established a school in Madras, India, for orphans of British soldiers and Indian mothers. Bell modified the ancient Hindu tutoring system and in a 1797 report described the successful application of individual and group peer tutoring as a method of instruction and discipline. Bell's methods were enthusiastically adopted by an English educator, Joseph Lancaster, who strongly advocated tutorial or "monitorial" methods of instruction. In what came to be called the Bell–Lancaster system, professional teachers instructed older students who in turn instructed younger students, with the younger students teaching still younger students. Although variations of the Bell–Lancaster system spread to other European countries in the early 1800s, popularity of the system was short-lived, since increasingly teaching was being viewed as a profession requiring training and talent and more moneys were being devoted to public education. Nevertheless, peer tutoring was an accepted practice in the "one-room schoolhouses" of the early colonial period in American history.

Renewed interest in peer tutoring as a teaching method in the United States began in the early 1960s due to concerns over shortages of teaching personnel and the belief that some children (for example, the disadvantaged) might learn more effectively from another child than from an adult. One of the first and most extensive large-scale tutoring programs was the High School Homework Helpers Program started in 1962–63 in New York City. In this program approximately 1,000 16–18-year-old students served as paid tutors to approximately 6,000 ninth and tenth graders (age 14–16) with reading problems from disadvantaged backgrounds. A second major project designed to improve the reading skills of children from impoverished, inner-city homes was the Youth Tutoring Youth Program. This project was originated by Mary Kohler who operated an independent agency in New York City called the National Commission on Resources for Youth. Youth Tutoring Youth programs were started in several large cities including Washington, DC, and Chicago, and Mary Kohler is credited with having trained more than 3,500 persons in student tutoring techniques. A third noteworthy program was the cross-age tutoring project of Lippitt and Lippitt which was instituted in schools in Michigan and California to improve the achievement and self-esteem of elementary-school students. Each of these projects is described by Allen (1976).

Although tutoring is not a unitary practice that is similar across programs, numerous anecdotal reports and controlled studies indicate the effectiveness of tutoring. One of the first studies was the 1967 evaluation of Homework Helpers Program where it was found that students who received reading tutoring for four hours a week for five months gained more in reading comprehension than did a group of nontutored children. This study also found that tutors improved in reading even more than did the tutees. This was one of the first studies to show the benefits of tutoring for the tutor as well as for the tutored student.

Devin-Sheehan et al. (1976) reviewed several years of research on children tutoring children and concluded that several different tutoring procedures were effective in improving the academic achievement of tutees, and depending upon the particular procedure, found that tutoring was beneficial in improving the achievement of tutors. Tutoring was also noted as being effective in improving the self-concepts and other similar attitudes of program participants, although this was not found as often as achievement gains. The vast majority of these studies were done with children who were of school age and who were not in special education. Recent studies have documented the value of tutoring programs for preschoolers and for handicapped children (Osgothorpe 1984). Also, there has been considerable interest in the variables or processes that serve to increase the likelihood that tutoring will be effective. Among the variables studied have been the attitudes and perceptions of tutoring participants, the status of participants, and the teaching style of the tutor.

2. Tutoring of Adults

Tutoring is used widely with adults in need of academic and/or vocational instruction. This type of tutoring is provided by colleges and universities for students who are unable to do certain college-level work because of limitations in their previous education or background; for veterans who enter college without formal training; for older adults who have forgotten what they learned in high school or college many years before; for adults and students undertaking nonformal educational programs; for the handicapped; or just for students who need additional instruction to keep up with the subject matter.

There are at least three basic varieties of college tutoring. In "course tutoring," a tutor provides a tutee with additional assistance and explanation of material that is covered by the professor. This type of tutoring is a key component of Keller's (1968) Personalized System of Instruction (PSI). In the PSI method students are provided with lessons or units of instruction and allowed to progress through the lessons at their own pace. Each student must attain a certain level of proficiency (commonly 90 percent mastery) before being allowed to proceed to a more advanced unit. PSI tutors are called proctors and are students who have previously taken the course and received a high grade. The role of the proctors is to grade the students' test answers and provide immediate feedback; to clarify and review course material; to provide support and encouragement to the students; and to provide administrative help to the course professor. Many studies have documented advantages of PSI relative to traditional lecture formats (see *Keller Plan: A Personalized System of Instruction*).

"Emergency tutoring" is the kind provided to students who need help quickly because of an impending examination, anxiety, or a personal crisis. Finally, in "structured tutoring," the tutor makes use of computer-structured material and programmed learning. The tutor assists the tutee to learn to operate teaching machines and make use of recorded lessons.

Within the last few years there have been great advances in computer-aided tutoring. Computer programs have been designed that function as active, intelligent agents that seek to make their knowledge base available to both children and adult students. The use of computers as tutors is expected to greatly increase in the next decade.

3. Some Guidelines for Tutoring

The effectiveness of tutoring as a teaching method, whether directed toward a child or toward an adult, greatly depends upon the quality of the tutorial relationship and the way the tutoring is organized and strucured. Although few definitive statements can be made regarding how to select participants, how best to pair tutors and tutees, and how to choose the most beneficial tutoring methods, some basic guidelines can be offered.

First, the attitude of the tutor toward the tutee is very important. The tutor should be encouraging, accepting, reassuring, and the tutor and tutee should genuinely like one another. In a sense, the tutor should attempt to emulate many of the behaviors of a good counselor.

Second, the tutor must be trained in basic instructional techniques including the proper use of feedback and drill. Although older tutors are generally more effective than younger ones, this is mostly a function of their greater mastery of the material and teaching skill rather than age per se. Some tutoring programs have allowed tutors flexibility in devising instruction, whereas other programs follow a set format. Two programs of the latter variety are Harrison's "structured tutoring" and Ellson's "programmed tutoring" (Allen 1976).

Third, the tutoring lesson must be limited to a reasonable amount of time to prevent the tutee from getting restless and frustrated.

And finally, the success of formalized tutoring programs in public schools depends on administrative support, monitoring, and appropriate evaluation. Excellent descriptions of practical tutoring techniques and ways to set up and structure peer tutoring programs are provided by Allen (1976), Rauch (1969), and Ehly and Larsen (1980).

Bibliography

Allen V L (ed.) 1976 *Children as Teachers: Theory and Research on Tutoring.* Academic Press, New York

Devin-Sheehan L, Feldman R S, Allen V L 1976 Research on children tutoring children: A critical review. *Rev. Educ. Res.* 46: 355–85

Ehly S W, Larsen S C 1980 *Peer Tutoring for Individualized Instruction.* Allyn and Bacon, Boston, Massachusetts

Gartner A, Kohler M C, Reissman F 1971 *Children Teach Children: Learning by Teaching.* Harper and Row, New York

Keller F S 1968 "Good-bye teacher . . ." *J. Appl. Behav. Anal.* 1: 79–89

Osgothorpe R T 1984 Handicapped students as tutors for nonhandicapped peers. *Acad. Ther.* 19: 473–83

Paolitto D P 1976 The effect of cross-age tutoring on adolescence: An inquiry into theoretical assumptions. *Rev. Educ. Res.* 46: 215–37

Rauch S J 1969 *Handbook for the Volunteer Tutor.* International Reading Association, Newark, Delaware

Formality

Open Versus Formal Methods

R. M. Giaconia

The debate about whether open education is superior to formal or traditional education has existed for centuries, since at least the time of Socrates. But what evidence is there about the effectiveness of open education programs relative to formal education programs? In recent times, the logical analysis and anecdotal evidence that characterized the earliest debates have yielded to systematic empirical research. Horwitz (1979) identified over 200 of these empirical studies, that is, correlational, quasiexperimental, and experimental studies that contrasted pupil achievement and attitudes under open and formal education programs.

This article first describes three major reviews of the studies of open education that attempted to identify general effects that held across all open education programs. Second, this article describes a more recent review that analyzed which specific features of open education programs were most related to program effectiveness.

1. What is Open Education?

Over the years, a plethora of terms has emerged for innovative educational programs that all seem to share at least some common philosophical assumptions and observable features of open education, for example, progressive education, British infant school, informal education, free school, open space school, open corridor school, integrated day plan, and alternative school. But unlike many specific educational innovations [e.g., personalized system of instruction (PSI) (see *Keller Plan: A Personalized System of Instruction*), or computer-assisted instruction (CAI)] or even long-standing teaching methods (e.g., the lecture method, the classroom recitation), open education programs vary widely in emphasis and implementation. Figure 1 uses portions of a model for the study of classroom teaching (Dunkin and Biddle 1974) to illustrate how open education programs have been variously conceptualized as presage, context, or process variables.

Some open education programs have been defined

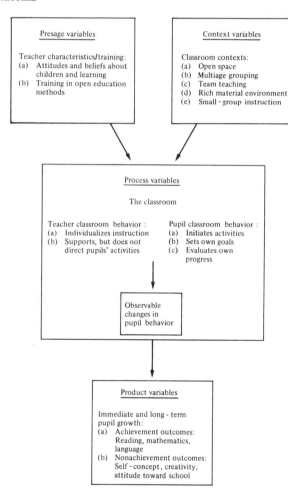

Figure 1

Various conceptualizations of open education as presage, context and process variables[a]

a Source: Dunkin and Biddle 1974

imply as a set of teacher attitudes and beliefs about children and learning (presage variables), whereas other open education programs have emphasized context variables, such as open space, multiage grouping, and team teaching. Many open education programs emphasized specific teacher behaviors, such as individualizing instruction, or pupils' behaviors, such as setting their own goals. Still other open education programs have relied on some combination of these presage, context, and process variables (Horwitz 1979, Hedges et al. 1981, Giaconia and Hedges 1981).

The reasons for this variability in the ways open education has been (and is) conceptualized and implemented are complex and probably determined by many factors. But it is not surprising that open education programs are so heterogeneous, for at least two reasons. First, a common set of philosophical beliefs about children and the nature of learning does not guarantee a common set of educational practices. For example, many investigators acknowledged Rousseau's notions of the free and unfree child or Montessori's or Piaget's views about how children learn as important in the development of a particular open education program. But such ideas do not uniquely define an educational program; how a particular investigator translates these ideas into educational practices is probably mediated by factors such as personal predilections, the zeitgeist, economic and social constraints, and so on.

For example, the British infant schools that arose from a particular set of historical and social factors in the United Kingdom differ in some ways from the more recent versions of these programs imported by the United States. Giaconia and Hedges (1981) observed that studies of open education programs that defined open education as *only* open space, multiage grouping, and team teaching were more likely to be found in the United States than in the United Kingdom. Similarly, the recent rise of minimum competency testing in the United States may impact on the nature of pupil evaluation in open education programs; open education programs that shun standardized testing in favor of written anecdotal evaluations of pupil progress may be faced with the need to prepare their pupils for such standardized tests.

Second, open education programs are heterogeneous because they cover so many different aspects of teaching and learning, from teacher attitudes and training, to the physical layout of the classroom, to specific teacher behaviors during instruction. And different investigators have chosen to emphasize different aspects of open education.

Open education, then, has been conceptualized and operationalized as any or all of the following: a set of teacher beliefs and attitudes about children and the nature of learning; teacher training in the principles of open education; the classroom context such as open space, multiage grouping, and team teaching; teacher behaviors, such as supporting but not directing student activities; pupil behaviors, such as goal setting and self-

evaluation. A review (Giaconia and Hedges 1981) described later in this article lists some specific features of open education found in the studies of open education and analyzes how these separate features are related to program effectiveness.

2. What is Formal Education and How Does it Differ from Open Education?

Most of the studies of open education compared a particular open education program to a traditional education program. Thus, the terms "effects of open education" or "effectiveness of open education" should be understood to mean the extent to which pupil achievement and attitudes in the open education program exceeded or fell below pupil achievement and attitudes in the traditional education program. Within-method studies, that is, studies that examined which variations among open education programs are most effective, are scanty. Emphasis has been on comparing open education to prevailing educational practices (traditional education).

Just as there is a good deal of heterogeneity in the open education programs, there is much heterogeneity in the traditional education programs used in the comparisons between open and traditional education. Some investigators failed to explicitly define the traditional education program; many defined the traditional education program in juxtaposition to their particular definition of the open education program. For example, if the open education program was described as one which involved the flexible use of space and furnishings, the traditional education program was described as one in which the students' desks were arranged in rows. If the open education program was defined as a score above a certain level on the Dimensions of Schooling measure (Traub et al. 1972), then the traditional education program was defined as a score below a certain level on the Dimensions of Schooling. While such descriptions serve to illustrate that the open and traditional programs were different in some respects, they may not capture all the salient features of the traditional education program.

The long discussions of the philosophical origins of assumptions that accompanied the descriptions of the open education programs were singularly lacking in the descriptions of the traditional education program. Traditional education was taken as the given standard to which the open education program was compared.

Traditional education, then, is probably best defined as the "current educational practices in a particular region." How traditional education practices differ from open education depend on the investigator's particular conception of open education. Similarly, the features of open education shown in Fig. 1 and Table 2 are certainly not unique to open education programs, for example, individualized instruction and small-group instruction can also be found in traditional education programs.

3. *Identifying General Effects for Open Education*

The persistence of the open education debate and the large number of empirical studies that have been generated by this debate both suggest the importance of attempts to search for meaningful ways to summarize the empirical findings. Although some individual studies of open education have been particularly controversial or influential in shaping public opinion, it should be remembered that such studies are only a small part of a large body of research. For example, a study by Bennett et al. (1976) generated much heated debate among educational researchers and the general public, both in the United Kingdom and abroad. A recent reanalysis of the data from this study (Aitkin et al. 1981) similarly resulted in a spate of newspaper articles. But the convergence of evidence about open education from many studies might prove more useful than the results of a single study.

The 200 studies of open education identified by Horwitz (1979) are as heterogeneous as the conceptions of open education. They include a mixture of books, monographs, published journal articles, and unpublished doctoral dissertations. These studies represent investigations carried out in the United Kingdom, Canada, Australia, and the United States and include a variety of methodologies: correlational, experimental, quasiexperimental, and to a lesser degree, case studies.

Investigators have studied open education programs in preschools, elementary schools, and junior-high schools. These open education programs have ranged in duration from a few weeks to several years.

Three reviews of the open education studies will be described briefly: a review by Horwitz (1979), a meta-analysis by Peterson (1979), and a meta-analysis by Hedges et al. (1981) (see *Synthesizing Research Evidence*).

3.1 *The Review by Horwitz*

Horwitz (1979) identified about 200 empirical studies that evaluated open education programs. Most of these studies involved comparisons of an open education program with a traditional education program. Studies were included in the review if the educational treatment had either been explicitly labeled by the term "open" or if it had been described as having characteristics generally ascribed to open education, such as flexibility of space, student choice of activity, richness of learning materials, integration of curriculum areas, and more individual and small-group than large-group instruction.

Nine student outcome variables were reported in this review: academic achievement, self-concept, attitude toward school, creativity, independence and conformity, curiosity, anxiety and adjustment, locus of control, and cooperation. Horwitz was primarily interested in the effects of open education on nonachievement outcomes, so specific academic achievement outcomes such as mathematics achievement, reading achievement, and language achievement were not reported.

Horwitz used a "box score" method to summarize findings across the studies on the basis of the statistical significance of the reported results. That is, for each student outcome variable, he tallied the number of studies whose results could be classified as either "open better," "traditional better," "mixed results," or "no significant differences." Conclusions were drawn about the effects of open education on the basis of which category received the most tallies. Horwitz found that in many instances the studies showing no significant differences or mixed results outnumbered those studies showing open better or traditional better.

For the student outcome variables—academic achievement, self-concept, anxiety and adjustment, and locus of control—the "no significant differences" category received the most tallies. For the student outcome variables attitude toward school, creativity, independence and conformity, curiosity, and cooperation, the "open better" category contained the largest number of studies.

Horwitz concluded, "At this time, the evidence from evaluation studies of the open classroom's effects on children is not sufficiently consistent to warrant an unqualified endorsement of that approach to teaching as decidedly superior to more traditional methods" (p. 83).

3.2 *The Meta-analysis by Peterson*

Peterson (1979) completed a meta-analysis of the studies reviewed by Horwitz and other studies that she located. She used only those 45 of the studies that contained enough information to permit calculation of "effect sizes" (means and standard deviations of open and traditional education groups). Peterson did not retrieve the doctoral dissertations reviewed by Horwitz and found that the abstracts of these dissertations often contained too little information to compute effect sizes. Thus Peterson's sample of 45 studies was only about one-fourth of the size of Horwitz's original sample.

Peterson's rationale for undertaking a meta-analysis of a sample of the same studies that Horwitz had already reviewed was to eliminate two major problems inherent in the box score or vote-counting method that Horwitz used. First, the box score procedure may tend to compound the problem of the low statistical power of many studies of the effects of open education. Sample sizes in most studies of teaching (including studies of open education) are small, and effects for any single teaching variable are expected to be small (Gage 1978 pp. 26–27). Thus, the statistical test for a treatment effect in the study has a large probability of incorrectly yielding no statistically significant difference between open and traditional education when a true difference may have existed. That is, most studies would thus tend to automatically fall into the "no significant differences" category.

Second, the box score method used by Horwitz provided no indication of the magnitude of the open education treatment effect. Glass (1978) argued that the box score procedure does not allow the research integrator to determine whether a treatment "wins by a nose or a walkaway." Glass recommended calculating an "effect size" for each study, as a measure of the strength of the treatment effect. Peterson used Glass's procedure, which consists of estimating the population effect size δ by

$$(\overline{X}_E - (\overline{X}_C)/\overline{S}_C$$

where $\overline{X}_E$ = sample mean of the experimental (open education) group; $\overline{X}_C$ = sample mean of the control (traditional education) group; $\overline{S}_C$ = standard deviation of the control group. In general, an effect size can be interpreted directly as the difference between the average performance in the experimental (open education) and control (traditional education) groups, in z-score units. Alternatively, because z-scores can be translated into percentile ranks, an effect size can be interpreted as the percentile rank corresponding to the performance of the average person in the experimental (open education) group relative to the average (traditional education) control subject's performance. For example, an effect size of +0.50 indicates that the average performance in the open education group is one-half of a standard deviation higher than the average performance in the traditional group, that is moderate to large advantage for open education. Similarly, an effect size of +0.50 indicates that if we consider the performance of the average person in the traditional education group to be at the 50th percentile, the performance of the average person in the open education group is at the 69th percentile since a z-score of +0.50 corresponds to the 69th percentile.

Peterson computed an estimate of effect size for each study using Glass's procedure. She then averaged the effect sizes for all studies on each of the following student outcome variables: composite achievement, mathematics achievement, reading achievement, creativity, problem solving, self-concept, anxiety, and independence. She based conclusions about the effects of open education on both the direction and magnitude of the average effect sizes; a positive effect size meant average performance was higher in the open education groups, while a negative effect size indicated that average performance was higher in the traditional education groups.

Peterson noted that for most of the student outcomes, effect sizes were quite small, indicating little advantage for either open or traditional education. Average effect sizes for mathematics achievement, reading achievement, and composite achievement were negative and showed about 0.1 of a standard deviation (or slight) advantage for the traditional education groups. Average effect sizes for locus of control and anxiety were near zero, showing no advantage for either open or traditional education.

For the student outcomes creativity, attitude toward school, and curiosity, average effect sizes were positive and indicated a slight advantage for open education students between 0.1 and 0.2 of a standard deviation.

Independence and attitude toward teacher yielded relatively larger effect sizes that showed an advantage for the open education students of between 0.33 and 0.5 of a standard deviation.

Peterson concluded (about the main effects of open education) ". . . although a more direct or traditional approach appears to be better than a more open approach for increasing students' achievement, an open approach appears to be better than a more direct approach for increasing students' creativity, independence, curiosity, and favorable attitudes toward school and learning" (p. 67).

3.3 The Meta-analysis by Hedges, Giaconia, and Gage

Hedges et al. (1981) undertook yet another meta-analysis of research on open education. This meta-analysis was designed to improve upon the meta-analysis by Peterson in at least three ways. First, doctoral dissertations were retrieved and used in the analysis. Peterson had excluded these from her meta-analysis. These dissertations numbered about 90 and constituted over half of the total sample of studies used by Hedges and his co-workers.

Second, the statistical analyses were based on improved statistical theory for effect size estimation. For example, the development of statistical theory for effect size estimation (Hedges 1981) led to the conclusion that Glass's estimator was biased, tending to overestimate the true (population) effect size. Hedges et al. used an unbiased estimator of effect size given by

$$c_m \frac{\overline{X}_E - \overline{X}_C}{S_{\text{pooled}}}$$

where $\overline{X}_E$ = sample mean of the experimental (open education) group, $\overline{X}_C$ = sample mean of the control (traditional education) group, S_{pooled} = pooled estimate of the within-group standard deviation, c_m = constant for m degrees of freedom, where $m = n_E + n_C - 2$.

The exact formula for c_m is given by Hedges (1981), but a good approximation is given by

$$1 - \frac{3}{4m - 1}$$

where $m = n_E + n_C - 2$.

The third way in which the meta-analysis by Hedges et al. improved upon the meta-analysis by Peterson was by taking into account various characteristics of each study. These characteristics included subject characteristics, experimental design characteristics, experimenter characteristics, and experimental context variables. This information was used to look for differences in the magnitude of effect sizes for various configurations of these study characteristics. For example, were the effects of open education greater for younger students than for older students; for open education programs that included open space than for those that did not?

249

Hedges and his colleagues used a sample of 153 studies that included most of the studies reviewed by Horwitz. A few studies that had been published after Horwitz's bibliography was prepared were also added. Several studies that Horwitz had reviewed were excluded because complete reports could not be obtained, because the studies did not compare open education students to any other group (e.g., case studies), or because it appeared that the open education group was not receiving any open education treatment.

An unbiased estimator of effect size (Hedges 1981) was used to compute an effect size for each comparison of open and traditional education, in each study, for each student outcome variable. When a study did not provide enough information to permit calculation of an effect size, only the direction of the differences was recorded (favors open, favors traditional, or favors neither).

Hedges et al. identified 38 student outcome variables and reported average effect size for 16 of these: achievement motivation, adjustment, anxiety, attitude toward school, attitude toward teacher, cooperativeness, creativity, curiosity, general mental ability, independence and self-reliance, locus of control, self-concept, language skills achievement, mathematics achievement, reading achievement, and miscellaneous achievement.

The average effect sizes for each of these student outcomes were based on the unweighted average of the comparisons across studies. Averages weighted by the number of students in each group were also computed but the pattern of results using weighted averages did not differ. Hedges and his co-workers also reported the percentage of studies for which the direction of the effect favored open, favored traditional, or favored neither educational treatment.

The average effect sizes for the student outcomes adjustment, attitude toward school, attitude toward teacher, curiosity, and general mental ability, were all positive and showed a small advantage for the open education group of about 0.2 of a standard deviation. The direction of the effect for the majority of studies also favored open education for these student outcomes.

The average effect sizes were positive, but near zero, for the student outcomes locus of control, self-concept, anxiety, and miscellaneous achievement. The direction of the effect for the majority of the studies favored traditional education for locus of control, anxiety, and miscellaneous achievement. For self-concept, the direction of effect for the majority of studies favored open education.

For cooperativeness, creativity, and independence, average effect sizes were positive and indicated a small advantage for open education of between 0.25 and 0.33 of a standard deviation. The majority of the studies showed a direction of effect that favored open education for all of these student outcomes.

The average effect sizes for language achievement, mathematics achievement, and reading achievement were negative, but near zero, indicating no particular advantage for either open or traditional education. The direction of effect for the majority of studies, however, favored traditional education.

Hedges et al. concluded that some of the claims of proponents of open education had been supported, but that open education did not produce consistent effects across the different student outcomes. Open education made its strongest showing for the student outcomes creativity, cooperativeness, independence and self-reliance, attitude toward teacher, curiosity, attitude toward school, and adjustment. Open education made its weakest showing for reading, mathematics, and language achievement.

3.4 Summary of the Reviews of Open Education

Table 1 summarizes the results reported in the three reviews of open education by Horwitz, Peterson, and Hedges et al.

Two major conclusions seem warranted from the results reported in Table 1. First, in general, open education is somewhat more effective than traditional education for nonachievement outcomes. Traditional education is only slightly more effective than open education for the traditional academic achievement measures. For many student outcomes, there are near zero differences between open and traditional education.

Second, these general conclusions about the effectiveness of open education must be tempered by the fact that the variability of the effects of open education programs is often quite high. The ranges of effect size reported by Peterson for each student outcome were quite large. For example, mathematics achievement yielded an average effect size of -0.14, (small advantage for traditional education) but the range was -1.01 (large advantage for traditional education) to $+0.41$ (moderate advantage for open education). Similarly, the standard deviations of effect size reported by Hedges and his co-workers were large. For example, mathematics achievement yielded an average effect size near zero (-0.034), but the standard deviation was 0.383. Thus, while the average effect sizes across studies were in most cases quite small, some studies produced particularly large positive (favors open education) or particularly large negative (favors traditional education) effect sizes.

4. Identifying Features of Effective Open Education Programs

The idea that there are some general effects of open education that hold across most open education programs is unsupported by the three reviews just described. In addition, a series of statistical analyses by Hedges et al. (1981) demonstrated that for every student outcome variable, the set of effect sizes was not homogeneous. That is, the variability in effects for open education was too large to be explained by chance

Table 1
Summary of the results reported in three reviews of open education

Student Outcomes	Review by Horwitz (1979) Percentage of studies classified as					Meta-analysis by Peterson (1979) Effect size			Meta-analysis by Hedges, Giaconia, and Gage (1981)					
	N of studies	Open better	Traditional better	Mixed results	No sig. diff.	N of studies	M	Range	N of comparisons	M	SD	Favor open	Favor trad.	Favor neither
Academic achievement composite	102	14	12	28	46	25	−0.12	−0.78 to +0.41	—	—	—	—	—	—
Language achievement	—	—	—	—	—	18	−0.14	−1.01 to +0.58	32	−0.053	0.581	36	57	7
Math achievement	—	—	—	—	—	20	−0.13	−0.72 to +0.44	62	−0.034	0.383	47	48	5
Reading achievement	—	—	—	—	—	—	—	—	73	−0.083	0.362	42	54	4
Miscellaneous achievement	—	—	—	—	—	1	0.98	—	23	0.014	0.889	38	55	7
Problem solving	—	—	—	—	—	—	—	—	13	0.178	0.434	61	35	4
General mental ability	—	—	—	—	—	—	—	—	11	−0.278	0.285	27	60	13
Achievement motivation	—	—	—	—	—	—	—	—	19	0.167	0.578	58	42	0
Adjustment	22	31	0	50	19	—	—	—	30	0.026	0.599	51	49	0
Anxiety	17	18	29	6	47	5	0.07	−0.63 to +0.69	68	0.166	0.447	68	31	1
Attitude toward school	57	40	4	25	31	15	0.12	−0.43 to +0.48	20	0.199	0.497	67	25	8
Attitude toward teacher	—	—	—	—	—	2	0.42	+0.29 to +0.56	6	0.214	0.481	78	11	11
Cooperativeness	9	67	0	11	22	11	0.18	−0.23 to +0.50	23	0.302	0.403	71	17	12
Creativity	33	36	0	31	33	3	0.14	−0.17 to +0.52	5	0.169	0.430	57	29	14
Curiosity	14	43	0	36	21	3	0.30	+0.07 to +0.55	26	0.258	0.659	68	30	2
Independence	23	78	4	9	9	5	0.03	−0.34 to +0.70	20	0.023	0.336	41	54	5
Locus of control	24	25	4	17	54	—	—	—	—	—	—	—	—	—
Self-concept	61	25	3	25	47	14	0.16	−0.14 to +1.45	84	0.056	0.420	53	41	6

variation. Some factor or factors other than chance were contributing to the variability in effect sizes across studies. Hedges et al. (1981) assessed the extent to which factors such as student characteristics (e.g., age, sex, entering ability), or study characteristics (e.g., duration of treatment) could account for the variability in effects. In general, none of these factors, taken individually or together, adequately explained the variability of effects across student outcomes.

A more recent review (Giaconia and Hedges 1981) examined the relation of the observed variability in effect sizes to the observed variability in the numbers and types of open education features implemented. That is, they tried to identify which features of open education programs distinguished between relatively effective and ineffective open education programs.

The 153 studies of open education that were used in the meta-analysis by Hedges et al. served as the database. For each of the 16 student outcomes, studies were sorted into one of three categories on the basis of the magnitude and direction of the unbiased estimate of effect size for the study.

"Larger effect" studies were the one-third of the studies with the largest positive effect sizes, that is, those studies that showed the larger advantage for open education. "Smaller effect" studies were the one-third of the studies with the smallest effect sizes, including those less than zero, that is, those studies that demonstrated the largest advantage for traditional education. "Medium effect" studies were the one-third of the studies remaining after the larger effect and smaller effect studies had been identified. Only larger and smaller effect studies were used in the subsequent analyses.

The student outcome variables used in this review were those for which there were at least seven studies in each of the larger effect and smaller effect categories. These outcome variables were self-concept, creativity, attitude toward school, reading achievement, mathematics achievement, and language achievement.

4.1 Descriptions of the Features of Open Education Programs

The careful identification of a complete and representative set of features of open education programs on which to compare larger effect and smaller effect studies was crucial to the review by Giaconia and Hedges. Two major decisions had to be made: which features of open education would be included in the analysis and how information about these features would be coded.

The first decision involved a tradeoff between compiling an exhaustive, detailed list of features that would fully capture all the nuances of different open education programs and the practical constraint that most studies included too little information about the open education treatment to conduct this fine-grained analysis.

The features of open education that were used in this review to compare larger effect and smaller effect studies were based partly on the general categories proposed by Traub et al. (1972), partly on the categories described by Walberg and Thomas (1972), and largely on general impressions gathered in the course of reading the 153 studies reviewed in the meta-analysis by Hedges et al. (1981).

Traub and his co-workers developed a teacher questionnaire (Dimensions of Schooling) which categorized several features that were found to distinguish open education programs from traditional education programs. Two criteria were used by Traub and his co-workers in identifying these features of open education programs. First, the feature could not contradict any of the assumptions about the way children behave, develop, and learn that Barth (1969) had identified as central to open education. Second, the feature had to have two or more program manifestations that could be easily ranked in degree of openness.

Ten dimensions of schooling were proposed by Traub and his co-workers:

(a) Setting instructional objectives—process by which instructional objectives are set, that is, participation of students in this process.

(b) Materials and activities—diversity of material, activities, and media.

(c) Physical environment—flexible use of space and furnishings.

(d) Structure for decision making—student choice in assignment to teachers.

(e) Time scheduling—no fixed timetables, time for independent study, unstructured time, no attendance requirements.

(f) Individualization of learning—small-group instruction, individually-paced instruction, student choice in method of learning.

(g) Composition of classes—multiage grouping of students.

(h) Role of teacher—teacher as resource person, teacher as diagnoser of student problems and progress, teacher guides but does not force students, teacher works with individuals or small groups of students.

(i) Student evaluation—little or no use of conventional tests, purpose of evaluation is to direct student learning, student also provides self-evaluations, continuous evaluation, use of observations, work samples, and anecdotal evidence.

(j) Student control—role of student in rule formulation and rule enforcement.

Walberg and Thomas (1972) identified eight themes of open education which they used as the starting point for the development of a 50-item open education observation scale and a parallel teacher questionnaire. The eight themes proposed by Walberg and Thomas were based largely on the ten themes that Bussis and Chittenden (1970) had arrived at from their interviews with open education teachers. These eight themes and sample indicators include:

(a) Provisioning for learning—diversity of manipulative materials, freedom of movement for students, students group themselves for instruction.

(b) Humaneness, respect, openness, and warmth—environment includes materials developed by students, students' activities and ideas are reflected in the classroom.

(c) Diagnosis of learning events—test results not used to group students, tests used to find out what student knows.

(d) Instruction, guidance, and extension of learning—individualized instruction, small-group instruction, little use of curriculum guides or textbooks.

(e) Evaluation of diagnostic information—teacher writes individual histories of each student's development, tests not used to compare students, teacher collects samples of student's work, evaluation used to guide instruction.

(f) Seeking opportunities for professional growth—use of teacher aides, teacher relies on colleagues.

(g) Self-perception of teacher—teacher tries to keep all students in view in order to make sure they are doing what they are supposed to.

(h) Assumptions about children and learning—student involvement, warm and supportive emotional climate, clear set of rules and regulations.

Giaconia and Hedges (1981) identified seven general features of open education for their review: open space, materials to manipulate, multiage grouping of students, individualized instruction, role of the child in learning, team teaching, and diagnostic evaluation.

Table 2 gives the definitions of each of these seven features of open education programs. The table also lists key words or descriptive statements reported in some of the studies that are examples of each of the seven features.

Table 3 shows the correspondences among the features of open education identified for the review by Giaconia and Hedges, the dimensions of schooling described by Traub and his co-workers, and the open education themes reported by Walberg and Thomas. The table shows some evidence of convergence among the three sets of features, although some of the features differ in specificity and some of the categories do not overlap perfectly.

A second decision, after choosing the features of open education on which to compare large effect and small effect studies, was how to code information in the 72 studies. The choice was between coding only the presence or absence of a feature in each open education program and coding qualitative aspects of each feature. The former approach was chosen because most of the studies contained too little information for a finer-grained analysis and because the number of studies examined for any one student outcome variable was small.

4.2 Results and Conclusions

One way that Giaconia and Hedges assessed the relationship between the seven features and effect size was by comparing the average number of features implemented in larger and smaller effect studies. Table 4 reports the mean number of features of open education that were implemented in larger effect and smaller effect studies for each student outcome variable. The results of t-tests for the difference between means are also shown.

For the nonachievement outcomes of self-concept, creativity, and favorable attitude toward school, the more effective programs had a larger number of features (on the average) than the less effective programs. The opposite was true for the achievement outcomes of reading, mathematics, and language achievement; the less effective programs had more features than the more effective programs. The difference in number of features between larger and smaller effect studies was largest for the outcomes of self-concept and creativity, where the more effective programs had an average of one to two more features than the less effective programs.

Because some of the seven features are represented more often in conceptualizations of open education, it was useful to examine the occurrence of each of the features individually. The percentages of larger effect and smaller effect studies for which each feature of open education was present or absent were determined and are shown in Table 5.

For the nonachievement outcomes, the first four features (role of the child, diagnostic evaluation, materials to manipulate, and individualized instruction) tended to differentiate the studies that yielded larger effects from the studies that yielded smaller effects. The open education programs that produced larger effects on these nonachievement outcomes were much more likely to include these four features than the programs which produced smaller effects. For example, all of the more effective programs on the outcome of self-concept included these four features and the vast majority of larger effect studies on the outcomes creativity and favorable attitude toward school included these four features. On the other hand, only about half of the studies yielding smaller effects on nonachievement outcomes included the first four features. Overall, the larger effect studies were about 30 percent more likely than the smaller effect studies to have included each of the first four features.

Table 2
Descriptions of the features of open education on which larger effect and smaller effect studies were compared

Feature	Definition	Indicators and descriptive statements
Role of child in learning	Child is active in guiding its own learning; child actively chooses materials, methods, and pace of learning; role of teacher as resource person; less teacher-centered instruction and more student-centered instruction	Voluntary action on the part of the child Active agent in his or her own learning process Self-motivated learning Student initiates learning Active participant rather than recipient of commands Trust in the student's ability to choose his or her own learning experiences Child-centered environment Child's freedom and responsibility for his or her learning and development Democratic learning atmosphere Student sets rate of learning High degree of child contribution to the learning environment Teacher as resource person Teacher is authoritative not authoritarian
Diagnostic evaluation	Purpose of evaluation is to guide instruction; little or no use of conventional tests, but extensive use of work samples, observation, and written histories of the student	Charting of progress toward specific individual goals Evaluation used to facilitate and guide learning Child's performance not compared to that of other children Teacher's record-keeping combines constant jotting in class and thoughtful writing about each child Less standardized concept of student progress Nongraded approach to evaluate student's performance
Materials to manipulate	Presence of diverse set of materials to stimulate student exploration and learning	Sensory materials Exploration and discovery-oriented materials Use of natural materials Rich material environment Alternative modalities for learning Diversity of materials Abundance of instructional aids Tactile confrontation with manipulative materials Real world materials
Individualized instruction	Instruction based on the individual needs and abilities of each student; individualization of rate of, methods, and materials for learning; small-group as opposed to large-group instruction	Individualized instruction Individualized approach Individualized work Environment responsive to individual learner needs Individualizing the curriculum Individualized goal setting Learning in accord with their own rate and style Small-group or individual instruction
Multiage grouping of students	Grouping students for instruction in which grade labels are not applied; two or more grades may be housed in the same area	Family grouping Nongraded school Heterogeneous age grouping Children from different grades work together in same classroom Ungraded classrooms Vertical grouping Continuous progress education
Open space	Physical environment of the classroom involving flexible use of space and furnishings	Open area classroom Open space architecture Flexible school architecture Open instructional area Activity centers Fluid space Decentralized classroom Small-group instruction

Table 2—(continued)

Feature	Definition	Indicators and descriptive statements
Open Space (continued)		Open plan facility No interior walls or movable walls School without walls Flexible seating arrangements Physically unstructured
Team teaching	The sharing in planning and conducting instruction offered to the same group of students by two or more teachers; use of parents as teaching aides	Team teaching organization Team teaching units Teachers work together in teams with a team leader Large spaces with two or more teachers

For the achievement outcomes, the pattern of differences between larger and smaller effect studies in the inclusion of the first four features was not the same as for the nonachievement outcomes. With the exception of the materials to manipulate feature, the more effective programs were no more likely to include these features than were the less effective programs.

The last three features reported in Table 5 (open space, multiage grouping, and team teaching) did not consistently differentiate between more effective and less effective open education programs. This was true for both achievement and nonachievement outcomes.

Thus, the process variables (role of child, diagnostic evaluation, individual instruction) were more likely than the context variables (open space, multiage grouping, team teaching) to distinguish relatively effective from ineffective open education programs.

The observed relationship between the first four features and program effectiveness on nonachievement outcomes is understandable given the relationship between these features as educational treatments and the outcomes as psychological constructs. Some elements of these features would probably be a part of any systematic intervention designed to influence self-

Table 3
Comparison of the categories of open education features proposed in three studies

Giaconia and Hedges (1982)	Traub, Weiss, Fisher, and Musella (1972)	Walberg and Thomas (1972)
Open education features	Dimensions of schooling	Open education themes
Role of child in learning	Student control; setting instructional objectives; role of teacher	Provisioning for learning; humaneness, respect, openness, and warmth
Diagnostic evaluation	Student evaluation	Diagnosis of learning events; evaluation of diagnostic information
Materials to manipulate	Materials and activities	Provisioning for learning; humaneness, respect, openness and warmth
Individualized instruction	Individualization of learning	Instruction, guidance, and extension of learning
Multiage grouping of students	Composition of classes; structure for decision making	Provisioning for learning
Open space	Physical environment	—
Team teaching	—	—
—	Time scheduling	—
—	—	Seeking opportunities for professional growth
—	—	Self-perception of teacher

Table 4
Differences between larger effect and smaller effect studies in the mean number of features of open education that were implemented[a]

| | Larger effect studies | | | Smaller effect studies | | | |
Student outcomes	M	SD	n	M	SD	n	t
Self-concept	6.12	0.81	16	3.88	1.78	16	4.60[b]
Creativity	4.71	1.80	7	3.71	1.38	7	1.17
Favorable attitude toward school	4.15	1.68	13	3.92	1.75	13	0.34
Reading achievement	4.47	1.46	17	4.53	1.46	17	−0.12
Mathematics achievement	4.43	1.02	14	4.71	1.77	14	−0.52
Language achievement	4.75	1.75	8	5.00	1.69	8	−0.29

a Maximum number of features is 7   b $p < 0.01$

concept, creativity, or attitude. Indeed, the reason that the first four features are most central to conceptions of open education is that most conceptualizations of open education have emphasized outcomes such as self-concept, attitude, and creativity.

For example, the self-concept measures used in these studies assess self-appraisal, self-security, and self-acceptance. And, the feature called diagnostic evaluation emphasizes the positive progress of each child. Therefore the child in a program that emphasizes diagnostic evaluation experiences positive self-referenced evaluations rather than potentially negative norm-referenced evaluations. Given this experience it is plausible that the child will rate himself or herself more positively

on measures of self-appraisal, self-security, and self-acceptance.

On the other hand, the relationship between the first four features of open education and academic achievement as measured by standardized tests is more tenuous. For example, although individualized goal setting may lead to greater mastery of goals set by the child, this may not lead to greater mastery of the objectives required for success on a standardized achievement test. In fact, standardized achievement tests that served as the outcome measures are often alien to open education programs.

The last three features of open education programs (open space, multiage grouping, and team teaching) are

Table 5
Percentages of larger (L) and smaller (S) effect studies on each outcome variable that have each open education feature[a]

Feature		Self-concept	Creativity	Favorable attitude toward school	Non-achievement average[b]	Reading achievement	Mathematics achievement	Language achievement	Achievement average[b]
Role of the child	L	100	86	85	90.3	75	71	86	77.3
	S	50[d]	67	69	62.0	75	69	88	77.3
Diagnostic evaluation	L	100	100	73	91.0	82	80	86	82.7
	S	46[d]	50[c]	50	44.3	77	83	83	81.7
Materials to manipulate	L	100	80	82	87.3	77	67	83	75.7
	S	27[d]	50	56	44.3	50	54	67	57.0
Individualized instruction	L	100	83	80	87.7	85	83	86	84.7
	S	44[d]	67	75	62.0	77	86	100	87.7
Multiage grouping	L	81	83	46	70.0	71	57	57	58.3
	S	75	33	46	51.3	65	79	75	7.30
Team teaching	L	67	40	36	47.7	73	62	71	68.7
	S	69	57	62	62.7	50	54	38	47.3
Open space	L	87	71	54	70.7	75	71	88	78.0
	S	81	71	85	79.0	94	79	88	87.0

a Studies for which there was no information on a particular feature and for which an informed judgment could not be made were excluded from the analysis for that feature. Median percentage of cases excluded for all features, for all student outcomes, was 7 percent of total sample   b This column is an unweighted average, calculated for descriptive purposes. No significance tests were performed   c $p < 0.10$ d $p < 0.01$ for chi-square test or Fisher's Exact Test administrative or organizational features, or context variable. The relationship between these features and outcomes is probably indirect. For example, open space may be conducive to the child's self-initiation of activities and learning. But the effects of open space per se are probably less direct in this regard than the effects of an open education program where the role of the child as self-initiator of learning is an explicit part of the program. Therefore it is not surprising that these features were not strongly related to program effectiveness for either achievement or nonachievement outcomes.

5. Directions for Future Research on Open Education

Although there are over 200 empirical studies of the effects of open education relative to the effects of traditional education, there are few general conclusions that can be drawn about open education. Indeed, the review of Giaconia and Hedges (1981) suggests that it is not appropriate to talk about "the effects of open education" as if open education were a single, well-defined educational treatment.

Despite the large number of empirical studies of the effects of open education that have been conducted to date, even more studies of open education are needed. What are needed are studies to systematically test the causal efficacy of various configurations of the open education features that Giaconia and Hedges (1981) identified as related to larger program effects. Studies of this sort can determine the relative contribution of each feature to overall program effects. This information can then be used to identify a set of necessary and sufficient features of effective open education programs.

See also: Architecture; Synthesizing Research Evidence; Seating Patterns; Structuring

Bibliography

Aitkin M, Bennett S N, Hesketh J 1981 Teaching styles and pupil progress: A reanalysis. *Br. J. Educ. Psychol.* 51: 170–86

Barth R S 1969 Open education assumptions about learning. *Educ. Philos. Theory* 1(2): 29–39
Bennett N, Jordan J, Long G, Wade B 1976 *Teaching Styles and Pupil Progress*. Harvard University Press, Cambridge, Massachusetts
Broudy H S, Palmer J R 1965 *Exemplars of Teaching Method*. Rand McNally, Chicago, Illinois
Bussis A M, Chittenden E A 1970 *Analysis of an Approach to Open Education*. Educational Testing Service, Princeton, New Jersey
Dunkin M J, Biddle B J 1974 *The Study of Teaching*. Holt, Rinehart and Winston, New York
Gage N L 1978 *The Scientific Basis of the Art of Teaching*. Teachers College Press, New York, pp. 26–27
Giaconia R M, Hedges L V 1981 *Identifying Features of Effective Open Education Programs*. Paper presented at the meeting of the American Educational Research Association, Los Angeles, April 13–17, 1981. ERIC Document No. ED 208 513
Glass G V 1978 Integrating findings: The meta-analysis of research. In: Schulman L S (ed.) 1978 *Review of Research in Education*, Vol. 5. Peacock, Itasca, Illinois
Hedges L V 1980 *Combining the Results of Experiments Using Different Scales of Measurement*. Final Report, Stanford University Program on Teaching Effectiveness, Meta-Analysis Project, Vol. 1, Stanford, California
Hedges L V 1981 Distribution theory for Glass's estimator of effect size and related estimators. *J. Educ. Stat.* 6: 107–28
Hedges L V, Olkin I 1980 Vote-counting methods in research synthesis. *Psychol. Bull.* 88: 359–69
Hedges L V, Giaconia R M, Gage N L 1981 *Meta-analysis of the Effects of Open and Traditional Instruction*. Final Report, Stanford University Program on Teaching Effectiveness, Meta-Analysis Project, Vol. 2, Stanford, California
Horwitz R A 1979 Psychological effects of the "open classroom". *Rev. Educ. Res.* 49: 71–86
Marshall H H 1981 Open classrooms: Has the term outlived its usefulness? *Rev. Educ. Res.* 51: 181–92
Peterson P L 1979 Direct instruction reconsidered. In: Peterson P L, Walberg H J (eds.) 1979 *Research on Teaching: Concepts, Findings, and Implications*. McCutchan, Berkeley, California
Silberman C E (ed.) 1973 *The Open Classroom Reader*. Random House, New York
Traub R E, Weiss J, Fisher C W, Musella D 1972 Closure on openness: Describing and quantifying open education. *Interchange* 3: 69–84
Walberg H J, Thomas S C 1972 Open education: An operational definition and validation in Great Britain and United States. *Am. Educ. Res. J.* 9: 197–208

Direct Instruction

B. Rosenshine

The term direct instruction has appeared in educational literature since at least 1920. Earlier authors have not given a specific, detailed definition of the term. In general, the term has been used to refer to explicit, step-by-step instruction directed by the teacher.

Because the term has been around so long, and because definitions can change from time to time, it would be inappropriate for anyone to provide an "official" definition of direct instruction. Instead, this article will describe the term as it exists in the United States in 1986. Direct instruction in 1986 is used interchangeably with other similar terms such as systematic teaching, explicit instruction, explicit teaching, and active teaching. All these terms refer to explicit, step-by-step instruction, in which there is an emphasis upon all students practicing successful responses and achieving academic success. Direct instruction and the similar terms can be summarized in the phrase: if you want students to learn something, teach it to them—directly.

Thus, if a teacher wants students to learn study skills, map skills, or critical reading skills, the advocates of direct instruction claim that such skills should be taught—directly. Simply asking comprehension questions or higher cognitive level questions is not enough; students need to be taught—directly—how to answer such questions.

Similarly, research on classroom management has found that effective managers (Evertson 1982, Emmer et al. 1980, Evertson et al. 1980) were those who directly taught classroom behavior skills—lining up, sitting down, moving from group to group. And these skills were taught in small steps, with active student practice, correction of student errors, and review and repetition when necessary.

The findings on direct instruction are most relevant when the objective is to teach explicit procedures, explicit concepts, or a body of knowledge. Specifically, these results are most applicable when teaching math concepts and procedures, English grammar, sight vocabulary, historical knowledge, reading maps and charts, and science knowledge and procedures.

These findings are less relevant when teaching in implicit areas, that is, where the skills to be taught cannot be broken down into explicit steps. Such areas include math problem solving, analysis of literature, writing term papers, or discussion of social issues. Still, competency in explicit areas is necessary, although not sufficient, for learning these implicit skills.

1. An Overview of Direct Instruction

On the basis of correlational and experimental classroom studies conducted since 1974, it can be concluded that, in general, students taught with structured curricula do better than those taught with more individualized or discovery learning approaches, and those who receive their instruction directly from the teacher do better than those expected to learn new material or skills on their own or from each other (see *Individualizing Teaching*). In general, to the extent that students are younger, slower, and/or have little prior background, teachers are most effective when they:

(a) structure the learning experience;

(b) proceed in small steps but at a rapid pace;

(c) give detailed and more redundant instructions and explanations;

(d) have a high frequency of questions and overt, active practice;

(e) provide feedback and corrections, particularly in the initial stages of learning new material;

(f) have a success rate of 80 percent or higher in initial learning;

(g) divide seatwork assignments into smaller segments or devise ways to provide frequent monitoring;

(h) provide for continued student practice (overlearning) so that they have a success rate of 90–100 percent and become rapid, confident, and firm.

For younger students, the key concept is mastery to the point of overlearning. Basic skills—arithmetic and decoding—are taught in hierarchically organized strands, so that success at any given level requires application of knowledge and skills mastered at earlier levels. Typically, students are not able to retain and apply knowledge and skills unless they have been mastered to the point of overlearning—to the point where they are automatic (see *Mastery Learning Models*). Thus, it is necessary to help students achieve this level so that they can proceed to the next step with success. The high success rates seen in the classrooms of highly effective teachers and programs is obtained because the initial instruction proceeds in small steps that are not too difficult and also because teachers see that students practice new knowledge and skills sufficiently to obtain this point of overlearning.

This overlearning and automaticity of skills is also necessary for higher processing. In discussing beginning reading, Beck (1978) noted that the data support the position that the brain is a limited capacity processor and that if a reader has to spend capacity decoding a word (whether through phonics or context) then there is less energy available to comprehend the sentence.

2. Demonstration-guided Practice and Independent Practice

When teaching a class, or a group of students within a class, a three-step process appears to be most efficient: this three-step process might be called direct instruction. The first step is the demonstration of what is to be learned. This is followed by guided student practice in which the teacher leads the students in practice, checks for student understanding, provides prompts, and provides corrections and repetitions when necessary. When the students are firm in their initial learning, the teacher then moves them to independent practice where the students work with less guidance. The objective of the independent practice is to provide sufficient practice so that students demonstrate quickness and competence.

An example of these three steps would be teaching two-digit multiplication (e.g., 54 times 7). The first step would be teacher-led demonstration of the steps to be followed in solving these types of problems. This is followed by guided practice in which the students work two or three problems and the teacher circulates and checks on how well the students are doing. Those students who need additional instruction (or demonstration) receive it at this time. If necessary, the teacher repeats the demonstration or parts of the demonstration. When the students are firm in the guided practice, and are making few errors, they are moved to independent practice where they practice learning how to do the skill accurately and rapidly.

Sometimes demonstration and guided practice are combined. For example, when teaching a word list a teacher could demonstrate how to pronounce the first word, then conduct guided practice, then demonstrate the next word, then lead guided practice, and continue this mixture of demonstration and guided practice. Or, in teaching two-digit multiplication the demonstration could be broken into small steps where each step consists of student practice and repetition. Whether or not one mixes, the important points are the clarity of the demonstration of each step, and the adequacy of the guided practice.

Although the above three components—demonstration, guided practice, and independent practice—appear obvious and common sense, they are not always common practice. Frequently the time spent in demonstration is too short; the students do not receive enough guided practice; the teacher does not circulate, correct student errors, and reteach where necessary; and frequently, too much time is allocated to student independent practice and too little time to demonstration and guided practice.

There is evidence that these skills are not "obvious." In experimental studies (Anderson et al. 1979, Good and Grouws 1979, Evertson et al. 1982, Emmer et al. 1982, Becker 1977) where one group of teachers received training in direct instruction and another group did not receive training, each investigation found that (a) the trained teachers used more of the direct instruction skills in their classrooms and (b) the students of the trained teachers had higher achievement scores or had more time on task. Thus, although almost all teachers are using parts of direct instruction, experienced teachers who received specific training showed the results of this training in their own behavior and improved achievement (and/or engagement) of their students.

Now, the discussion will move to some specific items within demonstration, guided practice, and independent practice.

2.1 Demonstration

The first area—demonstration or presentation—unfortunately, has not received much attention in the classroom research literature. Current research is taking place under the general titles of task analysis and instructional design. However, the following suggestions for effective demonstration have emerged from the experimental and correlational classroom literature:

(a) Stating lesson goals.

(b) Focusing on one thought (point, direction) at a time. Completing one point before beginning another.

(c) Giving step-by-step directions using small steps.

(d) Organizing material so that one point is mastered before the next point is given.

(e) Giving detailed and redundant explanations for difficult points.

(f) Having many and varied examples.

(g) Checking for student understanding on one point before proceeding to the next point.

When demonstrations are not clear the main problems appear to be giving directions too quickly, assuming everybody understands because there are no questions, and introducing more complex material before the students have mastered the early material.

2.2 Guided Practice

Teacher presentation is followed by guided practice. Because the presentation represents new material, the purpose of the guided practice is to help the students become firm in the new material. This is effectively done by:

(a) guiding students in practicing the new material;

(b) checking for student understanding and areas of hesitancy and/or confusion;

(c) correcting errors;

(d) providing for a large number of successful repetitions.

One common method for achieving these instructional functions is through teacher questions. Both correlational and experimental studies have shown that a high frequency of teacher-directed questions was important for acquisition of basic arithmetic and reading skills. Stallings and Kaskowitz (1974) identified a pattern of factual question–student response–teacher feedback as most functional for student achievement. Similar results favoring guided practice through teacher questions were also obtained by Stallings et al. (1977, 1979), Soar and Soar (1973), and Coker et al. (1980).

During successful guided practice two types of questions were usually asked by the teacher: questions which called for specific answers, and those which asked for an explanation of how an answer was found.

Two experimental studies (Anderson et al. 1979, Good and Grouws 1979) used controlled practice as part of the experimental treatment. In each study, the teachers who received the additional training were taught to follow the presentation of new material with guided practice. The practice consisted of students responding to teacher questions and doing exercises on their own. In each study, the teachers in the trained group asked more questions and had more guided practice than did the control teachers who continued their normal teaching. And, in each study, the students in the experimental groups had higher achievement than the students of teachers in the regular control groups. Furthermore, the Anderson et al. study found strong positive correlations for the amount of time spent in question–answer format and for the number of academic interactions per minute. Thus, it is not only useful to spend a lot of time in guided practice, it is also valuable to have a high frequency of questions and problems.

Of course, all teachers spend time in guided practice. However, the more effective teachers and their students spent more time in guided practice, more time asking questions, more time correcting errors, more time repeating the new material which was being taught, and more time working problems under teacher guidance and help.

(a) *The importance of frequency*. Note that in all of these studies, the consistently positive results are not being obtained merely by the type of teacher question being asked but by the frequency of direct convergent teacher questions and by the frequency of student responses. Elementary students, like adults, need a great deal of practice, and factual convergent questions provide a form of controlled practice whose frequency has consistently been correlated with student achievement.

Frequency is particularly important in primary grades because no matter how quick a learner is, it takes a large number of repetitions before she or he can recognize words rapidly. For example, Beck (1978) showed that among first grade children, words that were recognized in less than four seconds appeared more than 25 times in the instructional materials, whereas words which were recognized in five seconds or longer appeared less than 10 times.

(b) *High percentage of correct answers*. Not only is the frequency of teacher questions important, but the percentage of correct student responses is also important. One of the major findings of the Beginning Teacher Education Study (Fisher et al. 1980) was that a high percentage of correct answers (both during guided practice and when working alone) was positively correlated with achievement gain.

Similarly, Anderson et al. (1979) found that the percent of academic interactions where the student gave the correct answer was positively related ($r = 0.49$) to achievement gain. Gerstein et al. (1981) also found that teachers who obtained high reading achievement from their students had student accuracy rates near 90 percent, whereas those with lower class achievement had accuracy rates of less than 75 percent.

This principle, a high percentage of correct responses given rapidly and automatically, is a relatively new finding in research on classroom instruction. Specific answers on how high this percentage should be can probably never be given. As a reasonable benchmark for now, it is possible to recommend that the success rate be at least 80 percent during the instruction and at least 90 percent at the end of the new unit.

(c) *Checking for understanding*. With older students, guided student practice also includes teacher "checking for understanding." That is, the teacher attempts to determine whether all the students have mastered the major points in the presentation. Checking for understanding appears in the training manual developed by Good and Grouws (1979) and as part of the training manual developed by Emmer et al. (1980). The term has been in common use for a long time.

It is best that checking for understanding take place frequently so that the teacher can provide corrections and do reteaching when necessary. Because checking for understanding involves teachers asking questions, it is best that these questions be prepared beforehand. Some suggestions for conducting checking for understanding include:

(a) asking students to repeat directions, procedures, or main points;

(b) asking many brief questions on main points with oral responses;

(c) having everyone write the answer (on a small chalkboard or a piece of paper) while the teacher circulates and then having everyone show their answer to the teacher;

(d) having everyone write the answer and check the answer with a neighbor.

When working with younger students in small groups (i.e., 4 to 10) there are times when it is useful to have students respond in unison (see Becker 1977). Unison responses seem particularly appropriate when students are repeating word lists, word sounds, or number facts. Unison responses enable each student to make a larger number of responses. When doing unison responses in word lists (for example) the teacher should be sure that all students respond together, to a signal. Without a signal, the slower students tend to wait a fraction of a second and echo the faster students. When conducting unison responses, it is useful to give individual turns to the slower students to check whether they are firm and quick or whether they need additional repetitions.

The wrong way to do checking for understanding is to ask a few questions, call on volunteers to hear their (usually correct) answers, and then assume that all the class either understands or has now learned from hearing the volunteers. Another error is to ask "Are there any questions?" and, not hearing any, assume that everybody understands. The teacher's error, in the above cases, is in not having prepared enough questions (or problems) to use in checking for understanding.

(d) *Calling on students*. First in a correlation study (Brophy and Evertson 1976) and then in an experimental study (Anderson et al. 1979) it was found that in primary grade reading groups it was better for student achievement if the teacher called on students in ordered turns. Such ordered turns were for new words and when reading a story out loud. In explaining the results, the authors claimed that ordered turns insure that all students have opportunities to practice and participate, and ordered turns simplified group management by eliminating hand waving and other student attempts to be called on by the teacher.

Anderson et al. (1979) note that although the principle of ordered turns works well in small groups, it would be inappropriate to use this principle with whole class instruction in most situations. They suggest that when a teacher is working with a whole class it is usually more efficient to select certain students to respond to questions or to call on volunteers than to attempt systematic turns.

(e) *Feedback and correctives.* During guided practice, during checking for understanding, or during any recitation or drill part of a lesson, how should a teacher respond to a student's answer?

If a student is correct but hesitant, then it is important for the teacher to tell the student that the answer is correct. If the student is correct and firm then the research suggests that the teacher can simply ask a new question, maintaining the momentum of the practice. There is also value in short statements of praise (e.g., "very good") which do not disturb the momentum of the lesson.

There are two related schools of thought on handling an incorrect response. Some research (Stallings and Kaskowitz 1974, Anderson et al. 1979) suggests that the teacher should help the student arrive at the correct answer by asking simpler questions and providing hints. Other research (Good and Grouws 1979, Becker 1977) suggests that the teacher should reteach the material using small steps. Thus, one line of development suggests using hints and helps, and another suggests reteaching. The important point, in either approach, is that errors should not go uncorrected, and that there should be specific procedures to be sure that the student learns the new material. The wrong method is to give the student the answer and then move on.

2.3 Independent Practice

During the guided practice phase, students (a) have begun to work the new problems or apply the new skills, (b) receive additional process explanations, if necessary, and (c) receive corrections and reteaching when necessary. If the prompted practice is done successfully, the students can now move into the independent practice phase.

Providing time for students to independently practice new skills to the point of mastery is an important component of effective instruction. When doing this practice, students usually go through two phases. They begin with "unitization" (Samuels 1981) where the students are first putting the skills together. The early stages of reading or of mathematics computation are examples of unitization: the students are successful, but they are also quite slow. After a good deal of practice, students achieve the "automatic" stage where they are successful and rapid and no longer have to "think through" each step. When students are learning two-digit multiplication and are hesitantly working the first few problems, the students are in the unitization phase. When they have worked sufficient problems correctly so that they are confident, firm, and automatic in the skill, then the students are in the automaticity phase.

The advantage of automaticity is that students who reach it can now give their full attention to reading comprehension or mathematics problem solving. Thus, when learning new material, it is important that students continue their practice to the point of overlearning, where they are rapid, quick, and firm in their responses.

(a) *Managing independent practice.* Studies have shown that when students are working alone during seatwork they are less engaged than when they are being given instruction by the teacher. Therefore, the question of how to manage students during seatwork, in order to maintain their engagement, becomes of primary interest.

One consistent finding has been the importance of a teacher (or another adult) monitoring the students during seatwork. Fisher et al. (1980) found that the amount of substantive teacher interaction with the students during seatwork was positively related to achievement and that when students have contacts with the teacher during seatwork their engagement rate increases by about 10 percent. Thus it seems important that teachers not only monitor seatwork, but that they also provide academic feedback and explanation to students during their independent practice. However, the research suggests that these contacts should be relatively short, averaging 30 seconds or less. Longer contacts would appear to pose two difficulties: the need for a long contact suggests that the initial explanation was not complete and the more time a teacher spends with one student, the less time there is to monitor and help other students.

Another finding of Fisher et al. was that teachers who had more questions and answers during group work had more engagement during seatwork. That is, another way to increase engagement during seatwork was to have more teacher-led practice during group work so that the students could be more successful during the seatwork.

A third finding (Fisher et al. 1980) was that when teachers had to give a good deal of explanation during seatwork, then student error rates were higher. Having to give a good deal of explanation during seatwork suggests that the initial explanation was not sufficient or that there was not sufficient practice and corrections before seatwork.

Another effective procedure for increasing engagement during seatwork was to break the instruction into smaller segments and have two or three segments of instruction and seatwork during a single period. In this way, the teacher provides an explanation (as in two-digit multiplication), then supervises and helps the students as they work a problem, then provides an explanation of the next step, and then supervises the students as they work the next problem. This procedure seems particularly effective for difficult material and/or slower students.

(b) *Students helping students*. Researchers have also developed procedures for students to help each other during the seatwork. In some cases the students in the groups prepare a common product, such as the results of a drill sheet, and in other situations the students study cooperatively in order to prepare for the competition which will take place. Research using these procedures usually shows that students who do seatwork under these conditions achieve more than students who are in regular settings. Presumably, the advantages of these cooperative settings come from the social value of working in groups, and the cognitive value gained from explaining the material to someone and/or having the material explained to oneself. Another advantage of the common worksheet and the competition is that it keeps the group focused on the academic task and diminishes the possibility that there will be social conversation (see *Small Group Methods*).

3. Summary

Direct instruction (or similar terms such as systematic teaching or explicit teaching) is not new. Examples of every one of the above points can be found which go back hundreds of years. But examples of the opposite points, also going back hundreds of years, can be found too.

What is new is that the above ideas have a research base. The research base comes from experimental studies conducted in regular classrooms with regular teachers teaching regular subject matter. The results have consistently shown that when teachers modify their instruction so that they do more systematic teaching, then student achievement improves with no loss in student attitudes toward school or self.

See also: Structuring; Technical Skills of Teaching

Bibliography

Anderson L M, Evertson C M, Brophy J E 1979 An experimental study of effective teaching in first-grade reading groups. *Elem. Sch. J.* 79: 193–222

Beck I L 1978 *Instructional Ingredients for the Development of Beginning Reading Competence*. Learning Research and Development Center, University of Pittsburgh, Pittsburgh, Pennsylvania

Becker W C 1977 Teaching reading and language to the disadvantaged: What we have learned from field research. *Harvard Educ. Rev.* 47: 518–43

Brophy J E, Evertson C M 1974 *Process–Product Correlations in the Texas Teacher Effectiveness Study: Final Report*. University of Texas, Austin, Texas

Brophy J E, Evertson C M 1976 *Learning from Teaching: A Developmental Perspective*. Allyn and Bacon, Boston, Massachusetts

Coker H, Lorentz C W, Coker J 1980 Teacher behavior and student outcomes in the Georgia study. Paper presented to the American Educational Research Association Annual Meeting, Boston, Massachusetts

Emmer E T, Evertson C M 1981 *Teacher's Manual for the Junior High Classroom Management Improvement Study*. Research and Development Center for Teacher Education, University of Texas, Austin, Texas

Emmer E T, Evertson C M, Anderson L M 1980 Effective classroom management at the beginning of the school year. *Elem. Sch. J.* 80: 219–31

Emmer E T, Evertson C, Sanford J, Clements B S 1982 *Improving Classroom Management: An Experimental Study in Junior High Classrooms*. Research and Development Center for Teacher Education, University of Texas, Austin, Texas

Evertson C M 1982 Differences in instructional activities in higher and lower achieving junior high English and math classes. *Elem. Sch. J.* 82: 329–50

Evertson C M, Anderson C W, Anderson L M 1980 Relationship between classroom behaviors and student outcomes in junior high mathematics and English classes. *Am. Elem. Res. J.* 17: 43–60

Evertson C, Emmer E T, Sanford J, Clements B S 1982 *Improving Classroom Management: An Experimental Study in Elementary Classrooms*. Research and Development Center for Teacher Education, University of Texas, Austin, Texas

Fisher C W, Berliner D C, Filby N N, Marliave R, Cahen L S, Dishaw M M 1980 Teaching behaviors, academic learning time, and student achievement: An overview. In: Denham C, Lieberman A (eds.) 1980 *Time to Learn*. United States Government Printing Office, Washington, DC

Gerstein R M, Carnine D W, Williams P B 1981 Measuring implementation of a structured educational model in an urban school district. *Educ. Eval. Policy Analysis* 4: 56–63

Good T L, Grouws D A 1979 The Missouri mathematics effectiveness project: An experimental study in fourth-grade classrooms. *J. Educ. Psychol.* 71: 355–62

Good T L, Grouws D A, Beckerman T M 1978 Curriculum pacing: Some empirical data in mathematics. *J. Curric. Stud.* 10: 75–81

Samuels S J 1981 Some essentials of decoding. *Excep. Educ. Q.* 2: 11–25

Soar R S, Soar R M 1973 *Classroom Behavior, Pupil Characteristics, and Pupil Growth for the School Year and the Summer*. Institute for Development of Human Resources, College of Education, University of Florida, Gainesville, Florida

Stallings J A, Kaskowitz D 1974 *Follow Through Classroom Observation Evaluation, 1972–73*. Stanford Research Institute, Menlo Park, California

Stallings J A, Gory R, Fairweather J, Needles M 1977 *Early Childhood Education Classroom Evaluation*. Stanford Research Institute International, Menlo Park, California

Stallings J, Needles M, Stayrook N 1979 *How to Change the Process of Teaching Basic Reading Skills in Secondary Schools*. Stanford Research Institute International, Menlo Park, California

Lesson Formats

M. J. Dunkin

Lesson formats are accepted or recommended patterns for conducting interactions within classrooms involving teachers and students. For example, a lecture is a solo performance usually by the teacher, in which verbal communication is one way. A discussion is an interactive format featuring a considerable amount of two-way verbal communication. Demonstrations, role plays, student-led seminars, buzz sessions, and seatwork are further examples of different lesson formats.

The field of educational innovation is full of advocacy to dispense with some lesson formats and to adopt new ones. However, there is surprisingly little information about the nature of some prescribed formats when observed in practice. Furthermore, there has been disagreement in many cases about the meaning of terms applied to lesson formats. For example, the term "discussion" probably means different things to different users. To some it might include situations in which the teacher asks the questions and the pupils are permitted merely to respond, while to others discussion might refer only to situations in which students engage in free and open exchanges, perhaps even excluding the teacher.

The most systematic attempt to analyse lesson formats was conducted by Herbert (1967). His method of viewing lesson formats is shown in Fig. 1. Herbert suggested that to decide the type of format used in a lesson three matters need to be settled. First, it has to be determined whether the teacher alone is working on the subject matter, whether the teacher and the students together are working on it, or whether the students alone are involved. Decisions at lower levels of the diagram depend upon which of these three alternatives is applicable. If the teacher works alone on the subject matter, then it must be decided whether verbal or nonverbal materials are used. If there is teacher–student interaction, the pattern of that interchange has to be inspected. If the students alone are working on the subject matter, then the role played by the teacher towards the student must be analysed.

From Herbert's diagram, a lesson can be described in which the teacher alone modifies subject matter using words as either a lecture or a verbal performance. Where the teacher alone modifies subject matter using nonverbal behaviour there is either an exhibit or a demonstration. Note the various ways in which seatwork can take place depending upon whether it is voluntary or assigned, supervised or nonsupervised (private).

Some interesting similarities and differences concerning lesson formats among teachers in the United States, England and Wales, Australia, and New Zealand were reported by Adams (1970). Teachers from all four countries claimed to emphasize communication between teachers and students first, free communication among all members of the classroom second, and exclu-

sive teacher communications least. Australian and United States teachers agreed in ranking undifferentiated whole-class activity first, differentiated activities for groups second, and the same activity for different groups third. However, New Zealand and English and Welsh teachers agreed in placing undifferentiated activities for groups first but disagreed in placing whole-class teaching second and third respectively.

At least two other approaches have been made to the conceptualization of lesson formats. One approach is intuitive using commonsense terms without concern for conceptual overlap. Perkins (1964, 1965), for example, used six categories to classify lesson formats. Perkins' attempt was based on the principle that lessons should be described in terms of student rather than teacher activity. Teachers might be highly active or utterly quiet during a large-group discussion but that would not affect how the lesson was classified. Perkins' categories are as follows:

(a) Large-group discussion: entire class discusses an issue or evaluates an oral report.

(b) Class recitation: teacher questions, student answers—entire class or portion of it participating.

(c) Individual work or project: student works alone on task that is not a common assignment.

(d) Seatwork, reading or writing, common assignment.

(e) Small-group or committee work: student is member of group working on assignment.

(f) Oral reports—individual or group: student reports orally on book, current affairs, or research.

Perkins' investigation of fifth grade (age 10–11) lessons in United States classrooms revealed that most time was spent on seatwork and class recitation with only small amounts of time devoted to individual work, group work, large-group discussion, or oral reports. Flanders (1964) also devised a six category system for classifying activities in the classroom, as follows:

(a) *routine* administration—such as taking roll, distributing or collecting materials, and so forth; (b) *evaluation* of the products of learning—such as discussion of homework, test results, or student reports; (c) introducing *new material*—such as a class discussion of a new formula (or new facts about a country); (d) *general discussion* of old material or current problems; (e) *supervision of seat work*—periods when students were busy doing homework or projects . . .; (f) *teacher–pupil planning*—or class discussions about the organization of work. (p. 211)

Flanders found in the midwest United States seventh- and eighth-grade (age 12–14) classrooms he studied that teachers were more likely to be indirect in their influence

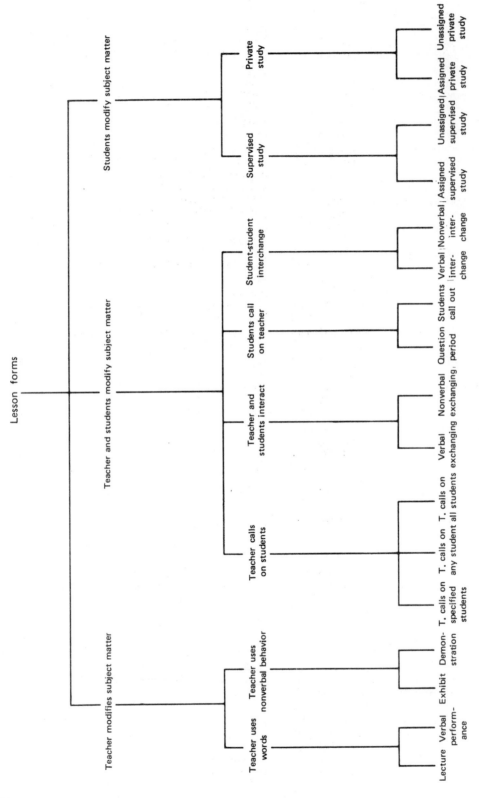

Figure 1
Herbert's scheme for classifying lesson formats[a]

technique during planning, new material, and general discussion formats than during the others.

In Sweden, Lundgren (1972) developed a system designed to apply particularly to the 11th grade (age 16–17) mathematics lessons he was researching. He referred to his concepts as "themes". They included: going through theory; going through type examples; working with exercises; examination and control of homework or written tests; classroom management; and not subject relevant and not relevant to the tasks of the teacher.

Gump (1967) adopted a somewhat different approach in his study of third grade (age 8–9) classrooms in the midwest of the United States. For him, lesson format had at least five independently defined components: lesson concern; teacher leadership pattern; group quality; pupil activity demand; and action sequencing. Lesson concern referred mainly to the subject matter of the lesson. Teacher leadership pattern concerned "the basic persistent pattern of the teacher's relationship to the maintenance of the [format]". Teachers could be participators, watcher–helpers, action directors, recitation leaders, instructors, readers, testers, or not be involved in any of those. Group quality dealt with the subgroup structure of the format and involved distinguishing among activities conducted with the whole class or with subgroups, where members might work privately or interdependently. Pupil activity demand concerned what it was that pupils were expected to do during the format. It included reading, working with own materials, singing, attending to class events, and getting ready. Action sequencing provided categories for judging whether students managed themselves (as in self-pacing), or whether they were managed externally, and whether they engaged in mass performances, took turns, and the like.

Gump found that certain combinations of the above facets occurred more frequently and took up more time than others. The most time-consuming "format" was one in which the teacher was not involved, the students worked with their own materials on a task, at their own pace as members of subgroups but privately. This might be recognized as "isolated seatwork" and took up 21 percent of the time. Other combinations of Gump's facets might be seen to constitute "supervised study" (8 percent), "whole-class recitation" (19 percent), "reading circle" (10 percent), "teacher reading" (4 percent), and "getting ready" (8 percent). He found that lesson formats involving supervised study by students seemed to generate more deviancy control for the teacher; that teachers were more active during whole-class recitation, reading circle, and music formats than during supervised study and isolated seatwork; that student involvement was highest in reading-circle formats, less high during tests, instruction, and whole-class recitation, and lower during supervised study, isolated seatwork, and student presentations. One particularly interesting discovery was that these 9- and 10-year-old students touched themselves much more during formats that might be

described as passive such as teacher reading or instruction, than during such formats as reading circle.

For Adams and Biddle (1970) at any one time the classroom consisted of one or more groups each having a structure and a function. By group structure they meant whether the class was a single communicating group or was fractioned into subgroups and, if so, how many; who the members of those groups were and the kinds of roles members performed in the communicative patterns of the group(s). Members could be disengaged concerning any particular communication. They could be part of a central group attending to a communication, or they could belong to a peripheral group. Group members as well as being audience members, could be emitters or specific targets of messages.

By group function, Adams and Biddle meant variations in the content and mode of classroom communications. Content might be scheduled or nonscheduled subject matter, sociation (instances where the message is about sociability or is itself a social convention, for example "Good morning"), or organization of the classroom. Mode had to do with the level of sophistication of a group's proceedings. It could consist of operation, that is, motor activity such as handwriting, singing, miming, and the like. It could be information dissemination and therefore concern the transmission of facts, dates, definitions, and so on. Or it could be intellectualization involving explanations, inferencing, synthesizing, and other "higher" level processes.

The possible combinations of the categories of structure and function developed by Adams and Biddle could be regarded as a system for describing lesson formats. Their research, which was conducted in the midwest of the United States, was one of the first attempts to use television cameras and recorders in the study of classrooms. After gathering data at first, sixth, and eleventh grades in social studies and mathematics, they found that most lessons were dominated by a central group engaged in teacher lecturing, single pupil responding to the teacher, and teacher questioning or directing a single pupil. However, they also found that lesson formats varied systematically depending upon subject matter, teacher age, and teacher sex.

Apart from a great deal of inconclusive and much criticized research on lecture versus discussion methods, there has been little research on lesson formats. This survey of attempts to analyse and conceptualize lesson attributes indicates some of the characteristics of classrooms that might be considered in planning for teaching. Highly elaborated approaches, such as those by Gump, and Adams and Biddle, offer insights into the complexities of lesson formats that other approaches do not. Those more sophisticated efforts should be particularly useful to teachers who are prepared to learn the technical terms involved.

See also: Activities: Structures and Functions; Teacher Roles; Student Roles

Bibliography

Adams R S (ed.) 1970 Symposium on teacher role in four English-speaking countries. *Comp. Educ. Rev.* 14: 50–59

Adams R S, Biddle B J 1970 *Realities of Teaching: Explorations with Video Tape.* Holt, Rinehart and Winston, New York

Flanders N A 1964 Some relationships among teacher influence, pupil attitudes, and achievement. In: Biddle B J, Ellena W J (eds.) 1964 *Contemporary Research on Teacher Effectiveness.* Holt, Rinehart and Winston, New York

Gump P V 1967 *The Classroom Behavior Setting, Its Nature and Relation to Student Behavior.* Final Report, Project No. 2453, Contract No. OE-4-10-107. Dept. of Health, Education, and Welfare, Office of Education, Washington, DC

Herbert J D 1967 *A System for Analyzing Lessons.* Teachers College Press, New York

Lundgren U P 1972 *Frame Factors and the Teaching Process: A Contribution to Curriculum Theory and Theory on Teaching.* Almqvist and Wiksell, Stockholm

Perkins H V 1964 A procedure for assessing the classroom behavior of students and teachers. *Am. Educ. Res. J.* 1: 249–60

Perkins H V 1965 Classroom behavior and underachievement. *Am. Educ. Res. J.* 2: 1–12

Pacing and Sequencing

G. J. Posner

Pacing and sequencing decisions are two of the most important decisions made at the classroom level. Together they determine to a large extent both the depth and breadth of classroom learning. Pacing refers to the crucial decision of how quickly to move through a series of classroom activities. Sequencing refers to the relationship that should exist between members of the series.

Taken together, both decisions reflect an attempt by the teacher to solve partially the unavoidable coverage/mastery dilemma facing classroom teachers. Teachers have a large body of subject matter to cover. They also want as many students as possible to gain as much from the material as possible. If they attempt to cover too much, they risk the loss of mastery. If they dwell on any particular aspect or take very small instructional steps so that mastery by all students is assured, they run the risk of sacrificing breadth of coverage (see *Mastery Learning Models*).

Much of the recent attention given to pacing and sequencing, and to the terminology itself, and thus one theory guiding much of the research and development in this area derives in part from work originally done on teaching machines and programmed instruction by Pressey in the 1920s, Skinner in the 1950s, and Crowder, Mager, and Gilbert in the 1960s. Teaching machines and then programmed texts involved learners in active response as they moved through successive frames of small steps proceeding from the known to the unknown in a straight-line sequence. The programs were based on the theory that learning is aided by knowledge of progress and by the minimization of errors. The Keller plan (1968) or Personalized System of Instruction (PSI) is analogous to programmed instruction and represents an application of the general theory to the instructional management of a whole course. Two features of the PSI, in particular, are relevant here: (a) the individualized or self-pacing feature, and (b) the organization of the course into small steps in order to minimize error (see *Keller Plan: A Personalized System of Instruction*).

Problems of pacing and sequence, particularly the organization and ordering of educational activities, have also concerned many of the greatest educational practitioners and theorists throughout educational history. The writings of Aristotle, Plato, St. Thomas Aquinas, Alfred North Whitehead, John Dewey, William Kilpatrick, Jerome Bruner, and many others, attest to this fact. Thus, the current attention and the divergent perspectives on pacing and sequencing derives from a rich and varied set of historical antecedents.

1. Pacing

Much of the current interest in pacing can be traced to recent attention given to time as a key factor affecting learning. John Carroll's model of school learning considers time the basic constraint on learning. Degree of learning is determined by the ratio of time actually spent to the time needed (see *The Carroll Model*; *Time*).

Pacing decisions can be considered three dimensionally as described by three questions: Who decides? For whom is the decision made? On what basis is the decision made? The agent of the decision, be that the learner or the teacher, constitutes the first dimension. The object of the decision, be that the individual, subgroups, or the whole class, constitutes the second dimension. The referent used for judging sufficient attainment, be that norm referenced or criterion referenced, constitutes the third dimension. Figure 1 summarizes this analysis.

Who decides the pace has been the subject of much debate in programmed instruction. In the early days of programmed instruction and teaching machines, it was believed that for instruction to be effective the learners themselves must determine the rate at which they proceed. Currently, self-pacing is seen by some as somewhat less mandatory.

The issue of whether pacing decisions should be made for groups or for individuals has not been resolved. Benjamin Bloom's (1976) mastery learning strategies

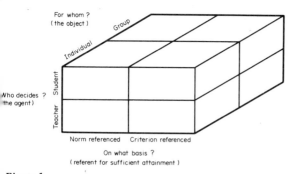

Figure 1
Three dimensions of pacing decisions

attempt to vary the amount of time the individual receives, while allowing the whole class to progress uniformly through the course (see *Mastery Learning Models*). The Keller Plan, as was mentioned above, allows for an individualized pace and, therefore, results in the completion of different numbers of course units by different students.

When considering more typical classrooms, a simpler group-based approach to pacing is found. The teacher moves from one activity to the next when he or she believes that a sufficient number of learners have gained a sufficient grasp of the material. However, what constitutes a "sufficient" number of learners and a "sufficient" grasp of the material is far from obvious. What constitutes mastery has received relatively less attention from researchers than the topic of who the teacher uses as a steering group.

Swedish researchers, particularly Dahllöf (1971) and Lundgren (1972), have found that teachers identify a group of learners, termed the "criterion steering group," to whom the teachers refer when making pacing decisions. When the teacher believes that this group of learners has reached the expected level of performance, the teacher moves on to the next unit, thereby proceeding within the syllabus. Dahllöf and Lundgren found this group of learners to be between the 10th and 25th percentiles in achievement, although the importance and the level of the curriculum unit treated may alter these numbers. It is possible that the steering criterion would be especially low in basic units, in which the teacher expects almost all learners to perform well, but somewhat higher in more advanced units.

The issue in pacing concerned with the referent for acceptable levels of attainment may be viewed as centering on norm- versus criterion-referenced performance. That is, does the teacher use as a standard of achievement the level of attainment reached by other learners (norm referenced) or does the teacher use an absolute standard (criterion referenced)? Norm referencing might pertain to other members of the current class for pacing decisions about individuals within the class. For example, the teacher might decide that whenever a pupil understands an idea as well as the three

brightest pupils in the class, that pupil should move on to the next unit. With regard to whole class, rather than individual pupil-pacing decisions, the teacher might use the performance of pupils from previous years as the basis for a standard.

Criterion-referenced standards are based on a judgment by the teacher of the performance levels necessary for ultimate success. For situations where individuals are prepared to perform defined functions in a predictable situation, the criterion is determined by an analysis of the subsequent situation for which the individual is being trained. Job analyses, for example, generate both the functions (or tasks) for which the individual is being trained and also the necessary standards of performance for success on the job. In a similar manner, when it can be determined that a particular curriculum unit is necessary for successful completion of a subsequent unit, then there is also an objective basis for setting absolute performance standards. In both of these cases, the criterion level can be set in a nonarbitrary manner. However, in situations designed to equip individuals to perform undefined functions in unpredictable situations, criterion levels may risk being more arbitrary, unless the curriculum unit is instrumental for a subsequent unit.

2. Sequencing

It seems natural to think of teaching as a sequence of classroom activities. But in order to describe fully teaching in this way, the description must recognize at least two dimensions of classroom activities and, therefore, two dimensions of activity sequences. Classroom activities can be described in terms of what students and teachers do or in terms of the content of the activities. Descriptions of activity sequence can, therefore, focus on the pattern of interaction between students and teachers (i.e., what they do in the classroom) or on substantive aspects of those interactions. The former is commonly termed "teaching method" or "approach" and the latter the "subject matter," "curriculum," or "content of instruction." A variety of sequencing schemes focusing first on teaching method, then on instructional content will be examined.

Throughout history, educational thinkers have proposed and practiced a wide variety of teaching methods and, therefore, divergent approaches to sequencing educational activities. For example, the Hebrews, the Spartans, and the American Indians practiced the memorization method. The modern-day equivalent of this method might consist of a sequence of three activities (or steps): (a) the student reflects upon the material, (b) the material is repeated by the student until learned, and (c) the content is recited by the student to determine whether any parts of the material require further work. The Socratic method consists of two stages: (a) the "ironic" stage uses teacher questioning to reveal to students their ignorance regarding a concept; and (b) the "maieutic" stage uses a second series of teacher

Table 1
Principles of sequencing activities: focus on instructional content

Principles	Key ideas	Examples
1.0 World related	World-related sequences are those sequences in which there is consistency between the ordering of activities on the one hand, and relationships between phenomena as they exist or occur in the world on the other hand	
1.1 Space	Sequences based on spatial relations are those in which activities can be ordered in accord with the physical arrangement or position of the phenomena of interest. Sequencing principles of this subtype include closest-to-farthest, bottom-to-top, east-to-west, and so on	Teach the parts of a plant from the root, to the stem, to the leaves and flower, or the reverse
1.2 Time	Activities can be ordered in accord with the order of events in time, typically from the earliest to the most recent events	Teach the major ideas of Marx before teaching about the nature of the Russian revolution. Teach the names of the kings of France from the earliest to most recent
1.3 Physical attributes	Activity sequences may be based on physical characteristics of the phenomena of interest such as size, age, shape, number of sides (e.g., in geometry), brightness (e.g., in astronomy), hardness (e.g., in geology), physical complexity (e.g., in comparative anatomy), and countless other characteristics (chemical properties are included)	Teach the names of the continents in size order. Teach the structure of a primitive society before teaching about a complex industrial society
2.0 Concept related	While world-related sequences presumably reflect the organization of the empirical world, concept-related sequences reflect the organization of the conceptual world	
2.1 Class relations	A class concept is a concept which selects or groups a set of things or events as instances of the same kind of thing in that they share common properties. Activities can be organized either by teaching the characteristics of the general class before teaching about the members of the class or vice versa	Teach about mammals before teaching about specific animals in that group. Define "discrimination" before examining racial and sex discrimination. Compare sound and light before teaching the concept of wave motion
2.2 Propositional relations	A proposition is a combination of concepts which asserts something. Sequences of this sort include teaching evidence prior to the proposition which the evidence supports, teaching a theory prior to the facts which the theory explains, or teaching microlaws prior to teaching macrolaw. This sequencing principle focuses on the relation between propositions rather that what one does with propositions (see 3.1, Logic of inquiry)	Teach an overview of the theory of natural selection before studying the adaptation of Darwin's finches (theory instance). Teach in deductive order the steps in a geometric proof. Teach the volume of a gas at several temperatures and pressures before teaching Boyle's law
2.3 Sophistication	Concepts and propositions can differ in their level of precision, conceptual complexity, abstractness, vagueness, range, and level of refinement, etc. The concept of sophistication here is similar to Bruner's "spiral" curriculum which returns periodically to concepts at higher and higher levels of sophistication	Teach the real numbers before teaching about imaginary numbers. Teach what "acceleration" means before teaching it as "v/t." Teach the concept of "stimulus" before the concept of "conditioning"
2.4 Logical prerequisite	A concept or proposition is a logical (i.e., a priori) prerequisite to another concept or proposition when it is logically necessary to understand the first concept or proposition in order to understand the second	Teach what "velocity" means before teaching that "acceleration" is a change in velocity. Teach the concept of set before the concept of number

Table 1—(continued)

Principles	Key ideas	Examples
3.0 Inquiry related	Inquiry-related sequences are those which derive from the nature of the process of generating, discovering, or verifying knowledge. Therefore, such sequences reflect the nature of the logic or methodology of a given area of thought	
3.1 Logic of inquiry	Sequencing principles rooted in logic will reflect views of valid inference. Different logics yield differing sequencing principles; e.g., a view that considers discovery to be a matter of generalizing over numerous instances (i.e., induction) will provide instances of a generalization prior to attempting to have the student discover the generalizations. A view which considers discovery to be a matter of testing bold conjectures will seek to elicit hypotheses and then turn to a process of evidence collection	Explain how Galileo arrived at the hypothesis that the change in velocity per unit of time for a freely falling object is a constant; then have students find that the acceleration of any object allowed to fall freely is 9.8 m/sec., as long as air resistance is not a factor. Discover ways to light a bulb with a battery, then generalize a rule
3.2 Empirics of inquiry	Some features of proper inquiry are rooted in descriptions of how successful scientists actually proceed or in the social or psychological conditions of fruitful inquiry. Suppose, for example, that successful inquirers were found to study a problem area before working on specific problems. This might lead to sequencing activities in such a way that they emphasize the need for a general survey of an area prior to consideration of special problems	Teach what other researchers have discovered about reinforcement schedules before teaching pupils to frame hypotheses about optimal reinforcement schedules. Have students write grant proposals before having them collect data
4.0 Learning related	Learning-related sequences draw primarily on knowledge about the psychology of learning. Most psychologists, although they might disagree about the particular instructional approach to be used, argue that the nature of the subject matter is not as relevant to sequencing activities as are empirical claims about the way people learn	
4.1 Empirical prerequisite	If it can be determined empirically that the learning of one skill facilitates or makes possible the learning of a subsequent skill, the first skill can be termed an empirical prerequisite of the second	Teach discrimination between initial consonants; then teach the use of work attack skills; then teach reading
4.2 Familiarity	Familiarity refers to the frequency with which an individual has encountered an idea, object, or event, i.e., how commonplace it is to the individual	Teach the various occupations in the local community before teaching about careers in other communities and in other nations
4.3 Difficulty	Factors affecting difficulty include (a) how fine a discrimination is required, (b) how fast a procedure must be carried out, and (c) the mental capacity required for learning	Teach long vowel sounds before short ones. Teach weaving slowly, then teach the pupil to speed up. Teach the spelling of short words before longer words. Teach rhymes before blank verse
4.4 Interest	Activities that are intrinsically interesting are commonly those that involve phenomena about which the learner has had some limited experience but remain a challenge, retain the potential for surprise, or can arouse curiosity. Sequences of this subtype begin with those activities which are more likely to evoke pupil interest	Teach pupils how to pick a lock before teaching them how a lock works. Teach pupils to dig out a local cellar before teaching archeology

Table 1—(continued)

Principles	Key ideas	Examples
4.5 Development	The work of Piaget has served as a focus for much of the current dialogue on sequencing. Developmental psychologists such as Piaget contend that an activity is best used when the learner is developmentally "ready" for it	Teach pupils to base their concept of morality on authority, then on democratically accepted law, and finally on individual principles of conscience. Teach mathematics first through concrete objects before dealing in abstractions
4.6 Internalization	If the educational intent of a sequence is to have the student internalize an attitude or value, then activities can be ordered in accord with an increasing degree of internalization	Have students listen to Christian ideas, then have them interpret events in terms of a Christian ideology, then show them the implications of a world view based on a Christian value system. Have students recognize certain behaviors in others, then in themselves
5.0 Utilization related	The subject matter taught in classrooms is ultimately utilized in three possible contexts: social, personal, and career. Within each of these three utilization contexts activities can be sequenced (a) in a way that reflects procedures for solving problems or fulfilling responsibilities, or (b) according to the utilization potential for the content of the activity	
5.1 Procedure	When each activity in a training program represents a step in a procedure or process, it is often appropriate for the sequence to reflect the order in which the steps will be followed when carrying out the procedure. Sometimes, however, one may start with the completion of the procedure, and work backwards, always completing the task at each stage	Analyze the effects of air and water pollution (i.e., establish a phenomenon as a "problem"), then analyze the causes and then decide how to eliminate or correct the factors that cause pollution (i.e., suggest solutions)
5.2 Anticipated frequency of utilization	Often we teach the most important things first and by "most important" we mean that which the student is likely to encounter most often	Teach the use of means and standard deviations before analysis of variations. Teach compound interest before stock transactions
6.0 Implementation related	Many decisions regarding the sequencing of activities are based on factors related to the implementation of programs in specific situations. Such contextual factors which Dahllöf terms "frame factors," include the materials and facilities available, availability of funds, time schedules, weather and climate, location of the school, transportation needs, and teachers' and students' background, interest, and competencies. Implementation-related principles are dependent not on relationships among the activities but on relationships between the activities and the administrative, physical, personal, societal, and time frames of teaching	
6.1 Temporal frame factors	The duration and distribution of time are two of the most powerful influences on the nature and success of the educational process. Time of day and season of year also significantly affect the scheduling of classroom activities	Observe migratory patterns of birds in autumn, animal tracks in winter, and nest building in spring. Schedule outdoor activities during times of day and seasons of year that permit them. The availability of flexible scheduling leads to the provision for science laboratory periods
6.2 Physical frame factors	Geographical location, characteristics of the school site, climate, amount and type of instructional space and facilities all affect the sequencing of classroom activities	Practice time is added to the sequence of music activities after a classroom is converted into a set of practice rooms. Science activities are provided when the science room is available

Table 1—(continued)

Principles	Key ideas	Examples
6.3 Organizational frame factors	Class size, school size, departmentalization, as well as more remote factors such as the overall configuration of educational levels all have some affect on activity sequence	Activities are grouped by subject matter when teaching is departmentalized. Activities requiring movement around the classroom become de-emphasized as the class size increases
6.4 Personal frame factors	Characteristics of the teaching staff and the student body are two important influences on activity sequence. What students already know, their background, their learning style, and their capabilities must be taken into account by the teacher. Similarly the teachers' competencies, teaching style, and background mediate any educational intervention	Discuss with children their views about the Earth as a cosmic body, then use demonstration and homework to provide counter evidence for their views and evidence for a more sophisticated view. Give students subtraction exercises, then analyze their work, identifying systematic errors, then give some individual instruction on just those procedural errors, then give more exercises, and so on

questions to guide the students to discover for themselves a concept.

The Jesuit approach known as "prelection" begins with (a) the teacher reading a passage he or she has chosen. The teacher then (b) reads it again at a slow enough speed for the students to transcribe notes, (c) explains the meaning of the passage, (d) analyzes it word by word, (e) correlates it with other related disciplines, (f) assigns students to memorize it, (g) assigns monitors to check the correct repetition of the passage from each student, (h) leads a discussion of the passage's interpretation, and (i) offers prizes and rewards to the best students.

The Herbartian approach provides for five activities: (a) preparation, in which the teacher arouses the students' interest and prepares them for understanding of the new material; (b) presentation, in which the teacher presents the material in a concrete manner using examples, illustrations, and so on; (c) association or comparison, in which the teacher helps students compare and contrast the new material with the old ideas students have; (d) generalization, in which the teacher derives general principles abstracted from the previous concrete experiences; and (e) application, in which the teacher assigns the students to do something that uses or applies the general principle.

Kilpatrick's project method entails four activities carried out by students themselves: (a) setting a purpose for a project, (b) planning the project, (c) executing the project, and (d) judging the success of the project (see *The Project Method*).

Other approaches could be mentioned but the approaches outlined above sufficiently illustrate the range of approaches to sequencing educational activities that have been practiced over the span of human civilization.

These approaches focus on what teachers and students do. On the other hand, it might be desirable to describe sequences of activities on the basis of the activities' content. In such a case, one could construct a set of categories for all content sequencing principles. Table 1 presents a categorization scheme consisting of sequencing types and subtypes. The major epistemological distinction on which the scheme was constructed is the distinction between the world and the language and concepts used to think or talk about the world, that is, between the empirical and the conceptual. It should be noted that the scheme is presumed to be comprehensive for the major types but not for the subtypes. Furthermore, the types and subtypes, although conceptually distinct, are rarely found in practice in their "pure" form. For example, it is unlikely to find any whole course that is a "pure" world-related type, much less a pure example of a world-related subtype (e.g., "space"). However, it is not unreasonable to find particular sequences that emphasize a particular type or even subtype.

These categories of sequencing principles are intended as a comprehensive overview of the topic and should help the reader to sort out competing claims in the educational literature regarding activity sequence. For example, some argue that activities should be sequenced psychologically rather than logically. The problem with claims of this sort is their ambiguity and vagueness. The category scheme suggests that there are several different principles that could reasonably count as psychological or logical. The scheme thus serves as a set of rather precise concepts for thinking about and discussing activity sequence when focusing on instructional content. The scheme also provides the planner with a set of alternatives to increase the range of choices available in sequencing decisions. For example, perhaps the planner has only considered organizing the teaching of history chronologically and never conceptually. One caution is important in this regard. Decisions about sequence cannot be made in isolation. They must be based on aims. For example, if it is decided to organize history content conceptually (around such concepts as nationalism, urbanization, and revolution), a decreased appreciation for the temporal flow of events is being risked so that the students' understanding of historical trends and themes may be increased. Since the way teaching is organized communicates a particular substantive emphasis, sequencing decisions almost always involve a trade off. Thus, the category scheme is not simply intended as a shopping list for selecting sequencing principles. Sequencing principles, like most other considerations about teaching, must be consistent with educational aims.

See also: Planning; Frame Factors

Bibliography

Bloom B S 1976 *Human Characteristics and School Learning.* McGraw-Hill, New York
Colman J E 1967 *The Master Teachers and the Art of Teaching.* Pitman, New York
Dahllöf U S 1971 *Ability Grouping, Content Validity, and Curriculum Process Analysis.* Teachers College Press, New York
Hartley J, Davies I K (eds.) 1978 *Contributions to an Educational Technology*, Vol. 2. Kogan Page, London
Lundgren U P 1972 *Frame Factors and the Teaching Process: A Contribution to Curriculum Theory and Theory on Teaching.* Almqvist and Wiksell, Stockholm
Lundgren U P 1981 *Model Analyses of Educational Processes*, 2nd edn. Stockholm Institute of Education, Department of Educational Research, Stockholm
Posner G J, Rudnitsky A N 1986 *Course Design: A Guide to Curriculum Development for Teachers*, 3rd edn. Longman, New York

Homework

F. Coulter

There are few issues in education which are as controversial as homework. Its advocates claim that it encourages student initiative, develops independent learning skills, and allows time for practice and application of what has been learned in school. Its critics argue that it encroaches upon children's leisure time and denies them access to community activities. They also see homework as a powerful instrument of class discrimination in the sense that children from lower income groups often do not have conditions appropriate for home study and must compete on unequal terms with their middle-class peers.

Although there is little consensus about the value of homework there is general agreement about its nature and purpose. It is generally regarded as school work formally assigned for completion outside school time. It is seen as embracing a number of activities including revision and preparation for future class work, extended research and project work, and private study. Because it also serves to help teachers cope with pupils' different work rates, finishing off class work represents one of the most important categories of homework. It is thus the slower students who are often left to work independently on tasks not fully understood or completed in class. The range of activities which might comprise homework is often not fully acknowledged. This is because it is generally perceived as sedentary "home" work rather than as independent learning which may involve a great variety of activities either in the home or in the wider community.

1. Homework as a Neglected Area of Research

Although there have been ample statements of opinion and numerous reports of practices, there have been surprisingly few well-designed studies that provide substantial evidence of the kind or amount of homework which should be assigned. Major reviews of homework research over the past 50 years have noted a dearth of experimental research and a lack of firm and comprehensive evidence on the various facets of homework. Rosenshine (1971) noted that there had been no study of teachers' or pupils' actual classroom behaviour related to homework. Rosenshine's comment has not quickened much research interest; fewer than 30 theses or reports of research on school homework have appeared since then and only one has involved any direct observation of classroom activities related to homework. Significantly also, homework remains largely unmentioned in the writings of time-on-task researchers even though it represents an increasingly significant aspect of school time as students grow older. Although teachers and pupils place heavy reliance on homework, especially in secondary school, researchers remain more concerned with teacher and pupil behaviour as it relates to school-based learning. To assume that it is the classroom where all the action is may be quite inappropriate. Crowded curricula, cumulative assessment, competitive examinations, and independent assignment or project-based learning cause an overflow of work from school time into out-of-school time. Indeed, the fact that much formal (and informal) learning occurs outside the classroom may help to explain why demonstrated relationships between teaching behaviours and pupil achievement have been so persistently weak. The virtual exclusion of out-of-school learning from teaching–learning models employed by researchers suggests that an insufficient range of teaching and learning activities relevant to achievement have been considered.

In view of the significance of homework in the lives of pupils, their parents, and their teachers, the lack of research evidence is surprising. Although in-school and out-of-school learning are intimately related they have been researched in isolation of each other, with in-school learning receiving most of the attention. This illustrates the manner in which boundaries can be drawn arbitrarily between research areas according to the interests and expertise of different groups of investigators.

Apart from studies which have surveyed attitudes of parents, teachers, and pupils toward homework, the research falls into three broad categories. The first includes those studies which have investigated the persistent and popular question of the effect of homework on school achievement. Studies in the second category have examined how homework is best structured and sequenced, while those in the last group have investigated the efficacy of different feedback and grading strategies.

2. Homework and School Achievement

Research into the relationship between homework and school achievement was stimulated by the homework debate in the United States during the 1930s. Because this early research was conducted in a climate of controversy, its guiding hypotheses tended to define the issue somewhat crudely as one in which homework, whatever its nature, did or did not affect school achievement. Both the findings and the quality of these early American studies varied and are discussed in detail in such reviews as Goldstein (1960). On the whole, the data supported the view that regularly assigned homework enhanced school achievement. However, the researchers and school administrators who interpreted the research argued that it offered little support for the retention of homework. Together with considerations relating to the problems experienced by children of low-income families, this interpretation of the research contributed to a shift in the United States toward less homework and more school-based study.

A major weakness of these early studies was that homework was usually seen in quantitative rather than qualitative terms. It was considered as a treatment which, regardless of its quality or the conditions under which it was carried out, would affect school learning. Little concern or interest was shown by researchers in the kind of homework set or in the manner in which it was structured or followed up. More recent research was focused on the kind of homework involved and has offered clearer support for the view that there is a relationship between school achievement and certain kinds of regularly assigned homework. Most studies have focused on mathematics and have generally reported significant achievement differences in favour of homework groups over no-homework groups, although relationships have generally been stronger and more consistent for high achievers. The weaker relationships between mathematics achievement and homework for low achievers may arise from the fact that many of

the homework assignments involved have been revision exercises to consolidate work covered in class. It is possible that lower achievers did not understand the concepts introduced in class and the homework represented a task far more difficult than revision and drill. This tendency for higher ability students to profit more from homework was reported by Ten Brinke (1967). In a study of upper-elementary mathematics students randomly assigned to either a homework or supervised study treatment, there was some evidence that higher ability students achieved better under the homework condition than in supervised study, and that lower ability students profited more from supervised study than from homework. Certainly many teachers consider that it is only the middle and high achieving groups who can profit from homework. Coulter (1981) reported that low achieving groups in secondary school were set little or no homework because teachers believed that they did not possess the skills or motivation to work independently, and that they could cover their less demanding curriculum during the school day. This attitude toward low achievers contrasted sharply with the expectations of parents who considered that low achievers were the very children who needed additional time-on-task, and that by failing to recognize this, and by assigning homework only to high achievers, teachers widened the difference between high and low achievers.

The largest scale investigations of relationships between homework time and school achievement have been those of the International Association for the Evaluation of Educational Achievement (IEA), which include homework time as one variable. These studies treat homework in quantitative terms and have not considered its nature or the context of its introduction or follow-up. However, time was one of many factors studied in comparisons between the educational achievement of children in more than 20 countries, in seven subject areas, across a number of different age levels. Taken as a whole the IEA studies have indicated positive relationships between time spent on homework and school achievement in certain subjects, the strongest relationships being for mathematics and science. In the case of mathematics (Husén 1967), the relationship between time spent on homework and achievement was strong in some countries (England, Scotland, Australia, and Belgium) for junior secondary- school students, but weak at the terminal secondary level. In other countries it was stronger for lower than for higher mental processes, especially for younger children. The nature of the relationships between homework time and achievement for mathematics were therefore complex, varying between different countries, pupil age groups, and the kind of task involved. In the case of science (Comber and Keeves 1973) the studies of children in 19 countries also revealed complex relationships. Homework was associated with between-school differences in science achievement in 8 of the 14 countries involved at the 14-year-old level. However, at the terminal secondary level the relationships were inconsistent and weak.

When the student rather than the school was used as the unit of analysis at the 14-year-old level there were positive simple correlations between total time on science homework and science achievement in the majority of countries, although they weakened in multiple regression analyses. At the terminal secondary level, however, the dominant variable in accounting for different levels of science achievement in all but one country was a composite of time given to science study and science homework. This underscores the importance of defining homework as one aspect of overall curriculum time.

The equivocal nature of many of the IEA findings arises partly from the methods of analysis. First, the analyses assumed a linear relationship between time and school achievement. It is likely that the relationships are in fact curvilinear with some ability groups profiting more than others from additional time on certain tasks. Second, the dependent variable was overall school achievement in the different subject areas. The effects of homework on the specific aspects of the subject area for which homework was assigned is difficult to assess. Finally, the analyses did not control for pupil ability. The effects of homework time might be more clearly demonstrated if children of similar ability were compared in terms of the amount of homework time and level of achievement at tasks related to the homework. Such controlled analyses would overcome the problem that slower students may devote more time but still achieve at lower levels than their higher achieving peers who may need to commit less time to master a similar task.

Few researchers are still interested in testing a global homework versus no homework hypothesis. Interest has turned to the relationships between certain kinds of homework and the school achievement of particular kinds of students. Aptitude–treatment interaction studies of this kind promise more useful insights than did those which persisted for so long with the question of whether much, some, or no homework affected school achievement. Common sense suggests that some students will profit from additional time on certain tasks. The real questions relate to which students, which tasks, which sequences, and which structures. A handful of studies in the following section have addressed themselves to the latter question of how homework may be most appropriately structured and sequenced.

3. The Introduction and Structuring of Homework

The majority of studies in this section have considered the manner in which homework may be best organized to introduce students to new work, or to review work already covered in class. Most of these have been comparatively recent, short duration, experimental studies in which achievement differences between control and experimental groups have been attributed to particular homework structures. All have been in the area of mathematics. Typical are studies which have investigated the effects of "massing" homework problems pertaining to a particular topic as distinct from distributing the identical problems over several assignments. These studies have reported differences in initial learning and retention which favoured the experimental or "distributed" groups, especially for middle- and low-ability students.

Several studies have also examined the effects of exploratory mathematics homework exercises. Achievement differences in junior-high-school mathematics have favoured students who had exploratory home exercises before the class teaching of the topic and review exercises after instruction. The "exploratory" groups out-performed control groups which followed a traditional programme of homework both on textbook chapter tests and longer term retention tests. These findings are consistent with research which has reported gains in mathematics achievement through the use of "semi-oblique" organizational patterns in which students began exploring the next topic before completing the previous one.

This small group of studies relating to the distributive patterns of homework indicates that achievement may be enhanced by:

(a) revision exercises that are spaced over time, particularly in the case of low-ability students who may be less able to meet the shorter and more intensive demands of massed review exercises; and

(b) exercises of an exploratory nature that provide an intuitive base for new class work.

It is clear that the structure and content of homework assignments should be varied according to pupil ability. This need for individualizing homework is highlighted by the findings of a Belgian study by Hotyat (1968) who reported enormous variation in the time which different children spent on the same homework task. In that survey of 2,000 students from age 12 to the last year of teacher training, the maximum time taken over homework assignments was considerably more than twice that of the minimum time at all grade levels. In a study of nearly 1,000 students in Nottingham schools (UK) Cole and Lunzer (1978) also reported huge time variations. Students took anything from 15 to 90 minutes to write a short composition, from 10 to 45 minutes to complete a volume calculation and from 10 to 30 minutes to draw a simple diagram in science. These findings discredit the popular assumption that homework assignments are blanket rather than individualized tasks. Much more work needs to be done to determine how content is best structured and sequenced for students of widely differing capacities for independent study. A useful starting point might be for teachers to make a clearer definition between general ability in a subject area on the one hand, and ability to study independently, on the other. Having drawn such a distinction a more careful analysis might be made of the extent and nature of independent study skills demanded by various homework tasks. Only one homework study has attempted to relate school achievement to an estimate of students' independent study skills, and even in that case it was only a crude estimate derived from students' own perceptions of their capacity for independent study.

Although this group of studies points to the importance of the teacher's role in structuring and sequencing homework assignments there is scarcely any evidence of attempts to observe directly the manner in which they go about this task. Little information is available about the time that teachers devote to explaining the objectives of homework, the nature of their follow-up, or the manner in which homework is related to further class work. What teachers actually say or do to prepare their students for home study has rarely been reported. Perhaps more importantly, there is little evidence of direct observation, whether from diary records, interviews, or home visits, of the kind of support structures that parents, neighbours, and older siblings provide. In one of the few studies in this category Coulter (1981) reported that there was great variation in teachers' homework-related behaviour and that this variation was reflected in pupils' participation rates. Where teachers planned and introduced homework as an integral part of the lesson or series of lessons, spent time structuring and explaining the exercises, and ultimately followed them through and used them as a basis for diagnosis or assessment, student participation rates tended to be higher. In that study teachers' homework-related behaviour was a more significant predictor of homework participation than was students' social class background.

4. Studies of Different Homework Grading and Feedback Strategies

Studies in this third area relate to feedback research generally and have been largely experimental. Achievement differences between control and experimental groups have been attributed to various experimental grading and feedback treatments. Illustrative of this

research is a study by Austin and Austin (1974), who assigned students from two junior-high-school mathematics classes to two treatments in which they either received grades on every homework problem or on a random half of the problems. After seven weeks they found no achievement differences between the two groups. In a later study Austin (1976) extended this by randomly assigning pupils from nine high-school mathematics classes to two treatment groups in which their homework was either corrected and graded without comment, or in which it was given a grade plus written corrective information, praise, or encouragement. In only two of the nine classes involved did the "comment" group score significantly higher on teacher-constructed tests. Other research has reported no difference in the maths achievement of students whose homework was collected and graded four times weekly, and those who received only spot checks and daily quizzes. Before accepting the proposition which is implicit in the above findings, that correction, praise, and other feedback have no consequence for achievement, several questions should be asked about the research. The first relates to the difficulty of assessing the quality of the comments and their impact on particular students. The assumption is that all comments within a broad category are equal. This is inappropriate because various students may perceive the same comment differently, depending on their attitudes toward the subject, toward the teacher or toward themselves. Moreover, the absence of any comment may convey to some students a far stronger nonverbal message than any perceived by a "comment" group. A further problem is that the nonsignificant differences reported in these studies may have been artefacts of achievement tests that were not logically related to the feedback and grading strategies. For example, in Austin's (1976) study, the effect of feedback was related to regular teacher-constructed examinations of the work concerned in class and at home over the six-week period of the study. Homework averages were not included. It

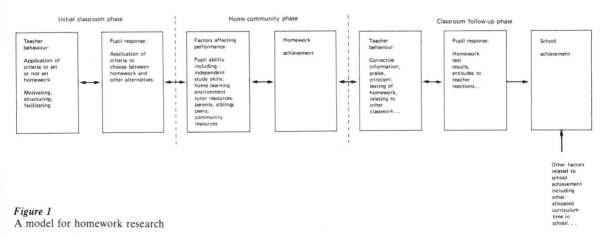

Figure 1
A model for homework research

may have been more appropriate to have related homework feedback strategies to homework achievement and to certain aspects of pupils' affective responses to the teachers' comments and to the homework assignments concerned. This tendency for homework strategies to be related to general school achievement rather than to homework achievement is difficult to understand. Where the teachers' homework strategy relates to specific structuring and feedback approaches, it would seem more appropriate to compare treatment groups on homework performance. The long-term interest could still be in summative evaluation as referenced by school performance over a longer period of time; but in the shorter term, which is only a matter of weeks in the majority of these experimental studies, the relationships might better be investigated as part of a formative process that might ultimately affect more general achievement.

5. A Model for Homework Research

Much of the preceding discussion implies that the model within which homework research has proceeded is incomplete. Many of the teaching behaviours relating to the introduction and structuring of homework remain unconsidered. Similarly, little attention has been given to students' responses to the expectations which teachers set for homework. For example, little is known of the student's decision-making process regarding homework, including the criteria which are applied in choosing between homework and various other alternatives which occupy leisure time. Also, home learning conditions have been narrowly defined within the concept of social class. These various facets of homework are articulated within Fig. 1 which summarizes the discussion and represents a more parsimonious model which might provide some guidelines for further research.

Like all models it is propositional rather than descriptive of what is known actually to be the case. Moreover, although homework performance is seen as being affected by a far wider range of factors than have hitherto been considered, the variables listed in the model do not exhaust the possibilities. They are merely examples of the behaviours and conditions which might apply in various phases of homework activity. For example, the motivating, structuring, and facilitating teacher behaviours in the initial classroom phase are only suggestive of the general categories of behaviour which might be considered. The model locates the pupil in a position of primacy in the sense that he or she is seen as making a deliberate choice between homework and other alternatives which out-of-school time may present. It recognizes that this choice may be influenced by such factors as the student's perceptions of the resources available in terms of home environment, tutors, or personal ability. However, it also allows for the possibility that a decision not to participate in homework may be reached without reference to such factors, but simply by an assessment of the importance of the task

against other personal priorities. In some cases, therefore, home environment may only become relevant when and if the student decides to acquiesce. This proposition is contrary to the traditional social class view that the child is passive and that homework participation and achievement is determined primarily by such factors as home environment and parental attitudes. It allows for the fact that some children at all social class levels reject various aspects of the school curriculum and exercise choices about the use of leisure time. The student's responses are also seen as interacting with and affecting the teacher's behaviour, as there is some evidence that students negotiate with teachers on the nature and extent of homework assignments. In the classroom follow-up phase the model also suggests a wider range of teacher behaviours such as testing, reacting, and relating homework to other classroom activities. These teacher behaviours are seen as being influenced to some extent by pupils' responses, as students negotiate homework grades and presumably influence other follow-up behaviours. A final observation about the model is that it distinguishes between two different outcomes which are homework achievement and more general school achievement. Homework achievement is seen as being one of a large number of factors which may relate to school achievement.

6. Conclusion

The significance of homework as a factor in school learning has been obscured by two things. The first is emotional argument which has tended to embed homework in a cluster of educational practices widely regarded as contrary to the best educational and social interests of children. Such arguments derive strength from the fact that homework often is a dull, repetitive, sedentary task which makes excessive demands on pupils' time, and fails to establish its relevance to the in-school programme. The second thing which has obscured the significance of homework for school learning is the research itself. Although on balance the findings support the view that homework contributes to school achievement, the designs have often inhibited any likelihood of demonstrating such a relationship. There is a need to disentangle the homework issue from emotional argument and to see it in its true perspective; as an aspect of overall time-on-task which, by the end of secondary school, apparently contributes as much to achievement in some subjects as the time allocated during regular school hours.

See also: Time

Bibliography

Austin J D 1976 Do comments on mathematics homework affect student achievement? *Sch. Sci. Maths.* 76: 159–64

Austin J D, Austin K A 1974 Homework grading procedures in junior high mathematics classes. *Sch. Sci. Maths.* 74: 269–72

Cole J, Lunzer E A 1978 *Reading for Homework*. University of Nottingham, Nottingham

Comber L C, Keeves J P 1973 *Science Education in Nineteen Countries: An Empirical Study*. Wiley, New York

Coulter F 1981 *Secondary School Homework*, Cooperative Research Series No. 7. Education Department of Western Australia, Perth

Goldstein A 1960 Does homework help? A review of research. *Elem. Sch. J.* 60: 212–24

Hotyat F 1968 Homework at secondary school level: A Belgian study. *Educ. Res.* 10: 154–55

Husén T (ed.) 1967 *International Study of Achievement in Mathematics: Comparison of Twelve Countries*. Wiley, New York

Rosenshine B 1971 *Teaching Behaviours and Student Achievement*. National Foundation for Educational Research, Slough

Ten Brinke D P 1967 Homework: An experimental evaluation of the effect of achievement in mathematics in grades seven and eight (Doctoral dissertation, University of Nebraska) (University Microfilms No. 71–19,521)

Thinking Aloud

A. Bonboir

The technique of thinking aloud permits an observer to follow, step by step, the unfolding of a subject's thought while the latter is engaged in certain learning activities and working under normal conditions.

Subjects are invited to say aloud everything that crosses their minds while they are reacting to situations which are suggested to them, or while they are acting upon existing situations and questioning themselves about them.

Teaching situations may consist of problems to be solved, tasks to be carried out, or the discovery of new problems. They may require already-acquired material or skills to be made use of, or the construction of new knowledge and skills, or the achievement of an understanding leading to the reorganization of the basic situations.

The observer of a subject's intellectual progress may be a practising teacher; or an observer of the process of teaching, anxious to know individual subjects in order to shape and guide them more efficiently; or a researcher who wants to know and understand the processes of thought common to, or most frequent among, a defined population engaged in specific learning tasks.

1. Origin and Evolution of the Method

Envisaged as a necessary complement to the method of objective tests, this technique originates from the conviction that, in order to assist the learning subject, it is often more important to grasp the structure of a line of reasoning or behaviour than to measure its results.

The origin and development of this technique explain why it has been used especially in research. Practising teachers realized its usefulness in the late 1960s when emphasis was laid on the importance of formative evaluation for continuous adjustments in the dynamic learning process.

In the United States, Winch (1914), Courtis (1916), Monroe (1918), Buswell and Lenore (1926), and Burger (1932) suggested general means of making use of this technique, which would make it possible to diagnose pupils' difficulties in various areas of arithmetic (Buyse 1935). Numerous research projects carried out by Buyse and his collaborators at the University of Louvain in Belgium, and many other studies later derived from the experimental tradition of teaching, made use of it when studying the learning of various subjects.

The label "thinking aloud" (or *réflexion parlée*) seems to have been coined by Claparède (1917). Studying adult thought processes, he saw this method as a way of reducing the inconveniences of introspection (in which one thinks, and observes one's self-thinking, at the same time) and the inconveniences of retrospection (which presupposes that one can retrace the steps of reasoning which one has followed) (Claparède 1934).

The technique of directly recording thinking aloud is close to the clinical method invented by Piaget and applied to children, yet is clearly distinct from it. Piaget's method (Piaget 1935, Johannot 1947) consists of setting subjects problems, leaving them alone for a short time to seek out solutions and then trying (irrespective of the result obtained) to follow the paths and the detours their thoughts have taken, and the obstacles they have met. This method has to take into account children's inability to reflect upon their own thoughts. It is, however, still noticeable that the child is liable to invent afterwards an artificial path, taking the point arrived at for the point of departure (Piaget 1935), and that this is hard to avoid.

It is clear that if the subject—child, adolescent, or adult—is asked to verbalize what comes into the mind during the development of reasoning, this procedure may avoid such an obstacle. But there are still other difficulties which make it impossible to isolate and study the complete process: hesitations and silences are difficult to interpret.

2. Precision in Methodology

The subject being observed in the process of thinking is considered as an active researcher, capable of imposing a direction on his or her other actions and of continuously adjusting them, capable also of anticipation, control, and correction.

Thinking aloud is the expression of the dynamic exchanges between the knowing subject and the object of knowledge, between the subject and the task. It describes a subject's way of learning or progressing in a discipline. For the subject it is a method of learning. For the observer it is a technique of investigation or of continuous formative evaluation of the interaction between the teacher and learners in the dialogue which the process of learning to teach presupposes. Learning can be monitored by an observer–teacher, who by a skillful interplay of questions and answers, suggestions and counter-suggestions, leads the learner–discoverer to construct his or her knowledge (Denis-Prinzhorn and Grize 1966). Thinking aloud thus appears as a dialogue between the observer and the subject observed, a Socratic dialogue, a truly maieutic method.

In this, the technique recalls Piaget's method in its critical aspect, which demands the systematic application of doubt to everything the subject affirms (Vandenplas-Holper 1979).

The subject's thinking aloud is immediately recorded, in order that it may then be methodically analysed in both form and content, in the organization and structure of its development.

3. Use Made of the Technique in Research and in Practice

The study of the recorded process is firstly descriptive; secondly, it acquires a diagnostic value.

Although it is essentially individual, it can furnish information of value for statistical study, when cases are studied in large numbers. This information concerns difficulties which may explain certain errors occurring in subjects who have failed to complete the proposed task, for whom a corrective treatment can then be worked out and experimentally applied. It also concerns the particularly successful processes which have brought about the completion of the task. These must be made easier by a teaching which takes care to foresee errors and to establish efficacious methods of procedure (Bonboir 1970a, 1970b).

The technique of thinking aloud is of immediate service to teaching because it has in view the optimum exploitation of the processes of learning either directly in practice or by way of applied research which employs it. This is what differentiates it from Piaget's method. In the latter, clinical interrogation has taken an increasingly heuristic and experimental turn. It involves the verification of hypotheses deduced from theoretical logicomathematical models, and the conjunction of an observing action and a deducing action brings about the elaboration of descriptive and explanatory models of intellectual development. These are fundamental researches into the spontaneous processes of subjects who are confronted with situations meaningful in terms of their educational backgrounds.

Thinking aloud is the study for the purpose of applying the results in practical teaching, of purposive processes which are intentionally directed towards certain objectives in the cognitive domain.

Bibliography

Bonboir A 1970a *La Pédagogie corrective*. PUF, Paris
Bonboir A 1970b *L'Observation rationnelle des écoliers*. Vander, Louvain
Buyse R 1935 *L'Expérimentation en pédagogie*. Lamertin, Bruxelles
Claparède E 1917 La psychologie de l'intelligence. *Scientia* 22: 353–68
Claparède E 1934 La genèse de l'hypothèse: Etude expérimentale. *Archives de Psychologie Genève* 24: 1–155
Denis-Prinzhorn M, Grize J B 1966 La méthode clinique en pédagogie. In: Bresson F, de Montmoulin M (eds.) 1966 *Psychologie et Épistémologie génétiques: Thèmes Piagétiens*. Dunod, Paris, pp. 319–25
Johannot L 1947 *Le Raisonnement Mathématique de l'Adolescent*. Delachaux et Niestlé, Neuchâtel
Piaget J 1935 *Le Jugement et le raisonnement chez l'enfant*. Delachaux et Niestlé, Neuchâtel
Vandenplas-Holper C 1979 *Vers une Pédagogie des processus de socialisation*. Ministère Education Nationale, Direction des études, Bruxelles, pp. 77–110

Written Instruction

F. Richaudeau

The first section of this article devoted to the writing of educational texts, moves from the word to the sentence and then to the way in which sentences are linked together. The second section, devoted to typography, moves from the letter to the word and then to the make-up of the text. A reductionist approach to the process of reading is adopted for ease of presentation.

1. The Writing of the Text

1.1 The Words of the Text and Readability Formulas

Communication theorists tell us that for a message expressed by a "transmitter" to be effectively received and recorded by a "receiver", the transmitter and the receiver must use the same "code". This is the same as saying simply that they must use the same words and the same syntactic structures and that the author of a text must use words and choose the grammatical constructions with which the reader is already familiar. However, the situation becomes more complex in the case of teaching materials and especially in that of school textbooks. Indeed, one of the aims of these textbooks is precisely to introduce new concepts to the pupils who read them, very often words or grammatical structures previously unknown to them. Therefore a distinction must be made in the vocabulary of textbooks between words which the pupil should already know and which are used as tools in order to transmit new concepts to him or her, and words which are new to the pupil and which it is intended that he or she should learn.

The basic vocabulary of a pupil will vary with age, cultural background, and ethnic group. It may happen that basic vocabulary is minimal so that the language of the classroom is different from that used at home. The language of the classroom will then function as a second language. It is, therefore, hardly rational and of little use to supply, for example, the same history book to the pupils of a school integrated in a scientific community and to those of a school attended by the children of immigrant workers. Readability formulas generally take account of the influence of the choice of words on the readability of a text. They do so in any of the following ways:

(a) By measuring the length of words (expressed in syllables), the readability of words being inversely proportional to their length [this is, for example, the technique adopted in Flesch's (1951) formula];

(b) by having recourse to the proportion of words presented in a standard list of everyday words [for example in the formulas of Henry (1975)];

(c) or by taking into account the "pregnancy" of the words used: their "personal" (Flesch 1951) or "concrete" (Coleman and Miller 1968) nature.

In addition there are numerous basic vocabularies drawn up by educationalists or psychologists which indicate, for each age-group, the words generally known and used by young pupils.

Very simply, two procedures may enable the young reader to learn the meaning of new words.

(a) The words may be inserted directly in the text to be read, but presented in sentences which give good examples of their use, whilst at the same time explaining them in terms of situations known to the pupils.

(b) Pupils can be asked to learn the meaning of these words first, by more rigid methods: for example, by comparison with synonyms, inclusion in categories of other words, or use of the dictionary.

Experience shows that the first method proves to be the more effective (Gipe 1978, Kameenui et al. 1982).

Using the first method, it is in the course of writing the teaching text that the author should explain the meaning of new words used. This conforms to the principles which follow and which show the importance of meaning at all stages of the comprehension and memorization of linguistic information.

1.2 Sentences and Text

Just as short and everyday words are on average perceived better—and memorized better—than long and unusual words, so short sentences with a simple and known structure are generally memorized better than long sentences with a complex structure. The lower the educational level of the person concerned—for example, the younger he or she is—the shorter and simpler the sentences must be. One feels this intuitively and psycholinguistic research confirms it, but, as shall be seen, with certain qualifying conditions. The readability formulas described above all take into account the length of sentences, the readability of the texts tested being inversely proportional to the length of the sentences, expressed in words. Although statistically their scores generally prove to be accurate, it is nevertheless appropriate to refine and extend this criterion. Imagine, for example, a text consisting of a series of sentences composed of three syntagmas and with an identical structure: the subject followed by the verb, then by the complement with its adjective; all these words would be in everyday use. The text would receive a maximum readability score and yet its monotony and the conciseness of its sentences would make it unreadable in real terms by the end of a few lines.

Psycholinguistics experiments highlight certain other factors which combine to make sentences more comprehensible and easier to memorize. In simple terms they point to two parameters: meaning and visualization. Without having the thread of meaning to follow, the short-term memory of a child, like that of an adult, cannot retain a group of more than five to seven words (Miller 1956); whereas it can retain three to four times as many if they are linked by threads of meaning: syntactic thread according to the laws of syntax and semantic thread according to the meaning of the message. The reason why the cloze test scores can be considered a criterion gauge of the readability of texts is precisely because the principle on which it is based (in a text in which one word in five has been deleted and the proportion of words restored by a reader is calculated) covers both meaning and readability. Indeed, if the cloze test were applied to a random list of words the score would be nil. It has been shown (Dunn-Rankin 1978) that of the eight factors used in reading to recognize a word, it is meaning which comes first (before morphological or phonetic features); this result has been found not only with adults but also with third, second, and first graders.

Meaning enables the reader not only to recognize the

words read but also facilitates a function inseparable from the process of reading—anticipation, both syntactic and semantic. Experiments carried out on child readers of 9 years of age show that they understand a message better if it is expressed in one sentence rather than two or three sentences (Pearson 1974), where all the sentences under consideration are short, for example; "Because John was lazy, he slept all day." is remembered better than: "John was lazy. So he slept all day." Similarly "The man who was tall liked the short woman." is remembered better than: "The man liked the woman. He was tall. She was short." The same researcher notes that the presence of cueing conditions clearly helps in the memorization of sentences read, through the use of functional words such as: because, as, for, so, etc. He also notes that quite often linguistic chains of the effect–cause type are remembered by young readers in the cause–effect form; and even that linguistic chains which do not include a link between cause and effect are actually remembered with the inclusion, in fact the invention, of a cause–effect link.

This research converges with that of others working in this area (Richaudeau 1969, 1974, 1979, 1981); it shows that any factor in the writing which emphasizes the syntactic and semantic threads of meaning and assists in anticipation of the message, facilitates understanding and memorization of that message.

The writer of teaching texts must then be careful to take these principles into account. While sentences which are too long and too ponderous must be removed, equally, many very short sentences—even when writing for young children—must be avoided. One must not be afraid to punctuate sentences with functional words such as because, so, for, who, or why, which emphasize causal links and assist the process of anticipation. On the other hand sentences whose structure is enumerative should be avoided as these make anticipation difficult.

These same principles should be applied both when composing sentences and when constructing text; dry enumerations and unmotivated statements should be avoided. In order to facilitate memorization, the summary of a text should be placed at the end rather than the beginning of that text (Hartley 1976).

1.3 Visualization

Many experiments have shown that visual memory is the most effective form of memory. This is true both for short- and long-term memory; for adults, but also for children; as has been shown, for example, by Hargis and Gickling (1978) for children aged 5 to 6; Wolpert (1972) for pupils aged 11; Steingart and Glock (1979); and by Bahrick et al. (1974) for older students. The author of teaching texts is then well-advised to give preference to concrete terms, easily visualized by the young reader. If the themes or concepts are abstract in nature an effort should be made to try to clarify them with examples or even metaphors. At the same time, the difficulty which young children have in understanding certain transfers of meaning must be borne in mind.

According to Gardner and Winer (1979), while children under about 8 years of age may be very good at associating physical concepts (e.g., the setting sun put on his red pyjamas), they cannot cope with associations of a psychological nature (e.g., the prison guard has a heart of stone).

2. The Composition of Texts

In Western countries, the shapes of the letters making up the words of text have been more or less definitely fixed for centuries, and there is freedom to choose only the size and style of letters most likely to benefit young readers.

2.1 The Size of the Characters

Although the results of different researchers are not identical, all agree that there is an inverse correlation between the age of the reader and the size of the characters: the younger the reader, the larger the minimum size of the letters should be. Tinker (1965) at the University of Minnesota, assisted by Donald Paterson, devoted several dozen years to the problem of legibility. He found that legibility thresholds were as shown in Table 1. The different type bodies mentioned correspond to average typeface sizes of the order of 3 mm (18 point), 2.3 mm (14 point), 2 mm (12 point), 1.7 mm (10 point), 1.3 mm (8 point). It is very important to note that beyond these legibility thresholds, further increase in the size of the characters has no effect on reading. A text composed of characters three times as big as the threshold size will neither be read more quickly nor be better understood.

Table 1
Legibility thresholds of character sizes

Year of schooling	Age	Size of type body
1	6	14 to 18
2–3	7 and over	14 to 16
4	9	12
5 and over	10 and over	10 to 12
	Adults	8

It should, however, be pointed out that if it is no longer a question of reading a running text, but rather one organized into a hierarchy, the text composed of large characters will attract more attention from the young reader and will thus be taken as more important.

2.2 The Design of Characters: Outline

The letters of Western writing may be composed as follows:

In Roman lower case
(or small letters)— a b c d e...
In Roman upper case
(or capitals)— A B C D E...

In Italic lower case
(or small letters)— *a b c d e...*
In Italic upper case
(or capitals)— *A B C D E...*

It is very difficult to compare the "absolute" legibility of these four forms, as the results of tests carried out on readers are influenced not only by the pattern of the words but also by what the readers are accustomed to. For instance, a text composed in Gothic letters 𝔞𝔟𝔠𝔡𝔢... will be read with great difficulty by a French or British person, and easily by a German academic.

By taking into account the reading habits of the contemporary Western reader it may be maintained that:

(a) words composed of small letters (or lower case) are significantly more legible than those composed of capitals;

(b) words composed in italics are slightly less legible than those composed in Roman letters.

In practical terms this leads to the following usage:

(a) Roman lower case for the main body of principal texts;

(b) Italic lower case for:
   (i) certain special expressions, such as proper names, technical terms, and so on.
   (ii) relatively short, special texts (prefaces, boxes, legends, notes, etc.);

(c) Roman capitals for titles and subtitles;

(d) Italic capitals for certain subtitles of secondary importance.

Having said this, it must be noted that there is an extension of the use of capitals for running texts in two sectors:

(a) that of typed letters: some modern typewriters, so-called executive typewriters, having only capital letters;

(b) that of the strip cartoon: the great majority of the texts of "balloons" are written in capitals. This second factor may prove to be particularly important in forming the habits of future readers; it is possible that in a few years legibility tests will reveal that capitals are just as legible as lower case letters.

2.3 The Design of Characters: Detail of Execution and Style

The characters used for the principal texts of school books are chosen from the six families below:

(a) venetians— a b c d e

(b) goraldes— a b c d e

(c) transitionals— a b c d e

(d) moderns— a b c d e

(e) slab serifs— a b c d e

(f) sans serif— a b c d e

Experiments do not show any significant differences in reading speeds between these six styles. In particular it has been shown that the presence or absence of serifs has no influence on legibility.

2.4 Spaces Between Words and Breaking Words

In all running texts which are mechanically composed, the distances or spaces separating the words are inserted automatically and according to criteria of legibility. Frequently, however, lines of titles or subtitles presented in large letters are composed manually, often using sheets of transfer letters. The layout designer is then completely free to choose both the spaces between letters and those between words. And he or she is sometimes tempted, on aesthetic grounds, to reduce the spaces between words. However, it should not be forgotten that for young readers, the words of a language are not always clear and self-evident entities, and it is practice in reading which helps them to define these entities. It is therefore necessary in all cases to maintain appreciable spaces between words; these may be fixed using an em quad, that is to say, a basic space whose width is equal to the body size of the characters.

2.5 Justified or Unjustified Margins

A text may be composed either with a justified right-hand margin or with unjustified lines. In the first case, the lines composed are of equal length, which often involves breaking the last word in the line and inserting a hyphen. In the second case, words are not broken, which automatically leads to uneven, "jagged" right-hand margins. Experiments carried out on adults show no difference in reading performance between the two types of composition, although the opposite might have been expected.

Nevertheless, educationalists recommend that for very young learner-readers, rather than experienced readers, texts should be composed without breaks in words, that is, with unjustified margins.

2.6 Other Factors Affecting Legibility

Do short lines or long lines hinder the reading process— as once again might be expected? It seems not, at least if one keeps within the normal lengths found in the press and in books (Hartley et al. 1973). Similarly, spacing, the distance between lines, does not seem to be a determining factor, except—again—in extreme cases, such as when the composition is too cramped and the tails of certain letters (e.g., p) overlap with the stems of other letters (e.g., h), or, on the contrary, when the space between lines is exaggeratedly big. To end this brief discussion consider the problem of paper and ink: texts composed of black print on white paper are the most legible; for preference the paper should be matt (bulky paper with a slightly granular structure), or very slightly shiny (machine coated paper). It is best to avoid excessively shiny paper which in certain reading positions and lighting conditions may partly dazzle the reader. Also, it is better to avoid paper which is too transparent.

3. The Make-up of Texts

If all the sentences of the text of a school book were of equal importance and equally easily understood by the pupils, and if all these sentences were destined to be read in a continuous manner and in the order in which they were composed, it would suffice to compose the sentences of this same text one after another, using the same type, the same body size, and with the same justification, simply taking account of the recommendations below concerning the composition of running texts.

However, this is obviously not what happens in the case of teaching texts. Notions presented in books are not all of equal importance: some are essential, others secondary, others are even useless as far as direct learning is concerned but are designed to amuse or appeal to the young reader. These notions are not all equally easy to understand. Some are easily grasped and memorized, while others are more difficult to assimilate and remember.

Finally, the powers of perception, understanding, and concentration of young readers are limited, and it is necessary to allow for pauses and rest from reading, to emphasize certain information which it is essential to understand and memorize, to "sacrifice" other useful but not essential information, and to check on the acquisition of all this information. The designer of a school textbook must therefore naturally take into account the different levels of these texts (and of the illustrations), and integrate them in a structured presentation, organized in a hierarchy, which guides the young reader and helps him or her to make good use of the book.

It is not possible in this article to study even briefly the rules governing the make-up of school books. Some principles or recommendations on this subject are:

(a) The first factor which enables the reader to recognize hierarchies within the text is visual contrast. But the idea of contrast is relative; in other words, in make-up it is not so much the body size or thickness of type used for text that is being emphasized which are important, but the difference between them and the body size and thickness of type of a secondary text.

(b) The most striking contrast, that between black and white, is also the most economic to achieve. This means, for example, that a text in medium type framed in white will be more striking than the same text in larger type inserted in a text in small type.

The use of blank spaces to make blocks of text stand out, to separate paragraphs, and to indicate a hierarchical arrangement of paragraphs is the most economical method—and often the most elegant.

In particular, this method allows texts simply produced on a typewriter, in a single type, to achieve a relatively sophisticated and functional make-up.

(c) Having said this, the typographic variety made possible by modern composition procedures (photocomposition and computers), the use of italics, of underlining, of various styles of characters, of the many sizes of characters, with several thicknesses of type for each one, of special signs, and so on, must not be forgotten.

Two further points must be taken into consideration:

(a) The eye of the young reader is less experienced than that of the typographer or layout designer, and differences (e.g., between two sizes of type) must be clearly marked.

(b) The discriminatory memory of this young reader (just like that of the adult reader) is limited. It is therefore sensitive to only a limited number of different typographical factors, seven according to Richaudeau. Just as a driver is confused by too many road signs at a junction, so the reader of a textbook will not perceive hierarchies marked by too many typographic factors.

Bibliography

Bahrick H P, Bahrick P O, Wittlinger R P 1974 Long-term memory: Those unforgettable high-school days. *Psychol. Today* 8(7): 50–56

Coleman E, Miller G 1968 A measure of information gained during prose learning. *Read. Res. Q.* 3: 369–86

De Landsheere G 1973 *Le Test de closure mesure de la lisibilité de la compréhension.* Nathan, Paris

Dunn-Rankin P 1978 The visual characteristics of words. *Sci. Am.* 238(1): 122–30

Flesch R F 1951 *How to Test Readability.* Harper, New York

Foucambert J 1976 *La Manière d'être lecteur.* Sermap–Hatier, Paris

Gardner H, Winer E 1979 The child is father to the metaphor. *Psychol. Today.* 12(12): 81–91

Gipe J P 1978 Investigating techniques of teaching word meanings. *Read. Res. Q.* 14: 624–43

Hargis C H, Gickling E E 1978 The function of imagery in word recognition development. *Read. Teach.* 31: 870–74

Hartley J 1976 Is there a "best place" for the summary. *Keele Staffs.* University of Keele, Keele

Hartley J, Burnhill P, Fraser F 1973 Typography communication and learning. *The Visual Presentation of Technical Data.* ERS/SIAD, University of Keele, Keele

Henry G 1975 *Comment mesurer la lisibilité.* Nathan, Paris

Kameenui E J, Carnine D W, Freschi R 1982 Effects of text construction and instructional procedures for teaching word meanings on comprehension and recall. *Read. Res. Q.* 17: 367–88

Miller G A 1956 The magical number seven, plus or minus two: Some limits on our capacity for processing information. *Psychol. Rev.* 63: 81–97

Pearson P D 1974 The effects of grammatical complexity on children's comprehension, recall, and conception of certain semantic relations. *Read. Res. Q.* 10: 155–92

Richaudeau F 1969 *La Lisibilité.* Retz, Paris

Richaudeau F 1974 6 phrases, 200 sujets, 42 lapsus, 1 rêve. *Commun. Langages* 23

Richaudeau F 1979 *Conception et production des manuels scolaires.* UNESCO, Paris

Richaudeau F 1981 *La Linguistique pragmatique.* Retz, Paris

Richaudeau F (ed.) 1984 *Recherches actuelles sur la Lisibilité.* Retz, Paris

Steingart S K, Glock M D 1979 Imagery and the recall of connected discourse. *Read. Res. Q,* 15: 66–83

Tinker M A 1965 *Bases for Effective Reading.* University of Minnesota Press, Minneapolis, Minnesota

Vezin J F, Berge O, Mavrellis P 1973 Rôle du résumé et de la répétition en fonction de leur place par rapport au texte. *Bull. Pschol.* 27: 309

Wolpert E M 1972 Length, imagery, values and word recognition. *Read. Teach.* 26: 180–86

Higher Education

Lectures and Lecturing

G. A. Brown

In essence, a lecture consists of one person talking to many about a topic or theme. The talk may be augmented by the use of audiovisual aids and by occasional questions. When several questions are asked by the lecturer or by recipients, the format is more appropriately known as a discussion class. In a lecture, notes are usually taken by the recipients and it may be supplemented by handouts provided by the lecturer. The purposes of the lecture are usually considered to be to convey information, to generate understanding, and to stimulate interest. The emphasis given to each of these purposes may vary between lectures, between lecturers, and between academic subjects.

The processes of lecturing include structuring and conveying ideas, procedures, and facts to a group which receives, interprets, and responds to the messages received. Attitudes and values may also be transmitted, intentionally or unintentionally, by the lecturer and by the students. It therefore follows that the processes of lecturing are cognitive *and* social activities. Hence in considering lecturing one has to take account of interpersonal skills as well as intellectual skills.

In the remainder of this article, a historical sketch of lecturing, a model for exploring lecturing, a brief review of relevant research, and a discussion of implications are provided.

1. A Historical Sketch

Lecturers may be traced back to the Greeks of the fifth century. In medieval times lectures were the most common form of teaching in both Christian and Moslem universities. The term lecture was derived from the medieval Latin *lectare*—to read aloud. Lectures consisted of an oral reading of a text followed by a commentary.

The method of reading aloud from a text or script is still used by some lecturers in the arts even though the conventions of written and oral language are different in all cultures.

Lecturers in medicine and surgery have long used the demonstration as part of the lecture. By the nineteenth century, demonstrations, pictures, and chalkboards were used by lecturers in science as well as medicine. Today it is still the lecturers in sciences, engineering, and medicine who are the more active users of audiovisual aids in their lectures.

Lectures are still the most common method of teaching in universities throughout the world. Their continued use may be attributable in part to tradition and in part to economics. Classes of 1,000 or more are not uncommon in countries which are anxious to minimize costs in higher education. In some countries the lecture may be the major source of information and only the lecturers may have access to texts and articles in the major languages of the world.

These simple facts suggest that lectures are likely to be widely used well into the twenty-first century, hence the importance of exploring ways of making lectures more effective as well as economical in the years ahead.

2. A Model for Exploring Lectures

The key features of the process of lecturing are intention, transmission, receipt of information, and output. There are likely to be gaps between a lecturer's intention, the transmission, and the receipt of information. A common error is to close the gap between intention and transmission by reading aloud from a prepared script thereby widening the gap between transmission and receipt. Other important features are the objectives and expectations of the recipients (the students) and their intended applications and extensions of the information received. All of these features influence considerably the overall quality of the lecture as a method of teaching and learning.

2.1 Intentions

The lecturer's intentions may be, as indicated in the introduction to this article, to provide a coverage of a topic, to generate understanding, and to stimulate interest. These goals are not always compatible within the same lecture. Undue attention to coverage can obscure understanding. A stress on understanding may require deliberate neglect of detail. A stress on interest *per se* may lead to inadequate understanding. Of course, handouts and carefully selected readings can be used to augment coverage and not all lectures within a course need be concerned equally with all three goals. In addition other teaching methods may be used to generate understanding and interest. Consideration of the three goals of lecturing together with a knowledge of the earlier learning of the students are essential constituents of lecture preparation.

2.2 Transmission

A lecturer sends messages verbally, extraverbally, nonverbally, and through his or her use of audiovisual aids. The verbal messages may consist of definitions, descriptions, examples, explanations, or comments. The "extraverbal" component is the lecturer's vocal qualities, hesitations, stumbles, errors, and use of pauses and silence. The "nonverbal" component consists of his or her gestures, facial expressions, and body movements. All of these types of messages may be received by the students who may sift, perhaps store and summarize, and note what they perceive as the important messages.

A lecturer transmits not only information. His or her nonverbal cues may convey meanings and attitudes which highlight, qualify, or distort the essential messages.

2.3 Receipt

The information, meaning, and attitudes conveyed by the lecturer may or may not be perceived by the students. Attention fluctuates throughout a one-hour lecture. After 20 minutes there is a marked decline in attention followed by a peak of attention just before the lecture ends. This decline in attention is less likely to occur if the lecture includes some short activities for students such as *brief* small-group discussions or simple problem solving. Any change of activity is, in fact, likely to renew attention. Messages that are received by the students are filtered and stored temporarily in the short-term memory. They are forgotten after about 30 seconds if they cannot be kept in mind or noted, or if they cannot be transferred to the long-term memory. The long-term memory most readily receives messages which are closely related to the network of concepts and facts which are already stored in the long-term memory. The long-term memory will also store new messages which are only loosely associated with existing facts and ideas. Facts and concepts that are incomprehensible are most likely to be forgotten. Competing verbal and audiovisual messages are difficult to cope with.

2.4 Output

A student's response or "output" is not only a set of intelligible notes which may be understood and, if necessary, restructured and learnt; it also consists of reactions to the lecture and the lecturer. The immediate reactions are usually nonverbal signals and these may be received, interpreted, and perhaps acted upon by the lecturer. Herein lies an important difference between televised and live lectures.

More important than the immediately observable responses to a lecture are the long-term changes in attitudes and understanding which may occur in a student. These changes are not easily disentangled from other learning experiences but it is likely that a student's attitudes towards a subject and towards lecture methods are influenced markedly by the quality of lecturing he or she experiences as well as by the student's own personality characteristics. A lecture *may* change a student's perception of a problem or theory, it *may* increase a student's insight, and it *may* stimulate him or her to read, think, and discuss ideas with others. The probabilities of these events are dependent upon the student's knowledge, attitudes, and motivation to learn and on the lecturer's preparation, lecture structure, and presentation.

3. Some Research on Lecturing

Studies of lecturing have been the subject of many reviews during the past 60 years. Amongst the most useful are those by Spence (1928), McLeish (1976), Bligh (1980), and Dunkin (1983). Other useful sources are Beard and Hartley (1984), Brown (1978), Brown and Bakhtar (1983), and Brown (1985). This brief review may be supplemented by reference to the above texts and articles.

3.1 Lecturing and Other Methods of Teaching

A common question asked is "Is lecturing as effective as other methods of teaching?" The evidence indicates that lecturing is at least as effective as other methods at presenting information and providing explanations. Practical skills are obviously taught more effectively in laboratories but the underlying methodologies and theories may be taught as effectively and perhaps more efficiently in lectures. Problem-solving skills appear to be taught more effectively in small groups. However even these results depend upon the quality of the discussion or lecture. The few studies of attitude change also favour the small group although it is likely that a skilful lecturer does achieve attitude changes in a lecture.

Comparisons between lectures and newer methods of teaching should also be treated cautiously. Whereas newer methods such as computer-assisted learning, games, and tape–slide programmes are prepared carefully and evaluated systematically, lecture methods are rarely subject to such rigorous planning and analysis. Comparisons between the lecture and other forms of teaching mask the rich variety of lecture methods and lecturing styles that are available. Such comparisons are often based on imprecise objectives and unsuitable criteria. The results, even in well-designed experiments, may depend upon inadequacies in the preparation, presentation, and structure of a particular lecture rather than upon the lecture methods per se.

Comparisons of live lectures and televised lectures have also yielded equivocal results. On the whole there are no statistically significant differences in learning but there is an apparent tendency for live lecturers to be more effective and students do prefer live lectures (MacKenzie et al. 1970, pp. 141–46). The lack of differences may be due to defects in experimental design and to inadequacies in television production.

A distinction should be made between live lectures, live lectures which are televised but not recorded, televised lectures which are prerecorded, and televised lectures which are produced and prerecorded. Only the last category is likely to be more effective than live lectures. The costs of television production and technical assistance should be borne in mind by any intending user.

Despite the equivocality of the studies comparing lectures and other forms of teaching, it does appear that lectures do have a role in higher education but they should not be the only method used. As Spence (1928) observed in the first review of research on lecturing:

> The decrying of the wholesale use of lectures is probably justified. The wholesale decrying of the use of lecturing is just as certainly not justified.

3.2 Views of Students and Lecturers

Generally speaking students and lecturers appear to like lectures although students do comment frequently on poor lecturing technique. Students' main dissatisfactions with lectures appear to be inaudibility, incoherence, failure to pitch at an appropriate level, failure to emphasize main points, difficulty in taking notes, reading aloud from notes, and poor chalkboard work. The five most common weaknesses in lecturers reported in one study were saying too much too quickly, assuming too much knowledge, forgetting to provide summaries, not indicating when making an aside (rather than a main point), and difficulty in timing the length of a lecture (Brown and Bakhtar 1983).

Both students and lecturers value highly clarity of presentation, structure, and interest. However there are differences between arts and science students on valued characteristics and between arts and science lecturers. Science students value detailed, logically structured notes more highly than arts students. Science lecturers value logical and structured characteristics more highly than arts lecturers, and science lecturers consider that features of lecturing, such as logical presentation, structure, use of aids, selection of apt examples, can be learnt whereas many arts lecturers do not (Brown 1985). In an interesting study of 33 "gifted" lecturers, Sheffield (1974) concluded that the most important aspect of lecturing was "to stimulate students to become active learners in their own right". The group of lecturers and their former students also stressed in their essays and comments the importance of caring for students, love of subject, preparing properly, and conveying principles rather than details.

The views of lecturers identified by Sheffield are echoed in the "good" and "bad" stories of lectures told by science students in discursive interviews (Ogborn 1977, Bliss and Ogborn 1977). Good stories contained descriptions of involvement, enthusiasm, and of generating understanding and human interest. Bad stories described the opposite.

3.3 Intentions and Planning

Studies of specific intentions and planning are neglected research topics. Whilst Beard and Hartley (1984) and Brown (1978) provide guidelines for preparing lectures, there are no published studies extant of how lecturers actually prepare their lectures.

3.4 Transmission

The key variables identified by researchers are clarity and expressiveness. Land has summarized the main studies of clarity of explanations as measured by student achievement since the mid 1970s (see *Vagueness and Clarity*). The results show that higher student achievement scores were obtained when explanations had fewer verbal mazes (false starts, redundant phrases, tangles of words), greater use of specific emphasis, and clear transitions from one subject to another.

Expressiveness, which includes enthusiasm, friendliness, humour, dynamism, and even charisma, have long been regarded as essential ingredients of lecturing. A meta-analysis of 12 experimental studies of expressiveness (Abrami et al. 1982) suggests that expressiveness is more likely to influence students' responses to a lecturer and their attitude towards their subject of study than it is to produce marked changes in achievement. However the studies reviewed were rather extreme in their use of expressiveness and variation in content. Furthermore, favourable changes in attitude may be an important long-term goal of lecturing (see *Student Evaluations of Teaching*).

The sequence and organization of lectures has not been studied in detail. Lecturers report that their most common method of organizing lectures is the "classical" approach of subdividing topics and then subdividing subtopics (Brown and Bakhtar 1983). Linguistic analyses of lectures appear to have focused upon microstructure and as yet they have not considered larger units of discourses in lectures.

The skills of lecturing have at their heart the complex skill of explaining. Other important skills are demonstrating, narrating, using audiovisual aids, comparing and contrasting, and generating student interest. These skills may all be improved upon through training—as may students' skills of learning from lectures. However there is a dearth of experimental studies on training in lecturing and learning from lectures (Brown 1985).

Styles of lecturing have been identified and these appear to be closely associated with subject content but not with length of experience or status. In one study (Brown and Bakhtar 1983) five styles were identified.

These were the "visual information giver", the "oral presenter", the "exemplary" who used successfully a blend of visual and oral approaches, the "eclectic" who was less successful at blending visual and oral approaches, who has self-doubts but a strong commitment to his or her subject, and the "amorphous" whose main characteristics are vagueness and arrogance.

3.5 Receipt and Output

Studies of note taking in lectures are reviewed succinctly in Beard and Hartley (1984). In general it appears that note taking aids learning and recall and that reviewing one's notes soon after a lecture aids subsequent recall and understanding. There are a wide variety of approaches to note taking and it appears that students in different subjects tend to have different approaches. Science, engineering, and medical students tend to take fuller, more structured notes than their peers in the arts. This may be in part because objectives and expectations of learning from lectures vary across subjects.

There are also likely to be differences between students according to their personality characteristics, motivation to learn, and learning styles. For example, Hodgson (1984) used the technique of stimulated recall to study how students had reacted during lectures. Three broad sets of reported experiences were identified: extrinsic, intrinsic, and vicarious relevance. The first two appear to be related to the learning styles of surface and deep processing and the third is related to the students' perception and understanding of the lecturer's view. Vicarious experience occurs when the lecturer is enthusiastic, committed, and provides illustrations and metaphors which strike home.

Vicarious experience provides a link between studies of expressiveness and student attitude change. It is as if the student begins to identify and incorporate the lecturer's view into his or her own mode of thinking and appreciation of the subject.

4. Implications and Issues

Lecturing and lectures are clearly portmanteau terms which require closer scrutiny. The term lecture may have a quite different meaning for science and arts lecturers and students. The experiences of receiving or giving lectures in different subjects have not been fully explored, yet it is clear that the structure and content of subjects have a marked influence upon the mode of lecturing. Students' learning styles may also have a marked effect upon note taking and learning from lectures. The experiences of preparing, giving, receiving, and learning from lectures could, with advantage, be explored further using a wide variety of methodologies including linguistic, ethnographic, and phenomenological approaches.

Such research would make a contribution to cognitive and social psychology as well as to teacher education.

It would perhaps provide a deeper understanding of how a lecturer's expressiveness generates interest and attitude changes in students and how clarity of presentation is translated into student understanding.

However, it is not necessary to await the answers to these questions before attempting to improve lecturing and learning from lecturing. Three readily implementable approaches would almost certainly improve the quality of lecturing and learning from lectures. First, provide lecturers and students with more information on how lectures may be structured and presented. Secondly, give lecturers specific training in the skills of lecturing, and thirdly, train students in the skills of listening, observing, and note taking from lectures. So far there have been very few studies of the effects of training on lecturers and students so it would be worth mounting a research training programme in which data are collected in experimental or naturalistic settings on the skills and processes of lecturing as well as data on training.

In summary, research over the past 60 years indicates that for some tasks lectures are at least as good as other methods of teaching. They are economical and fairly efficient but they should be augmented by other forms of teaching. The research has also shown that clarity of presentation, structure, and expressiveness are key factors in effective lecturing. However, it is not yet clear how these factors operate upon the student's perception, understanding, and attitudes. Given that they do operate, it is worth providing some training in lecturing to lecturers and in learning from lectures to students. After all, a nation's economic growth depends in part upon the potential of its students. Since the tradition of lecturing is so deeply embedded in most subjects and cultures it is worth attending to ways of improving lectures as vehicles of learning as well as continuing the search for more effective, economical, and stimulating ways of promoting learning.

Bibliography

Abrami P C, Leventhal L, Perry R P 1982 Educational seduction. *Rev. Educ. Res.* 52: 446–64
Beard R, Hartley J 1984 *Teaching and Learning in Higher Education*, Heinemann, London
Bligh D A 1980 Methods and techniques in post-secondary education. *Educational Studies and Documents*, No. 31. UNESCO, Paris
Bliss J, Ogborn J 1977 *Student Reactions to Undergraduate Science*. Heinemann, London
Brown G A 1978 *Lecturing and Explaining*. Methuen, London
Brown G A 1985 Explaining, explaining. In: Hargie O (ed.) 1985 *Handbook of Communication Skills*. Croom Helm, London
Brown G A, Bakhtar M (eds.) 1983 *Styles of Lecturing*. Loughborough University Press, Loughborough
Dunkin M J 1983 A review of research on lecturing. *Higher Educ. Res. Dev.* 2(1): 63–78
Hodgson V 1984 Learning from lectures. In: Marton F, Hounsell D, Entwistle N (eds.) 1984 *The Experience of Learning*. Scottish Academic Press, Edinburgh

MacKenzie N, Eraut M, Jones H 1970 *Teaching and Learning: An Introduction to New Methods and Resources in Higher Education*. UNESCO and International Association of Universities, Paris

McLeish J 1976 The lecture method. In: Gage N L and Berliner D (eds.) 1976 *The Psychology of Teaching Methods*, 75th Yearbook of the National Society for the Study of Education, Chicago, Illinois

Ogborn W (ed.) 1977 *Understanding Science Teaching*. Heinemann, London

Sheffield E F (ed.) 1974 *Teaching in the Universities: No One Way*. Queen's University Press, Montreal

Spence R B 1928 Lecture and class discussion in teaching educational psychology. *J. Educ. Psychol.* 19: 454–62

Group Teaching

D. Jaques

The experience of working together in small groups has long been one of the most cherished features of learning in tertiary education. Discussion of academic work affords students the opportunity to organize their thinking by comparing ideas and interpretations with each other, and to give expression and hence form, to their understanding of a subject. Small group discussion is important for wider purposes too. There is an increasing need for professionals to demonstrate oral skills in committees and in more general communication with clients and colleagues. Cooperation and teamwork have become essential features of most work situations, as have skills in listening, drawing out information, and persuading. Industry and commerce have greater expectations of the graduates' ability to communicate and this is further underlined by the high standards set by radio and television which make for more critical audiences (Beard et al. 1978). But perhaps most importantly, small group discussion can or should give students the chance to monitor their own learning and thus gain a degree of self-direction, and independence of the tutors, in their studies. All these purposes have excellent pedigree. Yet often they are not realized to a satisfactory level and both tutors and students may end up with a sense of frustration.

In all human interactions there are two main ingredients—content and process. Content relates to subject matter or the substantive task on which people are working. Process refers to the dynamics of what is happening between those involved. Perhaps because content is more readily definable, or at least examinable, it commonly receives more attention from all concerned. Process, on the other hand, being less tangible, is rarely attended to; yet it is usually what causes a group to work effectively or ineffectively. Group members are often half-aware of the ways in which physical environment, size, cohesion, climate, norms, liaisons, organizational structure, or group goals affect discussion. These properties are common to all groups and an awareness of them, as they become evident, should enhance a participant's worth to the group. For no-one is this more true than the leader or tutor, who has a crucial position in determining the "success" or "failure" of a discussion group.

1. Theory

Group process, or group dynamics as it is more frequently called, has been the subject of much theorizing and research. In many ways theory and research have informed one another though they do lead to separate strands of explanation for group behaviour. One important theory, interaction analysis (Bales 1970), is based on the assumption that what happens in a group can be seen as the sum of observable skills and behaviours. Bales identifies 12 categories of behaviour: seems friendly, dramatizes, agrees, gives suggestion, gives opinion, gives information, asks for information, asks for opinion, asks for suggestion, disagrees, shows tension, seems unfriendly; and these provide a fairly straightforward descriptive and nonevaluative feedback.

The Tavistock theory on group experience, however, views the group as a corporate entity and stresses the emotional and largely unconscious processes that derive from the attitudes and habits developed in the first and usually most important group in a person's life—the family. Bion (1961) suggests that a group operates simultaneously at two levels: the "work group" and the "basic assumption group". The work group meets to perform a specific and overt task but is frequently diverted or obstructed by the powerful emotional undercurrents of the "basic assumption activity". The basic group behaves as if it shared the following tacit assumptions or motives:

(a) that some sort of magic resides in the leader who is endowed with authority and expertise: the group feels an undue sense of "dependency" on the leader;

(b) that it can cope with difficult problems by "fight": making a scapegoat of some other person or group; or by "flight": indulging in withdrawal, passivity, dwelling on the past, or jesting;

(c) two individuals form a bond which excludes the other members and renders the group inactive: this "pairing" may be mutually supportive in nature or take the form of an intellectual conflict. The tutor may himself "pair" with the whole group in a collusion with them to avoid work.

The basic group which operates under these assumptions is of course the same one that is engaged in the work task; they are the same members operating under different modes with varying degrees of intensity. Conflict is likely to arise when the subversive motives of the basic group enmesh with the reality task of the work group.

A more detailed understanding of these processes may be obtained from *Group Tutoring* (Bramley 1979). Bramley stresses the tutors' responsibility not to be drawn inadvertently into the unconscious processes but to confront the group about, or to explain what they appear to be doing. She also draws attention to "valency"—the tendency of all tutors to "fix" a group in the basic assumption activity with which they feel most comfortable (e.g., authority and dependency). Readers will find other theoretical approaches to learning groups in Bramley including the focal conflict theory and theme-centred interactional method. This latter method, described also in Shaffer and Galinsky (1974), provides a commendably simple and effective model for classroom and seminar practice. Shaffer and Galinsky also draw comparisons between various approaches to group therapy including the T-groups, Gestalt, Psychoanalytic and Tavistock models. Rudduck (1978) deals with some of the practical implications of the Tavistock approach in the context of teaching and learning.

2. Research and Experience

Research into group behaviour, while sometimes criticized (Reason and Rowan 1981) for its artificiality and reductionism, does provide evidence of great value.

Cartwright and Zander (1968) and Shaw (1972) give full accounts of the evidence from this research; for an up-to-date account the reader could refer to the various journals of social psychology. Knowles and Knowles (1972) provide a practical resumé of research findings in their excellent primer on group dynamics, upon which much of the succeeding section is based.

Both research and common sense suggest that group work has several advantages over individual work: the presence of others increases motivation, group judgments are more reliable, and groups usually produce more and better solutions to problems. Of great importance from the teaching point of view is the evidence that groups learn faster than individuals (Shaw 1972). What is more, as Bligh et al. (1980) conclude in a survey of research into teaching methods, group discussion, while no more effective than either reading or lectures in the transmission of information, is significantly better for the teaching of thinking skills and attitudes.

Given that learning is facilitated in these important ways through the use of groups, it may be asked: "What makes a group a group?" "What makes a group work effectively?" "What factors contribute to satisfaction and productiveness, especially in a teaching and learning environment?" and finally, "What does the teacher need to do to achieve these goals?"

3. Characteristics of Groups

A gathering of people is a group when its members are collectively conscious of their existence as a group; when they believe it satisfies their needs; when they share aims, are interdependent, want to join in group activities, and to remain with the group.

Though groups occur in many forms and sizes, there seems to be a set of characteristics fairly common to them all. Certainly the following features are of consequence to any teacher involved in group teaching.

3.1 Time Boundaries

Past: Members of a new group bring with them sets of expectations arising out of what they know of the origins, history, or composition of the group—which significant people are to be in it? They build up expectations from any statements they have heard about the group's purpose and task. Members may also bring with them attitudes to other members born out of prior relationships outside the group, and the group itself may carry a reputation for a particular style, climate, or level of achievement. In education, students will probably have picked up comments about how well or badly the group went in the previous year. The formation of a group requires that someone make prior decisions about place, resources, and the size and composition of the group. Whoever undertakes this task, for example the tutor, will have considerable influence in the success of the group, at least in its initial stages.

In an established group, members may carry with them feelings derived from previous meetings; they may look forward to the resumption of an exciting interchange or may dread the re-enactment of conflicts and time-wasting tactics. They may have to do preparatory work, such as a paper or a report, and their anticipation of what will happen may cause them to approach or engage with the group in a predetermined way. New members may need careful briefing on the group's norms and procedures.

Present: While a meeting is in progress members may be taken up with thoughts about what may be happening concurrently elsewhere: an important external event, what is happening in another, possibly similar, group; why an absent member is not there, and so on.

The agreed duration of the discussion group imposes another time boundary. The tutor's awareness of time constraints in terms of the achievement of certain aims, the appropriateness of tasks, when to intervene, curtail, summarize, and so on, is of great importance. Conflicts often arise between "coverage" of topics and completion of tasks on the one hand and the need to finish on time on the other.

Future: Whatever matters are discussed, decisions made, or problems solved, the minds of group members will at some stage turn to what will happen when the meeting ends. They may be thinking of what they have to communicate and to whom, of resuming former roles and relationships outside the group. They may also have it in mind that they may be answerable later for what they said or did within the confines and culture of the meeting, especially to other members with whom they may have a less democratic relationship in the wider world. Finally, there will undoubtedly be an anticipation of the end of the meeting which will bring with it a sense of relief, if it has been tedious or tense, and of sadness if it has been exciting and involving.

Questions to ask about time boundaries are:

(a) What do students need to know beforehand—place, time, aims, membership, roles, prior tasks?

(b) What expectations are they likely to have—from previous studies, from other students?

(c) What prior experience of group discussion are they likely to have had? What external distractions might occur?

(d) Should there be any rules about openness and confidentiality?

(e) What are students expected to do after the meeting?

(f) How acceptable are these tasks?

3.2 Physical Environment

Several critical factors in group dynamics—flow of communication, perception of status, emergence of leadership, for example—are affected by things like the physical position of group members, their distance apart, and their body orientations. These in turn are strongly influenced by the shape and size of the room in which a group meets, and the spatial arrangement of chairs and tables. A long, narrow room will probably limit eye contact along its length and impel members to talk to others across the room, but not along it. Anyone who sits at the end of a long table or behind the only desk in the room is likely to be accorded leadership status. Dominant members will tend to choose the more central seats in any group situation, and reticent ones may even try to sit outside the group. The further apart members are, the less talkative and more formal is the interaction likely to be. Tables create a physical barrier which may be reassuring in groups where formality is of the essence, or where there is a wish to maintain personal distance or space. They may also be invaluable as a writing surface. A lack of tables may be threatening to some but it usually encourages openness and informality.

Personal space, the area around a person which he or she regards as private, will of course vary from individual to individual, but it is clear that people of higher status often prefer, or are accorded, greater distance between them and others. (The seats on either side of a tutor in an otherwise undifferentiated circle of chairs are often the last to be filled by students.)

The location of a group meeting has its effect too. The tutor's room is his or her territory and underlines the authority role. The student union bar on the other hand is a more egalitarian venue but has the drawback of invasion by others, not to mention licensing limitations. Just as groups may assume territorial rights over physical space and objects, so may members act territorially about positions in a room. The work of Sommer (1969) is of great interest in this regard.

Questions about physical environment might include:

(a) What associations does the room have in the minds of the students?

(b) Is it the tutor's room, a formal classroom, or some neutral area?

(c) Is the room to be a regular venue?

(d) Might discussion be vulnerable to noise or interruption?

(e) Can everyone be equally spaced?

(f) Is anyone (especially the tutor) likely to have a special position e.g., behind a desk or at the head of a table?

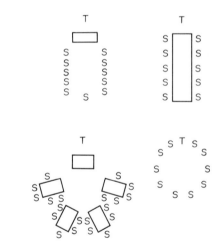

Figure 1
Commonly used "layouts" of chairs and tables for group situations in higher education

(g) What can be done by moving furniture, to improve communication in the group?

(h) Can everyone make eye contact with each other?

(i) How possible is it to rearrange the grouping of chairs and tables?

Figure 1 shows some commonly used "layouts" of chairs and tables. The reader might like to consider which alternative he or she might choose for a discussion group of any particular kind.

3.3 Group Size

There are two opposite tendencies with regard to the number of people in a group. The larger the group, the greater is the pool of talent and experience available for solving problems or sharing the effort; on the other hand as the size increases, fewer members have the chance to participate, and indeed the differences in relative participation increase to the point where one or two members begin to dominate. It thus becomes more likely that reticent members will fail to contribute, though they may well enjoy the relative anonymity a large group affords them.

The smaller the group, the greater is the likelihood of close relationships, full participation, and consonance of aims; leadership and other roles will probably be shared or rotated. With larger numbers the formation of subgroups, and the increasing differentiation of roles in a large group will lead to the emergence of a leader. Where there is an agreed leader (e.g., the teacher) the need to counteract the above tendencies places special demands on his or her awareness of the problems and skills in coping with them.

When does a group become "large" and does it still have any merits? Most theorists, researchers and practitioners agree that five to seven members is the optimum for leaderless groups. In the case of led groups, as for academic discussion, the maximum for member satisfaction according to students (NUS 1969) is 10 to 12. Larger groups are an advantage when it requires the combining of individual efforts as in brainstorming. They are of less value when everyone must accomplish the task, which is the general situation in most discussion groups. If the group is small (i.e., two or three in number), the tutor is likely to be dominant from the start. With a large group (eight or more) the divergence of aims and the need for role differentiation may push the tutor into a dominant position. However, the use of subgroups can overcome some of the difficulties of large group discussions.

If the tutor has any choice in the matter the tutor might ask:

(a) What size of group is appropriate to the aims?

(b) How many people can be fitted into the room and still have good eye contact?

(c) Will the tutor take a leadership role or will students take responsibility for the process?

(d) Does the tutor intend to split the group into subgroups?

(e) Is the group large enough to avoid total dominance by the tutor?

(f) Will the group still be large enough if one or two members are absent?

3.4 Group Composition

As a general rule, a heterogeneous mix of students in each group provides the best chemistry for interaction and achievement of task. Such qualities as age, sex, nationality, and personality may be taken into account, though one can never be sure what mixture might lead to good participation. Individual students will contribute differently according to which other students they are grouped with. There occurs what is known as an "assembly effect" which is often impossible to predict. Indeed the tutor may be part of this, for example when a group of dependent students are led by an assertive tutor.

From the point of view of cognitive learning, in problem solving for example, there are good reasons for mixing quicker or more intelligent students with their slower counterparts, thus enabling a teaching process *between* the students to take place. Yet often the most powerful influences are the personal likes and dislikes of fellow members. People tend to agree with individuals they like and disagree with those they dislike even though both may express the same opinion. By and large, groups composed of compatible people learn well when they want to learn. The opposite may often be the case with a disaffected group.

In allocating students to groups, the tutor may want to ask questions like:

(a) What are the main differences between students?

(b) What kinds of task are suitable?

(c) Which students seem to identify with and support each other?

(d) Which students are likely to be continually at loggerheads?

(e) What exclusive cliques do there seem to be?

(f) How well do the personalities enmesh, trigger each other in a positive way?

3.5 Communication

It is through communication that members of a group learn to understand one another and to influence, or be influenced by, each other. Yet communication is not just a matter of expressing ideas clearly. It is often suffused with unintended effects, fears and dislikes, and unconscious motives. Often the nonverbal part of communication is the most eloquent. A great deal is revealed about what a person is really thinking and feeling by their facial expression, posture, and gestures.

The content of communication is important too. In every subject area there is a specialized vocabulary which a newcomer may find off-putting. A clique within the group may sustain a private joke which intentionally excludes the rest.

For any communication to take place, speaking must be complemented by listening. Students may often, through preoccupation with their own thoughts or scorn for another's opinions, fail to hear what is being said. Ground rules in which each speaker in turn has to summarize what the previous one said can encourage more purposeful listening.

Questions about communication that can be asked are as follows:

(a) Were members expressing their ideas clearly?

(b) Were they evidently listening to each other?

(c) Did they make connections to or build on each others' contributions?

(d) Did they check for understanding or ask for clarification when they were not sure of what somebody else meant?

(e) Was there good eye contact round the group?

(f) Were feelings as well as thoughts communicated?

3.6 Participation

The degree of participation in a group is dependent to a large extent on its size and the physical environment. The pattern of interaction may also vary. For instance, it may take the form of a one-way "mini" lecture by the leader or tutor, or be a two-way question-and-answer format, again directed by the tutor. In some cases, comments may be channelled through a member, not officially the leader, because of his or her dominant role outside the group, and in others a small clique may set up an interaction to the exclusion of the rest of the members. As a general rule attention is directed upwards in the status hierarchy and the upward communication tends to be more positive than that directed downwards. Consequently, the tutor may receive more rosy information than is appropriate: an important fact to remember in conducting an evaluation of the group or the tutor.

Patterns of interaction in a group may be consistent over time or may vary. They can certainly be changed through the structuring of discussion with subgroups or by introducing helpful ground rules. The more widespread the participation in discussion, the better will be the interest and involvement.

Questions the tutor may wish to ask are:

(a) Did everyone appear involved, either verbally or nonverbally?

(b) Were quieter students encouraged to participate? How?

(c) To whom were questions usually addressed: the whole group, the tutor, particular members?

(d) For what proportion of time did the tutor talk?

(e) If a chart of the participation pattern is drawn, how does it look? (see Fig. 2).

Figure 2
Participation patterns between student and teacher in higher education group settings

3.7 Cohesiveness

Cohesiveness is a measure of the attraction of the group to its members (and the resistance to leaving it), the sense of team spirit, and the willingness of its members to coordinate their efforts. Compared with members of a low-cohesive group, those in a high-cohesive group will, therefore, be keen to attend meetings, be satisfied with the group, use "we" rather than "I" in discussions, be cooperative and friendly with each other, and be more effective in achieving the aims they set for themselves. The low-cohesive group will be marked by absenteeism, the growth of cliques and factions, and a sense of frustration at the lack of attainment.

Questions for the tutor to ask on group cohesiveness are:

(a) How satisfied are members with the group and their part in it?

(b) Did members seem glad to see each other again?

(c) Did there seem to be a sense of shared purpose or was everyone "doing their own thing"?

(d) Did any subgroup or private conversations develop?

(e) Was the quality and quantity of communication high or low?

(f) Did members turn up on time and stay to the end without looking distracted?

(g) What evidence was there of interest or lack of interest among members in what was happening or where the group was going?

(h) Did members talk inclusively about the group— "our group", "we", and "each one of us" rather than "the group", "I", or "you"?

3.8 Norms

Every group has a set of norms: a code of conduct about what is acceptable behaviour. Such norms may apply to everyone in the group or to certain members only, and some will be strictly adhered to while others permit a wide range of behaviour. The group usually has sanctions (e.g., disapproval) which it may apply in the case of "deviation". Common norms in groups involve: taboo subjects, open expression of feelings, interrupting or challenging the tutor, volunteering one's services, avoiding conflict, length and frequency of contributions. Most norms will be hidden or implicit and new members may find it difficult to learn and adjust to them. Over the first few meetings of a group there may be confusion about what the norms are with consequent frustration, discomfort, and lost momentum. It may be helpful to invite a group to break into subgroups to discuss its norms and perhaps to discard some of those which seem counterproductive.

Questions about norms may be:

(a) Are there any taboo subjects?

(b) How do norms appear to be enforced? Who does it?

(c) Does anyone consistently break the norms? How does the group respond?

(d) Are there norms about breaking or not breaking norms?

(e) Are the norms well-understood by everyone?

(f) Do the norms seem to help or hinder progress?

3.9 Procedures

Procedures are really metarules or conventions for ensuring that what a group wants to happen, does in fact happen. They are the means of handling problematic events like making decisions, conflict, distribution of tasks, assessment, and evaluation; and they may be invoked by, or applied to, any member or the whole group. Procedures may also be seen as devices for ensuring the smooth running of the group and the achievement of agreed aims. They may be formal and strictly codified, as in many committees, or informal and loose as for teams and working groups. The main virtue of a procedure is that it is usually set up before the event and this detaches discussions of how the group should handle problems in general from the process of tackling any particular problem. Typical rules and procedures for groups may be:

(a) All decisions should be made by consensus.

(b) Anyone may call "time-out" at any stage in order to review progress.

(c) The group starts and finishes on time.

(d) The first five minutes of every meeting are spent miliing around the room and chatting.

(e) The group follows an agenda like that proposed by Hill (1969).

(f) Members take on functional roles like timekeeper, summarizer, and so on (again see Hill 1969).

(g) Each member has a maximum time-limit for contributions.

A very sophisticated group might also agree a meta-procedure which determines how any of the above rules or procedures might be changed.

Rules and procedures may be invented in response to questions like these:

(a) How will the group decide on aims, tasks, and agendas?

(b) How is the group to make decisions?

(c) What regular process problems are likely to arise?

(d) How can it make best use of the resources of its members?

(e) How is it going to ensure full involvement in discussion?

(f) How will it monitor and evaluate its progress?

(g) How will it coordinate the various activities outside the group or in subgroups?

3.10 Structure

When a group comes together for the first time and begins to interact, various differences between the members begin to appear: differences in status, influence, role, ability, and so on. The pattern of relationships that is thus established is known as the group structure. The pattern will, of course, change according to the nature of the task or the stage of discussion and the most influential person for one purpose may not be so for another. Where there is no appointed leader, as in tutorless groups, the leadership may therefore move round different members of the group. A structure that emerges in these ways is known as an invisible structure.

A visible structure exists when the group agrees a division of labour, roles, and responsibilities, in order to get essential tasks performed. Hill (1969) proposes a set of roles to be distributed in the group: initiating, giving and asking for information, giving and asking for reactions, restating and giving examples, confronting and reality testing, clarifying, synthesizing and summarizing, gatekeeping and expediting, time-keeping, evaluating and diagnosing, standard setting, sponsoring and encouraging, and group tension relieving. Such a method, though it is valued by some students, is found by others to be too socially demanding. Northedge (1975) describes another kind of structure to encourage participation: a sequence of stages involving individual work, followed by discussion in pairs, then in fours, and a final session with the whole group or class.

Questions to ask about structure include:

(a) What kind of pecking order(s) emerged among the students?

(b) What kind of group roles or functions (see Hill above) were missing, and what effect did this have?

(c) What role did the tutor adopt—instructor, facilitator, chairperson, resource, consultant? Was it clear?

(d) Did students have any specified roles?

(e) Was the assessment role of the tutor clear to the students?

(f) How did the invisible structure match any visible one?

(g) How was the invisible structure manifest? Who influences whom, who volunteers, defers to others, etc.?

(h) Was the group structure visible or invisible, appropriate to the task?

3.11 Aims

Aims are implicit in most, if not all, groups though they are not often thought about and even less often discussed. These aims may be intrinsic in nature: "to enjoy each other's company", "to discuss environmental pollution", or they may be extrinsic: "to make decisions about the course" or "to prepare for an examination". Aims also have social and task dimensions. Social aims include "to develop group loyalty and a sense of belonging" while task aims refer to qualities like judging ideas and checking progress. Social and task aims are complementary. If the social dimension is not given due regard, students may feel cool about the group and have no sense of commitment. If the task dimension is missing they may become dissatisfied and feel frustrated at not achieving anything worthwhile. The social dimension has an additional educational scope. It includes qualities like self-awareness, the ability to work independently yet cooperatively in a team—all important aspects of the students' personal development.

Members of any group are likely to have their own personal and, sometimes, hidden aims and these may have little to do with the aims of the group as a whole, where these are known. Sometimes these personal aims, for example, impressing the tutor, scoring off another student, wanting approval of the group, capitalizing on other students' ideas, may undermine the intended aims of the tutor. It is the tutor's job to somehow accommodate or mobilize the personal aims within the overall aims; and there is usually no better way to do this than through as open a discussion as possible of all the aims arising from the group.

Some questions about aims are:

(a) What were the aims of the group?

(b) Were they clear to the students?

(c) Were they acceptable to the students?

(d) To what extent did everyone inside (and outside) the group share the aims?

(e) What separate aims did the students have?

(f) Was the method/technique/interaction appropriate to the aims? What was the evidence?

(g) What unintended outcomes were there?

(h) Did the group evaluate its progress during and at the end of the meeting/series of meetings?

3.12 Tasks

If an aim is to represent a bit more than good intentions, it must be related to a corresponding task. The task specifies the activity in which the students individually or collectively are engaged. It is what must be done in order to achieve an aim. Not enough attention or imagination is usually given to specifying tasks in group teaching. The tendency is to assume the task is simply one of discussing a topic. Yet a wealth of stimulating tasks, or their key verbs, may easily be found if one of the taxonomies of educational objectives is referred to, for example: identify, contrast, predict, select, differentiate, organize, judge, criticize, and so on. If the aim for a group meeting is to develop awareness of different strategies for solving problems, a suitable set of group tasks might be:

(a) to try to solve a given problem;

(b) to monitor the strategies used;

(c) to share the findings and compare with research evidence;

(d) to draw up a set of guidelines on problem-solving strategies.

Tasks will vary in quality and quantity. Some are too difficult or too lengthy to be tackled in a given time; others are best done individually rather than by the group. There are tasks which demand no more than a "surface" approach of students while others require a "deep" or "holistic" style of argument. It is part of the tutor's job to select tasks accordingly. Questions to ask might be:

(a) What prior tasks, for example, writing, reading, consulting, and so on, were required?

(b) How thoroughly were they done?

(c) What tasks were set at the meeting? Were they clear and attainable within the time allowed?

(d) Did the tasks take into account the students' developmental needs? Did they encourage imaginative and deep thinking?

(e) What tasks were agreed at the end to be done for the next meeting?

3.13 Climate

Though it may be difficult to define, the social climate in which group discussion takes place is of enormous importance, and is usually fairly easy to sense. The tutor has an important role to play in creating a climate in which warmth, spontaneity, openness, and informality exist. A positive climate can not only release more energy and imagination in a group, but affect the way students feel about belonging to it.

Questions to ask about climate include:

(a) Was the group harmonious or dissonant, warm or cool, relaxed or tense, free or constrained?

(b) Was there a sense of competition—how did it arise?

(c) Did students seem willing to take risks—for example, express uncertainty and half-formed ideas, reject the tutor's ideas, express feelings?

4. The Tutor's Skills

Even when tutors are conversant with group dynamics and have prepared well for a particular meeting, they still have the more tactical problem of knowing if, when, and how to make interventions in the discussion. Heron (1975) suggests six categories of intervention for group leaders: prescribing, informing, and confronting (the "authoritative" mode), and releasing tension, eliciting, and supporting (the "facilitative" mode).

Each of these interventions covers a set of verbal and nonverbal behaviours. The tendency in many styles of group leadership is to exhibit either the authoritative or the facilitative modes, but not both. A competent tutor should be versatile, able to use all the interventions, and to judge when to make them. Jaques (1985) gives detailed examples of the ways in which such interventions may be enacted.

4.1 Asking Questions

Tutors have the power to open or close down discussions through the way in which they ask questions. The following guidelines for tutors asking questions are adapted from UTMU (1978):

(a) Try to have some idea of the mental processes students are going through, and adjust your questions to the way they respond rather than thinking up good questions beforehand as though the quality of a question was independent of the time, place, and person involved.

(b) Try to avoid questions which suggest one answer is expected more than another, for example, "do you think Wordsworth had a great influence on Coleridge?" Rather ask: "What sort of relationship do you see between the works of Wordsworth and Coleridge?"

(c) Try to avoid playing the game, an elaboration of the above, in which you invite students to guess what is in your mind, as in the children's party game "Hunt the Thimble". If you do not want students to arrive at a predetermined answer or you have your own favourite solution, it is probably better to draw out a range of possible answers from students and then to encourage discussion of their merits. This often produces ideas which you had not thought of. You may then reveal your own list for comparison.

(d) Try to ask questions which give informative answers. Not "Did you calculate the mean?"; "Did you subtract the mean from each reading?". Rather ask: "Tell me exactly what you did.", followed by "What about . . .?" "What else?" "Uh-huh".

(e) Ask questions which elicit responses at the higher end of Bloom's Taxonomy, for example, "Could you put those ideas together for us?" "How does that theory compare with the other?" "How important do you think this scheme is?" "How do you feel about it?"

(f) Be very cautious about showing approval and disapproval in evaluating answers. Sometimes it may help reticent students to have their one and only contribution approved, but disapproval is likely to change what a student is willing to say. An honest attempt to contribute should be welcomed. If you feel a comment is irrelevant to the discussion (remember it may not be irrelevant to the student concerned or to the other students), you may respond with "that's very interesting—could we come back to it later once we have settled the issue of . . .?" It is important to recognize that the apparent irrelevance of a comment may be an indication that the student is feeling confused or has had to wait so long to speak that the contribution has become out of date.

(g) Once you have asked a question, be prepared to wait for an answer. Short silences are not necessarily a bad thing—they often get students talking more freely in the long run once they know you require (and appreciate) an honest answer to an honest question. If every question is greeted with silence then it might be of value to discuss with the group why this is so.

(h) If you fail to get the answer you want, consider the possibility that the answer a student gives may be the answer he or she wants, or that you have asked the wrong question.

(i) Sometimes it can be useful to encourage individual thought about a question by asking students to write some brief notes which might then be compared with a neighbour's. As well as allowing students to stand back from the discussion for a while, it can encourage participation by quieter members. Notes may sometimes be transferred to a board or over-

295

head projector so that they may be shared more easily.

(j) Remember you can often ask questions with little more than the raising of an eyebrow (if you can do it!). Facial expressions are frequently a more direct and less threatening means of querying someone's contribution.

For further ideas on what tutors can do in seminars and tutorials see Habershaw et al. (1984).

5. Variety in Group Teaching

The term "group teaching" usually conjures up a picture of the traditional seminar or tutorial in which students discuss a topic under the leadership of a knowledgeable and expert tutor. The seminar is generally regarded as "subject-centred" and discussion is usually based on prior reading and the presentation of an analysis, critique, or summary by the tutor or a student. The tutorial is supposedly "student-centred", with a distinct emphasis on the student's problems in learning to write essays, or solve problems. In recent years there has been a growing interest in a number of less traditional group techniques; techniques which serve a broader range of aims and give both teacher and student a more varied and stimulating experience of group teaching.

The following list of techniques is not exhaustive and one or more may be combined with or incorporated in others. Broadly, they are organized in a progression from tutor control to student freedom.

(a) Controlled discussion—students raise questions or make comments under the strict control of the tutor.

(b) Step-by-step discussion—a handout or videotape is presented and, at chosen points, there is a break for discussion as a whole group or in subgroups.

(c) Seminar—a generic title for most discussion groups of 8 to 20 students led by a tutor. An excellent critique of the standard seminar and suggested improvements is given in Jaques (1985).

(d) Case discussion—a case history or problem is presented; students analyse and offer solutions. Can be used (but not often) in science and engineering. Easton (1982) is an excellent reference.

(e) Tutorial—discussion centred on students' work: in small groups the tutor tends to dominate especially when in the assessment role.

(f) Buzz groups—an invaluable way of easing communication when it gets sticky or as a break in lectures. Students are asked to turn to a neighbour and discuss problems, applications, and so on for 2 to 5 minutes.

(g) Snowball groups—a development of the buzz group: individuals write down points, then form pairs to share thoughts, and finally merge into progressively larger groups with a plenary discussion at the end.

(h) Cross-over groups—in the first phase, students work in subgroups and are each given a letter, number, or colour which allocates them in the second phase to another group comprising one person from each of the first set.

(i) Syndicates—the class is divided into groups of about six who are given reading and writing assignments to complete on a cooperative basis over a period of weeks (see Collier 1980).

(j) Horseshoe groups—students are grouped round tables in a large classroom; the ends of the tables closest to the board are left vacant. This enables the class to alternate between small group discussion on a given task, plenary discussion on outcomes, and a short lecture from students or teacher.

(k) Associative discussion—the topic and direction of discussion are controlled by the student group; the tutor observes, intervening at agreed times with comments on anomalies and inconsistencies in the arguments helping students "see themselves as capable of change" (Abercrombie 1979).

(l) Brainstorming—a problem-solving technique involving creative thinking in which ideas are generated freely. Four ground rules apply: no criticism or evaluation; everyone must "free wheel" ideas; quantity is preferred to quality; ideas should be built upon and combined.

(m) Synectics—a development of brainstorming in which devices like metaphor, making the strange familiar or the familiar strange, and fantasy are used to extend the bounds of imagination. Stein (1975) gives a full critique of both these creative-thinking techniques.

(n) Simulation and gaming exercises—a contrived but stimulating situation is enacted in the classroom with a set of prescribed rules and a "scenario"; this can also be used to stimulate more openness and cohesiveness in a group.

(o) Role play—a kind of simulation in which participants try themselves out in different roles in prescribed or agreed situations.

(p) Fishbowl—half the group sit in an inner circle while the remainder sit round the outside and observe patterns of interaction, styles of argument, and so on.

(q) T-groups—a method of teaching self-awareness and interpersonal relations in which group members, under a trained leader, discuss their "here and now" relationships with each other. (See Smith 1980, Shaffer and Galinsky 1974.)

(r) Peer-tutoring—of great value for distance learning. The informal exchanges that go on between students in laboratory groups or over coffee are formalized into teaching and learning tasks, as for example in a "learning cell" where students ask and answer questions on commonly read material (Goldschmid and Goldschmid 1976, Boud 1981).

Most of these techniques are described in greater detail in Jaques (1985), as is their organization within a structured sequence in a course.

6. Groups in Context

Wherever group teaching occurs—in the seminar, the laboratory, or the project, there are two further factors which the alert tutor will want to consider: the social and educational context in which the group meets, and how to evaluate the work of the group. Students can be profoundly affected by aspects of institutional life outside the formal curriculum: departmental norms, the structure of the buildings, and the accessibility of various people to each other (see Parlett and Simons 1976). The value of chance encounters and space for ad hoc groups to meet should not be underrated. In the educational sense, group teaching has to form an integral part of a sometimes complex and, to the student, bewildering curriculum. Tutors need to ask themselves, how does this group link to the lectures/laboratory work/field trips? How can some group work be included in lectures (Gibbs et al. 1984), and how do the norms and requirements of groups marry with those of other tutors?

Many interesting examples of the ways groups have been used in the curriculum are summarized in Jaques (1985).

7. Evaluation

To many teachers, the very notion of their teaching being evaluated induces a defensive reaction. It is often seen as an all-or-nothing judgment, "good" or "bad", and they are rightly sceptical that the intricate network of their experience in groups can be gauged in any way which produces clear and unambiguous answers. Evaluation of any teaching, particularly in groups, is of greater value to all concerned when it is not seen as a unilateral judgment but as a creative source of learning that informs both students and tutor about their respective parts in the work of the group. Students in group discussion are not consumers: they are participants in, and contributors to, an evolving process of mutual enrichment.

The most effective kind of evaluation for group teaching is, therefore, one which develops the students' awareness of the way groups work, and increases their sense of responsibility for each other and for the quality of work they do together. In this way the evaluation itself can become a vehicle for the students to learn many of the valued social aims of group work.

There are some fairly simple methods of evaluating groups in this way.

(a) *Questionnaires*. Students (and tutor) complete a process questionnaire or checklist of the kind shown in Jaques (1985), discuss the results, and decide on what needs to be done to effect improvements.

(b) *"Do-it-yourself" checklist*. Using the "Snowball" technique (see above) individual students are asked to write down three statements about the class, which, after successive pooling as the groups combine, are written on a board and given a rating in turn by everyone.

(c) *Reporting back*. At the beginning of each meeting, 5 minutes are devoted to a critique of the previous meeting. Discussion evolves naturally from this.

(d) *Diaries*. Students and tutor spend a short time towards the end of each meeting to record impressions, feelings, and what they learned about the dynamics of the group. Diary comments are shared at a later, designated meeting.

(e) *Fishbowl*. Students from another group are invited to sit round and observe the group in question as it conducts a discussion and to reveal their observations afterwards. A questionnaire or checklist may be used. If subsequently the inner group and outer group reverse positions, the evaluation can be made reciprocal.

(f) *Self-made evaluation*. Two or more subgroups devise an evaluation technique to use on the other subgroups, and then administer it.

(g) *Video or audio playback*. The camera may be obtrusive but the recorded playback does give the opportunity to witness live action and for members to contemplate their own behaviour.

For any of these techniques to be really productive there must be a shared commitment to them, and to acting on the results, by all members of the group and they must be employed at a time which is neither too early for the group to have "gelled" nor too late for it to benefit from any resulting improvements.

See also: Discussion Methods

Bibliography

Abercrombie M L J 1969 *The Anatomy of Judgement: An Investigation into the Processes of Perception and Reasoning*. Penguin, Harmondsworth

Abercrombie M L J 1979 *Aims and Techniques in Group Teaching*, 4th edn. Society for Research into Higher Education, Guildford

Abercrombie M L J, Terry P M 1978 *Talking to Learn*. Society for Research into Higher Education, Guildford.

Applbaum R L, Bodaken E, Sereno K, Anatol K 1979 *The Process of Group Communication,* 2nd edn. Science Research Associates, Chicago, Illinois

Bales R F 1970 *Personality and Interpersonal Behavior.* Holt, Rinehart and Winston, New York

Beard R, Bligh D, Harding A 1978 *Research into Teaching Methods in Higher Education.* Society for Research into Higher Education, Guildford

Bion W R 1961 *Experiences in Groups, and other Papers.* Tavistock, London

Bligh D (ed.) 1986 *Teach Thinking by Discussion.* Society for Research into Higher Education and NFER/Nelson, Guildford

Bligh D, Jaques D, Piper D W 1981 *Seven Decisions when Teaching Students.* Exeter University Teaching Services, Exeter

Boud D 1981 *Developing Student Autonomy in Learning.* Kogan Page, London

Bramley W 1979 *Group Tutoring: Concepts and Case Studies.* Kogan Page, London

Cartwright D, Zander A (eds.) 1968 *Group Dynamics, Research and Theory,* 3rd edn. Harper and Row, New York

Collier K G 1980 Peer-group learning in higher education: The development of higher order skills. *Stud. Higher Educ.* 5: 55–62

Easton G 1982 *Learning from Case Studies.* Prentice Hall, New York

Entwistle N (ed.) 1976 *Strategies for Research and Development in Higher Education.* Swets and Zeïtlinger, Amsterdam

Gibbs G, Habershaw S, Habershaw T 1984 *53 Interesting Things to Do in your Lectures.* TES Publications, Bristol

Goldschmid M L, Goldschmid B 1976 Peer teaching in higher education: A review. *Higher Educ.* 5: 9–33

Habershaw S, Habershaw T, Gibbs G 1984 *53 Interesting Things to Do in your Seminars and Tutorials.* TES Publications, Bristol

Heron J 1975 Six Category Intervention Analysis. Human Potential Research Project, University of Surrey, Guildford

Hill W F 1969 *Learning Thru' Discussion: A Guide for Discussion Group Leaders and Members.* Sage, London

Jaques D 1985 *Learning in Groups.* Croom Helm, London

Johnson D W, Johnson F P 1975 *Joining Together*: *Group Theory and Group Skills.* Prentice Hall, Englewood Cliffs, New Jersey

Klein J 1961 *Working with Groups.* Hutchinson, London

Knowles H, Knowles M S 1972 *An Introduction to Group Dynamics,* rev. edn. Association Press, Follett, Chicago, Illinois

McKeachie W J 1969 *Teaching Tips: A Guidebook for the Beginning College Teacher.* Heath, Lexington, Massachusetts

McLeish J, Matheson W, Park J 1973 *The Psychology of the Learning Group.* Hutchinson, London

Miles M B 1981 *Learning to Work in Groups,* 2nd edn. Teachers College Press, Columbia University, New York

Napier R, Gershenfeld M K 1981 *Groups: Theory and Experience,* 2nd edn. Houghton Mifflin, Boston, Massachusetts

National Union of Students (NUS) 1969 Report of Commission on Teaching in Higher Education. NUS, London

Northedge A 1975 Learning through discussion in the Open University. *Teaching at a Distance,* No. 2, Open University, Milton Keynes

Parlett M, Simons H 1976 *Learning from Learners: A Study of Students' Experiences of Academic Life.* Nuffield Foundation, London

Reason P, Rowan J (eds.) 1981 *Human Inquiry: A Sourcebook of New Paradigm Research.* Wiley, New York

Richardson E 1967 *Group Study for Teachers.* Routledge and Kegan Paul, London

Rowan J 1976 *Psychological Aspects of Society, Book 3: The Power of the Group.* Davis-Poynter, London

Rudduck J 1978 *Learning Through Small Group Discussion: A Study of Seminar Work in Higher Education.* Society for Research into Higher Education, Guildford

Schmuck R A, Schmuck P A 1979 *Group Process in the Classroom,* 3rd edn. Brown, Dubuque, Iowa

Shaffer J, Galinsky M 1974 *Models of Group Therapy and Activity Training.* Prentice Hall, Englewood Cliffs, New Jersey.

Shaw M E 1972 *Group Dynamics: The Psychology of Small Group Behavior.* Tata McGraw-Hill, New Delhi

Smith P B 1980 *Small Groups and Personal Change.* Methuen, London

Sommer R 1969 *Personal Space: The Behavioral Basis of Design.* Prentice Hall, Englewood Cliffs, New Jersey

Stein M I 1975 *Stimulating Creativity,* Vol. 2: *Group Procedures.* Academic Press, New York

Thelen H A 1965 *Dynamics of Groups at Work.* University of Chicago Press, Chicago, Illinois

University Teaching Methods Unit (UTMU) 1978 *Improving Teaching in Higher Education.* University of London Institute of Education, London

Science Laboratory Teaching

E. Hegarty-Hazel

Within a science course, the term practical work may be taken to include any activity involving students in real situations using genuine materials and properly working equipment. In many of the physical and biological sciences, practical work takes place in a laboratory and thus is often known as laboratory work (although in the United Kingdom and some other European countries practical work remains the preferred term). Field work in animal behaviour or geology would be an example of practical work which does not take place in a laboratory.

Laboratory work has long been considered the hallmark, the unique feature, of education in a science discipline. The reason for this tradition is that most of the physical and biological sciences are essentially empirical in nature—research is conducted, knowledge is produced, and progress is made in the professional laboratories of scientists. It has seemed logical to science educators that the features of student science should reflect those of professional science and thus that science students should be taught for at least part of the time in laboratory classes. This view is supported by research on learning which suggests that scientific knowledge can be most effectively learned from texts, lectures, or discussions but that the methods and spirit of enquiry in a discipline are learned in the laboratory. However, a point which has often been overlooked is that the degree to which it is important for the methods and spirit of enquiry to be learnt cannot be decided in general but rather must be decided separately for groups of students in different contexts.

Laboratory teaching is now an umbrella term which can cover one or various combinations of the following activities (Dunn 1986):

(a) controlled exercises, experiments, demonstrations;

(b) audiotutorial/laboratory method;

(c) Keller plan (personalized system of instruction, PSI) (see *Keller Plan: A Personalized System of Instruction*);

(d) computer-assisted laboratory instruction;

(e) experimental investigations;

(f) project work (see *The Project Method*);

(g) participation in research.

Despite the variety of approaches available, much of current thinking is influenced by the great tradition of university laboratory work (Ogborn 1977 p. 2). Traditional laboratory work contains a number of experiments, many of them ingenious and elegant, each in some way a microcosm of the art of experimentation though the emphasis may be laid more on one aspect than another. Each is more or less equivalent to the others in the thinking it demands, the time it takes, and the difficulties it presents. Often there is no special order in which students do the experiments.

Hegarty (1982) described three aspects of science laboratory teaching with findings of particular relevance for classroom practice as well as for theory and research: the educational goals pursued, the type of classroom life which eventuates, and the effects of enquiry-oriented curriculum materials. Each of these and the relationships between them was further explored by Hegarty-Hazel (1986) and throughout Boud et al. (1986).

1. Goals of Laboratory Teaching

Statements of goals of science teaching can be considered within one of six major categories (based on the scheme proposed by Klopfer 1971):

(a) knowledge and comprehension;

(b) manual skills;

(c) processes of scientific enquiry:

    (i)   observing and measuring
    (ii) interpreting data
    (iii) identifying problems
    (iv) seeking ways to solve problems;

(d) appreciation of the ways in which scientists work;

(e) scientific attitudes and interests;

(f) application of scientific knowledge and methods.

The literature on science goals for secondary-school students stresses (a), (c), (d), and (e). Similar goals are stressed for university students not majoring in science (e.g., arts or commerce students). For university students in applied fields such as medicine or dentistry the goals stressed are (a), (d), and (f). For science and engineering majors at universities, the goals stressed are (a), (b), (c), (d), and (e).

Which of these goals is laboratory teaching best suited to achieve? The outcomes of comparative learning research provide guidance. These studies of the effectiveness of laboratory work have been of the method A versus method B variety where outcomes of laboratory teaching are compared with outcomes of instruction by lectures/discussions/demonstrations. From reviews (Bradley 1968, Bates 1978) where the results of large numbers of such studies have been accumulated two generalizations emerge.

Firstly, laboratory work is superior in teaching manual skills and in increasing understanding of the apparatus involved. It is valuable in giving practice in processes of scientific enquiry and certain problem-solving skills, developing appreciation of ways in which scientists work, developing scientific attitudes and laboratory resourcefulness, and providing for individual differences.

Secondly, lecture/discussion/demonstration is superior for the presentation of complex material and more efficient for the presentation of large amounts of factual information and concepts. It can be effective in teaching applications of scientific knowledge and methods.

Thus, the need to use laboratory teaching for university science and engineering majors would seem extremely clear. The need for its use with all the other groups of students discussed above would depend on local circumstances.

1.1 Knowledge and Comprehension

Laboratory teaching is not efficient for the presentation of factual information. Reception of knowledge via texts or lectures is superior. However, when new concepts are introduced, laboratory teaching can provide concrete experience which gives meaning to the concept. In this way laboratory teaching seems especially suited to the promotion of meaningful learning as distinct from rote learning (memorization without understanding). One of the most potentially powerful uses of laboratory teaching is currently being explored in physics and chemistry—its use in creating cognitive conflict, in confronting students' misconceptions, and encouraging students to accommodate a new conception of the subject matter. If experience has taught students misconceptions, then it is unlikely that formal instruction will overcome them. A laboratory setting could provide the link with prior experience. It is likely that peer-group discussion and specific teacher challenges would be required for a student to clarify the difference between his or her notion of a science concept and the expert or desired notion.

The Keller plan or personalized system of instruction (PSI) and the audiotutorial approach are two systems of individualized instruction which can incorporate laboratory work and which seem well-matched to the goal of joining knowledge and comprehension. The emphasis on mastery learning (see *Mastery Learning Models*) with PSI means, in principle, that all laboratory materials would need to be available throughout the course. This is less likely to cause organizational problems in the physical sciences than in the biological sciences where animals, plants, micro-organisms, enzymes, and other biologically active extracts have limited life spans.

1.2 Manual Skills

It may be safely asserted that laboratory skills can be well learned in suitably designed laboratory classes. Examples of such skills include techniques such as diluting, titrating, preparing chemical solutions, dissecting, preparing and staining smears and sections of animal and plant tissues, together with the use of equipment such as balances, microscopes, spectrophotometers. When mastery of laboratory skills is required, teacher demonstrations, films, television, computers, and simulations cannot substitute for individual laboratory work. However they can complement it in many effective ways including methods overviews, showing fine details of technical manoeuvres, and providing introductions to equipment which is especially complex, fragile, or expensive.

Studies with adult learners have shown that effective learning of technical skills requires both practice, and feedback on the success of attempts. As well, it requires that the experimenter have an overview of the method (the order and purpose of the steps in the method). Some examples from chemistry show how the conditions for effective learning can be met. Students who used techniques-kits obtained practice in weighing, titrating, preparing standard solutions, and using a spectrophotometer before testing the success of their practice by completing exercises which required precise execution of the technique and where errors were measured. This practice and feedback reduced average student errors by five- to ten-fold. A different approach which proved successful in chemistry volumetric analysis was to provide students with methods overviews for the use of analytical balances, pipettes, and burettes together with structured exercises where students were

required to go through mental practice of the steps of each procedure.

1.3 Processes of Scientific Enquiry

Over the period 1960 to 1980 the impetus for encouraging students to act as scientific enquirers came not from universities but from secondary-school science programmes. Major restructuring resulted in the production of the Nuffield enquiry-based science curricula in the United Kingdom, and BSCS Biology (Biological Sciences Curriculum Study) and other enquiry-based science curricula in the United States and other countries.

As a result, there was some development of enquiry skills by students in especially attuned contexts. Studies using questioning on goals and learning environment inventories have shown that such high-school students in the United Kingdom, the United States, Australia, and Israel, were aware of the enquiry orientation and the experience of investigating scientific problems although they had not necessarily become more scientifically curious as a result. By comparison, studies of university students in the same countries have shown significantly less awareness of scientific enquiry.

The conclusion of the major United States national report, *Case Studies in Science Education* (Stake and Easley 1978) was that for very many high-school students, the enquiry-oriented science curricula had somehow failed in practice to materialize. Some reasons offered by the researchers for the nonappearance of enquiry skills as student outcomes were: (a) lack of time, overcrowding, understaffing, and preoccupation with laboratory management activities; (b) difficulties in incorporating laboratory experiences as part of a meaningful enquiry; (c) use of teachers' authority to overcome discipline problems discourages problem solving and scientific enquiry. In response to the *Case Studies in Science Education* and three other major assessments of the actual status of school science in the United States, Welch et al. (1981) proffered an entire reassessment whereby they suggest it is no longer feasible to hope for development of science enquiry skills in all high-school science students. Rather, it would be recognized that enquiry objectives would only be achieved when consistent with a student's psychological needs, and personal goals and in a school and community environment which is conducive.

University laboratory teaching has suffered from widespread failure to introduce enquiry-oriented curricula in the first place. For example, content analysis of some 500 exercises in commercially available laboratory manuals for university science students in one discipline failed to locate any exercises where students were required to play any role in recognizing a problem or designing an experiment or the methods and materials needed to investigate a problem (Hegarty 1979). Students cannot conduct meaningful enquiries in areas in which they have no background. Thus the change required would not be the provision of unguided student discovery learning (a discussion of dimensions of guidance, discovery, and enquiry may be found in Shulman and Tamir 1973). Rather it would be a change towards sequences of laboratory work where exercises involving enquiry skills follow prior learning of basic concepts and the learning of the skills with techniques and apparatus required for the enquiry (Dunn and Boud 1986, Hegarty-Hazel 1986).

At universities, the use of short or long projects in science laboratory teaching is a time-honoured way of providing some experience of scientific enquiry (Ogborn 1977). This is usually restricted to final year students although it is sometimes used in the final segments of more junior courses. Despite acknowledged high cost, uncertain efficiency, and difficulties of management and assessment, projects have found quite wide acceptance especially in the United Kingdom. Criticisms of projects on grounds other than cost-effectiveness include the uncontrolled nature and variability of experience of scientific enquiry skills. There are many occasions in which the learning–challenge sequences described above could provide experience with a similar range of enquiry skills under more circumscribed circumstances. Finally, it is worth pointing out that if students are to conceptualize the processes of scientific enquiry as conducted by professional scientists, there should be explicit instruction on the topic as well as any implicit instruction which may be embedded in enquiry-oriented laboratory exercises or projects.

2. Life in Laboratory Classes

Life in laboratory classes is a constantly changing balance between private engagements of students with phenomena and encounters whereby they learn from teachers or other students. Possible teacher roles can vary correspondingly from facilitator, manager, and supplier of materials to provider of information, and demonstrator of techniques or to questioner, challenger, and promoter of enquiry. Most observational studies suggest the former roles are most favoured. At school level, studies show busy teachers who do a great deal of telling and demonstrating, who may have little or no technical assistance, and who spend a disproportionately large amount of time on laboratory management activities (Stake and Easley 1978). At university level, the report of the Higher Education Learning Project (Ogborn 1977) gives an overwhelming impression of laboratory classes considered by science students and staff alike as valuable places of learning but not especially enjoyable or stimulating. Teachers tend to play shepherding roles caring for their students and making certain that equipment is safe and functioning smoothly. Indeed university teachers seem to regard ensuring smooth functioning of all aspects of students' laboratory work as perhaps their major role.

Quantitative data on behaviour in high-school science laboratories was obtained for biological and physical sciences by Parakh (1968), Evans and Balzer (1970),

Eggleston et al. (1975), Guy (1982), and reviewed by Hegarty (1982). It was found that in laboratories as well as lecture classrooms, teachers were the source of activity for most of the time. However, the level of teacher talk in laboratories (35–50 percent) was much lower than in lecture classrooms where teachers talked for some 70 percent of the time. Dominant teacher behaviours were the development of substantive content (30–50 percent) and laboratory activities and organization (40–55 percent). Of the cognitive behaviours, there was approximately equal emphasis on low level talk about subject matter and procedures (10–15 percent each) with less emphasis on scientific processes (about 8 percent). Discussion of the nature of scientific enquiry was rare, as was reflection of scientific enquiry in behaviours such as problem identification and hypothesis formulation. Lower level enquiry processes such as data interpretation, prediction, and formulation of conclusions were also uncommon. Teachers seldom asked pupils for new approaches to a problem or the design of an experiment to help solve a problem. The science laboratories were primarily neutral in tone with time spent on verbal affective behaviours being 5 percent or less. Of the limited data presented about students, behaviour classified as cognitive occupied about 13 percent of class time with most of that being taken by asking questions about laboratory techniques and procedures and by responding to questions by providing facts and definitions. Significantly more studies have been made of behaviour in school science classes with no laboratory component and for comparisons, reference may be made to the review by Power (1977).

At university level, Hegarty (1978) reported an account of the commonplaces of laboratory behaviour in final year microbiology classes at two Australian universities. The observation scheme used had four major divisions, cognitive, laboratory activities, laboratory organization, and class unrelated. Using this scheme, results showed that at both institutions, students' time was divided approximately equally between the first three of the major divisions with the remaining 10–15 percent of time spent on activities unrelated to classwork. The university teachers spent about the same proportion of their time (28 percent) on organization as their students. Time spent on laboratory activities was low (4–14 percent) and time spent on behaviours classified as cognitive was higher (40–60 percent) than that reported in most other studies. This difference was mostly attributable to heavy emphasis on talk about laboratory procedures and, at one of the universities, a great deal of talk at low cognitive levels stressing recall of knowledge and definitions. Totals of categories for verbal behaviour showed that at this second university the teachers spent the greatest part of their time in the laboratory talking (72 percent)—questioning and lecturing to small or large groups of students.

Comparable results were reported from a study carried out at the University of Iowa, in the United States, to analyse the behaviours of students and instructors in the introductory and advanced level laboratories of five science disciplines—botany, chemistry, geology, physics, and zoology (Kyle et al. 1979, 1980). Effects such as the large proportion of teachers' time spent on talk at low cognitive levels and of students' time spent on passive activities such as listening, reading, and writing, seemed even more marked in this study considering that observations were made only during the central "hands-on" portion of the laboratory (i.e., excluding any prelab or postlab lectures or discussions). There were no consistent differences between disciplines (which may be an artefact of the type of observation scheme and sampling system used). Differences between introductory and advanced levels included less teacher talk in introductory classes (average 20 percent vs. 30 percent) and more student experimentation (average 43 percent vs. 22 percent). The authors suggested that their data supported the conclusion that instructors were randomly reacting to situations as they arose in the laboratory and did not show evidence of systematic teaching and especially not of enquiry-oriented teaching. The results for students were described as consistent with performance of knowledge-oriented "cookbook" laboratories.

Studies at university level and their implications were reviewed by Hegarty-Hazel (1986).

3. Effects of Enquiry-oriented Curriculum Materials on Behaviour in Science Laboratories

Many of the newer school science curricula (such as BSCS, Biological Sciences Curriculum Study) and some university science courses have claimed to place more emphasis on scientific enquiry than did traditional curricula. Evans and Balzer (1970) reported the results of observations in classrooms where BSCS (enquiry-oriented) materials and "non-BSCS" were in use although they did not clearly differentiate between periods with and without laboratory work. When data for the major category "management" in their observation scheme were analysed in detail, there was an increase (with BSCS) in teacher time spent on laboratory management, and when data for the major category "content development" were analysed, it was found that BSCS teachers placed more emphasis on scientific enquiry. There was a decrease in the percentage of time spent on lower cognitive behaviours (knowledge), a substantial increase in time spent on behaviours reflecting scientific enquiry, and a decrease in time spent on discussion of laboratory procedures. Some similar findings were reported with the Australian Science Education Project (ASEP) (Power and Tisher 1976). Process–product studies showed that there was a strong negative correlation between teachers' time spent on management activities and student achievement and that there was greater variability in achievement (possibly better performance by more able students) in classes where there was frequent teacher–student interaction

and less frequent lecturing by the teacher to the class as a whole. However, strategies which showed positive effects when used with one ASEP unit did not necessarily produce similar effects with another unit.

In one study, a comparison was made of behaviour in laboratory classrooms at high school and university levels (Tamir 1977). The school students were using an enquiry-oriented biology curriculum (BSCS) whilst students at the Hebrew University (Israel) were using locally designed course offerings in chemistry, biology, histology, and physiology. Investigative indices were calculated as the sum of scores for all enquiry-oriented behaviours divided by the scores for all verification-oriented behaviours. The average investigative index at high-school level was 1.2 compared with 0.5 at university level, (i.e., at university level, verification dominated enquiry behaviour). In school science laboratories high scores for enquiry-orientation were associated with the use of "postlab" discussion on analysis of data and interpretation of results (range 7–29 percent of time). Postlab discussions were uniformly nonexistent in the university laboratories and Tamir was critical of the lack of emphasis on enquiry in the university classes and the approach where every measure was taken to ensure smooth and safe completion of the task by providing detailed instructions and, as far as possible, eliminating difficulties and mistakes which might lead students to unpredicted results.

The studies quoted above provided indirect evidence on the effects of introducing enquiry-oriented curricula. Most were of the method A versus method B type where an enquiry laboratory at one institution may vary in many uncontrolled respects (besides enquiry-orientation) from a conventional laboratory in a different course or institution. More direct evidence was provided by Hegarty (1978) who reported on changes in laboratory behaviours within a single university science course. These were observed when laboratory work changed in enquiry emphasis from low to high. Levels of openness for enquiry were allocated as 0, 1, 2, or 3 using the scheme developed by Herron (1971). This is a scheme where Level 0 exercises provide practice in techniques or are confirmatory exercises with the answer already provided for students. Exercises at levels 2 and 3 are those which provide opportunity for scientific enquiry. At level 2, the problem is defined by the teacher, but the students are responsible for its investigation. Hegarty (1978) subdivided this level into 2A and 2B (2A exercises being structured by the teacher to the extent of specifying the materials available but requiring students to design the methods, and 2B being more open projects). The laboratory observation study reported by Hegarty compared behaviours during classes designated at level 0, level 2A and level 2B.

Time spent on talk about scientific processes was used as one indicator of enquiry orientation. Although this was low in all classes (maximum 3 percent for students and 5 percent for teachers) there were highly significant changes associated with change of laboratory exercises from level 0 to level 2. For students, talk on scientific processes increased some thirtyfold for the change 0 to 2A and tenfold for the change 0 to 2B. Most of this was accounted for by talk with fellow students, not teachers. This is worth noting since it is often assumed desirable that the introduction of enquiry-oriented curricula should be accompanied by a decrease in students' dependence on the teacher and an increase in peer group interaction. Opportunities for students to compare observations and discuss interpretations is thought to facilitate self-regulation (in Piagetian terminology) and the acquisition of abstractions (Lawson and Renner 1975). With the change in exercises from level 0 to level 2 there was a fivefold increase in teachers' talk at low cognitive levels and a concomitant marked increase in students' time listening to such talk. But the expected increase in teachers' talk on scientific processes did not occur. There was a small increase to level 2A but during extended exercises and projects at level 2B, the talk on scientific processes dropped below the score for level 0. This suggests that the university teachers took a dominant role in the development of substantive content and knowledge of procedures but took the role of resource person/manager when dealing with students' bench work (Hegarty 1978).

Other effects accompanied the change in levels from 0 to 2. These were an increase in students' time spent planning and organizing (11 percent at levels 0 and 2A, but 21 percent at level 2B) and a decrease in time spent using techniques, making observations, and taking measurements. Teachers' laboratory management activities increased to a total of some 20 percent of time and the increase was especially marked for those activities where the teacher left the laboratory room entirely in order to locate glassware and equipment for unexpected requests associated with students' projects. There was a sixfold increase in these out-of-lab management activities. The effect was far more pronounced for the projects at level 2B than for the more structured exercises at level 2A. Similarly there was an increase in time spent by students on laboratory organization (twofold to a total of some 20 percent) when students were pursuing exercises at level 2B over that at lower levels (Hegarty 1978).

These results give an idea of the types of "trade-offs" (in the sense they were discussed by Good and Power 1976) which resulted from an increase in enquiry orientation in a university science laboratory course. Enquiry-related behaviours of both teachers and students were more noticeable at level 2A than at 2B. This presents a challenge to the practice of offering project work (which is at level 2B, or occasionally 3) in university science. Projects are notoriously expensive of time and money and it is likely that some of them could be replaced with more structured exercises at level 2A (which apparently present more opportunities for enquiry within a compressed time span). The only obvious loss would be students' unlimited choice of materials.

In general, research reviewed in this section suggests that enquiry-oriented teacher behaviour (such as questioning, challenging, encouraging hypothesis formation, design of experiments) was expected by investigators but seldom found. If the underlying assumptions are warranted, the data suggest that many science teachers have limited understanding of scientific enquiry or of the teaching skills likely to promote students' understanding of scientific enquiry in a laboratory classroom setting.

Bibliography

Bates G C 1978 The role of the laboratory in secondary school science programs. In: Rowe M B (ed.) 1978 *What Research Says to the Science Teacher*, Vol. 1. National Science Teachers Association, Washington, DC

Boud D J, Dunn J G, Hegarty-Hazel E 1986 *Teaching in Laboratories*. Society for Research in Higher Education and NFER/Nelson, Guildford

Bradley R L 1968 Is the science laboratory necessary for general education science courses? *Sci. Educ.* 52: 58–66

Dowdeswell W H, Harris N D C 1979 Project work in university science. In: International Council of Scientific Unions Committee on the Teaching of Science (eds.) 1979 *Learning Strategies in University Science*. University College, Cardiff

Dunn J G 1986 Strategies for course design. In: Boud et al. 1986 Chap. 2

Dunn J G, Boud D J 1986 Sequencing and organization. In: Boud et al. 1986 Chap. 3

Eggleston J F, Galton M J, Jones M E 1975 *A Science Teaching Observation Schedule*. Macmillan, London

Evans T P, Balzer L 1970 An inductive approach to the study of biology teacher behaviors. *J. Res. Sci. Teach.* 7: 47–56

Good T L, Power C N 1976 Designing successful classroom environments for different types of students. *J. Curric. Stud.* 8: 45–60

Guy J J 1982 Quantitative classroom observation illustrated by a study of chemistry practical teaching. In: Royal Society for Chemistry 1982 *Chemical Education Research: Implications for Teaching*. Report of a Symposium. Royal Society for Chemistry, Birmingham.

Hegarty E H 1978 Levels of scientific enquiry in university science laboratory classes: Implications for curriculum deliberations. *Res. Sci. Educ.* 8: 45–57

Hegarty E H 1979 The role of laboratory work in teaching microbiology at university level. Unpublished Ph.D thesis, University of New South Wales, New South Wales

Hegarty E H 1982 The role of laboratory work in science courses: Implications for college and high school levels. In: Rowe M B (ed.) 1982 *Education in the 80s: Science*. National Education Association, Washington, DC

Hegarty-Hazel E 1986 Research In: Boud et al. 1986 Chap. 6

Herron M D 1971 The nature of scientific enquiry. *Sch. Rev.* 79: 171–212

Klopfer L E 1971 Evaluation of learning in science. In: Bloom B S, Hastings J T, Madaus G F (eds.) 1971 *Handbook of Formative and Summative Evaluation of Student Learning*. McGraw-Hill, New York

Kyle W C, Penick J E, Shymansky J A 1979 Assessing and analyzing the performance of students in college science laboratories. *J. Res. Sci. Teach.* 16: 545–51

Kyle W C, Penick J E, Shymansky J A 1980 Assessing and analyzing behavior strategies of instructors in college science laboratories. *J. Res. Sci. Teach.* 17: 131–37

Lawson A E, Renner J W 1975 Piagetian theory and biology teaching. *Am. Biol. Teach.* 37: 336–43

Ogborn J M (ed.) 1977 *Practical Work in Undergraduate Science.* Heinemann, London

Parakh J S 1968 A study of teacher–pupil interaction in high school biology classes, Part II: Description and analysis. *J. Res. Sci. Teach.* 5: 183–92

Power C N 1977 A critical review of science classroom interaction studies. *Stud. Sci. Educ.* 4: 1–30

Power C N, Tisher R P 1976 Relationships between classroom behavior and instructional outcomes in an individualized science program. *J. Res. Sci. Teach.* 13: 489–97.

Shulman L S, Tamir P 1973 Research on teaching in the natural sciences. In: Travers R M W (ed.) 1973 *Second Handbook of Research on Teaching: A Project of the American Educational Research Association.* Rand McNally, Chicago, Illinois

Stake R E, Easley J A (Codirectors) 1978 *Case Studies in Science Education.* Prepared for the National Science Foundation Directorate for Science Education. Center for Instructional Research and Curriculum Evaluation, University of Illinois at Urbana-Champaign, Illinois

Tamir P 1977 How are the laboratories used? *J. Res. Sci. Teach.* 14: 311–16

Welch W W, Klopfer L E, Aikenhead G S, Robinson J T 1981 The role of inquiry in science education: Analysis and recommendations. *Sci. Educ.* 65: 33–50

Clinical Teaching

P. A. Cranton

Clinical teaching may be defined as an instructional process which occurs in a natural health-related environment (medicine, dentistry, nursing, social work, physical therapy, etc.). Students observe and participate in clinical activities which are intended to provide opportunities for the application of facts, theories, and principles to the practice of the profession. Clinical teaching differs from classroom teaching in that it occurs in a setting which is not primarily designed for instruction. Individuals (staff, patients, or clients) and activities (patient care, institution management) which are not directly involved in the instructional process are present and do influence the nature of the instruction.

The literature in the area of clinical teaching tends to be varied in nature and scope. Many authors describe techniques that have been developed for a particular program or school, and education writers often attempt to apply principles of classroom teaching and learning to the clinical setting. When research has been conducted, it has tended, with few exceptions, to be concerned with isolated aspects of clinical instruction, such as techniques for evaluating student performance in a specific area.

Clinical teaching methods can be discussed under four headings: (a) the use of orienting stimuli (e.g., objectives, clinical orientation) in order to inform the student of what is expected; (b) the sequencing of instruction; (c) teaching roles, techniques, and materials; and (d) the evaluation of student performance.

1. Orienting Stimuli

It has been demonstrated repeatedly in educational research that when students know what they are expected to learn, their learning is facilitated. In the area of clinical teaching, most authors advocate the use of objectives (Stritter 1972) and most clinical instructors use some orienting technique (Kiely 1981). Students generally perceive some type of orientation as a factor which enhances clinical learning (Miller 1976, Stritter et al. 1975); however they may place less emphasis on clearly defined objectives than do instructors (O'Shea and Parsons 1979), perhaps due to a lack of knowledge of the utilization of objectives (Kiely 1981). When programs are designed to train clinical instructors, some emphasis is usually placed on defining learning objectives; this is illustrated in the University of Manchester's comprehensive clinical teacher training effort (Byrne 1974).

Although the use of objectives, goals, and orientation sessions is stressed by authors and practitioners in the clinical area, no systematic attempt has been made to investigate their effectiveness in facilitating student learning.

2. Sequencing Instruction

Educational researchers and instructional design experts generally agree that the sequence and organization of instruction is important in facilitating student learning. Taxonomies of learning objectives have been developed in the cognitive, affective, and psychomotor domains; the structure is a hierarchical one, beginning with low level, simple tasks, and moving to higher level, more complex tasks. In the clinical setting, the sequencing of instruction is affected by the daily activities of the institution and an instructional design approach is often not possible. Quint (1965) reviews the nature of unexpected events that interfere with planned instruction. However, particularly in nursing education, many authors present guidelines for planning clinical assignments (Hayter 1967), with an emphasis on providing opportunities for students to apply knowledge after it has been learned. In general, the sequencing principles suggested in the clinical teaching literature follow the taxonomies developed for classroom instruction. A taxonomy developed specifically for clinical education (Dudley 1970) includes factual knowledge at the lowest level, and "clinical systematics" (mental strategies for problem solving) at the highest level.

Some research has investigated the type of sequencing principles which are actually used in the clinical setting. Kiely (1981), for example, found that 84 percent of a sample of nursing instructors used the principle of simple to complex nursing care to plan instruction. The effect, however, of specific sequences of instruction on student learning has not been investigated.

At a more general level, the sequence of clinical rotations through different disciplines (such as surgery, pediatrics, psychiatry) has been investigated (Cranton and Patel 1981, Patel and Cranton 1981) and has been found to influence student learning, particularly in the affective domain.

In summary, most writers and instructors in the clinical area advocate and follow sequencing principles similar to those implemented in traditional instruction; however there is no evidence of the effectiveness of this approach.

3. Roles, Techniques, and Materials

Instructor roles, teaching techniques, and materials used are aspects of the clinical instructional process which necessarily differ considerably from classroom instruction. Consequently, a great deal of descriptive literature is available, providing discussions of how clinical teaching is actually done, or advocating methods that should be used.

3.1 Instructor Roles

In most clinical areas, instructors perceive themselves to be role models. Although the types of role models tend to vary with the profession and the level of learning, authors argue that modeling is an essential component of student learning. It is interesting, however, that when students' perceptions are investigated, a discrepancy is found: O'Shea and Parsons (1979) noted that faculty indicated role modeling as a facilitative behavior five times as often as students did. Kiely found that students perceived instructors as resource persons nearly 60 percent of the time, and as models only 10 percent of the time.

3.2 Teaching Techniques

The environment within which clinical teaching occurs dictates to a large extent the teaching techniques which can be utilized. The most frequently used methods tend to be instructor demonstration, peer teaching, discussion (either between one instructor and one student, or with a small group of students and the clinical instructor), and clinical conferences (Kiely 1981). Using the critical incident technique and factor analysis of rating scales, several researchers have investigated students' perceptions of effective clinical teaching behavior (Stritter et al. 1975). Results of this research have tended to agree that active student participation, student-centered activities, applied problem solving, and opportunity to practice skills are among those components of teaching behavior which facilitate student learning. Students tend to perceive the more passive situations, such as observational learning and didactic learning as less effective (it should be noted that the frequent use of instructor demonstration is inconsistent with these results).

3.3 Instructional Materials

Materials utilized in the clinical setting are determined most often by the nature of the profession and the institution. Examples of commonly used materials include: professional books and articles, the *Compendium of Pharmaceuticals*, drug cards, patient charts, nursing cardex, medication cardex, and hospital procedure or policy books. Unfortunately researchers have not investigated the effectiveness of various instructional materials in the clinical area.

4. Evaluation of Student Performance

An integral part of any instructional process is the evaluation of student learning, both in terms of providing ongoing feedback to the student in order to facilitate learning, and assessing student competence for the purpose of grading or certification. In clinical instruction, the concern is most often with the actual performance of skills and with the affective domain, two areas which are relatively difficult to evaluate. The literature in this area includes descriptions of techniques for evaluation which have been developed in various disciplines, as well as studies of the reliability and validity of specific instruments.

Although the literature on the evaluation of clinical competence is vast, some general themes emerge. It is usually suggested that student performance be divided into categories of behavior to permit a more objective observation and recording process (Litwack 1976). In recent years, a criterion-referenced approach to the assessment of competence within behavioral categories has been advocated (Newble et al. 1978) and implemented in most institutions (Patel 1981). The measurement techniques most often described are a combination of paper and pencil multiple-choice or problem-solving tests, and observation of clinical performance in a real or simulated setting using checklists or rating scales (Holmes et al. 1978). Student performance may be videotaped and more than one observer may be used. Harden and Gleeson (1979) describe the design and implementation of one such technique, called the "objective structured clinical examination": students rotate through stations, each representing one component of clinical competence, and are evaluated by checklists and multiple-choice questions related to the station activity.

The assessment of clinical competence in the affective domain (interpersonal skills, attitude, integrity) is probably the most difficult aspect of the evaluation process. Grayson et al. (1977) describe one possible technique, in which students observe videotaped interview segments and answer multiple-choice questions after each segment. Attitudes have been assessed by questionnaire (Patel 1981), and often communication skills, professionalism, and other affective areas are judged while the student is performing other tasks. Generally, it has been found that measures of affective learning do not correlate with other areas of clinical performance (Willoughby et al. 1979).

Although much has been written about the evaluation component of clinical instruction, it continues to be an area of concern for both instructors and researchers. The deficiencies of traditional clinical examinations have been identified; however relatively few attempts have been made to improve the assessment of clinical skills.

5. Summary

The study of clinical teaching is a relatively new area in educational research. Consequently, although there is a large descriptive literature, much work remains to be done in the investigation of effective instructional techniques. To some extent, the knowledge that has been gained in research on the teaching and learning process in the classroom can be applied to the clinical area, but the unique environment in which clinical teaching takes place leads to the necessity to conduct further investigations on all aspects of the process.

Bibliography

Byrne P S 1974 Training teachers of general practice. *Lancet* 11: 568–70

Cranton P A, Patel V 1981 Improving teaching in the clinical area. Paper Presented at the Annual Meeting of the American Educational Research Association, Los Angeles, California

Daggett C J, Cassie J M, Collins G F 1979 Research on clinical teaching. *Rev. Educ. Res.* 49: 151–69

Dudley H A F 1970 Taxonomy of clinical educational objectives. *Br. J. Med. Educ.* 4: 13–18

Grayson M, Nugent C, Oken S L 1977 A systematic and comprehensive approach to teaching and evaluating interpersonal skills. *J. Med. Educ.* 52: 906–13

Harden R M, Gleeson F A 1979 Assessment of clinical competence using an objective structured clinical examination (OSCE). *Med. Educ.* 13: 41–54

Hayter J 1967 Guidelines for selecting learning experiences. *Nursing Outlook* 15: 63–65

Holmes F F, Baker L H, Torian E C, Richardson N K, Glick S, Yarmat A J 1978 Measuring clinical competence of medical students. *Med. Educ.* 12: 364–68

Kiely Y An investigation of effective clinical teaching (M.Ed. Thesis, McGill University, Montreal, 1981)

Litwack L 1976 A system for evaluation. *Nursing Outlook* 24: 45–48

Miller M D 1976 Student evaluation of clinical teaching. Paper Presented at the Annual Meeting of the American Educational Research Association, San Francisco, California

Newble D I, Elmslie R G, Baxter A 1978 A problem-based criterion-referenced examination of clinical competence. *J. Med. Educ.* 53: 720–26

O'Shea H S, Parsons M K 1979 Clinical instruction: Effective and ineffective teacher behaviors. *Nursing Outlook* 27: 411–15

Patel V The effects of a clinical clerkship program on the clinical competence of senior medical students. (Doctoral dissertation, McGill University, Montreal, 1981)

Patel V, Cranton P A 1981 Changes in interpersonal skills and attitudes of senior clerks during the final clerkship year at McGill. Paper Presented at the Annual Meeting of Research in Medical Education, Association for Canadian Medical Colleges, Ottawa, Ontario

Quint J C 1965 The hidden hazards in patient assignments. *Nursing Outlook* 13: 50–54

Stritter F T 1972 The teacher as manager: A strategy for medical education. *J. Med. Educ.* 47: 93-101

Stritter F T, Hain J D, Grimes D A 1975 Clinical teaching re-examined. *J. Med. Educ.* 50: 876–82

Willoughby T L, Gammon L C, Jonas H S 1979 Correlates of clinical performance during medical school. *J. Med. Educ.* 54: 453–60

Keller Plan: A Personalized System of Instruction

J. A. Kulik

The Keller Plan or Personalized System of Instruction (PSI) is an individualized teaching method developed for use in college-level instruction during the early 1960s by psychologist Fred Keller and his associates. Like other individualized teaching methods, PSI allows students to move through course material at their own rates, and requires that they show mastery of all major course objectives. What distinguishes PSI from other individualized approaches is its use of peer proctors as aides to a course instructor. The primary job of these proctors is to evaluate student performance on unit quizzes, but proctors also contribute to the interpersonal atmosphere in a classroom and provide some tutorial assistance for students.

Interest in PSI stems in part from its popularity as a teaching method. Thousands of teachers have offered courses using Keller's method since the early 1970s, and hundreds of thousands of students have taken such courses. The approach has been used by teachers in almost every discipline and in most parts of the world. But interest in PSI also comes from its record of success in evaluation studies and from its value as a tool in educational research. Few teaching innovations in the history of education have inspired so much research in so short a period of time.

1. Background

The Personalized System of Instruction has a short history but a long past. The formal history of the method goes back to 1963 when two American psychologists, Fred Keller and J. Gilmour Sherman, and two Brazilian psychologists, Carolina Bori and Rodolfo Azzi, devised the method as a way of offering psychology courses at the newly established University of Brasilia. In 1964 Keller and his associates offered the first PSI course, and in 1968 Keller presented the first formal description of the method in a classic paper "Good-bye, Teacher . . .."

But the Keller Plan also belongs to a long tradition of experiments in individualized instruction (Kulik 1982). This tradition goes back at least to the turn of the century when Frederic Burk of the San Francisco State Normal School began work on the first clear-cut plan for individualized instruction for use in his institution's elementary school. Like Keller's plan, Burk's approach called for abandoning class recitations and daily assignments. Burk and his teachers divided school work into units, constructed self-instructional materials for each unit, and tested each pupil for mastery as the pupil completed the work outlined for a unit. During the 1920s Burk's student Carleton Washburne developed the internationally acclaimed Winnetka Plan as an extension and refinement of Burk's methods (see *The Winnetka Scheme*).

In the *Twenty-fourth Yearbook of the National Society for the Study of Education* (Whipple 1925), Washburne and his colleagues described the work on individualized instruction from this period: the procedures that were used, the rationale for these procedures, and the evaluation results that were achieved. The yearbook was perhaps meant to stimulate further interest in individualized instruction, but instead it served as a monument to an educational era that was coming to an end. For this first flowering of interest in individualized instruction did not survive the cold years of the Great Depression and the Second World War. By the end of the 1920s, meaningful experimentation on individualized instruction virtually stopped, and individualized systems began to fade from view.

The stimulus for the reinvention of individualized systems came from psychologist and inventor B. F. Skinner, who in 1954 argued in "The science of learning and the art of teaching" that programmed mechanical devices, used individually by learners at their own rates, could make teaching more effective. Skinner's basic idea was that the learning of any behavior, no matter how complex, rested on the mastery of a sequence of less complex component behaviors. Theoretically, Skinner asserted, students could master even the most complex skill if a teacher divided the skill into a chain of component behaviors and then had students master each link in the chain. Skinner's programmed devices, which embodied this idea, presented instructional materials in a sequence of brief presentations, "frames," or small steps of about a sentence or a paragraph in length. The devices required learners to make an active response by correctly answering the question or solving the problem presented in each frame. And finally, the programmed devices gave learners immediate feedback about their mastery or nonmastery of the material presented in the frame.

Enthusiasm about programmed instruction has died down in recent years, and Skinner's machines and programmed texts are no longer a major focus of educational research or practice. One problem was that some of the premises of programmed instruction did not hold up well in experimental studies. Another was that the contributions of programmed devices to school learning turned out to be less dramatic than originally expected. But Skinner's teaching machines and programmed texts still seem important today because of the later work they inspired. For it was programmed instruction that rekindled interest in individualized instruction in the 1960s. Skinner's emphasis on short units, step-by-step progress, learner activity, frequent evaluation, immediate feedback, and mastery led directly to the reinvention of individualized systems by Skinner's students and colleagues. Among the individualized systems developed during the 1960s, the method devised by Skinner's friend and colleague Fred Keller holds an important place.

2. Description of PSI

In his 1968 paper "Good-bye, Teacher . . .," Keller identified five features that distinguish PSI courses from conventional ones. PSI courses are (a) mastery oriented and (b) individually paced courses that use (c) a few lectures to stimulate and motivate students, (d) printed study guides to communicate information, and (e) student proctors to evaluate quizzes. Together these five features form a "system." Given the goal of mastery—feature (a), the other features seem to follow directly. To achieve mastery in any part of a course, each student must be given the necessary time. Individual pacing—feature (b) thus seems necessary. Lecturing on required information to groups of students is incompatible with individual pacing, but optional lectures for "stimulation" are possible—feature (c). Required information must be packaged, usually in written form, for use at the student's individual rate—feature (d). Finally, since the teacher's time is limited, undergraduate proctors are needed to help with quiz evaluation and occasional one-to-one tutoring—feature (e).

To college students, Keller courses look different from other courses. The student beginning a PSI course first notes that the course is carefully divided into topics or units. In a simple case, the content of the units may correspond to chapters of a course textbook. At the start of a course, the student receives a printed study guide to direct work on the first unit. Although study guides vary, a typical one introduces the unit, states objectives, suggests study procedures, and lists study questions. The student may work anywhere—including the classroom—to achieve the objectives outlined in the study guide.

Before moving on to the second unit in the sequence, the student must demonstrate mastery of the first by perfect or near-perfect performance on a short examination. Students are examined on units only when they feel adequately prepared, and they are not penalized for failure to pass a first, second, or later examination. When the student demonstrates mastery of the first unit, the student receives the study guide for the next unit. Students thus move through PSI courses at their own rates. They may meet all course requirements before a term is half through, or they may require more than a term for completing a course.

The staff for implementing the Keller Plan includes the instructor and undergraduate proctors. The instructor selects and organizes material used in a course and usually writes study guides and constructs examinations for the course. PSI instructors give fewer lectures and demonstrations than do teachers in conventional courses (perhaps six during a semester), and these lectures are not compulsory and no examinations are based on them. Proctors evaluate readiness tests as satisfactory or unsatisfactory. Since proctors are chosen for their mastery of course content, they can prescribe remedial steps for students who encounter difficulties with course material. Proctors also offer support and encouragement for beginning students.

3. Evaluation

Evaluation studies that compare the educational outcomes of PSI and conventional classes provide important evidence about the effectiveness of PSI as an instructional system. Kulik et al. (1979) summarized results from 75 studies of this sort, reported in 72 different papers. This section is based on their findings.

3.1 Final Examinations

A total of 61 of these 75 studies compared the final examination averages of students taught the same content in PSI and conventional classes. In 57 of the 61 studies, final examination scores were higher in the PSI class; and in 48 of the studies, the examination difference in results from PSI and conventional classes was large enough to be considered statistically reliable. In no case was the examination average from a con-

ventional class significantly higher than that from a PSI class.

In the typical PSI class, the average final examination score was 74 percent; in the typical conventional class, the average score was 66 percent. A difference of eight percentage-points may be large enough to have some practical significance. In statistical terms, it amounts to a separation of approximately one-half standard deviation unit. A difference of this size suggests that PSI raises the final examination score of a typical student in a typical class from the 50th to the 70th percentile.

The 61 studies differed from one another in many ways—in study design, setting, discipline, and so on. The reviewers classified the 61 studies according to such study features, and tried to determine whether PSI produced especially clear effects in studies of certain types. They reported that PSI added to instructional effectiveness in all types of studies. A few settings and research designs, however, produced especially sharp differences between PSI and conventional classes. Differences in results were very clear, for example, when different teachers taught PSI and conventional classes; differences were less clear when the same teacher taught the two types of classes. The discipline in which a course was given also influenced results; studies from the social sciences produced the clearest results.

3.2 Follow-up Examinations

Eight studies investigated student retention of what was learned. In these studies investigators looked beyond the final examination for effects of instruction by Keller's method. In each of the studies, PSI students performed better on follow-up examinations than did students from conventional classes, and in each study the difference between groups reached statistical significance. In most of the studies, differences were greater at the time of follow-up than at the time of the final examination. For the eight PSI classes in these comparisons, average performance was 77 percent on the final examination and 69 percent on the retention test; for the average conventional class, typical scores were 68 percent on the final examination and 55 percent on retention examination.

3.3 Student Attitudes

Evaluation studies also reported on student attitudes toward personalized instruction. Some of the studies asked students to compare their PSI class to the typical class that they had taken in college. In a representative study at the College of Engineering at the University of Texas at Austin, about 70 percent of the students in a PSI class considered this method to be superior to the lecture approach; about 20 percent considered the two methods about equal; and about 10 percent preferred the lecture method. Other studies compared student responses from PSI and conventional classes on items rating the overall quality of a course. PSI ratings were higher than conventional ratings in 10 of 11 studies that secured ratings of overall quality. In eight of the studies, the difference between PSI and conventional ratings was large enough to be considered statistically reliable.

3.4 Other Reviews

These findings are consistent with findings in seven other major reviews of the PSI literature cited by Kulik et al. (1979). Each of the seven reviews noted that the vast majority of evaluation studies report PSI outcomes that are superior to those from conventional teaching. Kulik et al. (1979) so noted that PSI effects are stronger than those usually reported for other alternative college teaching methods. Of five technologies examined by these reviewers, Keller's PSI had the strongest effects on student achievement and the most pronounced effects on student ratings of instruction.

4. Essential Components

Researchers have also tried to determine which features of PSI are necessary for its distinctive effects on student achievement. Four of the ingredients of PSI seem especially important. PSI seems to work well because it involves: (a) a mastery requirement; (b) small units of work; (c) immediate and specific feedback on quiz performance; and (d) a requirement for review work. Kulik et al. (1978) summarized research results on each of these features. This section presents their major findings.

4.1 Mastery

Most PSI teachers see the unit-mastery requirement as a cornerstone of the system. They feel that a mastery requirement inevitably leads to higher levels of student achievement since with this requirement, each student must answer correctly, at least once, each important type of question raised in a college course. Research studies tend to support this line of thought. In seven studies reviewed by Kulik et al. (1978), remediation was required for some students whenever unit-quiz performance failed to reach a predefined level of excellence (usually 90 percent); remediation was not required for other students when they failed to reach this level. In each of the seven studies, students for whom mastery was required scored at least slightly higher on final examinations; in four of the studies, students for whom mastery was required scored significantly higher on examinations. The evidence, therefore, seems good that the strong remediation requirement in PSI courses is one factor that contributes to superior student achievement.

4.2 Unit Size

In PSI courses, units are short in size but large in number, and students therefore must take many unit quizzes. At least three reasons are usually given for the use of short units in PSI courses. First, with short units, teachers can usually quiz students on every course objective; with large units, teachers are less likely to be comprehensive in their testing. Second, with short units, student study time is more likely to be evenly distributed over the

term; with longer units and fewer quizzes, students are more likely to "cram." Finally, with short units and frequent quizzes, student errors can be corrected immediately before they propagate so that students in PSI courses always build on firm foundations. Research studies also tend to show that small units are more effective than large ones. Kulik et al. (1978) summarized results from three studies of short versus long units. Two of the studies reported that student achievement was significantly higher with short units.

4.3 Immediate Feedback

The main function of proctors in PSI courses is to provide immediate feedback on student performance on unit quizzes. Several researchers have provided convincing evidence of the importance of such immediate feedback. Kulik et al. (1978) summarized results from four studies comparing achievement of students who received immediate feedback with achievement of students who received delayed feedback. The studies showed that delaying feedback in PSI courses interfered with student learning of course material. It was not clear, however, why timing of feedback affected student learning so dramatically. The same mastery standard was required of students who received immediate and delayed feedback. Yet students who received delayed feedback performed less well on final examinations. The finding was especially perplexing because there is good evidence that for some kinds of learning tasks, delayed feedback is superior to immediate feedback.

4.4 Amount of Review

Many instructors feel that review is an important element in PSI courses. In arranging course material, therefore, they provide occasions for students to review and integrate what they have learned. Review materials are designed to show students what they know, to provide an overview of a subject, and to help students relate ideas covered separately in previous units. Some instructors put review materials into individual units, and write one review unit for every four or five regular units. Other instructors prefer to add a few review questions to each study guide and quiz in a PSI course. Kulik et al. (1978) summarized results from three studies on the importance of review units and review questions in PSI courses. Each of the studies reported that review procedures, either review units or review items on unit quizzes, enhanced student learning and retention.

4.5 Other Components

The more distinctive and controversial features of PSI have apparently played a less important role in its instructional successes. Amount of tutorial help available from proctors, for example, seems unrelated to overall student achievement. As long as quizzes are graded immediately, students perform at high levels in PSI courses. Additional actions taken by proctors— discussion of individual quiz answers, individual troubleshooting—seem not to add to the success of PSI courses. Restrictions can also be placed on self-pacing in PSI courses without affecting student achievement. Finally, lectures may be used for transmitting information in PSI courses without negative or positive effects on student achievement.

5. *Theory of PSI Learning*

The components that contribute most to PSI's effectiveness are the ones that increase the number of quiz items that students answer in college courses: short units, a high mastery requirement, and special review units or items. With short units, students usually have to take many quizzes and thus answer many quiz questions. With a high mastery requirement, students take alternative forms of quizzes until they demonstrate mastery, and they thus have to answer additional quiz items. With review units, students answer still more quiz questions. Any change in PSI which reduces the amount of quizzing seems to reduce PSI's impact. Thus, it seems possible that amount of quizzing is the key variable in PSI's effectiveness.

Even if this is so, much more needs to be known about the effects of frequent evaluation of students. The important question is, how do frequent evaluations affect student performance? At least two types of influence are possible. First, the amount of evaluation in personalized instruction may affect student use of study time. The requirement of frequent evaluation and re-evaluation may affect how much and how often students study. Second, the requirement may affect the content that students attend to in college courses. The numerous evaluations in PSI courses may serve to direct students toward the content that teachers consider to be most important.

Examining how students use time in PSI courses seems especially appropriate today when many educational researchers emphasize the critical importance of time as a variable in school learning. Berliner (1979), for example, has proposed a general model relating the amount that classes learn to the amount of time that teachers and students in the classes spend on the learning task. According to Berliner's model, differences in the amount that students learn about a subject are closely related to differences in the amount of time their teachers allocate to the subject. The differences in amount learned are even more closely related to the amount of "engaged" time on a task, or the amount of time that students in a class actually spend working on the subject. Finally, differences in amount learned are most closely related to the amount of time students spend working on material of an appropriate level of difficulty. This model suggests that PSI students learn more because they spend more time engaged on relevant work (see *Time*).

Is this suggestion correct? Do students spent more time on PSI courses than on other courses? Early, self-report studies suggested that students did put more time and effort into PSI courses (Kulik et al. 1976). One early study, for example, reported that 90 percent of all students in a PSI class said that they were working harder than they did in comparable lecture classes. A more complex picture emerged from later, more carefully controlled studies. In one especially well-designed investigation, a teacher deposited in a special study center all the materials for a course in beginning psychology, and then monitored the amount of time spent on the course by students in PSI and lecture sections. The teacher found that students in the two groups spent the same amount of time on the course, but they spent their time differently. Students in the lecture group used about one-third of their time attending lectures and two-thirds of their time studying individually. Personalized System of Instruction students spend nearly all of their time in individual study. Although total amount of time was about the same for the two groups, amount of "engaged" time may have been different.

Teachers have also reported other differences in the way students use time in PSI and conventional classes. First, student work may be more evenly distributed over time in PSI classes. With 15 to 20 quizzes to pass in a semester in a typical PSI class, work must necessarily be spread out. Students may cram for one or two major examinations in a conventional course; it is hardly possible to cram for the 15 to 20 separate quizzes in a PSI class. Second, in PSI classes, differences among individuals in study time may more accurately reflect differences among these individuals in aptitude and background for the course. Because of the requirement of mastery on short units of material in PSI classes, students with poor backgrounds may soon learn how much they have to study to overcome their deficiencies; students with strong backgrounds may soon learn that a small amount of work is sufficient for them. Thus, variation among individuals in study time may be greater in PSI classes than in other classes, and the correlation between student aptitude and amount of effort may also be different with the two types of teaching.

Another factor to consider in PSI classes is *what* is learned. Instruction by Keller's method is meant to keep student attention on course essentials and direct attention away from incidental and irrelevant matters. It is possible, of course, for teachers of conventional classes to publish lists of detailed course objectives and thus share with their students their ideas about course essentials. Some teachers of conventional classes and most PSI teachers, in fact, distribute lists of such objectives. But PSI teachers also do much more. They especially emphasize testing as a means of directing student attention. PSI teachers quiz students on every essential point, again and again, until students reach the standard set by the instructor. Even after students reach this standard, PSI teachers ask students the same types of questions on review items. The result is that students in PSI classes learn very well those things that instructors consider important. On measures of incidental or irrelevant learning, PSI students may not do so well, but on tests that measure mastery of course essentials, PSI students show what they have learned.

See also: Mastery Learning Models

Bibliography

Berliner D C 1979 Tempus educare. In: Peterson P L, Walberg H J (eds.) 1979 *Research on Teaching: Concepts, Findings and Implications*. McCutchan, Berkeley, California

Johnson K R, Ruskin R S 1977 *Behavioral Instruction: An Evaluative Review*. American Psychological Association, Washington, DC

Keller F S 1968 "Good-bye, teacher . . ." *J. Appl. Behav. Anal.* 1: 79–89

Keller F S, Sherman J G 1974 PSI: *The Keller Plan Handbook: Essays on a Personalized System of Instruction*. Benjamin, Menlo Park, California

Kulik J A 1982 Individualized systems of instruction. In: Mitzel H E (ed.) 1982 *Encyclopedia of Educational Research*. Macmillan, New York

Kulik J A, Jaksa P, Kulik C-L C 1978 Research on component features of Keller's personalized system of instruction. *J. Personalized Instruc.* 3: 2–14

Kulik J A, Kulik C-L C, Cohen P A 1979 A meta-analysis of outcome studies of Keller's personalized system of instruction. *Am. Psychol.* 34: 307–18

Kulik J A, Kulik C-L C, Smith B B 1976 Research on the personalized system of instruction. *Program. Learn. Educ. Technol.* 13: 23–30

Sherman J G 1974 PSI: *Personalized System of Instruction: 41 Germinal Papers*. Benjamin, Menlo Park, California

Skinner B F 1954 The science of learning and the art of teaching. *Harvard Educ. Rev.* 24: 86–97

Whipple G M 1925 Adapting the schools to individual differences. In: *Twenty-fourth Yearbook of the National Society for the Study of Education*. Society for the Study of Education, Chicago, Illinois

SECTION 4

Classroom Processes

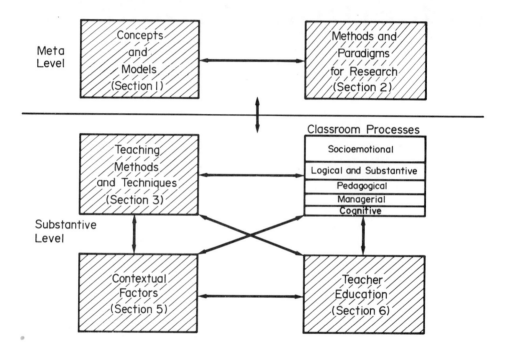

Schematic representation of Section 4 in relation to other Sections

SECTION 4

Classroom Processes

INTRODUCTION
TO SECTION 4

The organization of this section implies that an observer viewing classrooms would become aware of five major facets of activity. First, it would emerge that classrooms are places where students and teachers form interpersonal relationships involving praise, acceptance, criticism, feelings of satisfaction, likings for one another, initiation, response, competition, cooperation, and many other aspects of a *socioemotional* variety. Second, the observer would probably quickly conclude that the events of the classroom are very different from events in other social settings in terms of their content. That is, the subjects of the talk, writing, listening, and watching are different from those at the sports club, the family meal, the church gathering, or the disco. The *substance*, or content, of communications in the classroom and the ways in which that content is *processed intellectually* would bear considerable analysis by the observer.

The observer would also notice patterns in the ways in which the teacher and the students share activities in pursuit of learning tasks. In particular, it would be seen that questioning, answering, correcting, commenting, reviewing, recapitulating, and similar "pedagogical" behaviours are performed to different extents by teachers and students and apparently according to rules for classroom behaviour.

Depending upon such factors as the size of the class, the motivation of the students, and the suitability of the learning tasks, teachers find the establishment and maintenance of law and order in classrooms easy or difficult. The observer would quickly identify problem children, efficient teachers, difficult contexts, and the like by watching the state of orderliness in classrooms. This *management facet* is an important component of classroom life and involves skills that have much to do with the success teachers have in implementing the teaching methods presented in Sect. 3.

Not all of the processes of the classroom are immediately and directly available for observation. Thought, either by teachers or students, is a covert process. Nevertheless, thinking attracted a good deal of interest by researchers in the 1970s and 1980s and so is an important area for this section of the Encyclopedia.

1. Socioemotional

In the first article in this subsection, Withall, himself a pioneer of research into this aspect of classrooms, writes from a historical and theoretical perspective about teacher-centred and learner-centred education. In many ways, his article is associated with the historical article by Connell in the previous section (see *History of Teaching Methods*). Withall's article includes a section on the thought of John Dewey, with special mention of the principles of continuity of accumulated wisdom and knowledge and interaction between the student and the environment. He also discusses Freire's "pedagogy of the oppressed", with emphasis on "banking" education, "conscientization", "necrophilic" education, and "problem-posing" education, before turning to a presentation of Illich's contributions.

Withall writes that the concept of learner-centred education derives from Carl Rogers' client-centred therapy where "the ultimate aim is to help human beings to tap their latent and frequently unused urge for growth en route to becoming self-directed, self-responsible, and autonomous persons". His introduction of psychological theory here leads to a discussion of the social psychology of group processes, especially as developed by Kurt Lewin, to "attribution", theory, and research led by de Charms, and finally to consideration of theories of human needs and motivation as expounded by Maslow.

Withall's comprehensive exploration of the bases of thought and research on teacher-centred and learner-centred education provides an important starting point for the articles on the socioemotional processes of the classroom.

The article by Soar and Soar which follows is about the concept of "classroom climate". They trace the development of knowledge and thought concerning this phenomenon from the 1920s and show its connections with the concepts of "dominative" and "integrative" teacher behaviour, "learner-centred" and "teacher-centred" behaviour, and "direct" and "indirect" teacher influence. They review empirical research relating positive and negative affect to student achievement and noncognitive outcomes, giving special attention to praise which seems to have different effects from other types of positive affect. Most of the research reviewed employed live observational techniques but there is also included a review of research using paper and pencil instruments. The authors conclude by noting that the research of more recent years raises issues underlying the concerns of the mental hygienists of earlier decades.

The next two articles in this subsection are about *Cooperation* and *Competition* in classrooms and are written by Owens. Owens discusses the theses that competition is instructive in humans and that cooperation and competition are mutually exclusive. He distinguishes among three main referents for the two terms: cooperation and competition as structures, as traits, and as behaviours. In further considering cooperation, he writes about teaching strategies for encouraging student cooperativeness and distinguishes between those which see cooperation predominantly as "helpfulness" and those which see it as "mutuality". In this discussion Owens considers the methods presented in the previous section in the articles by Slavin and Medway (see *Small Group Methods*; *Tutoring*). His article on competition takes up the issue of its desirability in the classroom. He lists the pros and cons of competition and reviews research on its effects, concluding that "for school-age students the prevailing competitive individualistic ethos in which one person is encouraged to strive against all others may be counterproductive".

Much of what goes to make up classroom climate seems to be the teacher's use of rewards and punishments. In the final article in this subsection, Bates writes about the behaviourist concept of reinforcement. His article is, therefore, related to that on *Behavioral Models* in the first section of this Encyclopedia. Bates begins by distinguishing between positive and negative reinforcers and then discusses primary, secondary, and activity reinforcers and the potential for their use in the classroom. Next he considers schedules of reinforcement, including the fixed-ratio, fixed-interval, variable-ratio, and variable-interval schedules.

After discussing important issues such as the need to identify critical components within broader learning goals, to plan specific contingencies of reinforcement for them, to maintain a consistent reinforcement schedule, and to encourage generalizing desired responses in the longer term and outside the classroom, Bates considers negative reinforcement and punishment as alternatives to positive reinforcement. Among the many important points he makes here is the following: "Despite frequent demonstrations that consistent, immediate punishment is the most efficient means ever devised to eliminate unwanted behaviours, it has never been demonstrated that punishment alone will teach an organism the correct behaviour". Bates concludes his article by summarizing five principles of reinforcement and by drawing attention to gaps in knowledge about response maintenance, generalization, and the effects of reinforcement on internal sources of motivation.

2. *Logical and Substantive*

What are lessons about? According to Leinhardt in the first article in this subsection, research has tended to neglect the description of lesson content and so such information has to be deduced from other research. After discussing elements of lesson preparation such as the time frame, control and planning, scheduling, and grouping, the author describes typical lessons in elementary mathematics, reading, and social studies. In mathematics the typical sequence of activities begins with monitoring homework and reviewing the previous lesson, then proceeds with a more general review or the presentation of new material through either one-way or two-way interaction, followed by practice involving diagnosis, and assessment and further tutoring. In reading, however, much more reliance is placed on work in small groups within which phases like those in mathematics lessons are followed while the rest of the class does seatwork. In social studies there is more emphasis on teacher lecturing to present information followed by question and answer sessions.

Leinhardt discusses three main causes of lost time in classrooms: interruptions, transitions, and practice work that is too difficult; she then takes up the topic of time on task which is discussed later in this section by Anderson and by Smyth. Leinhardt also introduces research on teacher and student thought during lessons, thus providing useful introductions to the more detailed coverage of those topics in the final part of this section.

In the next article, Barr reviews evidence of the relationship between content coverage in classrooms and student achievement, first, by examining research using indirect measures of content coverage, such as teachers' ratings, and then research in which coverage was measured directly through observations of lessons given and the counting of, for example, the number of concepts introduced.

After introducing opposing viewpoints of the teacher versus the context as determining content coverage, Barr presents the interesting concept of the "steering group", which some research suggests influences the pace of progression during lessons (see *Frame Factors*). Further exploration involves research findings about the influence of textbook content, ability grouping, and teacher preferences upon content coverage. Barr concludes thus:

> The amount of material covered, then, pertains to the problem of matching instruction to the range of individual characteristics represented within groupings, and individual learning represents the by-product of collective instruction along with the influence of individual characteristics.

Anderson's article on *Opportunity to Learn* continues the exploration of content in classrooms. He distinguishes between two definitions of "opportunity to learn" in the literature and clarifies the link between one of those definitions and the Carroll model of school learning which is discussed in the first section of this Encyclopedia. To make the distinction between the two definitions clear, Anderson chooses the terms "allocated time" and "content overlap" for his review of research. While both variables were found to be correlated with student achievement in the relevant research studies, content overlap was generally found to be more strongly correlated with achievement in studies using both. In concluding his article, Anderson calls for a merging of the two conceptualizations in the belief that the regular inclusion of such a merged variable in classroom research would contribute greatly to understanding of classrooms.

Time is the subject of the next article, by Smyth, who attributes the increased interest in the topic by researchers of the 1970s and 1980s to the influence of the Carroll model of school learning. After discussing some of the dimensions of time in school learning, Smyth reviews research using four time variables in relation to student achievement: nominal amount of schooling; quantity of schooling per student; time allocated to curriculum content; and engaged learning time. He then focuses upon early and more recent research on engaged learning time, student attention, or academic learning time (ALT). Important distinctions are made between the last of these and the opportunity to learn concept of classroom time explained by Anderson in the previous article. Smyth finds strong evidence of the relationship between ALT and student achievement and between teacher behaviour and ALT. This suggests that ALT can be controlled by teachers through effective classroom management, which is the subject of several articles in a later subsection of this work. Smyth cites research demonstrating that teachers can be trained in the behaviours which enhance student engagement "without too much trauma".

Another approach to the description of classroom processes requires analysis of the intellectual properties of the content and activities occurring there. These cognitive components are the focus of the next two articles. In the first, Sutton and Ennis write about *Logical Operations*. After referring to applications of the Bloom taxonomy of educational objectives and Piaget's concepts to classrooms, the authors explain the deductive logic approach and dimensions of deductive logic ability. Included in the latter are the abstractness/concreteness of the content and the complexity of logical operations, both of which are explored in articles to follow in this section of the Encyclopedia. After reviewing research on the above and on the question of teachability of logic to students at various levels, the authors discuss the implications for the classroom of the deductive logic approach in handling deductively invalid arguments, in understanding the relationship between evidence and hypotheses, in suppositional thinking, in identifying assumptions, and in defining.

Next, Sutton and Ennis describe the "logic-of-teaching" approach in which transcripts of actual lessons were analysed to study the logic of verbal interactions in classrooms. This approach produced findings about the types and frequency of different logical operations and suggested much about the structure of logic in teaching. Similarly, Sutton and Ennis describe the "critical-thinking" approach which focuses upon the goal of enhancing "the mental ability to deal reasonably with questions about what to believe". After listing the types of judgments, inferences, skills, habits, tendencies, and criteria involved in critical thinking, the authors consider studies conducted involving them and discuss the implications for schooling.

The next article, by Dunkin, takes up the question of abstractness and concreteness that Sutton and Ennis introduced. Dunkin notes the particular notions of abstractness/concreteness as they appear in the theories of Piaget, Bruner, and in the Bloom taxonomy, and concentrates on observational research on variations among classrooms in this dimension. After noting the presence in earlier writing of the assumption that as logical complexity increased so did abstractness, Dunkin cites research evidencing that the opposite is the case. He concludes thus:

> Classrooms, it appears, continue to be highly verbal, and, therefore, highly abstract venues for learning. Theories of cognitive development that advocate greater use of concrete experiences still have plenty of scope for influence, it appears.

While the previous two articles discussed the complexity and abstractness of lesson content, the final article in this subsection, by Land, discusses the issue of vagueness and clarity in the classroom. Land introduces the topic by arguing that "vagueness occurs as speakers commit themselves to present information they cannot remember or never really knew". He then reviews research using low-inference measures of vagueness and of both correlational and experimental designs. After distinguishing among such variables as "vagueness terms", "verbal mazes", other single clarity variables and clusters of variables, Land considers students' perceptions of teacher clarity and cites evidence that student perceptions mediate the effect of clarity on student achievement. He concludes by summarizing what has been learned from the research on vagueness and by identifying areas for future research.

3. Pedagogical

Pedagogy is the art and science of teaching. It concerns the knowledge and skills that practitioners of the profession of teaching employ in performing their duties of facilitating desired learnings in others. In the third group of articles in this section on classroom processes there are several articles whose titles derive mainly from research into the language of classrooms conducted under the leadership of Arno Bellack during the 1960s. Bellack and his colleagues delineated four "pedagogical moves" as parts of the "language game" of the classroom. They were "structuring", "soliciting", "responding", and "reacting".

In the first two of these articles, Doenau writes about *Structuring* and *Soliciting* in the classroom. In relation to structuring he points out that "while there is some kind of general agreement about the aspects of behaviour encompassed by the term, there is by no means a consensus about its particulars". After a detailed consideration of the concept of structuring and instances of its occurrence, Doenau reviews early and later research on it and associated concepts, concluding with a consideration of the concept's theoretical importance.

The second article by Doenau is about "attempts by teachers or students to elicit a verbal or nonverbal behaviour from a classroom member". The term "soliciting" is applied in preference to "questioning" because such attempts are not always in the interrogative mood. Doenau discusses the early research on soliciting and its usage in the Bellack study but then goes further to review research on questioning. He focuses on the cognitive requirements of questions, thus establishing links with the article by Sutton and Ennis in the previous subsection, and reviews research on the frequencies of question types, on increasing the use of higher order questions and on the relationships between these variables and student achievement. Similarly, he presents evidence relating to the frequency of questioning, probing, multiple questions, questioning by students, and wait-time.

The reciprocal of soliciting is responding, that is "any verbal or nonverbal act designed to fulfil the expectations implicit in the questions, commands, or requests of others", according to Power in the third article in this subsection. Responding occupies between 20 and 30 percent of verbal moves, and 90 percent of responding is performed by students. Power points out that attention is selective, and that teachers' solicitations have to be interpreted so that covert processes precede students' overt responses which may be correct, erroneous, or incongruous. These responses, in turn, lead to inferences by the teacher about the students. Power describes research concerning the responding process and individual response patterns before relating this research to attentiveness and engaged time. He concludes by arguing that more careful research into students' classroom responding would help in the design of learning tasks that enhance student thinking and learning.

The fourth pedagogical move conceptualized by Bellack and his colleagues was reacting. In the next article, Zahorik writes about reactions and feedback in the classroom. He links the feedback move to reinforcement that strengthens the response it follows to motivation for future learning, and points to the cognitive information often contained. He then reviews research of the 1960s and early 1970s noting particularly the contradictory findings reached. He summarizes the outcomes of the 1970s research effort as follows:

> Presently, it can be said that teacher verbal feedback is helpful in regard to student learning, some types appear more helpful than others, and its contribution to learning seems to be related to its function in the direct instruction pattern of teaching.

That final comment should be seen in the light of Rosenshine's article on *Direct Instruction* in Sect. 3 of this Encyclopedia.

Zahorik concludes his article by presenting suggestions for future research on teacher reactions. Among these are calls for a balance of experimental and descriptive studies, for "qualitative", holistic studies using intensive observation to enhance the description of reacting behaviour, particularly of nonverbal feedback, of the effectiveness of reacting in relation to outcomes other than student achievement, such as classroom control and classroom climate, of the most useful units of analysis for understanding reacting behaviours, and contextual influences, such as class size and grade level, on reacting behaviour.

In Bellack's conceptualization of pedagogical moves, structuring was seen only as a "launching" or "halting" move and necessarily preceded responding and reacting moves. Other researchers, however, found evidence of other types of structuring which Nuthall describes in the next article in this subsection entitled *Reviewing and Recapitulating*.

After presenting several meanings of "review", Nuthall selects the following as the focus of this article:

> The teacher, or students and teacher in discussion, might summarize or abstract the main points or conclusions to be drawn from a previous learning activity. Or at the beginning of a new activity or topic, they might briefly recapitulate the main points of previous learning as preparation for a new topic.

Nuthall comments on the neglect of these teaching behaviours in some of the best known reviews of research in spite of evidence that they are "important components in effective teaching". In describing six correlational studies he shows that review and recapitulation were shown to be related to student achievement in some but not in others. However, experimental studies showed more consistently that reviewing is an important influence on student achievement.

In an effort to explain why reviewing and recapitulating might have inconsistent effects on learning, Nuthall considers initial presentations of material that vary in structure and clarity, suggesting that where there is lack of them (with accompanying misunderstanding on students' parts), reviewing might come into its own. He also makes a connection with direct instruction described by Rosenshine in Sect. 3. Nuthall concludes by calling for research into occasions when review and recapitulation are important and Power writes about these sequences and patterns as *Teaching Cycles and Strategies*. He extends his coverage beyond research in the Bellack tradition to include studies of teaching "episodes", "incidents", "tactics", "ventures", and "strategies", as well as ethnographic research on complex sequences in an urban classroom. He mentions the persistence of the "recitation" format in American classrooms during this century and seeks explanations for that in terms of frame factors (see *Frame Factors*), teachers' coping strategies, and sheer teaching effectiveness. In pursuing these, Power reviews research and discusses many important insights into classroom life arising from both micro- and macro-level analyses of sequential patterns.

In the final article in this subsection Tisher writes about *Student Roles*, defining "roles" as "behaviours that are characteristic of persons in a context". Tisher gives particular emphasis to contextual influences upon student behaviour and provides valuable tabulations of norms for students in conventional, open area, self-paced, primary and secondary school environments. He reviews research on these variables and then pursues the question of the influence of students' characteristics upon their classroom behaviour. In particular, he finds that prior achievement level and ability affect student behaviour in interaction with teachers. Similarly, Tisher cites evidence that teachers' attitudes towards students are associated with the latters' classroom roles. Section 5 of this Encyclopedia contains many articles elaborating upon personal and environmental influences upon classrooms.

4. Managerial

The next group of articles have in common a particular relevance to the ways in which classroom groups maintain themselves for the purposes of achieving educational goals. Since traditionally the teacher is the leader of the classroom group, much of the material in this subsection focuses upon the strategies adopted by teachers to minimize deviancy and to deal with behaviour problems that arise. Some of the articles are not so directly focused upon problems, however, and are attempts to understand how these important social entities called classrooms work.

In the opening article, Emmer writes about management in the elementary school. He begins by discussing criteria for effective management and considers the possibility that the shorter term objectives of management strategies, such as securing attentiveness and reducing noise level, may not always be conducive to the attainment of longer term goals. Emmer finds theoretical bases for management activities mainly in the behavioural model of instruction which was discussed in Sect. 2. He is careful to point out that "preventing disruption is not sufficient for good management; the teacher must also create conditions to engage and maintain students in classroom activities". He then analyses three main management tasks of teachers: identifying expected student behaviour, translating those expectations into procedures and routines, and room arrangement. There follows consideration of principles of implementing management plans during the first part of the school year and the longer term maintenance of the classroom management system. Here Emmer emphasizes the importance of careful monitoring, prompt and appropriate handling of deviancy, use of sanctioning behaviour, establishing accountability, and maintaining lesson or activity flow. He concludes by discussing the role of contextual factors such as school organization, team teaching, and student ability in classroom management.

Although successful classroom management is more than dealing with disruptive students, these are major challenges to the teacher. Cairns takes up the topic of *Behaviour Problems* in the classroom. He begins by considering different approaches to the definition of deviancy, including that which focuses upon the personality of the student and that which focuses upon the social system which labels some behaviours as "problems". He points to sex differences and stereotypes and mentions teachers' tolerance as an important variable in what constitutes problem behaviour. Teacher attributions of intentionality on the part of students as well as changes in standards over time are also discussed. After considering influences such as personality, socioeconomic status, intellectual capacity, heredity, peer groups, domestic values, television, and characteristics of the school, classroom, and teacher, Cairns concludes that no unique set of psychological, sociological, or educational factors can account for all the problem behaviour in the classroom.

He then proceeds to discuss behaviour problems in relation to learning. Behaviour problems are claimed to be threats to optimal time-on-task not just of the problem student but of others as well. Teachers' efforts to deal with such problems can damage teacher–student relationships and create unwanted expectations and perceptions by students of the teacher. Cairns argues that the teacher needs to keep in mind eight key points in deciding upon reactions to behaviour problems: intensity, duration, frequency, context, contiguity, generality, normality, and effect on others. He then lists several recommendations arising from research on teachers' "desists" or reprimands. After recommending that careful consideration also be given to the audience students' reactions to problem behaviour, Cairns concludes by suggesting that problem situations be seen from the viewpoints of the problem student, the teacher, and the peer groups and that teachers be more sensitive to the "miscreants" and audience students' views.

The third article in this selection concerned with classroom management is by Gump who presents the results of careful observation of the structure and functions involved in class activities. Gump introduces the notion of "classroom segments" which "consist of physical and activity aspects joined together to support desired inhabitant behaviour and experience". In elaborating upon the concept of classroom segments, he explains that segments have *physical features*, such as furniture, *action structures* which determine goals, rules for behaviour and interpersonal relationships, as well as *temporal and spatial boundaries*. After illustrating the way in which segments change during a day in a classroom, he introduces a number of dimensions for describing segments. First there is the activity/passivity dimension; then the independence/interdependence dimension; and finally the matter of transitions from one segment to another.

In the rest of his article Gump discusses these dimensions, research associated with them, and its implications for effective classroom management. He concludes as follows:

> Teachers must do much more than teach; they select, establish, and maintain segments and they become content sources of action in some of these segments. The success of their efforts is much dependent upon the vigor and the appropriateness of the settings they establish.

The next two articles also emphasize the importance of appropriate teacher decisions in relation to classroom management. In them Rohrkemper and Good argue that good management is important for optimizing time-on-task and also that "similar behavior underlies both effective management and effective instruction". In the first article they introduce the term "proactive teaching" to apply to teachers' decisions featuring positive goal orientation", "deliberate planning", and "a preventive focus". After reviewing correlational and experimental research relevant to this form of teaching, the authors write that no clear prescriptions for effective teaching emerge but that the research provides helpful "heuristics".

In their second article the same authors explore a contrasting type of teaching behaviour known as "reactive teaching", that is, "those teacher behaviours that occur in the 'interactive' or ongoing phases of instruction in response to unanticipated events". While they argue in favour of proactive rather than reactive instruction the authors acknowledge that both are required in teaching, so that good teaching requires skills in both. After discussing research associated with the topic and theoretical advances about the use of reinforcement (see *Reinforcement*), the authors conclude that the effectiveness of reactive instruction is associated with teachers' perceptions and interpretations of student behaviour and intentions.

In the next article, Flanders writes on the topic of *Flexibility*. He locates the origins of research on this topic in the early research on the socioemotional facet of classroom behaviour discussed by Soar and Soar previously in this section but finds relevance also in research reviewed by others under the category of "variability". Flanders argues that reviewers have tended to misinterpret his own research and to ignore his concern with flexibility of influence in favour of focusing upon results obtained for indirectness of influence. After considering the question of flexibility in the sense of adapting to individual differences among students, Flanders discusses training in flexibility for teachers and concludes that "the only realistic approach to instruction is to prepare teachers who are capable of establishing and maintaining their own dynamic equilibrium with the fluctuating demands on the school. This is a balancing act that requires flexibility in instruction".

Classrooms are usually described as settings in which the predominant type of activity is verbal involving combinations mainly of talking, listening, reading, and writing. Yet, clearly there are other forms of communication present in the form of facial expressions, tones of voice, gestures, and so on. In the final article in this subsection, Smith writes about *Nonverbal Communication*. He provides a brief historical background to the study of these forms of communication and then proceeds to discuss the contributions of various channels of influence to teaching effectiveness.

His discussion of environmental factors is related to the article by Giaconia in the previous section of this Encyclopedia and to the article by Bennett in Sect. 5, and concerns research on the "open plan" classroom. Proxemics involves the study of locations and seating patterns in classrooms; kinesics involves the study of gestures, eye contact, facial expressions and so on. Other categories discussed are touching behaviour or "haptics"; physical traits, such as body size, attractiveness, and skin colour; paralanguage consisting of voice tone, loudness, hesitations, and so on; and artefacts such as spectacles, perfume, and make-up.

Smith then pursues a number of key questions involving nonverbal behaviour in classrooms. They are: How do teachers develop impressions from the nonverbal behaviour of their students? How do teachers communicate those impressions in their own nonverbal behaviour? How do students interpret variations in teachers' nonverbal behaviour? And how do teachers use nonverbal behaviour in instruction and management? Some of the findings related to these questions and presented by Smith are: "students who sit toward the front of the classroom . . . are viewed by the teacher as more attentive and likeable"; "teachers tend to stand further away from 'rejected' students . . ."; "teachers who conduct their classes from among the students are viewed more positively than those who teach from beside, behind, or seated on their desks"; "when teachers are closer to the students they tend to show more permissive and interactive verbal communications". Smith warns that these findings are the fruits of initial research in these areas and that they should be received cautiously. He concludes his article by considering the need for future research and implications for social skills training, multicultural education, special education, and teacher education.

5. Cognitive

The information processing model of teaching presented in the first section of this Encyclopedia requires that teachers' and students' thoughts about teaching and learning be investigated in attempts to understand their behaviour in classrooms. This subsection contains articles about attempts to research and theorize about both teachers' and students' thinking. There are six articles beginning with the article by Taylor on *Implicit Theories*, that is, "teachers' beliefs about the purposes of teaching as well as their beliefs about the institutionally bound acts of teaching". Taylor organizes his article in terms of teaching as an enterprise, teaching as an act, planning teaching, interaction in teaching, the educational institution and teachers' implicit theories, and perceived influences and constraints on teaching. He reports research findings that teachers both past and present believe the enterprise of teaching has both moral and instrumental purposes and that a balance has to be struck between individual and societal goals. Furthermore, the acts of teaching (informing, explaining, describing, and exemplifying, as well as controlling the other managerial acts) are the subjects of teacher theorizing.

When it comes to the principles teachers apply in planning for teaching, Taylor finds that teachers seldom employ the recommendations of educational theorists. Instead, they take a great deal of information about the particular context into account, including the students, the subject matter, the physical milieu, and teaching style. Teachers' theories of planning, he writes, "possess an existential quality; for teachers a plan is a scene in being". Taylor's discussions of teachers' theories about classroom interaction focuses upon the results of research with science teachers on preferred styles of teaching, of which eight were discovered ranging from a "face-to-face" style to a "laboratory assistant" style. Each of the eight styles, he claims, is an implicit theory of science teaching effectiveness.

In his consideration of influences and constraints on teaching, Taylor distinguishes between forces that push teachers in particular directions and forces which inhibit and circumscribe goal attainment. After delineating five types of the former and two of the latter, he concludes by suggesting further study of the beliefs teachers have about themselves and their self-improvement.

Taylor's comments on teachers' planning are followed up in the second article in this subsection by Shavelson who also points out that teachers typically do not follow the prescriptions for planning as learned in teacher education programmes. According to Shavelson, the basic planning unit is the "task" which has several elements: content; materials; activity, including sequencing, pacing, and timing; goals; students; and the sociocultural context. He tabulates the findings of research and reports results concerning the foci of teachers' planning. Some contradictory results appear, particularly concerning the importance of objectives in teachers' planning, and concerning possibly undesirable side-effects of long-term and thorough planning in the form of insensitivity to student needs.

Much of teaching is dependent upon teachers' judgments about students' characteristics, such as their abilities, behaviours, and needs. In his second article Shavelson defines judgment as "the process of evaluating or categorizing a person or an object", and describes attempts made over the decades to conceptualize teachers' judgments. He finds attribution theory in particular to be highly relevant to the judgment process. Attributions concerning the causes of student achievement may underlie judgments about abilities, behaviour, and attitudes. Heuristics too, are seen to play crucial roles in the judgment process, as does "conflict-stress". Shavelson reviews research on the accuracy of teachers' judgments about students' intelligence, achievement, reading interests, and reading difficulties and concludes that additional research would facilitate the development of training programmes to improve teachers' judgments.

In his third article on *Interactive Decision Making* Shavelson points out that the decisions teachers make "inflight" are influenced by their plans. Plans function to minimize the number of such decisions so that monitoring can be devoted to particular students and to deviations from the plan. When faced with choices about continuing with a plan or changing the lesson, research indicates that teachers tend to stay with the plan. Shavelson considers reasons that might explain teachers' reluctance to alter plans and concludes that their main concern during interaction with students is "to maintain the flow of the activity" lest management problems develop. He reports research that found several principles used by teachers in reacting to unexpected student responses. These are the principles of compensation, strategic leniency, power sharing, progressive checking, and suppressing emotions. Shavelson concludes by reviewing research on the number of interactive decisions teachers typically make during lessons and the bases for decisions they make about grouping students.

The study of teachers' epistemologies, writes Young in the next article, "is an attempt to understand their theories of knowledge and the implications of these for their practice". Young describes philosophers' attempts to research teachers' epistemologies as "highly rationalistic" and claims that the results of their efforts did not fall neatly into pre-existing categories and that their epistemologies were not always consistent with other aspects of their educational theories. Young interprets these results as indicating a need for "exploratory" research and for more adequate theory relating epistemologies to other beliefs and practices. He then reviews some attempts to explore teachers' epistemologies and concludes by discussing implications arising from them.

In the final article in this section, Winne explores students' thinking in the classroom. He sets about attempting to adapt a general model of cognitive processing for use as a model of students' cognitive processing in the classroom, and begins with two general principles. (a) "Cognitive processing can be applied to any kind of information"; (b) "Cognitive processing is neither just a response to events in a student's environment, nor is it a complex internal determinant of a student's performance. Cognition is both an effect caused by previous events, including cognitive ones, and a cause of future events."

After considering some implications of these principles, Winne comments on research on the cognitive qualities of teachers' questions and notes the neglect of students' cognitive responses in such research. This leads him to explain the "cognitive–mediational paradigm" (see *Paradigms for Research*) in which students' cognitive processing is central.

His consideration of cognitive processing leads Winne to discuss "sites" in the cognitive processing system, as well as structures of information, processes and functions, and parameters of the cognitive system. Next he discusses sites, structures, and parameters of the curriculum, and structures, functions, and parameters of instructional cues. The final element in the system is student tasks of which there are two broad types: learning the curriculum and using instructional cues.

Winne summarizes the model as follows:

> Students' cognitive processing during teaching consists of reciprocal interactions among their cognitive processing system on the one hand, and the curriculum and instructional cues on the other. The setting within which this interaction occurs is a task. By specifying a goal and a set of initial conditions, a task establishes a framework within which students carry out cognitive processing according to a plan.

Socioemotional

Teacher-centered and Learner-centered Teaching

J. Withall

A fact that evades many educators and learners is that nobody can learn for anyone else. However, others can help learners to initiate and develop coping skills, abilities, facts, and principles to use in their everyday lives. That realization, if fully comprehended, leads to these questions: What behaviors, values, and principles can educators utilize to enhance the probabilities of learners achieving more information, abilities, and coping skills? What behaviors and values expressed vis-à-vis learners tend to impede their learning and development?

Some answers to these queries have been proffered by distinguished and pioneering thinkers including Dewey, Lewin, Rogers, Illich, Weiner, and associates. This article will draw upon their views as it examines teacher-centered and learner-centered instruction.

What follows will be sketches of the philosophy and theory of certain key contemporary psychologists, educators, and researchers regarding teacher-centered and learner-centered instruction. The time line will run from the turn of the century to 1980, encompassing scholars listed above.

1. Philosophy and Theory of Dewey

Perhaps the most far-reaching, earliest, yet astonishingly current analysis of education was made by Dewey at the turn of the century. This is set forth in such classics as *Democracy and Education* and *Experience and Education*. The latter (Dewey 1963) was an exceptionally succinct, straightforward, and comprehensive statement of this theory and philosophy. It made it eminently clear that education and instruction can be viewed either as a leading out of potential and competence from the learners, or as an externally controlled molding that overrides the learners' aims and interests that are replaced by ideas and goals prescribed by others. Dewey used the label "traditional" for the format that is dubbed "teacher-centered" and "new" for the "learner-centered" procedure. In his view, traditional education aimed mainly at transmitting societal and cultural values, attitudes, and ideas less for use

in the here and now and more for utilization in the unpredictable future.

In the traditional or teacher-centered mode, Dewey pointed out that the standards, content, and methods are determined by educators not learners. Participation by students in deciding on processes and purposes is minimal. The major aim seems to be to ensure mastery of what is in books and in the educators' minds mostly through verbal communication.

Dewey stated that the learner-oriented processes ensured the students' analysis of their experiences and encouraged learners to become more self-directed and self-responsible. Instead of processing facts from books and teacher talk, learning emerges from the learners' processing of their direct experiences. Skills are not acquired by drill and rote memorization but by activities that the learners, with the aid of educators, employ to serve their interests and needs. As a result, current dilemmas and tasks are met and dealt with rather than anticipated demands and problems in the future. Educators, Dewey reminded us, have to help individuals to capitalize on the demands of current happenings. It is an article of faith with Dewey that valuable educative outcomes emerge from ongoing day-to-day activities. He does not overlook, however, the fact that the past can make a substantial contribution to the job of dealing with the present effectively and equipping people for tomorrow's responsibilities.

1.1 Principle of Continuity

Although Dewey deprecated exclusive dependence in education on information from those who have preceded us, it would be folly, he said, to ignore the facts, insights, and principles gleaned from the past. He urged instructors who base their teaching on learners' first-hand and vicarious experiences to draw on the tested wisdom that has been accumulated. This necessitates giving considerable opportunities for meaningful dialogue between learners and learners, and learners and mentors, accompanied by thoughtful analysis and interpretation of the findings of our forerunners. He emphasized that the self-same process has to be used by students in deriving benefits, meaning, and principles from their own activity and experience. As regards a culture's accumulated wisdom and knowledge, Dewey insisted that mere transmission of facts is not a major end of education but a means to the attainments and development of human beings.

Dewey seemed, from an examination of his writings, philosophy, and theory, downright prescient. He was anticipatory in taking out insurance, so to speak, against people's imagining that activity and experience per se were educative, regardless of their quality. He cautioned against this misperception by pointing out that when one contends that true education derives from undergoing and analyzing experience this ". . . does not mean that all experiences are genuinely or equally educative . . ." (p. 25). In fact some experiences may be miseducative. Only activities that lead on to richer and wider ones and have continuity with prior and upcoming events lead on to learning and growth. Any benefits derived from learning situations are a function of the quality of the experience.

The principle of continuity, Dewey explained, has to do with the pervasive connectedness of events since every experience draws on past events and modifies those encountered later.

1.2 Principle of Interaction

It was Dewey's view that educators have to cultivate the ability to put themselves into the learners' shoes, and take the phenomenological view. There has to be an awareness of the interplay between the external conditions (environment) and the internal conditions that consist of the learners' needs, purposes, and capacities. On the basis of this interaction of internal and external factors arises the educator's responsibility to: (a) identify some of the environmental conditions they can bring about to enhance the probabilities of growth and learning; and (b) appreciate as fully as possible some of the unique perceptions, purposes, and concerns of each learner.

The trouble with traditional education, in Dewey's view, was the almost exclusive attention given to external factors such as the teacher's purposes and the basic physical environment of books, lighting, and the like with minimal attention to the needs and feelings of the students. The psychic and physical needs of the learners have been viewed as givens that are comparable for all persons. These are to be addressed and molded to the expectations and norms of society and educators.

The two guiding principles of continuity and interaction are intimately interwoven in Dewey's theory. Since continuity involves relating current experience with prior learning and foreseeing their probable utility in future learning, the issue of transfer of learning is implicit in the model. Interaction encompasses the integration by the learner, with the help of mentor or peers, of his/her affective and cognitive needs with the environmental variables that include the behaviors of peers and teachers, instructional artifacts, and teaching facilities.

As one rereads and analyzes Dewey's formulations one is surprised and impressed by his astonishing perspicacity and farsightedness. The timeliness and relevance of his educational philosophy and theory for current educational malaise is obvious.

He foreshadowed Lewin's $B = f(P \times E)$ equation, that behavior is a function of interaction between person and environment. He underscored the importance of incidental or peripheral learning or, as he called it, collateral learning. He anticipated our awareness of the impact of verbal and nonverbal behaviors on the social-emotional climate of learning and problem-solving settings as well as on communication and interpersonal relationships in all situations. He anticipated Bruner's aphorism regarding the feasibility of teaching young learners in an intellectually honest way, using complex concepts and ideas so that they can master them at their level of maturity. This is by no means an exhaustive list of indicators of Dewey's prescience in educational theory, research, and practice. Sarason (1981) commends Dewey's foresightedness concerning the proper focus of psychology on the social order and human welfare. Dewey in his 1899 presidential address to the American Psychological Association had expressed concern about the asocial direction psychology was taking. Sarason says Dewey saw clearly that psychology cannot be independent of, or ignore, the social order.

Dewey cast far-reaching beams of enlightenment on the behavioral and social sciences.

2. Pedagogy of the Oppressed

The potency of a pedagogy that drew the content of education from the problems and opportunities of day-to-day experience was extolled by Dewey. Freire (1973) born, educated, and teaching in Latin America urged, even more passionately, that educational content be drawn from the everyday life experiences of the learners. Freire's students were illiterate and oppressed peasants first in Brazil and then in Chile. It was with and for them that he formulated his "pedagogy of the oppressed". Thus Freire's educational philosophy and methods were developed in the context of human and social degradation visited on an economically and politically disadvantaged segment of the Third World in Latin America.

On the strength of his implementation of his values and methodology with groups of peasants, Freire envisioned the possibility of groups and individuals improving their self-image and their socioeconomic and political lot. As with all learners, a key need in working with these disadvantaged people was a cadre of instructors who respected, trusted, and cared for them and who, in helping them learn, themselves learned. Through thoughtful dialogue with the teachers and their peers the learners began to comprehend their condition and its causes. They were helped to analyze and appreciate the inequity of their situation. Beyond this they were helped to realize that they could plan, initiate, and consummate actions that not only reduced their sense of powerlessness but also mitigated their deprivations.

Freire spelled out the ethics, strategies, and values of his pedagogy. Basically it did not manipulate and control the students but involved them fully in the process. Coupled with this was the goal to help the learners, through sharing and analyzing their experiences and thinking with peers and mentors, to realize some of their purposes through tapping their individual and group potential.

2.1 "Banking" Education

Freire, like Dewey, deplored the superordinate–subordinate relationship that frequently exists between the teacher and students in many educative settings. In such settings, Freire charged, learning is hindered by 'narration sickness" wherein the instructor monopolizes, as the research has indicated, three-quarters of the talk time. It seems to indicate that most educators believe that sharing their perceptions and ideas with the learners will benefit them. In many cases, Freire stated, reality is presented as static, unchangeable, and dissociated from the students' experience. This occurs because the educator's task is perceived as being one of filling the students with others' facts and beliefs. These "deposits" disbursed by the teacher are to be taken in by learners, filed, and stored. Under this dispensation the deposits are to be accounted for and brought forth on signal. Freire labeled this "banking education."

The deposits of information are often viewed as gifts from those who strive to project an image of considerable knowledgeability enabling them to dispense intellectual largesse to the unfortunate. The changing of this banking model is possible and achievable, Freire contended, when all parties to the learning–teaching situation are enabled to be ". . . simultaneously teachers and students . . ." (p. 59).

Banking education is implemented when the instructor (a) talks most of the time and the learners listen; (b) chooses and enforces his or her choices; and (c) chooses the content and the students adapt to it. Freire lists seven more items similar to the preceding. His list parallels to some extent a list of 10 assumptions, (Rogers 1969), guiding graduate education. Instructional regimens based on these kinds of practices and values are seen by Freire as lessening the students' creative and critical powers and preventing them from perceiving the world accurately and seeing it as alterable. Worst of all, from Freire's standpoint, it deprives learners of achieving conscientization, ("*conscientização*").

2.2 Conscientization

"Awareness" and "realization" are words that catch the import of Freire's term; it means realization of the social, political, and economic contradictions in the world and the initiating action individually or with peers to change matters. Along with this goes an awareness of one's beliefs, purposes, and potential in bringing about change. Conscientization is conceived by Freire as a process and an attitude that aids persons to develop appreciation for autonomy and self-responsibility. The process and its context aid students to unveil—Freire's verb—the repressive conditions that militate against development of self-responsibility and self-affirmation. In short, conscientization, as Freire delineates it, helps people to better understand themselves and their potential and to initiate action against society's shortcomings and ills.

If educators want to enable students to be inquirers and thinkers regarding themselves and the environment, they need to view learners as partners in the instructional procedures and themselves as colearners in the learning process. Under the traditional teacher-oriented regimen, Freire claimed that learners have been exposed to "schooling" and conditioning that equips them to fit themselves to the world and to conform. As conformists and adapters they have little ability or urge to press for change or to question things as they are. The conscientization process, on the other hand, impels the learners to examine and inquire about themselves, their situation, and their environment. They thereby begin to comprehend their responsibilites for initiating moves not only in their own but in others' interests.

It is through communication in its encompassing sense of a two-way traffic of information, ideas, and feedback between peers and with the instructor that liberating education occurs. Such communication, Freire contended, can bring about humanizing, lasting, and utilizable learning. Such communication leads to conscientization.

2.3 Necrophilic Education

Gibran (1966) eloquently reminded one that teachers cannot learn for the learners, cannot confer their understandings and values on them, and cannot transfer their wisdom to them. But teachers can create learning conditions that enable students to process what they are encountering and with the help of caring mentors, derive personal meaning, and knowledge. Freire deplored the static, other-controlled, normative educational system and labeled it "necrophilic." He saw it as restricting experimentation and creativity by replacing first-hand experience with others' beliefs and notions. The result, he claimed, is schooling that domesticates and emasculates individuals and renders them more susceptible to indoctrination and external control. Over against this, Freire placed instructional strategies that lead on to liberation and praxis, namely, ". . . the action and reflection of men upon their world in order to transform it . . ." (p. 66).

2.4 Problem-posing Education

Freire recommended abandoning "banking education" and replacing it with "problem-posing" education. In problem-posing pedagogy, learners and teachers conjointly address issues of moment to them while sharing, turn and turn about, the roles and functions of both learner and teacher. Whereas ". . . banking education anesthetizes and inhibits creative power, problem-posing education involves a constant unveiling of reality . . ." (p. 68).

Students who consistently confront problems drawn from experience and that are related to their aims and interest will be cognitively and affectively challenged but not psychologically threatened by personally significant issues.

Learner-oriented instruction and education aims at specifying the parameters of reality. Teacher-centered instruction tends to mask reality by restricting learner–learner and learner–teacher dialogue. The problem-posing model capitalizes on interpersonal interaction in order to enhance skills in communication and critical thinking. Dewey's (1963) philosophy of education anticipated Freire's. He urged that free, self-directed activity for learners be encouraged and that externally enforced controls be delimited; that learning be through first-hand experience and not be sought exclusively from textbooks and teachers; that all educational activities be beamed at capitalizing on present opportunities and challenges and not be focused on anticipated future events and problems.

Speaking, as it were, for the southern and developing segment of the globe, Freire, in unison with Dewey speaking for the northern and technologically developed segment, proposed that education be directed toward humanization of people, advancement of human well-being, and the development of critical discrimination and ability to reason. Learner-centered or problem-posing education is carried on neither for nor about the learners but *with* them.

In order to identify the content of education Freire urged:

> It is to the reality which mediates men, and to the perception of that reality held by educators and people, that we must go . . . . (p. 86)

In a similar vein Dewey wrote:

> . . . education in order to accomplish its ends both for the individual learner and for society must be based upon experience—which is always the actual life experience of some individual . . . . (p. 89)

Learners in the view of Dewey and Freire have to participate fully in selecting the issues to examine, analyze, and initiate action on. Educative processes and content emerge primarily with them. Spinoff issues appear and are shared with others, then findings, interpretations, and implications for action developed. The culmination is action intended to resolve problems, assuage needs, and serve the aims of individuals and society.

Dewey spoke not only for himself but for Freire too when he expressed unbounded confidence in the potential of education grounded in ". . . directed devel-

opment of the possibilities inherent in ordinary experiences . . ." (p. 89).

3. Convivial Tools and Manipulative Institutions

Educators and educational institutions, Illich contended, have laid claim to being the major channels or vehicles for worthwhile education. This claim slights the home, peers, and community as potent educative milieux—not to mention the learning opportunities arising from life experiences.

While emphasizing the dehumanizing effects of industrialization and technology, Illich (1971, 1973) delineated the manner and the institutions that contribute to the dehumanizing of human beings and their lives. He exemplified this by reference to the field of medicine which, in his opinion, instead of bringing health and freedom from disease to more people had rendered its services less available. This, he explained, was a function of the profession's making physicians' service a monopolistic domain accessible primarily by the well-to-do. Illich asserted that the same kind of situation pertains to education. It too is a closed guild that caters to, and serves more fully, the privileged.

He cited China as having responded to the domination of the field of medicine by specialists and physicians through preparing and sanctioning services rendered by "barefoot doctors." These paraprofessionals were prepared by means of short courses, work in laboratories, and apprenticeships with medical personnel to equip them to give basic medical services to the public. In addition, they offer preventative health services such as environmental sanitation, immunization, primary medical care, gynecological assistance, as well as birth control and abortion education.

3.1 Conviviality

In industry, medicine, and education, Illich (1973) counseled, society must be reoriented in their attitudes and perceptions so that the facilities of those institutions would be made more accessible to, and manageable by, either individuals or primary groups. Tools and equipment used in the reoriented settings would be "convivial" in the sense that they would convey a sense of autonomy to people and lead to joyfulness and more satisfying interpersonal relations.

The term "convivial" is descriptive of the tools or agencies utilized and "conviviality" is applied to the productive and gratifying atmosphere that surrounds the activities and interactions between human beings and with the environment. These outcomes and benefits emerge when people are involved in self-selected and self-directed undertakings. The spontaneous and people-oriented activities and interactions are contrasted with the usual reactions of persons to the traditional, compulsory attendance school setting. Traditional institutions ensure that society's requirements are met so that qualifications, status, and rewards can be readily determined and dispensed.

Illich construed conviviality ". . . to be individual freedom realized in personal interdependence . . ." (p. 11). He argued for the full use and enjoyment of the one resource at the disposal of each human being: personal energy under personal control. This required arrangements that ensure the full participation of each individual in the planning and conduct of endeavors related to their and society's well-being and interests. The endeavors involve institutions such as industry, education, transportation, medical services, and social services. When a convivial climate arises it would be a function of social arrangements ". . . that guarantee for each member the most ample and free access to the tools of the community . . ." (p. 12).

Three values would undergird this kind of society; they are survival, justice, and self-defined work. These values would result from the elimination of enforced education, enforced labor, and compelled consumption.

Insofar as education is concerned, conviviality would entail the recognition of the uniqueness and worth of each person and appreciation that learning occurs in the events, environments, and activities of each person. Learning occurs within the context of significant groups such as family, neighborhood, peer, ethnic, geographic, and recreational units.

3.2 Manipulative Education

Comenius is credited or blamed by Illich (1971) for the delimited view of education as 7 to 12 grades of compulsory attendance in classrooms accompanied by assembly-line exposure to predetermined facts and activities. Comenius, Illich implied, had aims that paralleled those of the alchemists who hoped to change base metals into precious ones. Comenius hoped that through 12 levels of school the dross of young learners could be converted to gold.

Education, instead of being an exciting and challenging undertaking, has been heavily tainted and continues to be tainted, Illich believed, by a Pavlovian conditioning outlook. The result is that the wonder, adventure, and delight in learning is lost. A large proportion of the products of our schools—kindergarten through graduate school—have been innoculated by their schooling against learning.

In a similar vein, Illich saw machines and technology as highly damaging to human beings and society. Illich explained that he was not urging rejection of all machines. He does, however, object to tools and facilities that are not controllable by the effort and energy of one person or a few individuals. Hand tools such as hammers, pocket knives and awls, looms, pedal-driven sewing machines, and bicycles are all deemed to be convivial tools. He emphasized that it was a mistake to imagine that all large tools would be eliminated in a society imbued with conviviality. Rather, there should be a balance between the enormous human-dominating tools and agencies, and the enhancing and humanizing tools and facilities that foster self-esteem in people and an atmosphere of conviviality.

3.3 Hidden Curriculum and Myths in Manipulative Education

It should be obvious that education as presently structured is not perceived by Illich as a convivial institution. Schools and education are lumped with mental hospitals, nursing homes, law enforcement, and modern warfare as decidedly nonconvivial. They are viewed by him as coercive and dehumanizing agencies that dominate societies worldwide. In addition, schools communicate a hidden agenda of social attitudes and perceptions. These congeal to the point where people believe that the way institutions operate is correct and the manner in which human beings behave is a function of human nature. Incidentally, Illich did not employ these descriptions only in reference to agencies and people in Latin America and the rest of the Third World, but also to people and institutions in the developed world.

Illich stated that manipulative schools purvey, besides a hidden curriculum, a number of educational and societal "myths." These include the notions that (a) the most valuable learning comes from instruction; (b) grading and ranking people measures everything of importance; and (c) increasing productivity and consumption of goods and services yields more benefits to all.

The ills of our society and world, Illich believed, are the product of a number of complex and interacting factors. However, he maintained that a large measure of the responsibility for ecological damage, danger of war, poverty, and the energy crisis lies with the educators, schools, and the regimented type of education they offer, hence he urged deschooling society.

In calling for deschooling, Illich (1971) was not inviting a start to that process. Rather, he expressed the belief that it was already underway. There seems to be some truth in the assertion in view of the dissatisfaction being expressed and new departures—alternative schools, parents using home-based instruction, and religious denominational schools—being tried. However, the movement seems to be regressive in that there is frequently a call to return to the basics, in pressing for more "discipline" and greater conformity to "abiding" truths. This seems hardly a liberating or humanizing bent.

The format for a humanizing and liberating educational system would, Illich contended, encompass networks or webs of people who would provide instructional resources that would be available to each potential learner on a voluntary basis. As such it would be quite different to the funnel model of traditional schooling where information and beliefs are poured into learners perceived as empty vessels devoid of ideas and information.

A learner-centered style of instruction as envisioned by Illich would afford opportunities and procedures that enabled learners to pursue freely, in consultation with mentors who trust and respect them—ideas, concepts, skills, and values.

Three functions of the reconstructed, learner-oriented system that Illich (1971) proposed would be to

... provide all who want to learn with access to available resources at any time in their lives; empower all who want to share what they know to find those who want to learn it from them; and, finally, furnish all who want to present an issue to the public with the opportunity to make their challenge known. (p. 108)

To implement this model he identified four convivial webs that the learners control and that are used to address their needs and goals: (a) reference services to provide information on facilities and processes; (b) skills exchanges to serve as clearinghouses for sharing and learning a skill; (c) peer-matching to link people according to mutual interests; and (d) reference service to educators at large comprising directories of professional and nonprofessional educators and their specialties. Illich feared that if the kind of educational processes he has suggested are not promptly implemented, a system will emerge where freedom of choice and self-directed people would be supplanted by puppet-like creatures manipulated by authority figures and decision makers.

4. Learner-centered Education

The concept of learner-centered education (Rogers 1969) derives from client-centered therapy (Rogers 1965). The essence of client-centered therapy and learner-centered education is the enabling of clients in either context to assume full responsibility, with the aid of an acceptant and empathic therapist or mentor, for decisions, actions, and their consequences. The ultimate aim is to help human beings to tap their latent and frequently unused urge for growth en route to becoming self-directed, self-responsible, and autonomous persons.

This development is encouraged by the therapist or educator initiating, in a one-to-one or a small group situation, a pattern of communication that creates a climate of trust and security. This type of milieu helps the client and learner to focus on the issues, goals, and problems that confront her or him. It also facilitates the marshalling of the diverse cognitive, affective, and psychomotor resources required to resolve or reduce the concerns and problems. This facilitative setting is initiated and maintained by the facilitator's communicating a nonjudgmental, acceptant, and caring appreciation for the learners and clients.

The therapist and the educator both address the same task. Both are striving to help bring about changes in behavior. The processes and strategies used in therapy are to aid the clients to see themselves and their interactions with others and their environment from new vantage points. This is achieved through discussion with the therapist followed by reflection and experimentation with behaviors between sessions. This results in modest changes in perceptions, attitudes, and behaviors that the client elects to test in day-to-day encounters and interactions. The philosophy and theory guiding learner-centered educators will now be examined.

4.1 Philosophy and Theory of Learner-centered Education

Rogers (1969) has described the philosophy and theory that guide his behaviors in facilitating learning in education as well as in therapy. He spelled out an orientation that seems essential for the model he has developed and used. Simply put: educators must be aware of, and take into account, the affective needs of the learner as well as the cognitive.

Implementation of this necessary condition for learning, Rogers has insisted, requires the educator to evidence realness or genuineness by consistent and spontaneous patterns of behavior. This requires that the facilitator take risks and be prepared to admit to herself or himself and to the learners—when appropriate—biases, hopes, concerns, and distress. At the same time the educator has to focus unremittingly on the learners and their goals and strivings. The educator–facilitator needs to communicate by words and actions acceptance, trust, and caring for the learners. Teachers who want to increase the likelihood of learning, have to communicate empathic appreciation of their charges' concerns and aims.

Concomitant with being genuine and empathic, an educator who is learner-centered utilizes these procedures: he or she makes known and available a wide range of resources and sources; indicates that the educator views herself/himself as an inquirer and colearner with the students; recognizes his/her own limitations. Above all, learner-centered instructors attend to, and thoughtfully entertain as fully as possible, all the verbal and nonverbal behaviors of the learners. These are construed as indicators of the learners' needs, concerns, and goals.

Rogers and associates have analyzed and tested the philosophy and theory he has set forth, and have been impressed with their potency and validity. Those who have been served by him as educator or therapist (Rogers 1965, 1969) vouch for the efficacy of the methods. Better still, when those former clients and students thoughtfully and sensitively guide and monitor their own behaviors by these attitudes and insights, the predicted outcomes and benefits accrue to both the clients and the helper, whether in a one-to-one or group setting.

4.2 Strategies of Learner-centered Educators

A learner-centered educator helps learners with strategies similar to those used by therapists. In the educational situation, the instructor employs a variety of behaviors (Withall 1975a, 1975b) to initiate, nurture, and maintain a facilitative learning climate. The behaviors may include: arranging the physical environment for face-to-face, same eye-level dialogue between educator and learners and learners and learner; reducing social distance and unfamiliarity by everyone's hear-ng, at the outset, basic facts about each other, such as name, hometown, family status, hobbies, field of study, and recreations; taking a census of purposes of individuals and the group insofar as the course is concerned; giving a choice of modes of offering evidence of thought and effort being expended by learners on topics of their choosing; the instructor's consistently inviting learners' input by honoring their questions, comments, demurers, and objections and concomitantly reining in her or his urge to lecture; respecting the desire of those who are reticent with oral input and prefer to serve as silent participants. These strategies are implemented in the context of verbal and nonverbal reinforcement directed to the learners. By encouraging choices and participation of learners in goal setting, procedures determining, and evaluation processes, involvement and commitment may be augmented.

Giving learners "a say in" what they want to achieve and how they will get there, having learners help determine the agenda from meeting to meeting, inviting learners to tackle questions raised by peers, and enabling students to establish criteria for assessing their progress and achievement—all these group processes are hypothesized to enhance the probabilities of learning. Furthermore, these strategies help learners to feel more secure and adequate. As a result they are somewhat abler at marshalling their resources and skills in processing and using information that will have increased personal meaning. Lewin has been recognized as a pioneer in, and an outstanding proponent of, group processes strategies and theory for developing the facilitative climate and skills required in educational and other settings.

5. Group Processes and Learning Theory

The early writing and research of Lewin (1947, 1948) demonstrated the value and utility of interpersonal communication in group contexts for learning and changes in perception, values, and conduct. His group processes model underscores the strength of person-oriented strategies to enable a disparate collection of individuals to coalesce into a maturing group of interdependent people with which they can identify—a referent group. Changes in behavior are brought about by changes in perception, attitude, and information. Such changes, Lewin showed, are best accomplished by changing the "culture" of the referent group or groups. Any attempt to force new values and behaviors on an individual or group rouses resistance. How then can changes be brought about? Lewin (1948) indicated that changes start and come to fruition if the individual or group were afforded choices and assisted in identifying the probable consequences of the possible choices and decisions. This is best realized once the individuals in the group have a sense of belongingness, security, and freedom to make choices. He emphasized, furthermore, that ". . . voluntary attendance, informality of meetings, freedom of expression in voicing grievances,

emotional security, and avoidance of pressure . . ." (p. 65) all contribute to the conditions that nurture change. He pointed out, in passing, Rogers' emphasis on self-decision by clients in therapy.

5.1 Learning Through the Agency of Groups

A fundamental fact in helping people learn is that by inviting them to learn an idea, fact, concept, or skill they are being asked to alter their perceptions and thereby change themselves and their behavior. This can be psychologically threatening to the person's integrity. Each individual has striven in the context of a referent group or groups to build an integrated self-concept and self. The significant groups in the development of this unity of the person include the family, peers, and neighborhood unit. Resistance to change is basically resistance to being asked to betray oneself, one's referent group, and change one's perceptions.

It is imagined, Lewin (1947) wrote, that it is easier to bring about change in one individual than in several individuals comprising a group. Such is not the case. The behaviors and values of an individual are identified with and imbedded in some group or groups. Therefore, in order to help alter the attitudes, perceptions and behaviors of an individual, the group as a whole has to be helped to examine and choose revised values and behaviors. Examination of issues, group discussion, and commitment to change has to be agreed on by the group and public commitment made to that effect.

It appears that the first order of business for learner-centered instructors is the task of melding a collection of persons into a cohesive and compatible group that collaborates to achieve individual goals in the framework of group processes and purposes. The rapport, esprit de corps, and effective communication needed is arrived at by affording full partnership to members in setting goals and procedures.

5.2 Impact of Groups on Learning

Group processes properly exploited in learning–teaching situations provide a setting and opportunities for developing coping and interpersonal relations skills that are needed to fulfill adequately the many roles each of us is expected to assume. Group processes in classrooms make a significant contribution, for good or for ill, to the development of a person's self-concept. The self-image emerges out of the reactions and interactions between people in varied circumstances. The self-concept is based on the processing and interpreting of others' cues and signals and on the individual's self-assessment in the light of those data.

The groups with which people are associated and in which they move give them their sense of significance and status. The family, the peer group, and groups formed in educational contexts are the more important groups for each one of us. These groups provide opportunities at all age levels to acquire and hone skills needed for effective social interaction and roles in family, community, recreational, and work settings.

Peer groups at any maturity level play crucial roles in giving support to their cohorts and in shaping one another's attitudes, opinions, information, and social behaviors. Members of peer groups also serve as gate-keepers and monitors of their fellow-members' activities, affiliations wherein new skills and content may be absorbed from learning opportunities. Peer group members have a considerable effect, next only to the the family, on the socioeconomic, vocational, and value orientations of one another.

All groups, again at all age levels, affect and require roles that address the task-focused responsibility and functions inherent in them. At the same time roles and processes that fulfill or meet maintenance or succorance needs of group members have to be present. The maintenance needs and roles include mediation, tension reduction, reinforcing, humor infusing, and process analysis behaviors and functions by various members. When both maintenance and task roles are implemented by the members, task and security responsibilities of the group are fulfilled.

6. Causality, Attribution, Motivation

The research of deCharms (1968, 1976) has made significant contributions to the values and theory of learner-centered education. His focus has been the striving of human beings to be the source or origin of their own behavior. His major hypothesis being that ". . . Man strives to be a causal agent, to be the primary locus of causation for, or the origin of his behavior, . . ." (deCharms 1968 p. 269). The terms "origin" and "pawn" are used to distinguish two motivating conditions that individuals may experience. As origins, they perceive themselves as choosers and controllers of their behaviors and responsible agents for the consequences. As pawns they have a sense of being puppets controlled by external pressures and forces.

Since learners in a learner-centered milieu participate in determining goals, procedures, and processes for evaluation, they tend to have a sense of commitment, involvement, and personal agency. They perceive themselves as origins. Situations which enable one to have this perception enhance achievement and the feeling of responsibility for what is done and for the outcomes.

In reporting on the programmatic research he and his associates undertook, deCharms (1976) indicated they had rejected the traditional route of curriculum and materials development. Instead, they developed strategies and exercises *with* teachers to help them achieve a fuller understanding of motivation in the framework of the origins and pawns model along with strategies that enable students to have the motivational experience of being origins. Under such circumstances learners invest more of themselves, their skills, and energy in the learning process and enjoy the satisfactions of seeing themselves as responsible for the goals, procedures, and outcomes.

Part of the rationale of deCharms is that human beings need to be, or have a sense of being, initiator of their behaviors and not be subject to the dictates of others. As a result, each educator is confronted with the complex task of introducing the kind of structure in the learning–teaching situation that will provide the optimum climate for learners to experience a feeling of autonomy and responsibility.

Educators have to be attuned to the motivational implications of their methods. This involves their responsibility for: (a) nurturing readiness in the learners for the facts, concepts, and experiences they are encountering; (b) assisting the learners to realize how the content and concepts relate to their needs; (c) encouraging input by the learners at all stages; and (d) alerting learners to resources and facilities they might find useful. A further responsibility of instructors is to act on the premise of the learners being full participants in all facets of the learning–teaching program—including the instructional aspect.

The work of deCharms dovetails well with the research of Weiner (1972, 1974, 1980). The latter studied the perceptions of people regarding causality for outcomes and the conditions that produce the sense of personal responsibility. The contributions by Weiner and associates to attribution theory have been considerable, especially in terms of motivation, causality and attribution. Their investigations were aimed at the effect on individuals' seeing themselves as origins of behaviors and instigators of the results.

Attribution theorists hypothesize that human beings want to perceive themselves as the authors of behavior whereby they make changes in the environment around them. In this quest, freedom to act and liberty to choose seem essential to an individual's sense of causation and self-attribution for outcomes. Making choices and enjoying freedom to act links persons to their action and the outcomes of those actions.

In the educational situation, the learners' perceptions of freedom and opportunities to make choices in terms of their particular needs and interests will have a large impact on the quality of their performance, feelings about the learning process, and self-attribution for the results. This being so, in the light of Weiner and associates' research, a heavy responsibility falls on the educator to structure learning conditions and environment so as to facilitate the learners' making of choices, implementation of individual learning styles, and identification of causal attribution. The involvement, committment, and sense of personal causation or responsibility taps motivation, enhances the quality of outcomes as well as feelings toward the learning process and tasks. Thus more of the well-springs of intrinsic motivation are made accessible to the learners.

7. Basic Human Needs and Motivation

It would seem that many instructors at all levels of sophistication on the educational ladder have misconstrued the concept of motivation both as to its source nd its energizing basis. The view of many is that the mentor has the capability to motivate or supply motivation to others. This is revealed in questions: "How can we motivate these people?" or "What can we do to increase Paul's motivation?" If the question were posed as to the manner in which teachers may help students up their intrinsic motivation, it would be more valid and implementable. Each individual has urges and needs that move him/her to act and to cope. It is inferred from personal knowledge that all human beings behave from motives that are yoked to unfulfilled drives, purposes, or needs. Through activities, experiences, and behaviors energized from within, the constantly emerging needs are assuaged or mitigated.

Maslow (1962, 1970, 1971) has postulated a hierarchy of basic human needs that encompass physiological needs for food, shelter, and sexual activity, through needs for safety and security, needs for belonging and social activity, needs associated with self-esteem and status, to the highest need for self-fulfillment. In the light of Maslow's proposed hierarchy of needs, it seems reasonable to believe that each person's motivation and energy used for fulfilling those needs, derive from the tension and urges associated with them.

Clearly, within the boundaries of Maslow's needs model, no-one can give or augment anyone's motivation other than their own. Educators, however, can help students cope with their needs by arranging the environment and creating a climate that enables the learners to marshall resources and employ strategies that aid in fulfilling some of their needs.

The burden of this article has been that there are at least two sets of variables in play in all learning–teaching situations. They comprise the internal conditions embodying the needs, urges, purposes, and perceptions of each learner and the external conditions of the environment that provide the degree of security, safety, and openness that the learners perceive in it. The educator has a major impact on the environmental conditions and thereby affects the internal conditions that influence the learners.

The literature and scholars who produced it have emphasized that educators have the opportunity and challenge of trying to influence the motivational, emotional, and perceptual conditions of the learners at the same time that they affect the external environmental conditions. The educators by their strategies, along with the learners' peers, constitute the major factors contributing to the meaningfulness, retrievability, and utility of skills, facts, principles derived from the activities, and content to which the learners are exposed.

Both learner-centered educators and therapists use appropriate communicative and acceptant procedures to create conditions that enhance the probabilities of mastering and using the skills needed to fulfill the functions that people are required to assume during their lives. This article has explored and specified some of the strategies and principles by which educators guide the

and carry out their task of creating a learning climate that encourages learners to master the ideas, skills, concepts, and processes needed to fulfill various roles. These include being a member of a family, a citizen of a country, a consumer and a conserver of world resources and products, a recreator seeking healthful and self-fulfilling activities, and a worker producing goods and services.

Within the framework of a person-oriented environment and appropriate instructional processes, learners can be helped to develop through day-to-day experience, communication and problem-solving skills, competence in social relations, empathic ability, positive attitudes toward information, learning and their fellow-learners, a positive self-concept, and behaviors energized by intrinsic motivation.

There seems to be a myth that once individuals step into classrooms they are no longer affective beings. It appears that their basic human needs were to be left outside on the doorstep. Learner-oriented educators, however, attempt to address the interests, concerns and needs of the total person, in accordance with Maslow's postulated basic human needs.

There is a significant pertinence to this for educators who prepare tomorrow's teachers. When teacher–educators model and implement the behaviors and the values believed by Dewey et al. to enhance learning, teachers-to-be will not only learn from such modeling the strategies and moves that will enhance their effectiveness as educators but they may also acquire skills needed to be fully functioning persons in all their other roles.

It seems to this writer that the concepts and principles disseminated by Lewin, Dewey, Rogers, Illich et al. encompass many of the instructional strategies and variables that either enhance or impede learning. An additional perspective that might be added is that of Bandura (1971, 1977a, 1977b, 1978). Bandura emphasizes the power of modeling behaviors and implementation by mentors of skills, attitudes, ideas, and principles being commended to learners. His research deals with the constructs of self-efficacy, (an estimate of a person's personal competence in varied situations), the self-system (encompassing the gamut of a person's skills, facts, needs, and concepts), the reciprocal interaction of the person, the environment, and the resultant behaviors in every social interaction. These notions enhance the development of strategies and theory for effective instruction and lasting learning.

Bibliography

Bandura A 1971 *Psychological Modeling: Conflicting Theories*. Aldine Atherton, Chicago, Illinois
Bandura A 1977a Self-efficacy: Toward a unifying theory of behavioral change. *Psychol. Rev.* 84: 191–215
Bandura A 1977b *Social Learning Theory*. Prentice-Hall, Englewood Cliffs, New Jersey

Bandura A 1978 The self-system in reciprocal determinism. *Am. Psychol.* 33: 344–58

deCharms R 1968 *Personal Causation: The Internal Affective Determinants of Behavior.* Academic Press, New York

deCharms R 1976 *Enhancing Motivation: A Change in the Classroom.* Irvington, New York

Dewey J 1916 *Democracy and Education: An Introduction to the Philosophy of Education.* Macmillan, New York

Dewey J 1963 *Experience and Education.* Collier, New York

Freire P 1973 *Pedagogy of the Oppressed.* Seabury Press, New York

Gibran K 1966 *The Prophet.* Knopf, New York

Illich I D 1971 *Deschooling Society.* Harper and Row, New York

Illich I D 1973 *Tools for Conviviality.* Harper and Row, New York

Lewin K 1947 Frontiers in group dynamics: Concept, method, and reality in social science: Social equilibria and social change. *Hum. Relat.* 1: 5–41

Lewin K 1948 *Resolving Social Conflicts: Selected Papers on Group Discussion.* Harper, New York

Maslow A H 1962 *Toward a Psychology of Being.* Van Nostrand, New York

Maslow A H 1970 *Motivation and Personality*, 2nd edn. Harper and Row, New York

Maslow A H 1971 *The Farther Reaches of Human Nature* Viking Press, New York

Rogers C R 1965 *Client-centered Therapy: Its Current Practice, Implications, and Theory.* Houghton Mifflin, Boston Massachusetts

Rogers C R 1969 *Freedom to Learn: A View of What Education Might Become.* Merrill, Columbus, Ohio

Sarason S B 1981 An asocial psychology and a misdirected clinical psychology. *Am. Psychol.* 36: 827–36

Weiner B 1972 Attribution theory, achievement motivation and educational process. *Rev. Educ. Res.* 42: 203–16

Weiner B (ed.) 1974 *Cognitive Views of Human Motivation.* Academic Press, New York, pp. 1–100

Weiner B 1980 *Human Motivation.* Holt, Rinehart and Winston, New York

Withall J 1975a Personalized and participatory learning and teaching. In: Maas J B, Kleiber D A (eds.) 1975 *Directory of Teaching Innovations in Psychology.* Division of the Teaching of Psychology, American Psychological Association, Washington, DC

Withall J 1975b Teachers as facilitators of learning: A rationale. *J. Teach. Educ.* 26: 261–66

Classroom Climate

R. S. Soar; R. M. Soar

Early measures of classroom behavior attempted simply to describe classrooms on the basis of observations, with later work assigning different values to different behaviors. This trend broadened after a time to examine relations between classroom measures and measures of pupil outcome. Along with this change in focus there was a trend toward increasing differentiation of the concepts used to measure classroom behavior. Early work used a single broad concept of climate such as social behavior or democratic vs. autocratic processes, but later work moved toward increasingly refined and narrow concepts, such as emotional climate vs. classroom management.

1. Major Reviews

Three reviews will be particularly useful to the reader who wishes to pursue the background of the topic further. Medley and Mitzel (1963) review the development of observational measures of classroom behavior in careful detail, presenting numbers of the early instruments, and with considerable attention to methodological detail. Dunkin and Biddle (1974) review the development of the concepts which were emerging, and present an extensive review of substantive findings with methodological commentary. The latest and perhaps the most useful review of substantive findings is that of Medley (1977), since it includes several large-scale studies which appeared after the Dunkin and Biddle review. He developed several quality-control criteria which reduced the number of studies to be reviewed, presumably lessening confusion by eliminating less well done studies. He also tabulated the findings of the studies by dimensions of teacher or pupil behavior, separately for subject matter and affective outcomes, by the socioeconomic status (SES) and grade level of pupils, and by the cognitive level of outcome. As a consequence, findings which had seemed to be inconsistent were sometimes seen to be consistent. For example, relations between a given classroom behavior and pupil outcome were sometimes consistent within each SES level, but opposite from one to the other.

2. Early Development

2.1 A Study of Social Behavior

An early study by Thomas (1929) was primarily concerned with describing the social behavior of preschool children. The recording procedure initially consisted of charting the movements of a given child around the playroom, timing each activity, and noting its nature. Thomas identified problems which still plague researchers. She noted that times for each activity were highly correlated across observers, ". . . but the extent o which this activity is concerned with persons or things s still in non-quantitative form . . ." (p. 8), and again, ". . . when a given child approached another the recorder made his own interpretation of whether it was a genuine social contact. These low coefficients of correlation are a beautiful example of how unreliability creeps in when interpretation is permitted the recorder" (p. 9). The problem of reliability when observer judgment is involved is still with us.

Later, she devised a set of categories for coding social behaviors and commented that there was no difficulty in agreeing on the number of contacts, but there was considerable difficulty in categorizing their kind. When two observers recorded the same activity "One recorded the situation as consistently 'conflict between William and Edward,' whereas the other observer recorded 'William embraces Edward'" (p. 11). The emotional tone of the contacts was not a major issue, although it was involved; rather, the primary concern was whether the behavior was social or not.

2.2 Integrative–Dominative Behavior

The work of Anderson et al. (1946) is a classic from which most observational research since then has drawn. It summarizes research over a number of years by a number of people, using the organizing principle of the freedom which the child is given to make decisions which affect him/her. Although Anderson and his colleagues used the terms "dominative" and "integrative" they equate the terms with democratic vs. autocratic processes, and state that ". . . whatever contributes to the democratic interplay between human beings is ipso facto a contribution to mental hygiene" (p. 31).

The categories in their observation system scale from active expression of motivation by both teacher and pupil in opposition to each other, to the teacher using imagination and resources to carry out educational objectives, but adapting to an expressed interest or activity of the child. Again, emotional climate is not a primary organizing feature, although aspects of it are clearly being recorded.

They concluded that observers agreed well in coding both teacher and pupil behaviors. After observing the same two teachers for two successive years, with different pupils the second year, the authors found similar patterns of pupil behavior both years, suggesting that teachers establish the patterns of behavior in their classrooms, rather than just respond to pupils. In integrative classrooms pupils showed more spontaneous behavior, both voluntarily and in response to others. In more dominative classrooms pupils showed more looking-up (distractability) and more of both conforming and nonconforming behavior.

Again, it is clear that the major focus was on authority relationships between teacher and pupils and how they were implemented. Different behaviors were valued differently because of their implications for democratic living and for mental health, with aspects of emotional climate embedded in the data being collected.

2.3 Learner-centered—Teacher-centered Behavior

Withall's (1949) categories clearly build on the work of Anderson et al., with the term "climate" appearing for the first time. The work was characterized as the development of a climate index, with the opening sentences of the definition indicating that it was ". . . to represent the emotional tone, which is a concomitant of interpersonal interaction" (p. 348). However, the set of categories was characterized as lying on a teacher-centered vs. pupil-centered continuum. They deal only with teacher statements: (a) learner supportive, (b) accepting and clarifying, (c) problem structuring, (d) neutral (formalities and administrative comments), (e) directive or hortative, (f) reproving or deprecating, and (g) teacher self-supporting. If the teacher's statements fell primarily in categories (a), (b), and (c), the teacher was said to be learner centered; in categories (e), (f), and (g), teacher centered; if the statements falling in category (c) outweighed the others, the teacher was characterized as problem centered. Statements in the neutral category (d) were ignored.

Reliability was established by having judges code statements from three transcripts, and was found to be generally satisfactory. Validity was studied by comparing transcripts coded with his categories with coding using the Anderson et al. categories and by judgments of raters as learner centered, problem centered, or teacher centered.

Although Withall's terms were learner centered vs. teacher centered, they parallel the terms integrative vs. dominative of Anderson et al. The term "climate" does appear, however, and "emotional tone" is used in the definition.

2.4 Climate in an Eclectic Approach

The work of Cornell et al. (1952) explicitly identified climate as an aspect of the data being collected. The purpose of the study was again a descriptive one, intended to identify differences between schools and school systems by examining the nature of the activities that occurred in classrooms. The major headings of their observation schedule were differentiation, social organization, pupil initiative, content, variety, competency (presentation and development of subject matter), climate-teacher, and climate-pupil.

There were 103 items altogether, of which 34 were climate items, further broken down into positive and negative. Although some of the behaviors identified as climate appear to deal with motivation and management, it is clear that communication of affect, both positive and negative, by both teacher and pupil, was explicitly being recorded. These distinctions, which current work suggests are important, were first made in their instrument.

Reliability was assessed by an analysis of variance procedure which results in intraclass correlations—a procedure whose sophistication is still not widely recognized. In effect, it identifies the reliability of the score which describes a given classroom by treating the variation which occurs from time to time and from observer to observer as error. In recording the climate behaviors, the authors commented that originally they checked each time one of these behaviors occurred during an observation period, but discovered that more reliable results were obtained if an item was checked only once regardless of how many times it occurred. This is the first test where the sign coding procedure was used. The reliabilities of the climate scores were in the 70s. The "validity" of the instrument was studied by establishing that it distinguished between classrooms at different grade levels and in different systems.

Among the contributions of the work of Cornell et al. were the separation of items into major headings reflecting many aspects of classroom behavior, among which was climate broken up into four components, the test of sign coding procedures, and a sophisticated reliability assessment. But perhaps as much as anything else, this instrument provided the largest number of items and definitions developed at that time, which provided a basis for the development of later observation schedules.

Later studies of classroom climate were carried out in other countries, most often of a descriptive nature. They are reported by Campbell (1970) and Chanan (1973).

3. *Major Influences on Current Work*

The late 1950s and early 1960s were a watershed for research on classroom climate. New observation instruments were developed, and concepts for describing classroom behavior were differentiated and refined. But these were extensions of previous work. The major innovation was that researchers went beyond mere description and began to relate the classroom behavior measures to pupil outcomes, most often to gain in achievement. The publication of Medley and Mitzel's Observation Schedule and Record (OScAR) and Flanders's Categories, both drawing heavily on past work, set the procedures for later work, began the process of relating measures of classroom behavior to measures of pupil outcome, began the process of differentiating concepts based on factor analysis, and provided instruments which have probably been used in more studies than any other.

The Observation Schedule and Record (Medley and Mitzel 1958) drew heavily on the items developed by Cornell et al. It also incorporated Withall's categories, with some change—specifically, the addition of categories to reflect teacher nonverbal expression of positive and negative affect. The instrument was not organized around a central theme, as some of the earlier instruments had been; rather, like Cornell et al., it was an eclectic gathering of items to describe a wide variety of teacher and pupil activities in the classroom.

One of the innovative aspects of their work was the way in which items were assembled into scales. Initially, items were assembled into keys on a rational basis; for example, the key "teacher manifest hostility" was made up of the items teacher uses sarcasm, teacher yells, teacher reproving statement, and teacher hostile behavior (nonverbal). Twenty such keys were developed and tested for reliability. Following this, the 14 keys which showed significant reliability were factor analyzed and produced three scales (factors). The factor "emotional climate" identified as polar opposites teacher and pupil expressions of affection and support vs. teacher and pupil expressions of negative affect. "Verbal emphasis" reflected the degree to which verbal activities were predominant in the classroom. "Social organization" reflected the amount of social grouping and pupil autonomy in the classroom.

In retrospect, the distinction which these factors made between emotional climate and pupil autonomy was notable, particularly in the light of other instruments both earlier and later in which these two aspects of the classroom were conceived of as part of the same concept. This use of statistical methodology to identify independent aspects of teacher–pupil behavior in the classroom is clearly a step forward in clarifying concepts and provides a basis for further work.

Flanders's (1970) system, originally published in 1960, is almost surely the other of the two instruments which has been most influential in the development of classroom observation. It is a clear outgrowth of the Anderson et al. work, and of Withall's categories, and codes only verbal interaction in the classroom. Although the organizing concept which Flanders used scaled classrooms from indirect to direct, he described these terms as expanding pupil freedom and limiting pupil freedom, so it seems to parallel the autocratic/democratic dimension of Anderson et al., and the pupil-centered/teacher-centered dimension of Withall. Again, as in both of those earlier systems, emotional climate is not named as such, but it is clear that at least two categories deal explicitly with climate, along with categories which reflect classroom management and substantive interaction between teacher and pupils.

The indirect categories (numbered as Flanders did) were: (1) teacher accepts feelings; (2) teacher praises or encourages; (3) teacher accepts or uses student idea; and (4) teacher asks question. The direct categories were: (5) teacher lectures; (6) teacher gives directions; and (7) teacher criticizes or justifies authority. The student categories were: (8) student responds; and (9) student initiates. The system was completed with category (10) which was used to code silence and/or confusion.

A notable development with the Flanders system was the method of tabulating the categories into a 10×10 matrix in such a way that one step of sequence was retained. Each cell in the matrix simultaneously represented the current activity and the activity which immediately preceded it. This permitted asking questions such as "What does a teacher do most often after a pupil stops talking?" Accept feelings? Criticize? "Does a teacher praise, accept, or use ideas initiated by pupils as often as she/he does answers to questions posed by the teacher?'' This appears to be a powerful advance, and has been incorporated into other category systems.

Medley and Mitzel and Flanders were pivotal in changing the focus of classroom observation by relating measures of classroom behavior with measures of pupil gain, introducing a new conception of validity. Until then, interest had been in recording classroom behavior for its own sake.

Overlapping with this development of classroom observation and measures of climate, research on teaching effectiveness was being carried out, but was primarily concerned with characteristics of the teacher which were correlated with administrator ratings. Little attention was paid to what actually happened in classrooms, or how much pupils learned. These deficiencies, which now seem obvious and compelling, were filled by the work of Medley and Mitzel, and Flanders, and their work set the pattern for work which followed. This work relating classroom behavior to pupil gain became known as process–product research and mushroomed in the decades which followed, with instruments for measurement of classroom behavior appearing literally by the hundreds, with emotional climate often represented. The focus of the remainder of this review will be on findings which relate climate with pupil outcomes from a number of these studies, particularly studies which meet Medley's quality-control criteria, and the large-scale federally funded projects.

4. Empirical Findings

Since findings are often variable, trends across studies will be sought; also the attempt will be made to identify and present studies which suggest reasons for apparent inconsistencies.

For observational studies, only results from low-inference measures will be reviewed, since higher inference measures suffer from multiple weaknesses. High- and low-inference measures are distinguished by how well they provide a record of the specific behaviors which occurred (low inference) in contrast to providing merely an abstraction from, or evaluation of, the behavior (high inference). For example, if a teacher is rated as enthusiastic (high inference) does the teacher move around, use gestures, dramatic pauses, varied facial expressions, express warmth? It is not possible to tell from the rating, and as a consequence the meaning of the rating is not clear, and comparisons from study to study are uncertain. As a further problem, are these behaviors (and perhaps others) all equally weighted in arriving at a composite, or are some given heavier weights than others by the rater? Finally, how enthusiastic is enthusiastic—that is, what are the norms or standard against which the rater makes a comparison in order to make the rating? In short, (a) the behavior which occurred, (b) the weights applied in arriving at a composite view, and (c) the norms or standard against

which the composite is compared, all reside in the rater's head and are not part of the record. All that is recorded is the consequence of comparing the rater's composite with his/her standard.

High-inference measures have the further problem that commonly held conceptions of teaching often combine unrelated dimensions. For example, indirectness includes teacher control of pupils as well as warmth, which are relatively unrelated. This problem can be present in any high-inference rating and not be identifiable. For all these reasons, the major focus here will be on findings from low-inference measures.

4.1 Positive Affect and Pupil Achievement

An early study which related a low-inference measure of climate to pupil achievement was that of Medley and Mitzel using OScAR (1959). They studied the relations of its three factors with supervisor ratings of teacher effectiveness as well as with measures of pupil attitude and gain in reading. The measure of emotional climate was positively related to ratings of teachers' effectiveness and pupils' perceptions of rapport, but none of these was related to pupil reading gain. Although supervisors believed that a warm emotional climate was important to pupil learning, neither the rating nor the low-inference measure supported that belief.

In 1960, shortly after this study of Medley and Mitzel's, Flanders published the results of the first process–product research with his instrument (Flanders 1970). Although Flanders's results for indirectness and those of others are mixed, Gage's (1977) meta-analysis (statistical synthesis) of the studies reviewed by Dunkin and Biddle found a significant positive relationship between indirectness and student achievement. Interpretation of the results is uncertain, however, since indirectness involves both teacher control and warmth, as discussed above.

Research since then—particularly applications of factor analysis—has identified narrower, more specific dimensions of classroom behavior than were used in earlier studies, but which are at the same time more inclusive than individual items. Following this line of development, the remaining portions of this review will focus on the narrower definition of climate defined as teacher and pupil affect expression, positive and negative, and more specifically, praise.

Probably the most helpful single source for such results is that of Medley (1977). In his summary of relationships between positive affect and student achievement, negative relationships are about as frequent as positive relationships. As another way of synthesizing these results, Wilkinson (1980) did a meta-analysis of findings from those studies and obtained an overall correlation of 0.07 between positive affect and student achievement. This is probably the clearest evidence of the usefulness (or lack of usefulness) of positive affect expression as employed by teachers.

Although somewhat speculative, there are some suggestions in the literature that the context in which positive affect is used, the nature of the pupil, or the nature of the outcome measure makes a difference. In one study in which a negative relation was found, positive affect occurred in a context in which there was considerable pupil activity but little learning activity. Tisher (1970) found greater achievement gain for pupils low in need achievement where warmth was high; but greatest gain for pupils high in need achievement where warmth was low. With respect to the nature of the outcome measure, Stallings and Kaskowitz (1974) found positive affect to be related positively with gain in Raven's Progressive Matrices (a measure of complex problem solving), but negatively with reading. Clearly the relation between positive affect and achievement is complex, and the overall correlation may represent too great an oversimplification.

4.2 Praise as a Specific Positive Affect

It may be helpful in clarifying the mixed relationships for positive affect to examine praise separately. In Medley's review, praise is often related positively to achievement, in contrast to the mixed results for positive affect. One of the individual findings offers a provocative contrast, however. Praise was related positively with math and reading, but negatively with the Raven's Progressive Matrices (Stallings and Kaskowitz 1974). This is opposite to their results for positive affect in general (see below for further discussion of this point).

In a review of the ways in which teachers use praise Brophy (1981) reports that teachers in general do not use praise systematically in support of the attainment of classroom objectives—that is, praise is not contingent on a particular behavior nor is that behavior clearly specified. However, Rowe (1974) found that teachers did praise high-achieving pupils contingently, but not low-achieving pupils even though they were praised as often. It should be noted that some teachers in the Stallings and Kaskowitz study had been trained to use praise systematically as reinforcement, so contingent use was likely.

4.3 Negative Affect and Pupil Achievement

In the Medley review, expression of negative affect in the classroom is more consistently related to student achievement, in the negative direction as expected, but even here the results are short of being completely consistent. However, Gage's meta-analysis found criticism and disapproval significantly negatively related to achievement.

It seems possible that some of the inconsistency of findings for both positive and negative affect may also be accounted for by interactions between pupil socioeconomic status and affect expression. Two studies indicated that negative affect had stronger negative effects for low SES pupils than for high, or even that the relationship reversed for high SES pupils (Brophy and Evertson 1974, Soar and Soar 1975). Further support for the suggestion that SES makes a difference comes from Wilkinson's meta-analysis. She compared results for

positive affect for groupings by grade level, SES, and subject matter, and one of the few differences was the suggestion that positive affect was positively related with learning for low SES first-grade pupils but not for middle and higher SES pupils.

One interpretation of these findings is that a major problem for the teacher of primary grade disadvantaged pupils is that of maintaining sufficient motivation for pupil task activity. If so, this may be why negative affect is more destructive of gain and positive affect more helpful for these pupils.

4.4 Results for Noncognitive Outcomes

While achievement is the most frequently used outcome, different kinds of noncognitive outcome measures have been used in a smaller number of studies. Medley's review reports that only positive relations were found between positive affect and pupil self-concept and attitude toward school; negative affect was negatively related with the same outcomes; praise showed no relations with these noncognitive outcomes. Campbell (1970) in Australia found warmth (positive affect) to be positively related with pupil need to excel, but that teacher dominance (negative affect) was negatively related to need to excel and positively related to need to avoid failure. So the studies show parallel results for positive affect in general (but not praise) in supporting wholesome self-concept, attitude toward school and motivation, with opposite results for negative affect.

However, for praise, Stallings and Kaskowitz found a strong negative relationship with pupil independence. Similarly Rowe found that pupils from classrooms in which there was relatively little teacher praise tended to rely on their own observations and judgment, whereas pupils from classrooms high in praise were more likely to rely on the authority of the teacher as a way of answering questions. Soar (1966) found that criticism was positively related to increase in pupil dependence. So these three studies agree in indicating that both praise and criticism may not be useful, and may increase pupil dependence.

4.5 Praise vs. Positive Affect

The discrepant results for praise and positive affect suggest the need to separate them conceptually. Praise was related positively with achievement gain but negatively with Raven's Progressive Matrices, pupil independence, and pupils' reliance on their own thought processes. Positive affect was unrelated to achievement gain overall, but was related positively to Raven's Progressive Matrices and attitude toward self and school. A possible interpretation is that praise places authority and control in the adult, which hinders pupil development of independence, self-reliance in thought, and complex thought processes. Positive affect on the other hand, more generally extends teacher support and acceptance which encourages pupil independence, complex thought processes, and more positive attitudes. With such different results, it seems imperative to separate praise from positive affect, conceptually, as measures in research, and as desirable teacher behaviors. For further discussion, see Soar and Soar (1983).

5. A Questionnaire Approach

A different approach for measuring classroom climate is that of collecting student perceptions by pencil and paper instruments and relating these to measures of outcome. Walberg (1969) has conducted work based on probably the most extensive and intensive developmental studies, carried out in the context of Harvard Project Physics.

Three cognitive measures of science knowledge used as a composite and three noncognitive measures of attitude toward science, also as a composite, were used as outcomes. The climate variables were 14 measures of student perception of the nature of the classroom derived from a single inventory.

Difficulty ("The class is best suited for the smartest students") was the only significant predictor of gain on the cognitive composite. The noncognitive composite was predicted positively by satisfaction ("The students enjoy their class work"), and negatively by friction ("Certain students are responsible for petty quarrels"), cliqueness ("Certain students stick together in small groups") and apathy ("Members of the class do not care what the class does"). Interestingly, the measure nearest to positive affect, intimacy ("All the students know each other very well"), did not relate to either outcome composite.

The study illustrates a different, much less expensive data collection procedure, and also presents results at the secondary-school level, which are scarce in the observational literature. Other studies suggest that measures of student perception are probably useful down to sixth grade, and perhaps even lower.

6. Concluding Comment

Over the years, the definition of climate and its focus have changed. The initial concern was with a broad concept of climate of interest in itself. As observational methodology developed, a more differentiated definition of climate emerged which had independent dimensions within it. Emotional climate was differentiated from control, and was broken up into positive and negative; and positive affect, in turn, into praise vs. positive affect in general. As the focus has changed from description to examining relations between classroom measures and pupil outcomes, it has become clear that some beliefs about the effects of climate are in error.

In general, negative affect is negatively related with both cognitive and noncognitive pupil outcomes. Positive affect broadly defined does not relate consistently with achievement, and relations apparently depend on specifics such as context, pupil socioeconomic status, and the nature of the outcome. On the other hand, praise related positively with achievement, but negatively with higher level cognitive outcomes and negatively with pupil independence. The implications for learning as a lifetime process seem critical and argue for distinguishing praise from other positive affect. Ironically, these findings take us back to the mental hygiene concerns of Anderson et al. except that research in the intervening years suggests that praise has an effect which is counter to outcomes which they valued.

See also: Evolution of Research on Teaching; Teacher-centered and Learner-centered Teaching; Psychological Environment

Bibliography

Anderson H H, Brewer J E, Reed M F 1946 Studies of teachers' classroom personalities. III Follow-up studies of the effects of dominative and integrative contacts on children's behavior. *Appl. Psychol. Monogr.* 11

Brophy J 1981 Teacher praise: A functional analysis. *Rev. Educ. Res.* 51: 5–32

Brophy J E, Evertson C M 1974 *The Texas Teacher Effectiveness Project: Presentation of Non-linear Relationships and Summary Discussion*, Report No. 74-6. Research and Development Center, University of Texas, Austin, Texas

Campbell W J 1970 Some effects of affective climate on the achievement motivation of pupils. In: Campbell W J (ed.) 1970 *Scholars in Context: The Effects of Environments on Learning*. Wiley, New York

Chanan G (ed.) 1973 *Towards a Science of Teaching*. Humanities Press, New York

Cornell F G, Lindvall C M, Saupe J L 1952 *An Exploratory Measurement of Individualities of Schools and Classrooms*. University of Illinois, Urbana, Illinois

Dunkin M J, Biddle B J 1974 *The Study of Teaching*. Holt, Rinehart, and Winston, New York

Flanders N A 1970 *Analyzing Teacher Behavior*. Addison-Wesley, Reading, Massachusetts

Gage N L 1977 *The Scientific Basis of the Art of Teaching*. Columbia University, New York

Medley D M 1977 *Teacher Competence and Teacher Effectiveness*. American Association of Colleges for Teacher Education, Washington, DC

Medley D M, Mitzel H E 1958 A technique for measuring classroom behavior. *J. Educ. Psychol.* 49: 86–92

Medley D M, Mitzel H E 1959 Some behavioral correlates of teacher effectiveness. *J. Educ. Psychol.* 50: 239–46

Medley D M, Mitzel H E 1963 Measuring classroom behavior by systematic observation. In: Gage N L (ed.) 1963 *Handbook of Research on Teaching: A Project of the American Educational Research Association*. Rand McNally, Chicago, Illinois

Rowe M B 1974 Relation of wait-time and rewards to the development of language, logic, and fate control: Part II Rewards. *J. Res. Sci. Teach.* 11: 291–308

Soar R S 1966 *An Integrative Approach to Classroom Learning*. Temple University, Philadelphia, Pennsylvania. ERIC Document No. ED 033 749

Soar R S, Soar R M 1975 *Classroom Behavior, Pupil Characteristics, and Pupil Growth for the School Year and the Summer*. Institute for Development of Human Resources, University of Florida, Gainesville, Florida

Soar R S, Soar R M 1983 Context effects in the teaching–

learning process. In: Smith D C (ed.) 1983 *Essential Knowledge for Beginning Educators*. American Association of Colleges for Teacher Education and ERIC Clearinghouse for Teacher Education, Washington, DC

Stallings J A, Kaskowitz D H 1974 *Follow Through Classroom Observation Evaluation*. Contract OEC-0-8522480-4633 (100). Office of Education, Department of Health, Education and Welfare to Stanford Research Institute, Menlo Park, California

Thomas D S 1929 *Some New Techniques for Studying Social Behavior*. Columbia University, New York

Tisher R P 1970 Association between verbal discourse and pupils' understanding in science. In: Campbell W J (ed.) 1970

Walberg H J 1969 Social environment as a mediator of classroom learning. *J. Educ. Psychol.* 60: 443–48

Wilkinson S S 1980 The relationship of teacher praise and student achievement: A meta-analysis of selected research (Unpublished doctoral dissertation, University of Florida)

Withall J 1949 The development of a technique for the measurement of socio-emotional climate in classrooms. *J. Exp. Educ.* 17: 347–61

Competition

L. Owens

For most of the twentieth century, competition has been seen as a cornerstone of cultural advancement. Schools are frequently given a central place in training the young in competitive–individualistic striving for success, frequently in material terms. The appropriateness of this competitive training is currently being scrutinized carefully by philosophers, social psychologists, and cultural analysts. Attention is being directed to questions of definition and conceptual clarification. The arguments for and against the desirability of competition in school learning are now frequently being voiced, with the sceptics loud and persuasive. Finally, the evidence regarding the effectiveness of interpersonal competition in learning is being examined carefully by social scientists who have devised and tested numerous variations and alternatives.

1. The Concept of Competition

It has been argued philosophically that there are three general conditions which must be met if "competition" is to occur (Dearden 1972). Two individuals or groups are in competition when:

(a) both want the same goal or object,

(b) the accomplishment of the goal by one thereby excludes the other from it,

(c) knowing that one or the other must be excluded, both persist in their efforts to reach the goal.

In "competition", therefore, a participant consciously persists in attempts to achieve superiority, that is, a better relative position with regard to the goal than an opponent can achieve. It differs from "rivalry" because the striving is focused on achieving the goal rather than on humiliating the opponent. It differs from "emulation" because one participant achieves the goal by excluding the other from reaching it rather than simply by matching the other's example.

Competition can be seen as a form of conflict in which observance of certain rules and conventions by the competing parties precludes total ruthlessness. It thus seems possible to conceive of fair and unfair competition, depending on the extent to which ethics are shared by all of the competitors. Indeed, in this regard it has been argued that competition necessarily includes cooperation (Perry 1975):

Competitions require us to assume the capacity to cooperate if they are to run at all. (p. 128)

"Unfair competitions", then, would be characterized by an absence of agreed-upon conventions, or by a bias in the rules themselves. In this conception of competition, the notion of "competing with oneself" is not logically possible, since a single person cannot both win and lose at the same time. Striving within oneself for improved performance is commonly referred to as competition nevertheless. Ruben (1980) calls these situations "autocomps" and observes that they are typically used as internal training for subsequent external interpersonal competition. There is no doubt that the desire for self-improvement is a powerful motive in learning and that it is, for example, put to use in numerous strategies for individualized instruction. For clarity, nevertheless, such a motivational state is excluded from being labelled as competition in the present discussion.

It is plain that the term "competition", through varied common and educational usage, has acquired a number of meanings. In classroom settings, therefore, it is important to distinguish among three main senses in which the term is used.

1.1 Competition as Structure

"Competition" is used to refer to an overall goal structure established for learning. As for other goal structures, (for example, see *Cooperation*), the interdependence among teacher and students will be influenced by the general nature of the goal, the specific tasks devised for achieving the general goal, and the amount and type of interaction among participants in the tasks. Inevitably, too, the atmosphere of the school and the overall ethos of the culture make an impact on the goal structure for learning. As a result of the arrangement of task, learners, and materials:

> A competitive goal structure exists when students perceive that they can obtain their goal if, and only if, the other students with whom they are linked fail to obtain their goal. (Johnson and Johnson 1975 p.7)

Competition is the overall organization that enables and encourages a limited number of students to succeed at the highest level (however defined) while the majority do not.

1.2 Competition as Trait

"Competition" is used to refer to a personality trait of the learner. The attitude of the participant to the arranged goal structure is an essential consideration. A learner who is simply present within a competitive goal structure is different from one who enters knowingly and willingly into the striving for superiority. Thus, "to take part in a competition" does not necessarily mean "to act competitively", and it is the internal motivational state of the learner which makes the difference. School attendance is compulsory for a specified age group, but the knowing/willing competitive motive is not compulsory. Therefore, it is not appropriate to call all school attenders who are apparently caught up in competitive goal structures competitors.

1.3 Competition as Behaviour

"Competition" is used to refer to the observable behaviour by the student in the classroom. From the forgoing discussion it would seem that competitive behaviour is a composite of three types of action. The first is a stated intention to achieve superiority over an opponent (or an unstated but visible eagerness to enter into the process of striving). The second is persistence in striving during the complete period of time allocated to the contest, even in the face of discouragement or weariness. The third is the experience (and possibly display) of a positive emotion such as pleasure at a successful outcome. At the very least, a competitor is not indifferent to the outcome. The obverse to this positive emotion is, of course, some degree of dismay at an unsuccessful outcome.

2. The Desirability of Competition

It is a commonplace observation that "Western" cultures which embody a high level of materialism are characterized by high competition, achievement, and profit drives. The school systems in such cultures are apparently integral in the training of young people to accept the appropriateness of these drives, and to strive willingly to seek the rewards offered. The arguments are increasingly being voiced, however, that such drives are sociably devised exaggerations of natural human urges to survive and thrive, and that other equally natural human qualities for sociability and mutual support are being thwarted. Johnson and Johnson, for example, conclude that schools promote "irrational competition" (1975 p. 10), and Slavin further observes that:

> Schools are one of the very few areas of human endeavour in which cooperation is relatively rare, and is in fact often defined by the system as "cheating". (1981 p. 1)

It is therefore appropriate to list some of the current arguments for and against the desirability of using competition in the classroom (Grenis 1975, Lynn 1977, Sapon-Shevin 1978, Wax 1975). They are presented here without comment or counterargument.

2.1 In Favour of Competition

(a) Competition is associated with the development of such personal characteristics as self-reliance, perseverance, and industry.

(b) On a larger scale, the progress and productivity of a society is enhanced, and indeed a country's economy may prosper in direct relation to the level of domestic competitive activity.

(c) Progress is a result of a diversity of competing ideas.

(d) Unimpeded individualistic achievement is a cornerstone of democratic freedom.

(e) Competition is a powerful motive in stimulating effort and ambition, in school and in wider social experience.

(f) Comparative excellence is rewarded in society, and this should therefore begin at school.

(g) Guidance for vocational or personal purposes requires comparative information regarding aptitudes and motivations, best obtained from competitive situations.

(h) "Ideally every child is a winner—who doesn't win *every* time" (Grenis 1975 p. 200), but with a sufficiently broad curriculum in schools, the range of competitive situations will accommodate most aptitudes.

(i) Competitive activity is a source of self-confidence and self-esteem.

2.2 Against Competition

(a) Aspects of personal identity such as self-esteem, self-acceptance, and feelings of competence are integral to human welfare and are therefore personal rights; these should not be apportioned in limited supply as a result of the arranged competitions of schooling.

(b) Competition is essentially selfish and promotes excessive self-regard to the exclusion of the legitimate rights of others.

(c) Competition promotes secrecy, greed, subterfuge, and hatred.

(d) Education ought to be a joyful experience; furthermore, it is unethical to arrange the public humiliation of some students for the benefit of others.

(e) Competition leads to a deterioration of: sensitivity to others; feelings of affiliation; communal concern; and willingness to negotiate.

(f) The only students motivated by competition are the relatively few who believe they have a chance to win.

(g) Handicapped and disadvantaged children who are placed intentionally in heterogeneous classes (mainstreaming) are frequently destined for failure despite their earnest performance.

(h) Economic and industrial success, and in a larger view the progress of civilizations themselves, are attributable not to competitive activity but rather to cooperation and teamwork.

(i) Competition is a source of insecurity, self-doubt, and personal unhappiness for the large proportion who do not win.

Rebuttals to some of these arguments, both pro and con, are featured in Johnson and Johnson (1975) and in Kleinig (1982). There is also a noteworthy pair of contrasting philosophical analyses (Fielding 1976, Prvulovich 1982). The sensitivity of the issues regarding the appropriate level of competition in the classroom attracts partisans to one side or the other. It is worth noting, though, that a well-known pair of these outspoken protagonists firmly agree that a mixture of competitive and cooperative goal structures should be used in classrooms, while they disagree on which should predominate—Johnson and Johnson (1975) favour cooperation but Lynn (1977) opts for competition.

3. The Effectiveness of Competition

In order to appreciate the evidence about the effectiveness of competition in learning, it is necessary first to ask "learning by whom?" and "in what society?" The sex-role stereotype in most Western, industrialized nations links boys with competitiveness and girls with cooperativeness. In the United States, for example, Ahlgren and Johnson (1979) found that in a large sample of children from a midwestern city, boys expressed more positive attitudes to competition than girls did (see *Students' Sex*). This difference between the sexes was consistent across a wide age range from 7 to 18, and was especially marked between the ages of 13 and 16.

The results were identical for an equally large sample of Australian schoolchildren, with entry to high school (age 12) coinciding with an increase in between-sex differences (Owens and Straton 1980, Owens 1985). The cultural context is crucial, however. In the 45 "Anglo–American" studies analysed by Strube (1981), the same sex-typed pattern was evident for young children in their actual behaviour and not simply in their expressed attitudes. At preschool and primary school ages, boys acted significantly more competitively than girls did in the experimental situations. Mexican and Mexican–American children seemed similarly inclined, but a number of Israeli studies revealed the opposite— girls seemed more competitive than boys or there were no detectable differences. The mores and values of a society, and the early socializing experiences which make an impact on the psychosocial development of children, play a large part in the eventual receptiveness of students to competition as a learning mode.

There is American evidence that interpersonal competition as a goal structure is associated with effective academic learning (Michaels 1977). After reviewing a select group of studies in which individual competition was compared with one or more of group competition, individualization, and group cooperation, Michaels concluded that "the most striking finding was the consistent superiority of individual competition" (1977 p. 95). Seven of the ten studies reviewed were concerned with postsecondary students, however, leaving unclarified the appropriateness and effectiveness of the competitive goal structure for primary and secondary students.

With regard to these younger students, a large-scale analysis of research has indicated that interpersonal competition, while facilitating subject learning for college-age students, is less effective at primary and secondary level than goal structures utilizing cooperative methods (Johnson et al. 1981). Although this conclusion appeared valid for all subject areas, the analysis also found that interpersonal competition is more useful for rote, drill, or mechanical correcting tasks when compared with problem-solving and concept-attainment tasks, which is also consistent with older evidence (Johnson and Johnson 1975). Group competition, involving within-group cooperation as well as between-group striving for superiority, was also found to be superior to interpersonal competition. In a recent analysis Slavin (1983) has argued that the positive effect of group competition on achievement may be due to two features: clear procedures for providing rewards to a group for the learning of members, and the high visibility of these rewards. It may not be competition *per se*, therefore, which is crucial; a non-competitive process with an equally clear reward allocation system might serve just as well. An additional benefit from methods using group competition for school-age students is not only that subject achievement is demonstrably enhanced but also that the affective and social aspects of learning are acknowledged and developed (Slavin 1980). In the American social context, there is evidence that group-competitive methods promote mutual concern generally, and specifically improve relationships between antagonistic racial and national subgroups. As well, the use of the natural social inclinations of children has an impact on motivation and concentration, and on general liking for school.

For school-age students, therefore, the prevailing competitive—individualistic ethos in which one person is encouraged to strive against all others may be counterproductive. Methods of competition using groups or teams enable students to assist one another cooperatively while at the same time striving for comparative success. This seems especially apt for outcomes in which the product is complex or in which the thinking is complicated, and in addition, in which positive interpersonal attitudes are involved.

See also: Cooperation; Small Group Methods

Bibliography

Ahlgren A, Johnson D W 1979 Sex differences in cooperative and competitive attitudes from the 2nd through the 12th grades. *Dev. Psychol.* 15: 45–49
Dearden R F 1972 Competition in education. *Proc. Philos. Educ. Soc. Great Britain* 6: 119–33
Fielding M 1976 Against competition. *Proc. Phil. Educ. Soc.* 10: 124–46
Grenis M 1975 Individualization, grouping, competition, and excellence. *Phi Delta Kappan* 57: 199–200
Johnson D W, Johnson R T 1975 *Learning Together and Alone: Cooperation, Competition, and Individualization.* Prentice-Hall, Englewood Cliffs, New Jersey
Johnson D W, Maruyama G, Johnson R T, Nelson D, Skon L 1981 The effects of cooperative, competitive, and individualistic goal structures on achievement: A meta-analysis. *Psychol. Bull.* 89: 47–62
Kleinig J 1982 Competition. In: Kleinig J 1982 *Philosophical Issues in Education.* Croom Helm, London, pp. 162–74
Lynn R 1977 Competition and cooperation. In: Cox C, Boyson R (eds.) 1977 *Black Paper 1977.* Temple Smith, London, pp. 107–13
Michaels J W 1977 Classroom reward structures and academic performance. *Rev. Educ. Res.* 47: 87–98
Owens L 1985. The learning preferences of students and teachers: An Australian–American comparison. *Teaching and Teach. Educ.* 1(3): 229–42
Owens L, Straton R G 1980 The development of a cooperative, competitive, and individualised learning preference scale for students. *Br. J. Educ. Psychol.* 50: 147–61
Perry L R 1975 Competition and cooperation. *Br. J. Educ. Stud.* 23: 127–34
Prvulovich A 1982 In defence of competition. *J. Phil. Educ.* 16: 77–88
Ruben H L 1980 *Competing: Understanding and Winning the Strategic Games We All Play.* Harper and Row, Sydney
Sapon-Shevin M 1978 Another look at mainstreaming: Exceptionality, normality, and the nature of difference. *Phi Delta Kappan* 60: 119–21
Slavin R 1980 Cooperative learning. *Rev. Educ. Res.* 50: 315–42
Slavin R 1981 A policy choice: Cooperative or competitive learning. *Character* 2(3): 1–5
Slavin R E 1983 *Cooperative Learning.* Longman, New York
Strube M 1981 Meta-analysis and cross-cultural comparison: Sex differences in child competitiveness. *J. Cross Cult. Psychol.* 12: 3–20
Wax J 1975 Competition: Educational incongruity. *Phi Delta Kappan* 57: 197–98

Cooperation

L. Owens

Recent years have seen a surge in popularity of methods of teaching that promote student–student interaction. Young teachers are being increasingly urged in their preservice education to consider the possibilities for using cooperative groups in classrooms. Curriculum packages (e.g. *Man: A Course of Study*) are being designed so that group work is integral to achieving the aims. Numerous open plan schools have been built on the assumption that flexible groupings of learners will promote achievement. Students of the social psychology of learning are increasingly being sensitized to the group processes inherent in interaction in the classroom. Educational researchers are being exhorted to investigate various types of group methods and their impact on achievement and attitudes. Like mother and the national flag, cooperation is difficult to criticize. Precisely because the desirability of cooperation seems beyond doubt, there are three key questions for educators to consider: What are the alternatives to cooperation in learning? What differences in meanings are associated with the term? What variety in kinds of cooperative teaching strategies is available for classroom use?

1. Cooperation and Competition

One of the legacies bequeathed by Charles Darwin to the scientists of the twentieth century has been the thesis of the inherent naturalness of human striving for superiority. Adopted by the "social Darwinists", this qualified biological observation became a credo of those arguing for instinctive competition in humankind in all social and economic interaction. Though scientists like Ardrey and Lorenz also place important restrictions on the generalized assertions about competition, nonetheless they stand as recent and respected protagonists in this line of thinking from Darwin to the present. Cooperation as a human characteristic, therefore, has been seen until fairly recent years as the relative absence of competition. The more competition in a person, necessarily, then, by logical and biological argument, the less cooperation in that person. This thinking was typically embodied in the type of classroom survey question for students illustrated by the following:

Choose (a) or (b)
What I enjoy in this class is:
(a) the group work and helping each other learn
(b) the chance to come first in a test and be the best

The assumption plainly is that a student can enjoy (a) or (b), but not both.

Notable resistance to the idea of the mutual exclusiveness of cooperation and competition came from Margaret Mead, who, at the level of total culture, was able to show that a human society is a functional blend of both cooperation and competition. As with all such blends, the balance between the two varies from culture to culture, with some being markedly cooperative and some markedly competitive. It is important to note, in addition, that this coexistence does not necessarily diminish the cohesion nor reduce the continuance of the culture. From these data it is but a short step to the point of view of Montagu that, in contrast to the prevailing beliefs, it is not competition but rather it is cooperation that is the predominant characteristic of human beings. People are bonded together by love and cooperation, and it is this quality on which the survival of humankind is based.

A student's attitudes toward cooperation and competition in the classroom, therefore, need not be in mutual disagreement. A student can favour both cooperation and competition in classroom learning, or one of them, or neither. The independence of these attitudes has been demonstrated by Johnson and Ahlgren (1976) with a sample of American schoolchildren and has been replicated with Australian children by Owens and Straton (1980). An additional outcome from the latter study is a learning preference scale in which expressed attitudes to cooperation, competition, and individualization can be tabulated independently of each other, though with a common conceptual basis. Students indicate agreement/disagreement with items such as the following:

(a) I like to work in a group at school
(b) I like to try to be better than other students
(c) I like to work on my own without paying attention to other people

In keeping with the modern theory, a student may agree with one, or two, or all three of these statements. They are not opposite ends of the same dimension of character, and students are not expected to choose one and thereby exclude others.

2. The Concept of Cooperation

The term "cooperation" is frequently used, both casually in conversation and specifically in educational writing. The term has acquired a variety of meanings and there is the definite possibility of semantic confusion between user and listener. In classroom settings, it is important to distinguish among three main referents for the term.

2.1 Cooperation as Structure

"Cooperation" is used to refer to an overall goal structure established for learning. Components of this goal structure include the general nature of the goal, the value of the specific tasks in achieving this goal, the amount of interaction expected among participants in the task, the actual responses of others to the goal structure (e.g., approval or disapproval), and the types of interdependence to be created among participants. In addition, the ethos of the total culture impinges inescapably on the classroom goal structure, especially in the perceived relevance to students' broader concerns and their interaction with others outside school. As Johnson and Johnson (1975) succinctly state:

A cooperative goal structure exists when students perceive that they can obtain their goal if, and only if, the other students with whom they are linked can obtain their goal. (p. 7)

Although some individual differences may exist, the overriding goal is a mutual one and concern for achieving it is shared generally among the students. This mutual goal may be limited and the tasks may occupy just a few lessons, or the scope may be extensive and the tasks lengthy and complicated.

2.2 Cooperation as Trait

"Cooperation" is used to refer to a personality trait of the learner. Such a trait is fundamental to the response by the learner to the goal structure being employed. The significance or value of the procedure will be seen differently by students whose personal dispositions to enter into cooperative learning are dissimilar. Their motivation and willingness to participate, too, are associated with cooperation as a trait. The interaction between trait and structure is complex. Just as the trait of cooperation enhances a student's receptivity to a cooperative goal structure, so also the actual experience of cooperative learning reinforces and extends the cooperative disposition of the student. On a larger scale, though some of the tendency toward cooperation may be inborn in humans, there is no doubt that much of it is learned through experience. Girls, for example, seem more inclined to cooperation in school learning than boys, and the evidence is that contrasting socialization pressures by parents, teachers, and media at very early ages are responsible. In cross-cultural comparisons, research in Sydney indicates that Australian aboriginal schoolchildren express much less personal preference for competition than whites, and aboriginal adults express much more personal preference for cooperation. Kagan's samples of Mexican–American children score more cooperatively and less competitively on social motive personality measures in comparison with Anglo–American children (Sharan et al. 1980). Both schoolchildren and teachers in the United States express stronger preferences for cooperation in learning than equivalent groups in Australia (Owens 1985). The cultural patterns in which a child grows up make great impressions on the developing personality.

2.3 Cooperation as Behaviour

"Cooperation" is used to refer to the observable behaviour by the student in the classroom learning situation. Logically, it would seem reasonable to assume that, given a cooperative goal structure, a student with a cooperative disposition or trait would act in an altruistic and/or group-enhancing fashion. That is, the mutual goal would be accepted and the actions would clearly advance progress toward that goal. In practice, there are two conditions that may interfere with this harmony. First, a student possessed of cooperation as a trait, faced with cooperation as a goal structure, may nonetheless act individualistically in response to the prevailing stress of preparing for a forthcoming major examination (an extrinsic condition). Second, this same student may nonetheless act competitively if faced with other group members acting in this way, whose success would be threatening (an intrinsic condition). In planning and carrying out cooperation in the classroom, therefore, a teacher cannot assume that cooperative behaviour follows automatically from the association of cooperative organization with a socially-oriented personality. The actions must be observed, recorded, and analysed for intent and impact on others. It may require some sensitivity to distinguish between cooperative and noncooperative behaviour, and it may require considerable effort to train students in the social skills that are inherent in successful cooperative learning. Such skills in human relationships include general abilities such as unambiguous communication, giving and receiving feedback, sharing and trusting, and listening (Johnson and Johnson 1975). Particular cooperative learning schemes have been developed that require specialized social skills.

3. Teaching Strategies that Use Cooperating by Students

There is little doubt that cooperation generally as a teaching strategy has positive outcomes on achievement (Johnson et al. 1981) and on social relationships (Sharan 1980, Slavin 1980, 1983). The difficulty in interpreting the results of the research studies is created by the different kinds of cooperating that are employed in the teaching strategies. Just as the concept of cooperation has a number of possible meanings, outlined briefly in the preceding discussion, so also the techniques for

cooperating vary and can be classified by selected criteria.

A quite simple, yet very useful, distinction between cooperation and helpfulness is made by Mead:

> In cooperation, the goal is shared and it is the relationship to the goal which holds the cooperating individuals together; in helpfulness, the goal is shared only through the relationship of the helpers to the individual whose goal it actually is. (1961 p. 17)

In "helpfulness", therefore, the emphasis is on the association between individuals, frequently occurring as a form of tutoring in which one person directly assists another. In contrast, the emphasis in "cooperation" is on the mutual attractiveness of the goal to all of the participants and the shared willingness to work together to achieve that goal.

3.1 Cooperating as Helpfulness

Most of the teaching strategies in which the cooperating among students can be characterized as "helpfulness" employ a form of tutoring. Peer tutoring occurs when classmates or agemates aid each other in the process of learning. The relationship between helper and helpee(s) is usually directed by the teacher, if not in person, then by means of carefully selected and structured information to be learned and/or specified tasks to be accomplished. Communication is typically dyadic and involves a role difference between participants (i.e., one teaches and the other listens). The outcome of the tutoring is the quality of the individual performance of the tutee (a good test result, a well-written essay, a drawing in proper perspective). The helpfulness, therefore, occurs in the (shared) means or procedures by which one person assists another to achieve (unshared) goals or objectives. If more than one tutoring relationship occurs in a given classroom, these need not necessarily be of a uniform type nor need they necessarily be coordinated systematically beyond the desire for reasonable order.

An aggregate of tutoring relationships in a classroom, therefore, has an individualistic character in that each tutor–tutee team may differ from its neighbour. Within this overall relative individuality, however, certain specific forms of programmed interdependence can be arranged by the teacher.

First, there is interdependence in task, in which students must depend on each other so that each presents a portion of the work and all can thereby learn the whole of the work. A clear example of this interdependence is found in Jigsaw Learning (Aronson et al. 1978). As the title implies, a learning task is "jigsawed" or cut into pieces that, when fitted together, recreate the total picture. Each group of five or six students gets a complete set of task sections, and each student in the group takes the responsibility for one of these sections. After learning the section of material, the student tutors the other members of the group, and is tutored in turn by them. Tests are taken individually over the whole of the material (see *Small Group Methods*).

Second, there is interdependence in reward, in which students must depend on each other so that the performance of each group member contributes to the reward received by the group. The most highly organized strategies of this type are Teams–Games–Tournament (TGT) learning and Student Teams–Achievement Divisions (STAD) (Slavin 1983). In STAD, classroom teams of four or five students study together, and frequently quiz and tutor each other, with specifically assigned material for the current topic. At designated times the students take individual tests, and each student, on the basis of improvement from previous tests, contributes points (reward) to the study-team total. Team totals are then tabulated and compared competitively with each other. The motivation is for students to assist team-mates to improve their personal test scores so that the total study-team is rewarded. In TGT the procedure is identical in all respects save one. The testing is carried out in a "game" composed of three students, each drawn from a different original study-team. The students ask each other questions in turn and allocate points for correct answers. The earned points for each student are contributed to the total for the study-team, and team totals are compared competitively.

Third, there is interdependence in both task and reward, in which students must rely on each other both to accomplish the work and to be recognized for it. Two strategies are available, both variations of existing schemes. A variation of Jigsaw Learning (Jigsaw II) introduces to the basic tutoring process an individual testing phase at the end (as in STAD), with the points awarded to team members tabulated for the team and team totals compared competitively. A variation of STAD (Team Assisted Individualization) replaces the common learning task for the team with individualized programmes for each team member. Students assist each other to accomplish the personal objectives of each programme. Individual testing occurs as for STAD with team points accumulating from individual performance scores.

Cross-age tutoring differs from the tutoring schemes described above in that there is an age difference between tutor and tutee, and the helpfulness almost invariably occurs in dyadic interaction. Tutors can be chosen from a wide range of ages and backgrounds. The essential prerequisite is that the tutor actually has the skill to be taught. The qualities of patience and being able to perceive the tutee's abilities realistically are also important. There is some evidence that a minimum age difference of two to three years between tutor and tutee is beneficial, and that too large an age difference (e.g., an adult assisting a primary-school child) may leave the tutor "out of touch" or perhaps too didactic with the tutee. Some training of the tutors is desirable, though the evidence about the type and length of training is equivocal (Devin-Sheehan et al. 1976). As a minimum, though, tutors should have:

(a) a specific task to accomplish

(b) clear instructions about the task and how to accomplish it
(c) a visible model of effective tutoring behaviours
(d) an opportunity to practice tutoring behaviours with feedback
(e) the responsibility to choose, and perhaps transform, the tutoring materials in response to the actual situation. (Bloom 1976)

There is some disagreement about the appropriate degree of structure and invariant specificity of the tutoring procedure [point (e) above] (Ellson 1976). There is no disagreement, though, that the impact of the cooperating is nearly as great on the achievement of the tutor as it is on that of the tutee (Bloom 1976, Cohen et al. 1982). The effort of organizing and comprehending the subject matter so that it can be communicated leads to demonstrably greater facility with the skill/information by the tutor. Thus, although the tutor's stated goals frequently differ from the tutee's (e.g., to receive payment, to satisfy a school service requirement, to experience prevocational training, or to exercise unspecified feelings of altruism), the learning outcomes are frequently the same.

3.2 Cooperating as Mutuality

The essential characteristic of cooperating considered as "mutuality" is that the aims and overall objectives as well as the procedures to accomplish these aims are shared by all participants. From the beginning of the learning task, students take the responsibility for sifting and sorting the important information from the unimportant information. This independence of judgment is frequently associated with an active problem-solving orientation to learning and with the cognitive skills of interpretation and synthesis of facts from diverse sources. Interaction is flexible and varied, and features mutual exchange by participants. Evaluation may be based on the performances of individuals but is more likely to be an assessment of a collective effort (report or project) to which everyone has contributed. Finally, the whole class may function as a "group of groups" with between-group relationships being coordinated and labour-sharing rather than competitive.

A teaching strategy that features mutual cooperativeness gives a close and unique learning atmosphere. A strategy that can be called Learning Together (LT) has been developed and promoted by the Johnsons and their students (Johnson and Johnson 1975). Learning Together utilizes a "cooperative goal structure" that requires mutual acceptance of a common goal by group members and that minimizes individualistic striving. There are two features of LT that distinguish this cooperative approach from others: (a) students are sensitized toward and receive training in human relations skills necessary for group functioning, and (b) only one completed product or outcome is submitted from each working group, and the participation of each group member in that product is expected. Learning Together has been successfully used to integrate mainstreamed and handicapped students into the work of heterogeneous classes, and to promote interracial friendship and social attractiveness.

A second strategy using mutual cooperativeness which incorporates the features of LT, but which extends the level of group interaction even further, is the Group-investigation method (GI) developed by Sharan and his collaborators (1976, 1980). Given a multifaceted general learning area, students propose research on selected subtopics and form common interest groups. Cooperative planning proceeds so that, as the information is gathered and analysed, the groups relate to each other as a coordinated system rather than as independent units. Two additional features give the GI approach distinctiveness among generally cooperative strategies. First, each student group is expected to present a report, demonstration, or display to the rest of the class. Second, in addition to the teacher's evaluation of the group's work, the students themselves are involved in the assessment procedure either by direct comment on their peers, by contributing questions to a common test, or by self-evaluation of their own efforts.

One clear indication of the differences between helpful cooperating and mutual cooperating is evident in the complexity of the teacher's role. The originators of Jigsaw, TGT, and STAD have devised one-day inservice workshop programmes to instruct teachers in these techniques. With relatively simple information and neatly prepared record-keeping sheets it is possible to employ these methods without lengthy reorientation of either students or staff. On the other hand, the more involved strategies for cooperating (LT and GI) require a thorough and wide-ranging preparation by teachers. Not only do teachers need the organizational and trouble-shooting skills for establishing new social systems in the classroom, but also they need a reflective capacity to evaluate cooperativeness, competitiveness, and individualization in schooling and society generally. If the effect of the cooperative strategy is to be long-lasting, then teachers must have plenty of time to discuss and practise the new behaviours. The Johnsons, for example, use a 10-day inservice programme in two stages, allowing in-school practice and consolidation of skills as a crucial intermediate step. Sharan's team in Israel provided 60 hours of inservice instruction for teachers over the period of a year. The message seems plain. First, mutuality in group work is more complicated for students and more demanding on teachers. Second, the potential for long-lasting change is proportionately higher than with other methods of cooperating.

See also: Competition

Bibliography

Aronson E, Blaney N, Stephan C, Sikes J, Snapp M 1978 *The Jigsaw Classroom*. Sage, Beverley Hills, California

Bloom S 1976 *Peer and Cross-age Tutoring in the Schools: An Individualized Supplement to Group Instruction*. United States Department of Health, Education, and Welfare, Washington, DC, Report no. HE19.202: T88

Cohen P, Kulik J, Kulik C-L 1982 Educational outcomes of tutoring: A meta-analysis of findings. *Amer. Educ. Res. J.* 19: 237–48

Devin-Sheehan L, Feldman R, Allen V 1976 Research on children tutoring children: A critical review. *Rev. Educ. Res.* 46: 355–85

Ellson D 1976 Tutoring. In: Gage N L (ed.) 1976 *The Psychology of Teaching Methods*. 75th Yearbook of the National Society for the Study of Education, University of Chicago Press, Chicago, Illinois

Johnson D 1980 Group processes: Influences of student–student interaction on school outcomes. In: McMillan D (ed.) 1980 *The Social Psychology of School Learning*. Academic Press, New York

Johnson D, Ahlgren A 1976 Relationship between student attitudes about cooperation and competition and attitudes toward schooling. *J. Educ. Psychol.* 68: 92–102

Johnson D, Johnson R 1975 *Learning Together and Alone: Cooperation, Competition, and Individualization*. Prentice-Hall, Englewood Cliffs, New Jersey

Johnson D, Maruyama G, Johnson R, Nelson D, Skon L 1981 The effects of cooperative, competitive, and individualistic goal structures on achievement: A meta-analysis. *Psychol. Bull.* 89: 47–62

Mead M (ed.) 1937 (enlarged edn. 1961) *Cooperation and Competition Among Primitive Peoples*. Beacon Press, Boston, Massachusetts

Montagu A 1967 *On Being Human*, 2nd edn. Hawthorn, New York

Owens L 1985 The learning preferences of students and teachers: An Australian–American comparison. *Teaching and Teach. Educ.* 1(3): 229–42

Owens L, Straton R G 1980 The development of a cooperative, competitive, and individualised learning preference scale for students. *Br. J. Educ. Psychol.* 50: 147–61

Sharan S 1980 Cooperative learning in small groups: Recent methods and effects on achievement, attitudes, and ethnic relations. *Rev. Educ. Res.* 50: 241–71

Sharan S, Sharan Y 1976 *Small Group Teaching*. Educational Technology, Englewood Cliffs, New Jersey

Sharan S, Hare P, Webb C, Hertz-Lazarowitz R (eds.) 1980 *Cooperation in Education*. Brigham Young University Press, Provo, Utah

Slavin R E 1980 Cooperative learning. *Rev. Educ. Res.* 50: 315–42

Slavin R E 1983 *Cooperative Learning*. Longman, New York

Reinforcement

J. A. Bates

Reinforcement is the process of increasing the frequency of occurrence of a low-frequency behavior, or maintaining the frequency of occurrence of a high-frequency behavior. Two general procedures may be applied to achieve either of these goals. The first and more common approach involves pairing participation in, or level of performance on, the target (desired) behavior with presentation of a (usually) pleasant or satisfying event. For example, an autistic child might be offered a small bit of his or her favorite food immediately upon making a desired verbal response (for example, saying, "mother," when shown her picture). In this case, receiving the food is said to be contingent upon verbalizing the target response. If presentation of the food has the desired effect—that is, if it leads to an increase in the frequency of occurrence of the desired behavior—then that act is called positive reinforcement. The consequential event responsible for increasing target frequency—the bit of food itself—is called a positive reinforcer.

The second general method of reinforcement involves pairing participation in, or level of performance on, target behaviors with removal of (usually) unpleasant or aversive events, or removal of the threat of such events. For example, an anxious youth might be fearful of receiving low marks on an examination, perhaps because of anticipated parental disapproval. If studying for the examination is maintained at an appropriate level in order to avoid this expected aversive consequence, the cessation of the threat is called negative reinforcement, and the threat itself is a negative reinforcer.

Two important points must be understood regarding these general procedures. First, reinforcement is defined solely in the context of its effects on the target behavior. Any consequence that leads to an increase in low-frequency behavior or maintenance of high-frequency behavior carries the label of reinforcement, no matter how irrelevant or insubstantial that consequence may appear to a neutral observer. Second, the terms "positive" and "negative" do not imply relative worth or desirability. They are not synonymous with "good" and "bad." Rather, these terms are used to make explicit the direction of the contingency between a target behavior and its consequence. Positive reinforcement simply means that something is given to the individual when the target behavior occurs. In contrast, negative reinforcement means only that something is taken away from the individual upon occurrence of the target. In both cases, the goal is to maintain or to increase the frequency of a desired behavior.

The general principles of reinforcement have long been recognized as useful, if informal, tools to modify the behavior of humans and lower organisms alike. However, it has only been since the 1950s that their formal applications in the classroom have been systematically investigated. Prior to that time, traditional instruction was dominated by the rote drill-and-practice model of associationism, with its emphasis on strengthening the memorial bonds between environmental events (stimuli) and physical behaviors (responses). From about 1950 onwards, a growing number of Western educators, led by the Harvard psychologist B. F. Skinner, have exhorted their colleagues to pay greater attention to the consequences of classroom behaviors,

primarily by controlling the sources and availability of reinforcement. What has resulted is a true technology of learning, comprising what have been demonstrated to be some of the most reliable and powerful strategies available to the classroom teacher for maintaining discipline and increasing academic achievement.

1. Types of Positive Reinforcers

Although reinforcement is operationally defined as being entirely dependent on behavioral outcomes, and is thus a totally person- and situation-specific phenomenon, it is possible to distinguish among broad categories of generally reinforcing events. Three such categories and some attendant subcategories that have varying applicability in classroom contexts will be discussed next: primary, secondary, and activity reinforcers.

1.1 Primary Reinforcers

All living organisms have certain fundamental needs that must be met to insure individual and species survival, among them being food, water, shelter, and the ability to reproduce. For the human organism, the need for psychological as well as physical well-being may be included, as well as the need for sensory stimulation, and the need for social approval. Objects or events that naturally satisfy any of these needs are called primary (or, sometimes, unconditioned) reinforcers. The adjective "primary" indicates that the relationship between such objects or events and need satisfaction is unlearned. That is, a hungry person does not need to learn that food will alleviate hunger, and will usually quite naturally engage in behaviors that lead to food acquisition. Similarly, an infant will actively seek out sources of sensory stimulation without being taught to do so, as will an older child attempt to behave in such a way as to earn parental or peer approval.

Several primary reinforcers are available to the classroom teacher, although their effectiveness will vary dependent upon the individuals and target behaviors involved. Edible reinforcers, such as small pieces of candy, breakfast cereal, or other sweets, have been demonstrated to be extremely effective reinforcing consequences for preschool-aged children and for children and adults with severe learning handicaps (such as autism, Down Syndrome, etc.). For older children and adults of more nearly normal ability, the presentation of edibles may not be so powerful, especially when the teacher is not the sole source of these reinforcers, or when they are contingent on unpleasant, albeit educationally relevant, behaviors.

Tangibles are a second type of primary reinforcer, and may include toys, games, puzzles, books, or other sources of sensory stimulation. Tangibles frequently are effective reinforcers for all manner of educational activities, for students of all ages. The major pragmatic disadvantage of a dependence on tangibles as reinforcing consequences is the variability of individual preference. That is, although sensory stimulation appears to be a fundamental human need, and although appropriate generic primary reinforcers may thus be identified, nevertheless, the specific objects and events that an individual may regard as stimulating are largely a function of that individual's experiential, social, and cultural heritage. Therefore, the classroom teacher must have access to a wide variety of tangibles in order to meet individual needs. As a result, reliance on tangible reinforcers may become prohibitively expensive.

Consequences of behavior need not be edible or otherwise tangible to be primary reinforcers. The need for social approval, to be accepted by significant members of one's social sphere, and thus to maintain a psychologically healthy level of self-esteem, also seems to be a part of our genetic endowment as human beings. Intangible events that may satisfy this need are among the least expensive and most powerful of reinforcers within the classroom and without. Some examples of social reinforcers are verbal praise for a job well done, an approving smile or nod of the head in recognition of a correct response, or any other culturally appropriate, intangible indication of acceptance as a person.

The most important factor determining the effectiveness of social approval relative to alternative reinforcers is the importance of the source of this approval to its recipient. Who is and who is not a valued source seems to be both culturally and longitudinally variable. For example, most preschool and primary-school children in the United States (i.e., aged 3 to 10 years) will actively work to receive approval from their teachers, perhaps because of an association between parents and other adults in positions of authority. However, beyond about age 11 or 12 the same children often engage in behaviors that, if not explicitly disapproved of by their teachers, are at least not followed by teacher approval. What has probably happened in such cases is not a reduction in the need for acceptance, but rather a shift in its preferred source from teachers (and other adult authority figures) to the peer group. In fact, some adolescents in this society will often engage in behaviors intentionally that result in teacher reprimands, apparently solely to earn the concurrent consequence of peer approval and admiration. Upon reaching adulthood, however, the same individuals may once again value teachers and other authority figures as sources of approval. It seems likely that other societies possessing a similar structure will manifest similar patterns of student behavior, and that those societies expressing greater or lesser regard for authority will engender other behaviors.

Primary reinforcers are satisfactory choices as consequences for classroom behavior provided that the teacher has adequate control over their availability. As has been noted, however, this may often not be the case, especially in the use of social approval with older children and adolescents. In any event, it must be remembered that no reinforcer, no matter how powerful for a given student in a given context, will be an effective consequence for everyone in all contexts.

1.2 Secondary Reinforcers

If primary reinforcers such as food and social approval were the only stimuli to which humans would respond, it would be relatively easy to account for all types of human behavior. However, people often work hard to obtain not primary reinforcers themselves, but rather otherwise neutral objects and events that have somehow come to acquire desirable, reinforcing qualities. Such objects and events are called secondary (or, sometimes, conditioned) reinforcers, indicating that the relationship between them and need satisfaction is an artificial, learned arrangement.

Secondary reinforcers acquire their reinforcing quality by having been repeatedly paired with other stimuli that directly satisfy basic needs, due either to the vagaries of personal experience or to the structure of society. As an illustration of the former process, consider an infant whose primary caretaker nearly always wears the same blue apron when giving the child her daily meals. The infant, when grown to adulthood, may demonstrate a clear preference for articles of clothing or works of art colored blue, and may work harder to obtain such objects than to obtain similar objects of any other color. Blueness has thus acquired reinforcing properties due to association with the primary reinforcer, food. An even more straightforward example may be used to illustrate society's effect on secondary reinforcers. Humans cannot consume paper or metal, nor do they usually construct shelter or clothing from small pieces of these materials. Nevertheless, bits of paper and metal have become (arguably) the most powerful reinforcers imaginable in most modern social systems: money. People will engage in every sort of endeavor to earn those objectively impotent scraps of matter because society has arranged things such that, without them, very little primary reinforcement is possible.

The classroom teacher has no control over which neutral objects and events will have become secondary reinforcers for her students due to the more-or-less random effects of personal experience. However, knowledge of their existence is extremely valuable, for they may be used as reasonable alternatives to direct primary reinforcement. In order to be so used, they must first be identified by keeping a careful and objective record of the consequences that maintain day-to-day classroom behavior for each student. There will doubtless be some repetition of usable reinforcers across students, due to common backgrounds and environments. Nevertheless, considerable time expenditure for observation and record keeping is to be expected if the teacher wishes to make extensive use of these "natural" secondary reinforcers.

A more efficient classroom procedure for secondary reinforcement is possible, and is based on the observation of society's structuring of these stimuli. This is the use of a system of exchangeable reinforcers—that is, neutral objects that may be earned, accumulated, and exchanged for whatever other secondary or primary reinforcers the student may choose. One such system has already been mentioned: legal currency with which one may purchase available goods and services. However, the use of money to pay for academic efforts or appropriate classroom behavior is likely to be economically (and, perhaps, ethically) unfeasible for most school systems.

An alternative system of exchangeable reinforcers has been developed and refined since the early 1960s that makes full use of the same principles and that has been demonstrated repeatedly to be very successful. This system is called the token economy. To use it, the teacher presents students with a few small, neutral objects (such as wooden or plastic chips or beads), called tokens, contingent upon successful completion of some desired behavior. The number of tokens "paid" depends on the skill level of the student and the level of difficulty of the target behavior. For example, sitting quietly in one's seat for five minutes might earn a preschool child five tokens, whereas 30 minutes might be required for an adolescent to receive the same reward. One token might be earned for each simple addition problem correctly solved by a child just learning arithmetic, but 10 problems might be required when the basic principles of arithmetic have been mastered.

At regular intervals, perhaps once or twice a week, students who have accumulated tokens are permitted to exchange them at a classroom "store" for any of a variety of preferred objects or events. The range and nature of goods made available for purchase is limited only by the teacher's creativity, and need not require a large monetary investment. Many manufacturers market inexpensive novelties, such as small toys, pencils, erasers, and colorful trinkets, expressly for use in token economies with young children. Older students respond well to puzzles, games, books, magazines, and tickets to athletic events. Some thrifty teachers require that each student who wishes to make a purchase must also remit a contribution to the classroom "store" in the form of some second-hand but usable object that might be desired by someone else. Thus, expense is further minimized while at the same time maintaining the "store's" inventory. Other effective choices may be readily available that cost little or nothing, including free selection of classroom seating, extra play or study time, and access to school athletic equipment. Even access to school textbooks and to advanced assignments may be purchased in order to have the opportunity to earn tokens at a faster rate. Whatever particular goods are made available, it is important to maximize their variety in order to be certain that each student's personal needs may be met.

The effectiveness of token economies as means of modifying both academic and social behavior is well-documented (Ayllon and Azrin 1968, O'Leary and Drabman 1971, Sulzer-Azaroff and Mayer 1977). If these systems are open to any major criticism, it is that

they may be, in some cases, too effective. That is, students who experience an efficiently managed token economy often become reluctant to engage in other desirable academic endeavors that do not earn tokens, or to maintain behaviors that are rewarded within the classroom when they are in other, nonrewarding environments. If access to tokens suddenly stops because of a halt to the program, behaviors that have been maintained at desirable levels may become inappropriately infrequent and difficult to remotivate. What will have occurred is a well-known behavioral phenomenon called extinction: behavior previously reinforced will decrease in frequency when the opportunity for reinforcement is withdrawn. Although this is not a problem exclusive to token economies, the very effectiveness of such systems may make it more pronounced. Therefore, teachers who choose to apply the token economy technique in their classrooms would do well to observe two cautions: first, gradually increase the frequency or quality of behaviors necessary to earn tokens, in order to make them gradually less available; and, second, increase the availability of social approval or other more "natural" reinforcers at the same time as the tokens are being withdrawn.

Another form of secondary reinforcer is also available to the teacher that, while not as powerful as the token economy, may at least avoid some of its drawbacks. This is called the symbolic reinforcer. One type of intangible symbolic reinforcer has already been discussed. Consider the particular words that may be used in the reader's native language to indicate recognition of a job well done. None of these arbitrary sequences of phonemes, nor any other such arrangement, is likely to possess intrinsically reinforcing properties, yet each may serve, in the appropriate context, as a powerful social reinforcer. Although social approval may be considered to be a primary reinforcer, the words that come to represent that approval in any given culture are clearly secondary, symbolic reinforcers.

Grades or marks recorded on examination papers, classroom assignments, and term reports are the most common symbolic reinforcers systematically used in most schools. High marks are intended to represent the teacher's recognition of superior achievement, to thereby enhance the student's self-esteem, and therefore to act as reinforcing consequences for continued academic excellence. In contrast, it is usually hoped that low marks are interpreted by the student as aversive symbolic consequences to be avoided at all reasonable cost, and thus to act as effective negative reinforcers. Unfortunately, most research on grades and marks indicates that they are usually only very weak reinforcing consequences for academic behavior, and that their effectiveness is often limited to maintaining the performance of those students who are already operating at satisfactory or superior levels. Students who have a history of unsatisfactory academic accomplishment often show no apparent concern over whatever grades or marks they receive. For these students, grades and marks are not reinforcers at all, either positive or negative.

Other objects and events intended to be symbolic of academic accomplishment such as certificates of achievement, trophies, and the like, may be of similar limited usefulness when the goal is to increase the occurrence of low-frequency academic behaviors. However, teachers should not reject these approaches before evaluating them in their own classrooms. It has been noted repeatedly that objects and events are categorized as reinforcers dependent on their observed effects on behavior, and that the power of reinforcers will vary between individuals and contexts. If a group of students is observed to expend reasonable academic effort to earn symbolic awards, then continued use of these awards carries with it at least two important benefits. Such reinforcers cost virtually nothing, and they are so well-ingrained into the routine of most schools as to be considered a natural part of the school environment. It is a guiding maxim in the application of behavioral principles to real-world problems that one use the least powerful and artificial consequences necessary to get the job done.

Whereas symbolic reinforcers may not be well-suited to the enhancing of academic behaviors, they are often effective consequences for prosocial classroom conduct. One example of this technique is the consistent pairing, early in a term, of praise and public recognition for especially kind and considerate student behavior with presentation of a small figurine, trophy, or even a piece of stone bearing the hand-painted inscription, "Good Citizen." After a short time, presentation of the symbol alone may become sufficient consequence to maintain high levels of prosocial behavior. This apparently simplistic technique has been used with great success by many elementary-school teachers in the United States. It has been reported to be effective even when used in adolescent classrooms, provided that the teacher allows the students to present the award themselves.

The fact that people respond to secondary as well as primary reinforcement complicates the task of accounting for a particular behavior engaged in by a particular person. At the same time, however, an understanding of the sources and scope of this phenomenon can expand the teacher's arsenal of potential tools to modify classroom activity.

1.3 Activity Reinforcers

In 1959, David Premack, a behavioral psychologist then at the University of Missouri, published a research report demonstrating that rats, monkeys, and humans will expend considerable effort in the performance of one task in order to earn the opportunity to perform a different task. More specifically, Premack found that organisms will often freely choose to engage in some behaviors rather than others. For example, a laboratory rat may prefer chewing a piece of wood over running through a maze. Once the relative preference of activities is recognized, one activity may be used as a conse-quence to modify the frequency of occurrence of the other. That is, the events may be organized for the rat such that its access to wood-chewing is contingent upon its first running the maze. When events are so arranged, the less-preferred behavior will be positively reinforced by the more-preferred behavior. This functional relationship between behaviors has come to be called the Premack principle.

That people respond to the Premack principle has been informally recognized probably for as long as people have existed. Most parents know, for example, that their children will be more likely to do their daily chores if they are not permitted to play with their friends until the chores are completed. Premack's contribution, therefore, was not the discovery of a mysterious new behavioral phenomenon, but rather the first systematic, across-species analysis of a well-known but informal observation.

In order to appropriately apply the Premack principle of activity reinforcers in the classroom, teachers must first observe and record very carefully both the behaviors that students will freely choose to perform more often than other behaviors, and the relative frequencies of those competing behaviors. Once the more- and less-preferred activities are identified, those that are academically desirable but infrequent may be reinforced by constructing a contingency link between them and some more frequently selected activity. For example, a teacher might note that his or her mathematics students spend nearly all of their free class time playing available mathematical board-games rather than completing their daily assignments. Some typical teacher responses might include insisting that the game-playing stop, threatening the students with aversive consequences if the assignments are not completed, or removing the games from the classroom. None of these responses may increase the frequency of assignment completion, and all may increase ill feelings between students and teacher. Consider the alternative response of announcing that all students who complete their assignments during the first half of the free period may use the remaining time to play the game of their choice. If game playing is in fact a behavior more preferred than assignment completion, then the Premack principle tells us that controlled access to the former activity will act as a positive reinforcer for the latter.

All sorts of activities may serve as reinforcers for classroom behaviors. Conversation time, athletic contests, artistic endeavors, and even simply being permitted to do nothing at all, have been used with success. Such activities need not intrude into classroom time if their availability is yoked to a token economy. That is, target behavior may earn tokens that can be exchanged for desired activities when formal instruction is completed. Nor need activity reinforcers be non-academic to be effective. Students frequently prefer one content area over another (e.g., reading rather than arithmetic), or have a favorite method of learning (e.g., seeing a motion picture rather than hearing a lecture).

Knowledge of such preferences will permit the teacher to sequence instruction such that student effort is maintained at an optimum level, while fostering the notion that learning, itself, may be an enjoyable activity worthy of pursuit.

As with all other approaches to reinforcement, accurate knowledge of students' preferences is the key to success. Teachers must not select activities as potential reinforcing consequences based on their own preference. Although it is possible that a teacher's likes and dislikes may coincide with those of the students, it is also possible that even more effective activities may be available. Alternatively, the students may have no greater preference for the teacher-selected activities than for the targets, in which case no change in behavior would be forthcoming. Worse still, the students may actually enjoy the teacher-selected consequence even less than the target. The logical opposite of the Premack principle suggests that a more-preferred activity will decrease in frequency if its consequence is a less-preferred activity, which is hardly a desirable outcome in this context. As ever, the safest course for the teacher is to determine what consequences are maintaining or increasing student behaviors in the present, without artificial inducements or threats, and to make use of those natural reinforcers as consequences for low-frequency targets.

2. Schedules of Reinforcement

Selection of appropriate reinforcers is a necessary but not a sufficient precondition for efficient modification of behavior. One must also consider the nature of the contingency link between target and consequence—that is, the specific amount and degree of availability of the reinforcer. Behavioral researchers have identified numerous methods of presenting reinforcers, called schedules of reinforcement. Each schedule specifies a particular response–reinforcer relationship, and is characterized by a particular pattern of reinforced behavior. The four broadest categories of schedules are discussed next, and examples are provided of their applications in the classroom. (For a more detailed treatment of reinforcement schedules, especially as they pertain to problems in education, the reader is recommended to see Sulzer-Azaroff and Mayer 1977.)

2.1 The Fixed-ratio Schedule

The simplest method of presenting reinforcers is to make them available only after the organism has emitted some fixed number of desired responses. For example, a student in a token economy classroom might earn one token for each homework assignment completed and submitted when required. This illustrates the most basic form of fixed-ratio schedule, continuous reinforcement, so called because of the one-to-one relationship between targets and consequences. The continuous reinforcement schedule is most appropriate when a target

behavior is nonexistent or is occurring at a very low frequency. Because any organism will usually tire of all but the most powerful reinforcers if they become too easily accessible, one should not maintain a continuous reinforcement schedule beyond a point at which it is clear that the target behavior is occurring at a stable rate. Then, the schedule of reinforcement should be gradually lengthened by requiring more and more correct responses before the consequence is forthcoming. Care must be taken not to lengthen the schedule too rapidly, or the target behavior may cease altogether. Rather, each increment of the schedule should itself be maintained long enough to assure that the target has again stabilized.

Fixed-ratio schedules generally result in steady, although moderate levels of behavior. They have the advantage of being based on a relatively easily monitored event: the occurrence of a fixed number of targets. However, they also have an inherent weakness. Behaviors maintained by means of fixed-ratio schedules are more susceptible to extinction than are behaviors maintained by alternative methods. This means that such behaviors are likely to demonstrate a rapid drop in frequency of occurrence when the reinforcers are no longer available. This may occur whenever students leave their classrooms, and it is clearly an undesirable outcome when the behaviors are ones that should transfer to other environments. Therefore, continuous reinforcement and other fixed-ratio schedules should be maintained only until target behaviors are occurring at stable and appropriate levels.

2.2 The Fixed-interval Schedule

Just as a student who is contingent upon a fixed number of desired behaviors may be reinforced, so may he or she also be reinforced contingent upon the occurrence of a desired behavior after the passing of a fixed period of time. For example, a teacher may notice that one of his or her students spends considerably more time staring out a window than doing assigned in-class reading. After ascertaining that the student tends to respond favorably to social approval, the teacher might choose to observe him after every five-minute interval of the in-class reading period. If, immediately at the end of each interval, the student is observed to be attending to his or her textbook rather than looking out the window, the teacher could then give him or her a friendly pat on the head or a smile of approval. What is important in this case, as is characteristic of all fixed-interval schedules, is the occurrence of the target behavior after the passing of a specified amount of time, rather than the occurrence of a specified number of targets.

Fixed-interval schedules are usually not appropriate for the acquisition of new behaviors, but can engender and maintain low–moderate levels of previously infrequent activities. They are especially useful when the teacher is not able to monitor every instance of target behavior, as would be necessary for fixed-ratio chedules, or when the target is not easily quantifiable (e.g., attending to one's textbook). Just as with fixed-ratio schedules, fixed-intervals may be gradually lengthened to meet the specific needs of a situation.

Two disadvantages inhere to fixed-interval schedules. The first is that which was noted for fixed-ratios—susceptibility to rapid extinction if the reinforcing consequences are suddenly withheld. The second is the peculiar pattern that often characterizes fixed-interval behavior. An organism that becomes accustomed to reinforcement contingent only on the occurrence of a specific behavior at the end of specific time intervals may come to engage in that behavior only at or about the end of those intervals. One all-too-typical classroom example of this phenomenon may be observed when examinations are scheduled to follow regular units of time, such as once a week or once a month. If good/poor marks are effective positive/negative reinforcers, many students may quickly acquire the pattern of studying not at all until a few days before the examination, increasing their study time to a high point immediately before the examination, and studying not at all for a few days after the examination. Although this "scallop" effect may not be a problem in some situations, it is probably not appropriate for study behaviors, and its occurrence is indicative of a need to change reinforcement schedules.

2.3 The Variable-ratio Schedule

Rather than reinforcing a fixed number of responses, one may instead reinforce an average number of responses, thereby varying the ratio of responses to reinforcers. For example, some tangible reinforcer might be contingent upon the students' correctly answering oral questions from the teacher. On some occasions, only one or two answers might be sufficient to earn the reward. On others, eight or ten might be required. On the average, however, reinforcement would be forthcoming after every five responses, although the students would never be certain which particular response might achieve the goal.

Variable-ratio schedules provide several advantages over their fixed-ratio counterparts. One is that they generally yield much higher rates of responding. Individuals performing some act on a variable-ratio schedule demonstrate far fewer and briefer pauses between behaviors. This characteristic makes such schedules especially useful for many desirable classroom behaviors, such as the completion of homework assignments, and prosocial interactions with peers and teachers. Variable-ratio schedules are also far more resistant to extinction than are fixed ratios, and behaviors acquired under such schedules may be maintained long after external reinforcement has ceased.

The power of variable-ratio schedules to maintain high-frequency, extinction-resistant behavior is illustrated by their widespread use in gambling establishments to insure a steady, rapid shift of money from their patrons to the house. A similar application may be made in the classroom, where assignments may be randomly spot-checked for accuracy as a prerequisite for reinforcement. Teachers using this procedure often find that their students actually perform better, in terms of frequency and correctness of responses, than do those students whose every response is monitored.

2.4 The Variable-interval Schedule

Not only may the number of targets required for reinforcement be varied, but also the time intervals between reinforcements. That is, correct responses that occur after the passing of an average amount of time may be reinforced, while the exact amount of time between any two reinforcements may differ considerably. A variable-interval schedule of social approval would be quite appropriate for the previously mentioned child who spends too much time looking out the window during in-class reading. Rather than observing the child after every five-minute interval of the reading period, the teacher might instead make some observations only one or two minutes apart and others eight or ten minutes apart, while maintaining an average nonobservation interval of five minutes. One likely outcome of such a procedure would be a higher rate of the desired reading behavior than would be expected under the fixed-interval schedule, owing to the fact that the child could never be certain which instant might be a potential occasion for reinforcement.

The above example illustrates one advantage of variable-interval schedules—high rates of target behaviors (although not usually so high as might be achieved with variable-ratio schedules). Moreover, the pattern of responses generated by a variable-interval schedule is likely to be fairly steady, without the peaks and valleys associated with fixed intervals. Finally, variable-interval behaviors are also highly resistant to extinction. These characteristics of the variable-interval schedule make it extremely useful when linked with academic behaviors of long-term importance, such as studying. Teachers who give examinations or collect homework assignments at random rather than regular intervals report that their students tend to study at a more uniform rate, resulting in improved achievement and superior retention of learned material.

Two notes of caution should be observed by teachers considering the use of either the variable-ratio or the variable-interval schedule. First, they are usually not appropriate for the acquisition of new behaviors. In such cases, a continuous reinforcement schedule would probably be more effective, and could be modified into a longer variable-ratio or variable-interval schedule once the target behavior has stabilized. Second, a variable schedule of reinforcement can lead to a deterioration in the quality of the target behavior at the same time as it increases target frequency, especially if the reinforcer is a powerful one. This outcome can be avoided if quality of response, in terms of some absolute standard, is consistently combined with response frequency as a necessary precondition for reinforcement.

3. Additional Considerations

Throughout the preceding discussion of classroom reinforcement procedures, it has been implicitly assumed that target behaviors are straightforward and well-defined by the teacher. This assumption is probably at least somewhat inaccurate in many, if not most, situations. What may, on the surface, appear to be the specific desired behavior—say, increasing the frequency of satisfactory assignment completion—will often on closer examination be revealed as a broad goal comprising several critical components—for example, acquisition of basic skills, attending to instructions, ignoring distractions, and so on. If the teacher fails to recognize these components and constructs contingencies only for the broader goal, both the teacher and the students are likely to meet with frustration and disappointment.

The only way to avoid this and other pitfalls of reinforcement procedures is by careful, rigorous objectification of target behaviors. That is, all targets must be broken down into their critical subcomponents, each of which must be defined in observable, measurable terms, before reinforcement contingencies are instituted. One example of this careful objectification may be observed in the personalized system of instruction (PSI) procedures first outlined by Fred Keller of the University of Kansas (1968, Keller and Sherman 1974) (see *Keller Plan: A Personalized System of Instruction*). The PSI approach is to break down a content area into units of instruction that are further broken down into sets of objectives. Each objective describes specific behaviors (e.g., defining important terms, providing original examples of abstract concepts, etc.) that are to be acquired by the student at whatever rate is comfortable for him or her. At regular intervals, examinations are given on the objectives for each unit, and the student must have successfully mastered those objectives before he or she will be permitted to proceed to the next, usually more complex, unit (see *Mastery Learning Models*). Reinforcement in the form of grades/marks, tokens, or other desirable consequences is contingent upon a systematic progression through the content area, rather than solely on reaching a broad terminal goal. Application of the PSI approach to content objectification has been consistently demonstrated to yield superior achievement and longer retention of learned material.

As time consuming as such a method may be for objectifying cognitive target behaviors, it may prove even more difficult for the teacher to generate adequate definitions of physical targets, such as attending, proper seating behavior, or prosocial classroom conduct. The difficulty lies not so much in the complexity of such events as it does in the ambiguity of their appropriate expression. Consider, for example, proper seating behavior. Must both feet be on the floor, or may a leg be crossed? May one straddle the seat backwards, or must one sit only forwards? How long must one remain in the seat to be reinforced? These questions may appear facetious, but they will not be if the student population is a group of anxious preschoolers on their first day of class. Once again, the proper strategy is for the teacher to define these targets in observable, measurable, and nonambiguous terms before instituting reinforcement. Otherwise, inappropriate behaviors may be inadvertently reinforced and thus come to interfere with efficient classroom management.

Another consideration is the maintenance of a consistent reinforcement schedule, whatever the specific parameters of that schedule might be. If a student is to earn a consequence on a fixed interval of five minutes, then the target behavior must be monitored at these intervals. Erratic monitoring of targets will almost inevitably lead either to the inadvertent reinforcement of unwanted behaviors or to the extinction of the target, or to both. Avoiding these outcomes requires an accurate system of recordkeeping. A variety of observational techniques and devices have been developed by behavioral researchers to serve this need, including event- and time-sampling procedures, wrist-band event counters, alarm timers, charts, and graphs. It is beyond the scope of this entry to review the details of the myriad of methods available to insure accurate records. The reader should see other sources for this information (for example, Bijou and Ruiz 1981, Sulzer-Azaroff and Mayer 1977). More critical than the particular technique selected are the teacher's commitments to reliable definition of targets, objective observation of student behaviors, accurate recording of target occurrences, and consistent administration of appropriate reinforcers.

One final consideration must be discussed, and that is what to do when the target behavior reaches the level of occurrence that has been predefined to be appropriate. In the behavioral literature, this is known as the issue of response maintenance and generalization. One of the foremost goals of educators is to transmit to students a body of skills and knowledge that may be put to use in environments outside the classroom. It is known, however, that behaviors tend to be maintained only when they are reinforced. If exclusive use has been made of artificial consequences for behaviors—such as edibles, tangibles, tokens, or grades—that are not likely to be similarly associated with those behaviors when students leave classrooms, then it is possible to be certain that many of those behaviors will not be maintained and will not generalize to new situations. In short, the larger, long-term goal will not have been met because of an overenthusiastic pursuit of short-term gains.

Unfortunately, the guidelines for avoiding this outcome are not so straightforward as those previously discussed. One sure if somewhat general suggestion is to never artificially reinforce behaviors that are already occurring at satisfactory levels. If a student reads easily and with enjoyment, do not give him or her tokens for reading. No tokens for reading will be forthcoming when that student leaves the classroom. If a student is completing homework assignments satisfactorily, do not induce the student with extra play time for continued effort. To do so would risk shifting the control of her behavior from internal sources to external and not omni-present consequences. A second suggestion has already been mentioned: make full use of whatever objects and events are maintaining student behaviors without teacher intervention. Such consequences, like social approval and the self-satisfaction that inheres in making the correct response, are more likely to be continually available outside the classroom. Finally, when artificial consequences have of necessity been used, begin shifting to more natural reinforcers as soon as the target reaches an appropriate level. This shifting of control must be gradual, and is accomplished by lengthening the schedule of artificial reinforcement while at the same time increasing the availability of the natural consequences.

4. Negative Reinforcement and Punishment as Alternatives to Positive Reinforcement

Most of the emphasis in this article has been placed on the use of positive reinforcement to alter classroom behaviors. It might be argued, however, that the bulk of human activity is more likely to be the product of negative reinforcement—that is, working to avoid unpleasant or aversive consequences. One might wonder if negative reinforcement might therefore be a more effective technique to achieve classroom goals. Certainly, there are situations where negative reinforcement may seem to be necessary to induce desired behavior. For example, a student may refuse to complete any assignments at all, thereby rendering impotent whatever schedule of positive reinforcement might be associated with that behavior. In order to encourage at least one reinforceable response, the teacher may threaten that student with removal from the class or a note sent home to parents if there is a continued lack of effort. Indeed, there are many similar cases where available reinforcers may be of insufficient power to produce target behaviors, but where threat of an aversive consequence may yield the desired effect.

There are, however, major drawbacks to the widespread use of negative reinforcement procedures in place of positive reinforcement. One of these is that behaviors other than those designated as targets may be discovered to be effective means of avoiding the aversive consequence. For example, the student threatened with a note to parents may simply destroy the note or forge the parents' signatures on it rather than completing that target assignments. The creativity of organisms faced with aversive consequences is nicely illustrated by a common laboratory demonstration. A rat may be placed in an enclosed chamber (called a Skinner box) that has a wire-mesh floor attached to an electrical source. Inside the Skinner box is a lever that the rat must press to turn off a painful electric current flowing through the floor. Most rats will quickly learn to press the lever, that behavior then becoming negatively reinforced. Occasionally, however, a rat will completely ignore the lever and simply roll over on its back, thereby insulating itself from the shock. Humans are certainly at least as clever as rats, and may similarly discover many alternative, unwanted methods to avoid unpleasant consequences. In short, negative reinforcement, by itself, does not guarantee acquisition or maintenance of target behaviors.

Another problem with negative reinforcement is that its extensive use in the classroom is likely to increase the anxiety level of the students. This may occur even when positive reinforcement is also provided for correct responses, especially if the negative reinforcers are extremely aversive (e.g., threats of public ridicule or physical pain). Psychologists have known since the beginning of this century that high levels of anxiety yield inferior levels of performance, whatever the organism. In addition, the morality of constructing a classroom environment with the foreknowledge that it will produce anxiety in its students may be seriously questioned.

All this is not to say that negative reinforcement should never be used by the classroom teacher. Rather, it is suggested that this procedure be used only in conjunction with positive reinforcement of targeted behaviors when they finally do occur, and that the negative reinforcement be eliminated entirely as soon as the targets have stabilized.

Punishment is also considered to be an alternative to positive reinforcement, especially in cases of classroom discipline. Punishment is defined as the process of reducing the frequency of a behavior. Just as there are procedures for positive and negative reinforcement, there are also procedures for positive and negative punishment. Positive punishment refers to the presentation of an aversive stimulus immediately following the occurrence of an unwanted response. Negative punishment involves the removal of a pleasant stimulus upon occurrence of an unwanted response. Although both punishment and extinction decrease response frequencies, the procedures are not identical. Extinction means that nothing whatsoever is done to the organism when it emits a response. In contrast, punishment means that some usually aversive consequence follows a response. Extinction is passive, but punishment is active.

It should be clear, then, that the goals of reinforcement and of punishment are completely reversed. Therefore, it would be a mistake to assume that these techniques are true alternatives. In fact, despite frequent demonstrations that consistent, immediate punishment is the most efficient means ever devised to eliminate unwanted behaviors, it has never been demonstrated that punishment alone will teach an organism the correct behavior.

The greatest value of punishment to the classroom teacher is as a means of quickly eliminating behaviors that may compete or interfere with a student's acquisition of more desired behaviors, or that may be physically harmful to the student or his peers. If, for example, a student always talks to a neighbor while the teacher is giving instructions for assignments, then that student will not be able to correctly complete those assignments, no matter what the associated reinforcer may be. Swift punishment for inappropriate talking, in the form of verbal disapproval, loss of tokens, or other suitable consequences, may be necessary to permit reinforceable behavior to occur. Similarly, if an autistic child engages in self-mutilation (a common event for such children), a painful electric shock may be a necessary and justifiable consequence to prevent serious injury.

Although punishment is an effective method of controlling behavior, it has drawbacks even more serious than those of negative reinforcement. A person who has experienced frequent punishment in a particular environment may attempt to escape from that environment. If no escape is possible, the person may become sullen and withdrawn to the point of being entirely uncommunicative. Alternatively, it has been experimentally demonstrated that people who experience frequent punishment with no apparent means of escape may become increasingly aggressive and hostile, striking out at friends and foes alike (Oliver et al. 1974).

In general, the best way for the teacher to minimize the undesirable outcomes associated with punishment is to use that procedure as little as possible. Frequently, an extinction technique may be equally as effective, in the long run, for keeping problem behaviors at a tolerable level. That is, one can simply ignore unwanted responses completely while at the same time providing frequent opportunities for reinforcement of correct behavior. If punishment must be employed, it must always be yoked with access to reinforcers for more appropriate responses.

5. Summary and Conclusions

The principles of reinforcement may be applied at all levels of education, and can help to solve educational problems ranging from the maintenance of classroom discipline to the acquisition of complex cognitive skills. To make full use of their potential, the teacher must remember to (a) define target behaviors in observable, measurable, nonambiguous terms; (b) select as reinforcers those objects and events that are observed to maintain student behaviors without teacher intrusions, and the access to which may be placed under teacher control; (c) choose schedules of reinforcement that are compatible with the nature of the targets, and that are likely to produce appropriate patterns of behavior;

(d) monitor target occurrences by means of a reliable data-collection and recordkeeping procedure, to insure that reinforcement is provided as scheduled; and, (e) gradually phase out artificial consequences when target behaviors stabilize at appropriate levels, and phase in reinforcers that are more likely to be available for similar behaviors in other environments.

Despite the utility of reinforcement techniques, their formal application in the classroom should be accompanied by some teacher caution. The issue of response maintenance and generalization has not been resolved satisfactorily by behavioral researchers, and is of critical importance to most educational goals. In addition, recent investigations into the relations between reinforcement and internal sources of motivation indicate that the former can be damaging to the latter, although how severely and for how long have not been established with certainty (Bates 1979). As with all other instructional techniques and classroom strategies, reinforcement has both its place and its drawbacks. Ultimately, it is up to the classroom teachers to determine where and how these procedures may best be applied to benefit their students.

See also: Reacting

Bibliography

Ayllon T, Azrin N H 1968 *The Token Economy: A Motivational System for Therapy and Rehabilitation.* Appleton-Century-Crofts, New York

Bates J A 1979 Extrinsic reward and intrinsic motivation: A review with implications for the classroom. *Rev. Educ. Res.* 49: 557–76

Bijou S W, Ruiz R 1981 *Behavior Modification: Contributions to Education.* Erlbaum, Hillsdale, New Jersey

Keller F S 1968 "Goodbye, teacher." *J. Appl. Behav. Anal.* 1: 79–89

Keller F S, Sherman J G 1974 *PSI: The Keller Plan Handbook.* Benjamin, Menlo Park, California

O'Leary K D, Drabman R S 1971 Token reinforcement programs in the classroom: A review. *Psychol. Bull.* 75: 379–98

Oliver S D, West R C, Sloane H N Jr. 1974 Some effects on human behavior of aversive events. *Behav. Ther.* 5: 481–93

Premack D 1959 Toward empirical behavior laws: I. Positive reinforcement. *Psychol. Rev.* 66: 219–33

Skinner B F 1954 The science of learning and the art of teaching. *Harvard Educ. Rev.* 24: 86–97

Sulzer-Azaroff B, Mayer G R 1977 *Applying Behavior-analysis Procedures with Children and Youth.* Holt, Rinehart and Winston, New York

Logical and Substantive

Types of Content

G. Leinhardt

The structure and content of a "typical" lesson have been gradually developing and changing over the last century. Prior to the twentieth century, lessons, regardless of subject or grade level, had a remarkable similarity—material was presented orally or in writing on a chalk board, it was copied, and then studied. Studying consisted of recitation and memorization. The teacher's role was to present prescribed sequences and monitor students. With the emergence of both a more expanded curriculum and an enlightened view of the learning and instructional processes, dramatic changes have taken place.

Since the late 1950s, researchers have been examining a variety of features of lessons. The heaviest concentration of research has been in the area of teacher effectiveness and process–product studies (see *Proactive Teaching*). In this research, the student's academic growth has been the dependent variable of interest, while a wide variety of independent variables (engaged time, content covered, motivation, teacher and student verbalization, and action patterns) have been mined for a possible strong influence. This research has begun to be somewhat more fruitful than earlier reviews had assumed in terms of prediction; however, it has not shed very much light on the nature of the phenomenon under study. In some sense, the research has skipped the important naturalistic stage of description and leaped to causal analysis. Thus the description of lesson content and structure must be deduced from information obtained for other purposes.

This article focuses on lesson content in reading, mathematics, and social studies at the elementary level. A lesson can be described in terms of its structural elements, including the classes of activities and group arrangements, or in terms of its content, or in terms of its plans and objectives. These three aspects will be woven through the discussion on the background planning of lessons, lesson presentation, time utilization, and teacher and student thought.

1. Lesson Preparation

1.1 Behind the Scenes

A lesson does not just happen, it is rather the product of long- and short-term planning, specific class history, and the routines used in that particular lesson type. Jackson (1968) has made an important distinction between preactive and interactive aspects of teaching. Preactive teaching includes all of the components of instruction that must go on other than the actual discourse between teacher and students (preactive is a slight misnomer as some of the actions come after teaching), and the interactive stage of teaching involves the actual lesson presentation. Preactive teaching includes planning the action, content, and purpose of a lesson, selecting and gathering materials, and an evaluation of the previous lessons in the sequence in order to plan for any review or recapitulation necessary in the next lesson. The plan can cover as much as an entire year or simply a single lesson.

1.2 Time Frame

The planning of a lesson is dependent on the particular time frame used. Yinger (1977) identified five basic time frames: yearly, by term, monthly, weekly, and daily. Mathematics teachers' plans seem to be framed by a combination of important temporal markers and major blocks of material to be taught. Thus, teachers are observed to plan by the year, taking into account external test barriers (standardized or district-based tests), and major holidays such as Thanksgiving, Christmas, and Easter (in the American calendar). They also plan by lesson presentation (daily), topic duration (variable), and unit tests (often landing on Thursdays or Fridays). Berliner (1982) and Shavelson and Stern (1981) assume a considerable amount of planning on the part of teachers. Other evidence suggests that teachers engage less in formal external planning and more in on-line planning (Leinhardt and Greeno in press). Regardless of which position is correct, teachers have several areas of influence and control beyond the sample lesson interactions.

1.3 Control and Planning

The most significant areas of control and hence planning for teachers are material selection, time allocation, group formation, and activity structures (Berliner 1982). While teachers employ some of these consciously and regularly, others, such as time allocation and material selection, are used rarely or not at all. Some teachers do not follow prescribed preselected texts, while others teach in a manner that is consistent with the text. Thus, while content covered is a vital aspect of instruction in terms of influence on what is learned, the issue of conscious control of content by the teacher is in somewhat greater debate (Leinhardt and Seewald 1981, Schwille et al. 1979).

1.4 Scheduling

Scheduling the lesson in terms of its duration and location in the day is under the control of those teachers who have a self-contained classroom and teach all subjects. Duration, the length of lessons per day and frequency per week, is significant because it alters opportunity to learn (see *Opportunity to Learn*; *Time*). Location in the daily schedule may be important because student attitudes and restlessness vary during the day. Schedule is not under the control of teachers when students rotate through different classes. In such cases, schedules are planned by administrators. The variation, intentional and unintentional, in the time allocated to a subject is remarkable (Cooley and Leinhardt 1980, Fisher et al. 1978, Harnischfeger and Wiley 1977).

1.5 Grouping

Teachers must also plan the formation of groups, usually for reading, but occasionally for other subjects as well. Grouping refers to the practice of splitting up an entire class into subgroups which work on and are taught different material at different rates (see *Grouping for Teaching*). The advantage of grouping is that it permits more intensive diagnosis and instruction. The disadvantages of grouping are that it is often done for arbitrary and capricious reasons, it can be inflexible, and if done too early may leave a child doomed to the bottom track for their academic career. Teachers make decisions about grouping based on previous teachers' opinions, prior academic history, and occasionally totally irrelevant criteria (Borko and Niles 1982, Rist 1973, Salzen 1981).

Preparation for the presentation of lessons involves a complex weaving of all of these factors. Teachers can be thought of as juggling multiple constraints and engaging in a form of opportunistic planning (Hayes-Roth and Hayes-Roth 1978). Teachers conduct the lessons through the execution of plans which include scenarios of both their actions and the students' actions and by the skillful use of routines or activity structures. These routines become established during the first few weeks of school and can be considered a part of the preactive phase of teaching; however, because they act as the skeletal frame for the lesson actions, they may more fruitfully be thought of as part of the interactive portion of a lesson (Emmer et al. 1980, Leinhardt et al. in press).

2. Lesson Presentation

An actual lesson will contain different routines and substance depending on the subject matter being taught. This simple fact has gone unrespected in many research studies of classroom processes. Not only is the content different but so also is the basic class organization. For example, most mathematics is taught around a core of review, new presentation, and practice. It is taught to the entire group of students. Most reading instruction involves a teacher and a small group of students, with the core made up of introduction, discussion, and students reading aloud. Social studies, on the other hand, is taught to the whole group through lecture and recitation. These differences lead to distinctive patterns of verbalization and socialization. Naturally, the rate of teacher and student verbalization is quite different. In reading and mathematics the proportions of time spent on management and individual discourse are quite similar, as is the percentage of time (60 percent) spent on on-task behavior. However, the ratio of cognitive to management verbal behavior is twice as high in reading as in mathematics; the small-group exchanges are twice as high and the whole-class exchanges are one-quarter as frequent in reading as in mathematics (Cooley and Leinhardt 1980). The cognitive exchanges in social studies lessons are quite high but very shallow: teacher requests facts, a student responds, the teacher assesses and continues (Korth and Cornbleth 1982, Stodolsky et al. 1981, Stodolsky 1983). A mathematics lesson, a reading lesson, and a social studies lesson will be considered briefly below.

2.1 A Mathematics Lesson

A typical mathematics lesson is organized around a topic, for example, fractions, which takes from one to eight weeks to complete. The topic is divided into subtopics, such as equivalent fractions, which take from one to three classes to complete. The 40 to 50 minute class starts with a review of homework which serves two functions. First, it monitors homework completion and second, it is a review of the content of the prior lesson. The next activity is either review or presentation of new material. This is the heart of the lesson, the time when new material is presented or generic misconceptions are corrected. The presentation lasts from 3 to 10 minutes and may either involve straight one-way or two-way presentation. A two-way presentation involves asking a question, getting a response, and evaluating or qualifying the response. Until students are about the age of 10 or 11 two-way presentation is the most common approach (Good et al. 1983, Leinhardt and Greeno in press).

After the presentation phase the teacher moves the

class toward a production or practice phase. The purpose of this phase is to permit the children to try out what has been taught and to inform the teacher of how successful the lesson has been. This phase is itself broken down into several different elements. The first tests the ability of the students to carry out the operations. This element is used as a diagnostic device, to assess individual and group comprehension of the lesson. It has a semipublic nature, often involving work at the chalkboard or on "scratch" paper. The second phase of practice is less public but has the teacher acting as a guide and publicly responding to students' less public practice. This phase is usually when problems from the text or worksheets are handed out. The first few problems are closely monitored and the remainder are done with more independence. This element permits the monitoring of on-task behavior as well as some in-depth tutoring. This pattern of presentation and practice is followed by the teachers who are most successful in teaching mathematics; however, it is by no means uniform—some elements may never occur or the order may be changed (Good and Grouws 1983, Leinhardt 1983).

2.2 A Reading Lesson

Reading instruction follows a different course. Each lesson lasts from 60 to 90 minutes. The class is divided into as few as two or as many as five reading groups. One group works with the teacher while the other groups do "seat work." The lesson with the teacher consists of a brief review/introduction followed by a presentation of vocabulary and theme to be encountered in the lesson. This serves to focus attention and also to head off errors before they occur. The presentation, which lasts under five minutes, is followed either by discussion of the topic or by practice of the vocabulary. Children are then instructed to read a section and look up. The teacher waits until one-third to one-half of the small group (5–8) are finished and then asks each child to read aloud in turn. This is followed by a question and answer segment on the meaning of the portion read. The cycle is then repeated one or two more times. The teacher then has the children finish on their own and answer questions or write a summary. During this last phase (about 10 minutes) the teacher may dismiss the first group and call another group to the area, or may monitor the silent reading. The seatwork carried out by the remainder of the class consists largely of students completing mimeographed sheets which drill grammar, phonics, and occasionally spelling, or sometimes require silent reading. One of the most difficult tasks for teachers in this context is to keep content covered, time spent in instruction, and style of interaction reasonably consistent across ability groups. Research suggests that they are often unsuccessful in this attempt. The tendency is to spend more time, have more in-depth discussion, and more fluid reading in the top group while less time is spent and the discussions are more trivial in the lower groups (Allington 1982, 1983).

Two aspects of these different lessons are important to consider: planning and the efficient use of time. Obviously the planning required for the reading lesson is more complex and its execution more easily disrupted than that required for mathematics. Both classes require clear understanding of the scripts or routines to be used on the part of the teacher and on the part of the child. Further, both situations require a smooth consistency of timing in the exchanges between teacher as lecturer, poser of questions, and guide for learning. The degree to which the structure of a lesson can be well-handled has an impact on the time available for learning.

2.3 A Social Studies Lesson

Social studies follows a rather different course of instructional patterning than that observed in mathematics or in reading. In social studies the teacher conveys information to the class for large portions of the time. This is done in a lecture format. Following the lecture, which is given to the entire class, two types of pattern are observed. In one, individual students read portions of the text aloud and then are questioned, usually on an individual basis, on various points of fact or theory associated with the passage. The students sit and listen as the teacher goes around the room, calling on one child after another. Interestingly, on-task behavior is observed to be very high in social studies classrooms. However, boredom is also observed to be very high. In another pattern, students are given worksheets and they write in the answers for the remainder of the class. In social studies, the three primary student actions are listening, reading aloud or responding, and writing. The social studies lesson involves much less movement, shifting, or different types of exchanges between teacher and students than does either the mathematics or the reading lesson (Stodolsky 1983). This is not as teacher educators or theoreticians would like it to be but as it seems to appear in actual situations most often.

3. Time Utilization

Recent work has emphasized the tremendous value in preserving every possible moment of available instructional time. Unfortunately this has been misinterpreted as "time-on-task." Clearly the percentage of time a child spends on-task influences the total amount of learning time the child can accumulate. However, most studies show that students are on-task from 60 to 90 percent of the time (e.g., Leinhardt et al. 1981). Further, allocated (assigned) time for reading has been steadily on the rise since the early 1960s, at least in the United States. An important but overlooked area that affects both the quality and effectiveness of a lesson is time lost. The sources of loss are: interruptions, transitions, and work assigned at an incorrect level (see *Time*).

3.1 Interruptions

Interruptions occur in a class with surprising frequency. An external interruption comes in several forms: supply delivery, student transfer, a stray student from the halls, announcements on the loud speaker, a visiting parent (or researcher). There appears to be an erosion in the norm that a lesson is sacred or inviolate. Most interruptions are brief, one minute or less, but their after effects influence all but the most effective teachers. In some classes there are at least two interruptions per lesson—assume four minutes lost per lesson—totaling two lessons per month in mathematics, roughly one subject topic missed per month. As the teacher falls behind in his or her larger plan, the reason for the loss is not at all apparent and either the students or some other uncontrolled external cause are blamed (McCutcheon 1981).

3.2 Transitions

The second area of potential time loss is transitions, the time taken to change from one activity to another within or between lessons. As the mathematics lesson was described, there are a number of interfaces between lesson segments that take some time to execute. Homework gets corrected, then handed in or put away, blank paper and pencils are passed out for lesson practice, a subgroup moves to the board, and books are removed. Each segment change can take from 30 seconds to three minutes, depending on the clarity of the signals and the previous rehearsals of the switch. The transitions in reading are fewer, but involve much more movement with groups of children moving from the reading area, taking all possessions, and another group moving to the area, remembering books, pencils, and so on. Transitions in social studies are few, hence the high time-on-task estimates.

Transitions occur between lessons as well. Frequently when a lesson comes after lunch or recess, or the children change classrooms, time is lost in reorganization. As much as five minutes can be lost at the start of a lesson. The cost in time of between lesson transition must be weighed against advantages of subject matter teachers and special groupings. However, Berliner (1982) recounts considerable time saving by having a language arts teacher record the expected assignment for each of the groups on the blackboard rather than waiting for everyone to "get settled." Other research has shown that experts use time effectively (Fisher and Berliner 1985, Leinhardt and Greeno in press).

A third area of time loss involves incorrect level of practice work. Incorrect level of work refers to the practice and homework portion of the lesson. In mathematics this time is 50 to 70 percent of the lesson, in reading it is 60 to 80 percent, and in social studies 50 to 70 percent. After being presented with the new material the student practices by doing problems or reading or writing. When this practice is too hard, the child either stops working or, more commonly, diligently fakes it, believing that answering each item or scanning each line, in essence getting through, is the most important task. Then when the child is "on-task" but is not rehearsing, learning, or absorbing any of the points of the

lesson, he or she is losing time in a very particular way. The problem arises from several sources: the inability of the teacher to select correct material; the inability to model how the task is to be done; and the inability of both teacher and student to keep the correct objective (learning the lesson) in mind. The consequence is a severe loss in the opportunity to learn.

3.3 Time-on-task

Having described the potential interruptions or loss of time devoted to learning of instruction, it is useful to return briefly to descriptions of time-on-task. The time-on-task literature is enormous and has been well-reviewed. What is relevant here is to consider the various activity structures and the percentage of time spent on task in each of those structures as observed in various settings. The work of Berliner et al. (1981) describes in detail 12 activity structures, and in addition, analyzes those activity structures for several important features, for example, the potential of the teacher to give feedback to the students, and the amount of engaged time observed in each of those activity structures.

The two predominant modes of instruction in reading and mathematics are the reading circle, or small-group instruction, and two-way presentations. In both cases it is observed that there is considerable opportunity for teachers to give feedback to students, and in both cases there is a very high percentage of on-task behavior. That is, the dominant mode of interactions or activity structures that occur in mathematics and reading provide for both on-task behavior and the opportunity for feedback. In social studies the recitation mode provides for less on-task behavior, although the seatwork mode tends to be accompanied by high on-task behavior. Essentially, in social studies a disproportionate period of time is spent with students giving simple close-ended, or short answer responses to teachers' questions, with very little generalization or expansion made possible to either the style of the questioning or the circumstances of the lesson structure (Korth and Cornbleth 1982).

4. Teacher and Student Thought During Lessons

The early work on teacher behaviors grew out of the impetus, already described, to predict student achievement. Recently a shift has occurred that focuses interest on those things that produce student behavior, as opposed to student academic growth. The reason for this is that a variety of studies (Leinhardt et al. 1981, Fisher et al. 1978) have shown that teacher behavior is related to student behaviors which in turn are related to achievement. In pursuing the question of what is going on or what guides behavior, many researchers have turned to the area of teacher and student thought. It is assumed that differences in behavior have traceable origins in differences in thought. Early studies of teacher thought focused on the preactive, planning phases because they were easier to capture. Later work focused more attention on the interactive portions of teaching

Anderson-Levitt and Hertweck 1982, Clark and Peterson 1986, Leinhardt 1983, Morine-Dershimer 1982). Systematic studies contrasting the thinking of teachers at different levels of different subjects, and different levels of competence have not yet been carried out, however.

4.1 Teacher Thought

Some researchers, notably Shavelson, have viewed the teacher as continuously making branching decisions between one or another alternatives (Shavelson and Stern 1981). A challenge to that perspective can be posed by the notion of a teacher following a single path which has built into it information gathering nodes, points at which the teacher stops and assesses new information. There are significant implications for teacher training and class management, depending on the perspective one takes. If the decision-making model is taken, then training in decision making should be encouraged as well as lesson structures that reduce the number of decisions to a manageable size. If an information processing and script-notion is used as the model, then script design (or the significance of establishing useable routines) and information-gathering techniques would be useful for beginning teachers to learn.

Consider, as an example, a mathematics teacher of a class of 9-year-olds leading a lesson on two digit multiplication within the constraints of a 40 minute class period. Some of the resources and demands embedded in the task can be examined. There may be 25 to 30 children; the teacher is using a standard curriculum series but may have rearranged the order of presentation. The teacher is using a preplanned agenda. The agenda consists of a series of goals, subgoals, and actions for both the teacher and the student. Proceeding through the agenda, the teacher is bombarded with massive amounts of information: social and management information carried by student behaviors; temporal concerns due to the fit, or lack of it, between the clock and the sequence of actions; students' grasp of the academic presentation, reflected by the errors and correctness of student responses and questions; random external interruptions such as supply deliveries, principal's announcements, and the like. The skilled teacher filters and selects carefully from this rich array of information in order to maximize the chance of accomplishing the agenda; the newer teacher may be more distracted and pulled away (Putman 1985). Teachers move through the system of activity structures that define the particular lesson, using information that will help accomplish a series of goals and related subgoals. For example, in correcting or returning homework, the teacher is trying to get homework corrected as well as to reinforce the importance of doing the work.

4.2 Student Thought

A logical corollary to teacher thought is student thought (Anderson 1981, Peterson and Swing 1982). Unlike the study of teacher thinking which has been done in highly naturalistic settings, the study of student thought has been conducted in laboratory settings. From this work it seems that students have little comprehension of the purpose of seatwork. Further, students who both attend (concentrate) during lesson and rehearsal of practice and engage in conscious problem solving do considerably better than those who "listen." A recent review of student thought is presented by Wittrock 1986; a model of student thought has been proposed by Leinhardt 1985.

Lessons are affected by both the long-term and short-term planning of teachers. In the plans the teacher can control scheduling, content, and the basic structure of a lesson. Lessons in different subject areas and at different levels have distinct patterns of teacher and student interactions, both in terms of quantity of verbal exchanges and in terms of the types of activity structures. With respect to activity structures, mathematics and reading are seen to have more dynamic patterns of activities than social studies. The particular of activity structures is also seen to affect the frequency of internal interruptions and time gained or lost for instruction. Teacher and student thought during lessons not only affects behavior but involves both successful and unsuccessful responses to the multiple constraints of the setting.

See also: Interactive Decision Making; Planning; Teachers' Judgments; Time; Opportunity to Learn; Content Coverage

Bibliography

Allington R 1982 Amount and mode of contextual reading as a function of reading group membership. Paper presented at the annual conference of the National Council of Teachers of English, Washington, DC
Allington R 1983 The reading instruction provided to readers of differing reading abilities. *Elem. Sch. J.*
Anderson L M 1981 Student responses to seatwork: Implications for the study of students' cognitive processing. Paper presented at the annual meeting of the American Educational Research Association, Los Angeles, California
Anderson-Levitt K M, Hertweck A 1982 Teachers' interpretations of students' behaviors in French and American classrooms. In: Greeno J (Chair) 1982 *Teacher Cognitions: Research and Theory from Multiple Perspectives.* Symposium presented at the annual meeting of the American Educational Research Association, New York
Berliner D C 1982 The executive functions of teaching. Paper presented at the annual meeting of the American Educational Research Association, New York
Berliner D, King M, Rubin J, Fisher C W 1981 Describing classroom activities: A pilot study. Unpublished manuscript, University of Arizona, Arizona
Borko H, Niles J A 1982 Factors contributing to teacher's judgements about students and decisions about grouping students for reading instruction. Unpublished manuscript, Virginia Polytechnic Institute and State University, Virginia
Clark C M, Peterson P L 1986 Teachers' thought processes. In: Wittrock M C (ed.) 1986 pp. 253–96
Cooley W W, Leinhardt G 1980 The instructional dimensions study. *Educ. Eval. Policy Analysis* 2: 7–25
Emmer E, Evertson C, Anderson L 1980 Effective man-

agement at the beginning of the school year. *Elem. Sch. J.* 80: 219–31

Fisher C W, Berliner D C (eds.) 1985 *Perspectives on Instructional Time*. Longman, New York

Fisher C W, Filby N N, Marliave R, Cahen L S, Dishaw M M, Moore J E, Berliner D C 1978 Teacher behaviors, academic learning time and student achievement. Final report of Phase III-B, *Beginning Teacher Evaluation Study*. Technical Report V-1. Far West Laboratory for Educational Research and Development, San Francisco, California

Good T L, Grouws D A, Ebmeier H 1983 *Active Mathematics Teaching*. Longman, New York

Harnischfeger A, Wiley D E 1977 Conceptual issues in models of school learning. *Studies of Educative Processes,* No. 10. CEMREL, Chicago, Illinois

Hayes-Roth B, Hayes-Roth F 1978 *Cognitive Processes in Planning*. A report prepared for the office of Naval Research (R-2366-ONR)

Jackson P W 1968 *Life in Classrooms*. Holt, Rinehart and Winston, New York

Korth W, Cornbleth C 1982 Classroom activities as settings for cognitive learning opportunities and instruction. Paper presented at the annual meeting of the American Educational Research Association, New York

Leinhardt G 1983 Novice and expert knowledge of individual student's achievement. *Educ. Psychol.* 18 (3): 165–79

Leinhardt G 1985 Tracing students' mathematical knowledge from intuition to competence. Paper presented at the annual meeting of the American Educational Research Association, Chicago, Illinois

Leinhardt G, Greeno J G in press The cognitive skill of teaching. *J. Educ. Psychol.*

Leinhardt G, Seewald A M 1981 Overlap: What's tested, what's taught? *J. Educ. Meas.* 18: 171–77

Leinhardt G, Weidman C W, Hammond K M in press Introduction and integration of classroom routines by expert teachers. *Curric. Inq.*

Leinhardt G, Zigmond N, Cooley W W 1981 Reading instruction and its effects. *Am. Educ. Res. J.* 18: 343–61

McCutcheon G 1981 Elementary school teacher's planning for social studies and other subjects. *Theory and Res. Soc. Educ.* 9: 45–66

Morine-Dershimer G 1982 Tying threads together: Some thoughts on methods for investigating teacher thinking. In: Greeno J (Chair) 1982 *Teacher Cognitions: Research and Theory from Multiple Perspectives*. Symposium presented at the annual meeting of the American Educational Research Association, New York

Peterson P L, Swing S R 1982 Beyond time on task: Students' reports of their thought processes during direct instruction. *Elem. Sch. J.* 82: 481–91

Putnam R T 1985 Teacher thoughts and actions in live and simulated tutoring of addition. Unpublished doctoral dissertation, Stanford University

Rist R C 1973 *The Urban School: A Factory for Failure*. MIT, Cambridge, Massachusetts

Salzen J A 1981 The effects of instructional grouping on the mathematics achievement of male and female elementary students. Paper presented at the annual meeting of the American Educational Research Association, Los Angeles, California

Schwille J, Porter A, Gant M 1979 *Content-decision Making and the Politics of Education*. Michigan State University, Institute for Research on Teaching, East Lansing, Michigan

Shavelson R J, Stern P 1981 Research on teachers' pedagogical thoughts, judgments, decisions, and behavior. *Rev. Educ. Res.* 51: 455–98

Stodolsky S S 1983 *Classroom Activity Structures in the Fifth Grade*. Final Report. National Institute of Education (NIE), Washington, DC

Stodolsky S S, Ferguson T L, Wimpelberg K 1981 The recitation persists, but what does it look like? *J. Curric. Stud.* 13: 121–30

Wittrock M C (ed.) 1986 *Handbook of Research on Teaching*, 3rd edn. Macmillan, New York

Yinger R J 1977 A study of teacher planning: Description and theory development using ethnographic and information processing methods (Doctoral dissertation, Michigan State University) *Dissertation Abstracts International* 1978 39: 207A-208A (University Microfilms No. 7810138)

Content Coverage

R. Barr

The empirical literature on content coverage can be separated into two main strands. In one, investigators are concerned with the influence of the curriculum on students' opportunities to learn concepts measured by achievement tests. In the second, researchers view content coverage as an instructional condition and ask about its determinants as an element of instruction and about its effects manifest in learning.

Although content coverage serves as a major construct in some theoretical formulations, it has received little conceptual treatment in its own right. Further, as used descriptively, it refers to a complex of related conditions. Porter et al. (1979) distinguish between content covered and content emphasized. The first refers to actual counts made of the concepts introduced, whereas the latter includes such proxies for content coverage as time allocated to different content areas, textbook length, and test content. There is little quarrel about using actual counts of concepts introduced during instruction to represent content coverage, although exactly how such counts should be made in science, social studies, and literature appears to be more problematic than in beginning reading and mathematics. But there is a class of indices that Porter and associates refer to as content emphasized, some of which appear to be more closely associated with the content of instruction than others. For example, number of pages covered in mathematics or reading, content analyses of curricular programs, and evaluations of test items in terms of what was covered during instruction seem to be closer approximations of content coverage than unspecified measures of instructional time allocated to different content areas and the number of pages in textbooks. In this review, studies that include direct measures of content coverage and those involving closer approximations of coverage are considered, whereas those entailing measures of curricular time allocations, the length of textbooks, and the like are not because of their relative imprecision as indices.

The most striking characteristic of the literature on content coverage is its recency. Only since the early 1970s has the concept received serious empirical attention. How might this neglect be understood? Rosenshine (1979) suggests that it is "because different classrooms use different materials and texts and we have not developed a technology for studying content covered in such situations" (pp. 32–33). While it is true that different classes may use different texts, these texts have been subject to content analyses, however primitive in nature, and it would appear that similar analyses could have been made of the content of class instruction.

Alternatively, failure to consider coverage may have a conceptual as well as a methodological basis. Prior to the Coleman Report (1966), it was taken for granted that since what was covered was learned, there was no need to demonstrate the obvious. However, as arguments raged over the ineffectiveness of schooling, educational researchers felt impelled to specify the conditions of learning. Hence, in the late 1960s and the 1970s there were an increasing number of researchers who addressed the central role of textual materials and the influence of content coverage on learning.

1. Curricular Content and Achievement

The International Association for the Evaluation of Educational Achievement (IEA) study of mathematics achievement (Husén 1967) represents a landmark not only in the evaluation literature but also in research on content coverage. Teachers from 12 participating nations were asked to judge whether students had had the opportunity to learn the type of problem exemplified by each test item. The relationship between teacher reported opportunity to learn and mathematics achievement was substantial; the level to which scores were aggregated, however, influenced the strength of the relationship.

The level of mathematics instruction (based on a rating of the courses students reported they had taken) represents a second measure of content coverage in the IEA analysis. Level of mathematics instruction and opportunity to learn, along with student interest, accounted for more than half of the total variation in mathematics achievement in a multiple regression analysis involving a total of 26 independent variables (Husén 1967 p. 263).

The opportunity students have to learn material tapped by achievement test items has been shown to be an important condition in other research as well. For example, a second IEA study reported substantial association between teacher reported opportunity to learn and achievement in various areas of science (Comber and Keeves 1973). Chang and Raths (1971) also had

teachers evaluate test items according to whether or not they had spent very little to very much time teaching relevant content, and found that differences in achievement between middle- and lower-class schools were associated with the degree of emphasis on content as reported by teachers. Leinhardt et al. (1981) found that the overlap between the content of instruction and test items was second only to reading achievement measured prior to instruction in accounting for the posttest reading achievement of primary level, learning disabled students.

Some investigators have compared the content of curricular programs with that of achievement test items. Walker and Schaffarzick (1974) examined 23 curricular evaluations. They found that groups studying from innovative curricula scored higher on tests favoring those curricula than did students using traditional programs. Reciprocally, those studying from traditional curricula achieved higher scores on a substantial number of comparisons when test material was similar to what they had covered than did those studying from the innovative programs. Because more of the tests favored innovative curricula, the appearance that they were more effective was illusory.

Researchers have also examined the grade placement of textbook content in relation to achievement test results. Pidgeon (1970) compared the mathematics achievement of 11-year-olds from California, Australia, and England and found that students in the latter two countries scored substantially higher; indeed, the score achieved by a third of the English sample was attained by less than 1 percent of the California sample. He compared the English and American textbooks and found that most of the content measured by the test items was introduced one or two years later in American than in English books. An earlier comparison by Buswell (1958) reported similar achievement and curricular findings: while American children were finishing arithmetic in seventh and eighth grades, English children were covering algebra and geometry.

The challenge of textbooks may also influence the performance of students on scholastic aptitude measures. Chall (1977) analyzed the readability of selected textbooks used by students taking the Scholastic Aptitude Tests (SAT) from 1947 to 1975 and found that the declining difficulty of textbook passages paralleled the declining performance of students on the SATs measured at six points during this period.

These studies involving teacher estimates of coverage and analyses of curricular materials suggest a direct relationship between what is covered and what is learned. Nevertheless, direct evidence is not presented, and to the extent that tests do not tap content actually covered, the true relationship between content coverage and learning is underestimated. On the other hand, to the extent that teacher estimates reflect knowledge of learning as well as coverage and to the extent that curricular content is not presented during instruction, the relationship may be overestimated. Research evidence involving direct measures of content coverage presented in the following section clarifies the strength of the relationship. More importantly, studies of instruction enable us to understand the nature of content coverage. Is it a condition that acts upon learning autonomously or is it a reflection of a complex set of instructional components that jointly affect learning?

2. Content Coverage as an Instructional Condition

Most studies of content coverage focus on beginning reading or mathematics instruction. Coverage in reading has been variously measured by the number of concepts introduced (Barr 1973–74), the number of words assigned during a three day period (Leinhardt et al. 1981), the number of books read (Anderson et al. 1979, Harris et al. 1968), and the difficulty of books read (Anderson et al. 1979). Coverage in mathematics has been measured by the range of content or skills taught (McDonald 1976) and the number of pages covered (Good et al. 1978). The degree to which coverage is associated with achievement ranges from substantial covariation ($r = 0.93$) when coverage is measured as the number of concepts presented and outcome measures are directly related to covered content (Barr and Dreeben 1983) to moderate ($r = 0.36$ to 0.49) when less content specific measures of coverage and general achievement tests are used.

It is clear from this evidence that what teachers cover does have a substantial bearing on what is learned. Nevertheless, there is debate about how this finding should be interpreted. Good and his colleagues (1978) argue that coverage should be treated as an independent variable that can be manipulated to enhance learning; and evidence exists in support of the notion that teachers do have some degree of freedom in determining how much should be covered. For example, Good found that some mathematics teachers covered 50 percent more pages than others. Barr (1973–74) reports that reading groups of comparable ability differed by as much as a factor of three in the amount of reading content they covered.

Other researchers, by contrast, argue that coverage is a varaible that is responsive to and limited by other conditions, most importantly, the aptitude of students. Two major theoretical formulations have been proposed in which the relationship between aptitude and coverage holds a central position. Dahllöf (1971) argues that frame conditions—the physical setting, school administration, grouping, class size, structure and objectives of the syllabus, school year, and number of lessons a week—set temporal and spatial limits on educational processes within schools (see *Frame Factors*). As the mechanism through which frame factors influence instruction, the teachers, he contends, in traditionally instructed classes monitor the progress of a small group of students at the lower end of the aptitude distribution to determine when to proceed from one unit to the next. He calls this group, which he tentatively defines as including students from the 10th to the 25th percentile

in the aptitude distribution, the criterion steering group. He argues that grouping students into classes affects the ability composition of classes, and this, through the influence of the steering group, affects the number of units covered and the class level of achievement and variation.

In a test of this formulation involving 46 sophomore classes in five subject areas studied for the duration of a school year, Lundgren (1972 p.184) found little relation between the average aptitude of the steering group and content coverage. By contrast, he reports that "the textbook, by its sequence of units and massive content, governs the planning of the teaching and the way it is carried out and to what extent. For these two aspects, the textbooks show marked variations between each other" (p. 175). Accordingly, the aptitude of a class may be a less important influence on what gets covered than the textbook. Further, as suggested by case studies undertaken by Schwille et al. (1983), whereas most teachers follow their mathematics text materials closely, other influences such as district guidelines and teacher preferences provide the rationale for content decisions.

By contrast, Barr and Dreeben (1983) find both textbook and aptitude influences on content coverage in beginning reading instruction. Their conceptual model of schooling distinguishes between productive activities occurring at different levels of school systems. They view the work of teachers as facilitated and limited by the student, material, and temporal resources made available to them through activities at the district and school levels of organization. At the class level, teachers must determine how a diverse collection of students should be organized for instruction, and the particular grouping pattern developed is viewed as a class level outcome that has immediate consequences for the design of instruction. At the group level, teachers match instructional materials and their teaching over periods of time to the characteristics of instructional groups in order to achieve instructional goals. Content coverage is treated as the main outcome of group level instruction, and one that is responsive not only to the mean aptitude of groups but also to the nature of textual materials, allocated instructional time, and teacher preferences. Content coverage, in turn, becomes a primary influence on individual learning.

Barr and Dreeben provide evidence that when ability groups are established in classes, the coverage of basal reading materials is associated more closely to group mean aptitude than to other conditions such as the difficulty of the reading curriculum. By contrast, coverage of phonics is found to be influenced more by the difficulty of the reading materials (the total number of phonics concepts they contain) than by the mean aptitude of the instructional group. They also report that teachers using more demanding materials allocate proportionately more time to reading activities than those with less; thus, textbook content and allocated time work together to influence content coverage. Consequently, differences in coverage among groups comparable in ability are in part a reflection of materials and time and not simply teacher preference.

In their analysis of instructional conditions influencing individual learning, content coverage is the only condition that accounts for a significant proportion of the variance in word learning; by contrast, although coverage accounts for a significant proportion of variance in phonics learning, other conditions such as the length of the school day and curricular material difficulty account for additional variance. Although coverage is closely associated with learning, this is not to say that children learned all they covered. They learned from 57 to 98 percent of what they were taught, with those of lower initial readiness learning proportionately less than those of higher readiness.

The formulative work of Dahllöf and of Barr and Dreeben poses the problem of how an adequate match can be obtained between the aptitudes of learners and content coverage in the collective setting of the classroom. Particularly, when classes are not grouped on the basis of ability and when a total class instructional strategy is employed, there are bound to be substantial numbers of students who are exposed to too much or too little instructional material.

Yet relatively little research has explored the question of how much mismatch students can tolerate. Gates and Russell (1938) studied the effective limits of content coverage by exposing 6-year-old children to reading materials that varied in vocabulary burden. High readiness children learned more when they were exposed to a medium or large number of different words. By contrast, those of average or low readiness learned more when they encountered the smallest number of words; they learned more of a small set of different words and less of larger sets so that their total learning was highest when the vocabulary burden was small.

From the Gates and Russell work, the size of vocabulary that is appropriate for children of different levels of readiness is known in relative terms. Unfortunately, it is not known exactly how many different words were presented during their study, and accordingly, there is no way of identifying the range within which the relationship between coverage and learning ceased to be linear for different aptitude groups.

Begle (1973) provides interesting evidence on this question. Junior-high-school students who achieved below average in mathematics were given two years to cover what more capable students had covered in a year. Below average 12-year-olds nearly equaled and below average 16-years-olds outperformed the more capable students on the final test. The results suggest that it is not the inherent difficulty of the content but the pace of introducing new content that is problematic for some students.

3. Conclusions

The evidence from this limited body of research supports the conclusion that content coverage is an impor-

tant condition demanding attention, but it needs clear definition and a place in a constellation of related concepts. It has implications for at least three related areas of classroom research: evaluations of program effectiveness, studies of instruction, and investigations of student learning.

Inappropriate correspondence between curriculum and test content can seriously bias the results of evaluation studies. Such studies attempt to establish a connection between curriculum and learning. But if they are to be valid, one needs to have not only good test results, but solid documentation that they tap the curriculum. Determining and measuring the content covered, thus, must be one important element in evaluation.

From one perspective, content coverage is an instructional condition and it should be viewed as part of the more general problem of how instruction takes the form it does. Indeed, coverage is particularly important because of its responsiveness to such conditions as the ability of the group for which instruction is planned, whether the materials are easy or difficult, and how much time is available for instruction. Used in this capacity, content coverage is a useful indication of the potential of instruction to influence learning.

At the same time, from an alternative perspective, content coverage is a condition of learning, one that facilitates learning up to a point but may then depress it if too much is crowded into too short a time. Individual learning is influenced by a range of instructional conditions, time and materials as well as coverage, and also by characteristics of the individuals themselves, such as ability, interest, motivation, and so forth. In classroom settings, however, it is important to distinguish instructional and individual influences because instruction is overwhelmingly geared to groupings of one kind or another, and only rarely to individuals directly. The amount of material covered, then, pertains to the problem of matching instruction to the range of individual characteristics represented within groupings, and individual learning represents the by-product of collective instruction along with the influence of individual characteristics.

See also: Opportunity to Learn; Time

Bibliography

Anderson L M, Evertson C M, Brophy J E 1979 An experimental study of effective teaching in first-grade reading groups. *Elem. Sch. J.* 79(4):193–223

Barr R 1973–74 Instructional pace differences and their effect on reading acquisition. *Read. Res. Q.* 9(4):526–54.

Barr R, Dreeben R 1983 *How Schools Work.* University of Chicago Press, Chicago, Illinois

Begle E G 1973 Some lessons learned by SMSG. *Maths Teach.* 66:207–14

Buswell G 1958 A comparison of achievement in arithmetic in England and central California *Arithmetic Teach.* 5:1–9

Chall J S 1977 An analysis of textbooks in relation to declining SAT scores. In: Wirtz W W et al. (eds.) 1977 *On Further Examination. Report of the Advisory Panel on the Scholastic Aptitude Test Score Decline.* College Entrance Examination Board, Princeton, New Jersey

Chang S S, Raths J 1971 The school's contribution to the cumulating deficit. *J. Educ. Res.* 64:272–76

Coleman J S et al. 1966 *Equality of Educational Opportunity.* United States Government Printing Office, Washington, DC

Comber L C, Keeves J P 1973 *Science Education in Nineteen Countries: An Empirical Study.* Wiley, New York

Dahllöf U S 1971 *Ability Grouping, Content Validity, and Curriculum Process Analysis.* Teachers College Press, New York

Gates A I, Russell D H 1938 Types of material, vocabulary burden, word analysis, and other factors in beginning reading. *Elem. Sch. J.* 39:27–35, 119–28

Good T L, Grouws D A, Beckerman T M 1978 Curriculum pacing: Some empirical data in mathematics. *J. Curric. Stud.* 10:75–81

Harris A et al. 1968 *A Continuation of the CRAFT Project.* Division of Teacher Education of the City University of New York, New York. ERIC Document No. ED 010 297

Husén T (ed.) 1967 *International Study of Achievement in Mathematics: Comparison of Twelve Countries.* Wiley, New York

Leinhardt G, Zigmond N, Cooley W W 1981 Reading instruction and its effects. *Am. Educ. Res. J.* 18(3):343–61

Lundgren U P 1972 *Frame Factors and the Teaching Process: A Contribution to Curriculum Theory and Theory of Teaching.* Almqvist and Wiksell, Stockholm

McDonald F J 1976 *Research on Teaching and its Implications for Policy Making: Report on Phase II of the Beginning Teacher Evaluation Study.* Educational Testing Service, Princeton, New Jersey

Pidgeon D A 1970 *Expectation and Pupil Performance.* National Foundation for Educational Research in England and Wales, Slough, Berkshire

Porter A et al. 1979 *Teacher Autonomy and the Control of Content Taught* (Res. Ser. No. 24). Institute for Research on Teaching, Michigan State University, East Lansing, Michigan

Rosenshine B 1979 Content, time and direct instruction. In: Peterson P L, Walberg H J (eds.) 1979 *Research on Teaching: Concepts, Findings, and Implications.* McCutchan, Berkeley, California

Schwille J et al. 1983 Teachers as policy brokers in the content of elementary school mathematics. In: Shulman L S, Sykes G (eds.) 1983 *Handbook of Teaching and Policy.* Longman, New York

Walker D F, Schaffarzick J 1974 Comparing curricula. *Rev. Educ. Res.* 44:83–111

Opportunity to Learn

L. W. Anderson

Opportunity to learn as an important variable influencing, and possibly explaining, the effectiveness of classroom instruction was introduced into the educational literature during the decade of the 1960s. Carroll (1963) included opportunity to learn as one of five central variables in his model of school learning (see *The Carroll Model*). Opportunity to learn was also examined in a major international study of mathematics achievement described in two volumes edited by Torsten Husén (1967). Despite the use of the same variable label, however, Carroll's opportunity to learn and Husén's opportunity to learn are conceptually distinct. The purposes of this entry are to (a) describe the conceptual distinctions, (b) explore the ways in which opportunity to learn has been measured, (c) summarize briefly the research evidence concerning opportunity to learn, and (d) speculate on the future of opportunity to learn as a key variable in classroom instructional research and practice.

1. Conceptual Distinctions

Carroll (1963) defined opportunity to learn as the amount of time allocated to the learner for the learning of a given task. If, for example, the task assigned to a learner is to understand the concept of noun, opportunity to learn is simply the amount of time the learner has available to learn what a noun is.

In Carroll's model, opportunity to learn is contrasted with the amount of time the learner needs to spend in order to learn. This latter variable is primarily dependent on the learner's aptitude for the task. Thus, while teachers have virtually no control over the time needed for learning, they do have some control over opportunity to learn.

Carroll also contrasted opportunity to learn with the amount of time the learner actually spends actively engaged in the process of learning. This latter variable, frequently referred to as engaged time, active learning time, or time-on-task (see *Time*) is believed to be influenced by the perseverance of the learner, the quality of the instruction, and opportunity to learn. In this context opportunity to learn places an upper bound on engaged time.

In contrast with Carroll, Husén (1967) defines opportunity to learn in terms of the relationship between the content taught to the students and the content tested by the achievement test. Thus opportunity to learn from the Husén perspective is best understood as the match between what is taught and what is tested. Put simply, the greater the match, the greater the opportunity to learn.

Two major distinctions exist between Carroll's and Husén's conceptualizations of opportunity to learn. First, while Carroll's conceptualization clearly suggests that opportunity to learn is an instructional variable (one under the direct influence of administrators and teachers), Husén's conceptualization implies that opportunity to learn is mainly a measurement variable (one akin to content validity).

Second, Carroll's opportunity to learn is a continuous variable while Husén's opportunity to learn is essentially a dichotomous variable. The issue from Carroll's perspective is how much time a learner has available to learn a particular task. The issue from Husén's perspective is whether or not a learner (or particular groups of learners) have been provided with any instruction relative to the content included on the achievement test(s).

The distinctions between the two conceptualizations have been noted by several researchers since the early 1960s. Poyner et al. (1977), for example, included two opportunity to learn variables in their *Instructional Dimensions Study*. One variable, which they termed "quantitative," is identical to Carroll's opportunity to learn. The other variable, termed "qualitative," is the same as Husén's opportunity to learn.

Increasingly, researchers have begun to use labels other than opportunity to learn to highlight these conceptual distinctions. Allocated time (Wiley and Harnischfeger 1974, Fisher et al. 1980) has replaced Carroll's opportunity to learn. Content coverage (Cooley and Leinhardt 1980) and, perhaps most appropriately, content overlap (Leinhardt and Seewald 1981) have replaced Husén's opportunity to learn. Since the labels "allocated time" and "content overlap" seem to best capture the conceptual distinctions mentioned earlier, these labels will be used in place of opportunity to learn in subsequent sections of this article.

2. Allocated Time: Measurement and Research

One of the reasons Carroll placed time in such a central position in his model of school learning was the properties of time as a metric. Time is relatively easy to measure, has an absolute zero point, and is expressed in commonly understood and equal units (e.g., seconds, minutes, hours, days, and years). These three properties make it quite easy to conduct research on allocated time.

In fact, research has been conducted using several of the time units. Carroll's (1974, 1975) research has focused primarily on the number of years students have studied a particular subject matter. In the earlier study the subject areas were reading and mathematics. Several successive levels of the Comprehensive Tests of Basic Skills (CTBS) were equated for the purpose of examining student progress from ages 6 to 17. Using a memory test as a measure of mathematics aptitude, a vocabulary test as a measure of reading aptitude, and grade level as an indicator of opportunity to learn, Carroll was able to partially test his model of school learning. The fit of the data to the model was quite good, providing strong support for the inclusion of opportunity to learn (defined in terms of number of years of schooling) in the model.

Carroll's (1975) second study provided additional support for the importance of opportunity to learn as measured by the number of years of schooling. In this study Carroll reported the results of an international study of the teaching of French as a second language. Eight countries participated in the study. One of the variables examined in relationship to differences in student achievement among the various countries was the number of years during which students received instruction relating to the learning of French. Of all the instructional variables included in the study, this opportunity to learn variable was most clearly related to between-country differences in the learning of French.

Quite clearly the number of years of instruction is the most global indicator of allocated time. Wiley and Harnischfeger (1974) studied a slightly less global indicator, average daily attendance. This is defined as the proportion of students who are able, because of their attendance, to receive *any* instruction on a typical school day. In one sense, then, average daily attendance can be viewed as the number of days per year on which students received instruction pertaining to a variety of subject areas. Wiley and Harnischfeger found a small, but statistically significant, relationship between average daily attendance and student achievement differences between schools.

The Beginning Teacher Evaluation Study (Fisher et al. 1980) brought the unit of allocated time to the level of hours and minutes. In addition, estimates of allocated time were based on classroom observations rather than written records (as was the case in both the Carroll, and Wiley and Harnischfeger research). One of the most intriguing aspects of the study was the great differences in the amount of time allocated to particular subject areas and to specific topics within various subject areas. For example, in an early study report, Dishaw (1977) reported large differences in the amount of time per day devoted to the teaching of reading in 25 second grade classrooms (age 7). While the most reading-oriented teacher spent 127 minutes per day teaching reading, the least reading-oriented teacher spent only 34 minutes. If this difference remains consistent over a 180-day school year, the first group of students would receive an additional 279 hours of reading instruction in the second grade. Similar differences were found for second grade mathematics and for fifth grade (age 10) reading and mathematics. As in the case of the Wiley and Harnischfeger (1974) study, these differences in allocated time were slightly but statistically significantly associated with achievement differences between classes.

One final point needs to be raised before moving on to content overlap. In the Beginning Teacher Evaluation Study, engaged time or time-on-task was more highly related to achievement than was allocated time. This finding is in line with the predictions that can be made based on Carroll's model. In Carroll's model engaged time or time-on-task is hypothesized to directly influence learning. Allocated time, on the other hand, is expected to have only an indirect influence on learning.

The direct influence of allocated time is on engaged time or time-on-task, not on learning.

In summary, then, allocated time, expressed either in years, days, or minutes, is related to student achievement. This relationship tends to be stronger for years than for either days or minutes. This stronger relationship for more global indicators of allocated time makes sense from two perspectives. First, more global indicators allow for cumulative effects of learning (or failure to learn). That is, three years of French instruction is one more than two years. This is not necessarily true of minutes of instruction where the differences found by Dishaw in second grade reading instruction can be compensated for by differences in first or third grade reading instruction.

Second, fairly global indicators of allocated time are more likely to be related to fairly global indicators of achievement. The more specific the indicator of allocated time, the more likely that content overlap interferes with the allocated time–achievement relationship.

3. Content Overlap

Content overlap has been measured in several ways. In the Husén (1967) study and in a subsequent study by Comber and Keeves (1973) content overlap was estimated in the following manner. Each teacher was asked to examine each item on the international achievement test. For each item the teacher was to estimate the percentage of students in his or her class who received instruction relating to the content or skill tested. The teacher then selected one of three percentage categories for each item: less than 25 percent, 25 to 75 percent, and more than 75 percent. The ratings were scaled by assigning the midpoint of each category to each estimate. For each teacher a content overlap score was computed by summing the values of the midpoints corresponding to the responses made to each item.

Borg (1979) asked teachers to examine each test item and indicate on a five-point scale the degree to which they had emphasized the content or skill tested. For each item, teachers were to choose from among the following five response options: "E—teacher emphasized content related to the given item; DC—teacher definitely covered content, PC—teacher probably covered content; DR—teacher did not remember whether content was covered; NC—teacher did not cover content" (Borg 1979 p. 638). Each response option was assigned a numerical value from 5 (E) to 1 (NC). These numerical values were summed to arrive at a content overlap score. Borg (1979) contends that his procedure for estimating content overlap "is likely to produce more accurate teacher estimates than would be obtained by asking what percentage of pupils had an opportunity to learn each concept, as was done in previous studies" (p. 638). No evidence is presented to support this contention, however.

Despite the differences in procedures, both Husén and Borg used teachers to provide the estimates of content overlap. Other researchers, however, have relied on an examination of the curriculum to yield such estimates. The techniques used in these studies are quite similar. For example, Jenkins and Pany (1978) examined the overlap of five standardized achievement tests and seven commercial reading series. Their focus was on word recognition of first and second grade students (age 6 and 7). Two sets of word lists were formed. The first set of word lists consisted of all words included on the word recognition subtest of each standardized achievement test. The second set of word lists consisted of all words included in each of the seven commercial reading series. Each time a word included on an achievement test was also included in a reading series, one point was assigned. In this way, each achievement test was assigned an overlap score with each of the seven reading series. Armbruster et al. (1977) used a similar technique in exploring content overlap in terms of reading comprehension. Sixteen categories of reading comprehension were identified to aid in the analysis. Similarly, Porter et al. (1978) and Schmidt (1978) developed a taxonomy for classifying the content included in mathematics curricula and on standardized mathematics achievement tests.

Despite the differences in measuring content overlap, the results are quite similar. Jenkins and Pany (1978) did not examine differences in achievement test scores. Instead, they considered each "match" as one correct item, computed a raw score on each of the five tests for a hypothetical "average" student, and transformed these average raw scores to grade equivalent scores. The grade equivalent scores for the average first grade student studying the various curricula were estimated to range from less than 1.0 to approximately 2.3 for five tests. For the average second grade student the grade equivalent scores were estimated to range from less than 1.0 to approximately 3.5. The Jenkins and Pany results suggest that differences in content overlap can result in achievement differences as large as 1.5 grade levels in grade 1 and 2.5 grade levels in grade 2.

Both the Husén study and the Borg study included actual student achievement as the dependent variable. Since the Husén study predates the Borg study it will be discussed first. Furthermore, since the Husén study was in many ways the first study of opportunity to learn, the results will be discussed in some detail. In the Husén study the results pertaining to content overlap were analyzed both within countries and between countries. Median within-country correlations between content overlap and student achievement in mathematics were computed separately for each of four samples: (a) a sample of 13-year-old students, (b) a sample of students enrolled in the grade in which the majority of 13-year-olds are enrolled, (c) a sample of students enrolled in one or more mathematics courses during their final year in secondary school, and (d) a sample of students not enrolled in a mathematics course during their final secondary year. Since students in this last sample would not have had any opportunity to learn mathematics during their final secondary year, this sample is not relevant to the present discussion.

The median within-country correlations for the three samples of interest ranged from 0.10 to 0.18. These relatively low correlations were attributed in part to the homogeneity of teachers' ratings within certain countries. That is, the countries with the lowest correlations were those countries in which the teachers had the least influence on the content actually covered in a given year.

When the data were analyzed between countries the results were quite different. For the three samples of interest the correlations between content overlap and student achievement ranged from 0.64 to 0.81. This difference in within-country and between-country results led to the conclusion that "a considerable amount of the variation between countries in mathematics scores can be attributed to the differences between students' opportunities to learn the material which was tested" (Husén 1967 pp. 168–69).

The results of Borg's (1979) study generally supported the results of the Husén study while at the same time identifying conditions under which the content overlap–student achievement relationship would be more and less likely to hold. Perhaps the conditions affecting the relationship are more informative than the magnitude of the relationship itself. Borg found that the magnitude of the content overlap–student achievement relationship depended on (a) the nature of the material being learned, (b) the type of achievement test administered (i.e., multiple choice, essay), and (c) the type of students being taught (i.e., white, minority). For example, for white students learning particular types of material tested by a multiple-choice test, the correlation between content overlap and student achievement was approximately 0.40. Furthermore, the magnitude of this relationship did not depend greatly on student ability or socioeconomic status.

In summary, then, content overlap has been found to be significantly associated with student achievement in several studies. The magnitude of the relationship depends on several factors including, but not limited to, the amount of variation in content taught, the type of material being taught, the students being taught, and the test used to assess learning.

4. A Comparison of Allocated Time and Content Overlap

Only a few studies have examined allocated time and content overlap. One of the largest studies to investigate both was the Instructional Dimensions Study (Poyner et al. 1977), a study involving approximately 4,500 students and 350 teachers. Students in both first and third grades (ages 6 and 8) were included in the study. Both reading and mathematics achievement of the students were examined. Although results pertaining to several subsamples were presented, only the results pertaining to four samples will be discussed. These four samples are: (a) total sample of first grade reading students, (b) total sample of first grade mathematics students, (c) total sample of third grade reading students, and (d) total sample of third grade mathematics students.

In all four samples the correlation between allocated time and content overlap was quite small, ranging from 0.03 to 0.18. Thus, empirically speaking, the two conceptualizations of opportunity to learn are quite independent. Furthermore, in all four samples, the content overlap–student achievement relationship was stronger than the allocated time–student achievement relationship. The correlations between content overlap and student achievement ranged from 0.31 to 0.44. In contrast, the correlations between allocated time and student achievement ranged from −0.11 to 0.12.

The magnitude of the correlations found in the Instructional Dimensions Study parallel those found in studies examining either allocated time (e.g., Fisher et al. 1980) or content overlap (e.g., Borg 1979) separately. In general, then, it appears that content overlap is more strongly related to achievement than is allocated time. Of course, this conclusion is based on studies conducted within a single academic year. If multiyear studies are considered, the importance of allocated time may increase while that of content overlap may decrease. This latter conclusion is based primarily on the quasilongitudinal research conducted by Carroll (1974, 1975).

5. The Future of Opportunity to Learn

Based on the information presented in this entry two generalizations concerning the future of opportunity to learn can be proffered. First, opportunity to learn will emerge as a key extraneous variable in future instructional research. Second, a composite "opportunity to learn" variable will be formed from the present, conceptually distinct variables of allocated time and content overlap. Each of these generalizations will be briefly discussed.

If differences in curricula, instructional programs, or teaching are to be examined validly, differences in opportunity to learn must be controlled or estimated. In this context opportunity to learn is best considered an extraneous variable. The potential impact of opportunity to learn as an extraneous variable has been addressed from both the allocated time and content overlap perspective.

Walker and Schaffarzick (1974) reviewed some 23 studies on the basis of curriculum type and resultant student achievement. They concluded that the extent to which the innovative curriculum was superior depended on the nature of the achievement test administered. Students studying an innovative curriculum displayed higher achievement gains only when the content tested matched the innovative curriculum more than the traditional curriculum. In those cases in which the content tested more closely matched the traditional curriculum, students studying the traditional curriculum outperformed their innovative curriculum counterparts.

In a reaction to the results of a large-scale study conducted by Bennett (1976), Gray and Satterly (1978) suggested that the differences in the effectiveness of formal and informal teachers described by Bennett can be attributed to time allocations. "Formal teachers not only allocate more time to the basic skills but also ensure (because they believe such skills are overridingly important) that their pupils [spend more time] by maintaining stricter discipline and by being less tolerant of what they perceive as pupil 'time-wasting'" (Gray and Satterly 1978 p. 141). Both of these reviews (i.e., the Walker and Schaffarzick, and the Gray and Satterly) clearly indicate the potential confounding of opportunity to learn with curriculum, instructional, or teaching variables.

Finally, despite the different conceptualizations of opportunity to learn some merger of the two conceptualizations seems worthwhile. Such a merger could conceivably result in a more powerful variable if the merger could maintain the strengths of both conceptualizations. This new conceptualization would focus on the amount of time allocated to the teaching of content underlying each of the items included on the achievement test.

A modification of Borg's approach could be used to measure this new variable. Each teacher would be given a copy of the test and asked to indicate the number of lessons (or class periods) spent teaching the content tested by each item. The length of each lesson (or class period) also could be ascertained by asking the teacher. The total number of hours and minutes spent teaching content directly related to the achievement test could be estimated by multiplying the total number of lessons by the number of minutes per lesson. Other measurement approaches, some of which involve direct observation of teachers, also could be used in this regard.

A single conceptualization of opportunity to learn coupled with the inclusion of the variable in classroom instructional research on a regular basis could have profound effects on our understanding of life in classrooms. This entry has provided some insights to guide researchers and practitioners in this direction.

See also: Content Coverage; Time; The Carroll Model

Bibliography

Armbruster B B, Stevens R J, Rosenshine B 1977 *Analyzing Content Coverage and Emphasis: A Study of Three Curricula and Two Tests*. Technical Report No. 26. Center for the Study of Reading, University of Illinois, Urbana, Illinois

Bennett N 1976 *Teaching Styles and Pupil Progress*. Open Books, London

Borg W R 1979 Teacher coverage of academic content and pupil achievement. *J. Educ. Psychol.* 71: 635–45

Carroll J B 1963 A model of school learning. *Teach. Coll. Rec.* 64: 723–33

Carroll J B 1974 Fitting a model of school learning to aptitude and achievement data over grade levels. In: Green D R (ed.) 1974 *The Aptitude–Achievement Distinction: Proceedings of the 2nd CTB/McGraw-Hill Conference on Issues in Educational Measurement, Carmel, California, 1973*. CTB/McGraw-Hill, Monterey, California

Carroll J B 1975 *The Teaching of French as a Foreign Language in Eight Countries*. Wiley, New York

Comber L C, Keeves J P 1973 *Science Education in Nineteen Countries: An Empirical Study*. Wiley, New York

Cooley W W, Leinhardt G 1980 The instructional dimensions study. *Educ. Eval. Policy Anal.* 2: 7–25

Dishaw M 1977 *Descriptions of Allocated Time to Content Areas for the A-B Period*. Beginning Teacher Evaluation Study (BTES) Technical Note Series, Technical Note N-2a. Far West Laboratory for Educational Research and Development, San Francisco, California

Fisher C W et al. 1980 Teaching behaviors, academic learning time, and student achievement. In: Denham C, Lieberman A (eds.) 1980 *Time to Learn*. National Institute of Education, Washington, DC

Gray J, Satterly D 1978 Time to learn? *Educ. Res.* 20: 137–41

Husén T (ed.) 1967 *International Study of Achievement in Mathematics: A Comparison of Twelve Countries*. Wiley, New York

Jenkins J R, Pany D 1978 Curriculum biases in reading achievement tests. *J. Read. Behav.* 10: 345–57

Leinhardt G, Seewald A M 1981 Overlap: What's tested, what's taught? *J. Educ. Meas.* 18: 85–96

Porter A C, Schmidt W H, Floden R E, Freeman D J 1978 *Impact on What? The Importance of Content Covered*. Educational Resources Information Centers (ERIC), National Institute of Education, Washington, DC. ERIC Document No. ED 155 215

Poyner H et al. 1977 *Final Report on the Instructional Dimensions Study*. National Institute of Education, Washington, DC

Schmidt W H 1978 *Measuring the Content of Instruction*. Educational Resources Information Centers (ERIC), National Institute of Education, Washington, DC. ERIC Document No. 171 783

Walker D F, Schaffarzick J 1974 Comparing curricula. *Rev. Educ. Res.* 44: 83–111

Wiley D E, Harnischfeger A 1974 Explosion of a myth: Quantity of schooling and exposure to instruction, major educational vehicles. *Educ. Res.* 4: 7–12

Time

W. J. Smyth

Time has always fascinated poets, philosophers, romantics, and science fiction writers. Educationists, however, are only just beginning to discover the full significance and impact of time as a variable in the education process. It is proving to be far more complex than first thought. Power (1980) expressed it neatly when he said:

. . . time is the coin of the realm in education. Education is a process which takes time, and which can and does occur at points in time. (p. 99)

He points out that time in learning has a transactional quality:

Time is what teachers must give if they are to help others learn. Time is what learners must spend if they are to "buy" the education they want. (p. 99)

Jackson's (1977) warning to proceed carefully should also be heeded. He argues that as the possibility is tested out that time may be the culprit that it is suspected to be in schools, it should also be remembered that time itself is valueless. Accordingly:

It acquires value chiefly because it marks the expenditure of a precious commodity: human life. Even though we often speak as though time were an object—something to be saved, wasted, spent, and so on—we must not lose sight of the fact that true wastage, at least in educational contexts, must be measured in terms of life experiences gained or foregone. (p. 38)

This article starts by sketching some of the possible dimensions and perspectives of time in school learning. Consideration then focuses on studies that have examined the relationship between learning time and pupil achievement, along with the predictability of this relationship in natural classroom settings. Specific attention is given to an interesting amalgam of variables known as "academic learning time" (ALT). Discussion highlights the robustness of academic learning time as a variable, particularly its relationship to achievement, as well as to teaching behaviours and aspects of classrooms that seem to have an impact on student achievement. Instructional time is, therefore, envisaged as providing a common frame in which to study both the actions and intentions of teachers, as well as the learning pursuits of pupils.

1. Dimensions of Time in School Learning

Bloom (1974) noted that while time has been a variable in the laboratory study of animal and human learning since the turn of the century, it is only recently that time has emerged as important in classroom studies. Both economists and instructional psychologists have begun to realize its usefulness in classroom research. Economists, for example, regard time as a resource or input into classrooms, and are interested in aspects of its productivity and substitutability. Psychologists, on the other hand, are interested in the way time features as a determinant in the learning process.

Current interest in time as a psychological learning variable in the classroom is directly attributable to Carroll's (1963) "Model of School Learning" (see *The Carroll Model*). Carroll proposed a model with five elements, three of which were time related: time needed, time allowed, and time spent on learning. According to Bloom (1974), by placing time as a central variable in school learning, Carroll generated a major

shift in emphasis in research on teaching. Indeed, as a way of describing classroom events and processes, time has a number of attractive features for classroom researchers. Bloom (1974) claims among the advantages the fact that time can be used with whatever macro (years and months) or micro (minutes and seconds) precision desired by the researcher. As a unit of measurement, time has also been said to have equality of units, an absolute zero, and a facility to permit comparisons, between individuals. Referring specifically to "engaged time", or the time during which a pupil is recorded as being actively occupied with ideas or educational materials, Marliave (1978) noted its utility in these words:

It offers immediate feedback on the strengths and weaknesses of instructional events. It pinpoints those student behaviours (or the lack thereof) that obstruct learning. Furthermore, it allows for continuous monitoring of learning events without disrupting or actually displacing those events (as testing does). (p. 20)

Learning time as conceived in recent classroom studies has the additional advantage of providing a language and a way of talking about events occurring in classrooms. It has facilitated the avoidance of the unfortunate aspect of many earlier studies of teaching which, while they looked closely at the teacher's behaviour, largely ignored the impact on pupils and learning.

Despite its obvious appeal as a research variable, instructional time is complex. Research by Karweit (1978), for example, found that, far from the relationship between time and learning being linear, under certain conditions for some kinds of pupils, the relationship is curvilinear. Put simply, researching the relationship between time and teaching/learning variables will not alone provide an understanding of classroom processes. Notwithstanding, there is a clear need for studies that provide detailed descriptive accounts of how teachers and schools allocate teaching time, how pupils are allowed to utilize that time qualitatively, and the classroom settings and associated teacher behaviours.

Much of the research on instructional time has been concerned with establishing connections between quantity of instruction and ultimate pupil achievement. Although the research has proceeded on a broken front the overall effect has been a "nested" approach (see Fig. 1). Attempts have been made to relate achievement and gross measures of learning time (years of schooling, number of days of schooling), through progressively more discrete measures of learning time (allocations of hours and minutes to specific content), to the most proximal indicator of achievement, pupil engagement on meaningful learning tasks, and content. The most significant research findings have occurred at the engaged time ("active learning time", "time-on-task") end of the nested spectrum. In particular the concept of "academic learning time", which is a subset of overall allocated learning time, and which is defined as "the time a pupil is engaged with instructional materials or

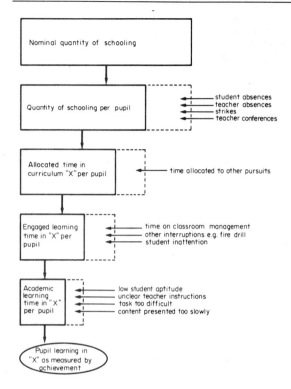

Figure 1
To show "nested" approach to research and instructional time[a]

a Adaptation of the Harnischfeger and Wiley model (1976)

---

activities that are of an easy level of difficulty (or produce few errors) for that student" (Berliner 1978), is a variable that has displayed a consistent relationship with both pupil achievement and certain teaching organization and behaviour.

Section 2 addresses some of the actual research findings within the context provided by Harnischfeger and Wiley's (1976) conceptualization.

2. Learning Time and Pupil Achievement

2.1 Nominal Amount of Schooling

Studies in various countries have pursued the conceptually simple presumption that more time produces higher levels of achievement. These studies show that the nexus between time and achievement is complex.

Several studies have found considerable variation between schools in the amount of instructional time, measured by length of school year. Harnischfeger and Wiley (1977) discovered variations in total school hours from 710 to 1,150 hours per annum. Clearly, pupils in some schools receive up to 50 percent more school time than others. Stallings and Kaskowitz's (1974) study of 120 United States schools found length of school day to

vary by up to two hours. Similar findings have emerged in the United Kingdom and elsewhere. The cumulative effect of these variations in exposure to schooling can amount to some students receiving substantially more schooling in a year than do other students.

Research that has sought to establish a connection between gross amount of school time and subsequent pupil achievement has produced some conflicting results. Harnischfeger and Wiley (1976) found the average number of hours of schooling per year to be positively and significantly related to reading and mathematics achievement. A study of high poverty United States schools by Lee et al. (1981), while finding considerable variation in the length of the school year (from 119 to 157 days), was unable to show a consistent relationship between gross amounts of school time and pupil achievement.

In summary, while macro measurements of time such as length of school year, term, and week, appeal to a sense of logic as being related to achievement, the available research does not bear out this proposition. It may be an illustration of where "more of the same" makes little difference. Part of the explanation for the apparently anomalous findings may have to do with the unit of analysis, rather than providing support for the view that time makes no difference. Many of the above analyses have used the school, rather than the classroom or individual pupils as the unit of analysis. Because of the possibility of compensating effects when using such macro measurements of instructional time, it just may be possible that modular studies conceal more than they disclose about the precise nature of "time" as an independent variable. What really matters, in the final analysis, is how effectively teachers are able to bring individual pupils into contact with learning materials and sustain that engagement.

2.2 Quantity of Schooling per Pupil

Several factors that make substantial inroads into the effective quantity of schooling received by pupils, such as student and/or teacher absences and school interruptions, have also been the subject of research studies. Again, the nature of some of this evidence is difficult to interpret because of mixed findings.

Studies have reported findings both for and against the effect of absenteeism on achievement. A series of United States studies in the 1960s focused on reading achievement in the first two years of schooling and all reported negative correlations between teacher and/ or student absences and achievement. A British study found that upper-middle-class children were unaffected by absences, while lower-middle-class children achieved less as a result of absences (see *Students' Social Backgrounds*). A more recent British study by Fogelman (1978) discovered attendance at school did affect achievement in reading, comprehension, and mathematics for students between the ages of 7 and 15 years. The study concluded that pupils with higher levels of school attendance achieve higher, and that social class was not a factor.

While studies have found a wide dispersion of absent days to be less harmful to achievement than prolonged absences, others have disclosed that absences from school affected achievement only when excessive. From their research, Summers and Wolfe (1975) claimed that achievement gains were affected by an amalgam of days present, unexcused absences, and lateness to classes. Absences were found to have a greater negative impact on student growth as the achievement levels of pupils increased. Other ̄researchers have argued about the difficulty of disentangling the interactive effects of community and student variables, from absences. Commenting on the directionality of the relationship between student absences and low achievement, even where it has been shown to exist, Karweit (1978) highlighted a salient point:

> Students could achieve poor marks because they missed important work during their absence. Alternatively, because students achieve poor marks and find school less rewarding, they could choose to be absent fairly often. Most likely poor marks and absenteeism are mutually reinforcing. (p. 213)

Although strong suspicions may exist, there is little to substantiate claims about the possible reduction of school time as a result of the actions of school administrators. Some of the evidence in the United States suggests that actual instructional time may be as little as two hours per day in some schools. Case study work by Tikunoff and Ward (1976) concluded that organizational restrictions on teacher time may be so substantial as to limit the effective school year to as little as 2.5 months of teaching, in some schools.

One particular study by Fredrick (1977) found that where high-achieving schools wasted 25 percent of available instructional time through student/teacher absences, interruptions, and student inattention, the low-achieving schools lost an alarming 49 percent of time through the same factors.

In summary, the evidence on quantity of schooling per pupil is encouraging albeit difficult to interpret on occasions. The relationship between time, as reflected in school attendance, and achievement, is generally in the direction that would have been expected even though it is not yet possible to make confident statements about the strength of that relationship. It would seem that pupil absences have differential effects depending on the age and ability levels of pupils, as well as upon the number and exact timing of absences. The nature of the reciprocating relationship between student absences and achievement is also still unclear. More research is also required on the extent to which school organizational arrangements cut into instructional time and how this impacts on achievement. A real problem with the interpretation of instructional time research at this level is the implicit, although somewhat unjustified presumption, that because school time is provided, learning does in fact occur. Obviously this aspect requires further investigation by refining "quantity of schooling" to the level of particular pupils within classrooms.

2.3 Time Allocated to Curriculum Content

One of the earliest reported educational research studies in the United States was conducted in 1897 to investigate whether spending 10 minutes or one hour had any noticeable impact on spelling achievement. Despite a finding of no difference, a large number of studies have since pursued the allocated time–achievement relationship.

One reason for the continuing research interest in this area has to do with the discretionary decision-making power vested in schools and individual teachers, and the way they spread time across various curriculum areas. Studies have in fact revealed substantial variability in school time allocated to particular subjects. Research by Fisher et al. (1980) found some teachers allocated twice as much testing time to some activities, compared with other teachers. This research also suggested that some second-grade pupils (aged 7) may be receiving, on average, less than 130 hours combined in reading and mathematics in a school year. During an eight week observational period some students received as much as 39 hours more instruction in basic skill subjects, than did other students. Other United States studies have confirmed the existence of what amounts to quite inequitable treatment in terms of instructional time allocations to certain areas of the curriculum. Harnischfeger and Wiley (1977) reported that children in some fifth-grade reading classes (aged 10) were receiving twelve-fold more instructional time on certain "fundamentals" than others, and that classrooms with higher achievement scores also tended to be the ones with greater allocated reading time. Studies in the United Kingdom have revealed similar disparities in the amount of instruction received by students across curriculum areas. Not to be overlooked also in this discussion of allocated time, is the likely impact of out-of-school time, or homework. Coulter (1979) has made the point that in the renewed interest in time as a factor in school learning, researchers have paid little attention to time spent learning outside of school as a factor in achievement.

Quite apart from the variation problem, research seeking a connection between allocated time and subsequent achievement has produced conflicting findings. Guthrie et al. (1976), for example, found no relationship between time allocated to reading and reading achievement. Similarly, Welch and Bridgman (1968) found that the amount of time a teacher spent on a unit of instruction did not necessarily act as an accurate indicator of likely student success on that unit of work. Felsenthal and Kirsch (1978) also reported no significant difference between time allocated, and reading performance in elementary classrooms. Smith (1976) too was unable to demonstrate that students who received greater allocations of time performed any better in social studies than other students. While these results may appear rather puzzling at first, it may at least partially reflect the fact that achievement may be closely connected to student ability rather than simply being dependent on amount of time allocated to instruction.

Several studies have found a positive correlation between allocated time and achievement. A forerunner of the Fisher et al. (1980) study reported "qualified support" for the hypothesis that time allocated to particular content leads to more learning. Both Vivars (1976) and Kidder et al. (1975) found a positive relationship between allocated instructional time, and reading scores. The problem with a number of other studies that have found a relationship in the same direction is that it is difficult to assess their importance because of the impact of an amalgam of variables (school attendance, length of school week, homework time) reflecting "opportunity to learn".

In summary, it is difficult to make firm statements about the allocated time–achievement nexus. This is due, in part, to the fact that many of these studies have relied on teacher self-reports of time allocations. Some doubt surrounds the validity with which teachers can report the way they allocate time to specific curriculum areas, and to components within those areas. Teachers are invariably so busy handling the multiplicity of classroom interactions, that their absorption with this task effectively prevents them from accurately estimating how they allocate class time. The studies reviewed here support the conclusion reached by Rosenshine and Berliner (1978) that ". . . in studies which consider allocated time, most of the results tend to be non-significant" (p. 6).

This is not to suggest that time makes no difference; rather, it points to the need to refine our research methodology and be somewhat more discrete in the way we examine time as a learning variable. As one commentator noted, the teacher may be analogous to a broadcasting station where not everyone is "tuned in". It may be more realistic to regard the teacher as communicating with various pupils for sporadic periods, with pupils responding to other stimuli for the remainder of the time. To find out how pupils learn while teachers teach, it is necessary to look more closely at what occurs during those periods of time when learners are known to be actively engaged on learning tasks.

2.4 Engaged Learning Time

A point sometimes overlooked is the fact that the definition of instructional time is important. Indeed, engaged time appears to be a more valid estimate of instructional time than allocated time because time made available for inspection may or may not be used efficiently and may or may not be spent on appropriate instructional tasks.

Focusing on pupil engaged time has long held appeal for both teachers and researchers. As Jackson (1968) noted:

> From a logical point of view few topics would seem to have greater relevance for the teacher's work. Certainly

no educational goals are more immediate than those that concern the establishment and maintenance of the student's absorption in the task at hand. Almost all other objectives are dependent for their accomplishment upon the attainment of this basic condition. (p. 85)

Furthermore, the mere volume of research on engaged time extending from the early 1930s, underscores its perceived importance as a variable in the teaching/learning process. The persistence with it speaks not only about the importance of the variable, but also attests to its robustness. This becomes apparent when the three broad historical phases of research on pupil engagement are looked at:

(a) An early era in which both the problem and the approach were mechanistic and concerned with issues of efficiency and effectiveness as they related to teaching.

(b) A modern era where the preoccupation was with establishing a correlational association with the outcome measure of pupil achievement, and where the methodology reflected the need to verify data collected by observational means.

(c) A recent era where the nexus with achievement has been generally established, and where current efforts are being directed at isolating associated teaching and classroom-related variables (Smyth 1981a p. 135).

Although this categorization is arbitrary, it does serve to demonstrate the changing focus on pupil engagement as a research variable.

3. Early Studies

During the early part of the twentieth century a number of studies in the United States focused on pupil engagement (or attention) as a serious object of research concern. A point that emerges clearly from these studies is that they were certainly a "product of their time". Arising as they did during the "scientific management" era of the 1920s these particular studies of pupil engagement were pursued for reasons relating to efficiency, effectiveness, and productivity. The search was fairly obviously for a reliable index of teaching effectiveness. Pupil attention appealed as a logical, measurable, and plausible way of rating teaching performance. Notwithstanding their underlying purpose, these studies did succeed in making an important methodological contribution to research in the area.

The emphasis in these pioneering studies was on the use of group attention scores as an indicator of teacher effectiveness. Correlations were established between principals' assessments of teachers' classroom abilities, and recorded class attention scores. The researchers focused upon the eye movement and body position of pupils during normal class lessons, and from this they developed informative attention-score profiles of students who were, or were not learning. The other major development was a start on research on pupil attention aimed at predicting likely student achievement. Even as early as the 1930s there were encouraging indications from the research that pupils who were inattentive performed poorly on tests.

As the technique of measuring pupil attentiveness grew, along with the calculations of class attention scores, so too did the number of studies challenging whether observational means could conclusively establish pupil attention and indeed whether such data were robust enough to be used as indications of teacher effectiveness. Details of these studies are reported elsewhere (Smyth 1980, 1981a).

In summary, while the purpose for which they were undertaken may be questioned, there were a number of interesting early studies of pupil attention. Their intent was not to establish a nexus between attention per se and achievement, but rather to expand the repertoire of methods for measuring the effectiveness of teaching performance. As a by-product, these studies made some salient methodological findings, as well as underscoring the importance of pupil attention as an indicator of classroom activity.

4. Modern Studies

A criticism often levelled at education is its notorious susceptibility to fads. Educational research is no exception in that it tends to focus on issues that are fashionable, only to be replaced when new trends or concerns emerge. What is refreshing about research on engaged time is the fact that it has persisted despite changes in ideology and philosophy. Admittedly, this research area has undergone substantial changes in direction and emphasis.

The 1950s represented an important phase in the development of research on pupil engagement or attention, with two thrusts becoming evident. There was one group of studies that explored the connection between pupils' observable classroom pursuits and after-the-event self-reporting of mental processes. These studies were significant because of their attempt to establish congruence between the overt and covert aspects of learning, using novel introspective research methods. The other research thrust at this time aimed to establish a relationship of a different kind; namely, the connection between pupil task engagement and subsequent achievement.

Impetus for the first of these developments came from Bloom (1953) and his students who used a stimulated recall technique to explore whether student thoughts were on-task or off-task during lessons. It was argued that by observing students while keeping an audio recording of the lesson (video in later studies) and replaying this to students after the lesson with intensive interviewing about their recollections of their thoughts, it would be possible to obtain a more accurate indicator of cognitive attention. Although Bloom claimed success

with this as a method of gauging attention, others disputed it.

Also beginning during this period were a number of studies aimed at conclusively establishing the nexus between engagement and achievement. These studies were remarkably successful in that the hypothesis that time actively engaged on learning tasks would predict achievement, held for pupils of varying ages, at different levels of schooling, and across varied subject matter. Although there were variations in the strength of this relationship between studies, there was no longer any serious questioning of the impact per se of engagement on achievement.

Several recent studies have both broadened and deepened the engagement–achievement nexus, although there are still unanswered questions about the strength of the relationship and its consistency across all kinds of pupils, in all curriculum areas, and at all grade levels. Fisher et al. (1980), in one of the longest and most extensive pieces of educational research undertaken anywhere (the Beginning Teacher Evaluation Study), found a consistent positive relationship between engagement and achievement in reading and mathematics at the elementary-school level. In the Beginning Teacher Evaluation Study where engagement was one of a cluster of variables described as academic learning time (ALT), Fisher et al. (1980) found the variable of ALT accounted for between 11 percent and 20 percent of residual variance in achievement. Lee et al. (1981), in another United States study reported support for their hypothesis that greater attentiveness during lessons enhances achievement, although many other factors operated to affect the strength of this connection.

Although interesting, what these correlational studies fail to explain is the precise nature of pupil engagement and the variables which promote, and are otherwise associated, with it.

What a number of these studies uncovered was that pupil ability was a confounding factor when considering engagement and achievement. One study that found little difference between engagement levels of high- and low-achieving pupils prompted the suggestion that engagement alone is insufficient to account for success and that task appropriateness and difficulty may be salient variables. Rusnock and Brandler (1979) and Smyth (1979) both found quite distinct patterns of off-task behaviour between high- and low-ability children. Where low-ability students tended to interrupt academic pursuits with off-task behaviour, high-ability students tended to finish an academic task prior to engaging in distractions. Other studies have shown engagement to vary substantially according to ability level, curriculum content, type of activity, and class grouping.

Understanding engagement and its variability will possibly come as comprehensive profiles of learning students are developed (Fisher et al. 1980). Ecological studies of pupil engagement by Stodolsky (1979), Grannis (1978), and Smyth (1979), have helped to develop a clearer understanding of how pupils react to and interpret different kinds of classroom settings in ways that influence engagement. Other studies are interesting because of the finding that even after allowing for ability levels, engagement did not consistently relate to achievement. These particular studies highlight a number of important teaching behaviours.

5. Academic Learning Time: An Alterable Variable

In contrast to earlier educational research, recent efforts have tended to focus on variables that have both a demonstrated impact on learning, and which can be altered by classroom teachers. To change the length of the school year, or the hours available per day or week, requires major legal and policy decisions; even then, research considering such variables is equivocal about their impact on achievement. However, active learning time or pupil time-on-task has been shown to be both a potent influence on pupil achievement, and a readily controllable variable. Clearly, available or allocated time is important because it represents the opportunity for pupils to learn; but it is not a crucial variable on its own. It is also clear that time-on-task alone is not sufficient for learning to occur. Some consideration must be paid by the teacher to the appropriateness of the task so that engagement is meaningful and can constitute a valued learning experience.

Fisher et al. (1980) in the Beginning Teacher Evaluation Study have conceptualized and researched at the elementary-school level an amalgam of variables described as "academic learning time" (ALT). They define it simply as the amount of time a pupil spends attending to academic tasks while performing at a high rate of success. Because of the demonstrated relationship between ALT and achievement, the more ALT a pupil accumulates, the more the pupil can be presumed to be learning. The components of ALT are: (a) allocated time; (b) engagement rate, and (c) success rate. Allocated time is the amount of time the pupil has available to work, and it is this aspect within the classroom which constitutes the pupil's opportunity to learn. Engagement rate represents the percentage of allocated time during which the pupil appears to be attending to the learning task. That portion of engaged time during which the pupil experiences a high success rate (i.e., with few errors) amounts to optimal learning conditions. Success rate is defined as the percentage of available instructional time that the pupil spends experiencing "high", "medium", and "low" levels of success on learning tasks. This cluster of variables has been shown to be quite consistently and positively related to pupil achievement (Fisher et al. 1980).

An important implication emerging from the Beginning Teacher Evaluation Study research is the highlighted need for teachers to be sensitive to the variables comprising ALT and the way in which they influence learning. How teachers allocate learning time in class,

the way they allow pupils to utilize the available time, and the meaningfulness or value of that time to individual pupils, are important ingredients in the total learning process. Fisher et al. (1980), for example, found that teachers who monitored short-term outcomes of pupil classroom learning, were able to enhance levels of pupil ALT and thus learning. In particular, high levels of interactive teaching, in contrast to seatwork, were found to relate consistently to high ALT. Teacher feedback to pupils about the correctness of responses was found to relate to enhanced ALT, as was the clarity of teacher directions on how to proceed with assigned learning tasks. Other predictors of high ALT were the teacher's emphasis on academic goals in class, and the teacher's ability to assess pupil skill levels and prescribe learning tasks of appropriate difficulty. Variables found by Fisher et al. (1980) to relate negatively to pupil ALT were teacher provision of explanation in response to pupil need once an activity had commenced, and frequent teacher reprimands to misbehaving pupils.

The encouraging aspect to these findings is their teacher controllable nature. Structuring lessons so pupils are aware of aims and objectives, communicating these so pupils understand the teacher's work expectations and contingency plans upon completion of set work, are aspects that successful teachers have always practised. This research confirms the desirability of preactive rather than reactive teaching (see *Proactive Teaching*; *Reactive Teaching*), the communication of clear directions to students, with adequate attention to feedback on progress. When students are unclear where the lesson is headed, where there are continual exhortations to "get back to work", these are hallmarks of structural deficiencies in the lesson that reflect a need to look at the level of interactive teaching, task difficulty, and feedback being provided to students.

Experimental research by Arlin (1979) confirmed that "activity flow" in the way teachers handle transitions from one teaching activity to the next, holds important implications for levels of pupil engagement. Off-task behaviour by pupils tended to be higher during transitions than at any other time during the lesson. This is another area where teachers can clearly monitor their own practice. Further support for the importance of teacher behaviour as a determinant of pupil engagement was found in a study by Bell and Davidson (1976). After allowing for student ability, what the teacher did was found to be the most important factor associated with level of pupil activity.

Anderson (1981) summed up the importance of these teacher controllable variables in the phrase "timing as managing". His argument is that teachers who employ certain teaching strategies at the correct moment, are effective classroom managers (Smyth 1981b) who have classes that learn (see *Classroom Management*). Utilizing Kounin's (1970) research, Anderson suggests that effective teachers display "withitness", or are able to prevent disruptive class situations by intervening with the right student(s) at the right time. Likewise, being able to maintain lesson "momentum" really amounts to diagnosing the right time or the teachable moment for students. The provision of "group alerting" comments designed to maintain student suspense in the lesson, is another aspect of timing. According to Anderson bad timing results in more time on disciplinary aspects, and hence less for instructionally productive tasks. In brief, his thesis is that better timing on the part of the teacher will reduce the amount of time students need in order to learn.

Studies of the relationship between learning, achievement, time on-task, and teacher behaviour assume added significance in the light of studies that suggest teacher behaviour *can* be changed to enhance levels of on-task engagement. Borg and Ascione (1979) found in a "controlled" experiment that teachers could be trained to alter their teaching styles so as to increase levels of pupil engagement. Berliner (1978) confirmed that 12 hours of workshop contact were sufficient to produce changes in teaching behaviour of this type. Ingersoll et al. (1980) also reported success in training teachers to change their behaviour so as to monitor pupil behaviour in respect of learning tasks. Indeed, there are increasing proliferations of materials that provide training for teachers on how to alter and monitor levels of class engaged time.

6. Conclusion

This article has attempted to highlight the importance of time in school learning. Although time has emerged as a prominent variable in educational research it is increasingly evident that it is a much more complex variable than initially thought. Research studies cited here were viewed within the context of a "nested" approach that started with gross measurements of time (such as nominal amount of schooling, actual quantity of schooling per pupil, and allocated time per pupil in curriculum areas) through to progressively more refined indicators (such as academic learning time). While predictable relationships were found to exist between macro measurements of time and pupil achievement, the consistency and strength of these relationships are still problematic.

On the other hand, the large number of studies that have pursued the connection between pupil engaged time and achievement, have established remarkable consistency between pupil engagement and achievement-related outcome measures of learning. This appears to be so for a variety of pupil ability levels, grade levels, and curriculum areas.

Coupled with the pupil engagement–achievement research has been that which has isolated alterable teaching behaviour and classroom variables that enhance pupil engagement. Research in the areas of teacher development and training has also demonstrated that teachers can, without too much trauma, change their teaching styles to achieve these ends. The overall utility of tracing alterable causal variables such

as the ones looked at here, was summed up by Berliner (1979):

> Without turning classes into authoritarian factories of learning, many teachers can improve their effectiveness by attending to these variables and re-organizing classroom practices to maximize teaching time and learning time—resources over which they have considerable personal control. (p. 134)

See also: The Carroll Model; Opportunity to Learn; Planning

Bibliography

Anderson L 1981 Time and timing. Paper presented to Invitational Conference on Instructional Time. Northwestern University, Chicago

Arlin M 1979 Teacher transitions can disrupt time flow in classrooms. *Am. Educ. Res. J.* 16: 42–56

Bell M, Davidson C 1976 Relationships between pupil on-task performance and pupil achievement. *J. Educ. Res.* 69: 172–76

Berliner D C 1978 Changing academic learning time: Clinical interventions in four classrooms. Paper presented to the Annual Meeting of the American Educational Research Association, Toronto

Berliner D C 1979 Tempus educare. In: Peterson P L, Walberg H J (eds.) 1979 *Research on Teaching: Concepts, Findings and Implications.* McCutchan, Berkeley, California

Bloom B S 1953 Thought process in lectures and discussions. *Gen. Educ.* 7: 160–9

Bloom B S 1974 Time and learning. *Am. Psychol.* 29: 682–88

Borg W R, Ascione F R 1979 Changing on-task, off-task and disruptive pupil behavior in elementary mainstreaming classrooms. *J. Educ. Res.* 72: 243–52

Carroll J B 1963 A model of school learning. *Teach. Coll. Rec.* 64: 723–33

Coulter F 1979 Homework: A neglected research area. *Br. Educ. Res. J.* 5: 21–33

Felsenthal H, Kirsch I 1978 Variations in teachers' management of and time spent on reading instruction: Effects on student learning. Paper presented to the Annual Meeting of the American Educational Research Association, Toronto

Fisher C, Berliner D C, Filby N, Marliave R, Cahen L, Dishaw M 1980 Teacher behaviors, academic learning time, and student achievement: An overview. In: Denham C, Lieberman A (eds.) 1980 *Time to Learn.* National Institute of Education, Washington, DC, pp. 7–32

Fogelman K 1978 School attendance, attainment and behaviour. *Br. J. Educ. Psychol.* 48: 148–58

Fredrick W 1977 Use of classroom time in high schools above or below the median reading score. *Urban Educ.* 11: 459–64

Grannis J C 1978 Task engagement and the consistency of pedagogical controls: An ecological study of differently structured classroom settings. *Curric. Inq.* 8: 3–30

Guthrie J, Martuza V, Seiffert M 1976 *Impacts of Instructional Time in Reading.* International Reading Association, Newark, Delaware

Harnischfeger A, Wiley D E 1976 The teaching/learning process in elementary schools: A synoptic view. *Curric. Inq.* 6: 5–43

Harnischfeger A, Wiley D E 1977 Time allocations in 5th grade reading. Paper presented to Annual Meeting of the American Educational Research Association, New York

Ingersoll G, Gliessman D, Lund J, Ghassemloian M 1980 Training in monitoring classroom behavior. Paper presented to the Annual Meeting of the American Educational Research Association, Boston

Jackson P W 1968 *Life in Classrooms*. Holt, Rinehart and Winston, New York

Jackson P 1977 Looking into education's crystal ball. *Instructor* 87: 38

Karweit N 1978 The organization of time in schools: Time scales and learning. Paper presented to National Invitational Conference on School Organization and Effects, San Diego, California

Kidder S, O'Reilly R, Kiesling H 1975 Quantity and quality of instruction: Empirical investigations. Paper presented to the Annual Meeting of the American Educational Research Association, Washington, DC

Kounin J S 1970 *Discipline and Group Management in Classrooms*. Holt, Rinehart and Winston, New York

Lee D, Carriere R, MacQueen A, Poynor L, Rogers M 1981 Successful practices in high-poverty schools. Technical Report No. 16 from The Study of the Sustaining Effects of Compensatory Education on Basic Skills, System Development Corporation, Santa Monica

Marliave R 1978 Academic learning time and achievement: The validation of a measure of ongoing student engagement and task difficulty. Paper presented to Annual Meeting of the American Educational Research Association, Toronto

Power C 1980 Ab initio ad finem: Dr Who and alternative ways of organizing time in education. In: Australian Council for Educational Administration (eds.) 1980 *Alternative Ways of Organizing Education*. Australian Schools Commission, Canberra

Rosenshine B V, Berliner D C 1978 Academic time engaged. *Br. J. Teach. Educ.* 4: 3–26

Rusnock M, Brandler N 1979 Time off-task: Implications for learning. Paper presented to the Annual Meeting of the American Educational Research Association, San Francisco

Smith N M 1976 The relationship between time allotted to social studies instruction and student achievement in fifth grade classes of the tri-county area of Southern Maryland (Unpublished doctoral dissertation, University of Maryland 1976) *Dissertations Abstracts International* 1977 28: 3274A (University Microfilms No. 77-26,539)

Smyth W J 1979 An ecological analysis of pupil use of academic learning time. Unpublished doctoral dissertation, University of Alberta

Smyth W J 1980 Pupil engaged learning time: Concepts, findings and implications. *Aust. J. Educ.* 24: 225–45

Smyth W J 1981a Research on classroom management: Studies of pupil engaged learning time as a special but instructive case. *J. Educ. Teach.* 7: 127–48

Smyth W J 1981b Teacher-as-executive: Managing pupil engagement during learning. In: Lomas L et al. (eds.) 1981 *Classroom Processes*. Deakin University, Geelong, Victoria

Stallings J, Kaskowitz D 1974 Follow-through classroom observation evaluation, 1972–3. Stanford Research Institute, Menlo Park, California

Stodolsky S 1979 Ecological features of fifth grade math and social studies classes and their relation to student involvement. Paper presented to the Annual Meeting of the American Educational Research Association, San Francisco

Summers A, Wolfe B 1975 Which school resources help learning? Efficiency and equity in Philadelphia public schools. *Business Rev.*

Tikunoff W, Ward B 1976 Some selected findings from three studies. Far West Laboratory for Educational Research and Development, San Francisco, California

Vivars T 1976 The effect of a fixed lower student-staff ratio utilizing paraprofessionals and variable fixed time changes on reading scores of grade six students with deficiencies in basic reading skills. Unpublished doctoral dissertation, Virginia State University

Welch W W, Bridgman R G 1968 Physics achievement gains as a function of teaching duration. *Sch. Sci. Math.* 8: 449–54

Logical Operations

R. E. Sutton; R. H. Ennis

There are a variety of ways of viewing logical operations in the classroom. In this entry three approaches will be discussed: deductive logic, logic-of-teaching, and critical thinking.

In deductive logic the primary concern is whether arguments are valid, that is, whether a conclusion follows necessarily from its premises. Deductive logic permeates other classroom operations that are logical in the broad sense of the word. For example, it is involved in testing hypotheses, some types of explaining, and identifying assumptions. The logic-of-teaching approach focuses on verbal transactions in the classroom, and categories include definition, explanation, and justification. Critical thinking is concerned with the ability to deal reasonably and reflectively with questions about what to believe or do. Emphasis here is on dispositions and abilities that critical thinkers need. These provide possible goals for classroom instruction.

There are at least two other important approaches to logical operations in the classroom: the Piagetian approach, and Bloom's *Taxonomy* approach. Piaget created a new discipline of study called genetic epistemology. The aim of this discipline is to discover psychological structures that underlie the formation of concepts fundamental to science. Logic plays a central role within Piagetian epistemology. It is the underlying link which connects the diversity of sciences. Piaget believed that logic is the key to the individual's understanding of nature. It is the presence of logical structures in children which permits them to reconstruct and understand the physical, biological, and social worlds. The logic of infants is much more primitive than that of nursery- or elementary-school children. It is only in adolescence that a true formal logical system comparable to that constructed by logicians develops, according to Piaget.

Piaget believed that age-related differences exist in the cognitive and logical capacity of individuals. To account for these he proposed a series of distinct, but interrelated cognitive models which are commonly called stages. It is the last two stages, concrete and formal operations, which have the most relevance to logical operations in the classroom. There is a large body of theoretical and empirical literature based on the Piagetian approach, and this is presented in other sections in this Encyclopedia, so it will not be examined in detail here. However, the Piagetian approach is an important one in considering logical operations in the classroom.

Bloom's *Taxonomy of Educational Objectives* (1956) provides a taxonomy of "intended (goal) behaviors." "Intended behaviors" are units which consist of a problem and correct response. The aim of this work was to provide a comprehensive taxonomy that would reflect levels of thought in teachers. Six levels of behavior were delineated. These are knowledge (interpreted as recall), comprehension, application, analysis, synthesis, and evaluation. These levels are assumed to possess a cumulative, hierarchical structure increasing in complexity.

One could use Bloom's *Taxonomy* to classify logical operations in at least two different ways. First, it can be used as a scheme for classifying logical operations that are goals. For example, the logical operation "judging the bearing of information on the credibility of a source," would be classified at the highest level, evaluation. Second, the *Taxonomy* has been used as a basis for classifying classroom dialogues. In this approach the actual occurrence of these logical operations in the classroom is reported.

Bloom's *Taxonomy* is one of the best-known works on education and is important in considering logical operations in the classroom. Because it is examined elsewhere in this Encyclopedia it will not be discussed in detail in this article.

For each of the three approaches that will be considered in greater detail (deductive logic, logic of teaching, critical thinking) its conceptual framework will be presented first. Then studies relevant to the conceptual framework will be summarized. Finally, prescriptive elements, which include educational goals associated with the approach and implications for curriculum and instruction will be presented.

1. Deductive Logic Approach

1.1 Conceptual Framework

The fundamental question in deductive logic is whether a conclusion follows necessarily from its premises. If it does, the argument is deductively valid. If not, then it is deductively invalid. There is a strong tradition in education and psychology that distinguishes between two types of logic: class and conditional logic.

(a) *Class logic*. This type of logic is concerned with inferences based on relationships among classes and their members. The following argument is a deductively valid class logic argument. (The line separates the premises from the conclusion and the symbolic form of the argument is given on the right.)

Example 1:
(All) thin rods are flexible. (All) *A*'s are *B*'s.
The rod labeled "*S*" is not flexible. *n* is not a *B*.

So, the rod labeled "*S*" is not thin. So, *n* is not an *A*.

There are two classes mentioned here: thin rods and flexible things. (Note that the predicate adjective "flexible" is converted to the class, "flexible things," represented by "*B*'s" in the symbolic form.) The first premise holds that the first class (thin rods) is included in the second class (flexible things), assuming that the word "all" is intended at the beginning. The second premise holds that the rod labeled "*S*" is not a member of the second class. Because of these two relationships the rod labeled "*S*" cannot be a member of the first class (thin rods). The conclusion follows necessarily from the premises. The argument, therefore, is deductively valid.

(b) *Conditional logic*. This type of logic is concerned with the relations between subject–predicate units (henceforth "S–P units"). They are often joined together by logical operators like "if," "then," and "or," and can be negated by "not." For example, "The rod labeled '*S*' is thin" is an S–P unit, as is "The rod labeled '*S*' is flexible." These units can be joined together by "if" and "then" as follows: "If the rod labeled '*S*' is thin, then the rod labeled '*S*' is flexible." This can be shortened to "If the rod labeled '*S*' is thin, it is flexible" without changing the meaning.

The following is a deductively valid conditional argument:

Example 2:
If the rod labeled "*S*" is thin, it is flexible. If *p*, then *q*.
The rod labeled "*S*" is not flexible. Not *q*.

So, the rod labeled "*S*" is not thin. So, not *q*.

Examples 1 and 2 differ in the first premise. In example 1 the first premise relates two classes. In example 2 the first premise relates two S–P units by using the words "if" and "then."

The first premise in example 2 makes a statement about only one rod. This argument would still be conditional logic if the first premise were replaced by the generalization, "If any rod is thin, then it is flexible." This generalization contains two S–P units joined by logical operators.

In common logical terminology the S–P units of the first premise of example 2 are called "propositions." The S–P units of the parallel generalization are called "propositional functions." Piaget's formulation of what he calls "propositional logic" actually deals with propositional functions.

1.2 Dimensions of Deductive Logic Ability

Three different dimensions of deductive logic ability will be delineated: a logical–principle dimension, a content dimension, and a complexity dimension.

(a) *The logical–principle dimension.* To be proficient in the logical–principle dimension is to be able to tell whether four basic moves are deductively valid. A variety of names and classifications of principles exist. Examples 1 and 2, which are valid moves, can, because of their similarities, be grouped together under the label, "particular contraposition," though one is class logic and the other conditional. (Example 2 has two other names: "*modus tollens*" and "denying the consequent.")

The following are examples of deductively invalid arguments:

Example 3 (class logic):

(All) thin rods are flexible.	(All) *A*'s are *B*'s.
The rod labeled "*R*" is flexible.	*n* is a *B*.
So, the rod labeled "*R*" is thin.	So, *n* is an *A*.

Example 4 (conditional logic):

If the rod labeled "*R*" is thin, then it is flexible.	If *p*, then *q*.
The rod labeled "*R*" is flexible.	*q*.
So, the rod labeled "*R*" is thin.	So, *p*.

Because of their similarities, one can call both example 3 and example 4 "particular conversion," but again there are a variety of names. Arguments of the form of example 4 are also sometimes called "affirming the consequent."

Table 1 gives the four basic moves in their class and conditional versions. Two are deductively valid and two deductively invalid. The forms of examples 1–4 can be located in Table 1: examples 1 and 2 are particular contrapositions, class and conditional respectively (the second row). Examples 3 and 4 are particular conversions, class and conditional respectively (the third row).

Deductively valid reasoning is airtight, and thus always acceptable. Some deductively invalid reasoning is acceptable as well. Most scientific conclusions, interpretations of a text, historical interpretations (and even claims about what happened) are supported by arguments that are deductively invalid, even though they usually contain parts that are deductively valid.

(b) *The content dimension.* The content of the premises and conclusions influences our ability to handle arguments. Individuals can sometimes understand and use logical principles when the content is concrete and innocuous, but are not able to do so with other types of content. One aspect of the content which is important is the individual's belief in the premises. A premise can be believed, considered as a hypothesis without belief or disbelief, or can be disbelieved. The individual's prior commitment to the conclusion is another aspect which may be important. A third is the presence or absence

Table 1

The forms of four basic class and conditional moves[a]

Class	Conditional	Name
Valid moves:		
All *A*'s are *B*'s *n* is an *A*	If *p*, then *q* *p*	Detachment
So, *n* is a *B*	So, *q*	
All *A*'s are *B*'s *n* is not a *B*	If *p*, then *q* no *q*	Particular contraposition
So, *n* is not an *A*	So, not *p*	
Invalid moves:		
All *A*'s are *B*'s *n* is a *B*	If *p*, then *q* *q*	Particular conversion
So, *n* is an *A*	So, *p*	
All *A*'s are *B*'s *n* is not an *A*	If *p*, then *q* not *p*	Particular inversion
So, *n* is not a *B*	So, not *q*	

a For the sake of brevity the table does not include basic moves employing the logical operators, "or" and "not both," which can be defined in terms of those given (assuming conjunction)

of symbolic material, a fourth the degree of familiarity of the content to the individual, and a fifth aspect is the presence of irrelevant content. A final aspect is the degree of abstractness of the content. Competent deductive reasoning involves the ability to operate with all types of content.

(c) *The complexity dimension.* A third dimension of logical operations is complexity. Two elements of complexity are the number of connections and intricacy. Consider examples 5 and 6:

Example 5:

If this thermometer is put in that liquid:	If *p*;
then, if the temperature is 20° C,	then, if *q*,
then the thermometer will read 20.	then *r*.

Example 6:

If this thermometer is put in that liquid, then it will read 20;	If *p*, then *r*;
and if the thermometer reads 20,	and if *r*,
then you will find it comfortable.	then *s*.

Example 6 has three connections: two "if-then" connections and one conjunction connection. Example 5 has only two connections: two "if-then" connections. So example 6 has a greater number of connections. However, example 5 has greater intricacy because of the embedding of one "if-then" within the other. This embedding is clearer if implication is represented with arrows: $p \rightarrow (q \rightarrow r)$.

The move from the conjunction of two "if-then"

connections, as in example 6, (i.e., if p, then r; if r, then s) to a third "if-then" connection, "if p, then s," is called transitivity. It is more complex than the detachments of which it is mostly comprised.

In addition to the number of connections and intricacy, other elements of complexity include the extent of nonstandard order of the parts of an argument (e.g., the appearance of the conclusion in the middle of an argument, and a reversal of the order of premises in the just-given transitivity move), and the extent of inclusion of negatives.

Understanding complex arguments is essential in modern life. This can be seen by examining such things as insurance policies, income tax forms, almost any contemporary law, a will, a loan or mortgage agreement, and rules of eligibility for social welfare benefits.

In the next section some studies concerning individual's performance on deductive logical arguments will be summarized. Another thorough review from a different perspective appears in Evans (1982).

1.3 Studies

(a) *Class and conditional logic.* Several studies suggest that class logic is somewhat easier than conditional logic. Roberge and Paulus (1971) tested 263 students in grades 4, 6, 8, and 10 (age range: 9 to 16 years) and found scores significantly higher ($p < 0.05$) on class logic items. Ennis and Paulus (1965) reported class logic scores higher than conditional logic for 4th through 12th graders (ages 9 to 18). Hill (1961) tested 6 to 8-year-olds and reported the same trend. However, Kuhn (1977), using 1st through 4th graders (ages 6 to 10) as subjects found no significant difference in class and conditional logic.

While class logic appears to be easier than conditional logic, performance on both types of logic increases gradually with age (Ennis and Paulus 1965, Roberge and Paulus 1971). First graders do appear to have some understanding of conditional and class logic (Hill 1961, Kuhn 1977) and this understanding increases until at least adolescence (Ennis and Paulus 1965, Roberge and Paulus 1971). However, even late adolescents have not fully mastered conditional and class logic (Evans 1982).

(b) *Logical–principle dimension.* One of the best established findings is that principles of invalidity (e.g., conversion) are more difficult than principles of validity (Ceraso and Provitera 1971, Donaldson and Withrington 1963, Ennis 1971, Evans 1982). This finding applies to all of the studied ages (ages 6 through the late teens).

While the principles of validity are easier than the principles of invalidity, there are differences in difficulty among valid principles. Studies have shown that detachment is easier than particular contraposition and transitivity (Ennis and Paulus 1965).

Performance on the principles of detachment, transitivity, particular inversion, and particular conversion increases through childhood and adolescence (Ennis and Paulus 1965, Wildman and Fletcher 1977). This is not the case for contraposition. Increases have been found up to about 3rd grade (age 8) (Kodroff and Roberge 1975, Taplin et al. 1974), but a leveling off or decrease has been observed from early to late adolescence (Ennis and Paulus 1965, Wildman and Fletcher 1977). Wason (1968) found college students had special difficulty with particular contraposition. Why such difficulty occurs in older adolescents and young adults is not known.

(c) *Content dimension.* The research shows fairly consistently that prior beliefs about premises and/or conclusions tend to reduce success in judging arguments when the belief is in conflict with the direction of the argument (e.g. Roberge and Paulus 1971, Wason and Johnson-Laird 1972). The research does not distinguish between difficulty introduced by the lack of belief in the premises and the lack of belief in the conclusions.

Arguments containing unfamiliar and abstract content and symbolic content have generally been found to be more difficult than material without such content (Wilkins 1928, Wason and Johnson-Laird 1972). As abstract content is usually unfamiliar, it is difficult to know whether the abstractness itself creates difficulty, or whether the difficulty is with the associated unfamiliarity.

Burt (1919) found in his various studies of children's reasoning ability that irrelevant content made deductive judgments more difficult. However, Kodroff and Roberge (1975) found having an implication's antecedent and consequent unrelated to each other made no difference in difficulty for young children.

(d) *Complexity dimension.* Transitivity has more operators than detachment since it has two "if-then" statements whereas detachment has only one. This could partly explain why transitivity is more difficult. Burt (1919) found that the number of connections was positively related to difficulty of deductive logic problems. To date, intricacy has not been directly studied by empirical researchers. Logic teachers known to the authors attest to the difficulty of the intricacy resulting from embedding connections within connections. Similarly, logic teachers report that nonstandard ordering may be more difficult. However, Roberge (1970) found that reversing the premise order in a two-premise implication made no difference. A number of studies have indicated that the presence of negatives makes reasoning more difficult (Evans 1982, Wason and Johnson-Laird 1972).

(e) *Teachability.* It is difficult to conduct studies which test the extent to which students at various levels can be taught logic in classroom settings. In addition to the standard problems of conducting research in schools, there is the possibility that the teaching was not done properly. That is, if a group of students does not learn logic, it cannot automatically be concluded they are unable to learn. One possible explanation is that the teaching was inappropriate. It does appear, however, that students above age 12 can be taught both class and conditional logic (Stewart 1978). Students aged 6 to 12 do have considerable knowledge of validity principles

(Ennis 1971, Shapiro and O'Brien 1970) but the extent to which they can be taught logic needs further study.

1.4 Implications for the Classroom

Because of the scarcity of research on teaching deductive logic in the classroom, these implications focus on what students need to be taught, rather than on how or when to go about the teaching.

Goals of elementary and secondary schools in the area of logic could include ability to handle deductively invalid arguments, the understanding of the relationship between evidence and hypotheses, suppositional thinking ability, ability to employ deduction in identifying assumptions, and defining ability.

(a) *Deductively invalid arguments*. Although many good arguments are deductively invalid (e.g., arguments in support of scientific laws), deductive invalidity can be a serious flaw in an argument. This is the case when an arguer acts as if a single simple reason is sufficient to establish a conclusion. Here is an example of class particular conversion:

Example 7:
The Nazis are patriotic Germans.
Hans is a patriotic German.

So Hans is a Nazi.

The two reasons offered are not sufficient to establish the conclusion and students should learn to recognize that in this situation deductive invalidity is a defect. This sort of thing can be learned by most adolescents and many preadolescents.

(b) *Bearing of evidence on a hypothesis*. In a variety of forms of inquiry, hypotheses are formulated, predictions are made, and evidence is collected to determine whether the predictions are true or false. Deductive logic plays a role in drawing conclusions concerning the bearing of evidence on hypotheses.

If the evidence indicates the predictions are false, two conclusions are possible: the hypothesis is false, or one of the assumptions used in deriving the predictions is false. This is a case of particular contraposition complicated by the conjunctive connection between the hypothesis and the assumptions. Students who consider the bearing of evidence on explanatory conclusions in science, social science, history, literary criticism, and many practical matters of the everyday world need to understand this particular contraposition move. Adolescents and preadolescents appear to be marginal in their understanding of particular contraposition though adolescents have achieved significant improvement under instruction. This suggests the possibility of successfully teaching adolescents about the bearing of a denied prediction on a hypothesis.

If the evidence indicates the prediction is correct, the situation is more complex. Using this evidence to accept the hypothesis requires accepting a (deductively) invalid argument (it is a case of particular conversion). In this case, the deductive invalidity is not a fatal flaw, as hypotheses derive their support from being the best available explanation of the facts, rather than only being supported by (deductively) valid arguments. However, deduction plays a loose role in explanation so a general grasp of deduction is useful in understanding the support of evidence for hypotheses, even though the hypothesis does not necessarily follow from the evidence. Deduction, then, is a prerequisite for classroom instruction about the bearing of evidence on hypotheses.

(c) *Suppositional thinking ability*. Suppositional thinking is the ability to think and reason with propositions without believing them, and is a crucial aspect of deductive thinking. This ability is required in many practical situations (e.g., in the testing of hypotheses, and in the consideration of the implications of what one thinks to be a false view). Suppositional thinking is one element of the content dimension of deductive logic ability. Some people find it difficult to do this and must be helped.

(d) *Assumption identification*. Identifying assumptions is an important aspect of reasoning. One common type of assumption is an unstated premise that would convert an argument into a deductively valid one. For example, consider the simple argument, "She is not guilty, because she was temporarily insane." One likely assumption of this argument is, "A person who is temporarily insane is not guilty." This assumption makes the argument a deductively valid one (by the principle of detachment). Thus, understanding of deductive logic is a prerequisite for assumption identification.

(e) *Defining*. Many definitions present a logical equivalence relationship between the term to be defined and the defining material. An example: "A triangle is a closed figure with three straight sides." Deductive logic is useful in grasping, formulating, and testing such definitions. It is similarly useful for operational definitions, which present implications. An example (that defines temperature): "If a mercury thermometer is put in a liquid; then the reading of the thermometer is X, if and only if, the temperature is X."

2. Logic-of-teaching Approach

Logic-of-teaching approaches provide classification systems for classroom dialogue and behavior. Major categories used include definition, explanation, and justification. A variety of logic-of-teaching approaches exist, some of which are described in *Mirrors for Behavior* (Simon and Boyer 1970). The system developed by B. Othanel Smith et al. (1970) was developed on the basis of intensive study of a large set of classroom transcriptions, and the exposition is thorough and generally clear; so this system will serve as a paradigm of the logic-of-teaching approach.

2.1 Conceptual Framework

The aim of Smith et al. (1970) was to study the logic of verbal transactions in the classroom. They sought to identify logical operations which they defined as "the forms which verbal behavior takes as the teacher shapes the subject matter in the course of instruction. For example, the teacher reduces concepts to linguistic patterns called definitions" (p. 3).

Their research is descriptive and analytic in the natural history sense. They described and analyzed the transcripts of five consecutive class periods of 14 teachers in five high schools. They divided the verbal teaching behaviors into pedagogically significant units and labeled the units in logically meaningful ways. The units chosen were called "episodes" which are "one or more exchanges which comprise a completed verbal transaction between two or more speakers" (Smith et al. 1970 p. 14). Monologues by teachers were not analyzed. Here is an example of an explanation episode in a discussion of a novel (p. 155):

Example 8:
Teacher: *Why did he—Jarvis—leave (the) room?*
Student: To go down and see what was the matter.
Teacher: All right, he heard the noise, he heard the servant calling and went down.

Episodes are classified by their opening phrases or "entry" characteristics. In example 8 the opening phrase is italicized. The entry shapes the character of the episode and may be made by the teacher or by a student.

Smith et al. (1970) describe 13 different kinds of entry. The name of each type of entry, along with a brief description and an example are given in Table 2. The relative occurrence of each type of entry is also given.

2.2 The Study

The date in Table 2 are averaged across the 14 high-school classrooms. The most common logical operation was "describing." One-quarter of the items were classified in this category. An analysis of the individual classrooms shows that "describing" occurs at least 20 percent of the time in 10 of them. Thus, this pattern is consistent. The two classrooms with the lowest percentage of this category were English classes.

The two next most common categories were designating and explaining. Together these two accounted for a little more than 25 percent of the episodes. This means that just three categories, describing, designating, and explaining, accounted for over half of the logical transactions in the classrooms studied. The fourth most common category was classroom management.

The other categories, listed in order of decreasing occurrence in the Smith study, were conditional inferring, stating, opining, evaluating, defining, comparing and contrasting, classifying, reporting, and substituting.

It appears that most of the episodes in these classroom dialogues were not aimed at higher cognitive processes, or independent creative and critical thinking. They instead seemed aimed at routine mastery of the subject matter.

2.3 Implications

The aim of the Smith study was descriptive and analytic and it provides a baseline for study (using some standard United States classrooms). No attempt was made to suggest what patterns of occurrence would be most suitable in classrooms. While the investigators collected data from different age groups, they did not present results separately for each grade or age. Further research is needed to determine if age-related trends exist, and if some patterns are more beneficial than others. For those interested in promoting the higher cognitive and logical processes in the schools, one implication is that there is much further study to be done.

3. Critical-thinking Approach

Critical thinking, a third approach to logical operations in the classroom, has long been advocated as a goal of the schools, though often in not enough detail to provide sufficient guidance. In what follows, some details will be supplied and tied together under a broad definition of "critical-thinking ability."

3.1 Conceptual Framework

"Critical-thinking ability" may be defined as "the mental ability to deal reasonably and reflectively with questions about what to believe or do." The focus on questions about belief and action appears to capture conceptually the concerns of people who advocate critical thinking. It also provides a basis for analyzing the decision (since action assumes belief) and for identifying items that should be included in a critical-thinking curriculum.

Decisions about what to believe require at least two judgments. One is associated with the acceptability of grounds for the belief and the second concerns the inference from these grounds to the prospective belief. Furthermore there are at least three major types of inferences possible: deductive, inductive, and evaluative. This grounds-inference way of viewing the decision process (suggested by Weston 1982, among others) provides a basis for identifying dispositions and abilities to serve as goals in education. Table 3 provides a list of dispositions and abilities, together with criteria (based on Ennis 1980, Ennis 1986).

There are 14 major types of critical-thinking dispositions listed and 12 abilities. Their relationship to the grounds-inference way of viewing the critical-thinking decision process calls for some explanation.

A ground for a belief, when the ground is not itself based on an inference, but is based on something, is either an observation or statement made by a source, or both. Hence the skills of observation (Table 3, Sections B, 5) and judging credibility (B, 4) are major ones in this approach to critical thinking.

The three major types of inference, deductive (B, 6), inductive (B, 7), and evaluative (B, 8), because they are significant and quite different, call for a corresponding listing of three ability areas. Auxiliary skills of argument analysis (B, 2), definition (B, 9), and assumption identi-

Table 2
Smith's logic-of-teaching categories

Category	Description	Examples of entries	% of total number of entries
Defining	The entry implicitly or explicitly asks for the meaning of terms	Who are the Magi? What is the Monroe Doctrine?	4.1
Describing	Describing involves telling about something, or representing something by words or drawing	Where are the kidneys located? Can you tell us anything about the schools in New Zealand?	25.3
Designating	Something is identified by name—a word or another symbol	Name some words which have the same form for both plural and singular What is the longest bone in the body?	14.8
Stating	Entries in this category ask for statements of issues, steps in proofs, rules, theories, conclusions, ideas, beliefs, and so on. It does not include asking for names, descriptions, and so on	What is the formula for the area of a square? What criticism did they make of Harding's administration?	6.8
Reporting	This involves asking for a report on what a book or document says, for information in the text, or for a summary or review	Tell us what is given What did we say about public control of business?	2.9
Substituting	A student is asked to perform a symbolic operation, usually of a mathematical nature	Substitute for us in this equation	0.3
Evaluating	Estimating the worth of something	Was the sit-down strike a sensible thing? Is that a safe argument?	4.6
Opining	The student (or teacher) is asked to form a conclusion, but no explicit conditions are given on which the conclusion is to be based	Does a fish have to live in water? How do you think the Romans felt about foreign conquests?	5.3
Classifying	A given instance is put in a class where it belongs, or a class is placed in a larger class to which it belongs as a subclass	What group of animals does the starfish belong to? What special type of triangle did you find it to be?	3.0
Comparing and contrasting	Two or more things—actions, factors, objects, processes, and so on—are compared	Is the state the same thing as the government? How does murder differ from culpable homicide?	3.3
Conditional inferring	These entries contain the antecedent, or conditional part of a statement. They may also contain the consequent, and the students are asked to make an inference	Is he a good judge if he sentences the man to hanging? If the two lines are parallel, what is the altitude of the two triangles?	7.3
Explaining	A particular consequent is given and the student is asked to supply an antecedent	Why does iron rust? What is the cause of juvenile delinquency?	12.9
Directing and managing a classroom	These entries are designed to keep classroom activities going	Who is to lead the group today? Who has problem no. 4?	9.4
			100%

fication (B, 10), are needed in the belief-decision process for the sake of being clear about what is being considered. Two general application skills round out the 12: deciding on an action (11), and interacting with others (12). These 12 ability areas should be accompanied by certain critical-thinking dispositions (like open-mindedness), which are listed under A and complete this brief elaboration of the suggested definition of critical thinking.

These dispositions and abilities are interdependent and not as sharply differentiated as the separate listings might suggest. For example, identifying the conclusion and unstated reasons (part of argument analysis) are skills that call for best explanation inference (classified under "induction"); best explanation inference involves some deductive inference; and judging inferences requires argument analysis. Furthermore, they all require the exercise of good judgment, open-mind-

Table 3
Critical thinking dispositions and abilities

A. Dispositions

1. Seek a clear statement of the thesis or question
2. Seek reasons
3. Try to be well-informed
4. Use credible sources and mention them
5. take into account the total situation
6. Try to remain relevant to the main point
7. Keep in mind the original and/or basic concern
8. Look for alternatives
9. Be sensitive to the feelings, level of knowledge, and degree of sophistication of others
10. Be open-minded
    (a) Consider seriously other points of view than one's own ("dialogical thinking")
    (b) Reason from premises with which one disagrees—without letting the disagreement interfere with one's reasoning ("suppositional thinking")
    (c) Withhold judgment when the evidence and reasons are insufficient
11. Take a position (and change a position) when the evidence and reasons are sufficient to do so
12. Seek as much precision as the subject permits
13. Deal in an orderly maner with the parts of a complex whole
14. Employ one's critical thinking abilities

B. Abilities (Classified under these categories: Elementary Clarification, Basic Support, Inference, Advanced Clarification, and Strategy and Tactics)

Elementary Clarification
1. Focusing on a question
   (a) Identifying or formulating a question
   (b) Identifying or formulating criteria for judging possible answers
   (c) Keeping the situation in mind
2. Analyzing arguments
   (a) Identifying conclusions
   (b) Identifying stated reasons
   (c) Identifying unstated reasons
   (d) Seeing similarities and differences
   (e) Identifying and handling irrelevance
   (f) Seeing the structure of an argument
   (g) Summarizing
3. Asking and answering questions or clarification and/or challenge, for example:
   (a) Why?
   (b) What is your main point?
   (c) What do you mean by "_____"?
   (d) What would be an example?
   (e) What would not be an example (though close to being one)?
   (f) How does that apply to this case (describe case, which might well appear to be a counterexample)?
   (g) What difference does it make?
   (h) What are the facts?
   (i) Is this what you are saying "_____"?
   (j) Would you say some more about that?

Basic Support
4. Judging the credibility of a source; criteria:
   (a) Expertise
   (b) Lack of conflict of interest
   (c) Agreement among sources
   (d) Reputation
   (e) Use of established procedures
   (f) Known risk to reputation
   (g) Ability to give reasons
   (h) Careful habits
5. Observing and judging observation reports; criteria:
   (a) Minimal inferring involved
   (b) Short time interval between observation and report
   (c) Report by observer, rather than someone else (i.e. not hearsay)
   (d) Records are generally desirable. If report is based on a record, it is generally best that:
       (1) The record was close in time to the observation
       (2) The record was made by the observer
       (3) The record was made by the reporter
       (4) The statement was believed by the reporter, either because of a prior belief in its correctness or because of a belief that the observer was habitually correct
   (e) Corroboration
   (f) Possibility of corroboration
   (g) Conditions of good access
   (h) Competent employment of technology, if technology is useful
   (i) Satisfaction by observer (and reporter, if a different person) of credibility criteria (see No. 4 above)

Inference
6. Deducing, and judging deductions
   (a) Class logic—Euler circles
   (b) Conditional logic
   (c) Interpretation of statements
       (1) Double negation
       (2) Necessary and sufficient conditions
       (3) Other logical words: "only", "if and only if", "or", "some", "unless", "not", "not both", etc.
7. Inducing, and judging inductions
   (a) Generalizing
       (1) Typicality of data; limitation of coverage
       (2) Sampling
       (3) Tables and graphs
   (b) Inferring explanatory conclusions and hypotheses
       (1) Types of explanatory conclusions and hypotheses
           (a) Causal claims
           (b) Claims about the beliefs and attitudes of people
           (c) Interpretations of authors' intended meanings
           (d) Historical claims that certain things happened
           (e) Reported definitions
           (f) Claims that something is an unstated reason or unstated conclusion
       (2) Investigating
           (a) Designing experiments, including planning to control variables
           (b) Seeking evidence and counterevidence
           (c) Seeking other possible explanations

Table 3—(continued)

(3) Criteria: given reasonable assumptions,
  (a) The proposed conclusion would explain the evidence (essential)
  (b) The proposed conclusion is consistent with known facts (essential)
  (c) Competitive alternative conclusions are inconsistent with known facts (essential)
  (d) The proposed conclusion seems plausible (desirable)

8. Making and judging value judgments
  (a) Background facts
  (b) Consequences
  (c) *Prima facie* application of acceptable principles
  (d) Considering alternatives
  (e) Balancing, weighing, and deciding

Advanced Clarification

9. Defining terms, and judging definitions; three dimensions:
  (a) Form
    (1) Synonym
    (2) Classification
    (3) Range
    (4) Equivalent expression
    (5) Operational
    (6) Example—nonexample
  (b) Definitional strategy
    (1) Acts
      (a) Report a meaning ("reported" definition)
      (b) Stipulate a meaning ("stipulative" definition)
      (c) Express a position on an issue ("positional", including "programmatic" and "persuasive" definition)
    (2) Identifying and handling equivocation
      (a) Attention to the context
      (b) Possible types of response:
        (i) "The definition is just wrong" (the simplest response)
        (ii) Reduction to absurdity: "According to that definition, there is an outlandish result"
        (iii) Considering alternative interpretations: "On this interpretation, there is this problem; on that interpretation, there is that problem"
      (iv) Establishing that there are two meanings of key term, and a shift in meaning from one to the other
  (c) Content

10. Identifying assumptions
  (a) Unstated reasons
  (b) Needed assumptions: argument reconstruction

Strategy and Tactics

11. Deciding on an action
  (a) Define the problem
  (b) Select criteria to judge possible solutions
  (c) Formulate alternative solutions
  (d) Tentatively decide what to do
  (e) Review, taking into account the total situation, and decide
  (f) Monitor the implementation

12. Interacting with others
  (a) Employing and reacting to "fallacy" labels (including)
    (1) Circularity
    (2) Appeal to authority
    (3) Bandwagon
    (4) Glittering term
    (5) Name-calling
    (6) Slippery slope
    (7) Post hoc
    (8) Non sequitur
    (9) Ad hominem
    (10) Affirming the consequent
    (11) Denying the antecedent
    (12) Conversion
    (13) Begging the question
    (14) Either–or
    (15) Vagueness
    (16) Equivocation
    (17) Straw person
    (18) Appeal to tradition
    (19) Argument from analogy
    (20) Hypothetical question
    (21) Oversimplification
    (22) Irrelevance
  (b) Logical strategies
  (c) Rhetorical strategies
  (d) Presenting a position, oral or written (argumentation)
    (1) Aiming at a particular audience and keeping it in mind
    (2) Organizing (common type: main point, clarification, reasons, alternatives, attempt to rebut prospective challenges, summary—including repeat of main point)

---

edness, taking into account the total situation, and the other dispositions listed in Sect. A.

3.2 Studies

It would be desirable to have information on at least these five questions. (a) To what extent do students acquire the various aspects of critical thinking on their own? (b) Can critical thinking (or each aspect thereof) be taught? (c) At what level can it be taught? (d) How can it be taught? (e) How can a curriculum be organized to include the various aspects of critical thinking? Unfortunately research relating to these questions has been minimal.

Among the various aspects of critical thinking, deduction (including its suppositional aspects) and the isolation-of-variables part of induction have received the largest amount of attention. Other aspects that have received attention include observation, nondeductive suppositional thinking, and seeing alternatives and possibilities.

Deduction has been considered in an earlier section. A critical-thinking-oriented summary is in order here. The evidence indicates that even without deliberate deduction instruction, students gradually develop deduction skills, except contraposition. It also appears that deliberate instruction in deduction can be effective for adolescents and older individuals. Suppositional content, unfamiliar content, symbolic content, abstract content, and irrelevant content make deduction more difficult, as do the complexities introduced by negations, intricacy, more logical connections, and necessary condition language.

Instruction in a combination of deduction and argument analysis was shown to be effective for a group of gifted 12-year-olds (Tomko 1980). This instruction extended over a period of four months for one 50-

minute class period per day. Its appropriateness for lower levels was not tested. Some evidence suggests that instruction in isolation of variables can be effective (Anderson 1965, Linn 1980). The planning of investigations and controlled experiments appears to be more spontaneously done by adolescents than children and to be more successfully accomplished by adults and older adolescents than by younger adolescents (Siegler and Liebert 1975).

Inhelder and Piaget (1958) demonstrated that older children and adolescents are better at some aspects of observing than younger children. Young children often let their preconceived ideas influence their observations. In the floating and sinking experiment children are asked to predict whether objects will sink or float. Then they actually perform the experiment. Young children often behave as Mic (age 5) who predicted that the plank would sink. The experiment did not change his mind as he leaned on the plank with all his strength to keep it underwater and said "You want to stay down, silly" (Inhelder and Piaget 1958 p. 22). The ability to observe more correctly appears to increase with the onset of concrete abilities (Inhelder and Piaget 1958). However, even in adults it has been demonstrated that prior beliefs, theories, or impressions frequently bias observation (Nisbett and Ross 1980).

Seeing alternatives and seeing possibilities appear to be more prevalent among adolescents than children, who seem to be more tied to the concrete and to what exists (Keating 1980). Suppositional ability, especially the ability to think about the impossible, also is more typical of adolescent thought than that of children (Elkind 1974).

Further work is obviously needed, but it seems reasonable to claim that individuals cannot become critical thinkers until at least adolescence. Even after adolescence the probability of uninstructed individuals having all the proficiencies seems small. Recent work by social and cognitive psychologists has found that adults use many flawed inferential strategies (for a review see Nisbett and Ross 1980). These flawed inferential strategies would affect the ability to infer generalizations, to make predictions, and to evaluate, indicate reasons, and give explanations and definitions.

3.3 Implications

If one thinks that a goal of the schools should be to help students improve their critical-thinking ability then one implication would be to actively pursue this goal. Broadly speaking, this is not done at the time of writing.

Since deductive logic ability appears to be a significant part of a number of other critical-thinking abilities, deduction instruction (or assessment of proficiency) might well appear in the early stages of a critical-thinking curriculum. Another early-appearing feature might be instruction in identifying conclusions, since the formulation of one's own arguments and the appraisal of others' cannot succeed without its being clear just what is the conclusion.

Evidence that would suggest an appropriate place to begin critical thinking is sparse. However, it does appear that instruction at least in deduction, argument analysis, isolation and control of variables is feasible for adolescents.

The interdependence of the various aspects of critical thinking means that a simple building-block approach to instruction is unlikely to be successful. Mixture with spiral and problem approaches would probably be more appropriate.

Because of the severe lack of information about what is possible at various levels and how to go about teaching critical thinking, the most important implication is that much further research is needed. It should include the development of tests and other evaluation instruments and approaches, so that results can be replicated and widely understood.

4. Summary

Of five prominent approaches to the topic, logical operations in the classroom, only three were examined here in any detail: the deductive logic, logic-of-teaching, and critical-thinking approaches. The other two, the Piagetian and Bloom *Taxonomy* approaches, are treated elsewhere in this Encyclopedia, and so are not discussed here.

A three-dimensional analysis of deductive logic was offered: logical principle, content, and complexity. The four basic principles are detachment, particular contraposition, particular conversion, and particular inversion. The first two of these are validity principles, the other two, invalidity principles. Elements of the content dimension are belief in premises, commitment to conclusion, symbolic, familiarity, irrelevance, and abstractness. Elements of the complexity dimension include the number of connections, intricacy, nonstandard order, and negation.

Students without deliberate logic instruction gradually improve in deductive logic as they grow older, except in contraposition. At all ages, they are considerably better at employing the validity principles than the invalidity principles. By and large, the elements of the content and complexity dimensions increase the difficulty of deductive logic.

Deductive logic is useful in the classroom in the following areas: judging some arguments for their validity, evaluating the bearing of evidence on a hypothesis, practicing suppositional thinking, identifying assumptions, and defining.

A logic-of-teaching approach analyzes the logical aspects of classroom dialogue, categorizes them, and counts instances. Assuming the classrooms Smith et al. (1970) studied are typical it appears that there is not a great deal of higher cognitive activity in classrooms.

The critical-thinking approach presented here is based on the following definition of critical-thinking ability: the mental ability to deal reasonably and reflectively with questions about what to believe or do. This ability requires a number of dispositions and abilities. Twenty-six major ones were presented.

Minimal research on the teaching of and testing for critical thinking has been conducted. But it does seem that in general not a great deal can be accomplished prior to adolescence. The interdependence of aspects of critical thinking makes such teaching especially difficult and any critical-thinking curriculum must confront this problem.

See also: Students' Cognitive Processing; Soliciting

Bibliography

Anderson R C 1965 Can first graders learn an advanced problem-solving skill? *J. Educ. Psychol.* 56: 283–94

Bloom B S (ed.) 1956 *Taxonomy of Educational Objectives: The Classification of Educational Goals, Handbook 1: Cognitive Domain.* Longmans, Green, New York

Burt C 1919 The development of reasoning in school children. *J. Exp. Pedag.* 5: 68–77, 121–27

Ceraso J, Provitera A 1971 Sources of error in syllogistic reasoning. *Cognit. Psychol.* 2: 400–10

Donaldson M, Withrington D 1963 *A Study of Children's Thinking.* Tavistock, London

Elkind D 1974 *Children and Adolescents: Interpretive Essays on Jean Piaget,* 2nd edn. Oxford University Press, New York

Ennis R H 1971 Conditional logic and primary school children: A developmental study. *Interchange* 2: 126–32

Ennis R H 1980 A conception of rational thinking. In: Coombs J (ed.) 1980 *Philosophy of Education 1979.* Philosophy of Education Society, Normal, Illinois

Ennis R H 1986 A taxonomy of critical thinking dispositions and abilities. In: Baron J, Sternberg R (eds.) 1986 *Teaching Thinking Skills.* Freeman, New York

Ennis R H, Paulus D H 1965 *Critical Thinking Readiness in Grades 1–12, Phase 1: Deductive Reasoning in Adolescence.* Cooperative Research Project No. 1680. Cornell Critical Thinking Project, Ithaca, New York. ERIC Document No. ED 003 818

Evans J St B T 1982 *The Psychology of Deductive Reasoning.* Routledge and Kegan Paul, London

Hill S A 1961 A study of logical abilities of children. (Doctoral dissertation, Stanford University) *Dissertation Abstracts International* 21: 3359 (University Microfilms No. 61–1229)

Inhelder B, Piaget J 1958 *The Growth of Logical Thinking from Childhood to Adolescence: An Essay on the Construction of Formal Operational Structures.* Basic Books, New York

Keating D P 1980 Thinking processes in adolescence. In: Adelson J (ed.) 1980 *Handbook of Adolescent Psychology.* Wiley, New York, pp. 211–46

Kodroff J K, Roberge J J 1975 Developmental analysis of the conditional reasoning abilities of primary-grade children. *Dev. Psychol.* 11: 21–28

Kuhn D 1977 Conditional reasoning in children. *Dev. Psychol.* 13: 342–53

Linn M C 1980 Teaching students to control variables: Some investigations using free choice experiences. In: Modgil S, Modgil C (eds.) 1980 *Toward a Theory of Psychological Development Within the Piagetian Framework.* National Foundation for Educational Research, Slough

Nisbett R, Ross L 1980 *Human Inference: Strategies and Shortcomings of Social Judgment.* Prentice-Hall, Englewood Cliffs, New Jersey

Roberge J J 1970 The effect of reversal of premises on children's deductive reasoning ability. *J. Psychol.* 75: 53–58

Roberge J J, Paulus D H 1971 Developmental patterns for children's class and conditional reasoning abilities. *Dev. Psychol.* 4: 191–200

Shapiro B J, O'Brien T C 1970 Logical thinking in children ages six through thirteen. *Child. Dev.* 41: 823–29

Siegler R S, Liebert R M 1975 Acquisition of formal scientific reasoning by 10 and 13 years olds: Designing a factorial experiment. *Dev. Psychol.* 11: 401–02

Simon A, Boyer E G (eds.) 1970 *Mirrors for Behavior 2: An Anthology of Observation Instruments Continued: Summary.* Research for Better Schools, Philadelphia, Pennsylvania

Smith B O, Meux M O, Coombs J, Eierdam D, Szoke R 1970 *A Study of the Logic of Teaching.* University of Illinois Press, Urbana, Illinois

Stewart B L 1978 *Teaching Logic in Grades 7–12: A Literature Review.* Illinois Thinking Project, Champaign, Illinois

Taplin J E, Staudenmayer H, Taddonio J L 1974 Developmental changes in conditional reasoning: Linguistic or logical? *J. Exp. Child Psychol.* 17: 360–73

Tomko T N 1980 *Brief Evaluation of Logic I at University High School, 1979–1980.* Illinois Thinking Project, Champaign, Illinois

Wason P C 1968 Reasoning about a rule. *Q. J. Exp. Psychol.* 20: 273–81

Wason P C, Johnson-Laird P N 1972 *Psychology of Reasoning: Structure and Content.* Harvard University Press, Cambridge, Massachusetts

Weston A 1982 A pattern for argument analysis in informal logic. *Teaching Philosophy* 5(2): 135–39

Wildman T M, Fletcher H J 1977 Developmental increases and decreases in solutions of conditional syllogism problems. *Dev. Psychol.* 13: 630–36

Wilkins M C 1928 The effect of changed material on ability to do formal syllogistic reasoning. *Arch. Psychol.* No. 102

Abstractness and Concreteness

M. J. Dunkin

It has long been argued that learning proceeds most effectively if students are actively engaged and if the learning tasks themselves are selected or planned so as to relate closely to the students' experiences. Thus, teachers are urged to introduce students to new concepts or ideas by the use of materials that directly stimulate the sensory mechanisms of the students. Objects that can be touched, seen, smelt, and even tasted are common in modern classrooms and include such educational materials as Cuisenaire rods, Dienes' attribute blocks, form boards, jigsaw puzzles, modelling clay, and the like. Whole teaching methods, such as the Montessori Method, are based upon the perceived importance of concrete experience. To the extent that a learning experience involves direct sensory experiences of actual objects, it is said to be concrete. Learning experiences that involve only the use of symbols, such as words or numbers, are said to be abstract.

This article is about abstractness and concreteness in classrooms. It deals with attempts to define and measure abstractness and concreteness for the purposes of research. It examines the relationship between abstractness/concreteness and other dimensions of instruction, especially logical complexity, and it presents some evidence about the occurrence of abstract, concrete, and other categories of behaviour in schools.

1. Concepts of Abstractness and Concreteness

Both Piaget, with his theory of developmental stages proceeding from sensory-motor to formal operations, and Bruner, with his theory of developmental levels proceeding from enactive to symbolic, implied a continuum ranging from concreteness to abstractness. The *Taxonomy of Educational Objectives* in the cognitive domain (Bloom et al. 1956) also included some reference to abstractness and concreteness. Much more attention was given to them in the work of Hilda Taba (1966) who classified the types of thought processes involved in classroom discourse according to their abstractness/concreteness. Thought processes that involved giving specific pieces of data, relating, comparing, or contrasting them and providing factual explanations were classified as concrete. Making inferences from data, giving inferential explanations, inferring generalizations, drawing analogies, and stating logical relationships among inferences were all classified as abstract. Taba seemed to be distinguishing between concrete and abstract mainly on the basis of whether the thought unit was factual or inferential.

A somewhat different approach to the conceptualization of the abstractness/concreteness continuum was adopted by Solomon (1970) who was attracted particularly by Bruner's suggested iconic level of development. Solomon substituted the term "representational" for iconic and argued that verbal pictures or images such as are found in similes and metaphors and colourful vocabulary are significant in rendering classroom discourse more concrete for learners. Solomon devised an observational instrument called the Taxonomy of Image Provocation (TIP) consisting of five major categories as follows:

(a) Concrete without imagery.

(b) Concrete to provoke imagery, where the teacher uses concrete experiences to provoke imagery of

visual, auditory, kinesthetic, olfactory, or gustatory types.

(c) Representational, where the teacher uses models, pictures, diagrams, maps, etc., to provoke imagery of the above types.

(d) Abstract to provoke imagery, where symbols such as language are used in ways that evoke images appealing to senses of the above kinds.

(e) Abstract without imagery.

Imagery was defined by Solomon as "a conscious mental representation of a perceivable, absent, or nonexistent object, process or concept" and was thought to be significant in cognitive development because it "is necessary in order to relate an iconic 'representation' to that which it represents" (Solomon 1970 p. 53). Solomon tried to advance a continuum of cognitive growth incorporating and adding to the developmental stages of Piaget's and Bruner's imagery-related stages.

2. Research on Abstractness/Concreteness in the Classroom

Earlier attempts by Bloom and his colleagues (Bloom et al. 1956) and Taba (1966) to represent the abstract/concrete dimension in thought about educational objectives and classroom behaviour, implied that abstractness/concreteness covaried with logical complexity such that as the type of thinking engaged in became more complex, so the level of abstraction necessarily rose.

Dunkin and Biddle (1974), in reviewing research on this matter, discussed evidence that, particularly among the more complex types of thinking such as synthesis and evaluation, the relationship between abstractness/concreteness and complexity was negative. That is to say, as the more complex logical operations engaged the teachers' and students' attention, the content of the discourse became more concrete. Dunkin and Biddle suggested that classroom participants might find operating at high levels of complexity with highly abstract content too difficult and that either the level of complexity or the level of abstraction is lowered to reduce the difficulty.

Solomon and Wood (1970) reported findings concerning the incidence of the various categories of TIP in a sample of 22 elementary and 49 secondary student teachers in West Virginia. Within the total group there were large variations in the extent to which the five categories were observed but by far the most common were the abstract with and without imagery categories, with very little difference between the elementary and secondary levels. Imagery appealing to the visual sense was almost twice as common as the other senses together, whether concrete, representational, or abstract.

In his study of classrooms in the Western Highlands

of Papua New Guinea, Dunkin (1977) found that the relationship between abstractness/concreteness and logical complexity varied with grade level and subject area. In grade 4 social studies and mathematics and in grade 1 mathematics the more complex logical operations of evaluation, classification, comparing and contrasting, conditional inferring, and explaining were accompanied by representations and concrete objects more often than were simpler logical operations. In grade 6 social studies and mathematics the reverse was the case. Dunkin also found that abstract experiences were by far the most frequent in grades 4 and 6 in both subject areas. Only in grade 1 mathematics were concrete experiences the most frequent.

3. Implications for Teaching and Research

As yet there has been very little research conducted on the question of abstractness/concreteness in classrooms. In particular, no one seems yet to have investigated relationships between abstractness/concreteness and student learning. The small amount of evidence concerning the frequency with which students encounter concrete and representational, as distinct from abstract, learning experiences suggests that there may need to be some shift of emphasis towards concreteness, especially

in the lower grades. Classrooms, it appears, continue to be highly verbal, and, therefore, highly abstract venues for learning. Theories of cognitive development that advocate greater use of concrete experiences still have plenty of scope for influence, it appears.

See also: Logical Operations

Bibliography

Bloom B S, Engelhart M D, Furst E J, Hill W H, Krathwohl D R (eds.) 1956 *Taxonomy of Educational Objectives: The Classification of Educational Goals, Handbook I: Cognitive Domain.* McKay, New York

Dunkin M J 1977 A study of classroom interaction in Papua New Guinea. *Papua New Guinea J. Educ.* 13(2): 1–11

Dunkin M J, Biddle B J 1974 *The Study of Teaching.* Holt, Rinehart and Winston, New York

Solomon G 1970 The analysis of concrete to abstract classroom instructional patterns utilizing TIP profile. *J. Res. Dev. Educ.* 4(1): 52–61

Solomon G, Wood S 1970 Classroom behavior accompanying TIP profile measures. Unpublished manuscript, West Virginia University

Taba H 1966 *Teaching Strategies and Cognitive Functioning in Elementary School Children*, United States Office of Education Co-operative Research Project No. 2404. San Francisco State College, San Francisco, California

Vagueness and Clarity

M. L. Land

Teacher clarity is the term used to describe how clearly a teacher explains subject matter to students. This article focuses on recent research on the effects of low-inference variables of teacher clarity on student achievement and makes recommendations for additional research.

The most recent research in teacher clarity has been both correlational and experimental research in the field and laboratory, with single variables and clusters of low-inference variables. This research has begun to yield relatively unambiguous knowledge concerning causal connections between variables of teacher clarity and student achievement. A description follows of the low-inference variables of teacher clarity about which the most is known.

1. Teacher Clarity Variables

1.1 Teacher Vagueness Terms

Vagueness occurs as speakers commit themselves to present information they cannot remember or never really knew (Hiller 1968). Hiller et al. (1969 p. 670) defined vagueness as "a psychological construct which refers to the state of mind of a performer who does not sufficiently command the facts or understanding

required for maximally effective communication." They placed vagueness terms into nine categories of impreciseness (Table 1). Based on observations of teachers in natural classroom settings, teachers average from two to five vagueness terms per minute of teacher talk (Smith and Land 1981). In his original study, Smith (1977) reported a mean of 2.18 vagueness terms per minute of teacher talk with 40 percent of the teachers averaging between 2.5 and 4.0 such terms per minute.

In studying the relationship between teacher vagueness terms and student achievement, two basic approaches have been used—the field or correlational approach, and the laboratory or experimental approach. Teachers taught lessons in natural classroom settings (the field approach) and students were then administered achievement tests. In the experimental approach, lesson scripts were prepared and videotaped so that the only difference between lessons was the frequency of vagueness terms. Students, randomly assigned to groups, then viewed the videotaped lessons and took a test over the lesson contents. The unit of analysis was the teacher in the correlational research; in the experimental research, the unit was the student. Table 2 indicates that the effect of vagueness terms in

Table 1
Categories of vagueness terms

	Category	Examples
(a)	Ambiguous designation	Conditions, other, somehow, somewhere, someplace, thing
(b)	Approximation	About, almost, approximately, fairly, just about, kind of, most, mostly, much, nearly, pretty (much), somewhat, sort of
(c)	"Bluffing" and recovery	Actually, and so forth, and so on, anyway, as anyone can see, as you know, basically, clearly, frankly, in a nutshell, in essence, in fact, in other words, obviously, of course, so to speak, to make a long story short, to tell the truth, you know, you see
(d)	Error admission	Excuse me, I'm sorry, I guess, I'm not sure
(e)	Indeterminate quantification	A bunch, a couple, a few, a little, a lot, several, some various
(f)	Multiplicity	Aspect(s), kind(s) of, sort(s) of, type(s) of
(g)	Negated intensifiers	Not all, not many, not very
(h)	Possibility	Chances are, could be, may, maybe, might, perhaps, possibly, seem(s)
(i)	Probability	Frequently, generally, in general, normally, often, ordinarily, probably, sometimes, usually

all cases cited was negative, and was significant (0.07 to 0.001) in eight of the ten studies cited. The percent of variance in student achievement that could be accounted for by teacher vagueness terms ranged from 18 to 34 percent in the correlational studies and from 2 to 17 percent in the experimental studies.

Smith (1977), Dunkin (1978), and Dunkin and Doenau (1980) reported negative correlations between frequency of teacher vagueness terms and degree of lesson content coverage. Dunkin and Doenau (1980) also reported negative correlations between teacher vagueness terms and (a) general ability and knowledge of students, (b) student initiations other than initiations of student questions, (c) long student utterances, and (d) student use of vagueness terms. They also reported a positive correlation between teacher vagueness terms and degree of student dogmatism, and between frequency of student vagueness terms and the general ability and knowledge of students.

Why would vagueness terms interfere with learning?

Table 2
Vagueness terms and student achievement (unadjusted)

	Significance	% of Variance	Content	Grade level	N	Reference
Correlational:	0.01 to 0.001	23 to 34	Social studies	High school	32 teachers 672 students	Hiller et al. 1969
	0.05	24	Mathematics	High school	20 teachers 455 students	Smith 1977
	ns	—	Social studies	Elementary	29 teachers 827 students	Dunkin 1978
	0.05	18 to 24	Social studies	Elementary	28 teachers 723 students	Dunkin and Doenau 1980
	ns	—	Social studies	Elementary	26 teachers 741 students	Dunkin and Doenau 1980
Experimental:	0.05	2	Mathematics	College	204 students	Smith and Edmonds 1978
	0.05	8	Mathematics	College	50 students	Land and Smith 1979a
	0.07	2	Mathematics	College	160 students	Land and Smith 1979b
	0.001	17	Mathematics	Elementary	100 students	Smith and Cotten 1980
	0.05	8	Biology	High school	48 students	Smith and Bramblett 1981

No one knows for certain, but speculation based on student perceptions indicates that students may get the idea that the teacher is uncertain about the lesson because of the impreciseness of the words used. This may cause the student to feel uncertain about the ideas to be learned and interfere with learning.

Two studies have attempted to reduce the number of vagueness terms in teacher speech. Hiller (1971) demonstrated experimentally that increased teacher knowledge of subject matter reduces the use of vagueness terms, and Smith (1982) reported a training procedure that was significant in reducing vagueness.

1.2 Teacher Verbal Mazes

Smith (1977) operationally defined a verbal maze as a false start or halt in speech, redundantly spoken words, and tangles of words. Following are two examples of verbal mazes (italicized):

(a) "Here are three *types, no, uh,* examples of generalizations."

(b) "A concept is a word or *phase,* phrase, or symbol ..."

Smith reported an average of two to three verbal mazes per minute of teacher talk, based on observations of teachers in natural classroom settings. More than 35 percent of the teachers he studied, however, used between three and six verbal mazes per minute of teacher talk.

There are three published studies on the individual effects of teacher verbal mazes on student achievement. Smith (1977) reported a negative correlation (−0.28, $p > 0.05$) between the average number of teacher verbal mazes per minute and student achievement in high-school mathematics. Land and Smith (1979a) reported a significant ($p < 0.02$) negative effect with college students, and Land and Combs (1981) reported a significant ($p < 0.005$) negative correlation between verbal mazes and achievement, with college students. In the latter two studies, the percent of variance in student achievement that could be accounted for by teacher verbal mazes was 3 percent and 5 percent, respectively. That amount of variance seems very small until one puts into perspective that verbal mazes are only one of numerous variables comprising teacher clarity, which itself accounts from 14 to 50 percent of the variance in student achievement in high-inference studies of clarity.

Why would verbal mazes interfere with learning? In comparison with lessons containing no mazes, the perceptions of students learning from lessons containing mazes were as follows: the teacher was perceived as being less confident, the students were less confident, the explanations were perceived as unclear, the speech of the instructor was irritating, and the teacher was perceived as being nervous and unprepared. The net effect seemed to be increased student frustration and less efficient student achievement. In contrast with vagueness terms, students perceive a more deleterious effect for mazes than vagueness terms (Smith and Land 1980).

1.3 Other Single Clarity Variables

Although the majority of research on low-inference clarity variables has been with vagueness terms and mazes, there has been a limited amount of research with at least five additional variables: length of utterances/sentences; utterances of "uh," "ah," "um"; utterances of "OK"; additional unexplained content; and transitions. No significant effects have been reported for length of utterances (Denham and Land 1981); utterances of "uh" (Smith 1977); nor additional unexplained content (Land and Smith 1979b, Land and Combs 1982). Smith (1977), however, did report a significant positive correlation ($r = 0.46$, $p < 0.05$) between average number of "OK's" per minute of teacher talk and student achievement in mathematics. Smith and Cotten (1980) reported a significant effect, $F(1,96) = 10.62$, $p < 0.01$, for transitions, which they labeled as continuity/discontinuity. They defined two types of discontinuity. One type referred to the teacher's interruption in the lesson flow with an announcement irrelevant to the stimuli in the lesson. The second type referred to the teacher's interjection of relevant stimuli at inappropriate times in the lesson.

1.4 Clusters of Low-inference Variables

There have been at least 11 studies on the relationship between a cluster of low-inference variables and achievement (Table 3). Hiller et al. (1969) reported significant correlations (0.38 and 0.42) between student achievement and teacher verbal fluency, defined as a combination of average sentence length (teacher), comma proportion, and utterances of "uh." This variable accounted for 14 and 18 percent, respectively, of the variance in achievement.

The variable referred to as teacher structuring has been defined as a combination of reviewing main ideas and facts, stating objectives, outlining lesson content, signaling transitions, indicating important points, and summarizing as the lesson proceeds. Clark et al. (1979) reported results in favor of high structuring, but not significant results. Dunkin (1978) reported a significant correlation (0.41, $p < 0.05$) between structuring (coverage) and unadjusted achievement, accounting for 17 percent of the variance in student achievement.

Land (1979, 1980) and Denham and Land (1981) reported significant effects for a cluster of five clarity variables (mazes, vagueness terms, emphasis, transitions, and additional unexplained content) on achievement. In these three studies, the percent of variance in student achievement that could be accounted for by this cluster of variables was 8 percent, 6 percent, and 20 percent, respectively.

Working with a cluster of vagueness terms and mazes, Land (1981) reported significant results on achievement in mathematics, accounting for 6 percent of the variance in student achievement. Land and Smith (1981),

Table 3
Clusters of low-inference clarity variables and student achievement

Variables	Reference	Significance	% of Variance	Content	Grade level	N
Teacher verbal fluency: (average sentence length, comma proportion, utterances of "uh")	Hiller et al. 1969	0.01	18	Social studies	High school	32 classes
	Hiller et al. 1969	0.05	14	Social studies	High school	23 classes
Teacher structuring: (reviewing main ideas and facts, stating objectives, outlining lesson content, signaling transitions, indicating important points, summarizing)	Clark et al. 1979	ns	—	Science	Elementary	408
	Dunkin 1978	0.05	17	Social studies	Elementary	827
Clarity: (verbal mazes, vagueness terms, emphasis, transitions, additional unexplained content)	Denham and Land 1981	0.001	20	Psychology	College	129
	Land 1979	0.01	8	Psychology	College	78
	Land 1980	0.02	6	Psychology	College	77
	Land and Smith 1981	ns	—	Social studies	College	80
	Land 1981	0.05	6	Mathematics	College	84
Clarity: (29 variables)	Hines et al. 1982	0.03	52	Mathematics	College	32

IET-N

Table 4
Direct and indirect effects of clarity

		Direct effect— % of variance		Indirect effect— % of variance
		Clarity on perception	Clarity on achievement	Perception on achievement
(a)	Vagueness terms			
	Smith and Bramblett 1981	29	8	a
	Smith and Cotten 1980	17	7	a
	Smith and Land 1980	3	2	a
(b)	Verbal mazes			
	Land and Combs 1981	35	5	10
	Smith and Land 1980	27	3	a
(c)	Cluster of vagueness terms and mazes			
	Land 1981	59	6	a
	Land and Smith 1981	32	—	a
(d)	Cluster of 29 variables Hines, Cruickshank, and Kennedy 1982	49	40	28

a not available

however, reported no significant effect for this cluster on social studies achievement. In the former case, achievement was measured above the knowledge level, while in the latter case, the test items were written at the knowledge or recall level only.

In a study with a cluster of 29 variables, Hines et al. (1982), reported a significant relationship ($R = 0.72$, $p < 0.03$) between observer estimates of clarity and student achievement, accounting for 52 percent of the variance in student achievement.

2. Perception of Teacher Clarity

Educational researchers have rarely studied student mediating processes in relation to teacher behavior effects. Student perception of teacher clarity is such a process that may mediate the effect of teacher clarity on student achievement. Reference to Table 4 indicates the percent of variance in student perception and achievement that can be accounted for by various teacher clarity variables, and the percent of variance in achievement that can be accounted for by perception. In every case cited, the percent of variance accounted for by clarity was greater for perception than for achievement. In the Land and Combs study (1981), the percent of variance in achievement that could be accounted for by student perception was greater than that accounted for by teacher clarity, while the reverse was true in the Hines et al. study (1982). Hines et al. showed student perception of clarity to mediate strongly

the effect of clarity on student satisfaction (path coefficient = 0.51, $p < 0.001$), and to mediate moderately the effect of clarity on achievement (path coefficient = 0.13).

3. Conclusion

What has been learned about teacher clarity from recent studies? On the basis of natural classroom studies, low-inference variables of clarity can be broadly divided into those that inhibit learning (e.g., vagueness terms), and those that facilitate learning (e.g., signaling transitions). More is known about two of these variables—vagueness terms and verbal mazes—than is known about other low-inference clarity variables. Additional research in delineating other low-inference clarity variables and their effects (singularly and in combination) on student perception and achievement is needed. In addition, research is needed such as that by Hines et al. (1982) using path analysis procedures to study the direct and indirect causal effects of clarity variables on achievement. Then what is known about clarity needs to be applied to educating preservice teachers; that is, to decreasing the frequency of inhibiting clarity variables in a teacher's repertoire, to increasing the occurrence and frequency of facilitating clarity variables, and, finally, to studying the effects of these procedures on the achievement of the pupils of these preservice students.

See also: Technical Skills of Teaching; Synthesizing Research Evidence; Definitions of Teaching

Bibliography

Clark C M, Marx R W, Stayrook N G, Gage N L, Peterson P L, Winne P H 1979 A factorial experiment on teacher structuring, soliciting, and reacting. *J. Educ. Psychol.* 71: 534–52

Denham A, Land M L 1981 Research brief: Effect of teacher verbal fluency and clarity on student achievement. *T. Tech. J. Educ.* 8: 227–29

Dunkin M J 1978 Student characteristics, classroom processes, and student achievement. *J. Educ. Psychol.* 70: 998–1009

Dunkin M J, Doenau S J 1980 A replication study of unique and joint contributions to variance in student achievement. *J. Educ. Psychol.* 72: 394–403

Hiller J H 1968 An experimental investigation of the effects of conceptual vagueness on speaking behavior. Paper presented at the annual meeting of the American Educational Research Association, Chicago, Illinois

Hiller J H 1971 Verbal response indicators of conceptual vagueness. *Am. Educ. Res. J.* 8: 151–61

Hiller J H, Fisher G A, Kaess W 1969 A computer investigation of verbal characteristics of effective classroom lecturing. *Am. Educ. Res. J.* 6: 661–75

Hines C V, Cruickshank D R, Kennedy J J 1982 Measures of teacher clarity and their relationships to student achievement and satisfaction. Paper presented at the annual meeting of the American Educational Research Association, New York

Land M L 1979 Low-inference variables of teacher clarity: Effects on student concept learning. *J. Educ. Psychol.* 71: 795–99

Land M L 1980 Teacher clarity and cognitive level of questions: Effects on learning. *J. Exp. Educ.* 49: 48–51

Land M L 1981 Combined effects of two teacher clarity variables on student achievement. *J. Exp. Educ.* 50: 14–17

Land M L, Combs A 1981 Teacher clarity, student instructional ratings, and student performance. Paper presented at the annual meeting of the American Educational Research Association, Los Angeles, California

Land M L, Combs N 1982 Teacher behavior and student ratings. *Educ. Psychol. Res.* 2(1)

Land M L, Smith L R 1979a Effect of a teacher clarity variable on student achievement. *J. Educ. Res.* 5: 19–22

Land M L, Smith L R 1979b The effect of low inference teacher clarity inhibitors on student achievement. *J. Teach. Educ.* 30: 55–57

Land M L, Smith L R 1981 College student ratings and teacher behavior: An experimental study. *J. Soc. Stud. Res.* 5: 19–22

Rosenshine B 1971 *Teaching Behaviours and Student Achievement.* National Foundation for Educational Research, Slough

Smith L R 1977 Aspects of teacher discourse and student achievement in mathematics. *J. Res. Math. Educ.* 8: 195–204

Smith L R 1982 Training teachers to teach clearly: Theory into practice. Paper presented at the annual meeting of the American Educational Research Association, New York

Smith L R, Bramblett G H 1981 The effect of teacher vagueness terms on student performance in high school biology. *J. Res. Sci. Teach.* 18: 353–60

Smith L R, Cotten M L 1980 Effect of lesson vagueness and discontinuity on student achievement and attitudes. *J. Educ. Psychol.* 72: 670–75

Smith L R, Edmonds E M 1978 Teacher vagueness and pupil participation in mathematics learning. *J. Res. Math. Educ.* 9: 228–32

Smith L R, Land M L 1980 Student perception of teacher clarity in mathematics. *J. Res. Math. Educ.* 11: 137–46

Smith L R, Land M L 1981 Low-inference verbal behaviors related to teacher clarity. *J. Cl. Inter.* 17: 37–41

Pedagogical

Structuring

S. J. Doenau

Structuring is a term that frequently occurs in the literature dealing with observational studies of classroom processes. It refers to the attempts by teachers and students to supply the content of lessons and to provide both the long-term and the moment-by-moment frameworks that guide the course that those lessons take. While there is some kind of general agreement about the aspects of behaviour encompassed by the term, there is by no means a consensus about its particulars. An exposition of differences in usage will form a substantial part of this article.

1. The Structuring Move

1.1 Definition and Identification

Perhaps the most widely known approach to the analysis of structuring has been that developed by Arno Bellack and his associates at Teachers College, Columbia University, and described in detail in *The Language of the Classroom* (Bellack et al. 1966). In their analysis of the form and content of classroom discourse, Bellack et al. identified four "basic verbal actions" which they named "pedagogical moves": two initiating moves and two reflexive moves. "Structuring" was one of the initiating moves.

Two aspects of teaching suggested to Bellack et al. that the general metaphor of language games proposed by the philosopher Ludwig Wittgenstein was appropriate to the particular case of teaching. These were that the roles of teacher and student were complementary and that their activities seemed to be governed by rules. The term "move" adopted by Bellack et al. reflected their view that classroom discourse or "verbal interplay" could be thought of as a kind of language game. Within this conceptual framework, structuring was presented as a move in the classroom game.

Structuring moves are "pivotal points" which determine the direction of classroom discourse. Their function is "setting the context for subsequent behaviour by (a) launching or halting–excluding interactions between teacher and pupils and (b) indicating the nature of the interaction in terms of the dimensions of time, agent, activity, topic and cognitive process, regulations, reasons, and instructional aids" (Bellack et al. 1966 pp. 16–17). A structuring move may occur at any point within the classroom discourse, and may be made by either teacher or a student. It may occupy the whole of an utterance, or may share an utterance with one or even two other types of moves. Its length may vary from a single word to many consecutive words or lines of transcript. The context which it sets may relate to an overarching classroom game (such as a unit of work that spans a single lesson or a series of lessons) or a component segment or subgame (such as a student debate, pupil report, class discussion, or observation of a film). Sometimes a single structuring move may relate to both the total classroom game and one or more subgames. It may be a "single component" move presenting one set of "directives" for the game or subgame, or a "multicomponent" one presenting more than one set ("directives" are any indicators of the course to be taken, as distinct from orders or commands).

The following lesson excerpt contains illustrations of structuring moves. The moves have been italicized. The first structuring move is quite a complex multicomponent one. It launches the topic of the overarching classroom game and indicates later component subgames (activities of examining pictures, subgrouping, and reassembling). It also contains information about the dimensions of time (for the total game and some of the subgames), agent (teacher and students), cognitive process (telling and giving opinions), and instructional aids (pictures). The second structuring move is less complex. It halts one interaction and launches another, and contains a proposition about Japanese cities. The third structuring move is an example of a short simple move which merely announces the topic for the next part of the classroom discourse. Like the second structuring move, it is located in an utterance containing two other moves: a reacting move and a soliciting move.

Teacher: *This afternoon we're going to push ahead with cities. We'll get as far as we can this afternoon, but I think we'll have to continue tomorrow. I have some pictures here and I am going to ask you to tell me some of the things that you see and maybe your opinions about some of the problems that come out. After that we'll break up into discussion groups for 20 minutes or so, and then we'll all meet again to see what came out.* In this first picture I'm holding up, what do you notice?

Student: It's modern.

Teacher: Yes, that picture does tell you something about that, it's modern. What else do you notice?

Student: It has a lot of pollution.

Teacher: Yes, it does, a lot of pollution. *But there's something else. Remember last week we talked about population figures. We met the idea of population density. And as a matter of fact I saw an article in this morning's paper about the high population density of some Japanese cities. Perhaps some of you saw it too.* Now what did we decide about population density? What does it mean?

Student: The number of people.

Teacher: The number of people.

Student: The number of people in a place.

Teacher: OK. But could someone give me something accurate, an accurate definition?

(The discussion continues for several minutes, and then the teacher says)

Teacher: I think you've made some very good points there, Jannine's especially. *They suggest another one to me. Transport.* What could you tell me about population density and transport?

Distinguishing between structuring and other neighbouring moves in classroom discourse is often uncomplicated. Boundaries may be sharply defined; linguistic forms may be noticeably different; or speakers may change. Nevertheless, difficulties of recognition occur from time to time, particularly where a reacting move might be involved. For example, as Bellack et al. pointed out, some structuring moves may contain elements referring to a previous discussion, and some reacting moves may contain an implied introduction to a future topic. For Bellack et al., solutions to the consequent problems lay in using manifest content, especially a "distinct shift to another substantive area", and providing comprehensive definitions and numerous examples in their explanations of the system of analysis. Residual difficulties were handled by choosing the category that forwarded the discourse: that is, structuring.

1.2 The Directive Meaning of Structuring Moves

In addition to their concept of the structuring move, Bellack et al. provided a complementary set of concepts about the "directive meaning" of the structuring move. The members of this set were predominantly called "dimensions", but on some occasions the terms "directive functions", "features", and "directive features"

were applied to them. The term "components" was also used in relation to dimensions, although there was no clear indication whether the reference was to the dimensions as such or their subaspects.

The concept of directive meaning and its major dimensions were borrowed from Carl Wellman and adapted for application to classroom discourse. Wellman had proposed three basic features of directive meaning—indication (agent, object, and time reference), quasicomparison (specification of action), and prescription–prohibition. From these and their subaspects, Bellack et al. derived seven dimensions: function, method, activity, topic, cognitive process, agent, and time. These were supplemented by three further dimensions not derived from Wellman—reason giving, instructional aids, and regulations—to give a total of 10. Each of these dimensions was then analysed into subaspects appropriate to classrooms.

Many of these dimensions and subaspects were incorporated in the comprehensive discourse analysis system designed to encompass the four pedagogical moves and referred to by Bellack et al. as the "content analysis system" or simply the "coding system". There were differences but no incompatibilities between the structuring system and the comprehensive system. The main difference between them was that the former included subaspects not specifically identified in the latter, particularly with the subaspects of function, method, agent, time, regulations, and instructional aids.

1.3 Research Results from Bellack et al.

The first application of the system devised by Bellack et al. was in an analysis of four standard-content lessons taught to each of 15 upper-high-school classes studying a course on problems of democracy. The following were the main findings of this investigation, in so far as they related to structuring:

(a) Structuring moves occurred with less frequency than any of the other three pedagogical moves; 5.5 percent of the total moves and 18.1 percent of the total transcript lines were occupied by structuring. The mean length of teachers' structuring moves was 9.1 lines of transcript.

(b) Structuring was performed by students, but to a much lesser extent than its performance by teachers; 86 percent of structuring moves were made by teachers, and 12 percent by students.

(c) The function of launching was more frequent than the function of halting–excluding, 95.4 percent being launching. Of these 85.2 percent were performed by the teacher. Halting–excluding was an exclusively teacher function. The method of launching was announcing in 45.2 percent of instances, announcing and stating propositions in 34 percent of instances, and stating propositions in 16 percent of instances. While announcing was the most common launching method in both teachers' and the total discourse, the most common method in students' discourse was stating propositions (45 percent of instances).

(d) In 85 percent of instances, structuring was a single-component move; in 85 percent of these moves, the speaker was the teacher. Almost all multiple-component moves were spoken by the teacher.

(e) In about 20 percent of the components in which a topic was announced, the logical process to be used was also specified.

(f) The most common activities announced were general oral, reporting, and questioning–answering. Combined, these accounted for 78 percent of instances.

(g) In 84 percent of instances, the move following a teacher structuring move was a teacher question. With student structuring moves, a teacher reaction was the immediately following move in 49 percent of cases, a teacher solicitation in 22 percent of cases, and a student solicitation in 26 percent of cases.

2. The Structuring Move in Later Research

2.1 Important Research

The analysis system developed by Bellack and his associates has been used in a number of investigations in the United States, Sweden, Finland, Australia, New Zealand, and Papua New Guinea. Power (1971), citing advice from Bellack, indicated that the number of such studies at that time was about 25. Sometimes, the Bellack system has been the only analytic technique used; at other times, it has been used in association with other observational systems. Among the studies in more readily available primary or secondary sources have been Hoetker (1967), Power (1971), Lundgren (1972), Karma (1972), Dunkin (1977), Gustafsson (1977).

2.2 Modifications

In all of these named studies except Hoetker's, some modifications of aspects of the original instrument have been made, by way of subclassifications of categories, reinterpretations of demarcation procedures, changes in nomenclature, or shifts in an underlying conceptual stance. Power (1971), Lundgren (1972), Gustafsson (1977), and Dunkin (1977) are given below as examples of pieces of work illustrating modifications affecting the structuring move.

Power (1971) attempted to account for some of the nonverbal correlates of moves. For structuring, the subscript D was coded to indicate "when a predominantly verbal move is accompanied by a demonstration".

Lundgren (1972) reinterpreted the method of analysing some instances of the Bellack reacting move, which the originators (Bellack et al. 1966 p. 36) had nominated as one of the problematic aspects of analysis. His

approach was to code reacting followed by structuring when an utterance contained information that was additional to that contained in the preceding student response, even though the function of the additional information was not to change the substantive direction of the discourse. In explaining his approach, Lundgren used the example of a teacher saying "Yes, but we never actually send gold bullion to these foreign countries." The Bellack code for this utterance was reacting. Lundgren's dissenting usage was that "Yes" is a reacting move, but that the remainder of the utterance is a structuring move. Lundgren noted (1972 p. 234) that this deviation is marginal, though its effect is to increase the number of total moves and the number of structuring moves. It would also have an effect upon the number of cycles initiated by structuring.

Gustafsson (1977) identified four subtypes of structuring moves which, for comparative purposes, could be combined into a single structuring move equivalent to that of Bellack et al. The four subtypes were as follows:

(a) "Methodological administrative structuring action" organizes the practicalities of the teaching situation (e.g., "Okay, you can sit down like the rest and let's keep our books closed. And then we'd like all of you to sit in the same place each time you come here. . .").

(b) "Instructional structuring action" typically refers to a concrete situation such as the teacher's demonstration of a cognitive or practical operation accompanied by commentary by the teacher (e.g., "And then let's look closely and I'll teach you how we figure this out. I do exactly as before and write 15 just like before, and then I write the next number. . .").

(c) "Structuring action which lacks pedagogical content" is a comment without substantive content. One of the functions might be tension release (e.g., "Now let's see how John can cope with this problem"). Rhetorical questions are allocated to this subcategory.

(d) "'Telling' action" imparts substantive content (e.g., "We've never done anything like that before. Most of what we've learned has been something times 10. But we're now going to learn times 12").

In explaining her subclassifications, Gustafsson has included several paragraphs of description and one example for each of the types of structuring moves. Some problems, however, remain. The descriptions and examples are not substantial enough to allow the ready solution of equivocal cases. The distinctions between the command form of a methodological administrative structuring action and the Bellack imperative solicitation (e.g., "Turn the lights out Bobby," Bellack et

l. 1966 p. 95) are not clear. Her practice with respect to the Lundgren reinterpretation of some instances of the Bellack reacting move remains uncertain.

Dunkin (1977) used two interchangeable sets of terminology for his pedagogical moves: "statements, questions, answers, and comments" and "structuring, soliciting, responding, and commenting". Structuring or statement moves were defined as those which "provide information before a question or during discussion after a question, so long as they are not comments on or additions to a pupil's answer". Dunkin's inclusion of postquestion information is not necessarily inconsistent with the usage of Bellack et al. although their chapter on teaching cycles has presented no explicit consideration of the possibility. Nor is it necessarily inconsistent with Lundgren's reinterpretation which divided some of Bellack's reacting moves into reacting and structuring moves. But, whilst inconsistencies are not necessarily implied, caution about equating these coding conventions should be exercised.

Dunkin also identified an additional type of pedagogical move—the monologue—which was "an extended period of talk by a teacher without questions or requests directed to pupils". The criterion for coding speech as monologue was five or more lines of transcript.

2.3 Contexts and Results

In the studies utilizing the Bellack system, a variety of contexts has been represented: 45 hours of discourse from nine junior high-school (ages 11–13) English classes in the United States (Hoetker 1967); 57 lessons from eight grade 11 (age 16) mathematics classes in a large Swedish city (Lundgren 1972); 20 lessons from four grade 8 science classes in the metropolitan area of a large Australian city (Power 1971); 96 lessons devoted to Finnish, arithmetic, civics, drawing, religion, and music in one Finnish classroom of grades 3 and 4 students (Karma 1972); 40 short lessons covering mathematics and social studies taught by 10 teachers in grades 1, 4, and 6 of three schools in the highlands of Papua New Guinea (Dunkin 1977); 6 arithmetic lessons taught to the middle-ability subgroups of two classes in a Swedish large-city suburban school; and 9 lessons (460 minutes) covering mathematics, Swedish, and general subjects in a single grade 5 classroom in the same school (Gustafsson 1977).

Basing their comments on several combinations of findings, Hoetker (1967), Power (1971 p. 231), Lundgren (1972 p. 274, 1977 p. 148), Dunkin (1977), and Gustafsson (1977 p. 101) were impressed by the similarity of findings across cultures, grade levels, and subject areas. As far as the structuring move is concerned, the following regularities were apparent:

(a) The structuring move is the least frequent of all the moves. The mean percentages of moves that were structuring were 3.9 (Hoetker), 5.7 (Power p. 232), 10.0 or 11.0, depending on the basis of the calculation (Lundgren pp. 260, 274), 8.0 (Dunkin), 12.0 and 11.0 for grades 4 and 5 respectively (Gustafsson p. 100).

(b) The teacher was the predominant agent of structuring. The mean percentages of structuring moves made by the teacher were 92 (Hoetker), 96.5 (Power), 96 (Lundgren), 100 (Dunkin), 100 and 94 for grades 4 and 5 respectively (Gustafsson).

(c) Within studies which reported the incidence of pedagogical moves in different subject areas, the findings about structuring were generally maintained across subject boundaries. In Dunkin's study, 8 percent was the mean for the number of structuring moves in each of the set of mathematics and social studies lessons. In Gustafsson's grade 5 study, a reconstruction of the results shows that the percentages of structuring moves were 12.5, 10.5, and 6.5 for general subjects, mathematics, and Swedish respectively (Gustafsson 1977 p. 189). Structuring by the teacher accounted for 100 percent of the structuring moves in mathematics and Swedish and 90 percent of structuring moves in general subjects.

This general profile of results, however, was not evident in all studies. In Karma (1972), 17.5 percent of all moves were structuring moves. This was still the lowest percentage of moves in comparison with other types of moves, but was higher than the percentage reported in the majority of studies. A notable difference in Karma's study was that 43 percent of structuring moves were registered by students. An even more extreme result was recorded in Bernardini's (1974) study of eight lessons conducted in a series of adult classes in computer programming, where over half of the discourse was reported to have been devoted to the structuring move.

Other important results in the Swedish research reveal the differentiated roles of student subgroups. Lundgren (1972 p. 315) found that students in the "steering group" (students in the 10–25 percentile according to general ability) received fewer structuring moves than other class members: 3 percent of the moves they received were structuring, compared with 16 percent for entire classes. Gustafsson (1977 pp. 194–214) identified clusters of students who displayed similarity in their patterns of verbal actions during class lessons. Separate analyses of these patterns revealed marked differences between clusters in the number of structuring moves which they received. In the grade 4 study, the percentages of structuring moves for the two main clusters were 15 and 3 respectively; in the grade 5 study, the percentages for the two main clusters were 17 and 11 respectively in mathematics lessons, 5 and 11 respectively in Swedish lessons, and 10 and 18 respectively in lessons on general subjects.

3. The Structuring Move and Similar Variables

3.1 Types of Variables

The terms "structuring", "structures", "structure", and "structured" are common occurrences in the literature of teaching and teaching research. For example, the Adams (1972) analysis of concepts appearing throughout the observational studies of 150 researchers contained 14 separate instances of the word "structures". Some behaviours designated by these terms manifest little or no relationship with the Bellack structuring move. There are others where the relationship is strong, although the precise degree of equivalence with original or modified Bellack usage is frequently difficult to establish. Further, in some observation systems, there are behaviours which are identified by labels that omit any reference to "structure" but which, nevertheless, closely resemble the Bellack move or certain of its manifestations. In the following paragraphs the usage by Bellack et al. provides a stable and convenient reference point for comparison. There is no implication, however, that theirs is the only legitimate usage.

Concepts denoted by such terms as "structure", but unrelated to the structuring move of Bellack et al., are beyond the scope of the present article. Examples of such concepts are "highly structured question", "structuring feedback", "low structure instruction" (an equivalent of nondirective instruction), "discourse structure" or the "structure of lessons" (as in Sinclair and Coulthard 1975), "kinetic structure analysis", "unstructured class time", "structured learning", and "structuring behaviours" as an equivalent of "direct instruction" (see *Direct Instruction*).

3.2 Structuring

Descriptions of structuring that are related to identifiable acts of teaching and to the usage of Bellack et al. may be grouped into several clusters dependent upon the number of behaviour types comprehended and the extent of divergence from Bellack et al:

(a) reductions of the scope of the Bellack structuring move,

(b) expansions which include the possibility of some aspects of the Bellack reacting move,

(c) expansions which additionally include some aspects of Bellack soliciting or responding moves, including the possibility of Bellack cycles,

(d) conglomerates of teaching strategies which include diverse combinations of Bellack moves.

There are two main types of reductions. The first consist of those diffuse descriptions which can be interpreted as having less scope than Bellack's structuring move. Examples of this type are:

(a) "Structure: examination of 'old' knowledge as an end in itself, as in review; or a clearcut break during development of a new relation or during application of new or old concepts" (Wright 1970 p. 25).

(b) Rowe's (1974 p. 218) characterization of structuring as "moving to a new topic".

(c) Turney et al. (1973 p. 40) equated lecturing and structuring, "that is, expository statements by the teacher".

(d) Berliner and Tikunoff (1977 p. 287), working within an ethnographic framework, identified 61 dimensions of effective classrooms. One of these was structuring: "teacher prepares students for lessons by reviewing, outlining, explaining objectives, and summarizing". Good and Brophy (1980 p. 445) described structuring in exactly the same terms. The reduction lies in the emphases upon the teacher and upon preparation for lessons.

(e) McCaleb and White (1980 p. 27) conceptualized organization as consisting of two major components, structuring and sequencing. Structuring includes the aspects that "promote a clear presentation: stating the purpose, reviewing the main ideas, and providing transitions".

The other main type of reduction is the explicit decomposition of the concept of structuring into separately named subaspects. Zahorik and Brubaker (1972 p. 19) proposed two subtypes of informing: relating and structuring. "Structuring can be defined as those acts which establish the setting in which teaching and learning will occur. Relating refers to the stating of substantive facts, generalizations, opinions, values, ideas, and the like." In much the same way, Duthie (1978) separately identified "structures" and "informational statements". It should be noted that Gage and Unruh's (1967) comparison of live and programmed instruction, based on their interpretation of Bellack's results, made a similar distinction.

Expansions including the possibility of some aspects of the Bellack reacting move are consistent with the Lundgren modification and are represented by a set of researchers and reviewers who include, under structuring, such behaviours as summary and review. Under the conventions of Bellack et al., summary would frequently, though not necessarily, be included in the reacting move: "substantive reactions serve to modify (by clarifying, synthesizing, or expanding) what was said substantively in the occasioning move" (p. 172) or, to put it another way, may be used "to clarify, expand, or synthesize statements of preceding speakers" (p. 169). Examples of structuring which include aspects of Bellack's substantive reaction are:

(a) A series of studies by Corno and her associates featured structuring (Stayrook et al. 1978, Corno 1979, 1980). This behaviour was reported as explicitly "derived" from Bellack et al. (Stayrook et al. 1978) and "adapted directly from Peterson's behavioural specifications" (Corno 1980), and included "reviewing, stating goals, summarizing, and marking important points" (Corno 1980).

(b) For Arlin (1979), transitions between one classroom activity and the next were designated as structured if they were marked by an established set of procedures; explanatory pretransition comments and comments about students' off-task behaviour were both manifestations of structured transitions.

(c) Wright and Nuthall (1970 pp. 482–89) identified two types of structuring: the "content-relevant information during the course of discussion" frequently occurring either before a significant question (prequestion structuring) or after it (postquestion structuring), and terminal structuring "at the completion of an episode initiated by a question" (i.e. "information following pupil responses" or "an informative summary at the end of an episode of discussion").

(d) An experimental study conducted by the Stanford Center for Research and Development in Teaching (Program on Teaching Effectiveness 1976) manipulated combinations of high and low structuring, soliciting, and reacting to form a set of "strategy variations". High structuring consisted of "reviewing the main ideas and facts covered in a lesson, stating objectives at the beginning of a lesson, outlining the lesson content, signalling transitions between parts of a lesson, indicating important points in a lesson, and summarizing the parts of the lessons as the lesson proceeded". Low structuring was the absence of these behaviours.

(e) Structuring was described in an important series of reviews by Rosenshine, and Rosenshine and Furst in the early 1970s. Though similar, these descriptions were not identical. One description appeared in Rosenshine (1971 p. 110), where structuring referred to "the teacher comments made at the beginning or at the end of a lesson, and the teacher comments made before or after the teacher asks a question". The emphasis in Rosenshine and Furst (1973 p. 157) was upon structuring as the provision of overviews rather than mere informative comments: "Structuring statements which provide an overview for what is about to happen or has happened have been identified and counted at the start and end of lessons, and at the start and end of sequences of questions". This set of descriptions of structuring should be sharply distinguished from the "structuring behaviours" of Rosenshine's later series of reviews dealing with direct instruction (e.g., Rosenshine 1976 p. 365).

Expansions including Bellack soliciting components and perhaps Bellack cycles are represented in the following examples:

(a) Predating Bellack et al., the Aschner–Gallagher System for Classifying Thought Processes (Gallagher and Aschner 1963) contained four components of structuring. Self-structuring consists of remarks signalling the content and purpose of one's own next remarks on behaviour. Structuring others is the engineering of the next speech or actions of others, monitoring performance or "pump-priming". Future structuring is a forecast of behaviour and activities in subsequent class sessions. Class structuring is the focusing of attention on a particular point, including laying the groundwork for a problem or question and "probing, pushing, adding data for bogged-down class".

(b) Peterson's (1977) four synthesized approaches to teaching utilized two levels of each of structuring and pupil participation. "Structuring included goals, verbal markers, transition signals, advance organizers, teacher summaries, student summaries, teacher reviews, student reviews, and teacher previews." In the high structure/high participation treatment, such behaviours as goal setting, reviewing, and summarizing are performed by students as a consequence of questioning by the teacher. In addition, in the high structure/high participation treatment, "teacher asks many questions and uses questions and student responses to structure lessons". In contrast, the low structure/low participation teacher "asks few questions and does not use those few questions to tie the lesson together". That is, participation level strongly affects the extent to which Peterson's structure behaviours are able to be equated with aspects of Bellack's structuring move on the one hand, or other Bellack moves or cycles on the other.

(c) In the Sydney Micro Skills Manuals (Turney et al. 1975 p. 64) structuring consists of "statements by the teacher which provide pupils with information on the purpose and direction of the lesson and which provide content-relevant information to assist pupils to reach the goals which have been established for the lesson". Structuring includes statements of aims and procedures at the beginning of a lesson (initial structuring), prequestion comments, and ongoing teacher comments designed to keep the lesson within bounds (procedural structuring). Structuring may also be "particularly with regard to setting objectives or suggesting ways to proceed . . . a joint teacher–pupil venture" (Turney et al. 1975 p. 87).

(d) Tisher and Power's (1975 p. 133) "additional structuring" included reference to both the beginnings and ends of lessons. It thus bore a similarity to the outlining, stating objectives, and reviewing of other authors. However, its inclusion of class discussions as structuring components extended the term to encompass Bellack cycles as well as Bellack moves.

They described "additional structuring" in this way: "At the beginning and end of each lesson the teachers led a class discussion on the salient points which had been covered previously and indicated points that would arise in the ensuing lesson: thus they involved the whole class in review and overview at the beginning and end of each lesson."

Extensive conglomerates are found particularly in commentaries and texts. An example is the description of "teacher structuring behaviour" in Gage and Berliner (1975 pp. 690–95). Included in the description were the rate of teacher initiation and structuring (in both the Bellack et al. and the Wright and Nuthall usages of the term), signal giving (another form of "instructional structuring" or "structuring move" that includes indicating transitions and using verbal markers of importance), organization, and directness (in the Flanders use of the term) which is "akin to structuring". The Gage and Berliner analysis contained one instance where "structuring" and "information giving" were conceptually distinguished, but this was not consistent with their typical interpretation.

3.3 Specific Structuring Behaviours

There is a group of studies which have not used the term "structuring", but have used terms that might apply to particular manifestations of the Bellack structuring move. For example, *British Mirrors* (1978), which contained very few instances of the term "structuring" or "structures" in the 41 instruments reported, contained many instances of such behaviours as: "teacher tells, requires nothing of class but attention" (Alexander); "task statements (i) of facts (ii) of ideas, problems" (Boydell); "representation" as an aspect of "general initiating utterances" (Breen and Goodall); "teacher makes statements (i) of fact and principle, (ii) of problems, (iii) of hypothesis or speculation, (iv) of experimental procedure" (Eggleston, Galton, and Jones); "giving an opinion" and "giving information" (Powell); and "marker", "informative", the statement form of "clue", "silent stress", metastatements" which function to indicate the "structure of the lesson" (Sinclair and Coulthard).

Other examples are found in such researchers as Borg (1975) and Kounin and Doyle (1975):

(a) Apart from his "terminal structure" ("near end of lesson, teacher adds content-relevant information which has not been covered previously") at least three of Borg's 12 behaviours could be classed as specific manifestations of the structuring move. "Cueing" occurs when the teacher "calls students' attention to important points by using phrases such as 'this is important' or 'be sure to remember this'" [a different usage from Sinclair and Coulthard's "cue", which is the teacher's attempt to evoke a response bid, and from Corno's (1979) "verbal cues" which include stating goals, marking important points, summarizing, and reviewing]. "Voice modulation" refers to the teacher's use of voice tone and inflection to emphasize main points. "Open review" is where "at start of lesson, teacher reviews or elicits student review of relevant past learning"; the statement form of this behaviour is similar to Wright and Nuthall's "recapitulation".

(b) Kounin and Doyle (1975) presented the proposition that there are "external provisions of lessons" which orient and support the behaviours of pupils during lessons. These provisions, which may commonly be specific verbal communications (such as "Let's see which things stick to a magnet and which don't") or lesson props, are called "signal systems".

3.4 Process–Product Relationships

Relationships between the several versions or particular manifestations of structuring and student achievement have been explored in a number of studies. Most of these have been correlational, although several important experimental studies have been undertaken.

Rosenshine (1971) and Rosenshine and Furst (1973) have summarized the results of the earlier process–product studies on structuring. From their analyses, they concluded that "structuring" was then one of the 11 strongest variables in classroom research, although the results were not conclusive enough to warrant inclusion in their list of the strongest five.

In all, these reviewers were able to identify only eight pertinent classroom studies. Three of these were high-inference studies which used observer or student ratings of the teacher's mode of beginning and ending a lesson. For "beginning the lesson", significant positive correlations were found in two studies, and a combination of significant and nonsignificant in the third. For "ending the lesson", results were mixed—significant in one study, not significant in another, and both significant and nonsignificant in the third. Five low-inference studies were identified, including one without significance tests. The variables used in these were transition signals (one study), emphasis (two studies), number of statements before questioning (one study), number of seconds lecturing before questioning (one study), and Wright and Nuthall's (1970) five forms of structuring (prequestion, postquestion, episode-termination, review/recapitulation at beginning of lesson, review/revision at end of lesson). Significant positive relationships were reported for number of statements before questioning (nonlinear relationship), number of lecturing seconds before questioning, emphasis through verbal markers of importance, episode-termination (terminal structuring), and review at the end of a lesson.

Although the reviewers were impressed by the number of significant positive relationships in both the low- and high-inference studies, they were nevertheless cautious about the validity of including such diverse and sometimes imprecisely defined behaviours under a common label (e.g., Rosenshine and Furst 1973). Additionally, they were interested in making recommendations that would more accurately identify the operation of structuring in future research. In particular, Rosenshine (1971) recommended three types of analysis: the placement of structuring, the relationship between questioning quality and prequestion structuring statements, and the use of nonlinear analyses as adjuncts to the more frequent linear techniques.

Structuring has continued to be a target of process–product classroom research in the period since the Rosenshine review series. The rate of production has continued to be slow, the diversity of definitions of structuring has persisted, and Rosenshine's own use of the term "teacher structuring" has dramatically expanded in his later review series on direct instruction (e.g., Rosenshine 1976). Against this background, however, the body of research has reflected several of the recommendations that Rosenshine had made.

The highlight of the period has been the contribution of the Stanford group, with its large-scale experimentation, its use of aptitude-treatment interaction (ATI) concepts and analyses, and its rigorous approach to statistical analysis. Five studies warrant particular mention:

(a) In an experimental study from the Stanford Center for Research and Development in Teaching (Program on Teaching Effectiveness 1976) four experienced teachers were trained to produce eight combinations of recitation behaviours formed from either high or low amounts of structuring, soliciting, and reacting. These combinations were used with groups of grade 6 students (aged 11) in a nine-lesson ecology unit. The behavioural specifications for high and low structuring were those included in an earlier section of this entry. The major result from the analysis of structuring was that high structuring groups performed only marginally better than the low structuring groups on both the immediate and the retention tests of achievement. The investigators interpreted this difference as being perhaps due simply to chance.

(b) Stayrook et al. (1978) analysed the behavioural, student perception, and achievement data from the 1975 Program on Teaching Effectiveness study, using separate path analyses for each of the three manipulated teacher behaviours. For teacher structuring, the correlation with achievement was 0.32. Decomposition revealed a direct causal effect of 0.04, an indirect causal effect of 0.10, and a non-causal effect of 0.18. The authors' interpretation of this finding was that the indirect perception-mediated effect was greater than the direct teacher-implemented effect of structuring.

(c) Peterson (1977) used one teacher to teach a two-week social science unit to four 9th-grade classes (aged 14). Each class received a different experimental treatment consisting of a high or low level of each of structuring and participation. On a range of achievement and attitudinal measures, the experimental treatment alone was not significant. But several complex and significant ATIs involving structuring effects were found. The finding that has attracted the most interest in those who have cited Peterson (e.g., Corno 1979 p. 393) is that the low-structuring/low-participation treatment was unfavourable for students either low or high in both anxiety and general ability, and favourable for students with high/low combinations of both aptitudes.

(d) Corno (1979), within an ATI framework, conducted extensive observations on the structuring and participation demands of 33 3rd-grade teachers, taking account of behaviours directed both to the whole class (teacher focus) and to individual students (child focus). Analyses of results showed a significant general ability × structure ATI for the vocabulary measure, indicating a strong increase in achievement for classes of high ability under a low structure treatment.

(e) A further ATI analysis of teacher structuring and participation demands was undertaken by Corno (1980) in an experimental study of a parent-mediated instructional programme (the Learning Skills Program) designed to sensitize 3rd-grade students to the role of these two variables conceptualized as "memory support strategies". The results of the study showed that those who used the programme performed significantly higher than controls on a test of knowledge about the "tricks for making ideas orderly" and "tricks for sharing your ideas". The main ATI findings were that high-ability classes showed the highest acquisition of the programme concepts; high-anxiety class groups appeared to profit most from the programme in terms of vocabulary test scores; and a general ability × anxiety × programme analysis showed that, on nonverbal reasoning tests, all configurations except the high-ability/low-anxiety classes did best without the programme.

Other research since the Rosenshine and Furst review has included the following:

(a) Nuthall (1974) conducted nonlinear analyses of the data from Wright and Nuthall (1970) for prequestion (beginning of episode) structuring. The original 1970 analysis had found a significant positive relationship between terminal structuring and achievement, but no relationship between prequestion structuring and achievement. The reanalyses found curvilinear relationships for both variables at each of three levels of pupil ability.

(b) Borg (1975) used protocol modules to train 25 teachers to use or avoid 12 specified behaviours, including several that related to structuring: voice modulation, cueing, terminal structure, summary review, and opening review. Posttraining teaching of a set of four standard-content lessons was followed by achievement testing. Cueing (calling attention to important points), terminal structure (an addition, near the end of a lesson, of information not previously covered), and opening review showed significant positive relationships with achievement.

(c) Dunkin's (1978) correlational process–product study of 29 grade 6 (age 11) standard-content social studies lessons was essentially an analysis of several models of apportioning variance in student achievement. Among the process variables were two measures of teacher structuring: teacher structuring coverage (the number of posttest items for which relevant information occurred at least once in teacher structuring moves) and teacher structuring repetition (the number of posttest items for which relevant information occurred at least twice in teacher structuring moves). Teacher structuring coverage showed a significant positive correlation with the three postlesson measures of achievement.

(d) Dunkin and Doenau (1980) conducted a similar study with two standard-content lessons in grade 6 social studies; one of the lessons involved 28 classes, and the other 26. A critical thinking test and short-term and longer-term knowledge tests were administered after each lesson. Included in the classroom process measures were two global informing measures: content coverage in teacher informing and content repetition in teacher informing. There were also three more specific structuring variables: initial informing (before the primary question of an episode), terminal informing (after the final student response in an episode), and intervening informing (between the episode's primary question and its final student response). In the first lesson, content coverage in teacher informing showed a strong pattern of significant positive correlations with various measures of the knowledge test; and terminal informing showed a strong pattern of negative correlations with residualized measures of knowledge and critical thinking. In the second lesson, the only structuring variable to show significant results was content coverage in teacher informing, which was positively correlated with two measures of short-term knowledge.

4. Structuring and Theory

The approach of Bellack et al. to the analysis of classroom discourse owed a considerable theoretical debt to the views of Wittgenstein and Wellman. Since the publication of the influential *Language of the Classroom* in 1966, however, other attempts to embed structuring into a theoretical framework have received a low priority, either by way of deriving stringent hypotheses from theoretical postulates or utilizing empirical findings in the construction or refinement of well-integrated theories of teaching. This state of affairs is not unique to structuring but has been common to teaching research in general. As far as structuring is concerned, the most notable attempts at providing theory-based or theory-generating research have been the frame factor studies conducted by the Swedish group (e.g., Lundgren 1972) and the ATI studies, which utilize anxiety and general ability as major student aptitudes, conducted by the Stanford group (e.g., Peterson 1977).

See also: Direct Instruction; Activities: Structures and Functions; Teaching Cycles and Strategies

Bibliography

Adams R S 1972 Observational studies of teacher role. *Int. Rev. Educ.* 18: 440–58
Arlin M 1979 Teacher transitions can disrupt time flow in classrooms. *Am. Educ. Res. J.* 16: 42–56
Bellack A A, Kliebard H M, Hyman R T, Smith F L 1966 *The Language of the Classroom.* Teachers College Press, New York
Berliner D C, Tikunoff W 1977 Ethnography in the classroom. In: Borich G D, Fenton K S (eds.) 1977 *The Appraisal of Teaching: Concepts and Process.* Addison-Wesley, Reading, Massachusetts
Bernardini D D F de 1974 A descriptive study of teacher–student verbal behavior in selected computer programming language classrooms in an adult education environment (Ed.D. thesis, Columbia University) *Dissertation Abstracts International* 35: 6566A–6567A (University Microfilms No. 75–7831)
Borg W R 1975 Protocol materials as related to teacher performance and pupil achievement. *J. Educ. Res.* 69: 23–30
Corno L 1979 A hierarchical analysis of selected naturally occurring aptitude-treatment interactions in the third grade. *Am. Educ. Res. J.* 16: 391–409
Corno L 1980 Individual and class level effects of parent-assisted instruction in classroom memory support strategies. *J. Educ. Psychol.* 72: 278–92
Dunkin M J 1977 A study of classroom interaction in Papua New Guinea. *Papua New Guinea J. Educ.* 13: 1–11
Dunkin M J 1978 Student characteristics, classroom processes and student achievement. *J. Educ. Psychol.* 70: 998–1009
Dunkin M J, Doenau S J 1980 A replication study of unique and joint contributions to variance in student achievement. *J. Educ. Psychol.* 72: 394–403
Duthie J H 1978 Primary school technological instrument. In: Galton M (ed.) 1978
Gage N L, Berliner D C 1975 *Educational Psychology.* Rand McNally, Chicago, Illinois
Gage N L, Unruh W R 1967 Theoretical formulations for research on teaching. *Rev. Educ. Res.* 37: 358–70
Gallagher J J, Aschner M J 1963 A preliminary report on analyses of classroom interaction. *Merrill–Palmer Q.* 9: 183–94
Galton M (ed.) 1978 *British Mirrors.* School of Education, University of Leicester, Leicester
Good T L, Brophy J E 1980 *Educational Psychology: A Realistic Approach*, 2nd edn. Holt, Rinehart and Winston, New York

Gustafsson C 1977 *Classroom Interaction: A Study of Pedagogical Roles in the Teaching Process*. Department of Educational Research, Stockholm Institute of Education, Stockholm

Hoetker W J 1967 Analyses of the subject matter related verbal behavior in nine junior high school English classes (Unpublished Ed.D. Dissertation, Washington University) Cited in: Hoetker J, Ahlbrand W P (eds.) 1969 The persistence of the recitation. *Am. Educ. Res. J.* 6: 145–67

Karma K 1972 *Investigations into the Instructional Process: Experiences with the Bellack Classification System*. Institute of Education, University of Helsinki, Helsinki

Kounin J S, Doyle P H 1975 Degree of continuity of a lesson's signal system and the task involvement of children. *J. Educ. Psychol.* 67: 159–64

Lundgren U P 1972 *Frame Factors and the Teaching Process: A Contribution to Curriculum Theory and Theory on Teaching*. Almqvist and Wiksell, Stockholm

McCaleb J L, White J A 1980 Critical dimensions in evaluating teacher clarity. *J. Classroom Interaction* 15: 27–30

Nuthall G A 1968 Studies of teaching, II: Types of research on teaching. *N. Z. J. Educ. Stud.* 3: 125–47

Nuthall G A 1974 Is classroom interaction research worth the effort involved? *N. Z. J. Educ. Stud.* 9: 1–17

Peterson P L 1977 Interactive effects of student anxiety, achievement orientation, and teacher behavior on student achievement and attitude. *J. Educ. Psychol.* 69: 779–92

Power C N 1971 The effects of communication patterns on student sociometric status, attitudes and achievement in science (Unpublished Ph.D thesis, University of Queensland, Australia)

Program on Teaching Effectiveness SCRDT 1975 *Preliminary Report of a Factorially Designed Experiment on Teacher Structuring, Soliciting and Reacting*. Stanford Center for Research and Development in Teaching, Stanford, California

Rosenshine B 1971 *Teaching Behaviours and Student Achievement*. National Foundation for Educational Research, Slough

Rosenshine B 1976 Classroom instruction. In: Gage N L (ed.) 1976 *The Psychology of Teaching Methods: The Seventy-fifth Yearbook of the National Society for the Study of Education, Part 1*. University of Chicago Press, Chicago, Illinois

Rosenshine B, Furst N 1973 The use of direct observation to study teaching. In: Travers R M W (ed.) 1973 *Second Handbook of Research on Teaching: A Project of the American Educational Research Association*. Rand McNally, Chicago, Illinois

Rowe M B 1974 Pausing phenomena: Influence on the quality of instruction. *J. Psycholinguistic Res.* 3: 203–24

Sinclair J M, Coulthard R M 1975 *Towards an Analysis of Discourse: The English Used by Teachers and Pupils*. Oxford University Press, London

Stayrook N G, Corno L, Winne P H 1978 Path analyses relating student perceptions of teacher behaviour to student achievement. *J. Teach. Educ.* 29: 51–56

Tisher R P, Power C N 1975 A study of the effects of teaching strategies in ASEP classrooms. *Aust. J. Educ.* 19: 127–45

Turney C, Clift J C, Dunkin M J, Traill R D 1973 *Microteaching: Research, Theory and Practice: An Innovation in Teacher Education Especially as it Relates to the Australian Context*. Sydney University Press, Sydney

Turney C, Cairns L G, Williams G, Hatton W, Owens L C 1975 *Sydney Micro Skills Handbook*, Series 1: *Reinforcement, Basic Questioning, Variability*. Sydney University Press, Sydney

Turney C, Owens L C, Hatton N, Williams G, Cairns L G 1975 *Sydney Micro Skills Handbook*, Series 2: *Explaining, Introductory Procedures and Closure, Advanced Questioning*. Sydney University Press, Sydney

Wright C J, Nuthall G 1970 Relationships between teacher behaviors and pupil achievement in three experimental elementary science lessons. *Am. Educ. Res. J.* 7: 477–91

Wright E M J 1970 Wright System. In: Simon A, Boyer E G (eds.) 1970 *Mirrors for Behavior II*, Vol A.

Zahorik J A, Brubaker D L 1972 *Toward More Humanistic Instruction*. Brown, Dubuque, Iowa

Soliciting

S. J. Doenau

In observational investigations of classroom processes, the term "soliciting" is applied to attempts by teachers or students to elicit a verbal or nonverbal behavior from a classroom member. Many authors use the term only with reference to questioning and to verbal responding; but a minority apply it both to questioning and to a variety of managerial or directive statements or activities.

1. Bellack's Soliciting Move

One of the broadest usages of the term "soliciting" has appeared in the pioneering research of Bellack et al. (1966). Soliciting was one of the four "pedagogical moves" identified by those authors, and was described as a move "intended to elicit (a) an active verbal response on the part of the person addressed, (b) a cognitive response, for example, encouraging persons addressed to attend to something, or (c) a physical response." The sequence of a "response-expectant" soliciting move followed by "expectancy fulfilling" responding move—"the soliciting–responding act"was considered to be the "core of classroom discourse."

For the analysis of classroom discourse as a whole, Bellack et al. developed a system which they referred to as "the basic system," "the content analysis system," or simply "the coding system." In texts and reviews it is usually identified as the Bellack System. When applied to soliciting, this instrument has been used to generate information about the number and source of soliciting moves, the cognitive processes involved in them—analytic (defining, interpreting), empirical (fact-stating, explaining), and evaluative (opining, justifying)—and the proportion of a lesson devoted to each.

In addition to the basic system, Bellack et al. developed a more detailed, though overlapping, approach to the analysis of soliciting. It was directed towards three major aspects: who solicits whom, what expectations are conveyed by the solicitor (the indicative meaning), and how the expectations are conveyed (the stylistic meaning). The subcategories within these three aspects are so extensive that the analysis system is clearly one of the most comprehensive in the entire research literature on solicitation. It has, however, attracted far less attention from the research community than the more versatile basic system.

The basic and detailed systems were applied by Bellack et al. to a set of four standard-content lessons taught to each of 15 upper-high-school classes. Subsequently, the basic system has been used, though not necessarily in its complete form, in a number of studies (see *Structuring*). As far as the soliciting move is concerned, analyses within the Bellack framework have typically been confined to source, frequency, and logical processes. The major exceptions since the comprehensive work of Bellack et al. (1966) have been Gustafsson (1977) and the less accessible investigation by Power (1971).

The most common findings from studies within the Bellack framework are as follows:

(a) The soliciting move is generally the most frequent of the four pedagogical moves. Mean percentages of soliciting moves in various studies range from 29 to 42.

(b) Soliciting is a move made predominantly by teachers rather than students. Mean percentages of teacher soliciting moves range from 76 to 97, with percentages over 90 being most frequent.

(c) In the analysis of formally ordered teaching cycles—that is, interrelated series of moves commencing with either a structuring or soliciting move—two cycles account for a major proportion of cycle types. These cycles were soliciting–responding–reacting (with percentages ranging from 17 to 37) and soliciting–responding (with percentages ranging from 14 to 22) (see *Teaching Cycles and Strategies*).

Other less common findings concern the logical processes demanded by solicitations (e.g., Bellack et al. 1966, Karma 1972), the differential experiences of classroom subgroups (e.g., Lundgren 1972, Gustafsson 1977), and the indicative and stylistic meanings of solicitations (e.g., Bellack et al. 1966, Power 1971).

2. Research Beyond the Bellack Framework

Beyond the Bellack framework, the observation-based analysis of classroom questioning has had a relatively short history. The pioneering work of Stevens (1912) (in Wragg et al. 1976) who used both live observation and shorthand records to study the frequency and nature of questions, has been described in the very useful historical overview in *Classroom Interaction* (Wragg et al. 1976). Such a research interest in questioning, however, remained extremely rare until at least the 1950s.

The extent of the developing interest in questioning is apparent in instrument anthologies such as *Mirrors for Behavior* and *British Mirrors* (1978). In the 1970 edition of *Mirrors for Behavior*, 52 of the 69 observation systems contained references to questioning or its components; in *British Mirrors*, 30 of the 41 systems contained such references.

From these instruments, the analyses of questioning by such major reviewers as Gall (1970), Rosenshine (1971), and Dunkin and Biddle (1974), and the research output since the middle 1970s, it is clear that the aspects of questioning of interest to instrument developers and system-based researchers have been cognitive level or intellectual demand, frequency, probing, questioning by students, post-question wait-time, and multiple questions. Of these, frequency and cognitive demand have been predominant. But it should be noted that, despite the robust role of questioning in textbooks for teachers, the volume of research into classroom questioning has been quite small.

3. Cognitive Features of Questions

The three main topics of observation-based research into the cognitive levels of classroom questioning have been the relative frequencies of types of questions, the extent to which cognitive demand of questioning is responsive to training, and the relationship between the cognitive demand of teachers' questions and student achievement. This research has been thoroughly described and assessed in the reviews of Gall (1970), the earlier Rosenshine series (especially 1971), Dunkin and Biddle (1974), the later Rosenshine series on "direct instruction" (e.g., 1976), and Winne (1979).

3.1 Analysis Techniques

Dunkin and Biddle have presented a comprehensive description of the main systems used in the analysis of the cognitive levels of classroom questions: the Bloom-based systems (such as Davis and Tinsley); the Guilford-based system of Aschner and Gallagher; Taba; Smith and Meux; and Bellack. Of these five ways of conceptualizing the cognitive features of questions, Bloom-based systems have continued to be the most common. Other conceptualizations are reflected in the range of terms identified by Rosenshine (1971) or contained in the instrument anthologies.

3.2 Frequencies of Question Types

Studies about the cognitive status of teachers' questions have frequently shown a preponderance of lower order questions. An interpretation that lower order questions are typical of teaching is one which many reviewers would adopt. For example, Gall (1970) concluded that, in the half century since Stevens' classic study, the types of questions emphasized by teachers seemed not to have changed, with about 60 percent requiring recall of facts, 20 percent requiring thinking, and the remainder requiring procedural activities. Drawing on a more extensive and diverse set of investigations, and more cautious about global generalizations, Dunkin and Biddle (1974) identified eight Bloom-based studies in which "knowledge" was more commonly used than any other category, two studies using Gallagher and Aschner's approach which revealed the use of more cognitive memory than other categories (though behaviors other than questioning were included), and three studies based on Smith and Meux in which describing was used more than any other single category and the seven categories designated by Tisher as "higher level" accounted for between one-quarter and one-third of all teacher questions.

Studies additional to those cited by Dunkin and Biddle have produced mixed evidence about the incidence of various types of questions. On the one hand, for example, three studies included in Chanan's (1973) collection reported that a combination of Bloom's categories 1 and 2 accounted for approximately 75 percent of all questions or all cognitive questions. On the other hand, these three studies also reported a greater percentage of comprehension than knowledge questions, whilst the Saunders et al. (1975) training study found mean pretreatment percentages of higher cognitive (that is, nonfact) questions of about 75 percent and the Galassi et al. (1974) training study found a mean pretreatment percentage of Bloom's five categories of about 55. Such findings are enough to curb any excessive enthusiasm for claims about the demonstrated generally "low level" of teacher classroom questioning. They also indicate the value of more careful consideration of what might constitute "lower order" questions.

3.3 Increasing the Teacher's Use of Higher Order Questions

The set of teacher-training studies and experimental investigations of teacher questioning have generally demonstrated that higher order questioning under various guises is susceptible to significantly increased usage by various styles of training or instruction. Illustrative of this body of evidence are the training studies cited by Dunkin and Biddle for the Bloom and Taba orientations, the later Bloom-based training studies of Galassi et al. (1974) and Saunders et al. (1975), and the experimental studies reviewed by Winne (1979).

3.4 Question Types and Student Achievement

Of all the aspects of research into classroom questioning, the one that has most attracted and intrigued reviewers is the investigation of relationships between cognitive features of teachers' questions and student achievement. For all their importance, such studies have been relatively scarce. Gall (1970) noted that fact, and based the relevant part of his review solely on Hunkins' work in the late 1960s. Even so, the cited work of Hunkins was text-based rather than teacher-based.

Rosenshine's (1971) thorough analysis took account of 15 studies: nine of these used only two classifications of questions, four used three or more classifications as a basis for the development of ratios, and two used the separate categories of detailed cognitive coding systems. For these studies, achievement was reported as positively related to higher order questions in four, negatively related to higher order questions in two, positively related to lower order questions in one, and positively related to medium usage of higher order questions in two. With the exception of the investigations using detailed cognitive systems, Rosenshine characterized the collection of investigations as presenting a pattern of "inconsistent, nonsignificant results . . . too diverse to permit any synthesis."

To the set reviewed by Rosenshine, Dunkin and Biddle added three more studies. One of these (Rogers and Davis) showed no relationship between higher level categories and student achievement; another showed a direct relationship between the incidence of lower level questions and student achievement on abstract–complex tasks, and the third (Tisher's analysis for low-ability students) found a positive relationship between student achievement and low-frequency use of higher cognitive questions. The conclusion reached by Dunkin and Biddle was that process–product research had not produced strong evidence of a positive relationship between teachers' use of higher order questioning and student achievement. For studies based on Bloom and Guilford models, the evidence was "spotty if not negative"; for studies based on Bellack and Smith and Meux, it seemed that "logical complexity probably does not bear a simple relationship with pupil achievement."

In one of his major "direct instruction" reviews, Rosenshine (1976) examined the findings of three major correlational studies and two major experimental studies [Gall et al. (1978) and the Stanford Program on Teaching Effectiveness investigation of structuring, soliciting, and reacting]. Rosenshine's interpretation of the total pattern of findings was that "the effects of higher order questions are nowhere to be seen, nor are the effects of lower order questions as clear as one would wish . . . . The results are best stated as trends: lower order questions tend to be positively related to achievement, higher order questions tend to be unrelated, and personal questions tend to be negatively related."

In Winne's (1979) comprehensive review of experimental studies into cognitive levels of teacher questions, nine training and nine skills investigations were analyzed. In the training studies, teachers undertook training in using higher cognitive questions and subsequently taught lessons, though without constraints on what types of questions they asked. In the skills experiments, the research objective was to have teachers perform predetermined cognitive patterns of questioning. Some treatments utilized patterns of 30 percent to 70 percent (e.g., 30 percent lower cognitive and 70 percent higher); others used more extreme patterns (e.g., 100 percent lower). Adopting the definition of "lower cognitive" ("facts or knowledge") as those closely corresponding to Bloom's knowledge and comprehension categories, Winne concluded that, regardless of the methodological soundness of various studies, the review indicated that "whether teachers use predominantly higher cognitive questions or predominantly fact questions makes little difference in student achievement." However, Redfield and Rousseau (1981) performed a meta-analysis of 14 appropriate experimental studies, including 13 from Winne's set. The effect size statistic was calculated by a variant of Glass's (1977) formula. Unlike the conclusion reached by Winne's socalled box score or voting procedure, the effect size calculated by Redfield and Rousseau indicated a positive effect for higher cognitive questions.

Redfield and Rousseau pointed out that conclusions drawn from a set of studies are critically affected by the review methodology. Other explanations for the relatively poor empirical performance of higher order questions in individual studies and in traditional box score reviews have been definitional problems, difficulties in operationalizing the concepts higher and lower cognitive questions, inappropriate or insensitive criterion measures, and the complexities introduced by such dimensions as abstractness–concreteness.

4. Questioning Frequency

4.1 Occurrence of Questioning

Evidence about the frequency of questioning has been produced by studies representing a number of orientations to teaching research. Dunkin and Biddle (1974) reported three FIAC-based studies which included individual category frequencies in their results and concluded that, in the total sample of 189 United States elementary and secondary classrooms, one-tenth to one-sixth of the classroom interaction time was occupied by teacher questions. In the United Kingdom, Wragg's study—reported in Chanan (1973)—collected FIAC data from four to six lessons delivered by each of 56 male and 46 female student teachers, for a total of 578 lessons and more than 330,000 category tallies. In the total set, questioning occupied 7 percent of the tallies for males and 9 percent for females. For individual subjects the percentages devoted to teacher questioning ranged from 5.9 in physics lessons to 9.3 in history lessons. It should be noted that there are certain circumstances where FIAC category 3 is nominated as the appropriate category for recording teacher questioning based on student ideas, and the above percentages may marginally underestimate the incidence of all teacher questions.

As for studies conducted outside the FIAC framework, a useful secondary source for the pre-1970 period is Gall's (1970) review. Gall reported what he termed "high frequencies" of question means per teacher of 395 per day, 348 per day, 180 per lesson and 64 per 30-minute lesson in four studies which he cited. Since Gall and Dunkin and Biddle, consolidated reviews about questioning frequency have not appeared in readily available sources, although evidence of questioning percentages and rates of emission have continued to appear. For example, in the United Kingdom the small-scale study of Boydell (1974) and the large-scale study of Galton et al. (1980) found question-to-statement ratios of 1 : 2.7 and 1 : 3.7 respectively.

4.2 Questioning Frequency and Student Achievement

One of the relatively important areas of research into questioning has been the investigation of relationships between questioning frequency and student achievement or attitude. In his review of this body of research, Rosenshine (1971) identified 14 relevant studies, representing kindergarten to grade 12 (ages 4–18). Of these, seven showed significant relationships between teacher–student interactions (frequency of questions) and at least one criterion measure. The effective teacher variable was high questioning frequency in four studies and moderate frequency in two studies; one study showed moderate frequencies to be negatively associated with the outcome measure. The inconsistency of the results, and the many difficulties which Rosenshine had encountered in determining the precise nature of the independent variable (questioning frequency) in the studies, led him to conclude that interpretation of the results was extremely difficult. It is noteworthy that questioning frequency was not one of the 11 variables which the well-known review of Rosenshine and Furst (1971) nominated as the strongest in the literature. Consistent with the position of Rosenshine and Furst was the conclusion by Dunkin and Biddle (1974) that questioning frequency was a "weak variable."

Investigations since the 1970s have produced no simple consolidation of evidence about the correlates of effects or questioning frequency. For example, Stallings (see Borich 1977 pp. 105–13) found no significant relationships between adult questioning and children's independence, task persistence, cooperation, and question-asking. Dunkin and Doenau (1980) found no significant relationships between five questioning measures and nine achievement measures. In the longitudinal study of Good and Grouws (see Borich 1977 pp. 121–29) "high effective" teachers used direct questions and process questions with significantly less frequency than "low effective" teachers. On the other hand, in the painstaking experimental study of Nuthall and Church, included in Chanan's (1973) collection, it was found that teaching content through a strong reliance on questioning was more effective than teaching it predominantly through information. An additional complexity was revealed in the ATI studies of Peterson (1977) and Corno (1979) where teaching styles involving relatively high rates of questioning were linked in some nstances with superior student achievement. In both studies, however, the contribution of questioning per se was impossible to determine.

5. *Probing*

There is general agreement in the literature that probing is a follow-up teacher behavior that seeks a student response superior to the one already given. Frequently, the required improvement involves clarification, justification, precision, or elaboration. However, there is no unanimity about the exact behaviors denoted by the term. Conceptual distinctions are commonly made between "probing" and "prompting." But some authors make no such distinctions and use "probing" to encompass all follow-up behaviors. Among those who make the distinction, some present prompting as a subclass of probing, whilst others present them as separate unrelated terms. A further complication is that "prompting" may enjoy a range of definitions: "giving hints" is common, but some use it exclusively for rephrased questions or a replacement series of smaller scale questions. The occasion of probing shows considerable difference from one author to another. It has been variously linked solely or predominantly with higher order questions, correct answers, incorrect answers, or merely inadequate answers. A final complication in usage concerns identification of the target of probing. In some formulations, it is only the preceding respondent; other formulations readily include redirecting to another student; still others include redirecting, but only after the probe has first been directed to the preceding respondent.

The two major concerns of research into probing have been the impact of training upon its acquisition and its relationship with student achievement. The success of microteaching training for probing (variously defined) or its specific components has been documented in a number of studies such as Galassi et al. (1974) and Saunders et al. (1975). The evidence about its relationship with achievement, however, is considerably more tentative. The Rosenshine review series of the early 1970s (e.g., Rosenshine 1971 pp. 134–36) identified three studies of "probing," each showing significant relationships with achievement. However, the behaviors were a disparate collection which were, at best, specific aspects of Rosenshine's very broadly defined "probing" or perhaps no more than distantly related to it. Rosenshine and Furst (1971) nominated probing as one of their 11 most promising variables, though not one of their strongest five. Its inclusion, however, was accompanied by a caution that there was no basis in the available evidence for any confident conclusions about it.

Since the middle 1970s, "probing" has been a much less popular variable in process–product research than in teacher-training programs and training research. Several studies have produced mixed results. Investigations by Cameron-Jones and Morrison (see Chanan 1973) and Anderson et al. (1979) found evidence of significant relationships between "probing" and achievement. On the other hand, the studies of Gall et al. (1978) and Evertson et al. (1980) found no significant relationships.

Rosenshine's claim, that probing is a variable that merits attention, still seems appropriate. But further progress in understanding its function would seem to depend upon more precise definition, the identification and separate analyses of its subtypes and related behaviors, and the use of contextual variables (e.g., grade, subject, and student ability) in research designs.

6. *Multiple Questions*

Multiple questioning, which is frequently represented as an undesirable behavior, has attracted a small amount of research attention. Wright and Nuthall (1970) found significant negative correlations between student achievement and utterances with two or more questions, and a significant positive correlation between achievement and utterances with one question. Borg (1975), defining multiple questions as "teacher asks two or more questions before seeking a student response," found that its incidence could be significantly reduced by training but that it was not significantly related to achievement. Dunkin and Doenau (1980), who applied a tight definition of multiple questions (a teacher utterance containing two or more complete questions, such that the response required by each would be appropriate for any other question in the utterance), found no significant relationships between multiple primary questions and student achievement, and a consistent pattern of positive though not significant correlations between multiple secondary questions and achievement for one of the two lessons in their series.

7. *Questioning by Students*

Reviews containing some attention to student questioning have been Gall (1970), Rosenshine (1976), Medley (1978), and Borich (1979). These indicate the rarity of studies linking student questioning and achievement. Rosenshine (1971 pp. 156–59) was surprised to find only four studies using student talk in process–product analyses, none of which isolated student questioning. Dunkin and Biddle (1974) reported no process–product studies involving any form of student initiation. Rosenshine (1976) reported three important studies of the middle 1970s and offered two conclusions about student questioning: that for relevant student questions, a negative correlation with achievement was shown by one study and nonsignificant and mixed correlations by two, and that for irrelevant student questions negative correlations with achievement were shown by two studies and nonsignificant and mixed correlations by one. Medley's (1978) exhaustive analysis of research enabled him to identify characteristic behaviors of "effective" and "ineffective" teachers of low socioeconomic status students. Included in his list for ineffective teachers was

411

"more pupil-initiated questions and comment." The two main process–product studies since Medley's analysis seem to be Dunkin and Doenau (1980) and Evertson et al. (1980). The former found a consistent pattern of negative correlations, including four statistically significant ones, between "student initiating questions" and a battery of achievement measures for the first lesson in their series, but mixed nonsignificant correlations for the second lesson. In Evertson et al., significant positive correlations were found between achievement in mathematics and English and "student-initiated relevant questions integrated into class discussions as a proportion of all student questions and comment." However, in English, "student initiated relevant called out questions ignored as a proportion of all student questions and comment" showed a significant negative correlation with student attitude.

8. Wait-time

Despite the popularity of pausing as a behavior valued in many teaching textbooks and training programs, it was not until the work of Rowe that serious empirical investigations began to appear. In several related articles (e.g., 1974) Rowe reported on a seven-year project about the influence of wait-time on the development of children's language and logic. Over the span of the project, she utilized the audio recordings of more than 900 naturalistic, microteaching, and manipulated lessons. Two wait-times were studied: postquestion and postresponse. The claimed outcomes of extended postquestion wait-times (3 to 5 seconds) were, for students, more appropriate unsolicited responses, fewer inflected responses, more speculative thinking, more student questioning; and for teachers, increased flexibility scores, decreased questioning rates, and increased variability of questions.

Since Rowe, the postquestion pause denoted by such terms as wait-time and lapse time has attained further exposure in the research literature. Representative investigators have been Arnold et al. (1974), Attwood and Stevens (1976), Rice (1977) and Chewprecha et al. (1980). In such studies, which have been typically small-scale, common findings have been that postquestion pauses can be extended by training and that larger pauses are correlated with higher cognitive questioning. However, as Rowe found, the research designs have been unable to separate wait-time or lapse time from a complexity of other variables. Until stronger designs have been utilized, conclusions about the impact of postquestion pausing should be held in abeyance, although it should be regarded as a variable meriting further serious study.

See also: Logical Operations; Students' Cognitive Processing

Bibliography

Anderson L M, Evertson C M, Brophy J E 1979 An experimental study of effective teaching in first grade reading groups. *Elem. Sch. J.* 4: 193–223

Arnold D S, Attwood R K, Rogers V M 1974 Question and response levels and lapse time intervals. *J. Exp. Educ.* 43(1) 11–15

Attwood R K, Stevens J T 1976 Relationships among question level, response level, and lapse time: Secondary science *Sch. Sci. Math.* 3: 249–54

Bellack A A, Kliebard H M, Hyman R T, Smith F L Jr 1966 *The Language of the Classroom.* Teachers' College Press, New York

Borg W R 1975 Protocol materials as related to teacher performance and pupil achievement. *J. Educ. Res.* 69: 23–30

Borich G D 1977 *The Appraisal of Teaching: Concepts and Process.* Addison-Wesley, Reading, Massachusetts

Borich G D 1979 Implications for developing teacher competencies from process–product research. *J. Teach. Educ.* 30(1): 77–86

Boydell D 1974 Teacher–pupil contact in junior classrooms. *Br. J. Educ. Psychol.* 44: 313–18

Chanan G (ed.) 1973 *Towards a Science of Teaching.* NFER/ Nelson, Windsor

Chewprecha T, Gardner M, Sapianchai N 1980 Comparison of training methods in modifying questioning and wait-time behaviors of Thai high school chemistry teachers. *J. Res. Sci. Teach.* 17: 191–200

Corno L 1979 A hierarchical analysis of selected naturally occurring aptitude-treatment interactions in third grade. *Am. Educ. Res. J.* 16: 391–409

Dunkin M J, Biddle B J 1974 *The Study of Teaching.* Holt, Rinehart and Winston, New York

Dunkin M J, Doenau S J 1980 A replication study of unique and joint contributions to variance in student achievement. *J. Educ. Psychol.* 72: 394–403

Evertson C M, Anderson C W, Brophy J E 1980 Relationships between classroom behaviors and student outcomes in junior high mathematics and English classes. *Am. Educ. Res. J.* 17: 43–60

Galassi J P, Gall M D, Dunning B, Banks H 1974 The use of written versus videotape instruction to train teachers in questioning skills. *J. Exp. Educ.* 43: 16–23

Gall M D 1970 The use of questioning in teaching. *Rev. Educ. Res.* 40: 707–21

Gall M D, Ward B A, Berliner D, Cahen L S, Winne P H, Elashoff J D, Stanton G C 1978 Effects of questioning techniques and recitation on student learning. *Am. Educ. Res. J.* 15(2): 175–99

Galton M J, Simon B, Croll P 1980 *Inside the Primary Classroom.* Routledge and Kegan Paul, London

Glass G V 1977 Integrating findings: The meta-analysis of research. In: Shulman L S (ed.) 1977 *Review of Research in Education*, Vol. 5. Peacock, Itasca, Illinois

Gustafsson C 1977 *Classroom Interaction: A Study of Pedagogical Roles in the Teaching Process.* Department of Educational Research, Stockholm Institute of Education, Stockholm

Karma K 1972 *Investigations into the Instructional Process: Experiences with the Bellack Classification System.* Institute of Education, University of Helsinki, Helsinki

Lundgren U P 1972 *Frame Factors and the Teaching Process: A Contribution to Curriculum Theory and Theory on Teaching.* Almqvist and Wiksell, Stockholm

Medley J 1978 Research in teacher effectiveness: Where it is and how it got there. *J. Classroom Interaction* 13(2): 16–21

Peterson P L 1977 Interactive effects of student anxiety, achievement orientation, and teacher behavior on student achievement and attitude. *J. Educ. Psychol.* 69: 779–92

Power C N 1971 The effects of communication patterns on student sociometric status, attitudes, and achievement in science. (Unpublished postdoctoral thesis, University of Queensland)

Redfield D L, Rousseau E W 1981 A meta-analysis of experimental research on teacher questioning behavior. *Rev. Educ. Res.* 51: 237–45

Rice D 1977 The effect of question-asking instruction on preservice elementary science teachers. *J. Res. Sci. Teach.* 14: 353–59

Rosenshine B 1971 *Teaching Behaviours and Student Achievement.* NFER/Nelson, Windsor

Rosenshine B 1976 Classroom instruction. In: Gage N L (ed.) 1976 *The Psychology of Teaching Methods.* The Seventy-fifth Yearbook of the National Society of Education, Part 1. University of Chicago Press, Chicago, Illinois

Rosenshine B, Furst N F 1971 Research on teacher performance criteria. In: Smith B O (ed.) 1971 *Research in Teacher Education: A Symposium.* Prentice-Hall, Englewood Cliffs, New Jersey

Rowe M B 1974 Wait-time and rewards as instructional variables, their influence on language, logic and fate control, Part 1: Wait-time. *J. Res. Sci. Teach.* 11: 81–94

Saunders W, Gall M, Nielson L, Smith G 1975 The effects of variations in microteaching on prospective teachers' acquisition of questioning skills. *J. Educ. Res.* 69: 3–8

Winne P H 1979 Experiments relating teachers' use of higher cognitive questions to student achievement. *Rev. Educ. Res.* 49: 13–50

Wragg E C, Oates J, Gump P 1976 *Classroom Interaction.* Open University Press, Bletchley

Wright C J, Nuthall G 1970 Relationships between teacher behaviors and pupil achievement in three experimental elementary science lessons. *Am. Educ. Res. J.* 7(4): 477–91

Responding

C. N. Power

In teaching situations, responding refers to any verbal or nonverbal act designed to fulfil the expectations implicit in the questions, commands, or requests of others. Thus instances of responding moves include occasions on which the teacher provides help at the request of a pupil, a pupil answers a question posed by the teacher, or the class complies with a command to begin working through problems in a textbook. Almost all systems for analysing classroom interaction recognize responding as a basic unit of behaviour. For example, Bellack et al. (1966) define responding in terms of its pedagogical function in relation to soliciting moves: responding moves "fulfill the expectation of soliciting moves and are, therefore, reflexive in nature" (p. 18).

1. Examples

(a) Teacher: Now what do we mean, Elizabeth, when we say something floats?   Teacher solicits
Pupil: It stays on top of the water   Pupil responds

(b) Pupil: Please, Miss Jones will you help me?   Pupil solicits
Teacher: In a minute   Teacher responds

In classroom discussion, responding moves account for between 20 and 30 percent of all verbal moves. Typically, it is the pupils who respond: over 90 percent of the moves made by them are responding moves. On the other hand, in 10 studies using the Bellack system, between 3 and 6 percent of moves made by the teacher were responding moves. Studies using other systems for classifying verbal interaction which include a pupil responding category (e.g., the pupil talk–response category 8 of the Flanders system) confirm that in classrooms, the primary role of the pupils is to respond to the demands of the teacher (Dunkin and Biddle 1974). With the emergence of new paradigms for research on teaching, the importance of the processes and patterns of student responding has been highlighted. Students do not simply stand between a teaching process variable and an outcome variable as passive recipients of stimuli. Rather what is attended to, what is processed, how it is processed and, therefore, what is learned are a function of their mediating responses (see *Paradigms for Research*).

2. The Responding Process

Generally the rewards for attending to teacher solicitations outweigh the costs. Nevertheless, attention is a selective, filtering process. If teacher solicitations are to elicit responses, they must attract the attention of students. Students, like all human beings, take in data from the outside world through a variety of sensory organs, each linked to a temporary storage system allowing brief retention of a substantial amount of information. However, the capacity of the human processing system is limited, so that the bulk of the sensory inputs are filtered out. Few messages are attended to and decoded. Whether a covert or an overt response is made to a teacher solicitation then depends both on the properties of the message and on the physiological states and motivational predispositions of the students.

Experienced teachers are only too well-aware of the

difficulties some students have in paying attention during lectures and whole class discussion. By the addition of unexpected questions, gestures, changes in pitch and volume, the random distribution of questions, increasing the time between question and calling on a pupil for a response and other strategies, teachers seek to arouse and maintain attention in order to ensure that students respond actively to the tasks of the lesson.

Provided that the student attends, the next stage in responding involves the decoding of the message. The teacher's question is stored in short-term memory and the longer-term store of organized information (facts, concepts, principles, etc.) searched to retrieve relevant associations in memory, initially in order to interpret the meaning of the question. Given an appropriate level of motivation and the location of some relevant knowledge, information processing continues. Information is retrieved and rules and programmes for processing this information are activated in order to construct a response which fits the student's perception of the requirements of the teacher's solicitation.

As a result of these covert processes, students either will or will not have constructed a response to the teacher's solicitation. If given the opportunity to speak or write, some students then will be in a position to respond with an answer thought to have the correct content and form. Of course, the student's belief may or may not be justified: the response may prove to be incongruent, incorrect, or incomplete. Other students will have attended to the solicitation, attempted to decode the message and/or to construct a response, but been unable to do so either because the question was unclear or because of gaps or defects in their knowledge structure. Still others may have filtered the question out entirely and not even know what the question was, let alone have a response ready.

In classroom discussion, if a student is selected as a response model by the teacher, the overt response given can be assumed to be a product of a covert responding process similar to that described above. It is generally assumed by teachers that majority of pupils will attend to solicitations and be in a position to make a response, even if not called upon to do so. On the basis of the overt responses made, teachers make inferences about the abilities, knowledge, and attitudes of individual pupils and the progress of the class. The pupils too make inferences about their relationship to the teacher and their capacity to cope with schooling on the basis of what teachers call on them to do and how their responses are handled.

3. Oral Response Patterns

With studies of verbal discourse in classrooms, the content and appropriateness of student responses to teacher questions can be examined in more detail. Approximately two-thirds of teacher solicitations demand a substantive–logical response, most commonly either the recall of a fact or the construction of an explanation. But how do students respond? Bellack et al. (1966) analysed the degree to which the overt responses of pupils selected as targets meet the demand implicit in the eliciting solicitations. In their coding system, solicitations and responses are classified according to whether the task is a substantive or an instructional (i.e., procedural) one; the substantive–logical (i.e., cognitive) process and instructional–logical process involved; and the information-process activity (e.g., selecting from given alternatives versus constructing a response) called for. On all three dimensions, it was found that on about 90 percent of occasions, the response was congruent with the expectations of the solicitation. Overall, pupil responses match very closely the demands of the questions asked by the teachers; teachers also normally respond in ways which match the expectations implicit in pupil requests, but their responses quite regularly involve a more complex logical process than that expected. For example, a pupil may ask for a fact but the teacher may give an explanation as well. The form of teacher solicitation affects the number of responses as well as their content. Often, challenging higher cognitive questions elicit a lower audience response (as measured by hands raised) but lead to a sequence of related responses. Closed, easy, factual questions elicit a high audience response, but usually only a single response opportunity.

With few exceptions, classroom researchers have relied on the teacher's reaction to pupil responses to judge the correctness of the response. In the teacher's judgment, most pupil responses (70–80 percent typically) are acceptable. Whereas oral responses tend to provoke confirmation or failing that, redirection to another pupil, written pupil responses are more likely to be followed by teacher corrective information and probing questions. Analyses of pupil oral responses indicate that pupils selected to respond rarely are unable to offer any response, give an erroneous answer about 15 percent of the time; and incomplete, incongruent, or imprecise responses about 15 percent of the time; a correct response about two-thirds of the time; and a response giving additional relevant information or a novel, but acceptable, answer less than 3 percent of the time.

Teacher–pupil talk is mainly public and meanings are therefore shared. In a class which has been together for some time, particular terms and events can assume meanings which are both rich and complex. Several of the ethnographic studies reported in Stubbs and Delamont (1976) suggest that it is difficult to understand the meaning of pupil responses in an absence of a conception of teacher and pupil definitions of the situation and of how they present themselves in particular activity settings. It is important then to seek to understand the meaning of student responses in the social context of the classroom. Approaches which might be, but as yet rarely have been, used include a microsociological approach which tries to interpret why and how pupils respond in different situations; an anthroological approach, in which language is seen as an integrating part of cultural patterns; a linguistic–philosophical approach which tries to analyse responses as integrated acts with specific intentions; a text–linguistic approach which analyses responses using methods of linguistic description in units such as text and speech; and a sociolinguistic approach which examines the relationship between linguistic structures and social structures.

Early attempts to link achievement with the response opportunities given by the teacher during lessons yielded inconsistent results. However, more recent analysis suggests the possibility of a weak curvilinear relationship between the mean class achievement and class responding rates (Doyle 1979).

4. Individual Response Patterns

Studies which have looked at the response opportunities given to individual students reveal that at this level, opportunities are not only limited, but are highly variable (Brophy and Good 1974). While most pupils spend most of their time as passive audience members, a small number frequently become the target of teacher questions. While the frequency and content of pupils responding at the collective classroom level is fairly much under the control of the teacher and his or her decision-making processes and teaching style, individual pupils adapt to the demands of the classroom in different ways, adopting distinctive patterns or styles of responding. For example, Galton et al. (1980) found about 20 percent of pupils are the focus of most teacher contacts with individuals on routine matters ("attention seekers"); 36 percent tend to avoid contact with the teacher and are easily distracted ("intermittent workers"); 32 percent prefer to work quietly and to avoid frequent direct interaction ("solitary workers"); and the remainder have moderate levels of interaction, responding most actively during class discussion ("quiet collaborators"). Galton et al. have explored how the distribution of these styles varies with style of teaching. For example, in classes taught by teachers classified as "individual monitors", the proportion of intermittent workers was about 47 percent, but only 9 percent in classrooms taught by teachers classified as "class enquiries". Power (1973) studied the origins and consequences of four patterns of pupil responding in the classroom. He found evidence indicating that each pattern is closely related to the background, ability, and personality of the pupil. Moreover, the cognitive, affective, and social outcomes of classroom interaction are closely associated with the observed patterns of pupil responding as well as pupil characteristics. His data, as well as that of Galton et al., indicate that academically and socially successful pupils are actively engaged intellectually in responding to teacher demands (covertly if not overtly), are more often correct, and are more likely to be given precise feedback about the nature and source of errors than other pupils. The "intermittent workers" tend to

be academically unsuccessful, while the "attention seekers" generally are rejected by their peers and perform at a mediocre level.

The relationships between responding patterns and instructional outcomes are complex. Hence, the effects of attempting to increase a student's involvement during classroom discussion by calling on the student to respond more frequently may depend on the characteristics of the student, the task, and the setting. Certainly, studies by Hughes (1973) and Power (1977) suggest that increasing the mere quantity of pupil responses is unlikely to raise pupil achievement.

5. Attentiveness, Engaged Time, and Responding

Given that pupils are expected to respond covertly and to produce overt responses only when called upon, it becomes pertinent to ask what the majority of pupils are really doing during various classroom activities. For much of the first half of this century, recitation and seatwork were the dominant activity in the classroom. Given the prevailing industrial and business ethic of "scientific management", a major concern of administrators and researchers has been with the efficiency of teachers. Provided pupils appeared "attentive", it was assumed they were learning and that the teacher was effective. Observers scanned the pupils row by row noting on a group attention score card how many pupils were inattentive. Typically, group attention scores ranging between 80 and 95 percent were noted. In time, however, interest in pupil attention declined as the limitations of the procedure became evident and management models with explicit control overtones fell into disfavour.

In the current economic and political climate, interest in the cost-effectiveness of schooling and in what pupils are doing in classrooms has been rekindled. Within research, the early work of Bloom on university students' thoughts during lectures and discussions in the 1950s, his concept of mastery learning (see *Mastery Learning Models*), and Carroll's (1963) Model of School learning have focused attention on the amounts of content covered in the classroom, pupil academic engaged time, and student achievement. The research which followed suggests that there are wide variations at the national, system, and classroom level in the time allocated to different areas of the curriculum and in the amounts of time pupils are actively engaged in meaningful academic tasks in the classroom (Rosenshine 1979). While there is evidence of a link between the amount of time pupils are engaged actively on a task and their mastery of the task (indeed it would be very surprising if there were no such link), it is still uncertain as to what pupils are doing when they are "engaged" and as to the contextual, presage, and process variables which influence time-on-task (see *Time*).

Analyses of the major activities of classroom indicate that pupils, particularly in primary schools, spend a good deal of their time (often up to two-thirds) working alone or in small groups responding to the solicitations deriving from the teacher or curriculum materials. For something like 68 percent of the time during seatwork and small group activity, pupils are "academically engaged" (compared with on average, about 85 percent when the teacher is interacting with the class as a whole). Most of the off-task time during seatwork, pupils are waiting for the teacher to correct their answers or to tell them what to do next. The level of task involvement during seat work and small group activity appears to be a function of the variety and challenge of tasks assigned, their degree of structure and difficulty and the management decisions and strategies of the teacher (Doyle 1979, Power and Tisher 1979, Rosenshine 1979).

Over the years, much experimental research has concentrated on the relationships among the characteristics of texts and academic tasks on the one hand, and pupil information-processing strategies and responses on the other. In comparison, relatively little is known about the characteristics of the seatwork tasks assigned by teachers in classrooms and how students respond to the demands of these tasks. What little ecological evidence is available seems to suggest that pupil responses may be, at times, the product of attempts to achieve "successful performance-grade exchanges by using strategies that effectively short-circuit the intended learning process." (Doyle 1979 p. 202). As Doyle notes, the ecological framework opens up a number of lines of inquiry concerning student response variables that function to modify and transform classroom processes initiated by the teacher and the text.

6. Conclusion

The research reviewed reveals that the tasks assigned by, and actions of, the teacher activate response processes on the part of pupils which, in turn, can be linked with the outcomes of instruction (both intended and unintended). It would seem then that any attempt to understand how the teaching effects occur must look seriously at the ways in which pupils respond to classroom tasks, instructional formats, and teacher strategies. The incorporation into classroom research of more careful analyses of student responses to the demands of classrooms can be expected to help refine and extend understanding of what is involved in designing classroom tasks that enhance student thinking and learning.

See also: Paradigms for Research; Soliciting; Structuring; Reacting; Teaching Cycles and Strategies; Time

Bibliography

Bellack A A, Kliebard H M, Hyman R T, Smith F L 1966 *The Language of the Classroom*. Teachers College Press, New York

Brophy J E, Good T L 1974 *Teacher–Student Relationships: Causes and Consequences*. Holt, Rinehart and Winston, New York

Carroll J B 1963 A model of school learning. *Teach. Coll. Rec.* 64: 723–33

Doyle W 1979 Classroom tasks and student abilities. In: Peterson P L, Walberg H J (eds.) 1979 *Research on Teaching: Concepts, Findings, and Implications*. McCutchan, Berkeley, California

Dunkin M J, Biddle B J 1974 *The Study of Teaching*. Holt, Rinehart and Winston, New York

Galton M J, Simon B, Croll P 1980 *Inside the Primary Classroom*. Routledge and Kegan Paul, London

Hughes D C 1973 An experimental investigation of the effects of pupil responding and teacher reacting on pupil achievement. *Am. Ed. Res. J.* 10(1): 21–37

Power C N 1973 The unintentional consequences of science teaching. *J. Res. Sci. Teach.* 10: 331–39

Power C N 1977 Effects of student characteristics and level of teacher–student interaction on achievement and attitudes. *Contemp. Ed. Psychol.* 2: 265–74

Power C N, Tisher R 1979 A self paced environment. In: Walberg H J (ed.) 1979 *Educational Environments and Effects: Evaluation, Policy, and Productivity*. McCutchan, Berkeley, California

Rosenshine B 1979 Content, time, and direct instruction. In: Peterson P L, Walberg H J (eds.) 1979 *Research on Teaching: Concepts, Findings and Implications*. McCutchan, Berkeley, California

Stubbs M, Delamont S (eds.) 1976 *Explorations in Classroom Observation*. Wiley, Chichester

Reacting

J. A. Zahorik

Four major categories of instruction, according to Bellack and his colleagues (1966), are structuring, soliciting, responding, and reacting. Structuring and soliciting are initiatory behaviors. They serve to begin classroom activity. Structuring behavior sets the context for classroom activity by launching or halting/excluding interaction between the teacher and students (see *Structuring*). Soliciting behavior is intended to elicit a verbal or physical response (see *Soliciting*). Teacher questions and commands are solicitations. Responding and reacting are reflexive behaviors. They are always generated by a preceding behavior. Responding behavior is used in relation to soliciting behavior. Student answers to teacher questions are responding acts. Reacting behavior is used in relation to any of the other three behaviors, but it is not directly elicited by them. Reacting behaviors serve "to modify (by clarifying, synthesizing, or expanding) and/or to rate (positively or negaively) what has been said previously" (Bellack et al. p. 4). Praising of a student's answer by a teacher is a reacting behavior.

These four behaviors occur in various types of cycles or patterns (see *Teaching Cycles and Strategies*). A complete cycle is illustrated in Fig. 1. Other cycles ranging from one to three behaviors are possible.

The focus of this section is reacting behavior. As illustrated in Fig. 2, reacting behavior can take a variety of forms as it rates or modifies. Reacting behavior can consist of direct rating, repeating the response, correcting the response, developing the response, repeating the solicitation, and ignoring the response by moving the lesson on to new areas through structuring or soliciting. In addition, reacting acts can occur in pairs or triplets such as "Good, radiation poisoning." (rating and response repetition) or "Accidents in nuclear plants are very rare. What do you think is a disadvantage, Vicki?" (correcting and repeating the solicitation).

Reacting behavior that teachers use following student responding or other acts carries feedback information. It can communicate to students the extent to which their responses or other acts are correct, adequate, or appropriate and thereby help them to adjust and gain a measure of control over their future behavior. Some forms of reacting behavior provide feedback in a direct way, such as direct rating and correcting the response,

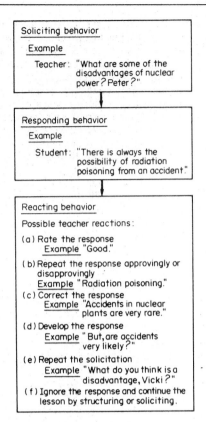

Figure 2
Possible reacting behaviors

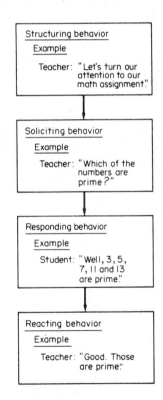

Figure 1
A complete teaching cycle

while others provide feedback in an indirect way, such as developing the response or moving the lesson on to new areas.

Theoretically, feedback can have considerable effect on student learning and behavior. It can reinforce student behavior and, consequently, strengthen the response that it follows; it can motivate students for future learning; and it can provide cognitive information that confirms meanings and associations, corrects errors, clarifies misconceptions, and indicates the current state of learning task mastery.

The purpose of this article is to examine research on the feedback function of teacher reacting behavior. Research will be examined in three categories: the recent past, the present, and the future.

1. Recent Past

Reacting behavior, along with other teacher classroom behavior, began to receive attention during the 1960s. Some of the studies examined the total teaching act of which teacher reacting was usually a part while others concentrated on a particular teacher behavior, such as teacher reacting behavior. Also, some of the studies, especially the early studies, only sought to describe the teaching act while others attempted to reveal the relationship of teaching to student academic achievement as well as to provide descriptions.

Representative of the studies that sought to investigate the total teaching act of which teacher reacting was a part are those of Flanders (1970), Gallagher (1965), Bellack et al. (1966), and Wright and Nuthall (1970). Each of these studies, as most studies of teacher behaviors in the 1960s, made use of observation systems or sets to record and categorize teacher behavior. Flanders' observation system consists of seven teacher behaviors, two student behaviors, and one general category. Of the seven teacher behaviors, three are reacting behaviors that provide direct feedback: praises or encourages, accepts or uses ideas of student, and criticizes or justifies authority. The Gallagher observation system consists of five types of teacher behavior: routine, cognitive memory, convergent thinking, evaluative thinking, and divergent thinking. The routine subcategories of verdict, personal verdict, and agreement are reacting behaviors that provide feedback. In the research by Bellack et al., as has been seen, reacting behavior is one of the four major types of teacher behavior. The subtypes of reacting contained in the observation system consist of substantive reactions, precedural reactions, and substantive–procedural reactions. Within the procedural reactions section are positive, admitting, repeating, qualifying, not admitting, and negative rating reactions. The observation system developed by Wright and Nuthall is similar to the Bellack et al. system. The specific types of teacher reacting behavior that it contains are simple affirmative and negative comment, indefinite and complex comment, reflecting comment, thanks and praise, managerial comment, challenging comment, and repetitition of pupil response.

Studies that focused specifically on reacting behavior are those by Zahorik (1968), Mueller (1973) and Hughes (1973). Zahorik's observation system contains 14 types of reacting or feedback behavior: praise–confirmation; reproof–denial; praise–confirmation and reproof–denial; positive answer; negative answer; positive answer and negative answer; positive explanation; negative explanation; response–extension—development; response–extension—improvement; solicitation–repetition—several answers; solicitation–repetition—one answer; lesson progression—different topic; and miscellaneous feedback. Of these reacting behaviors, the first eight are direct feedback and the remaining six are indirect feedback. The observation system that Mueller developed also consists of 14 types of reacting behavior: no comment, conventional comment, negative feedback, positive feedback, verdict, neutral comment, repeats question, supplies answers, amplifies, asks for repeat, managerial comment, structures, probes, and other. The Hughes observation system consists of eight

categories: praise, confirmation, positive answer, supportive denial, denial, negative answer, urging–reproof, and answer.

The descriptive data about teacher reacting behavior that have emerged from both the general studies of teaching and from the specific studies of teacher reacting are not extensive. The completed research reveals that feedback is a major teacher behavior. About one-third of the behaviors that occur in classrooms are reacting behaviors of one type or another, and most of the reacting behavior that occurs is that of the teacher. It also reveals that reacting behavior is usually positive rather than negative and simple rather than elaborate. In terms of quantity of usage, it has been found that praise accounts for a maximum of 6 percent of the classroom time, accepting student ideas a maximum of 8 percent, and criticism a maximum of 6 percent.

In addition to these general data, some research has found differential usage of reaction behavior in relation to teacher characteristics, student characteristics, and setting variables.

The question of the relationship of various types of teacher reaction or feedback to student learning has been pursued by many of the previously mentioned studies and by others. Thorough summaries of these studies have been prepared by Rosenshine and Furst (1973) and by Dunkin and Biddle (1974).

Rosenshine and Furst identified nine variables related to student achievement that emerged from correlational research. Two of these concern reacting behavior of the teacher: criticism and teacher indirectness. Of 17 studies on the relationship of criticism to student achievement, significant negative correlations were found in six. When only the direction of the relationship was considered, 12 of the studies were found to have negative correlations with more harsh criticism yielding higher negative correlations than more mild criticism. Teacher indirectness consists of several related variables such as praise, use of student ideas, and direct/indirect ratios (a greater use of student feelings, praise, student ideas, and questions than lecture, directions, and justifying authority). Although significant results were not found for teacher indirectness, positive correlations were found in seven of eight studies for use of student ideas and in 11 of 13 studies for high indirect/direct ratios. Interestingly, teacher reactions that were found to be unrelated to student learning were praise, nonverbal approval, and warmth.

The comprehensive Dunkin and Biddle summary reveals some similar findings and some contrasting findings. They found that greater teacher indirectness (use of student ideas, praise, student ideas, and questions) was related to greater student achievement in 10 studies, unrelated to student achievement in 15 studies, and related in a complex way in three studies. In experimental studies they found that indirectness was unrelated in five studies and related in a complex way in three studies. In terms of student affect, they found that indirectness was related to more positive student attitudes in nine studies and unrelated to student attitudes in five studies.

Summaries of studies that focused specifically on praise reveal, according to Dunkin and Biddle, that praise is related to greater achievement in three studies and unrelated in 11 studies, and that it is related to more positive student attitudes in one study and unrelated to student attitudes in four studies. Dunkin and Biddle also show that use of student ideas is related to greater achievement in one study and unrelated in six studies, and that it is related to positive student attitudes in three studies and unrelated in three studies.

Criticism was found by Dunkin and Biddle to be related to lower student achievement in six studies, unrelated in seven studies, and related in a complex way in one study. It was also found to be related to more negative student attitudes in two studies and unrelated to attitudes in three studies.

Some might view the yield of the 1960s concerning understanding of reacting behavior and other teaching behavior as meager. Certainly the descriptions of reacting behavior are not complete. The effects data are, in several instances, contradictory and difficult to interpret. However, the research results of this period do represent a major advancement from previous knowledge about teaching and these suggest research needs for the future. Although more thorough description was needed, researchers appeared to be more intrigued by the conflicting effects results and devoted extensive effort to this puzzle in the following decade.

2. Present

The seemingly contradictory results of the effects studies appear to be related to the diffuse research efforts of the 1960s. The studies that Rosenshine and Furst, and Dunkin and Biddle summarized were done at a variety of grade levels and in a variety of subject matter areas. Summaries of studies conducted in a wide variety of settings were destined to produce some inconsistencies. In the 1970s, the issue of the impact of variable settings on the relationship of teacher behavior to student achievement was addressed.

Encouraged by government financial support and citizen discontent with poor achievement of students in basic skill areas, a number of large-scale, comprehensive research efforts were begun in the United States. These projects had two qualities in common. They all studied the relationship of teacher behavior to student learning in basic skill areas and they all focused on the elementary-school level. Chief among these studies, each of which examined the effects of teacher reacting or feedback behavior, are those conducted by Fisher et al. (1978), Brophy and Evertson (1974), Stallings and Kaskowitz (1974), and Good and Grouws (1975, 1979).

The study that Fisher et al. conducted is known as the Beginning Teacher Evaluation Study (BTES). This long-term project began in 1972 and issued its final report in 1978. The original impetus for the study was the California Commission for Teacher Preparation and Licensing. However, the actual research was carried out by various groups with Phase 3, the final phase, being conducted at the Far West Laboratory for Educational Research and Development. The objective of the study was to conceptualize and assess instructional factors that promote student learning. The researchers developed an instructional variable known as academic learning time (ALT) and set about determining its relationship to student achievement, to teaching processes, and to student attitudes. Academic learning time refers to that portion of time in classrooms when students are engaged in tasks in which few errors are committed and where the task is relevant to an academic outcome (see *Time*).

In their focus on the teaching process they identified and examined the effects of two reacting behaviors: academic feedback and task engagement feedback. Academic feedback refers to informing students about the correctness of their responses or comments. Task engagement feedback refers to informing students about the acceptability of their classroom conduct.

The subjects in this study were 25 teachers of 7-year-olds and 22 teachers of 10-year-olds and their classes. A target sample of students in each classroom was administered achievement tests in reading and mathematics at the beginning, middle, and end of one school year. During the year a number of other types of data were collected including data on teacher interactive behavior. Each classroom was observed for a full day approximately once each week during which time teacher behavior and other classroom data were recorded. Data analysis consisted of correlating teacher behavior with student residual achievement.

Results indicate that academic feedback at both age levels and in both subject areas is a strong, positive correlate of achievement. The correlation is significant at the 7-year-old level and nearly significant at the 10-year-old level. Of the teacher variables investigated it was the most consistently related variable at both grade levels. The researchers attribute this relationship, in part, to student engagement. Academic feedback was positively corelated with engagement at both grade levels and in both subject areas.

Results also indicate that task engagement feedback correlated negatively with achievement for the 10-year-olds in reading and mathematics but not for the 7-year-olds. Further, it correlated negatively with engagement at both levels and in both subject areas. In this study, task engagement feedback usually consisted of criticism intended to make students attend to the task at hand.

Brophy and Evertson (1974) also sought to determine the relationship of teacher behavior to student achievement at the elementary-school level in basic skills areas. Their four-year study focused on the behavior of experienced teachers who had a record of consistency in their relative success in producing achievement gains as measured by standardized achievement tests in reading and mathematics. A total of 31 teachers of 7- and 8-

year-olds and their classes were used in the first year of data collection, and 28 in the second.

Data concerning teacher–student interaction were collected with a modification of the Teacher–Child Dyadic Interaction System (Brophy and Good 1970). This instrument contains several teacher reaction categories: praise, criticism, giving no feedback reaction at all, giving the answer, giving process feedback, calling on another student to answer, call out, rephrase or cue, repeat, and new-question. Each teacher was observed for approximately 10 hours during the first year of data collection and for approximately 30 hours during the second year. Data analysis consisted of correlations and regression analysis to determine relationships between teacher behavior and student residual gain achievement scores.

Brophy and Evertson found that immediate corrective feedback was associated with student learning, particularly in low socio economic status schools. Successful teachers in these schools used feedback on an individual basis in conjunction with skill practice that was preceded by group demonstration. Apparently students in low SES schools are more dependent on the teacher as a source of feedback than are students in high SES schools. Pre-existing knowledge of students in high SES schools makes teacher feedback less important.

Brophy and Evertson also found that teachers' attempts at getting students to improve their responses correlated positively, but mildly, with learning gains in low SES schools, but it correlated negatively with learning gains in high SES schools. The researchers point out that high SES students typically give a complete response when they are asked to respond and, therefore, see the teacher's attempt to get them to improve or change their response as needless coercion. Low SES students, in contrast, often make incomplete responses. For them, teacher reaction was of benefit.

In relationship to praise, Brophy and Evertson again found a differential effect for low SES and high SES students. Praise correlated positively with achievement gains for low SES students quite frequently. These correlations were weak, however, and they varied with the context in which praise was used. In general, praise correlated negatively with achievement gains for high SES students. High SES students appear to benefit more from challenge and high standards as a means of motivation than they do from praise. In terms of context variables, Brophy and Evertson found that the strongest negative correlations occurred in student initiated contacts (e.g., student shows completed work to the teacher), but positive correlations occurred in teacher initiated contacts (e.g., student answers a teacher's question). The researchers suggest that praise in the second instance is often more specific and, therefore, more effective.

Findings about criticism from the Brophy and Evertson study were that criticism does correlate with achievement gains in certain situations. Although teach-

ers in the study did not use criticism frequently, when it was used in relation to inadequate student performance on academic tasks it correlated positively with achievement. Criticism used in other situations did not correlate positively.

The purpose of the Stallings and Kaskowitz (1974) study was to determine how well various Follow Through education programs were being implemented and to examine the relationship of classroom instructional practices to student achievement gains and other outcome measures). Of the 22 Follow Through programs that were established by the United States Congress in 1967 to reinforce and extend academic gains from Head Start and other preschool programs into the primary grades, seven were selected for observation. Represented in the study were programs based on reinforcement theory, cognitive development theory, open education theory, and other theories.

After verifying that the treatments were being implemented appropriately, the researchers examined the relationship of classroom processes to student achievement in reading and mathematics and to problem-solving skill, absences, task persistence, independence, and other measures. Data were collected from students in 105 first grades and 58 third grades. To determine classroom processes that were being employed, each teacher was observed for three days with an instrument based on the work of Flanders (1970). The categories that deal with teacher reactions are acknowledgment, praise, positive corrective feedback, neutral corrective feedback, and negative corrective feedback.

Both positive and negative correlations were found between teacher reacting behavior and student achievement. Most of the positive correlations occurred between academic reactions and achievement, and most of the negative correlations were related to reactions associated with student behavior and other tasks. At the first-grade level academic acknowledgment, praise, positive corrective feedback, neutral corrective feedback, and negative corrective feedback all correlated positively. At the third-grade level the correlations were similar except that a low negative correlation was found in regard to academic acknowledgment in mathematics, and positive correlations in regard to academic positive corrective feedback and neutral negative corrective feedback in mathematics were all low. Stallings and Kaskowitz concluded that feedback, either positive or negative, as a part of systematic instruction involving giving information and asking questions about it, is clearly associated with higher achievement test scores. Reactions associated with music or science, for example, or those focusing on student conduct are associated with lower achievement test scores.

Good and Grouws (1975, 1979) examined the relationship of teaching to learning in the area of mathematics at the fourth-grade level. They conducted two related investigations. In the first study, 41 teachers from the same school district were identified who taught mathematics using the same textbook and for whom student achievement test data were available for three consecutive years. Each teacher was observed at least six times over a three-month period by trained observers to determine how time was utilized, how teachers and students interacted, and how teachers managed classroom learning. Data about teacher–student interactions were collected with the Teacher–Child Dyadic Interaction System (Brophy and Good 1970). This instrument, as we have seen, identifies nine types of teacher reacting behavior. Selected for concentrated study were 18 teachers who were consistent in their effectiveness over a two-year period. Nine of the teachers were relatively effective and nine were relatively ineffective. That is, nine of the teachers had relatively stable and high student residual achievement gain scores and nine had relatively stable and low residual achievement gain scores. The results of this study in relation to teacher reacting behavior were that relatively ineffective teachers use disciplinary questions (questioning an inattentive student), give the correct response, correct the wrong response, give no response, give praise, negate the wrong response, repeat the question, and give warnings or criticism to teacher-initiated behavior-related contacts more frequently than do relatively effective teachers. Relatively effective teachers give process feedback and feedback to student-initiated work-related contacts more frequently than relatively ineffective teachers. Good and Grouws concluded from these results that a nonevaluative climate consisting of comparatively little use of praise and criticism is functional in terms of student achievement gains.

The second investigation was an experimental study. Twenty fourth-grade teachers were trained to use the behaviors that were associated with relatively effective teachers from the first study. Twenty other fourth-grade teachers served as a control group. Observation revealed that the experimental teachers satisfactorily implemented the behaviors that they were trained to use. Results based on pre- and post-testing indicated that after two and a half months of the program, the performance of students in experimental classrooms was considerably better than that in control classrooms. It was better as measured by a standard achievement test and by a criterion referenced test. Also, an attitude scale revealed that experimental students had more favorable attitudes at the end of the experiment than control students.

From these four large-scale, naturalistic studies concerning the relation of teaching to student achievement in which variation in both subject area and grade level of students was substantially reduced, several conclusions about teacher reacting behavior can be made.

First, feedback that reacting behavior provides is consistently related to increases in student achievement in basic skills at the elementary-school level. It has been known both in theory and from research on learning that feedback is an essential element in learning. These studies show that feedback in the form of teacher verbal remarks is related to learning that takes place in the classroom.

Second, although feedback seems to have a favorable impact on learning, exactly how it impacts and under what conditions is not clear. Reducing the variability in the setting in which reactions and other behaviors are used was beneficial in revealing knowledge about the feedback function of reacting and about other reaching behaviors, but these studies also introduce a new round of variability. Rather than simplify and clarify the issue of feedback, they have illustrated that the relationship between feedback and learning is complex. The complexity relates to type of feedback, degree of feedback, SES of students, grade level of students, and other variables. For example, Fisher et al. (1978) found that academic feedback correlates positively with achievement, but task engagement feedback does not. At the fifth-grade level task engagement feedback correlates negatively. Brophy and Evertson found that several kinds of feedback correlate positively with achievement including negative feedback with low SES students, but the same types do not correlate positively for high SES students. Further, they found that praise is only weakly related to achievement for low SES students and not at all for high SES students. Stallings and Kaskowitz found that corrective feedback relates to student achievement even when it is negative feedback, and Good and Grouws found that neither praise nor criticism should be used to any extent for most effective learning.

Third, feedback seems to be most beneficial as an integral part of a teaching pattern associated with what Rosenshine (1976) calls direct instruction. This pattern involves the giving of information through lecturing, explaining, or demonstrating; asking related, factual questions; and providing feedback on the adequacy of the response. It is this sequence which appears to be related to achievement of basic skills at the elementary-school level.

In summary, research of the 1970s on teacher reacting behavior has been productive, but it has only begun to answer important questions about this major classroom behavior of teachers. Presently, it can be said that teacher verbal feedback is helpful in regard to student learning, some types appear more helpful than others, some types are more effective in some settings than others, and its contribution to learning seems to be related to its function in the direct instruction pattern of teaching.

3. Future

The type of research that will be conducted on teacher reactions in the future and the nature of the knowledge that will be uncovered is, of course, unknown. Analysis of past research and results, however, suggests several conceptual and methodological considerations that may be useful in inceasing understanding of this important classroom event.

An overall suggestion is that researchers should

extend their research both forward to experimental studies and backward to descriptive studies. How teacher reaction occurs in classrooms needs greater description. The description thrust of the 1960s needs to be reaffirmed and pursued. Our knowledge of the nature of teacher verbal feedback is not strong. Early efforts at description used quantitative techniques in which reactions or other teacher behaviors were isolated, categories or types of reacting were developed prior to observation, and frequencies of occurrence were tabulated. What might increase understanding of teacher verbal feedback is the utilization of qualitative research in which a holistic approach is used and types of reactions and other behaviors are permitted to emerge naturally through intensive observation.

At the same time, experimental studies of teacher feedback and other behaviors are needed. In addition to Good and Grouws (1979), Stallings et al. (1979), Crawford (1978), and others have turned to experimental research. Some might argue that the correlational studies examined here have been put to inappropriate use. That is, the purpose of mass correlational studies is to discover relationships for more intensive experimental study. The purpose is not to identify practices and prescribe them for teacher use under the claim that they bear a causal relationship with student learning.

Another suggestion is that teacher verbal feedback be investigated in relationship to the other types of feedback that students receive. The assumption in much of the research that has been conducted is that teacher verbal feedback is the major, if not only, source of feedback students receive. This myopia needs to be corrected. Teacher nonverbal feedback as well as feedback that students receive from their peers and from instructional materials needs to be studied. Further, feedback from marks, the display of work, the assigning of work, and also the feedback received at the school level, such as that investigated by Rutter et al. (1979) needs study. The relative importance of the various types of classroom feedback needs to be ascertained.

The study of teacher verbal feedback in aggregate form is a questionable practice. It stresses quantity at the expense of quality and credibility. The meaning of the same verbal feedback across a range of teachers can differ considerably. When a teacher who rarely reacts at all uses the word "good" after a student's response, it probably means something quite different from the teacher who routinely uses the term "good" for every student response that is uttered. Researchers need to find a way to adjust teacher reacting behavior in terms of the teacher's characteristic ways of reacting prior to aggregating reacting behavior across teachers. Another approach would be to conduct indepth qualitative studies of how individual teachers react and provide feedback. Qualitative research would be sensitive to the phenomenological meaning of feedback.

It is assumed that reacting behavior, and the feedback function that it can serve, is related in some way to

student learning. This assumption is based on the belief that all teacher behaviors and actions are aimed at student learning. This may be a valid assumption, but it is possible that learning is not always the goal of the teacher or at least is not always the immediate goal. Some researchers (Jackson 1968, Doyle 1979, Zahorik 1982) suggest that student cooperation is a more central drive of teachers than is learning. Because social control is a more urgent goal of teachers and the effect of teachers' efforts to achieve it are immediately knowable, teachers may stress it over or prior to student learning.

Brophy (1981) also makes the point that feedback is not always or only directed at learning. He contends that teacher praise is frequently not intended as reinforcement. If it were, he argues, it would be used with contingency, specificity, and credibility. The function of praise that Brophy identifies are (a) to express spontaneous surprise, (b) to balance criticism, (c) to identify exemplary behavior, (d) to avoid criticism, (e) to establish communication, (f) to satisfy students who elicit praise, (g) to signal a transition, and (h) to encourage slower students. Most of these functions serve to control the classroom or to maintain a positive classroom climate.

If teacher reacting behavior serves many functions in addition to or instead of learning, to examine only its effect on learning is inappropriate. Its broad effects need to be studied including its intermediate effects on classroom control, classroom climate, and other variables as well as any ultimate effect it may have on student learning.

Another suggestion is that researchers attempt to find the appropriate level at which to analyze teacher reacting behavior. Breaking down reacting behavior into all of its conceivable varieties and examining the relationship of each variety to learning or some other variable may not be productive. This analysis may be too molecular because many of the specific types of reactions serve similar functions. On the other hand, examining classroom warmth or reinforcement in an effort to understand reactions may be too molar. Intermediate, meaningful units of analysis are needed. The unit would have to be one which permitted researchers to answer several questions: How are students receiving feedback in this setting? Why is it occurring in the way that it is? What does it mean for the classroom participants? Some of the contradictions or inconsistencies in findings regarding teacher feedback are attributable to differences in level of analysis. Fisher et al. (1978), for example, examined two general types of feedback, but Brophy and Evertson (1974) examined a whole range of types of feedback.

Attending more to the situational use of feedback is another research suggestion. Most of the research on teacher reacting behavior cited here studied differential usage of feedback in relation to grade level and subject area. In addition, Brophy and Evertson investigated student SES differences. Important knowledge was provided by these studies concerning contextual variation n the use of feedback, but more attention to situational use is needed. Teacher reacting behavior needs to be studied with more advanced students and in other subject matter areas such as science, history, music, and literature. Further, a closer look must be taken at where and how feedback fits into the structure of the lesson. Teacher feedback may vary with the type of lesson such as a problem-solving lesson or a review lesson, and it may vary with the phase of the lesson in which it occurs, such as the beginning phase where the teacher may be concerned with motivation and the development phase where the teacher may be concerned with understanding.

A closer look also needs to be taken at the composition and size of the instructional group. More able groups of students may receive different feedback than less able. With small groups or individuals, teachers may react differently than with large groups. The work of Hawkins and Taylor (1972) indicates that teachers of large groups do behave differently from teachers of intermediate size groups.

Examination of instructional group characteristics will, appropriately, lead to a focus on individual students. Just as a way needs to be found to adjust teacher feedback in relation to the teacher's typical ways of providing feedback, a way needs to be found to adjust the effects of the feedback in relation to the individual student's typical ways of interpreting feedback. The word "good" surely does not carry the same meaning for all students. Some students may view it as insufficient, others as perfunctory, and still others as real commendation.

Teacher reacting behavior, like teaching itself, is intricate and involved, perhaps more so than was once believed. Present research has made significant progress in improving understanding of this important teacher action. This progress has come through narrowing the range of teaching situations in which it was studied and studying it in relation to other teacher behavior rather than studying it in isolation. At this point, however, there is little knowledge about reacting behavior that can be used to improve teaching. Modifications in research are needed to come to understand the nature and effects of this behavior sufficiently to identify prescriptions for practice.

See also: Direct Instruction; Responding; Reactive Teaching; Reinforcement

Bibliography

Bellack A A, Kliebard H M, Hyman R T, Smith F L 1966 *The Language of the Classroom*. Teachers College Press, New York

Brophy J E 1981 Teacher praise: A functional analysis. *Rev. Educ. Res.* 51: 5–32

Brophy J E, Evertson C M 1974 *Process–Product Correlations in the Texas Teacher Effectiveness Study: Final Report*. University of Texas, Austin, Texas

Brophy J E, Good T L 1970 Brophy–Good system. In: Simon A, Boyer E G (eds.) 1970 *Mirrors for Behavior: 2. An Anthology of Classroom Observation Instruments*. Research for Better Schools, Philadelphia, Pennsylvania

Crawford J 1978 *An Experiment in Teacher Effectiveness and Parent-assisted Instruction in Third Grade*. Center for Educational Research, Stanford, California

Doyle W 1979 The tasks of teaching and learning. Paper presented at the American Educational Research Association Annual Meeting, San Francisco, California

Dunkin M J, Biddle B J 1974 *The Study of Teaching*. Holt, Rinehart and Winston, New York

Fisher C, Filby N, Marliane R, Cahen L, Dishaw M, Moore J, Berliner D 1978 *Beginning Teacher Evaluation Study, Technical Report Series*. Far West Laboratory for Research and Development, San Francisco, California

Flanders N A 1970 *Analyzing Teacher Behavior*. Addison-Wesley, Reading, Massachusetts

Gallagher J J 1965 *Productive Thinking of Gifted Children*. Institute for Research on Exceptional Children, University of Illinois, Urbana, Illinois

Good T L, Grouws D 1975 *Process–Product Relationships in Fourth Grade Mathematics Classrooms*. University of Missouri, Columbia, Missouri

Good T L, Grouws D 1979 The Missouri mathematics effectiveness project: An experimental study in fourth grade classrooms. *J. Educ. Psychol.* 71: 355–62

Hawkins W H, Taylor S 1972 Teacher reactive behavior related to class size and to the teaching of mathematics, social studies and English. Paper presented at the Australian Association for Research Annual Meeting, Canberra

Hughes D C 1973 An experimental investigation of the effects of pupil responding and teacher reacting on pupil achievement. *Am. Educ. Res. J.* 10: 21–37

Jackson P W 1968 *Life in Classrooms*. Holt, Rinehart and Winston, New York

Mueller D L 1973 The second-round question or how teachers react to student responses. *Urban Educ.* 8: 153–65

Rosenshine B 1976 Classroom instruction. In: Gage N L (ed.) 1976 *The Psychology of Teaching Methods*. 75th Yearbook for the National Society for the Study of Education. University of Chicago Press, Chicago, Illinois

Rosenshine B, Furst N F 1973 The use of direct observation to study teaching. In: Travers R M W (ed.) 1973 *Second Handbook of Research on Teaching: A Project of the American Educational Research Association*. Rand McNally, Chicago, Illinois pp. 122–83

Rutter M, Maughan B, Mortimore P, Ouston J, Smith A 1979 *Fifteen Thousand Hours: Secondary Schools and their Effects on Children*. Harvard University Press, Cambridge, Massachusetts

Stallings J A, Kaskowitz D H 1974 *Follow Through Classroom Observation Evaluation, 1971–73*. Stanford Research Institute, Menlo Park, California

Stallings J A, Needels M, Stayrook N G 1979 Identifying efficient strategies for teaching basic reading in secondary schools: An experiment. Paper presented at the American Educational Research Association Annual Meeting, San Francisco, California

Wright C J, Nuthall G 1970 Relationships between teacher behaviors and pupil achievement in three experimental elementary science lessons. *Am. Educ. Res. J.* 7: 477–91

Zahorik J A 1968 Classroom feedback behavior of teachers. *J. Educ. Res.* 62: 147–50

Zahorik J A 1982 Learning activities: Nature, function, and practice. *Elem. Sch. J.* 82: 308–17

Reviewing and Recapitulating
G. Nuthall

Often, at the beginning or end of a class lesson, the teacher will remind the students of what they have just learned, or summarize the main points of the previous discussion. When this review or recapitulation occurs at the beginning of a new topic or lesson it may involve drawing together the relevant points of several previous lessons. Where it occurs at the end of a unit of work, it may involve selecting and highlighting the most important aspects of the material the students are expected to remember.

This article is concerned first with defining what is usually meant by reviewing and recapitulating in teaching, and then with the research which looks at how these teaching practices affect student learning.

1. What is Reviewing and Recapitulating?

Examination of the literature on "reviewing" starting with an entry by Suzallo in the 1913 edition of the *Cyclopedia of Education* (Monroe 1913 Vol 5 p. 172) suggests that there are three different meanings which have been the focus of research and discussion.

First, there is the concept of "review" as repetition of a previous learning activity. This is the use of the term which is found in research on rote-learning activities (e.g., in the debate between massed versus spaced review) and on programmed or computer-based instruction. In this latter context, a branching programme which recycles the student through the same frames a second time is seen as providing for student review (literally reseeing).

Second, there is the concept of "review" as classroom discussion or recitation. This comes from a traditional model of classroom teaching in which students are first set to read new material from a text and that material is later discussed by the teacher in class. This discussion and any subsequent treatment of the material is described as "review". For example, in a standard text on teaching methods, Harley (1973) discusses 10 different methods of review including: students writing their own summaries, getting students to transfer their newly acquired knowledge to new problems, taking students on field trips, and so on.

The third concept of "review" is the one outlined at the beginning of this article. The teacher, or students and teacher in discussion, might summarize or abstract the main points or conclusions to be drawn from a previous learning activity. Or at the beginning of a new activity or topic, they might briefly recapitulate the main points of previous learning as preparation for a new topic.

This third concept is the one that will be the focus of this article. It should be noted, however, that it is not a precisely defined aspect of teaching. The practice of reviewing seems to vary a great deal depending on the type of teaching, the type of topic being taught, and the age of the students. Many studies of teaching make no reference to it at all and those that do, show significant variation in the teaching behaviours they associate with it. Review and recapitulation are often seen as part of the more general teacher behaviour of structuring. Associated terms include summarizing, synthesizing, outlining, terminal structuring. Often included within these behaviours are signalling, highlighting ("markers of importance"), and providing an overview.

2. Relationship to Teaching Effectiveness

It is not clear from recent reviews of research on teacher effectiveness what the role of reviewing and recapitulating is in determining the outcomes of teaching. The *Second Handbook of Research on Teaching* (Travers 1973) does not list either review or recapitulation in the index and includes no reference to these activities in the relevant chapters. Dunkin and Biddle (1974) in their comprehensive review of research on teaching make reference to only one relevant study. Brophy (1979) in an analysis of those teaching behaviours which appear, from recent research, to be clearly related to student achievement, makes no reference to review or recapitulation. Similarly when Rosenshine (1981) attempts to draw out the parallels between the findings of research on teaching effectiveness and the content of specially developed teaching programmes with known effectiveness (e.g., Bloom's Mastery Learning model) he does not include anything like review or recapitulation among his 32 most significant variables.

However, a careful examination of those studies which have looked at the relationship of review to student outcome, or have included review as part of an experimental teaching procedure, indicates that there is, in fact, good evidence for seeing reviewing and recapitulation as important components in effective teaching.

2.1 Correlational Studies

Six studies have looked at the relationship of review to student learning in naturally occurring classroom situations. Fortune (1967) tried to identify teacher "presenting" behaviours which would discriminate between more and less effective elementary grade teachers across three different subject areas—English, mathematics, and social studies (Fortune 1967). He failed to find any teaching behaviours which distinguished the good teachers across all three subject areas, but he did find five behaviours which discriminated across at least two of the subject areas. Two of these five were: (a) introductions involving an overview or analogy, and (b) the use of review and repetition.

Wright and Nuthall (1970) described a study in which

audiotaped recordings of teachers teaching a three lesson science topic to 8-year-olds were used to identify teaching practices that correlated with student learning. Of the 28 different teacher behaviours analysed, the one with the highest correlation (+0.67) with student achievement was time spent on revision at the end of lessons.

Pinney (1970) made use of videotape recordings of trainee teachers to examine the effects of a range of nonverbal as well as verbal behaviours on the achievement of 13- and 14-year-old students. He concluded that "the high scoring teachers in general did a better job of conveying the essential points of the lesson by emphasizing them through the use of repetition, verbal statements of importance, and reinforcement of pupil responses" (p. 37).

These three studies seem to provide support for the importance of review as an effective teaching practice. However, the remaining three studies throw doubt on that conclusion.

Madike (1980) carried out a study of alternative methods of training teachers at the Institute of Education in Benin, Nigeria. As part of that study he looked at the relationship of selected teaching skills to high-school student achievement in mathematics. A group of 36 teachers were videotaped and the frequency of their use of nine teaching skills was recorded. Among these was "planned repetition" which was apparently derived from the studies of Pinney and Wright and Nuthall described above. Madike found, however, that "planned repetition" made no significant contribution to the multiple correlation of the nine teaching skills to student mathematics achievement.

Brophy and Evertson (1974) reported a long-term study of the characteristics of elementary-school teachers with a consistent record of producing high (or low) gains on standardized achievement tests in several different areas over two or three years. They recorded the frequency of a number of "presenting" behaviours in the classrooms of these teachers. Among these were "summarizing review" and "review of old material". The correlations between these behaviours and several measures of student achievement were low and inconsistent.

A study by Clark (1976) was primarily concerned with the extent to which teachers change their behaviour and effectiveness as a result of practice. As part of that study, however, he looked at the correlations between the frequency of certain teaching behaviours and student achievement on a social studies topic. Two of these behaviours: structuring and summarizing, showed low negative relationships with achievement.

It is always difficult with studies carried out in natural settings, with very limited control over what is happening in each of the classrooms, to know what to do with contradictory findings. It might be argued that the six studies described above are not equally reliable and that the least reliable studies should be discounted. However, each study has different strengths and weaknesses and discounting any of them would involve a complex critical analysis. The more sensible conclusion is to take them at their face value. Review and recapitulation have been shown to be related to student achievement in some studies but not in others. The discussion turns now to a set of more carefully controlled, but consequently less natural, experimental studies.

2.2 Experimental Studies: Testing Review Alone

There have been two experimental studies in which the use of review has been the major focus of the experiment.

Vickery (1971) recorded a 13-minute lecture on "Listening" which he presented to groups of college students. He also recorded a short review consisting of a summary of the main ideas in the lecture which he added to the beginning or end of the recording. Student comprehension of the lecture was assessed with a 31-item test administered immediately afterwards. Analysis of the results showed no effect of hearing the review either before or after the lecture.

In a longer and more successful study, Zeiss (1979) looked at the positioning of review periods during an eight week (15 session) English course in a community college.

Two existing classes were randomly divided into four groups. One group received no reviews, the second group received immediate reviews, the third group received delayed reviews, and the fourth group received both immediate and delayed reviews. For this experiment, a review consisted of a 10-minute period during which the teacher summarized the main points covered in a session and discussed these points with the students. Immediate review occurred after each class session and delayed review occurred at the beginning of a class two to four sessions after the original presentation. Class tests consisting of objective items were given as part of the 7th and 15th class sessions. The results indicated that the groups receiving reviews did better than the group receiving no review, and that the immediate review was more effective than the delayed review.

2.3 Experimental Studies: Review as Part of a Teaching Pattern

In recent years there have been a number of carefully designed experimental studies in which control has been exercised over the way teachers interacted with students and carried out their teaching. Two of these studies have included review and recapitulation (or closely related behaviours) as part of the cluster of teacher behaviours being studied.

The first of these was a complex factorial experiment carried out at the Stanford Center for Research and Development in Teaching (Program on Teaching Effectiveness, SCRDT 1976). Teacher behaviour was controlled by having four experimental teachers carefully trained to follow a detailed "script" for each lesson. Scripts for a nine-lesson sequence on "ecology" were prepared in eight different versions. These versions varied according to whether they contained high or low amounts of structuring, soliciting, or reacting. Scripts which contained high amounts of structuring included frequent use of reviewing, stating objectives, outlining the lesson, signalling transitions, indicating important points, and summarizing.

The four teachers taught each of the eight versions to a different class of 11-year-olds. Detailed analysis of student outcome scores did not reveal more than a slight direct effect of the structuring behaviours on student learning or attitude change. However, it was possible to show that structuring did have an effect when students reported that they were aware that the teacher was using these behaviours. This finding is probably better described the other way round. Students who do not seem to be aware that the teacher is using structuring behaviours (reviewing, summarizing, etc.) do not learn from them.

The second experimental study to include review and recapitulation is the Missouri experiment on teaching mathematics to 9-year-olds reported by Good and Grouws (1979). In this study the authors trained 20 teachers to implement a package of teaching procedures which had been selected from previous correlational studies of teacher effectiveness. The experimental training programme focused on five "key" clusters of instructional behaviours. These were: (a) daily review (first eight minutes daily), (b) development of new material (next 20 minutes), (c) seat work (final 15 minutes), (d) homework (15 minutes daily), and (e) special reviews (weekly and monthly).

The implementation of the programme lasted for four months and the 20 experimental teachers and the 20 control teachers were observed on six occasions each. As predicted, the students in the classes of the experimental teachers did significantly better on several measures of mathematics achievement and had retained their advantage several months later.

In both of these multiple-variable experimental studies it is difficult to tell whether review should be identified as contributing to the experimental results, or whether the other variables associated with it had the more important effect. In the Stanford experiment there is no question about whether review was included in the programme. The scripted nature of the treatments ensured that. In the Good and Grouws experiment, observation indicated that the experimental teachers were very good at including daily reviews but frequently failed to include a summary of the previous day's work.

3. How Does Reviewing and Recapitulating Affect Student Learning?

In the previous section it was noted that few recent reviews of effective teaching include reviewing and recapitulating as significant practices. However, the studies described above make it clear that there is some substantial evidence that they can have a significant effect on student learning. But why are reviewing and recapitulating not always related to student learning, and how, if they do have an effect, does this effect occur?

Two related areas of research help to provide answers to these questions. One of these is research on understanding and remembering text and narrative material. It is now clear that memory for text or narrative is strongly affected by the structure contained in the material, or the structure that the reader (or listener) imposes on it. For example, Meyer (1975) has shown that the presence of signals in a text which make the reader aware of its structure and purpose affect the degree to which the text is remembered. These "signals" include such things as summaries, specification of structure, pointers to the author's intentions, and so on. Ross and Di Vesta (1976) have shown that requiring students to provide their own oral summaries of a text increases their ability to recall it. Hearing another student's oral summary also increases recall but not to the same extent.

The second line of research is more closely related to classroom teaching. Several studies have shown that the clarity of a teacher's presentation is an important determinant of what students learn (e.g., Smith and Cotten 1980) and that the students' understanding of what the teacher is trying to do is an equally important variable (e.g., Anderson 1981, Peterson et al. 1981).

What these lines of research suggest is that there are important connections between the clarity of the presentation, the structure of the content, identification of what is important, and the students' understanding and learning of the material. Material which is not clearly and logically presented, or is not well-structured, may be easily misinterpreted or misunderstood and stored in memory in inappropriate or inadequate ways.

If this is true, then review and recapitulation may be one important method of providing students with a clear picture of the meaning and purpose of an instructional activity, and a structure to use in storing and recalling the content of instruction at a later date.

It should be noted, however, that instruction which is otherwise clear and well-structured may not need to include much in the way of review or recapitulation. When the teacher has evidence that the students understand the purpose of their activity and the meaning of what they are learning, then review and recapitulation may be unnecessary. This is why in some research studies (e.g., Madike's study of teaching skills) the teachers' use of review had no direct effect on student achievement, while in other studies (e.g., Good and Grouw's mathematics teaching experiment) it was an important variable.

In the studies described above, review and recapitulation occur in association with other variables. Pinney notes that review is most effective in combination with "markers of importance". In the Wright and Nuthall study the frequency of review is correlated with the frequency of closed questions, questions which students answer correctly, and with the number of times the teacher speaks. This suggests a pattern of more direct, active teaching. Good (1981), in an analysis of why the Missouri mathematics teaching experiment succeeded, focuses on the importance of active, clearly directed teaching.

What is now needed is further research to help a teacher identify those occasions when review and recapitulation are important, and to help determine what kinds of review are likely to be most effective in promoting student understanding and learning.

See also: Structuring; Soliciting; Vagueness and Clarity

Bibliography

Anderson L M 1981 Student responses to seatwork: Implications for the study of students' cognitive processing. Paper presented at American Educational Research Association (AERA) Meeting, Los Angeles
Brophy J E 1979 Teacher behavior and its effects. *J. Educ. Psychol.* 71: 733–50
Brophy J E, Evertson C M 1974 *Process–Product Correlations in the Texas Teacher Effectiveness Study: A Final Report.* Report No. 74-4, Research and Development Center for Teacher Education, University of Texas, Austin, Texas
Clark C M 1976 *The Effects of Teacher Practice on Student Learning and Attitudes in Small Group Instruction.* Technical Report No. 47, Stanford Center for Research and Development in Teaching, Stanford, California, pp. 1–109
Dunkin M J, Biddle B J 1974 *The Study of Teaching.* Holt, Rinehart and Winston, New York, pp. 1–490
Fortune J C 1967 *A Study of the Generality of Presenting Behaviors in Teaching.* United States Office of Education, Project No. 6-8468, Memphis State University, Memphis, Tennessee
Good T L 1981 Classroom research: Past and future. Unpublished paper, University of Missouri, pp. 1–95
Good T L, Grouws D A 1979 The Missouri mathematics effectiveness project: An experimental study in fourth-grade classrooms. *J. Educ. Psychol.* 71: 355–62
Harley B 1973 *A Synthesis of Teaching Methods.* McGraw-Hill, Sydney
Madike F U 1980 Teacher classroom behaviors involved in micro teaching and student achievement: A regression study. *J. Educ. Psychol.* 72: 265–74
Meyer B J F 1975 *The Organization of Prose and Its Effect on Memory.* North Holland, Amsterdam
Monroe P (ed.) 1913 *A Cyclopedia of Education*, Vol. 5. MacMillan, New York
Peterson P L, Swing S R, Braverman M T, Buss R 1981 Students aptitudes and their reports of cognitive processes during direct instruction. Paper presented at American Educational Research Association (AERA) Meeting, Los Angeles
Pinney R H 1970 *Teacher Presentational Behaviors Related to Student Achievement in English and Social Studies.* Technical Report No. 16. Stanford Center for Research and Development in Teaching, Stanford, California
Program on Teaching Effectiveness, SCRDT 1976 *A Factorially Designed Experiment on Teacher Structuring, Soliciting and Reacting.* Memorandum No. 147 Stanford Center for Research and Development in Teaching, Stanford, California
Rosenshine B 1981 The master teacher and the master developer. Unpublished paper, University of Illinois, Champaign-Urbana, Illinois
Ross S M, Di Vesta F J 1976 Oral summary as a review strategy for enhancing recall of textual material. *J. Educ. Psychol.* 68: 689–95
Smith L R, Cotten M L 1980 Effect of lesson vagueness and discontinuity on student achievement and attitudes. *J. Educ. Psychol.* 72: 670–75
Travers R M W (ed.) 1973 *Second Handbook of Research on Teaching: A Project of the American Educational Research Association.* Rand McNally, Chicago, Illinois
Vickery J F 1971 An experimental investigation of the effect of previews and reviews of orally presented information. *Southern Speech J.* 36: 209
Wright C J, Nuthall G 1970 Relationships between teacher behaviors and pupil achievement in three experimental elementary science lessons. *Am. Educ. Res. J.* 7: 477–91
Zeiss P A 1979 A comparison of the effects of temporal positioning of reviews on the retention of meaningful material (Ed. D Dissertation, Nova University, Florida) ERIC Document No. ED 180 450

Teaching Cycles and Strategies

C. Power

Teaching is an intentional activity which assumes its distinctive character and meaning not in isolated behaviours, but in sequences of interrelated acts. Whereas there have been many normative theories prescribing what these sequences ought to look like, there have been relatively few attempts to describe and to account for the sequential patterns of interactive behaviour which actually occur in classrooms—despite Dunkin and Biddle's (1974) timely warning to classroom researchers that "any meaningful analysis of teaching *must* involve sequential elements" (p. 353). The concept of "teaching cycles" is the product of one attempt to describe communication patterns in the classroom in terms of sequences of smaller units of verbal behaviour.

In the Bellack et al. (1966) study, teaching was conceived as a type of "language game" in which the player's (teachers, pupils) make "pedagogical moves" comparable to moves in a game of chess. Moves are classified according to their function in classroom discourse, these classifications being soliciting, structuring, responding, and reacting. As in a game of chess, teachers and pupils employ tactics and strategies to achieve their purposes.

Hence, moves tend to occur in logical sequences or cyclic combinations which Bellack et al. designated "teaching cycles". Teaching cycles then are distinctive sequences of interrelated pedagogical moves which can be described in terms of certain patterns of moves and the relationship of moves to each other.

Logically, a teaching cycle must begin either with a structuring move or with a soliciting move, both of which are initiating manoeuvres, that is, they serve the function of getting a cycle underway (see *Logical Operations*). In contrast, responding and reacting moves are reflexive in nature, being elicited or occasioned by a preceding move. Therefore, reflexive moves cannot begin a teaching cycle. Given the Bellack model, there are 21 possible types of formally ordered teaching cycles, each representing a somewhat different pattern of verbal interaction. The Bellack model then provides a basis for the identification and classification of sequential patterns of classroom behaviour.

Analyses of the rate, source, and types of teaching cycles undertaken by Bellack et al. (1966), Lundgren (1972), Power (1973), and others reveal that cycles are typically short in duration (averaging two cycles per minute) and initiated by the teacher (85–90 percent of cycles). Of the 21 possible sequences of pedagogical moves, the most commonly observed are shown in Table 1.

It is also possible to describe the teaching style of each teacher in terms of the rate, source, and the dominant types of teaching cycles used. Unfortunately, as has been so often the case in classroom research, there have been few attempts to build upon Bellack's pioneering work. What little is known about the forces which influence the rate, source, and types of teaching cycles used in classrooms and their effects has been reviewed comprehensively by Dunkin and Biddle (1974). Factors influencing the rate, source, and type of cycle used include lesson format, cultural context, subject, and social background of the class; higher achievement appears to be associated with a moderate cycle rate, the incidence of teacher-initiated simple reciprocation cycles (SOL–RES, SOL–RES–REA), and terminal structuring.

Table 1
Possible sequences of pedagogical moves in teaching cycles

Teaching cycle	Bellack	Power	Lundgren
SOL RES REA	26%	37%	22%
SOL RES	22%	18%	16%
SOL	10%	4%	6%
SOL RES REA REA	9%	1%	4%
SOL RES REA RES . . . REA . . .	7%	14%	3%
STR SOL RES REA	6%	9%	6%

Key: SOL—Soliciting, STR—Structuring, RES—Responding, REA—Reacting. . .—additional moves of the kind designated e.g., RES . . . means one or more additional responses to the same solicitation

1. Other Attempts to Describe Teaching Sequences

A confusing diversity of terms and approaches have been employed in the study of sequential patterns of interaction. The conclusion by Dunkin and Biddle (1974 p. 353) that researchers interested in studying such patterns are "groping toward solutions to complex problems" remains as true today as it did then. The literature is still couched in intuitive, analogistic phrases. The flow of discourse is dissected linguistically, logically, empirically, interpretatively, or whatever into sequences, small (cycles, episodes, tactics, etc.) and large (grand strategies, ventures etc.); and segments are described in murky terms (informal style, rotating charges, free-wheeling). The breakthrough looked for by Dunkin and Biddle is no closer, but the sequential concepts and research undertaken do hint at the forces which shape discourse and the immediate and larger consequences of patterns of teaching. In this section, two attempts to explore the relationships between shorter and longer sequential patterns in classroom discourse are reviewed.

Smith and Meux (1962) conceived of short tactical sequences used by teachers as "episodes", defined as exchanges which comprise completed verbal interactions, which deal with a single topic, which are initiated by an opening question demanding one of 12 cognitive operations, and which include a sustaining and a terminal phase. The most common episodes identified were describing (25 percent), designating (15 percent), and explaining (13 percent). One problem with this analysis is that episodes are defined in terms of the initiating question—subsidiary questions are ignored. Nuthall and Lawrence (1975) introduced the notion of an "incident" to enable them to analyse sequences within an episode. In a second study, Smith et al. (1967) set out to study longer strategic sequences they called "ventures". A "venture" is defined as a "segment of discourse in dealing with a single topic and having an overarching content objective". Eight such ventures were identified—causal, conceptual, evaluative, interpretative, particular, procedural, rule, and reason. Ventures were analysed in terms of 36 major categories of moves. For example, moves within conceptual ventures include descriptive, comparative, and instantial moves; the most common concept development strategies used by teachers involved ventures containing sequences of descriptive moves only, alternating sequences of descriptive and comparative moves, and alternating sequences of descriptive and instantial moves. In an experimental study, Nuthall (1968) found that ventures containing descriptive *and* instantial moves were more effective than ventures containing comparative moves in inducing concept learning. Unfortunately, however, no further studies exploring the consequences of different strategies used in ventures have appeared.

At this stage, it may be helpful to illustrate how a segment of discourse would be analysed using the systems discussed above. Alongside the segment from a

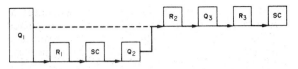

Figure 1
Segment of discourse showing two designating incidents

grade 8 lesson on magnets shown in Table 2 are simplified Bellack and Nuthall codings.

In the Bellack coding, the segment is divided into three cycles: C_1 = STR–SOL–RES–REA; C_2 = SOL–RES–REA. Had the entire system been used, it would have been possible to describe the source, rate, and content of each cycle. The analysis would show that cycles were teacher-initiated, short, demanded facts about magnets, and that pupil responses were rated positively.

In the Smith and Meux analysis, the segment would be described simply as a designating episode. In the Nuthall analysis, the segment would be depicted as containing two designating incidents as shown in Fig. 1. In addition, it could be described as part of a conceptual venture involving a sequence of instantial moves.

With the emergence of the "interpretative paradigm" as a major force in educational research, symbolic interactionists, ethnographers, phenomenologists, and case study workers have adopted a less atomistic and molecular approach to the analysis of sequences. In their attempts to understand the underlying patterns of classroom life, the subjective meanings ascribed to situations and patterns by teachers and pupils are sought.

The ethnographic study of Smith and Geoffrey (1968) reveals something of the complexity of the sequenced patterns of behaviour in one urban classroom. This study provided a context within which Westbury (1973) and his students have sought to formulate an organic conceptualization of the task of teaching. Their analysis begins with the assumption that teaching takes place in an organizational context which makes its own universal demands, that is, teachers are expected to (a) cover a body of content; (b) engender mastery of that content by their students; (c) create affect on the part of students to ensure compliance to the demands of the setting; and (d) manage the class. Westbury argues that teachers opt for a "grand strategy" with respect to the ends demanded (e.g., they may opt to "give deference to all", "omit one or two", or "fudge on mastery"). In addition, the teacher's "basic approach" as manifested in the observed teacher–pupil interaction format (e.g.,

seatwork, recitation, lecture, discussion) and the "supplementary manoeuvres and tactics" (e.g., humour, bantering, contracts) used to complement the "basic approach" and to remedy its defects are described.

This line of studies has identified two overarching "coping strategies" used by teachers. One group, designated "craftsmen", opted for a strategy giving even-handed emphasis to all four classroom demands by using conventional recitation and seatwork formats as the basic approach, and tackling problems using supplementary manoeuvres and tactics. The second group, designated "artists", seemed to cope by interpreting the teaching task in ways which corresponded with their own personal views of a "proper education", and by choosing a basic approach which depended more on their personal capabilities than on efficiency.

2. A Persistent Cycle

In the first systematic coding of classroom discourse, Romiett Stephen in 1912 found that teachers talked about 64 percent of the time. The major pedagogical strategy to which more than 80 percent of classroom talk was devoted, appeared to be a rapid-fire, question and answer session. Because teacher's questions rarely called for anything other than rote responses, Stephen called this pattern "recitation". So common was this impression of early classrooms that it is almost the only kind of teaching pattern which one finds in novels which deal with life in schools in some way. Historically, as well, in most ancient classrooms similar regularities seem to have existed. Apart from the Socratic method

Table 2
Analysis of a segment of discourse to show different strategies

	Transcript	Bellack	Nuthall
T	One thing we found out about magnets last week is that they attract some metals.	T/STR	O_1
	Now do they attract all metals? Greg?	T/SOL	
P_1	No.	P/RES	R_1
T	No, not all.	T/REA	SC
	Which ones? Steven?	T/SOL	O_2
P_2	Aluminium.	P/RES	R_2
T	It does or it doesn't?	T/SOL	O_3
P_2	It doesn't.	P/RES	R_3
T	Right, it doesn't.	T/REA	SC

(Bellack column bracketed: T/STR, T/SOL, P/RES, T/REA = C_1; T/SOL, P/RES = C_2; T/SOL, P/RES, T/REA = C_3)

Key: T = Teacher, P = Pupil, C = Cycle, Q = Question, R = Response, SC = Simple comment which aimed to teach by inquiry into what might be accepted as valid knowledge, the emphasis seems always to have been on transmission of knowledge, on imitation, repetition, memorization, and on obedience.

Reviewing research on teaching in the first half of this century, Hoetker and Ahlbrand (1969) concluded that the studies show a remarkable stability of verbal behaviour patterns—despite the fact that successive generations of would-be reformers have condemned the rapid-fire, question–answer pattern of instruction which predominates. More recent studies also suggest that recitation persists (Stodolsky et al. 1981). It seems as if there is a high degree of regularity in the outer form of verbal discourse in classrooms. Regardless of subject area, grade level, type of school, or cultural context, and no matter where the language game is played, the rules regulating the roles occupied by teachers and pupils are much the same: the teacher structures and solicits, pupils briefly respond, and the teacher reacts.

Why has the rapid-fire, teacher-centred pattern of instruction persisted, despite the condemnation of successive generations of would-be reformers? Its survival in the evolutionary struggle with other, more highly recommended patterns has generally been attributed to the conservatism of teachers, but three other possibilities may be entertained.

(a) External "frame factors" constrain, regulate, and govern the teaching situation such that teachers must control the content of teaching and maintain order.

(b) Recitation is a "coping strategy" which enables teachers more or less successfully, to attend to organizational demands and pupil needs, within the existing constraints and limited resources of the classroom.

(c) For some instructional purposes and pupils, a teacher-centred question–answer pattern may be more effective than more open, pupil-centred approaches.

Lundgren (1977) argues that to explain any educational process, one must have a conceptual apparatus that relates the economic and social structure of society to the teaching process. He is developing a "frame" theory which links the micro and macro levels of analysis of teaching. The concept of "frame" includes factors which specify the limits on the teaching process on one level, and which express decisions within the administrative frame system, the curriculum goal system, and the legal rule system (which reflect past and present economic, social, and political structures) on the other. In all societies, it is necessary to select out of the culture what is to be transmitted in order to maintain production and social order. In order to ensure this occurs, decisions are made within the legal, resource, and curriculum systems. These decisions in turn regulate, constrain, and govern the internal functioning of classrooms. The

tighter the frame systems, the more likely it is that teachers will adopt a recitation pattern, since this is one of the few strategies which enables teachers to control the content of teaching and maintain social order. A variant of recitation which Lundgren identified when teachers face problems in covering the prescribed content in the time available is called "piloting". Piloting involves the use of short, simple chains of leading questions which students can answer even if they have not fully mastered the prerequisite knowledge and relationships. With the help of a "steering group" of pupils, the teacher adjusts the pace of instruction so as to pilot the class as a whole through the curriculum. The content is "covered" and order is maintained. One consequence is that as well as learning, to a greater or lesser degree, aspects of what they are supposed to learn, pupils also learn about their capacity to learn and hence to engage in mental work (meta-learning). In Lundgren's theory, the stable outer forms of classroom communication are a consequence of a broader social, political, and economic context within which the processes of the classroom take "gestalt".

Others have attempted to account for the persistence of dominant teaching cycles in terms of the demands and constraints inherent in the nature of schools and classrooms as they are known. Westbury (1978) argues that teaching needs to be viewed as a "sociotechnology" by means of which the activities of the collectivity of pupils who make up the class are directed towards learning. This focus on the demands of the classroom context directs attention away from specific behaviours and methods believed to foster individual learning, and places the emphasis on teaching strategies and cycles which teachers use to manage the class, behaviour settings, and activities. Recitation then is a teaching cycle which enables the teacher to cope with the realities of classroom organization and its conflicting demands.

In that classrooms are mass transmission-processing systems, there is a limited degree to which the level of information and flow of exchanges in any of the commonly used teaching cycles or styles necessarily matches the interests or abilities of individuals or groups. The problematic nature of the classroom environment and of three patterns of teaching (recitation, group work, and individualized instruction) is highlighted in Good and Power's (1976) analysis of the task of designing classroom environments which maximize the achievement and satisfaction of different "types" of pupils. Even effective teachers, whose flexible use of a variety of strategies enables them to achieve a reasonable balance, are forced into trade-offs among competing demands because of limitations on time and resources. Recitation may be a strategy which enables teachers to attend, directly or indirectly, to the most pressing demands of most types of pupils and classroom tasks, most of the time.

Not all educators concede that recitation is primarily dedicated to control and should be replaced by patterns which allow for the sensitive, participatory exploration of topics by groups and individuals. The shift from the progressive concerns of the 1960s and early 1970s towards the neoconservative position has given space to researchers whose studies have been interpreted as vindicating traditional emphases. While studies whose prime purpose has been to validate some ideology often turn out to be flawed, several studies of "conventional" versus "open" teaching styles (see *Open Versus Formal Methods*) and of "direct instruction" do seem to suggest that a teaching sequence resembling recitation is a reasonably effective means of keeping pupils on task, providing controlled practice, and promoting achievement in basic skills areas in primary schools (Rosenshine 1979). Conceptual models and instructional programmes synthesizing this work are now appearing (Bennett 1978). This does not mean, however, that the "new" sociotechnology of "direct instruction" or its older counterparts are as universally effective as some of its advocates claim.

Other reviews of the literature (Peterson 1979) provide support for the assumption that the effectiveness of any given pattern of teaching depends on the pupils being taught, the goals sought, and the resources available. Most teachers recognize this, and opt to vary the dominant pattern to prevent it from degenerating into a limited and impoverished ritual. Furthermore, teachers classified as "progressive" almost invariably turn out to employ some teacher-directed, structured sequences in their classrooms. The reality is that each style of teaching represents a subtle blending of teaching cycles and approaches, and each turns out to have its strengths and limitations (Egglestone et al. 1976, Galton et al. 1980). Such studies challenge the claims and counterclaims about what is happening in schools put forward by both traditionalists and progressives, and point out the ironies of educational ideologies which ignore what does and what cannot happen in classrooms.

However regular the outer form of discourse may appear to be, it has an inner form which reflects, in subtle and not so subtle ways, social and cultural differences between and within classrooms. It is possible then to detect differences in the pedagogic codes used by teachers in regulatory and instructional discourse, differences which are associated with the attitudes, expectations, and values of teachers and the social and intellectual backgrounds of pupils. Individual pupils then extract different meanings from the same pattern of discourse and adapt to its demands by adopting distinctive pupil styles. These styles have been described in terms of the sequencing and content of their interactions with the teacher, peers, and materials (Galton et al. 1980, Power 1973). Each pattern or style of teaching makes possible the evolution of a set of pupil strategies for accommodating to its demands, strategies which lead to varying degrees of academic and social success at school. These studies, together with studies of working class pupils like those of Willis (1977), seem to suggest the possibility that pupil strategies of resistance lead to teaching cycles of policing and conflict

avoidance whereby some pupils come to reject or fail to profit from the school. These longer term cycles and patterns implicate both pupils and teachers in the processes of reproduction and production in society, processes which cannot be accounted for solely in terms of models which rely on some form of cultural or economic determinism.

3. Conclusion

Initially the study of teaching cycles began by exploring how single units of teacher and pupil behaviour fit into small sequential patterns of behaviour, and how these in turn fit into longer sequences of interactive behaviour. The linkages between these sequences, the meanings which teachers and pupils assign to the events and sequential patterns, and their consequences have only just begun to be explored, leading to a series of models which attempt to account for some of the more commonly observed teaching cycles. Some attempts have also been made to fill the space between the sequential patterns revealed by microlevel analyses and the macro-patterns which, it is claimed, stem from the wider functions served by schools in society. But to do so would demand more intensive studies of sequential patterns of teaching across the school year, in different contexts, and at different levels of education than have been conducted to date (Power and Cotterell 1981).

See also: Soliciting; Structuring; Responding; Reacting; Frame Factors; Technical Skills of Teaching

Bibliography

Bennett S N 1978 Recent research on teaching: A dream, a belief and a model. *Br. J. Educ. Psychol.* 48: 127–47

Bellack A A, Kliebard H M, Hyman R T, Smith F L 1966 *The Language of the Classroom.* Teachers College Press, New York

Dunkin M J, Biddle B J 1974 *The Study of Teaching.* Holt, Rinehart and Winston, New York

Egglestone J F, Galton M J, Jones M E 1976 *Processes and Products of Science Teaching.* Macmillan Education, London

Galton M J, Simon B, Croll P 1980 *Inside the Primary Classroom.* Routledge and Kegan Paul, London

Good T L, Power C N 1976 Designing successful classroom environments for different types of students. *J. Curr. Stud.* 8: 45–60

Hoetker J, Ahlbrand P 1969 The persistence of recitation. *Am. Educ. Res. J.* 6: 145–167

Lundgren U P 1972 *Frame Factors and the Teaching Process: A Contribution to Curriculum Theory and Theory on Teaching.* Almqvist and Wiksell, Stockholm

Lundgren U P 1977 *Model Analysis of Pedagogical Processes.* Liber Läromedel/Gleerup, Lund

Nuthall G A 1968 An experimental comparison of alternative strategies for teaching concepts. *Am. Educ. Res. J.* 5: 561–584

Nuthall G A, Lawrence P J 1975 *Thinking in the Classroom: The Development of a Method of Analysis.* New Zealand Council for Educational Research, Wellington

Peterson P L 1979 Direct instruction reconsidered. In: Peterson P L, Walberg H J (eds.) 1979 *Research on Teaching: Concepts, Findings and Implications*. McCutchan, Berkeley, California

Power C N 1973 The unintentional consequences of science teaching. *J. Res. Sci. Teach.* 10: 331–340

Power C, Cotterell J 1981 *Changes in Students in the Transition from Primary to Secondary School*. Australian Government Publishing Service, Canberra

Rosenshine B 1979 Content, time, and direct instruction. In: Peterson P L, Walberg H J (eds.) 1979 *Research on Teaching: Concepts, Findings and Implications*. McCutchan, Berkeley, California

Smith B O, Meux M O 1962 *A Study of the Logic of Teaching*. University of Illinois Press, Urbana, Illinois

Smith B O, Meux M O, Coombs J, Nuthall G A, Precians R 1967 *A Study of the Strategies of Teaching*. University of Illinois, Urbana Illinois

Smith L, Geoffrey W 1968 *The Complexities of an Urban Classroom*. Holt, Rinehart and Winston, New York

Stodolsky S S, Ferguson T L, Wimpleberg K 1981 The recitation persists but what does it look like? *J. Curric. Stud.* 13: 120–30

Westbury I 1973 Conventional classroom, open classrooms and the technology of teaching. *J. Curric. Stud.* 5: 99–121

Westbury I 1978 Research into classroom processes: A review of ten years work *J. Curric. Stud.* 10: 283–308

Willis P E 1977 *Learning to Labour: How Working Class Kids Get Working*. Saxon House, Farnborough

Student Roles

R. P. Tisher

In this discussion of student roles in the classroom, the concept of role will be centred upon behaviours that are characteristic of persons in a context. Consequently, the article begins with a general and simple portrayal of students' characteristic classroom behaviours. The term classroom includes laboratories, self-paced learning environments, and open-area situations, each of which has differing contextual features which may affect the nature of students' behaviours. The general portrayal is, then, refined with a description of the characteristic classroom behaviours of students in differing contexts. That description is followed by an account of the differences in behaviour patterns of students when they are categorized according to achievement level and teachers' attitude toward them. The article concludes with a discussion on the variety of student roles in the classroom, the need to establish well-conceived typologies of students' roles, and to discover more relationships between the nature of these roles and student learning and attitudes.

1. A General Portrayal

In conventional (or traditional) classrooms as well as in more informal ones or ones where self-paced curriculum materials are used, students will be talking for about 30 percent of the time. In the more informal situations there is not generally a higher proportion of student verbal behaviour but there are many more non-oral activities, for example, reading, writing, and watching (Tisher 1981). A survey of a number of research findings about student behaviours in conventional learning environments, self-paced learning environments, and open-area situations reveals the following situation: Students may spend up to 60 percent of their time in class working alone and when they are working alone, or

even, for that matter, working in groups, the greater proportion of their behaviours are non-oral ones, especially reading, writing, and watching. When talking does occur it is highly likely to be initiated by the teacher and the students will be listening. On average each student listens more often to someone than he or she talks. When a student talks it is more likely to be in response to a factual question. On occasions verbal interactions between pupils comprise up to 20 percent of all types of interactions in class but then pupils discuss other than class work in 50 percent of the instances. In about one-tenth of the interactions, students ask questions and they respond on a corresponding proportion of occasions.

This fairly general picture is congruent with Dunkin and Biddle's (1974) assessment that students' roles in the classroom are much more passive than teachers' roles (see Table 1). They also noted that students spend most of their time in listening and watching and in reading and writing. The picture is a very simple portrayal and does not indicate important differences which may occur in behaviours for different students in learning contexts which in turn differ from each other in specific ways. It is the case that student behaviours are affected by contextual specifications as the summary of research in Table 2 shows.

2. Influence of Contextual Variables

It is generally accepted that the introduction of a new curriculum with its ancillary materials will alter the characteristic behaviour patterns of students from what these were before. Certainly this was what Tisher and Power (1978) found to be the case in a series of studies involving the Australian Science Education Project (ASEP) materials in secondary schools. In the newly

Table 1

Student roles in the classroom: Some general information on student behaviour

(a) In conventional and open area situations students work alone for about 60 percent of the time

(b) In self-paced learning environments in secondary schools student–student interactions are not frequent: they may constitute up to 20 percent of all interactions

(c) In open area situations there are higher proportions of student–student interaction

(d) Students spend up to two-thirds of the time listening to teachers talk

(e) For about 90 percent of the questions directed to them, students have to respond in a manner which reproduces textbook information

(f) Students can be interrupted often by teachers and other students during responses

(g) In self-paced environments about 70 percent of all student activities are nonverbal ones

(h) Watching (60 percent) and writing (20 percent) are proportionately the most frequent nonverbal activities in secondary science and social science classes

(i) Grade 5 students (age 10) spend most of their time in lessons watching (30 percent) and reading and writing (30 percent)

(j) Secondary school students, aged 14, are less frequently the source of a verbal move (40 percent of instances)

created self-paced learning environments students interacted much more with curriculum materials (e.g., student workbooks) than was the case in the more conventional science classrooms. Also students initiated more interactions with peers and with teachers and, as a consequence, both types of initiated interactions constituted a higher proportion of the total interactions in class than was the case for the more conventional science classroom. The greater interaction with the curriculum materials is to be expected since the conventional science classrooms did not contain student workbooks, but it is interesting to note that in the self-paced environments students initiated more contacts with others. However, the introduction of a new curriculum does not always affect student roles in the classroom. According to Oakley and Crocker (1980) new primary-school science curricula often have a negligible effect, and this may be linked to the nature of the ancillary curriculum materials. Certainly when there is a rich array of reading materials, student workbooks, and equipment, behaviour patterns are altered and, as might be expected, there is a higher proportion of "off-task" behaviour in those self-paced learning environments than in a teacher-centred classroom (Tisher and Power 1978). There can also be variations in student behaviours between self-paced learning environments depending on the topic or the subject matter under

study. For example, in one comparison between self-paced secondary-school classrooms (Tisher 1981) it was noted that students in science classes spent more time in reading their curriculum materials than corresponding groups of students in social science classes. On the other hand the social science students were watching or looking at someone or something more often than the science pupils, but in both types of classes there were comparable proportions of nonverbal to verbal activities. The latter accounted for about 30 percent of all pupil activities.

Table 2

Student roles in classrooms: Contextual variables

(a) In self-paced secondary science classrooms student–student interactions may comprise up to 20 percent of all interactions

(b) Students in open classrooms ask three times as many higher cognitive questions as pupils in traditional classrooms

(c) Off-task verbal behaviour of secondary-school students in self-paced learning environments constitutes over 50 percent of all student verbal behaviour

(d) When teachers set clear goals, student on task behaviour and attention are increased

(e) When students work in small groups there is a greater amount of interaction between the students when no teacher is present at the group

(f) In informal primary-school settings there is a predominance of teacher questions and interactions between students and teacher are brief

(g) In primary schools the introduction of new science curricula can have negligible effects on student roles

(h) In open-area schools there is more movement of students, a greater variety of behaviours, and a higher proportion of student–student interaction than in traditional schools

(i) There is more student–student interaction in affiliation-oriented classrooms than in control-oriented ones: there are also fewer student initiated behaviours in the latter

(j) There are more student initiated behaviours in classrooms using computer assisted instruction than in traditional classrooms

Some research workers who have compared traditional classrooms with open-area ones report that there are differences between pupils' behaviours in the two environments (see *Open Versus Formal Methods*). For example, there are higher proportions of student–student interactions in the open environments, as well as higher proportions of higher cognitive questioning and off-task behaviours. In informal settings in the English primary school Resnick (1972) noted a predominance of teacher questions directed at students and that generally interactions between student and teacher were quite brief. But, then, not all the research on open areas has found marked differences between student behaviours in those situations compared to student behaviours in conventional classrooms. In one national study of Australian open-area primary schools (Angus et al. 1975, 1979) only minor differences were detected between student behaviours in these and in the conventional situations. The research workers noted that independent study was not more frequent in the Australian open areas nor was there a higher proportion of student–student interaction. There was in fact a corresponding variation in the range of behaviours in each of the different types of classrooms. That only minor differences were documented in the Australian open-area schools study cannot be accounted for simply in terms of cultural or national factors. Other features may be more salient, for example, the "tone" or "climate" of the classroom. In a study of 200 secondary-school classrooms Moos (1978) reported that those whose social environment was affiliation oriented were characterized by more student initiation and participation and interaction between students than was the case for control-oriented classrooms. Furthermore, the presence of the teacher, or the proximity of the teacher alters students' behaviour patterns. The mobility of different teachers in various classrooms could account for some variations in student behaviours. It has been observed (Oakley and Crocker 1980) that there will be more student–student interactions in group learning situations when there is no teacher present in the group.

In addition, some of the strategies teachers use can affect student behaviour patterns quite markedly. In particular, when teachers specify clear lesson goals for students there are more on-task behaviours by students and greater attention to class work (Schunk and Gaa 1981). As was noted earlier when teachers introduce self-paced curriculum materials to guide students' classroom activities, students behaviour patterns can change. Similarly, the use of other educational media can have an effect.

So, even though there are characteristic behaviours of students in classrooms, for example, reading, writing, responding, questioning, reacting, and watching, the relative proportions of each can vary depending upon the nature of the classroom context. But the proportions are also influenced by other features, including the perceptions that students and teachers have of each other and what may have been designated overtly or covertly as appropriate or inappropriate behaviour by teachers, students, or parents.

3. Influence of Student Variables

Differences in behaviour patterns, and consequently in student roles occur between individuals who are more or less successful in class. In a detailed study of some Australian primary classrooms, Canning (1980) recorded that the high-achieving students raised their hands more often in response to a question, were called on more frequently to respond, and initiated more work-related interactions with others than did their low-achieving peers. On the other hand they received less

praise for correct answers but they were also subject to less criticism for incorrect answers than their low-achieving classmates. This is not meant to imply that Australian primary-school teachers discriminate against low-achieving pupils. On the contrary, when Canning (1980) compared and contrasted his findings with those from comparable North American studies (Brophy and Good 1970) he concluded that the Australian teachers appeared to discriminate more in favour of the low-achieving students than their American counterparts, who, according to Mitman (1982) distribute more praise overall to the high achievers and interact more with them.

There are other ways in which high-achieving students' behaviours differ from the low achievers—they talk more as a group (Williams and Pellegreno 1975), initiate more talk on divergent and evaluative questions, and are treated favourably by having their ideas (initiations) accepted and used more by teachers. But then not everything happens to their advantage: they have to wait longer than their low achieving peers when they initiate evaluative or divergent type questions. Perhaps as a compensation they then initiate more talk on these types of questions (Campbell 1977).

In his study of school students in the United Kingdom, Bennett (1976) reported on the differences in classroom behaviours between students he categorized as low, average, and high ability. The amount of work-related interactions between students was greatest for the highs, and least for those classified as average, whereas the amount of social interaction between students varied in an expected direction from the low, to the average, to the high ability students. These students also fidgeted much more in class than the other two groups and as might be predicted, the high ability students fidgeted the least. Perkins (1965) noted that a distinction has to be made between low-achieving boys and girls with respect to their work-related interactions since the girls, more so than the boys, interacted more on work-related matters. However when the low achievers interact with the teacher they appear to be cut short, that is, receive terminal feedback, more frequently than their high-achieving peers. Certainly this appears to be the case in some reading lessons (Clements and Hoffman 1982).

Differences in students' characteristic classroom behaviours have also been noted when students are grouped or categorized according to the affective attitudes teachers have toward them. Brophy and Good (1974) have summarized quite a number of teacher–student interaction studies involving four basic teacher attitudes toward pupils: attachment, indifference, concern, and rejection; and from their excellent review a number of roles of students can be identified. For example, "rejection" students create a lot more procedural and work-related interactions than other peers, and they call out and interrupt ongoing activities without permission much more frequently than other peers. As a consequence they are involved in a large number of interactions with the teacher on procedural matters. In contrast, students regarded as indifferent initiate fewer work-related contacts and do not respond as frequently to questions, which is probably related to the fact that they are not given as many response opportunities as others, especially the students classified as attachment ones, who raise their hands frequently, volunteer to answer questions, and initiate more interactions with the teacher regarding assigned class work.

4. Differing Student Roles

In the preceding discussion it was stated that differences have been noted in students' characteristic classroom behaviours when they are categorized according to achievement level or the attitude of the teacher toward them, that is, differences have been noted when students are playing roles of high or low achievers or indifferent or rejected individuals. But they may be categorized in numerous other ways. In fact teachers and others talk about a variety of student roles in the classroom, for example, receivers and senders, cooperators, concealers, reinforcers, workers, manipulators, mediators, screeners, creators, and consumers. These are not determined primarily by the prevalent classroom behaviour of the students, even though, as indicated above, there are some differences between the behaviour patterns of different student groups. There are probably other factors which also influence teachers' categorizations of students and students' roles. These most likely include the nature and intensity of the various student behaviours, when these occur in the general flow of lesson activities, whether they are sanctioned by classroom rules or expectations, whether they are work-related or not, or whether they conform to teachers' perceptions of the ideal student. Science teachers maintain that the ideal student is one who is stable and unemotional, conforms, fits in with established classroom procedures, is thorough and punctual with work, is highly motivated, and reveals a creative element in his or her thinking (Wilkinson 1972). By implication, students who interrupt classroom discourse, initiate frequent off-task interactions, ask numerous procedural questions, do not respond to science teachers' questions, are not "ideal", and may be regarded as playing uncooperative or disruptive roles. Generally teachers expect students to be cooperative in class or to comply, that is, conform to classroom rules, fit in with classroom procedures and organization, and be punctual with assigned work. So those who appear to be doing these things, who are frequently on-task when reading, writing, and talking, and who initiate work-related contacts with teachers and peers are likely to be regarded as playing the roles of cooperators.

Most of the preceding categorizations of students' roles were derived from the perspectives of teachers or other adults (e.g., research workers) but not from students who also have their own interpretations of classroom events, and form expectations about these, the teacher, and other peers. Boser and Poppen (1978)

for example have shown what some of the effects of students' interpretations may be: teachers with whom students believed they had poor relationships were characterized as confronting them often and asking what was being done. Allender et al. (1981) reported that when students believed the teachers trusted them, they participated more and were more involved in classroom activities. Students' classifications for, and views about, their classroom roles are rarely compared and contrasted with teachers' categorizations of student roles and there is not much information about the educational significance of high or low congruences between the respective categorizations.

For that matter, there has been, very little well-conceived research that has established typologies of student roles in the classroom, taking into account the multifaceted nature of those roles, and what links the nature of those roles with student outcomes. Some workers have taken the first steps to establish typologies of students using a number of dimensions such as measures of pupil ability, personality, motivational variables, and records of classroom interaction and have shown how these typologies might be used to inform teachers and heighten their awareness regarding the effectiveness of various teaching strategies. These are encouraging developments which could be applied with profit to research on student roles, bearing in mind that roles are not only behavioural but limited in some ways by contextual specifications including teachers' and students' perceptions and expectations of classroom situations. Perhaps when more researchers take up the challenge to establish typologies of students' roles using a number of dimensions and sophisticated clustering techniques more relationships will be found between student learning or attitudes and student roles in the classroom. This is a needed area of research that was highlighted by Dunkin and Biddle (1974), yet there are still no outstanding findings to report. Nevertheless, the research associated with student roles does draw attention to factors which affect the nature of these roles and consequently provides valuable information which can be used to heighten teachers' awareness about their classroom procedures and perceptions of students.

See also: Teacher Roles; Students' Ethnicity; Responding; Students' Sex; Affective Teacher Education; Psychological Environment

Bibliography

Allender J S, Seitchik M, Goldstein D 1981 Student involvement and patterns of teaching. *J. Classroom Interaction* 16(2): 11–20
Angus M J, Evans K W, Parkin B 1975 An observation study of selected pupil and teacher behaviour in open plan and conventional design classrooms. Australian Open Area Schools Project, Technical Report No. 4. Education Department of Western Australia, West Perth
Angus M J, Beck T, Hill P, McAtee W 1979 *A National Study*

of Open Area Schools. ERDC Report No. 21, Australian Government Publishing Service, Canberra

Bennett N 1976 *Teaching Styles and Pupil Progress*. Open Books, London

Boser J, Poppen W A 1978 Identification of teacher verbal response roles for improving student–teacher relationships. *J. Educ. Res.* 72: 90–94

Brophy J E, Good T L 1970 Teachers' communication of differential expectations for children's classroom performance. *J. Educ. Psychol.* 61: 365–74

Brophy J E, Good T L 1974 *Teacher–Student Relationships: Causes and Consequences*. Holt, Rinehart and Winston, New York

Campbell J R 1977 Science teachers' flexibility *J. Res. Sci. Teach.* 14: 525–32

Canning L 1980 The communication of teacher expectations for pupil performance a longitudinal study in two Victorian primary classrooms. (M.Ed. thesis, Monash University, 1980)

Clements R, Hoffman J 1982 Student reading miscues and teacher feedback as a function of students' reading achievement level. Paper presented at the Annual Meeting of the American Educational Research Association, New York

Dunkin M J, Biddle B J 1974 *The Study of Teaching*. Holt, Rinehart and Winston, New York

Flanders N 1967 Teacher influence in the classroom. In: Amidon E, Hough J (eds.) 1967 *Interaction Analysis: Theory, Research, and Application*. Addison-Wesley, Reading, Massachusetts

Mitman A 1982 Teachers' differential behavior toward higher and lower achieving students and its relationship with selected teacher characteristics. Paper presented at the Annual Meeting of the American Educational Research Association, New York

Moos R H 1978 A typology of junior high school classrooms. *Am. Educ. Res. J.* 15: 53–66

Oakley W F, Crocker R K 1980 An exploratory study of teacher interventions in elementary science laboratory groups. *J. Res. Sci. Teach.* 17: 407–18

Perkins H 1965 Classroom behavior and underachievement. *Am. Educ. Res. J.* 2: 1–12

Resnick L 1972 Teacher behaviour in the informal classroom. *J. Curric. Stud.* 4: 99–110

Schunk D H, Gaa J P 1981 Goal-setting influence on learning and self-evaluation. *J. Classroom Interaction* 16(2): 38–44

Tisher R P 1981 *Teaching Strategies: A Research Report*. Monash University, Melbourne

Tisher R P, Power C N 1978 The learning environment associated with an Australian curriculum innovation. *J. Curric. Stud.* 10: 169–84

Wilkinson W J 1972 Science teachers' opinions of the pupil and the measurement of pupil role. *Educ. Rev.* 25: 46–53

Williams W C, Pellegreno D 1975 Gatekeeping and the student role. *J. Educ. Res.* 68: 366–70

Managerial

Classroom Management

E. T. Emmer

Classroom management includes the set of teacher behaviors and activities that are primarily intended to foster student cooperation and involvement in classroom tasks. The concept spans a very broad range of activities, encompassing such things as arranging the physical setting, establishing and maintaining classroom procedures, monitoring pupil behavior, dealing with deviant behavior, keeping students accountable for work, and conducting lessons that keep students on task. In addition to their broad scope, management behaviors are central to the teaching role, usually regarded as necessary for the achievement of classroom goals and tasks (Duke 1979). The intention of this article is to try to organize into a coherent framework those teacher behaviors that are related to indicators of successful management.

1. Criteria for Effective Management

The management criteria of student involvement or cooperation in classroom tasks (or related variables such as absence of disruption, attentiveness, student engagement) have the advantage of a clear relation to the teacher's role. Few educators would argue the relevance of these criteria for management effectiveness. However their use does not imply that they are the sole criteria for effective teaching. Other criteria, such as pupil achievement and affective outcomes, must also be considered when specifying good teaching practice. Furthermore, the effects of particular management strategies may be moderated by context features such as student characteristics or subject matter. Additional features of the context, such as school organization or variation in student ability levels, may also influence the teacher's behavior and activities. In reviewing research on management, an emphasis was placed on seeking characteristics of good management that were identified in various contexts, rather than relying on single studies in restricted populations.

The criteria for evaluating management practices emphasize the immediate day-to-day workings of the classroom. Are children engaged productively in classroom activities? Is there an absence of conflict and deviant behavior? Is time used wisely with the major share available for achieving the curricular goals? This emphasis on the immediate and proximal goals of management raises the question of compatibility with the superordinate goals of education. It is not difficult to identify circumstances in which a single-minded concern for eliciting high levels of task engagement would interfere with important learning or affective outcomes. For example, Dreeben (1973) has argued that teachers choose particular activities or lesson formats (e.g., recitation) primarily because student attention is easier to maintain in them, rather than for their superiority in promoting student learning. Indeed, unless teachers have compelling evidence for superior learning gains of particular teaching methods, lesson formats, behaviors, and so on, it is likely that teacher decision making will be influenced by more immediate concerns for task involvement. Certainly the crowded classroom setting itself, the custodial function, the multiplicity of activities to be conducted, makes it likely the teacher's information processing will be strongly influenced by evidence of student cooperation or deviation (Doyle 1979). Fortunately, evidence on the relationship of management criteria and learning outcomes indicates that better management is associated with greater achievement. When adjusted for entering achievement, correlations between student achievement measures and indicators of management effectiveness are usually positive and significant. The picture with respect to affective criteria such as student attitudes or self-concept indicates that certain teacher behaviors (for example, punishment and personal criticism) associated with poorer student affect are also associated with less student involvement and more disruptive behavior; that is, with poorer management results. Thus, concerns for management outcomes can be compatible with, and frequently are complementary to, the primary achievement and affective goals of schools. That generalization does not rule out the possibility that excessive zeal for a well-managed classroom might interfere with other educational goals. Furthermore, in most research studies the strength of the relationship between management variables and learning outcomes is no more than moderate, so that an exclusive concern with management outcomes is inappropriate.

2. Theoretical Perspectives

Much of the writing on classroom management derives from three major lines of inquiry or perspectives. These are a functional perspective, a behavior modification orientation, and a humanist–interactionist perspective. Functional approaches focus on criteria for management, searching eclectically for teacher behaviors that help accomplish these outcomes. These approaches are frequently atheoretical and use concepts derived from many different theories or disciplines, including common sense or "naive" viewpoints. The behavior modification perspective, which focuses on the use of reinforcement and punishment to establish, maintain, or eliminate specific behaviors, is narrower than the functional approaches in its selection of predictor variables. Although behavior modification research has been criticized because of its laboratory orientation, many field studies have also been conducted in recent years. Because the dependent variables in behavior modification research are often related to management outcomes, such as time-on-task, and amounts of disruptive or deviant behavior, this body of research, augmented by its recent concern for cognition, provides sources of evidence for good management. A third approach found in writing on management, the humanist–interactionist perspective, has been described as having a psychotherapeutic base (Brophy and Putnam 1979). This approach places a positive value on particular types of teacher behavior, such as acceptance of student feelings or active listening, because they are believed to promote growth of students' self-concept, personal adjustment, or responsibility. Teacher behaviors advocated by this perspective may indeed promote pupil growth in affective areas; however, there is little classroom research supporting the use of these techniques as good management practices. Thus, their use as models of classroom management depends on the assumption that they produce changes in student affective characteristics that then result in better classroom management outcomes. Because the research evidence linking humanist–interactionist approaches with management outcomes is much thinner than either the functional or behavior management areas, most of the components described below will reflect the first two perspectives.

3. An Analysis of Management Tasks of Teachers

Research using criterion variables such as high task engagement or low disruptiveness has identified a number of teacher behaviors and activities that contribute to better managed classrooms. Research from this perspective allows for the analysis of management tasks as a series of activities performed by the teacher to promote engagement and cooperation.

Two major types of activities form the core of the teacher's management skills. First, the teacher must establish standards for behavior that discourage disruption or at least keep the levels of such behavior very low. However, preventing disruption is not sufficient for good management; the teacher must also create conditions to engage and maintain students in classroom activities. Thus, a second area of management competence encompasses skills relevant to the maintenance of lesson and activity flow. In the following sections, the skills that contribute to these management facets will be described. In these sections, the concern with establishing and maintaining a well-managed classroom should not be interpreted as a lack of concern with substantive content. Instead a well-managed classroom is created in conjunction with content activities.

3.1 Identifying Expected Student Behavior

Much research indicates that in order to manage classrooms effectively teachers must play a central role in defining expected student behavior. This implies that teachers must have a clear idea of what behaviors are and are not appropriate in advance of instruction. However, identifying expectations for behavior is not a simple matter because of the complexity of the elementary-school classroom. Children are engaged in learning many different subjects, often working in a variety of formats including whole class, small groups, and individual seatwork. Within these formats different activities occur such as recitations, pupil presentations, teacher presentations, and discussion. Children leave the classroom at various times to go to different instructional areas, lunch, recess, and so on. Most of these activities require different student behaviors. Thus, the teacher cannot depend on a few general expectations (e.g., "respect others") to carry the day; students need to know what is expected of them in these different settings. The complex behaviors required of students can be seen in the descriptions below of expected behavior during activities commonly used in elementary classrooms.

(a) *Beginning the school day*. Children need to know what to do when they first enter the classroom or teaching area. Some signal such as ringing a bell may be used to cue in-seat behavior and cessation of talking. Teachers often use a whole class activity, for example a song, to reestablish group responsiveness or cohesion. A brief seatwork activity that all students are expected to perform may also be used at this time to enable the teacher to attend to administrative matters such as checking attendance.

(b) *Whole class activities*. Expected student behavior frequently includes listening attentively when the teacher or a student speaks, raising one's hand and waiting to be recognized before speaking, and following directions. "Call outs" by students during certain activities such as a fast paced recitation may be permitted, but the context or the teacher must provide cues to discriminate when such behavior is acceptable from situations in which hand raising is required.

(c) *Small-group activities*. This format is commonly used for teaching reading and, less frequently, for mathematics and other subjects as a way to cope with a wide range of achievement entering students in while at the same time allowing sustained interactive contact of the teacher with the students. The format requires an identification of what is appropriate for two sets of students: those in the group under the immediate supervision of the teacher and those out of the group. For students in the supervised group, the teacher needs to decide how to manage their responses, that is, whether or under what circumstances to allow call outs and whether hand raising or patterned turns will be used to control recitation. For students out of the group several things must be decided, such as whether students are allowed to talk to each other and under what circumstances (e.g., to help, to socialize, to seek help) and in what manner (e.g., whisper or use "classroom voices"). Students not in the group must have assigned or chosen tasks. The teacher also needs to consider what these students will do when they are unable to continue with their work. Can they interrupt the teacher? If so, under what circumstances? Should they be able to seek help from other students? If so, can they ask anyone or should the teacher identify special monitors? Although many systems are feasible depending upon the setting, the teacher's availability, and the complexity of the task, it is clear that the teacher must have some system covering most of the preceding areas. Otherwise, for example, whenever students out of the supervised group encounter difficulty with the assignment, they will either go off task or they will interfere with the teacher or other students' work when seeking help (see *Small Group Methods*).

(d) *Out-of-room activities*. Often teachers are responsible for supervision of students out of the classroom, for example, lunch period, library, play or recess, and passing to and from other areas of the building. Not only are teachers concerned with efficient use of time in these settings and activities, but safety is also a major consideration. Planning should include an identification of appropriate behavior in nonclassroom settings and any related school policies that might affect expectations.

(e) *End-of-day routines*. Behaviors appropriate for this important time also need to be planned. Common expectations include getting work spaces and desks ready for the next day and organizing materials to take home. Some teachers like to use this time to discuss the day's activities with their class and to foreshadow upcoming activities and events that are likely to be of special interest to the children.

In addition to these common activities, several other formats call for different student behavior and, therefore, careful planning.

(f) *Transitions*. The time between two activities is a transition period. Many transitions occur during the school day, for example changing from reading group to an arithmetic lesson, or from story time to art, or from small group to seatwork activity. If the teacher is not clear about what is permitted, each transition may turn into a period of noise and confusion, an excuse for task avoidance, and a struggle on the teacher's part to restore order. Providing some structure to transitions makes them run smoother with less disruption (Arlin 1979). Structure can be provided by making it clear to students what they should or should not do during the transition, and by setting a time limit for completing the transition. Movement through transitions can also be improved by teacher monitoring and by citing positive examples; for example, "I see six students who are ready to begin," or "I like the way tables one and two are carefully putting the supplies away."

(g) *Use of centers, equipment, and shared materials*. Frequently classrooms contain items which must be shared. Teachers must decide how such use will occur. Important considerations include time of use, proper care, and return of items.

(h) *Planning for personal needs*. Children need to know how to use toilet facilities, get a drink of water, find lost objects, store food or other items brought from home, and maintain their personal belongings. The teacher should be able to explain to children how these matters will be handled in their classroom.

The areas outlined above encompass the major types of activities occurring in most elementary-school settings, and for which the teacher will need to have clear expectations for appropriate student behavior. Although the list of areas is long and some aspects may appear to be trivial, it is through the accumulation of such pieces that the mosaic of classroom management is constructed.

3.2 Translating Expectations into Procedures and Routines

The process of identifying expectations is accompanied by the formulation of classroom procedures and routines to promote behavior in accordance with the expectations. Sometimes this process may be very direct. For example, if a teacher wants children to be seated quietly during attendance check, a workable procedure is to require that children be seated when the last morning bell rings and to refrain from speaking unless called upon. Other procedures may be more complex. For example, if children are expected to line up and pass through the halls in an orderly manner, a procedure to facilitate this behavior might include identifying a signal for lining up, how and when to leave seats (e.g., by rows or tables in a prespecified order), and appropriate behavior in line (e.g., hands off others, talk in whispers only, walk rather than run). The point of such procedures is not to regiment classroom life unduly, but rather to allow large numbers of children to coexist, move about, and do what is needed in order to preserve time and energy for accomplishing schools' primary goals. Failure to develop a workable set of procedures and routines will result in poor conditions for constructive use of time.

The formulation of classroom procedures should parallel the functional analysis of classroom behavior described earlier. Important areas for procedures include the common activity types found in elementary-school settings: whole class, small group, and individual seatwork, transitions, opening and closing routines, and room and materials use. Also, accountability procedures require definition in aspects such as taking up and returning assigned work, checking, providing feedback, and making up work after a period of absence. For example, a workable system for giving assignments to all but the youngest elementary children is recording them on a chalkboard or poster and having students copy the assignments into a notebook or onto an assignment sheet. The teacher may also provide oral directions for the assignment; however, the written procedure will eliminate confusion about what is required, will provide a record in case work needs to be done out of the classroom, and will prevent interruptions and delays caused by inattention to the oral instructions.

Part of the process of translating expectations into procedures is to formulate some general rules governing conduct. These rules may be displayed on a bulletin board or a wall poster, allowing them to serve as a reminder for correct behavior. Classroom rules are often stated in general positive terms such as "Treat others with respect," or "Complete assignments on time." However, some rules may prohibit certain behaviors, for example, "No fighting, pushing, or shoving" or "No chewing gum allowed." A common feature of classroom rules is their incorporation of schoolwide rules. When this is done, the rules have the added weight of the authority of other teachers and the principal. Classroom rules need to be consistent with the procedures the teacher plans to use. For example, if the teacher intends to allow children to help each other during seatwork, then a rule prohibiting talking without permission will be inconsistent unless the teacher limits the rule to whole class activities or otherwise clarifies the exceptions. Classroom rules are usually introduced during the first day or two of class. They are not, however, a substitute for a more detailed and carefully planned set of procedures. Instead, rules should function as general guidelines for behavior rather than directions for accomplishing specific classroom tasks.

3.3 Room Arrangement

Ease in moving about the room, uncomplicated access to supplies, and clear lines of sight for both teacher and students are examples of room conditions that may contribute to more efficient use of time and better instruction. Conversely, blocked aisles, crowding, poorly stored items that are difficult to retrieve, and areas of the room that are difficult to monitor may contribute to a loss of time for instruction, delays, and off-task student behavior. Thus, an important part of planning for classroom management is the arrangement of the physical setting (see *Seating Patterns*). To some extent the existing facilities will shape the teacher's choices. For example, if the room contains tables and chairs rather than individual desks for the children, then the teacher will have to plan for storage space for children's personal belongings. Important physical features to take into account include visibility, access to frequently used areas, and traffic patterns. Providing clear lines of sight is important both for the teacher and for the students. For the teacher, good visibility allows careful monitoring of children. Visibility for the teacher is not usually a problem during whole class activities; however, care should be taken when planning where to conduct small-group activities to allow the teacher to be able to observe the rest of the class. Other characteristics of the classroom layout such as traffic flow and access to work areas or materials are important because of the varied activity patterns and curriculum materials used in the modern classroom. Desirable results include open lanes of movement between frequently used activity areas, separation of group work centers from seatwork areas, and easy access to frequently used facilities such as the pencil sharpener, bathroom, and sink (if these are in the room). In addition, space for teacher's and children's belongings should be provided.

4. Implementation During the First Part of the School Year

The preceding section presented several topics that must be considered in the preactive phase of classroom management. In this section, attention is given to how the teacher can use the beginning of the year to establish effective classroom management practices. The beginning of school is an important time for classroom management because it is at this time that student behavior patterns and expectations are established. During the first week of classes, the amount of disruption usually will be at a low point and the level of cooperation will be high. The teacher's management goal is to keep matters this way by teaching children what behaviors are desirable and what should be avoided. It is far easier at this time to establish patterns of appropriate behavior than later to extinguish inappropriate behaviors and to substitute desired ones in their place. Of course, children do not enter classrooms *tabula rasa*. Some children may bring with them bad habits acquired at home or in an earlier grade. However, the new grade, with its new teacher, room, materials, and classmates, offers sufficient novelty to create a favorable condition for acquiring appropriate behavior.

An important principle to use in guiding the choice and sequence of activities during the first part of the year is to be aware of the child's perspective and concerns (Anderson et al. 1980). Most children, like many adults entering a new setting, have strong self-concerns. The child wants information about how to negotiate the classroom environment and how to succeed in accomplishing classroom tasks. If the teacher can plan the beginning-of-year activities to be responsive to the child's needs for security and success, then there is a higher probability that the management plan will succeed. Furthermore, the teacher by virtue of his or her position is responsible for planning an orderly environment in which children work and learn. Thus, at the beginning of the year the teacher's task is to be the children's source of information about the classroom. The teacher should assume a leadership role, anticipating the problems children might encounter or that may interfere with the adoption of good behavior patterns. The principles of anticipating children's concerns and perspectives and assuming a proactive role translate into a number of management strategies associated with better managed classes (Emmer et al. 1980).

At the beginning of the year, better managers emphasize the learning of procedures and rules. This does not imply an absence of substantive content, but content is initially a vehicle for establishing classroom procedures and work habits. The process of learning procedures and routines is emphasized on the first several days of instruction and attention to this facet continues as long as there are new procedures to be learned. Better managers do not try to teach all their classroom procedures immediately; instead, they are introduced gradually as they are needed. For example, procedures for small group activities or for learning centers can be taught when these activities are first used, which may not be for several weeks.

On the first school day, name tags may be used for easy identification. The teacher commonly starts with some whole class or seatwork activity, the purpose being in part to establish the teacher as direction giver and information source and to prevent confusion or the necessity of children seeking help from each other at this time. After the initial activity, which allows for late arrivals to be seated and for minor adjustments in name tags and recordkeeping, the teacher and class frequently will have a short "get acquainted" activity. In addition to helping the children feel more secure with the teacher and classmates, the teacher can use the opportunity to suggest procedures for the activity, such as raising hands to be called upon (see *Responding*). During or after this activity, the teacher can begin showing students the room and how to use it. Only those aspects of more immediate concern need be shown, and procedures associated with parts of the room which are not going to be used soon do not need discussion at this time. The children's perspective is important here: they need to know where the lavatory is, where to put their lunch sacks, what to do with milk money, the areas of the room to which they have access, and so on. This initial look around the room is usually accompanied by a discussion of procedures for each area that will be used soon. For example, the teacher may explain procedures for using art supplies and materials or lavatory procedures. The point of these activities is to help the

child learn to function in the classroom, to get his or her needs met, and to avoid confusion and disruption.

After the initial activities, teachers may engage children in a discussion of general classroom and school rules, or they may continue a presentation of procedures associated with activities that are planned for the day. Teachers frequently combine a discussion of classroom rules with a discussion of general procedures. Participation by the children in the establishment of classroom rules varies considerably across classrooms. The teacher may present rules individually and ask students to help supply a rationale for them, or the teacher may engage students in a discussion of why rules are necessary and ask students to offer suggestions for rules. When the latter is done, the teacher must be ready to help students form general principles from the list of specific and frequently negative suggestions sure to be produced by the students. Note that the teacher cannot rely on students to define procedures; such a process would be inefficient and, furthermore, students cannot be expected to have thought through the best choices among the many available procedures to accomplish particular classroom tasks. It is, after all, the teacher's role to do the planning of these details. However, some student participation in discussing rationale for major rules is desirable from two perspectives. First, such discussion will help make general rules more concrete. Second, stage theories of moral development (i.e., those of Piaget and Kohlberg) suggest that elementary-age children accept a rule-oriented system even if it is externally defined when it is perceived as a means of maintaining positive relations with teachers and peers. A discussion of reasons for having and following rules is likely to reinforce the idea that such a system helps everybody get along with one another and get work done, and is likely to strengthen the possibility that the rules will be viewed as normative by the class.

Teachers need to plan substantive activities for the time periods after the initial discussion of room, rules, and beginning procedures. Remaining procedures can be taught along with substantive activities either interspersed among them or as a part of the activities. Substantive activities at the beginning of the year should be carefully designed to possess a number of characteristics that enhance good management results. First, the activities should use simple formats and avoid those that require complex procedures. Usually whole class and individual seatwork activities are the easiest to set up at this time of year. The problem with complex formats (e.g., student choice of activities, small-group projects, centers) during the first few days of school is that they require even more time to teach than simpler and more familiar procedures. Once appropriate behavior in simpler formats has been learned, then more complex formats can be introduced. A second characteristic of beginning-of-year activities is that they should be interesting and easy, so that all the children will achieve success. This will reassure them and increase the amount of cooperation the teacher is likely to receive in subsequent activities. When seatwork activities are planned, some extra work of a stimulating and enjoyable nature should be planned for those who finish early. A third characteristic of early substantive activities is that the teacher should maintain contact with the class as a whole as much as possible. This means remaining in the room at all times, keeping eye contact during presentations or discussions, and moving around the room to check progress during seatwork. Maintaining close contact serves two purposes. It allows the teacher to monitor and to detect problems before they become crises. It also maintains the teacher's role as the source of information about procedures and behavior, thus preventing confusion or inconsistency resulting from conflicting student perceptions or misinformation. If it becomes necessary for the teacher to work for a period of time at his or her desk, a not uncommon event during the first few days of school, then it is important to plan for the occasion and have seatwork activities for students that they can complete independently without difficulty. During such time it is still very important for student activities to continue to be monitored.

The teaching of classroom procedures is similar to the teaching of any skill, with explanation, demonstration, practice, and feedback. Generally, the younger the children and the more complex the skill, the greater the need for demonstration and practice. To continue with an earlier example, suppose the teacher wants to teach children how to line up properly. At an earlier time the teacher will have formed expectations for how lining up should be done. A reasonable goal for this procedure is that children will, upon being given a verbal signal, go quietly from their seats to the proper position and wait there until given another signal to leave. To teach this set of behaviors to older children, the teacher can simply explain the correct behavior immediately before the procedure is first used. After giving a signal, the teacher must then carefully monitor how the children respond. Feedback to the class and a repetition of the process, if it is not performed satisfactorily, might also be necessary. With younger elementary-grade children or with any age group that lacks "going to school" skills, the above procedure can be augmented by demonstration and practice. For example, the teacher might model the correct way to walk from one's seat to the door, or the teacher could ask several students to demonstrate the behaviors. This exercise should continue until the teacher is satisfied that the procedure can be correctly performed.

Once taught, procedures cannot be assumed to be learned permanently. During the first several weeks of the year, teachers should continue to monitor carefully, providing feedback and reteaching procedures when necessary. The small amount of time required to teach major procedures is well spent because once in place the system will contribute to the smooth functioning of the classroom throughout the year. In comparison to poorly managed classrooms, better managed classrooms

use more time for procedures at the beginning of the year, but require less time for procedures during the rest of the year.

The process of establishing a well-managed, smoothly functioning class is a gradual one, with the greatest emphasis during the first few days of instruction. As the children learn more procedures and demonstrate the ability to follow them, the teacher can introduce additional and more complex procedures. Within a few weeks the children will have "settled in," and most procedures will have become routines that require only prompting by the teacher. Generally, children in early elementary grades will take longer to reach this stage.

5. Maintaining the Classroom Management System

Once in place a system requires maintenance and, at times, alteration. The following skills have been found to be related to good management results.

5.1 Careful Monitoring

This maintenance skill, related to Kounin's (1970) concept of "withitness," means that teachers observe classroom events carefully. During whole class presentations, the teacher maintains good eye contact; in seatwork activities the teacher frequently scans the class to verify task engagement and to find children who may need assistance. When working with a small group, a good monitor will continue to be aware of the rest of the children. Because teachers who are good monitors of student behavior are more likely to detect inappropriate behavior before it becomes disruptive, the importance of this behavior for management is apparent.

5.2 Prompt and Appropriate Handling of Inappropriate Behavior

This skill is concomitant with careful monitoring. However, detecting problems is not sufficient. The teacher also needs to take some action to alter unacceptable behavior, provide needed assistance, or to prevent disruption from spreading. The teacher's reaction, of course, depends upon the nature of the problem and the activity during which it occurs. For example, talking out is more likely to interrupt the flow of a recitation or a discussion format than individual seatwork activities. Thus, teachers tend to be more sensitive to and react more quickly to such behavior during whole group modes of instruction. In seatwork activities, off-task behavior by an individual student is less likely to disrupt other students, and so the teacher need not be as concerned with immediate handling of the incident. Furthermore, the response to the individual in seatwork activities can be private and relatively unobtrusive, whereas a public reaction may be the only alternative for ending disruption during whole class formats. The response of the teacher also depends upon the nature of the inappropriate behavior. Many inappropriate behaviors are the result of students not following a classroom procedure. In such cases, reminding the student of the correct procedure is often sufficient. The teacher can also ask the student to state the correct procedure or to practice it once or twice. If the teacher observes several children failing to follow a procedure, it probably should be retaught.

When working in a whole class format such as a recitation or in a small group, the teacher will interrupt the flow of the lesson if he or she reacts to each instance of inappropriate behavior. Constant teacher interruptions then will give rise to less involvement in the lesson and may even reinforce the children who are behaving inappropriately. To avoid interrupting lesson flow, a common tactic is to continue instruction while making eye contact with the student and holding the contact until the inappropriate behavior ceases. Another tactic is to move closer to the student until the behavior terminates. The teacher may couple eye contact with a signal such as a finger to the lips or saying the student's name. When inappropriate behavior persists, the teacher needs to intervene directly, and a penalty may be necessary to deter future occurrences (penalties are discussed in the next section).

Under certain circumstances it is best to ignore inappropriate behavior. When the student's behavior neither interferes with instruction nor attracts attention and if it is likely to be short-lived, there is usually no point in reacting to it. Also, inappropriate behaviors intended to attract the teacher's attention can be ignored unless they persist or receive rewarding attention from other children. Thus, a child who calls out rather than raising a hand during discussion can be safely ignored if the teacher is certain that the child knows the correct procedure. The teacher should, of course, recognize the child when his or her hand is raised.

The two skills of monitoring and quickly stopping inappropriate behavior go hand in hand. By effective monitoring the teacher can detect problems before they escalate. Good monitoring also allows the teacher to find children who do not understand the task, enabling corrective action to be taken before frustration and avoidance develop. Note that monitoring alone is not sufficient. The teacher who does not take action to deal with the problem behavior risks its spread to other students, and may communicate mixed signals or inconsistency about what behavior is actually appropriate for the activity.

5.3 Use of Reward Systems, Penalties, and Other Consequences

Well-managed classrooms are predictable environments in which children know what is expected and how to succeed. Such predictability occurs because the consequences of following procedures and rules and engaging in academic tasks are clear. Ideally, the natural consequences of engaging in classroom work (e.g., task accomplishment and learning) should be rewarding to children, and often this happens (Dreikurs et al. 1982).

At times, however, young children may not comprehend the connection between the task and the consequence, or it may be too distant to be effective. Furthermore, other activities that interfere with learning might be equally or more rewarding. Thus, good management frequently calls for use of rewards to help promote appropriate behavior. Reward systems may be simple or complex. Easy to use rewards include expressions of personal approval or interest such as a smile, praise, a note on an assignment, or a privilege. In order to avoid attributions of unfairness, privileges such as line leader, teacher's aide, or first row or table to leave for recess are best used when they are a logical consequence of the rewarded behavior (e.g., having desks cleared and materials properly stored clearly indicates that one is ready to leave for recess). Some other rewards require only a little more effort to use. These include symbols of approval such as stars or happy faces, a nice note to parents, awards, or allowing extra time for certain activities. An effective and commonly used system is to display a daily record of behavior. For example, a bulletin board may be used to show a monthly calendar for each child, who receives a star for each day on which all assignments are completed or class rules are followed. A treat at the end of the week or a special activity can then be provided to students who receive a pre-established number of stars. Very elaborate systems, such as token economies and charting individual student behaviors, are possible, but these systems invariably require extensive commitments of teacher time and energy. Consequently, teachers in regular elementary-school classrooms without extra personnel usually rely on simpler reward systems.

When reward systems are used, an extensive body of research in the behavior modification literature indicates that they will be more successful when the desired behaviors are clearly described and when students understand what procedures must be followed in order to meet the expectations. Thus, the teacher who has carefully considered his or her expectations for behavior and who has made these clear to students early in the year will be in a good position to use positive consequences to help maintain good behavior.

Negative consequences are also a part of classroom life and need to be used appropriately in order to benefit the classroom management system and to avoid harmful effects. Some common negative events—they are negative because most children do not like them and avoid them when possible—are expressions of teacher disapproval, a low mark or grade, withdrawal or withholding of a privilege or a desired activity, detention, engaging in a repetitive activity, sitting in a "time-out" seat, and being sent to the principal's office. Appropriate use of negative consequences means that they should be contingent on, and in proportion to, the inappropriate behavior. In order to avoid denial of responsibility through attributions of unfairness, it is desirable that the use of negative consequences be a logical outgrowth of the inappropriate behavior. For example, a student who talks out of turn should lose his or her turn; failure to complete an assignment will result in a lower grade; poor effort on an assignment causes the student to remain in from recess until the work is completed satisfactorily. Such consequences help the student perceive the connection between his or her behavior and its effects, thereby helping students learn to avoid undesirable behavior. When the negative consequence is not the naturally occurring one, then it usually involves some kind of penalty. Common penalties include after school detention, a low grade for conduct, or "paying a fine" such as an extra assignment or copying sentences. Often school policy will prescribe a penalty for a particular behavior such as fighting. When used, penalties should be clearly explained to students, connecting them to the behavior the penalty is intended to deter. Thus rationalized, penalties are more likely to be accepted as a legitimate extension of institutional authority and not subject to arbitrary use.

Consistency is a critical factor in the effective use of negative consequences. When inappropriate behavior is not followed by the negative consequence or when the teacher interferes with the naturally occurring negative consequence (e.g., extends a deadline for a student who has been lax in completing work), then the credibility of the system is reduced. More inappropriate behavior is likely to occur, especially if other children have observed the inconsistency.

The dictum "Be consistent" is common advice to the new teacher. Unfortunately, its meaning is not usually clear to the novice. What appears to be important is that the teacher has a clear idea of what behavioral expectations and consequences are appropriate. Consequently, the planning stage for management described earlier is especially crucial. Next, the students must have clearly understood what penalties are to be used and under what conditions. Then, the teacher must follow through when necessary. If the teacher's goals or expectations are very unrealistic and the children's behavior does not achieve the expected level, then the teacher is trapped in a dilemma. On the one hand, the inappropriate behavior calls for the prescribed consequences. Unfortunately, so much misbehavior may be occurring that the teacher must be excessively punitive in order to follow through consistently. On the other hand, not following through risks giving the impression of inconsistency and inviting a subsequent round of limit testing and great difficulty in re-establishing order. The only effective solution to this problem is to redefine expectations, identify appropriate procedures, and reteach this aspect of the management system to the students. Even with a well-planned management system, however, total consistency is not possible. The effects of inconsistencies can be minimized by keeping such events private when possible, or by acknowledging and explaining exceptions to the class. Such acknowledgment by the teacher communicates that the rule/consequence connection is still in force generally, even though exceptions may be made. In this circumstance the exception is then defined by the teacher and is less subject to speculation and future limit testing by students.

The importance of consistency in the use of penalties and the need to avoid a punitive and threatening climate suggests that penalties should be established as a consequence only for a limited number of easily observable behaviors. The behaviors must be easily observed in order to provide a reasonable chance for consistency in delivering the penalty. They must be limited in number in order to prevent an overemphasis on punishment. Therefore, penalties are best reserved for major infractions of classroom rules. Minor infractions, such as talking out of turn, occasional incomplete assignments, or not following a procedure, are best handled by invoking more natural consequences; for example, losing one's turn, completing the assignment during free time, or repeating the procedure correctly (see *Reinforcement*).

5.4 Establishing Accountability for Completion of Assignments

The child's school day is filled with seatwork assignments interspersed among whole class and small-group activities. Assignments such as completing a worksheet, solving a set of arithmetic problems, writing answers to questions, and drawing maps are frequently designed to supplement instruction, to provide practice, and occasionally to introduce new material. Establishing and maintaining engagement in assignments is clearly a major management goal that has important implications for student learning. Because children must work independently during many seatwork activities, the task of establishing and maintaining engagement deserves special attention. Important considerations in choosing and managing seatwork activities include insulating the activities from the intrusions of others and, when possible, programming the activities in a step-by-step manner. Such activities produce more on-task behavior because they have clearer and stronger cues to elicit the appropriate responses (Kounin and Gump 1974, Kounin and Doyle 1975). In addition, the amount of variety and challenge exhibited by seatwork assignments is positively related to engagement (Kounin 1970). Several other features of effective management of seatwork assignments, termed accountability procedures, have been identified (Worsham and Evertson 1980). First, requirements for assignments, including deadlines for completion, are carefully communicated to students. For complex assignments particularly, written directions supplement oral instruction. Once an assignment has been given, teachers monitor behavior during the transition to the seatwork. When feasible, a good strategy is to begin working on the seatwork assignment as a whole class activity led by the teacher. This gives greater assurance of a successful start for all of the students. Once work on an assignment is under way, the teacher needs to monitor carefully to detect problems; long periods of time spent helping one student can interfere with monitoring and should be minimized. Routines also need to be established for turning in and checking work. Helpful procedures include a designated time and place to turn in completed assignments and to retrieve corrected ones; an established procedure to pass in papers; and procedures for identifying and making up assignments missed because of absence. As with any other classroom procedure or routine, these accountability procedures should be carefully planned and thoroughly taught to students. Other considerations in establishing accountability for assignments are monitoring student progress and provisions for feedback, which can be provided by prompt and regular checking of student work. Unit projects or other assignments that take several days to complete need to be checked in progress. Older students can be encouraged to engage in self-monitoring by having them keep a daily or weekly record of completed assignments. When assignments are graded, students can record the grade on the record sheet. In addition to self-monitoring, the student's record can be used to communicate student progress to parents.

5.5 Maintaining Lesson or Activity Flow

Well-paced lessons that proceed smoothly are conducive to high levels of student engagement. Loss of momentum or progress in a lesson invites student disengagement because it permits a competing distraction for student attention. A number of teaching behaviors that contribute to lesson flow have already been discussed, including careful monitoring, prompt handling of inappropriate behavior, accountability procedures, and so on. In addition, activity flow can be enhanced by clarity of communication and by avoiding behaviors that interrupt, slow down, or deflect lesson progress. Clear communication can be aided by planning that identifies and organizes component parts of lessons and supporting materials. Lesson features that support clarity include providing step-by-step directions, using an outline to organize and sequence complex content presentations or activities, and frequent checking to verify student understanding. Avoiding behaviors that interfere with lesson momentum means that the teacher stays on the topic, avoiding digressions and resisting the urge to interrupt students or an activity by adding "just one more" thought. The teacher who has the lesson objectives and activity sequence clearly in mind, focuses student attention on the task, screens out competing stimuli, and does not initiate irrelevant activity will have the best chance for maintaining a smooth lesson flow.

6. Contextual Features

Several factors external to the teacher influence classroom management. The organization of the school—for example, whether each teacher is solely responsible for a group of students or whether responsibility is shared as in team teaching—will alter certain management features. For example, a common problem

in team teaching is the loss of instructional time produced by lengthy transitions between classrooms. Another problem common to some variations in organizational patterns is reduction of student accountability for completion of work. Whenever responsibility for children is shared among teachers, it may be more difficult to keep track of a child's progress and to maintain communication with the child and parents. Such problems can be minimized by careful coordination and communication among teachers. Any change in classroom unit structure is likely to be better managed when the expectations for student behavior are clearly communicated to students and shared among teachers. This process will make monitoring of behavior easier and promote greater consistency in the environment. In addition to effects on management of school organizational patterns, the presence or absence of good leadership by the school administrator can be influential. Some systems for classroom management (e.g., Glasser's application of reality therapy to schools) recognize and incorporate the use of schoolwide procedures as part of an overall management plan. The use of schoolwide systems is especially helpful for inexperienced teachers, because they permit the use of shared expectations about behavior. Such expectations are frequently not well thought out by the beginning teacher, whose training experiences generally are limited to one or two sites and often omit the formulation of expectations for a new setting.

Student characteristics, particularly the ability or achievement levels of the students, also influence classroom management procedures and outcomes. At least two types of contexts are important: the overall achievement level of the students relative to their grade and the range or heterogeneity of achievement levels within the class. That these features have important implications for management is not surprising because of the relationship between ability and task involvement. The presence in a classroom of children whose entering achievement levels prevent their successful completion of classroom work will clearly have a major impact on the degree of involvement of those pupils and thus upon classroom management. The existence of a wide range of student ability within a classroom is usually accommodated by grouping for reading instruction, and to a lesser extent for mathematics and other subjects. Such grouping practices add to the complexity of the classroom management system because of the need to maintain the involvement of students not in the small group under the direct supervision of the teacher. Management tasks whose importance is heightened by grouping for instruction within a classroom include monitoring of students outside the group, maintaining their accountability for work, and establishing procedures for work in and out of the group. Student heterogeneity also affects the success of whole class activities. During whole class instruction, lower achieving students in highly heterogeneous classes can be helped by seating them where they can be monitored more easily and by providing supplemental instruction and directions when needed. These supplemental contacts should be brief so as not to prevent the teacher from monitoring the whole class (Evertson et al. 1981).

Classes that are distinctly below grade level in achievement also pose special challenges to management. Research and much case study evidence indicate that on average students in low-ability classes are less involved and more disruptive. The teacher's ability to match tasks to students' levels is a critical skill in these settings. Whereas in higher ability classes the teacher's perceived competence in subject matter is a more important factor in maintaining student cooperation, in lower achieving classes student acceptance of teacher authority is more a function of the teacher's being perceived as someone who can explain clearly and respond to students' concerns for support (Metz 1978). In the lower achieving class, a history of student frustration is associated with generally lower success levels. Low-ability students often exhibit sensitivity to low teacher expectations, along with a well-developed set of avoidance responses to activities or settings in which failure seems probable. The management characteristics required to cope with these special problems include a strong sense of personal efficacy or ego strength on the part of the teacher, a clearly defined set of appropriate expectations for student behavior, the expression of these expectations in the classroom management structure, and a high level of affective support for the students' attempts to master the curriculum (Brophy and Evertson 1976).

7. Summary

Classroom management is the process of creating conditions favorable to the engagement of students in classroom activities. Three phases of establishing good management are distinguishable: planning before the school year begins; implementation; and maintenance. Components of good management include identification of clear expectations for student behavior in a wide array of classroom activities; establishment of procedures and rules; consequences; monitoring; prompt handling of inappropriate behavior; student accountability for assignments; and maintaining lesson or activity flow.

See also: Reacting; Grouping for Teaching

Bibliography

Anderson L M, Evertson C M, Emmer E T 1980 Dimensions in classroom management derived from recent research. *J. Curric. Stud.* 12: 343–56
Arlin M 1979 Teacher transitions can disrupt time flow in classrooms. *Am. Educ. Res. J.* 16: 42–56
Brophy J E, Evertson C 1976 *Learning from Teaching: A Developmental Perspective.* Allyn and Bacon, Boston, Massachusetts
Brophy J E, Putnam J 1979 Classroom management in the elementary grades. In: Duke D L (ed.) 1979
Charles C M 1981 *Building Classroom Discipline.* Longman, New York
Doyle W 1979 Making managerial decisions in classrooms. In: Duke D L (ed.) 1979
Doyle W 1986 Classroom organization and management. In: Wittrock M C (ed.) *Handbook of Research on Teaching,* 3rd edn. Macmillan, New York
Dreeben W 1973 The school as a workplace. In: Travers R M W (ed.) 1973 *Second Handbook of Research on Teaching: A Project of the American Educational Research Association.* Rand McNally, Chicago, Illinois pp. 450–73
Dreikurs R, Gunwald B, Pepper F 1982 *Maintaining Sanity in the Classroom: Classroom Management and Techniques.* Harper and Row, New York
Duke D L (ed.) 1979 *Classroom Management.* 78th yearbook of the National Society for the Study of Education, Part 2. University of Chicago Press, Chicago, Illinois
Emmer E T, Evertson C, Anderson L 1980 Effective classroom management at the beginning of the school year. *Elem. Sch. J.* 80(5): 219–31
Evertson C, Sanford J, Emmer E 1981 Effects of class heterogeneity in junior high school. *Am. Educ. Res. J.* 18: 219–32
Kounin J S 1970 *Discipline and Group Management in Classrooms.* Holt, Rinehart and Winston, New York
Kounin J S, Doyle P H 1975 Degree of continuity of a lesson's signal system and the task involvement of children. *J. Educ. Psychol.* 67: 159–64
Kounin J S, Gump P V 1974 Signal systems of lesson settings and the task-related behavior of preschool children. *J. Educ. Psychol.* 66: 554–62
Metz M 1978 Clashes in the classroom: The importance of norms for authority. *Educ. Urban Soc.* 11: 13–47
Woods P (ed.) 1980 *Teacher Strategies: Explorations in the Sociology of the School.* Croom Helm, London
Worsham M, Evertson C 1980 *Systems of Student Accountability for Written Work in Junior High School English Classes* (Research and Development Report No. 6105). Research and Development Center for Teacher Education, University of Texas at Austin, Texas

Behaviour Problems

L. G. Cairns

Misbehaviour of pupils in the classrooms of schools has been a major concern of teachers, principals, and parents for as long as schools have existed. Even a brief glance through many of the publications on teaching and schools will quickly reveal reference to "misbehaviour", "discipline" and "pupil control". Studies of the nature, extent, and influences of pupil misbehaviour, and possible teacher reaction to pupil misbehaviour have become important areas of applied educational research and writing this century with particular contributions by educational psychologists and sociologists.

1. What is a Behaviour Problem?

Initially, it would appear relatively easy to define a behaviour problem as behaviour of a pupil that causes problems in the classroom. The "problems" so caused often include interrupting other pupils, disrupting class activities, or conflicting with the rules and legitimate expectations of the teacher and the school. On further consideration however, a number of factors emerge that show the concept of a behaviour problem to be a far from simple commonsense notion.

First, there is the consideration of the source of the behaviour—the pupil. Usually the child is discussed by teachers, principal, and school counsellors within a psychological framework. The misbehaving child is showing "deviant" behaviour that can be classified across a wide range of "types". Categories usually refer to problems associated with morality (stealing, inflicting injury), reaction to authority (obscene language, temper tantrums), aggressive personality behaviours (stubbornness, resentfulness), classroom work-related behaviours (inattention, laziness), and inappropriate coping responses (withdrawal or shyness). Implicit in such systems of categorization is a psychological model relating underlying causes and personality dimensions to the behaviours exhibited by the child. This tradition has led to a great deal of research on deviant children and the causes of their problem behaviours and has provided many lists of the possible categories and causes.

Another view, more recent and with fewer examples of classroom research work, is that of a group of sociologists who advocate an application of "labelling theory" to classroom deviance (e.g., Hargreaves et al. 1975). This approach is concerned with studying all parties to classroom deviance to describe and analyse the system that labels such behaviours as "problems". Of concern in this type of analysis are the answers to some of the following questions rather than the search for personality defects in the misbehaving child. The questions include, "Who makes the rules?" "How are they formulated?" "Do some teachers and children view the rules in different ways?" "Are some rules seen as illegitimate by some teachers and some pupils?" It can be seen that this focus can lead to a very different interpretation of what constitutes problem behaviour and how to handle the situation in the classroom. It is important that some aspects of both these views be kept in mind in any discussion of pupil behaviour problems.

In considering pupil variables in misbehaviour, notice should also be taken of age-group related problems (e.g., preschoolers, adolescents) and such aspects as the developmental psychologists' view of the "normalcy" of such behaviours as testing authority and sexual exploration.

As well, there have been consistent findings in research since the early 1960s that there are sex differences in problem behaviour and the expectations of teachers about such behaviour. Boys are expected to present more boisterous and unruly behaviour and they fulfil those expectations (see *Students' Sex*). The stereotypes about the school behaviour of boys and girls are accentuated and maintained by teacher expectations (see *Teachers' Expectations*). In classrooms, boys receive a greater number of reprimands than girls (and of a more severe kind) as well as receiving differential treatment in codes of corporal punishment. (Girls are often excluded but boys are not.) This maintenance of sex-role stereotypes is a long-standing aspect of schooling that needs to be noticed and broken down. The question of whether boys by some stroke of nature *are* more prone to misbehave at school is not the appropriate point of departure. The important questions are rather why boys have been socialized into such a role and how teachers perpetuate the difference. Pupil behaviours are seen as problems to the extent that others (teachers, peers, parents) perceive them as such and react by deciding that the pupil has a behaviour problem.

This leads to an additional consideration—the "perceivers" or "reactors" to behaviour problems. Most definitions and discussions of behaviour problems begin by examining how a pupil has interfered with, disrupted, or upset the teacher and/or pupils in the context of an expected classroom orderliness. Parents are not usually directly involved, as they are not frequently part of classroom interaction. The repercussions of classroom misbehaviour often reach the home however, either as a teacher's call for discussion or as a child's complaint to parents about being disciplined. An important factor in the extent to which a pupil's behaviour in a classroom is perceived as a problem is related to the tolerance levels of the audience. A teacher with a low level of tolerance for classroom noise may identify reasonable talking aloud as a misbehaviour and only slightly louder exchanges as quite significant and disruptive problems. The degree to which a behaviour is identified as a problem is then directly related to the prevailing opinions of other pupils and (usually more importantly) the teacher as to what constitutes a violation of acceptable "normal" behaviour within the rules. Classroom rules may be explicit expressions—even displayed on a chart—or more usually, implicit understandings of what the teacher allows, expects, and will tolerate. This teacher-centred nature of classroom rules may be less a feature of some school systems but is frequently the norm in most Western societies.

Another important element in the consideration of problem behaviour is the question of "Who owns the problem?" This concept arose in the work of Gordon (1974) who claimed that the ownership of problems in classroom interaction was a significant consideration in understanding and resolving conflicts and problems. In an elaboration and application of this concept, Brophy and Rohrkemper (1981) grouped classroom behaviour problems into three types: (a) teacher-owned, in which the pupil's behaviour frustrates the teacher's needs and causes the teacher to be upset or annoyed; (b) pupil-owned, in which the pupil's needs are frustrated by events or people other than the teacher; and (c) shared, in which the pupil and the teacher frustrate each other's needs and goals to the same extent. Brophy and Rohrkemper asked elementary-level teachers to respond in detail to a series of fictional incidents involving behaviour problems from each of the three groups. The responses were also examined for attributions made by the teacher about the pupils involved, the causes of the problem, and how they would respond to the situation. It was evident that problem behaviour designated as teacher-owned led to teacher attributions of pupil intentionality and control (i.e. pupils were seen as being deliberate and knowing in their misbehaviour) and the teacher's responses were more severe and more motivated by short-term control than in the other two situations. Student-owned problems were seen by the teachers as not within the direct control of the pupils and the teachers' responses were more encouraging and focused on helping pupils to cope. With shared problems, the teachers tended to respond to the pupils with rewards and positive techniques to change the behaviour and attributed controllability to the pupils but not intentionality. These findings clearly indicate the importance of both problem ownership and teacher attributions of pupil intent and control in classroom behaviour.

It is not enough merely to identify that a problem behaviour exists in the classroom since the "ownership" of that problem and the related attributions by the teacher about the degree of deliberate intent and control the pupil has over the problem lead to differing responses by the teacher to that behaviour.

In addition, the mores relevant to acceptable standards and patterns of behaviour in a society and a culture change over time. Behaviours such as "lateness to school" are not treated as severely as they were in the first quarter of the twentieth century, nor are matters of "talking in class" necessarily seen as misbehaviour by many teachers today. What was outspoken insubordination in the late nineteenth century may be seen by some today as evidence of divergent thinking. As patterns of acceptable and nonacceptable behaviour have changed, so have teacher reactions. Teachers in many educational systems no longer use corporal punishment or subject pupils to ridicule and severe punitive tasks. Punishments and sanctions have given way to somewhat more positive emphases and the use of praise, encouragement, and rewards—though some systems still operate a punishment code.

What has emerged from theory and research in recent years is an understanding that behaviour problems are no simple matter of teachers identifying transgressions against their authority and punishing accordingly. Problem behaviours are the result of a number of influences and require care in definition, identification, and reaction.

2. Influences on Behaviour

It needs to be stressed that the influences on pupil behaviour in the classroom are many and varied. An examination of the range of influences may facilitate better understanding of behaviour problems.

Various psychological influences are related to problem behaviours in the classroom. Extreme behaviours such as violence, property destruction, and physical assault on fellow students by high-school-aged pupils have been the subject of clinical and empirical investigations since the early 1960s (Feldhusen 1979).

Many of these problems have been found to be associated with personality problems, attitudinal and motivational patterns, socioeconomic status, and intellectual capacity. Aspects of both heredity and environment are frequently mentioned as significant influences, but there is no clear-cut profile of the behaviourally disturbed child. Certainly the developmental changes children undergo from early childhood until the end of their school years are frequently quite dramatic and traumatic. The emergence of strong peer group pressures, resistance to authority, growing independence, physical stress, and uncertainty all add up to possible predictions of future difficulties. How some children cope and others do not is still the subject of considerable debate in the literature. The fact that developing children and the norms of their social and cultural backgrounds may differ from the expectations of the school and teacher often leads to direct clashes. Homestyle and domestic values may be in contrast to school mores—a child may be used to certain language and behaviour conventions at home which are not permissible at school and a clash of values seems inevitable—unless the child can adapt to both systems. For those failing to adjust, a clash is inevitable.

A further influence, beyond the basic psychological considerations and sociological patterns, is the possible impact and modelling of television. In modern television-orientated societies, children watch many hours of programmes daily. It has been suggested that the violence and mayhem so vividly depicted in many television programmes can have a deleterious effect on pupil behaviour in school, home, and society. Links have been made between television violence and teenage incidence of violent behaviour. It appears that if pupils view violent and aggressive behaviour on television in depicted surroundings similar to their own environment, then they are more likely to copy that behaviour (Feldhusen 1979).

Many of the behaviour problems in classrooms are, however, not of the violent and dangerous kind. Some are quite simple yet still disruptive manifestations of annoyance, defiance, anger, or frustration with people, objects, tasks, or rules. At other times pupils may be unwell or suffering some discomfort that coincides with a distraction, rebuke, or disruption and they then show signs of misbehaviour. The child who has come to school after an angry scene at home with a parent or sibling may find it difficult to settle to a task set by the teacher and can appear to be distracted or even defiant. Such problems vary across the age/grade range of schooling and need to be carefully considered. Physiological problems of ill-health (whether short term or long term), developmental stress, fatigue, and malnutrition all influence behaviour. Assuming that a problem behaviour is demonstrating only some underlying maladjustment in psychological terms is a limited view of the problem.

In addition to the influences already mentioned are those associated with school organization and demands. School-related influences may include aspects such as the size of the school. Very large, impersonal, and regimented school organizations can alienate some pupils who seek attention and rebel against the order imposed. This is more frequently a factor associated with high schools rather than elementary or primary schools. In addition, pupils who have histories of academic failure and low streaming may negatively value education and school experience. Syndromes of "learned helplessness" where some pupils feel trapped with little control of their progress and success and behave as if they do not care about school and its consequences have been identified as common in inner-city and rural isolated children. Children with these types of experiences are frequently identified as having behaviour problems.

Another school-related influence on behaviour problems is the teacher and the way classroom teaching is structured and presented. The research of Kounin (1970) highlighted the fact that a teacher who does not present material at an adequate pace and who jumps from one activity to the next without smooth "transitions" is asking for pupil loss of task involvement and disruption. In this formulation, the teacher's lack of "withitness" (being "on the ball" and aware) and inability to overlap (handle more than one thing simultaneously) may also be associated with pupil problems. If the teacher appears to pupils as inept, slow, or jerky in presentation and locked in on one thing at a time, then pupils will be more likely to be off task and disruptive. This idea may not be very acceptable to some teachers but it appears to have been supported in research studies carried out since the early 1970s (Brophy and Putnam 1979). The conclusion is that teachers can contribute to behaviour problems by their lack of preparation, organization, and low levels of presentation competence.

Influences on pupil behaviour and problem behaviour in particular are multifarious and interrelated. No unique set of psychological, sociological, or educational factors can account for all the problem behaviour in the classroom. It is a complex and involved area of study.

3. Learning and Behaviour Problems

Pupils who manifest behaviour problems in the classroom are not only viewed with concern by teachers because they represent some disruption to the otherwise orderly proceedings in which the teacher is engaged. Certainly, there is an element of frustration and threat to power when the teacher is faced with a misbehaving pupil. The main area of concern for many teachers however, is with the deleterious effects behaviour problems have on pupil learning and psychological development.

Recent research in the area of teacher effectiveness has shown the crucial importance of "time-on-task" (i.e., pupils' time effectively engaged in their class work) for learning and achievement (see *Time*). It is self-evident that pupils who misbehave and are active in ways not associated with school work are going to spend less time on the expected tasks. Decreases in "time-on-task" have been shown to be related to lower levels of learning. It is not just a simple equation of more time equals more learning but it is apparent that time *off* task leads to problems in pupil achievement.

It is not only the misbehaving pupil's learning that is interfered with by problem behaviour in the classroom. One pupil's misbehaviour can, and usually does, lead to some disruption to the learning of others in the classroom. This may be through the simple matter of causing another pupil to be off task or by the spread of the problem to involve a number of pupils in similar misbehaviour. This is often referred to as "contagion" and the spread of disruption across a class group is a common (and feared) sight for many teachers. Most often it is the teacher who is disrupted or annoyed by a pupil's misbehaviour and this can lead to the teacher interrupting or stopping class activities to issue a reprimand. Sometimes this in turn leads to more severe clashes with the pupil(s) involved in the problem. In addition, other pupils may respond to a pupil's misbehaviour with aggressive reactions to being disrupted in their activities and in turn cause even greater class disruption.

Teacher reprimands (or desists) can account for a good deal of lost time and learning interference in the classroom. Some teachers approach misbehaviour with long and frequent reprimands and even spend lengthy periods explaining (or justifying) their actions to the class. Some regard their role here as showing up their response to a behaviour problem as an example to other pupils and thereby justify nagging, prolonged reprimands. Very often what is communicated to pupils by such teacher behaviours is a lowering of positive expectations and a heightening of a belief that the teacher is watching for and expecting problem behaviour. Occasionally, severe reactions by the teacher can lead to pupils being resentful or fearful and generally losing respect for the teacher. Constant resentment or fear of the teacher may cause pupils to become too preoccupied to work effectively in the class.

Another aspect related to teacher expectations and reprimands is that some pupils misbehave in order to gain the teacher's attention. In addition, such misbehaviour can gain a good deal of peer attention and/or approval. This observation shows the need for teachers to be aware that their reprimands and responses to pupil behaviour problems may be acting as reinforcement to increase the behaviour rather than reduce it. If pupils gain more of the teacher's attention by misbehaving than spending time effectively engaged then they are likely to increase that misbehaviour, reduce time-on-task and learning, and achievement will suffer.

There are other issues that need to be considered in relation to the effects behaviour problems have on children's learning at school. Pupils who frequently misbehave may be signalling a number of important facts about themselves and their attitudes to an aware teacher. Frequent minor pupil inattention and off-task behaviour can indicate that the tasks and teacher presentations are not appropriate, that the pupil is less than motivated or has some minor problem with the particular material/tasks. Such behaviour could also indicate a more general lack of interest in the school situation. As previously mentioned, some pupils may have passing problems of health, peer disagreements, personal worries, or excitement that reduce their concentration and on-task behaviour on occasional days. It is the child who frequently and severely shows problem behaviour that signals most to the teacher. In most schools there are some children who have been described as "disturbed" or have emotional and psychological problems that affect their school and classroom behaviour and learning. Such children may behave in ways ranging from very unusual "acting out" behaviour such as barking or screaming for no apparent reason to sitting and rocking back and forth, to complete withdrawal and voluntary mutism and even perhaps flight from school (frequent running away). The behaviours may be attention seeking, attention rejecting, responses to stress, indicators of psychological disturbance, or maladaptive coping strategies in relation to school, teacher, peers, or self. Many of the pupils who show these behaviours need long-term and careful diagnostic (and specialized) treatment. Others are often not apparently so severe as to need special placement but still cause other pupils and the teacher considerable anguish.

4. Reactions to Behaviour Problems

When problem behaviours occur, there are a number of aspects to consider about the reactions of the various classroom participants. First, the pupil who is behaving in a "problem" manner expects some reaction from the teacher and/or peers. Second, the teacher, as the responsible adult charged with the supervision of the class of pupils, may choose to ignore the problem, rebuke or desist the pupil, or undertake some form of remedial action. Third, the audience of pupils in the classroom may react to the problem behaviour.

The misbehaving pupil, given that he/she is not so disturbed as to be unaware of the behaviour, can expect some reaction to the behaviour. Often the pupil has needs which the "problem" behaviour may satisfy. The particular task or situation in the classroom may be annoying or unacceptable to the pupil who wishes to express that feeling and finds some way to breach the norms of classroom behaviour to show the frustration or displeasure felt. A fellow pupil may be disrupting and/or annoying a pupil and manage to avoid any reprimand so the victim takes an action that breaches the norms and in turn becomes a disruptive problem. Alternatively, a pupil may find that one of the only ways to attract teacher and fellow pupil attention is to misbehave in the classroom. In some of these cases, the pupil who initiates the deviance may gain some satisfaction and resolution of his/her needs in carrying out the behaviour but in other situations the reaction of peers and teacher in the classroom may cause additional frustration, aggression, and/or further disruption and misbehaviour.

The teacher, when faced with problem behaviour, can, as already mentioned, either ignore or act on that behaviour. There are however, a number of factors to be carefully considered in this situation. Initially, the teacher needs to be conscious of his/her own abilities to handle certain pupil behaviours and the complexity of the situations that can arise. An early decision as to how severe or difficult the problem is (or could become) should influence whether the teacher takes personal action or brings in others—be it the principal, counsellor, or parents. There are at least eight key points for the teacher to consider when assessing possible reaction to pupil behaviour (based on Leach and Raybould 1977):

(a) Intensity—to what extent does the behaviour interfere with the pupil's other activities?

(b) Duration—how long does the behaviour episode last?

(c) Frequency—how often does the behaviour occur?

(d) Context—is the cause obvious and is the behaviour reasonable given the circumstances?

(e) Contiguity—does the behaviour problem occur contiguously with other specific behaviours?

(f) Generality—does the problem behaviour occur across a number of situations?

(g) Normality—does the problem behaviour depart from the norm for the age group of the pupil?

(h) Effect on others—how does the behaviour disrupt others?

Consideration of these points (and any others relevant to the circumstances and the pupils involved) will lead the teacher to a better informed decision as to what action should be taken. Other entries in this encyclopedia deal more specifically with teacher behaviours relevant to effective classroom management (see *Classroom Management*) and responses to pupil misbehaviour but some discussion, albeit brief, is necessary here. If the teacher decides that the pupil problem behaviour is not one requiring specialist assistance in the first instance then a number of actions are possible. The teacher may reprimand the pupil, ignore the behaviour, or take some more deliberate action involving a specific remedial strategy or programme.

A good deal of research has been completed on teacher's "desisting" (i.e. reprimanding) behaviour since the early 1950s and an examination of the research leads to the following recommendations to be considered when formulating desists (Cairns 1981):

(a) desists should be clear and firm ("I mean it") rather than rough or threatening;

(b) desists should indicate precisely which pupil is being reprimanded and emphasize the positive behaviour expected rather than the negative aspects occurring;

(c) desists should have a task focus (what is to be done) rather than merely a disapproval focus (what is not liked in the behaviour);

(d) the teacher should avoid harsh and emotional desists;

(e) the teacher may deliberately capitalize on the "ripple effect", which is the name given to the way a reprimand's effect can spread across the class of pupils even though the original teacher desist was aimed at only one pupil;

(f) the teacher should aim to use simple reminders to pupil self-control as the main desisting behaviour (e.g. once an expected behaviour has been discussed with a pupil the teacher may simply remind that child of the agreed-upon behaviour by saying "Scott, remember?" or some such phrase).

Research on the teachers' use of rewards, and other sanctions (including punishment) has occurred largely within the field of behaviour modification. Teachers can and do make systematic use of rewards and punishments to react to and change pupil behaviour problems.

Other more involved (in terms of time and effort) teacher reaction strategies have been proposed by many researchers and writers. Gordon's Teacher Effectiveness Training (TET), as previously referred to, is one popular and useful strategy. Other significant approaches based on different theory and practice have been proposed since the early 1930s. In particular, the work of Glasser (1969), Canter (1976), and Dreikurs et al. (1982) are among the most popular systematic approaches. A decision to implement one of these strategies with a group of pupils will certainly depend on the

answers to the eight key points raised above as well as the teacher's views on the philosophies inherent in the approaches.

The audience of pupils within the classroom is another source of reaction to problem behaviour. The consequences of disruption in relation to learning in the classroom were discussed earlier on in the article, but an important aspect of reaction to behaviour problems is the extent that fellow pupils find the problems amusing or disruptive. Some groups of pupils may offer strong peer support to pupils who cause problems. Adolescents, in particular, may support behaviour that is at odds with the school/class rules and norms as a way to demonstrate peer control and solidarity. The incidence of amusement at problem behaviour may also reinforce the problem and lead to consolidation of the "class clown" type of behaviour. In other circumstances, peer groups may act as inhibitors to problem behaviour. Some behaviour modification research has even systematically manipulated peer pressure as a successful means of changing pupil misbehaviour.

In considering reactions to problem behaviour in the classroom, all three perspectives need to be employed. How does the problem student see the situation? How does the teacher react? How does the peer group react? Teachers, in particular, need to be more sensitive to the miscreant's and peer's views than they have generally been in the past.

Behaviour problems in the classroom are an important concern for teachers and all involved in education. What constitutes problem behaviour or misbehaviour is not answered by simple classifications of all the inappropriate or psychologically maladaptive behaviours traditionally discussed. What is needed is a broad range consideration of all the participants in the classroom, the various factors that impinge upon the pupils and teacher, their interaction and the rules, norms, or mores they operate within. How the teacher and pupils together can arrive at, understand, and accept those norms and then manage the behaviour problems that can and will emerge in their classroom groups should be of concern to all the participants. Educators have tended to be preoccupied with the classification of "deviant" behaviours and the search for simple solutions that took little or no account of the social system that is the classroom. This approach also emphasized the teacher as the centre in terms of specification, alteration, and enforcement of the rules or "control" of the classroom.

See also: Behavioral Models; Classroom Management; Environmental Influences

Bibliography

Brophy J E, Putnam J G 1979 Classroom management in the elementary grades. In: Duke D L (ed.) 1979 *Classroom Management*. National Society for the Study of Education 78th Yearbook, Part 2. University of Chicago Press, Chicago, Illinois

Brophy J E, Rohrkemper M M 1981 The influence of problem ownership on teachers' perceptions of and strategies for coping with problem students. *J. Educ. Psychol.* 73:295–311

Cairns L G 1981 Managing the classroom. In: Turney C (ed.) 1981 *Anatomy of Teaching.* Novak, Sydney

Canter L 1976 *Assertive Discipline: A Take Charge Approach for Today's Education.* Canter, Los Angeles, California

Dreikurs R, Grunwald B B, Pepper F C 1982 *Maintaining Sanity in the Classroom: Classroom Management and Techniques.* Harper and Row, New York

Feldhusen J 1979 Problems of student behavior in secondary schools. In: Duke D L (ed.) 1979 *Classroom Management.*

National Society for the Study of Education 78th Yearbook, Part 2. University of Chicago Press, Chicago, Illinois

Glasser W 1969 *Schools Without Failure.* Harper and Row, New York

Gordon T 1974 TET *Teacher Effectiveness Training.* Wyden, New York

Hargreaves D H, Hester S K, Mellor F J 1975 *Deviance in Classrooms.* Routledge and Kegan Paul, London

Kounin J S 1970 *Discipline and Group Management in Classrooms.* Holt, Rinehart and Winston, New York

Leach D J, Raybould E C 1977 *Learning and Behaviour Difficulties in School.* Open Books, London

Activities: Structures and Functions

P. V. Gump

Classrooms are environments for learning. Over a school day, a number of subsettings or segments of environment are established to be inhabited by teachers and pupils. The classroom segments consist of physical and activity aspects joined together to support desired inhabitant behavior and experience. The qualities of classroom segments can be identified and the effect of these qualities upon teacher and student behavior can be determined. Effective learning and other worthwhile school experience are much conditioned by the qualities of classroom segments. Presented here are the available conceptualizations and research findings regarding classroom segments and their relation to pupil and teacher behavior.

1. The Nature of Classroom Segments

Classrooms have physical features: enclosure, furniture, tools, and supplies. These furnish the physical environment, but not the operating environment. The operating environment additionally possesses an action structure which utilizes the physical environment. An action structure is easiest to appreciate by considering children's games. In a simple game of hide-and-seek one player (the *It*) shuts his or her eyes at the home base and permits others to hide within a bounded area. Then the *It* searches for each member and tries to "call them out" by running back to the goal ahead of them. The last person found becomes the new *It* and the action just described runs through a second cycle.

The game action structure, once it is accepted by participants, determines important aspects of their subsequent behavior and experience. For example, this structure determines action goals (to successfully hide or to successfully search out); it establishes means to these goals (it states how hiding shall occur and how game cycles shall proceed), and it determines action relationships among participants. (The *It* is in a competitive relationship against each member of the group; members of the group are "against" *It* but not "for" one another as they would be in a team game.)

The action structure of the game heavily influences the context, the environment, of participants. Physical milieu and action structure are fitted together. Appropriate patterns in each make such a fit possible. The hiding and seeking behavior requires a milieu with open spaces (for running) and sheltered spaces (for hiding). The situation is similar in the classroom. If a teacher wishes a small group to share one another's contributions in a social discussion, he or she often arranges children in a circle of inward facing chairs. Sharing ideas (action structure goal) is presumed facilitated by face-to-face communication (action structure behavior) which, in turn is supported by chairs arranged in a small circle (physical milieu).

Seating arrangements are just one aspect of the physical milieu of the classroom; others include: presence or absence of library areas, extent of visual display space, and differentiation of space into "learning centers." An important fact about the physical milieu is that various arrangements and provisions are rarely good or bad, in themselves; their usefulness depends upon the particular action structure to be employed. For example, there are occasions when children's immediate sharing of ideas is not desirable. If the teacher wishes to make a rather extended clarification of a process in arithmetic, the ideas of the children should not be shared in the process—many may be in error. For the clarifying period, a row and column seating arrangement would be more appropriate than the sharing–inviting small circle. The relation of physical milieu to action structure goals and procedures has been explicated by Weinstein (1981). For our discussion here, the appropriate physical patterns for given action structures are assumed, so that the structures and their effects can be emphasized. In reality, one does not assume that the most fitting physial arrangements have actually been established for the action structures in operation.

Not only do classroom segments manifest physical facilities, action structures, and a fit between the two, these segments also exhibit temporal and spatial boundaries. Particular segments begin at a certain time and end at another; over time, transitions must be made between segments. Segments also have their spatial boundaries; in a total class presentation, the boundaries are the room walls, but for other activities (reading circles, learning centers) the space is more circumscribed. [The conceptualization of segments described here is consistent with that laid down by Barker (1968) for behavior settings.]

2. Classroom Segments in Groups

The units of the classroom operate in sequence throughout a school day. They are comprehensive; teachers and students will be involved in one or another segment (or temporarily between them) throughout the time in school. A part of a classroom day, described schematically, appears in Fig. 1. Mrs Apple's third grade (age 8) day began with a kind of free period for early arrivers at 8.30. Children were free to visit about the room so long as reasonable decorum was maintained. Some children preferred working on assignments left over from the previous day.

At 8:45, the school bell signaled the official start of the day. After an en masse flag salute, two children had

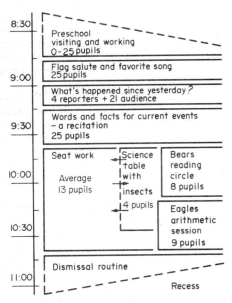

Vertical distances show time duration of segment; horizontal distances indicate children per segment; fluid lines reveal a shifting population

Figure 1
Classroom segments for Mrs Apple's morning

the privilege of picking the songs for the day. The teacher accompanied on the piano. At a little before 9:00, the first academic segment operated. Four children who had been given the assignment, reported the major news stories given in the previous evening or early morning television news. This segment was followed by a brisk review of all key words for the previous week of current events. Each reciter was to give the proper spelling and one important fact for each key word.

At 9:40, the class broke into three simultaneously operating segments: seat work, a science table with insects, and a reading aloud group at the rear of the classroom. The science table was a specially established learning center with four simple and preset microscopes to examine three common insects. After examining each insect, pupils were to "write a brief description of each insect." Pupils left seat work for the science table as spaces at the microscopes became available. The reading circle and the arithmetic session were teacher led while students worked on their own at the seat work and science table. The first morning session ended with structured (row-by-row) dismissal routines.

The segments represented on Fig. 1 can be described along a number of dimensions. First, there is the question of whether activity is paced by continual active external stimuli or by the decisions of the participants working with more passive contexts; secondly, segments may provide for interdependent or independent action of pupils; and, finally, the establishment of segments means that transition between segments must be made. Other dimensions of classroom segments are identifiable and of interest but the three just presented can provide an outline for a description of segments, and their relation to aspects of pupil and teacher behavior.

3. Segments with Active Versus Passive Inputs

When the teacher managed a "brisk review" of words from current events (Fig. 1), the action structure in this segment presented active, intrusive, external pacing of student behavior. What pupils were to do, moment-by-moment, was made clear by teacher questioning, pupil responding, and teacher response to pupil contribution. Most other segments in Fig. 1 present an action structure with external pacing. In the Flag Salute and Song segment, any one student is surrounded by stimuli which indicate what is to be done when. The active input structure tends to "pull participators along."

Major exceptions to the action input structure in Fig. 1 are the seat work and the science table segments. In these activities, participants pace themselves; when they act and how, depends upon their own plans, understanding, and persisting motivations.

It is important to note that the active versus passive input dimension is a property of the classroom environment, not of responding pupils and teachers. Once the arrangements for active or passive inputs are accepted, the signals determine further participant behavior. This active–passive dimension has important relationships to the degree to which students are involved in classroom activity and to the management behavior of teachers. A variety of independent studies has shown that pupil attention to task is substantially higher under active rather than passive input. A study by Kounin et al. (1966) showed that, in grades 1 to 5 (ages 6–11), the recitation segments (active input) yielded 85 percent pupil involvement and the seat work segments (passive input) only 65 percent; furthermore, deviancy (misconduct beyond inattention) was almost four times as frequent in the passive input segments.

The success of most active input segments depends upon clear and continuous signals to action. The professional teacher knows how to keep signals coming, how to move a recitation forward without undue empty spaces in the flow of external input. Other active input segments which may involve films, television, tapes, or audio presentations are usually constructed by professionals who also know how to keep the pacing moving along. However, under other circumstances, it is possible for active input to operate in a more faltering fashion. Child performers may be responsible for active input (the four reporters in "What's Happened Since Yesterday?" segment in Fig. 1.); these inputs may lack continuity and forward thrust. Often when young children are sources of active input, the involvement of audience children is quite low compared to the same children in other types of segments. However, when children are older (9 years and up) and have some instruction in presentation, they can often hold listener's attention (Silverstein 1979).

3.1 Management of Active Input Segments

Teaching behaviors which can improve student involvement in active input segments (such as recitation) have been identified by Kounin (1970). One set of behaviors, labeled group alerting, was significantly associated with good attention and low deviancy. The alerting might consist of a little prelude statement such as "Let's all think about this next one; it may fool you." A second set of teacher behaviors related to higher involvement in active input segments were those which maintained forward movement. Teacher actions which can break forward movement or momentum are: immersion in one reciter; overdwelling on just how to handle materials or carry out assignments; and making intrusive or prolonged behavior corrections. In the active external input segments, participants must depend on the input source. If this is teacher behavior, it is important that he or she "get on with it." On many occasions, pupils in active input segments have been judged by observers to be "off task." But sometimes the input source (usually a teacher) is off task and pupil off-task behavior is inevitable.

3.2 Management of Passive-availability Segments

Segments may provide stimuli which do not intrude upon participants but can be selected and used by participants. Seat work usually provides materials for reading, computing, and writing but these materials do not "call" participants to immediate attention and possible action. Other passive input segments include arts and crafts where, again, the materials are available in the environment but they do not press themselves on the participants. Management of the passive input segment depends upon recognition of what is required to sustain effective pupil action. Such moment-by-moment calls to action do not exist in the action structure where participants must depend upon their own interest and their own clarity about how to proceed. Such clarity is improved by adequate preparation; teachers may not only explain procedures but invite a few steps of the study process practiced before releasing the students to work on their own. Clarity can also be improved by guides for study.

Perhaps the most pervasive problem in passive input segments is boredom. If the external world offers little active input and if one's own self-paced activity does not create arousing stimulation—as is often true in seatwork—boredom and subsequent uninvolvement can result. Variety of materials, tasks, or intellectual challange can be programmed into segment action structures to counteract boredom. A well-replicated study by Kounin (1970) demonstrated that segments with variety yielded much improved task involvement for younger children (ages 6 and 7). However, there was some evidence that too many changes within the passive input segments was associated with lower involvement by older children (ages 8–11). Unfortunately, there was no replication for the older children study. Kounin speculated that the changes might have interfered with the "felt progress" which motivated the more academically serious older pupils.

A nursery-school study reported by Kounin and Sherman (1979) analyzed 596 taped lessons and identified six different lesson types. While active input lessons involving a "reliable" input source (teacher, not children) yielded high pupil involvement, one passive availability action structure, individual construction, produced even significantly higher involvement. In individual construction children made, from readily available materials, their own collages, valentines, and so on. In this activity, children developed ideas on what to do from teacher suggestions *and* from direct interaction with materials. The child's relation to his activity in individual construction can be appreciated if one considers the "paper face project." Children were given a paper pie plate, pieces of colored paper, paste and scissors. As the child began he or she might have cut a blue piece for one eye, pasted it on, and inspected the result. Clearly a second eye was required and was produced. Another inspection suggested a nose and so the activity proceeded. What was created here was a tight cycle of: action–feedback–second action–feedback, and so on. Immersed in this cycle, children were not only highly involved but insulated from distraction.

In group construction (i.e., several children cooperate

on a mural), the signals came not only from materials but from other children; now the tight action–feedback–further action had more difficulty becoming established. Pupil involvement scores in group construction were much lower than in individual construction.

The reader will have noted that what is good management action by teachers is much dependent upon the segment action structure in operation. For example, variety of action was significant in the passive input segments but not in the active input segments. Group alerting and momentum maintenance are highly relevant to active input segments but not to passive input arrangements.

4. Action Structures with Interdependence of Pupil Participants

An example of an action structure with high pupil–pupil interdependency is provided by Aronson's "jigsaw" format (Aronson et al. 1978). Students are divided into small groups. At the first small-group meeting each child is assigned a section of the lesson, and the responsibility for teaching that section to other children in the group. If the lesson involved the life of a famous person, for example, one pupil might be asked to teach about that person's childhood, another his or her early adulthood, and so on.

Each child in the group then goes to a "counterpart" group—one composed of those children with the same assignment as his or her own. In this small group, all work together deciding on how to present material, how to answer anticipated questions, and so on. After helping one another prepare, the children return to their original group to teach. As each child offers his or her section, the lesson is put together as a "jigsaw." Important in this operation is the essentiality of each person. Grades for group members depend on mastery of the entire lesson. Pupils are thus pressed to encourage, and to listen to, one another. The jigsaw method has resulted in a number of improvements in interpersonal relationships—less need to "beat classmates at school work," more liking for, and being liked by, other students.

The jigsaw technique was devised to yield better social integration of minority groups; follow-up research has shown improved relationships between children of different races (Aronson et al. 1978). As an added bonus, children in the jigsaw arrangement reported they were less bored by school and liked it more. The jigsaw arrangement is one of a number of interdependency formats researchers have employed (see *Small Group Methods*).

The importance of activity structure in affecting not only pupil–pupil social relationships but pupil–teacher relationships has been documented by Bossert (1979). Using the interdependency formats, teachers can put children into action structures that require extensive cooperative actions, which develop more personal cooperative feelings and actions.

5. Transitions Between Segments: Issues and Options

In principle, there are three phases of transitions between one segment and another: the closeout of the first segment, some kind of "moving over" (physical or psychological), and an entering into the second segment.

When transitions do not go well, they can consume much educational time. In one study of open-space and traditional schools, the overall amount of time that was not invested in educational activity amounted to 21 percent (Gump 1974). Most of this noneducational time went into transitions. And when the programs of the school involved frequent changes of site, the noneducational time rose to 27 percent.

The fact that transitions can create managerial problems is suggested by changes in teacher behavior. In a study of six third-grade teachers for two days, each teacher on both days increased his or her behavior-corrective activity during transitions. Teachers deal with children on a one-to-one basis much more frequently during transitions between segments than during the segments themselves (Gump 1969).

One reason the teacher behaves differently at transitions is that the children change their behavior. In a study of 59 classes managed by student teachers, Arlin (1979) found that off-task behavior in transitions was almost double the rate occurring in nontransition activities. The data were consistent over five different sets of schools studied.

What is involved in the problems that accompany transitions? First, there may be problems in detaching students from the interests and actions of the first segment. Arlin noted that if students come from a physically stimulating segment, such as recess or gym, into a more sedentary segment, much off-task behavior may result.

A second transition problem involves losing the structure that deterred deviancy and off-task behavior during the first segment. Without a second structure, children are likely to do what comes naturally.

A third factor is that students have "saved up" problems or tensions during the first segment and deal with them during the more open transition period. (Children seem to wait for this opportunity to ask something, show something, move about, talk to their neighbor, and so on.) Saving up requests to the teacher is often a part of the classroom rule system established to free the teacher from interruptions during times when he or she must actively lead a subgroup. Extension of transition periods for this purpose is probably legitimate; however, the possible loss of activity momentum is a consideration.

A fourth transition problem may arise in the beginning of the second segment if there are delays. The teacher may be dealing with individual children or assembling materials. In some cases, the teacher is held up because he or she is still involved with another group.

455

Delay in starting the second segment is much more often responsible for excessive transition time than is the time required to move pupils and materials to the second segment.

There are two solutions to these problems. For example, children may need some help in detaching themselves from the first segment; obviously the more interested they are, the more they need a kind of advance warning and a "wrap up" to move away from the first segment and into the next. For some problems, the second segment needs a different introduction. When Krantz and Risley (1977) found that going from recess directly to story time produced a 37 percent off-task behavior in the beginning of story time, they inserted a "rest period" before the story and reduced off-task behavior to 14 percent.

Not all transitions must involve a temporary loss of any action structures that guide behavior. Although Arlin (1979) found that transitions, overall, yielded much higher off-task behaviors than other periods, he established an important second finding. He examined a subgroup of student teachers who managed both structured and unstructured transitions. (In structured transitions, procedures of transition were present.) Arlin discovered that structured transitions yielded significantly less disruption than unstructured ones; in fact, there was no significant difference in off-task behavior between structured transitions and nontransitional periods. The structured transition maintains a behavior-guiding action system; the momentum of activity is preserved.

6. Classroom Structures in Conceptions of the Education Enterprise

Presented here were three major aspects of classroom structure: active or passive inputs in action structure; interdependence of participants as required by action structure; and issues of transitions between segments. Illustrative implications of these aspects of structure, for pupil behavior and/or teacher management action, have been described.

Consideration of all researchers who have contributed to the emphasis upon classroom ecology or environment is beyond our scope but mentions might be made of a thorough work on preschool ecology by Smith and Connolly (1981). Contributions of many others have been outlined by Gump (1980) and Berliner (1983).

The segment unit, and similar conceptions (classroom activities, instructional groups, etc.) provide for an integration of three aspects of the educational environment often considered separately: physical facilities and resources, curricula, and teacher behaviors.

Physical facilities can have independent impact upon events in the classroom. However, when these physical provisions are coupled with an action structure, the resulting environmental unit influences behavior much more.

Curricula might be thought of as the learning content aspect of classroom environments. But curricula are essentially purposes and plans. Teachers and pupils do not live in curricula, they live in ongoing segments of the classroom. The segment structure makes the curricula operational. Realistic evaluation of curricula comes down to description of the subsettings in which it impacts students and teachers.

Elementary-school teachers engage in one to two thousand acts per school day. The segment structure idea makes it possible to understand this mass of activity in a holistic fashion. Teachers must do much more than teach; they select, establish, and maintain segments and they become content sources of action in some of these segments. The success of their efforts is much dependent upon the vigor and the appropriateness of the settings they establish. Their many behaviors often reflect the requirement of classroom segments they have established, both managerial and pedagogical actions by the teachers are conditioned by the operating classroom structure.

The fact that teachers as well as pupils are influenced by segments has implications. If a change in classroom events (including teacher behavior) is desired, such change might be better achieved by selection of different segments than by attempts to change teacher or pupil behavior within existing segments.

See also: Environmental Influences; Frame Factors; Classroom Management; Equipment and Materials

Bibliography

Arlin M 1979 Teacher transitions can disrupt time flow in classrooms. *Am. Educ. Res. J.* 16: 42–56
Aronson E, Bridgeman D L, Geffner R 1978 The effects of a cooperative classroom structure on student behavior and attitudes. In: Bar-Tal D, Saxe L (eds.) 1978 *Social Psychology of Education: Theory and Research*. Halstead, New York
Barker R G 1968 *Ecological Psychology: Concepts and Methods for Studying the Environment of Human Behavior*. Stanford University Press, Stanford, California
Berliner D 1983 Developing conceptions of classroom environments: Some light on the T in classroom studies of ATI. *Educ. Psychol.* 18: 1–13
Bossert S T 1979 *Tasks and Social Relationships in Classrooms: A Study of Instructional Organization and its Consequences*. Cambridge University Press, New York
Gump P V 1969 Intra-setting analyses: The third grade as a special but instructed case. In: Willems E, Raush H (eds.) 1969 *Naturalistic Viewpoints in Psychological Research*. Holt, Rinehart and Winston, New York
Gump P V 1974 Operating environments in schools of open and traditional design. *Sch. Res.* 82: 575–93
Gump P V 1980 The school as a social situation. *Am. Dev. Psychol.* 31: 553–82
Kounin J S 1970 *Discipline and Group Management in Classrooms*. Holt, Rinehart and Winston, New York
Kounin J S, Sherman L W 1979 School environments as behavior settings. *Theory Pract.* 13: 145–51

Kounin J S, Friesen W V, Norton A E 1966 Managing emotion-ally disturbed children in regular classrooms. *J. Educ. Psychol.* 51: 1–13

Krantz P J, Risley T R 1977 Behavioral ecology in the class-room. In: O'Leary K D, O'Leary S G (eds.) 1977 *Classroom Management: The Successful Use of Behavior Modification*, 2nd edn. Pergamon, New York

Silverstein J M 1979 Individual and environmental correlates of pupil problematic and nonproblematic classroom behavior (Doctoral dissertation, University of New York) *Dissertation Abstracts International* 1980 40: 2567A (University Microfilms No. 7925292)

Smith P K, Connolly K J 1981 *The Ecology of Preschool Behaviour*. Cambridge University Press, Cambridge

Weinstein C S 1981 Classroom design as an external condition for learning. *Educ. Tech.* 21 (8): 12–19

Proactive Teaching

M. M. Rohrkemper; T. L. Good

Recent teacher effectiveness research has consistently found an interrelationship between teachers' man-agement skills (see *Classroom Management*) (typically measured by frequency, intensity, and duration of inap-propriate student behavior) and achievement (Brophy and Good 1986, Good 1979, 1981, Good and Brophy 1986). Teachers who are effective managers also tend to be effective instructors. This relationship between managerial and instructional skill is likely to exist because teachers who are more effective classroom man-agers have to contend with less inappropriate student behavior thus subsequently a greater proportion of class time is allocated to instruction (Doyle 1986).

Recent research on "time-on-task," the amount of time students actually spend engaged in productive learning activity, has found a positive relationship between the amount of time students spend on instruc-tional activity and long-term student achievement (see *Time*). Similarly, research on "direct" (Rosenshine 1979), "active" (Good and Grouws 1979), or "inter-active" instruction has also substantiated a positive relationship between the amount of instructional time and end-of-the-year student achievement (see *Direct Instruction*). The more effective classroom manager then, is apt to be able to increase both the time students are engaged in their work, and the amount of time he/she is able to spend on actual instruction, both of which are associated with increased student achievement.

A second factor likely to be associated with the relationship between managerial and instructional skill is that a similar behavior underlies both effective man-agement and effective instruction. This more pervasive teacher behavior has been termed proactive behavior, indicating an active teacher decision-making process that is characterized by: (a) a positive goal orientation (vs. mere control/desist goals); (b) deliberate planning (vs. nonreflective habit or reaction); and (c) a preventive focus (vs. remedial orientation). Proactive teacher behavior operationalizes a broader philosophical frame-work that includes the expectation that students can, and will, learn and that the teacher is key to the arrange-ment of that learning. Such positive expectations have been associated with increased student achievement at both the level of the individual teacher (Brophy and Good 1974, Good 1980, 1981, Weinstein 1982) and the school (Brookover et al. 1978, Rutter et al. 1979).

1. Approaches to Researching Proactive Behavior

Research on teacher effectiveness has proceeded along two main approaches, termed by Rosenshine as "master teacher" and "master developer" approaches. In the master teacher tradition teachers found to be effective in producing a particular student outcome, typically achievement as measured on standardized tests, are compared in their classroom behavior with teachers who are less effective in promoting student achievement. In these process–product investigations (Dunkin and Biddle 1974) the differences found in the more and less effective teachers' classroom behavior is believed to be associated with improved student learning. The data obtained from these investigations are inherently correlational, however, and as has been argued else-where (Slavin 1982), those behaviors found associated with effective classroom instruction are limited to those already in the teachers' repertoire. Thus, not only is this research limited by an inability to argue causal direction of a given teacher behavior and student out-come (i.e., does an effective teacher bring out the best in students, or do successful students bring out the best in their teachers?), but it is also bounded by current pedagogical practice.

The master developer approach to research on teacher effectiveness differs from the above in that it undertakes to learn about classroom instruction through experimental implementation of a complete instruc-tional program. These programs are developed from prior research, accumulated wisdom, and theories of human learning and behavior. This approach lends itself to both experimental manipulations that allow more confident statements concerning the causes of student achievement and the observation of teacher behavior that may not have occurred otherwise.

Both the master teacher and master developer approaches are represented in the study of proactive instruction. The construct of proactive instruction as it emerged from key master teacher investigations will be discussed first, followed by the articulation of proactive instruction as it appears in three master developer programs of research. Before doing so, however, it is important to stress that the research cited in this review involves teachers at the elementary-school level. The application of these findings to the junior-high and secondary levels has been speculated upon but researched little (Evertson and Emmer in press). It is likely that the developmental differences among students, the range and concentration of student preparation and ability, and differences in subject matter and educational goals all play a role in the determination of proactive instructional behavior. The nature and extent of these differences are only beginning to be examined.

2. Master Teacher Investigations

Perhaps the most influential study of proactive teacher behavior was conducted by Kounin (1970). He attempted to describe the differences between more and less effective teachers in terms of their ability to respond to inappropriate student behavior. Toward this end, videotapes of teacher–student classroom interactions were made and analyzed for distinctions among the teachers' management responses. Research findings were unable to identify teacher reactions to students that differentiated the more from the less effective teachers. What they did find, however, was a relationship between the frequency of student misbehavior and the effectiveness ratings of teachers. This investigation pointed to the importance of those behaviors that prevented inappropriate behavior from occurring in the first place, and in doing so fundamentally changed the construct of effective management in the next decade of research.

Kounin describes preventive teacher behaviors as those which maintained student engagement in tasks and encouraged student cooperation in general. They included constructs of "withitness," "overlapping," smoothness of transitions, both between lessons and between activities within lessons, and group alerting and accountability strategies. These teacher behaviors have been investigated in subsequent research and generally found associated with better classroom management and increases in student learning. Exceptions include some qualifications due to context factors and resulting curvilinear relationships associated with group alerting and accountability strategies (Anderson et al. 1979, Brophy and Evertson 1978, Good and Grouws 1979). More recently, some concern with difficulties in replication of teacher withitness has emerged, but has thus far been confined to a single investigation (Irving and Martin 1982).

A more recent investigation of preventive or proactive teacher behavior was that conducted by Emmer et al. (1980). This large-scale investigation examined teacher management strategies at the beginning of the school year and thus was able to examine the relationship of initial teacher strategies with long-range outcomes in student classroom behavior and achievement. These investigators were able to identify teachers who, from the very first day of school differed dramatically in their ability to establish a smooth-running learning environment, and to compare their effectiveness as managers and instructors at the end of the school year. They found that teachers who were more effective classroom managers acted in significantly different ways from the less effective managers from the very start of the year. These differences included ". . . the quality of leadership exhibited by the teacher in managing behavior and instruction, planning for student concerns, and coping with constraints . . ." (Emmer et al. 1980).

Surprisingly, the specific management system did not appear to be as important as was the teaching of that system to students. Effective managers took the time to teach their students the classroom rules, and to consistently and predictably monitor and respond to student behavior. Effective teachers then, in effect socialized their students into a classroom setting with instructions on procedures that were designed to help the classroom run efficiently and to meet the students' needs as members of participants in the classroom. As in the Kounin work, more and less effective managers were not distinguishable by their responses to student misbehavior but rather by their ability to prevent it from occurring in the first place and by stopping it sooner when it did occur. Thus, more effective teachers were proactive in their approach to classroom management, and more "withit" when student disruption did occur. Emmer and Evertson and staff are currently examining these data and other findings in experimentally designed master developer research in an attempt to validate and elaborate these correlational data.

Currently, similar data have been associated with junior-high-level classrooms, with some differences in emphasis evident with the older students (Emmer and Evertson 1981).

3. Master Developer Research

The above studies are informative in that they point to teacher behaviors that are associated with more effective classroom management, and subsequently with more time on instructional activities. These studies are correlational, however, and as such are unable to discuss data in causal terms. The master developer investigations cited in this section are programmatic attempts to experimentally examine proactive teacher behavior and its effects on student achievement. Three research efforts will be examined: the first-grade reading group study (Anderson et al. 1979); the cooperative learning programs developed by Slavin and others (see *Small Group Methods*); and the Missouri Mathematics Project (Good and Grouws 1979).

The first-grade reading study involved an experimental manipulation with an instructional model containing organizational, instructional, and management strategies to be used during reading. The data obtained are based on classroom observation and student achievement. Strategies which were found significantly correlated with effective instruction were consistent with the constructs postulated by Kounin with the exception of the optimal accountability procedures. Instead of random turns, Anderson et al. found that calling on students in an orderly pattern was associated with increases in student learning.

The authors caution that their data is based on a white, middle-class sample and that optimal teacher behavior may well vary with the socioeconomic status and ability levels of students. In addition attention should be paid to the age level of the students. The developmental level of first graders (age 6) may underlie the effectiveness of some of the behaviors found to be successful. Further, the fact that the subject under study was reading and that as such, the number of children involved at any one time with the teacher was less than that which is typical in whole class instruction, may partially explain the effectiveness of pattern as opposed to random turns. What the data do underscore, however, is the necessity of efficient classroom management, particularly teacher monitoring and smoothness of transitions, in the establishment and maintenance of an appropriate learning environment.

Programmatic research by the Slavin group at the Johns Hopkins University differs from that described above in that it involves an instructional program that includes curricular materials, teacher instructional behavior, and organizational strategies designed to enhance student motivation. Thus, the focus of these programs is to enhance student achievement through increased student independence from the teacher, and simultaneously increased interdependence with one another through the development of a team spirit in pursuit of an academic goal.

Slavin's research differs from the reading study described above in that it has been conducted in a variety of socioeconomic climates, ability and grade levels, and subject matter areas. Results have indicated support for these programs in terms of student achievement, self-concept, and attitudes toward minorities and mainstreamed students. What is lacking in this research, however, is a concern for the processes which result in these outcomes. Slavin's data provide support for practices not typically found in classrooms, but it is not possible to discuss the process underlying particular teacher behaviors or organizational factors which appear to be more or less important in effecting the student outcomes. For instance, the increases in student achievement associated with these approaches may be due to the subsequent reduction in risk and ambiguity for the students, rather than due to cooperation per se. Process data are clearly needed to provide explanatory constructs.

A final investigation to be described, the Missouri Mathematics Project (Good and Grouws 1979), combined in its program instructional and managerial strategies obtained from prior process–product research of more and less effective, or "active" teachers. Like the Anderson et al. reading prescriptions, this project included strategies for maintaining student attention and using alerting and accountability principles appropriately. In addition, it stressed instructional issues in teaching mathematics involving distributed practice and review, particularly stressing the appropriate ratio of lesson development to seat work practice. Of special concern were the establishment of a meaningful context for any lesson and practice activity, and the encouragement of student involvement and success.

Observational data indicated that, in general, teachers implemented the program very well and pre- and post-testing with standardized achievement tests and content specific tests indicated the experimental groups performed higher than the control. Experimental students' attitudes toward mathematics were also higher. Other research on this program conducted by Keziah (1980) and Andros and Freeman (1981) also supports the success of the program.

4. Conclusions

Taken together, the master teacher and master developer investigations underscore that some teachers do obtain more student achievement than other teachers, and that effective proactive teacher behavior can be taught. It is equally clear, however, that there are no universal, specific teaching behaviors that can be labelled proactive. Differences in contextual factors, including students, instructional goals and subject matter, all restrict the ability to describe specific teacher behavior. What research can and does provide, however, are heuristics that function to reduce the teacher's "problem space" and thus facilitate the identification of appropriate teaching strategies. The proactive teacher is best described as an active information processor and decision maker who believes that students can and will learn through appropriate instruction, and who filters general strategies and principles for effective management and instruction through the particular demands of the teaching context. Thus, research on proactive instruction provides important information to the teacher, but cannot now, or likely ever, provide the teacher with explicit prescriptions.

See also: Reactive Teaching; Teachers' Expectations

Bibliography

Anderson L M, Evertson C M, Brophy J E 1979 An experimental study of effective teaching in first grade reading groups. *Elem. Sch. J.* 79: 193–233
Andros K, Freeman D 1981 The effects of three kinds of feedback on math teaching performance. Paper presented at the annual meeting of the American Educational Research Association, Los Angeles, California
Brookover W B, Schweitzer J, Schneider J, Beady C, Flood P, Wisenbaker J 1978 Elementary school climate and school achievement. *Am. Educ. Res. J.* 15: 301–18

Brophy J E, Evertson C M 1978 Context variables in teaching. *Educ. Psychol.* 12: 310–16

Brophy J E, Good T L 1974 *Teacher–Student Relationships: Causes and Consequences*. Holt, Rinehart and Winston, New York

Brophy J E, Good T L 1986 Teacher behavior and student achievement. In: Wittrock M C (ed.) 1986 *Handbook of Research on Teaching*, 3rd edn. Macmillan, New York

Doyle W 1986 Classroom organization and management. In: Wittrock M C (ed.) 1986 *Handbook of Research on Teaching*, 3rd edn. Macmillan, New York

Dunkin M J, Biddle B J 1974 *The Study of Teaching*. Holt, Rinehart and Winston, New York

Emmer E T, Evertson C M 1981 Synthesis of research on classroom management. *Educ. Leadership*, 38: 342–43

Emmer E T, Evertson C M, Anderson L M 1980 Effective classroom management at the beginning of the school year. *Elem. Sch. J.* 80: 219–31

Evertson C, Emmer E in press Effective management at the beginning of the school in junior high classes. *J. Educ. Psychol.*

Good T L 1979 Teacher effectiveness in the elementary school: What we know about it now. *J. Teach. Educ.* 30: 52–64

Good T L 1980 Classroom expectations: Teacher–pupil interactions. In: McMillan J H (ed.) 1980 *The Social Psychology of School Learning*. Academic Press, New York

Good T L 1981 Classroom research: Past and future. Paper presented at the Conference on Teaching and Educational Policy, National Institute of Education, Washington, DC, February, 1981

Good T L, Brophy J E 1986 *Educational Psychology: A Realistic Approach*, 3rd edn. Longman, New York

Good T L, Grouws D A 1979 The Missouri mathematics effectiveness project: An experimental study in fourth grade classrooms. *J. Educ. Psychol.* 71: 355–62

Irving O, Martin J 1982 Withitness: The confusing variable. *Am. Educ. Res. J.* 19: 313–19

Keziah R 1980 Implementing instructional behaviors that make a difference. *Centroid* (North Carolina Council of Teachers of Mathematics) 6: 2–4

Kounin J 1970 *Discipline and Group Management in Classrooms*. Holt, Rinehart and Winston, New York

Rosenshine B 1979 Content, time, and direct instruction. In: Peterson P L, Walbert H J (eds.) 1979 *Research on Teaching: Concepts, Findings, and Implications*. McCutchan, Berkeley, California

Rutter M, Maughan B, Mortimore P, Ouston J, Smith A 1979 *Fifteen Thousand Hours: Secondary Schools and Their Effects on Children*. Harvard University Press, Cambridge, Massachusetts

Slavin R 1982 Cooperative learning and the alterable elements of classroom organization. Paper presented at the annual meeting of the American Educational Research Association, New York, 1982

Weinstein R 1982 Expectations in the classroom: The student perspective. Invited address at the annual meeting of the American Educational Research Association, New York, 1982

Reactive Teaching

M. M. Rohrkemper; T. L. Good

Reactive instruction concerns those teacher behaviors that occur in the "interactive" or ongoing phase of instruction in response to unanticipated events. Reactive instruction involves primarily teacher response to student behavior that is typically seen as inappropriate, although unanticipated student events can also be positive events. A second restriction on the construct is that teacher reactive behavior is usually viewed from the perspective of management rather than instruction. The need for appropriate assessment and adequate response to student questions and responses during instruction are clearly important teaching skills, but are not addressed in this review.

Reactive instruction differs from proactive instruction (see *Proactive Teaching*) in terms of the amount of time available for decision making and the timing of the subsequent strategy. In reactive instruction then, the time available for assessment of the situation and construction of a strategy is brief and the event is already in process. The interrelationship between proactive and reactive instruction is evident. The more proactive decision-making and behavioral strategies that a teacher engages in, the more predictable the classroom environment becomes. Proactive behavior in general then, increases the ability to anticipate problem spots associated with particular subject matter, lesson formats, and individual students (Morine-Dershimer 1979). As such the need to respond to unexpected student behavior is markedly reduced. Kounin (1970) and others (Anderson et al. 1980) have found that it is proactive behavior that distinguishes teachers who differ in effectiveness. In their reactive behavior these teachers are much alike. Effective teaching however, requires both proactive and reactive strategies. No matter how thorough the plan for a given day, or how effective the monitoring and "withitness" (Kounin 1970), there are bound to be unanticipated events that require an immediate and reasoned response from the teacher. Some of these responses are clearly more desirable than others. The issue is therefore not whether to use proactive or reactive instruction, but how to optimize both.

Surprisingly little research has been undertaken on what constitutes effective reactive teacher behavior. With the general exception of research on behavior modification approaches, much of the advice on responses to inappropriate student behavior remains unexamined. Many of these approaches are derived from psychological theories of human disturbance, behavior, and motivation, and involve complete programs of diagnosis and response that are derived from therapeutic settings, or from laboratory settings. As yet, the relative lack of research and evaluation of these programs means that there is little systematic information regarding the assumed overall effectiveness of these approaches. Neither are there data on the relative effectiveness of individual program components (Slavin 1982). A related issue concerns the outcome criteria studied. Reactive instruction research would benefit from examination of the short-term effects of a given teacher behavior, in addition to the concern with long-term outcomes which is typical of "process–product" research (Anderson 1981).

Until and unless such research is undertaken, these approaches do little to further our understanding of what constitutes optimal reactive behavior and what types of heuristics are more or less useful to teachers in the construction of their reactive strategies (see *Models of Heuristic Teaching*). As will become evident, the research that has employed principles derived from some of these theories, either directly or indirectly, has been very useful in providing information on the contextual constraints that elaborate and qualify a given strategy.

Research on responses to inappropriate student behavior has primarily been concerned with elementary- or primary-school children. It is likely that the nature of reactive strategies fluctuates across the elementary grades, as the ratio of the teacher's role as instructor and socializer varies. Thus, teachers of younger children are apt to encounter fewer difficulties with children that cannot be handled within an instructional role. This pattern changes significantly from the ages of about 9 to 14 where the shift from an adult to a peer orientation, and the accumulation of experiences in the student role, combine to result in proportionately greater management concerns (Brophy 1979, Good and Brophy 1986).

The fact that younger, adult-oriented elementary or primary students are often the focus of reactive management research is perhaps the reason that behavior modification programs have received such unquestioned support in the reactive instruction research literature. As has been argued (Brophy and Putnam 1979), behavior modification approaches to inappropriate student behavior do appear quite successful in changing discrete behaviors, especially in younger students, but they are much less effective with diffuse problems and with older students for whom the teacher does not function as an important reinforcer.

Much research has been undertaken to examine the theoretical constructs of reinforcement, punishment, extinction, and schedules of administration in the classroom. Useful qualifications of these general strategies have resulted, as have conflicts with the theoretical constructs of extinction and reward. Kounin (1970) and others (Brophy and Evertson 1976) have found that extinction frequently is not feasible in a group setting. Typically, systematic ignoring results in escalation of the problem behavior, student confusion as to rules and

teacher intention, and continued distraction of the other students. Immediate response to the inappropriate behavior seems the more effective strategy in that it consistently communicates that certain behavior will not be tolerated and that the teacher is "with it," that is, aware of student behavior. These concerns led to the Tanner (1978) criteria for the appropriate use of extinction: when the problem behavior is nonserious and momentary, involving a generally well-behaved student, and when calling attention to it would increase the disruption for the rest of the class.

A second area of disagreement concerns the usefulness of rewards and praise when motivation is already evidenced. Research in the laboratory and classroom setting has indicated that rather than increasing motivation, rewarding motivated students can result in decreases in motivation as indicated by reduced desire to resume an activity, less task persistence, decreased quality of performance, and less successful learning in general (Lepper and Greene 1978).

These findings are indeed startling, and need to be examined within the context of intrinsic motivation. They do not speak to the situation where motivation does not exist in the first place. In these situations, where a student is not motivated in the classroom, research by Deci (1976, 1978), has provided valuable insights into the informative as opposed to controlling aspects of reward use. Similarly, Brophy (1981) has discussed caveats in the use of praise as a means of controlling and reinforcing student behavior. Perhaps the most important issue these researchers underscore is the need to understand the perspective of the recipient in using *any* strategy, including those derived from behavior modification. Concern for student perception and involvement appears to account for the more recent use of contingency contracting and cognitive behavior modification approaches (Meichenbaum 1977, Meichenbaum and Asarnow 1979).

Concern for how behavior is perceived from the teacher perspective is the focus of the interview portion of the Classroom Strategy Study (Brophy and Rohrkemper 1981, Rohrkemper and Brophy 1982). As part of a larger investigation, teachers were interviewed about their responses to a series of written vignettes depicting a range of troublesome student behavior. The vignettes were clustered by level of problem ownership portrayed (teacher owned, student owned, teacher–student shared) (Gordon 1974), and teacher self-reports were analyzed for attributional knowledge and behavioral strategies. The data confirmed the usefulness of problem ownership in examining teacher–student situations in the classroom and indicated that the role of perceived intention underlying behavior, and the assumed ability for self-control over that behavior were key in determining the teacher reactive behavior with that student. The differences in perception–cognition–behavior patterns associated with the varying levels of problem ownership are a promising source of further investigation of reactive teacher behavior. It was clear from these data that some reactive strategies are more appropriate than others. Thus, teacher behavior with students exhibiting student owned or teacher–student shared problems appeared to be generally successful, but these same teachers' responses to students who were perceived as acting intentionally and capable of self-control if they chose, (i.e., they presented teacher owned problems) were at least counter-productive and more likely part of a self-fulfilling prophecy cycle in their focus on short term control through punishment and minimal communication.

As evident in the relative scarcity of investigations of teacher reactive strategies, more research is needed. Data from the research described above indicates that some teacher reactive strategies are more appropriate than others and that effectiveness is associated with teacher perceptions and interpretations of student behavior and intention. The role of the perceptions of the participants, both teachers and students, needs to be further investigated if useful heuristics for teachers are to be identified as they construct reactive strategies. Finally, acknowledgement of the interrelationship of reactive and proactive instruction would facilitate examination of the role of teacher expectation in dealing with unanticipated student behavior; the usefulness of proactive strategies in teacher assessment of the effects (intended and otherwise) of a reactive strategy (Rohrkemper 1982), and the dynamics involved in the simultaneous pursuit of both long and short term goals.

See also: Reinforcement; Reacting; Proactive Teaching

Bibliography

Anderson L M 1981 Student responses to classroom instruction. *Elem. Sch. J.* 82: 97–108
Anderson L M, Everston C M, Emmer E T 1980 Dimensions in classroom management derived from recent research. *J. Curric. Stud.* 12: 343–56
Brophy J E 1979 Teacher behavior and its effects. *J. Educ. Psychol.* 71: 733–50
Brophy J E 1981 Teacher praise: A functional analysis. *Rev. Educ. Res.* 51: 5–32
Brophy J E, Evertson C M 1976 *Learning from Teaching: A Developmental Perspective.* Allyn and Bacon, Boston, Massachusetts
Brophy J E, Putnam J 1979 Classroom management in the early grades. In: Duke D L (ed.) 1979 *Classroom Management.* 78th Yearbook of the National Society for the Study of Education, Part 2. University of Chicago Press, Chicago, Illinois
Brophy J E, Rohrkemper M M 1981 The influence of problem ownership on teachers' perceptions of and strategies for coping with problem students. *J. Educ. Psychol.* 73: 295–311
Deci E L 1976 *Intrinsic Motivation.* Plenum, New York
Deci E L 1978 Applications of research on the effect of rewards. In: Lepper M R, Greene D (eds.) 1978
Good T L, Brophy J E 1986 *Educational Psychology: A Realistic Approach*, 3rd edn. Longman, New York
Gordon T 1974 *Teacher Effectiveness Training.* Wyden, New York
Kounin J S 1970 *Discipline and Group Management in Classrooms.* Holt, Rinehart and Winston, New York
Lepper M R, Greene D (eds.) 1978 *The Hidden Costs of Reward: New Perspectives on the Psychology of Human Motivation.* Erlbaum, New York
Meichenbaum D 1977 *Cognitive-behavior Modification: An Integrative Approach.* Plenum, New York
Meichenbaum D, Asarnow J 1979 Cognitive-behavioral modification and metacognitive development: Implications for the classroom. In: Kendall P C, Hollon S D (eds.) 1979 *Cognitive-behavioral Interventions: Theory, Research and Procedures.* Academic Press, New York
Morine-Dershimer G 1979 *Teacher Plan and Classroom Reality: The South Bay Study, Part IV.* Research Series No 60. Institute for Research on Teaching, Michigan State University, East Lansing
Rohrkemper M M 1982 Teacher self-assessment. In: Duke D L (ed.) 1982 *Helping Teachers Manage Classrooms.* Association for Supervision and Curriculum Development, Alexandria, Virginia
Rohrkemper M M, Brophy J E 1982 Teachers' thinking about problem students. In: Levine J M, Wang M C (eds.) 1982 *Teacher and Student Perceptions: Implications for Learning.* Erlbaum, Hillsdale, New Jersey
Slavin R 1982 Cooperative learning and the alterable elements of classroom organization. Paper presented at the annual meeting of the American Educational Research Association, New York
Tanner L N 1978 *Classroom Discipline for Effective Teaching and Learning.* Holt, Rinehart and Winston, New York

Flexibility

N. A. Flanders

Flexibility in instruction refers to the different patterns to be found in the flow of instructional events. Pattern variation may be due to a change of the immediate instructional objectives, or a rearrangement of the class formation, or a shift to different learning activities. A change may also occur when a sensitive teacher is working with a single pupil and makes a quick adjustment in response to some cue the pupil exhibited. These changes may be planned and therefore expected, or they may be unplanned and unexpected, but the central idea is that of a teacher who can make adjustments quickly and competently and/or whose style of teaching shows variation and variety.

Planned changes are relatively easy to recognize. When a teacher says, "Boys and girls, please put away your art work, we have to get ready for arithmetic," it is a signal that a planned change in subject matter is about to take place. During the arithmetic lesson the teacher may say, "Now that we've tried these problems together, I'd like you to continue working on them by yourselves, at your seats." The subject matter has not changed, but total class discussion has changed to individual seatwork. Later the teacher may say, "Most of you are having trouble with this step (the teacher demonstrates on the chalkboard), everyone go to the chalkboard, please, so we can have a short drill period. Please help your neighbor if asked." At this point the class formation has changed and so has the communication network. During a single hour in almost any classroom, there will be expected variation in the immediate instructional goals which result in a different role for the teacher and the students, a different class formation and change in communication, a different noise level, and different learning activities. These variations in learning activities are usually planned and expected in the classroom of a flexible teacher.

There are planned differences in how a flexible teacher works with individual students, although these may be harder to detect. A teacher may consistently call upon certain students only after some other student has first demonstrated what is to be done. A teacher may challenge some students and be careful not to challenge others. These planned variations in approaching a student are based on teacher expectations and they mark a flexible teacher providing that such expectations are not rigidly held and can be modified to match individual growth patterns or incidental moods.

Unexpected changes may occur when a teacher notices a cue exhibited by a student and therefore modifies his or her approach, or sees group interest lag and decides to terminate an activity sooner than expected. Some teachers make use of particular students, such as one whose attention span is short, to provide "early warnings" about the need for a change. This latter kind of flexibility requires sensitivity and the ability to recognize cues that may be almost imperceptible to a stranger.

By now it should be clear that every teacher possesses some degree of flexibility, some of it planned, some unplanned, and it should be obvious that degree of flexibility varies greatly between teachers and probably varies for the same teacher on different occasions. In turn, this means the labels "flexible teacher" or "inflexible teacher" are ambiguous. Nevertheless, like the term "intelligence," which everyone possesses to one degree or another, different degrees of flexibility can be discussed and the labels can be useful if they are assigned consistently.

1. A Brief History and Rationale of Instructional Flexibility

The rationale behind flexibility in instruction flows from three sources: first, it is a "good" thing because it reflects desired social values; second, it is associated with the personality of the teacher; and third, it is a characteristic of effective teaching and the best way to manage a classroom.

A positive regard for others and concern for the welfare of each person has had a long history in education appearing and reappearing in cycles illustrated by Rousseau, progressive education, and Carl Rogers. Flexibility of instruction can be seen as a current expression of this tradition. One example is the work of Anderson (1939) who saw "dominative" social contacts as the opposite of more flexible "integrative" contacts. Another is the work of Lippitt and White (1943) who investigated the social climate of small groups in which leaders were "authoritarian," "laissez-faire," or "democratic." The "democratic" was the most flexible and sensitive leadership style. Withall and Lewis (1963) provide an extensive summary of this research and interpret the results as if they were based on compelling objective evidence. On the other hand, Dunkin and Biddle (1974 p. 100) have been more cautious describing this line of research as a genuine commitment which, if held strongly enough, could survive the inevitable controversy to follow.

The assertion that some teachers have a knack of adjusting to "the vicissitudes of the chalk pits" suggests that flexible teaching is itself a personality characteristic. In fact Anderson and Brewer (1946) entitled their early work an investigation of "teachers' classroom personalities." The notion that personality strongly influences behavior has quickened the pulse of many researchers, but such research is difficult. It is relatively easy to administer personality inventories to fairly large samples, but it is much more difficult to obtain reliable measures of behavior from large samples. McGee (1955) found a correlation of 0.58 (for 150 relatively young teachers with less than three years teaching experience) between scores on the Authoritarianism F-Scale and logically related classroom observation variables. For a summary of research on the personality measures of teachers and various correlates, Getzels and Jackson (1963) is most helpful.

The issue of whether the most flexible teachers are also the most effective has not been resolved by evidence from research. There are several reasons. The most important is lack of agreement on the definition of flexibility and how to measure it. With this disagreement, comparisons between projects are not productive and replication is not available. In their review of "variability" Rosenshine and Furst (1973 p. 156) included separate studies in which (a) students or an observer determined if the teacher was "flexible in procedure," (b) the degree to which extra materials, displays, and resource materials were in the classrooms, and (c) the degree to which a teacher used a greater variety of cognitive levels in class discussion. All of these indices might be associated with flexibility. But before these possibilities can be tested, field studies and experiments must be designed, researchers must decide what flexibility is, and propose a tentative explanation about why it helps to make teaching more effective.

The following paragraphs explore flexibility in terms of its relation to social values, to the personality of the teacher, and more effective patterns of teaching. This will be done by discussing flexibility in classroom management, flexibility in individual contacts, and training teachers to be more flexible.

2. Flexibility in Classroom Management

One of the earliest studies employing a form of inter-action analysis is Stevens' (1912) study of teacher questions. The main thrust of his conclusions was that teachers ask so many questions so rapidly (235 per hour in one drill period for German), that the students do not have time to think. Two comments are related to flexibility:

> Any teacher who attempts to follow a rigid sequence of questions is hopelessly lost, and all spontaneity is swallowed up in "method."
>
> With the scientific [thoughtful] teacher, [class discussion] is the time for *versatility in effort* to establish ideals, to form habits of thought and action, to do any of the many things pertinent to the development . . . of the youthful mind. (Stevens 1912 pp. 10 and 11, emphasis added)

Was Stevens reacting to relatively inflexible recitation?

Some 50 years later, work by Flanders (1960a, 1960b) was concerned with how teacher influence changed when instructional purposes changed. (Note: most references to Flanders' work on interaction analysis report the relationship between teacher "indirectness" and student achievement, as if a simple process–product relationship was involved. However, Flanders' purpose was to investigate variation in teacher indirectness.)

It was clear as early as 1956 (Flanders and Amidon 1981 p. 30) that some teachers, who appeared to be more effective, sometimes "moved in closely to supervise (direct) student work and other times were more indirect and solicited student initiatives in the conduct of work." How did the teachers decide? Was there an explanation for this flexibility? To answer these questions, the following theory was proposed. A teacher would be more direct or less direct depending upon how clearly the students perceived the immediate learning task. If the student knew what the task required, the teacher could be more direct without increasing unwanted "student dependence on teacher direction." If the student was unsure of the task requirements, the teacher should ask for and react to the student's perception of the task before giving, or perhaps before not giving, directions. To be direct when the task was not clear would increase student dependence. Two kinds of data were collected to test these hypotheses (Flanders 1965 pp. 102–08).

It was assumed that goals would be less clear during the first two days of a 10-day unit of study, especially compared with the fourth, fifth, or sixth working days. To make comparisons, 16 eighth grade (age 13), single period, mathematics classes and 15 double period, seventh grade (age 12), social studies classes were split into two contrasting groups: those in which students learned more and had more positive attitudes and those that were the opposite. In the classrooms in which students learned more and liked learning better, more time was spent on planning during the first two days and the teachers were more indirect, supporting the hypotheses. The second kind of data indicated that more effective teachers had a greater range of directness and indirectness, showing greater flexibility, than the less effective teachers. Correlations between this last index of flexibility and the outcome variables were: (a) eighth grade achievement, 0.43; (b) eighth grade attitude, 0.43; (c) seventh grade achievement, 0.37; and (d) seventh grade attitude, 0.13. When this study was replicated at the fourth grade level (age 9), the correlation with achievement was 0.46 and with attitude was 0.08. The data on achievement provide support in three out of three independent studies, but for attitude, in only one out of three

It is informative to compare these results with the field study conducted by Bennett (1976) in England whose work on formal and informal teaching styles showed a general superiority of student achievement in the formal classes. If the contrast between formal and informal teaching is similar to inflexible–flexible teaching, then Bennett's results are the opposite of those just reviewed. It is most difficult to compare an index of flexibility based on interaction analysis data with the opinions of teachers even when teacher opinions are shown to be related to classroom practice. Bennett summarized the perceptions of teachers regarding formal and informal teaching (Bennett 1976 p. 63) and some of the perceptions seemed especially inconsistent with the teaching patterns that separated flexible from inflexible teachers in the United States fourth, seventh, and eighth grade samples. For example, teachers in Bennett's sample thought informal teachers more likely to "leave pupils unsure of what to do," yet the flexible teachers spent more time in planning and were more likely to check on the students' understanding of work plans than the inflexible teachers. In a similar comparison, the perception that informal teachers were "likely to encourage wasting time and day dreaming," would be just the opposite in the Flanders' distinction between flexible and inflexible teachers since students with more flexible teachers learned more and liked the learning activities better compared with classes with inflexible teachers. The distinction between flexible and inflexible teachers, based on the ratio of indirect to direct teacher statements, did not necessarily separate teachers who are more "content oriented" from those who were less so (Flanders 1965 p. 80) since both types appeared among the more flexible seventh grade teachers. This discussion illustrates how difficult it is to compare studies of teaching effectiveness and flexibility.

3. Flexibility and Individual Students

Besides scheduling changes in the pattern of instruction, should the concept of flexibility include adjusting teacher behavior to individual students? Hunt (1981 p. 59) makes the assertion, "Teachers' adaptation to students is the heart of the teaching–learning process." Other researchers would agree. It is no accident that many of the most frequently used systems of interaction analysis include one or more categories to code teacher reactions to student statements. A most remarkable feature of teaching is that every time a teacher contacts a student, there is a choice. Should the teacher respond or initiate? Is it time to clarify, or is it time to move on? A flexible teacher is free to make this choice and not only sees, but can embellish the alternatives.

Hunt reviews a number of interesting experiments in which it was possible to observe the tendency of teachers to ignore or react to student behavior. He describes (Hunt 1981 p. 63) an experiment in which a teacher was given a task, such as "explain the balance of power in the Federal government," and a student was trained to interject, according to schedule, specific obstacles or misconceptions. The purpose was to find out whether the teacher ignored this behavior or tried to adjust to the awkward and unexpected turn of events. An analysis of the performance of several hundred adults (some student teachers, some teachers, some parents) suggested that awareness was one component of the behavior, that is, seeing the interjection as an obstacle. A second component was "modulating the approach to the student's requirements"—in short, to sense and to adapt.

Peck and Joyce (1981) designed additional experiments to investigate sensitivity by creating more extreme conditions. In one treatment, the difficulty of the "student" was more subtle, almost obscure, and difficult to sense. In another treatment, students were instructed to create more persistent and more aversive resistance to the teaching goals. These investigations led to the concept "strength" which referred to the teacher's ability to persist in conducting the lesson, in spite of resistance. Thus, both the sensing and the adapting became more difficult. Is strength necessary for sensing? Can a strong person be sensitive? The researchers found scores on strength and sensitivity correlated, which suggests the possibility that growth in one may be associated with growth in the other.

Elsewhere in this Encyclopedia are essays on information processing models and the mastery learning model (see *Mastery Learning Models*). These require a teacher to sense cues from students and to adapt teaching behavior in terms of these cues. Another example is the work of Renner and Lawson (1973) in adapting science laboratory instruction to students who function at different cognitive levels. This adaptation has two requirements: first, either through tests or interviews a teacher develops a tentative estimate of a student's reasoning power; and second, by asking questions, the teacher discovers the kind of reasoning the student is using at the moment. With these insights, a teacher can then adapt the next move to the needs of the student.

There has been very little research on the difference between planned and unplanned flexibility. If knowledge of this kind is developed, it is likely to come from research on teacher decision making while teaching. Meanwhile an insightful discussion of this topic can be found in Smith and Geoffrey (1968 pp. 111–21) where spontaneous "skirmishing," "banter," and "getting off the hook" are discussed.

4. Training Teachers to be Flexible

The book *Flexibility in Teaching* (Joyce et al. 1981) marks the first time an entire book has been devoted to a discussion of why flexible teacher behavior is a rational response to the complexity of teaching. A teacher must be able to control:

(a) intellectual strategies for making curricular and instructional decisions;

(b) his or her own teaching behavior;

(c) procedures for the analysis of teaching;

(d) the interpersonal contacts and complex relationships among the individuals in the classroom; and

(e) procedures of evaluation so knowledge about education can be revised and adapted.

Since at any given moment the consequences of exercising control in these five areas cannot be predicted with precision, Joyce and Hodges assert:

We [are] concerned, then, with . . . teachers who would have great flexibility and who could modify their teaching behavior in order to experiment effectively in the classroom.

This is a call for not one, but a variety of models to guide the professional activities of a teacher. The book *Models of Teaching* (Joyce and Weil 1980) explains 24 different models of teaching. A model is more than a description of teaching behavior, it is a curriculum design in which instructional materials, learning activities, special objectives, class formations, and patterns of teaching behavior are synthesized into a coherent, understandable *Gestalten*. Models, therefore, can be used in three ways: for making curriculum plans, as a guideline for teacher–pupil interaction, and as a rationale for selecting and arranging instructional materials. Each model is based on the ideas of a primary theorist. Some of the names are: Ausubel, Bruner, Dewey, Piaget, Rogers, Schwab, Skinner, and Taba. Models, once learned and stored in repertoire, provide a resource for planned flexibility and an instant retrieval system to resolve unexpected emergencies. Joyce et al. (1981 p. 140) have summarized as follows:

To develop repertoire means to develop flexibility. Part of this flexibility is clinical and professional, and part is emotional and personal . . . a wide range of models . . . offers more creative and imaginative solutions to problems. . . . Repertoire requires the ability to grow as a person and expand one's potential . . .

The authors argue that both experienced and novice teachers can learn models, provided they have adequate resources and time.

5. The Current Status of Flexibility

All teachers show some degree of flexibility. The phrase "flexible teaching," however, refers to a pattern of instruction with more variety, variation, and teacher adaptation than is to be found in the average classroom. Evidence in support of above average flexibility from research on teaching is inconsistent.

Some researchers who have conceptualized teaching in terms of flexibility, such as Joyce and his colleagues, are not actively concerned with this inconsistency. They believe that research on teaching is unlikely to locate or construct a single model of teaching that will be superior to all others and, in their view, teaching is a craft that requires not one but several models. They see the classroom as an extremely complex social situation continuously buffeted by all the forces of a pluralistic culture. They expect the configuration of these forces to continue changing, one decade to another, for the foreseeable future. Thus, the only realistic approach to instruction is to prepare teachers who are capable of establishing and maintaining their own dynamic equilibrium with the fluctuating demands on the school. This is a balancing act that requires flexibility in instruction.

See also: Human Interaction Models; Teachers' Judgments; Interactive Decision Making; Planning

Bibliography

Anderson H H 1939 The measurement of domination and of socially integrative behavior in teachers' contacts with children. *Child Dev.* 10: 73–89
Anderson H H, Brewer J E 1946 Studies of teachers' classroom personalities, II. Effects of teachers' dominative and integrative contacts on children's classroom behavior. *Appl. Psychol. Monogr.* No. 8
Bennett N 1976 *Teaching Styles and Pupil Progress.* Open Books, London
Dunkin M J, Biddle B J 1974 *The Study of Teaching.* Holt, Rinehart and Winston, New York
Flanders N A 1960a *Teacher Influence, Pupil Attitudes, and Achievement.* Final Report, Cooperative Research Project, No. 397. University of Minnesota, Minneapolis, Minnesota
Flanders N A 1960b Diagnosing and utilizing social structures in classroom learning. In: Henry N B (ed.) 1960 *National Society for the Study of Education*, 59th Yearbook, Part 2: *The Dynamics of Instructional Groups.* University of Chicago Press, Chicago, Illinois
Flanders N A 1965 *Teacher Influence, Pupil Attitudes, and Achievement.* United States Department of Health, Education, and Welfare, Cooperative Research Monograph, No. 12. United States Government Printing Office, Washington, DC
Flanders N A, Amidon E J 1981 *A Case Study of an Educational Innovation.* Amidon, St. Paul, Minnesota
Getzels J W, Jackson P W 1963 The teacher's personality and characteristics. In: Gage N L (ed.) *Handbook of Research on Teaching: A Project of the American Educational Research Association.* Rand McNally, Chicago, Illinois
Hunt D E 1981 Teachers' adaptation: "Reading" and "flexing" to students. In: Joyce B R, Brown C C, Peck L (eds.) 1981
Joyce B R, Hodges R E 1981 Flexibility as repertoire. In: Joyce B R, Brown C C, Peck L (eds.) 1981
Joyce B R, Weil M 1980 *Models of Teaching*, 2nd edn. Prentice-Hall, Englewood Cliffs, New Jersey
Joyce B R, Brown C C, Peck L (eds.) 1981 *Flexibility in Teaching.* Longman, New York
Lippitt R, White R K 1943 The "social climate" of children's groups. In: Barker R G, Kounin J S, Wright H F (eds.) 1943 *Child Behavior and Development: A Course of Representative Studies.* McGraw-Hill, New York
McGee H M 1955 Measurement of authoritarianism and its relation to teachers' classroom behavior. *Genet. Psychol. Monogr.* 52: 89–146
Peck L, Joyce B R 1981 Strength and sensitivity: The battleground of explicit matching behavior. In: Joyce B R, Brown C C, Peck L (eds.) 1981
Renner J W, Lawson A E 1973 Promoting intellectual development through science teaching. *Phys. Teach.* 11: 273–76
Rosenshine B, Furst N 1973 The use of direct observation to study teaching. In: Travers R M W (ed.) 1973 *Second Handbook of Research on Teaching: A Project of the American Educational Research Association.* Rand McNally, Chicago, Illinois
Smith L M, Geoffrey W 1968 *The Complexities of an Urban Classroom: An Analysis Toward a General Theory of Teaching.* Holt, Rinehart and Winston, New York
Stevens R 1912 The question as a measure of efficiency in instruction: A critical study of classroom practice. In: Simon A, Boyer E G (eds.) 1967 *Mirrors for Behavior: An Anthology of Classroom Observation Instruments*, Vol. 14. Research for Better Schools, Philadelphia, Pennsylvania
Withall J, Lewis W W 1963 Social interaction in the classroom. In: Gage N L (ed.) *1963 Handbook of Research on Teaching: A Project of the American Educational Research Association.* Rand McNally, Chicago, Illinois

Nonverbal Communication

H. A. Smith

The present review of nonverbal communication in teaching has several major objectives: (a) to provide a brief historical sketch of the general area of nonverbal communication; (b) to summarize some of the major research findings of educational investigations into nonverbal phenomena; and (c) to outline possible directions or future theory and research. In view of the intended aims and scope of this presentation, the number of references have been held to a minimum. However, many of the original studies upon which the article is based are outlined in the references shown at the end of the text.

One ongoing source of difficulty for investigators involves definition of the term "nonverbal communication." In the present context, nonverbal communication will be defined broadly as the area of study which includes all essentially nonlinguistic phenomena which impinge on and influence the process of human interaction. Accordingly, physical structures, facial expressions, body postures, conversational silences, and human adornments such as clothing may all qualify as legitimate topics of nonverbal research. In addition, the present definition of nonverbal communication assumes neither a conscious intent to communicate on the part of the sender nor the "correct" decoding of a message by the receiver.

1. Historical Developments in Nonverbal Communication Research

Topics relating to nonverbal communication have been addressed since the beginning of recorded history. The dances and rituals of the ancient Aztecs, the Roman and Greek writings on gesture, mime, and dance, the sign language of the Australian Aborigines, the gestures and postures of Chinese theater, and the courtesy books of Renaissance Italy have all predated more contemporary efforts to investigate nonverbal phenomena in a scientific manner (see Davis 1972, Davis and Skupien 1982, and Key 1977 for brief historical treatments and for comprehensive lists of classical works on nonverbal communication).

The publication in 1872 of Charles Darwin's *The Expression of the Emotions in Man and Animals* initiated serious interest in the nonverbal domain as a viable research area and yielded a variety of data and conclusions which are still valid today. The research topics begun by Darwin have been characterized since by both active and dormant periods of activity (for example, research on human facial expression was active during the 1920s and 1930s, faded away in the 1940s, and began again with renewed vigor in the 1950s) and by a fragmentation into a number of parallel streams of research. Present investigations in ethology, cross-cultural comparisons, developmental patterns, emotional expression, and personality psychodiagnosis can each trace their beginnings to Darwin's seminal work. Research areas of more recent development include communication, interaction, ecology, and the psychological interpretation of actions. The overlapping academic disciplines encompassing the theory and data of all of these research foci include ethology, communications, sociology, anthropology, psychology, and education.

Comprehensive treatments of the nonverbal domain

from a primarily psychological perspective have been presented in several texts (for example, see Knapp 1978 for an American perspective) and journal articles (see Ellgring 1981 for an overview of German research). Concurrently, a number of publications aimed at the popular market have served to make the general public more aware of nonverbal topics. Unfortunately, many of the speculations contained within these books have received only ephemeral support from research findings. One of the more substantial contributions to the latter category of publications is a recent handbook on human actions and gestures (Morris 1977).

2. Nonverbal Channels and Teaching Effectiveness

In teaching, only minor notice was paid to nonverbal elements before 1960. Some early suggestions regarding use of the eyes and forms of "proximity control" were advanced, but deliberate study of the area is a product of the period since the early 1960s and particularly since the early 1970s.

For research and discussion purposes, nonverbal communication has been divided typically into a number of channels which vary with the perspective and research interests of the individual researcher. However, the common elements of these divisions invariably involve use of one's body within the dimensions of space and time and usually result in a list of from six to ten channels of influence. For example, the facets of the nonverbal domain may consist of: environmental factors (the effects on communication of the physical attributes of settings), proxemics (the use and perception of social and personal space), kinesics (the influence on communication of gestures, body movement, posture, and eye and facial behavior), sensory communication (involving touch, taste, smell, sight, and hearing), paralanguage (the nonverbal characteristics accompanying speech such as voice pitch, volume, tempo and intensity, intruding sounds, and silent pauses), physical characteristics (the influence of varying physiques, degrees of attractiveness, body odors, and hair or skin colour) and artifacts (the adornments of human beings such as clothes, jewelry, and assorted beauty aids).

Additional separate channels of nonverbal influence might include chronemics (involving the use of time) and silence, both of which are subsumed here under kinesics or paralanguage. However, the nature of the research question being asked usually determines whether use of any of these categories is appropriate. For purposes of the present report, the major research findings will be summarized in the first instance under each of the above topics. (School-based investigations in areas of nonverbal communication have been reviewed more extensively by Weinstein 1979, Smith 1979, and by Woolfolk and Brooks 1983. Various aspects of nonverbal communication in teaching have been presented in special issues of *Theory into Practice* published in 1971, 1977, and 1985.)

2.1 Environmental Factors

Within this category, the focus of study involves effects of the physical attributes of settings on communication. Environmental factors are considered relevant because they help to define the contexts within which human interaction takes place and thus help to determine the appropriateness of behaviors manifested by the participants.

For present purposes, the most global level of interest involves the physical qualities of the school itself. Unfortunately, relatively little work has been done to examine the effects on behavior of school size and design. Currently, there is no strong evidence to indicate that building plan in and of itself has a major influence on student or teacher attitudes or interactions. However, some results suggest that secondary schools in the medium-size range of about 300 to 450 students per grade produce the fewest personnel problems and the greatest amount of student and teacher integratedness. It seems that particular combinations of design and utilization patterns are more critical to communication than size or design alone. For example, in contrast to central plans, extended school layouts contribute to smaller moving masses of students who interact in ways more supportive of the goals of the administration. In addition, many very large schools are now characterized by "school within school" arrangements that foster close relationships within the distinctive elements of the school (see *Architecture*).

More research has been conducted on the design and physical characteristics of the individual classroom. The most obvious feature in this regard involves differences in behavior resulting from placement within either the traditional classroom or the more recently constructed "open" areas (see *Open Versus Formal Methods*). The respective achievement and attitude data suggest that one setting is not inevitably superior to the other. The increased amounts of noise and visual stimulation in the open classrooms are distracting to some students but not all. However, open areas seem to provide more privacy for students and more personal study space than the traditional setting. Unfortunately, research attempting to compare the two types of classroom is accompanied by several major difficulties. Firstly, the problem of defining degree of openness is of no small consequence, especially when classrooms originally constructed as "open" gradually manifest increased numbers of physical barriers such as screens, chalkboards, bookshelves, and coat racks (see *Equipment and Materials*). Secondly, and more substantially, open areas do not automatically provide open education. Since the latter entity is more closely related to a particular philosophical outlook than to a physical structure, "openness" may occur in traditional classrooms as easily as in open areas. Hence, differences among classrooms in levels of student achievement, attitude, and interaction may reflect contrasts in educational philosophy rather than in classroom design.

Several investigations have examined the effects of windowless classrooms on student and teacher communication. Although few influences have been reported, results suggest a tendency toward increased student aggression or activity levels relative to those of students placed in the traditional classroom. These heightened levels of arousal may be revealed by increased student participation in classroom activities. In settings where the environment outside the school is full of visual and auditory distractions, the windowless classroom may serve an important educational need.

A variety of additional environmental factors influence classroom life. For example, illumination and temperature are usually maintained at average maximum comfort levels and furniture size is generally matched with student size. Various studies have shown that an abundance of color, flexible lighting, and comfortable seats substantially influence pupil attitudes and related behavior even when effects on academic performance cannot be observed. Also, the availability and organization of equipment and materials seem to be important for a good quality program. At the elementary level, it appears that achievement and interaction are enhanced when a small number of students can work together, when numerous sound-proof barriers exist, and when the teacher moves among the students instead of directing class activities from the desk.

Hence, environmental factors permit or deny a variety of classroom activities. Although a number of environmental effects have been observed, many other potential influences await examination in future investigations.

2.2 Proxemics

For purposes of nonverbal communication, environmental factors are closely related both to the social uses made of them and to their perceived relevance in the social situation. These latter aspects characterize the channel of proxemics, which is generally defined as the meaning and use of one's social and personal space. Although proxemic variables have been examined in a variety of settings, the present review will focus on major results concerning classroom seating arrangements, student and teacher proximity, and teacher use of space.

Several relatively consistent findings have emerged from studies of classroom seating and spatial arrangements and their effects on classroom behavior. The first set of findings involves the increase in student participation with a decrease in distance between teacher and student or with an increase in the directness with which teachers and students face each other (the latter variable is usually accompanied by an increase in teacher gaze, a kinesic variable to be examined later). That is, highest amounts of student participation occur from the front to back rows in a crowded seminar room or in a laboratory with student benches arranged parallel to the front of the classroom. In addition, if the teacher remains at the front center of the traditional classroom with its rows of desks, a "triangle of participation" can often be observed extending across the front row of seats and along the front two-thirds of the center column of student desks. Similar triangles may be created in other parts of the classroom whenever the teacher chooses to remain in one location for a substantial period of time.

Among other class arrangements, highest student participation has been observed at the base of a U-shaped configuration whenever the teacher is seated opposite in the "gap" of the U. Apparently, the influence of direct orientation between teacher and student, with enhanced levels of mutual eye contact, promotes increased student involvement with classroom activities.

In general, students seem to dislike the standard class arrangement with rows of student desks overseen in front by a large teacher's desk. Some evidence suggests that less academically able students prefer to have the teacher's desk placed among their own, while more academically able students prefer the "freer" learning environments consisting of circles of desks or horseshoe-shaped configurations (see *Seating Patterns*).

One question arising from studies examining the uneven distribution of student participation asks whether more verbal or otherwise active students choose the high participation areas of the classroom, or whether placement in the classroom affects student verbalization. Some data suggest that both effects occur. When compared with moderate or low verbalizers, high verbal students tend to choose more central classroom areas. On the other hand, high or moderate verbalizers tend to participate more when placed in central areas than when assigned to more peripheral regions of the classroom. However, the participation levels of low verbalizers seem relatively unaffected by classroom placement. In general, when students are placed centrally, other nonverbal behaviors such as looking, blinking, turning around, and writing also tend to increase in frequency.

At least one study has reported some advantage in letting students choose their own desks from one occasion to the next. The results indicated that higher test scores were obtained from students allowed to change their seats from class to class than from those required to remain in single locations. Hence, there may be a need to recognize variations in individual moods and energy levels by allowing students to withdraw somewhat or to participate more fully in class activities according to their own desires.

Several other features characterize the use of space. For example, more controlling behavior has been observed in elementary teachers provided with inadequate amounts of classroom space (less than 2.80 m² per child) than in teachers given additional space (more than 4.55 m² per child). Therefore, crowded classrooms may result in patterns of behavior which are less than maximally productive. It has also been observed that many teachers do not use all of the classroom space available to them. One study found that 45 percent of all class activity took place in one-twelfth of the floor space. In general, there appears to be a general reluctance of teachers to move around the classroom and to maximize use of all of its areas.

An additional aspect related to spatial arrangement involves the classroom organization of desks, bookshelves, other furniture, and equipment. When these physical elements are arranged so as to allow orderly flow patterns and sufficient room to move, students exhibit more productive and fewer disruptive behaviors.

Use of the teacher's own space relative to that of the students is another important feature of proxemics. In general, the closer the teacher is to the student (up to within 1 to 2 m), the better the student's attitudes and performance seem to be. Particularly at the elementary level, teacher proximity is seen to indicate liking, approval, and friendliness toward the student.

In the traditional classroom, students consider themselves more included in class activities when the teacher makes a habit of standing in front of the desk rather than behind it. If the teacher works customarily from among the students, then the students consider themselves liked. In general, the teacher is seen to be less warm as the distance from the students increases, while teacher placement behind the front desk is related negatively to teacher affection and inclusion. However, some evidence suggests that boys at the elementary-school level may be more tolerant than girls of increased teacher distance.

The important influence on communication of distance between teachers and students may be explained to at least some degree. As interpersonal distance decreases, the quality of the interaction appears to change markedly. From further away there is more lecturing and one-way communication on the part of the teacher, while more two-way interactions of a permissive nature occur when teachers and students are closer together. Further, when teachers are closer, students feel themselves to be more "included" in class activities and they behave in ways that are valued by teachers: they look at the teachers more, they write more, and they speak more.

Finally, some proxemic differences have been observed between traditional classrooms and open-space areas. In the latter settings, teachers seem to move around the classrooms more frequently and, at the elementary level, to change positions from standing to kneeling to sitting more often than teachers in the regular classroom.

2.3 Kinesics

An additional important area of nonverbal communication is that of kinesics, defined as the study of body movement, posture, and facial and eye behavior. Of the categories considered here, kinesics is the one which has received the most research and the greatest amount of public attention during recent years.

A major component of kinesics involves the use of gestures. In teaching, a more frequent use of gestures has been associated with a more affiliative classroom style which elicits liking and cooperation from others. Although gestures are influenced by personality style and cultural background, they also reflect the amount of involvement that the teacher brings to a task. Hence, some moderate level of gestural activity (between the extremes of lethargic and hyperkinetic activity) seems to be associated with the rather nebulous concept of "enthusiasm," which has sometimes been related in turn to teacher effectiveness.

Kinesics in general, and gestures in particular, are influenced strongly by cultural norms and therefore should be of special interest to the teacher. Various physical motions, but notably the meanings assigned to them, can vary widely from culture to culture. Accordingly, foreign-language teachers or teachers of students from different cultural backgrounds bear an extra responsibility to become familiar with differences in kinesic expression. Although it may be unrealistic to expect teachers to change their own basic behavioral patterns and cultural assumptions, they should have a working knowledge of the kinesic differences represented in their students and an empathy for children from dissimilar cultural environments.

Gestures play an especially important role for racial or cultural groups which minimize the amount of verbal communication in which they engage. For such groups, sign language in context may have its own grammatical and situational rules and be the essential means of communication. In these cases, gestures alone may convey the entire message but both sender and receiver need to know the language codes involved.

Cultural differences are also reflected in the usual interpersonal distances adopted by the interacting parties. For example, northern European teachers placed in a southern European classroom may be perceived by the students as cool, distant, and not liking them. In contrast, a southern European teacher may cause initial discomfort in northern European students by standing uncommonly close to them and by making physical contact with them (for example, by placing a hand on the student's shoulder).

An additional body movement variable is that of posture. Teachers who are more accessible to students tend to manifest a relaxed and open bearing and usually lean toward the students. Research has demonstrated that teachers who characteristically lean forwards are seen as accepting the students, involved with them, and liking them. In general, students prefer the closer teacher and think that he or she is better than one who displays less apparent involvement.

Use of the eyes, or gaze, has been implicated repeatedly in considerations regarding effective teacher behavior. The type and amount of gaze is considered important for purposes of classroom management and instruction. Increased numbers of disruptions are observed whenever the average amount of teacher eye contact with the class declines. In order to restore classroom order most teachers are aware of the effec-

tiveness of a "cold stare" directed at offending individuals. For instructional purposes, looking at the students promotes their attentiveness, involvement, and positive regard for the teacher. These elements are particularly important when the teacher is working with a single student.

The type and amount of eye contact is another area in which cultural differences occur. In the majority North American culture, students are expected to look directly at the teacher when speaking or when being spoken to. However, in other cultures, eye contact is considered either as an invasion of privacy, or an act of defiance, or a demonstration of lack of trust.

Some highly anxious students find the teacher's gaze too anxiety provoking, and so avert their gazes or avoid direct eye contact altogether. The teacher who is sensitive to this phenomenon should either reduce the amount of his or her own gaze or ask the student if eye contact is distressing.

Relatively little attention has been paid to the effects of the teacher's facial behavior on student attitudes and achievement. However, it is generally taken for granted that teachers who have grown up in a particular cultural milieu are familiar with the usual messages transmitted by the varying arrangements of facial muscles. The use and interpretation of frowns, grimaces, and smiles are presumed to be similar both inside and outside the classroom. Further, evidence suggests that facial expressions reflecting the emotions of anger, happiness, and sadness, among others, may be universally shared.

Although most beginning teachers in North America are advised to not smile until December so as to help establish classroom control, the presence of teacher smiles seems to play an important role in classroom behavior. For example, one study found that student teachers who smiled and used verbal probing were associated with thoughtful and responsive students over a variety of performance measures. Supplementary research has found that smiling is related to the ephemeral quality called warmth. In general, it appears that smiling fosters a supportive and nonthreatening classroom climate which promotes the development of positive student attitudes and achievement. However, for some experimental situations, a major problem consists simply of defining a smile.

Some differences in kinesic behavior between traditional and open-area classrooms have been reported. In the open setting, teacher gestures and body movement seem to be more informal and spontaneous and to consist of more kneeling, squatting, and associated behaviors. Since no work has been done on the relationship among kinesic, personality, and situational variables, the effects of such altered kinesic activity on student achievement and attitudes remains undetermined. One study found that instructional moves by the teacher were similar in the two settings, since cyclical patterns involving surveying the class, pointing, and nodding did not seem to differ. Similarly, student kinesic movements such as raising the hand did not vary from the traditional to the open classroom. However, since most of the research has focused on the elementary grades, different results may be obtained at the secondary-school level.

Implicit in a consideration of kinesic variables is the notion of rhythm, which involves performance of an action within the dimensions of both time and space. Most skilled teachers have a sense of rhythm or pacing which allows appropriate time for the performance of actions as well as for smooth transitions from one instructional activity to the next. In these cases, flow or momentum is maintained together with a lack of redundant action and loss of time. Unskilled teachers with deficient rhythms seem to produce uneven transitions with increased probabilities of student confusion and misbehavior. However, in the absence of systematic inquiry into the effects of teacher rhythm on classroom management and instruction, no firm conclusions can be drawn.

Thus far, the focus in the review has been on behaviors performed. However, a behavior which is not manifested when expected or considered appropriate can also be seen by a potential recipient as carrying a significant message. Not returning a greeting, not looking at one individual in a small group that is being addressed, and not reaching out for an extended item can all be considered as messages that may affect the future relationship between the people involved. For obvious reasons, this aspect of nonverbal communication is a difficult one to research.

2.4 Touching Behavior

The study of touching behavior, also called haptics, focuses on a nonverbal element considered essential to normal human development. However, only limited work has been done to relate teacher touch with student attitudes and achievement. In one investigation at the first and second grade levels (ages 6 and 7), no significant relationship was observed between the type of touch used and student achievement in reading. In a second study where both teacher touch and smiling were used together in a one-to-one teaching situation, students receiving both nonverbal cues showed increased learning when compared with students receiving neither.

Although firm evidence remains to be obtained in educational settings, the important role played by touch has been outlined elsewhere. For example, it seems that some children prefer touch to verbal or visual communication in their daily encounters. In addition, in so-called "contact" cultures where touch is used regularly and frequently in interaction, the total absence of touch may trigger negative reactions toward both speaker and situation. Whenever touch is employed in the classroom setting, it should appear to be a natural part of the communication and should be conducted only by teachers who feel comfortable using it.

2.5 Physical Characterisics

Thus far it appears that almost no research has been done to relate the physical characteristics of students or teachers with achievement or success in the classroom. Hence, the influence of physique, physical size and weight, body odors, degree of attractiveness, and hair or skin color remains essentially unspecified in this context. Nevertheless, it seems that different cultural groups place different values on particular manifestations of these characteristics which, for the most part, cannot be altered significantly by the individual.

In North American populations, research has demonstrated that children rated as more attractive are also more popular with their peers and have a better self-image. Additional work has revealed that teachers make attractiveness judgments about young children and treat the attractive ones with more numerous and more positive comments. Thus, teachers and students who possess a number of culturally valued physical attributes may enjoy more success in their daily encounters than those lacking this advantage.

2.6 Paralanguage

This category of nonverbal communication consists of the nonlinguistic accompaniments of speech such as voice volume, tempo, pitch, and intensity as well as intruding sounds, hesitations, and pauses. However, as was the situation for several previous areas, the effects of paralinguistic cues on the teaching situation remain to be investigated.

Other work may have some implications for the classroom setting. For example, one study found that voice tone was not a reliable index of interpersonal warmth. In addition it seems that sarcasm, whereby the true meaning of a message is transmitted by paralinguistic elements rather than by words, is generally not understood by children in elementary school. Apparently, this age group relies heavily on the spoken word to interpret intended meaning.

Additional research indicates that voice quality and manner of speaking reveal much about the speaker. However, it is still unclear as to whether this information can alter the listener's perceptions of the speaker over time or whether it serves simply to reinforce initial impressions. In the classroom setting, it is generally presumed that lack of teacher confidence or knowledge of the subject is disclosed by these paralinguistic variables, but research has yet to confirm these judgments.

Another variable which can be considered as paralinguistic is silence, the total absence of a verbal input. Depending on when and where it occurs in an interpersonal interaction, silence can communicate the full range of emotional expression from scorn and dislike to indifference to love and sympathy. Research thus far has yet to examine the role of silence in teaching, particularly for possible differing effects with various age groups.

However, it has been suggested that traditional classroom teachers are silent too little and often fail to comprehend the existing class situation before speaking. From the instructional perspective, silence can play an important role by virtue of the amount of time provided for students to respond to questions or problems and the time required to move from one activity to the next.

2.7 Artifacts

The category of artifacts defines items in contact with the interacting persons which can be varied at will such as clothes, perfumes, eyeglasses, hair pieces, and other assorted beauty aids. In general, it seems as though these items play some role in establishing initial impressions of individuals but wane in significance once the persons become known. Also, artifacts can disclose to others one's present mood and desired image. In educational practice, unwritten (and sometimes written) guidelines concerning use and type of artifact exist for both students and teachers and generally reflect existing social norms or ideals. However, the relationship between changes in artifacts and levels of teaching and learning performance remain undetermined.

3. Effects of Nonverbal Behavior Patterns on Teaching

Up to this point in the review, each of the seven categories, or channels, of nonverbal communication has been treated separately and given a status which may not be justified in practice. Unfortunately, there are several severe limitations in studying the influence on communication of the independent channels. First of all, the entire constellation of behaviors displayed determines the function and meaning of a communication except when specific gestures or movements are intended to substitute for spoken words. Second, and related, the context in which the communication takes place is critical in order to make sense or meaning of the behaviors. Hence, although study of the individual channel can serve a useful function, future investigations should strive to comprehend effects of the total behavior cluster for the particular context being examined.

A recent report (Woolfolk and Brooks 1983) has taken several steps in this direction by reviewing the relevant literature under four questions of interest to educational researchers: (a) How do teachers use the nonverbal behavior of their students to form impressions, expectations, and attitudes? (b) How do teachers reveal these expectations and attitudes in their own nonverbal behavior? (c) How do students interpret variations in their teachers' nonverbal behaviors? (d) How do teachers use nonverbal behaviors in instruction and class management? Although these researchers then subdivided each of the questions into the three channels of proxemics, kinesics (called "coverbal" by Woolfolk and Brooks), and paralinguistics, some interesting findings emerged. Several of these results will be considered next.

3.1 Teacher Impressions of Student Nonverbal Behaviors

A variety of student behaviors has been found to affect the impressions, expectations, and attitudes of teachers. For example, students who sit toward the front of the classroom rather than at the back are viewed by the teacher as more attentive and likeable. Also, more attractive students with good voice qualities are considered more intelligent, enthusiastic, and academically successful than students who are unattractive and have poor voice qualities. In general, the more the student shows positive nonverbal behaviors (for most North American settings, reflected in higher levels of gaze and more frequent smiling and head nodding), the more the teacher reciprocates with positive nonverbal behaviors and more favorable written evaluations of the student's intellectual and social abilities. At this time, however, these results should be accepted with some caution since teacher assessments may vary with the culture, race, age, and gender (see *Students' Sex*) of both students and teacher.

3.2 Teacher Expectations as Reflected in Nonverbal Behavior

Several studies have suggested that expectations and attitudes held by teachers about their students are displayed by the teachers' nonverbal behaviors in the classroom. For example, teachers tend to stand further away from "rejected" students than from the other class members. Evidence also indicates that low-ability students may be placed in more distant regions of the classroom for much of the school year. In these remote classroom areas, it is often difficult to see what is written on the board, to hear the teacher, and to feel included in ongoing class activities.

It is evident that teachers tend to reciprocate the nonverbal behaviors of their students, whether these behaviors are highly positive or less so. Teachers, particularly females, tend to use more words and to speak in more positive voice tones when addressing nonverbally positive rather than nonverbally negative students. Some related data show that teachers display more positive nonverbal behaviors toward children of their own races, but that these differences are usually detectable only to other persons of the same race. Racially prejudiced teachers tend to reflect their attitudes nonverbally.

Some differences in nonverbal behavior have emerged between experienced teachers (those with more than five years of experience) and inexperienced teachers (those with five or fewer years' experience). The former group may be more nonverbally encouraging of both upper and lower class students while the latter group may be more nonverbally encouraging of upper class students alone. However, both experienced and inexperienced teachers seem to exhibit the least amount of encouragement toward the majority of the class membership, the middle class students.

Teachers reveal positive nonverbal behaviors in several ways: by leaning forward or reaching toward the students and by increased amounts of eye gaze, affirmative head nods, and smiling. More positive behavior is displayed toward the atypical students in the class (that is, the bright and the slow or mentally retarded) and more nonverbal encouragement is shown toward both the gifted and the delinquent child than toward regular-elementary or secondary-school students. However, the function of the nonverbal displays may be more critical than the frequencies of occurrences when comparing teacher behaviors directed toward gifted and slow students, for example. Although both groups receive high amounts of positive behavior, an examination of the class context reveals that the teacher does much more pointing toward the instructional materials or directing of activities when working with the slower students.

3.3 Student Perceptions of Teacher Nonverbal Behavior

Relatively little work has been done to examine student perceptions and understandings of teacher nonverbal behavior in the classroom situation. However, some relevant findings have been obtained, together with those from tutoring sessions or from studies where the "teacher" has appeared on videotape.

In general, it appears that teachers who conduct their classes from among the students are viewed more positively than those who teach from beside, behind, or seated on their desks. When compared with the latter group of teachers, the former are perceived as warmer, more friendly, and more effective. However, young male students tend to view more distant teacher behaviors less negatively than female students, a difference which increases with student age. Further, at the high-school level, very close teacher distances are considered more acceptable when female teachers are close to female students instead of male students. Students also like teachers who smile more often and who hold up books for the whole class to see.

In a one-to-one tutoring format, students prefer the "close" (as opposed to "distant") teacher who displays more forward lean, head nods, eye contact, and smiles. The close teacher is considered more friendly and understanding and to like children, and the individual child, more. Also, the close teacher is seen to enjoy being near the student and to be the significantly better instructor.

Some evidence suggests that, in the United States at least, gender of the teacher can affect student perceptions of teacher nonverbal behavior. In the study in question, female teachers were viewed more positively and received higher student attraction scores when they were nonverbally positive instead of nonverbally negative. However, the corresponding nonverbal behaviors of male teachers did not affect student perceptions or attraction scores. Perhaps cross-cultural research should be conducted to examine more thoroughly the influence of teacher gender on student perceptions.

The ability of students to perceive teacher nonverbal behavior, and the types of judgments rendered, seems to be related in part to student age. In general, younger students are less able than older ones to decode affect which is expressed paralinguistically, and so are less able to detect "mixed messages," that is, communications which are inconsistent across the verbal and nonverbal domains. Even when younger children are paying attention to both words and tone of voice, they attend less to facial expressions which may reflect incongruent messages. It is possible that the ability to comprehend simultaneous behaviors in several channels demands a level of cognitive functioning which the younger child has yet to attain.

3.4 Teacher Nonverbal Behavior in Instruction and Management

The fourth problem of interest to educational researchers and practitioners involves the effectiveness of various teacher nonverbal behaviors for purposes of classroom instruction and management. Although many pertinent questions remain unanswered, the existing data suggest that some constellations of behavior are more effective than others in certain settings.

As indicated previously, students who are closer to the teacher (within limits which are in part culturally determined) are more involved in class proceedings, participate more, and behave more in accordance with the teacher's goals. Closer students tend to look at the teacher more and to write more, and therefore tend to foster more positive teacher impressions. On the other hand, when teachers are closer to the students they tend to show more permissive and interactive verbal communications. As the interpersonal distance increases, teachers engage more in one-way communications and lectures.

Teacher assertiveness, particularly in the vocal channel, seems to play an important role in matters affecting classroom management. However, the content of the verbal messages should be positive in nature for superior instructional advantage. Research supports the common assertions that teachers, particularly beginning teachers, should give the appearance of being firm and business-like and that this appearance is depicted primarily through nonverbal means.

The influence of kinesic variables on instruction and management remains unclear, particularly where facial behavior and eye contact are concerned. Perhaps the latter variables are less important when the focus is on instruction, mainly a cognitive concern, and more important when the major issue is discipline, primarily an affective matter. Certainly there are many testimonials concerning the effectiveness of a stern, unsmiling face and a determined stare when class control is at stake. In related work, one study found that junior-high-school students preferred teachers who smiled and gestured more frequently while a second project found that students learned more and liked the teacher better when the teacher (shown on videotape only) was nonverbally active. In the latter study, nonverbal activity was reflected in measures of eye contact, amount of gesturing, and dynamic voice tone.

Some work has shown that student expectations may have as much influence on teacher nonverbal behavior as teacher expectations do. It seems that when students have confidence in the teacher's ability they behave more positively by increasing their amounts of eye gaze, forward lean, and direct orientation. In turn, and presumably as a result of the students' behaviors, the teacher performs more adequately.

Several major areas involving instruction and management matters require additional research. The influence of the teacher's nonverbal behaviors on students' affective behaviors remains essentially unspecified. Similarly, except for the small number of results outlined above, the teacher nonverbal behaviors which promote student involvement, participation, and ultimately learning deserve further attention.

4. The Nature and Concerns of Future Research

As reported above, a variety of questions concerning nonverbal communication in teaching remain unanswered and therefore deserve further investigation. However, in addition to specific questions, there are several entire areas which hold particular promise for future research and development. Some of these areas will be surveyed next, together with a brief overview of research methodology and instrumentation. Even though theoretical issues concerning the structure and function of nonverbal communication will be implied, these issues will not be considered in depth at this time.

4.1 Research Methods in Nonverbal Communication

The roots of experimental educational psychology and, by extension, classroom nonverbal processes lie in laboratory-designed procedures and laboratory-based experiments. However, dissatisfaction with the validity of many experimental findings has produced a growing movement of researchers into the live classroom since the late 1960s. Many of these researchers have then employed observational techniques similar to those used by ethologists, with a minimum number of preconceived notions concerning what phenomena one should look at and how one should look at them.

With the trend toward naturalistic observation, many of the category systems used to classify nonverbal behaviors were found to be inadequate. Presently, frequency counts of discrete behaviors are often seen to be of less importance than the patterns of behavior and their intended functions or meanings in the context within which they occur. Accordingly, the problem of what to look at, and how, has become particularly vexing. Most researchers are left with little choice but to isolate the specific behaviors of interest to themselves and to devise their own meaningful units of analysis.

Since observation alone is inadequate to account for many behaviors when the plans or intentions of the actors are unknown, there is an obvious need to use a wide variety of research techniques and methods of data collection. Hence, many studies combine observational methods with ethnographic techniques and traditional paper–pencil tests. Fortunately, technological advances have kept pace with these more sophisticated research demands. Today and increasingly in the future, permanent videotaped records will be obtained for repeated viewing and for analysis by assorted systems of computer support.

4.2 Patterns of Nonverbal Interaction

The traditional method of examining nonverbal behavior in the classroom has been to collect frequency counts of discrete behaviors regardless of their order or distribution. However, during the past few years, increased attention has been paid to patterns of behavior which emerge and evolve over time. Several clusters of related work have prompted this change in research emphasis. First of all, simple frequency counts of observed behaviors have been found to be inadequate to gain an understanding of significant classroom events. This inadequacy is reflected best in rarely occurring events which nevertheless have significant implications for classroom life.

Secondly, a variety of data have demonstrated that teachers and students influence each other over time, an aspect already considered previously. Therefore, teacher nonverbal behaviors at a particular point in time reflect both previous history and present events. In addition, these behaviors may have a substantial influence on future behavior. Frequency counts alone are inadequate to capture the evolving nature of a teacher–student relationship.

Thirdly, recent work outlining both the classroom structure and the way in which structuring takes place (Mehan 1979) has implications for the study of nonverbal communication. Mehan has demonstrated how the initiation–reply–evaluation sequence is an important feature of classrooms and how this sequence is created and later manifests itself. Clearly, nonverbal messages play an important role in creating this structure but the precise nature of their involvement requires further delineation.

Related research in social psychology has focused on interaction and interaction sequences as important contributing factors in personality development. Relevant work has been done to study mother–infant interactions but the corresponding influence of teachers on students, and vice versa, remains to be investigated.

4.3 Social Skills Training

One important area for applying research on nonverbal communication involves the training of social skills. Interest in this field has been prompted by recent findings that some students with classroom behavior problems are simply unaware of the existing, but unwritten and unspoken, rules for classroom demeanor. Teachers too are often unable to detect the nonverbal messages being emitted by their students or to adequately transmit their intended cognitive and affective signals.

Accordingly, it should be possible to instruct both

teachers and students in skills related to physical and vocal expression and behavioral interpretation. Some methods already in use for these purposes include photo analysis, live observation, and role playing or discussion sessions. However, this work should proceed with some caution since social skills training is usually conducted by representatives of the dominant culture who may strive to eliminate unique but functional behaviors of minority cultures.

4.4 Cultural Considerations

Cultural aspects have already been considered but deserve further attention in the present context. Although several universal nonverbal behaviors have been isolated, a majority of those observed in social settings appear to be culturally influenced or determined. These behaviors, particularly those involving differences in use of space and time, should be more specifically isolated for recognition by teachers. It is possible that many atypical and apparently dysfunctional classroom behaviors are simply expressions of dissimilar cultural backgrounds (see *Students' Ethnicity*).

In addition, teachers of foreign languages should be aware of and impart the unique characteristics of the cultural or linguistic groups which they represent. Because kinesic and proxemic qualities often characterize languages, foreign-language teachers bear an important responsibility to relay these cultural–linguistic features to their students. Perhaps more attention should be paid to using foreign languages and their nonverbal accompaniments in actual situations.

4.5 Brain Functions and Nonverbal Behavior

The fundamental role played by nonverbal behaviors in human performance and communication suggests that there is an integral link between nonverbal elements and capacities of the human brain. For example, some evidence indicates that the body participates in cognitive activities, since complex mental processes may be reflected in patterns of body movement. Further, movement may support the learning of concepts. It has been observed that children's learning is often enhanced by the use of rhythm and that many younger children move their bodies before producing words in cognitive assignments. More recently, bodily involvement has been observed in children who are seated at computer terminals and engaged in thinking tasks. These relationships are reinforced by current data which suggest that motor behavior is integrated by electrical oscillations in the brain and that similar oscillations are related to the brain rhythms which underlie information processing.

The associations between brain functions and nonverbal behavior may have particular relevance for special education. For instance, it seems that severe mental retardation is accompanied by deficits in physical movement and that some students requiring remediation in learning have benefited from forms of movement education. In the latter cases, increased body awareness and movement of limbs in space have prompted gains in levels of both cognitive and physical performance. Perhaps movement education can be used at times to supplement skills deficits. However, much more research is required in these areas and present applications should be conducted with the closest of care and attention.

4.6 Teacher Education

Despite the not insignificant number of results relating teacher nonverbal behaviors with effectiveness in the classroom, very little work has been done to transmit this information to future teachers. Some efforts have been made to instruct preservice teachers in discrete elements of nonverbal behavior (such as forward lean, eye gaze, and proximity) but the effects of these interventions have been mixed. Elements of the more substantial nonverbal constellations which underlie "enthusiasm," "rapport," and "warmth" have been difficult to isolate and therefore to use for instructional purposes. However, attempts to develop the teacher's sensitivity to nonverbal behaviors have proved to be slightly more successful. The related problem of whether or not to select teachers according to their degree of nonverbal sensitivity remains essentially unanswered.

In conclusion, the major aspects concerning nonverbal communication in teaching have been considered in this article. One method of specifying the channels of nonverbal communication has been presented, several questions relating nonverbal behavior and classroom practice have been raised, and areas of significant research and development potential have been outlined. One caution is worth emphasizing at this point: most of the work reported here has been conducted in Western societies by Western investigators and so the ability to generalize results to other societies and cultures remains questionable. Hopefully, work in the future will help to overcome this deficiency.

See also: Synthesizing Research Evidence

Bibliography

Burgoon J K, Saine T 1978 *The Unspoken Dialogue: An Introduction to Nonverbal Communication.* Houghton Mifflin, Boston, Massachusetts

Davis M 1972 *Understanding Body Movement: An Annotated Bibliography.* Arno Press, New York

Davis M, Skupien J 1982 *Body Movement and Nonverbal Communication: An Annotated Bibliography, 1971–1981.* Indiana University Press, Bloomington

Ekman P (ed.) 1973 *Darwin and Facial Expression: A Century of Research in Review.* Academic Press, New York

Ellgring H 1981 Nonverbal communication: A review of research in Germany. *Ger. J. Psychol.* 5: 59–84

Key M R 1977 *Nonverbal Communication: A Research Guide and Bibliography.* Scarecrow, Metuchen, New Jersey

Knapp M L 1978 *Nonverbal Communication in Human Interaction*, 2nd edn. Holt, Rinehart and Winston, New York

Mehan H 1979 *Learning Lessons: Social Organization in the Classroom.* Harvard University Press, Cambridge, Massachusetts

Morris D 1977 *Manwatching: A Field Guide to Human Behavior.* Abrams, New York

Scherer K R, Ekman P (eds.) 1982 *Handbook of Methods in Nonverbal Behavior Research.* Cambridge University Press, Cambridge

Smith H A 1979 Nonverbal communication in teaching. *Rev. Educ. Res.* 49: 631–72

Weinstein C S 1979 The physical environment of the school: A review of the research. *Rev. Educ. Res.* 49: 577–610

Wolfgang A (ed.) 1979 *Nonverbal Behavior: Applications and Cross-Cultural Implications.* International Conference on Non-verbal Behaviour, Ontario Institute for Studies in Education, 1976. Academic Press, New York

Wolfgang A (ed.) 1984 *Nonverbal Behavior: Perspectives, Applications, Intercultural Insights.* Hogrefe, Toronto

Woolfolk A E, Brooks D M 1983 Nonverbal communication in teaching. *Rev. Res. Educ.* 10

Cognitive

Implicit Theories

P. H. Taylor

Teaching is both an act and an enterprise. The enterprise of teaching is widely dispersed throughout society. The act(s) of teaching are institutionally bound. They take place in different types of educational establishment—in primary and secondary schools, in colleges and universities, each of which share with one another common roles, rules, and definitions of purpose. Each school or college has, through the organization of teaching, the power to influence the lives and behaviour of their students.

The influence exercised by teachers through the institutional arrangements to which they contribute—either directly by the positive enforcement of organizational rules and regulations, or indirectly by their passive acceptance of the necessity for their enforcement, and by teaching—is nested within an ideological framework which defines both the ends and the justifications of their actions, and links these actions to the social enterprise of teaching.

It is to the examination of teachers' beliefs about the purposes of teaching as well as their beliefs about the institutionally bound acts of teaching that this article is devoted; to what Doyle (1979) terms "the implicit theories of teaching", though set here against a broader canvas. It will be quickly seen that teachers' implicit theories of teaching are not grounded theories (Glaser and Strauss 1967). At best, the evidence will suggest, they possess a prima facie validity and (which is more important) a capacity to sensitize people to the nature and meaning of teaching. It may also be argued, though not here, that though they are inadequate as scientific theories, they are not without interest as hermeneutic ones (McDonald 1981).

1. Teaching as an Enterprise

An important function of teaching as an enterprise is to provide the act(s) of teaching with both an educational meaning and a professional justification, both of which are socially acceptable. The meaning and the justification will possess moral overtones because they denote reason for the intervention "for the better" in the lives of children and young people. The moral character of the meaning and justification, of the ideology of the enterprise of teaching, allows in some degree for the inevitable gap between the rhetoric of schooling, including teaching, and the reality of what is taught and what is learned (Foxwell 1973, Lodge 1975).

Teachers readily accord meaning and purpose to the enterprise of which they are a part, and have this century done so with increasing confidence (Musgrove and Taylor 1969). They develop their beliefs about the purpose and meaning of the enterprise of teaching from those generally valued areas of human endeavour commonly conceded to lead to human betterment; to becoming educated—the development and enhancement of the intellect, of moral awareness, of social insight, of instrumental, and of interpersonal skills. It is generally considered that such human characteristics or qualities are necessary both to the maintenance of a human (and humane) social organization possessing political, economic, technological, legal, and interpersonal subsystems, as well as to the establishment for the individual, of a sense of personal self-esteem.

Waller (1932), in one of the earliest empirical studies of teaching, characterized schools as "museums of virtue" and thus cast teachers in the role of custodians of most that is worthwhile in human endeavour—love of truth, beauty, and justice. In this he was doing no more than confirming those qualities of the enterprise of teaching which mostly determine teachers' beliefs about the purposes that should govern and justify their actions.

Later studies serve to confirm Waller's view. Musgrove and Taylor (1969) in a study of English secondary-school teachers found that teachers stressed moral training: the inculcation of such values and attitudes as honesty, kindness, tolerance, courage, and the like, to a much greater extent than citizenship, social training, education for family life, and social advancement (preparing children to get on in life) though only marginally more than instruction in subjects. They also indicated their view that their beliefs about the purposes of the enterprise of teaching would not be shared by parents whom they believed would most strongly emphasize the training of children to get on in life. In this, teachers were, in fact, wrong.

The idealistic quality of teachers' beliefs surrounding the enterprise of teaching persist. A national study of the value to be placed on schooling by parents, pupils, and teachers showed teachers to hold the view that character qualities and moral attributes should be the salient purposes of schooling, not instrumental and marketable skills (Schools Council 1968).

In a later study of the opinions of primary-school teachers, (Ashton et al. 1975), teachers were asked to weight relatively, two antithetical purposes of primary education; one a societal purpose and one an individual purpose. Each of these purposes has considerable durability in the rhetoric of English primary education. The result, not surprisingly, showed almost three-quarters of the teachers responding were balanced in their weighting of the two views, holding both views to have comparable validity.

A later replication with a much smaller sample (Ashton 1981) showed an overall similarity with the earlier findings with a slight shift among those teachers giving complete weight to one of the two purposes with a bias toward the societal purpose of primary education; that is, toward education as the development of social competence and useful skills, rather than individuality and personal independence.

Such evidence as there is suggests that the system of beliefs that teachers hold about the enterprise of teaching possesses both a moral tone and a broad functional justification (Lortie 1975). As theory, these beliefs serve to dignify and elaborate the teachers' occupational role, giving it worth as well as meaning.

2. Teaching as an Act

The acts of teaching are many. They include the logical acts of teaching—informing, explaining, describing, exemplifying, instancing, showing, and the like—and those quite different acts of controlling, motivating, and evaluating which are managerial in nature and which are essential ingredients of teaching as enacted in the interactions of teacher and taught, made necessary by the institutional context of teaching. There are also those acts involved in the planning of teaching—diagnosing, selecting, and prescribing what is to be taught. Figure 1 sets out details of the parameters of the subsystems of teaching about which teachers hold implicit theories.

3. Planning Teaching

The general character of teachers' implicit theories of planning for teaching, as is evidenced from a number of studies, are hardly in dispute, though as Clark and Yinger (1979) have shown, there remains much detail to be settled, not least how the process of routinization in the implementation of planning works.

The work of Taylor (1970) and Beeson and Gunstone

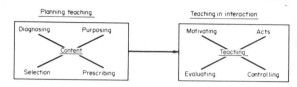

Figure 1
The subsystems of teaching[a]

a Source: Denham C, Lieberman A 1980 *Time to Learn*. State Commission for Teacher Preparation, Sacramento, California

(1975) show that for secondary-school teachers neither the objectives model (Tyler 1949, Bloom 1956, and others) nor the decision theory model (Stufflebeam et al. 1971, Shavelson 1976) represent teachers' implicit theories for the planning of teaching. Zahorik (1975) and McCutcheon (1980) show the same to be true for teachers at the primary-school level. As Taylor's (1970) empirical study suggests, teachers' views of planning do not possess the systematic qualities of planning advocated by educational theorists. Teachers' views are both more holistic and more rule of thumb. As McCutcheon (1980 p. 20) puts it:

Teachers' planning, then, involves a complex, simultaneous juggling of much information about children, subject-matters, school practices, and policies. Teachers' planning does not follow the objectives-first model . . . . Rather, teachers' planning takes into account far more information and follows different paths of thinking and a different order.

The model which Taylor (1970) developed in his study was based on the perceptions of planning courses of study held by secondary-school teachers. This model (Fig. 2) suggests that all the information which needs

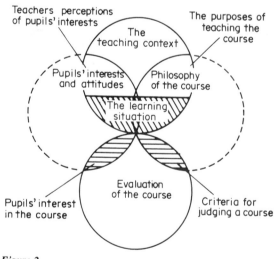

Figure 2
Grounds for the development of a methodology for curriculum planning by teachers

to be taken into account when teaching is planned—students, their interests in and attitudes to learning, and their abilities, the content or subject matter to be taught and understood, the milieu or setting in which teaching is to take place, and the style to be employed by the teacher—is taken into account not sequentially but altogether with the main focus on the learning situation which the teacher has to enact through the processes of teaching.

From this model and the work of others (Good and Brophy 1973, Goodlad and Klein 1970) for example, several characteristics of teachers' implicit theories of planning may be discerned:

(a) they focus on the context, on the arena for teaching;

(b) parts possess multiple meanings which are not necessarily clearly discriminated between by teachers. For instance, student interests may refer at one point to what will interest students (i.e., hold their attention, involve them in learning) and at another to what is in their interest (i.e., what will benefit or be of profit to them). In an analogous way the purpose of teaching, its aims, are perceived by teachers both as a guide to teaching *and* a justification of teaching;

(c) they possess an existential quality; for teachers a plan is a scene in being.

4. Interaction in Teaching

For teachers, the act of teaching needs to be as with the planning of teaching, taken as a whole. Teachers' implicit theories of teaching are set in a different world with different frames of reference from that which has prompted the many psychological studies of teaching, especially those which start from behaviourist assumptions and purport to be part of the search for a science of teaching. The study of science teachers' opinions about effective science teaching is especially illustrative here (Taylor et al. 1970).

A sample of secondary-school science teachers were asked to rate descriptive statements of teaching for the degree to which they considered they were important elements in effective teaching.

The statements were culled from the literature on science teaching and from recorded discussions with science teachers. The rated statements were factored producing eight descriptions or styles of effective science teaching. Each style of effective science teaching, as will be seen in the example below, brings into view teacher, student, the subject matter of science, and the ambience of the setting of enactment together as a whole; each style a balanced correlated composite of the commonplace of teaching—teacher, student, content, and milieu.

For example, in the style described as "face-to-face science teaching" teacher and students are to be seen to have an easy, warm, and direct relationship, with the main vehicle of content being teacher talk. The ambience of the context of teaching and learning is bookish and academic rather than practical and experimental; there is an absence of scientific materials and equipment, though the ideas of science are being carefully explored with the teacher demonstrating a sound knowledge of the ways in which the young come to an understanding of scientific concepts. The general impression which this style of science teaching gives is of considerate and concerned teaching through which students will learn about the nature of science, though little of its methods. Students will enjoy such teaching, feeling involved as persons, realize that the teacher understands their difficulties in learning science, be willing to continue to participate in his or her teaching having in fact learned something about science, not as an academic mystery, but as related concrete ideas about the natural world accessible to their intellects. An important quality of the students' understanding of science is that they will appreciate the essentially refutable and open-ended nature of scientific knowledge.

In contrast, the style described as "laboratory assistant science teaching" teaches science as a rule-governed, closed system of facts which students are to learn from experiments performed by them following a set of instructions and writing up the results of the experiments after a given pattern—aim of the experiment, description of the apparatus used, results observed, and conclusions arrived at. The medium of teaching (and learning) is part teacher's talk, mainly concerned with the teacher giving instructions, and part observation and recording by the students. Relationships between teacher and students in this style of science teaching are impersonal; the teacher's concern is more with the nature of science, especially the processes through which scientific knowledge is acquired, than with the difficulties the young may have in understanding scientific concepts. Some students will enjoy this style of science teaching. Its routines will given them security and the intellectual demand to acquire, rather than understand, the facts of science and will be well-within their competence. Other students will find this style arid, dulling their interest in science, though they will not refuse to participate in the teaching if only because participating in experiments brings with it an apparent degree of personal enhancement.

Each of the eight perceived styles of science teaching, of which the above are but examples, represents an implicit theory of teaching which may be held by teachers to account for effectiveness in teaching science. Other theoretical positions are entirely possible. Whatever qualities they incorporate will account for a particular disposition toward science teaching as well as toward students. Figure 3 sets out the major parameters, and locates the two styles discussed above.

Others have focused attention on alternative variables in teaching: on style of control and for gaining coop-

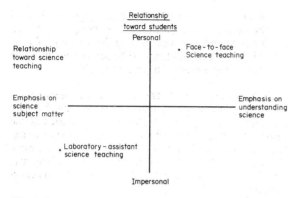

Figure 3
Styles of effective science teaching

Figure 4
Teachers' perceived influences on teaching

eration, on style of decision making in the classroom, and on styles of characterizing the content of teaching. Each conception of style offers a vantage point from which to view the qualities of teachers' implicit theories of teaching and so become sensitive to the complexities of the teacher's art.

5. The Educational Institution and Teachers' Implicit Theories

Teaching, as was pointed out earlier, takes place both as an enterprise and an act in the institution of the school and college and it is finally to those aspects of teachers' implicit theories of teaching which take account of the larger institutional setting than the classroom or laboratory that the discussion now turns through studies of those variables which are seen by teachers to influence or constrain their teaching.

Empirical studies of teachers' perceptions of factors which influence their teaching and of those which set limits to their best efforts (constraints) are relatively recent but the existence of influences and constraints on teachers have long been presaged in the literature.

6. Perceived Influences on Teaching

In the studies of primary-school teachers' perceptions of influences on what separately was taught in the school and what they taught in their classrooms [or in the case of studies at the secondary level, influences on the content (curriculum) of a course and on the teacher's teaching of it], a remarkable consistency of general findings emerges. Figure 4 provides an updated model derived from a study of a Mid-Western elementary-school system in the United States which will stand as a surrogate model for all the enquiries undertaken (Taylor et al. 1974, Taylor, Reid and Holley 1974, McConnellogue 1975, Taylor 1975, Oram 1976).

Five interlocking, correlated subsystems of influence are evident in the perceptions of the teachers:

(a) an administrative–bureaucratic, allocative subsystem concerned with the fiscal and managerial support for the enterprise of teaching;

(b) a school-based, client-focused political subsystem concerned with educational issues which become matters of conflict and controversy. Sex education and corporal punishment have in recent years been such issues as have the voucher system and bussing;

(c) a classroom-based, collegial, professional, and normative subsystem concerned with the ways in which teachers, ought to conduct themselves in relation to the principal, their colleagues, and their students;

(d) an expert: advisory (of expertise) subsystem concerned with the development of professional knowledge and understanding, and its communication;

(e) an ideological: values subsystem concerned with defining and redefining the meanings that shall adhere to being educated in a particular society.

Influences arising from these five loci of influence are seen by teachers to affect both the enterprise of teaching and teaching itself. The force of their influence varies, though collegial, professional, and normative influences are consistently of powerful effect on the teachers' work setting. Currently, with the economic recession, administrative–bureaucratic, allocative influences are having a marked effect.

7. Perceived Constraints on Teaching

Influences "push" teachers and teaching in particular directions. They form and mould what teachers do and the reasons they give for acting as they do. Constraints, on the other hand, inhibit and circumscribe the extent to which, despite their best efforts, teachers can achieve the goals which they set themselves. Seen through the eyes of teachers constraints arise from:

(a) Beyond the boundaries of the school (or college), in the students' home environment, in the expectations held of what teachers should achieve held by parents and public, and in their own professional preparation and training.

(b) Within the school (or college), in the functioning of the staff; the task group whose relationship as professionals has the job of making the institution

work; in the know-how or technology of teaching—the methods and materials of teaching available to them as well as from their understanding of how children learn; and from the beliefs or theory which gives direction and purpose to teaching.

Each of these major centres or loci of constraints—task group, technology, and "theory"—may be seen modelled in relationship within the boundaries of the institution in Fig. 5. Much in the model remains tentative, though a commonsense appreciation of teachers' work settings suggests that the model goes a long way toward representing the reality which teachers experience.

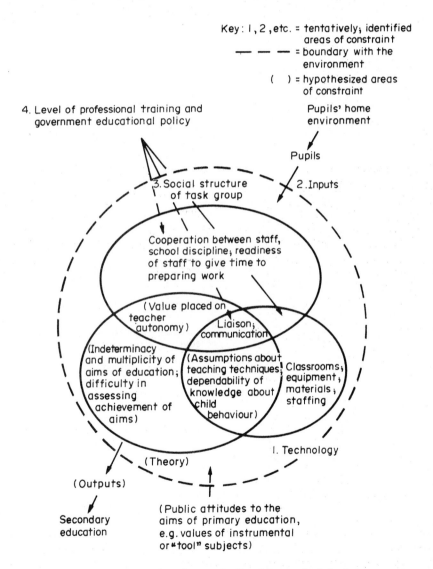

Key: 1, 2, etc. = tentatively identified areas of constraint
— — — = boundary with the environment
( ) = hypothesized areas of constraint

4. Level of professional training and government educational policy

Pupils' home environment

Pupils

3. Social structure of task group

2. Inputs

Cooperation between staff, school discipline; readiness of staff to give time to preparing work

(Value placed on teacher autonomy)

Liaison; communication

(Indeterminacy and multiplicity of aims of education; difficulty in assessing achievement of aims)

(Assumptions about teaching techniques; dependability of knowledge about child behaviour)

Classrooms; equipment; materials; staffing

1. Technology

(Theory)

(Outputs)

Secondary education

(Public attitudes to the aims of primary education, e.g. values of instrumental or "tool" subjects)

Figure 5
Tentative schema of sources of constraint on the primary school's achievement of aims[a]

a Source: Taylor et al. 1974 *Purpose, Power and Constraint in the Primary School Curriculum.* Macmillan, London, p. 36

8. Concluding Summary

Teachers' implicit theories of teaching represent the attempts of those caught up in the enterprise and acts of teaching to confer meaning on their experience and their efforts. That they do not account for all the facts of the world to which they relate should not be surprising. No theories do, and perhaps ever can. But there is much yet to be done before the theories which teachers use to make an ordered world out of their beliefs is exhausted. Much still needs to be known about how teachers account for its mechanisms and make it rational in their terms. Of special importance is a need to understand what teachers believe is important for effective learning. As Buchmann (1981) has pointed out, the commonsense beliefs which teachers cherish about how to affect learning may well be wrong, though Richards (1975) showed that teachers' beliefs about discovery learning were complex and many sided. More also needs to be known about how teachers regard content and choice of content. Swille et al. (1979) offer an interesting hypothetical model. Empirical data may suggest others and Clark's (1980) model for research on teacher thinking promises a way forward.

But it is not only out of beliefs about the purposes of the enterprise to which they contribute, the acts of teaching in which they daily engage, or the influences and constraints to which they are subjected that teachers develop embedded theories. It is also out of beliefs about themselves, beliefs about how they learn to be more effective, and what it is that renders constant increments of improvements in their performance. It is here that an examination of the implicit theories of teachers could promise most in professional development.

See also: Definitions of Teaching; Planning; Teachers' Judgments

Bibliography

Ashton P 1981 Primary teachers' aims 1969–77 In: Simon B, Willocks J (eds.) 1981 *Research and Practice in the Primary Classroom.* Routledge and Kegan Paul, London
Ashton P, Kneen P, Davies F, Holley B J 1975 *The Aims of Primary Education: A Study in Teachers' Opinions.* Macmillan Educational, London
Beeson G W, Gunstone R F 1975 The teachers' role in curriculum decision. *Aust. Sci. Teach. J.* 21: 5–19
Bloom B S et al. (eds.) 1956 *Taxonomy of Educational Objectives, Handbook 1: Cognitive Domain.* Longman, London
Buchmann M 1981 Can traditional lore guide right choice in teaching. *J. Curric. Stud.* 13: 399–48
Clark C M 1980 Choice of model for research on teacher thinking. *J. Curric. Stud.* 12: 41–48
Clark C M, Yinger R J 1979 Teachers' thinking. In: Peterson P L, Walberg H J (eds.) 1979 *Research on Teaching: Concepts, Findings and Implications.* McCutchan, Berkeley, California
Doyle W 1979 Making managerial decisions in the classroom. In: Duke D L (ed.) 1979 *Classroom Management.* 78th Yearbook, National Society for the Study of Education. University of Chicago Press, Chicago, Illinois
Foxwell K J 1973 A comparative analysis of art and craft teaching in four middle schools. Unpublished Diploma of Education dissertation
Good T L, Brophy J E 1973 *Looking in Classrooms.* Harper and Row, New York
Goodlad J I, Klein F 1970 *Behind the Classroom Door.* Jones, Worthington, Ohio
Glaser B G, Strauss A L 1967 *The Discovery of Grounded Theory: Strategies for Qualitative Research.* Weidenfeld and Nicolson, London
Lodge P A 1975 What is taught in English lessons. Unpublished M.Ed. dissertation, University of Birmingham
Lortie D C 1975 *Schoolteacher: A Sociological Study.* Chicago University Press, Chicago, Illinois
McConnellogue P T 1975 Tradition and change in the primary school curriculum in Northern Ireland. In: Taylor P H (ed.) 1975 *Aims, Influence, and Change in the Primary School Curriculum.* NFER–Nelson, Windsor
McCutcheon G 1980 How do elementary teachers plan? The nature of planning and influences on it. *Elem. Sch. J.* 81: 4–23
McDonald J B 1981 Theory, practice and the hermeneutic circle. *J. Curr. Theory* 3: 130–38
Musgrove F, Taylor P H 1969 *Society and the Teacher's Role.* Routledge and Kegan Paul, London
Oram R 1976 Curriculum development in first-cycle education. Some implications of a study of teacher opinion in a developing country. *J. Curric. Stud.* 8: 171–81
Richards C 1975 Primary school teachers' perceptions of discovery learning. In: Taylor P H (ed.) 1975 *Aims, Influence and Change in the Primary School Curriculum.* NFER–Nelson, Windsor
Schools Council 1968 *Enquiry 1: Young School Leavers.* Series No. 88-5367. Her Majesty's Stationery Office, London
Shavelson R J 1976 Teachers' decision-making. In: Gage N L (ed.) 1976 *The Psychology of Teaching Methods.* 75th Yearbook of the National Society for the Study of Education, Part 1. Chicago University Press, Chicago, Illinois
Stufflebeam D L et al. 1971 *Educational Evaluation and Decision-making.* Peacock, Itasca, Illinois
Swille J, Porter A, Gant M 1979 Factors influencing teachers' decisions of what to teach: Sociological perpsectives. In: Blalock H M (ed.) 1980 *Sociological Theory and Research: A Critical Appraisal.* Annual American Sociological Association meeting, Boston, Massachusetts, 1979. Free Press, New York
Taylor P H 1970 *How Teachers Plan Their Courses: Studies in Curriculum Planning.* NFER–Nelson, Windsor
Taylor P H 1975 A study of the curricular influences in a mid-Western elementary school system. In: Taylor P H (ed.) 1975 *Aims, Influence and Change in the Primary School Curriculum.* NFER–Nelson, Windsor
Taylor P H, Christie T, Platts C V 1970 An exploratory study of science teachers' perceptions of effective teaching. *Educ. Rev.* 23: 19–32
Taylor P H, Reid W A, Holley B J 1974 *The English Sixth Form: A Case Study in Curriculum Research.* Routledge and Kegan Paul, London
Taylor P H, Reid W A, Holley B J, Exon G 1974 *Purpose, Power and Constraint in the Primary School Curriculum.* Macmillan Educational, London
Tyler R N 1949 *Basic Principles of Curriculum and Instruction* Chicago University Press, Chicago, Illinois
Waller W 1932 *The Sociology of Teaching.* Wiley, New York
Zahorik J A 1975 Teachers planning models. *Educ. Leadership* 3: 134–39

Planning

R. J. Shavelson

Teachers' planning refers to that aspect of teaching where teachers formulate a course of action for carrying out instruction over a school year, a semester, a month, a day, or a lesson. Planning is one important component of teaching that is typically carried out without the presence of students.

The importance of planning cannot be overestimated. Decisions made by teachers while planning instruction have a profound influence on their classroom behavior and on the nature and outcomes of the education children receive. Teachers' instructional plans serve as "scripts" for carrying out interactive teaching. Scripts exert such a strong influence on teachers that they tend not to deviate from them once they have begun teaching (see *Interactive Decision Making*). By knowing a teacher's script for a particular lesson, much of the teacher's behavior in the classroom can be predicted. Stern and Shavelson (1981) found this to be true of reading instruction and Smith and Sendelbach (1979) found this to be true of science instruction using ethnographic studies of single classrooms.

Teachers' planning decisions influence the content, materials, social climate, and activities of instruction. For example, decisions about curriculum adoptions, or at least selections from and modifications to adopted curriculum, affect the process of teaching as well as what children learn. Also decisions about grouping students for reading have been shown to have such a profound effect that children in the highest reading group may be paced 13 times as fast as children in the lowest reading group with reading test scores reflecting this difference in pacing (Shavelson and Borko 1979).

1. Teachers' Instructional Plans

Most teachers are trained to plan instruction by: (a) specifying (behavioral) objectives, (b) specifying students' entry behavior (knowledge and skills), (c) selecting and sequencing learning activities so as to move students from entry behavior to objectives, and (d) evaluating the outcomes of instruction in order to improve planning. While this prescriptive model of planning may be one of the most consistently taught features of the curriculum of teacher education programs, the model is consistently not used by teachers in planning instruction. Obviously there is a mismatch between the prescriptive planning model and the demands of classroom instruction. This mismatch arises because teachers must balance multiple educational goals (e.g., content instruction, behavior control, social interaction), must take into account students' goals (peer relations, learning), and must maintain the flow of activity during a lesson or face behavioral management problems. Activities, then, and not the prescriptive model are the focus of teacher planning.

As Taylor (1970) pointed out, most planning appears unsystematic and general in nature. Teachers appear uncertain as to what the planning process requires. To date, research on teacher planning has not led to the formulation of a model of teachers' planning; rather, it has identified components that such a model must incorporate to be descriptive and to be realistically prescriptive.

The instructional activity is the basic unit of planning and action in the classroom. The basic, structural unit of planning is termed the "task." A task is comprised of several elements which have individually been identified in the planning literature. One element is content, the subject matter to be taught. Once a curriculum has been selected, teachers accept the textbook as the major, usually only, source of content. A second element of a task is materials, those things that children can observe and/or manipulate. A third element of a task is activity, the things the teacher and students will be doing during the lesson. The concept of activity includes sequencing, pacing, and timing the instructional content and materials. A fourth element is goals, the teacher's general aim for a task, usually learning, affect, or both. Goals are not the same as behavioral objectives; they are much more general and vague, but functional. A fifth element is students, especially their abilities, needs, and interests. The last element is social–cultural context of instruction. This refers to the class as a whole and its sense of "groupness" or a specially created community, as well as teachers' groupings of students for instruction.

The conception of teachers' planning presented here is one in which instructional tasks are created by the teacher. In creating tasks, it is known that teachers juggle some or all of the elements described above. In addition, it is also known that any conception of planning must include a time dimension. One aspect of the time dimension is the hierarchical organization of planning; Yinger (1977 p. 172) identified five levels:

(a) Long range yearly—basic ideas for social studies, science—some for math and reading—basic structure of what will be done but not specific time;

(b) Term—planning on a term basis for social studies, science, and for movies;

(c) Monthly—deciding on basic units for social studies, science, and math. I decide on what I need librarian to get or what movies I need;

(d) Weekly—use teacher's plan book—specific units and time element added—more detailed;

(e) Daily—put schedule on board, getting actual materials out.

A second aspect of the time dimension is that planning decisions made early in the academic year exert a profound influence on teachers' planning for the remainder of the year. According to Joyce (1978–79 p. 75):

> Most of the important preactive decisions by teachers are long-term in their influence as opposed to the influence of lesson by lesson planning. Relatively early in the year, most teachers set up a series of conditions which were to be powerfully influential on the possibilities of decision making thereafter. Lesson planning, to the extent that it goes on consciously, involves the selection and handling of materials and activities within the framework that has been set up by the long-term decisions.

2. Studies of Teacher Planning

Researchers studying teacher planning have used a variety of methods including questionnaires/interviews, ethnography, simulations, and "think aloud" protocols. Not surprisingly, different methods reveal different aspects of the planning process. Nevertheless, for the most part, the findings, as summarized above, have been consistent or complementary. Namely, teachers focus on tasks and embedded in these tasks are teachers' concerns about content, activities, students, goals, and the like.

The results of research on teacher planning are summarized in Table 1. Most of the research has found that teachers are concerned with subject matter in planning instruction. Their concern, however, is less with the structure of the subject matter and more with the selection of content for the purpose of building tasks.

Research has also found that teachers consider information about students, especially student ability, when planning instruction. Both Morine-Dershimer (1978–

Table 1
Studies of teacher planning[a]

Study	Method of investigation	Content focus: Subject matter and materials	Student focus	Activities focus	Specifying goals or objectives during planning unimportant or secondary	Teachers have long-term preactive plans
Borko (1978)	Laboratory	X	X		Contradictory findings	X
Carnahan (1979)	Literature review	X	X			
Clark and Elmore (1979)	Classroom					X
Clark, Wildfong and Yinger (1978)	Laboratory	X	X			
Clark and Yinger (1979)	Laboratory		X	X		X
Cooper et al. (1979)	Literature review	X	X	X		
Joyce (1978–79)	Theoretical			X		X
Mintz (1979)	Laboratory	X	X	X	X	X
Morine (1976)	Classroom/ laboratory	X	X	X	X	X
Morine-Dershimer (1978–79)	Classroom/ laboratory	X	X	X		
Peterson et al. (1978)	Laboratory	X	X	X	X	
Peterson and Clark (1978)	Laboratory					
Russo (1978)	Laboratory	X	X		Contradictory findings	
Shavelson et al. (1977)	Laboratory	X	X			
Smith and Sendelbach (1979)	Classroom				X	X
Stern and Shavelson (1981)	Classroom	X	X	X	Contradictory findings	X
Taylor (1970)	Classroom	X	X		X	
Yinger (1977)	Ethnography	X		X	X	X
Zahorik (1975)	Laboratory	X		X	X	

a A blank space indicates the topic of the column was not a focus of the study

79) and Mintz (1979) pointed out that teachers' concerns about students in their planning were greatest early in the year when teachers were "getting to know" their students. Once teachers had reached a judgment about their students, less attention (i.e., conscious concern) was given to students in verbal reports. In contrast, Peterson et al. (1978) reported that verbal protocols showed little mention of students during planning. However, these contradictory findings may be an artifact of the methods used. First, in the Peterson et al. study, students (unknown previously by the teacher) were randomly assigned to teachers. These teachers, then did not have information about their students. Second, Morine-Dershimer (1978–79) has pointed out that "while the . . . teachers rarely mentioned pupil ability, specific objective, teaching strategy, or seating arrangement in response to the general question (to state their lesson plans), their ready responses to the probes indicated that the mental plans or images of the lesson . . . did include such aspects of instruction" (p. 85).

A central focus of teachers is the activity developed in the lesson plan (see Table 1). Activity refers to the allocation of time, the sequencing, and the timing (or pacing or flow) of content and materials during the lesson. While most research has found the activity to be of central importance in plans, little is known about how activities are constructed or what routines or "scripts" teachers bring to the planning process which are filled out monthly, weekly, and daily to provide the routine for interactive teaching. Yinger's (1977) study provides some insight into activity planning. The teacher he studied approached the activity as a three-stage problem-solving task including: (a) problem finding where content, goals, knowledge, and experience combined to yield an initial conception of the activity worthy of future consideration; (b) problem formulation and solution involving progressive elaboration of the activity; and (c) activity implementation emphasizing "evaluation and routinization to the teacher's repertoire of knowledge and experience, which in turn play a major role in future planning deliberations" (Clark and Yinger 1979 p. 238). Research, having established the task as a central focus in planning, needs to move on to describing the variety of routines or scripts teachers have for planning activities and under what conditions they are used.

Most naturalistic research reports that objectives do not play a major role in the planning process while laboratory simulation studies report that teachers do take objectives/goals into consideration. This conflicting finding might be resolved on methodological grounds. Apparently teachers' verbal reports and lesson plans do not emphasize objectives. However, in laboratory simulations asking teachers to make decisions about goals or objectives, teachers do so and report that doing so is consistent with their classroom planning. While objectives are not part of their verbal reports about lesson plans, they are part of the teachers' mental image or plan. Probing, done either directly or indirectly as in simulations or interviews, is apparently needed to find this out.

Finally, several studies have shown that teachers, at the beginning of the academic year, set forth plans and make decisions that guide subsequent planning over the remainder of the year. This means that, unless researchers examine planning at the beginning of the year, they are liable to miss some aspects of planning. They are also liable to conclude that teachers do not, for example, consider student characteristics or objectives when, during most of the year, such information is part of the teacher's planning script or routine. Moreover, these long-term plans have a profound influence on classroom teaching. "In effect, the selection of materials and the subsequent activity flow establishes the 'problem frame'—the boundaries within which decision making will be carried on" (Joyce 1978–79 p. 75).

There are a few findings, not reported in Table 1, that deserve attention. Several studies have found that management of students is a primary concern in planning, especially in grouping students. And Zahorik (1970) observed that teachers who planned thoroughly were less sensitive to their students (i.e., encouraged student ideas and discussion less). Peterson et al. (1978a, 1978b) found that teachers who were prolific planners had students with lower attitude scores than the students of teachers who did not plan extensively. These last two studies suggest planning may be counterproductive if teachers become single-minded and do not adapt their lesson to student needs.

See also: Information Processing Models; Teachers' Judgments; Implicit Theories

Bibliography

Borko H 1978 An examination of some factors contributing to teachers preinstructional classroom organization and management decisions. Paper presented to the annual meeting of the American Educational Research Association, Toronto, Ontario

Carnahan R S 1979 Planning. In: Romberg T A, Small M, Carnahan R S (eds.) 1979 *Research on Teaching from a Curricular Perspective.* Conceptual Paper No. 6, Wisconsin Research and Development Center for Individualized Schooling, Madison, Wisconsin

Clark C, Elmore J L 1979 *Teacher Planning in the First Weeks of School.* Research Series No. 55, Institute of Research on Teaching, Michigan State University, East Lansing, Michigan

Clark C, Wildfong S, Yinger R 1978 *Identifying Cues for Use in Studies of Teacher Judgment.* Research Series No. 23, Institute for Research on Teaching, Michigan State University, East Lansing, Michigan

Clark C M, Yinger R J 1979 Teachers' thinking. In: Peterson P L, Walberg H J (eds.) 1979 *Research on Teaching: Concepts, Findings and Implications.* McCutchan, Berkeley, California

Cooper H M, Burger J M, Seymour G E 1979 Classroom context and student ability as influences on teacher perceptions of classroom control. *Am. Educ. Res. J.* 16: 189–96

Joyce B R 1978–79 Toward a theory of information processing in teaching. *Educ. Res. Q.* 3: 66–77

Mintz S L 1979 *Teacher Planning: A Simulation Study.* Paper presented at the annual meeting of the American Educational Research Association, San Francisco, California

Morine G 1976 *A Study of Teacher Planning.* Beginning Teacher Evaluation Study, Far West Laboratory, San Francisco, California

Morine-Dershimer G 1978–79 Planning in classroom reality: An in-depth look. *Educ. Res. Q.* 3: 83–99

Peterson P L, Marx R W, Clark C M 1978a *Teacher Planning, Teacher Behavior, and Student Achievement.* School of Education, University of Wisconsin, Madison, Wisconsin

Peterson P L, Marx R W, Clark C M 1978b Teacher planning, teacher behavior, and student achievement. *Amer. Educ. Res. J.* 15: 417–32

Russo N A 1978 Capturing teachers' decision policies: An investigation of strategies for teaching reading and mathematics. Paper presented to the annual meeting of the American Educational Research Association, Toronto, Ontario

Shavelson R J, Borko H 1979 Research on teachers' decisions in planning instruction. *Educ. Hor.* 57: 183–89

Shavelson R J, Stern P 1981 Research on teachers' pedagogical thoughts, judgments, decisions, and behavior. *Rev. Educ. Res.* 51: 455–98

Smith E L, Sendelbach N B 1979 *Teacher Intentions for Science Instruction and Their Antecedents in Program Materials.* Paper presented to the annual meeting of the American Educational Research Association, San Francisco, California

Stern P R, Shavelson R J 1981 The relationship between teachers grouping decisions and instructional behaviors: An ethnographic study of reading instruction. Paper presented to the annual meeting of the American Educational Research Association, Los Angeles, California

Taylor P H 1970 *How Teachers Plan Their Courses.* National Foundation for Educational Research, Slough

Yinger R J 1977 A study of teacher planning: Description and theory development using ethnographic and information processing methods (Doctoral dissertation, Michigan State University) *Dissertation Abstracts International* 1978 38: 207A–208A (University Microfilms No. 7810138)

Zahorik J A 1970 The effect of planning on teaching. *Elem. School J.* 3: 143–51

Zahorik J A 1975 Teachers' planning models. *Educ. Leadership.* 33: 134–39

Teachers' Judgments

R. J. Shavelson

Judgment refers to the process of evaluating or categorizing a person or an object. Often the process of judgment is called classification, selection, or estimation. This process is not simply the application of a rule; judgment goes beyond the available information, adding information as the process progresses.

Teachers classify students. Teachers, for example, classify students according to ability. This classification can be seen in the membership of different reading groups, teams, and so on. Teachers select students for referrals to special education, to tasks such as taking attendance, reading an essay, and the like. And teachers estimate students' ability, class participation, independence, self-concept, and so on.

Judgment, then, permeates teaching. It is an important process that, until recently, has been given little systematic attention by researchers on teaching, and even less attention by teacher educators.

1. Conceptualizations of Teachers' Judgments

Perhaps one of the first attempts to conceptualize the judgmental processes used by teachers was reported by Varner in 1923. Actually Varner was studying the accuracy of teachers' ratings of students' intelligence because, in the absence of measurements of traits other than intelligence, teachers' ratings of these traits would have to be used. In the case of intelligence, a criterion—

the IQ test—existed. Teachers' rating of students' intelligence could be compared with this criterion. From this comparison, Varner reasoned, a generalization could be drawn about the accuracy of teachers' rating of other traits.

Varner (1922, 1923) assumed that teachers' ratings (i.e., estimates of students' intelligence, hence judgments) were inaccurate. He identified five factors that contributed to this inaccuracy and, by doing so, developed a conceptualization of the judgmental process not unlike some aspects of present-day conceptualizations.

One factor influencing teachers' judgments was that teachers tended to be influenced by traits other than intelligence in rating intelligence (e.g., industry, personality, appearance). This factor, then, is akin to a halo effect in the judgmental process (see heuristics below).

A second factor was that some teachers failed to take students' ages into account when rating their intelligence. Varner presented evidence that, as expected, teacher ratings correlated more highly with an intelligence quotient than with mental-age scores. In other words, teachers failed to consider available information which could increase the accuracy of their ratings.

Third, the accuracy of teachers' ratings was lower for younger children than for older children. For example, Varner (1922) found that teachers' classifications of children into the highest and lowest 20th percentiles more closely approximated a classification based on intelligence test scores for 13-year-old students (42 percent correctly classified in the highest group; 63 percent correctly classified in the lowest group), than for second grade students (22 percent and 53 percent, respectively). This finding is consistent with current psychometric data; measurements on very young children are less reliable than measurements on older children due, in part, to differences in rates of intellectual, emotional, and experiential growth.

A fourth factor was the inability of teachers to compare their pupils with pupils in general of corresponding grade levels. Put in more modern terms, teachers' relative judgments (ordering of students within their classes) were more accurate than their absolute judgments on their students' IQ scores. This finding is consistent with psychometric theory and empirical findings that errors of measurement associated with absolute judgments are greater than or equal to errors associated with relative judgments (e.g., Shavelson and Webb 1981).

The fifth factor was the teachers' tendency to rate students too high. Teachers tended not to want to rate children too low. This is consistent with recent findings of leniency in, for example, grading.

Varner (1923) conducted a series of studies which provided a test of this conceptualization of teacher judgment. He constructed detailed instructions and a rating form which addressed each factor. He demonstrated, under a variety of conditions, that teachers' ratings using his rating instrument were more accurate than ratings made without it. For example, in one study, correlations of teachers' ratings of IQ without the instrument with IQ test scores ranged from 0.31 to 0.71 with a median of 0.58, while these ratings with the instrument ranged from 0.63 to 0.70 with a median of 0.64. Correlations with mental-age (MA) scores of ratings of MA without the instrument ranged from 0.23 to 0.66 (median = 0.42) while with the instrument, the correlations ranged from 0.39 to 0.81 (median = 0.64).

About 50 years later, Shavelson (1976, see also Shulman and Elstein 1975) developed a model of teachers' judgments and pedagogical decisions as a heuristic for organizing and conducting research on teaching. The model suggested a set of questions and conjectures about what information teachers use in making pedagogical judgments, how this information is integrated to reach judgments, and how institutional constraints and individual differences between teachers affect these judgments (see Fig. 1).

The model assumes that teaching is a process by which teachers make reasonable judgments and decisions with the intent of optimizing student outcomes (Shavelson 1976). While teachers' judgments and decision making do not always match this description, it seems to apply to many goal-oriented teaching situations. For example, in recalling their thoughts while viewing a videotape of their teaching:

Teachers were most affected by their concern for the pupil and based many of their decisions on what they surmised

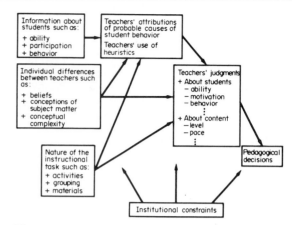

Figure 1
Some factors contributing to teachers' pedagogical judgments and decisions

was happening with the individual student . . . . Content accounted for the bulk of the remaining concerns voiced. Teachers apparently focused much of their attention on what was occurring during the lesson, i.e., what the students were hearing, saying, doing, and feeling. (McNair 1978–79 p. 32)

Teachers are seen as active agents with many instructional techniques at their disposal to help students reach some goal. In order to choose from this repertoire, they must integrate a large amount of information about students from a variety of sources. And this information must somehow be combined with their own beliefs and goals, the nature of the instructional task, the constraints of the situation, and so on, in order to reach a judgment.

More specifically, the model (Fig. 1) identified some important factors which may affect teachers' judgments. Teachers have available a large amount of information about their students. Teachers usually seek information about their students' general ability or achievement, class participation, self-concept, social competence, independence, classroom behavior and work habits. This information comes from many sources such as their own, informal observations, anecdotal reports of other teachers, standardized test scores and school records. In order to handle the information overload, teachers integrate this information into judgments about the student's cognitive, affective, and behavioral states. These judgments, if relevant, are used in making pedagogical decisions.

The attributions and heuristics section of Fig. 1 posits that information is selected and integrated by teachers to reach a judgment, in part, on the basis of a few heuristics and their attributions for the causes of events. Teachers' attributions for the causes of achievement may serve as the basis for teachers' judgments about students, such as student ability, effort, and classroom behavior. Thus, the literature on attribution theory in general and achievement attribution in particular is pertinent; it has been reviewed by Kelley and Michela (1980) and Weiner (1977) and so will not be reviewed here.

Because they cannot handle, simultaneously, large amounts of information, people use heuristics for selecting information (salience and vividness heuristic), judging the frequency or probability of an event (availability), classifying persons and objects (representativeness), and revising their initial judgments (adjustment and anchoring). While these heuristics lead to accurate judgments in many situations, they may also lead to predictable errors (Nisbett and Ross 1980). The representativeness heuristic, for example, states that people decide whether or not some person or object belongs to a particular category by judging the similarity between the attributes of the person or object and the attributes of the category (Tversky and Kahneman 1974). For example, when a description of a student matches the stereotype of a slow learner, even if the description is unreliable, incomplete, or outdated, people often predict with high certainty that the student is a slow learner. Dusek (1975) and Smith and Lugenbuhl (1976) have shown that, in laboratory studies, teacher–student interaction is influenced by unreliable information about the student.

The anchoring heuristic states that

> people make estimates about events and other people by starting from an initial value that is adjusted to yield a final answer. The initial value, or starting point, may be suggested by the formulation of the problem, or it may be the result of a partial computation. In either case, adjustments are typically insufficient. That is, different starting points yield different estimates, which are biased toward the initial values. (Tversky and Kahneman 1974 p. 1128)

For example, subjects were asked to estimate percentages of African countries in the United Nations. They were given an initial percentage determined at random and asked to estimate the actual percentage. Groups of subjects beginning at either 10 percent or 65 percent estimated actual percentages of 25 and 45, respectively. Shavelson et al. (1977) suggested that this heuristic might be one mechanism underlying the teacher expectancy phenomenon in that a teacher's initial expectation may serve as an anchor for a subsequent estimate of the student's ability. In a number of studies reviewed by Dusek (1975), for example, initial but not necessarily valid information about students influenced ("anchored") the way in which tutors taught students. Brophy and Good (1970) found that teachers' estimates of student ability influenced teacher–student interaction.

Shavelson et al. (1977), in a laboratory simulation, examined subjects' estimates of a student's ability based on either reliable or unreliable information, and their willingness to revise these estimates on the basis of subsequent information, which was either reliable or unreliable. They reported that:

> . . . the subjects did consider the reliability of the information, adjusting their estimates in the direction predicted

by . . . [a normative] Bayesian model. Furthermore, the anchoring heuristic and research on teacher expectancy suggest that initial estimates are difficult to overcome, even in the face of conflicting information. Nevertheless, the data show that the subjects did revise initial probability estimates, as expected by Bayes' Theorem. (p. 95)

These findings are in contrast to much of the judgment literature on the use of heuristics (e.g., Einhorn and Hogarth 1981, Slovic et al. 1976). There are a number of possible explanations. One is that the research in most of the literature has used undergraduate students making judgments in areas outside their expertise. Experts may not fall prey to these errors. Hence, subjects in the Shavelson et al. study (teachers and students in a graduate school of education), being professionals, may have not fallen prey to errors based on the anchoring heuristic. A second possible explanation is that the laboratory simulation was so highly structured that the subjects could only act rationally. Further research is needed to decide which of these or some other explanation is most plausible.

Attributions refer to the processes by which people integrate information to arrive at causal explanations for events. To make attributions, the perceiver (e.g., teacher) is assumed to know the generality of an actor's (e.g., student's) behavior across contexts (consistency information), across entities (distinctiveness information), and the generality of the reaction across other actors (consensus information). Various patterns of this information give rise to different attributions. Attributions to the actor (student) arise when there is high consistency (Sally always passes this particular mathematics test), low distinctiveness (Sally passes most other mathematics tests), and low consensus (hardly any other student passes this particular mathematics test). Under these conditions teachers would perceive Sally as a good mathematics student. Attributions to the test (stimulus attribution) occur when Sally always passes this test (low distinctiveness), and everyone else passes this test (high consensus). When a perceiver has limited information, the individual will try to find the pattern most consistent with the information available.

Finally, conflict–stress refers to psychoemotional processes. These processes may affect the choice of information teachers use to construct their psychological reality.

By generalization, heuristics, attributions and conflict–stress might be expected to influence teachers' judgments about students, instructional activities, and institutional constraints. Depending on the focus of the research, these judgments may take the form of expectations, hypotheses, or inferences.

2. Research Modeling Teachers' Judgments

Much of the research on teachers' judgments and decision making has used a policy-capturing approach. With this approach, for example, a teacher makes judgments about a number of students based on their observations of the students in their classroom or based on information provided by the researcher. Then the teacher's judgments are predicted on the basis of information available to the teacher (e.g., achievement, work habits, classroom participation, classroom behavior). The result is a statistical model which weights each piece of information in order to maximize prediction of the teacher's actual judgments.

Research in the literature on human judgment has found that people's policies can be represented by an additive model with about three pieces of information in the model. Research on teachers' policies for judging ability, motivation, and the probability that a student will have a behavior problem supports these findings in the more general literature. Laboratory simulations have found that, in judging student ability, teachers primarily use information about student achievement but also may use information about problematic behavior. In judging motivation (effort), teachers rely heavily on information about achievement, problematic behavior, and work habits. And estimates of behavior problems rely on information about classroom behavior and, to a lesser extent, achievement.

Research on human judgments has found that people are generally unaware of the nature of their judgment policies. Hence, they report using more information in more complex ways than is suggested by the statistical model of their policies (e.g., Shulman and Elstein 1975, Slovic et al. 1976). Studies of teachers' policies parallel these findings. For example, Clark and Yinger (1979) reported that teachers were unaware of their judgment policies.

2.1 Accuracy of Teachers' Judgments of Students' Intelligence

Research on the accuracy of teachers' judgments of their students' intelligence typically has correlated intelligence-test scores with teachers' ratings or rankings of their students. This research shows that teachers are, in general, reasonably accurate in spite of what might be asserted by critics. In eight studies reported before 1930, the median correlation was 0.54 with a range from 0.31 to 0.70. In six studies reported since 1930, the median correlation was 0.54 with a range from 0.42 to 0.81.

How high should this correlation be? Critics might consider a correlation of 0.54 between teachers' judgments and intelligence-test scores too low. In contrast, some researchers consider this degree of accuracy credible. In making a decision, the following should be considered. First, most "strong" validity coefficients (correlations between predictors such as teachers' judgments and criterion scores such as intelligence test scores) are, in magnitude, 0.50. It is unusual for validity coefficients to rise above 0.60. Second, teachers' implicit definitions of intelligence do not correspond to the definition that guides intelligence-test construction, something Varner recognized in 1923. Hence, teachers' ratings are not measuring exactly the same trait as

are intelligence tests. This fact will tend to reduce the correlations.

Coverage of this topic would be incomplete without noting the large variability between the accuracy of different teachers' judgments of their students' intelligence. Accuracy, as measured by correlations, generally ranges from lows in the 0.20s to highs in the 0.80s. Few studies have examined what accounts for this variability; Varner's (1923) is a notable exception.

2.2 Accuracy of Teachers' Judgments of Students' Achievement

Research on the accuracy of teachers' judgments of their students' achievement typically has correlated teachers' ratings or grades assigned to students with achievement-test scores. This research shows that teachers are reasonably accurate in making this judgment. The median correlation from over 15 studies was 0.71 with a range from 0.33 to 0.96.

2.3 Judgments and Diagnoses Regarding Reading

Byers and Evans (1980) studied the accuracy of teachers' judgments of students' reading interests. Teachers judged their students' reading preferences; students' actual reading choices served as the criterion measure. They found that students' reading interests fluctuated widely over grade level and gender, and that teachers, on average, inaccurately predicted students' reading preferences (overall range of accuracy was −0.23 to 0.69 with a mean of 0.23), because they lacked knowledge about students' interests.

Teachers' and expert clinicians' diagnoses of children with reading problems have been studied extensively by Vinsonhaler and his colleagues (e.g., Vinsonhaler 1979, see also Gil 1980, Weinshank 1980). They have conducted three types of studies: (a) laboratory and classroom studies of reading specialists, special education personnel and classroom teachers diagnosing children's reading problems; (b) computer simulation studies; and (c) training studies.

Four laboratory and classroom studies have examined the degree to which reading clinicians and classroom teachers agree on the diagnosis of reading problems. The Agreement Corollary of their Inquiry Theory states that (a) individuals' diagnoses are more closely related to the "average diagnosis" based on a group of clinicians ("group agreement") than are diagnoses among individuals, and (b) agreement between diagnoses made by one individual on equivalent cases ("intraclinician agreement") should be greater than agreement between clinicians ("interclinician agreement").

The results of the studies indicated that there was a reasonable level of group agreement on diagnosis. However, the intraclinician agreement coefficients and the interclinician agreement coefficients, were very low. Reading clinicians, special educators, and classroom teachers did not agree with themselves or with each other on diagnosis. Neither did they agree on remediation. In addition, a correlation of zero was found between diagnosis and remediation at the individual level.

Gil (1980) observed and interviewed teachers about their diagnoses. He found that the 10 teachers: (a) lacked systematic strategies for collecting and using information to reach diagnostic decisions, (b) differed on a number of process variables such as the length of their interaction with a case and the number of cues collected, and (c) used general and incomplete diagnostic strategies both in the laboratory and in the natural classroom setting. Teachers appeared to lack information-processing strategies to make complete, specific diagnoses. In addition, Weinshank (1980) found that individual clinicians interacting with a case tended not to follow their stated plans of action regarding data collection procedures, diagnosis, and remediation.

Computer simulation studies examined diagnostic accuracy as a function of (a) having a specific routine for collecting information on a case; and (b) generating a few or many hypotheses, depending on the certainty of the hypotheses. These studies found that simulations that used routine cue collection procedures and generated hypotheses early performed significantly better than those that did not. However, the simulations did not perform as well as the human clinicians who diagnosed the same cases. Finally, training teachers to conduct a systematic diagnosis of a reading problem increased the accuracy of their diagnoses. Nevertheless, the accuracy for most trainees was below that considered appropriate.

3. Conclusions

Teachers' judgments are a critical component of the teaching process. Their judgments of general ability traits—intelligence and achievement—are reasonably accurate. However, the accuracy of their judgments of students' behavior on particular tasks—or of students' reading problems—is considerably lower than would be hoped for. While there is some evidence that training can overcome, to some degree, these inaccuracies, additional research on teachers' judgmental processes is needed. Such research would serve as the basis for training teachers to improve their judgments. By doing so, it might just be possible to improve the effectiveness of teachers in helping students reach valued educational goals.

See also: Interactive Decision Making; Planning; Implicit Theories; Teachers' Expectations; Information Processing Models

Bibliography

Brophy J E, Good T L 1970 Teachers' communication of differential expectations for children's classroom performance: Some behavioral data. *J. Educ. Psychol.* 61: 365–74

Byers J L, Evans T E 1980 Using a lens-model analysis to identify factors in teaching judgment. Research Series No. 73, Institute for Research on Teaching, Michigan State University, East Lansing, Michigan

Clark C, Yinger R 1979 Teachers' thinking. In: Peterson P L, Walberg H J (eds.) 1979 *Research on Teaching: Concepts, Findings, and Implications.* McCutchan, Berkeley, California

Dusek J B 1975 Do teachers bias children's learning? *Rev. Educ. Res.* 45: 661–84

Einhorn H J, Hogarth R M 1981 Behavioral decision theory: Processes of judgment and choice. *Annu. Rev. Psychol.* 32: 53–88

Gil D 1980 The decision-making and diagnostic processes of classroom teachers. Research Series No. 71, Institute for Research on Teaching, Michigan State University, East Lansing, Michigan

Kelley H H, Michela J L 1980 Attribution theory and research. *Annu. Rev. Psychol.* 31: 457–501

McNair K M 1978–79 Capturing inflight decisions: Thoughts while teaching. *Educ. Res. Q.* 3: 26–42

Nisbett R E, Ross L 1980 *Human Inference: Strategies and Shortcomings of Social Judgment.* Prentice-Hall, Englewood Cliffs, New Jersey

Shavelson R J 1976 Teachers' decision making. In: Gage N L (ed.) 1976 *The Psychology of Teaching Methods.* 75th Yearbook of the National Society for the Study of Education Pt. 1. University of Chicago Press, Chicago, Illinois, pp. 372–414

Shavelson R J, Stern P 1981 Research on teachers' pedagogical thoughts, judgments, decisions and behavior. *Rev. Educ. Res.* 51: 455–98

Shavelson R J, Webb N M 1981 Generalizability theory: 1973–1980. *Brit. J. Math. Stat. Psychol.* 34: 133–66

Shavelson R J, Cadwell J, Izu T 1977 Teachers' sensitivity to the reliability of information in making pedagogical decisions. *Am. Educ. Res. J.* 14: 83–97

Shulman L S, Elstein A S 1975 Studies of problem solving, judgment, and decisionmaking: Implications for educational research. In: Kerlinger F N (ed.) 1975 *Review of Research in Education*, Vol. 3. Peacock, Itasca, Illinois

Slovic P, Fischoff B, Lichtenstein S C 1976 Cognitive processes and societal risk taking. In: Carroll J S, Payne J W (eds.) 1976 *Cognition and Social Behavior.* Halstead, New York

Smith F J, Lugenbuhl J E R 1976 Inspecting expectancy: Some laboratory results of relevance for teacher training. *J. Educ. Psychol.* 68: 265–72

Tversky A, Kahneman D 1974 Judgment under uncertainty: Heuristics and biases. *Science* 185: 1124–31

Varner G F 1922 Can teachers select bright and dull pupils? *J. Educ. Res.* 6: 126–31

Varner G F 1923 Improvement in rating the intelligence of pupils. *J. Educ. Res.* 8: 220–32

Vinsonhaler J F 1979 The consistency of reading diagnosis. Research Series No. 28, Institute for Research on Teaching, Michigan State University, East Lansing, Michigan

Weiner B 1977 An attributional approach for educational psychology. In: Shulman L S (ed.) 1977 *Review of Research in Education.* Peacock, Itasca, Illinois

Weinshank A 1980 An observational study of the relationship between diagnosis and remediation in reading. Research Series No. 72, Institute for Research on Teaching, Michigan State University, East Lansing, Michigan

Winkler R L, Murphy A H 1973 Experiments in the laboratory and the real world. *Org. Beh. Human Performance* 10: 252–70

Interactive Decision Making

R. J. Shavelson

Teachers' interactive decision making refers to decisions teachers make while interacting (e.g., lecturing, discussing, tutoring) with their students. These decisions have been characterized as "inflight" or "real-time" decisions since teachers typically do not have the luxury of time to reflect upon these decisions or to seek additional information before deciding upon a course of action.

Teachers' interactive decisions are greatly influenced by their plans (see *Planning*). Instructional tasks—including the goals, content, materials, activities, and timing of instruction—constitute a large part of teachers' planning activity. These instructional tasks serve as a mental plan for carrying out interactive teaching. These images or plans are routinized so that once begun in the classroom they typically are played out (Joyce 1978–79, Morine-Dershimer 1978–79), much as a computer subroutine is. Routines minimize conscious decision making during interactive teaching (Clark and Yinger 1979) and so the "activity flow" (Joyce 1978–79) is maintained. Moreover, from an information-processing perspective, the routinization of behavior makes sense. Routines reduce the amount of information teachers have to consider and the number of decisions they have to make by rendering the timing and sequencing of activities and students' behavior predictable within an activity flow. Hence, conscious monitoring of instruction can then focus on particular students (MacKay and Marland 1978) and on deviations of the lesson from the original plan (Clark and Yinger 1979).

Decision making during interactive teaching, then, usually arises when the teaching routine is not going as planned (Clark and Yinger 1979). Usually on the basis of lack of student involvement or behavior problems, teachers judge that the lesson is problematic (e.g., Peterson and Clark 1978) and may choose to: (a) continue the lesson or (b) change the lesson (Joyce 1978–79). Typically, teachers choose not to change the lesson (Clark and Yinger 1979). In some cases, this choice is based on a decision to deal with the problem in future plans (Joyce 1978–79). This tactic seems reasonable since, if the expectation is set up that the teacher will continually change a lesson, management of students and instructional tasks may become problematic.

Morine-Dershimer (1978-79 p. 86) has aptly captured the nature of decision making during interactive teaching.

For the lessons examined in detail here, when there was little or no discrepancy between teacher plan and classroom reality, teacher information processing was "image-oriented," with teacher recall of previous knowledge about pupils playing an important part. Decision points were handled by established routines. When there was a minor discrepancy between teacher plan and classroom reality, teacher information processing was "reality-oriented," with a fairly narrow range of pupil behavior being observed.

Decision points were handled by "in-flight" decisions. When a more pervasive discrepancy between teacher plan and classroom reality was perceived, then teacher information processing was "problem-oriented," with teachers tapping a broader spectrum of information about pupils. When a large discrepancy existed, decisions were postponed to a later time.

1. A Model of Teachers' Interactive Decision Making

A model of teachers' interactive decision making is presented in Fig. 1. It posits that teachers' interactive teaching may be characterized as carrying out well-established routines. In carrying out the routine, the teacher monitors the classroom, seeking cues, such as student participation, for determining whether the routine is proceeding as planned. This monitoring is probably automatic as long as the cues are within an acceptable tolerance. However, if unacceptable behavior occurs (e.g., student out-of-seat behavior during discussion), the teacher has to decide if immediate action is called for. If so, the teacher has to decide if a routine is available for handling the problem. The teacher may take action based on a routine developed from previous experiences. If no routine is available, the teacher reacts spontaneously and then continues the teaching routine. If an immediate action is not called for, the teacher considers whether delayed action, say after the lesson or in future planning, is necessary. The

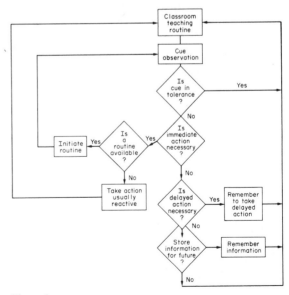

Figure 1
Model of teachers' decision making during interactive teaching (from Shavelson and Stern 1981)

teacher notes the action in memory and carries on his or her teaching routine. If no action is necessary, the teacher decides whether or not to retain the information and continues with the teaching routine.

2. Research on Teachers' Interactive Decision Making

Most of the research on teachers' decisions and behavior during interactive teaching has employed the method of stimulated recall. With stimulated recall, the researcher either audio- or video-tapes a lesson. After the lesson (or after school, depending on scheduling), the tape is played back to the teacher by the researcher and the teacher is asked to describe covert mental activities that accompanied the overt behavior.

Research using stimulated recall has consistently found that teachers' plans serve as a mental script or image which guides their interactive teaching. These images or scripts are routinized. Once begun, they are typically carried out. Hence, interactive teaching has been described in many studies as primarily carrying out a routine.

Moreover, this research has found that teachers are reluctant to change their routines, even if they are not proceeding as well as expected. When changes do occur, they typically are minor adjustments in the routine and not major revisions. However, this research does not reveal why the teachers are reluctant to change their plans (Peterson and Clark 1978). One possible reason is that the routine chosen during planning was judged, on the basis of experience and the nature of the task, to be better than any alternative routine available to the teacher. A second possible reason is that the current routine was the only one available and any hastily developed routine might not be expected to fare as well. A third possible reason is that changing routines during a lesson introduces uncertainty, both for teachers and students. For teachers, this constitutes an information-processing burden and a decrease in their ability to monitor participation and behavior in the class. For students, shifting routines might lead to their having difficulty following the flow of instruction and result in learning and classroom management problems.

In sum, teachers' main concern during interactive teaching is to maintain the flow of the activity. To interrupt this flow to reflect on an alternative and consider the possibility of changing a routine drastically increases the information-processing demands on the teacher and increases the probability of classroom management problems.

Studies of teachers' reports of their thoughts while teaching reveal that teachers attend to their mental script or image while teaching, and this focus of attention is broken only when their monitoring of the classroom indicates a potential problem or unexpected event. When a problem or unexpected event arises, teachers report becoming "aware of reality" (e.g.,

McNair 1978–79, McNair and Joyce 1978–79). Their attention then focuses on student behavior.

A very common script used by teachers during interactive teaching is one of structuring, soliciting, responding, and reacting (Bellack et al. 1966), where teachers ask questions and students respond. Teachers using this script attend to subject matter in the script and to students. A decision is required when a student gives a somewhat unexpected response. In carrying out this script, teachers apply certain principles or routines regarding their interaction with students (MacKay and Marland 1978). One principle is termed compensation. The teacher attempts to compensate the alleged "have-nots" in their classes by favoring the shy, or low-achieving student in, for example, selecting respondents to their questions. A second principle is strategic leniency, which entails being lenient with a student in need of special attention. A third principle is power sharing, where the teacher uses the informal power structure for dispensing his or her influence. A fourth principle is progressive checking, where the teacher checks on especially low-ability students' progress during interactions or on assigned tasks. And the fifth principle is suppressing emotions. Teachers systematically suppress their emotions in front of students because: (a) their emotions might be a catalyst for unmanageable student behavior; (b) their emotions, especially negative reactions toward students' responses, might harm the students' self-concepts; or (c) their emotions might lead to unjust treatment of different students.

Teachers regularly monitor the classroom as a way to evaluate a routine. A problem with a routine is often signaled by a lack of student participation or by unsanctioned behavior such as out-of-seat or noise. If the problem is serious enough, it may interrupt the routine (see Fig. 1). This is the occasion for most decision making during interactive teaching.

Most studies report that teachers' decision making is not pervasive during interactive teaching (MacKay 1977). However, MacKay reported that teachers made about 10 interactive decisions per hour and Morine-Dershimer and Vallance (1975) reported between 9.6 and 13.9 decisions per lesson. Clearly, teachers make decisions during interactive teaching. In making decisions, teachers tended to consider only a few alternative courses of action. MacKay reported that teachers seldom considered more than two alternatives and Morine-Dershimer and Vallance reported means of between 2.2 and 3.2 alternatives per lesson for four different groups of teachers. Moreover, teachers tended not to evaluate critically the alternatives; rather, they sought confirmation for their choice.

Few studies have traced the teaching process from initial information, through teacher characteristics and cognitive processes, to planning and interactive teaching and the effects of these components of teaching on students' achievements and attitudes. One notable exception is a study by Peterson and Clark (1978). Twelve teachers taught a social studies unit (not previously taught by the teachers) to three different groups of eight junior-high students whom they did not know and on whom they had no other information. They found that teachers used information about student participation and involvement in the lesson to judge how well their lesson was going. They considered alternatives only when teaching was going poorly and changed strategies in about half the problematic situations. However, these changes usually were not major ones; rather, they were more like fine tuning of the original plan.

Peterson and Clark (1978) also found that teachers high in verbal ability (measured by a vocabulary test) were more likely to generate alternative courses of action and to use a more complex decision strategy than were teachers low in verbal ability. Moreover, teachers high on reasoning ability and conceptual level were very likely to use a more complex decision strategy than teachers who scored low on these measures.

Correlations between measures of planning and interactive teaching replicated Zahorik's (1970) finding that planning exclusively directed to content and objectives may produce rigid instruction. That is, process-oriented teachers were more likely to change plans than content-oriented teachers.

Correlations between a measure of the complexity of teachers' reported interactive decisions and measures of student achievement and attitude were negative. Teachers who considered alternative teaching strategies and even changed strategy during teaching were associated with students lower in achievement and attitude. Note, however, that these teachers also experienced problems with their normal teaching routine and so had to consider alternatives. In contrast, teachers reporting that their teaching went as planned were associated with high student achievement. Those routines which maintained the flow of activity, then, were associated with higher student achievement.

In a review of four studies, Shavelson and Borko (1979) examined teachers' policies about grouping students for reading and traced the grouping decision through interactive teaching and student achievement. They reported that most teachers grouped students for reading on the basis of ability. However, a few teachers did not group students primarily due to a lack of materials and other resources. Once grouped, the group and not the individual student became the unit for planning instruction. Teachers' plans for low-ability groups differed considerably from their plans for high-ability groups. Procedures, decoding skills (reading aloud), and highly structured assignments were planned and carried out for low-ability groups while flexibility in procedures and assignments and an emphasis on comprehension skills were planned and carried out for high-ability groups. During interactive teaching, the high-ability groups were paced as much as 15 times faster than the low groups. And student achievement in the high-ability groups was correspondingly higher than in the low groups.

See also: Information Processing Models; Planning; Teachers' Judgments; Implicit Theories

Bibliography

Bellack A A, Kliebard H M, Hyman R T, Smith F L 1966 *The Language of the Classroom.* Teachers' College Press, New York
Clark C M, Yinger R J 1979 Teachers' thinking. In: Peterson P L, Walberg H J (eds.) 1979 *Research on Teaching: Concepts, Findings and Implications.* McCutchan, Berkeley, California
Joyce B R 1978–79 Toward a theory of information processing in teaching. *Educ. Res. Q.* 3: 66-77
MacKay A 1977 The Alberta studies of teaching: A quinquereme in search of some sailors. *CSSE News.* 3: 14–17
MacKay D A, Marland P 1978 Thought processes of teachers. In: Fyans L J (ed.) 1980 *Symposium on Achievement Motivations: Recent Trends in Theory and Research.* Plenum, New York
McNair K M 1978–79 Capturing inflight decisions: Thoughts while teaching. *Educ. Res. Q.* 3: 26–42
McNair K M, Joyce B R 1978–79 Thought and action, a frozen section: The South Bay study. *Educ. Res. Q.* 3: 16–25
Morine-Dershimer G 1978–79 Planning in classroom reality: An in-depth look. *Educ. Res. Q.* 3: 83–99
Morine-Dershimer G, Vallance E 1975 *A Study of Teacher and Pupil Perceptions of Classroom Interaction.* Technical Report 75–11–6, Beginning Teacher Evaluation Study, Far West Laboratory, San Francisco, California
Peterson P L, Clark C M 1978 Teachers' reports of their cognitive processes during teaching. *Am. Educ. Res. J.* 15: 555–65
Shavelson R J 1976 Teachers' decision making. In: Gage N L (ed.) 1976 *The Psychology of Teaching Methods.* 75th Yearbook of the National Society for the Study of Education. University of Chicago Press, Chicago, Illinois
Shavelson R J, Borko H 1979 Research in teachers' decisions in planning instruction. *Educ. Hor.* 57: 183–89
Shavelson R J, Stern P 1981 Research on teachers' pedagogical thoughts, judgments, decisions and behavior. *Rev. Educ. Res.* 51: 455–98
Zahorik J A 1970 The effect of planning on teaching. *Elem. Sch. J.* 71: 143–51

Epistemologies

R. E. Young

The study of teacher epistemologies is an attempt to understand their theories of knowledge and the implications of these for their practice. This is a different quest from the classical philosophical search for an understanding of the nature of human knowledge, although, obviously, knowledge about teacher epistemologies must be warranted in the light of research methods whose validity rests on some epistemological assumptions.

The study of teachers' epistemologies is related to the study of metacognition, because epistemological beliefs are beliefs about other beliefs: epistemological "knowledge" is knowledge about knowledge, just as metacognition is. Epistemological beliefs may function to control or modify the processing of other beliefs which are more directly related to "the way the world works". Similarly, metacognitive beliefs about memory strategies, or about study and examination skills may control the way in which a student processes information from lectures or encyclopedias such as this one. In the case of epistemological beliefs, the process which is controlled is the process of forming truth or falsehood judgments about say, propositions, or theories, which purport to explain aspects of human experience and the experienced "world". Thus, one way of studying teachers' epistemologies would be to focus on epistemologies-in-action: the epistemic practices of teachers, in making their own validity judgments and in recapitulating these in the classroom.

One should be wary, though, of assuming that the link between epistemology and validity-forming practices is a clear cut, logically valid application of epistemological theory to specific instances. This assumption is based on a further assumption of rational behaviour and a cognitively clear set of epistemological beliefs. But peoples' metaepistemic views may be hazy; they may be affectively charged rather than dispassionate. Research must be open to the possibility that there may not be a clear demarcation between philosophically "acceptable" epistemological views and a range of half-beliefs, attitudes, feelings, values, and hunches about knowledge.

1. Research by Philosophers

Most early research on teacher epistemologies was characterized by a highly rationalistic view of both the link between epistemologies and other areas of thought and practice, and of the internal composition of teacher epistemologies themselves. This work was carried out almost exclusively by philosophers, borrowing the methods of the behavioral sciences. The link between theory of knowledge and epistemic practice was theorized as if it were a rational philosophical process; that is, the philosophers' model of the teacher was the teacher as philosopher.

There was a tendency to assume that a teacher's views about education in general, and about curriculum and pedagogy would be consistent with his or her epistemology. Scheffler (1965) provides one of the clearest and most explicit examples of this kind of theory although he himself did not fall into the trap of believing that teachers generally thought consistently along such lines. Scheffler argued that an understanding of knowledge involved a series of logically independent but

related questions, the answers to which had to be reconciled with one another, more or less "laterally":

"What is knowledge?"

Given an answer to this question, "What knowledge is most reliable or important?"

"How does knowledge arise?"

"How ought the search for knowledge be conducted?" and

"How is knowledge best taught?"

One influential view tended to divide epistemologies into four categories on the basis of "conceptual" analysis: realism, pragmatism, existentialism, and idealism. These were then expected to relate to appropriate views of curriculum and pedagogy, the connection between epistemology and theory of education being essentially one of "lateral" consistency at a philosophical level rather than one of "vertical" effects of epistemology or everyday knowledge processing.

Questionnaires were devised to identify the four epistemologies (e.g., the Ross Epistemology Inventory) which were then administered to samples of teachers along with questions concerning related areas of teachers' theory of education (e.g., Abbas 1949, Erlich 1963, Ross 1970, Starkey and Barr 1972).

The results of more than a decade of this kind of research tend to confirm two things: first, teachers' epistemologies do not appear to fall neatly into the four postulated categories; and, second, that there is little "lateral" consistency between teachers' epistemologies and other aspects of their educational theory. Teachers typically displayed "mixed" epistemologies in terms of the philosophical–conceptual categories applied, and the pattern of correlations between teachers' epistemological views and other beliefs was weak and inconsistent from one study to another.

Two conclusions could be drawn from these results. First, that there was a need for exploratory research to discover something about the nature and variety of teachers' epistemological views; and second, that there was a need to develop a more adequate theory of the relationship between teachers' epistemologies and other beliefs and practices.

2. Exploratory Research

The first systematic attempt to discover the nature of the epistemological beliefs of teachers (and other professional groups) was carried out by Royce (1959, 1964). Royce carried out interviews with subjects from a number of occupational backgrounds, identifying the occurrence of four types of epistemological validity criteria in varying contexts and combinations: "rationalism–thinking", "empiricism–sensing", "intuitionism–feeling", and "authoritarianism–accepting".

However, in attempts to construct a summated rating scale Royce found that the four groups of criteria did not form mutually exclusive categories. Respondents typically endorsed more than one kind of validity criterion. But instead of questioning the mutual exclus-

iveness of his categories, Royce switched from an agree/
disagree questionnaire format to a rank order method,
forcing respondents to assign statements to ranks. A
weak rank order scale was produced after the "authoritarianism–believing" dimension was dropped. A
later study of the construct validity and reliability of
the scale was not encouraging. A more ethnographic
orientation to the exploratory study of epistemologies
might have led to a means of making sense of Royce's
categories. On a purely historical basis one might have
expected that the two categories "empiricism–sensing"
and "rationalism–thinking" would have been combined
for respondents with a logical—empirical view of knowledge, a view which many writers have argued is very
common in advanced, industrialized societies (e.g.,
Radnitsky 1968).

A more thoroughgoing ethnographic study was carried out by Young (1981a). Data were collected through
participant observation, nondirective interviews, written protocols, and classification experiments, from a
sample of Australian secondary teachers. The data from
interviews, protocols, and experiments were exhaustively rather than anecdotally analysed to produce complete lists of epistemological vocabulary and categories,
and the way in which the categories formed systems was
also explored.

Analysis of the data revealed that most teachers in
the sample (around 80 percent) spoke about knowledge
as a state of mind characterized by at least a strong
belief, expressible in statements, based on some kind
of evidence. Where teachers differed was in respect of
the kinds of experience which they believed could count
as evidence and in the degree of validity they assigned
to these. Most of the differences among teachers could
be located on a dimension from "scientism" to "her-
meneutics", with a "pluralist" position in the middle.
To some, the natural sciences in their logical—empirical
guise were the epitome of knowledge; to others it was
the cultural studies and the arts, while some believed
there was a range of different forms of knowledge, each
based on its own kind of evidence.

Of the remaining 20 percent of teachers perhaps 10–
15 percent possessed a view which stood outside this
science–arts dimension. A variety of dialectical, critical,
and relativistic views could be found in this latter group.

Analysis of the majority of teachers' talk about knowledge revealed the presence of four kinds of epistemological rules: rules about the definition of the concepts, or entities, about which knowledge statements
could be made (mainly boundary maintaining rules concerning clarity and meaning); rules about the syntax of
meaningful statements (e.g., logic/mathematics versus
metaphor/analogy); rules about the validating relationship of statements to experience (e.g., sensory observation versus inward feelings); and other derived rules
about the usefulness or objectivity of different kinds of
knowledge. The range of rules identified concerning
the relation of statements to experience was generally
consistent with the criteria Royce had discovered.

3. Implications of Teachers' Epistemologies

It was clear from the form taken by teachers' talk about
knowledge that it was likely to be useful to theorize
about the implications of teachers' epistemologies in
relation to the role played by a logical–empirical view
of science in modern society. Earlier theory had tended
to operate in a social vacuum relying instead on testing
for conceptual and logical consistency across a teacher's
various areas of belief.

Following a great deal of recent research on the
nature of the teacher's task, Young (1981b) argued that
a teacher's epistemology was likely to make its presence
felt in three main ways. It would be felt in the process
of selecting, and justifying selection of, the knowledge
that should be included in the curriculum. It would
affect the process of managing the presentation of this
knowledge in the classroom and, in particular the justification or otherwise of a teacher-managed pedagogy.
And it would also be felt in the process of assessment,
including the social legitimation of assessment
processes. Basil Bernstein's theory of "visible" and
"invisible" pedagogies was modified to include this epistemological dimension (1975). It was argued that in
advanced industrial societies, a scientistic view of knowledge would lend support to a didactive view of teaching
(stresses the teacher's active role), a discipline-based or
"collection" view of overall curriculum organization, a
teacher-centred view of control, and a psychometric/
normative approach to assessment. It was felt that this
technicist view of education was in the process of replacing "traditional" educational philosophies.

Scales were developed to measure each of these four
areas of teacher's beliefs (knowledge, curriculum organization, control, and assessment) and a survey of the
staff of a sample of five urban secondary schools was
carried out. The results indicated that the four areas of
belief formed a coherent ideology with a strong tendency towards consistency in terms of a sociological
rather than a philosophical theory of the implications
of a teacher's epistemological beliefs.

Other work by Young (1980) focused on epis-
temologies-in-use. Working from transcripts and videotapes of classroom talk, Young attempted to identify
the epistemology-in-use as teachers shaped epistemic
discourse in classrooms. An earlier study by Prusso
(1972) paved the way for analysis of this kind, but
Prusso's study was confined to science teachers' views
of science and based on a predetermined set of types
of epistemology, in a manner similar to other studies
discussed above.

Essentially, Young argued on the basis of a review of
observational and linguistic studies of classrooms, that
the most common structures of classroom discourse
involved validational practices which constructed, and
appealed to, an implicit context, or background of
unproblematic, already-resolved validity claims, rather
than practices which lead to discursive exploration of
validity claims. That is, the knowledge-oriented aspects

of classroom talk were underpinned by an unspoken background of cognitive assumptions to which the structure of the talk itself closed off all possibility of critical access.

If one's philosophy of education coincides with Scheffler's it would be necessary to define teaching in terms of a rational dialogue and to argue that:

> Insofar as the teacher is teaching, he is, in any event, risking his own particular truth judgments, for he is exposing them to the . . . general critique . . . and to the free critical judgment of the student's mind. (Scheffler 1965 pp. 12–13)

However, if this is teaching in the believed-in epistemology of many teachers, it is not necessarily found in their epistemology-in-use. There, other factors, deriving from the demands of curriculum coverage, future assessment goals, and control of pupil conduct, compete with educational ideals in shaping the concrete discourse of teaching and learning.

Bibliography

Abbas A A 1949 A method to determine a science teacher's philosophy of education (Ed.D dissertation, Colorado State University) University Microfilms No. 00-01591

Bernstein B B 1975 Class and pedagogies: Visible and invisible. In: Bernstein B B (ed.) 1975 *Class, Codes and Control,*

Vol. 3: *Towards a Theory of Educational Transmissions.* Routledge and Kegan Paul, London, Chap. 6

Erlich E 1963 Opinions of citizens, teachers and students about certain philosophical statements of education (Ph.D. dissertation, Ohio State University) University Microfilms No. 63-2637

Prusso K W 1972 The development of a scheme for analyzing and describing the epistemological criteria adhered to in secondary school natural science classroom communication (Doctoral dissertation, Temple University) *Dissertation Abstracts International* 33: 1972 1595A (University Microfilms No. 72-27207)

Radnitsky G 1968 *Contemporary Schools of Metascience,* Vol. 1: *Anglo–Saxon Schools of Metascience.* Akademiförlager/Gumpert, Göteborg

Ross C 1970 *Ross Educational Philosophical Inventory.* ERIC Document No. ED 053 995

Royce J R 1959 The search for meaning. *Am. Sci.* 47: 515–35

Royce J R 1964 *The Encapsulated Man: An Interdisciplinary Essay on the Search for Meaning.* Van Nostrand, Princeton, New Jersey

Scheffler I 1965 *Conditions of Knowledge: An Introduction to Epistemology and Education.* Scott, Foresman, Glenview, Illinois

Starkey J D, Barr R L 1972 *The Philosophical Nature of Teachers: Graduate and Undergraduate.* ERIC Document No. ED 072 018

Young R 1980 The controlling curriculum and the practical ideology of teachers. *Aust. and N.Z. J. Sociol.* 16(2): 62–70

Young R 1981a The epistemic discourse of teachers: An ethnographic study. *Anthrop. Educ. Q.* 12(2): 122–44

Young R 1981b A study of teachers epistemologies. *Aust. J. Educ.* 25(2): 194–208

Students' Cognitive Processing

P. H. Winne

Cognitive processes are unobservable mental actions used to manipulate information. Like other kinds of processes, cognitive processes produce outcomes, or cognitive products. Cognitive products may be processed again, or they may be manifested in performance. For example, a student may rehearse (cognitive process) the spelling of an irregular word over and over to learn (cognitive product) to spell it correctly on a test (performance).

Presently, research on human cognitive processing outside classroom settings greatly exceeds that on students' cognitive processing in classrooms. Only recently have researchers begun to explore students' cognitive processing during teaching and describe the way this relates to what they learn in classrooms. A synthesis of the two areas must reflect the relative proportions of research in these two areas. Thus, one major task undertaken here is to transpose general models of cognitive processing (Bower 1975) onto a model of students' cognitive processing in classrooms. Following this, the

present state of research on students' cognitive processing in the classroom will be described.

Before beginning this transposition, two general principles characterizing both areas of research warrant mention immediately. Because these principles are consistently descriptive of cognitive processing in diverse situations, they help justify translating findings from research not done in classrooms to classroom settings. Also, these principles give rise to several key issues that need to be addressed when considering relations among students' cognitive processing, curriculum, teaching, and learning.

The first principle is that cognitive processing can be applied to any kind of information. Information can include visual forms like the patterned lines that form letters of the alphabet, organized verbal data like stories, motivational events like students' evaluations of their performance on arithmetic problems, and plans for accomplishing tasks like composing an essay. The significance of this principle is that students' cognitive systems have the potential to process not only the various kinds of information found in educational curricula, but also information that acts of teaching provide to students to help them achieve educational objectives. Thus a single unified model can be used to analyze how students learn concepts, create and use cognitive strategies, and acquire and demonstrate motivation.

The second principle is that cognitive processing is neither just a response to events in a student's environment, nor is it a complete internal determinant of a student's performance. Cognition is both an effect caused by previous events, including cognitive ones, and a cause of future events. The relation between cognitive processing and events in the instructional environment is reciprocal. Over time, each shapes the other. The principle of reciprocity has two important implications. First, students cannot be passive recipients of teaching. They participate in creating what teaching means to them, even if it appears that all they do is listen. Second, the principle of reciprocity makes it improper to declare teacher behaviors as the sole cause of students' achievement. Since students' cognitive processing creates cognitive products that they manifest as learning, cognitive events like rehearsing a concept are among the causes of learning. This cognition may have been stimulated by the teacher's utterance, "That's important for tomorrow's quiz." In turn, the teacher's behavior may have been triggered by a student's prior question that reflected earlier cognitive processing, and so on. Depending on how one defines the units of interaction within the dynamic flow of classroom events, what one labels as cause and as effect can vary. The more general characterization is one of reciprocity.

To describe students' cognitive processing during teaching, it will be useful to develop a model. The model presented here (see Fig. 1) synthesizes mainstream research from cognitive and instructional psychology with very recent research on teaching. The central part of this model, the student's cognitive processing system, can be described in terms of three major facets. The first facet represents static aspects of the system, sites where cognitive processing works on different forms of information. The second facet reflects dynamic features of the system, namely the cognitive processes and their functions. The third facet, called parameters, describes boundaries of the cognitive processing system.

Three major additions to this representation of a student's cognitive processing system are needed to create a model relevant to classroom teaching. The first is a conceptualization of curriculum that is compatible with the student's cognitive processing system. When a curriculum is delivered to students in classrooms, instruction is taking place. Describing instruction in terms of its reciprocal interactions with a student's cognitive processing system is the second addition. Finally, because it is students who work at learning from instruction, a characterization of student tasks will summarize how students learn from teaching according to a cognitive processing framework. Before building a model of

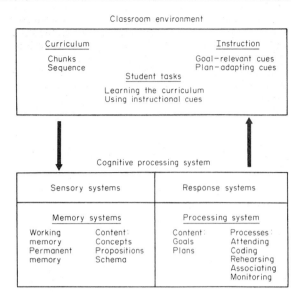

Figure 1
A cognitive model of learning from teaching

the student's cognitive processing system that integrates curriculum, instruction, and the way these culminate in student tasks, a rationale for considering students' cognitive processing in the classroom is presented.

1. The Cognitive Mediational Model

During the first six decades of this century, research on how teaching affects students' learning changed substantially. Early studies of teaching effectiveness typically characterized teaching quite globally. For example, classrooms were labeled democratic or laissez faire, and teachers' interaction with students was described by terms like helping or providing corrections. Slowly, these descriptions became more detailed as researchers recognized the need to analyze specific behaviors that teachers used to act democratically or give help. As this focus sharpened, it became apparent that students' cognitive processing during lessons bridged or mediated the relation between how teachers were behaving and how students ultimately demonstrated learning and motivation. Thus, studies in the 1950s and early 1960s characterized most teacher behaviors in two parts: behavioral features that allowed observers to distinguish one kind of teacher activity from another, and a student's hypothesized cognitive response to each kind of teacher behavior. In these studies, students' cognitive processing was pivotal in hypothetical explanations about how teaching affected learning.

This view is clearly illustrated in studies relating types of teachers' questions and students' achievement (see Dunkin and Biddle 1974). In the middle 1950s,

Guilford's model of human intelligence and a taxonomy of educational objectives developed by Bloom and his colleagues provided early frameworks for describing students' cognitive processing. Guilford's system used three facets simultaneously describing the content being processed, the cognitive operation being performed, and the cognitive product that resulted. There were four kinds of content: figural, symbolic, semantic, and behavioral. The cognitive processes Guilford posited were cognition (awareness), memory, convergent production, divergent production, and evaluation. Six types of products were hypothesized: units, relations, classes, systems, transformations, and implications. For example, a teacher's question, "What might happen if the polar ice caps melted?" was presumed to call for students' divergent production (process) of semantic (content) implications (product). Bloom and colleagues' taxonomy was simpler. It identified only six major cognitive products: knowledge, comprehension, application, analysis, synthesis, and evaluation.

Using these frameworks, many systems were developed to observe teachers' use of questions in lessons. Each system categorized teachers' questions in terms of the cognitive processing students were believed to engage in as they answered various questions. These cognitive processes, presumed to be stimulated during teaching, were theorized to promote different amounts and varying qualities of learning. Specifically, researchers and educators shared a commitment that teachers' questions requiring more complicated cognitive processing by students, called higher cognitive questions, promoted more and better learning than questions which asked students merely to recognize or remember information. However, a critical review of experiments testing this commitment showed it was not justified (Winne 1979). Similar conclusions have been reached about other instructional behaviors, such as praise, whose effects on achievement also were explained in terms of students' cognitive responses (Brophy 1981).

In research like this, called process–product research, each category of teacher behavior, say a teacher's synthesis questions, was tacitly assumed to affect all students equivalently during teaching. In studies, researchers changed a teacher's use of synthesis questions in one classroom but not in another. They assumed that differences in students' achievement test scores across the classrooms could be explained by the effect synthesis questions had on students' cognitive processing during teaching. This reasoning failed to recognize that different students might cognitively process a single question differently, and that several equivalently phrased questions might be cognitively processed differently by a single student (Winne 1982). Students' cognitive variations were not examined directly, nor were there means for bringing them under control in the studies.

This problem was not remediable at the time. Models for describing students' cognitive processing during teaching were just being developed and tested experimentally. Although research in the 1960s and 1970s relied on students' cognitions to explain how teacher behaviors affected students' achievement, the nature of this mediation was obscure. It was a black box that needed opening. In response to this weakness, a cognitive mediational model was proposed to supplement the earlier process–product model that related teaching processes to student products. The cognitive mediational model defined general characteristics of this black box by combining the findings of previous research on teaching with models that were emerging from other research on learning (Doyle 1978, Winne 1982, Winne and Marx 1977).

In its simplest form, the cognitive mediational model characterizes learning from teaching as a series of interactions between events in the instructional environment and a student's cognitive processing system. It is hypothesized that there are instructional cues or stimuli in lessons that have a potential to influence each student's cognitive processing. Given a cue, such as a synthesis question (e.g., "What might explain why it rains less on the lee side of a mountain range than on the windward side?"), the model identifies at least four ways that a student may fail to respond appropriately. First, a student may not have attended to the question. This student does not cognitively process either the question or curricular information needed to answer the question. Second, if the question was attended to, a student may not know what kind of answer is required. This student misperceived information in the cue about the goal to be achieved. Thus, cognitive processing that is engaged produces the wrong kind of cognitive product on which to base an answer. Third, a student may lack curricular information needed to produce the cognitive product on which a good answer depends. Even though this student carries out appropriate cognitive processing, a good answer will not result. Fourth, a student who attends to the question, appropriately perceives how to answer it, and has the curricular information needed, may choose not to pursue the task. This student is said to lack motivation. In each of these four cases, the question will not affect the students' learning as intended by the teacher or as theorized by a researcher. Only when students successfully carry out all four cognitive mediating steps can the synthesis question influence students' learning as the process–product model of teaching said it would (Winne 1982).

The four parts of the cognitive mediational model—instructional cues, cognitive processes, cognitive products, and students' performance—link observable events in classrooms (teachers' questions, students' answers) to the cognitive processing students use to learn from teaching. By specifying these four steps, the cognitive mediational model highlights the principle of reciprocity. For instance, if a student misperceives the kind of answer the teacher requires of a synthesis question, the teacher may probe the student to improve the answer. The teacher's probe is an instructional cue that may stimulate particular kinds of further cognitive processing for this particular student. Whereas process–product research treated teachers' questions and teachers' probes as two distinct independent variables, the cognitive mediational model illuminates their joint impact by taking into account the way that they interact with students' cognition. This interaction between teacher behaviors, students' cognitive processing, and what students learn is the focus of analysis according to the cognitive mediational model. To perform such analyses, however, the black box of the learner's cognitive processing system must be opened.

2. The Cognitive Processing System

The cognitive processing system lies inside the black box of the cognitive mediational model. Though research has explored this system since the late nineteenth century, the greatest part of our understanding about cognition has emerged since the early 1960s. Fundamentally, models of the cognitive processing system are hypothetical descriptions of what information is, and of the ways that information is perceived, transformed, learned, and used. Within the overall system for cognitive processing, there are four major sites (see Fig. 1).

2.1 Sites in the System

The four major sites through which information is moved and processed are the sensory system, the memory system, the central processing system, and the response system. The sensory system is the gateway through which information from the environment enters the cognitive system. Here, energy from the environment, such as light reflected from print on a page, is transformed into a neurally coded representation of the print. This representation is maintained for a very brief period (in the order of tens to a few hundreds of milliseconds) and then transferred to the memory system. The sensory system does not select the information it receives. For purposes of examining students' cognitive processing in classrooms, this system is not addressed further. Although the sensory system is important in analyzing some instructional events, like the perception of letters and shapes, these are outside the mainstream of classroom phenomena.

The memory system is the most researched site for cognitive processing. It contains two sites itself: permanent or long-term memory, and working or short-term memory. Permanent memory is theorized to be the repository of all information that has been learned. The information stored here is permanent, and the amount of information that can be stored is immeasurably large, at least insofar as it can be measured. Structures of information stored in permanent memory are described in a later section.

As its name implies, working memory is the cognitive site where information is stored after it has been processed. Working memory's alternate name, short-term memory, describes a prime characteristic of information at this site. Information stored here is short lived, available for cognitive processing only for about 10 to 30 seconds. If cognitive processing of some kind is not undertaken, the information is lost. When the information that is lost originated in the environment, this loss is permanent unless the environment provides the information again or unless the student reinvents it on the basis of a plan (described later). On the other hand, if the information was originally transferred from permanent memory, its loss is only temporary because, under the right conditions, it can be retrieved again from permanent memory.

The third major site for cognitive processing is the processing system where cognitive processes actually manipulate information. The processes used at this site are described in the next section.

The fourth major site in the cognitive processing system, the response system, is the gateway for the products of students' cognitive processing to be manifested as performances. It consists of a storage area that temporarily holds information before it is translated into neural messages for motor action. While there is much research about the response system and its role in the cognitive processing system, this knowledge is outside the domain of most classroom phenomena and therefore is not addressed further.

2.2 Structures of Information

Research suggests that information in permanent memory is stored in codes that reflect different modalities in the environment. The primary codes are: images for visual information about actions, shapes, and colors; auditory codes for sounds; and abstract language codes for verbal, logical, and mathematical information. Other codes like tactile and olfactory ones also exist, but these are less well-researched and less relevant to most classroom teaching. An important exception, though, would be teaching situations where people have sensory limitations, such as instructing the blind in braille.

Information in permanent memory is highly organized. It can be pictured as a complex network or a hierarchical array. Three basic forms of information are theorized: concepts, propositions, and schemata (Wickelgren 1979). A concept is a basic unit of information that represents a category. Beyond this simple description, it is difficult to specify precisely what concepts are. Some concepts, especially ones from artificially created systems such as mathematics, are best described in terms of a label (e.g., circle), a set of criterial or defining features that are necessary to fully describe any instance of the concept (continuous line, all points equidistant from a point "inside" the line), and a set of unessential or potential features (color of the line, size of the circle). Other concepts are better described by prototypes or "best" examples. A ball (as in baseball, ball of mud, ball-and-socket joint) fits this model. Concepts can be concrete (a ruler), abstract (energy), static (the number 2), dynamic (revolving), and even procedural (solving equations). Whatever their type, concepts exist and become meaningful by being related to other concepts. The parts or features of a concept are called its constituents. Constituents are themselves concepts. It is unknown whether there exists a set of primitive, unanalyzable constituents from which all other concepts can be created.

A second form of information in permanent memory is the proposition. Propositions are like sentences that relate two or more concepts. The number and kinds of primitive relations (equivalent to, part of, acts on, causes, precedes, etc.) are not agreed on, but this is not a major problem in studying students' cognitive processing in classrooms. The following are all propositions: (a) The word "cat" can be decoded by assigning a sound to each letter and saying the sounds quickly in sequence; (b) If a piece of land is surrounded by water, it is an island; (c) I like science; (d) After I give a complicated answer to the teacher's questions about themes in short stories, she usually leaves me alone; (e) When my laboratory results are not exactly like the text's, I can't explain them; (f) I passed the test because I was lucky.

These examples illustrate several important features of propositions. First, propositions can contain factual information like (b) or (e), or can reflect feelings like (c) and probably (f). Second, propositions can describe static relations like (b), procedural knowledge like (a), and conditional relations like (d) and (e). Third, propositions can describe relations along a dimension of predictability. For instance, (a) expresses certainty while (d) describes a less probable relation. Finally, although propositions may be difficult for students to articulate, as (d) probably would be, propositions are learned. Learning may be deliberately guided by the teacher, as during instruction, or it may emerge from the student's inherent cognitive activity.

Propositions like (a) and (b) make up the majority of academic curricula. Knowledge of procedures and strategies like decoding words in (a), borrowing in subtraction, locating a book in a library, or creating a first-letter mnemonic like FACE for notes in the treble clef also are key elements in almost every subject area. Acquiring verbal knowledge like (b) also is a well-accepted goal of education.

Propositions like (d) and (e) describe expectations students have about the instructional environment. When an expectation relates a student's performance to a consequence that follows that performance, as (d) does, it is called an outcome expectation. A different kind of expectation is illustrated by (e). It is a prediction about being able to perform depending on conditions antecedent to the performance, labeled an efficacy expectation.

Proposition (f), which described a student's explanation about why cognition or performance turned out as it did, is called an attribution. Attributions have been categorized along three dimensions: stable–unstable

(e.g., ability–mood), internal–external to the student (e.g., immediate effort–luck), and controllable–uncontrollable (e.g., getting help from others–difficulty of the task). These dimensions combine to describe an attribution. For instance, proposition (f) is an attribution to an unstable, external, uncontrollable cause.

The kind of proposition illustrated by (c) is a value, attitude, or predisposition. It describes the student's emotional constituents of a concept. These kinds of propositions are theorized to build up from experiences beginning at the earliest stages of life when infants make associations between physiological needs and things (people, behaviors) that satisfy those needs. Over the course of development, students learn to like or dislike mathematics, sharing stories, being in front of the class, or studying.

Attributions, attitudes, and both types of expectations combine to account for motivation that influences students' performances in classrooms. For example, suppose a student has an efficacy expectation like (e) and an attitude like (c). Suppose further that this student attributes the cause of whether laboratory experiments yield results like those in the text to the amount of extra effort applied to the exercise. An instructional cue delivered by the teacher might be: "This experiment is tricky, so be extra careful setting up your apparatus and recording your data." This cue sets the stage for the student to appear highly motivated from the teacher's point of view. In the student's plan for doing the experiment, extra effort increases the probability of getting results like those in the text. Such results can be explained, that's what science is all about, and so there is a high incentive to apply extra effort because the student likes science. But to achieve such results, the student must follow the teacher's cue and be extra careful to produce results that are explainable. The student's behavior that manifests these cognitions is likely to be what the teacher labels high motivation. Note that the student must possess some verbal and procedural knowledge about this task to appear highly motivated. Thus, performance also depends on reciprocal interactions among several forms of information.

Classroom performances of nearly every kind require students to integrate many varied propositions. Thus, to learn from instruction, students must draw on the "right" concepts and propositions so they can rearrange information already stored in permanent memory and add new concepts and propositions to this network of information. Helping students to do this is one way to characterize teaching (see Sect. 4.1).

Consider now the third major form for information in permanent memory, a schema (also called a script or frame). Schemata are collections of propositions organized to describe prototypes of phenomena or events. They might be compared to blueprints: schemata provide some information directly, like the dimensions of a building; identify slots where information about the current context should be incorporated into the schema, like empty rooms that will be filled with particular types of furniture; and provide an organizational structure for representing the overall phenomenon, like different perspectives of the complete building. Two examples, one about a structure of information to be processed and one concerning an activity, illustrate the concept of a schema.

Students frequently read stories in school. Stored in permanent memory as the product of prior learning is a schema for stories. It specifies the overall nature of a story, categories of information to be filled in while reading a particular story, and relationships among these categories. One model of a schema for stories portrays these categories as a hierarchy. At the highest level are categories for the story's setting, theme, plot, and resolution. The story setting has slots for characters, location, and time. As a student reads a particular story, the setting is defined (slots are filled in) by the particulars of the story. Usually, the setting is described early in the story. Knowing when information is provided in a story is also a part of this schema. Research has shown that students whose schema for stories is underdeveloped often fail to comprehend fully stories that they read. This suggests that teachers may need to teach a schema for stories.

A schema for an activity can be illustrated by characterizing a student who is studying several pages of biology text for an upcoming quiz. A schema for this task probably contains several parts. One part might be that sentences having the form of a definition (e.g., "A chromosome is . . .") present propositions that should be rehearsed. There are two requirements for success here: knowing what a defining sentence looks like, and knowing which cognitive process should be engaged when defining sentences are located. Another part of this schema might be to generate and practice answering questions like short essay items that might appear on a quiz. In addition to rehearsing information, this entails several other propositions such as: prior knowledge about the kinds of short essay questions the teacher might include on the quiz ("What is crossbreeding?"), a procedure for recognizing this kind of information in the text, another procedure for generating a question about this material, and a third procedure for checking the adequacy of answers to such questions.

To review the structures of information in permanent memory, then, there are three increasingly complex forms of information—concepts, propositions, and schemata. These forms of information are organized, and they achieve meaning by their relationships to one another. One goal of teaching is to add properly organized information of all three forms to students' permanent memories. However, information rarely travels directly from the instructional environment to permanent memory. An intermediate stopover is working memory.

Information in working memory can take any of the three forms described earlier and can be represented in any of the earlier mentioned codes. One very general schema frequently found in working memory is a plan.

Plans are cognitive designs for accomplishing tasks that students undertake. To understand what plans are requires first some analysis of what a task is.

A task is something the student must do. The examples presented earlier about reading a story for comprehension, doing an experiment, and studying a text for a quiz are illustrative school tasks. Tasks begin with a set of conditions and a goal. Some conditions are determined by the instructional environment, and some are determined by a student. For example, the number of definitions to be studied for a quiz and the degree to which some definitions are embedded in other definitions are initial conditions determined by a text. The time available for study is determined by another aspect of the instructional environment, the teacher. The extent to which the student can identify definitions in the text is determined by the student's ability. These and other initial conditions of the task define an initial status.

A second status of any task is a goal, the conditions that define when the task is done. Some conditions of the goal are determined by the instructional environment, and some are set by the student. For instance, the teacher fixes the relation between grades and the number of definitions that must be learned to achieve different grades. The student decides how many definitions will be rehearsed, probably by weighing a trade-off between grades for different amounts of learning and work that must be done to learn varying amounts. If there is a discrepancy between the initial status and the goal, cognitive processing to study the text may be engaged if the student is "motivated." If there is no discrepancy from the student's point of view, another task (e.g., playing with a friend) will be pursued.

The notion of a plan can now be described as a set of sequenced cognitive operations that the student applies to information to complete a task. In essence, a plan is a schema the student activates to perform a particular task. The plan progresses through a succession of cognitive operations on information. Each successive operation produces a cognitive product that is an updated blend of information from the instructional environment and from the student's permanent and working memories. These intermediate cognitive products are stored in working memory. Also stored in working memory is a record of the student's place in the plan. This record most likely represents two propositions: the discrepancy between the current status of the task and the immediately preceding status, and the discrepancy between the current status and the goal.

To sum up the sites and structures of information, the two major sites for cognitive processing relevant to instruction are the memory system and the central processing system. The memory system is divided further into two major parts: permanent memory and working memory. Information throughout the system is theorized to be coded in one or more modalities (visual, semantic, etc.) and in forms of increasing complexity ranging from concepts through propositions to schemata. Information also varies over other dimensions like concrete to abstract, and factual to attitudinal. Schemata that are activated to accomplish tasks are called plans. When working through plans, students keep track of their place in the plan in terms of discrepancies between initial, intermediate, and goal states.

2.3 Processes and Functions

Discovering the nature of cognitive processes has been one of the most difficult tasks in pursuing theories about how cognition affects students' performance. The forms and codes for information just described are somewhat amenable to observation by asking students to tell or draw what is being worked on mentally. How information was manipulated, however, can only be inferred from changes in these observable products rendered by cognitive processing. Nonetheless, a powerful model of cognitive processes has been generated over the course of thousands of experiments. As will become apparent, most cognitive processes are carried out on information that has been stored in working memory.

It will also emerge that the set of cognitive processes is not invariantly sequenced. Rather, the processes interweave in complex, purposeful ways according to plans and the successively updated cognitive products that plans produce. Though it seems that the various cognitive processes do not all operate simultaneously, several may operate nearly simultaneously, and it is clear that their resulting cognitive products can trigger more cognitive processing. The principle of reciprocity applies here too.

One basic cognitive process is focusing on information or paying attention. Attending to information in permanent memory, say a concept, activates the particular concept being focused on, thereby automatically transferring it to working memory. Because the concept attended to is associated with other information in permanent memory, it is hypothesized that the activation spreads along these relations, diminishing in potency as it fans out in the hierarchy or network of information. Metaphorically, attending to a concept can be imagined as hitting a target of information that becomes fully activated. The target reverberates to produce a halo or periphery of partially activated information, while the remainder of information in permanent memory remains unactivated or quiet. Thus, the result of attending to information in permanent memory is to activate it, to transfer it to working memory so it can be processed further.

Coding information is another basic process. It functions in two ways. First, coding renders information in the sensory system into a form that is manipulable by the cognitive system, such as a visual representation of a circle. Second, coding can change information in working memory into another code, i.e., recode information. The reverse of coding is responding.

A third basic cognitive process is forming propositions or associating. When the proposition formed relates

several concepts (say meteorology, astronomy, and biology) on the basis of a shared feature (method of study), associating is referred to as chunking. Part of the new proposition, the concept that labels the chunk (science), may be information already present in permanent memory or it may be a new entry. Chunking is one way students learn new concepts. Associating new information with information in permanent memory is called encoding. Encoding is usually a necessary precursor to learning new information meaningfully.

Another basic cognitive process is rehearsing. When information is in an auditory code, rehearsing is like mentally whispering the information over and over. Rehearsing is practice without feedback. It maintains the activated state of information, keeping it available in working memory, but it does not change the information. Rehearsing seems to transfer information to permanent memory by a method of brute force, but this may produce information that is less interconnected with the other information stored there. Rote learning will be addressed later.

The fifth basic cognitive process is monitoring, a process of determining the match between a prototype for information and the current nature of information. When monitoring consistently reveals discrepancies among concepts or propositions, a discrimination is achieved. When successive discrepancies are revealed between the goal of a task and the products of cognitive processing according to a plan, it is theorized that an "executive" plan is activated. This is a very general routine that contains a structured set of propositions about whether information other than that currently activated should be attended to, or whether another cognitive process (e.g., associating, recoding) should be applied to the presently activated information. Theoretically, if successive monitoring of the executive plan reveals discrepancy after discrepancy, the student will use trial-and-error to continue with the task or will quit the task.

Varying integrations of these five basic cognitive processes applied to concepts, propositions, and schemata can describe the everyday cognitive events that students engage during teaching. Here is a compressed analysis of cognitive processing for a student who is asked: "What might explain why it rains less on the lee side of a mountain range?" (see also Gagné 1978). First, the student must understand the question. This entails encoding it as a set of concepts within propositions where the propositions have particular relations to one another. This operation is called parsing. Several things happen next. Attending to concepts in the encoded propositions (an explanation, rains, lee side) activates target and peripheral information in permanent memory. The concept of an explanation probably has a schema for a cause-and-effect relation as a constituent. Particular information must be sought to fill the schema's slots for the cause and for the effect. Also, the schema for cause-and-effect relation provides several constituents that the student can use as criteria when monitoring whether an explanation that is synthesized fits this schema. For instance, the cause must precede the effect, and the effect cannot occur if the cause is absent.

Meanwhile, the task of answering the question has been encoded. The goal of the task is to explain. Some of the initial conditions of the task are the concepts, propositions, and schema in the question that the student has activated and transferred to working memory. Activating the schema for explaining creates a plan for directing the work to be done. One proposition in this plan says that a concept can be found in the parsed question that is either a cause or an effect. So the propositions are examined (monitored) for a fit to either of the concepts of cause or of effect. The proposition "it rains less" fits the concept of an effect. This information then fills the slot in the schema for "explain" corresponding to "the effect." The task now shifts to filling the remaining slot for "cause" in the schema. At this point, the student understands the question and is ready to try to answer it.

Filling the slot for "cause" is the heart of this synthesis question. How might it be done? While the question was being encoded and the plan was being created, both target and peripheral information in permanent memory were activated. For instance, activating the concept "rain" and the "explain" schema probably partially activated the constituent "causes of rain." These causes (drop in temperature, drop in barometric pressure, etc) now are attended to as targets because the student's monitoring revealed that information was needed to fill the slot for the "cause" in the "explain" schema. Monitoring whether any of these activated causes is also a constituent of the concept "lee side of a mountain range" determines whether it explains why it rains. Unfortunately, this is likely a wrong tack for the student's cognitive processing to take. The effect named in the question is that it rains less, not that it rains.

When this lack of fit is identified by the monitoring process, any of a number of things may happen. The student may give up. Perhaps a tentative answer will be offered: "Because the temperature is lower on the lee side?" Or, another round of cognitive processing may be initiated if the student's plan for answering questions in class includes a strong incentive for achieving a correct answer. Suppose the executive plan contains a proposition to associate opposites of concepts such as "lee side" and its peripherally activated opposite "windward side." Activating information about the causes of rain on the windward side of mountains and monitoring whether these are *not* constituents of the concept lee side has more potential to yield a correct answer. This is what makes a synthesis question seem harder and more complicated. The student must create a cue for activating information in permanent memory that was not activated automatically by encoding the question. In this example, the student needed to activate information about the opposite of "lee side" and monitor causes of rain that are absent on the lee side but present on the windward side. The probability that a student's cognitive processing leads to generating a retrieval cue like this depends jointly on information encoded from the question, the plan the student uses to guide how this information is processed, and propositions in permanent memory about the incentive for doing all this cognitive work.

To recap, there are five basic cognitive processes: attending, coding, associating, rehearsing, and monitoring. Variations in students' performance depend on how these cognitive processes are applied to concepts, propositions, and schema as guided by a plan (activated schema) for accomplishing a task. Cognitive products that result from cognitively processing information may trigger more cognitive processing or they may end the cycle, depending on the fit between these products and the goal for the task that is specified in the student's plan.

2.4 Parameters of the Cognitive System

Properties of the cognitive processing system that set conditions for how the system can operate are called parameters. Several parameters of the cognitive processing system warrant mention because they limit or impose boundaries on what can be accomplished, and because they have direct implications for teaching.

Perhaps the most well-known parameter is that a limited amount of information can be held in working memory for processing. Depending on the code and form of the information, this span of memory ranges from approximately three to eight items. One of the major problems students face as they cognitively process information delivered during instruction is to avoid overloading the capacity of the system. Chunking is one procedure that alleviates overload. Taking notes is another.

The way students work to avoid exceeding capacity can affect their immediate performance and ultimate learning in important ways. For instance, a student who chunks information may create concepts that a note taker may not. The number of bits of information in the chunk may not include all that the teacher presented, however, if creating the chunk borrowed cognitive resources that were needed to attend to all the information that was being presented. Thus, exercising extra cognitive processing may lower the capacity for other processing to be engaged. How students allocate resources for cognitive processing can affect the amount, the structure, and the durability of learning.

A second parameter of the cognitive processing system relates to the degree of automaticity of processing. As a student writes, the cognitive processing engaged to recode internal language codes into letters and words is extremely automatic. One might describe this level of automaticity by saying that this recoding does not require that one pays attention to what one is doing (though deciding what to write certainly does!). Five- and six-year-old students learning to write a simple word like cat, however, lack this automaticity even though all the components of the task are stored in permanent memory.

Automaticity of cognitive processing accounts for the speed with which complicated tasks can be accomplished. The primary ingredient in achieving automaticity is extensive rehearsing of the plan for a task. Not only does this "strengthen" the information rehearsed, but according to the principle of spreading activation, it can have peripheral benefits as well. There are two implications for teaching. Extensive practice is necessary to achieve automaticity. Second, drill results in rote or nonmeaningful learning only when the information being drilled is not integrated with other propositions that could be peripherally activated during drill. When material being drilled is meaningful, drill should enhance partially activated propositions, thereby partially drilling them as well. Thus, it is what is drilled, and not drill as such, that influences whether learning is meaningful.

A third set of parameters describe aspects of information in permanent memory. Two examples of this set are the number of chunks of information stored in memory and the average number of propositions to which a concept is related. These are related to the meaningfulness of information. Since these indices describe what students should learn as a result of teaching, they are treated in the next section about curriculum.

3. The Curriculum

The information that students should learn in school is described in the curriculum. All the codes and forms of information that exist in permanent memory are used to represent curricula. These include auditory schema (a fugue), visual propositions (a tangent to a curve), plans (finding items in a library), verbal concepts (metaphor), and more. Also, it should not be overlooked that an important part of the total curriculum is learning how to learn from teaching. Since students' understanding of instructional cues mediates learning from teaching, teachers should instruct students about how to use instructional cues to learn from teaching, as well as teaching the subject matter as such. Issues relating to teaching students about instructional cues, which might be labeled an enabling curriculum, will be considered in later sections. In the present section, the concept of curriculum is restricted to mean subject matter.

3.1 Sites for Curriculum Information

Every medium that can convey information is a potential site for introducing students to the subject matter. Common sites are the teacher, texts, the chalkboard, physical models, flashcards, films, worksheets, and television. Classmates are also frequent sources of information, particularly in recitation lessons where the teacher and students exchange questions and answers.

With two exceptions, the site from which curricular information is introduced is not an important influence on students' cognitive processing. One exception is that students with particular sensory difficulties, such as poor hearing, will lose some auditory information that otherwise might enter the cognitive processing system. This well-known, almost trite fact nonetheless is not always heeded. The second exception is more a qualification that will be elaborated in the upcoming section on parameters. Briefly, it is that sites can influence cognitive processing when certain parameters are not under students' control. Specifically, when parameters take on values that are mismatched to students' cognitive processing, detrimental effects may result.

3.2 Structures of Curriculum Information

The concepts, propositions, and schemata that make up curricula are an external representation of a part of the curriculum creator's permanent memory. Almost certainly, any packaged curriculum flexes and changes during teaching as it is modified by the teacher and students to fit with information in their permanent memories. Again, the principle of reciprocity emerges: students, as much as teachers, determine some of the information and its structure that constitutes "the" curriculum.

Two descriptions of information are useful for describing curriculum: chunks and sequence. As described earlier, chunks are made up of individual concepts associated on the basis of one or several shared constituents. A chunk labeled "literary devices" might include the concepts of metaphor, hyperbole, alliteration, and so on. Chunks in curricula are the curriculum designer's preferred structures for information.

The concept of sequence is the commonsense idea that there are some chunks of information that need to be learned (stored in permanent memory) before other chunks of information can be learned. Most often, sequence is imagined to be a constraint on whether information can be learned. This is not quite true. Almost any information can be learned by rehearsing it regardless of its sequential placement in a curriculum. As noted earlier, rehearsing information may or may not interconnect it with other information in permanent memory. Therefore, a 6-year-old could probably be taught to solve a few specific types of problems in integral calculus by repetitively rehearsing particular chunks of information. The child's ability to solve such problems would be very limited, obviously, owing to the isolated form of this information in permanent memory. For instance, the child almost surely could not explain why certain mathematical procedures were used. The important point about sequencing chunks of curriculum, then, is not whether information can be learned. Rather, sequence is important because it determines the number and nature of propositions that can be peripherally activated when a new chunk of curriculum is attended to. In other words, sequence importantly influences the quality of meaning (associations) available when learning new chunks in a curriculum.

3.3 Parameters Describing Curriculum

Parameters of curricula describe how well or how easily curricular information can be related to information in the student's permanent memory. Sequence closely approximates a parameter in this sense. Two other general parameters of curricular information can be distilled from research.

One commonsense parameter of curricula is meaningfulness. This is defined as the number of concepts in the curriculum that can and actually are associated to concepts in permanent memory. In other words, meaningfulness is measured by the number of propositions the student can create relating the new curriculum to previously learned information. One well-substantiated principle for teaching is that meaningfulness can be increased by elaborating curricular information with examples. This beneficial effect, corresponding to elaborative rehearsal on the student's part, is explained in terms of spreading activation, rehearsal, and chunking. Each example that students attend to activates target information plus peripheral information in permanent memory. Multiple examples involving overlapping information are equivalent to rehearsing target information by repeatedly activating it. Monitoring associations among target and peripheral concepts can lead to the creation of chunks of information that are rehearsed as the student processes further examples. When these chunks are attended to later in a lesson or because they appear on a test, the periphery surrounding the target information is informationally richer and stronger, that is, more meaningful.

A second family of curricular parameters relates to complexity. Information that is complex begins to challenge the capacity and automaticity parameters described earlier. One parameter of curricular complexity is the ratio of new information to old within the time interval that unrehearsed information remains activated in working memory. A high ratio strains the capacity of working memory in two ways: it approaches the maximum number of items of information (old plus new) that working memory can hold, and it increases the amount of cognitive processing required to achieve meaningfulness by associating new information to old. Old information may be information activated from permanent memory; or it may be information recently introduced by the curriculum and thus existing only in working memory, such as a character's name in a story. Research sometimes refers to a given-new contract between information in working memory and information just presented by the curriculum. When this contract is violated, students' learning is impaired because extra processing is needed to reinstate information in working memory, thereby limiting students' use of other forms of processing needed for learning.

Another parameter of complexity is the amount of cognitive processing that must be devoted to parsing curricular information into a set of structured propositions. In text or speech, the presence of lexically ambiguous words can tax processing capacity. For example, the referent for "they" is ambiguous in: "When numerators are unequal and denominators are equal, they must be factored before dividing fractions." Also, parsing complexity increases when new propositions are embedded in other new propositions, when words are not frequent in everyday language, and when concepts are unfamiliar.

Both meaningfulness and complexity for a particular sequence of chunks vary among students because the information in their permanent memories and their parameters for cognitive processing vary. This need not be a serious impediment, however, because curricular information can be designed to lessen these problems. To promote links between curricular information and information in students' permanent memory, however, designs for teaching must take three factors into account. The first is that curricular information should be chunked and sequenced for instruction in ways that do not exceed parameters governing students' abilities to create meaning for the curriculum. Students drawn through lessons without opportunities to integrate information through association and rehearsal will learn less. The second factor is that teachers should design instruction to provide feedback to themselves about how successfully students are coping with aspects of curricular complexity. Without such feedback, teachers will not know when and what kinds of adaptations to their designs are required. Finally, the instruction that delivers curriculum to students must assist students to cognitively process the information they are to learn during teaching by providing meaningful and timely instructional cues.

4. Instruction

When teachers deliver curricula to students in lessons and other settings, the events that occur are instruction. Research on students' cognitive processing during instruction has been done mostly by studying learning from text. Three strong lines of this research have examined the effects of providing students with instructional objectives, adjunct questions, and advance organizers (Gagné 1978).

In classrooms, relatively little research has directly investigated how students' cognitive processing interacts with instructional cues provided by teaching. This reflects the newness of thinking about teaching in terms of the cognitive mediational model. Previous sections on the student's cognitive processing system and the curriculum described the black box and how it interacts with information to be learned. This section analyzes how teaching events influence students' cognitive processing of curriculum. A position that is elaborated in the next section on student tasks is that teachers must influence students' cognitive processing of curriculum for instruction to be effective.

4.1 Structures and Functions of Instructional Cues

The cognitive mediational model proposes that, at any given instant, students' cognitive processing mediates instructional events and students' performance. Except for reflexes, students' cognitive processing is theorized to be governed by plans. Different plans require varying amounts of cognitive resources to carry them out and to keep track of their execution. In other words, plans are executed with varying degrees of automaticity. Two key cognitive processes in plans are monitoring and associating. Monitoring provides students with information about the fit between current status in a task and the goal state. Associating allows plans to adapt to a task midstream by linking target information to peripherally activated information during execution of the plan. Therefore, in addition to preparing curricular information for presentation, teachers who can help students carry out plans for learning the curriculum during teaching will be more effective. If this assistance were not necessary, teaching could be reduced to curriculum design. There is ample evidence that aiding students in executing their plans is beneficial (Brown 1978).

Instructional cues are stimuli in the teaching environment from which students can draw information to choose and adapt plans for learning. These cues provide information about the instructional goal to be achieved, and about how curricular information could be cognitively processed to reach this goal. As such, information provided by instructional cues is not part of the curriculum about which students will be tested. Rather, information in instructional cues enables students to learn the curriculum more effectively and efficiently than if instructional cues were absent. In this sense, students must learn to use instructional cues as input to plans if they are to profit from instruction. From the teacher's point of view, instructional cues are means for influencing how students learn.

Classroom research identifying the kinds of instructional cues students attend to and how their plans are influenced by instructional cues is scant. There is evidence that students do perceive instructional cues (Winne and Marx 1982), and that these perceptions are related to their achievement (Peterson and Swing 1982, Stayrook et al. 1978). Also, research has shown that students can be taught to identify and use instructional cues, but the effects of this training in classrooms are not yet consistently predictable. This unpredictability is probably due to the lack of empirical results describing how students' plans for accomplishing classroom tasks interact with instructional cues to influence their cognitive processing of curricular information.

The general nature of plans provides a framework for describing the features and functions of instructional cues in teaching. It seems logical that some instructional cues provide information about the goal state of a task. From this information, students can create a list of criteria against which intermediate cognitive products can be monitored. Two functions for goal-relevant instructional cues have been illuminated in research.

One function of goal-relevant instructional cues is to provide information from which the student judges incentive, the predicted value or gain for working at a task. If monitoring a plan reveals too wide a discrepancy between the student's current state and the goal, motivation to pursue the plan further is generally diminished. Some of the kinds of propositions illustrated earlier seem to be central in producing this product. First, if outcome expectations are weak (the consequence of achieving the goal is not clear), the student cannot judge the value of these consequences. Hence, incentives for pursuing the plan to achieve the goal are vague. Second, if outcome expectations are strong but efficacy expectations are weak (the prediction about being able to carry out cognitive processing is low), pursuing the plan will not seem worthwhile since what must be done to achieve the goal exceeds parameters. These propositions and other information, such as attributions that the student may make about the self (e.g., low ability), are most likely processed nearly automatically. Thus, instructional cues that provide students with information for assessing the incentive for accomplishing tasks may strongly influence whether they are motivated to learn (Thomas 1980).

The second function theorized for goal-relevant instructional cues is to provide students with information about the kind of performance required to manifest learning. Both casual comments by students and research show that students' beliefs about how they will be tested affects their execution of plans for learning (Gagné et al. 1977), thereby influencing which aspects of the curriculum are cognitively processed and how these are stored in permanent memory. For example, students process curriculum differently if told they will be tested by a multiple-choice test than by an essay test. Though the same basic set of propositions may be required to answer questions on both tests, multiple-choice items require information to be chunked differently than essay items. Similarly, various instructional cues appearing during verbal interaction in classrooms, such as exchanges of questions and answers in recitation lessons, may shape students' criteria for monitoring their success at learning since these, too, are occasions for demonstrating mastery of curricular information. Thus, goal-relevant instructional cues influence students' plans for mastering curricular information both during instruction and outside the classroom when they prepare for tests. If students' perceptions of goal-relevant instructional cues are inaccurate, they may learn less. An alternative hypothesis is that students use plans for learning within which the goal that guides monitoring is not the right goal. This, too, will appear to teachers and researchers as poor learning. If the performance required of students to demonstrate learning were changed to match the goal they sought, an importantly different result might emerge (Mayer 1979).

In addition to goal-relevant instructional cues, other instructional cues can guide students' executive plans. When a student struggles with new material, even an accurate perception of the goal the teacher has set for a task does not guarantee that the student's plan will flow unerringly toward that task's goal. When problems are encountered, students' executive plans search for eues about another avenue of attack. When students monitor how they are cognitively processing information, they are said to be engaged in metacognition. Thus, the instructional cues that help students adapt plans by providing useful information to executive plans are called metacognitive cues.

Research about metacognition and learning from teaching is very new. It is known that students can be taught how to adapt a current plan (Corno 1980), including plans relating to motivation (Thomas 1980), and to seek cues about whether to activate another plan. These studies, however, have focused more on defining students' executive plans than on how teachers might use metacognitive cues during instruction. The latter kind of research is emerging as the nature of students' plans for classroom tasks becomes better understood (Wittrock 1986).

4.2 Parameters of Instructional Cues

At this early stage of research, it seems logical that two parameters describe instructional cues. Timeliness of the cue, although only a speculation consistent with data at this point, is one parameter. The dynamic and interactive nature of plans logically suggests that instructional cues can be maximally useful only at particular points in executing a plan (Winne and Marx 1982). Instructional cues that are not available when they are needed obviously cannot help. Those presented and perceived by students after a critical juncture in a plan may not be attended to. Or, they may disrupt cognitive processing if the student needs to retrace the plan to reinstate a previous status.

A second parameter that may affect the utility of instructional cues is actually an initial condition of the task. It is the degree of freedom the student is allowed in defining the task to be accomplished. When instruction permits students wide latitude in defining the task, students probably do not pursue identical tasks. Therefore, in a class of students, different plans are being used by different students. Any particular instructional cue that the teacher provides thus has less probability of fitting into each one of the students' plans in an appropriate way and at an appropriate time.

5. Student Tasks—The Cognitive System at Work

Tasks are the environmental counterparts to students' cognitive plans. They are situations created by teachers (or any other site for curricular information) in which students work through a plan to acquire and demonstrate types of learning and motivation. Tasks present students with a collection of initial conditions and set a goal, either tacitly or explicitly. Among the initial conditions is information that the teacher judges students can associate with previously learned curriculum plus a structure governing the activities to be pursued. In addition to examples presented in earlier sections, two common tasks would be asking students to read some text and be prepared to discuss it, and observing a demonstration and lecture about how to solve arithmetic problems so that similar problems can be done in a seatwork activity.

At any point in a lesson, students are probably engaged in several tasks. Some tasks may be embedded concurrently within more global tasks, or tasks may form a sequence to be carried out in succession. Each task involves students in cognitive processing as they work through and keep track of their places in one or several plans. This suggests that the curriculum design and the instructional cues that are incorporated in teaching should accomplish four purposes (Winne 1985): to influence the schemata students activate so they can interact cognitively with information in the curriculum; to help students monitor their plans more effectively by explicitly providing criteria for monitoring; to offer feedback during instruction that guides executive plans; and to deliver teaching so that students can carry out tasks without exceeding parameters of their cognition (Case 1978). To the degree that teaching and students' cognitive processing harmonize in these four respects, instruction will be more effective than students' natural cognitive explorations of their world. These requirements for curriculum design and use of instructional cues correspond to two broad categories of tasks students face: learning the curriculum and using instructional cues.

5.1 Learning the Curriculum

This category of tasks has been researched widely (Calfee 1981), and many findings from these studies were mentioned in the course of earlier descriptions. Two particularly important points arise from the preceding characterization of tasks. First, because plans are designed and carried out to accomplish a particular goal, students' understanding of the goal will importantly influence the cognitive processing they undertake. In turn, this cognitive processing will shape the nature of what students learn and the ways they will be able to demonstrate their learning. The second point is that plans inherently entail propositions about attributions, outcome expectations and efficacy expectations, incentives, and attitudes related to the goal students perceive for a task. This is because activating target information about a goal and actions to be taken in pursuing a goal spread to peripheral propositions. Thus, tasks and the plans that are evoked for working with curricula are keys to teaching both knowledge and motivation. Moreover, according to the cognitive model, motivation is an integral aspect of curricula.

The cognitive model specifies the role that goals and propositions play in the plans that students use to accomplish tasks. It also outlines how plans are carried out and adapted. Thus, it provides teachers and researchers with a schema for designing curricular tasks and for analyzing why students' learning may be faltering. This greater analytic power was not possible when teaching was conceptualized in terms of the earlier process–product model. Future research in this vein, such as Brown's (1978) and that reviewed by Thomas (1980) will likely yield significant benefits for teaching.

5.2 Using Instructional Cues

From the student's perspective, learning curricular information under the guidance of instruction can either complicate or simplify cognitive processing. Complications arise when teaching includes instructional cues that require students to allocate cognitive resources to interpreting how to learn as well as applying cognitive resources directly to learning. In the short run, a student may view instruction as an unnecessary and even a confusing adjunct to usual ways of cognitive processing (Winne and Marx 1980). As the student's cognitive processing adapts to instruction, or as the teacher prepares and delivers better instruction, the benefits teachers and researchers ascribe to instruction can be realized. When this harmony is achieved, the information that instructional cues adds to the students' environment will enhance learning and motivation by increasing the appropriateness and effectiveness of their cognitive processing.

The tasks students face in using instructional cues are to achieve accuracy in understanding instructional cues, and then automaticity in using cues while being taught. Aiding students with both tasks is just as much a part of good teaching as designing and delivering curricula. But this appears to create a paradox. How can students learn to use instructional cues if teachers must use instructional cues to help them learn this in the first place?

This question is central to a philosophy of instruction, but it need not inhibit applications of instructional science to teaching. This is because, for whatever reasons, students at any age have already acquired plans well-suited to accomplishing some curricular tasks. Preschool children can follow simple directions because they have a broad and functional repertoire of language, among other things. Their existing capabilities provide a broad basis for designing instruction that addresses the four purposes of teaching. In other words, the aforementioned paradox is in fact paradoxical only at the very beginning of a student's lifelong interaction with information. Once some concepts, propositions, and schemata are available, these provide a basis for cognitive processing and further development, including students' cognitive processing of instructional cues.

5.3 Summary

Students' cognitive processing during teaching consists of reciprocal interactions among their cognitive processing system on the one hand, and the curriculum and instructional cues on the other. The setting within which this interaction occurs is a task. By specifying a goal and a set of initial conditions, a task establishes a framework within which students carry out cognitive processing according to a plan. If students were exposed to curricular information devoid of instructional cues, that is without instruction, they almost surely would learn something. This is because students already have well-developed plans for learning from their experiences. The intent of supplementing curricula with instruction is to improve the quality of students' cognitive processing beyond their natural levels. Thus, the objective of teaching is to influence the cognitive processing students use to learn. The model of students' cognitive processing developed here provides a basic framework for teachers and researchers to pursue this objective. Future research that provides more detail and that elaborates this model will advance our ability to reach this objective.

See also: Paradigms for Research; Information Processing Models; Logical Operations; Soliciting

Bibliography

Bower G H 1975 Cognitive psychology: An introduction. In: Estes W K (ed.) 1975 *Handbook of Learning and Cognitive Processes*, Vol. 1: *Introduction to Concepts and Issues.* Erlbaum, Hillsdale, New Jersey

Brophy J 1981 Teacher praise: A functional analysis. *Rev. Educ. Res.* 51: 5–32

Brown A L 1978 Knowing when, where, and how to remember: A problem of metacognition. In: Glaser R (ed.) 1978 *Advances in Instructional Psychology*, Vol. 1. Erlbaum, Hillsdale, New Jersey

Calfee R 1981 Cognitive psychology and educational practice. In: Berliner D C (ed.) 1981 *Review of Research in Education*, Vol. 9. American Educational Research Association, Washington, DC

Case R 1978 A developmentally based theory and technology of instruction. *Rev. Educ. Res.* 48: 439-63

Corno L 1980 Individual and class level effects of parent-assisted instruction in classroom memory support strategies. *J. Educ. Psychol.* 72: 278–92

Doyle W 1978 Paradigms for research on teacher effectiveness. In: Shulman L S (ed.) 1978 *Review of Research in Education*. Vol. 5. Peacock, Itasca, Illinois

Dunkin M J, Biddle B J 1974 *The Study of Teaching*. Holt, Rinehart and Winston, New York

Gagné E D 1978 Long-term retention of information following learning from prose. *Rev. Educ. Res.* 48: 629–65

Gagné E D, Bing S B, Bing J R 1977 Combined effect of goal organization and test expectations on organization in free recall following learning from text. *J. Educ. Psychol.* 69: 428–31

Mayer R E 1979 Can advance organizers influence meaningful learning? *Rev. Educ. Res.* 49: 371–83

Peterson P L, Swing S R 1982 Beyond time on task: Students' reports of their thought processes during direct instruction. *Elem. Sch. J.* 82: 481–91

Stayrook N G, Corno L, Winne P H 1978 Path analyses relating student perceptions of teacher behavior to student achievement. *J. Teach. Educ.* 24(2): 51–56

Thomas J W 1980 Agency and achievement: Self-management and self-regard. *Rev. Educ. Res.* 50: 213–40

Wickelgren, W A 1979 *Cognitive Psychology*. Prentice-Hall, Englewood Cliffs, New Jersey

Winne P H 1979 Experiments relating teachers' use of higher cognitive questions to student achievement. *Rev. Educ. Res.* 49: 13–49

Winne P H 1982 Minimizing the black box problem to enhance the validity of theories about instructional effects. *Instr. Sci.* 11: 13–20

Winne P H 1985 Steps toward promoting achievements. *Elem. Sch. J.* 85: 673–93

Winne P H, Marx R W 1977 Reconceptualizing research on teaching. *J. Educ. Psychol.* 69: 668–78

Winne P H, Marx R W 1980 Matching students' cognitive responses to teaching skills. *J. Educ. Psychol.* 72: 257–64

Winne P H, Marx R W 1982 Students' and teachers' views of thinking processes for classroom learning. *Elem. Sch. J.* 82: 493–518

Wittrock M C 1986 Students' thought processes. In: Wittrock M C (ed.) 1986 *Handbook of Research on Teaching*, 3rd edn. Macmillan, New York

SECTION 5

Contextual Factors

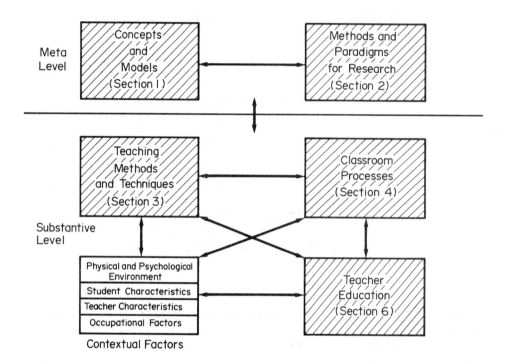

Meta Level

Substantive Level

Contextual Factors

Schematic representation of Section 5 in relation to other Sections

SECTION 5

Contextual Factors

INTRODUCTION
TO SECTION 5

Teaching and learning occur within a context. At every point of the process, contextual influences impinge on the teacher and the students. Most immediately these influences are the participants themselves, for teachers and students are parts of each other's surroundings. Curriculum and materials, the physical spaces occupied, the group feelings, indeed, the very temporal and cultural frames of the process, can be expected to have vital impacts through determining what are possible, acceptable, and desirable activities, as well as modes of communication, beliefs about reality, and so on.

This section contains articles about features of the context which impinge upon teaching and learning in classrooms. It is divided into four sections: the environment, student characteristics, teacher characteristics, and occupational factors.

1. The Environment

In the first article, Lundgren distinguishes three traditions of research into school and society relationships. First, he presents the habitus theory, second, the code theory, and third, the frame factor theory. After describing the first two, Lundgren elaborates upon the third, which is the focus of his article. He defines frame factors as "the measures taken by the state in regulating time, space, and personnel. Thus the frames are manipulated above the teachers and the taught and express a certain power relation to the state apparatus". He cites research demonstrating that policies about ability grouping in schools can, by way of a phenomenon known as "the steering group", create a strong influence on the pace at which curriculum units are completed. Next, he reviews research showing how pedagogical roles, such as those described in the previous section, can be affected by time constraints. He concludes thus:

> Frame factors are then factors that constrain the teaching process and which are not manipulated by the teachers. In studying the teaching process, it is important to determine what is possible or not possible within the frames given and how the frames have been built up . . . . Frame factors cannot be seen as simple functions of a rationalistic planning model; they must be understood as residuals of earlier school systems, as consequences of public expenditures, and as expressions of the wider economic and political context of education.

In the second article, Bennett discusses the influence of the architecture of schools and classrooms upon what goes on in them. After presenting data on the growth in popularity of open designs during the 1960s and 1970s, he explores alternative ways of designing the same amount of space. However, after discussing theory, research, and practice concerning openness in design, Bennett concludes "that physical differences in teaching spaces do not clearly differentiate teaching practices". His review of teachers' attitudes to aspects of working in open designs includes discussion of work loads, noise and distraction, cooperative or team teaching, the design of spaces, and staffing and training. From them he turns to students' attitudes and personality, and student achievement.

The central implications of Bennett's article are that assumptions linking architectural design with teaching methods are hazardous and that the use of a term such as "open plan" implying homogeneity in design is often inappropriate. Readers are urged to read the article *Open Versus Formal Methods* in Sect. 3 of this Encyclopedia in conjunction with this article by Bennett.

Teaching spaces are occupied by teachers and students. They are also occupied by the paraphernalia of teaching and learning. In the third article in this subsection, Ainley discusses the role of equipment and materials in classrooms. After considering theoretical perspectives about ways in which the physical environment influences human behaviour, he reviews research in schools, much of it in open plan classrooms, and although he cites findings that materials and equipment do influence behaviour, he identifies the same types of problems about research in open plan classrooms as Bennett does. He then turns to research in science classrooms and concludes his article by stating that there is a substantial amount of evidence of the effects of the physical environment upon behaviour in classrooms.

Class size is the subject of the next article in this subsection. After demonstrating concern with this issue as far back as Quintillian, Glass shows how significant it is in terms of expenditure on education and traces the history of empirical research concerning it in the twentieth century. The generally inconclusive findings reported were apparently more a function of the manner in which relationships between class size and variables such as school achievement were calculated. Glass reports the results of a series of meta-analyses (see *Synthesizing Research Evidence*) conducted by his colleagues and him. On the basis of a study of 725 comparisons of student achievement in smaller and larger classes, Glass concludes: "the relationship of class size to pupil achievement is remarkably strong. Large reductions in school class size promise learning benefits of a magnitude commonly believed not to be within the power of educators to achieve. And then there are the costs".

Glass continues with a discussion of class size in relation to affective outcomes, such as motivation, and concludes that affective outcomes are even more closely related to class size than are the cognitive outcomes of schooling. Glass's article is also valuable for the explanation it contains of the effect size statistic used in the meta-analyses.

Closely associated with the number of students in a class is the way in which their seating is arranged. Weinstein writes about the effects of various seating patterns in the next article. She looks first at conventional seating arrangements in rows in relation to personality variables, grades, participation, and attitudes, and reports findings that certain types of students are more likely to prefer the back of the classroom, that students with higher grades tend to sit at the front, that there is an "action zone" where students participate more actively, and that students at the front have more positive attitudes. After considering alternatives such as circular seating arrangements, Weinstein concludes that there is sufficient evidence to warrant serious consideration of seating patterns and to state several guidelines for teachers. She recommends that teachers move around the room to try to involve peripheral students, that students' seats be changed periodically, that students' seating preferences be used as indications of their self-esteem and liking for school, and that seating be arranged to capitalize upon principles of nonverbal communication, such as those involving eye contact and involvement.

Duke, in the sixth article in this subsection, discusses seven types of environmental influences particularly in relation to the management dimension of classrooms. The seven influences are as follows: technological, legal, political, economic, demographic, ecological, and cultural. Technological influences affect attitudes towards progress and the application of strategies such as reinforcement schedules, as well as equipment, materials, and architectural design. He points out that teachers are seldom consulted in the design of classroom technology.

Legal influences include the legal status of the teacher in relation to parents' and students' rights and involve disciplinary practices such as suspension from classes. They affect the rights of teachers' unions to negotiate in relation to such matters as class size. Political influences abound with regard to such issues as social integration and mainstreaming the handicapped. Economic influences obviously affect class size and teachers' workloads, which are also affected by demographic influences such as birth and migration rates, changes in family structure, and teacher age patterns.

After considering ecological influences, such as the existence of youth support agenices, and cultural influences, such as sex-role stereotyping and attitudes towards cooperation and competition, Duke concludes his article with a discussion of control and authority in education. He writes: "teachers are caught in the awkward position of witnessing their authority diminish . . . at the same time that they are urged to exercise greater control over student behaviour and achievement". Furthermore he concludes, "in jeopardy is the traditional belief that teacher interests and parent interests are compatible".

The final article in this subsection is about the psychological climate or atmosphere of the group of students and teacher(s) themselves. In it Walberg outlines the scope and history of research on the psychology of classroom groups and considers the relative merits of measurement techniques using student ratings as against direct observation by a researcher. Researchers using the student ratings methodology gather their data with paper and pencil instruments designed to sample such group characteristics as cohesiveness, cliqueness, democracy, friction, favouritism, and formality. Walberg concludes that "psychological perceptions of classroom environments have important influences on student achievement, performance, and self-concept as well as on other valuable educational outcomes".

2. *Students' Characteristics*

In the first article in this subsection, Sinclair writes first about a group of motives associated with students' self-concepts and self-esteem, then about motives concerned with exploratory behaviour and needs to know and understand, and finally about a group of social motives such as needs for praise, recognition, and attention.

In the first group, Sinclair distinguishes between striving to achieve and striving to avoid failure, the latter when aroused being experienced as anxiety. He then elaborates on anxiety and achievement motivation and introduces the notion of causal attributions, that is, students' explanations for their successes and failures. Sinclair sees scope for the employment of aptitude–treatment interaction approaches in forming appropriate links between teaching methods and student anxiety. He also comments on the potential effects of teacher feedback upon students' attributions of success and failure, noting sex differences in these regards.

Concerning curiosity and motivation to know and understand, Sinclair notes that highly curious students have been found to ask more and better questions in class and to display other differences, but he cautions that teachers need to minimize threats to students' self-esteem arising from curiosity arousing situations.

In discussing motives associated with one's relationships with other people Sinclair emphasizes the importance of teacher praise and the suggestion that students condition teachers to praise them. He goes on to discuss interrelationships among affective states in students and concludes that there is scope for much more research on them.

Next, Debus writes about cognitive or intellectual characteristics of students as part of the context of classroom behaviour. He traces relationships with classroom behaviour of students' ability levels and cognitive styles, noting that higher achieving students tend to be more attentive, and less dependent on teachers' praise and help. In mentioning other classroom behaviour differences between high- and low-ability students, Debus makes connections with students' perceptions of their abilities and thus with the previous article by Sinclair.

After reviewing theory and research on such cognitive styles as field dependence/ field independence and reflectivity/impulsivity, Debus sees important implications for classroom practice and research and concludes:

> Although the extent of actual classroom data related to cognitive-style variables remains rather limited, evidence does suggest that, like other cognitive characteristics of students, cognitive styles of students are reflected in classroom behaviour in ways which interact with patterns of teacher behaviour.

The remaining three articles in this subsection are about student characteristics that are quite different from those already discussed. Unlike students' affective and cognitive characteristics, students' ethnic background, sex, and social background are not likely to be affected by classroom events. This means that differences in classroom behaviour associated with these characteristics ought to be more easily attributed to the influence of the variables.

In the first of these three articles, Dunkin and Doenau report that most of the research on student ethnicity and classroom behaviour has been conducted in the United States and that the most common finding is that students from ethnic minority backgrounds have fewer interactions with teachers and have fewer positive and more negative contacts with teachers than other students have. However, they report that almost never has the research taken into account other variables associated with ethnicity, such as socioeconomic status, and the possibility that other variables, such as sex, or the combination of sex and ethnicity, might have more influence than ethnicity itself. Furthermore, they found only their own study to have attempted to look at differences in classroom interaction between ethnically different groups in relation to student achievement. They conclude their article by presenting implications for teachers arising from the research.

In the next article, Bank writes about sex of student and classroom behaviour. First, she presents research findings on the connection between student sex and student behaviour and discusses those findings in terms of biological determinism and differences in achievement between males and females in mathematics, the sciences, and other subjects. Next, she considers student sex in relation to teacher behaviours, and reports many differences in the way teachers behave towards males and females.

Her discussion of these differences includes the possibility that they are induced by "sex-linked interests and behaviours exhibited by students" rather than by teachers' biases. On the other hand, there is evidence that sex-role stereotypes are reinforced in subtle ways and there are claims by some that teachers do actively impose traditional sex roles.

Although the social background of students is frequently included in attempts to explain variations in attitudes towards schooling and school achievement, there is a relatively small literature on the difference social background makes to the ways in which students and teachers behave in classrooms. Kahl's article on *Students' Social Backgrounds*, makes clear that relationships between social background and education variables are complex. After discussing research problems associated with social background, different components of the concept, and results of research on its relationships with other student characteristics such as IQ, Kahl examines the classroom context. He distinguishes between the formal and informal aspects of the classroom social system and clashes that occur between them related to social status and demanding adaptation by some students. Next Kahl discusses learning processes associated with social status differences and interactions among them, school organization, and classroom behaviour. He concludes his article with some practical considerations including the observation "that the actual relationship between student social background and classroom behaviour turns out to be largely a result of social goals, ideologies, political priorities, and the like, since these determine what really happens at the school and classroom level".

3. Teachers' Characteristics

As Levis points out in the first article in this subsection, the personality characteristics of teachers tended to dominate the research on teacher effectiveness in the first half of this century. As Levis argues, this research did little to advance knowledge and understanding of teaching. Levis begins by describing the conceptual and theoretical problems underlying the research and then elaborates on them. First, he explains difficulties associated with meanings of the term "teacher personality" itself, distinguishing among behavioural definitions, social stimulus definitions, and depth-psychology definitions. He then discerns a more recent trend away from global concepts of teacher personality towards increased interest in cognitive aspects and teachers' attitudes toward teaching and students.

Another problem with earlier research on teachers' personalities, writes Levis, was with instruments used to measure them. A great variety of these were put to use apparently more on the grounds of their availability than their theoretical suitability, generating a great deal of empirical data that had little meaning and which defied synthesis. Next were problems arising from the criteria of teaching effectiveness applied in the research. Ratings by others such as school principals were common, and these were often flawed by subjectivity and unreliability. More acceptable criteria, such as gains in students' learning, were difficult to apply. But there were problems also in the notion that simple relationships would be found between teachers' personalities and their effectiveness, because this model ignores the context in which the teaching occurs and the ways in which the teachers actually behave. Furthermore, writes Levis, hypotheses tested were seldom justified on the basis of reasoned theories of interpersonal influence, and so explanatory and interpretative frameworks were missing.

Levis's review of research on teacher attitudes takes in some of the earlier research on teacher behaviours reviewed in Sect. 4 of this Encyclopedia. His conclusions about the variable teacher indirectness need to be seen in the light of the article by Soar and Soar in that section (see *Classroom Climate*). Further evidence of the influence of teachers' personality characteristics is the subject of other articles to follow.

Following Levis's article on teachers' personality characteristics is Coulter's article on the personality characteristics of those who are to become teachers. Coulter treats four main noncognitive dimensions of student teachers' personalities: their values, attitudes, and interests; their self-concept and self-esteem; their concerns and anxieties; and their commitment. Within the discussion on each of these dimensions, he reviews descriptive/comparative research, research on change as a consequence of teacher education, and, finally, research relating the dimension in question to effectiveness criteria such as student growth or supervisors' ratings. Two of the findings he reports are as follows:

(a) compared with other groups, student teachers have a stronger value commitment to people and personal relationships; and

(b) student teachers see themselves less positively after practice teaching.

Coulter discusses these and the many other findings he reviews in the light of theory and concludes his article by calling for "a comprehensive theory of teacher socialization". The article by Hoyle later in the subsection, and by Lacey in the next, take up this topic and explore it more fully.

In the next article, Braun writes on the topic of *Teachers' Expectations*. He introduces the term "self-fulfilling prophecy" and the suggestion that "teachers act on their perceptions about individuals so as to provide differential treatment to them and that such treatment can interact with pupil self-expectations to produce expected outcomes". After discussing the earlier studies of this phenomenon and the issues surrounding it, the author describes a seven-phase model of "the teacher expectancy cycle" and examines some of the mechanisms and linkages within the model.

Braun explains that teachers can begin to form expectations of students on the basis of such input as sex, physical attractiveness, intelligence, race, social class, and prior experience with the students' siblings. Such characteristics can lead teachers to form expectations consistent with stereotypes and labelling. Moreover, teachers' reactions to students' characteristics are likely to depend upon teachers' own personalities. The result of expectations developed by teachers is to be seen in such aspects of their treatment of students as grouping, tracking, or streaming decisions, and the allocation of praise and criticism. After a comprehensive review of research on these matters, Braun turns to the question of students' self-expectations as the outcomes of students' perceptions of differential teacher behaviour towards them. At this stage, prophecies in the form of teachers' expectations can become self-fulfilling through students' learning to behave as expected. On this basis Braun concludes with the caution that "teachers need to be sensitized to the personal biases and stereotypes they hold, and encouraged to examine these in relation to their classroom interactions with students".

The article by Bank in the previous subsection and the article by Braun on teachers' expectations leave little doubt that sex of student is an influential variable in classrooms and that the sex of the teacher might also be an important influence. In his article on this topic, Dunkin reviews the relevant research on classroom interaction and student learning outcomes. After noting that the deployment of male and female teachers in schools and school systems often assumes that one or the other is more suitable for teaching students of certain ages and other characteristics, and that sex differences in student achievement of certain types lead to hypotheses that teaching effectiveness is associated with sex of teacher, Dunkin reports the empirical evidence available from research.

Concerning differences in classroom behaviour, he concludes:

> On balance, the evidence supports the hypothesis that there are differences in classroom behaviour between male and female teachers. The impression that emerges most strongly is that the classrooms of female teachers tend to be warmer, more nurturant milieux while male teachers' classrooms are more highly organized and task oriented.

On the issue of whether teachers treat students of their own sex differently from others, Dunkin finds little or no evidence of favouritism for students of the same sex and some evidence of the reverse. Similarly, he finds little evidence that differences that might exist between male teachers and female teachers in their treatment of male students and female students affect the learning of those students. He concludes that there is little justification from this research for single-sex schools or for the placement of more male teachers in the lower grades.

The ways in which teachers behave are surely liable to depend upon their past experiences as teachers. Indeed, as Barnes argues in the next article, experience is often regarded as an asset and used as a criterion for appointment to teaching positions. Barnes discusses research on the use of experience in employment and alternative ways of measuring teaching experience. She then examines research on the relationship between teaching experience and student achievement, noting some results evidencing a nonlinear relationship, suggesting an optimal level of experience followed by a decline in effectiveness.

Whether teachers of more or less experience express different attitudes towards innovation, change, and minority groups, and whether more experienced teachers have less difficulty in classroom management are other issues included in Barnes's review. After discussing these, the value of experience outside teaching and how accumulated experience might be more effectively transmitted to the inexperienced, she concludes that the results of further research in this area could be beneficial to administrators, teachers themselves, and teacher educators.

Part of the experience of teachers has to do with their social origins and the status accorded to the occupation they have entered. Hoyle takes up these issues in his article on *Teachers' Social Backgrounds*. He begins his article by pointing out that status derives from such characteristics as age, sex, ethnic background, wealth, and occupation. In discussing the occupational prestige of teaching, Hoyle describes common methodologies for measuring prestige and the limitations they impose upon conclusions reached. He reviews relevant research in several countries and concludes that cross-national generalizations are suspect, especially across Western and Eastern European borders and in comparisons of developing with developed countries. Distinctions between primary-

and secondary-school teachers' prestige make the use of the blanket term "school teacher" as an occupational category meaningless, and the rarity of replications at different times makes it impossible to detect changes over time.

Similar problems confront those attempting to reach generalizations about the social origins of teachers. Here Hoyle discusses research in the United States, the United Kingdom, Australia, France, and Poland. He does, however, feel able to conclude as follows:

> Thus data from various countries show that although teachers are recruited from all social classes, the skilled working and white-collar groups tend to be more highly represented than the highest and lowest sectors, and middle-class representation in the teaching force becomes more pronounced as one moves from certificated primary school teachers to graduate secondary school teachers, expecially in the prestigious academic schools.

Hoyle goes on to discuss factors affecting the social status of teachers, including their social origins, the size of the teaching force, the proportion of women in teaching, academic qualifications, the childhood status of teachers' clients, and the teacher's relationship with those clients. These deliberations lead him to consider teaching as a profession and concepts of professionalization. His discussion forms a valuable link with articles to follow in the subsection on *Occupational Factors*.

4. Occupational Factors

Forces operating upon teaching and teachers arise partly from the intrinsic nature of the activity of teaching and partly from the milieu in which they are found. Teachers have expected and even prescribed roles to fulfil. They belong to an occupation which itself operates upon its members in order to socialize them into its ranks. Employers represent community interests in the selection of teachers and then, by the process of supervision of their work and granting or withholding credentials, attempt to ensure that their work is up to standard. All of this goes on within limitations imposed by economic, cultural, and demographic conditions that determine supply of, and demand for, teachers and the amount to be spent on them.

This subsection contains articles associated with those factors and issues. In the first of this set, Biddle provides a comprehensive analysis of *Teacher Roles*. He explains different approaches to the conceptualization of role and distinguishes among those which define roles in behavioural terms from those based on social position and those referring to expectations. He elaborates on each of these.

Research evidence on behaviourally defined teacher roles includes much that has been written about in Sect. 4 of this Encyclopedia. Thus, Biddle notes that teachers' behavioural roles include dominating the verbal interaction of the classroom, in particular the initiating roles of structuring and soliciting, and the role of reactor. Behaviourally defined roles involve teachers setting the cognitive tone of the classroom, responding to perceptions about students, and performing management tasks. In all, Biddle sees great development in knowledge of behavioural roles as a result of observational research during the 1960s and 1970s.

The social position concept of teacher role, writes Biddle, focuses on static characteristics of teachers, such as their status. He elaborates on two such aspects, status and the career of teaching, and covers some of the same ground written about by Hoyle in the previous subsection (see *Teachers' Social Backgrounds*). Biddle concludes that teachers have more prestige, wealth, and authority than most blue-collar workers but less than most professionals. His review of literature on the career of teaching includes the observation that "those who left teaching had greater analytical skills but those who remained were more expert organizers".

The expected role of the teacher is defined by Biddle as "the set of expectations that are held for teacher behaviours by both teachers and other persons". After outlining some of the complexities of this approach he gives special consideration to the issues of shared expectations, role conflict, strain, and resolution, and the relationship between role expectations and behaviour. This important last issue is one he finds seldom researched but often assumed.

Biddle's article is appropriately followed by Lacey's on *Professional Socialization of Teachers*. Lacey writes that the topic refers to "the process of change by which individuals become members of the teaching profession and then take up progressively maturer roles within teaching". This involves much more than learning to teach for it implies the acquisition of attitudes and values by a complex process sometimes viewed simplistically as a "filling of empty vessels". Lacey discusses critically the "crude functionalist" model of socialization with its static view of society and its assumptions of consensus. He also finds fault with Marx and other conflict theorists, mainly on the grounds that they leave "very little autonomy for individuals to influence their own development either collectively or individually".

These criticisms become dominant themes in the rest of Lacey's article during which he reviews research on teacher socialization, provides a penetrating critique of the consensual view of society, elaborates on areas of individual and collective autonomy, and considers in depth Becker's conceptual framework involving notions of internalized adjustment and strategic compliance. He then writes about career socialization noting that "career pressures clearly represent one of the most important socializing pressures felt by teachers". This is not only a process of being accepted into the existing structure of a school but also "the attempt by a particular teacher to make the school resemble more closely the sort of place in which that teacher would like to teach".

Being a member of the teaching occupation and being socialized in it follows being selected for it. Selection is not a process that applies only to student teachers, for there is mobility within teaching and many professionally socialized teachers submit themselves for selection to other teaching appointments. Eltis begins the next article by introducing questions involving teacher supply and demand, topics taken up more fully in later articles in this section. He points out that selection criteria and processes sometimes are adjusted to reflect prevailing conditions of supply and demand.

Several factors impinge upon initial selection for teacher training. Eltis discusses the needs of employing authorities and the incentives they offer to attract recruits, such as bonded scholarships. Among the needs are those for desired mixes of males and females, members of minority and majority groups, and specialists of various kinds. Another influencing factor is the resource pool from which recruits are available. He comments on a decline in academic quality towards the end of the 1970s and the implications of this for ways in which training institutions are funded.

Eltis's description of selection processes for initial training includes consideration of the difficulties of including criteria other than academic attainment and the need for a continuing rather than a once only selection process with appropriate screening and counselling facilities throughout the training period, especially where positive discrimination is desirable to ensure proper representation of some groups.

His discussion of selection of already trained teachers includes consideration of procedures for certification, a topic taken up in the article by Zimpher later in this section. This discussion leads Eltis to recommend that "collaborative working groups" consisting of teacher educators, employing authorities, researchers, and others professionally involved be set up to consider such matters as selection for training; criteria for selection; counselling; appointment to schools; initial certification; and subsequent approval of teachers as "professional scholars".

Eltis's discussion of supply and demand issues is followed by two related articles. The first, by Williams, focuses on the planning of teacher supply and demand, while the second, by Zabalza, concerns the economics of teacher supply. Williams lists four reasons for expecting that planning with respect to the teaching force should be less difficult than for other occupations. They are: first, the demand for teachers is determined by birth rates which are known; second, education is a single-occupation undertaking; third, there is usually one main employer of teachers, so that decisions about needs and employment are rather centralized; and, fourth, public authorities control the size of the education system. Nevertheless, shortages and surpluses of teachers are not uncommon.

Williams writes that major problems for forecasters have been volatile birth rates and changes in the employment opportunities for married women. The speed with which responses can be made to changes in demand is limited by constraints upon teacher training institutions, by variations in the need for teachers specializing in particular areas, and by promotion blockages that occur in contracting systems. Williams suggests ways in which shortages and surpluses might be better handled and concludes with the timely comment that "in the economically straitened circumstances of the 1980s the cost factor weighs as heavily as any with the decision makers in education", thus setting the scene for Zabalza's treatment of the economics of teacher supply.

Zabalza defines teacher supply as "the number of people who, under certain conditions, would be willing to offer their services to the teaching profession". He states that the economics of teacher supply is concerned with the ways in which pecuniary factors affect that number. Training costs and expected income are two basic elements in formulae used in making predictions of teacher supply, but, of course, nonpecuniary factors affect the accuracy of predictions based on pecuniary factors alone. Zabalza notes evidence that educational authorities have tended to ignore salaries as instruments for eliminating shortages while other evidence suggests that the supply of teachers responds to economic incentives, though the trend for males seems to be different from that for females. Furthermore, he concludes that teachers' willingness to move to unattractive locations is affected by "pecuniary differentials" between locations, though again, sex differences exist in this regard.

The article by Zimpher provides a description of the issues and procedures concerning the certification and licensing of teachers in the United States. She outlines the recent history of these practices, distinguishes between certification which applies to individual teachers and accreditation which applies to institutional programmes of teacher education, and describes recent trends concerning who controls the process of certification, and competency testing. She concludes by listing emerging issues which will shape future developments in this area. The reader is reminded that Eltis also discussed this topic in his article on *Selection for Teaching*.

The last two articles in this section are about two other occupational factors which affect teachers and teaching. One is the professional association of teachers, especially as it functions as a body which participates in negotiations with employers about working conditions, salaries, and the like. The other is about personnel other than teachers who participate in the process of schooling as ancillary staff and whose functions complement, and therefore affect, the functions performed by teachers themselves.

In the article on *Teachers' Organizations*, Colton lists the purposes and labels of such agencies and considers factors affecting membership of them, such as religious or ideological affiliations, social conditions, teachers' salaries, community support for teachers, social class background, and sex of teacher. Internal governance, goals, and activities, including teachers' welfare, pedagogical policy, and social issues are also discussed. The article concludes with a presentation of contending views about the effectiveness of teachers' organizations and the conclusion that they are in a precarious position.

Duthie's article on *Nonteachers and Teaching* concludes this section of the Encyclopedia. In it Duthie focuses on the roles of auxiliary staff in schools in Scotland. His article includes a report of attempts to define the responsibilities of nonteaching assistants, including a large number of "housekeeping" tasks such as escorting children inside from the playground, cloakroom supervision, collection of money, distribution and clearing of materials, objective marking, setting up and maintenance of audiovisual aids, and marking attendance rolls. He reports research findings that the presence of auxiliaries reduced by 10 percent the time teachers devoted to such activities, releasing them for more individual attention to students and more concentration on planning, evaluating, diagnostic, and other instructional tasks.

Duthie also reports on an enquiry into the use of nonteacher assistants in Scottish secondary schools. Here he discusses ways in which youth and community workers, librarians, and visiting experts from the community might contribute. Readers will find these ideas challenging, particularly in view of the financial situation in schools in the 1980s.

The Environment

Frame Factors

U. P. Lundgren

An educational system operates according to an explicit or implicit definition of its role in society. Clearly, all education has external effects in society. On a broad level these effects can be described as the fundamental reproduction of society. Behind the Anglo–Saxon research tradition there has been an assumption that the inner functions of education can be derived from the external functions. This assumption is of course rooted in a functionalistic approach to educational phenomena resulting in the notion that there is a correspondence between skills, knowledge, and personal disposition transmitted by education and the skills, knowledge, and dispositions demanded by production. In its most sophisticated way, this is expressed in the classical essay *The School Class as a Social System* by Parsons, in which the influence from Durkheim is clearly visible. With the expansion of educational systems after the Second World War, this notion of correspondence between external and inner functions of education received specific normative implications. Within economics of education, which was established as an interdisciplinary field, it concerned the relation between education and economics—its basis was the correlation between growth of the educational sector and the residual factor. (In neoclassical growth theories it was noted that besides the two main factors behind economic growth, fixed capital and labour, there was a third residual factor.) With the slowing down of the educational expansion and with the difficulties in reading off these expected correspondences, a criticism of the basic assumptions behind the expansion of school systems and educational reforms was formulated. In the United States this assumed gestalt in a renewal of the correspondence theory, perhaps best formulated in the following theoretical outlines:

> . . . the structure of education reflects the social relations of production. For at least the past century and a half, expansion of education and changes in the forms of schooling have been responses to needs generated by the economic system. The sources of present inequality in US education were found in the mutual reinforcement of class subcultures and social class biases in the operation of the school system itself. (Bowles 1977 p. 149)

Another more general type of theory directed towards the role of education to reproduce ideology was articulated by Apple (1982) and a more specific approach reflecting the neomarxist influenced research in Europe has been delivered by Giroux (1981).

In Europe this functionalistic research tradition was not as established as in the United States. The criticism of research within economics of education was directed towards the analyses of how the state administered the reproduction of fundamental economic and social relations.

> In Europe this was true of the "Prokla school", Elmer Altvater and others, who stressed inquiry into how the State secures the conditions underlying capital accumulation. In the area of education this means primarily how qualification of the labour force is undertaken. Second, French sociologists, such as Pierre Bourdieu, and political scientists, such as Nicos Poulantzas, have been more interested in reproduction of social classes and in the transmission of ideology. Third, "system theorists", such as Claus Offe, have attached relatively great importance to the fact that the State and the bureaucracy must legitimate their own actions as well as rectify "consequential problems" which result from prior state action or from the anarchy of capitalist economy. (Broady 1980 p. 3)

The research noted above has provided important contributions for the explanation of how education functions in relation to social production and to the understanding of how social and cultural reproduction is constituted as a consequence of how the forces and processes of production change (Lundgren 1981a, 1981b, 1982a, 1982b). At the same time as this research links the processes of schooling to the processes of production, it lacks in specificity concerning how this assumes gestalt at the very moment of teaching. Studies of teaching made for a lengthy period (Hoetker and Ahlbrandt 1969) over school systems and nations (Lundgren 1977, Gustafsson 1977, Pedro 1981), indicate that the process of teaching cannot be decoded in a simple one-to-one relationship to its social context (Callewaert and Nilsson 1980a, 1980b, Lundgren 1982b).

There are at least three lines of research aiming to uncover how in each moment of teaching there is a contextual meaning reflecting a wider cultural reproduction and a specific production. The main question for these three lines can be formulated in the following way: How can the internal work of the school be given form and configuration so that it can function internally and at the same time have, reflected against the society, predictable effects? These three lines of research will be called the habitus theory, the code theory, and the frame factor theory.

1. The Habitus Theory

The internal functions and effects of the school can obviously not be explained without a broader social theory. These effects do not appear by means of collecting and compiling data, as though the nature of the school in itself arranges these data in regular patterns and formations. It is of course necessary to proceed from a theoretically based explanatory model which supplies the determinants which are involved in the teaching process. The argument that the determinants for the process must be given, carries with it in turn a deeper analysis of what constitutes reasonable determinants in order, thus, to give a point of departure for empirical research. Such a theoretical framework is given in the research by Pierre Bourdieu and his colleagues at the *Centre de Sociologie Européenne* in Paris. In the book together with Passeron—*La Reproduction* (1970) he summarizes empirical research and formulates a series of theoretical propositions about schooling and cultural reproduction.

A central concept is habitus, which can be defined as a system of an enduring and transmittable state of dispositions which, at the same time as it integrates all previous experiences of the individual at any given moment, functions as a matrix for how the individual understands, evaluates, and acts (Bourdieu 1972 p. 178).

In order to analyse how socialization, of which teaching is a part, proceeds, it is necessary to clarify how it imprints a habitus which recreates itself. The imprinting of a habitus must thus take place in such a manner that it really works and becomes possible to transfer to various social fields, which makes outer control unnecessary, when the inner control takes over. To apply this concept and line of thinking to education, the nature of teaching processes must be determined, that is, the question of how teaching functions as a special case in order to form the habitus of various groups. Bourdieu aims to formulate a general theory of cultural reproduction. The educational system constitutes only a portion of the network of determinants which form and maintain a certain definite habitus.

Those who hold a social position embrace conceptions by means of relating to holders of other social positions with definite conditions of power springing from the economic and juridical–political levels. These power conditions are the basis for the symbolic relationship between social groups. The power that the economic and juridical–political conditions give some social strata or groups can get other social strata or groups to embrace certain values and conceptions. They have then the power to form the practices which determine and maintain the habitus for other social groups. This takes place on a symbolic level. In other words, dominating social groups can exercise a form of symbolic violence over dominated groups. They do this through the power of being able to determine the practices in which the symbolic violence is exercised. The school constitutes such a practice or such a social field. One of Bourdieu and Passeron's established assumptions is that "the power of symbolic violence adds its own forces, of symbolic nature, to the condition of force on which it is based". This can also be expressed in such a way that the force on which the power of symbolic violence is based is strengthened by means of the fact that it functions efficiently and thus establishes a definite habitus in specific social groups. In order for this to function, it is necessary that the dominating classes can get the dominated classes to understand certain concepts as legitimate. This takes place by means of concealing the nonsymbolic power conditions which the symbolic have as a basis.

The theoretical framework of Bourdieu and Passeron (1980) has been used in a study of teaching processes by Callewaert and Nilsson (1980a, 1980b). In relation to teaching, they transformed this line of thinking in the following way:

(a) The nonsymbolic power conditions are the basis for the symbolic power conditions.

(b) The dominating classes or groups can transmit their conceptions, values, and attitudes by means of presenting these as legitimate.

(c) Part of this transmission takes place within the schools. This means that education must appear as just and egalitarian, and that the actual teaching process must be seen by all as legitimate.

(d) The actual practice which takes place in education successively forms various phases of the internalization of a specific habitus.

(e) This habitus becomes enduring and steering for the ways in which other nonpedagogic practices are formed.

These points are, of course, simplifications, but they indicate the basic line of thinking. Following them and recording a series of lessons in the Swedish comprehensive school system, Callewaert and Nilsson tried to decode the teaching process. The basic classification system was built on the categories: manner of work, control, isolation evaluation, and balance. The interpretation of the data they deliver points out some fascinating mechanisms in the teaching process that reflects in an utterly sophisticated way how reproduction assumes gestalt in classrooms. They reveal in a new way the school class as a social system.

2. The Code Theory

The imaginative work of Basil Bernstein is intimately related to the work of Bourdieu. Both relate their theoretical systems to Durkheim. In Bourdieu's work, habitus is meaningful only in relation to the concept of social fields. In Bernstein's work the concept of code is isotopic to that of habitus but related to the concept of class not over the concept of social field but over the concepts of power and control. Bernstein uses the concept of code both as referring to principles according to which the individual creates an orientation to meaning and educational codes according to which educational institutions orientate their own meanings (Bernstein 1971, 1980). The relation between classes, says Bernstein (Bernstein 1980, Bernstein and Lundgren 1982) is built on the unequal distribution of power and social control. These class differences are realized in the creation, distribution, reproduction, and legitimation of physical and symbolic values. Thus class relations are articulated in the distribution of power and control. In order to explain how power and control are transformed in educational institutions, Bernstein uses the concepts of classification and framing. The concept of classification refers to the differentiation of contents, that is, to the principles according to which the curriculum is constructed.

"Curriculum defines what counts as valid knowledge. . ." (Bernstein 1971 p. 47). In making a distinction between strong and weak classified curricula, Bernstein identifies two types of curricula or educational codes.

> If contents stand in a closed relation to each other, that is, if the contents are clearly bounded and insulated from each other [strong classification, *my remark*] I shall call such a curriculum a *collection* type. Here, the learner has to collect a group of favoured contents in order to satisfy some criteria of evaluation. There may of course be some underlying concept as to a collection: the gentleman, the educated man, the skilled man, the non-vocational man.
>
> Now I want to juxtapose against the collective type, a curriculum in which the various contents do not go their own separate ways, but where the contents stand in an open relation to each other [weak classification, *my remark*]. I shall call such a curriculum an *integrated* type. (Bernstein 1971 p. 49)

Thus classification deals with the structure of the curriculum and is related to the concept of power. In order to analyse social control, Bernstein uses the concept of frame (Bernstein 1971). Later on, the same concept is called framing in analogy to classification (Bernstein 1980).

The concept frame is used to determine the structure of the message system, pedagogy. Frame refers to the form of the *context* in which knowledge is transmitted and received. Frame refers to the specific pedagogical relationship of teacher and taught. In the same way as classification does not refer to contents, so frame does not refer to the contents of pedagogy. Frame refers to the strength of the boundary between what may be transmitted and what may not be transmitted in the pedagogical relationship. Where framing is strong, there is a sharp boundary, where framing is weak, a blurred boundary, between what may and may not be transmitted. Frame refers us to the range of options available to teacher and taught in the control of what is transmitted and received in the context of the pedagogical relationship. Strong framing entails reduced options: weak framing entails a range of options. Thus frame refers to the degree of control teacher and pupil possess over the selection, organization and pacing of knowledge transmitted and received in the pedagogical relationship. (Bernstein 1971 p. 50)

In using this conceptual apparatus it is possible to identify how various contexts for reproduction are formed and positioned and constitute various codes. A code is a regulative principle tacitly acquired which selects and integrates: (a) relevant meanings—meanings; (b) form of their realizations—realizations; (c) evoking contexts—contexts (Bernstein 1980 pp. 2–3).

In analysing the "new pedagogy" Bernstein (1975) in a powerful way shows how codes are transmitted by various types of curricula and pedagogy and codes are related to the upbringing of the child in the home, that is, the code as a mechanism for positioning. The definition of the code given above indicates, as well as the development of the code concept, that a code is a specific semantic organization. It opens up, then, possibilities to study how classroom discourse is classified and framed in relation to the semantic competence of the students. In a study of Portugese education, Pedro (1981) has carried out one such study. In her work, Pedro shows how the class structure of Portugese society is reproduced in the use and regulation of language in single classrooms.

3. The Frame Factor Theory

The third line of research to be discussed has been labelled the frame factor theory. It represents from its beginning quite another tradition than the two earlier mentioned, but has been influenced by the work of Bernstein and Bourdieu as well as developed by collaboration with Callewaert and Nilsson. In discussing the last basic theory for this article it is hoped to be able to show both how the theory is related to more comprehensive theories of education and society, and how it has developed in an interplay with contemporary research.

Returning to educational research related to the expansion of educational systems in the 1950s and 1960s, it is possible to see how research was linked to educational reforms. Methodologically it is possible to identify two research lines that emerged.

527

On the one hand, much energy and many of the significant results have taken the form of empirical, usually quantitative, studies of the role of education in reducing or maintaining structures of inequality that coexist with widespread egalitarian ideologies. On the other hand there has been the development of action–research in the form of quasi-experiments, in most cases conducted under governmental auspices. (Karabel and Halsey 1978 p. 16)

Studies of the effect of ability grouping are examples of the latter type of research. The educational reforms after the Second World War, at least in Europe, can be characterized as directed towards educational systems that are comprehensive in the beginning and have a successive differentiation aiming towards various sectors of the labour market. The change from a differentiated school system on the lower and middle levels to a comprehensive system can, using Bernstein's conceptual apparatus, be described as a shift from a collective type of curriculum to a more integrated type. From an organizational point of view, this shift meant the transformation of the schools from differentiated classes to undifferentiated classes. From the planners' and the decision makers' point of view it became, then, important to know the pedagogical effects of nonability grouped classes. Most of the studies carried out as quasi-experiments yielded no clear indications (Heathers 1969, Goldberg et al. 1966, Esposito 1973, Dahllöf 1967, 1971, Bengtsson and Lundgren 1969, Lundgren 1972). This picture of a lack of consistent results was true both for studies using achievement tests as a dependent variable, and those using various measures of social and personal growth (Wrightstone 1957, Johannesson and Magnusson 1960). In relation to the comprehensive school reform in Sweden, one study was carried out— the Stockholm study (Svensson 1962, Husén and Boalt 1968). The main conclusion was that there were no demonstrable effects of grouping the students differently (Svensson 1962 p. 182). Using other data— time spent on various curriculum units—Dahllöf later reinterpreted the Stockholm study and showed that there were remarkable differences in time spent in order to reach the same achievement. Dahllöf explained these differences by means of what he called "the steering group hypothesis", which meant that a group of students steered the pacing through the curriculum units. In the Dahllöf study the data indicated that the steering group was located between the 10th and 25th percentiles concerning general ability. Methodologically, research into the effects of ability grouping were built on simple quasi-experiments, in which the independent variable was the composition of the school class and the dependent variable was achievement tests. Dahllöf suggested that studies of the effects of various organizational measures methodologically must be based on the relations among organizational frames, the teaching process, and results. The idea behind the concept of organizational frames was that, as frames, they merely delimit what is possible but do not determine the actual teaching process nor the outcome. The steering group hypothesis was then just an hypothesis suggesting the manner in which a specific set of frame factors facilitated a specific strategy for curriculum pacing. In a later study, Lundgren (1972) used different types of data, including classroom observations, and verified and developed the idea that frame factors influence the school class. According to Dahllöf, "frame factors have in common that they set a certain time and space limit for that part of the teaching process which takes place at school" (Dahllöf 1969 p. 60). Lundgren defined frame factors in a more general way, as the measures taken by the state in regulating time, space, and personnel. Thus the frames are manipulated above the teachers and the taught and express a certain power relation to the state apparatus. During an expansion, the frames are wider than during stabilization and decline. Thus the concept of frame factors must be understood in relation to how the state regulates education through allocating economic resources. It is also important to make a distinction between frames as objective measures and the subjective interpretation of frames (Lundgren 1973). In studying how the frames constrain the teaching process, it is then necessary to analyse how the curriculum is classified and how the pedagogy is framed, to use Bernstein's terminology (Kallós and Lundgren 1979). In the first empirical study (Lundgren 1972) the attempt was to show the pragmatic aspect of the classroom language in terms of how pedagogical roles were established as consequences of how teachers built up strategies for teaching within the constraints given. These pedagogical roles meant that the teacher directed questions and commands according to how the teacher codified the students' competence in relation to the goals and the frames. If, for example, the time was limited, the students were in the discourse grouped in fewer groups than if the time given was longer. This study of pedagogical roles has been followed up in an excellent work by Gustafsson (1977) and the structuring of the teaching process by time has been studied by Torper (1982). From these studies the frame factor theory expanded (Lundgren 1977). Distinctions were made between the curriculum and the classification of the curriculum and how this classification formed and regulated the way in which goals are perceived, and how the state controls the educational system by allocating resources regulated in an administrative apparatus that forms the constraints (the frame factors) and, finally, how the state juridically and politically regulates school laws realized in the formal rule system of education. This expansion of the frame factor theory lay in the direction of the work of Bernstein and of Bourdieu and meant a specific incorporation of the two research lines earlier discussed. The interest was then to study, not only how rules and roles in teaching were formed by the curriculum, school laws, and administrative regulations and constraints, but also how the actual transmission assumed gestalt. In a study of the teaching of arithmetic (Lundgren 1977) it was shown how the curriculum, concretized in textbooks, and the frame factors formed various specific mechanisms in the transmission process.

When teachers were constrained by time and by the variation in prerequisites among the children, they were forced to pilot the student through problems. Piloting meant that the discourse was reduced to a simple question–answer pattern, in which the answers were contextually given, so that the student solved a mathematical problem in the discourse but did not understand the solution from a mathematical point of view. In following the teaching over a lengthy period of time, the learning consequences of piloting were shown—metalearning, that is, when the pupil learned something about his or her capacity in relation to the curriculum more than the actual content. In that way, the pupils both consciously and unconsciously learn to select various courses. Metalearning opens up a possibility to study the transmission of a habitus and how various students by their semantic competence will acquire different types of metalearning. In doing that, the reproduction of social classes over a state-regulated school system can be explained. The first step towards such an analysis has been taken by Pedro (1981). In that study, which was done in Portugal, Pedro uses as her theoretical framework, an integration of Bernstein's theory and the frame factor theory as developed by Lundgren. Another step is taken in a study by Pettersson et al. (see Lundgren and Pettersson 1979).

4. Summary

The frame factor theory started as a methodological solution to studies of organizational measures and as a means of viewing organizational measures not as determining but as limiting educational processes. It has developed, influenced by more elaborated and broader theories about the relation between production and reproduction and state interventionism, in which the specific concept of frames indicates the general line of thinking in terms of how contexts constrain possible actions and how state-regulated resources for education constrain the teaching process (Lundgren 1982a, 1982b, Bernstein and Lundgren 1982).

Frame factors are then factors that constrain the teaching process and which are not manipulated by the teachers. In studying the teaching process, it is important to determine what is possible or not possible within the frames given and how the frames have been built up. The latter demands an historical analysis (Lundgren 1979). Frame factors cannot be seen as simple functions of a rationalistic planning model; they must be understood as residuals of earlier school systems, as consequences of public expenditures, and as expressions of the wider economic and political context of education.

The study of frame factors gives no sufficient structure for the explanation of how educational processes are constituted. They give some concepts of importance to see how the state regulates education. Thus, any study of constraints must also include the study of what actually is formed within the frames given, such as the content transmitted, the structure of the curriculum (classification and curriculum codes), the structure of the transmission process, and how social control is realized (framing). Using that conceptual apparatus, it opens up possibilities of finding the more delicate and sophisticated mechanisms in the socialization going on in the classroom; how habitus is imprinted; and how orientation to meaning is formed. Having found these mechanisms, it is then possible to relate these to social and cultural formation and to production processes. It is in this theoretical context that the frame factor is a subtheory, intended to explain one part of the relation between what goes on in classrooms and how the teaching process is independent of, and at the same time dependent upon, its broader social context.

Bibliography

Apple M W 1982 *Education and Power: Reproduction and Contradiction in Education.* Routledge and Kegan Paul, London

Bengtsson J, Lundgren U P 1969 *Utbildningsplanering och jämförelser av skolsystem* [Educational planning and comparisons of school systems]. Studentlitteratur, Lund

Bernstein B B 1971 On the classification and framing of educational knowledge. In: Young M F D (ed.) 1971 *Knowledge and Control: New Directions for the Sociology of Education.* Collier-Macmillan, London

Bernstein B B 1975 Class and pedagogics: Visible and invisible. In: Bernstein B B (ed.) 1975 *Class, Codes and Control,* Vol. 3. Schocken, New York, pp. 116–45

Bernstein B B 1980 *Codes, Modalities and the Process of Cultural Reproduction: A Model.* Department of Education, University of Lund, Lund

Bernstein B B, Lundgren U P 1982 *Makt, kontroll och pedagogik* [Power, control and pedagogy]. Liber, Lund

Bourdieu P 1972 *Esquisse d'une théorie de la pratique.* Droz, Paris

Bourdieu P, Passeron J C 1970 *La Reproduction: Eléménts pour une théorie du système d'enseignement.* Minuit, Paris

Bowles S 1977 Unequal education and the reproduction of the social division of labor. In: Karabel J, Halsey A H (eds.) 1977

Broady D 1980 *Critique of the Political Economy of Education: The Prokla Approach.* Reports in Education and Psychology, No. 2, 1980, Stockholm Institute of Education, Stockholm

Callewaert S, Nilsson B-A 1980a *Samhället, skolan och skolans inre arbete* [Society, the schools and the internal work of schools]. Lunds bok-och tidskrifts, Lund

Callewaert S, Nilsson B-A 1980b *Skolklassen som socialt system: Lektions-analyser* [The school class as a social system: Lesson analyses]. Lunds bok-och tidskrifts, Lund

Dahllöf U S 1967 *Skoldifferentiering och undervisningsförlopp* [School differentiation and the teaching process]. Almqvist and Wiksell, Stockholm

Dahllöf U S 1969 *Ability Grouping, Content Validity and Curriculum Process Analysis.* Reports from the Institute of Education, University of Gothenburg, Gothenburg

Dahllöf U S 1971 *Ability Grouping, Content Validity and Curriculum Process Analysis.* Teachers College Press, New York

Esposito D 1973 Homogenous and heterogeneous ability grouping: Principal findings and implications for evaluating and designing more effective educational environments. *Rev. Educ. Res.* 43: 163–79

Giroux H A 1981 *Ideology Culture and the Process of Schooling*. Falmer Press, London

Goldberg M, Passow A H, Justman J 1966 *The Effects of Ability Grouping*. Teachers College Press, New York

Gustafsson C 1977 *Classroom Interaction: A Study of Pedagogical Roles in the Teaching Process*. CWK/Gleerups, Lund

Heathers G 1969 Grouping. In: Ebel R L, Noll V H, Bauer R M (eds.) 1969 *Encyclopedia of Educational Research: A Project of the American Educational Research Association*. Macmillan, New York

Hoetker J, Ahlbrandt P A 1969 The persistence of recitation. *Am. Educ. Res. J.* 16: 145–67

Husén T, Boalt G 1968 *Educational Research and Educational Change*. Almqvist and Wiksell, Stockholm

Johannesson I, Magnusson D 1960 *Social- och personlig-hetspsykologiska faktorer i relation till skolans differentiering* [Social and personality psychological factors in relation to differentiation in the schools]. Statens Offentliga Utredningar, Stockholm, 42

Kallós D, Lundgren U P 1979 *Curriculum as a Pedagogical Problem*. CWK/Gleerup, Lund

Karabel J, Halsey A H 1977 *Power and Ideology in Education*. Oxford University Press, New York

Lundgren U P 1972 *Frame Factors and the Teaching Process: A Contribution to Curriculum Theory and Theory on Teaching*. Almqvist and Wiksell, Stockholm

Lundgren U P 1973 *Pedagogical Frames and the Teaching Process: A Report from an Empirical Curriculum Project*. Report from the Institute of Education, University of Gothenburg, Gothenburg

Lundgren U P 1977 *Model Analysis of Pedagogical Processes*. CWK/Gleerups, Lund

Lundgren U P 1979 *Att organisera omvärlden: En introduction till läroplansteori* [Organizing the world about us: An introduction to curriculum theory]. Liber, Stockholm

Lundgren U P 1981a Education as a context for work. Outlines for a theory on educational transmission. *Aus. Educ. Res.* 8: 5–29

Lundgren U P 1981b *Model Analysis of Pedagogical Processes*, Rev. edn. CWK/Gleerup, Lund

Lundgren U P 1982a The school class as a social system. *Acta Sociologica* 25: 187–94

Lundgren U P 1982b *Texts and Contexts in Curriculum*. Deakin University Press, Geelong

Lundgren U P, Pettersson S (eds.) 1979 *Code, Context and Curriculum Processes*. CWK/Gleerup, Lund

Pedro E 1981 *Social Stratification and Classroom Discourse*. CWK/Gleerup, Lund

Svensson N-E 1962 *Ability Grouping and Scholastic Achievement*. Almqvist and Wiksell, Stockholm

Torper U 1982 *Tid och tidsanvändning* [Time and the use of time]. Institution of Pedagogy, University of Lund, Lund

Wrightstone J W 1957 *Classroom Organization for Instruction*. National Education Association, Washington, DC

Architecture

S. N. Bennett

In the 1971 Yearbook of the National Society for the Study of Education Anderson wrote "It is almost axiomatic that the physical environment of a school is important as a factor in each child's learning; but solid proof of support of the proposition, especially in terms of assessing the amount of difference the environment makes is almost non-existent."

Despite lack of evidence, this belief in the link between the quality of teaching and learning and the design of instructional spaces has underpinned marked changes in the internal design of elementary schools in many parts of the world since the early 1960s. The educational rationale for such changes has been heralded for much of the century in various official reports but found its fullest expression in the Plowden Report of 1967. This report provided official endorsement for progressive teaching methods in the United Kingdom in which the individuality and uniqueness of each child is stressed. Pupils, it was claimed, would learn best when working at their own pace in a cooperative climate which allowed active discovery, freedom, and choice. Moreover such teaching approaches ideally required instructional spaces different from the self-contained

classroom which was too constraining. In other words, the design of teaching spaces should match the characteristics of the built environment to the flexibility perceived in contemporary teaching practices. Specialist activities required specialist spaces.

The spatial constraints of self-contained classrooms was also apparent in the United States where experiments with progressive methods under the banner of "open education" made use of corridors as teaching space and of open-door classrooms. Indeed the facilitation of movement between classrooms was seen as central to the learning environment created. It was a short move from this to the removal of classroom divisions altogether, embodying the concept of the elementary school as a single, though multidimensional, unit in which teachers and pupils made use of space and resources as these were required by the activities and experiences engaged in.

After a sporadic start, schools began to be built in the United Kingdom and the United States in the early 1960s which were characterized by the removal of internal walls, the integration of circulation areas such as corridors into the teaching space, and the provision of specialist spaces such as practical/wet areas for messy activities and quiet rooms for small group teaching. Since that time the growth in the number of such schools, variously categorized as open plan, open area, or open space, has been a worldwide phenomenon. During the period 1967 to 1969, for example, 50 percent of all schools built in the United States were of open design, and at the elementary level only 3 percent of schools built during this period were of conventional design. This pattern of growth was similar in Canada and the United Kingdom where now over one in 10 of all elementary schools are of open design. Australia and New Zealand began building a little later but growth has been substantial. In New Zealand, the first open school was built in 1971 but by 1978 one child in 12 was educated in one.

1. Open Designs

In the research effort which followed this innovation, one of the major weaknesses has been the erroneous assumption that open schools are architecturally homogeneous. Therefore before considering teaching practices in these schools, the attitudes of teachers towards them, and their impact on pupil outcomes, an elaboration on the diverse architectural features of teaching spaces seems necessary.

The variety of type, size, and orientation of spaces within schools is extremely great. Teaching units vary in size from the equivalent of two conventional classrooms to over 30, and the provision of specialist spaces varies widely as does the existence of shared teaching space. Figure 1 can only provide a limited understanding of this diversity. It is based on a space equivalent to four conventional classrooms. These classrooms are shown in Fig. 1(a) together with their associated corridor space.

Figure 1(b) shows the same space in a semiopen "bay" design. The classroom walls are retained but the doors are removed and the openings made substantially wider. Each bay opens onto a shared practical/wet area for project work and art and craft activities. In such a design each bay could be made somewhat smaller to allow the provision of a shared quiet room.

In contrast, Fig. 1(c) shows a totally open design with some four teachers and approximately 120 children sharing the space. A shared quiet room and practical/wet area are also provided. Such designs are fairly common but more typical, in the United Kingdom at least, are the two teacher units shown in Fig. 1(d).

Two alternative designs are presented. The upper unit is totally open being a scaled down version of that in Fig. 1(c). The lower unit is less open with a shared quiet room centrally sited, together with a partial wall divide. In a recent national study in the United Kingdom, it was found that this latter design is the most frequently built, but paradoxically, the design that teachers like least (Bennett et al. 1980).

This same study pointed to the importance of the

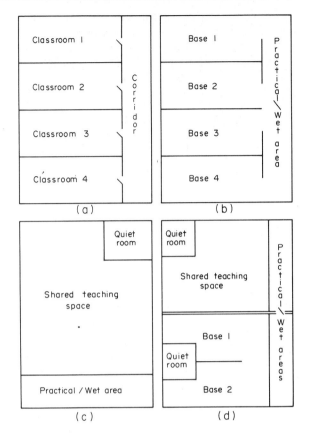

Figure 1
To show the diversity of possible designs for teaching units

extent of shared teaching space since it provides differential opportunity for teachers to implement alternative teaching arrangements. Cooperative or team teaching is certainly possible in the design in Fig. 1(c) since all teaching space is shared, but would be extremely difficult in the "bay" design where the only shared space is specialized. This is not meant to imply architectural determinism. Nevertheless, architecture certainly places limits on what can and cannot be implemented. Further evidence on the link between teaching practices and unit design is presented later.

2. Theory and Practice

It was argued earlier that the origins of open school design are to be found in the progressive tradition of elementary theory and practice. An additional expression of this can be found in a report on elementary education in Wales which posed the following questions. "Are children on the whole being instructed, or are they being trained to learn a great deal for themselves? Is their school day mainly a passive experience, or are they actively involved and seeking? Are they being regarded and dealt with mainly as a class, or is scope being given to the full range of individual variation? These are not idle questions. The evidence shows that the design of teaching space depends upon the answers one gives to questions of these kinds" (Gittins Report 1967).

The report postulates an explicit link between progressive or open education teaching approaches and school design, but is this link apparent in practice? Regrettably, many researchers have assumed the link instead of investigating it, a fact which makes much research on open schools of little value. Nevertheless, a number of studies have surveyed teaching practices in open schools in a number of countries using a variety of research techniques. Questionnaire surveys are considered first.

The largest study in the United Kingdom conceptualized teaching organization on an independent–cooperative dimension (Bennett et al. 1980). Independent teaching was defined as teachers operating on their own with no, or minimal, cooperation with other teachers in the unit. The majority of teachers claimed to be teaching in this way irrespective of the age of children taught. Approximately one-quarter claimed to teach cooperatively for some period during the day or week. However, differences were apparent when the design of teaching spaces was taken into account. Many more teachers were teaching cooperatively where shared teaching space was available. There thus appeared to be a relationship between the openness of the unit design and openness of teaching organization. Timetabling of space was also linked to unit design.

Idiographic research based on case studies of individual schools provides some elaboration on the theme of teacher independence. The phenomenon of teachers defining their territories within open designs has been commented on by researchers in a number of countries. One investigator in the United Kingdom was struck by the isolation of many teacher territories where linking doors between contiguous classrooms were bolted or plastered over with display materials and low furniture arranged down the middle of shared areas. This was also the case in a Canadian study where observers noted a variety of means to establish or maintain territories, most common being blackboards and bookshelves. And even where no physical barriers existed, imaginary lines were drawn over which children were not encouraged to cross.

It would seem from these observations that some teachers find it difficult to take advantage of the opportunities for flexible use of space and attempt to retain their "own" territory, that is, to retain their own personal space. Architects can remove walls but they can clearly be reinstated physically or psychologically.

Curriculum organization in schools in the United Kingdom is dominated by what is called the split-day where the basic subjects are taught in the mornings and project work, art and crafts, and other creative activities in the afternoons. Other popular organizations include various kinds of assignment system where pupils are assigned work at the beginning of the day or the week to be carried out either in a teacher-determined order or in pupil-chosen order. Only 10 percent of teachers place major emphasis on project or topic work.

A similar picture has been painted by all the surveys undertaken in the United Kingdom and can be summarized in the words of an educational adviser in Oxfordshire, a county well-known for its progressive practices, "to have an open plan building . . . means nothing in educational terms" (Jarman 1977).

Surveys in the United States and Canada present a mixed picture of practice dependent on the location and type of sample used. A study of schools in Toronto found more open teaching in open schools but other Canadian studies report very little difference in teaching practices in open and conventional buildings. The organizational climate in open schools has also been assessed. The largest of these studies reported that there were many more open schools with a closed climate than an open one and that this result was true irrespective of how long the school had been open.

Questionnaire surveys can only present reported practices which may or may not be accurate. Observational studies provide a more detailed record of the reality of classroom practice. The findings from such studies have not always been consistent but on balance the conclusion would seem to parallel that of the questionnaire surveys—that physical differences in teaching spaces do not clearly differentiate teaching practices. This would seem to be true of most countries. The conclusion from Canadian research is that open plan and open education are not synonymous and this is echoed by the major study in Australia. On the whole, instruction and learning experiences were being conducted along relatively traditional lines and the researchers concluded that the results "should discourage commentators from automatically associating a particular teaching style with a particular school design" (Angus et al. 1975).

Most observational studies have concentrated on more specific aspects of practice such as the balance of the curriculum, pupil involvement on tasks, and the amount of time spent in transition from one activity to the next.

Some parental concern has been expressed about the nature of the curriculum in open schools but this is not borne out by the evidence available. In the United Kingdom approximately one-half of curriculum time is devoted to mathematics and language activities. There were big differences between schools however, some devoting three times as much time to these areas than others. This is not a phenomenon restricted to open schools, however, since research in conventional schools shows the same pattern. This would appear to be a reflection of the high degree of teacher autonomy and lack of a central or local curriculum rather than school design.

Pupil involvement was also observed and although no

direct comparison was made with pupils in conventional schools, the levels would seem comparable on other evidence. This would not appear to be so in Australia where involvement was found to be higher in self-contained classrooms.

There does appear to be a greater danger in open schools that pupils might, without adequate supervision, display less involvement with their tasks. A survey undertaken by the Inspectorate in the United Kingdom commented on this and provided vivid examples of time wasting from their own observations. They also commented on time wasting in transitional activities, that is, moving, waiting, and clearing away materials between activities. Research in the United Kingdom and the United States has since supported this. The American study found that children used more spaces and came into contact with more teachers in open schools but spent more time in transitional activities. Among young children in the United Kingdom, such time amounted to nearly six hours per week, the equivalent of one school day. On this evidence, it would thus seem likely that transition time is greater in open schools since pupils often have to move space as well as activity.

The bulk of the evidence would indicate no clear link between teaching practices and the design of teaching spaces. Theory would not appear to be working in practice which is probably not surprising since the theory itself was based on inadequate evidence. The message that architecture can modify the environment but not the activities that take place in the environment may surprise few. As Drew (1970) notes "ultimately no architectural solution, no matter how brilliant, can be successful educationally without intelligent, imaginative, and committed teachers. If open space has done anything it has made us aware of the crucial role of the teacher".

Part of this mismatch between design and practice could be due to the lack of consultation and cooperation between architects and teachers. In the United Kingdom, at least, design policy has been fragmented and uncoordinated. Architects rarely observe the practice they are designing for and lack of evaluation of the final product is endemic. The opportunity for effective feedback from practitioner to designer has therefore been missed to the disadvantage of both. This in turn may explain the consistently poor design features apparent in teaching spaces. Notably, practical/wet areas tend to be sited such that they are used as major thoroughfares in the absence of specific circulation space, causing additional noise and distraction. In addition they are often sited out of sight of the teacher as are many quiet rooms. Inability to provide adequate supervision to children in such spaces has led to their underuse.

3. Teacher Attitudes

Many surveys have been undertaken of teacher attitudes to aspects of working within an open design. These have been grouped under five headings—work load; noise and distraction; cooperative teaching; design of teaching spaces; staffing and training.

3.1 Work Load

A large number of studies report adverse teacher comments relating to increased work load and insufficient preparation time. Ten Canadian studies all report that work loads are considerably higher in open schools largely because of increased planning time which in turn leads to stress. New Zealand teachers also stated that work load was their major problem and a large proportion of Australian teachers believed that work load had increased to a point where it was having an effect on their private lives. The same story is true of the United States and the United Kingdom. In the latter, teachers stated that demands on them were very high, quoting particularly the necessity for careful organization of methods of assessment and curriculum planning together with the physical exertion brought on by demands on their attention.

It is noteworthy however, that demands such as these have not led to low job satisfaction. The evidence is of reasonably high morale even though morale in conventional schools seems marginally better. Nevertheless, teachers in open schools show no great inclination to move back into the self-contained classroom although in the latest study in the United Kingdom, one-third of teachers wished to move back. It might be that some teachers are prepared to exchange some of the stimulation of the open situation for the lower demands evident in conventional schools.

There is also evidence of an interaction between teacher preference and the design of the unit such that the teachers who expressed the greatest preference for open schools were those who were teaching in the small open units, that is, those with shared teaching space.

3.2 Noise and Distraction

Only one study appears to have measured noise levels. An average of 63 decibels (db) was found in conventional classrooms and 70 db in open situations. The author felt that such differences were insufficient to differentially affect performance. Some architects would dispute this however. One report argued that 55 db should be the upper limit in buildings in which communication by speech is of great importance.

Research on the effect of noise on pupils and teacher performance has proved inconclusive to date but noise is a factor commented on in many surveys by both teachers and pupils. Some have reported that excessive noise levels constitute the most undesirable aspect of open designs and is cited as a factor which is related to distraction, disturbance, and teacher stress. Although noise is a feature in self-contained classrooms, teachers in open designs perceive it as a greater problem and believe that it can affect concentration. They also report that teaching approaches have to be compromised in order to avoid disturbing other teachers and classes.

Pupils have also been questioned on this topic and some are clearly distracted by it. There is also a suggestion that boys may be more adversely affected than girls. There would appear to be marked individual differences in noise tolerance. An excessive noise level to one may be acceptable to another. It would thus be a mistake to claim that all open schools are noisy and that all noise distracts.

One of the major mediating factors is the type of activity taking place in the teaching space. One study presented data to show that only 9 percent of pupils in an open school with a traditional teaching approach reported being distracted by noise compared to 27 percent in an open school with an individualized approach and 31 percent in a conventional school with the same programme.

Another factor frequently cited is density, and it has been claimed that crowdedness is more strongly related to all forms of distraction from all sources, and that providing more space per pupil is a better answer than elaborate acoustical treatments. This is an important consideration in some countries such as the United Kingdom where the amount of planned space per pupil has declined considerably since 1968.

A relationship has been hypothesized between noise, distraction, and discipline but there is little evidence to support this. Teachers' views on discipline in open schools present an inconsistent picture. Some have experienced few problems whereas others quote lack of discipline as a major problem. The evidence available would not lend itself to the conclusion that discipline is worse in open than conventional schools.

3.3 Cooperative/Team Teaching

Many believe that team organization and cooperation is of critical importance in open schools. Comparisons between teaching teams in open and conventional settings show that in the former, more teacher interaction related to work takes place and that such talk occurs in different contexts. Here, talk revolves around such issues as curriculum planning, teaching, and evaluation whereas in conventional schools teacher talk is limited to administration and routine. Increased teacher talk between teachers in open schools is reported in many countries, as is the teachers' belief that they appear to have more influence in decision making.

Team teaching appears to be more attractive in theory than in practice however. Teachers argue that cooperation should exist but the difficulties experienced in such efforts are frequently mentioned. In particular the quality of interpersonal relationships is stressed, and incompatibility is not uncommon. Factors which appear to be important for teacher satisfaction in teams include having no formal leader, being given a choice in the constitution of the team, a balanced status structure, and where possible a small team. Major obstacles to satisfaction include excessive teacher turnover, lack of consultation, incompatible philosophies, and discordant personalities.

3.4 Design of Instruction Spaces

For most teachers the design of teaching spaces is a *fait accompli*. Their major concern other than lack of consultation in the design process, is that the architecture should not dictate teaching organization, although many feel that it does. On more specific design issues the evidence from a number of countries is consistent. A general feeling is that there is a lack of space generally and that the specialist teaching spaces are inadequately sited and of an inappropriate size. Dissatisfaction with storage space and furniture is worldwide. In some countries there has been a call for enclosed spaces capable of housing an entire class, a feature which is fairly typical in many Canadian and American designs where there are both open and self-contained spaces in each school.

All comment is not adverse. The provision of activity areas and quiet rooms is welcomed when provided and well-sited, and the flexibility of some designs is praised.

3.5 Staffing and Training

Fitzpatrick and Angus (1974) have argued that "for any school to function at its peak it must have at least three factors operating in its favour. It must have a rationale or purpose that is clear to all its members; it must have a staff consistent in its appreciation and endorsement of the rationale; and it must have a staff equipped as fully as possible with the pedagogical skills that are required to operationalise the rationale". However, a number of studies testify to the fact that teachers are not always clear about the objectives, or that they disagree with them. The latter may thus find the open setting inappropriate since they may be unable to realize their teaching goals. Mobility of children between teachers and mismatch in professional expectations can leave considerable tensions and lead to teachers closing off their teaching areas as an act of withdrawal.

Teachers are not used to being visible and this often requires substantial adjustment. One-half of New Zealand teachers for example pointed to their openness to public scrutiny as being the biggest factor in their feelings of greater stress, and this feeling is echoed by teachers in other countries. Many teachers feel threatened in the absence of personal space defined by walls and may find working in an open space personally disastrous. There have thus been calls for the opportunity for teachers to opt out of teaching in open schools.

The selection of teachers has attracted considerable comment. Selection procedures vary widely but there is general agreement that teachers appointed should be committed to teaching in open designs and that this is most likely to result from appointing volunteers. They should also be appointed early so that staff development and curriculum planning can be achieved before the school commences operation.

The role of the school principal is considered vital in

open schools but the selection and training of such people has attracted little comment. This must be given priority in the future however, since lack of adequate leadership affects the whole school. This is exemplified in the New Zealand survey where teachers report frustration and confusion due to lack of leadership.

Preservice and inservice training of teachers is regarded as universally poor. In the national survey in the United Kingdom only 7 percent of principals stated that preservice training was adequate and complained that few colleges made any specific provision for teachers intending to seek employment in open schools.

Teachers have also expressed dissatisfaction with their preservice training and called for more inservice courses (see *Inservice Teacher Education*). The same message emanates from many studies with depressing regularity: "teacher training is not helpful for teachers in open plan"; "training for open plan is inadequate"; "insufficient"; "badly needed"; "a major problem".

The New Zealand survey is the only one found to sample college principals. These, it would appear, were uncommitted to open plan and held a cautious attitude to its development. Their sanguine comment was that there were insufficient open schools to allow practice. As a result most teachers in training leave college with no extensive knowledge, either practical or theoretical, of open schools. The report recommended that colleges should provide courses which include cooperative teaching, open plan organization and personal relationships, and similar lists of skills have been called for in Canada and Australia.

3.6. Summary

There is always the danger of overgeneralization from a mass of evidence of this type, particularly since teachers in open schools may to some extent be self-selected. Nevertheless, teachers seem to see advantages in teaching in a team or cooperatively, provided that there is agreement about its composition and size. When this is achieved, satisfaction among teachers is high. But there is also a great deal of concern about incompatibility due to problems of interpersonal relationships. These, together with frequent team changes can create low morale. The role of principals is seen as crucial. They should be concerned with the relationships among staff, have expertise in the organization of open plan schools, have the ability to delegate responsibility, giving the feeling of autonomy among teams and staff. Teachers do not always feel that sufficient leadership is provided.

Inadequate preparation time and heavy work loads are frequently mentioned as a fact of life but not ones which appear to affect morale, which, on the whole, appears to be reasonably high. It seems not to be as high as in conventional schools but a majority of teachers in open plan do not favour a return to self-contained classrooms.

Noise and distraction figure prominently in the hierarchy of problems of open plan both for teachers and pupils. However, individual perceptions of noise differ, perhaps indicating differing thresholds of tolerance. Noise levels appear to be related to certain kinds of activity, amount of space, and density. Overcrowdedness was seen as one of the greatest problems. To ease this requires sound absorbent surfaces, more space, or fewer pupils.

Noise also came up in opinions about school design, but the biggest plea is for more space generally, together with more withdrawal or quiet areas, and better designed practical areas. A plea for more consultation on planning is made.

There is agreement that the open plan teaching environment is not suitable for all teachers and pupils, who should be given the chance to opt out gracefully. Staff should ideally be committed volunteers, amply supported by inservice provision. There is universal condemnation of preservice training but little or no progress has yet been reported.

4. Pupil Attitudes and Personality

There is consensus among teachers that open schooling facilitates the social development of pupils by providing the opportunity for increased social contact with both peers and adults. However a note of doubt is expressed about the possibility of lack of security among pupils. Nevertheless, teachers feel that pupil responsibility is developed through greater independence and self-reliance and that pupils enjoy working in open areas.

Unfortunately, research evidence on those factors does not lend itself to coherent synthesis. Studies to date have been small-scale master's or doctoral theses and most have been inadequately conceptualized. Many have tested on only one occasion making it impossible to attribute any differences found to the type of school or teaching approach. To further confound matters most have also failed to differentiate between teaching approach and school design.

Research on pupil attitudes is totally equivocal. The two studies which were methodologically acceptable, tended to disagree partly, one suspects, because of the small and localized nature of the samples. Similarly, little can be said about differences in self-concept in schools of differing design, and nothing can be said about the development of self-concept. On the other hand, there is some evidence to show that pupils feel more secure in self-contained classrooms experiencing a traditional approach, and that under this approach creativity may be a little higher.

The most consistent picture is provided by studies of friendship patterns. Pupils in conventional schools tend to have more friends and to make friends more easily but from these studies it is not possible to assess whether this is a design or teaching effect. Evidence from research in conventional schools would indicate the latter.

Overall there appears to be no justification in accepting the generalizability of any of these trends, particularly since all were undertaken on the North American continent.

5. Pupil Achievement

Surveys of teacher perceptions of pupil achievement in open schools provide an inconsistent picture. Most studies report that teachers believe that standards of achievement are as high, or higher in open schools but a discordant view was struck in the national British survey where a majority of teachers felt achievement was better in conventional schools.

There is also a belief that only certain kinds of pupils benefit. Most isolate children of above average ability. Quiet, insecure, less able, and aggressive children are felt to be better in conventional schools since a sense of security is tied to a familiar room and a familiar place in it.

Research evidence would not seem to support the view that achievement is as high in open schools although methodological problems abound in this kind of research endeavour. Longitudinal studies which have followed children over time in open and conventional schools are limited by small samples. This is illustrated in a study by Bell et al. (1977) who samples pupils in one open, informal, and one conventional, traditional school in the same middle-class suburb, all of whom had attended kindergartens which followed the same curriculum. At the end of the first year there were no differences in arithmetic ability, but significant differences in reading favouring the conventional school. At this stage they were seven months ahead on word recognition, and twice as many of the open plan pupils were below reading norms. Since there had been no differences on preschool variables, or on age or socioeconomic status, the authors argued that the traditional learning situation was the cause of the difference, concluding that for a number of children the open environment provided an adverse educational situation.

The results of the second year revealed that the reading scores of the conventional group remained significantly better, but there were still no differences in arithmetic ability. At the end of the third year the conventional group was seven months ahead on reading, four months ahead in vocabulary, and five months in maths computation. The authors contended that both schools had dedicated, well-trained teachers and as such it was difficult to account for the differences except in terms of the more informal approach adopted in the open plan school, and the open design itself with its many distracting influences. Their impressions from observation were that children not under close supervision in small groups in the open plan school wasted much time aimlessly wandering about, watching the movements of other classes, and interacting without useful purpose with classmates.

The other longitudinal studies have tended to concentrate on reading achievement in a Canadian context.

All indicate higher achievement in conventional elementary schools although one reported the open school pupils catching up at the secondary stage. The longitudinal studies thus favour the conventional schools but none made any systematic attempt to describe teaching approaches, leaving it impossible to ascertain whether teaching methods or school design was the causal factor.

Only three studies appear to have classified both design and teaching approach, one of which was longitudinal.

Traub et al. (1976) report a study involving four designs and two kinds of school intake. Type 1 schools housed a high proportion of pupils from English-speaking homes. These tended to be of middle-class suburban background. Type 2 schools housed a higher proportion of pupils from homes where English was spoken as a second language. These tended to be of working-class inner-city background. Schools were also classified on school design into open, mixed, and closed, and teaching approach as less open and more open based on a questionnaire.

Children in type 1 schools showed no difference in achievement irrespective of school design and teaching approach. But in type 2 schools the achievement of pupils was consistently higher in schools with less open (more formal) teaching approaches. The differences were consistent across age levels and across all the subtests of the Canadian Test of Basic Skills (CTBS). "For every CTBS subtest at each grade level the students in schools with less open programmes substantially outperformed the students with more open programmes. This finding is the clearest and had the best statistical support of any finding in the present investigation." In terms of magnitude the differences amounted to about six months.

The importance of this study is that it points to an interaction effect between teaching approach and social class/ability. The benefits of a more structured approach for low ability or low socioeconomic status children have also been found in a number of other studies.

A recent Australian study found no interaction effects for pupil achievement but did so for self-esteem. This study related type of school design and teaching approach to pupil achievement and self-esteem among fifth-year primary children in 120 schools. Although the differences were not significant for written expression there were significant differences in maths and reading favouring conventional schools irrespective of teaching approach. On self-esteem it was found that conventional schools favoured pupils of low social status and open plan schools high social status.

The other study to classify teaching and design was a more limited investigation using a questionnaire and the CTBS test. Although in general little relationship was found between achievement and both design and teaching approach, the trends were for a traditional teaching approach in either an open or closed classroom for achievement in reading comprehension, and for a traditional teaching approach in a self-contained classroom for achievement in mathematics concepts.

The remaining studies have neither been longitudinal nor have they distinguished teaching approach or types of pupil. As such their value is limited. Six report findings favour conventional schools, two favour open plan, and another five report no differences.

From the research undertaken so far the trends favour higher achievement in conventional schools. But it would be rash to accept this as a final judgment. Samples have been small and unrepresentative and few have incorporated systematic observations of teaching practices in the schools making it extremely difficult to ascertain the factors which bring about differential achievement. To date those studies which have carried out intensive studies of teaching processes have not measured achievement and those that have tested achievement have collected little data on process.

6. Conclusion

Reviewers of research find themselves in a situation akin to that of ancient cartographers. They aim to map out an area as faithfully as possible from the information available, but are aware that incomplete information, and their own human fallibility, may distort the picture and become conscious that much is still to be discovered. Reviews, like ancient maps, are therefore always interim statements and a reflection of a particular historical context.

The information available would indicate that although there may be a symbolic link between open plan schools and open education practices, the link in reality is a tenuous one. The reasons for this are many—confusion about rationale and purpose, inappropriate staffing, inadequate preservice and inservice provision, inherent drawbacks of open design, and the heavy demands made on teachers, many of which could have been overcome early with constructive evaluation programmes. Nevertheless teachers must be given credit for resilience. Progress has been made with team and cooperative teaching approaches, morale is reasonably high, and few would wish to return to a self-contained classroom.

Studies so far carried out would indicate that the effect of open plan on pupil attitudes to school, self-concept, curiosity, and creativity is minimal, although there is a suggestion that security may suffer. The results of studies on pupil achievement are mixed but the overall trend appears to show that achievement on standardized tests favours pupils in conventional schools. But it is not possible to ascertain whether this effect is related to teaching approach or to school design, or indeed to an interaction of the two since rarely have they been differentiated. The acceptance of the assumption that open plan schools house a particular teaching approach has bedevilled the research, as indeed has the equally erroneous assumption that open

plan schools are as a group, homogeneous. In fact the layout of these schools, their size, amount, type, and orientation of space all differ to such an extent that it is inappropriate to regard them as a single group. Some researchers have recognized this and called for more precise ways of indexing architectural type. Future studies of the effects on pupils requires a more adequate conceptualization of the problem, including a longitudinal design incorporating a classification of both design and teaching approach, and allowing for interaction effects on pupil ability, social class background, sex, and race.

Finally, the evidence which indicates that open plan schools vary widely both in design and in teaching organization should serve to undermine general and often misconceived stereotypes, and lead to the recognition that each school is in a very real sense unique.

See also: Open Versus Formal Methods

Bibliography

Anderson R 1975 The school as an organic teaching aid. In: McClure R M (ed.) 1971 *The Curriculum: Retrospect and Prospect.* 70th Yearbook of the National Society for the Study of Education, Pt. 1. University of Chicago Press, Chicago, Illinois

Angus N I, Evans K W, Parkin D 1975 *An Observation Study of Selected Pupil and Teacher Behaviours in Open Plan and Conventional Designed Classrooms.* Technical Report 4. Australian Open Area Schools Project, Perth

Bell A E, Abrahamson D S, Growse R 1977 Achievement and self reports of responsibility for achievement in informal (open plan) traditional classrooms. *Brit. J. Educ. Psychol.* 47: 258–67

Bennett N, Andreae J, Hegarty P, Wade B 1980 *Open Plan Schools: Teaching, Curriculum, Design.* National Foundation for Educational Research, Slough

Drew P 1970 Open plan. *Canadian Architect* 15: 46–57

Fitzpatrick G S, Angus M J 1974 *Through Teachers Eyes: Teaching in an Open Space Primary School.* Technical Report 1. Australian Open Area Schools Project, Perth

Gittins Report 1967 Department of Education and Science Central Advisory Council for Education (Wales) *Primary Education in Wales.* Her Majesty's Stationery Office, London

Jarman C 1977 The organisation of open plan primary schools. The Oxfordshire experience. In: Bell S (ed.) 1977 *The Organisation of Open Plan Primary Schools: Report of a National Course on Organisation of Open Plan Primary Schools.* Jordanhill College of Education, Glasgow

New Zealand 1977 *Report on Open Plan Education in New Zealand Primary Schools.* Department of Education, Wellington

Plowden Report, Department of Education and Science Central Advisory Council for Education (England) 1967 *Children and their Primary Schools*, Vol. 1. Her Majesty's Stationery Office, London

Traub R, Weiss J, Fisher C 1976 *Openness in Schools: An Evaluation Study.* Research in Education Series 5. Ontario Institute for Studies in Education, Toronto, Ontario

Weinstein C S 1979 The physical environment of the school: A review of the research. *Rev. Educ. Res.* 49: 577–610

Equipment and Materials

J. G. Ainley

Equipment and materials constitute an important element of the physical environment for learning. It is often assumed that the physical environment of a school is important in student learning and this assumption is implicit in many programmes intended to improve the quality of schooling. A major review of research in this field suggests that the physical environment of the school does have effects upon patterns of behaviour of students and teachers and upon the attitudes of students even though substantial effects on achievement have not been consistently detected (Weinstein 1979).

1. Theoretical Perspectives

In the early 1970s, a review of research on the psychological and behavioural effects of the physical environment concluded that, even though there were studies which suggested environmental influences on behaviour, the mechanisms of those changes had not been elucidated and further theorizing was needed (Drew 1971). Since that review several new perspectives have helped to clarify issues in this area. These perspectives have concerned the types of dependent variables examined, the ways in which a physical environment might be described, and the mechanisms by which environmental influences might operate.

In terms of the outcomes considered to be influenced by the physical environment, an early distinction drawn between behavioural effects and psychological effects has continued (Drew 1971). Behavioural effects commonly can be considered in three categories: patterns of movement; other activity patterns (such as the use of materials); and patterns of attention and interaction. Psychological effects which are commonly examined include attitudes directly related to the physical environment (for example opinions about the pleasantness of the environment), more general attitudes (such as level of interest), and cognitive development. An important problem which needs further clarification is that of the relationship between behavioural and psychological effects of the physical environment. It is not clear to what extent changes in behaviour result from psychological effects, or vice versa.

It is now widely recognized that descriptions of the physical environment need to distinguish between the objective properties of the setting and the aesthetic properties of the setting. Several writers have argued for more systematic objective characterizations of the physical environment in terms of functional properties (Proshansky 1974). As an extension of this distinction it has been argued that an examination of the relationship between "the setting as it is" and the perceived setting "as it is experienced" constitutes an important part of research into the effects of environments on learning. Greater attention to the objective description of properties of the physical environment has also led to a more explicit consideration of materials and equipment as part of that environment in addition to more general design features. The distinction between the objective setting and the perceived setting has also served to emphasize the conceptual difference between the "physical environment" and the psychosocial "learning environment", and the importance of the study of the relationship between these two domains.

Consideration of the ways in which the physical environment influences student learning has led to two chains of influence being postulated. The first of these is the direct or pragmatic postulate that some features of the physical environment may simply impede certain activities. According to this view changes in the physical environment could change behaviour by removing impediments to activities which were considered desirable but not feasible. The second of the postulated chains of influence is that physical environments influence behaviour and attitudes through communicating a symbolic message or by being seen as "suggestive space". According to this postulate changes in the physical environment could cause changes in behaviour by suggesting possibilities which were not previously imagined. An extension of this argument might suggest that the influence of the physical environment on behaviour and attitudes might be transmitted through changes in the learning environment or classroom climate. Some of the research reviewed by Ainley (1981) suggests that this proposition is a plausible one and could prove to be a fruitful field of enquiry.

2. Research Studies in Schools

The expansion of most school systems during the 1960s and early 1970s was accompanied by major programmes of building and equipping schools. These programmes not only involved the construction of new schools which incorporated many architectural innovations, but frequently involved a reconsideration of the equipment and materials provided in schools. Accompanying this development was an arousal of interest in research into the influence of physical environments on learning. One particular area of interest was that of the relationship between "open-plan schools" (a design feature) and "open education" (a set of educational practices).

Some research studies were concerned only with architectural design but others involved consideration of the materials and equipment which constituted part of the physical environment. Weinstein (1979) reviewed a range of studies conducted in schools and concluded that, despite some inconsistencies and contradictory results, there was general support for the proposition that the abundance and quality of the materials and equipment in schools does influence the behaviour and attitudes of students and teachers. Evidence was drawn from both correlational and quasi-experimental studies. The correlational studies which were reviewed were concerned with a number of levels of schooling from day-care centres to college programmes and examined such effects as the involvement of students, levels of conflict, the rigidity of teacher restriction, sensitivity to individual requirements and patterns of movement, and use of materials. The review concluded that there was a noticeable influence of the physical environment on these types of variable at most levels of schooling. One experimental study was also reviewed. It reported changes in the behaviour of Year 2 and Year 3 students after an experimenter initiated intervention in the arrangement of equipment in an open-plan classroom (Weinstein 1977). After that change it was noted that students moved to areas which had been previously avoided (for example, the science room), a wider range of behaviours was exhibited (especially in the science and games areas), and changes occurred in the way materials were used.

Studies of open-plan schools have tended to produce conflicting results regarding the effect of these schools on students and teachers. Even though Weinstein was able to conclude that open-plan schools frequently lead to more interaction among teachers, greater feelings of autonomy, satisfaction, and ambition, and less time being consumed by routine procedures, it was considered that the evidence regarding effects on students was too fragmented to reach any firm conclusions. One of the problems of much research in this area appears to be the unspecific nature of the term "open-plan". Studies employing more detailed descriptions of the physical environment seem more likely to produce consistent results.

3. Studies in Science Classrooms

The use of special materials and specially equipped rooms for the teaching of science has generated an interest in environmental influences on teaching and learning in that field. Ainley (1981) concluded that research in science education suggested that even though the provision of good facilities might not dramatically alter teaching patterns it did seem that well-equipped science rooms in combination with adequate apparatus would foster science teaching practices which involved students in a wide variety of stimulating activities. The review considered studies which looked at the limitations in science materials perceived by teachers to restrict their teaching, studies of curriculum implementation, studies which used teacher reports of their practices, and studies which used student reports of science lessons in relation to external indicators of their physical environment.

A number of the articles reviewed by Ainley contained evidence that teachers believed that insufficient laboratory facilities, overuse of those facilities, lack of assistants, and large classes impeded the use of laboratory work in science teaching. Most of the evidence came from responses to questions concerned with whether these types of activities were restricted by a lack of materials and equipment. Another group of articles were concerned with the ways in which science curricula have been implemented in schools. These studies suggested that new programmes based on integrated science and enquiry learning have sometimes not been able to be fully implemented in schools with poor equipment. In such schools the new programmes were either viewed with disfavour or the programmes were so transformed that they retained little of the original concept.

Further evidence of the effects of materials and equipment on learning was reported from studies in which teachers were asked to report on their use of particular teaching methods, with these reports being related to the types of science teaching facilities available to them. One such study was reported by Englehardt (1968) in which it was noted that the use of enquiry methods in teaching science was significantly associated with having classrooms equipped for dual use as laboratories, especially when teachers had adequate preparation time and sufficient materials. Those results were interpreted as not only resulting from removal of limitations but from the creation of an environment which suggested the desirability of new activities.

Student reports have also been used as a source of information about what happens in science classrooms with varying standards of equipment. Ainley (1978) used student reports of aspects of science lessons as part of a study of the association between the resources available and the quality of science education experienced by Year 9 students. The resources available were measured in terms of the availability of science rooms in proportion to the school population, the quality of those rooms in terms of equipment and fittings, the abundance of apparatus, and the number of laboratory assistants. It was reported that better facilities were associated with an enriched learning environment (greater involvement, better organization, and more stimulation through variety in the methods used) and more varied activities in science lessons (more experimental work, greater encouragement to explore, and less learning from textbooks).

Even though the results above derive from studies concerned with the effect of materials and equipment in one specialized area of teaching they are congruent with those reported from more general research studies in elementary and secondary schools, and in a general sense probably apply to other areas of the school curriculum.

4. Summary

In the current research literature there is little consistent evidence of a strong effect of the materials and equipment in schools on achievement. Such evidence may accumulate as the design of studies in this area develops further. However there is already available a substantial amount of evidence that the physical environment of a school or classroom can affect the behaviour of people and their attitudes to school and learning. This evidence is relevant to the provision of schooling not only because it is important to foster a variety of types of learning, and to attend to a wide range of goals in schools, but because the development of interests through participation in varied activities may have long-term effects on cognitive and affective development.

See also: Architecture; Open Versus Formal Methods; Seating Patterns

Bibliography

Ainley J G 1978 *The Australian Science Facilities Program: A Study of Its Influence on Science Education in Australian Schools.* Australian Council for Educational Research (ACER) Research Monograph No. 2. ACER, Hawthorn

Ainley J G 1981 The importance of facilities in science education. *Eur. J. Sci. Educ.* 3: 127–38

Drew C J 1971 Research on the psychological–behavioural effects of the physical environment. *Rev. Educ. Res.* 41: 447–65

Englehardt D F 1968 *Aspects of Spatial Influence on Science Teaching Methods* (Doctoral Dissertation, Harvard University) ERIC Document No. ED 024 214

Proshansky H M 1974 Theoretical issues in environmental psychology. *Sch. Rev.* 82: 541–55

Weinstein C S 1977 Modifying student behaviour in an open classroom through changes in the physical design. *Am. Educ. Res. J.* 14: 249–62

Weinstein C S 1979 The physical environment of the school: A review of the research. *Rev. Educ. Res.* 49: 577–610

Class Size

G. V. Glass

School class size was surely a concern when Quintilian was young. It has been a matter of recorded scholarly opinion since the seventeenth century. Comenius said "I maintain that it is not only possible for one teacher to teach several hundred scholars at once, but that it is also essential. . . . The larger the number of pupils that he sees before him the greater the interest the teacher will take in his work. . . . To the scholars, in the same way, the presence of a number of companions will be productive not only of utility but also of enjoyment" (quoted in Fleming 1959 p. 35).

Comenius's opinion finds few adherents among contemporary teachers, who believe in little so fervently as they believe in the benefits of small classes. School officials, particularly those who do no teaching, often do not share this belief; they view class size as the chief economic issue to be resolved in meeting the education budget. The history of empirical research on the benefits of class size reduction is marked by contention and contradictory interpretations. An objective collating of the research evidence indicates that both teachers and school officials are correct: (a) class size reductions benefit pupils' learning and affective development; (b) the cost of effective reductions is great.

1. School Class Size: Past and Present

The United States began the decade of the 1980s with an elementary- and secondary-school budget of approximately US$150,000,000,000, or $750 for every person in the country. The comparable figure for the United Kingdom was approximately £10,000 million, or £180 per person. Roughly 85 percent of the net cost of education goes for teachers' salaries, and the $125,000,000,000 or £8,500,000,000 devoted to teachers' salaries is locked in one simple equation with pupil population and class size:

$$\text{No. teachers} = \frac{\text{no. pupils}}{\text{class size}}$$

The number of pupils who enter the school is largely a matter of birth rates and migration patterns; there is little that can be done to change materially the number of pupils a particular school must serve. When the number of pupils in the equation is fixed, the only variables are class size and number of teachers. Clearly, they are linked; an increase in one is accompanied by a decrease in the other. It costs 25 percent more per pupil if class sizes are set at 20 pupils instead of 25; and a reduction of class size by half (from 30 to 15, say) doubles the cost of education, or at least the 85 percent spent for teachers' salaries. When teachers and school officials meet to negotiate salaries and class sizes (the two most important issues in the opinion of both sides in the negotiation), costs of staggering proportions hang in the balance.

The ratio of the number of pupils to the number of teachers (a rough index of school class size) has been falling in virtually every industrialized nation. Year by year since 1900, the number of pupils for each teacher in the United States has declined. In 1900, the typical class enrolled over 35 pupils; by 1975, the class size had dropped to 21, a decrease of 40 percent. In the United Kingdom, the trend was remarkably similar, as shown in Fig. 1. Pupil-to-teacher ratios reflect the degree of individualization in education, but it would be slightly

Figure 1
Pupil-to-teacher ratios in the United States and United Kingdom from 1870 to 1975

inaccurate to imagine that because the ratio was 34.8 in 1925 that most teachers taught classes of 35 pupils. Because of special provisions that schools frequently extend to handicapped pupils or because of very low enrollments in some isolated rural schools, the typical classroom usually has a greater number of pupils than the pupil-to-teacher ratio might indicate. For example, in the United Kingdom in 1923, 48.6 percent of all classrooms had more than 40 pupils on the register (while the pupil-to-teacher ratio was 34.8). More than 20 percent of the classes had 50 or more pupils; this percentage dropped to 13.5 percent by 1927. Fifty pupils in a classroom seems remarkable, and one assumes there are few such classes in the United Kingdom today.

In Table 1, the ratio of pupils (roughly between the ages of 5 and 12) to teachers is recorded for 50 nations. From classroom to classroom within these countries, the numbers of pupils will vary. Nonetheless, these average figures are revealing. They range from 9.5

Table 1
Ratio of pupils to teachers at elementary-school level for 50 nations[a]

Nation	Pupil-to-teacher ratio	Nation	Pupil-to-teacher ratio
Afghanistan	36.7	Mexico	44.2
Algeria	39.5	Morocco	41.5
Argentina	17.9		
Australia	19.7	Netherlands	27.5
		Norway	9.5
Bangladesh	55.0		
Belgium	19.3	Pakistan	40.3
Brazil	21.7	Peru	40.0
Bulgaria	19.9	Poland	20.8
		Portugal	23.8
Colombia	32.4		
Cuba	21.6	Romania	20.8
Czechoslovakia	20.2		
		Saudi Arabia	19.5
Denmark	9.5	Sri Lanka	29.4
		South Korea	48.8
Ecuador	38.0	Soviet Union	13.7
Egypt	34.9	Sudan	36.0
		Sweden	18.5
Finland	16.0	Syria	32.7
France	17.7		
		Tunisia	39.5
German Democratic Republic	15.7	Turkey	33.5
Greece	30.2	Tanzania	51.2
Haiti	39.3	Uganda	34.8
Hong Kong	30.8	United Kingdom	20.5
Hungary	15.7	United States	20.0
Iceland	18.9	Venezuela	23.4
Iran	28.5	Viet Nam	35.6
Iraq	27.6		
Ireland	31.0	Yugoslavia	24.1

a Source: United Nations *Statistical Yearbook: 1978*. New York, United Nations, 1979 pupils per teacher in Denmark and Norway to 55.0 pupils per teacher in Bangladesh, a difference of over 500 percent. Northern Europe shows small ratios; Central and South America as well as the Middle East, Asia, and Africa average much higher, roughly more than 35 pupils per teacher. The pupil-to-teacher ratio appears to be determined in part by the wealth of the nation and the density (persons per unit of land area) of the population. The attention accorded students is extremely unevenly distributed around the world.

2. The Benefits of Smaller School Classes

Since before the twentieth century, since the beginnings of empirical research on education, researchers have sought to determine whether reductions in school class size benefit pupils' learning and attitudes.

2.1 Class Size and Learning

Scholarly opinion abounds on the question of whether smaller classes are better for learning, and it has been overwhelmingly negative. The treatment of class size in the third edition of the *Encyclopedia of Educational Research* (1960), where a mere 200 words were devoted to the subject, is typical: "There is nothing in the evidence to suggest that large classes materially affect attainment in subject matter . . . studies of the relation of class size to student attention, discipline, self-reliance, attitudes, and work habits failed to establish a research basis for decisions on class size" (Goodlad 1960 p. 224).

The first empirical study on educational processes and their effects on achievement included an examination of the class size question (Rice 1902 p. 287): "Equally surprising, if indeed not more incredible, may appear the statement that no allowance whatever is to be made for the size of the class in judging the results of my test." Rice reported virtually no numbers, and it is impossible to determine now whether the relationship Rice found was genuinely small or whether it was moderately large but only seemed small to Rice, who may have expected much more. Rice's study was followed by several similar studies published between 1900 and 1920. These studies are distinguished by their rugged nonexperimental logic. Cornman (1909) can stand as a typical example.

In the 1940s, class-size research went dormant. It was revived along with the rest of the field of educational research in the 1950s and 1960s. Researchers seemed intent on demonstrating, particularly at the secondary-school level, that lecture classes could be doubled or tripled in size without loss of effectiveness (see, for example, Haskell 1964).

By the late 1960s, huge empirical studies of education were undertaken to inform educational policy in many nations: the Coleman study (1966) of equality of educational opportunity in the United States; the Plowden Report (1967) in the United Kingdom; the International Association for the Evaluation of Educational Achieve-

ment (IEA) throughout the world (see Husén 1967). These huge statistical studies typically included data on the relationship of class size and pupil achievement. The Coleman study, for example, measured the achievement of tens of thousands of pupils in grades 1, 3, 6, 9, and 12 in United States schools. When pupil achievement was correlated with "school resources," including class sizes, the relationships observed were generally small and unimportant. The Plowden Report employed virtually the same methods and reached essentially the same conclusion. When Rutter and his colleagues (1979) countered the findings of the Plowden Report with new measures and finer analyses, they still could not find a relationship of class size and achievement: "School rankings on class size showed no significant association with outcome pupil achievement. What minimal trend there was indicated that attendance tended to be better in schools with *more* children per teacher . . ." (p. 103). The research relevant to class size that appeared in the 1970s showed a concern for establishing the benefits of individualization. Experiments were performed that involved radically reduced instructional group sizes, for example, one teacher with two or three pupils.

A recent study (Glass et al. 1982) was an attempt to perform an exhaustive and quantitative integration of the empirical research on the effects of class size. The approach taken followed the methodology of research meta-analysis, as described by Glass et al. (1981).

Glass et al. found 77 empirical research studies of the relationship between class size and learning. The studies spanned 70 years; they were performed in more than a dozen different countries and together incorporated test results of nearly a million pupils. The basic unit of the statistical analysis of the findings was a comparison of pupils' average achievement in classes of two different sizes. For example, the reading performance of pupils taught in classes of 15 might be compared with that of pupils in classes of 30. At this level, a single study could contain several comparisons: an experiment in which classes of 15, 25, and 35 pupils were compared with respect to reading and spelling would contribute six comparisons (15 vs. 25, 15 vs. 35, and 25 vs. 35 for both reading and spelling) to the analysis. From the 77 studies, there were recorded 725 comparisons of smaller (S) and larger (L) classes. The 725 comparisons of smaller and larger classes were divided almost exactly in half between junior school (elementary) or below, and secondary school.

From among the 725 comparisons of pupil achievement in smaller and larger classes, 435 or 60 percent favored the smaller class. That is, regardless of the pupils' ages, the school subject taught, or the sizes of the classes compared, the odds were 3 to 2 in favor of a study showing smaller classes having achievement superior to larger classes. Although two of five comparisons favored larger classes, the fact is not as significant as it first seems; the comparisons sometimes involved only very minor reductions in size (e.g., $S = 30$ and $L = 33$).

A more refined count sheds light on the relationship:

(a) In 111 of 160 instances (69 percent) in which classes of approximately 18 and 28 pupils were compared, the smaller classes achieved more than the larger classes.

(b) In 45 of 46 comparisons (98 percent) of class sizes of about 2 and 28 pupils, the smaller class achieved more than the larger class.

(c) At the other extreme, classes of over 30 and over 60 were equally likely to show a high achievement.

Small classes were very much better than large classes; large classes were hardly any better than very large classes. These preliminary analyses proved fruitful and suggested two further questions. Is the superiority of small classes over large classes a general phenomenon or does it disappear for certain types of student, certain subjects, certain ages, and the like? How great, in quantitative terms, is the superiority of small classes over large?

A simple statistic was defined to describe the relationship between class size and amount of achievement differential as determined by a study. No matter how many class sizes were compared, the data could be reduced to some number of pairs, a smaller class against a larger class. Certain differences in the findings had to be attended to if the findings were later to be integrated. The most obvious differences involve the actual sizes of "smaller" and "larger" classes and the scale properties of the achievement measure. The actual class sizes compared were preserved and became an essential part of the descriptive measure. The measurement scale properties were handled by standardizing all mean differences in achievement by dividing by the within-group standard deviation (a method that is complete and discards no information at all under the assumption of normal distributions). The eventual measure of relationship was:

$$\Delta_{S-L} = \frac{\bar{X}_S - \bar{X}_L}{\hat{\sigma}} \tag{1}$$

where
$\bar{X}_S$ is the average achievement of the smaller class which contains S pupils
$\bar{X}_L$ is the average achievement of the larger class which contains L pupils and
$\hat{\sigma}$ is the estimated within-class standard deviation, assumed to be homogeneous across the two classes

Suppose, for example, that $\Delta_{S-L} = +1$. Then assuming normal distributions within classes, the average pupil in the smaller class scores at the 84th percentile of the larger class.

By examining the Δ_{S-L} values separately for different subjects taught, levels of pupil ability, years of teachers' experience as well as for different properties of the studies themselves (e.g., type of achievement test, type of experimental design), it was found that only two

features of the research modified the basic relationship between class size and achievement: (a) studies in which pupils were taught in small classes for over 100 hours were more likely to show superiority than studies in which instruction lasted for fewer than 100 hours; (b) studies which exercised careful experimental control through random assignment of pupils to the classes of different size were more likely to show the superiority of smaller classes. For example, of the 725 comparisons, 109 came from experiments in which pupils were randomly assigned to the two classes; 81 percent of these 109 comparisons favored the smaller class. This finding is most revealing, and it places in clearer perspective the negative findings from nonexperimental surveys such as the Coleman and Plowden reports.

The contingency between the class size effects, experimental validity, and duration of instruction changed the analyses on which Glass et al. based their findings. Their principal findings were based on the 109 comparisons arising from the randomized experimental studies (14 of them in all), and they were reported separately for instruction of short and long duration (under vs. over 100 hours).

To portray the complete meaning of the results, Glass et al. sought to derive an empirical curve that summarized the information for the full spectrum of possible class sizes and did so in precise quantitative terms. Toward this end, a statistical model based on logarithmic relationships was derived mathematically and then shaped by the experimental data.

Figure 2 is a graph of the results of the mathematical curve fitting to the 109 experimental comparisons of smaller and larger classes. The curves were fitted separately to data arising from studies in which pupils were taught for more than 100 hours and from studies of fewer than 100 hours instruction; preliminary analyses indicated these two curves would be different. The curves in Fig. 2 portray the achievement of an average pupil, who in a class of 40 pupils would score at the 50th percentile on an achievement test. The curve then reveals how this average pupil's achievement would rise

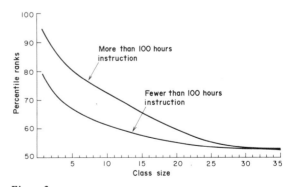

Figure 2
The relationship of class size and pupil achievement based on 109 experimental comparisons in the research literature

relative to the group of pupils taught in classes of 40 as this pupil is taught in smaller and smaller classes. For example, if he or she were taught for more than 100 hours in a class of 20 pupils, his or her achievement would exceed that of 60 percent of pupils taught in classes of size 40. Thus, he or she would have risen from the 50th to above the 60th percentile as a consequence of a reduction by half (from 40 to 20) of his or her class's size. In effect, his or her achievement would have benefitted by having passed 10 of 100 other pupils. The benefit of classes of 20 vs. 40 for fewer than 100 hours of instruction is not as dramatic, but it exists and equals about five or six percentile ranks. Further reductions of class size below 20 produce more dramatic benefits. Instruction of more than 100 hours in a group of five pupils moves the average pupil from the 50th percentile at class size 40 to beyond the 80th percentile, a gain of over 30 percentile ranks. The comparable gain for fewer than 100 hours of instruction (size 40 vs. size 5) is nearly 20 percentile ranks. The benefits grow as class size is reduced even further. The most effective instruction is tutoring: one pupil with one teacher.

The relationship of class size to pupil achievement is remarkably strong. Large reductions in school class size promise learning benefits of a magnitude commonly believed not to be within the power of educators to achieve. And then there are costs. We live in a world of what economists call "trade-offs," where not all things are possible. Figure 2 also shows that small (inexpensive) reductions in class size (say, from 30 to 25) return few benefits in terms of improved pupil achievement. Bringing about even a 10 percentile rank improvement in the average pupil's achievement by reduction of class size may entail cutting class size (and, hence, increasing schooling costs) by a third to a half.

2.2 Class Size and Affective Benefits

Learning and achievement is one aspect of education. Motivation, as reflected in pupils' attitudes and interests in their studies, is another. The relationship of these affective outcomes to class size has been studied for as long and as extensively as the relationship between class size and learning. Glass et al. (1982) attempted a quantitative integration of this research literature that paralleled their summary of the class size and achievement research.

Their literature search located approximately 60 published and unpublished research studies on the effect of class size reduction on such affective outcomes as pupils' motivation, interest in school, self-concept, enthusiasm, attention, creativity, and the like. In contrast to research on class size and achievement, the research literature on class size and affective outcomes was more recent. Over three-quarters of the studies were published after 1959; over one-third were published in the 1960s.

Bolander (1973) of Colorado State University published a study of college class size and students' motivation that gave findings favorable to small classes. Bol-

ander (1973) found five instructors who were simultaneously teaching a large class (average size 35) and a small class (average size 12) the same course. All 235 students were asked at the end of the semester to fill out questionnaires that measured their motivation to study and learn:

(a) Are classmates involved in their class as students? For example, do you and they try to do the job thoroughly, and take pride in the work accomplished?

(b) How much initiative do you and classmates show in the class?

(c) Do you and classmates try to improve yourselves to do a better job, such as extra research not assigned, to improve yourselves?

(d) Are you and classmates willing to adjust your effort in trying to perform well in the class instead of just trying to get by?

The students' answers to these questions were scored and analyzed, and it was learned that the students in the small classes exceeded by a substantial margin those in the large classes. They showed a greater degree of motivation, in the sense of the above questions. The discrepancy was so great, in fact, that only about 30 percent of the students in the large classes exceeded the average student in the small classes with respect to motivation.

From nearly 60 research studies, Glass et al. extracted 172 comparisons of pupils' affective outcomes in smaller versus larger classes. Of this number, 147 or 85 percent favored the smaller class, that is, pupil affective outcomes were more favorable in the smaller than in the larger class in 85 percent of the comparisons.

An attempt was also made to fit the Δ_{S-L} measure

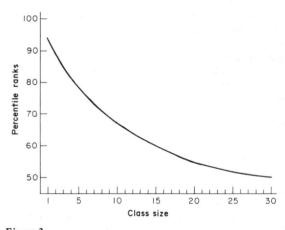

Figure 3
Relationship of class size to pupil affective outcomes based on 172 comparisons of smaller and larger classrooms

of outcome comparisons to a logarithmic curve so as to achieve a more complete quantitative description of how affective outcomes might vary as a function of class size. The best fitting curve is presented in Fig. 3. The curve has been positioned so that the average pupil in a class of size 30 fixes the 50th percentile. Increases and decreases in affective outcomes for the average pupil are measured in percentile units from the 50th percentile. For example, whereas the average pupil in a class of 30 is at the 50th percentile in attitude (toward school or a school subject, for example), the average pupil in a class of size 10 is at nearly the 70th percentile in attitude. For instruction in groups of size below 10, the gain in affective outcomes is even more dramatic; the average pupil in a group of five, for example, has gained 30 percentile ranks above the level of affective outcomes that would have been expected in a class of 30 pupils. Comparison with Fig. 2 shows that affective outcomes are even more closely related to class size than are the cognitive outcomes of schooling.

See also: Small Group Methods

Bibliography

Bolander S F 1973 Class size and levels of student motivation. *J. Exp. Educ.* 42(2): 12–17

Coleman J S 1966 *Equality of Educational Opportunity.* United States Government Printing Office, Washington, DC
Cornman O P 1909 Size of classes and school progress. *Psychol. Clinic* 3: 206–12
Fleming C M 1959 Class size as a variable in the teaching situation. *Educ. Res.* 1: 35–48
Glass G V, Cahen L S, Smith M L, Filby N N 1982 *School Class Size: Research and Policy.* Sage, Beverly Hills, California
Glass G V, McGaw B, Smith M L 1981 *Meta-analysis in Social Research.* Sage, Beverly Hills, California
Goodlad J I 1960 Classroom organization. In: Harris C W (ed.) 1960 *Encyclopedia of Educational Research.* Macmillan, New York, p. 224
Haskell S 1964 Some observations on the effect of class size upon pupil achievement in geometrical drawing. *J. Educ. Res.* 58: 27–30
Husén T (ed.) 1967 *International Study of Achievement in Mathematics: A Comparison of Twelve Countries.* Almqvist and Wiksell, Stockholm
Plowden Report 1967 *Children and Their Primary Schools: A Report of the Central Advisory Council for Education.* Her Majesty's Stationery Office, London
Rice J M 1902 Educational research: A test in arithmetic. *Forum* 34: 281–97
Rutter M, Maughan B, Mortimore P, Ouston J, Smith A 1979 *Fifteen Thousand Hours: Secondary Schools and Their Effects on Children.* Open Books, London.
Walker D A 1976 *The IEA Six Subject Survey: An Empirical Study of Education in Twenty-one Countries.* Wiley, New York

Seating Patterns

C. S. Weinstein

The traditional classroom, with its rows of desks facing the front of the room, has been a remarkably stable feature of educational systems. First grade or college, urban or rural, old or new, classrooms are generally arranged in much the same way. Since the early 1970s, several studies have looked at the impact of this traditional seating arrangement on grades, participation, and attitudes, and at the relationships between seat choice and various personality variables. A few studies have also examined the effects of alternative seating arrangements such as clusters and circles. This article reviews the empirical data on these topics and discusses the implications for teaching.

1. Conventional Row Arrangements

1.1 Seating Position and Personality Variables

In 1932, Willard Waller observed that the choice of a classroom seat did not appear to be random: "In the front row is a plentiful sprinkling of overdependent types, mixed perhaps with a number of extraordinarily zealous students. In the back row are persons in rebellion . . . . Quantitative investigation of these phenomena would be long and difficult, but not impossible" (p. 161). Fifty years later, a small body of empirical data exists that supports Waller's astute observation.

The most extensive study of the relationship between preferred seating position and individual characteristics was conducted in 1969 by Herbert Walberg. He administered a questionnaire to 817 high-school students asking about self-concept, attitudes toward school, interest, and seating preference. The results demonstrated that a student's choice of seat does, in fact, reflect his or her feelings about school. The students who preferred to sit in the front of the room generally expressed very positive attitudes toward learning, felt they had the capacity to succeed in school, and reported working hard to get good grades. Those who indicated a preference for a seat in the back expressed negative attitudes toward school, studying, and their own capacity for success.

More recent studies have found similar results. It has been demonstrated, for example, that high-school and college students with feelings of vulnerability, inadequacy, and low school self-esteem prefer to sit toward the back of the classroom, while students with the most positive self-concepts prefer the front.

1.2 Seating Position, Grades, and Participation

In a study of college classes, Becker et al. (1973) found that students sitting toward the front and the center of the room had higher course grades than those sitting toward the rear and the sides. This front–center phenomenon appears to hold true for participation as well. For example, Adams and Biddle (1970) observed 32 primary and secondary classes and recorded verbal interaction between the teacher and the students. They found that verbal interaction was concentrated in the front of the room and in a line directly up the center, an area of the room they called the "action zone." Adams and Biddle concluded that participation was primarily influenced by a student's seating position. Several other studies of seating and participation have found the same pattern of results, although the exact location of the action zone may vary.

There are two possible explanations for this front–center effect. One hypothesis is that more interested, more able students select seats in the front of the room, while less interested, less able students select seats in the rear. Opposed to this self-selection explanation is an environmental explanation, which posits that the characteristics of a front–center seat (such as greater opportunity for verbal and visual contact) influence participation and grades.

In an effort to determine which of these two explanations is correct, a number of investigators have compared the achievement and participation of students who were either assigned to seats or allowed to select their own. Unfortunately, the results of these studies are conflicting. Stires (1980) compared the test scores of two sections of a college course taught by the same instructors. Students in the choice condition selected permanent seats on the second day of class; students in the no-choice condition were seated alphabetically. In both sections, students in the middle of the room received higher grades than those at the sides, results that clearly support the environmental explanation.

In contrast, a very similar study by Wulf (1977) found a front–center effect only when students had chosen their seats, and even then, only for participation. Grades were unrelated to seating position in both the choice and no-choice conditions. Studies by Millard and Stimpson (1980) and Kinarthy (1975) were also unable to find any evidence that assigned seating position in college classrooms affects grades. An investigation by Levine et al. (1980) complicates the issue even further. These researchers found that when students selected their seats, those in the front had higher test grades than those in the rear, but participation was unrelated to seating position. (This is directly counter to Wulf's findings). When students were randomly assigned to seats, there were no differences in test scores as a function of seating position, but students in the front of the class participated more.

Thus, the question remains undecided. It is likely, however, that characteristics of the seat *and* the indi-vidual contribute to the front–center phenomenon. How this may happen is illustrated in a study by Koneya (1976) in which the participation of students previously judged to be highly or moderately verbal varied substantially according to assigned seat location: those randomly assigned to the action zone participated far more than those assigned to seats outside this area. The participation of students characterized as low verbalizers did not vary according to location; in other words, even a front-center seat was unable to alter the behavior of those who were unwilling to participate. These results suggest that environmental factors are most influential when the inclination to engage in the particular behavior is already present.

1.3 Seating Position and Attitudes Toward the Class

A number of recent studies have looked at the relationship between seating position in college classrooms and attitudes toward the class. The results are very consistent: a seat toward the front of the room is associated with greater enjoyment of the class, interest, feelings of involvement, and liking for the instructor. Moreover, these effects occur whether or not the seat has been assigned. The results thus support the notion that a front seat actually enhances these affective outcomes.

2. Conventional Row Arrangements Versus Alternative Arrangements

Only a few studies have compared the traditional row arrangement with other configurations. These have typically arranged students in rows, clusters, or horseshoes and examined the effects on a variety of student variables. Both Wheldall et al. (1981) and Axelrod et al. (1979) found that elementary students seated in rows exhibited greater on-task behavior than students clustered around tables. Gill (1977) observed greater peer interaction when elementary students were seated at tables than when they were seated in rows, but whether this was considered positive (as in the case of a cooperative activity) or negative (as off-task behavior) is not clear.

On the secondary level, Johnson (1973) compared the impact of seating arrangements such as rows, crescents, and circles on student–teacher interaction. Observations using Flanders Interaction Analysis indicated no significant differences in verbal interaction patterns. Finally, an investigation of various seating formations in college classrooms (Wang 1973) found no effect on students' level of anxiety, number of class acquaintances, or perceived social distance.

3. Circular Seating Arrangements

Teachers frequently arrange students in one large circle or in several smaller ones for discussions or interactive learning activities. Although the data are limited, there is evidence that a phenomenon parallel to the action zone exists: in arrangements where seats are facing inward, individuals will most likely speak to persons seated directly across from them, while they rarely speak to persons beside them (Steinzor 1950). Greater opportunity for eye contact and nonverbal communication appears to be responsible for this pattern of interaction.

In addition to influencing the flow of communication, seating position may affect an individual's perceived leadership ability. Howells and Becker (1962) seated five-person groups at a rectangular table, two people on one side and three on the other. Since the two individuals on one side could influence three individuals, and those on the three-seat side could influence only two, the investigators hypothesized that members of the two-person side would emerge more frequently as leaders. The data confirmed this prediction—14 people emerged as leaders from the two-seat side, compared with six from the three-seat side.

4. Implications for Teaching

The research on classroom seating arrangements is incomplete, inconsistent, and often contradictory. Nonetheless, there is sufficient evidence that seating position affects students' behavior and attitudes to warrant serious consideration by educators. A number of guidelines can be delineated for the benefit of teachers choosing to use a traditional row arrangement. First, since the action zone is presumably tied to the teacher's location, it is important for teachers to move around the room whenever possible and to direct comments to students seated on the periphery. Second, it is advisable to change students' seats periodically so as not to permanently relegate some students to seats outside of the action zone. Third, if students are allowed to choose their own seats, students' seat selections can be used as clues to their self-esteem and liking for school.

When clustering students in circular groups or around rectangular tables, teachers need to be aware that patterns of communication and leadership may be influenced by opportunities for eye contact and nonverbal communication. Thus, a teacher might place group leaders or those whose leadership potential they wish to develop in central positions where they are visually accessible to all members of the group. In order to encourage participation in a group discussion, a teacher could place a particularly quiet person opposite the leader or across from a more vocal group member. Finally, one might seat overly vocal members adjacent to the designated leader or next to each other, so that the reduced opportunity for visual contact may inhibit their participation.

Although there is little research comparing rows, circles, and other arrangements, it is clear that there is no single room arrangement that is ideal for all classes, all learning situations, and all people. While row arrangements may be preferable when teachers do not want students to interact (e.g., during a lecture, a demonstration, or testing), such arrangements may inhibit desirable interaction on a cooperative project. Musgrave (1975) suggests that teachers choose "home-base formations"—semipermanent arrangements that are suitable for a wide number of teaching situations—and move into "special formations" to provide needed variety and to meet the needs of a particular lesson. The crucial point is that teachers should use classroom seating arrangements to facilitate the achievement of their specific instructional and behavioral goals. Seating must be compatible with the nature of the activity and the needs of the persons involved.

See also: Structuring; Definitions of Teaching; Synthesizing Research Evidence

Bibliography

Adams R S, Biddle B J 1970 *Realities of Teaching: Explorations with Video Tape.* Holt, Rinehart and Winston, New York
Axelrod S, Hall R V, Tams A 1979 Comparison of 2 common classroom seating arrangements. *Acad. Ther.* 15: 29–36
Becker F D, Sommer R, Bee J, Oxley B 1973 College classroom ecology. *Sociometry* 36: 514–25
Gill W M 1977 A look at the change to open-plan schools in New Zealand. *N. Z. J. Educ. Stud.* 12: 3–16
Howells L T, Becker S W 1962 Seating arrangement and leadership emergence. *J. Abnorm. Soc. Psychol.* 64: 148–50
Johnson R H 1973 The effects of four modified elements of a classroom's physical environment on the social-psychological environment of a class (Doctoral dissertation, Oregon State University) *Dissertation Abstracts International* 1973 34: 1002A (University Microfilms No. 73-21,311)
Kinarthy E L 1975 The effects of seating position on performance and personality in a college classroom (Doctoral dissertation, University of Southern California) *Dissertation Abstracts International* 1976 37: 2078A
Koneya M 1976 Location and interaction in row and column seating arrangements. *Environ. Behav.* 8: 265
Levine D W, O'Neal E C, Garwood S G, McDonald P J 1980 Classroom ecology: The effects of seating position on grades and participation. *Personal. Soc. Psychol. Bull.* 6: 409–12
Millard R J, Stimpson D V 1980 Enjoyment and productivity as a function of classroom seating location. *Percep. Mot. Skills* 50: 439–44
Musgrave G R 1975 *Individualized Instruction: Teaching Strategies Focusing on the Learner.* Allyn and Bacon, Boston, Massachusetts
Steinzor B 1950 The spatial factor in face-to-face discussion groups. *J. Abnorm. Soc. Psych.* 45: 552–55
Stires L 1980 Classroom seating location, student grades, and attitudes: Environment or self-selection? *Environ. Behav.* 12: 241–54
Walberg H J 1969 Physical and psychological distance in the classroom. *Sch. Rev.* 77: 64–70
Waller W W 1965 *The Sociology of Teaching.* Wiley, New York
Wang Y T 1973 The result of differential seating arrangements

upon students' anxiety level, acquaintance volume, and perceived social distance (Doctoral dissertation, North Texas State University) *Dissertation Abstracts International* 1973 33: 4191A (University Microfilms No. 73-2932)

Wheldall K, Morris M, Vaughan P, Ng Y Y 1981 Rows versus tables: An example of the use of behavioral ecology in two classes of eleven-year-old children. *J. Educ. Psychol.* 1: 171–84

Wulf K M 1977 Relationship of assigned classroom seating area to achievement variables. *Educ. Res. Q.* 21: 56–62

Environmental Influences

D. L. Duke

Until the early 1960s it was not uncommon for individuals writing about life in classrooms to act as though schools were detached from the world around them. Classroom activities were treated as if they resulted exclusively from the intentions of teachers, school officials, and students. In recent years educators and researchers have begun to note that intentions are not always realized. Their efforts to explain this fact have led them to investigate the impact of environmental influences on classrooms.

Environmental influences can be divided into at least seven categories: technological, legal, political, economic, demographic, ecological, and cultural (Duke 1979b). These influences rarely operate in isolation from each other. Together they help to mold the expectations teachers and students bring to school, shape the nature of formal constraints on their conduct, and determine the resources to which they have access.

So consequential has the impact of environmental influences on schools become that researchers cannot fully understand an area such as classroom management without reference to them. Similarly, teachers cannot be trained to manage classrooms effectively without making them aware of these influences. An increasing amount of educational policy makers' time is devoted to the relationships between schools and external factors—government agencies, courts, communities, the economy.

Classroom management is defined as the provisions and procedures necessary to create and maintain an environment in which teaching and learning can occur (Duke 1979a). The remainder of this article consists of an analysis of some of the ways the seven environmental factors influence these provisions and procedures.

1. Technological Influences

As the numbers of students served by schools and the problems faced by educators have grown, more recommendations are heard that seek solutions from technology (applied science). While many teachers insist that teaching is more art than science, they nonetheless have come to rely heavily on technological developments.

Some technological influences on classroom management are so pervasive that it may be difficult for most teachers to realize they are taking place. These influences foster attitudes and predispositions which guide how teachers think about what they do. Consider, for example, the notion of progress. Spawned about two centuries ago and inspired by scientific theories and technological inventions, the belief in progress has become so ingrained in the thinking of many people—particularly in industrialized nations—that they cannot help expecting things to get better. Teachers may become disappointed when teaching and classroom management fail to grow easier from one year to the next. They frequently assume that, as they become more technically proficient and experienced, their jobs will be less taxing. What they may not realize, however, is that teaching is not completely analogous to production. Each cohort of students typically experiences a given grade or class only once. The uniqueness of being a second grader or taking algebra for each student suggests that expecting teaching to grow easier with each passing year can be unrealistic.

The way some teachers think about classroom management has also been subtly influenced by the "medical model." This model presumes that practitioners focus on diagnosing problems, prescribing treatments, and evaluating outcomes. Educational "specialists" are often needed to assist "general" practitioners with difficult classroom problems. The medical model sounds deceptively simple, but it implies a degree of clarity about desired outcomes that is less common in schools than hospitals. In addition, training teachers to look for problems may yield unexpected negative results. Individuals often find what they have been taught to see. The medical model can lead teachers to overemphasize problem management and ignore ways to define problems as opportunities. The proliferation of educational specialists has sometimes led to fragmentation of student instruction and coordination problems.

Another set of technological influences on classroom management takes the form of systematic, research-based strategies for dealing with student motivation and behavior problems. These strategies derive primarily from the work of behavioral and cognitive psychologists, sociologists, and psychoanalysts. Of all these approaches, behavior modification probably is the most widely used. Teachers are taught to apply the principles of systematic reinforcement and contingency management. Appropriate student behavior is reinforced, while inappropriate student behavior is modified through the use of token economies and other reward schemes or aversive reinforcement. Considerable evidence exists that behavior modification techniques are successful in reducing classroom management problems, at least on a short-term basis (Meacham and Wiesen 1974).

A third form of technological influence comes in the form of time-saving and labor-saving equipment. Computers are a current example. In class, microcomputers can be used to individualize student learning, thus reducing the likelihood of student frustration over the pace of instruction (see *Individualizing Teaching*). Teachers have more time to work intensively with particular students. At a school level, computers can be used for monitoring student attendance, grading, and other recordkeeping, thus reducing teachers' information-processing tasks. Japan has probably made greater use of computers in schools than any other nation.

New equipment, of course, may bring classroom management problems as well as benefits. Expensive computers invite vandalism or theft and thus require security precautions. Critics contend that computers serve to further impersonalize learning, thereby harming certain students who need direct contact and caring.

Television illustrates the mixed impact of new technology. Used extensively throughout the world as an instructional device, television has meant that students in underdeveloped nations can have access to new ideas, no matter how far they live from urban centers. At the same time, television, in its commercial operations, has been accused of undermining traditional cultures and modeling aggressive and disrespectful behavior for impressionable youth.

A final type of technological influence comes in the form of changes in the learning environment. Architects and design specialists exert a direct impact on classroom management by determining how comfortable, well-lit, vandal-proof, and conducive to teaching are schools and classrooms (see *Architecture*). In the late 1960s and early 1970s, for example, open-space schools were built throughout the United States and Canada. Designed to facilitate team teaching and reduce building costs by minimizing interior partitions between rooms, these new facilities fostered a host of classroom management problems (see *Open Versus Formal Methods*). Teachers often disliked working within clear view of neighbors and were bothered by peripheral noise. As a result, permanent walls were constructed in many of the open-space schools.

Of all these technological changes it can be said, in summary, that the persons most responsible for implementing and working with them—namely teachers—have rarely been involved in planning or developing them. Schooling in most countries is a big business, and technological changes represent potentially large economic gains for developers. New technology may not always be accompanied by the practitioner consultation, careful pilot-testing, and impact analysis so vital to the ultimate success of innovations.

2. Legal Influences

Courts of law have tended to play a more active role in schools in industrialized nations than elsewhere. Elementary and secondary education in many underdeveloped countries is subject to highly centralized federal and state authority. Centralized decision making minimizes local variations in school policy, thereby reducing the occasions when litigation may be necessitated. A second reason why legal influences seem to be less potent in some nations is the acceptance of the principle of *in loco parentis* for educators. In other words, teachers are accorded the broad discretionary authority of a parent in their classes. Teachers in the United States, Canada, and Scandinavia have seen their status as "surrogate parents" challenged in recent years by plaintiffs representing the interests of particular students.

Legal influences in the United States take several forms. Through the courts, pressure is brought to bear on educators perceived to be trespassing on the constitutional rights of students. Professional malpractice—once the concern of physicians and engineers—has become an issue with which teachers must reckon. Finally, the increase of labor negotiations, collective bargaining, and contract law has made an impact on how teachers act.

Courts have dealt with student rights on a collective and individual basis. The concerns of minority students, for instance, have been addressed in the form of lawsuits against school districts for denying equal educational opportunity and tolerating discriminatory disciplinary policies. Teachers who regard suspension from class and school as a mechanism for maintaining control must be careful that minority students do not receive a disproportionate number of suspension notices. Suspending a student from school has been interpreted as an abridgement of his or her constitutional right to an education. "In-school suspension" has been developed as an alternative by many United States schools.

Some of the ways in which teachers can deny students equal educational opportunity have been explored in an ethnographic study of three years in the schooling of a group of black elementary-school students (Rist 1970). Routine classroom management decisions, such as where a student can sit and with whom a student can interact, were found to seriously affect students' chances of success in succeeding grades. To date, however, courts have focused more on equity issues at the level of school and local educational authority than classroom.

Where classroom teachers have been directly challenged is in the area of freedom of expression and denial of due process rights. Teachers in the United States generally cannot prevent a student from expressing himself or herself verbally or symbolically, even if there is the chance problems will ensue. If a student must be suspended, he or she is entitled to due process, including a hearing at which charges are formally presented. The Supreme Court of the United States has made it clear that students do not "shed their rights at the schoolhouse door."

Malpractice suits have tended to be brought against school systems rather than individual classroom teachers, but it is likely that teachers increasingly feel legally vulnerable. Vulnerability breeds caution. Teachers express fear that any oversight or mistake may be interpreted as negligence or malfeasance. Thus the mere threat of legal action may be sufficient to influence the classroom management behavior of many teachers.

Litigation concerning interpretations of teacher contracts is another way in which courts can influence classroom management. Courts, for example, have upheld the right of teacher unions to negotiate a variety of pertinent issues, including class size and supervisory responsibility. On the other hand, administrative decisions to require ineffective teachers to obtain more training and to remove teachers who are unable to control student behavior in class have also been supported.

3. Political Influences

While the formal study of the politics of education is a relatively recent phenomenon, the fact is that schools have been shaped by political influences since their inception. Political decisions having a direct bearing on the nature of classroom management include the designation of a school-leaving age, the determination of how schools will be financed, and the specification of societal expectations for schools and students. The role to be played by schools in youth development is by no means commonly agreed upon. The absence of a coordinated youth policy in the United States and Canada has meant that secondary schools act as the primary socialization agents for adolescents. Many other countries have not permitted schools to exercise such pervasive influence. Israel and the People's Republic of China, for example, require large numbers of youth to become involved in extrascholastic work experiences (Boocock 1974).

A political decision with important implications for classroom management involves the role schools are expected to play in social integration. By regarding schools as prime elements in the effort to break down racial barriers, United States policy makers have created a need for teachers to become more sensitive to cultural influences on behavior and more aware of the subtleties of their own expectations. Recently integrated schools frequently report increased classroom behavior problems and teacher dissatisfaction.

The decision to "mainstream" handicapped students in regular classrooms is another political decision with major implications for classroom management. As a result of Public Law 94–142 (1975), United States teachers must work with students who previously were taught in small classes by specially trained instructors. Often these students have difficulty maintaining attention and conforming to class rules. Subject to ridicule by other students, they frequently necessitate considerable teacher intervention to maintain order. Teachers are uncertain about applying the same rules governing behavior to handicapped students that they apply to other students.

The fact that teachers traditionally have not been influential in shaping the political policies that, in turn, shape their classrooms has led to greater politicization of the teaching profession. Teacher unions have become major political forces in many nations. Where they have succeeded in winning the right to collective bargaining, teachers have begun to negotiate conditions of work in their contracts. As indicated in the preceding section, such matters as maximum class size and the limits of supervisory responsibilities are often spelled out in detail. In trouble-plagued urban schools, United States teachers concerned about personal safety have won provisions for greater security. It is clear that classrooms are unlikely to be orderly and productive if teachers are anxious and fearful. Where teachers join administrators in shaping school rules and sanctions, they are also more likely to enforce disciplinary policies consistently.

Involvement of students and community members in making decisions concerning issues related to student behavior has also been shown to reduce the likelihood of major discipline problems (McPartland and McDill 1976). Bronfenbrenner (1970) found that students in the Soviet Union handled almost all of the behavior problems in their schools, with quite positive results. There generally has been less willingness in most other countries, however, to accord students extensive authority over disciplinary matters.

4. Economic Influences

The quality of schooling available to a particular group of students is a function, in large measure, of the fiscal resources the community is willing to allocate to education. Money buys talented teachers and administrators, learning materials, and facilities. Classroom management is not immune to the economic behavior of the citizenry or to fluctuations in the economy.

Recent evidence of this relationship comes from case studies of urban high schools in the United States during the aftermath of budget cuts (Duke et al. 1981, Duke and Meckel 1980b). Any reduction in school funds that is more than marginal must be effected by removal of staff members. As teachers are let go, average class size grows, increasing the workload for teachers. As workload increases, teachers find less time to spend with individual students. Students who have difficulty keeping up with their lessons grow more restless and frustrated, and classroom behavior problems increase. The more time teachers must devote to handling behavior problems, the less time they have for direct instruction. The less direct instruction students receive, the less likely they are to achieve what is expected of them. As student achievement declines, teacher workload increases once again. This entire process can be compared to a steadily decreasing spiral, where each change serves to accelerate the downward movement, causing classroom management to become more difficult.

The downward spiral is further influenced by the withdrawal of students whose parents can afford nonpublic education. Often these students are high achievers. Their departure serves to increase the concentration of lower-achieving students with whom public school teachers work and make teacher dissatisfaction more likely. Ultimately, budget cuts in public education—particularly where urban schools are concerned—threaten to widen the gap between advantaged and disadvantaged students (Duke and Cohen 1983).

An economic influence related to the present mood of fiscal restraint is the accountability movement. As inflation continues and taxpayer resistance mounts, demands grow for careful review of how public education funds are spent. Teachers often watch helplessly as externally supported programs, upon which they have come to rely, are curtailed because evidence of dramatic changes in student achievement is lacking. Paraprofessionals, teacher aides, and support staff are the first to lose their jobs. Teachers are also subjected to closer scrutiny, supervision, and evaluation. As a result, they tend to spend time primarily on those activities which lead to measurable outcomes. Schools come to resemble commercial enterprises driven by concern for efficiency more than service organizations devoted to the care and growth of youth.

In the United States, recent concern over the rising costs of public education has occasioned debate—long common in other nations—over which students are most deserving of formal secondary education. Students who are chronically absent, disruptive, or unmotivated are no longer assured places in secondary schools. The fear, however, is that the economy cannot provide meaningful employment for those who fail to complete high school. The ultimate cost to society of having to deal with nongraduates is difficult to estimate.

5. Demographic Influences

Classroom management is subject to a variety of demographic influences, ranging from fluctuations in the birth rate to changes in the types of students with whom teachers must work. For example, following the Second World War, the birth rate rose dramatically in many industrialized nations. Unprepared for the rapid growth in students, school systems lacked adequate facilities and appropriately trained teachers. It is conceivable that part of the purported increase in student behavior problems during the 1960s and early 1970s can be attributed directly to overcrowding and lack of skilled personnel.

If these factors contributed to behavior problems, it might be expected that the declining enrollments of the 1970s would bring a proportional reduction in problems. That this situation has not occurred universally, suggests that other influences may be at work. In the United States, for instance, the 1970s were characterized by increasing concentrations of nonwhite students in city schools, the arrival of large contingents of non-English-speaking immigrants from Southeast Asia and Latin America, and the mainstreaming of handicapped youngsters in regular classrooms. Teachers thus were faced with management problems arising from the special needs of different groups of students. Frequently these problems stemmed from the teachers' lack of familiarity with or sensitivity to the behavioral norms of youngsters from different cultures. Educational researchers began to note the impact of teachers' differential expectations on the behavior and academic achievement of students from different cultures (Brophy and Good 1974).

Another reason why behavior problems did not necessarily subside as school enrollments shrank may have been the fact that the average age of teachers rose during the 1970s. Due to seniority rules, older teachers were able to retain their jobs as positions were eliminated. These teachers may have been less likely to be aware of the needs of new groups of students and receptive to changing their behavior to accommodate these students.

The problem of controlling the behavior of contemporary students has been exacerbated by several major changes in the types of homes from which students come (see *Students' Social Backgrounds*). More students today come from one-parent homes than ever before, a fact that is reflected in the difficulty many teachers find enlisting parental support and meeting students' emotional needs. Students living with both parents are not immune from problems, since they may lack proper supervision as a result of both parents working. A third concern involves the growing number of students who are new to a school during a given year. As the populations of industrialized nations become more transient, the likelihood decreases that students will remain in the same school system until graduation. As a result, it is harder for teachers and school officials to monitor the growth and development of individual students and to provide them with "personalized" guidance.

Demographic changes not only seem to have influenced the behavior problems with which teachers must deal and the nature of their relationships with parents, but the way classroom resources are allocated. Teachers faced with heterogeneous groups of students are expected to respond to the special needs of each group—a task for which adequate materials, time, and expertise is often lacking. Where sufficient funds exist, paraprofessionals are often hired to assist teachers in working with special students.

6. Ecological Influences

Ecological influences include, among other things, the organizations that interact with schools on a regular basis. Among the organizations that can potentially exert an influence on classroom management are large corporations, local businesses, foundations, interest groups, lobbies, and agencies at various levels of government.

The increase in reports of student behavior problems may signal growing ecological influences on the schools. Since the Second World War, a variety of agencies—public and private—have specialized in providing services to troubled youth. As a result, in many industrialized nations teachers can often turn for assistance to child welfare workers, probation officials, juvenile justice specialists, psychiatric social workers, and pediatricians specializing in behavior problems, as well as school-based guidance personnel, school psychologists, peer counselors, and community liaisons. With so much expertise available, it is tempting for many teachers to regard referral as their primary strategy for maintaining control. The proliferation of specialists in youth problems may actually serve to reduce the likelihood that any one professional—typically the teacher—assumes overall responsibility for handling a particular student's problems.

The availability of outside resources and expertise may have yielded a second undesirable by-product. Increasing reliance on extraclassroom assistance can contribute to "learned helplessness" on the part of teachers. When resources diminish, as they do during times of reduced government spending, teachers find themselves without specialists to whom to refer troubled students and without the skills to handle behavior problems themselves. The disappearance of government-supported alternative schools, clinics, work–study programs, dropout centers, and counseling activities may force teachers to deal with more nonacademic matters in a regular classroom context.

7. Cultural Influences

Cultural influences on classroom management, though often among the most pervasive and potent, are difficult to identify. They involve phenomena such as norms, values, and beliefs about the young, authority, society, and learning. Classroom management is subject to cultural influence through the expectations that teachers and students bring to class.

Studies of white elementary-school teachers in the United States, for example, find that mischievous behavior is tacitly condoned for boys but not for girls, reflecting conventional sex-role stereotyping (see *Students' Sex*). White teachers also may behave toward nonwhite students in ways that encourage these individuals to feel they are not expected to achieve as much as white students. "Double standards" of this kind are deeply rooted in many cultures.

Attitudes toward competition and cooperation offer another illustration of cultural influence. While many teachers expect students to take pride in knowing more than their peers, some American Indian cultures value cooperation so greatly that students learn to avoid any situation—such as answering a question that a peer cannot answer—which might embarrass another. Scott (1975 p. 200) maintains that the high incidence of criminal behavior in American society (and presumably misconduct in American schools) is attributable, in part, to the high value the dominant culture places on competition and conflict.

How a teacher defines a particular student behavior cannot be separated from the culture in which the teacher has grown up, received training, and worked (see *Teachers' Social Backgrounds*). White teachers thus may misinterpret as insolence the fact that black students tend not to look directly at adults when being corrected. Decisions regarding which students are considered handicapped, gifted, or emotionally disturbed may have less to do with objective, universal criteria than with the idiosyncrasies of local communities. Teachers who transfer from suburban or rural assignments to urban schools often discover that their students are accustomed to different ways of communicating and acting.

One of the few expectations characterizing most societies is that teachers should be in control of their classrooms. How this control is to be achieved, however, varies widely. In some societies teachers establish control by teaching students how to behave responsibly. In other societies teachers operate on the assumption that students cannot be trusted. They rely on rules and punishments to maintain order.

8. Control Versus Authority

Classroom management does not occur in a vacuum. The preceding analysis illustrates that how classrooms are organized and operated can be influenced by a variety of factors besides teachers' professional training and official school policies. In recent years many of these factors have had the collective impact of pressing for greater teacher control over classrooms. Of interest, though, is the fact that the desire for more control has not been accompanied by a corresponding push for greater teacher authority. Teachers are caught in the awkward position of witnessing their authority diminish—the victim of more rules, laws, fiscal constraints, technological changes, demands for accountability, and community involvement in schools—at the same time that they are urged to exercise greater control over student behavior and achievement. Such a trend may be part of a broader effort to deprofessionalize teaching. Functionaries and civil servants, unlike professionals, are typically expected to maintain order without exercising authority.

As behavior problems in classrooms grow and pressure for greater control mounts, teachers frequently counter with demands for more parental involvement n schools and stronger support for school disciplinary policies at home. As a result of this kind of interaction, the environment in which classroom management occurs is increasingly characterized by confrontation and adversarial relations. In jeopardy is the traditional belief that teacher interests and parent interests are compatible.

See also: Architecture; Behaviour Problems; Teachers' Expectations; Classroom Management

Bibliography

Boocock S S 1974 Youth in three cultures. *Sch. Rev.* 83: 93–111

Bronfenbrenner U 1970 *Two Worlds of Childhood: US and USSR.* Russell Sage Foundation, New York

Brophy J E, Good T L 1974 *Teacher–Student Relationships: Causes and Consequences.* Holt, Rinehart and Winston, New York

Dreikurs R, Grey L 1968 *A New Approach to Discipline: Logical Consequences.* Hawthorn, New York

Duke D L (ed.) 1979a *Classroom Management: Seventy-eighth Yearbook of the National Society for the Study of Education,* Pt. 2. University of Chicago Press, Chicago, Illinois

Duke D L 1979b Environmental influences on classroom management. In: Duke D L (ed.) 1979a

Duke D L, Cohen J S 1983 Do public schools have a future? *Urban Rev.* 15: 89–105

Duke D L, Meckel A M 1980a Disciplinary roles in American schools. *Br. J. Teach. Educ.* 6: 37–50

Duke D L, Meckel A M 1980b The slow death of a public high school. *Phi Delta Kappan* 61: 674–77

Duke D L, Cohen J S, Herman R 1981 Running faster to stay in place: Retrenchment in the New York City schools. *Phi Delta Kappan* 63: 13–17

King E J 1973 *Other Schools and Ours: Comparative Studies for Today,* 4th edn. Holt, Rinehart and Winston, Eastbourne

Lickona T (ed.) 1976 *Moral Development and Behavior: Theory, Research, and Social Issues.* Holt, Rinehart and Winston, New York

McPartland J M, McDill E L 1976 The unique role of schools in the causes of youthful crime. Report No. 216. Center for Social Organization of Schools, Johns Hopkins University, Baltimore, Maryland

Meacham M L, Wiesen A E 1974 *Changing Classroom Behavior,* 2nd edn. Intext Educational, New York

Rist R C 1970 Student social class and teacher expectations: The self-fulfilling prophecy in ghetto education. *Harvard Educ. Rev.* 40: 411–51

Scott J P 1975 *Aggression,* 2nd edn. University of Chicago Press, Chicago, Illinois

Skinner B F 1968 *The Technology of Teaching.* Appleton-Century-Crofts, New York

Psychological Environment

H. J. Walberg

The classroom psychological environment is the climate or atmosphere of the class as a social group that potentially influences what students learn. Because the classroom environment, as it has been investigated, refers to the less tangible aspects of the context of teaching and learning, it is often inferred by asking students to perceive and rate the psychological characteristics of their classroom group on questionnaire items. These items typically concern the affective and social relations among the class members, the emphasis given to efficient completion of learning tasks, and the implicit and explicit system of rules and organization of the class. The purpose of this article is to (a) describe the scope of the field of research on classroom psychological environments, (b) discuss its theoretical and historical underpinnings, and (c) synthesize educational research on the measurement of empirical relationships between psychological environments and learning. For recent comparisons of classroom psychological effects, see also Walberg 1984.

1. Scope of Research

Since the late 1960s, educational researchers and evaluators issued or published about 200 reports concerning student perceptions of the social–psychological dimensions of their classroom group such as cohesiveness, satisfaction, goal direction, difficulty, competitiveness, and friction. Reviews of this work (for example, Randhawa and Fu 1973, Shulman and Tamir 1973, Walberg 1974, 1976, Moos 1979a, 1979c) discuss theoretical, methodological, and practical issues and conclude that such perceptions are useful as independent, mediating, and dependent variables in educational investigations in natural settings. Items measuring these dimensions require the respondent to agree or disagree with such items as "Students enjoy their work in the class" and "Most students know the goals of the lessons." Much of the research shows that social–psychological perceptual scales provide statistically reliable sensitivity to variations in curriculum, teacher training, and instructional innovations as well as to efforts to increase teamwork, cross-sex/cross-ethnic-group cooperation, and similar group properties. Other work reveals that such perceptions reflect and mediate teacher and student characteristics and that they provide diagnostically valuable profiles of class and individual morale or climate that supplement conventional testing programs.

Educational evaluators throughout the world rely heavily and, in many cases, exclusively on conventional standardized tests of achievement and other outcomes of learning. Few responsible evaluators wish to discontinue their use, yet few claim that such tests give a complete picture of the educational process and outcomes. First, the tests themselves do not reflect such valued traits of the individual as good citizenship, ethical maturity, and creativity that educators try to foster; neither do they accurately predict, for groups with a given amount of education, indexes of adult success such as peer-rated competence, self-rated happiness, income, political participation in society, and prizes and awards. Second, even though they allow comparisons of individuals and groups with one another across time, they afford little indication by themselves of the causes of differences and changes in outcomes.

For these reasons, evaluators began several decades ago to collect data on the context and means of education to test causal explanations of how factors in the educational environment produce learning. Administrative, economic, and sociological measures (e.g., class size, expenditures per student, and social class) proved convenient enough to measure but explain little variance in learning. Counts of teaching behaviors account for a small to moderate amount of variance in learning but are time consuming and expensive to obtain.

In the late 1960s, however, three investigators and their colleagues began sustained series of programmatic investigations of educative environments of school-age children that resulted in several inexpensive and practical instruments and techniques for measuring variables that account for a considerable amount of the variance in learning outcomes. Kevin Marjoribanks, inspired by Chicago and British research and working in Toronto (Canada), Oxford (England), and Adelaide (Australia), developed parent-interview measures of the educatively stimulating qualities of the home environment. Rudolf Moos at Berkeley and Stanford, California (USA), measured the social environments of hospital wards, dormitories, and college and school classes, analyzed their common characteristics, and showed how profiles of comparative information can be used by leaders and groups to improve aspects of group climate such as perceived task orientation and satisfaction. At Harvard University and the University of Illinois at Chicago (USA), Herbert Walberg and his students developed and established the validity of student-perception measures of classroom social environment to predict cognitive, affective, and behavioral learning outcomes, and Walberg carried out or served as an advisor to a large number of educational evaluation projects making use of environmental assessments. Since 1975, evaluators and researchers in Africa, Australia, Asia, Europe, the Middle East, the United States, and South America have used or translated such measures, or developed similar ones and found them useful in a wide variety of educational evaluations. Recently, the Australian Barry Fraser and his students have implemented a substantial program of research on psychological environments in

relation to curriculum and instruction; and Australia is the most active center of educational research on this topic today.

A considerable number of review articles and collections of original studies are published. See Moos (1973) and Insel and Moos (1974) for an analytic treatment of psychological research on a variety of human settings; Campbell (1970) and Marjoribanks (1974) for valuable but neglected collections of substantive work on learning environments carried out in Australia, Canada, England, and the United States; Khan and Weiss (1973), Randhawa and Fu (1973), Shulman and Tamir (1973), and Walberg (1971, 1974a) for substantive and methodological reviews; and Walberg (1974b) for a source book of learning environment instruments and evaluations by several research groups. A review of the psychology of learning environments, including their historical antecedents, a framework for research on classroom perceptions, and developments in research are presented by Walberg (1976).

More recently, Moos's (1979b) book presented a conceptual model of interactions between people and their environments and reported findings based upon the administration of environment scales to nationally representative samples of 10,000 college students and over 10,000 junior- and senior-high-school students in more than 500 classrooms in the United States. Evidence of the impact of the teacher as a major force in educational environments is reviewed in Peterson and Walberg's (1979) volume which reports several inquiries into instruction which contribute to an understanding of how the actions of teachers influence environmental factors. Walberg (1979) edited 20 studies that provide data on the effects of environmental influences on scholastic achievement and deal with educational environments outside as well as within the classroom. The most recent works are Fraser's (1981) extensive review of learning environment research in curriculum evaluation published in *Evaluation in Education: An International Review Series*; his (1980) edited collection of studies and reflections in *Studies in Educational Evaluation*; and a meta-analysis of classroom psychological environments in relation to learning published in the *British Educational Research Journal* (Haertel et al. 1981).

2. Historical and Theoretical Underpinnings

It is said that large battalions are victorious; but, as Leibenstein (1976) notes, Leo Tolstoy in *War and Peace* maintained that, in military affairs, the strength of an army is the product of its mass and some unknown x, or the spirit of the army. The task of science, according to Tolstoy, is to discover the nature of x. Simply knowing the observable inputs such as the number of guns, men, and the commands of the generals is not enough; the group spirit or effort is crucial in determining outcomes. Beginning in the Second World War, psychologists began quantitative and qualitative documentation of teamwork in the military, business, and industry for outcomes and productivity.

Economists also have recognized that productivity depends not only on the factors that can be purchased (traditionally, capital, land, labor, and technology) but also on "*x*-efficiency," for example, effort and morale. In *Beyond Economic Man*, Leibenstein cites extensive evidence that output can be raised greatly by improved organizational arrangements, consultancies, and other efforts to improve industrial relations. Frequently, the ratio of best to worst output per worker is $4:1$ and can rise as high as $30:1$. Since it is difficult for managers to write completely detailed contracts for work to be performed even in simple jobs, general rather than close supervision, effective psychological incentives, and the encouragement of group and individual motivation often serve as keys to increased output.

Research on the sociopsychological environment of the classroom emphasizes perceptions and judgments of such morale factors. Investigators of learning environments often ask students to judge the suitability of their own classroom's psychological environment. As the primary consumers of educational efforts, students are at a good vantage point for making such judgments. Compared with a short-term observer, students can weigh in their judgments, not only the class as it presently is, but also how it has been since the beginning of the year. Students are able to compare from the student–client point of view their class with those in past grades, with others they are presently taking, or even with other social groups of which they are members. Students form a group of 10 to 40 sensitive, well-informed judges of the class; an outside observer is a single judge who has far less data and, though highly trained and systematic, may be insensitive to what is important for psychological incentives in a particular class.

Investigators of learning environments have tended to use general ratings of the environment, rather than counts of specific teacher or student acts. These subjective ratings of perceived behavior are referred to as "high-inference" measures. "Low-inference" measures, on the other hand, involve specific teacher or student behaviors.

Thus one way to find out about, say, the suitability of the learning environment is to ask the students, teachers, and trained observers to report their perceptions. Students, however, stand at a superior vantage point; what they take in makes the difference in learning. By the age of 10 they have encountered a variety of educational environments; they are with their teacher for many hours during the year; they are sophisticated judges with plenty of information to weigh. Their perceptions, as partakers of classroom social transaction, are of great value, and it is easy enough (and incrementally valid) to ask for them. Fiedler's (1975) study of classroom transaction showed that students' perceptions of their own influences on the class, but not observer estimates of the same, predict academic gains.

This is not to say that "objective" tests, counts of teacher behavior, and the like must be put aside, but only that by themselves they may be a narrow approach to understanding. Behavioral efforts to link classroom treatment with learning are numerous, expensive, and difficult. Investigating the links of perception with behavioral treatments and learning may yield more revealing clues to the puzzle of optimizing classroom learning.

3. Measurement and Validity

The most commonly used instrument for research on classroom psychological environments is the Learning Environment Inventory (LEI). Sample items and reliabilities of the 15 scales are shown in Table 1.

The LEI has been used to obtain scores not only for individual students but for entire classes as well. For classroom-level assessments, scores of all students are averaged for each scale. To establish the reliability of the LEI for each of these two applications, two types of reliability coefficients are required. At the individual level, the traditional alpha reliability coefficient is appropriate but, at the class level, intraclass correlations are more informative. Both of these indices have been computed for all the LEI scales. For the 15 scales, alpha measurements of internal consistency range from 0.54 to 0.85, with values above 0.70 for nine of the scales. Intraclass correlations range from 0.31 to 0.92, with values from 0.70 for 12 of the scales.

The 105 items on the LEI can be administered in approximately 25 minutes and produce, in most cases, reliable and valid estimates of the morale, climate, or learning environment of the class. The scales have been translated into several languages, and used in a number of countries of Africa, Asia, Europe, and South America, as well as Australia and the United States. Some investigators have omitted certain scales or reduced the number of items per scale to save student time. Occasionally, some scales have required modification to make them more suitable for a particular research setting (e.g., Fraser 1978).

The *My Class Inventory* (MCI) is an adaptation of the LEI for elementary-school research. It consists of 60 items and only five scales are included (cohesiveness, satisfaction, friction, competitiveness, and difficulty). The vocabulary level of the items has been simplified, but occasionally items must still be read and explained to poor readers.

Table 2 shows the relation of the LEI and the two other most carefully investigated measures of classroom environments, the Classroom Environment Scale (Trickett and Moos 1973) and the Individualized Classroom Environment Questionnaire (Rentoul and Fraser 1979). Numerous analyses (Fraser 1980) confirm that classroom perceptions cluster into dimensions of task orientation or completion of educational and personal tasks, affective and social relations among class members, and organization of the classroom work as shown in the table.

Table 1
Sample items, reliabilities, and consistencies of 15 subscales from the Learning Environment Inventory

Subscale	Sample item	Class reliability	Percent positive correlations learning[a]
Cohesiveness	All students know each other very well	0.84	86
Satisfaction	The students enjoy their class work	0.79	100
—Friction[b]	Certain students are responsible for petty quarrels	0.80	0
Apathy	Students don't care what the class does	0.77	14
—Cliqueness	Some students refuse to mix with the rest of the class	0.74	8
Democracy	Students have about equal influence on the class	0.61	85
Competitiveness	There is much competition in the class	0.56	67
—Diversity	Interests vary greatly within the group	0.36	30
—Favoritism	Certain students are favored more than the rest	0.65	10
Goal direction	Each student knows the goals of the course	0.73	73
Material environment	The room is bright and comfortable	0.79	86
Formality	The class has rules to guide its activities	0.87	65
Difficulties	Students find the course work hard to do	0.81	87
Speed	The course material is covered quickly	0.76	54
—Disorganization	The class is inefficient and not organized	0.87	6

a The learning criteria include cognitive, affective, and behavioral measures including higher mental processes and self-concept
b Subscales preceded by a minus sign measure aspects of the sociopsychological environment which are negatively related to learning outcomes

Studies in Australia, Brazil, Canada, India, the United States, and other countries demonstrate the substantial predictive validity of learning environment scales in general, and the LEI in particular. These scales are capable of predicting cognitive, behavioral, and affective gains that occur during instruction. The predictive validity of these scales was established by Anderson and Walberg (1974) in a review of the unique criterion variance accounted for by learning and by IQ. Using the LEI to operationalize the learning environment, Anderson and Walberg set out to answer the question "Is the Learning Environment Inventory a useful predictor of student learning?" To answer this question, they examined the results of other well-known predictors of student learning to determine whether or not such instruments as the LEI predict substantially more variance in learning than does IQ, and whether it predicts different variance from that predicted by IQ. Student perceptions of the social environment of learning accounted for a median of 30 percent (range = 13

Table 2
Classification of variables in three domains represented in three instruments

Instrument	Task	Affect	Organization
Learning Environment Inventory	Speed Difficulty Competitivenes Goal direction	Cohesiveness Friction Favoritism Cliqueness Satisfaction Apathy	Diversity Formality Environment Disorganization Democracy
Classroom Environment Scale	Task orientation Competition	Involvement Affiliation Teacher support	Order Rule clarity Teacher control Innovation
Individualized Classroom Environment Questionnaire	Independence Investigation	Personalization Participation	Differentiation

percent to 46 percent; all significant) of the variance in cognitive, affective, and behavioral postcourse measures beyond that accounted for by parallel precourse measures. By contrast, IQ accounts for only a median of 7 percent (range = 0 percent to 9 percent) of the residualized variance (Anderson and Walberg 1974). Efforts at generalizing these results suggest consistency across different school subjects and different languages and cultures (Anderson and Walberg 1974). Although in classroom research the usual treatment (aside from content opportunity) and its interaction with aptitude add little to the prediction of learning variation beyond that accounted for by aptitude, student perceptions of the social environment of learning add considerably.

Essentially the same conclusions were reached by Haertel et al. (1979) in a recent synthesis of research on the relation of sociopsychological environment to learning outcomes. A total of 734 correlations were analyzed, from a comprehensive collection of 12 studies of 10 data sets on 823 classes in eight subject areas, encompassing 17,805 students in four nations. All of these data were taken from studies carried out in naturalistic classroom settings, kindergarten through to 18-year-olds, and all were simple, part, or partial correlations between student perceptions of the sociopsychological climate and end-of-course learning. A tabulation of the signs of the relationships is shown in Table 1.

4. Conclusion

Psychological perceptions of classroom environments have important influences on student achievement, performance, and self-concept as well as on other valuable educational outcomes. Climate measures are practical, inexpensive, and valid; and they predict learning gains more accurately than do so-called objective variables such as students' social class, teacher behaviors and other characteristics, school and class sizes, and educational expenditures.

Constructive educational climates may be viewed as means to valuable educational ends or as worthy ends in their own right. Information on educational climates may be conveniently gathered and fed back to school staffs for the planning, execution, and evaluation of databased educational improvement programs. Climate measures can also be included along with standardized tests and other assessments in national, local, and school accountability, evaluation, and research efforts.

Because learning environment assessments are convenient, practical, and inexpensive, because of their demonstrated predictive validity and revealing, reliable sensitivity to educational innovations, and because research information from them proves interesting, meaningful, and suggestive to educational policy makers and practitioners, they are being used in a wide variety of evaluation and research projects in many countries. It seems likely that this thriving, young tradition of environmental assessment, because it balances and complements the older traditions of behavioral assessments and standardized cognitive measures, will continue to grow in size, theory, and utility.

See also: Classroom Climate; Cooperation; Competition

Bibliography

Anderson G J, Walberg H J 1974 Learning environments. In: Walberg H J (ed.) 1974b

Campbell W J (ed.) 1970 *Scholars in Context: The Effects of Environments on Learning.* Wiley, Sydney

Fiedler M L 1975 Bidirectionality of influence in classroom interaction. *J. Educ. Psychol.* 67: 735–44

Fraser B J 1978 Measuring learning environment in individualized junior high school classrooms. *Sci. Educ.* 62: 125–33

Fraser B J (ed.) 1980 Classroom learning environment, special issue. *Stud. Educ. Eval.* 3: 219–340

Fraser B J 1981 Learning environment in curriculum evaluation: A review. *Eval. Educ.* 5: 1–93

Haertel G D, Walberg H J, Haertel E H 1979 Social–psychological environments and learning: A quantitative synthesis. A paper presented at the American Educational Research Association Annual Meeting, San Francisco

Haertel G D, Walberg H J, Haertel E H 1981 Social–psychological environments and learning: A quantitative synthesis. *Br. Educ. Res. J.* 7: 27–36

Insel P M, Moos R H 1974 Psychological environments: Expanding the scope of human ecology. *Am. Psychol.* 29: 179–88

Khan S B, Weiss J 1973 The teaching of affective responses. In: Travers R M W (ed.) 1973 *Second Handbook of Research on Teaching: A Project of the American Educational Research Association.* Rand McNally, Chicago, Illinois

Leibenstein H 1976 *Beyond Economic Man: A New Foundation for Economics.* Harvard University Press, Cambridge, Massachusetts

Marjoribanks K (ed.) 1974 *Environments for Learning.* National Foundation for Educational Research, Slough

Moos R H 1973 Conceptualizations of human environments. *Am. Psychol.* 28: 652–64

Moos R H 1979a Educational climates. In: Walberg H J (ed.) 1979

Moos R H 1979b *Evaluating Educational Environments: Procedures, Measures, Findings, and Policy Implications.* Jossey-Bass, San Francisco, California

Moos R H 1979c Educational climates. In: Walberg H J (ed.) 1979

Peterson P L, Walberg H J (eds.) 1979 *Research on Teaching: Concepts, Findings, and Implications.* McCutchan, Berkeley, California

Randhawa B S, Fu L L W 1973 Assessment and effect of some classroom environment variables. *Am. Educ. Res. J.* 43: 303–21

Rentoul A J, Fraser B J 1979 Conceptualization of enquiry-based or open-classroom learning environments. *J. Curric. Stud.* 11: 233–45

Rentoul A J, Fraser B J 1980 Predicting learning from classroom individualization and actual-preferred congruence. *Stud. Educ. Eval.* 6(3): 265–78

Shulman L S, Tamir P 1973 Research on teaching in the natural sciences. In: Travers M W (ed.) 1973 *Second Handbook of Research on Teaching: A Project of the American Educational Research Association.* Rand McNally, Chicago, Illinois

Trickett E J, Moos R H 1973 Social environment of junior high and high school classrooms. *J. Educ. Psychol.* 65: 93–102

Walberg H J 1971 Optimizing and individualizing instruction. *Interchange* 2: 15–27

Walberg H J 1974a Educational process evaluation. In: Apple M W, Subkoviek M J, Lufler H S (eds.) 1974 *Educational Evaluation: Analysis and Responsibility*. McCutchan, Berkeley, California

Walberg H J (ed.) 1974b *Evaluating Educational Performance: A Sourcebook of Methods, Instruments, and Examples*. McCutchan, Berkeley, California

Walberg H J 1976 Psychology of learning environments: Behavioral, structural, or perceptual? In: Shulman L S (ed.) 1976 *Review of Research in Education*, Vol. 4. Peacock, Itasca, Illinois

Walberg H J (ed.) 1979 *Educational Environments and Effects: Evaluation, Policy, and Productivity*. McCutchan, Berkeley, California

Walberg H J 1984 Improving the productivity of America's schools. *Educ. Leadership* 41(8): 19–30

Walberg H J, Haertel G D 1980 Validity and use of educational environment assessments. *Stud. Educ. Eval.* 6(3): 225–38

Students' Characteristics

Students' Affective Characteristics

K. E. Sinclair

Affect is a term used to describe the feeling or emotional aspect of experience. Affective processes are associated particularly with the satisfaction of need states and with the motivation of behaviour including, in educational contexts, the learning and performance of students. Motivation signifies the causes or "why" of behaviour; it is concerned with questions about the energizing of behaviour and the direction that is given to behaviour.

Theory and research in educational contexts have focused on several groups of motives having particular relevance for classroom learning and behaviour. One important group is closely related to the maintenance and enhancement of self-esteem, and consists of anxiety and achievement motivation. A second group includes motives such as curiosity that are associated with exploratory behaviour and the need to know and understand. A third group consists of social motives such as the need for praise, recognition, and attention. For the most part, theory and research have concentrated on the problem of defining and measuring the various affective states involved and determining their separate influence on classroom learning tasks. To a lesser extent, although increasingly in recent years, studies have attempted to explore ways by which teachers and others can control that influence in order to facilitate the teaching–learning process.

1. Self-concept and the Need to Maintain and Enhance Feelings of Self-esteem

The self-concept has a central role to play in personality organization. A person's self-concept may be viewed as a store of self-perceptions; it consists of answers to such questions as Who am I? What do I believe in and value? What do I want to get out of life? What are my strengths and weaknesses? How capable a person am I? These self-perceptions are built up in a gradual fashion through experience and particularly reflect the perceived reactions of other people. In young children the reactions of parents, teachers, and friends are of particular importance and, increasingly with age, so are their own reactions to themselves as individuals. Studies indicate that the self-concept is not a unitary construct but consists of a number of distinguishable components. For instance, several factor-analytic studies indicate that the self-concepts of children can be differentiated into an academic self-concept with further sub-divisions into self-concept in particular subject matter areas such as reading and arithmetic, and a nonacademic self-concept with subdivisions into a social self-concept and a physical self-concept. Further differentiation is undoubtedly possible. Studies also reveal that a measure of academic self-concept is more closely related to the performance of children in academic situations than are measures of other components of self-concept or a general, summative measure of self-concept.

While self-concept is taken to refer to the store of self-attributes of a person, self-esteem has been used to refer to the extent to which individuals regard these self-attributes in positive or negative terms. Self-esteem particularly has to do with feelings of adequacy and inadequacy and with feelings of self-worth. It is associated with the extent to which people feel they can live up to expectations they hold for themselves or that are held for them by parents and other important persons in their lives. It is also influenced by the extent to which they perceive themselves to be accepted and loved by other people. A number of personality theorists have argued that the need to maintain and enhance feelings of self-esteem is one of the most basic of human needs and that people will go to considerable trouble to ensure that their feelings of self-esteem and self-worth are not damaged.

In educational situations particular attention has been directed towards the study of achievement strivings and anxiety and their role in maintaining and enhancing feelings of self-esteem. Self-esteem may be maintained and enhanced by succeeding in classroom learning tasks. Achievement motivation, reflected in a striving after academic success and competence is a learned drive directed towards that end. The other aspect of self-esteem, however, is the need to avoid failure which when aroused is experienced as anxiety. If the person is not able to achieve success and demonstrate competencies, the danger is that self-esteem will be eroded. These twin affective states of achievement motivation and anxiety have been found to be very important for understanding classroom performance and behaviour.

1.1 Anxiety

In attempting to understand the nature of anxiety, a distinction has commonly been made between anxiety as a trait and anxiety as a state. Anxiety-trait refers to the predisposition to be anxious. Anxiety-state refers to the anxiety reaction itself. Anxiety-states, as reactions to threats, are considered to have a number of components. On the one hand there are somatic responses that are aroused such as palmar sweating, dryness of the throat, increased heartbeat, and upset stomach. On the other hand there are worry responses that occur as the person ruminates about the difficulties faced in coping with the threat and the consequences of failure. When the level of anxiety aroused is high, these emotional and worry responses distract attention away from the task at hand. They may also be associated with defensive patterns of behaviour which may help preserve self-esteem but at the expense of successfully dealing with the task. The defensive behaviours may include daydreaming, careless and impulsive work, and sometimes avoidance of threats at school by feigning sickness or truanting.

Because of the distractive influence of anxiety feelings on attention and the avoidance character of most defensive coping manoeuvres, anxiety has commonly been found to interfere with performance at school. Because high levels of anxiety are a particularly unpleasant experience, they can also lead to a dislike of school and to a premature dropping out of school. At an extreme, the child may be completely unable to enter and remain in school because of feelings of dread and fear in which case the child is said to suffer from school phobia.

A number of recent studies, however, have suggested that the influence of anxiety will not always be debilitating but may vary with particular features of the task to be performed and the performance situation. Anxiety, for instance, appears to interact with task difficulty in influencing performance levels. When task difficulty is high, low-anxious students have been found to out-perform high-anxious students, but when task difficulty is low the high-anxious students are superior. A similar interaction has been found between anxiety and extent of ego involvement. When ego involvement is high, as in an important examination, anxiety acts to interfere with performance and low-anxious students are superior to high-anxious students. When ego involvement is low, however, as in a game-like performance situation in which failure does not have serious personal consequences, anxiety appears to have either little effect at all, or perhaps a slight facilitative influence.

These results suggest that the performance of low-anxious students is optimized by task situations in which anxiety and arousal are increased substantially, as when the task is difficult and performance important. The performance of high-anxious students on the other hand appears to be optimized by performance situations in which anxiety arousal is kept to a minimum. Important decisions about students, however, are often made on the basis of their examination performance on tasks that are high in difficulty level and under conditions of high evaluative stress. The interactions established between anxiety and both task difficulty and ego involvement support the view that high-anxious students will typically be disadvantaged in their performance on such examinations.

A further set of interactions has been established between anxiety level and the teaching method used in instruction. A characteristic of anxious students that has been frequently commented on is their strong dependency needs and preference for situations in which there are clear expectations about the task to be performed and about how they should go about performing it. This would suggest that high-anxious students would prefer a teacher-directed style of instruction rather than a student-centred style that requires them to use initiative and independence in finding things out for themselves. Support for this prediction has come from a number of studies involving subjects ranging from early elementary school to college age. High-anxious students were found to perform best when didactic teaching methods were used and were, in fact, superior to low-anxious students in that condition. The low-anxious students, on the other hand, performed best and were superior to high-anxious students when a student-centred teaching technique was used involving discussion and student discovery.

The interaction established between anxiety and teaching method suggests that teachers may optimize classroom performance by matching their teaching techniques to student characteristics. Rather than using a single teaching style that is either highly structured and directive or low in structure and direction, both styles may be made available creating a learning environment that is responsive to the particular needs of each student. This approach suggests that the performance of high-anxious students may be optimized by teachers using fairly directive teaching methods while that of low-anxious students may be optimized by less structured techniques.

The attribute–treatment–interaction approach is rather different from the more traditional approach of attempting to change student attributes to suit the teacher's method. Most commonly, high levels of anxiety have been regarded as an undesirable student characteristic and attempts have been made to reduce that anxiety level in order to facilitate performance. Such techniques as desensitization and relaxation training have been used successfully in reducing examination anxiety and anxiety in relation to specific school subjects such as reading and mathematics. Most often, however, these reductions in anxiety have not been accompanied by improvement in school performance.

The issue as to whether it is preferable to change the child to suit the teaching method or to adapt the teaching method to suit the particular needs of individual children is an important one and one that is in need of further research.

1.2 Achievement Motivation and Causal Attributions

Classroom achievement tasks offer the possibility of both success and failure for students. While fear of failure gives rise to anxiety feelings, the hope for successful achievement and the search for competence are associated with achievement needs. The concept of need for achievement was first suggested by Murray (1938) as part of his taxonomy of 20 human needs. It was McClelland and Atkinson (McClelland et al. 1953, Atkinson 1964) and more recently Weiner (1980), however, who developed the conceptual models and measuring instruments that have made a systematic study of achievement needs possible. Basic to these models is a strong cognitive assumption that achievement strivings and the tasks to which those strivings are directed are influenced by the person's expectancy of success and the value placed on success.

Achievement motivation is characterized by strong strivings after success based on high internalized standards of excellence. Pupils with high achievement needs tend to have high but realistic aspirations in relation to classroom learning and performance tasks and occupational goals, and reveal greater persistence in achievement situations. They have been found to be better able to delay gratification and perceive themselves as high in ability and as having high self-esteem. Despite these findings, however, studies have not been able to demonstrate a consistent superiority in classroom performance of students who have a high need for achievement. McClelland and Weiner have argued that this is not particularly surprising given the large number of factors that operate to influence performance.

Studies have also had only moderate success in attempting to increase need for achievement in students and, through this, classroom performance. McClelland found that little benefit was achieved through the use of short intensive training programmes for high-school and college students in which they received direct experience with how to think and act like a person with high need for achievement. Gains in need for achievement were typically found to be slight and nonenduring. Greater success was achieved by De-Charms (1976) in a longer term study in which student training in need for achievement was preceded by training of their teachers in need for achievement. When that training was conducted over an entire school year, quite dramatic increases in vocabulary, reading, language, and arithmetic were recorded with minority students from elementary schools in an American inner-city district.

In recent years researchers interested in achievement motivation have turned their attention to the study of locus of control and to attributions people make about, or reasons they cite for, successes and failures. It is assumed that achievement strivings will be related to student explanations for their successes and failures. Four attributions or reasons have commonly been discussed: ability, effort, task difficulty, and luck. These attributions have been conceptualized as varying with respect to such dimensions as locus of control, stability, and controllability. Locus of control may be either external to the person, signifying a belief that one has little personal control over learning and performance, or it may be internal, whereby personal responsibility is accepted for one's performance. Two attributions about success and failure indicative of an internal locus of control are ability and effort. The former is a stable but uncontrollable attribution which typically does not vary from situation to situation, while the latter is an unstable attribution which the person feels he or she can influence. Attributions indicative of an external locus of control are task difficulty and luck. Task difficulty is considered to be a stable attribution, and luck an unstable one, while both are felt to be outside of personal control.

Most often, students with high need for achievement tend to ascribe failure to lack of effort. This allows them to be optimistic about performance on similar tasks in the future, as amount of effort is within their control. Students with low need for achievement, however, tend to ascribe failure to their own lack of ability or to external attributions such as bad luck. Since ability is a stable attribute and the student has no control over external causes, motivation for future performance tasks will be reduced. The optimism and continuing achievement motivation of the high-need-for-achievement student is further sustained by a tendency to attribute success internally to ability. The low-need-for-achievement student on the other hand continues to deny personal control over success and attributes it to external causes. This has led some researchers to characterize students with this low need for achievement pattern as the "learned helpless". The beliefs of such students in achievement situations imply the inevitability or insurmountability of failure.

Relationships between these patterns of attributions and affective reactions of the individual have also been established. Generally speaking, affective reactions to success and failure, such as pride and shame, are likely to be greater if locus of control is internal. Such affective reactions also have strong implications for feelings of self-esteem and for the maintenance of self-concept. A high self-concept of ability will be maintained by ascribing failure to luck and success to ability. A low self-concept of ability will be maintained by ascribing failure to ability and success to luck. Students with a high need for achievement, therefore, are likely to have a high expectancy of future success together with affects such as pride and high self-esteem. Learned helpless students are likely to have a low expectancy of future success together with affects such as shame, guilt, anxiety, and low self-esteem.

Classroom studies suggest that teacher feedback about student success and failure may be important in shaping attributions. Feedback to girls has been found to differ from feedback to boys suggesting a reason for the observation that girls are more likely than boys to have the characteristics of learned helplessness. Reactions to girls who failed were almost entirely intellectual (e.g., that answer is wrong) and that would reinforce ability attributions about failure. For boys, most reactions were nonintellectual ones about lack of effort, neatness and so on; reactions centred less on ability and enabled attributions about effort and motivation to emerge. Success has also been attained in attempting to change the attributions of students to increase achievement motivation. In particular, training studies have been able to establish for students an association between effort attributions and performance.

2. *Curiosity and Cognitive Motivation*

The twin ego motives of anxiety and need for achievement appear to satisfy the traditional drive reduction view of human motivation fairly satisfactorily. School work is learned to reduce anxiety relating to failure or to satisfy drive states induced by achievement needs. Not all behaviour, however, appears to satisfy this drive-reduction model. Such behaviour as playing, exploring, and engaging in hobbies often seems to occur in the absence of pressing drive-related stimulation that needs to be reduced. Indeed it often seems that such behaviour induces greater arousal which is then regarded as pleasant.

Berlyne (1960) has proposed a theory to explain that class of behaviour which appears to be directed towards seeking stimulation and excitement. For Berlyne the objective of behaviour is not to rid the nervous system of stimulation but rather to keep the level of stimulation at a moderate level (or tonus level as he describes it) which is the level most conducive to effective behaviour. He draws particularly on the assumptions and research findings of arousal theorists in doing this. In his view small increases and decreases in stimulation in the region of the tonus level are sought after and are pleasurable, but large changes are not and will result in behaviour designed to return arousal to the tonus level. Thus small increases in arousal associated with turning attention to a hobby, engaging in an exciting pastime, daydreaming, or attempting to solve a problem may be as rewarding as experiencing a small decrease in arousal level by coming inside out of the cold, or satisfying achievement needs by learning a new skill.

Such small pleasurable increases in arousal level are often associated with curiosity and exploratory behaviour. Berlyne has identified two forms of exploratory behaviour, specific exploration and diversive exploration, as being of particular importance in education. Specific exploration arises in situations in which there is a conceptual conflict caused by novelty, uncertainty, ambiguity, or contradiction. In such a situation complete understanding is initially impossible; there is a missing link that needs to be identified if sense is to be made. Curiosity is often aroused as a result. Problem situations, therefore, will be important in the generation of feelings of curiosity. How does a bird fly or a fish breathe? Where would be the best place to set up camp on a deserted island? What kind of animal is a marsupial? The element of uncertainty or novelty generates a conceptual conflict, experienced as curiosity, which motivates specific explorations designed to resolve the conflict. Children may ask questions, read books, and apply directed thinking skills to resolve the conflict and through this, new knowledge will be gained. Such curiosity is called epistemic curiosity by Berlyne because of the knowledge seeking activities that are motivated.

Diversive exploration is exploration designed to ensure that there is sufficient variety in life's activities. It acts as a stimulant to play and entertainment and is often aroused in situations characterized by boredom. Because of having nothing to do, or the repetitive nature of a task, or the lack of challenge or interest involved in a task, arousal falls well below the tonus level. When this happens the person will search for activities to increase arousal level. At school when a lesson is boring the child may attempt to create a more stimulating situation by daydreaming, or by chatting with a neighbour, or by creating a diversion. Outside of the classroom the child may turn to a hobby, or to television, or a book, or may engage with friends in other novel and thrill-arousing activities.

Individuals differ widely in their tendency to become curious. Highly curious children have been found to ask more and better questions in class, show more persistence in problem solving and be more adventurous in their choice of activities than low-curious children. They are also more self-accepting, more secure, and less threatened by uncertainty. This latter result suggests an obvious relationship between curiosity and anxiety. Variables associated with curiosity arousal, such as uncertainty, ambiguity, and contradiction, are also common sources of threat and anxiety. Thus a situation may arouse curiosity through conceptual incongruity and at the same time arouse anxiety if success or failure is perceived as having strong implications for self-esteem. If curiosity is to be encouraged and used to advantage by the teacher it will be important that threats to self-esteem be kept to a minimum.

In the classroom, lessons designed to arouse curiosity as a primary motivator of learning commonly begin with a problem to be solved. Inductive–discovery learning methods, inquiry methods, the project method, and progressive child-centred approaches to instruction have all been advocated as ways by which learning may result from curiosity and intrinsic motivation. There is also evidence that curiosity and intrinsic interest in an activity may be diminished if extrinsic rewards are simultaneously available to motivate participation and performance. This will be particularly so if the extrinsic reward is used to ensure that participation takes place. If the reward, however, is used to signify a high level of performance on the activity, it does not seem to reduce intrinsic interest to engage further in the activity (Deci 1975).

3. Social Motives and Teacher Praise

The final group of motives to be considered is that associated with one's relationship with other people. In his list of human needs, Murray (1938) included the need for affiliation. Maslow (1970) also has identified the need to be accepted and to belong as a basic human need. In the classroom these needs express themselves as children seek out praise, attention, warmth, and nurturance from the teacher and classmates. These are important incentives for classroom learning and performance. The importance of incentives generally and of reinforcement based on the use of incentives is discussed in some detail in other entries in this encyclopedia.

There is a need here, however, to comment specifically on the use of praise as a motivator of student behaviour.

Praise and criticism, as Brophy (1981) points out in an important review and reappraisal of the concepts, differ from the usual reinforcers in terms of the strong affective information (surprise, delight, excitement or disapproval, disgust, rejection) that they contain. They are an important feature of teacher behaviour because of the belief that they may act as reinforcers in controlling student behaviour and also because praise is considered to be important in building student self-esteem and close teacher–student relationships.

In his review of studies, Brophy (1981) concludes that teachers use praise in a relatively infrequent and rather haphazard fashion so that its reinforcement value as a conditioning agent is likely to be slight. More important is the way in which some students successfully solicit praise from their teachers. Typically such students have high ability and are confident, sociable, and extroverted. These same students also have been found to reward their teachers for the praise received by reacting positively to it. In effect, as Brophy comments, they condition their teachers to praise them. Teachers, it appears, also use praise in an attempt to enhance the self-feelings of certain students. Students who appear to be lacking in confidence, unhappy, slow to learn, or unattractive but who are quiet and well-behaved in class are particularly likely to be praised. Again, such students often sustain the teacher's behaviour by reacting positively in response.

Teacher praise, therefore, may be seen to be an important factor involved in teacher–student interactions and relationships. Both teachers and students have needs to be accepted and belong and both seek out as well as react with praise. Teacher praise may be used to develop and enhance positive relationships with students that satisfy the teacher's own need to be accepted. Teachers may also distribute praise selectively to students who appear in need of praise to enhance self-feelings and to students who succeed in enticing the teachers to do so by approval seeking contacts.

4. Interrelationships Among Affective States

It should be clear from the discussion that the various affective states are rather closely interrelated. On the one hand, experience of success and failure and the setting of realistic expectations are important in determining the relative valence of need for achievement and anxiety. On the other hand, the encouragement and emergence of curiosity requires that classroom threat and anxiety be kept to a reasonably low level. The way teachers distribute success and failure and associated praise and criticism, and the extent to which they are able to create an atmosphere that keeps personal threat to a minimum will have an important bearing on the motivational states of students.

For the most part, researchers have failed to explore these inter-relationships or the patterning of affective states in particular groups of students, preferring, instead, to study the nature and effects of a particular affective state in isolation from others. There is some evidence, however, that low levels of self-esteem will commonly be associated with high levels of anxiety, with low levels of achievement motivation, and with attributions indicative of learned helplessness. One might expect, as well, that this motivational pattern would also be associated with low levels of curiosity. There is also evidence that this pattern of affective characteristics is more likely to be found in students living in disadvantaged circumstances than other groups of students. There is clearly a need for further research exploring such interrelationships and their effects on student behaviour.

See also: Aptitude–Treatment Interaction Models; Behavioral Models; Reinforcement; Effects of Teaching

Bibliography

Ames R E, Ames C (eds.) 1984 *Research on Motivation in Education. Volume 1: Student Motivation.* Academic Press, New York
Atkinson J W 1964 *An Introduction to Motivation.* Van Nostrand, Princeton, New Jersey
Berlyne D 1960 *Conflict, Arousal and Curiosity.* McGraw-Hill, New York
Brophy J 1981 Teacher praise: A functional analysis. *Rev. Educ. Res.* 51: 5–32
DeCharms R 1976 *Enhancing Motivation: A Change Project in the Classroom.* Irvington, New York
Deci E L 1975 *Intrinsic Motivation.* Plenum, New York
McClelland D C, Atkinson J W, Clark R W, Lowell E L 1953

The Achievement Motive. Appleton-Century-Crofts, New York

Maslow A H 1970 *Motivation and Personality,* 2nd edn. Harper, New York

Murray H A 1938 *Explorations in Personality: A Clinical and Experimental Study of Fifty Men of College Age, by the Workers at Harvard Psychological Clinic.* Oxford University Press, New York

Nicholls J (ed.) 1985 *The Development of Achievement Motivation.* JAI Press, Greenwich, Connecticut

Sarason I G (ed.) 1980 *Test Anxiety: Theory, Research and Applications.* Erlbaum, Hilsdale, New Jersey

Spielberger D C, Sarason I G (eds.) 1975 *Stress and Anxiety.* Halstead Press, New York

Weiner B 1980 *Human Motivation.* Holt, Rinehart and Winston, New York

Students' Cognitive Characteristics

R. L. Debus

In conceptualizations of teaching–learning situations, cognitive characteristics of students are seen as one cluster of determinants of the interactive and learning processes established in the classroom (Dunkin and Biddle 1974). Much research has demonstrated that such student cognitive characteristics as general mental ability or prior level of achievement do explain a substantial proportion of the variance in subsequent achievement, but only more recently has research focused on relationships between cognitive characteristics of students and the process variables of classroom behaviour.

Within a classroom setting individual students differ substantially in attention and task engagement, level of participation in classroom activities, and the extent to which they initiate contacts with the teacher and fellow students or participate more passively in response to opportunities afforded by the teacher. Some researchers have sought to explore the presence of relationships between (a) such cognitive characteristics of students as intelligence, prior achievement level, or cognitive-style variables, and (b) classroom behaviour. Such relationships, however, are unlikely to be direct and generalizable in view of the range of interacting variables contributing to the establishment of patterns of classroom behaviour.

1. Pupils' Ability Levels and Attentiveness

Some consistent relationships have, however, been demonstrated between pupil cognitive characteristics and pupil attentiveness in classroom activities. In an observational study with grade 6 pupils (aged 11), Lahaderne (1968) reported that higher intelligence pupils showed higher levels of attention in classroom activities than pupils of lower ability. Similar positive relationships existed between achievement level in several school subjects and pupil attention, although attention was unrelated to pupil attitudes to aspects of school life.

Other research has confirmed similar relationships at earlier grade levels (e.g., Cobb 1972, Luce and Hoge 1978). Levels of task-relevant attentiveness during reading activities in first graders (age 6) were also found to be associated with reading achievement as indexed by scores on a test of word recognition (Samuels and Turnure 1974), and such forms of inattentiveness as distractible behaviour and passive responding (inattention in group activities or passively waiting for directions or assistance) were more frequent in lower achieving second-grade pupils (aged 7) (McKinney et al. 1975). Lower achievers also tended to show a greater variability in levels of such behaviour as playing during class and neglecting to pay attention (Soli and Devine 1976) and these forms of behaviour are significantly associated with the relative level of achievement of such pupils.

Interpreting her findings, Lahaderne suggested that they probably reflected an interaction between the learner's cognitive abilities and the difficulty level of instruction. Inattention in lower ability learners, she suggested, would result when the instructional level became too difficult for the student. Levels of attention in classroom activities were thus seen as determined by an interaction between the general ability of students and instructional variables rather than by pupils' attitudes to school. More recent research has clearly confirmed relationships between appropriate levels of task difficulty and pupil task engagement.

2. Ability and Classroom Behaviour

Attempts to locate additional specific aspects of classroom behaviour associated with pupil IQ or levels of attainment have extended findings beyond the general attentiveness variables. Higher ability second graders showed less dependency on teacher praise and help and greater frequency of appropriate self-directed constructive play (McKinney et al. 1975). With fourth graders (aged 9), compliance with teacher requests and talking with other students about academic material in arithmetic lessons were found to be significantly associated with student level of achievement (Cobb 1972). For higher achieving students, who show less variability in attentional behaviours, such active task-relevant interaction with peers seems to play a more important role in influencing achievement level. Peer interactions which involve high-ability students in giving explanations to other students in a small group, seem to facilitate learning for the student doing the explaining (Peterson et al. 1981).

Most of the research which has indicated these differences in classroom behaviour between high- and low-achieving students (or high IQ and low IQ students) has been designed to show that these classroom behaviours have predictive value for later achievement, though as Hoge and Luce (1979) point out, their correlational and factorial designs have limitations as a basis for inferences concerning the direction of effects. In most cases, however, the studies demonstrate that the behavioural data do make a further contribution to prediction of achievement, independent of that shared with the ability measures (e.g., McKinney et al. 1975). Thus they have provided a basis for designing interventions to be used early in the school year to increase facilitative behaviours and thereby to enhance academic progress (Cartledge and Milburn 1978).

3. Teacher Reactions to Student Performance

Studies of classroom behaviour of seventh-grade students (aged 12) of high and low cognitive ability (as ranked by teachers) have shown high-achieving students to be more active classroom participants; they instigated more contacts with the teacher, initiated more comments and questions and called out answers more frequently than low-achieving students. Such behavioural differences were not, however, independent of the differences found in teacher behaviours directed towards high- and low-achieving students. Teachers gave high achievement students more response opportunities, asked them questions more frequently and were more likely to provide them with feedback about their responses than was the case for low achievers. High achievers received more praise and low achievers received much more criticism (Good et al. 1973).

These classroom-participation differences may thus be seen as emerging from the interaction of student characteristics and differential teacher responses to such characteristics. Other data (Brophy and Good 1974) lend support to these differences in teacher interaction with high- and low-achieving students and demonstrate that the rate of student-initiated academic contacts with the teacher is affected by the extent of criticism from the teacher (Cooper 1977). Nevertheless, despite higher levels of criticism and interaction with the teacher concerning classroom behaviour, lower ability learners may initiate more contacts with teachers when seeking guidance about procedures to be followed or help with difficulties in their work (Luce and Hoge 1978).

Teachers have been shown to vary distinctly in the extent of their differential behaviour towards high and low achievers (Brattesani et al. 1984, Mitman 1985). In classrooms in which teachers are perceived by low-ability students to differentiate substantially in their expectations and treatment of high and low achievers, there is evidence of negative effects on the achievement of the lower ability students (Brattesani et al. 1984). While these differences in classroom behaviour are correlated with the cognitive characteristics of students, they may substantially reflect student perception of their abilities relative to the reference group provided by their present class. Affective characteristics of students are substantially implicated in their classroom behaviour.

4. Effects of Mixed-ability Groups

Student cognitive characteristics may also be considered in a collective sense according to the ratio of high-aptitude students to low-aptitude students in a classroom group. A study of third and fourth graders (ages 8 and 9) learning mathematics found that classes in which high-aptitude students comprise more than one-third of the total number seemed to provide learning conditions that enhanced achievement levels for both high-aptitude and low-aptitude students (Beckerman and Good 1981). While the classroom processes which mediate these outcomes in high-aptitude-ratio contexts have not been demonstrated, they may well reflect higher levels of such classroom behaviours as task engagement, active participation, and positive peer interaction found to be more characteristic of high-ability students. Consistent with this suggestion is evidence that classes of greater heterogeneity of student ability show lower levels of student cooperation and task engagement (Evertson et al. 1981). In the high-aptitude-ratio setting, the behaviours modelled by the largest group in the classroom may be adopted by other students in ways that enhance their achievement also. Additionally, however, the enhanced outcomes may be mediated by patterns of teacher behaviour reactive to higher student-aptitude levels. Some evidence indicates that teachers may cover more relevant content and show less vagueness in explanation with classes higher in aptitude and prior achievement (Dunkin 1978), and also provide a higher proportion of positive reactions to students (Heller and White 1975). Adapting the pace of instruction and the content covered to the ability level of students may thus contribute to enhanced student achievement.

5. Age and Self-estimates of Ability

Some developmental progressions in children's understanding affect their classroom behaviour by influencing the way children of various ages interpret teacher behaviour and classroom events. Children of ages 5 to 8 for example, make less use of social comparison with peer performance in assessing their own ability at tasks (Ruble et al. 1980). Additionally, young children do not distinguish among such criteria as good performance, effort, or good work habits, which teachers use in giving praise or criticism. Thus, teacher praise in any of these areas seems to contribute to maintaining children's positive perceptions of their own ability, perceptions that may not always reflect the children's level of objective success (Stipek 1981). In the way they explain success and failure in tasks, younger children employ what has been termed a "halo schema" (Kun 1977) in considering how ability and effort contribute to task outcomes. They tend to see high ability and high effort as going together in determining success, while failure is seen as resulting from low ability and low effort. Only at ages 10 or 11 are more complex compensatory relationships between ability and effort recognized (Nicholls 1978).

With increasing age, however, children's estimations of their own abilities reflect more clearly the feedback resulting from their own performances and from comparisons with peers. Thus, pupils' perceptions of their own abilities progressively approximate more closely to teachers' ratings of their abilities (Nicholls 1979) and become more closely related also to their level of persistence on difficult tasks (Rholes et al. 1980).

In the later primary-school years, pupils recognize that additional effort may compensate for lower ability in producing success, and that some pupils who fail through making little effort may nevertheless have high ability. High-school students further recognize more complex ways in which teacher praise may imply differential assessment of student ability (Meyer et al. 1979). Teacher praise for success, combined with neutral feedback after failure, is interpreted by students as indicative of low ability, while neutral feedback after success together with criticism after failure implies high ability. High-school students recognize, too, that success despite low effort enhances one's reputation for ability and that low effort expenditure in study may obscure the causes of failure and provide a defence against the ascription of low ability as a cause of failure both by self and others (Harari and Covington 1981).

Developmental changes in student notions about the role of ability and effort in determining performance may thus have marked effects on students' responses to motivational strategies employed by teachers. At earlier age levels, praise for effort may instigate positive self-perceptions and higher levels of task engagement and persistence, while for the older child, praise for effort rather than performance may be seen as confirming self-evaluations of low ability and may have an opposite effect on task engagement and persistence.

6. Cognitive Style

Cognitive styles represent patterns of individual variation in modes of perceiving, remembering, and thinking which tend to be reflected with consistency in a wide range of learning and social situations. Cognitive styles are usually described in terms of polar opposites (field dependent/field independent; reflective/impulsive), though the presence of a continuum is recognized, and the differences are designated in terms of general behavioural dispositions rather than specific behaviours.

Field independent learners, for example, are characterized as responding to situations more analytically, perceiving a part of the field as discrete from the field as a whole. Field-dependent persons experience the environment in a more global fashion, being more influenced by the overall embedding context or the dominant organization of a field (Witkin et al. 1977).

Differing patterns in learning and in teacher–student interaction associated with the two styles have been revealed. Field-dependent learners are more attentive to the social aspects of learning situations, being more responsive to social cues, depending more on external referents, and being more influenced by criticism than field-independent students. Field-independent students respond better to material with impersonal content and can readily learn material that lacks structure and organization, while field-dependent learners respond better to social content and learn material best when it is structured and organized and they are provided with more explicit instructions in problem-solving techniques and defined performance outcomes. These patterns imply that differences in behaviours in various classroom contexts might be expected, but as yet the presence of such differences has not been explored through observational studies.

Some beginnings have been made in investigating consequences of matching (or mismatching) teacher and student cognitive styles. Differences in preferences for ways of teaching by field-dependent and field-independent teachers have been demonstrated. Field-dependent teachers favour teaching situations that allow interaction with students such as discussion approaches while field-independent teachers make more use of lecture and discovery methods. Evidence has indicated that students who are similar in cognitive style to their teacher report greater interpersonal attraction to the teacher than those with discrepant styles. It has been suggested that this positive attraction may reflect shared foci of interests and similarity in modes of communication (Witkin et al. 1977) but the specific classroom behaviours characterizing these interactions have not been distinguished.

While some positive consequences for learning outcomes from matching students and teachers on cognitive styles have been suggested, certain features of the learning environment provided by each group of teachers may also be seen to be facilitative for students with the other learning style. The provision of more explicit corrective feedback by field-independent teachers would, for example, probably be beneficial for the field-dependent student's need for structure, whereas the field-dependent teacher's emphasis on less structured discussion approaches may be less appropriate. As yet, sufficient evidence of achievement outcomes associated with a cognitive style match or mismatch of teacher and students is not available, though some evidence suggests that students with field-independent teachers may achieve better in basic skills areas (Saracho and Dayton 1980).

Teachers who have been provided with knowledge of their own and their students' cognitive styles and sensitized to the educational implications of cognitive styles apparently adapt their teaching in ways which produce learning gains in student self-concept and attitudes though the teacher and student behaviours which mediate these gains have not been identified (Doebler and Eicke 1979).

7. Reflective and Impulsive Styles

More specific behavioural differences between students characterized by reflective and impulsive cognitive styles have been identified (Kagan 1965, Messer 1976). This cognitive style dimension refers to the tendency to reflect on the validity of one's problem solving in situations in which several possible alternatives are available and there exists uncertainty as to which one is appropriate. The reflective style is characterized by a greater delay in making a response and a lower error rate, while the impulsive student responds more rapidly, making more errors. Such a cognitive style shows generality across situations characterized by uncertainty or ambiguity. Reflective children, for example, show longer response time in answering questions about their preferences and presumably also in response to teacher questions in classrooms where response uncertainty may be involved, though not in questions which relate to well-rehearsed information and skills. Reflective children are reported to set higher standards of performance and to persist longer with difficult tasks, though these differences were observed in individual testing rather than in classroom settings (Kagan 1965). Teachers rate the classroom behaviour of impulsive children as less attentive and more hyperactive than reflective pupils, and there may be a danger that teachers will wrongly interpret an impulsive response style with its accompanying tendency to error as indicating low ability (Kagan 1965). The teacher's demand for a quick response to questions or criticism of incorrect answers may have negative effects on impulsive learners. On the other hand, experienced reflective teachers who both model and encourage more reflective responding in young impulsive children may, in the course of a school year, influence their response style towards a more reflective pattern.

Although the extent of actual classroom data related to cognitive-style variables remains rather limited, evidence does suggest that, like other cognitive characteristics of students, cognitive styles of students are reflected in classroom behaviour in ways which interact with patterns of teacher behaviour.

See also: Time; Students' Sex; Students' Affective Characteristics; Students' Social Backgrounds; Grouping for Teaching

Bibliography

Beckerman T M, Good T L 1981 The classroom ratio of high- and low-aptitude students and its effect on achievement. *Am. Educ. Res. J.* 18: 317–27

Brattesani K A, Weinstein R S, Marshall H H 1984 Student perceptions of differential teacher treatment as moderators of teacher expectation effects. *J. Educ. Psychol.* 76: 236–47

Brophy J E, Good T L 1974 *Teacher–Student Relationships: Causes and Consequences.* Holt, Rinehart and Winston, New York

Cartledge G, Milburn, J F 1978 The case for teaching social skills in the classroom: A review. *Rev. Educ. Res.* 48: 133–56

Cobb J A 1972 Relationship of discrete classroom behaviors to fourth-grade academic achievement. *J. Educ. Psychol.* 63: 74–80

Cooper H M 1977 Controlling personal rewards: Professional teachers' differential use of feedback and the effects of feedback on the students motivation to perform. *J. Educ. Psychol.* 69: 419–27

Doebler L K, Eicke F J 1979 Effects of teacher awareness of the educational implications of field-dependent/field-independent cognitive style on selected classroom variables. *J. Educ. Psychol.* 71: 226–32

Dunkin M J 1978 Student characteristics, classroom processes and student achievement. *J. Educ. Psychol.* 70: 998-1009

Dunkin M J, Biddle B J 1974 *The Study of Teaching.* Holt, Rinehart and Winston, New York

Evertson C M, Sanford J P, Emmer E T 1981 Effects of class heterogeneity in junior high school. *Am. Educ. Res. J.* 18: 219–32

Good T L, Sikes J N, Brophy J E 1973 Effects of teacher sex and student sex on classroom interaction. *J. Educ. Psychol.* 65: 74–87

Harari O, Covington M V 1981 Reactions to achievement from a teacher and student perspective: A developmental analysis. *Amer. Educ. Res. J.* 18: 15–28

Heller M S, White M A 1975 Rates of teacher verbal approval and disapproval to higher and lower ability classes. *J. Educ. Psychol.* 67: 796–800

Hoge R D, Luce S 1979 Predicting academic achievement from classroom behavior. *Rev. Educ. Res.* 49: 479–96

Kagan J 1965 Impulsive and reflective children: The significance of conceptual tempo. In: Krumboltz J D (ed.) 1965 *Learning and the Educational Process: Selected Papers from the Research Conference on Learning and the Educational Process, held at Stanford University, June 22-July 31, 1964.* Rand McNally, Chicago, pp. 133–61

Kun A 1977 Development of the magnitude-covariation and compensation schemata in ability and effort attributions of performance. *Child Dev.* 48: 862–73

Lahaderne H M 1968 Attitudinal and intellectual correlates of attention: a study of four sixth-grade classrooms. *J. Educ. Psychol.* 59: 320–24

Luce S R, Hoge R D 1978 Relations among teacher rankings, pupil–teacher interactions, and academic achievement: A test of the teacher expectancy hypothesis. *Am. Educ. Res. J.* 15: 489–500

McKinney J D, Mason J, Perkerson K, Clifford M 1975 Relationship between classroom behavior and academic achievement. *J. Educ. Psychol.* 67: 198–203

Messer S B 1976 Reflection-impulsivity: A review. *Psychol. Bull.* 83: 1026–52

Meyer W-U, Bachmann M, Biermann U, Hempelmann M, Plöger F-O, Spiller H 1979 The informational value of evaluative behavior: Influences of praise and blame on perceptions of ability. *J. Educ. Psychol.* 71: 259–68

Mitman A L 1985 Teachers' differential behavior toward higher and lower achieving students and its relation to selected teacher characteristics. *J. Educ. Psychol.* 77: 149–61

Nicholls J G 1978 The development of the concepts of effort and ability, perception of academic attainment, and the understanding that difficult tasks require more ability. *Child Dev.* 49: 800–14

Nicholls J G 1979 Development of perception of own attainment and causal attributions for success and failure in reading. *J. Educ. Psychol.* 71: 94–99

Peterson P L, Janicki T C, Swing S R 1981 Ability X treatment interaction effects on children's learning in large-group and small-group approaches. *Amer. Educ. Res. J.* 18: 453–73

Rholes W S, Blackwell J, Jordan C, Walters C 1980 A developmental study of learned helplessness. *Dev. Psychol.* 16: 616–24

Ruble D, Boggiano A K, Feldman N S, Loebl J H 1980 Developmental analysis of the role of social comparison in self-evaluation. *Dev. Psychol.* 16: 105–15

Samuels S J, Turnure J E 1974 Attention and reading achievement in first-grade boys and girls. *J. Educ. Psychol.* 66: 29–32

Saracho O N, Dayton C M 1980 Relationship of teachers' cognitive styles to pupils' academic achievement gains. *J. Educ. Psychol.* 72: 544–49

Soli S D, Devine V T 1976 Behavioral correlates of achievements: A look at high and low achievers. *J. Educ. Psychol.* 68: 335–41

Stipek D J 1981 Children's perceptions of their own and their classmates' ability. *J. Educ. Psychol.* 73: 404–10

Witkin H A, Moore C A, Goodenough D R, Cox P W 1977 Field-dependent and field-independent cognitive styles and their educational implications. *Rev. Educ. Res.* 47: 1–64

Students' Ethnicity

M. J. Dunkin; S. J. Doenau

This article is about student ethnicity and whether or not it affects life in classrooms. The questions underlying the entry are as follows:

(a) Are students of different ethnic backgrounds treated differently by their teachers?

(b) Do students of different ethnic backgrounds behave differently in the classroom?

(c) Is ethnicity as influential as other student characteristics in affecting classroom behaviour?

(d) If students behave, and are treated, differentially according to ethnic background, is their success at school affected by such differences?

1. Theory

Students' background characteristics, such as sex and ethnicity, may influence the behaviour towards each other of teachers and students, first, by affecting directly the behaviour of the students themselves and, second, by acting as stimuli for the behaviour of teachers. Ethnic background may have direct effects upon student behaviour because of cultural learnings, acquired independently of the school through the family and other ethnically-oriented agencies. Attributes such as initial language, sex roles, religious values, and food preferences are cultural learnings usually brought to school by the students. Some of these learnings equip some students to accommodate more easily than others to the school setting. Difficulties in understanding and speaking the language of instruction, for example, can result in low verbal interaction rates, problems in maintaining concentration and in adhering to classroom rules. As well, learnings brought with children to school concerning appropriate ways for children to behave towards adults may influence the amount of interacting with teachers that children initiate.

Behaviours that may be exhibited in these ways as a result of ethnic differences become part of the complexity of the classroom environment and are stimuli for others—teachers and students. Given the special responsibilities that teachers have for their students, it is to be expected that ethnically determined differences in students are perceived, interpreted, and responded to by teachers, just as intellectual, emotional, and sexual characteristics are reacted to by teachers. In these ways, then, student ethnicity may affect the classroom behaviour of both students and teachers.

Student ethnicity may affect the way teachers behave even if it does not directly affect the behaviour of the student. Teachers acquire expectations of, attitudes towards, and feelings about ethnic groups that can be developed quite independently of the ways students belonging to those groups behave in classrooms. It follows, since phenomena like beliefs and expectations influence behaviour, that teachers' behaviour toward students may depend, at least partly, upon teachers perceptions of students' ethnic backgrounds. Such behaviours of teachers then become stimuli for the behaviour of students who might confirm or deny the teachers' beliefs or expectations. Again, it seems that, even indirectly, student ethnicity may affect the classroom behaviour of both teachers and students.

In attempts to conceptualize potential influences upon classroom behaviour, student ethnicity is simpler than some other student characteristics. This is because when a relationship is found between student ethnicity and a variable such as teacher praise, one can be confident that, if it is causal, the direction of influence is one way, from ethnicity to teacher praise. With other student characteristics such as achievement, self-concept, or anxiety, relationships found with teacher behaviour, even if causal, usually do not indicate whether the direction of influence is from the teacher behaviour to the student characteristics or vice versa. In other words, any amount or lack of teacher praise will not influence whether students are white Anglo, Mexican—American, Australian Aborigine, or Serbo—Croatian in ethnic background. But variations in teacher praise can influence whether students are high achievers in reading, think of themselves as competent students, or find the classroom a highly stressful setting.

2. Research

Although there has been considerable development within such fields as multicultural education and bilingual education in recent years, there have been relatively few studies conducted into classroom behaviour in multicultural settings. None of the major American studies of equality of educational opportunity investigated classroom interaction. Meyer and Lindstrom (1969) reported that observational studies of teacher behaviour towards black students and white students were unknown to them. Despite the national concern in the United States with school integration, Brophy and Good (1974) found only a paucity of relevant classroom research. Dunkin and Biddle (1974) found only one study that explored differences in teacher classroom behaviour towards students differing in ethnic background. By 1975, Gay had found only five such studies. Dunkin and Doenau's (1982) study, when added to those reviewed in their report, made a total of 14. Another three were identified in the preparation of this entry. In addition, there have been several studies in which classes composed of a particular ethnic group were observed, but analyses of differences between different ethnic groups were not conducted. In all then, the body of research available from which to seek evidence relating to the topic of this entry and the questions raised at its beginning is probably only about 20 studies.

Almost all of the research has been conducted in the United States and has involved comparisons among black Mexican—American, migrant (itinerant farm workers, usually Puerto Rican), and Anglo students. Observations of classrooms have most often been based on the Brophy-Good Dyadic Interaction System or the Flanders Interaction Analysis Categories (FIAC). Categories of teacher behaviour focused upon have included the amount of attention given to students, the number and types of questions asked, and the number and types of reactions to students' contributions. Student behaviours of greatest concern have been the number of initiations, the amount of participation, the degree of engagement in classroom activities, and the quality of the responses given in classroom interaction.

2.1 Teacher Behaviours

The most commonly obtained finding in this research is that ethnic minority group students have fewer interactions with teachers than other students (Gay 1974, Barnes 1973, Rubovits and Maehr 1973, Jackson and Cosca 1974, Mathis 1975, Ortiz 1976, Sayavedra 1976).

This is a reflection of the common findings that teachers tend to direct fewer questions to minority group students and that those students initiate interactions themselves less often than other students. One consequence of less frequent involvement in interactions with the teacher is that the student receives less information from the teacher about the acceptability or otherwise of his or her performance (Rubovits and Maehr 1973).

Perhaps more significant than the findings concerning sheer frequency of interactions are those concerning the quality of the interactions. Careful analysis by Barnes (1973) of the types of questions teachers directed towards minority group students revealed that white students were asked more questions for which there were single, correct, short answers, while black students were asked more questions for which a variety of answers were acceptable. Dunkin and Doenau (1982) analysed questions asked by teachers of Anglo and non-Anglo (predominantly Greek and Italian) students in Sydney, Australia. They found that the Anglo students received more questions that followed up earlier questions in the same interchange with the teacher and many more questions demanding complex thinking processes.

Students belonging to ethnic minority groups have also been found to receive teacher reactions that are different from those received by other students. They were found less likely to receive positive reactions of praise, acceptance, and encouragement (Rubovits and Maehr 1973, Mangold 1974, Gay 1974, Barnes 1973, Tyo 1972, Mathis 1975, Hillman and Davenport 1978) and more likely to receive negative reactions, such as criticism and disciplinary comments (Rubovits and Maehr 1973, Mangold 1974, Hillman and Davenport 1978, Tyo 1972, Mangold 1974, Gay 1974).

2.2 Student Behaviours

The nature of student classroom behaviour has also been found to differ according to ethnic background. Gay (1974) found that black students participated less in academic and substantive ways than white students. Hillman and Davenport (1978) found black students to give more incorrect and irrelevant responses than white students. Interestingly enough, Hess and his colleagues (Hess et al. 1973, Hess and Takanishi 1974) found no significant differences between ethnic groups in levels of student engagement, defined as "observable interest and/or attention to a learning task prescribed by the teacher".

2.3 Other Student Characteristics

One of the problems with most of the research cited above is that no control was exerted over other student characteristics such as socioeconomic background and prior school achievement which could just as easily have accounted for the differences in classroom behaviour observed and yet were attributed to the influence of ethnicity. Membership of minority ethnic groups, particularly those most frequently focused upon in research, usually has associated with it relative poverty and poor school achievement. Future research should be designed so that differences according to ethnicity are explored with groups that are similar in those other respects. Otherwise it is difficult to know whether differential teacher behaviour is stimulated by differences in ethnicity, socioeconomic status, school achievement, or combinations of those variables.

Some student characteristics operate in conjunction with ethnic background to affect classroom behaviour. Dunkin and Doenau (1982) found relatively few differences between students of Anglo and non-Anglo backgrounds in classroom behaviour. However, when their analysis was conducted according to sex within each ethnic group, non-Anglo females were found to be very different in classroom behaviour from the others. Non-Anglo females, although matched with Anglo female classmates in general ability, received about half as many teachers' questions and positive and informative reactions. They were much more likely to have what responses they did give rejected by the teacher than the Anglo females. In general, sex was found to be a considerably stronger determinant of classroom differences than ethnicity, with males receiving much more than their share of various types of teachers' questions and both positive and negative teacher reactions.

In short, ethnicity seemed to make some difference in the Dunkin and Doenau (1982) study, but sex made a bigger difference. Ethnicity and sex together had a combined effect such that to be a non-Anglo female, rather than just a non-Anglo or a female, made a tremendous difference.

2.4 Student Outcome

None of the research referred to in this entry was properly designed to test whether the differences between ethnic groups in classroom interaction affected the school achievement of those groups. However, Dunkin and Doenau (1982), having found some differences between Anglos and non-Anglos in classroom interaction found no corresponding differences in either subject matter knowledge or critical thinking outcomes in students. Their most challenging finding was that the non-Anglo girls who behaved and were treated very differently and in ways generally regarded as deleterious to learning, scored as well as the other students on subject matter knowledge and critical thinking tests. Dunkin and Doenau (1982) did find that non-Anglo students scored higher on a test of anxiety than their Anglo fellow students but were unable to test whether this difference was a cause or effect of differences in classroom interaction.

In summary, research has not demonstrated that the

learning outcomes for students of varying ethnic backgrounds are affected by differences in the ways they behave and are taught at school.

3. Conclusions

Research on ethnicity and classroom behaviour seems to lead to the following conclusions:

(a) Students of minority ethnic groups differ from others in the amount of positive and negative interactions they have with teachers. They tend to have fewer positive and more negative interactions.

(b) Students of minority ethnic groups tend to be called upon by teachers and to respond and initiate less often than others.

(c) Teachers tend to direct different types of questions to minority ethnic group students than to others.

(d) Other student characteristics, such as sex, may have stronger influences than ethnicity upon classroom interaction. The combined effects of ethnicity and other such characteristics might be particularly great.

(e) There is little or no evidence that differences in classroom interaction between ethnic groups are related to outcome learnings.

There has been a trend towards interpreting differential behaviour by teachers of minority ethnic groups as deliberate discrimination against those groups. Brophy and Good (1974) argued that such discrimination may not be consciously practised:

Teacher–student interaction is a two-way process, and often the student conditions teacher behavior as much or more than the teacher conditions student behavior . . . . Much teacher discrimination in the sense of treating two individuals or groups of students differently is not necessarily due to any conscious differential treatment on the part of the teacher but instead is due to unconscious conditioning of the teacher by differential behavior of the students. (p. 12)

The United States Commission on Civil Rights (1973) granted the possibility that differential teacher treatment of ethnic groups of students might be caused by differences in such student characteristics as language and culture. It then argued that it is still the responsibility of the teacher and the school to provide learning experiences appropiate to students' cultural and linguistic needs.

Dunkin and Doenau (1982) mentioned the possibility that teachers may consciously practise discrimination between majority and minority groups, not to favour one with respect to the other, but simply to acknowledge differences in the preferences of the two groups. Such differences might bear no relationship to differences in student achievement.

Implications for teachers of the research on ethnicity and classroom behaviour are as follows:

(a) Teachers should anticipate that students of different ethnic backgrounds are inclined to behave differently in classrooms.

(b) Because of those differences, and possibly other factors, teachers are prone to behave differently towards students of different ethnic backgrounds.

(c) Teachers need to be aware that ethnicity alone might not make as much difference to the way they behave towards students as ethnicity combined with some other student variable, such as sex.

(d) Teachers need to determine whether the differences they may display in the treatment of students of different ethnic backgrounds are in the best interests of the students concerned.

See also: Students' Affective Characteristics; Students' Social Backgrounds; Students' Sex; Students' Cognitive Characteristics

Bibliography

Barnes W J 1973 Student-teacher dyadic interaction in desegregated high school classrooms (Unpublished doctoral dissertation. University of Texas at Austin) *Dissertation Abstracts International* 1974 34: 5768A–5769A (University Microfilms No. 74-5193)

Brophy J E, Good T L 1974 *Teacher–student Relationships: Causes and Consequences.* Holt, Rinehart and Winston, New York

Cornbleth C, Korth H 1977 Teachers' perceptions of and interaction with students in multicultural classrooms. Paper presented at the Annual Meeting of the American Educational Research Association, New York

Dunkin M J, Biddle B J 1974 *The Study of Teaching.* Holt, Rinehart and Winston, New York

Dunkin M J, Doenau S J 1982 Ethnicity, classroom interaction and student achievement. *Aust. J. Educ.* 26(2): 41–59

Feldman R S 1977 Race of student and non-verbal behavior of teacher. *J. Classroom Interaction* 12(2): 20–6

Gay G 1974 *Differential Dyadic Interactions of Black and White Teachers with Black and White Pupils in Recently Desegregated Social Studies Classrooms: A Function of Teacher and Pupil Ethnicity.* Final Report OE-NIE Project No. 2F113. The University of Texas, Austin, Texas

Gay G 1975 Teachers' achievement expectations of and classroom interactions with ethnically different students. *Contemp. Educ.* 48: 166–72

Hess R D, Takanishi-Knowles R et al. 1973 *Teacher Strategies and Student Engagement in Low-income Area Schools.* Research and Development Memorandum No. 105. Stanford Center for Research and Development in Teaching, Stanford University, Stanford, California

Hess R D, Takanishi R 1974 *The Relationship of Teacher Behavior and School Characteristics to Student Engagement.* Technical Report No. 42 Stanford Center for Research and Development in Teaching, Stanford University, Stanford, California

Hillman S B, Davenport G G 1978 Teacher–student interactions in desegregated schools. *J. Educ. Psychol.* 70: 545–53

Jackson G, Cosca C 1974 The inequality of educational opportunity in the Southwest: An observational study of ethnically mixed classrooms. *Am. Educ. Res. J.* 11: 219–29

Mangold L C P 1974 Pupil-teacher dyadic interactions in desegregated elementary school classrooms (Unpublished doctoral dissertation, University of Texas at Austin) *Dissertation Abstracts International* 1974 35: 172A (University Microfilms No. 74-14, 730)

Mathis D W 1975 Differences in teacher interaction with Afro-American and Anglo-American students in the same classroom (Unpublished doctoral dissertation, University of Michigan) *Dissertation Abstracts International* 1976 36: 5950A (University Micro Films No. 75-29, 283)

Meyer W J, Lindstrom D 1969 *The Distribution of Teacher Approval and Disapproval of Head Start Children.* Syracuse University, Evaluation and Research Center, Syracuse, New York

Ortiz A A 1976 A study of teacher–pupil dyadic verbal interactions in four first grade classrooms (Unpublished doctoral dissertation, The University of Texas at Austin) *Dissertation Abstracts International* 1977 37: 5042A (University Microfilms No. 77-2310)

Rubovits P C, Maehr M L 1973 Pygmalion black and white. *J. Pers. Soc. Psychol.* 25: 210–18

Sayavedra L 1976 Teacher differential expectations and interactions with Mexican American and Anglo American secondary physical science students (Doctoral Dissertation, University of Texas at Austin) *Dissertation Abstracts International* 1977 37: 5016A-5017A (University Microfilms No. 77-3978)

Tyo A M 1972 A comparison of the verbal behavior of teachers in interaction with migrant and non-migrant students. ERIC Document No. ED 075 160 Center for Migrant Studies, State University of New York

United States Commission on Civil Rights 1973 *Teachers and Students. Differences in Teacher Interaction with Mexican–American and Anglo Students. Report V: Mexican–American Education Study.* United States Government Printing Office, Washington, DC

Students' Sex

B. J. Bank

A growing concern about the relative educational and economic disadvantages suffered by women in all contemporary societies has led to increased research into the ways in which classroom behaviors of students and their teachers foster or impede equality of opportunity and outcome across the sexes. The following review of this research is organized around three questions: In what ways are the classroom behaviors and achievements of students affected by their sex? In what ways do teachers treat boys and girls differently? What are the relationships among teacher behaviors and the sex-linked behaviors and achievements of students?

1. Student Sex and Student Behaviors

Observations of classroom behaviors reveal that boys are more active, independent, and assertive than girls. Although girls are somewhat more likely than boys to seek approval from teachers, boys successfully initiate a larger number of total contacts with teachers than girls do. Boys also have been observed to misbehave more than girls, to be more aggressive and disruptive, and to exhibit shorter attention spans and less emotional maturity. Questionnaire and interview studies tend to find that boys are more likely than girls to express negative attitudes toward school and teachers, but recent observational studies find that boys are no more sullen or likely to express negative affect in interaction with teachers than girls are.

Most of the studies on which the preceding findings are based were done in the United States. Studies that examine male–female differences in several countries, such as those conducted by the International Association for the Evaluation of Educational Achievement (IEA), focus upon student performance on standardized tests rather than upon classroom interaction. Reviews of IEA data (Finn et al. 1979) report that boys generally achieve higher average scores than girls in mathematics and the physical sciences, and several investigators have suggested a link between these sex differences and the tendency of boys to attain higher scores than girls on tests of spatial perception. Boys in most countries outperform girls in biology, but girls achieve higher scores in this subject in a few countries, notably New Zealand and England and Wales. Girls in most parts of the world achieve higher scores than boys in literature and French as a foreign language.

Although illiteracy rates are higher among females than males in every area of the globe, considerable national variation has been found in reading and verbal achievement among literate boys and girls (Bank et al. 1980, Stockard et al. 1980 pp. 20–22). Girls in the United States achieve higher average scores than boys in reading and such related areas as spelling, writing, word fluency, and language arts throughout their years of elementary and secondary education. A similar, but weaker, tendency has been found in Canada, but studies done in the Federal Republic of Germany, the United Kingdom, and Nigeria report higher levels of reading achievement for boys than for girls. The relative reading achievements of boys and girls do not seem to affect the general tendency for boys to be diagnosed as having more reading problems, and studies in the United States, Canada, the United Kingdom, the Federal Republic of Germany, and other central European countries have all found boys more likely than girls to be enrolled in remedial reading classes. It is possible,

however, that boys' reading problems cause more concern than equivalent problems exhibited by girls.

National context is only one of several variables that have been found to affect the directions and relative sizes of average sex differences in classroom behaviors and achievements. Other variables include age of students, social class (see *Students' Social Backgrounds*), race and ethnicity (see *Students' Ethnicity*), curricular content, teaching style, and various school characteristics such as coeducation versus single-sex education. Reviews of these findings by Finn et al. (1979), Good and Findley (in press), and Stockard et al. (1980) suggest that any successful attempt to explain the classroom behaviors and achievements of boys and girls must be able to account for differences not only between the sexes but also within each sex and across a variety of social contexts. Not surprisingly, therefore, explanations based upon simple notions of biological determinism have largely been replaced by more complex sociopsychological and cultural analyses (Bank et al. 1980, Bossert 1981, Finn et al. 1980, Stockard et al. 1980).

One set of explanatory variables included in these analyses consists of student perceptions, expectations, and interests. Studies of American students have found that young children of both sexes expect girls to be more successful in school and more well-behaved than boys; girls are more concerned than boys with pleasing others, following classroom rules, and being good; students consider reading, artistic and social skills to be feminine but athletic, mathematical, spatial, and mechanical skills to be masculine; boys and girls believe it is more important to do well in subjects associated with their own sex; boys are more confident than girls in their ability to learn mathematics; boys are more likely than girls to rate mathematics a useful subject; and the perceived usefulness of mathematics predicts whether students of both sexes plan to take more math courses. Studies from several other countries find that girls often have lower levels of aspiration than boys, and IEA data reveal that boys in most parts of the world are more likely than girls to express positive attitudes toward mathematics. In the United States, boys' greater interest in science has been found to precede their superiority over girls in scientific achievements which, like their superiority in mathematical achievements, does not occur until midadolescence.

2. Student Sex and Teacher Behaviors

Like their students, American teachers, especially at the preschool and elementary levels, have been found to perceive girls to be better students than boys. Data from a recent study by Brophy and Evertson (1981) show that teachers rated their female students as higher achieving, more persistent, calmer, more careful, more mature, happier, more attractive, more likely to maintain eye contact, and more cooperative than male students. These findings are consistent with results from other studies showing that boys are more likely than girls to be rated by teachers as "problem pupils," aggressive, independent, and "class clowns." Teachers also tend to underestimate the intelligence and abilities of boys and to overestimate the talents of girls in comparison to sex-linked performances on standardized tests.

Despite considerable evidence that teachers rate girls more favorably than boys, teachers have been found to expect high-achieving male students to have more successes in adulthood than high-achieving female students. Teachers have also been found to rate high-achieving students of both sexes as more "masculine" (e.g., independent, assertive, ambitious) and low-achieving students of both sexes as more "feminine" (e.g., kind, sensitive, concerned). With student achievements and behaviors controlled, teachers predict that "masculine" students will have more success at university than "feminine" students, regardless of sex. These latter findings result from studies of secondary-school teachers in the United States and other Western countries.

Very few studies have examined the relationships between sex-linked perceptions and expectations of teachers and the ways in which those teachers behave toward their male and female students. Observational studies of teacher–student interactions in American preschools and elementary schools reveal that teachers generally give more attention to boys than to girls. A higher proportion of teacher contacts with boys than with girls have been found to be of a managerial nature, and boys, in comparison with girls, have been observed to receive more frequent and intense disciplinary contacts from teachers, more disapproval, and more disciplinary referrals to school counselors and administrators.

Findings concerning teacher praise and instructional contacts between teachers and students are less consistent than those regarding teacher attention and disapproval. Although it is clear that American girls receive higher grades, on average, than American boys throughout their years of schooling, it is not clear whether girls also receive higher levels of other kinds of teacher approval. Some studies show girls receiving more praise and instructional contacts than boys, but other studies produce the opposite results. Some of these discrepancies may be due to variations in curricular content across the classroom lessons observed by different researchers. Support for this possibility has been presented by Leinhardt et al. (1979) who found that the second-grade teachers they studied made more academic contacts with girls than boys during reading lessons, but made fewer academic contacts with girls than boys during mathematics lessons.

Even though there were no initial sex differences in abilities of the students they studied, Leinhardt and her colleagues found that the girls achieved significantly higher end-of-year reading scores than the boys. This finding suggests that different teacher behaviors toward boys and girls produce differential achievement, but

Leinhardt et al. found no end-of-year differences between boys and girls in mathematics achievement. This latter finding does not necessarily negate the proposition that differential treatment of boys and girls produces sex-linked differences in achievement, however, because it may take more than one academic year for teacher behaviors to affect student test scores. Those effects also may depend upon the ways in which students interpret teacher behaviors, and several recent studies have found that students do not always understand or agree about the intent of teacher behaviors.

3. Relationships Between Teacher Behaviors and the Behaviors of Boys and Girls

Given the shortage of evidence demonstrating strong, direct effects of teacher behaviors on the differential behaviors and achievements of boys and girls, some investigators (e.g., Brophy and Evertson 1981) have argued that teachers play a relatively minor part in the process of sex-role socialization. In this view, teacher behaviors toward boys and girls result not from sex stereotypes or biases of teachers but rather from sex-linked interests and behaviors exhibited by students. Teachers reprimand boys more often than girls because boys misbehave more often; teachers give girls more reading instruction than boys because girls are more interested in reading; and so on.

To the extent that teacher behaviors are affected by teacher expectations, those expectations have less to do with sex roles than with notions about what constitutes a "good pupil." Extensive evidence exists showing that teachers in American preschools and elementary schools consider "good" students to be those who are high-achieving, dependent, conforming, orderly, and interested in school-type activities. The fact that young girls receive more favorable ratings from teachers than young boys results from the fact that the interests and behaviors of girls are more consistent than those of boys with teachers' profiles of the "good student." As noted above, secondary teachers tend to describe successful students using terms that are more stereotypically masculine. Presumably, this change is one reason why boys begin to outperform girls in midadolescence, but there is little evidence to support this supposition.

There is considerable evidence demonstrating that even very young children have well-established interests that are consistent with stereotypes of appropriate male and female behaviors. Experienced teachers have been found to reinforce preschool boys, but not girls, for cross-sex behaviors with the result that children of both sexes gain attention and approval for stereotypically feminine behaviors. Other studies find that, regardless of their sex, boys and girls perceived as orderly and conforming by teachers are given more praise and encouragement than students perceived as lacking these characteristics. Additional evidence for the importance teachers attach to appropriate student characteristics is provided by research showing that teachers' attitudes and behaviors toward students are more affected by student ability, achievement, and reading behaviors than by student sex.

Not all evidence supports the proposition that teachers tend to ignore sex-role socialization while focusing their efforts upon dealing with individual student differences and with the student-role socialization of both boys and girls. Bossert (1981) suggests that an overreliance by (American) researchers on verbal feedback as a major indicator of teacher–pupil interactions has led researchers to ignore the many other ways in which teachers convey sex-role messages. He places particular stress on the opportunity structure of classrooms which may preclude girls from enacting certain roles and boys from others, thereby creating a hidden curriculum of sex-role socialization.

Delamont (1980) provides compelling evidence from her studies of four schools in the United Kingdom to show the ways in which teachers use rivalry and differentation between the sexes as an integral part of their classroom management strategies; the ways in which teaching segregates and polarizes boys and girls; and the ways in which teachers differentiate between the sexes in their informal socializing. She acknowledges that students come to school with stereotyped ideas about boys and girls and often segregate themselves by sex, but she contends that teachers do more than reinforce pre-existing behaviors and preferences; they actively impose traditional sex roles on boys and girls.

Although Delamont notes that the sex-role socialization she observed is rarely a deliberate educational policy, such policies do exist in other countries where girls have fewer opportunities for schooling than boys. Throughout the world, girls are less likely than boys to be directed into subject areas that lead to relatively more possibilities for wage-earning employment (Finn et al. 1980).

To date there has been little research into the conditions determining whether teachers play the role of active socializers into traditional sex roles or function as reinforcers of preexisting behaviors and interests of boys and girls. Nor does much evidence exist supporting the plausible claim of a direct link between these teacher behaviors and the lifetime achievements of females and males. Nevertheless, the recent literature contains many calls for teachers to abandon these roles and to assume responsibility for destroying traditional sex stereotypes. Given the sex-linked interests children bring to classrooms, the support for those interests received from peers, the traditional portrayals of sex roles in curricular materials and the mass media, the lack of same-sex role models in nontraditional fields of study and employment, and the evidence showing resistance by students, teachers, and administrators to programs designed to change sex roles, it is clear that both teachers and students will need a great deal of support for current and future efforts to break through sex stereotypes, broaden opportunities, and equalize outcomes for boys and girls.

See also: Affective Teacher Education; Student Roles; Students' Cognitive Characteristics

Bibliography

Bank B J, Biddle B J, Good T L 1980 Sex roles, classroom instruction, and reading achievement. *J. Educ. Psychol.* 72: 119–32

Bossert S T 1981 Understanding sex differences in children's classroom experiences. *Elem. School J.* 81: 255–66

Brophy J E, Evertson C M 1981 *Student Characteristics and Teaching.* Longman, New York

Delamont S 1980 *Sex Roles and the School.* Methuen, London

Finn J D, Dulberg L, Reis J 1979 Sex differences in educational attainment: A cross-national perspective. *Harvard Educ. Rev.* 49: 477–503

Finn J D, Reis J, Dulberg L 1980 Sex differences in educational attainment: The process. *Comp. Educ. Rev.* 24(2): S33–S52

Good T L, Findley M J in press. Sex role expectations and achievement. In: Dusek J (ed.) in press. *Teacher Expectancies.* Lawrence Earlbaum, Hillsdale, New Jersey

Kelly A 1980 *Girls and Science.* Almquist and Wiksell, Stockholm

Leinhardt G, Seewald A M, Engel M 1979 Learning what's taught: Sex differences in instruction. *J. Educ. Psychol.* 71: 432–39

Stockard J, Schmuck P A, Kempner K, Williams P, Edson S K, Smith M A 1980 *Sex Equity in Education.* Academic Press, New York

Students' Social Backgrounds

T. N. Kahl

Teachers and other observers of classroom interaction often report that students can be roughly classified into different groups, according to certain features of their classroom behaviour. This article deals with the proposition that many aspects of the differences in behaviour stem, at least to a degree, from the social background of students. Typically, the relationship between students' social background and classroom behaviour is conceived of as leading to "problems", or as indicating the existence of "disadvantage" or "underprivilege". Thus, for instance, the tendency for children from unfavourable social backgrounds to obtain as a group lower IQ scores, to show lower levels of achievement, to have to repeat classes more frequently, to leave school at earlier ages, to be placed in special classrooms more frequently, to be more often identified as having "social" or "behaviour" problems, to attend universities and colleges less frequently, or indeed to make less use of all forms of postschool education, are all seen as, at least partly, problems of inequality arising from social background. Crucial questions to be examined in the present article are: What are the most important relationships between social background and students' academic behaviour, their nonacademic activities in class, their feelings about school, and so on? What are the crucial factors which determine the nature and consequences of these relationships? What kinds of dynamic interactions among such determining factors lead to outcomes such as those listed above?

Students' social background—to take a comprehensive definition—refers to the social context (consisting of people) students have lived in during their preschool life, and in which they live when not in the classroom. In this broad conception, student social background subsumes an extensive set of variables. The term "classroom behaviour" is also used here in a comprehensive sense: it refers not only to social behaviour in the classroom (which manifests itself in interactions with classmates and the teacher), but also to all kinds of academic and work-related behaviours, including participation in task-related activities and carrying out of cognitive operations, as well, of course, as to the outcomes of these behaviours. Such outcomes manifest themselves in scores on measures of achievement or of ability, as well as in success or failure in exams, which determine who participates in later selective learning activities such as higher education.

Although student social background is the main object of interest of this article, account will nonetheless be taken of the fact that the students' classroom behaviour is also influenced, even determined, by other factors such as genetics or certain characteristics of the school, the teacher, and classmates (see *Students' Sex*; *Students' Affective Characteristics*; *Students' Cognitive Characteristics*). These latter variables often interact with social background, for instance by supporting, ignoring, or suppressing certain behaviours whose source lies in pupils' social background. Discussion in this article of interrelationships between student social background variables and school variables will also assign special importance to the teacher's role (see *Teacher Roles*). It should be noticed, however, that a student's present or future social background can be affected or even drastically changed by the influence of the school itself.

1. Methodological and Research Problems

An initial major problem with this topic is that both student social background and characteristics of schools are heavily dependent on national and cultural conditions, so that they cannot be defined in universal forms. Rutter et al. (1979), for example, identified a number of characteristics of a "good" school in the United Kingdom, such as good attendance record or low levels of vandalism, indicators which might in other countries, for various reasons, be regarded as irrelevant. Further problems derive from the fact that discussions about the relevance of social background to students' success in school have political implications, and therefore often lead to emotional arousal. As a result, researchers either tend to be politically neutral or else to adopt an obvious partisan position, with the result that their scientific objectivity is often doubted. A third problem arises from the fact that it is impossible for a single individual or even a large group of researchers to be familiar with all of the relevant research with its—as it seems—often contradictory results. This reflects the fact that most empirical studies in the field of education include at least one variable which, in some way, touches upon aspects of student social background. It is also true that the first studies that dealt with student social background variables were published in the first decade of the twentieth century. In the light of these problems, this article mainly attempts to present a general overview of the key factors and the dynamic interactions between them, together with a theoretical framework for interpreting relevant literature and the results of empirical research.

2. Defining Students' Social Background

The problems mentioned above have led to a state of affairs in which there is no unanimously accepted definition of student social background. Nevertheless, two different general approaches can be distinguished: the roots of the first are often associated with Karl Marx's theory of social class, although it is not exclusively associated with Marxist thinking. This approach assumes that the socioeconomic conditions under which the parents of a student live are important factors which determine student social background. The second approach states that these socioeconomic conditions do not by themselves predict a child's behaviour and performance, whereas the parents' attitudes and motivations and the kinds of interaction that take place in the family (i.e., the family environment) do: consequently, variables of the latter kind should be used to define student social background. As a result of this controversy, empirical studies vary in the way variables associated with student social background are introduced and treated, with the consequence that reported results, and especially their interpretations, differ considerably.

As many studies have demonstrated, however, students' classroom performance can be predicted either by socioeconomic status (SES) variables or by family environment measures. If both are used, correlations between them are usually positive and large enough to indicate a considerable amount of covariance. It can thus be argued that SES can be regarded as an important aspect of student social background (Kagan 1977), and as a factor which—by determining certain aspects of family environment—indirectly influences students' classroom performance (Marjoribanks 1977). The relevance of SES as a predictor varies, nonetheless, according to the way it is defined and operationalized.

2.1 Socioeconomic Status

Socioeconomic status is usually defined by objective indicators that are readily observable by researchers. Because SES indices require only the answering of a few short questions, whereas measures of family environment demand greater effort—they are based on more complex information-gathering procedures/techniques such as interviews, observation, or long questionnaires—SES is more often employed in empirical studies. The most convenient indices of SES are (see, for instance, Guilford 1967):

(a) father's and/or mother's occupation;

(b) father's and/or mother's educational background;

(c) the family's material resources (what the family owns, level of income, etc.).

Sometimes further indices are used such as:

(a) family size;

(b) information about the region where the family lives (district or suburb; size of city, town, or village), information about home environment (e.g., number, size, and use of rooms; equipment: number of books, availability of mass media, etc.);

(c) information about the family's cultural background (race, ethnicity, and/or nationality of the parents; language used in family interactions);

(d) information about family structure (whether both parents live together; age of siblings, etc.).

Information concerning these variables is usually classified according to categories. Each of these can be used, either separately or in various combinations (multivariate methods), to indicate a family's SES.

As the term "status" implies, SES is regarded as a dimension on which persons can be rank ordered in various categories ranging from "low" to "high". What "low" or "high" means in detail is heavily dependent upon the ethos, mores, and values that are predominant in a specific culture: indices that are positively valued or are seen as desirable and useful confer high status, whereas people who lack these attributes or live in undesirable circumstances are assigned low status. According to cultural differences in what is valued, specific categories (for example, having a large number of children, owning a radio, being a skilled worker) can indicate a relatively high position on the SES dimension in one culture, whereas in another they indicate a low

rank. However, whatever the special characteristics that indicate SES or contribute to it in a particular society, position on the SES dimension has many implications for people's lives, as in every society it determines social standing, as well as possession of power and advantage, access to resources and privileges, and so on. The parents' socioeconomic status also typically leads to the acceptance of certain values and standards. In combination with enjoyment of the relatively objective advantages just discussed, SES thus helps to determine self-concept, self-esteem, aspirations for the future, and the like.

2.2 Family Environment

Indicators associated with SES can also be regarded as limiting factors which determine what kind of family environment parents can establish for their children. If, for example, in order to provide for the necessities of survival both parents are forced to work in full-time jobs, they have little time or energy left to spend with their children and to discover and satisfy their individual needs for contact and support. To do their homework adequately, students need sufficient time free of disruptions and a place where they can read, write, and think with some comfort. Furthermore, the parents' level of education and access to relevant information limits their ability to support their children's education, for instance by reducing their ability to function as models of "desirable" behaviour. Thus variables associated with SES exert what might be called a "direct" influence. In addition, however, SES-related factors such as parent's attitudes towards school and education in general also help to determine children's classroom behaviour, so that SES also exerts an "indirect" (but nonetheless potent) influence. The end effect is that SES indices and family environment characteristics are closely linked to each other. One important result is the frequent failure by researchers to make a clear distinction between the two ways of defining student social background, especially as correlational studies generally show a considerable amount of covariance.

Frequently used general family environment indices that predict a child's disposition to succeed in school (besides those mentioned above) are (see Vernon 1969):

(a) personal relations between the parents (e.g., congruency in attitudes and beliefs);

(b) amount and quality of interaction and communication between the parents and their child(ren);

(c) personal relations between the children;

(d) kinds and variations of parents' activities when children are with them (working, reading, writing, doing things outside the house such as shopping and sightseeing, and leisure activities such as playing, watching television, and so on);

(e) amount and kind of activities the child is permitted

to undertake on its own or without face-to-face contact or supervision by family members (playing alone, peergroup contacts, etc.);

(f) parents' attitudes towards school, interest in their child's school experiences, contact with school or teachers;

(g) parents' aspirations for their children.

The specific combination of family environment variables that is experienced by a child provides, among other things, a set of educational preconditions. Here the child learns what is right or wrong, good or bad, necessary or useless, and why this is so. In the family environment the child can develop personal dispositions to a greater or lesser degree, and become familiar with a variety of tasks and objects. The more dependent children are and the more able to adapt to expectations, the more their behaviour will be congruent with the behaviours and norms of family members. Further, as several studies have demonstrated, perceived age and sex-role differences and relations (distances) determine to a certain degree what a child views as personally appropriate and relevant and what, therefore, is internalized at various stages of development of the child's identity. As a result of these mediating factors, children who live in a particular family environment nonetheless often develop in dissimilar ways.

3. Social Background and Student Characteristics

Social background is an important source of a student's personal characteristics. Knowledge, verbal and non-verbal skills, cognitive styles, level and bias of abilities, as well as noncognitive factors such as self-image, self-esteem, personal identity, attitudes, motivations, interests, values, and so on are influenced by it. Differences in student social background are accompanied by measurable differences in some of these characteristics from the second year of life on, regardless of cultural background (Bloom 1976). Usually students from higher SES home backgrounds enjoy family environments that help them better to develop and make use of their gifts, talents, abilities, and genetic potentials, by providing direct support (see earlier discussion of "direct" and "indirect" factors) as well as by fostering the growth of personal orientations that make it easier for children to succeed under the conditions that are provided by school systems.

3.1 General Results

Generally, empirical research has shown that higher levels of SES go along with (see Vernon 1969):

a) higher IQ scores;

b) use of more complex and differentiated language structures;

c) possession of behavioural, affective, and cognitive

prerequisites that allow for personal mobility, efficient adaptation to new and unexpected situations, and ability to organize one's own behaviour with an eye to the future.

These latter characteristics are related to:

(a) the belief that a person's success is mainly dependent on the energy this person is ready to invest, and that this is more important than external forces such as fate, luck, and chance, or the influence of other people;

(b) the tendency to make plans not only for the near but also for the distant future, and readiness to forego gratification of immediate impulses, because delay of gratification in the long run yields more important or greater satisfactions;

(c) the ability to reconcile the necessity of being socially accepted with the achievement of individual concrete goals and/or to establish rational priorities;

(d) the ability to deal with symbolic representations of things as well as (or better than) with things in their concrete form;

(e) the tendency to value mental activities equally highly or higher than physical work;

(f) greater motivation to strive for higher and more abstract ideals, especially to reach academic success;

(g) greater familiarity with subjects, knowledge, and skills that are part of the conventional school curriculum (especially if the father or mother have had similar levels of formal education).

Although such results are frequently reported, so that they can be regarded as accurately reflecting the prevailing situation, it is important to notice that various studies yield differing findings, thus indicating that the relationship between social background and student characteristics (even at the preschool age) is rather complex.

3.2 Results in Subgroups

Studies have often shown that the student's characteristics can be readily and rather precisely predicted if the student's social background is particularly unfavourable, but that the making of valid predictions becomes more and more difficult when more favourable backgrounds are involved. Whereas in the case of lower-class to middle-class backgrounds there is a good deal of empirical support for the tendency just cited, the situation is different in the case of high and very high SES backgrounds. There, the relationship between student social background indices and student characteristics often becomes insignificant or even negative. Whereas extremely poor conditions (for example lack of adequate food and hygiene, with resultant frequent sickness and heavily restricted physical and cognitive activities) can often hinder children in developing all their gifts and talents, a phenomenon which makes predicting rather easy, the resources provided by a richer background need not necessarily be fully exploited and effectively used by students or their parents. If material, physical, and educational prerequisites in a family are adequate, the parents' knowledge, sensitivity, and communication skills, as well as the extent to which they make use of them in order to support the child's development, are of crucial importance. It should, nonetheless, be remembered that the effects of parental efforts are limited by a child's genetic potential.

As a result of the kinds of factor which have been described, different studies yield seemingly contradictory results concerning the "effects" of social background on student characteristics. It is often instructive in this context, to examine the student social background indices that have been used, as well as to look at their standard deviations and the magnitude of means obtained in the samples surveyed. It is also important to have objective information about the culture being studied.

3.3 Influence of Social Background on Student Characteristics

Educational and psychological literature provide many theories which are, to some extent at least, useful in understanding the relationship between social background and student characteristics. It is impossible here to discuss them all in more detail, but the two most important "sets" of theories can be described briefly.

The first set presupposes that student social background is associated with student characteristics in a symbolic way rather than by means of a cause-and-effect relationship. The main argument is as follows: as students and their parents share many common experiences, students' characteristics tend to be similar to their parents'. On the basis of common genetic potential, prenatal symbiosis with the mother, and processes of imitation and identification, the children adopt many characteristics of their parents. Social background variables can thus be regarded as indices used by researchers to label certain characteristics of parents which, because of the phenomenon just mentioned, usually turn out to be valid also for their children.

The second group of theories presupposes that students' social background consists of sets of objective stimuli that bring about specific environmental challenges for the student. By adjustment to these challenges the students develop certain personal characteristics that help them to survive in the environment in question. As a result, differences between students from different social classes reflect differences in the quality and quantity of stimulation.provided by their SES backgrounds. As for example Piaget's theory suggests, emergence of certain cognitive operations in a child requires certain kinds of experiences. Since higher SES backgrounds tend to promote the emergence of higher and more abstract thought processes, cognitive abilities correlate with SES.

The phenomena that are covered by each of these approaches show a considerable amount of overlap. Neither approach, however, answers all questions. Complex interactions must also be taken into account, while, if students' classroom behaviour is to be more fully explained, the influence of characteristics of the school and fellow students must also be considered.

4. Students Social Background and the Classroom as a Social System

Student social background and the classroom constitute two different social contexts or systems. Each can be characterized by the goals and specific sets of values that are predominant in it, and by the mechanisms of social control that are used to direct a person's behaviour towards these goals (for an introduction see Getzels 1969).

When children enter school at the age of about 6, each of them is strongly characterized by the predominant features of his or her family background. Each student has learned there that it is important to be accepted, or at least not rejected by other children and adults. Behaviour which previously served to satisfy one's own needs, may, however, even provoke rejection in the classroom setting. In the classroom each child is confronted with other children (who may come from different backgrounds and therefore have somewhat different characteristics) as well as with a teacher with expectations which may differ more or less markedly from those of the child's parents. Therefore a certain probability exists that a student's characteristics will be valued differently by various fellow students or by the teacher. The child prefers, either consciously or unconsciously, to have contact with those who show the greatest degree of acceptance; students who regard the teacher as a person whose acceptance is especially important may devote considerable effort to winning it. Since the teacher cannot satisfy the differing needs of different students simultaneously, immediately, completely, and continually, and since different student characteristics offer different chances of success, students are unequally successful in handling social interactions. One result is that formal rules for these interactions can be established, in order to reduce friction.

4.1 Formal and Informal Systems

Following this line of argument, the classroom is often regarded in sociology and social psychology as a social system with a formal and an informal structure. The formal structure mainly defines the student's role as a learner. It is strongly dependent on the school's educational philosophy as conveyed to the students by the expectations and behaviours the teacher demonstrates in the course of teaching. The extent to which a student's characteristics and behaviours fit this philosophy determines the amount of formal gratification the teacher awards to the student, especially in the form of marks.

Whereas these elements constitute the main basis of academic status and success, the informal structure of social interactions in the classroom is mainly defined by personal relationships. These are heavily influenced by the presence or absence of properties and characteristics of individuals regarded by others as valuable, desirable, and satisfying in face-to-face contacts in general (i.e., not only with regard to academic frames of reference but also—and often primarily—with regard to nonacademic properties and extracurricular activities). The informal structure of the classroom becomes explicit in the quality and degree of social status, honour, attractiveness, praise, and sympathy (versus neglect and rejection) that is assigned to each person by others. Thus, the formal and the informal social structures constitute two different dimensions that can be used to determine a student's position in the classroom, as well as providing two value systems a student has to cope with.

4.2 Clash Between Systems

Whereas the school as an institution is responsible for the features and structures of the formal system (i.e., the criteria by which student characteristics are evaluated and the means by which student behaviours are controlled and directed in terms of the school's general educational intentions), the structures of the informal system mainly derive from the opinions, needs, and behavioural strategies of the individuals who come together in the classroom. Thus the informal structure is heavily dependent on the specific combinations of personal characteristics in the classroom, and thus on social background variables.

From a psychological point of view the two systems are complementary to each other. If students feel that their personal needs and desires are not being sufficiently satisfied in the one system, they tend to seek satisfaction in the other. Thus, if students (or their parents) become dissatisfied with the classroom's formal aspects, they are inclined to support tendencies in the informal structure that are elitist, nonacademic, or even antiacademic in nature (establishing subgroups, cliques, etc.). This usually affects the children's academic success, and can lead to conflicts in the classroom, the desire to change classes or schools, or dropping out (Hargreaves 1967). Thus, the degree to which the formal system, both in quantity and kind, is adapted to each particular student's characteristics is of crucial importance in determining classroom behaviour.

The expectations of the formal system provide guidelines which make it possible, to a certain degree, to predict students' classroom behaviour, since these expectations define the student as a role incumbent. On the other hand, where formal regulations do not exist, students are free to choose their own behaviour and—on the basis of personal preferences—to adapt it to informal structures. By defining the formal structure, the school therefore directly determines the quality and quantity of personal satisfaction that can be obtained inside the formal system and, through this, indirectly determines the functions that particular individuals are likely to ascribe to the informal system. But as the main purpose of the formal system in schools is not to satisfy each student's momentary personal needs, students' general degree of satisfaction with school and their classroom behaviour mainly depend on their ability and motivation to understand and conform to the expectations and intentions of the formal system. When this conformity leads to severe conflicts with (or rejection by) elements of the informal system, which are also perceived as important, some students tend to attune their behaviour to the norms of the informal system and thus "misbehave" or even become "behavioural problems". This is particularly true of children of lower socioeconomic status.

5. Students' Social Background and the Formal System

As has already been pointed out, behaviour of students is affected by the values and expectations of different persons and groups in the classroom, which may cause conflicts and behavioural problems. The formal system also, however, defines certain contents, activities, and skills which have to be mastered by the students, and coping with these demands has further important consequences for classroom behaviour.

5.1 General Adaptation Problems

Although classrooms vary widely according to cultural conditions and students' age, some main features can be described in a universal form. Classrooms can generally be defined as places where a specially trained and educated person (the teacher) is expected to encourage emergence of certain behavioural dispositions in younger people (students), and to discourage others. These dispositions are expected to help the students successfully to master certain tasks which may occur in the present or future life in the society in question. Thus it is usually held that students should, among other things, become able:

(a) to earn their own living;

(b) to participate in the life of their community and in the political system, and therefore to know and understand important features of their culture;

(c) to take over the role of a father or a mother in an appropriate way;

(d) to behave according to certain social and legal norms;

(e) to make reasonable and responsible use of given leisure time, and of the society's resources.

What is meant by this, exactly and in detail, strongly depends on what is regarded as desirable by those who govern the schools. Usually their expectations and aspirations are more or less similar to those of people of middle-class SES in a given society, or at least significantly different from those of the lowest status categories, since these are usually seen as undesirable or lagging behind the society's ideals or objective needs and goals.

Students who come from low SES families are therefore confronted with important disparities between the norms of their particular social background and those of the classroom. They may, therefore, be exposed to typical problems:

(a) difficulties in understanding the meaning of certain items and subjects, organizational demands, behavioural rules, communication procedures, and so on;

(b) discrepancies in values and aspirations: What the student may value as "good" and "important" may be regarded as "bad" and "irrelevant" by fellow students or the teacher. This can be combined with a failure to give adequate reinforcement even to considerable individual effort and progress, because the visible results do not conform to a certain norm, or reach a certain minimum level;

(c) conflicting influences from the family and the school which may lead to uncertainty, disorientation, loss of self-esteem or self-confidence, or other unfortunate results, such as reduced motivation.

However, student social background variables not only contribute to the frequency and severity of such problems, but also determine the kinds of abilities and strategies available for coping with them. Children from lower SES groups frequently display lower levels of certain abilities (abstract thinking, willingness to delay gratification of impulses, etc.) while they often possess personal orientations that are primarily concerned with the quality of interpersonal and group contact (i.e., available sources of social support) rather than with rational, autonomous, matter-of-fact problem solving. These orientations are partly caused by the fact that their social background provides them with less school-related experience and school subject-related pre-knowledge. This makes it more difficult for them to identify with what is needed for success in school. When they enter school, for instance, these students find themselves at starting points that lie behind those of students from higher SES backgrounds (Bloom 1976). At the same time they are less well-equipped with strategies for mastering certain kinds of problems in a way that leads to success in the formal system. Their chance of overcoming initial relative deficits is consequently relatively low, and they run the risk of falling further and further behind, if special support is not provided.

5.2 Learning Processes

During instructional periods, students are expected to acquire knowledge and certain cognitive and behavioural skills. To do this, they work on content which is presented in various ways, for instance, with the help of various media, ranging from very concrete to symbolic and highly abstract forms. They are also required to carry out activities which can be purely physical and behavioural, affective, or cognitive in nature.

All students, regardless of SES, are familiar with certain physical objects and with concrete operations, as well as with certain abstractions that are derived from them. This makes it easy for them to deal with new examples of similar items which are presented in concrete forms. As a result, differences between students' abilities in this area usually show little covariance with SES variables. This is especially true for certain technical and practical activities (such as gymnastics, various kinds of artistic activity, and manual skills), as well as for concrete organizational activities and business affairs, indeed even for certain elements of mathematics and the natural sciences. Crucial in all cases is that tasks are clearly structured and the effects of one's efforts can be readily evaluated according to seemingly self-evident objective standards of what is right and wrong, good and bad, effective and ineffective. Sometimes, if most of their time and effort is dedicated to such contents and activities, students of low SES even show better achievement than students of higher SES, especially since members of the latter group (because of the influence of their family environment) often become acquainted with and interested in other forms and operations, and direct more time and energy to them.

In higher SES family backgrounds, students are usually also challenged to deal with things and problems on several metalevels:

(a) conveying information by means of language (instead of referring to concrete operations such as showing, demonstrating, or making use of non-verbal ways of expressing something);

(b) structuring open tasks and trying out things by themselves, with the result that different strategies are tried and used;

(c) working out reasons, meanings, sense, and outcomes of behaviours, processes, and objects.

In carrying out activities like these, students gradually acquire the ability to coordinate and integrate their perceptions, behaviours, affects, and cognitions, and to direct them to the effective management of complex tasks, such as reading. As (a) reading ability and language skills are extremely important prerequisites for effective participation in classroom learning activities (since language is the main medium of subject presentation, classroom interaction, and evaluation), and (b) the ability to concentrate, to stay on the task, to tolerate frustration, to show discipline and emotional stability, and so on, are strong predictors of classroom achievement, as well as being important sources of social acceptance (especially by the teacher), students' academic success in all subjects is influenced by these positively correlated "metalevel" factors. Nonetheless, the strength of their influence varies from subject to subject and also depends on the methodological and didactic approaches of the teacher, which can, in principle, be adapted to students' characteristics, for example, by making more or less use of language, concrete presentations, enquiry methods, physical versus symbolic operations, and so on.

6. School Organization, Students' Social Background, and Classroom Behaviour

The main features of educational techniques, philosophies, and school systems in different cultures, subcultures, states, and countries are dependent not only on what is known to be useful and efficient in the present, but also—and often to a greater degree—on the specific history and traditions of a certain society, its resources, perceived and accepted possibilities, ideals, and future needs.

Accordingly, schools can, to greater or lesser extents, be supported, run, even controlled by various agencies which determine the main structures of the educational environment that is offered:

(a) the national government, which hopes to provide equal schooling for all students throughout the country;

(b) local district or community authorities, which are mainly responsible for the adequacy of educational opportunities in their region;

(c) certain groups and organizations (such as the churches) which provide school systems where their own values and beliefs are supported, and where special requirements for admission and attendance sometimes have to be met.

Furthermore, to take account of students' characteristics and educational needs, as well as to meet certain demands of the society (especially training for certain sections of the labour market and for the reduction or limitation of social problems), the school system can be organized either in a selective way (students are assigned to different types of schools according to certain criteria of academic success) or in a comprehensive way (all students attend the same type of school where a wide variety of different activities is offered in order to do justice to individual characteristics and needs). These two sets of conditions affect the way in which a certain school in the system performs its tasks. They especially delimit the school's adaptability to certain student characteristics, and can, therefore, be regarded as sources of specific problems that arise in the classroom.

As students generally prefer to attend schools that are located near their family home, or in some cases are required to do so, the social structure and stratification of the population that lives in a certain region determines to some degree the nature of the school's student population, especially the proportion of students from different social backgrounds, as persons of similar background often live in proximity to each other. Students from low SES backgrounds show a particularly strong tendency to attend schools that are located near their homes, whereas students from higher SES backgrounds often feel free to go to a more distant location if it seems worthwhile. It is also true that more educational opportunities are usually available in larger cities than in rural regions. The result is that if the student populations in different schools are compared, there are often considerable differences between schools. As such differences can lead to educational provision which is inadequate for certain individuals, especially if schools are not free to adapt appropriately, various means (laws, busing, etc.) can be employed to equalize educational opportunity.

6.1 Homogeneity Versus Heterogeneity in Student Populations

In selective school systems—compared with comprehensive systems—classrooms generally consist of students with rather similar levels of prior academic success, and correspondingly similar indices of SES. But, of course, relative social homogeneity of a classroom's student population can also have other causes, such as the chance population structure of the region in which the school is located, parental freedom to choose a school, or certain strategies for assigning students to schools and classes. In homogeneous classrooms it is relatively easy for the teacher to proceed efficiently in a way that seems to be appropriate to all students (and also to their parents). Being exposed to such a homogeneous environment can, however, lead to lack of divergent experiences and the reinforcement of certain undesirable personal characteristics such as acceptance of biased social stereotypes or prejudice. Social heterogeneity, on the other hand, also provides valuable educational opportunities and challenges. Apparent differences can become subjects of instruction and discussion, the students and the teacher are forced to overcome conflicts and difficulties or to learn to live with them, students' different social background experiences can provide for a wider variety of approaches towards academic subjects, and so on.

Social homogeneity versus heterogeneity thus influences actual curriculum content, subject learning, and social interaction in the classroom. The definition of the formal system and the—complementary—features of the informal system are also affected. Whereas in homogeneous groups it is easy to establish rules and demands that are accepted as appropriate and can be successfully met by most children (with a resulting comparatively low level of importance of the informal system for personal support and satisfaction), in heterogeneous groups possible deviations from any norm are large. Thus, individual differences in formal and informal status become much more obvious; students tend to stick together in cliques that hold different informal values, and use various coping strategies in order to preserve their self-image (for example by fighting against other subgroups or the teacher)—the two status systems are more likely to interfere with each other (Hargreaves 1967).

With increasing heterogeneity it becomes more and more difficult to establish norms and rules that are accepted by all members of the class and can be met by them and their parents. Therefore, if in a certain classroom the limits of "tolerable" heterogeneity are passed, some students are usually sent to other classes or schools. In order to manage classrooms with a high degree of heterogeneity, the teacher not only needs effective means of social control (such as opportunities to reward and punish), but also adequate personality characteristics, special training and instructional skills, knowledge about students' personal characteristics and social background variables, as well as didactic freedom and social support from others, such as the headteacher, colleagues and parental groups, educational counselling agencies, social workers, and others.

6.2 Directions and Determinants of School Influence

It is the teacher's job to influence the students in certain directions that are regarded as educationally desirable. Therefore teachers have a considerable amount of power and authority. During teaching periods they can make use of this in different ways, often referred to in educational literature, as "leadership-styles". As cultures and subcultures hold strong views about the way in which power and authority generally are to be exerted, teachers are inclined to conform to these values and to believe that a certain—culturally accepted—style is adequate for all educational purposes. Therefore, empirical research on the effectiveness of different leadership styles or of other teacher behaviours which are viewed in a culture as "different" or "deviant" from what is positively valued are exposed to severe ideological criticism. Nevertheless, research findings have demonstrated (and often teachers know) that no single style serves all educational demands and purposes equally well. What may be optimal in a given situation and with a certain student population may be impossible, ineffective, or even harmful under different conditions, and may cause handicaps for certain students (Bennett 1976).

The decision in favour of a certain style is associated with a variety of influences on different students. Whereas some students are strongly influenced in educationally desirable directions by a given approach, influences on other students may be low or negative. As might well be expected, the relevant research has often shown that those teachers who produce optimal results in all students (i.e., they do not support some students at the cost of others) are able to diagnose the different demands of different students and different teaching or educational situations, and use the style that

is most appropriate under given conditions, that is, flexibly to change between different styles. But as culturally bound educational philosophies, mechanisms of social control, and personal dispositions of teachers generally favour certain behaviours and suppress others, the teacher's actual opportunities to support all students to the same degree are limited, and do not match theoretical ideals.

The actual influences in classrooms are strongly dependent on the students' individual reactions to the teacher's behaviour and presentations. On the basis of students' reactions, teachers develop feelings of attachment (pleasure), concern (sympathy that leads to support), indifference (associated with lack of involvement), or rejection (negative affect) towards individual students. They also formulate implicit personality theories (consisting of assumptions about a student's characteristics, such as maturity and ability), and develop expectations of students as well as propositions about the probable consequences of efforts to help a given student.

As the quality of stimuli that are presented in class initiates certain processes that determine what the teacher will feel and think about certain students, as well as how they actually behave, a wider variety of stimuli helps the teacher to get a broad and differentiated picture of the class and the students, to overcome prejudice, and to optimize instruction. It also helps the students to show more of their characteristics, strengths, and weaknesses. The teacher's opportunities to vary teaching style and forms of presentation of material thus mediate the direct influence of social background on students' classroom behaviour. With increasing restrictions on teachers, student social background characteristics will be expected to predict students' variance in classroom behaviour more strongly, especially in socially heterogeneous classes.

If a high degree of restriction of teachers' behaviour has to be taken into account, the following consequences are to be expected. Students who show characteristics and behaviours that do not hinder the teacher's efforts to proceed according to a particular instructional style, or who stimulate the teacher's efforts—this usually means students of middle-class (or even higher) SES background—are strongly influenced by teachers in directions that are generally regarded as desirable and, in turn, are rather successful in influencing the teacher in directions that they personally prefer. Here influence and interaction tend to be reciprocal, the frequency and quality of interaction (i.e., verbal, nonverbal) depending on the students' activities. Reciprocity of influence is supported by high levels of parental interest in their childrens' academic success and, correspondingly, frequent contact between them and the teacher. Under these conditions, relevant information can be conveyed in a circle that consists of the teacher, the student, the parents, and the teacher, and where information flows in several directions. This leads to a high degree of adaptation between school and family environment, both of them supporting the student in complementary ways.

Students who show characteristics and behaviours that do not suit the teacher's intentions are more likely to invoke highly directive behaviour, blame, and criticism as well as negative affect in teachers. This is also true if the teacher assumes that the student is, in principle, able to meet the expectations. If students feel that their actions are generally rejected by the teacher, they tend to evaluate the teacher's personality and professional ability negatively. Thus their chances of influencing the teacher in the way they wish are low, whereas the teacher's influence on them is very strong—in directions that run counter to what is generally seen as educationally desirable.

As students from low SES backgrounds are more likely to show behaviours that differ from what the teacher desires, they often belong to this group of students. If such a negative teacher–student relationship is accompanied by negative feelings towards the teacher on the part of parents, lack of contact between the teacher and the parents, or even conflict may result. This and additional factors, such as low interest in the student's academic career, negative academic self-concept, and perceived differences between student social background variables and demands of the formal system (which lead to feelings of distance and estrangement), help to explain research findings that often report a poor personal relationship between low SES parents and teachers. These parents often expect to have low influence on what happens in the classroom and—for this and several other reasons—tend to adopt an attitude of resignation. Their children thus receive low support from both parents and the teachers, and try to obtain it elsewhere—in the informal system where they ally themselves with peers and classmates who are in a similar position.

7. Practical Considerations

As has been outlined in this article, students from less favourable social backgrounds are usually exposed to many problems which together often lead to reduced academic success and—consequently—to poor chances of reaching higher positions in their society's SES structure. Nevertheless, as has hopefully already become obvious, there are large individual differences. Students' educational success is not preordained by something like a natural law. At least in theory, many possibilities exist of providing better or even optimal educational opportunities even for students from unfavourable social backgrounds. In fact, the degree to which they can be supported and helped to be successful largely depends on how much the school and the teacher are able and willing to adapt to their requirements. This topic is often neglected in empirical research, so that it has been almost impossible up to now to prove its importance by objective means. Indeed, it must be admitted that it is very difficult to master the relevant methodological problems, even though measurable indices exist, as may have become explicit in the present article. However, some evidence is available, especially in reports that show that the same students perform differently under different classroom conditions.

The fact that educational chances are to a considerable degree dependent on good luck, such as access to a "good" school, and contact with a competent and friendly teacher, is often perceived as unjust (Jencks et al. 1972). This not infrequently leads to the emergence of two radically different positions. Some writers claim that all of a society's resources should be mobilized to support those who are seen as "the disadvantaged". This article has shown that what would have to be done in order to realize this ideal on a wide scale could only be achieved by huge efforts and would take a considerable time to achieve. It would require, for example, huge expenditures for better educational facilities in schools, improved teacher education, and mobilization of long-term processes such as changes in personal and societal value systems. The opposite position takes the following form. If efforts to improve educational opportunities for children from unfavourable social backgrounds are to be undertaken, the society's present and future resources, properties, and demands should be taken into account. Educational reforms would have to supply the society with people who are willing and able to do the jobs that are available. To provide optimal educational opportunities for the disadvantaged is too expensive, and may produce consequences that are undesirable in certain other respects.

What these two arguments show is that the actual relationship between student social background and classroom behaviour turns out to be largely a result of societal goals, ideologies, political priorities, and the like, since these determine what really happens at the school and classroom level.

See also: Aptitude–Treatment Interaction Models; Students' Affective Characteristics; Students' Cognitive Characteristics; Students' Ethnicity; Student Roles; Students' Sex

Bibliography

Bennett N 1976 *Teaching Styles and Pupil Progress*. Open Books, London

Bloom B S 1976 *Human Characteristics and School Learning*. McGraw-Hill, New York

Getzels J W 1969 A social psychology of education. In: Lindzey G, Aronson E (eds.) 1969 *The Handbook of Social Psychology*, 2nd edn., Vol. 5. Addison-Wesley, Reading, Massachusetts, pp. 459–537

Guilford J P 1967 *The Nature of Human Intelligence*. McGraw-Hill, New York

Hargreaves D H 1967 *Social Relations in a Secondary School*. Routledge and Kegan Paul, London

Jencks C S, Smith M, Acland H, Bone M J, Cohen D, Gintis H, Heyns B, Michelson S 1972 *Inequality: A Reassessment of the Effects of Family and Schooling in America*. Basic Books, New York

Kagan J 1977 On cultural deprivation. In: Oliverio A (ed.) 1977 *Genetics, Environment and Intelligence.* North-Holland, Amsterdam, pp. 371–84

Marjoribanks K 1977 Socioeconomic status and its relation to cognitive performance as mediated through the family environment. In: Oliverio A (ed.) 1977 *Genetics, Environment and Intelligence.* North-Holland, Amsterdam, pp. 385–403

Rutter M, Maughan B, Mortimore P, Ouston J, Smith A 1979 *Fifteen Thousand Hours: Secondary Schools and Their Effects on Children.* Open Books, London

Vernon P E 1969 *Intelligence and Cultural Environment.* Methuen, London

Teachers' Characteristics

Teachers' Personality

D. S. Levis

There has long been strong popular support for the view that qualities of teacher personality are important determinants of successful teaching. Given this belief, it is not surprising that considerable research interest should have been shown in investigating the nature and measurement of personality and the relationship between teacher personality and instruction. In their comprehensive review of studies concerned with the teacher's personality and characteristics, Getzels and Jackson (1963) recorded that, over the previous two decades, some thousands of studies had attempted to predict teacher effectiveness from the personal characteristics of teachers. While acknowledging the prodigious research effort involved, the reviewers concluded that this research had been largely unproductive, leading to the reiteration of the self-evident rather than the discovery of specific features of teacher personality and of the effective teacher. They identified a number of major obstacles which had confronted researchers in this area and had limited the research outcomes. These included problems associated with (a) the wide range of meanings assigned to the term personality; (b) difficulties associated with the selection of appropriate measures of personality; (c) the difficulty of establishing teacher effectiveness criteria; (d) limitations of the criterion-of-effectiveness model as a basis for research; and (e) inadequate theoretical underpinning of the research. Each of these problems is worthy of consideration in the light of the studies reviewed by Getzels and Jackson and changes in the conception of teacher personality in subsequent research in the area.

1. Meanings of the Term Teacher Personality

The term personality has had widespread currency over a long period of time and various meanings have been ascribed to it. In what was probably not an all-inclusive list, Allport (1937) identified over 50 meanings. As a consequence, the concept of personality has proved elusive. Research studies based on different conceptions of personality have produced contradictory data and invalid conclusions where researchers have failed to recognize these differences in conception.

Getzels and Jackson attempted to effect some order by classifying definitions of personality according to three major categories: (a) behavioural definitions, in which personality is used to refer to the totality of a person's behaviour; (b) social-stimulus definitions, in which personality is the response made by others to the individual as a stimulus; and (c) depth definitions, in which personality is the dynamic organization within the individual that determines unique behaviour. In their selection and discussion of studies of teacher personality, Getzels and Jackson used the term personality to refer to the totality of a person's behaviour and included for consideration cognitive aspects of behaviour along with the affective aspects, such as attitudes, values, interests, adjustments, and needs. The inclusion of cognitive aspects was justified on the grounds that they filled out the portrait of the teacher as a functioning individual.

Since the early 1960s, educational theorists and researchers have tended to move from this inclusive conceptualization of personality and to make a more clear-cut distinction between the affective and cognitive aspects of teaching. This orientation seems to have flowed from the significant influences of Bloom and his associates (1956) and Krathwohl et al. (1964) in developing taxonomies of objectives in the cognitive and affective domains, and from recognition that, in the past, cognitive aspects of teaching had been relatively neglected by researchers. As a consequence, the 1960s and 1970s saw increased research activity relating to the cognitive aspects of teaching. Research on teacher personality tended to move from a broad base to more direct concern for investigating the effects of teachers' attitudes on their classroom behaviour and the achievement of their pupils. The spirit behind this research focus was captured by Smith (1971 p. 8) as follows:

There is little doubt that the attitudes a teacher has towards himself influence his behavior in the classroom. And there are strong reasons for believing that the teacher's attitudes towards his pupils—e.g. his expectations of them—will influence their achievement. There can be no doubt that personality in the attitudinal sense is a factor in teaching behavior. The question is what elements of personality make a difference in such behavior, and how those elements can be modified in directions that increased pupil growth.

2. Measures of Personality

Efforts to identify personality characteristics which "make a difference" have spawned a wide range of tests and projective procedures for measuring personality. Getzels and Jackson (1963 pp. 508–66) described in detail a number of well-known measures and reported their application for research of teacher personality. Included in their review were attitude measures, such as the Minnesota Teacher Attitude Inventory (MTAI) and the Authoritarianism (F) Scale; measures of values and interests, such as the Allport–Vernon–Lindsay Test of Values, the Kuder Preference Record, and the Strong Vocational Interest Blank; measures of adjustment and needs, such as the Minnesota Multiphase Personality Inventory (MMPI); personality inventories, such as the Guilford Personality Inventories and Cattell's Sixteen Personality Factor Questionnaire (16 P.F. Test); and projective techniques such as the Rorschach, Thematic Apperception Test, Word Association Test, and Draw-a-Teacher test. Regarding the application of such devices for assessing teacher personality Getzels and Jackson (1963 pp. 574–75) summarized as follows:

> The number of instruments available is legion, and indeed most have been tried in one study or another. If there is a test that promises anything at all, it has probably been administered to some group of practicing or prospective teachers. But the data provided by one instrument called a personality test are not necessarily the same as the data provided by another instrument also called a personality test. For example, data from self-report instruments are likely to represent a behavioral concept of personality; data from rating instruments a social-stimulus concept; and data from projective techniques a depth concept. The use of tests on the basis of availability . . . rather than on relevant personality concepts . . . has led to a "shot-gun" type of research yielding outcomes that are often inexplicable.

The British research literature of the 1960s contained a number of studies in which well-known tests were used to measure the personal characteristics of teachers and student teachers and to predict teacher effectiveness from them. Included in test batteries were a number of the measures listed above and such measures as the Eysenck Personality Inventory and the Maudsley Personality Inventory. Reviews of these studies were conducted by Garner (1973) and Lomax (1973). Garner (1973) concluded that together these studies produced a wide range of variables which may be determinants of teaching effectiveness and which substantiated Vernon's comment that "teachers are as diverse in their psychological traits as any other occupational group" and that "it is fallacious to talk of teaching personality as something distinct and consistent" (pp. 425–36).

3. Teacher Effectiveness Criteria

The most intransigent of difficulties has been to establish teacher-effectiveness criteria shown to be related to teacher personality. In his review, Lomax (1973) concluded that "even if past studies are given credit for helping to clear a little of the ground for future researchers, it must be recognized that very little is known about the relationship between personality characteristics and teacher effectiveness" (pp. 301–27). The most frequent criterion of teacher-effectiveness studies has been the rating made by a variety of judges such as supervisory teachers, principals, trained raters, experimenters themselves, and so on. This approach has been exposed to considerable criticism on the grounds of subjectivity and unreliability (Dunkin and Biddle 1974 p. 60). It has proved difficult to relate a more objective criterion, namely pupil gain, to teacher personality without reference to a wide range of variables within the school setting or the broader social and psychological context within which the pupil functions.

Garner (1973 pp. 427–29) expressed strong reservation about the criterion measure of teaching effectiveness. He argued that the concept of teaching effectiveness is basically a value judgment and he supported his view by reference to the statement by Rabinowitz and Travers (1953) that "the effective teacher does not exist pure and serene, available for scientific scrutiny, but is instead a fiction of the minds of men. No teacher is more effective than another, except as someone so decides and designates". Garner suggested that, if this point is accepted, any study of teaching effectiveness should state "what kind of teacher-produced effects are thought to be desirable and describe the extent to which these valued effects were deemed to have occurred". He observed that research into teaching had increasingly adopted a methodology which involved describing the events within classrooms of teachers possessing various personality attributes rather than rating their performance on some scale of excellence. While this approach sidesteps the values question, it does not avoid it completely since it might also be argued that a system for describing classroom behaviour is an embodiment of a set of values.

4. Criterion-of-effectiveness Model

The criterion-of-effectiveness model on which many of the research studies on teacher personality and instruction were based is an extremely simple one. As detailed by Gage (1972 pp. 85–86), it has involved the identification or selection of a criterion or set of criteria of teacher effectiveness. This criterion has become the dependent variable. The research task has been (a) to measure this criterion; (b) to measure potential correlates of this criterion; and (c) to determine the actual correlations between the criterion and its potential correlates. The model has implied that teaching behaviour is a function of teacher personality. It contrasts sharply with other psychological models of human behaviour which have asserted that behaviour is a function of both a situation and a person in that situation (Murray et al. 1938).

As stated earlier, teacher personality studies based on the simple criterion-of-effectiveness model have yielded disappointing results; correlations that have been non-significant inconsistent from one study to another, and usually lacking in psychological and educational meaning. Under these circumstances, researchers began to refine more comprehensive criterion-of-effectiveness models which included a wider range of variables beyond the personality characteristics on which teachers differ (e.g., Mitzel 1957, Biddle 1964) and gradually to develop teaching process models, which were not centred on criteria of teacher effectiveness, derived from outside the classroom, but which focused on the events occurring inside the classroom during the teaching process. Gage (1972 p. 96) gave two reasons for this change of direction: (a) to improve the yield of positive and consistent results; and (b) to examine intrinsically important phenomena. Process models such as those developed by Smith (1960) and Ryans (1963) viewed teaching as a complex interactive process involving both teacher and pupil behaviour. Referring to the complexity of interactions within classroom settings, Garner (1973 p. 433) commented as follows:

> The basic personality traits of individuals will interact with the kind of teacher education they will receive . . . to produce certain teaching styles. . . . These styles will in turn be affected by the conventions of the particular school and the particular subject that is to be taught. The resultant of this interaction will be the generally-observed behaviour of the teacher in the classroom. . . . At the final level of specificity this general classroom style will be varied from pupil to pupil, and from moment to moment, depending upon the interactions between the characteristics of specific pupils, specific problems that arise or specific kinds of interactions undertaken.

Garner presented the model illustrated in Fig. 1, showing suggested patterns of interaction, most of which he argued could be supported by research findings. The complexity of these patterns of influence and the distancing of teacher traits emphasize the inadequacy of the simple criterion-of-effectiveness model. On the basis of this model, Garner argued that the power of personality measures as predictors of teacher behaviour would depend upon the interacting conditions being held constant for the sample of teachers about whom the predictions are being made—an extremely difficult and unlikely possibility.

5. Theoretical Underpinning of Research

As implied in the previous section, many of the conceptual and experimental limitations of research on teacher personality and instruction resulted from the lack of explicit theorizing about the relationships that might be expected. In evaluating the studies of teacher personality and characteristics conducted in the 1950s,

Getzels and Jackson (1963 pp. 575–76) claimed that the research was conducted in a theoretical vacuum. Hypotheses were based on oversimplification of teacher personality and teaching context and were not grounded in learning theory or social–psychological theory. Theory was essential for providing dimensions for research, for serving an explanatory function, and to provide a framework for the interpretation of results. One exception among the early studies to a purely empirical approach was the extensive Teacher Characteristics Study conducted by Ryans (1960). This study paid great attention to the development of a theoretical framework as the basis for identifying some patterns of classroom behaviour, attitudes, viewpoints, and intellectual and emotional qualities which may characterize teachers. However, despite Ryans' systematic approach to theorizing, data gathering, processing, and interpretation, the Teacher Characteristics Study yielded limited entry points into the relationship between teacher personality and instruction. Subsequent evaluations of research on teacher personality and instruction (Gage 1972, Garner 1973, Lomax 1973) drew attention to the continuing lack of theorizing about relationships in studies conducted in this area through the 1960s.

6. Assessing Teachers' Attitudes

The earlier quotation from Smith (1971) asserted that teacher personality in the attitudinal sense is a significant factor in teacher behaviour and that the research tasks were to identify those elements of personality that affect teaching behaviour and to discover how they might be modified in directions to promote pupil growth. The research literature of the 1960s and early 1970s reported a number of studies that had investigated teacher attitudes and their relation to pupil achievement. In a review of studies supporting a relationship between teacher behaviour and student achievement, Rosenshine and Furst (1971) included four attitudinal variables: teacher enthusiasm, teacher business-like classroom behaviour, teacher indirectness, and teacher warmth. These were high-inference variables generally based upon rating scales. The research methods used and the findings reported in the studies of these variables did not inspire confidence that teachers' development of these variables would in itself enhance pupil achievement. Closer examination of each of these variables serves to illustrate the limited usefulness of knowledge gained through such research.

In the five studies of teacher enthusiasm reviewed by Rosenshine and Furst, data were gathered by (a) observer ratings on paired adjectives such as "stimulating vs. dull", "original vs. stereotyped", "alert vs. apathetic" (Fortune 1967, Kleinman 1964, Waller 1966); (b) observer estimation of the amount of rigour and power exhibited by the teacher during classroom presentation (Solomon et al. 1963); and (c) student ratings on the teacher's involvement, excitement, or interest regarding his or her subject matter (Solomon et al.

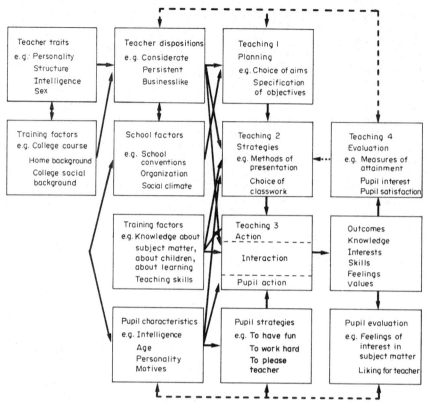

Figure 1
A model of teaching[a]

a Source: Garner 1973 p. 433

1963). Significant results relating teacher enthusiasm to student achievement on at least one criterion measure were obtained in all five studies; however, specific low-inference behaviours which comprise enthusiasm had not been identified.

Rosenshine and Furst reported seven studies in which various rating scales were used to estimate the degree to which a teacher was task-oriented, achievement-oriented, and/or business-like. The reviewers reported significant results on at least one of the criterion measures in six of the studies; however, they acknowledged that the combination of these studies under the one label was hazardous because there was no way of determining whether the different rating scales could be combined under one category.

Dunkin and Biddle (1974 pp. 105–133) carefully reviewed approximately 100 studies focusing on teacher indirectness and on teacher warmth. They evaluated the studies in terms of instrumentation, methods of gathering data, coding systems, units studied, reliabilities, designs, subjects, and contexts of research.

The notion of teacher indirectness was derived primarily from Flanders' conception of a continuum of

teacher behaviour exerting direct to indirect influence in classroom settings (Flanders 1967). In the Flanders Interaction Analysis Categories System (FIAC)`, indirectness consisted of the combined frequencies of teacher behaviours labelled acceptance of student feeling, praise or encouragement, and use of pupils' ideas. Most of the studies of teacher indirectness reviewed by Dunkin and Biddle were generated by the application of FIAC. On the basis of their careful evaluation, Dunkin and Biddle (1974 p. 132) concluded that "findings . . . appear to show relationships between indirectness and pupil growth, although the evidence is weak, contradictory, and the relations may be curvilinear or contextually bound. However, evidence from experiments is equivocal, suggesting that the apparent relationships . . . are not causative. Thus, the case for indirectness is not demonstrated!"

Three FIAC categories generated substantial findings that appeared to relate to the global concept of teacher warmth. These were teacher praise, teacher acceptance of pupils' ideas, and teacher criticism. Praise and acceptance were seen as positive components of warmth; criticism was seen as its antonym. In respect of teacher warmth, Dunkin and Biddle (1974 p. 132) concluded that "the classroom is usually neither warm nor cold but primarily neutral in tone" and that findings "show some relationships between these categories (particularly criticism) and pupil outcomes, although these effects are almost completely untested experimentally". They concluded that the case for warmth also was not demonstrated.

7. Summary

The conclusions reached about these four teacher attitudinal variables serve to illustrate the difficulties of research in this area and lend support to the pessimistic view expressed by Getzels and Jackson (1963 p. 574) that very little is known for certain about the relation between teacher personality and teacher effectiveness. Research studies carried out since the early 1960s do not provide evidence for a more optimistic view.

See also: Criteria for Evaluating Teaching; Definitions of Teaching; Human Interaction Models

Bibliography

Allport G W 1937 *Personality: A Psychological Interpretation*. Holt, New York
Biddle B J 1964 The integration of teacher effectiveness research. In: Biddle B J, Ellena W J (eds.) 1964 *Contemporary Research on Teacher Effectiveness*. Holt, Rinehart and Winston, New York
Bloom B S, Engelhart M B, Furst E J, Hill W H, Krathwohl D R 1956 *Taxonomy of Educational Objectives: The Classification of Educational Goals. Handbook 1: Cognitive Domain*. Longmans Green, New York
Dunkin M J, Biddle B J 1974 *The Study of Teaching*. Holt, Rinehart and Winston, New York
Flanders N A 1967 Teacher influence in the classroom. In: Amidon E J, Hough J B (eds.) 1967 *Interaction Analysis: Theory Research and Application*. Addison-Wesley, Reading, Massachusetts
Fortune J C 1967 *A Study of the Generality of Presenting Behaviors in Teaching Memphis State University* (United States Office of Education Project No. 6-8468). Memphis, Tennessee
Gage N L 1972 *Teacher Effectiveness and Teacher Education: The Search for a Scientific Basis*. Pacific Books, Palo Alto, California
Garner J 1973 The nature of teaching and effectiveness of teachers. In: Lomax D E (ed.) 1973 *The Education of Teachers in Britain*. Wiley, London, pp. 425–36
Getzels J W, Jackson P W 1963 The teacher's personality and characteristics. In: Gage N L (ed.) 1963 *Handbook of Research in Teaching: A Project of the American Educational Researsh Association*. Rand McNally, Chicago, Illinois pp. 506–82
Kleinman G S 1964 General science teacher's questions, pupil and teacher behaviors and pupils' understanding of science (Unpublished doctoral dissertation University of Virginia, Virginia) *Dissertation Abstracts International*, 1965 25: 5153–5154 (University Microfilms No. 65–3961)
Krathwohl D R, Bloom B S, Masin B B 1964 *Taxonomy of Educational Objectives: The Classification of Educational Goals. Handbook 2: Affective Domain*. McKay, New York
Lomax D 1973 Teacher education. In: Butcher H J, Pont H B (eds.) 1973 *Educational Research in Britain 3*. University of London Press, London, pp. 301–27
Mitzel H E 1957 *A Behavioral Approach to the Assessment of Teacher Effectiveness*. Division of Teacher Education, College of the City of New York, New York
Murray H A et al. 1938 *Explorations in Personality: A Clinical and Experimental Study of Fifty Men of College Age*. Oxford University Press, New York
Rabinowitz W, Travers R M W 1953 Problems of defining and assessing teacher effectiveness. *Educ. Theory* 3: 212–19
Rosenshine B, Furst N 1971 Research on teacher performance criteria. In Smith B O (ed.) 1971
Ryans D G 1960 *Characteristics of Teachers: Their Description, Comparison, and Appraisal: A Research Study*. American Council on Education, Washington, DC
Ryans D G 1963 Teacher behavior theory and research: Implications for teacher education. *J. Teach. Ed.* 14: 274–93
Smith B O 1960 A concept of teaching. *Teach. Coll. Rec.* 61: 229–41
Smith B O (ed.) 1971 *Research in Teacher Education: A Symposium*. Prentice-Hall, Englewood Cliffs, New Jersey
Solomon D, Bezdek W E, Rosenberg L 1963 *Teaching Styles and Learning*. Center for the Study of Liberal Arts for Adults, Chicago, Illinois. ERIC Document No. ED 026556
Vernon P E 1953 The psychological traits of teachers. *Yearbook of Education*, pp. 51–75
Waller N E 1966 *Relationships Between Teacher Characteristics and Student Behavior: Part Three*. United States Office of Education Cooperative Research Project No. SAE OE 5-10-181. University of Utah, Salt Lake City, Utah

Affective Characteristics of Student Teachers

F. Coulter

Induction into teaching is a challenging and often traumatic experience. It involves not only the acquisition of professional knowledge, but also the skills necessary to translate that knowledge into action. Failure to cope with this situation is a threatening prospect for the student teacher. This is because of a widely held belief that many teaching skills are innate, and that although they may be enhanced by training, teachers are born rather than made. These "innate skills", it is believed, arise from one's general personal competence which includes the ability to relate effectively to others, to motivate and lead, to be clear-minded, well-organized, well-informed, and intelligent. The implication for the student teacher is that failure as a teacher may be interpreted as personal failure and lack of wider personal competence in the sense that one or more of these traits is found to be lacking. Perceptions of this kind increase the pressures on students in an already demanding socialization context. Student teaching is therefore not only a period which may involve changes in values, attitudes and beliefs about education, schools, children, and the world generally, but also one which may involve stress and considerable personal reappraisal (see *Induction of Beginning Teachers*).

The situation is further complicated by the fact that student teachers must reassess their perceptions of the physical and social environment of the schools which previously they have known only as pupils. It is therefore not too surprising that student teachers' affective responses to these experiences have long held the attention of researchers. Studies have been made of a wide range of feeling states including values, attitudes, concerns and anxiety, commitment, and aspirations. Studies of student teacher affect have also embraced self-attitudes. These have included students' self-perceptions in particular contexts, and their more generalized or global concept of self as individuals or as teachers; their beliefs and assumptions about what kinds of people they are and what are their significant traits and characteristics. There has also been considerable interest in the related concept, self-esteem, which refers to student teachers' self-judgment or feelings of personal adequacy. This interest in self-attitudes arises from the acknowledgment that student teaching is a demanding social context likely to stimulate considerable introspection.

These various aspects of student teacher affect are unstable in the context of teaching experience and have thus attracted interest in the nature and direction of their change. However, such changes in feeling states have generally been studied in isolation of each other, and little attempt has been made to relate them within any general theory of socialization.

Research on student teacher affect has thus been wide ranging and for the present purposes it has been necessary to organize it somewhat arbitrarily around the following psychological constructs which relate to noncognitive aspects of the student teacher's personality:

(a) Values, attitudes, and interests

(b) Self-concept and self-esteem

(c) Concerns and anxiety

(d) Commitment

Although personality traits such as dogmatism, rigidity, and introversion have been included in earlier and more detailed reviews of teacher personality and characteristics (Getzels and Jackson 1963), they have been excluded from the present discussion except where they

have been directly associated with measures of student teacher affect (see *Teachers' Personality*). This is because they relate to behaviour styles rather than to feeling states.

Because there is considerable continuity between training and early teaching experience many studies of student teacher affect have extended into the first year of full-time teaching. Professional learning and personal change extend well beyond the college exit. The individual continues to formulate educational perspectives and to acquire the knowledge and skills necessary to cope with professional life.

Very broadly, teacher affect research may be grouped into three categories. The first is descriptive–comparative research which has sought to describe various affective states of student teachers and to compare and contrast them with those of other groups such as students preparing to enter other professions. The second category is socialization research which has considered the nature of change in students' affective states as they pass through their teacher education programmes and commence full-time teaching. The third category of studies is student teacher effectiveness research which has focused on relationships between affective characteristics and various measures of effectiveness such as pupil growth or supervisors' ratings. Studies in this category are part of a larger body of research which has sought to identify personality and other characteristics related to effectiveness, which could provide criteria for teacher selection and evaluation (see *Selection for Teaching*).

1. Student Teacher Values, Attitudes, and Interests

Student teachers have been described in terms of the general value orientations which underpin their attitudes toward specific professional issues. In reality many studies of student teacher attitudes are also studies of values in the sense that response patterns on attitude inventories reveal underlying value emphases such as conservatism, liberalism, or pragmatism. There is a close relationship between these wider personal value systems which students bring to teaching, and their professional attitudes. It has been suggested that knowing the life philosophy of student teachers might assist in decisions relating to their assignment to supervisors.

Other studies have sought to identify the nonvocational interests which distinguish student teachers from other groups. In general these have shown that the interests and leisure activities of student teachers are similar to those of other students. Part of this research has been guided by the hypothesis that if the individual is to be effective and happy in a profession such as teaching, then he or she might be expected to share many of the same interests such as nonvocational leisure pursuits and preferences as "average" individuals already successfully involved in the profession. There is much overlap between and within studies of values, attitudes, and interests of student teachers because the terms have been loosely defined and used with little consistency.

1.1 Descriptive–Comparative Research

(a) *Student teachers and other student groups*. Student teachers distinguish themselves from other student groups in terms of their values. Compared with other groups they have a stronger value commitment to people and tend to place greater emphasis on personal relationships. They place correspondingly less emphasis on economic success and what is seen by other groups as efficient or practical

Clear and consistent value differences between education and noneducation students have been indicated by Australian studies (Anderson 1974). Students in law, medicine, education, and engineering in several Australian universities were compared in terms of their intellectual and academic interests, political beliefs, and a number of personality characteristics. Education students (with law) scored highest on intellectual interests, and political–economic liberalism, but were lowest in terms of economic interests, or the desire to have a strong academic or research component in their work. Also, when compared with the other three professional groups, education students' images of the successful practitioner were less clear, as were their notions about the nature of their future profession in terms of the services to be provided. Although these differences have been identified between student teachers and other groups they are less significant than those which exist between different subgroups of student teachers, and students and experienced teachers.

(b) *Student teachers and experienced teachers*. There have been countless comparisons of student teachers and experienced teachers in terms of professional attitudes. A consistent finding is that students hold a far more liberal view of the relationship between school and society, and much more idealistic, progressive, supportive pupil-related attitudes, although these differences tend to diminish with practical teaching experience. A major weakness of much of this comparative research has been its failure to take account of the selective elimination or "winnowing" from training programmes of those students who hold attitudes which are at odds with those held by practising teachers. Longitudinal studies which have tracked the same students over time indicate that students most likely to leave teaching are those who hold more liberal educational attitudes. Attitude differences between student and experienced teacher groups may therefore diminish partly because student teachers' attitudes change with experience, and partly because the nature and composition of the student teacher group itself changes.

(c) *Males and females*. Female student teachers are more tender-minded and pupil-supportive, and less authoritarian than males. These differences tend to be stronger among secondary than primary student teachers. The most common explanations are that females have higher needs for nurturance and affiliation and

selectively enter primary teaching; and that secondary age children pose a greater threat to male teachers' authority and status and evoke more authoritarian responses.

(d) *Committed and noncommitted student teachers*. Student teachers who express satisfaction with, and commitment to, teaching as a long-term career hold attitudes which are more educationally conservative and less pupil-supportive than do less committed students. As a conservative value position aligns more closely with that exemplified by a majority of experienced teachers, lack of commitment to teaching has been interpreted as arising from students' perceptions of incongruity between their own professional values and attitudes and those they may be required to exemplify as practising teachers. Depending on the availability of work outside teaching such students have been able to resolve this perceived conflict by pursuing alternative careers.

1.2 Socialization Research

An overwhelming majority of socialization studies have focused on attitude change, particularly in the area of pupil control. A handful of studies has investigated the nature of change in student teachers' wider personal values during training. In a four year longitudinal study Anderson (1974), for example, found that education students, along with students preparing for law, medicine, and engineering, developed their intellectual interests, became less dogmatic, less pragmatic and cynical, and less conservative with respect to social and political issues. These value changes were interpreted as being in harmony with the liberalizing goals of university education.

Studies of attitude change are legion. The major concern has been to describe the nature of the change (usually within the limits of pupil control ideology), and then to explain it in terms of socialization theory. The repetitiveness of this area of research has been relieved only by a shift from functionalist to more interpretative approaches.

(a) *The nature of attitude change*. Socialization research has revealed a consistent pattern of change in professional attitudes. Whatever the attitude scales used, classroom experience during and after teacher training has been shown to bring with it the development of more custodial pupil-related attitudes as measured by the Pupil Control Ideology (PCI) Form (Willower et al. 1967); more tough-mindedness as indexed by the Manchester N R and T scales (Morrison and McIntyre 1967); and more conservatism and pragmatism according to the Minnesota Teacher Attitude Inventory (MTAI). As a group these studies suggest that the development of the student teacher's professional attitudes is a two-phased process in which idealistic, progressive attitudes during course work in the training institution are reversed after classroom experience. Several studies have reported that a peak in student teachers' progressivism and idealism occurs at the midpoint of training, when, in terms of time, they are furthest removed from the school situation.

Another group of studies has focused on the effects of training and early teaching experience on student teachers' racial attitudes. Australian research (Chambers 1981) indicates that attitudes toward Australian Aboriginals may be changed by preservice intervention courses in Aboriginal Studies. After these courses student teachers' attitudes shift from a simple acknowledgment of the need for equality in terms of civil rights, to a recognition of Aboriginals' rights to be separate if they wish, and to have access to differential provisions such as land rights. The effects of these courses are maintained, if not improved, once graduate teachers are in their teaching placements. Apparently full-time experience provides opportunities to directly observe such things as the extent of prejudice amongst children and how difficult it is to modify, indicating that their college courses were not theoretical and exaggerated, but practical and realistic. The flow-on effects of these attitudes on pupils' racial attitudes are less impressive because children's attitudes are a product of a complex set of environmental influences of which the teacher is but one part. Moreover, there is a predisposition by student teachers and their supervisors to avoid affective strategies in favour of information processing.

Patterns of attitude change have been examined for Australian student teachers in both urban and rural training colleges. There is a considerable body of evidence that the more negative racial attitudes held by rural people generally are reflected by rural student teachers. However, intervention programmes which include black lecturers, contact with black pupils, and other forms of "equal" status contact tend to eradicate negative stereotypes, and these positive effects are maintained during the first year of teaching. These findings are supported by the effects on student teachers of various humanities curriculum projects in the United States and the United Kingdom. These projects also emphasize the need for affective teaching strategies and equal status contact with minority racial groups.

(b) *Reality shock*. The increased custodialism, pragmatism, and conservatism which occurs as students approach the point of entry to the teaching profession has been explained in terms of "reality shock" which occurs after contact with the real teaching context during practice, and the concomitant realization that the real and ideal worlds of teaching are very different. Wright and Tuska (1966) describe this transition from the ideal to the real as one in which the student moves from "dream" at the time of decision to become a teacher, through the "play" of teacher training, to "life" as a full-time practitioner. As "life" begins with the end of training and the commencement of full-time teaching, attitudes are apparently influenced by what the students see and what they hear from experienced teachers. Senior colleagues are often not the community of scholars that had been expected, pupils often do not share their intellectual interests, and other experienced colleagues do not share their idealistic attitudes concerning teacher–pupil relationships. Reality shock has been similarly described for neophytes in other professions, including medical interns and law students. Students in various professions apparently bring to the training situation "lay images" of professional life. These prior conceptions of what the work will entail are often unrealistic in the sense that they fail to express the more humdrum routine components of the role and also fail to acknowledge aspects of the work place which ultimately force the student to assess more realistically his or her professional goals. Many students, for example, believe that the development of close interpersonal relationships with pupils is an essential aspect of good teaching. They discover, however, that the necessity of working with large classes forces them to deal with groups rather than individuals and that this often inhibits the development of close teacher–pupil relationships. This process of role clarification proceeds as students reinterpret earlier observations, and is a powerful factor in attitude change. It is also a functional aspect of the socialization process in the sense that it smooths students' transition into the teacher role by giving them a more realistic picture of the work place.

(c) *The influence of experienced teachers*. Early studies explained attitude change in terms of the organizational press on young teachers to change their professional attitudes in the direction of those held by more experienced teacher colleagues and supervisors. Typical of this early socialization perspective was the comment of Waller (1935), who observed that

> The significant people for a school teacher are the other teachers, and by comparison with good standing in that fraternity, the good opinion of students is a small thing and of little price. A landmark in one's assimilation to the profession is that moment when he decides that only teachers are important. (p. 389)

Later studies suggest that it is not just teachers in general who exert influence on younger teachers, but that it is older teachers who are prominent in the informal power structure who are significant in reshaping the beginning teacher's attitudes. Edgar and Warren (1969) argue that colleagues per se and the general attitudes of the work group are less important to beginning teachers than are the attitudes of significant evaluators. They conclude that in an organizational setting such as a school, where the greatest sanctions centre on work performance rather than on informal personal relations, student teacher attitudes are more likely to change in the direction of those held by evaluators who have the power to sanction. In addition, strong positive affect between the beginning teacher and the evaluator is a further motivational aspect of change.

(d) *Student teachers as active participants in the socialization process*. Early socialization studies defined teacher trainees as "empty vessels" to be filled with the professional perceptions of more experienced teachers.

They reflect the perspective expressed by Danziger (1971) who described the focus of socialization as being not upon "the active shaping of his life by the individual, but on the plasticity and passivity of the individual in the face of social influence" (Danziger 1971 p. 114).

More recently the student teacher has been acknowledged as an active participant who enters the socialization process not as an "empty vessel" but as an individual who, by virtue of his or her own experience as a pupil, already has a detailed and elaborate conception of the teacher's role. According to Lortie (1975), student teachers enter training with teaching models so strongly embedded in their consciousness that they reject those presented by the training institution which are at odds with their preconceptions of the role. Any changes in the direction of progressivism during training may therefore be only superficial or "managed" to meet the expectations of college lecturers. Far from being naive, passive objects to be easily moulded by college lecturers and practice teaching supervisors, the student teachers are already well along the socialization path through their own "apprenticeship of observation". Their attitudes and beliefs are not fixed or final. As student teachers they may actively reinterpret the data which they have collected in the past (Lacey 1977) and develop a "teacher perspective" in which familiar situations are seen in a new way. The initiative for this reinterpretation, however, derives largely from within the neophytes, rather than externally from agents who seek to influence them. Lacey (1977) further develops the notion of beginning teachers as actively participating in the socialization process by describing various strategies they employ to assert or retain their own professional values in the face of organizational pressure to change. Where values are consistent with their own there may be "internalized adjustment" in the sense that new teachers really believe in what they are doing. However, they may only "strategically comply" and merely seem to be conforming where they harbour reservations about particular organizational values, but seek to avoid confrontation; and in some circumstances they may seek to "strategically redefine" the situation by reshaping the attitudes and values of their more senior colleagues.

This redefinition of the student teacher as an active rather than passive agent reflects not only a disenchantment with earlier functionalist models, but also a recognition by researchers that there have been profound changes in attitudes toward authority and organizational participation more generally. The student teacher of the 1980s may be less susceptible to moulding than Waller's student of the 1930s. Accordingly it is now more necessary than ever that researchers employ conceptual frameworks which provide access to student teachers' views of the world, and which describe what they are doing to shape their role rather than simply being coerced by the expectations of others.

Most of the early research which sought to describe and explain student teacher attitude change within socialization theory tended to be gross in conception and to seek the collective student viewpoint rather than the diversity within it. This approach gave little opportunity of seeing issues qualitatively through student teachers' eyes. Moreover, the use of established attitude scales constrained student teachers' responses within predetermined limits. This approach contrasts sharply with microsocial analysis in which interviews and other participant observational methods have been used to describe the day-to-day routine and responses of medical interns and student nurses. It is only recently that student teacher research has more consistently used similar interpretive approaches. These approaches have revealed the complexity of professional socialization and the extent to which it is a more interactive, provisional and negotiated process than was suggested by earlier research models.

1.3 Teacher Effectiveness Research

(a) *Early studies.* These attempted to relate student teachers' values, attitudes, and interests to ratings of teaching performance. They are part of a much larger body of research which has investigated the relationships between teachers' personal characteristics and their teaching performance. This research has been reviewed by Getzels and Jackson (1963) in the *First Handbook of Research on Teaching.* That review revealed little evidence of relationships of any strength, consistency, or consequence between student teacher effectiveness and their values, attitudes, or interests. For example, from the findings of the many studies which used the Allport, Vernon, Lindzey Study of Values Scales, it was concluded that the usefulness of that instrument for discriminating between good and bad teachers (including student teachers) had not been established. A similar conclusion was drawn from the many attempts to relate student teacher effectiveness to vocational preferences and nonvocational interests and activities. Reported relationships were inconsistent and difficult to interpret in terms of their relevance to student teaching performance. Finally, scores on the most widely used professional attitude scale, the Minnesota Teacher Attitude Inventory, failed to relate consistently to student teaching performance. This is ironical in the sense that a high score on the MTAI has persistently been acclaimed as the hallmark of a good teacher. The failure of these early studies to demonstrate relationships between student teacher attitudes, values, interests, and performance may be attributable in part to the gross nature of the variables considered. For example, despite evidence that student teachers in various subject areas hold different values and interests, they have generally been considered together as one group of education students with homogeneous characteristics.

(b) *Attitudes toward different pupils and groups.* More recently research has focused on the effect on teaching behaviour of student teachers' attitudes toward particular pupils and groups. This is part of the teacher expectations research reviewed by Brophy and Good (1974) and which demonstrates clearly that student teachers, like experienced teachers, hold expectations for particular pupils which may influence their teaching behaviour in relation to them. These expectations may serve as self-fulfilling prophecies of achievement if they affect the quantity and quality of interaction with pupils. Student teachers who believe that some pupils are less able to achieve, may behave in ways which are likely to bring about failure by providing less reinforcement, corrective feedback, encouragement, and persistence in failure situations. Expectations of this kind may be derived from a student teacher's preconceptions about children of different race, socioeconomic background, sex, or their supervisors' comments and convictions about the potential of particular pupils or groups.

This latter group of studies represents a more successful attempt to relate student teacher attitudes to teaching behaviour and pupil achievement. They have proceeded within a much stronger theoretical framework developed by Brophy and Good (1974) and others, and have relied more heavily on direct observation of classroom behaviour.

(c) *The shift in research from student teacher affect to student teacher behaviour.* Since the early 1970s there has been a swing away from presage–product research; a disenchantment with attempting to predict effectiveness from characteristics such as values and attitudes which student teachers bring to the training situation. This change in emphasis has occurred in leadership research more generally, remembering that student teaching is a special case of leadership in which the concern is also to change a group's behaviour in some desired direction. Leadership research in other contexts such as industry, commerce, and the armed forces has also had limited success in identifying meaningful and consistent relationships between personal characteristics and leader effectiveness in terms of subordinate ratings, satisfaction, morale, or other criteria. This is because of the complexity of the relationships between traits within any one leader, and in turn, the complexity of the interactions between those characteristics and the leadership context, be it a classroom, school, or factory floor. Leadership research generally has thus focused more recently upon the question of which behaviours are effective in certain contexts. Likewise, student teacher effectiveness research has turned its attention from the question of which personal characteristics predict effective teaching behaviour, to a concern with identifying behaviours which might provide a list of competencies in which students might be trained to be effective. This shift in emphasis from traits to behaviours is well-illustrated by the increased emphasis which the *Second Handbook of Research on Teaching* (Travers 1973) gives to the effects of teacher training on student teacher behaviours and their consequences for pupil achievement; and by the sharply reduced emphasis on student teachers' affective characteristics compared with the *First Handbook of Research on Teaching* (Gage 1963) published a decade earlier.

2. Student Teacher Self-concept and Self-esteem

Despite the importance which theorists have attached to the self generally, and the evidence that self-concept relates to academic attainment and to professional performance, relatively little interest has been shown in self-concept or self-esteem among student teachers. Indeed, the *Second Handbook of Research on Teaching* (Travers 1973) does not contain a single entry on either student teacher self-concept or self-esteem. This may be explained partly by educational researchers' disenchantment with presage variables and their commitment to the direct observation of teacher behaviour. The shift from teacher characteristics research to classroom observational research occurred at the very time when empirical evidence began to point more clearly to the significance of self-concept for teaching behaviour. The lack of attention to self-concept may also have been due to the inordinate level of attention to student teachers' professional attitudes and values. This emphasis was encouraged by the ready availability of teacher attitude scales and a very narrow conceptualization of teacher socialization as encompassing change only in the area of attitudes and values. Consequently studies of student teacher self-concept are fewer in number and more recent than those concerned with attitudes.

They reveal that professional self-concept is multidimensional in the sense that student teachers are able to describe themselves along different dimensions such as creativity, lucidity, warmth–supportiveness, energy–enthusiasm, and orderliness. Student teacher self-concept is also unstable. Studies which have tracked students from one teaching context to another reveal that they see themselves differently with different pupil groups, although some dimensions of self-concept are more stable than others. For example, lucidity and orderliness are more stable than warmth–supportiveness and energy–enthusiasm, presumably because the latter two dimensions are more readily affected by the quality of the student teacher's relationships with different pupil groups. This instability of self-concept suggests that research designs which rely on one measure of global professional concept, or "self as a teacher in general", may oversimplify a complex construct.

A major area of confusion has been the inconsistency with which key terms have been used. Some investigators have used the term self-concept in a descriptive sense and have reserved self-esteem for evaluative purposes. It is not unusual, however, to encounter references to "high" and "low" self-concept scores where no distinction is drawn between self-concept and self-esteem. Whereas self-concept is used most often to refer to global self-view, it is used interchangeably with terms such as self-perception, self-attitudes, self-image, and self-view.

2.1 Descriptive–Comparative Research

(a) *Differences in teaching levels and specializations.* Student teachers of older age groups tend to see themselves more positively than do teachers of younger children. Also, students preparing to teach in special schools have been reported as having less positive self-concepts. The reasons for these differences are unclear, but the most common (although not necessarily the most acceptable) explanation has been that student teachers with less positive self-concepts are attracted to teach younger and handicapped children who are less likely to threaten their sense of adequacy. Other research supports the view that certain age groups may be more threatening than others to student teachers. For example, secondary student teachers assigned to middle-secondary-school classrooms tend to see themselves less positively after practice teaching than do students who complete practice with either lower- or upper-secondary classes where problems of pupil control are perceived as less challenging.

(b) *Student teachers and other professions.* Self-ratings by student teachers have been compared with those of other students including counsellor trainees, army officer cadets, high-school students, priests, and noneducation students generally. Higher levels of congruency between actual and ideal self-concepts (more satisfactory levels of adjustment) have been observed in groups such as counsellor trainees and army officer cadets than in student teachers. These differences have been attributed to stronger levels of occupational commitment and vocational interest within the nonteaching groups.

Predictably, studies which have compared education and noneducation students have revealed that student teachers picture themselves more clearly in the teacher role and have much readier access to educational imagery than do students in other professional groups. Studies which have used projective tests reveal that student teachers more readily use educational terms on sentence completion and word association tests, are able to draw more richly detailed pictures of themselves in teaching contexts and are more willing than noneducation students to defend the public status of the teaching profession. In "draw a teacher tests" student teachers tend to give greater emphasis to their status as authority figures in classrooms by drawing themselves larger and more centrally in the teaching context than do students in nonteaching programmes. However, not all student teachers are so ego involved in, and identified with, teaching. Not surprisingly, those who express a lack of commitment to teaching as a career produce responses on projective tests which are similar to noneducation students.

2.2 Socialization Research

Early studies suggest that student teachers see themselves less positively after practice teaching. This is especially the case for student teachers assigned to teach in difficult contexts including lower socioeconomic groups. Generally, these changes have been attributed to a sense of professional inadequacy arising from students' perceptions that they fail to cope. For example, decline in self-esteem after practice teaching in low socioeconomic areas has been explained in terms of students' belief that their inadequacies as teachers, and more generally as persons, are responsible for the failure to achieve by economically poorer children.

Practice teaching more generally is seen as promoting a conflict between student teachers' belief that they should establish close supportive relationships with children on the one hand, and maintain social distance and authority on the other. Their perceptions that they fail to satisfactorily resolve that particular conflict may cause a decline in professional self-esteem. A further explanation of these declines is that student teachers are often placed in practice teaching contexts which, in terms of the size of the pupil group and the knowledge of the curriculum which is required, demand a level of skill which they do not yet possess; declines in professional self-esteem thus arise from their inability to cope with the task.

Most studies of self-concept change during practice teaching have taken several measures, including self-ratings on various dimensions of professional and wider personal self-concept, self-esteem, and self-ideal congruence. Comparison of change in professional and nonprofessional self-concepts have revealed differences between elementary and secondary student teachers. Elementary students are more prone than secondary students to record declines in measures of both professional and personal aspects of self-esteem after practice teaching. Apparently secondary student teachers are more able to keep their professional and wider personal roles clearly separated. In the case of the elementary student teacher, where there is less emphasis on subject matter, and where the role involves closer and more continuous association with the same group of pupils, it may be more difficult to compartmentalize self and role; any perception of professional failure in the elementary student teacher may be more readily interpreted as arising from wider personal inadequacies.

Differences in professional self-concept change during early teaching experience are also associated with personality factors. Before practice teaching experience secondary student teachers who are socially extroverted, less flexible, and less anxious see themselves as being more professionally creative, lucid, organized and as more fully attaining their professional goals than do their more flexible, socially introverted, anxious peers. These differences become more pronounced after practice teaching experience. Social extroversion, rigidity and, to a lesser extent, lower anxiety are apparently personality characteristics which assist student teachers to adjust and survive better in teaching contexts which demand task oriented, highly structured and socially interactive teaching performances. Further evidence of these relationships derives from strong correlations between student teachers' scores on the extroversion scale of the Eisenck Personality Inventory and self-esteem, although the self-esteem measures have usually related to general rather than professional self-esteem.

The relationships between self-concept change and personality are complex. For example, there is a strong interaction between anxiety and flexibility. Anxiety is related to unsatisfactory professional adjustment and lower levels of professional self-esteem, provided that the student teacher is also flexible. Apparently anxiety is not a factor in professional adjustment if the student teacher is sufficiently inflexible to "shelter" within the tight structure which is afforded by highly task-focused, logically sequenced lessons. The relationship between professional self-concept change and anxiety is further complicated by the distinction between trait and state anxiety. It appears that there is a significant relationship between state anxiety and self-concept change during early teaching experience, but not between trait anxiety and self-concept change. Apparently student teaching may evoke anxiety in individuals who are not generally anxious, and does so to such an extent that some students (particularly the more introverted and flexible) perceive themselves as performing inadequately.

Whatever the reasons for declines in self-esteem after practice teaching, this phenomenon has stirred the interest of teacher educators since the early 1970s. The acknowledgment of the link between self-concept and performance has slowly led teacher educators to the conviction that positive self-concept should be promoted and enhanced rather than eroded by programme experiences. For this reason they have sought to identify training structures which maintain and promote positive self-concept in student teachers. Consequently, by far the largest number of student teacher self-concept studies relate to the exploration of links between training practices and self-concept change. These studies have revealed that supportive college supervisory practices are associated with the enhancement of self-concept; and that student teachers who are inducted gradually into large classes through small group practice teaching experience see themselves more positively than do students who are required to commence practice with large pupil groups. Other training programme characteristics associated with the development of a positive professional self-concept include tutoring, humanistic education courses, outward bound type experiences, and group counselling and guidance sessions in which student teachers share new teaching problems and experiences.

2.3 Teacher Effectiveness Research

As has been the case with student teacher attitude research, relationships have been sought between self-concept and effective teaching. Most investigations have shown a link between teaching performance and student teacher self-concept. For example, student teachers rated high on practice teaching hold positive self-attitudes, while student teachers rated low on teaching competence have low self-esteem and experience emotional stress during practice. The analysis in studies of this kind has been correlational and the direction of the relationship between self-concept and performance is never indicated; that is, high performance could have contributed to positive self-concept, or positive self-concept could have caused high achievement, in the sense that individuals who are confident and expect to be successful tend to behave in ways which are likely to bring it about.

Although the precise nature of the association between student teacher self-concept and teaching performance is still unclear, it is likely that the relationship is a reciprocal one; that is, each interacts with and directly influences the other. On the one hand students may feel positively because they have performed well and, in turn, positive self-concept may enhance the likelihood of successful subsequent performances in similar teaching contexts. Because of the reciprocal nature of the relationship between self-concept and performance it is generally argued as important that student teachers are placed in practice teaching contexts which maximize opportunities for success.

3. Student Teacher Concerns and Anxiety

3.1 Descriptive Research

There has been abundant research into the problems or concerns perceived by student teachers. Inventories of concerns reveal that student teachers worry most about their relationships with supervisors, their ability to maintain discipline, being liked by pupils, knowing their subject matter, having enough material to teach, and relating effectively to parents and other members of staff. Few studies have gone beyond simply identifying problems to the point of explaining why students are anxious in particular contexts, how much stress they experience, how they cope with their anxiety, and what are the implications of anxiety for pupil learning.

Early studies tended to define problems or concerns as equivalent to anxiety. Keavney and Sinclair (1978), in their review of teacher anxiety research, observed that any attempt to equate anxiety with concerns must necessarily fail to deal with the kind of anxiety which arises from the inability to identify the underlying problem or concern—the inability to trace the origin of anxiety. A further distinction between concerns and anxiety has been illustrated by the changes which take place in these two related phenomena during early teaching experience. While anxiety declines after teaching experience, concerns change in nature but do not diminish. This change in concerns is from worries about self-adequacy as a student teacher, to worries about pupils and the work as an experienced professional teacher. Perhaps these latter areas of concern are less anxiety evoking and, because of this, anxiety declines after teaching experience. In the absence of evidence to that effect, however, it is more fruitful to regard anxiety and concerns as related but discrete phenomena.

3.2 Teacher Effectiveness Research

Keavney and Sinclair (1978) discuss the consequences of teacher anxiety for pupil learning. They note that anxiety encourages the type of dogmatic stance as a means of defending the self. The outcome of such a stance is a more authoritarian classroom style with greater dominance by the teacher of interaction in talk, less verbal support, and less use of inquiry and open-ended discussion. This view has been supported by several studies which have detected increases in levels of dogmatism during teacher training. Further evidence of this relationship between anxiety and authoritarian practices as a coping strategy derives from research which has demonstrated that declines in student teacher anxiety are accompanied by increased custodialism as measured by the PCI Scales. This view is also supported by studies which show that anxious student teachers who see themselves as most satisfactorily coping with their role are those who are also inflexible and dogmatic.

Other studies of student teaching have revealed that pupil groups taught by anxious teachers obtain lower grades and are more hostile. However, it is also true that anxious teachers tend to give lower grades and this could explain the negative relationship between anxiety and pupil achievement. Moreover, all of the studies of student teacher anxiety are correlational and do not indicate whether it is anxiety which causes negative affect in the classroom, or whether pupil hostility causes the student teacher to be anxious. To clarify the direction of the relationship between anxiety and classroom climate it would therefore be necessary to directly observe the sequence of events between student teachers and their pupils to determine whether anxiety is in fact a cause rather than an effect. In the meantime, it is clear that anxiety arising from concerns relating to self-adequacy is commonly associated with the student teaching experience and that such anxiety is associated with classroom conditions which are not optimal for pupil learning.

4. Student Teacher Commitment

Most often commitment to teaching has been defined narrowly as anticipated length of stay in the teaching profession. It has been related to such factors as academic and practice teaching performance, professional attitudes, personality, sex, and perceived career prospects. Student teachers with strong academic performance backgrounds, especially in specialist subject areas which are in demand outside teaching, tend to be less committed. Students with weak and less specialized academic backgrounds have generally been reported as more committed, even where they are unsatisfied by teaching. This is presumably because they have little occupational mobility and see themselves as being locked into teaching. Another widespread finding is that male student teachers anticipate a much longer career in teaching than do females, who regard it as a contingent occupation; females generally perceive their continued participation in teaching as depending upon marriage, child raising, and the location of their spouses' work. This measure of commitment (anticipated length of stay) may say more about the state of the labour market outside teaching than it does about an individual's attraction to the profession. In times of economic growth, when opportunities for resignation and re-employment are favourable, this kind of commitment may be generally lower; in periods of economic recession, or in times of teacher oversupply, it may be generally high because of the attractiveness of any kind of employment. This particular measure of commitment is therefore unstable in terms of changing demographic, political, and economic factors which affect teacher supply and demand. Researchers have therefore sought measures which are less easily influenced by changing circumstances.

Recently commitment has been defined more broadly as the value attributed by the student teacher to the activity of teaching. Studies which have adopted this definition have revealed that student teachers' professional self-perceptions increasingly explain differences in level of commitment during the course of training; that is, the way in which student teachers view themselves in their professional role increasingly influences their evaluation of teaching generally. The degree to which young teachers perceive self-competence in behaviours associated with the professional role, and see themselves as fulfilling important professional goals rather than being frustrated and thwarted, is a major determinant of professional commitment. This area of research indicates that a student teacher is likely to be both committed to teaching and to have positive self-perceptions after teacher training (or to be uncommitted and to have less positive self-perceptions), irrespective of whether that student was committed and/or had positive professional self-perceptions prior to training. Because initial commitment is not necessarily related to commitment at the end of training, it is an inappropriate criterion to apply to the selection of student teachers into teacher education programmes. A further finding of research in this area is that there are no significant differences in commitment of this kind expressed by males and females.

5. Conclusion

Research in this area is characterized by lack of communication of two kinds. The first concerns research into different aspects of student teacher affect. Research into attitudes, for example, has generally proceeded along its own narrow path with little reference to work in related areas such as self-concept, commitment, or student teachers' concerns. This isolationism is surprising in the light of quite promising evidence that affective states of student teachers are closely interrelated, and that where there is change in one area there is often concomitant change in another. Such relationships have been indicated between self-concept, professional attitudes, and commitment.

There has also been a lack of communication between researchers in the areas of student teacher affect and student teacher behaviour. Although researchers in the latter area have claimed that antecedent or related feeling states have little importance for the study of teaching behaviour, there are clear linkages between what student teachers feel and how they perform. This is indicated by the complex relationships between self-concept and performance, and between anxiety and teacher behaviour. Perhaps the lack of communication has been encouraged by the failure of early teacher characteristics research to indicate relationships between certain aspects of affect and teaching effectiveness. More recent research which has involved different aspects of affect such as self-concept and anxiety, and which has used multivariate analysis within stronger theoretical frameworks has produced more promising results.

The development of a coherent picture of student teacher affect and its relationship to behaviour has thus been inhibited by a reluctance by researchers in different areas to communicate and build on the others' findings. Such coherence has also been discouraged by the lack of a comprehensive theory of teacher socialization. Professional socialization involves much more than personal change in one or more of the areas of affect; it concerns personal change across a wide range of affective and behavioural characteristics and includes not only the development of actual competence through the acquisition of professional knowledge and skills, but also the related development of self-competence which derives from a belief in the value of the activity of teaching and the conviction of one's capacity to perform adequately in the role. Recognition of the relatedness of these two aspects of professional socialization, the affective and the behavioural, is a precondition for a theory of teacher socialization which is sufficiently comprehensive to encourage researchers to move beyond a single and narrow area of focus.

See also: Professional Socialization of Teachers; Teachers' Personality

Bibliography

Anderson D S 1974 *The Development of Student-teachers: A Comparative Study of Professional Socialization.* Organisation for Economic Co-operation and Development (OECD), Paris

Brophy J E, Good T L 1974 *Teacher–Student Relationships: Causes and Consequences.* Holt, Rinehart and Winston, New York

Chambers B 1981 *Why Can't They be Like us?* Australian Institute of Aboriginal Studies, Canberra

Danziger K 1971 *Socialization.* Penguin, Harmondsworth

Edgar D E, Warren R L 1969 Power and autonomy in teacher socialization. *Sociol. Educ.* 42: 386–499

Gage N L (ed.) 1963 *Handbook of Research on Teaching: A Project of the American Educational Research Association.* Rand McNally, Chicago, Illinois

Getzels J W, Jackson P W 1963 The teacher's personality and characteristics. In: Gage N L (ed.) 1963

Keavney G, Sinclair K E 1978 Teacher concerns and teacher anxiety: A neglected topic of classroom research. *Rev. Educ. Res.* 48: 273–90

Lacey C 1977 *The Socialization of Teachers.* Methuen, London

Lortie D C 1975 *Schoolteachers: A Sociological Study.* University of Chicago Press, Chicago, Illinois

Morrison A, McIntyre D 1967 Changes in the opinions about education during the first year of teaching. *Br. J. Soc. Cl. Psychol.* 6: 161–63

Travers R M W (ed.) 1973 *Second Handbook of Research on Teaching: A Project of the American Educational Research Association.* Rand McNally, New York

Waller W 1935 *The Sociology of Teaching.* Wiley, New York

Willower D J, Eidell T L, Hoy W K 1967 *The School and Pupil Control Ideology.* Pennsylvania State Studies, No. 24. Pennsylvania State University, University Park, Pennsylvania

Wright B D, Tuska S A 1968 From dream to life and the psychology of becoming a teacher. *Sch. Rev.* 76: 253–93

Teachers' Expectations

C. Braun

"Teacher expectation," "self-fulfilling prophecy," and "teacher faith" are terms associated with the hypothesis that teachers create realities commensurate with their perceptions of students. The corollary is that the learner, in turn, makes his or her other reality—a reality substantially grounded in the reality of the teacher. This describes the mediating mechanisms that potentially bring about these expectancy phenomena. It is suggested that teachers act on their perceptions about individuals so as to provide differential treatment to them, and that such treatment can interact with pupil self-expectations to produce expected outcomes.

A landmark study by Rosenthal and Jacobson (1968) stimulated both interest and controversy when they announced to the educational world, findings that pupils mirror teachers' expectations in their school performance. The researchers submitted to elementary teachers a list of randomly selected "academic bloomers" who were given an intelligence test, ostensibly to norm the test. According to the researchers, this externally imposed information induced expectancies in teachers' minds which, in turn, were reflected in significantly greater intellectual gains in "academic bloomers" than in other children.

Publication of the Rosenthal–Jacobson study met with immediate enthusiasm from the educational community but methodological and generalizability concerns were raised by many about the study.

The concept of the self-fulfilling prophecy has generated volumes of research (Finn 1972, Brophy and Good 1974, Braun 1976, Darley and Fazio 1980). The concept continues to generate research, theory, and controversy. This is testimony to the importance of the construct, which is central to many of the practical implications of the sociopsychological dynamics in classroom settings.

While investigations continue to generate considerable evidence confirming the expectancy phenomenon in experimental settings, and in nonexperimental social interaction settings, the educator should bear in mind some of the problems which have clouded some investigations and many interpretations since the Rosenthal and Jacobson study. First, whether or not expectancies are artificially or naturally induced must be considered in any interpretation. It is reasonable to expect that self-generated expectancies are more potent than artificially induced expectancies (Braun 1976). Further, the results of some of the investigations remain equivocal partly because they have failed to examine teacher self-generated expectancies and children's academic performance in relation to different levels of the social environment of children, at different levels of the intellectual scale, and for different age cohorts of children.

Perhaps, the most critical caution is that the expectancy context should not be viewed as a simple, social dyad involving a student and a teacher as two non-interacting components. Much of the earlier research suggests a simplistic, direct "teacher-alone" effect on children. The expectancy relationships which might develop within the interactive dyad involve: (a) teachers' expectations about students' academic ability; (b) students' expectations about their own abilities; and (c) teachers' and students' combined expectations about the latter's abilities.

The purpose of the discussion here is to examine, in detail, the processes underlying the complexities of classroom interaction. Earlier discussions attempting to elucidate the process are those by Braun (1976), Cooper (1979), Brophy (1979), and Darley and Fazio (1980).

1. The General Teacher Expectancy Cycle

The mediating mechanisms by which a perceiver's (teacher's) beliefs and expectancies can ultimately be realized in differential outcomes can be conceptualized as a cyclic sequence of events. Such cyclic flow does not connote a consistent one-way process, but rather an interactive feedback flow. The general flow can be conceptualized as follows: (a) the teacher forms differential expectations about different learners as a result of observations, beliefs, and stereotypes which he or she has encoded about learners (input factors); (b) the teacher reconstructs or modifies expectations of particular learners on the basis of particular interactive constellations of "input" and develops a "set" for action; (c) the teacher acts toward different learners in accordance with the "set" developed (teacher output factors); (d) the learner interprets the meaning of the teacher's action based on his or her unique set of beliefs about self, and self in relation to the teacher and forms self-expectations; (e) the learner acts on the teacher's "output" in accordance with his or her perception of the total situation (pupil output); (f) pupil "output" provides new data for teacher "input" either to confirm original expectations, to modify, or to refute them; (g) the learner interprets his or her own action. This interpretation may vary from acceptance of the action as appropriate and caused by the teacher's action to a new inference about the self as a learner (Darley and Fazio 1980).

The cyclical sequence outlined above is a modification of an earlier process model (Braun 1976) and bears many similarities to the cycle suggested by Darley and Fazio. In fact, the latter provide a number of explanatory notes which help elucidate the complexities of the interaction sequence. First, they suggest that the sequence may represent a cyclical process in that the perceiver's (teacher's) expectancy may have developed from previous "passes" through the sequence, or it may represent the beginning of the interaction. Second, the authors point out that while one of the individuals involved in the interaction is designated as the perceiver and the other the target, such a process can be "symmetric" in nature. By the same token, the identification of who the perceiver is in the sequence is often non-arbitrary, in which case the interaction is "nonsymmetric."

Having presented the general flow of the expectancy cycle, some of the mediating mechanisms and intermediary linkages can now be examined.

2. Teacher Expectancy—Potential Sources of Input

The interactive sequence is initiated by the teacher's formation of expectancies about the behavior of the learner. There is no doubt that expectancies can be inferred from several "inputs," each with various possible sources of bias (Darley and Fazio 1980). It is these biasing sources that must be borne in mind when examining "input factors."

Sources of "input" into teachers' expectancies are well-documented. Elashoff and Snow (1971) summarize the impact of a few of these sources:

> Teachers . . . form impressions based on physical appearance and conduct . . . achievement, IQ scores, or general characteristics of older siblings or parents. These impressions

based on a day's or a week's experience may produce expectations about pupil behavior and future achievement . . . . When teachers characterize pupils they are likely to label them as "good," or "bad." Clean children "good," dirty ones "bad"; or they may be "fast" or "slow" learners. (p. 63)

It is interesting to note that physical appearance heads the list of "input" factors. Research studies have claimed varying degrees of potency for this factor. Clifford and Walster (1973) concluded that attractive children were perceived by teachers to possess a higher IQ, greater educational potential, and more interested parents than less attractive children. Further documentation is provided by Dion (1972) who found that attractive children were perceived as less likely to be antisocial than unattractive children. He reported that attractive children who commit unacceptable acts were perceived as more honest and pleasant than unattractive children. While several studies have reported contradictory evidence, these studies involved artificial settings.

The dynamics underlying the relationship between sex bias and achievement are less clear than the fact that the bias exists. Such bias appears to be operative for young children as well as older students.

The sex bias may, in part, relate to the common belief that girls' behavior in classroom settings is more compliant and more consistent with general academic expectations (Braun 1976). It is suggested that acts of disapproval may often be stimulated by an expectancy that boys will need correction. Felker (1974) has hypothesized that girls have more areas in which they can receive approval and positive feedback than boys in a school setting. An interesting and illuminating investigation by Leinhardt et al. (1979) adds an entirely new dimension. They found that teachers made more academic contacts with girls in reading and with boys in mathematics. Teachers also spent relatively more cognitive time with girls in reading and boys in mathematics.

Another "input" factor is that of the learner's general psychosocial environment including race and social class which have been shown to lead to differential assignment of personality traits or stereotypes.

It has been shown that middle-class students are expected to receive higher grades than lower-class students, and that white middle-class students are held more internally responsible for failure than other students.

The interactive nature of environmental "input" variables is further elaborated by Marjoribanks (1978). He concluded that if children come from a deprived social environment or have a low intelligence level, and are perceived by teachers as having unfavorable school-related behavior, then they suffer a compounded deprivation in school achievement. However, if children are perceived as having favorable school behavior, then they are able to overcome, at least in part, the restrictions imposed by environment and intelligence test performance.

Another important investigation is that of Rotter (1975). Her study took into account teacher variability in relation to race and socioeconomic status (SES). She found that previous performance of children was the most significant variable in controlling expectations. When such information was not available, race and SES effects were nonsignificant. The author noted a "leaning backwards" effect for race, that is, black teachers tended to grade white middle-class pupils higher than other types, and white teachers tended to grade black lower-class pupils highest. However, Cornbleth and Korth (1980) found that teachers rated white students higher than black students with respect to potential achievement and classroom behavior. They also rated white students as more efficient, organized, reserved, industrious, and pleasant while black students were rated as more outgoing and more outspoken. Overall ratings were higher for white than for black students.

Much research is needed to explicate the intricacies and complexities of social environment influences on expectations held for others and, more particularly, how such expectations translate into differential treatment.

There are a few findings from research regarding the impact of teachers' perceptions of the intelligence of students. Barnard et al. (1968) found that teachers tend to rate brighter pupils in a more favorable light, attributing more positive characteristics to high-ability than to low-ability children. Further, Willis (1972) found a positive relationship between teacher judgment of student ability and teacher evaluation of student attention, self-confidence, maturity, and ability to work without supervision. Kehle (1974) attested to the importance of test information in interaction with information on sex, attractiveness, and race.

There is a cluster of variables related to "input" which includes student past and present achievement and psychological reports and a fairly consistent body of research documenting differential teacher/pupil interaction based on the teacher's perception of high or low achievement (Braun 1976, Brophy and Good 1974, Good et al. 1980, Rosenthal 1974).

A study by Mason (1973) provides information regarding the potential biasing impact of psychological reports. This research directed its focus toward an examination of the effect of psychological reports containing fictitious material on teachers' perceptions of a child's performance and expectations for the child. A further purpose of the study was to investigate the impact of knowledge of the effect of biases on pupils' performance. Subjects after having heard a lecture on the effects of biases, observed a videotaped administration of the Boehm Test of Basic Concepts to kindergarten children. There were no significant differences on the observational variable due to the psychological report or lecture. However, the psychological report had a significant effect on expectations even in subjects who had just been warned against such biasing effects. One of the conclusions drawn by the author was that teachers are more influenced by negative information about students than by positive or neutral information.

The relationship between expectations based on record-type information (i.e., standardized tests, previous teachers, family, physical characteristics) and the quality of reported performance was investigated by Cooper (1979). He found a positive relationship between the variables. More interesting is the finding that the perceived accuracy of these expectations was relatively uninfluenced by the perceived reliability of the source that generated them. Further, expectations stated after more direct exposure to student performance continued to be influenced by preobservation expectations. While the study was conducted in a simulated setting, it does provide useful insights into potential ways in which reported information can be used.

At least two studies give credence to knowledge of siblings as a potential "input" source of teacher expectation. Seaver (1971) found that younger siblings of good students obtained higher achievement scores if they were assigned to the former teachers of older siblings than if they were assigned to other teachers. Seaver (1973) further substantiated the sibling effect. He obtained first grade achievement scores for 79 younger siblings who had been preceded in school by "bright" or "dull" older siblings. Again, he found that children taught by the same teacher as their older siblings performed better than those taught by a different teacher if their older siblings had been good students, and that they performed worse than the controls if their older siblings had performed poorly.

The forgoing "input" factors involve classes or categories of traits which trigger inferences about the actions an individual from these categories ought to display. These categories or stereotypes often become overgeneralized leading to degrees of inaccuracy in behavioral prediction (Brigham 1971). It is important to note that predictions are not necessarily based on observation of an individual's behavior but rather on inferences drawn from race, gender, ethnic, and other categories. Such a caution is particularly relevant when new categories and stereotypes are generated in the educational realm, categories which frequently have elusive, ill-defined, arbitrary designations. Such is the case with categories of handicapped children. A study of particular relevance is reported by Palmer (1979). He investigated regular classroom teachers' attributions and instructional prescriptions for normal achieving, educationally handicapped, and educationally mentally retarded pupils. Background descriptive information about pupils given to teachers affected teachers' failure but not success attributions as well as the manner in which they revised their failure attribution ratings. In addition, it was found that teachers' initial instructional prescriptions were anchored by descriptive information reflecting characteristics of normal achieving, educationally handicapped, educationally mentally retarded pupils. Pupils' subsequent achievement, however, did modify instructional decisions.

There is little doubt that the labeling process in education, and especially in special education, can serve to induce negative expectations. While most of the evidence to support this claim is impressionistic, a few recent studies lend empirical evidence (Foster 1975, Lee 1975). They demonstrated that teacher trainees in special education could be biased in their assessment of a child's behavior by applying different labels to the child prior to (or during) their observations. That such bias potentially affects performance is documented by Sutherland and Algozzine (1979).

It would be naive to assume that expectation "input" factors lead to direct, unqualified channels of "output" on the part of the teacher. It must be understood that most of the "input" studies base their findings on "average" reaction of teachers, and many of the conclusions are derived from correlational analyses. It is perhaps as dangerous to stereotype teachers on the basis of their perceptions as it is to stereotype their charges (Braun 1976). While "input" or "inputs" cue a set for action, or "output," teachers do not necessarily remain static in the implicit personality theories which they hold. Further, teachers may modify or reconstruct stereotypes which they hold. Then, too, there is wide variability with respect to teachers' inclinations to act on "input."

It would seem that teacher personality is a prime factor in orchestrating action or nonaction based on pupil "input." Suggestibility, or the degree to which teachers give credence to externally imposed information would appear to be one such factor, as would teacher sex and knowledge of behavioral theory.

Indeed, the link between teacher expectation and teacher "output" is not as direct as assumed by early expectation experimental studies. "Input" data are filtered through a complex of personality/dispositional, attributional, self-image, and knowledge variables.

3. The Instructional Environment—Teacher Output

While the impact of expectations held for different learners and groups of learners interacts with specific teacher variables, there is no paucity of research to support the fact that both quantitative and qualitative "outputs" are influenced by expectations. Teachers' expectations lead to "outputs" that often consist of grouping, tracking, or streaming students, usually to facilitate more appropriate treatment in the classroom. These are planned and explicitly reasoned outputs. There are, however, more subtle outputs. For example, the amount of attention and contact varies with students for whom differential expectations are held. It has been suggested that teachers pay less attention to low achievers, call on them less often, and interact differentially with high and low achievers at both elementary-, and secondary-school levels. Willis (1970) found that teachers ignored comments of low-efficiency students more frequently than comments from high-efficiency students. Even nonverbal behaviors emitted toward students labeled bright or dull have been shown to differ. Such behaviors include more smiling, leaning closer, more nodding, and more direct eye gaze for so-called bright than for dull students (Chaiken et al. 1974).

Further qualitative aspects of teacher contact include praise and blame. Evaluative feedback may well be the most potent classroom socializing and academic variable. Low-expectation students do receive less praise and more criticism than high-expectation students (Brophy and Good 1974). Cooper and Baron (1977) proposed that the teacher's sense of control over inter-actions might explain the linkage:

> Low expectations imply that future interactions with these students are more likely to be unsuccessful and more energy- and time-consuming. Since interactions initiated by the child are less controllable in both timing and content than teacher-initiated interactions, criticism may be dispensed more freely and praise less freely to low-expectation students to decrease these students' seeking out behavior. (p. 417)

It should be remembered that the distribution of praise and criticism is likely to vary widely among teach-ers. Consistent with attributional theory, praise and blame should be most pronounced when the causes of behavior are perceived to be personal in origin.

Task and performance expectations lead to dif-ferential treatment on the basis of high- and low-ability perceptions. Teachers may set tasks that either stifle or stretch the achievement of a group or individuals within that group. These differential expectations may be apparent in the range of comprehension questions posed to individual children. The group for whom expectations are low may have little opportunity to grapple with questions that require inferential and critical thinking. Brophy and Good (1969), for example, found that black children received more memory questions than did white children for whom higher expectations were held.

The treatment of children for whom the teacher has low expectations may have a dual effect. First, the teacher's treatment may reduce the motivation of the learner. Further, because the learner is exposed only to lower level tasks the teacher's low expectation is confirmed.

Pidgeon (1970) reports evidence of the relationship between expectancy and levels of tasks teachers set for children. In discussing the inferior arithmetic per-formance of California children compared with English and Welsh children, he attributes the difference in achievement to differential expectations reflected in the curricula:

> In California much less was expected of pupils in arithmetic; more limited objectives were formulated for children of primary school age and less emphasis was placed on rapid progress in mechanical arithmetic than was customary in England and Wales. (p. 84)

Perhaps more subtle interaction variables relate to the amount of prompting and probing that teachers do for individual children. Brophy and Good (1974) indicate that teachers' expectations clearly determine whether learners will be prompted to respond or whether they will be stifled by the impatience of the teacher. Rosenthal (1973) refers to "expectant voices" of teachers that are often fulfilled by the child's responses. He reports that 11 out of 12 studies support the notion that teachers encourage greater respon-siveness of students from whom they expect more. They call on such students more often, ask them harder questions, give them more time to answer, and prompt them toward the correct answer.

Closely related to prompting and probing is teacher interruptive behavior especially in reading. Allington (1980), for example, examined the incidence and type of verbal interruption behaviors of teachers with high- and low-ability readers. He found that not only do teachers interrupt poor readers more often than good readers but also that the type of interruptive behavior differed. Teachers tended to provide poor readers with remarks that directed attention to graphophonemic characteristics of the target word, whereas good readers were directed to semantic and syntactic information.

Further confirming evidence regarding differential task expectations of low and high achievers comes from student perception of teacher interactions with low and high achievers. Weinstein and Middlestadt (1979) found that student-perceived teacher treatment of male high achievers reflected high expectations, academic demands, and special privileges. Male low achievers were viewed as receiving fewer chances but greater teacher concern and vigilance.

Whether group assignment, labeling, or reinforce-ment comes first, it appears that the amount and quality of pupil–teacher interaction offer important clues to the mystery of possible expectancy cues which the learner internalizes, and ultimately translates into action.

Pupil–teacher and pupil–pupil interaction become a function of how both teachers and pupils perceive the individual child's status within the classroom social microcosm. Assignment to learning groups and special classes is often interpreted as a measure of status by both teachers and pupils. In a sociometric study of first-grade children, McGinley and McGinley (1970) found that lower reading group members chose significantly fewer than expected peers from their own group and significantly more than expected from the top reading groups. Middle group children made fewer than expected choices from lower reading groups and more than expected from top groups. The top group made significantly more than expected choices from their own group and fewer than expected from the lower two groups. The authors interpreted their findings as reflect-ing the principle that persons are generally attracted to successful persons, to persons sharing a successful experience, and to persons in a success–reward situa-tion. Further, they pointed to the probability of recipro-cal success–reward relationships between teacher and children from the top reading groups. These children read well, and were rewarded and attracted to the source of reward—the teacher. The teacher, in turn, was rewarded by the children's success. The opposite cycle of events was interpreted as occuring for the lower reading group children. Further apparent effects of group assignment involved teachers' expressed feelings about children. Five of the six teachers in the study expressed negative feelings toward children in the lower reading groups.

The effects of group assignment have also been investigated with older children. Stevens (1971) found that students assigned to remedial reading groups display specific behaviors which make them socially unacceptable. He concluded that remedial readers know how others feel about them.

Tuckman and Bierman (1971) studied the effects of grouping. They moved randomly selected junior- and senior-high-school students into higher ability groups. Students who were transferred to higher groups achieved higher on standardized tests than students who were not transferred. Further, more than half of the students transferred were recommended later by teachers to be retained in these groups. The authors suggested a possible "inertia" function related to the grouping process and commented on the frustration and disillusionment of grouping procedures that "lock students in and out."

There is evidence that the physical structuring of the classroom, on the basis of group assignment, may interact with other variables that will facilitate the permanent "locking-in" or "cementing-in" process. In a longitudinal study, Rist (1970) described how kindergarten children were ranked during the first eight days of their school life on the basis of mere guesses at their learning potential. On the basis of these guesses the children were designated to their social and academic destinies at three different tables—assignment which appears to have led to differences in performance. For example, children assigned to the nonacademic table were farthest from the teacher, so far away, in fact, that they had difficulty hearing the teacher. In addition, these children received considerably less attention than groups closer to the teacher. The author indicated that expectations, translated into group assignment "output," and consequently, differential treatment, were perpetuated as children advanced from first to second grade. Certainly, it is fallacious to generalize from a sample of one; however, variations of the dynamics of the Rist study are in evidence in at least some educational settings. Good and Brophy (1977) have supported the covariance of performance expectations with teachers' seating low achievers farther from themselves.

There appears little doubt that grouping, if employed on a long-term basis, affects achievement. Such implications pertain not only to in class grouping but also streaming. Burstall (1970) studied the achievement of children who scored low on tests designed to measure their performance in French. Schools where teachers expressed positive attitudes toward teaching French to low-ability children showed significantly higher achievement for such children than schools where teachers expressed negative attitudes. Moreover, children of low ability reached the highest level of achievement in French when they had been taught in heterogeneous classes.

Pidgeon (1970), has commented on the effects of streaming. He found standard deviations on test scores for the International Achievement Pilot Studies to be higher for students in England and Wales than for students in other participating countries. He suggested that homogeneous assignment to classes is probably responsible for the results. He surmised that when children are assigned to homogeneous classes, teachers assume that the students have been accurately placed and that within any classroom the ability of the students will be highly similar. Children are, then, treated differentially according to their assignment. Such treatment and the "culture of defeat," which is often prevalent in low stream classes, may account for many of the fulfilled prophecies. Vernon (1957) has postulated that expectancy, high or low, might be responsible for the underachievement of some pupils:

> Children who are relegated to a lower stream to suit their present level of ability are likely to be taught at a slower pace . . . . These initial differences become exaggerated and the duller children who happen to improve later fall too far below the higher streams in attainment to be able to catch up. (p. 72)

Just as teachers vary in their susceptibility to expectation "input" cues, so children vary in their susceptibility to the teacher "output." What are some of the variables that determine how potent this external imposition of cues will be?

The credibility of the source of "output" is perhaps one of the most potent variables. It is safe to make the generalization that, at least for primary-school children, the teacher's credibility rating is high. If teachers communicate to learners continuously that their performance is poor, this will undoubtedly influence the goals they strive to achieve.

The potency of specific expectancy cues also appears to be a function of the self-image of the learner. If a child already views itself as a competent learner, it may require a consistent bombardment of cues, and from credible sources, to change this image. Similarly, there is considerable evidence that a confirmed negative self-image is highly resistant to change and that part of this resistance results from the fact that the learner needs to be faithful to the picture of self or else be threatened with the loss of selfhood. Bettleheim (1961) commented on situations where children decided to think of themselves as failures in this way, making it virtually impossible for criticism for poor performance to hurt their self-images. Cues even of the most subtle type will help confirm this negative image, which is like a boundary that limits the learner's actions.

The degree to which one views such boundaries as fixed has critical educational implications. One could argue that individuals who attribute success or failure to effort (rather than to ability) are filtering their performance through an unstable as opposed to a controllable factor. This has implications for the interpretation of and reaction to teacher "output." If learners who perform poorly conclude that they are helpless in changing their performance, then their failure will undermine their motivation, satisfaction with self, and future performance. On the other hand, if learners are encouraged to associate failure with factors which are controllable, then the debilitating consequences of failure may be avoided. By emphasizing the importance of internal, controllable factors as causes, teachers may promote pupils' educational experiences that are both more satisfying and more effective.

4. Learners' Self-expectation—Pupil Output

If, indeed, children's perceptions of causes of present and past performance mediate their subsequent expectations of self, it seems logical that these self-expectations are the prime motivational energizers for pupil "output." It is this "output" which can be viewed as a significant mediating link between the teachers' original expectation of the child and the perpetuation (or modification) of the original expectation. Figure 1 presents

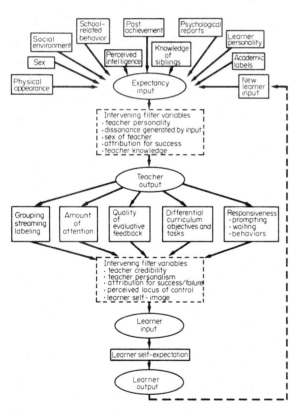

Figure 1
The mediating cycle between teacher expectation and learner output (after C Braun, A R Neilsen)

a graphic illustration that summarizes the cyclic flow of behavioral events.

It is reasonable that the factors which mediate the learner's interpretation of teacher "output" will, at least in part, determine pupil "output." Reference has been made to the significance of learners' perceptions of locus of control of their performance—unstable/controllable, internal/external. Such perception has implications, for example, for the degree to which learners take risks in responding and the degree to which they persist at a task even if success is not imminent. There certainly is a close relationship between self-expectation of failure in problem situations and withdrawal from such tasks. By the same token there is a close relationship between self-expectation of success in problem situations and persistence with such tasks.

A significant link that may account for the perpetuation of the cycle may be found in an interplay between expectation for success/failure and academic self-concept. If learners think of themselves as inferior, their actions will tend to be those of inferior persons and will confirm to the teacher and their peers the reasonableness of treating them as inferiors.

The cycle is probably maintained more than anything by the intellectual and affective constraints characteristic of the curriculum of the failing child. In the preoccupation to require every child to attain specific competencies, the need for children to explore widely to the point of discovering their own unique aptitudes has been forgotten. Curricular constraints frequently restrict the failing child to sterile, irrelevant, artificially contrived learning experiences.

The consequences for the individual learner of how the cycle (Fig. 1) is perpetuated or modified are staggering; the implications for the educator are sobering. Certainly, teacher personnel must become vitally concerned with preventative action. Perhaps the most logical step in this direction is a close examination of personal "input" factors relative to "teacher expectation of pupil." Teacher education courses and inservice programs must sensitize teachers to the potent dynamics of these "inputs," and their potential to trigger specific "output" for individual child treatment. Teachers need to be sensitized to the personal biases and stereotypes they hold, and encouraged to examine these in relation to their classroom interactions with students.

See also: Teachers' Expectations; Affective Teacher Education; Students' Sex; Students' Ethnicity; Students' Social Backgrounds; Teachers' Personality; Teachers' Sex

Bibliography

Allington R L 1980 Teacher interruption behaviors during primary-grade oral reading. *J. Educ. Psychol.* 72: 371–77
Barnard J et al. 1968 Teachers' ratings of student personality traits as they relate to IQ and social desirability. *J. Educ. Psychol.* 59: 128–32
Bettelheim B 1961 The decision to fail. *Sch. Rev.* 69: 377–412

Brandt L J, Hayden M E 1974 Male and female teacher attitudes as a function of students' ascribed motivation and performance levels. *J. Educ. Psychol.* 66: 309–14

Braun C 1976 Teacher expectation: Sociopsychological dynamics. *Rev. Educ. Res.* 46: 185–213

Brigham J C 1971 Ethnic stereotypes. *Psychol. Bull.* 76: 15–38

Brophy J E 1979 Teacher behavior and its effects. *J. Educ. Psychol.* 71: 733–52

Brophy J E, Good T L 1969 *Teacher–Child Dyadic Interaction: A Manual for Coding Classroom Behavior.* Report Series No. 27. Research and Development Center for Teacher Education, University of Texas, Austin, Texas

Brophy J E, Good T L 1970 Teacher's communication of differential expectations for children's classroom performance: Some behavioral data. *J. Educ. Psychol.* 61: 365–74

Brophy J E, Good T L 1974 *Teacher–Student Relationships: Causes and Consequences.* Holt, Rinehart and Winston, New York

Burstall C 1970 French in the primary school: Some early findings. *J. Curric. Stud.* 2: 48–58

Chaikin A L, Siegler E, Derlega V J 1974 Nonverbal mediators of teacher expectancy effects. *J. Pers. Soc. Psychol.* 30: 144–49

Clifford M M, Walster E 1973 The effect of physical attractiveness on teacher expectations. *Sociol. Educ.* 46: 248–58

Cooper H M 1979 Pygmalion grows up: A model for teacher expectation communication and performance influence. *Rev. Educ. Res.* 49: 389–410

Cooper H M, Baron R M 1977 Academic expectations and attributed responsibility as predictors of professional teachers' reinforcement behavior. *J. Educ. Psychol.* 69: 409–18

Cornbleth C, Korth W 1980 Teacher perceptions and teacher–student interaction in integrated classrooms. *J. Exper. Educ.* 48: 259–63

Darley J M, Fazio R H 1980 Expectancy confirmation processes arising in the social interaction sequence. *Am. Psychol.* 35: 867–81

Dion K K 1972 Physical attractiveness and evaluation of children's transgressions. *J. Pers. Soc. Psychol.* 24: 207–13

Elashoff J D, Snow R E 1971 *Pygmalion Reconsidered: A Case Study in Statistical Inference: Reconsideration of the Rosenthal–Jacobson Data on Teacher Expectancy.* Wadsworth, Belmont, California

Felker D W 1974 *Building Positive Self-concepts.* Burgess, Minneapolis, Minnesota

Festinger L A 1957 *A Theory of Cognitive Dissonance.* Row, Peterson, Evanston, Illinois

Finn J D 1972 Expectations and the educational environment. *Rev. Educ. Res.* 42: 387–410

Foster G G 1975 Expectancy and halo effects as a result of artificially induced teacher bias. (Doctoral dissertation, Pennsylvania State University) *Dissertation Abstracts International* 1976 37: 2738A (University Microfilms No. 76-24, 764)

Goebes D D, Shore M F 1975 Behavioral expectations of students as related to the sex of the teacher. *Psychol. Sch.* 12: 222–24

Good T L, Brophy J E 1977 *Educational Psychology: A Realistic Approach.* Holt, Rinehart and Winston, New York

Good T L et al. 1980 Classroom interaction as a function of teacher expectations, student sex, and time of year. *J. Educ. Psychol.* 72: 378–85

Kehle T J 1974 Teachers' expectations: Ratings of student performance as biased by student characteristics. *J. Exp. Educ.* 43: 54–60

Lee M 1975 Retention of stereotypes as a function of locus control and sources of information. (Doctoral dissertation, Michigan State University, Pennsylvania) *Dissertation Abstracts International* 1976 36: 7341A (University Microfilms No. 76-10,751)

Leinhardt G et al. 1979 Learning what's taught: Sex differences in instruction. *J. Educ. Psychol.* 71: 432–39

McGinley P, McGinley H 1970 Reading groups as psychological groups. *J. Exp. Educ.* 39: 36–42

Marjoribanks K 1978 Teacher perceptions of student behavior, social environment, and cognitive performance. *J. Genet. Psychol.* 133: 217–28

Mason E J 1973 Teachers' observations and expectations of boys and girls as influenced by biased psychological reports and knowledge of the effects of bias. *J. Educ. Psychol.* 65: 238–43

Palmer D J 1979 Regular-classroom teachers' attributions and instructional prescriptions for handicapped and nonhandicapped pupils. *J. Spec. Educ.* 13: 325–37

Pidgeon D A 1970 *Expectation and Pupil Performance.* National Foundation for Educational Research, Slough

Rist R C 1970 Student social class and teacher expectations: The self-fulfilling prophecy in ghetto education. *Harvard Educ. Rev.* 40: 411–51

Rosenthal R 1973 The Pygmalion effect lives. *Psychol. Today.* 7: 56–63

Rosenthal R 1974 *On the Social Psychology of the Self-fulfilling Prophecy: Further Evidence for Pygmalion Effects and their Mediating Mechanisms.* MSS Modular, New York

Rosenthal R, Jacobson L 1968 *Pygmalion in the Classroom.* Holt, Rinehart and Winston, New York

Rotter N G 1975 The influence of race and other variables on teachers' ratings of pupils (Doctoral dissertation, New York University, New York) *Dissertation Abstracts International* 1975 35: 7134A (University Microfilms No. 75–9694)

Seaver W B 1971 Effects of naturally induced teacher expectancies in the academic performance of pupils in primary grades. (Doctoral dissertation, North Western University, Evanston, Illinois) *Dissertation Abstracts International* 1971 32: 3426A-3427A (University Microfilms No. 71-30,945)

Seaver W B 1973 Effects of naturally induced teacher expectancies. *J. Pers. Soc. Psychol.* 28: 333–42

Stevens D O 1971 Reading difficulty and classroom acceptance. *Read. Teach.* 25: 52–55

Sutherland J, Algozzine B 1979 The learning disabled label as a biasing factor in the visual motor performance of normal children. *J. Learn. Disabil.* 12: 8–14

Tuckman B W, Bierman M L 1971 *Beyond Pygmalion: Galatea in the Schools.* Paper read at the American Educational Research Association Conference, New York

Vernon P E (ed.) 1957 *Secondary School Selection.* Methuen, London

Weinstein R S, Middlestadt S E 1979 Student perceptions of teacher interactions with male high and low achievers. *J. Educ. Psychol.* 71: 421–31

Willis B J 1970 The influence of teacher expectation on teachers' classroom interaction with selected children (Doctoral dissertation, George Peabody College, Nashville, Tennessee) *Dissertation Abstracts International* 30: 5072A (University Microfilms No. 70-7647)

Willis S 1972 *Formation of Teachers' Expectations of Students Academic Performance.* Unpublished doctoral dissertation, University of Texas, Austin

Teachers' Sex

M. J. Dunkin

Do male teachers differ from female teachers in their treatment of students? Do male teachers favour boys and female teachers favour girls? If so, should children be taught by teachers of the same sex? Should there be more male teachers in elementary schools? Is school achievement affected by the sex of the teacher? These are some of the questions considered in this entry which discusses evidence concerning the sex of the teacher in relation to classroom interaction, and student learning.

There are reasonable grounds for expecting that male and female teachers differ from one another in their treatment of students. After all, in most systems it is rare to find a male teaching preschoolers or kindergarteners and in many systems the majority of teachers are females, especially in elementary schools. Differences according to sex in the placement of teachers indicate that early childhood education and elementary education are more congenial to teachers of one sex than the other, and/or that school systems regard teaching at those levels as more appropriate for teachers of that sex. Presumably, there are some things about young students that warrant certain kinds of treatment that are more available from teachers of that sex.

Quite apart from their relative numbers in the teaching profession, there are other good reasons to expect that male and female teachers behave differently. Males are brought up differently from females. They are expected to, and generally do, acquire sex-role learnings that define the nature of socially acceptable behaviour for males differently from that for females. In addition, it would be surprising if the physical and physiological differences between males and females did not result in some differences in behaviour between the two.

1. Classroom Interaction

Research into the differences in classroom behaviour between male and female teachers has focused upon three aspects of behaviour. First, some researchers have asked whether the behaviour of male and female teachers differs in terms of the leadership style or classroom climate established. Second, differences of a pedagogical type involving questioning, answering, and correcting have been explored. Third, a few researchers have focused upon linguistic variables and gathered evidence of differences between men and women teachers in their use of language.

Studies of the leadership styles of male and female teachers have sometimes found that male teachers are more direct or dominant than female teachers. Adams and Biddle (1970) found that male teachers' classrooms were more centrally organized and teacher dominated than female teachers' classrooms. Griffin (1972) found that male teachers were more direct and authoritarian than female teachers. Good et al. (1972) concluded that female teachers in their study were "generally warmer", and more tolerant of misbehaviour. Their classes seemed more relaxed and disposed towards discussion. Male teachers seemed more active, more highly structured, and more oriented to mastery of content.

However, two studies concluded differently about the leadership styles of male and female teachers. Spaulding (1963) found that teacher sex was unrelated to the degree of indirectness displayed in classrooms, while McGee (1955) found that women teachers were, in fact, more direct in style than males.

Evidence of differences in pedagogical moves between male and female teachers comes mainly from Good et al. (1972). They found that students did more initiating, had more opportunities to respond, gave more incorrect answers, and seemed more willing to guess when unsure of answers in the presence of female teachers. Female teachers were found to give praise following correct responses more often than male teachers, while male teachers were more likely to comment on the processes by which responses were produced. Interestingly enough, male teachers were less likely to give feedback following correct responses while female teachers were less likely to comment on incorrect responses. Furthermore, male teachers were more likely to persist until a student gave an acceptable response while female teachers tended to supply the correct answer or redirect the question to another student.

Linguistic differences between male and female teachers were found by Loflin (personal communication, 1973) and Hays et al. (1971) in the same research team at the University of Missouri. Hays and his colleagues found that male teachers tended to emit longer utterances when they spoke than female teachers. Loflin found that male teachers used the first person less and the third person more, used first names less often, made more assertions, and used certain types of complex sentences more than female teachers. Male teachers also had students whose language use differed from the students of female teachers.

Finally, Adams and Biddle (1970) found that the male teachers in their study talked more than the female teachers and that the males were more likely to be disseminating information than were females. The latter gave more attention to intellectualizing than did male teachers.

On balance, the evidence supports the hypothesis that there are differences in classroom behaviour between male and female teachers. The impression that emerges most strongly is that the classrooms of female teachers tend to be warmer, more nurturant milieux while male teachers' classrooms are more highly organized and task oriented. The number of studies supplying the evidence is, however, quite small and generalizations about the effects of teacher sex upon classroom events are hazardous.

So far, the discussion has been concerned with evidence of general differences in classroom behaviour between male and female teachers. Some researchers have wondered whether there are differences of a more specific type involving links between the sex of the teacher and the sex of the student. This research inquires into the possibility that male teachers give special treatment to male students and that female teachers treat girls differently from boys.

Research on the interaction between sex of teachers and sex of student has been stimulated by attempts to explain the common finding that girls achieve better than boys at reading in the lower elementary grades. Since most elementary-school teachers are women, it has been argued that boys are disadvantaged. They are said to lack appropriate adult models of the same sex with whom to identify. It has also been argued that female teachers discriminate against boys by establishing a feminine environment and by invoking sanctions against typically masculine behaviour involving noise, aggression, activity, and the like. The result is, it has been claimed, that girls find elementary schools more congenial environments and achieve better in them. The answer to the problem for boys, then, might be to place more male teachers in elementary schools.

This controversy assumes that teachers favour students of like sex and that the favoured treatment results in enhanced achievement. Research on the first of these assumptions will now be considered.

Good et al. (1972) found no support for the claim that teachers favour students of their own sex. The only relevant significant difference they discovered was one that contradicted the claim. It was that female teachers initiated positive contacts with boys much more often than with girls.

Etaugh and Harlow (1973, 1975) found that male teachers favoured boys by calling on them more often than on girls, while there was no such difference for female teachers. However, female teachers praised boys more often than girls. Male teachers were even-handed in the allocation of praise to boys and girls.

Etaugh et al. (1975) and Lee and Wolinsky (1973) both detected a slight tendency for teachers to favour students of their own sex.

Thus, there is no strong support for the hypothesis that teachers treat students of their own sex more advantageously than others. Indeed, there is some evidence to suggest that if there is a bias it tends to favour boys.

2. Student Learning Outcomes

The second main area of research on the effects of the sex of the teacher has involved comparing performances of the students of male and female teachers on tests of various kinds. Some of the studies concerned produced evidence that teacher sex was related to student achievement but most did not.

Among the former was a study by Bennett (1967) who found that students taught by female teachers had higher overall achievement than students taught by males. Brophy and Laosa (1971) found that kindergarten children taught by a husband and wife team made greater gains in spatial ability than those taught by a lone female teacher. The latter children, however, made greater gains in verbal areas. There was some confounding of variables in the study and it is possible that the effects were due to special curricula materials rather than to sex of teacher.

Gross (1976) identified quite minimal differences in reading achievement between children taught by male as compared with female teachers. Lahaderne and Cohen (1972) found no differences on most of the measures used in their study. Students taught by female teachers were found to have higher scores on a test of science achievement and also to have more positive attitudes to school.

McFarland (1969) and Asher and Gottman (1972) found no effect of teacher sex on reading achievement. Peterson (1972) found no effect of sex of teacher on paired associate learning and Sweely (1970) found similarly with respect to students' self-concepts.

All of the above studies involved the application of standardized tests to students. Edmiston (1943) and Arnold (1968) query whether male and female teachers were different in grading students on the basis of normal classroom assessment data. Edmiston found no difference between men and women teachers but Arnold found evidence that males awarded higher grades than females.

In summary, the evidence is inconsistent that sex of teacher relates generally to student learning.

Could it be, however, that boys achieve better under male teachers and likewise for girls with female teachers? Not according to Clapp (1967), Asher and Gottman (1972), Bennett (1967), Sweely (1970), and Arnold (1968), all of whom found no evidence of such relationships. However, Smith (1970) found that boys taught by male teachers had higher scores on problem solving in mathematics, higher self-concept scores, and lower scores on psychological effeminacy than boys taught by female teachers. Finally, Shinedling and Pedersen (1970) found small differences in reading achievement in favour of boys taught by male as against female teachers.

Again, there is little support from research for the hypothesis that there is an interaction between the sex of the teacher and the sex of the student such that affects the learning of the latter.

3. Conclusion

There seems to be little basis in the research reviewed above for decisions such as to establish single sex schools, or to place more male teachers in the lower grades. Presumably, it is not sufficient merely to manipulate the proportions of male and female teachers in schools to remedy any achievement or other psychological shortcomings that pupils of one sex or the other might display. The explanation and control of such shortcomings are much more complicated than can be afforded by resort to a single variable such as teacher sex.

See also: Teachers' Expectations; Teachers' Social Backgrounds; Students' Sex; Teachers' Personality

Bibliography

Adams R S, Biddle B J 1970 *Realities of Teaching: Explorations with Video Tape.* Holt, Rinehart and Winston, New York

Arnold R D 1968 The achievement of boys and girls taught by men and women teachers. *Elem. Sch. J.* 68: 367–72

Asher S, Gottman J 1972 Sex of teacher and student reading achievement. Paper presented at the annual meeting of the American Educational Research Association. AERA, Washington, DC

Bennett D A 1967 A comparison of the achievement of fifth grade pupils having male teachers with those having female teachers (Doctoral dissertation, University of Denver) *Dissertation Abstracts International* 1967 27: 4032A–4033A (University Microfilms No. 67–3940)

Brophy J E, Good T L 1974 *Teacher–Student Relationships: Causes and Consequences.* Holt, Rinehart and Winston, New York

Brophy J E, Laosa L 1971 Effect of a male teacher on the sex typing of kindergarten children. *Proceedings of the 79th Annual Convention of the American Psychological Association,* pp. 169–70

Clapp R C 1967 The relationship of teacher sex to fifth grade boys' achievement gains and attitudes toward school (Unpublished doctoral dissertation, Stanford University) *Dissertation Abstracts International* 1968 28 2433A–2434A (University Microfilms No. 67–17,533)

Edmiston R W 1943 Do teachers' show partiality? *Peabody J. Educ.* 20: 234–38

Etaugh C, Harlow H 1973 School attitudes and performance of elementary school children as related to teacher's sex and behavior. Paper presented at the biennial meeting of the Society for Research in Child Development

Etaugh C, Harlow H 1975 Behaviors of male and female teachers as related to behaviors and attitudes of elementary school children. *J. Genet. Psychol.* 127: 163–70

Etaugh C, Collins G, Gerson A 1975 Reinforcement of sex-typed behaviors of two-year-old children in a nursery school setting. *Dev. Psychol.* 11: 255

Good T L, Sikes J N, Brophy J E 1972 Effects of teacher sex and student sex and student achievement on classroom interaction. Technical Report No. 61, Center for Research in Social Behavior, Univ. of Missouri at Columbia, Missouri

Griffin J 1972 Influence strategies: Theory and research: A study of teacher behavior (Unpulished doctoral dissertation, University of Missouri at Columbia, Missouri) *Dissertation Abstracts International* 1973 34: 1373A (University Microfilms No. 73-21,424)

Gross A 1976 The relationship between sex differences and reading ability: A study of children's performance in an Israeli kibbutz system. Paper presented at the Sixth World Congress on Reading of the International Reading Association (IRA), Singapore, August 17–19, 1976. IRA, Newark, Delaware

Hays D G, Kantor K N, Goldstein L 1971 Manifest characteristics of interactive sequencing in the classroom. Technical Report No. 41, Center for Research in Social Behavior, University of Missouri at Columbia, Missouri

Lahaderne H, Cohen S 1972 Freedom and fairness: A comparison of male and female teachers in elementary classrooms. Paper presented at the annual meeting of the American Educational Research Association, Washington, DC

Lee P C, Wolinsky A 1973 Male teachers of young children. A preliminary empirical study. *Young Children* 28: 342–53

McFarland W 1969 Are girls really smarter? *Elem. Sch. J.* 70: 14–19

McGee H M 1955 Measurement of authoritarianism and its relation to teachers' classroom behavior. *Genet. Psychol. Monogr.* 52: 89–146

Peterson J 1972 Effects of sex of E and sex of S in the first and fifth grade children's paired-associate learning. *J. Educ. Res.* 66: 81–84

Shinedling M, Pedersen D 1970 Effects of sex of teacher and student on children's gain in quantitative and verbal performance. *J. Psychol.* 76: 79–84

Smith D 1970 A study of the relationship of teacher sex to fifth grade boys' sex preference, general self-concept, and scholastic achievement in science and mathematics (Unpublished Ed. D. dissertation, University of Miami, Florida)

Spaulding R 1963 *Achievement, Creativity, and Self-concept Correlates of Teacher–Pupil Transactions in Elementary Schools.* Cooperative Research Project No. 1352, United States Dept. of Health, Education and Welfare, Office of Education, Washington, DC

Sweely H 1970 The effect of the male elementary teacher on children's self-concepts. Paper presented at the annual meeting of the American Educational Research Association, Washington, DC

Teaching Experience

J. Barnes

Teaching experience is conventionally regarded as an asset, presumably positively related to teaching success. In research it is seen as an easily accessible variable and tends to be included amongst background data in surveys and other empirical studies.

However, a sampling of some of the findings of studies since the early 1960s indicates that experience is neither easily nor effectively defined nor measured, and if not dismissed in the writing up of research findings, is considered very loosely, often being automatically treated as a dichotomous or linear variable.

Studies which have seriously considered the impact

of experience have frequently found a negative relationship with various desirable outcomes, and there seems to be considerable evidence of a curvilinear relationship. It appears that teachers get "better" during the first few years of their careers but after this their effectiveness levels off and probably declines.

Spady (1973 p. 152) concluded a review with the statement that "teacher experience must be regarded as an inadequately studied variable whose effect on student achievement remains obscure".

1. Experience and Employers

The previous experience of applicants for a teaching post, like their age, sex, and the nature and extent of their training, is included in any professional application and is presumably given at least some weight in appointment, tenure, and promotion decisions. Cook (1978) found that administrators considered teaching experience as a most important characteristic, although an Association for School, College, and University Staffing research report (Bryant et al. 1978) found that the characteristics considered important were the same for inexperienced as for experienced teachers. However, one of these was "successful previous employment" of whatever kind, and success in teaching may perhaps have been given priority over other employment experience.

2. Measurement of Experience

In the research area, the most widely used measure of teaching experience is number of years of teaching, but other criteria are often used and even years of teaching can be interpreted in a number of ways, for instance, years of actual teaching; number of years since commencing teaching regardless of breaks in service; or years at a particular school or in a particular type of school, environment, or system. Other measures encountered include age; salary (current or beginning); school expenditure (of which teachers' salaries usually form a large component); status in the institution or system; level, extent, or recency of training; and number of years since attainment of latest qualification.

Age may not be an appropriate alternative measure of experience. Berryman and Berryman (1981) analysed the effects of both age and teaching experience on teachers' attitudes to the mainstreaming of handicapped children, using a substantial sample of teachers, and found that while more experienced teachers were only a little less favourably disposed to the process than the less experienced, there was a very significant difference between attitudes of older and younger teachers, younger teachers being much more in favour. Brophy and Evertson (1976) found that a sample of teachers selected because they were consistent in achieving student success showed more "traditionalist" attitudes than an unselected sample of teachers, but they were also an average of 10 years older and more experienced because

of the criteria used to select the sample. When teaching experience was included in the analysis, there proved to be absolutely no relationship between degree of traditionalism and either age or years of experience, in either group.

3. Surveys and their Findings

Surveys within schools and education systems are widespread, and "experience" is usually included, generally as "years of teaching experience". Results of surveys are as varied as the systems and criteria, and critics have pointed out problems of questionnaire completion (e.g., Evertson et al. 1975, Spady 1973) and limitations on their usefulness because of the correlational nature of any analysis, even in cases when analysis is undertaken to establish effects. Good et al. (1975) suggest that much of the money currently invested in such research would be better used in identifying appropriate and inappropriate teacher behaviours clearly and unambiguously.

In justifying his research into the relationship between locus of control and experience, Leming (1980) wrote of a nationwide trend in the United States towards increasingly experienced instructors in public schools. This appeals to conventional wisdom in situations where an oversupply of teachers and general unemployment prevents newly qualified teachers from entering the system and causes those with experience to hesitate to move out. However, in the case of female teachers, resignations and long or short interruptions for child bearing or child rearing provide new openings and hold down the average number of years' experience in the whole system. There is no clear empirical evidence of trends. In 1966, Berkeley (1966) reported less than two years difference in mean age of male and female teachers in the whole of Australia, and no difference in their level of experience. At that time, 60 percent of teachers were under 35 years of age, and less than 20 percent over 50. McArthur (1980) quotes 1978 figures in Victoria indicating the age distribution of secondary teachers. Females made up 71 percent of those under 25 years of age, half of the 25–29 group, and 38 percent of those over 30. Cawthron et al. (1980), in South Australia, found an interesting situation in that, while status in the school was closely related to actual years of teaching experience, within a given type of school, male and female teachers with the same status tended to have the same amount of teaching experience but the females tended to be older, presumably reflecting broken service.

4. Experience and Student Achievement/Teacher Effectiveness

Longitudinal studies such as those by Fuller (1969) and Felder et al. (1979) which documented stages in the development of teachers, and focused particularly on their concerns, suggest that teacher effectiveness, while it may increase through the early years of a teaching career, probably does not continue to do so, certainly not in a linear fashion. Teacher "burnout" with its deleterious effects on both teachers and pupils has attracted attention from psychologists and is sometimes mentioned as a direct and disadvantageous effect of experience.

The overall impression seems to be of a curvilinear, but possibly an overall negative, relationship between years of teaching and effectiveness. This finding recurs in primary, secondary, and higher education settings of research.

In a comprehensive review of studies investigating the relationships between seniority and instructional experience of college teachers to their students' global and specific evaluations of them, Feldman (1982) concluded that there was no consistent finding. There does appear to be a tendency for an inverse or curvilinear relationship to emerge between experience and both general and specific evaluations, although a number of the studies reviewed reported no significant relationship and some found a positive one. Feldman discussed a number of possible contributing factors whose influence is supported by empirical research.

In the school setting, Ryans (1960) found an overall negative relationship which included a rise in effectiveness in the first five years, followed by levelling and a decline, and this seems to be supported in more recent studies, several of them associated with the Coleman inquiry into educational opportunity (Coleman et al. 1966, Mostellar and Moynihan 1972). Stated very simply, that inquiry found that home and family background variables made a much more significant contribution to student achievement than any school or teacher variables. "Years of teaching" was one of six factors contributing to the teacher quality variable in that study. Jencks (1972) in his reanalysis of the Coleman data found a small significant positive relationship between teachers' prior professional experience and students' achievement. However, he suspected that this finding probably reflected selective recruitment by the achieving schools. He found that the percentage of tenured teachers correlated positively with school mean level of achievement but when schools from similar backgrounds and with equally experienced teachers were compared, a 10 percent increase in the percentage of tenured teachers was associated with a significant *lowering* of the mean student achievement of the school. Smith (1972 p. 309) confirmed that the measured teacher characteristics in the Coleman study uniquely explained very little of the achievement variance. He considered that the small positive relationship found between experience and achievement when this subvariable was isolated was not overwhelming but suggested that a real relationship might have been masked by using a mean-experience variable common to every teacher and pupil within a school. It might be that a middle level of experience or a mix of experience and youthful enthusiasm might optimize achievement. Certainly more detai-

led study is needed. An overview of other research in the area reveals a similarly unclear picture.

In a controversial study examining the performances of groups taught by trained, experienced teachers and those taught by nonteacher-trained experts in the actual fields (motor mechanics, electronics, and social science research methods), Popham (1971) used very specific skills tests to measure students' skill acquisition, and consistently found no difference between the groups. The studies have been replicated by others but have also been widely criticized, particularly by Glass (1974) who denied claims that the skills tests were more objective or reliable than others. He argued that Popham's tests were too specific, and that the "teaching" conditions were so sterile that they eliminated any opportunity for teachers to display the benefits of experience.

A possible explanation of the nonpositive relationships between length of teaching experience and student achievement is that "poorer" schools, with lower mean student achievement and facilities (e.g., schools in poor inner-city areas, schools with high proportions of disadvantaged students of various kinds including those unfamiliar with the language of instruction, or rural schools in isolated communities) tend to have less appeal to teachers, so experienced teachers use their bargaining power to avoid appointment to or to obtain early transfers from those schools. Cawthron et al. (1980) found that South Australian metropolitan high schools had teachers with significantly longer service in the same school than did nonmetropolitan high or area schools, particularly in the case of male teachers. However, Jencks (1972) found that schools which hired teachers already experienced elsewhere demonstrated higher mean student achievement than those where the teachers' experience, while comparable in overall length, was largely at the current school.

5. Experience and Attitudes to Innovation, Change, and Minority Groups

In a review of a number of studies examining the effects of various school resources on teacher effectiveness in working with black students and others, Spady (1973) found an overall tendency for successful teachers of black students to be young, black, and inexperienced, with a preference for working with low-ability students. He quoted a number of studies, but commented on the poor quality of the research and lack of consistency among findings.

Experience and its relation to attitudes of teachers has attracted attention, and again there tends to be a negative relationship suggested. Teachers with fewer years of teaching tend to have higher expectations of disadvantaged students, to be more in favour of innovation or at least no less favourable than more experienced teachers, particularly if the teacher groups are of comparable age. However there does tend to be a positive relationship between the tendency to interialize decisions with regard to educational change and years of teaching experience.

6. Experience and Classroom Management

The dominance of concerns about classroom control amongst beginning teachers suggests that they at least see lack of experience as a disadvantage in this regard. However, Smith (1981) found no significant differences in classroom management approaches between experienced teachers and education majors without teaching experience although a gender group difference, while apparent in both groups, was much stronger in the nonexperienced group. Inexperienced males advocated sensitizing techniques in cases of aggressive behaviour much more than inexperienced females but this difference was much less marked amongst experienced teachers. Smith stressed the need to include both sexes in samples of teachers. The mean age differences between his groups may have contributed to some of his results, and he did not report any use of the wide range of experience within his "experienced" group. Within that group alone there might have been differences according to length of experience.

7. Experience Outside the Classroom

Experience other than in teaching may affect instruction. In Australia at least, few teachers have any experience of full-time employment outside the classroom (Cawthron et al. 1980) and this may affect their teaching style and their role. Exmilitary teachers who also had significant school teaching experience were seen by their secondary students as having significantly more authoritarian styles than career teachers without extensive military training but with comparable classroom teaching experience (Weaver and Stansel 1978). Studies examining the effectiveness of teachers returning after child rearing or other outside experience would be of interest.

8. Transmission of Experience

Watts (1980) suggested that writing and communicating with other teachers can be a useful means of overcoming the decline in effectiveness in a teacher's development, as well as helping less experienced teachers. She described the Resource Agent programme in Vermont where master teachers were encouraged and enabled to offer courses and workshops and be "identified as a resource" for other teachers. The consultancy schemes operating in Australian federal and state departments of education may provide an alternative approach. However, Newberry (1978) found significant barriers between new and experienced teachers, with experienced teachers hesitating to interfere by passing on advice and new teachers feeling unable to seek it.

9. Summary and Conclusions

Teaching experience is frequently included as a variable in educational research, but no clear picture of its effects has emerged. Reviewers consistently point to the need for clarification of the relationship with educational goals, with attention paid to obtaining an appropriate measure of the experience variable, as well as to measures of effectiveness.

If, as seems to be suggested in a substantial proportion of the studies surveyed, increases in teaching experience, at least after the early years in the classroom, are associated with lower student achievement levels and with a tendency for teachers to reject innovations and alterations in educational policy, the implications are considerable, although a resolution of the problem is by no means clear. If the innovations and criteria of effectiveness are unquestionably accepted as desirable, there is a need for changes in the selection or training of teachers, or in the classroom or administrative environments, so as to encourage teachers to continue to increase in effectiveness or at least maintain the highest level they have reached. If these criteria are inconsistent with the goals which experienced teachers set themselves, the question arises whether this is a result of complacency and a lack of enthusiasm or of a realistic acceptance of the classroom situation. Certainly, the field is open to high-quality research, the results of which could be of value to administrators as well as to teachers themselves and those involved in their selection and training.

See also: Classroom Management

Bibliography

Berkeley G F 1966 What the statistical survey reveals. *Teachers in Australia: An Appraisal Including the 1966 Buntine Oration.* Cheshire, Australian College of Education, Melbourne, Chap. 2, pp. 22–37

Berryman J D, Berryman C R 1981 *Use of the "Attitudes Towards Mainstreaming Scale" with Rural Georgia Teachers.* Paper to American Educational Research Association (AERA) annual meeting, Los Angeles, California

Brophy J E, Evertson C M 1976 *Learning from Teaching: A Developmental Perspective.* Allyn and Bacon, Boston, Massachusetts

Bryant B J et al. 1978 *What Employers Consider Important in Hiring Teachers.* Research Report. Association for School, College and University Staffing, Madison, Wisconsin

Cawthron E R, Craig R A, Menzies B 1980 Metropolitan and non-metropolitan secondary school teachers. *Pivot (A Journal of South Australian Education)* 7(3): 53–60

Coleman J S, Campbell E Q, Hobson C J, McPartland J, Mood A M, Weinfeld R L, York R L 1966 *Equality of Educational Opportunity.* United States Office of Education, Washington, DC

Cook R H 1978 Classroom interaction based on teacher ethnicity and experience (Ph.D. Dissertation, Walden University)

Evertson C M, Brophy J E, Crawford W J 1975 *Texas Teacher*

Effectiveness Project: An Investigation of Presage–Process Relationships. Report No. 75–16. Research and Development Center for Teacher Education, Texas University, Austin, Texas

Felder B D, Hollis L Y, Piper M K, Houston W R 1979 *Problems and Perspectives of Beginning Teachers: A Follow-up Study.* University of Houston, Houston, Texas

Feldman K A 1982 The seniority and instructional experience of college teachers as related to the evaluations they receive from their students. Unpublished manuscript. State University of New York, Stony Brook, New York

Fuller F 1969 Concerns of teachers: A developmental conceptualization. *Am. Educ. Res. J.* 6(2): 207–26

Glass G V 1974 Teacher effectiveness. In: Walberg H J (ed.) 1974 *Evaluating Educational Performance: A Sourcebook of Methods, Instruments, and Examples.* McCutchan, Berkeley, California

Good T L, Biddle B J, Brophy J E 1975 *Teachers Make a Difference.* Holt, Rinehart and Winston, New York

Jencks C S 1972 The Coleman Report and the conventional wisdom. In: Mosteller F, Moynihan D P (eds.) 1972

Leming J S 1980 *Efficacy and Experience: The Relationship between Locus of Control and Years of Teaching Experience.* Southern Illinois University, Carbondale, Illinois

McArthur J T 1980 *The First Five Years of Teaching.* Australian Educational Research and Development Committee, Canberra

Mostellar F, Moynihan D P (eds.) 1972 *On Equality of Educational Opportunity.* Random House, New York

Newberry J McI 1978 The barrier between beginning and experienced teacher. *J. Educ. Adm.* 16: 46–56

Popham W J 1971 Performance tests of teaching proficiency: Rationale, development and validation. *Am. Educ. J.* 8: 105–18

Ryans D G 1960 Prediction of teacher effectiveness. In: Harris C W (ed.) 1960 *Encyclopedia of Educational Research: A Project of the American Educational Research Association,* 3rd edn. Macmillan, New York, pp. 1486–91

Smith D K 1981 *Classroom Management Styles and Personality Variables of Teachers and Education Majors: Similarities and Differences.* Paper to American Educational Research Association (AERA) annual meeting, Los Angeles, California

Smith M S 1972 Equality of educational opportunity: The basic findings reconsidered. In: Mosteller F, Moynihan D P (eds.) 1972

Spady W G 1973 The impact of school resources on students. In: Kerlinger F N (ed.) 1973 *Review of Research in Education 1.* Peacock, Itasca, Illinois

Watts H 1980 *Starting Out, Moving On, Running Ahead or How Teachers' Centers Can Attend to Stages in Teachers' Development.* Occasional Paper No. 8. Far West Laboratory for Educational Research and Development, San Francisco, California

Weaver A M, Stansel P L 1978 Authoritarian-democratic attitudes and practices of retired military personnel employed as secondary school social studies teachers. *High Sch. J.* 62: 7–12

Teachers' Social Backgrounds

E. Hoyle

Status is the relative standing of an individual in the eyes of other members of society or some section of it. It is determined by the degree to which an individual has authority, exercises influence, and generates deference. These qualities derive, in turn, from such characteristics as age, sex, ethnic background, wealth, and occupation. This article considers the status accorded to the teacher on the basis of occupation. It is thus largely concerned with the occupational prestige of teachers in various societies However, although an individual's status is determined in an important way by occupation, the status-relevant qualities which teachers otherwise possess can influence the occupational prestige of teaching in a reciprocal manner. The social origins of teachers, that is the status of the families into which they were born, constitute an important influence on the occupational prestige of teaching. Thus two major sections of this article will deal with the issues of occupational prestige and social origins. The two other sections will consider the determinants of the status of teachers other than social background and the status of teaching as a profession.

1. The Occupational Prestige of Teaching

Occupational prestige is the position of an occupation relative to other occupations. All members of society have a general notion of prestige and this determines the degree of deference which they accord to individuals on the basis of their membership of an occupation. Social scientists operationalize this awareness of status differences by asking samples of people to assign a rank order to a range of occupations. The basic idea is simple; the actual procedures are much more complex. There is the perennial problem of validity of whether the rankings which individuals assign actually conform to the deference which they would in practice accord a member of a particular occupation. There is also the perennial problem of reliability, whether the rankings have at least a relative degree of permanence. Methodological problems include the wording of the instructions which raters are given, the representativeness of the sample of raters, the limits to the number of occupations which can be included, and the limits to the knowledge of raters about particular occupations. The generalizations made in this section are based upon data provided by investigations which vary considerably in size, sophistication, characteristics of raters, year of investigation, and so on, and they must therefore be treated with due caution. Data have been chosen for consideration partly on the basis of availability and partly on the basis of national variations in social, economic, political, and educational structure. The United States is the source of the majority of empirical studies of the relative prestige of teachers. In 1947 the National Opinion Research Center carried out a study of ranking of occupations in the United States. Respondents were asked to assign occupations to one of five categories: excellent, good, average, somewhat below average, and poor (along with a "don't know" category). The categories were assigned an arbitrary numerical weighting. In 1963 this study was replicated, using as far as possible the same occupations, categories, and method of data collection (Hodge et al. 1966). Table 1 gives the percentage responses in each category for the two studies.

Table 1

Percentage of respondents allocating teaching to prestige categories[a]

Occupation	Excellent	Good	Average	Below average	Poor
Public-school teacher 1947	26	4	24	3	2
Public-school teacher 1963	31	46	22	1	0

a Source: Hodge, Siegel, and Rossi (1966)

It can be seen that more respondents rated teaching as "good" in 1963 than in 1947 and as Table 2 shows, the rank order attained by teaching out of 90 occupations also improved. The occupations in Table 2 have been selected from the longer list for purposes of comparison.

Groff (1962) gives details of 15 studies reported between 1931 and 1958 dealing specifically with the relative prestige of teaching. The number of occupations with which teaching is compared ranges from 12 to 200. The location of teaching in the hierarchy varies between the second and fifth decile—higher for high-school teaching than for elementary-school teaching—but comparisons are difficult because of the influence on rank order of the other occupations chosen. The best generalization which one can make about "teaching" as a single category from these and other studies is that its modal position is in the fourth decile, below the elite professions of medicine and law, but above the other personal and public service semiprofessions.

In the United Kingdom, the Registrar General's Classification of Occupations, which is widely used for research purposes, ranks teaching as a single occupation in the second of six categories along with such occupations as nurse, police officer, Member of Parliament, and engineer.

A scale of relative occupational prestige in the United Kingdom, developed for use in the Oxford Occupational Mobility Enquiry, covered 124 occupations which included different categories of teacher. Table 3 contains a selection of occupations from that scale which locates these.

It can be noted that on this scale, although categories of headteachers are differentiated, both primary- and secondary-school teachers are included in the same group which is just outside the third decile of occupations and thus very close indeed to the ranking of "schoolteacher" in the United States study of Hodge et al. (1966).

A different picture presents itself in Table 4 which contains the ratings of teachers in a study conducted in Poland by Sarapata and Wesolowski (1961). Sarapata found the category "teacher" to be ranked third in a list of 29 occupations, an unusually high status. When the same occupations were ranked by agriculturally employed residents in rural areas, the top five occupations, in rank order were as follows: university professor; member in government cabinet; teacher; physician; industrial engineer.

Thus the general public in one Eastern European country assigns an exceptionally high status to teaching. However, when secondary-school students assign status

Table 2

Rank order of teaching and other selected occupations from a list of 90[a]

Occupation	Rank order (1947)	Rank order (1963)
US supreme court justice	1	1
Physician	2.5	2
College professor	8	8
Lawyer	18	11
Public-school teacher	36	29.5
Accountant for a large business	29	29.5
Police officer	55	47

a Source: Hodge, Siegel, and Rossi (1966, adapted)

Table 3
Rank order of selected occupational groups[a]

Rank order	Descriptive title and occupations of the greatest numerical importance in the group
1	Self-employed professionals I (Doctors, lawyers, accountants)
2	Administrators and officials 1 (Senior civil servants)
3	Salaried professionals I (Airline pilots)
5	Self-employed professions II (Dentists, architects)
15	Administrators and officials II (Headteachers, Senior police officers)
23	Administrators and officials VIII (Headteachers, managers in social welfare)
34	Self-employed professionals IX (Parochial clergy)
36	Technicians II (Draughtspersons, technical administrators)
38	Salaried professions V (Primary- and secondary-school teachers, social welfare workers, male nurses)
39	Self-employed professions X (Entertainers, artists, journalists)
40	Large proprietors VIII (Estate agents, travel agents, auctioneers)

a Source: Goldthorpe and Hope (1974, abridged)

in another Eastern European country, the Soviet Union, a very different picture emerges. Table 5 shows the different rankings assigned by male and female secondary-school graduates in an urban area (Novosibirsk) and a rural area (Novosibirsk region). The most relevant differences revealed in this table are the high ranking assigned to both primary and secondary teachers by girls, especially those living in rural areas. The other interesting findings is that boys rank miner above teacher and, in the rural area, even above physician. This ranking differs greatly from findings in Western countries.

Generalizations about the occupational prestige of teachers in developing countries are even more difficult. Those countries which are most comparable with developed societies are those which are themselves in the process of industrialization and/or have an enduring colonial legacy. Foster (1965), as part of a larger study of socioeconomic development in Ghana, had 25 occupations ranked by secondary-school students. The results are given in Table 6. Foster suggests that the unexpectedly low status of primary- and middle-school teachers has resulted from lower standards of entry caused by expansion, and an increased gap between these teachers and those in secondary school who have retained their status.

Hodge et al. (1966), using data from many sources, concluded that there was a remarkable degree of consistency between rankings across societies both devel-

oped and developing. This would seem to be broadly the case but variations do occur which may be due to a variety of factors which can now be considered. The nature of the group undertaking the task of ranking will clearly have an effect on the eventual hierarchy, although high correlations between raters from different social groups have been reported in many studies. Bolte (cited by Kob 1958), examined the different rankings allocated to 38 occupations by three groups of respondents in Schleswig–Holstein. The results are summarized in Table 7.

It can be noted that whereas adults rank secondary-school teaching well above primary-school teaching, both sets of students draw less distinction between the two categories but both, and especially the university students, rank secondary-school teaching below that accorded by the adult population. Kob takes this to imply that many university students would regard teaching as very much a second best occupation for them to enter. This factor must also be weighed when interpreting the data for the Soviet Union cited above.

Large-scale studies tend not to discriminate in any refined way between types of teacher. By and large, as seen in the data already considered, the only significant distinction made is between primary- and secondary-school teachers, yet different statuses in teaching enjoy different levels of prestige. In some developed societies there has been a trend towards a greater homogeneity of teaching in one sense with common salary scales and the exclusion of the unqualified, but at the same time the teaching profession has become more differentiated and stratified within the boundary separating teachers from nonteachers (Hoyle 1969a). In some systems (e.g., France) there still remain considerable prestige differences between teachers in elite secondary schools and other schools (Halls 1976). Thus the single category of "teacher" is a considerable oversimplification. However, there are relatively few studies of intraoccupational prestige and with the exception of the Oxford scale cited above (Goldthorpe and Hope 1974), research has tended to involve only small samples usually consisting of incumbents of educational roles. Nevertheless, some of these studies are instructive. Counts' pioneering study (Counts 1925) was based on the ratings of 45 occupations in which he distinguished different roles in education including college teaching, administrative posts, and different kinds of teacher: elementary, high school, and rural school. Deeg and Paterson (1947) partially replicated Counts' work taking 28 of his initial occupations and found virtually no change. Bernbaum et al. (1969) showed that a sample of student teachers in the United Kingdom perceived the general public as ranking lower than themselves all educational roles. The students differentiated between the prestige of various roles but although primary teachers and teachers in nonselective secondary schools were still given the lowest ranks, the gap between these roles and others was not as great as in the perceived rankings of the general public.

Table 4
Esteem ratings of occupations and positions by Warsaw residents[a]

Sequence	Occupations	Scale value[b]
1	University professor	1.22
2	Physician	1.44
3	Teacher	1.71
4	Mechanical engineer	1.78
5	Airline pilot	1.83
6	Lawyer	1.97
7	Agronomist	1.97
8	Minister of government cabinet	2.07
9	Journalist	2.13
10	Skilled steel worker	2.18
11	Skilled lathe operator	2.27
12	Priest	2.35
13	Nurse	2.38
14	Factory foreperson	2.53
15	Bookkeeper/accountant	2.54
16	Self-employed tailor	2.70
17	Self-employed locksmith/steamfitter	2.73
18	Office supervisor	2.77
19	Private farmer	2.78
20	Commissioned officer	2.79
21	Private storekeeper	3.01
22	Railway conductor	3.18
23	Militiaman (police)	3.21
24	Office clerk	3.43
25	Office secretary	3.50
26	Store clerk	3.59
27	Unskilled building worker	3.95
28	Charwoman in office	4.08
29	Unskilled worker on state farm	4.16

a Source: Sarapata (1966), reported in Fiszman (1972). See also Sarapata and Wesolwoski (1961) b Scale: 1—very high esteem; 2—high; 3—average; 4—low; 5—very low

Table 5
Rating of occupations by secondary-school graduates[a]

	Ranks (71 occupations)							
	Novosibirsk				Novosibirsk region			
	1963		1973		1963		1973	
Occupation	Boys	Girls	Boys	Girls	Boys	Girls	Boys	Girls
Pilot	3	3	1	1	1	1	1	1
Physician	16	6	22	2	35	5	25	3
Miner	25	—	28	—	24	—	18	—
Secondary-school teacher	39	25	38	14	39	2	32	4
Elementary-school teacher	51	31	49	25	51	9	40	9
Nurse	—	40	—	28	—	26	—	8
Fieldhand	63	61	59	50	48	46	36	52
Clerk	69	71	71	71	70	71	71	59

a Source: Shubkin, cited by Perevedentsev (1980, adapted)

Table 6
Ranking of 25 occupations in order of their perceived prestige made by Ghanaian secondary-school students[a]

	Rank order					
	Males			Females		
Occupation	Mean score	S.D.	Rank	Mean score	S.D.	Rank
Doctor	1.12	0.31	1	1.21	0.54	1
University lecturer	1.16	0.31	2	1.22	0.53	2
Lawyer	1.45	0.64	3	1.47	0.59	3
Chief	1.89	0.78	4	1.94	0.77	5
Author	1.97	0.80	5	1.86	0.86	4
Secondary-school teacher	2.05	0.51	6	1.97	0.53	6
Clergyman	2.06	0.84	7	2.14	0.82	7
Businessperson	2.50	0.73	8	2.45	0.70	9
Nurse	2.60	0.64	9	2.49	0.78	10
Political party worker	2.70	0.93	10	2.36	0.79	8
Government clerk	2.71	0.59	11	2.76	0.54	11
Soldier	2.78	0.81	12	2.84	0.76	15
Actor	2.81	0.90	13	2.79	1.01	12
Chief's counsellor	2.82	0.74	14	2.83	0.73	14
Police officer	2.94	0.73	15	3.00	0.62	17
Farmer	2.95	0.96	16	3.05	0.96	18
Office worker	2.96	0.60	17	2.81	0.54	13
Middle-school teacher	3.00	0.50	18	2.96	0.50	16
Primary-school teacher	3.25	0.67	19	3.27	0.69	19
Motor car mechanic	3.59	0.73	20	3.55	0.77	20
Petty trader	3.62	0.75	21	3.55	0.87	20
Shop assistant	3.80	0.66	22	3.63	0.64	22
Carpenter	3.84	0.73	23	3.77	0.69	23
Farm labourer	4.47	0.70	24	4.26	0.81	24
Street cleaner	4.74	0.56	25	4.62	0.70	25

a Source: Foster (1965)

Table 7
Rank order of occupations among a group of respondents[a]

	Adults	University students	Technical students
1.	University teacher	University teacher	University teacher
2.	Doctor	Factory director	Doctor
3.	Secondary-school teacher	Doctor	Municipal councillor
4.	Municipal councillor	Landowner	Secondary-school teacher
5.	Factory director	Municipal councillor	Factory director
6.	Minister of religion	Minister of religion	Landowner
7.	Landowner	Secondary-school teacher	Electrical engineer
8.	Major in the armed forces	Electrical engineer	Minister of religion
9.	Opera singer	Opera singer	Elementary teacher
10.	Electrical engineer	Elementary teacher	Major in the armed forces
11.	Elementary teacher	Major in the armed forces	Technical designer

a Source: Bolte (1955), cited Kob (1958)

There are very few studies of occupational prestige which involve regular replication to show changes in the status of occupations over time and studies must be drawn upon which were carried out according to different procedures at different points in time which tend to suggest a relative stability in the occupational prestige of teaching. Even in developed societies, changes could occur through policies which reduced existing divisions between teachers in systems which have had a stratified profession and changes in the labour market which affect the characteristics of those who enter teaching. However the problem is much more acute in developing societies where changes in prestige can turn on a variety of factors, which include the prestige of the teacher in a colonial era, the rapid expansion of primary education, the supply or oversupply of highly qualified but unemployable graduates, the combination of teaching with some other occupation such as farming, the degree to which teaching is a pathway to administrative or political status, and so forth.

2. The Social Origins of Teachers

The difficulties involved in making generalizations about the social origins of teachers must be pointed out. There are relatively few studies and these tend to have been conducted in developed societies. Existing studies vary in the categorization of social class and methods of analysis. Because there are considerable variations in the class backgrounds of teachers of various kinds, generalizations about the entire occupational group are

hazardous and most studies do not take account of the variance by sex, type of school, and so on. Nor do studies control changes in the occupational structure leading to changes in the distribution of social classes and rates of social mobility. Finally, changes in class background over time can only be fully understood in the context of changes in the labour market for teachers.

The largest number of studies of the social origins of teachers has been carried out in the United States (see Havighurst and Levine 1979 for a review). The broad picture would appear to be that there has been a gradual shift amongst those entering teaching away from the dominance of children of farmers and the emergence of a situation in which the social class background of teachers, especially in urban areas, is much more heterogeneous and embraces the full range. However, the lowest and the highest social classes are still considerably under represented compared with the general distribution of social classes in the population. Teachers tend to come predominantly from the middle groups of blue-collar and white-collar workers. Table 8 reports trends in the recruitment of teachers from different social backgrounds in England and Wales drawing on the detailed and sophisticated study of Floud and Scott (1961).

Entrants through the special postwar "Emergency Training Scheme" have been excluded from Table 8. For entrants through the normal channels the table shows the fluctuating trends for each group but, with an increased postwar recruitment compared with the beginning of the period studied, shows an increase in working-class male and lower-middle-class female

Table 8
Social origins of teachers entering the profession at various periods[b]

Period of entry to teaching	Father's occupation when teacher left school			
	Professional and administrative	Inter-mediate	Manual	All
(a) Men	%	%	%	%
Before 1919	11.3	49.5	39.2	100.0
1920–29	11.5	49.1	39.4	100.0
1930–39	7.0	47.6	45.4	100.0
1940–44	10.3	49.1	40.6	100.0
After 1945[a]	8.0	51.8	40.2	100.0
All	8.3	49.5	42.2	100.0
(b) Women				
Before 1919	10.9	56.2	32.8	100.0
1920–29	10.2	51.3	38.5	100.0
1930–39	9.0	58.1	32.9	100.0
1940–44	10.0	56.3	33.8	100.0
After 1945[a]	10.6	54.0	35.4	100.0
All	11.2	54.2	34.6	100.0

a These figures exclude teachers entering via shortened emergency training course after the war b Source: Floud and Scott (1961) entrants and a decrease in male entrants from the professional/administrative class.

Taylor and Dale (1971), as part of their study of new entrants to teaching in England and Wales, secured data on fathers' occupation from their national sample of probationers ($n = 3,598$). The results were as in Table 9 with a column added to show the distribution of classes in the total male population.

Table 9
Social class background of probationary teachers in England and Wales 1966[a]

Father's occupational status	Percentage	Percentage in total population
1. Professor	5	5
2. Intermediate	37	18
3. Skilled nonmanual	25	12
Total nonmanual	67	35
4. Skilled manual	17	38
5. Semiskilled manual	9	18
6. Unskilled manual	5	9
Total manual	31	65
Total probationers	100	100

a Source: Taylor and Dale (1971) (adapted)

Bassett (1958, 1971) has monitored changes in the social background of Australian teachers between 1944 and 1970 through studies of entrants to courses of teacher training in one university and one college of education. The major trend is the substantial increase in the proportion of students coming from the higher social classes. However, it is difficult to interpret these comparative figures without additional data on changes in the occupational structure, the job market, and changes in the organization of schooling such as a move away from selective secondary education.

One of the few studies which has attempted to control for changes in the occupational structure, with its increasing proportion of nonmanual, middle-class occupations, has been that of Betz and Garland (1974) for the United States. They did so by calculating a ratio of mobility. This study confirmed the growing accessibility of teaching to entrants from lower socioeconomic backgrounds.

There are differences in the social origins of different categories of teacher, particularly between men and women and between teachers in different kinds of school. In most systems for which data are available, the mean social class background of female teachers tends to be higher than that of male. Floud and Scott's data demonstrate the greater preponderance of women

teachers having middle-class origins. The oft-made comment that teaching is regarded as a suitable occupation for middle-class women to a greater degree than for middle-class men appears to have some basis.

Another general finding is that secondary-school teachers tend to have a mean social class background higher than that of primary-school teachers (see e.g., Floud and Scott 1961 for English data, and Organisation for Economic Co-operation and Development 1971a, Table 19 for French data).

In view of the fact that women constitute the great majority of primary-school teachers in most systems, and in view of the fact that they tend to come from a higher social class background than men, the overall lower social origins of primary-school teachers requires some explanation. Where data exist which allow an examination of this apparent anomaly, it would seem that the influence of the higher proportion of women in primary schools is more than offset by the considerably higher social class origins of both men and women in secondary schools. This is shown in the data on Chicago teachers collected by Havighurst (1964) given in Table 10.

It can be seen that if farm owners are categorized as middle class, whereas 53 percent of women teachers in elementary schools come from middle-class backgrounds, this is considerably lower than the 66 percent of women secondary-school teachers who do so.

The offspring of working-class families tend to have a lower average level of educational attainment than their middle-class counterparts. Thus working-class students, and men particularly, have found it possible to attain the academic requirements to become a primary-school teacher to a greater degree than a secondary-school teacher since this has only required a higher education in an institution other than a university, normally a teachers' college. Similarly, where a stratified system of secondary schools exists, both men and women from working-class origins find it easier to enter lower status secondary schools. There may be motivational factors operating independently of academic attainment, the preference of teachers from working-class backgrounds for posts in predominantly working-class schools, but there is little evidence to support this. The data in Table 11 from Floud and Scott's study shows the distribution of teachers by social class and type of school.

In connection with Table 11 it should be noted that both maintained and direct grammar schools are academically selective and, in the case of the latter, also involve parental fees.

Social class differences between teachers according to type of school reflect the different forms of higher education which they have experienced. Of the many pathways into teaching one can identify three modal patterns:

(a) university degree course followed by teacher training;

Table 10
Father's occupation of Chicago public-school teachers 1964[a]

Occupation of teacher's father	Percentage of teachers					
	Elementary school			Secondary school		
	Men	Women	Total	Men	Women	Total
Semiskilled and unskilled	26	15	17	20	9	14
Farm laborer or renter	1	1	1	1	1	1
Skilled worker, foreperson or similar	33	31	31	30	24	27
Farm owner	3	3	3	4	4	4
Clerical and small business	17	23	22	20	26	23
Professional and managerial	20	27	26	25	36	31
Number	720	4,430	5,150	1,123	1,250	2,373

a Source: Havighurst and Levine (1979), adapted from Havighurst (1964)

Table 11
Social origin of teachers in grant-earning schools, England and Wales 1955[a]

(a) Men					
Father's occupation when teacher left school	Primary %	Modern %	Technical %	Maintained grammar %	Direct grant grammar %
Professional and administrative	6.0	7.5	6.0	12.5	19.8
Intermediate	48.3	45.9	51.0	55.1	61.5
Manual	45.7	46.6	43.0	32.4	18.6
All	100.0	100.0	100.0	100.0	99.9

(b) Women					
Father's occupation when teacher left school	Primary %	Modern %	Technical %	Maintained grammar %	Direct grant grammar %
Professional and administrative	8.8	11.4	17.4	17.8	30.4
Intermediate	52.2	54.8	58.1	63.1	57.4
Manual	38.9	33.8	24.5	19.1	12.2
All	99.9	100.0	100.0	100.0	100.0

a Source: Floud and Scott (1961)

(b) a degree course in education in university or college with concurrent training;

(c) a certificate course in education in a teachers' college with concurrent training.

The academic qualifications gained at school by entrants to these courses vary, with university noneducation degree courses requiring the highest qualifications. But entrants also vary in social class background. Table 12 compares entrants to university and to colleges of education in the United Kingdom.

Similarly Fiszman (1972) reports that university places in Poland are filled disproportionately by children of the intelligentsia but that at institutions for teacher training the representation of the lower socioeconomic classes increases as one moves down the hierarchies of prestige and educational achievement. Table 13 compares the social class background of university students and students in schools of pedagogy, the equivalent of university schools of education. Data for France show similar class differences (OECD 1971b).

Class differences remain marked for those students having graduated from universities who enter teaching, and those who enter other occupations. Kelsall et al. (1972), in a follow-up study of students in the United Kingdom six years after graduation, show that education recruited more heavily from those graduates with lower social class origins.

Thus data from various countries show that although teachers are recruited from all social classes, the skilled working and white-collar groups tend to be more highly represented than the highest and lowest sectors, and

middle-class representation in the teaching force becomes more pronounced as one moves from certificated primary-school teachers to graduate secondary-school teachers, especially in the prestigious academic schools.

3. Factors Influencing the Social Status of Teachers

There are considerably more research data on the social status of teachers than on the factors which determine that status. Thus most of the studies of this issue have tended to be interpretive and, frequently, speculative. This section, therefore, summarizes some of the factors which have been held to affect the social status of the teacher. It is interesting to note that much of the literature on this issue implicitly, and often explicitly, addresses itself to the question of why the status of teaching is lower than it ought to be. There is little work which suggests that the status of teaching is higher than ought to be the case.

The discussion will follow the convention of the literature and consider those factors which are likely to account for the status of teaching being lower than the other professions. Six factors have been selected for discussion. They are all interrelated, but it is impossible in the present state of knowledge to give any order to the degree to which they separately influence status.

3.1 Social Origins of Teachers

Social origins have been considered in some detail in the preceding section. It was noted there that a reciprocal relationship probably exists between the status of an occupation and the social origins of its members: a high

Table 12

(a) Father's occupation of students on three-year courses in teacher training in the United Kingdom 1961/62[a]

	Higher profes- sional	Other profes- sional and marginal	Clerical	Skilled	Semi- skilled	Un- skilled	Not known	All students
Men	5	27	16	32	13	2	5	100
Women	8	36	14	27	7	2	5	99
Men and Women	7	33	14	28	9	2	6	99

(b) Father's occupation of university undergraduates in the United Kingdom 1961/62

	Higher profes- sional	Other profes- sional and marginal	Clerical	Skilled	Semi- skilled	Un- skilled	Not known	All students
Men	17	40	12	19	6	1	5	100
Women	20	43	11	16	6	1	3	100
Men and Women	18	41	12	18	6	1	4	100

a Source: Committee on Higher Education (1963) Tables 81 and 5

Table 13
Social class of students in Poland 1965–66[a]

Class background	Percentage of students	
	University	Higher-pedagogical school
Working class	26.1	35.6
Peasantry	14.1	20.9
Intelligentsia	53.3	38.3
Self-employed artisans	5.1	4.3
Other	1.4	0.7
Total	100.0	99.8

a Source: Fiszman (1972)

status profession recruits members from higher social origins who then, because of these origins, sustain the status of the occupation. Very broadly speaking, and with the necessary reservations which the discussion above would indicate as appropriate, it can be said that those who enter teaching at least retain and in many cases considerably improve their family-bestowed social status. Thus entrants are not bringing to teaching a social background which would enhance its status.

3.2 The Size of the Teaching Force

Teaching is by far the largest of those occupations which may claim to professional status. The size of the teaching force relative to other professional and quasiprofessional occupations varies in advanced societies and varies considerably in developing societies depending upon their educational policies, but teaching is considerably larger than other professions. It is held that the size factor detracts from the status of teaching. There is no inherent reason why this should be the case but perhaps two factors operate. One is that large size probably depresses salary levels compared with the small, elite professions and salary level is, in turn, likely to have a reciprocal effect on status: high salary bestows high status which commands high salary.

3.3 The High Proportion of Women in Teaching

This is a contentious issue and is advanced here only in the most tentative manner. There is a far higher proportion of women in teaching than in any of the high-status professions and it is possible that this affects the status of the profession as a whole. Insofar as teaching is regarded by the general population as "women's work" and insofar as the status of women's employment generally has been hitherto considered lower status than that of men, teaching thereby suffers.

3.4 The Academic Qualifications of Teachers

The academic qualifications of teachers are everywhere considerably higher than most other occupations and higher than the social service occupations with which they might be compared. But they are lower than the academic qualifications required for entry to the major professions. The following generalizations can be made about the academic backgrounds of entrants to teaching. Although the average length of the course of professional preparation for teachers has been steadily increasing in most countries, it has traditionally been of shorter duration than courses for the preparation of doctors and lawyers. The school-level academic achievements of entrants to teacher education have been lower than those required by most other professions. For many students, entry to courses of teacher education has been their only means of gaining entry to an institution of higher education. The final qualification of teachers, particularly elementary-school teachers, in many societies has been a certificate or diploma rather than a university degree. Specialist degrees in education are generally accorded lower status than degrees in arts or science subjects with teachers having such degrees and subsequently undergoing a brief period of teacher education having a higher professional status. This is something of a paradox in view of the fact that other professions require specialist degrees in their fields. It is explained, however, by the fact that more importance is often attached to the teacher's knowledge of a teaching subject than to educational or pedagogic theory and practice and by the fact that the possession of a specialist degree is offset by the other determinants of status referred to here and by the relatively low standing of professional schools of education in the prestige hierarchy of university departments.

3.5 The Childhood Status of the Teacher's Clients

This is a particularly speculative issue, but it may well be the case that the fact that the teacher's immediate clients are dependent and immature may be one of the determinants of the teacher's status. To be sure, other professionals have children as clients but their clientele does not consist exclusively of children. In some sense therefore the teacher is not wholly of the adult world and status is thereby depressed. The present writer has elsewhere speculated that the teacher's status is affected by being intermediate on a number of dimensions: the world of children and the world of adults; the world of schooling and the world of work; the moral order of the school and the different morality accepted in the wider world; and the academic world where knowledge is produced and the world of learning where knowledge is disseminated (Hoyle 1969b).

3.6 The Teacher's Relationship with Clients

The teacher's relationship with clients differs from that of the doctor or the lawyer. The teacher has a sustained relationship on a daily, weekly, and yearly basis. The teacher's clients are, at least during the ages of compulsory schooling, involuntary. They are normally taught in quite large groups and are not in the one-to-one relationship of the doctor's or lawyer's client. The teacher's clients are not usually in distress and do not have the individual problems which take the sick to the doctor or the prosecuted person to the lawyer. It is true that much of the work of the doctor, the dentist, and the lawyer deals with routine problems but there are also rare occasions when a dramatic intervention is necessary.

This different form of direct relationship takes from teaching much of the mystique which still attaches to other professions. With the disappearance of the teacher's gown, the raised dais, and various rituals, the classroom lacks the aura of the operating theatre or the courtroom or even the consulting room of the doctor or the lawyer. Everyone goes through school and therefore observes teachers at close quarters over many years which robs the teacher's role of any mystery. And, because clients are involuntary, the teacher faces the perennial problem of control, a struggle which all have observed during their school years and which is likely to detract from the teacher's status.

Thus there are factors which, at least hypothetically, reduce the teacher's status compared with that of members of other occupations. However, it should be stressed again that there is little hard evidence to support this account. Moreover, it is an account which relates particularly to complex industrialized societies. There are other societies where the teacher is much more revered, but in general teachers tend to have an ambivalent status.

4. Teaching as a Profession

This section considers briefly teaching as a profession. The discussion has much in common with the earlier discussion on the factors influencing status, but because the term profession has a symbolic significance its applicability to teaching can be separately considered. A review of recent literature on the teaching profession is to be found in Hoyle (1981).

The traditional sociological approach to the study of professions has been to identify the characteristics which are held to distinguish professions from other occupations and to use these collectively as a model against which to assess the degree to which various occupations approximate to professions. Lists of criteria abound in the literature and tend to have many elements in common.

Some of these common components are summarized by Lieberman (1956):

(a) a unique, definite and essential social service;

(b) an emphasis on intellectual techniques in performing this service;

(c) a long period of specialized training;

(d) a broad range of autonomy for both the individual practitioner and for the occupational group as a whole;

(e) an acceptance by the practitioner of broad personal responsibilities for judgments made and acts performed within the scope of professional autonomy;

(f) an emphasis upon the service rendered rather than the economic gain to practitioners;

(g) a comprehensive self-governing organization of practitioners.

Where teaching is matched against these criteria it is usually held to fulfil most of the criteria to some degree but to a lesser extent than, say, medicine, law, and architecture, therefore falling into the category of quasi- or semi-professions.

Three points can be made about the objective approach to the professions. One is that the criteria are derived from a study of those occupations which have high status and are currently referred to as "professions". The second is that the criteria are derived interpretatively from a variety of sources rather than generated impersonally from a systematic study of professional practice. The third is that they are often implicitly underpinned by certain assumptions which can be termed "functionalist".

An alternative approach to the professions has two main components. One is located in the symbolic interactionist rather than the functionalist perspective in sociology. It is less concerned with categorization, though there is an implicit assumption that there may be something relatively distinctive about occupations labelled professions, and more concerned with professional practice, professional ideologies, and the political influence of the organized profession (Hughes 1958, Dorros 1968, Leggatt 1970).

In the application of this approach to teaching, Waller's famous study (Waller 1965) stands out as an early contribution and, latterly, Lortie's work (Lortie 1973, 1975) and, although not taking a specifically sociological stance, Jackson's study of teachers and students (Jackson 1968). With this group the concept of "profession" is heuristic, used as an entry to substantive issues rather than a logical category. A related but ideologically more radical group of writers treats the term "profession" as an ideological weapon for the pursuit of status, power, and autonomy, and focuses on the procedures used by the established profession in their pursuit of self-aggrandizement (e.g., Bennett and Hokenstad 1973).

A related concept is that of professionalization. This is the process by which an occupation succeeds over time in meeting the criteria of a profession. This is usually treated as a unitary process, but it has been argued (Hoyle 1974) that two processes are involved which usually proceed *pari passu* but which could vary independently. These are professionalization as the improvement of status and professionalization as professional development or the improvement of professionality of the knowledge and skills involved in professional practice. Thus the elongation of the period of training for teachers constitutes professionalization, and it is assumed that this enhances professionality, but this cannot be treated as wholly axiomatic.

Because professionalization is likely to enhance status, it is vigorously pursued by teacher unions and associations. There is little doubt that in most societies teaching has been in the process of continuous professionalization. Some of the elements of this process have been: the extension of the period of initial training; an increase in the number of graduates in teaching; the growth of a body of theoretical knowledge underpinning educational studies; the growth of a research and development infrastructure; an increasingly strong boundary around teaching distinguishing the qualified from the unqualified; and so on. Increased professionalization should yield higher status and may well have done so, but it is difficult to demonstrate that this is the case to a degree which overcomes extrinsic determinants of status such as the social origins of entrants, the proportion of women in the profession, and so forth. Moreover, it may be the case that unless it is clear that professionality is enhanced, the teaching profession could be confronting the paradox of professionalization without status (Hoyle 1982).

Finally it should be noted that in taking a particular perspective on the teaching profession with status as the central concept, the article has thereby left unconsidered the alternative perspective which focuses on the class position of teachers and can do no more than alert readers to this other approach. In much of the literature, class and status are used interchangeably to denote relative positions in a social hierarchy. Indeed, class has been used in this way in this article. But the concepts have different sociological origins: the work of Weber in the case of status and the work of Marx in the case of class. In a Marxian usage, class refers to a position of a social group in relation to the economic structure and the distinctive consciousness to which this gives rise. Because occupation, an economic factor, is generally used as the best indicator of social status, class and status are easily conflated. However, class is also an indicator of the power which different social groups derive from their relationships to the means of production, distribution, and exchange. The class location of teachers is amongst those occupations which are involved in neither ownership nor production. The class position of teachers, the stance which they take in the class conflict which is central to Marxian analysis, is ambiguous. For an exploration of these issues the reader is referred to those works which undertake a Marxian analysis of teaching (e.g., Ozga and Lawn 1981, Harris 1982).

See also: Teacher Roles; Selection for Teaching; Professional Socialization of Teachers

Bibliography

Bassett G W 1958 The occupational background of teachers. *Aust. J. Educ.* 2: 79–90

Bassett G W 1971 The occupation background of teachers: Some recent data. *Aust. J. Educ.* 15: 211–14

Bennett W S, Hokenstad M C 1973 Full time people workers and conceptions of the professional. In: Halmos P (ed.) 1973 *Professionalization and Social Change.* Sociological Review Monographs, No. 20. University of Keele, Keele

Bernbaum G, Noble G, Whiteside T 1969 Intra occupational prestige differentiation in teaching. *Paedag. Eur.* 5: 1–59

Betz M, Garland J 1974 Intergenerational mobility rates of urban schoolteachers. *Soc. Educ.* 47: 511–22

Bolte K M 1955 *Wandlungen und Strukturen in unserer Gesellschaft: Untersuchungsbericht des Soziologischen Seminars der Universität Kiel.*

Committee on Higher Education 1963 *Administrative, Financial and Economic Aspects of Higher Education* (Robbins Report). Appendix 2B. Her Majesty's Stationery Office, London, Cmd 2154

Counts F A 1925 The social status of occupations. *Sch. Rev.* 33: 20–21

Deeg E, Paterson D G 1947 Changes in social status of occupations. *Occupations* 25: 205–07

Dorros S 1968 *Teaching as a Profession.* Ohio University Press, Columbus, Ohio

Fiszman J R 1972 *Revolution and Tradition in People's Poland: Education and Socialization.* Princeton University Press, Princeton, New Jersey

Floud J, Scott W 1961 Recruitment to teaching in England and Wales. In: Halsey A H, Floud J, Anderson C A (eds.) 1961 *Education, Economy and Society: A Reader in the Sociology of Education.* Free Press, New York

Foster P J 1965 *Education and Social Change in Ghana.* Routledge and Kegan Paul, London

Goldthorpe J H, Hope K 1974 *The Social Grading of Occupations: A New Approach and Scale.* Clarendon Press, Oxford

Groff P J 1962 The social status of teachers. *J. Educ. Sociol.* 3: 20–25

Halls W D 1976 *Education, Culture and Politics in Modern France.* Pergamon, Oxford

Harris K 1982 *Teachers and Classes: A Marxist Analysis.* Routledge and Kegan Paul, London

Havighurst R J 1964 *The Public Schools of Chicago: A Survey for the Board of Education, Chicago.* Board of Education, Chicago, Illinois pp. 417–18

Havighurst R J, Levine D U 1979 *Society and Education,* 5th edn. Allyn and Bacon, Boston, Massachusetts

Hodge R W, Siegel P M, Rossi P H 1966 Occupational prestige in the United States. In: Bendix R, Lipset S M (eds.) 1966

Class, Status and Power: Social Stratification in Comparitive Perspective, 2nd edn. Free Press, New York

Hodge R W, Treiman D J, Rossi P 1966 A comparative study of occupational prestige. In: Bendix R, Lipset S M (eds.) 1966 *Class, Status and Power: Social Comparative Perspective*, 2nd edn. Free Press, New York

Hoyle E 1969a Professional stratification and anomie in the teaching profession. *Paedag. Eur.* 5: 60–71

Hoyle E 1969b *The Role of the Teacher*. Routledge and Kegan Paul, London

Hoyle E 1974 Professionality, professionalism and control in teaching. *London Educ. Rev.* 3(2): 13–19

Hoyle E 1981 Sociological approaches to the teaching profession. In: Hartnett A (ed.) 1981 *The Social Sciences in Educational Studies*. Heinemann, London, pp. 214–76

Hoyle E 1982 The professionalization of teachers: A paradox. *Br. J. Educ. Stud.* 30(2): 161–71

Hughes E C 1958 *Men and Their Work*. Free Press, Glencoe, Illinois

Jackson P W 1968 *Life in Classrooms*. Holt, Rinehart and Winston, New York

Kelsall R K, Poole A, Kuhn A 1972 *Graduates: The Sociology of an Elite*. Methuen, London

Kob J 1958 *Das Soziale Berufsbewusstsein des Lehrers der Höheren Schule: Eine soziologische Lertstudie*. Werkbund, Wurzburg [1961 Definition of the teacher's role. In: Halsey A H, Floud J, Anderson C A (eds.) 1961 *Education, Economy and Society*. Free Press, New York]

Leggatt T 1970 Teaching as a profession. In: Jackson J A (ed.) 1970 *Professions and Professionalization*. Cambridge University Press, Cambridge, pp. 155–77

Lieberman M 1956 *Education as a Profession*. Prentice-Hall Englewood Cliffs, New Jersey

Lortie D C 1973 Observations on teaching as work. In: Traver R M W (ed.) 1973 *Second Handbook of Research on Training: A Project of the American Educational Research Association*. Rand McNally, Chicago, Illinois

Lortie D C 1975 *Schoolteacher: A Sociological Study*. University of Chicago Press, Chicago, Illinois

Organisation for Economic Co-operation and Development (OECD) 1971a *Conference on Policies for Educational Growth, Paris, 1970. Vol. 5 Teacher's Resources and Structural Change*. OECD, Paris

Organisation for Economic Co-operation and Development (OECD) 1971b *Training, Recruitment and Utilization of Teachers in Primary and Secondary Education*. OECD, Paris

Ozga J, Lawn M 1981 *Teachers, Professionalism and Class*. Falmer Press, Falmer

Perevedentsev V I 1980 *Choosing an Occupation*. [*Chelovek Uybirdet professiiu*]. Znanie Publishers [reprinted *Soviet Education* 23(1): 6–83]

Sarapata A 1966 Stratification and social mobility in Poland. *Empirical Sociology in Poland*. Polish papers collected and prepared for publication by Jan Szczepanski. Institute of Philosophy and Sociology, Polish Academy of Sciences PWN, Polish Scientific Publishers, Warsaw

Sarapata A, Wesolowski W 1961 The evaluation of occupations by Warsaw inhabitants. *Am. J. Sociol.* 66: 581–91

Taylor J K, Dale R 1971 *A Survey of Teachers in their First Year of Service*. University of Bristol, Bristol

Waller W 1965 *The Sociology of Teaching*. Wiley, New York

Occupational Factors

Teacher Roles

B. J. Biddle

The term, "teacher role", is a popular one, and hundreds of studies have now been published in which it appears. Chapters on teacher role may also be found in both theoretical and hortative works concerned with teaching, its contexts, and its effects. Unfortunately, use of this term is also vague, and several different concepts are intended by authors who write about teacher roles. Many who use this term seem unaware that it has other uses than the one they intend, so our first task is to distinguish some of the major concepts to which the term has been applied. Three such concepts are distinguished here, and each is then used as a basis for discussing relevant research and theory.

1. Concepts of Teacher Role

Technical use of the social role concept appeared in the 1920s and reflected the influence of at least three seminal contributors—Ralph Linton, Jacob Moreno, and George Herbert Mead. These three represented different disciplines in the social sciences and used the role concept somewhat differently. For simplicity three separate concepts will be distinguished that may be designated by the term teacher role. To avoid confusion, the discussion uses the standardized concepts and vocabulary developed for role theory by Biddle (1979).

1.1 Role as Behavior

Some authors use teacher role to refer to behaviors that are characteristic of teachers. Most who use role in this sense restrict their interests to teacher behaviors in the work context, that is, in the school or classroom. Nevertheless, teachers may also be found in nonwork contexts, and a few authors have discussed the role of teachers in their homes, the marketplace, or the political arena. Authors using role in this first sense presume that teacher behaviors are existential events and can be observed directly. Moreover, teacher roles may also be observed by other actors, hence are assumed to have the potential for affecting, and being affected by, the behaviors of pupils and other persons who interact with teachers.

1.2 Role as Social Position

Other authors use the term teacher role to refer to the identity or social position that is shared by teachers. In this usage the word role refers to the designating term ("teacher") and the set of persons who are designated by that occupational title. This second usage focuses on static characteristics of teachers—the recognition of teachers as having a separate social position, the composition of the teacher population, the status of the teaching profession, and conditions for entry into or departure from the field. Authors who intend this second meaning often speak of teachers as "occupying" their roles.

1.3 Role as Expectation

A third group of authors uses the term teacher role to refer to expectations that are held for teachers. Some of these expectations are held by teachers themselves, whereas others are held by parents, school administrators, pupils, politicians, or members of the public. Some expectations are normative in mode, but others may represent beliefs, preferences, or other modes of thought. Some may be widely shared, but others may reflect divergent opinions and generate role conflicts for the teacher. Authors who follow this third usage tend to view teachers as persons capable of rational thought. Expectations are learned through experience, and once they are formed, expectations will affect the behaviors of those who hold them in predictable ways.

None of these three concepts precludes the others, of course. None has precedence, and none has a corner on insight. Each represents a facet of the complexities that imbed the teacher, and each is capable of generating information for educators and other social scientists. Each has also generated research literature. Nevertheless, the fact that such different concepts are all designated by the same phrase poses problems for investigators and consumers alike. One must read each source carefully to establish the concept a given author intends with the phrase teacher role. And one must be prepared to discount confusion that is generated when some authors forget their conceptual definitions or misunderstand those of others.

2. *The Behavioral Role of the Teacher*

The behavioral role of the teacher may be defined as those behaviors that are characteristically performed by teachers. Like persons in other occupations and professions, teachers respond in characteristic ways. Most are regularly found in classrooms during the working day, and most spend much of that day supervising the instruction of pupils. When not in classrooms, teachers are likely to be found in the hallways or offices of the school building, or in the lunchroom or teachers' lounge. And during the evening, teachers are likely to be grading papers, preparing lessons, or attending school-related functions. This does not mean that all teachers behave identically, of course. But to learn that a person teaches for a living means that he or she is more likely to do certain things and less likely to do others, and it is the former that constitute the teacher's behavioral role.

The concept of teachers' behavioral role may be contrasted with two related concepts with which it is sometimes confused. The first of these is the profile of the teacher which may be defined as the characteristic, nonbehavioral features of teachers. Within the United States, for example, the Research Division of the National Education Association regularly surveys teachers to establish their profile for such nonbehavioral characteristics as sex, age, marital status, and years of education completed. Such information has intrinsic interest and may be useful for planning social policies concerning teachers. The second is the treatment of the teacher which consists of the characteristic behaviors that are directed towards teachers by others. Like all persons, teachers are the recipients of characteristic behavior from others with whom they interact, and their lives are made rewarding or galling depending on how they are treated by pupils, parents, principals, members of school boards, and even the press. Studies of these may be found, but neither treatment nor profile should be confused with role. The role of the teacher concerns how teachers themselves behave, and has its own data-base and interest.

Teachers characteristically do a great many things, so studies of the role of the teacher are normally limited in some fashion. Sometimes that limitation is contextual. For example, an investigator may examine the teacher's role in the classroom, the school, or in some other context in which membership in the teacher's social position is recognized and relevant. Sometimes, also, a sectoral limitation may be placed on the definition, in which case the investigator examines that portion of the teacher's role directed towards members of another social position, such as pupils. (Other sectors of the role are directed towards the school's principal, other teachers, or members of the public.) In contrast, if authors choose to discuss the teacher's role in non-educational contexts, usually that discussion focuses on behaviors that are presumed to be unique to teachers; that is, are not exhibited by other, comparable actors.

Sometimes, also, a functional limitation may be placed on the definition of the teacher's behavioral role. Like other professionals, teachers may accomplish a variety of things, and authors may single out one or more of those things for discussion. For example, many teachers are called upon to disseminate information to pupils, to serve as pupil counselors, and to grade pupils' performances on a regular basis. Each of these tasks requires somewhat different activities on the part of teachers, and simultaneous performance of these different activity sets may be difficult for the teacher to manage. The difficulty with functional analysis of the teacher's role is that no definitive set of functions is prescribed for most teachers, and behaviors characteristic of teachers may contribute to more than one identifiable function. As a result, many different lists of functions have been suggested for the teacher's role, and behavioral evidence concerning these functional distinctions is hard to find.

The issue of evidence raises another question concerning the behavioral role of the teacher. What is the best way to study such roles? Since behaviors are observable events, then surely the best way of studying them is to observe them directly. Up until about the middle of the twentieth century it was difficult to find studies of behavioral roles that were based on observation, but this has now changed (Dunkin and Biddle 1974). Literally thousands of studies have now appeared in which the classroom behaviors of teachers and pupils were observed, and these provide a wealth of data concerning the role of participants in that context. It is more difficult to observe behaviors elsewhere in the school, however, and more difficult still to study teacher activities in nonschool contexts. As a result, studies still appear in which the teacher's behavioral role is examined by asking teachers or others to discuss those activities in interviews and questionnaire responses. Technically, the latter forms of data are measures of what respondents *think* about the teacher's role and are more validly interpreted as measures of their expectations for teachers. To interpret them as measures of teacher role behavior means that a simple relationship must be assumed between role expectations and role behaviors, an assumption that is questioned below. Nevertheless, indirect evidence is better than no evidence, and much of what is presumed to be known about the teacher's behavioral role today is based on it.

Evidence concerning the behavioral role of the teacher is subject to two limitations that may be ignored by those who interpret that evidence. For one, the teacher's role varies somewhat depending on the grade level of the classroom and school. It presumably differs also depending on the curriculum and subject matter taught and may vary also depending on the composition of pupils in the classroom, the instructional equipment available, the age, sex, ethnicity, and disposition of the teacher, and the community or nation in which teaching is studied. As yet it is not well-understood how these variables affect the teacher's role, and to estimate those effects samples of teachers that represent specific subsets of the teacher population need to be studied. But collection and analysis of behavioral data is expensive, and most studies of the teacher's behavioral role are not conducted with representative samples. This fact may be forgotten by investigators who are sometimes tempted to make claims for broader segments of the teacher population than are warranted from the samples they have studied.

For a second limitation, teacher behavior is complex, various aspects of it may be chosen for study, and many techniques and observational instruments have now appeared that are used for such studies. Findings that are reported for any given technique or instrument may or may not be related to findings for another technique or instrument. To illustrate, findings for the teacher's nonverbal behavior (Smith 1979) bear unexamined relationships with findings for teacher verbal behavior (Bellack et al. 1966), and even the latter have questionable relationships with findings for another instrument that also expresses teacher verbal behavior (Smith and Meux 1962). In any strict sense, then, findings for the teacher's verbal role depend on both the actions of those teachers studied and the observational categories with which they are examined. The latter should always be kept in mind when thinking about claims made for the teacher's role, and attempts to examine variations in the teacher's role in different contexts should be considered valid only when they use identical (or at least similar) techniques and instruments.

2.1 Behavioral Role in the Classroom

Bearing the above strictures in mind, what are some of the major characteristics of the behavioral role of the teacher that have so far appeared in observational studies? For simplicity this article is confined to only a handful of research traditions where similar techniques and instruments have been applied to various classroom contexts.

An early and influential set of studies made use of an observational instrument developed by Flanders (1970). This instrument allowed observers to differentiate between teacher and pupils in the classroom and provided seven categories for classifying teacher talk: accepts feelings, praises or encourages, accepts or uses ideas of students, asks questions, lectures, gives direction, and criticizes or justifies authority. Moreover, the first four of these categories were said to constitute "indirect" teaching while the last three were "direct." More than 100 studies were conducted using this instrument in the 1960s and early 1970s (most of them in the United States), and classrooms observed covered all grades in primary and secondary schools and most subjects commonly taught.

The broad portrait of teacher role painted by these studies was of teacher verbal domination of the classroom. Talk was found to occur about two-thirds of the time in classrooms, and teachers did most of the talking. Most teachers talk was "direct" with lecturing being the dominant "direct" category, although quite a few directions were also given regularly. Among "indirect" behaviors, teachers were most likely to ask questions. Relatively few instances of praise and criticism were observed. Some of the role behaviors were also found to vary depending on pupil characteristics. "Indirectness" was more likely to appear with pupils who were higher in intelligence or social class. Boys were more likely to receive praise, criticism, and questions from teachers; minority pupils were also more likely to receive criticism but less likely to receive praise. Secondary-level classes were more likely to receive lecturing and less likely to be given directions. Research within the Flanders' tradition exhibited various problems and has declined since the early 1970s. Nevertheless, most of the findings for teacher role generated by this tradition have held up well. To illustrate, Brophy (1981) reports that recent studies continue to show little use of praise by teachers in classrooms.

A second set of studies was pioneered by research on language use in the classroom by Bellack et al. (1966). Taking insights from Wittgenstein, these authors consider classroom interaction to consist of a "game" whose procedural rules are well-understood by mature participants. Each verbal utterance in the classroom is considered to fall into one of four categories: structuring, soliciting, responding, and reacting. Moreover, sequences of moves can be recognized, called "teaching cycles," in which all of the moves have a common topic. Secondary classrooms in economics were studied in the United States by Bellack et al., with their procedures since replicated by investigators in Sweden and Australia (see *Teaching Cycles and Strategies*).

Findings from these studies paint a surprisingly similar role for the teacher. Teachers were found to make about 60 percent of the moves in the classroom. Teachers did by far the most structuring, soliciting, and reacting, whereas pupils did most of the responding. Most classrooms featured longish stretches of time when the teacher was emitting structuring moves, that is, the teacher was "lecturing." Such periods were interrupted by other stretches in which teachers and pupils interacted in predictable teaching cycles. Most such cycles were of short duration and consisted of a teacher solicitation, a pupil response, and (sometimes) a teacher reaction, but occasional longer cycles also appeared. Most classroom moves concerned relevant subject matter, and most teacher reactions were positive in tone. In short, most of the classrooms studied were reasonably orderly, focused on academic topics, and supportive. Given lack of familiarity with the rules of the classroom "game" among younger pupils, one would predict less orderliness and focus on academic topics in primary classrooms and more stress on learning the rules of the "game." These predictions were generally supported by Mehan (1979) who studied a multigrade primary classroom in the United States. In short, the teacher's role changes depending on whether the teacher is or is not faced with pupils who are competent at playing their own roles in the classroom "game."

A third set of studies concerned the logical analysis of classroom discourse and began with the work of Smith and Meux (1962). These authors proposed a set of 12 categories into which teaching cycles (which they called "episodes") could be sorted for purposes of logical analysis: describing, designating, stating, reporting, defining, substituting, evaluating, opining, classifying, comparing and contrasting, conditional inferring, and explaining. Six subtypes of explaining were also recognized. Smith and Meux studied several types of subject matter lessons in secondary schools in the United States, and their work has since been replicated in both New Zealand and Australia.

Each of these studies found that classrooms gave greatest emphasis to describing, thus classrooms tended to be focused on low-level, empirical concerns. Designating and explaining episodes were also popular, although frequencies for these latter categories varied depending on context. Science lessons often used defining and describing; geometry lessons emphasized stating; social studies lessons were high on opining; English lessons gave stress to stating and evaluating. Not surprisingly, then, teacher role was found to vary in logical emphasis depending on the demands of the subject matter taught.

A fourth set of studies was originally stimulated by discovery of "the Pygmalion effect" by Rosenthal and Jacobson (1968). In this work the authors showed that some teachers who expected pupils to be "bright" or "dull" inadvertently encouraged pupils to conform to those expectations in their achievements (see *Teachers' Expectations*). This effect was subsequently confirmed in literally scores of replication studies in the United States, although not all teachers were found to exhibit it. But how do teachers behave so as to encourage pupils to conform to expectations that are held for them by teachers? This question has now been investigated in a number of observational studies conducted in the United States, and a good summary of their methods and findings may be found in Brophy and Good (1974).

The latter studies found a number of teacher behaviors associated with expectations for pupils. Teachers were more likely to smile at and nod their heads toward "bright" pupils, to initiate more interactions with those thought to be "bright," to spend more time waiting for those thought "bright" to respond, to praise those thought to be "bright" more frequently, to respond more to the substance of what "bright" pupils said, and so forth. Not all teachers showed these reactions, however, and when those who did were alerted to their discriminatory behavior, they were likely to alter their behaviors. In this case, then, teacher role

was found to be associated with teacher expectations for pupils, although that relationship was not well-understood by teachers, and teachers were likely to alter their roles when alerted to it.

Having looked at some of the variables now known to affect teacher role, the consequences of variation in teacher role can now be examined. Does teaching make a difference, and if so, which aspects of teacher behavior matter? Several massive field studies have examined this question in the United States, and some of the major findings from them have already been confirmed in field experiments. Reviews of this American effort are already available (Brophy 1979, Good 1979, Rosenshine 1979), and a British study is also available (Bennett 1976). Much of this work has concentrated on primary-school teaching, although one or two studies at the secondary level are now beginning to appear.

Many such studies confirm Flanders' earlier conclusion that most teaching is "direct" in character. Moreover (and quite contrary to Flanders' advocacy), "direct" teaching appears to be more effective than "indirect" teaching, particularly for pupils of limited ability and from lower socioeconomic status homes. Despite strong calls for individualized instruction and the appearance of new educational curricula and instructional technology, most of the investigations found that teachers concentrate on whole-class instruction with lecturing, recitation, and seatwork alternating during the lesson. Studies also found that teachers with high-achieving pupils were good classroom managers. Their pupils spent a lot of time on task, motivation for learning was high, and teachers created the impression that they were fully "in charge" through strategies originally described by Kounin (1970). In short, variations in the teacher's role certainly *do* matter, and it is quite possible to establish aspects of that role that are associated with higher levels of pupil achievement for specific populations of pupils.

In summary, then, considerable information is now available concerning the teacher's behavioral role. The picture painted of that role is of a relatively stable and traditional form of behavior in which the teacher operates a classroom, maintains discipline, and manages the dissemination of subject matter to pupils by means of lecturing, interaction with pupils, and seatwork. The evidence suggests that these forms of social behavior are well-understood by both teachers and mature pupils. Variations in the teacher's role are associated with subject matter taught, grade level, teacher expectations, and populations of pupils taught. Variations in that role are also known to be associated with different levels of pupil achievement. Most of the evidence so far available concerning that role comes from American studies, although evidence has also appeared from a handful of other Western countries. Teacher behavioral roles probably differ in socialist and Third World countries, but few observational studies have yet appeared in the latter.

.2 Behavioral Role in Other Contexts

Little information is now available concerning teacher behavior in nonclassroom contexts. A fair number of anecdotal pieces have appeared on the topic, but observational research on teacher conduct outside of the classroom is hard to find, and even systematic reports of nonclassroom conduct are few. Hilsum and Cane (1971) collected data on "the teacher's day" from a random sample of 129 teachers in junior and primary schools in Surrey, England. They report that teachers spent nearly five hours per school day in classroom teaching, nearly two hours per day on "break" time (which were largely devoted to lesson preparation, conferences with colleagues, club activities, and lunch), and one or more hours per day on out-of-school work that was related to their jobs. The scene thus painted was of a busy and full professional week, albeit one that was subjected to many cross-pressures and frequent interruptions. Campbell (1970) studied supplementary employment among a sample of male teachers in the United States. He found that most teachers found it necessary to work at a second job to supplement their incomes, that the average teacher worked at his second job for 13 hours per week, and that most teachers also worked at supplementary, full-time employment during the summer. To the extent that these studies represent the wider population of teachers, then, teaching is not only a full-time occupation but is one that requires its participants to work at outside employment to make ends meet.

3. The Social Position of the Teacher

A social position consists of a set of persons who share some characteristic and who are given a recognized label within the society. Teachers regularly instruct pupils; thus the social position of the teacher may be defined as the set of persons who regularly instruct pupils and are given such designations as "teacher," "instructor," "master," and the like. Occasionally the concept of teacher is also extended to include persons who teach students in postsecondary education. However, the teaching of adults involves quite different activities than the teaching of nonadult pupils, and those who teach adults are normally recruited and trained for their occupations in quite different ways than are teachers. Consequently, most persons who write about the social position of the teacher confine their attention to those who teach at the primary and secondary levels.

Several confusions surround the social position concept. As mentioned, some authors use the term "role" to refer to social position, so one may find articles in which "teacher role" is used to designate those who teach rather than the activities of teaching or expectations for the latter. Other authors use the term "status" to refer to social position, which is also confusing because the word "status" has another, unambiguous meaning concerned with the ranking of social positions vis-à-vis one another. (The status-ranking of teachers is discussed below.) Finally, some authors define the social position concept as a "location" or "niche" in a division of labor. Such definitions are confusing because they presume that all positions are occupations. Whereas "teacher" is a recognized occupation in Western societies, teachers are not always paid for their services elsewhere but may still be recognized, even honored, for their activities.

3.1 The Status of Teachers

A number of characteristics of social positions have been studied over the years. One of these is status which concerns the ranking of social positions in terms of characteristics deemed desirable. As a rule, three criteria for status ranking have dominated the literature: prestige, wealth, and authority. Members of social positions have prestige when they are able to attract deferential behavior from others who are not members. They have wealth when they are given or are allowed to control commodities. They have authority when they can get others to follow their dictates. It is widely assumed that prestige, wealth, and authority go together and that social positions which have one of these qualities in abundance will also have the others. Although this is true on average, one can think of some social positions that are high on one or two of these criteria but not the others (church dignitaries, Mafiosi). Studies of the status of social positions may either focus on status as a (presumed) unitary concept or may involve separate investigations of prestige, wealth, and authority.

Relatively few studies of the prestige of teachers have yet appeared, but these tend to place teachers towards the lower end of middle-class occupations and at the bottom of those occupations deemed to be professions. Moreover, this status ranking tends to hold throughout Western countries and in at least some Eastern societies. A number of reasons have been suggested for the relatively low prestige of teachers: prevalence of women in the teaching profession, lack of specificity in the role expected of teachers, the fact that teachers work primarily with the young, devaluation of the knowledge deemed necessary to teach well, the large numbers of persons presently employed or available for employment as teachers, and others. Lortie (1975) views teachers as having a "special but shadowed" prestige position. On the one hand, their work is seen as having the aura of a "special mission," but on the other, teachers have largely lost whatever autonomy they once had to manage pedagogical theory and their classrooms because they have become functionaries in hierarchical organizations. Whatever may be the reason, teachers clearly do not attract as much deference as do the other, more secure professions: medicine, the law, the ministry, even politics. On the other hand, teachers receive more deference than do most blue-collar occupations.

Like all occupations, teachers are paid for their

services. Most teachers are also the employees of organizations that receive public funds, so their salaries are a matter of public record. Not surprisingly, then, many studies of the wealth of teachers have appeared and continue to appear on a regular basis. These studies suggest that teachers tend to be paid at about the scale appropriate to their prestige position—above the scale paid to blue-collar workers but below the scale paid to most professionals. In fact, the wages paid to many teachers are probably sufficient to support a single person but insufficient to support a family. Since many married women do not work, this fact presumably explains why most men teachers find it necessary to work at a second job to supplement their teaching incomes. The economic systems of most Western countries are capitalist, and not surprisingly the relative wages paid to teachers tend to rise during periods of teacher shortage. Thus probably the major reason why teachers are not paid better wages is that they have never formed cartels to prevent entry of "unqualified" persons into the profession—as is done widely in medicine. Recently teachers have begun to unionize, however, and teacher wages have sometimes been improved through collective bargaining and industrial action.

Studies of the authority of teachers are quite rare, but as a rule that authority is confined to pupils, the school, and curricular matters. Like the hospital, prison, or university, the school is a people-processing organization, and most school systems feature a bureaucratic hierarchy in which the teachers are the "workers." Given this low-authority position, teachers must take orders from most of the rest of the personnel: department heads, subject matter specialists, principals and their assistants, superintendents, school-board members. Teachers have traditionally been assigned great power in the classroom, but this has recently been eroded through laws that constrain teacher conduct, administrative control over the curriculum, and pupil violence. Despite these erosions, the teacher retains an authority in the classroom that is generated through custom, law, the teacher's expert knowledge, and the teacher's control over grades and promotions for pupils. Teachers also have some authority over parental conduct in matters relating to education, although relationships between the teacher and parent vary considerably among countries. (Within some countries, such as the United Kingdom, parents are often discouraged from "interfering" with the school whereas in others, such as the United States, they are usually urged to "involve themselves" in the education of their children.)

In summary, then, teachers have more prestige, wealth, and authority than do most blue-collar workers, although their status is clearly less than that of most professionals. One does not enter teaching if one is truly interested in high status. But the status of a teaching career may be seen as a step up for those from working-class backgrounds (see *Teachers' Social Backgrounds*).

3.2 The Teaching Career

A second characteristic of social positions frequently studied concerns the careers of position members as they enter, maintain themselves as members, and eventually depart from the position. Various concepts have been proposed for discussing entrance, maintenance, and exit conditions, of which the best known is Ralph Linton's distinction between ascribed and achieved positions. Ascribed positions are those one enters through accidents of birth, such as racial or sexual categories. Achieved positions, like teaching, are those one enters through effort and certification by others.

A recent and insightful discussion of entrance into teaching appears in Lortie's *Schoolteacher* (1975) which is based on interviews that were conducted with teachers in the United States. Like other commentators, Lortie differentiates between recruitment and socialization, the former referring to factors leading persons to choose to enter teaching, the latter concerned with experiences teachers have as they are inducted into membership. Five types of attractors for teaching were cited by Lortie: desire for contact with young people, desire to provide service to others, desire to provide cultural continuity for the next generation, material benefits such as working conditions or the typical long summer vacation, and the compatibility of the teacher's working schedule with personal needs. In addition, Lortie also notes two conditions that facilitate recruitment of teachers: the fact that candidates may make either an early or late decision to enter the profession, and the fact that licensing procedures are generally quite flexible in education. Most of Lortie's respondents cited positive reasons for becoming teachers, but a few spoke of blocked aspirations for other careers, economic pressures, and response to parental pressures. (Entrance into teaching for economic reasons may be more prevalent in other countries that provide bursaries for postsecondary teacher training.)

Four types of socialization for teaching are described by Lortie: the socialization everyone goes through when they first learn about teacher and pupil roles in the classroom, the curriculum to which prospective teachers are exposed in postsecondary education, practice teaching, and on-the-job training. Like many commentators, Lortie suggests that curricular, practice teaching, and on-the-job training influences are generally insufficient to provide teachers with the skills they will need to manage the classroom. Consequently, teachers enter their careers with many different expectations and skills which lead, in turn, to considerable variation in role behavior in the classroom.

Like persons in most occupations, teachers are required to perform their jobs with a certain degree of competence in order to keep them. A few school authorities also require teachers to take periodic "refresher" courses or to seek additional professional qualifications for higher pay or advanced certification. Apart from these requirements, however, few stages ppear in the teacher's career, and teachers with 25 years of experience are likely to be doing much the same kind of work that is performed by those with one or two years of experience. Nor are experienced or expert teachers generally given special recognition or honorific titles. Not surprisingly, then, substantial numbers of teachers eventually leave the profession, and those who remain are often subject to boredom, stress, and "burnout" (Kyriacou and Sutcliffe 1977).

Which teachers are more likely to leave their profession, and what are they likely to do thereafter? These questions were studied for teachers in the United States by Chapman and Hutcheson (1982) who found that those who left teaching had greater analytical skills but those who remained were more expert organizers. Those who left teaching assigned greater importance to job autonomy and to salary, while those who remained valued recognition of their work by other people. Whereas some of those who left teaching did so to take higher status jobs in education (school administrator or counselor), the majority left the field of education for other endeavors. Those who do not leave teaching for other occupations eventually retire, and most school districts set an arbitrary retirement age for teachers.

4. The Expected Role of the Teacher

The expected role of the teacher may be defined as the set of expectations that are held for teacher behaviors by both teachers and other persons. Like persons in other social positions, teachers are subjected to a number of expectations for their conduct that reflect law, custom, habit, desires, and theories concerning their activities. These expectations form a context in which teacher conduct is interpreted, and role expectations for the teacher are presumably a major motivator for teacher conduct. On the one hand, those who hold expectations for teacher behavior are presumed likely to pressure teachers to conform to those expectations; on the other, teachers presumably want to follow their own expectations as well as those they attribute to others.

The concept of expected role is a deceptively simple one and hides several issues that should be exposed. First, expectations may be expressed in at least three different forms. Some expectations are expressed verbally, some are written down in news accounts or codes of conduct, and some are presumably held as covert thoughts by participants. Most authors who write about expectations for the teacher have the last form in mind. But covert expectations cannot be perceived directly. One learns about them by listening to teachers talk about their behaviors or by asking questions about the topic. Consequently, studies of the expected role of the teacher are normally conducted by means of interviews or standardized questionnaires.

Second, at least three different modes of expectation appear in the literature on teacher role. Some inves-

tigators study norms for teacher conduct—statements that express what teachers ought to do. Others study preferences, likes and dislikes, for teacher conduct. Still others study beliefs—statements that express subjective probability for the appearance of teacher behavior. Many investigators confuse these three modes or presume that they are interchangeable. But what one wants another to do may or may not be what one prefers or thinks likely, and a good deal of evidence is now available indicating that these three modes of expectation are not interchangeable (Bank et al. 1977).

Third, expectations for teachers may either be held by persons themselves or may be attributed by those persons to other actors. To illustrate, teachers normally hold expectations for their own conduct and attribute expectations for it to the principal of their school. The principal also holds expectations, of course, and usually he or she also attributes expectations to the teachers. These four different types of expectations are sometimes confused by researchers, or researchers may presume that by measuring one of them, a good estimate is also obtained of another. As will be seen below, such presumptions are questionable.

Fourth, some authors assume that expectations for the teacher are largely shared within the school or society. Moreover, teachers or other actors in the school may make similar assumptions. Such assumptions are also unwise. Whereas some expectations are surely shared for teacher conduct, others are not. Moreover, teachers may be made quite uncomfortable when they are faced with contradictory expectations that are held for them by two or more persons who have authority over them. Such situations are called "role conflict" and have been widely studied for teachers and other employees of organizations.

Finally, some authors also assume a simple and direct relationship between expectations for the teachers and teacher role behavior. Sometimes it is assumed that expectations are formed largely from observing teacher conduct. Or it may be assumed that the latter is largely generated by the former. Such assumptions are also unwise. Persons involved with schools form their expectations from both observation of teachers and from other sources of information, and teacher conduct is generated by both expectations and by other motivating forces. To discover how expectations are related to behaviors it is necessary to conduct research in which both are measured.

To summarize, then, expectations for the teacher's role appear in several types and forms; are presumably held by most actors associated with the school; are generated by various forces; and have a variety of effects on teacher conduct. To say this does not mean that teachers are unaffected by role expectations. On the contrary, such expectations presumably have considerable impact on teacher behavior, and experienced teachers normally have well-formed ideas about both their own expectations and those of others in the school concerning teacher conduct.

4.1 Shared Expectations for Teachers

Teachers are employed to instruct pupils because of shared values concerning the importance of education and beliefs concerning the efficacy of schools for fulfilling those valued outcomes. Not surprisingly, then, various authors have presumed that agreement also appears on functions or tasks that teachers are expected to perform. Several lists of such functions have been proposed, many of them drawn from the insights of Waller (1932) and Parsons (1959). An example of such a list appears in Kelsall and Kelsall (1969) who argue that teachers are (consensually) expected to: emancipate pupils from their home environments, encourage achievement among pupils, sort out and socialize "winners" and "losers" in the achievement game, inculcate societal norms in pupils, teach technical skills, instill interpersonal sensitivity and discipline, and aid pupils in making decisions and training for occupations. The Kelsalls' list focuses on tasks associated with pupils. Other authors have stressed functions generated by structural properties of the school as an organization or values in the wider society. Thus, it is presumed that teachers are also expected to: maintain order in their classrooms, accept and promote a common curriculum, follow the orders of supervisors, maintain effective communication with parents, exhibit "loyalty" for their schools, and the like.

Several things may be noted about such lists. For one thing, some of the functions listed are inconsistent with others. To illustrate, teacher activities designed to encourage achievement among all pupils are probably different from those designed to persuade "losers" in the achievement game that they have "lost" and should accept their subservient status. This means that teachers are presumably subjected to contradictory task expectations for the performance of their role. For another, the expectations listed are for functions to be accomplished and not for behaviors that teachers might exhibit. For example, it is quite possible to encourage pupil achievement by rote instruction or by stimulating motivation through class discussion. The functions listed do not tell which of these two teaching techniques is the more appropriate behavior. Educational ideologies may encourage one or another such behavior, but few would argue that educators necessarily agree on ideologies, or that lay persons even understand the issues involved. For a third, it cannot be told from such lists whether the tasks enumerated are actually shared in the society or not. Chances are that parents are particularly concerned about some of these functions whereas school principals are worried about others, teachers have somewhat different concerns, and pupils have a still different list. Empirical research is needed to establish the actual concerns of persons for teachers' tasks, but such research has been hard to find.

This does not mean that research is unavailable concerning shared expectations for the teacher. On the contrary, many studies of expectations for teachers have now appeared, and some of these have reported findings that seem to apply to respondents from various social positions and contexts. Some of this research concerns beliefs or stereotypes about classroom conduct. To illustrate, Mackie (1972) reports that Canadians believe teachers are sympathetic and supportive to pupils but are also inclined to dominate the classroom. American studies summarized by Biddle (1969) have found teachers presumed to be nonaggressive, acquiescent, and to sin largely by omission rather than by commission. Other American studies have uncovered shared preferences for fairness in grading, neatness, and willingness to help pupils (Wright and Alley 1977) or shared norms that teachers should not discriminate among pupils, should be thoughtful and friendly and should maintain order and discipline in the classroom (Biddle et al. 1961). Such expectations may be fairly universal among Western countries, but the evidence so far available is insufficient to test this proposition. None of the studies so far reported seems to have been based on national samples, and some of the data reported were collected before 1960.

Other research on shared expectations has concerned teacher conduct in nonschool contexts. Teachers in the United States have traditionally been employed by local school boards and have been expected to uphold standards of virtue and to perform various duties in nonschool contexts. In addition, some local school boards responded to The Great Depression by restricting employment of teachers to a minority of those qualified (e.g., to unmarried women). These factors led to the appearance of shared, restrictive norms for teacher conduct in nonschool contexts that were reported in various American studies (Biddle 1969). These norms were resented by teachers and evidence suggests that they have been disappearing gradually in the United States. This problem seems not have been studied in other countries.

4.2 Role Conflict, Strain, and Resolution

Not all expectations for teachers are shared, of course, and many studies have reported nonconsensual expectations for teachers. Most such studies have focused on norms, and most authors have interpreted their findings as indications of role conflict. Several forms of role conflict have been suggested in this literature.

A common finding, interpreted as role conflict, concerns evidence that persons in various social positions hold differing norms for teacher conduct. Such disparities have been reported for both the United Kingdom and the United States between such social positions as teachers, school principals, parents, pupils, teacher trainees, teacher trainers, persons from differing social classes, persons from rural and urban communities, and so forth (Kelsall and Kelsall 1969, Biddle 1979). Most of this research has argued that these disparities will pose problems for teachers because those who hold differing norms will presumably bring conflicting pressures to bear on teachers for conformity. However, it is not clear from most of the studies that other people will actually produce such pressures, that teachers are aware of these disparate norms, or that teachers are actually made uncomfortable by their appearance.

Some teachers recognize that others hold disparate norms for their conduct, and this awareness is also interpreted by many authors as role conflict. Studies reporting such awareness have appeared in various countries, and a major investigation is available reporting equivalent findings for it from Australia, the United Kingdom, New Zealand, and the United States that were obtained from national samples of teachers (Adams 1970). This investigation found normative disparities in all four countries. Some findings were common in the countries studied; in particular, teachers everywhere were likely to view teachers as being at odds with principals and other school officials over such issues as willing acceptance of nonprofessional duties, and with parents over curricular matters. Other findings were unique to specific countries; presumed conflict between teachers and school officials was greatest in Australia, and conflicts involving parents were strongest in the United Kingdom. The fact that teachers perceive normative disparities among differing groups of persons does not mean that these perceptions are accurate. Biddle et al. (1966) provided data indicating that teachers, in systematic ways, distort the actual views of principals, parents, and other actors concerned with schools. On the other hand, perceived normative disparities have been found associated with indicators of strain among both teachers and members of other occupations (Biddle 1979).

So far normative disparities have been considered associated with differing groups of persons who may think about the teacher. Other disparities are generated when the teacher also holds membership in other social positions whose tasks are at odds with those of teaching. Studies have appeared reporting role conflict between norms associated with teaching and coaching, teaching and counseling, and teaching and administrative responsibilities, but most of the research has concentrated on the conflicting demands of teaching and homemaking. Most studies of this latter topic have appeared in the United States, where the bulk of teachers are women and interest in role conflicts involving women has blossomed recently. Such conflicts are also known to be associated with strain.

Finally, normative disparities may also be associated with the fact that teachers are called upon to perform tasks that are somewhat antithetical. This form of role conflict has been studied in both the United States and the United Kingdom, and a good summary of the issues involved may be found in Grace (1972). Role conflicts of this fourth form are also known to be associated with strain.

What does the teacher do when confronted by situations of role conflict? When serious and persisting, such experiences may interfere with the teacher's performance or may cause teachers to leave the profession.

However, many teachers manage to resolve role conflicts in one way or another, by choosing to conform to one of the disparate norms in their behavior, or by compromising among the alternatives advocated. A general theory of role conflict resolution was originally proposed by Gross et al. (1958) and has since been tested in many contexts. Dunkin (1972) examined reported role conflict resolution among Australian teachers and found that he could predict resolution strategies from personality characteristics. "Self-oriented" teachers appeared to be more likely to resolve conflicts in terms of their own needs whereas "other-oriented" teachers apparently paid more attention to the needs and authority of other persons to whom norms were attributed.

Strain associated with membership in a social position may be generated by other experiences in addition to role conflict. Teachers may experience stress because their lives are overloaded, because of a mismatch between their own needs and expectations that are set for teachers, because of inadequate salaries or poor physical conditions in the school, or because of ethnic conflict in the community or physical violence in the school or classroom. Given stagnation in the economies of many countries since the early 1970s, these latter problems seem to have escalated for teachers, and studies of role conflict have correspondingly declined in numbers. Nevertheless, role conflicts remain a source of strain for teachers, and various studies have shown such conflicts are a major correlate of low morale in the organizational context.

4.3 Role Expectations and Behaviors

Role expectations may be studied as a major indicator of the subjective culture of persons who are members of social positions. Thus, teachers may be asked about their own preferences, norms, and beliefs about teaching, as well as about the expectations of others, because researchers are interested in learning the thoughts of teachers about their professional role. However, most people who study role expectations do so because they presume that expectations predict behavior. Teachers are presumed to conform (or at least to "want" to conform) to expectations for their position, and others who hold expectations for teachers are thought to exert pressures on teachers for compliance.

The interesting thing about these "reasonable" propositions is that so little evidence is available to support them. Although hundreds of studies have now been reported on teacher role expectations and studies of teacher role behavior are even more numerous, little of a systematic nature is known about the relationships between these two realms of investigation. Many studies of conformity have been reported for other social positions, and the bulk of them suggest that conformity is by no means a simple, automatic response (Biddle 1979). Many investigations have also appeared concerning teacher expectations for pupils and teacher classroom conduct (Brophy and Good 1974), and a few authors have used instruments that measured expectations for teaching as a way of selecting teachers whose behaviors were subsequently observed (Bennett 1976). But systematic research on the relationship between teacher role expectations and teacher behaviors is hard to find. A fundamental attraction of role theory for educators is that it presumes that persons are capable of thinking rationally about their own and others' conduct, and that those rational thoughts will affect their behaviors in predictable ways. Unless people are willing to conduct research on the relationships between role expectations and role behaviors, that attraction will remain merely a speculation.

See also: Implicit Theories; Definitions of Teaching; Effects of Teaching

Bibliography

Adams R S (ed.) 1970 Symposium on teacher role in four English-speaking countries. *Comp. Educ. Rev.* 14: 5–64

Bank B J, Biddle B J, Keats D M, Keats J A 1977 Normative, preferential, and belief modes in adolescent prejudice. *Sociol. Q.* 18: 574–88

Bellack A A, Hyman R T, Smith F L Jr., Kliebard H M 1966 *The Language of the Classroom.* Teachers College Press, New York

Bennett N 1976 *Teaching Styles and Pupil Progress.* Harvard University Press, Cambridge, Massachusetts

Biddle B J 1969 The role of the teacher. In: Ebel R L (ed.) 1969 *Encyclopedia of Educational Research: A Project of the American Educational Research Association,* 4th edn. Macmillan, New York

Biddle B J 1979 *Role Theory: Expectations, Identities, and Behaviors.* Academic Press, New York

Biddle B J, Rosencranz H A, Rankin E F Jr. 1961 *Studies in the Role of the Public School Teacher.* University of Missouri Press, Columbia, Missouri

Biddle B J, Rosencranz H A, Tomich E, Twyman J P 1966 Shared inaccuracies in the role of the teacher. In: Biddle B J, Thomas E J (eds.) 1966 *Role Theory: Concepts and Research.* Wiley, New York

Brophy J E 1979 Teacher behavior and its effects. *J. Educ. Psych.* 71: 733–50

Brophy J E 1981 Teacher praise: A functional analysis. *Rev. Educ. Res.* 51: 5–32

Brophy J E, Good T L 1974 *Teacher–Student Relationships: Causes and Consequences.* Holt, Rinehart and Winston, New York

Campbell L P 1970 A study of moonlighting activities of male Jefferson County teachers. *Colorado J. Educ. Res.* 9: 2–5

Chapman D W, Hutcheson S M 1982 Attrition from teaching careers: A discriminant analysis. *Am. Educ. Res. J.* 19: 93–105

Dunkin M J 1972 The nature and resolution of role conflicts among male primary school teachers. *Sociol. Educ.* 45: 167–85

Dunkin M J, Biddle B J 1974 *The Study of Teaching.* Holt, Rinehart and Winston, New York

Flanders N A 1970 *Analyzing Teaching Behavior.* Addison-Wesley, Reading, Massachusetts

Good T L 1979 Teacher effectiveness in the elementary school: What we know about it now. *J. Teach. Educ.* 30: 52–64

Grace G R 1972 *Role Conflict and the Teacher.* Routledge and Kegan Paul, London

Gross N C, Mason W S, McEachern A W 1958 *Explorations in Role Analysis: Studies of the School Superintendency Role.* Wiley, New York

Hilsum S, Cane B 1971 *The Teacher's Day.* National Foundation for Educational Research, Slough

Kelsall R K, Kelsall H M 1969 *The School Teacher in England and the United States: The Findings of Empirical Research.* Pergamon, Oxford

Kounin J S 1970 *Discipline and Group Management in Classrooms.* Holt, Rinehart and Winston, New York

Kyriacou C, Sutcliffe J 1977 Teacher stress: A review. *Educ. Rev.* 29: 299–306

Lortie D C 1975 *Schoolteacher: A Sociological Study.* University of Chicago Press, Chicago, Illinois

Mackie M 1972 School teachers: The popular image. *Alberta J. Educ. Res.* 4: 267–76

Mehan H 1979 *Learning Lessons: Social Organization in the Classroom.* Harvard University Press, Cambridge, Massachusetts

Parsons T 1959 The school class as a social system: Some of its functions in American society. *Harvard Educ. Rev.* 29: 297–318

Rosenshine B 1979 Content, time, and direct instruction. In: Peterson P L, Walberg H J (eds.) 1979 *Research on Teaching: Concepts, Findings, and Implications.* McCutchan, Berkeley, California

Rosenthal R, Jacobson L 1968 *Pygmalion in the Classroom: Teacher Expectations and Pupils' Intellectual Development.* Holt, Rinehart and Winston, New York

Smith B O, Meux M O 1962 *A Study of the Logic of Teaching.* University of Illinois Press, Urbana, Illinois

Smith H A 1979 Nonverbal communication in teaching. *Rev. Educ. Res.* 49: 631–72

Waller W W 1932 *The Sociology of Teaching.* Wiley, New York

Wright R E, Alley R 1977 A profile of the ideal teacher. *Natl. Ass. Sec. Sch. Princ. Bull.* 61: 60–64

Professional Socialization of Teachers

C. Lacey

The professional socialization of teachers refers to the process of change by which individuals become members of the teaching profession and then take up progressively maturer roles within teaching. It is important to notice that the process of professional socialization does not end at the point of entry into the profession or at any arbitrary point during the early career of the teacher. For example, in the United Kingdom qualified teacher status (QTS) is usually acquired after a period of a year of probationary teaching. It marks a point in the career of the beginning teacher where substantial changes have taken place within the individual and have been recognized as being appropriate to becoming a fully fledged member of the profession by his or her training institution, his or her local authority, and senior teachers at his or her school. However, the process of individual change continues at a rapid pace as the beginning teacher consolidates his or her position within the school, reaches out for new responsibilities, and begins the climb for promotion.

The emphasis on socialization as a process which continues throughout the career of an individual is a modern development that owes much to the work of symbolic interactionists (Becker 1971).

It represents an extension to Merton's classic, functionalist definition of socialization . . . "the process by which people selectively acquire the values and attitudes, the interests, skills and knowledge—in short the culture—current in groups to which they are, or seek to become a member" (Merton et al. 1957).

It is clear from the definition that professional socialization entails more than just learning to teach. By including the selective acquisition of values and attitudes the definition immediately goes beyond the acquisition of the skills and knowledge implied by the phrase "learning to teach". However, Merton's definition mentions the selective acquisition of values and attitudes as though a profession can be adequately described as a culture, by the agreed values, and so on, held by the group. This has been described as a central value system or a central tendency form of analysis. The definition, therefore, glosses over and simplifies the searching and interactive process by which professional values are acquired and the manipulative, partial, and selective manner in which they are often held. The view adopted in this article implies that it is necessary to examine the profession to discover whether it can be treated as a whole, that is, as a consensual body.

Much of the early work on socialization by functionalist sociologists and psychologists assumed a simple "filling of empty vessels" mechanism by which the individual neophyte acquired those values and skills that were necessary to become a member of the profession. There were a number of dangers and distortions in this approach.

The main danger derives from what could be termed the crude functionalist model but there are similar problems associated with more sophisticated functionalist models. The crude functionalist model builds on the widely held notion that it is possible for experienced and responsible educationalists to recognize "good practice" or "good teachers". This assumption of a widely held and recognizable consensus made possible a research tradition in the 1950s and 1960s which "arose from practical interest in finding better methods for selecting persons who would make 'good' teachers and in improv-

ing the training and assessment of students and practitioners" (Morrison and McIntyre 1969).

The main elements in this model of socialization are clear. Society is viewed as a relatively stable entity in which there is a consensus on how the major roles within it are to be filled. The researcher's role becomes one of discovering this consensus and devising tests, usually of a psychometric variety, that will select those candidates who are most likely to take on the prescribed role.

This research tradition failed because of its underlying theoretical weaknesses. This became manifest through the failure of the prediction procedures and the lack of success in replicating any positive findings. There is always a danger, however, that political and administrative imperatives will give new life to this research tradition by funding research into new predictive tests. The element of political control that this implies is disguised by the scientific culture of test construction and the altruism implied by the aim of "improving teaching".

As the weaknesses of the "crude" model of socialization were exposed, a more sophisticated set of research devices were employed. The notion that there were several sets of acceptable, social and educational goals was introduced. The idea that studies of interpersonal behaviour between teachers and pupils would be more closely linked to teacher effectiveness was exploited and finally the effects on teachers' behaviour of demands by colleagues, parents, and others. These elaborations have been presented as three "basically different ways of thinking about the work of teachers, each with its own set of theoretical concepts, its implicit assumptions and its methodological techniques and problems" (Morrison and McIntyre 1969).

Viewed from the perspective of more recent work on socialization it is clear that these researches have in common a highly simplified view of the process of socialization which is not questioned by the research stance and more importantly they imply a consensual and essentially static view of society which is in turn unquestioned and promoted by the research stance.

A second way in which Merton's definition of socialization has been extended by the study of teaching has been to take into account the massive reorientation that student teachers experience as they move from being students to being teachers and by studying this more closely. For example, there is a difference between acquiring values and acquiring skills and knowledge. In the past there has often been the assumption that these processes of acquisition are similar, in other cases the differences have simply been glossed over. While there are some less visible professions in which the values and attitudes of the profession are practically unknown to the neophyte this is not likely to be the case with teachers. So that while many of the skills and much of the knowledge special to the profession may have to be acquired from scratch, many of the values and attitudes possessed by teachers are well-known to students who have experienced them as pupils in schools. What has changed for the neophyte teachers is not so much their knowledge of attitudes but their position with respect to these attitudes. As they become teachers their social position changes and with it the perceived responsibilities and duties associated with the classroom. That is, their perspective changes.

However, change in perspective is rarely a simple process. Many young people come to teaching with the idea that they will change some of the "old attitudes" that they resented when they were at school. The conflicts and dilemmas faced by the neophyte teacher are therefore considerable and make the professional socialization of teachers a critical case in the study of adult socialization.

This final point leads to a last modification of Merton's position. The functionalist model of society stresses the interrelatedness of the parts of society and the consensual aspects of society. Clearly, these are an important consideration in the study of socialization. More recent work by Marxist and other conflict theorists has highlighted the deep divisions within society deriving from class interests, racial and ethnic minorities, religious and political groupings, gender and other important subgroup characteristics. These conflicts cannot be ignored or treated as deviations from the normal. Conflict in society is a normal state of affairs, it is an important dynamic for change and highly relevant to the study of teacher socialization. The accommodation of conflicting positions about education within schools is currently an increasingly important aspect of school management. The traditional technique of insisting that the staff of a school are united and behind the administration on all major issues is increasingly ineffectual in schools in many countries where they are suffering educational cuts and a reassertion of central control over the curriculum and other school policies. The study of the professional socialization of teachers has developed in stages to provide models of socialization in keeping with the accelerating change in modern society and in particular the changes affecting education.

The use of conflict models of society is not without problems, however, and some of the problems are similar to the overdeterministic functionalist models. In stressing the role that schools play in reproducing the inequalities of wealth and power that characterize our society, many of the various forms of conflict theory fail to account for social change and the autonomy, albeit partial, experienced by individuals and institutions. The contribution of these theories has been to expose as class ideologies many of the functionalist theories of education.

In 1961 Dennis Wrong's speculative essay on the oversocialized conception of man in modern sociology crystallized a number of important developments and proposed a critique of classical socialization theory, the two main roots of which he summarized as follows:

> The first answer is summed up in the notion of the internalization of social norms. The second, more commonly employed or assumed in empirical research, is the view that man is essentially motivated by the desire to achieve a positive image of self by winning acceptance or status in the eyes of others. (Wrong 1961)

Wrong sees man as a neurotic discontended animal for whom culture is a violation of his socialized bodily drives. Wrong's picture of socialization is of an imperfect or partial process in which an essential element of man stays outside both the processes of internalization of social norms and the conforming needs of his personality (Lacey 1973).

In the same year as the publication of Wrong's essay, research carried out by Howard Becker, Blanche Geer, and Everett Hughes on the socialization of medical students brought together a number of concepts which for the first time could be considered sufficiently precise and integrated to form a conceptual framework, outside the work of functionalist theorists. Becker et al.'s use of concepts like culture, latent culture, perspective, side bets, and commitment in the study of adult socialization marks a breakthrough in the understanding of the processional aspects of socialization, the constraints affecting medical students, and their accommodation to an authoritarian system of education.

Nevertheless, Becker's approach falls short of satisfying both Wrong's critique and the emerging critique of functionalist socialization. Becker et al. take the position that since the students they studied seemed to be very much alike "We found it more useful to think and talk about one student culture than to think about many student cultures."

This fairly dogmatic statement is not tested against any evidence of homogeneity or heterogeneity and leads the researchers to treat the students as completely controlled by the faculty. "To the degree that the faculty actually exercises such power, students will have no opportunity to build their own perspectives . . ." (Becker et al. 1961) and by implication their own reactive subcultures.

In the later chapters of the book, the researchers modify this position but the modifications are circumstantial and do not affect the main conceptual framework proposed.

In other words although Becker et al. modify their highly deterministic model of socialization it remains similar to many functionalist models in leaving very little autonomy for individuals to influence their own development either collectively or individually.

Lacey's research into pupil socialization in schools carried out in the early 1960s led him to challenge this picture of socialization as being generally applicable. Within an intensive study of a grammar school and despite what he described as a "pressured academic environment" which would be expected to constrain pupil behaviour, a wide differentiation took place and opposed subcultures developed: proschool and antischool. These subcultures embodied different and opposed values relating to schooling and youth culture. It was also apparent that by the third and fourth years, when these subcultures were well-developed, some individual pupils were able to recognize the existence of both subcultures and manipulate their behaviour accordingly. In other words the "internalization" of values was at best partial.

1. The Study of Teacher Socialization

It is clear that much of the early work in the study of professional socialization took into account professions other than teachers, in particular medical students. In addition there has been a marked concentration on the training period. The middle and final years of professional life have been almost totally neglected. The reasons for this are fairly clear. The training period is the stage where the neophyte professional is being consciously shaped by others, the trainers. There is therefore an interest in the outcome of this process because in theory it can be altered to produce "better" or different results. The researcher is also drawn to study this period because it is a stage of massive personal reorientation and change, a *rite de passage*. Unfortunately, the concentration on this period has led to a neglect of the period of career socialization and the less spectacular but nevertheless important changes that occur as individuals take on positions of power within the profession, for example, heads of departments and heads of schools. In addition, teaching is a career that leads to other careers in further education, administration and teachers' unions, for example, and very little is known about this process.

The research into mid and late careers still remains to be carried out. This entry has concentrated on describing research that has led to the development of concepts and theoretical approaches that will facilitate this study when it is done and further understanding of the process of professional socialization in general.

In 1969 Lacey collaborated with Mary Horton and Peter Hoad in a four-year study of early teacher socialization. The research was based at Sussex University in order to centre the study on a new method of teacher training but it included as a comparative element the students from four other postgraduate certificate of education (PGCE) courses. The four other universities were chosen to compare and contrast with Sussex and therefore provide a known backcloth of results to help interpret the results at Sussex. For the Sussex and Southampton students the study spilled over to their first year at school (see Fig. 1).

The Sussex course provided an important base for this comparative study because it had developed a course which represented a radical departure from existing practice. The elements of the innovation can be summarized as follows:

(a) The traditional block teaching practice was changed to three days per week throughout the year. This was intended to enable the two major parts of the course, theory (sociology, psychology, and values) and teaching practice to be closely related in discussions both at the university and the school.

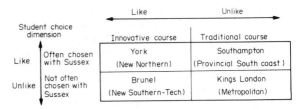

Note that York was chosen because it was like Sussex on both dimensions and Kings was unlike Sussex on both dimensions

Figure 1
Design of the Sussex study

(b) Two new roles were developed within the school, the teacher–tutor and the general supervisory tutor. The teacher–tutor was expected to be a senior subject teacher who was responsible for two student teachers in his or her subject. He or she organized their teaching within the department and gave them a weekly tutorial on their classroom teaching. The general supervisory tutor, usually a senior teacher organized the school experience of the group of students within the school.

(c) Within the university, the education tutor was responsible for liaison with schools and organizing a joint seminar in the spring term for all students and teacher–tutors in his or her subject.

The scheme therefore sacrificed variation within the school experience for the positive gain of continuity and depth in the student's relationship with his or her teaching practice school.

The research could be seen as having three purposes; the comparative study of an innovative scheme for the training of teachers; a study of the induction and training of teachers; and finally a study in grounded theory aimed at developing a model of the socialization process that would encompass the possibility of autonomous action by individuals and therefore the possibility of social change emanating from the choices and strategies adopted by individuals. It is the latter that is of particular interest here.

The study brought together three elements from the previous debates.

(a) A critique of functionalist theory with respect to its major components: the consensual and holistic nature of society and the model of socialization that assumes an unproblematic acquisition of central values.

(b) A commitment to seek out examples of individual and collective autonomy within a period of training and induction that is acknowledged to be a period of institutionally imposed constraints. Also to examine the relationship between individual autonomy and social change—if such a link could be traced.

(c) A desire to build upon Becker's conceptual framework for studying socialization and link a grounded research approach in this aspect of the study with theoretical considerations about the nature of society, derived from the critique of functionalism.

2. A Critique of the Consensual View of Society

An examination of teaching as a profession reveals a divided profession. It is divided by the subject disciplines and training that the professionals bring to the classroom; it is divided by the status and function of the institutions in which they serve; and by the training and social origins of its members and increasingly by disagreements over the aims and purposes of education. These divisions are in some cases interrelated and give rise to other divisions. For example the fragmented union or professional association representation of teachers in the United Kingdom and other countries relates in many instances to the separate traditions and differing statuses of the institutions in which they serve but also to differing values and policies which have emerged from these differing interests. These major divisions within the profession are clearly related to the class structure of society. In addition, sex and gender have given rise to an unequal distribution of opportunities for women within the profession and the career expectations for women are both inferior and differently specialized than for men. Despite this expectation, teaching represents a relatively favoured career structure for women compared with other professions which discriminate even more markedly against them. Table 1 illustrates some of these divisions.

Table 1 clearly demonstrates the way in which the teachers in the two categories of school are drawn differentially from different social classes. If data were available from a more recent study they would undoubtedly show that comprehensive schools within the United Kingdom had had some effect in reducing this aspect of class differentiation. The extent of this effect might, however, be smaller than expected if inner-city comprehensive schools were compared with suburban comprehensives. If data for public schools were available, this differentiation would appear even more extensive. Before leaving the table it is important to note the higher social class origins of women in each type of school illustrating the smaller number of alternative career opportunities for upper-class women compared with men. This feature of recruitment to teaching remains true today.

Disagreements over the aims and purposes of education have a history extending back to the origins of education as a separate function in society. Nevertheless after the 1944 Education Act and during the period of economic expansion in the 1950s and 1960s, there was an unusual agreement about the need for more education and more equal opportunities within education in the United Kingdom. The emergence of a varied system of comprehensive schools and new progressive methods of education including mixed-ability teaching and teacher-controlled examinations began to encroach on the traditionally elite grammar schools and the direct grant schools. When the special provisions supporting the direct grant grammar schools were abolished and they were asked to join the state system or the independent system, most opted for independence. The fight back of elitist educational philosophies espousing higher quality education for the few began in the late 1960s with the publication of the Black Papers (1968). Essays by Angus Maude attacking the "Egalitarian Threat" and other essays entitled "Progressive Collapse" and "Pernicious Participation" were at first dismissed as extremist and provocative. However, as the world economic recession following the oil crisis of 1973–74 affected government policies, and as education slipped down the list of priorities in the face of reduced government spending, these elitist philosophies gained ground. Within less than a decade they had replaced the expansionist Conservative philosophy and became the espoused philosophy of the Conservative government in power.

Table 1
Social origins of teachers in secondary modern and direct grant grammar schools in England and Wales 1955

Father's occupation	Secondary modern		Direct grant grammar schools	
	Men %	Women %	Men %	Women %
Professional and administrative	7.5	11.4	19.8	30.4
Intermediate	45.9	54.8	61.5	57.4
Manual worker	46.7	33.8	18.7	12.2
	100%	100%	100%	100%

Source: Floud and Scott 1961

The history of this period reveals education as a battleground of competing philosophies. Behind these philosophies lie the competing interests of classes and class factions and other interest groups.

It is not necessary for the purpose of this article to trace in detail the specific configuration of interests behind the debates of the early 1980s. It is clear that class structure and class interests are closely aligned to the structure of school provision and the period of expansion from 1944–74 represented a modification of the alignment of the middle class with grammar schools and an attack, however slight, on the privileges of elites. The reversal during the late 1970s and early 1980s marks a fight back by these elites to prevent further encroachments of reform and mark a return to previous policies which more efficiently reproduced the divisions of a stratified society.

It is on this battleground that new and intending teachers must make their careers. In the early 1970s their position was uncomplicated by the problem ot widespread unemployment and cutbacks in education. Nevertheless, becoming a teacher was impossible to characterize as an induction into a unified profession where agreement on values and procedures made induction an unproblematic process for willing and able students.

3. *Areas of Individual and Collective Autonomy*

The commitment to seek within the research for examples of individual or group action which exhibited autonomy did not derive from an intention to prove the existence of an open society free of constraint and compulsion. The analysis in the previous section shows this possibility to be an illusion. The intention was to move away from central tendency analysis which appears in both functionalist and conflict theory analysis and presents the social actor as a dupe, powerless to affect the outcomes of large-scale social processes. Behind this intention was the belief that the gradual, small-scale processes which are the result of choices made by large numbers of individuals over long periods of time, are the causes of rapid large-scale changes in society that are easily identified and described. These periods of revolutionary change or reform are often characterized as the outcomes of the actions of a few prominent individuals, the great names of history. In fact these major actors are often catalysts or "specks of dust" initiating the crystallization of a situation that was already saturated with the ingredients of change. Most actors do not have the opportunity to play the role of a major catalyst of social action but all do have the opportunity of making choices and of influencing the ingredients of change. If sociologists can refine their investigations of socialization to reveal some of the connections between individual social action and social change then democracy within institutions takes on a new meaning. Studying the possibilities in any situation (instead of the central tendency) enlarges the appreci-ation of choice and links these choices to larger-scale outcomes. Choice becomes informed and helps shape institutions. This exercise in the sociology of the possible is particularly appropriate in the study of adult socialization.

The first area of the investigation to reveal an area of student autonomy was the students' choice of university.

The analysis of the early questionnaires showed that even in the period before making the decision to join the teaching profession students were making choices that would influence the kind of teacher that they might become. The issue of subject choice of first degree for example has often been written about as if it constitutes a neutral decision aligned only with the individual's skills and abilities. In fact the research revealed orientations and sets of values closely aligned with subject subcultures that were related to ideas about teaching and education in general. In addition students revealed considerable knowledge of training courses and a wide variety of reasons for choosing the courses they attended. The first two items in Table 2 relate to aspects of the course, the next two items relate to the university, and the final three relate to reasons outside the course and university. If the first two items are combined they reveal a concern with the course among students opting for the newer innovatory courses:

	Sussex	York	Brunel	Southampton	Kings
Items 1 and 2 combined	57%	54%	42%	19%	15%

Other comparative indicators bear out this finding. The older universities attracted more students who had themselves gone to independent and direct grant schools and who intended to go on to teach in those schools. They also attracted students whose attitude could be characterized as less radical, naturalistic, tender minded, and progressive. The differences in opinion measured at the beginning of the courses tended to have increased by the end of the course. The graph of "naturalism scores" illustrates this pattern of change (see Fig. 2).

This part of the study therefore revealed a "select and be selected" mechanism that on the one hand gives students some control over the sort of teacher they wish to become and on the other provides a cohort of students biased in those qualities the university department of education wishes to encourage. This second feature is a neglected characteristic of open recruitment systems and it is also a factor affecting the possibility of change within a PGCE course or department of education. For example, those members of faculty wishing to promote change, within a course advertising itself as possessing certain characteristics will find support within the student body if the changes are in line with the students' expectations of the course.

At a more generalized level the research revealed two broad orientations or types of commitment to

Table 2
The most important factor influencing choice of university

	Sussex %	York %	Brunel %	Southampton %	Kings %
1. Content of course	11	50	36	17	9
2. Organization of teaching practice	46	4	6	2	6
3. Reputation of university	7	15	9	6	15
4. Familiarity with university	5	4	0	16	8
5. Desire for change	3	8	3	9	11
6. Geographical setting	8	11	25	16	18
7. Personal reasons	20	8	21	34	34
	100	100	100	100	100
Size of sample	62	74	33	196	105

teaching, a radical and a professional commitment that emerged early in the period of anticipatory socialization, and could be traced through the training period, and into the early years of teaching. There are in fact indications that these broad streams of progress through the early years of the profession continue in a modified way until the end of the career.

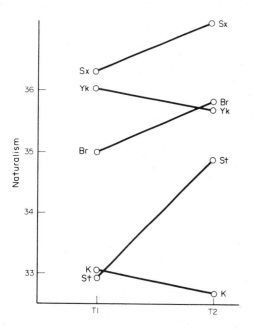

Figure 2
Naturalism attitude scores of Sussex, York, Brunel, Southampton, and Kings students

However, the lack of research into the mid and later careers of teachers means that this cannot be documented in any detail.

The analysis of these types of commitment emerged from an investigation of the changes in commitment that occurred during training. All university courses revealed a decrease in commitment as beginning teachers encountered the difficulties of the teaching situation. However, an examination of the kinds of teaching experienced by students and the reasons for commitment to teaching showed marked differences. This can be illustrated by taking Sussex and Kings as contrasting cases. Kings' students were more likely to have experienced the elite independent and direct grant schools as pupils (36 percent as compared to 21 percent); they were more likely to have experienced these schools during teaching practice (26 percent as compared to 8 percent) and they were more likely to apply to such schools for their first appointment (28 percent as compared to 3 percent). It follows that the levels of commitment measured in each course related to different types of teaching and it becomes necessary to examine the reasons the students had for their commitment to teaching.

A correlation matrix suggested that a radical commitment to teaching involved a low subject orientation; a tendency to choose teaching late rather than early; a low evaluation of the student's own teaching ability but a high commitment to teaching in comprehensive schools. The professionally orientated teacher on the other hand chose teaching early; had family connections in teaching; had high levels of commitment, satisfaction, and subject orientation. The professional commitment was strongly developed at Kings; the radical commitment appeared stronger at Sussex. A further difference emerged in attitude to career, the radically committed teacher saw teaching as a means to an end, to the realization of certain ideals. They were therefore more likely to see their career taking them outside teaching and education. It follows that becoming a teacher cannot be regarded as a single process. Student teachers become different types of teacher with different values and purposes. It is in this way that the major disagreements about society, its nature and future development, find their way into teaching and become central issues within schools where problems of pedagogy (learning) and discipline (behaviour) emerge and new solutions need to be found. There is a second perhaps more obvious sense in which the research demonstrated separate distinct strands of socialization. The subject discipline could be seen as giving rise to distinct strands of socialization within the course. Student teachers in each subject formed friendships together, experienced similar classroom difficulties, and developed recognizable teaching styles that differed between subjects.

Up to this point the process of socialization has been considered as a set of options presented to any individual at any one time; the choice of this course rather than another; the choice of this teaching practice school rather than another, and so on. This picture does not detail the finer processes in which these choices are embedded. It is necessary to achieve this level of detail if beginning teachers and practising teachers are to use the analysis to understand their own position and work towards controlling and changing it.

The analysis also fails to take into account what happens when students and beginning teachers make the wrong choices and find their intended direction of development blocked.

The unit of study that emerged as relevant to this purpose was the social strategy.

A social strategy involves the actor in the selection of ideas and actions and working out their complex interrelationships (action–idea systems) in a given situation. The selection of these action–idea systems as a student moves from situation to situation need not be consistent. For example, the student may select a permissive action–idea system for a university seminar but an authoritarian one for a school classroom. The justification for this change might be a consciously thought-out argument or it can be suppressed. It the first case, the social strategy is conscious, in the second case subconscious. The apparent contradiction in the selection of social strategies can only be resolved by reference to the student and his changing view of what represents the "real" world and his relationship to it. This can be illustrated by referring to a commonly occurring series of events experienced by the students we studied.

The first time the student teacher uses an authoritarian strategy within the classroom, shouting,

threatening, or demanding order, he or she often sees it as a last resort, a temporary solution and not "really them". They frequently report viewing themselves from outside: "Was that really me? It was horrible." As the student resorts more and more frequently to this strategy, he or she needs more and more to justify its use and to rehearse the arguments with others to obtain reassurance and support.

The frequent resort to a particular social strategy, colours the perception and world view of the student and eventually the qualified teacher (Lacey 1977).

4. The Development of Becker's Conceptual Framework

In their study of medical students, Becker et al. stressed the domination of students by the institution and the development of a single student perspective and culture. The mechanism that they described as producing this uniformity they called "situational adjustment": ". . . the individual turns himself into the kind of person the situation demands" (Becker 1971).

Clearly if this mechanism dominates totally then there is no choice for individual students and no chance of creatively expressing their talents and aspirations.

The research at Sussex revealed two other mechanisms, strategic compliance and strategic redefinition. They might well be less common than situational adjustment as defined by Becker but they need to be studied in concrete situations before they can be dismissed as unimportant strategies.

Situational adjustment can be defined as two types of strategy:

(a) Internalized adjustment, in which the individual complies with the constraints and believes that the constaints of the situation are for the best. He or she really is good. This is similar to Becker's situational adjustment.

(b) Strategic compliance, in which the individual complies with the authority figure's definition of the situation and the constraints on his or her action but retains private reservations about them. He or she is merely seen to be good.

A third variety of strategy, strategic redefinition, occurred when students found the situation to be contrary to their interests or expectations. In some cases students were able to bring new knowledge, new values, and new skills to the situation and "carry off" a new solution to the problem.

This last type of strategy was observed most frequently at the level of the classroom where students introduced small innovations or small deviations from the tutor's expectations. They also occurred in tutor groups and one group was able to transform its mode of operation from a tutor-centred one to a form of democratic participation with an elected chairperson and a collectively organized curriculum. The largest change occurred when the student body as a whole held several meetings and voted for a change in the course structure. Teaching practice in the summer term became optional as a result of this change.

Clearly the receptiveness of the organization and the skill of the students in bringing off the change in a responsible way were important factors in the success of these examples of strategic redefinition. The research also recorded (in the five courses) a number of unsuccessful attempts. In extreme cases this lack of success resulted in one student almost failing the Sussex course and a student in another university being suspended.

Strategic compliance appeared to be a much more common strategy. A large number of questionnaire responses made this clear.

Often it wasn't worth bringing conflict with teacher–tutor to a head, since there was a definite noncommunication and it was a waste of precious school time. It was more useful and peaceful to go away and do your own thing quietly.

Although I disagreed with my teacher–tutor, the only way to cope was to concur with her when she was present.

Introduction of Nuffield A-level biology syllabus, Education–tutor favoured. Teacher–tutor qualified enthusiasm, (he) favoured gradual incorporation of some (Nuffield) curriculum material but not change of exam syllabus. I agreed with Education–tutor in principle and with Teacher–tutor in practice.

The covertness illustrated in these quotations is an essential element of strategic compliance. It accounts for the fact that socialization studies have frequently failed to report this mode of situational adjustment and why the process of socialization is far less perfect and complete than most researchers, tutors, and headteachers have come to believe.

The set of examples of redefinition strategies that have been discussed so far relate directly to social change. They are examples of overtly negotiated change and although they do not necessarily become permanent features of organizations they have a clear relationship to organizational structure.

The relationship between organizational change and the examples of strategic compliance is less clear. The fact that an individual or group complies when they feel they have to makes for a problematic relationship with organizational change. It implies that a public display of solidarity could cover deep covertly held differences of opinion. It could even mean that the majority of a school staff are opposed to a particular practice or form of organization but that they will remain compliant until an incident or change of, say, the headteacher makes the practice open to change. It becomes an issue.

Socialization as described here can be characterized as the adoption or creation of appropriate social strategies. However, this characterization masks one important aspect of the process; its sequential nature. It would appear from the study that the development of a career falls into stages because certain perspectives and attitudes only arise after the student teacher has "processed" and "digested" the practical experiences which form the basis of the new perspective.

The research revealed four recognizable stages during the training year. The "honeymoon period" in which students experienced the euphoria of "being a teacher". During this period they felt released from the pressures of student life and enjoyed the status of being in control and doing something practical. The "search for material and ways of teaching" followed in which the emerging problems of the classroom were dealt with by looking for more interesting material and ways of presenting it. The "crisis" did not affect everyone to the same extent. It occurred as the problems of the classroom mounted and the search for material failed to stop the decline in classroom discipline. At this stage many student teachers felt like "giving it all up". Finally, "learning to get by or failure" marked the point where many of them felt more comfortable with the compromises and changes that had to be made. They could by this time present themselves as a teacher within the classroom without feeling guilty or uncomfortable within the role. If they failed in this then their prospective career as a teacher was in jeopardy.

During the period of "crisis" it is difficult to underestimate the pressures experienced by beginning teachers. They were now responsible, for short periods, for the learning in their subject of large groups of pupils. If they behaved in the classroom in a relaxed open way, characteristic of their university behaviour, then the classroom soon became a scene of chaos. They could actually observe individually pleasant and likeable children turn their lessons, which had involved hard work in preparation, into a situation where many children were not learning anything. If they attempted to stop the rot, they found themselves behaving in ways they could not easily condone, shouting, making examples of individual children, or giving out punishments. The guilt generated by this dilemma was discussed within the university seminars. It was often displaced in different ways, giving rise to two recognizable but contradictory positions. Some students felt the pupils were mainly to blame for their problems while others in a general sense put the blame largely on the system because it put the teachers and pupils into an impossible situation. This difference had theoretically discernible links with the major strands of radical and professional orientation to teaching described earlier. For example, displacement of blame onto the system is not easily reconcilable in the long term with a professional orientation to teaching. However, in the short term it was possible for individuals to hold mutually contradicting positions on even important issues like this.

The follow-up study in the first year of teaching was restricted to ex-Sussex and ex-Southampton students and restricted to a postal questionnaire. The analysis demonstrated that while the liberalizing and radicalizing trends of the training year were reversed, the different strands of orientation to teaching were still visible and therefore gave rise to a continuing differentiation within the profession. For example, a French teacher in a grammar school wrote "I now feel that only quite radical change will improve the education system . . . . Only when there is a complete restructuring of the curriculum will anything change really for the better"; while a primary school teacher wrote "I did not realize what a state education is in, thanks to unthinking innovation." To examine the socialization process as it develops deeper into the teaching career it is necessary to now turn to a different kind of study.

5. Career Socialization

There have been very few studies of teacher careers other than those of a purely descriptive nature intended for administrative purposes. Recent work by Lyons (1981), and Mardle and Walker (1980), has begun a more theoretically based enquiry. Geoffrey Lyons' study of teacher careers in five large comprehensive schools relies almost entirely on questionnaire data obtained through interviews and is based on Becker's conceptual model of career socialization. It analyses many of the major features of the process and usefully extends knowledge into some areas that are dealt with in detail.

It is immediately clear that becoming a teacher is only part of the process of professional socialization. Once the young teachers have passed through their probationary year, the difficulties of the classroom and the flood of new impressions, lesson preparation, and marking recede sufficiently for them to consider the longer term prospects and career.

To some this understanding comes quickly and easily, they develop what Lyons calls a career "map" that they use to guide their careers.

> Picked it up very quickly, then talked my way on. As soon as I realized that my peers were moving up a scale, I then realized what it was all about.

Others found this process more difficult.

> After 3–4 years in a school you become aware of the differentials in the pay scale and you can't realize how to get on—what is expected of you to get a scale post? How is your value assessed?. . . . (Lyons 1981 p. 42)

Lyons records that some teachers "reject entirely the value bases upon which 'successful' maps and timetables are predicted . . .". Unfortunately he does not pursue this line in any depth. Nor does he examine in any detail the alternative values or underlying purposes on which the careers are constructed. It is therefore difficult to pursue the differences that might emerge from following up "radically committed" teachers as opposed to "professionally committed" teachers. The reasons behind this omission are clear, Lyons works to a sophisticated functional model of teaching. Teaching is accurately described as a hierarchically or bureaucratically organized set of positions yielding a variety of possible careers. The teachers are then examined as unidimensional beings; whether or not they have a career "map" and how successful they have been in actualizing it. The deep purpose behind the research is to spread information about "timetables of promotion", "employable strategies", "recognizing gate keeping devices", "obtaining sponsors", and "holding alternative fulfillable goals" so that the system can work more smoothly and more people can have satisfying careers. Yet within this framework Lyons fails to explore adequately the question, what happens if as a result of more knowledge about how to construct a career more people become more career conscious and seek upward mobility in a system that is contracting and offering less chance of promotion? For example, Lyons shows that many teachers are tuned into the prospect of upward mobility by the promotion of their peers. He does not explore the possibility that in a situation where upward mobility is declining a possible result could be that less teachers will be afflicted with the pressure to "get on". The weaknesses of the research within its own functional rationality demonstrates the importance of exploring the multidimensional nature of teaching and situating the importance of career aspiration within the context of other competing and complementary aspirations. Lyons demotes these aspects of teaching and of life outside teaching to the "accumulation of valuables [that] could be a constraint on an individual's freedom of action, a restriction of his promotion opportunities".

The research adequately describes the differentiation of careers within teaching and the wide range of alternative careers that develop from a teaching career. In fact 17 percent of the sample envisaged a career in education outside teaching and another 6 percent saw themselves as moving outside education altogether. In addition, a number of teachers envisaged staying in teaching while developing outside interests. Yet others saw their satisfactions as deriving from the contact with pupils and resented the pressure to move up into the administration.

> There are pressures on you to go for deputy headship. But I fight it because I love teaching, for contact of minds and would therefore have lost job satisfaction. But where do I go from here?

Career pressures clearly represent one of the most important socializing pressures felt by teachers. Hierarchical structures with frequent points of promotion or gatekeeping devices effectively control the external or expressed characteristics of the development of teachers. In so far as these devices are effective in harnessing the energies and talents of aspiring teachers and in so far as the majority of teachers are aspiring to the next level they will be an effective form of control. The selective promotion of teachers supporting the traditional or conservative philosophies of education would give rise to a system of control that reached down to all levels of the profession, and create a situation similar to that described by Becker et al. (1961) for medical students. In such a situation there would be less space for experimentation and creativity and radical or innovative teachers would be isolated and forced back into their classrooms. The hierarchical structure of schools and the shape of teachers' careers therefore influence teacher professional socialization and it is impossible to gauge the effectiveness of strategic compliance and strategic redefinition in this long-term process. It is an issue that requires examination in a long-term study of teacher careers. At the present time this would be conducted in a climate of cutbacks in education and moves to curtail the autonomy of teachers.

6. Conclusion

This entry must be described as a theoretical and somewhat speculative attempt to describe the professional socialization of teachers. It is theoretical because it proposes a series of concepts that enables the process of socialization to be understood using new perspectives and insights. It is speculative because the development of the concepts has taken place in a study that concentrated on the training and probationary year of teachers. There has been no similar study of teachers in mid or late career. The process of promotion within schools has been studied in a narrow descriptive way and has omitted many of the considerations developed in this essay. The large number of teachers who actually leave the profession have also been substantially neglected but they might well have an important "selection" effect on the culture of those remaining.

The usual treatment of socialization by sociologists of education has been to work from an understanding of the structure of the school (a fairly static notion) and then to argue that socialization is the process by which individuals change to fit into the roles and positions identified in the structure. The approach contains a number of weaknesses. It assumes that the details of the structure of the school, noted and studied in the present, will still be a feature of the school in the future when a new cohort of teachers fills these positions. It therefore neglects an important mechanism of social change. In this essay the usual emphasis has been altered. The school now appears as the result, in part, of a process in which teachers strive to realize at least two goals. The first is the most obvious and most studied. It is acceptance into the existing structure of the school; the usual career orientation of a teacher. The second which has often been neglected is the attempt by a particular teacher to make the school resemble more closely the sort of place in which that teacher would like to teach. The importance of this second goal can vary enormously from time to time and place to place. While it is usually a secondary goal it can predominate and some teachers will give up the chance of promotion in order to pursue some pedagogic or organizational aim which supports their vision of making the school a better place. As the education system experiences cutbacks and declining standards of provision, and unemployment undermines pupil morale, this second aim can take on a defensive aspect. It can become a determination to preserve something of value in the face of increasing difficulty and outside hostility despite the possibility of damaging one's career in the process.

The careers of many individuals have exemplified this process. Gramsci, whose own career exemplifies it more than most, has captured this desire to understand and shape the relationships in which all as individuals participate.

> Man does not enter into relations with the natural world just by being himself part of it but actively by means of work and technique. Further; these relations are not mechanical. They are active and conscious . . . . Each of us changes himself, modifies himself to the extent that he changes and modifies the complex relations of which he is the heart. In this sense, the real philosopher is, and cannot be other than the politician, the active man who modifies his environment, understanding by environment the ensemble of relations which each of us enters to take part in. If one's individuality is the ensemble of these relations to create one's personality means to acquire consciousness of them, and to modify one's own personality means to modify the ensemble of these relations. (Gramsci 1971 p. 352)

It has been the task of this article to throw light on some important aspects of the professional socialization of teachers and promote understanding of the relationships that would otherwise limit or control human consciousness.

See also: Supervision of the Practicum; Implicit Theories; Teachers' Social Backgrounds; Teaching and Related Activities; Selection for Teaching

Bibliography

Becker H S 1971 *Sociological Work: Method and Substance.* Allen Lane, London (See in particular "Personal change in adult life")
Becker H S, Geer B, Hughes E 1961 *Boys in White: Student Culture in Medical School.* University of Chicago Press, Chicago, Illinois
Cox C B, Dyson A E (eds.) 1968 *Fight for Education: A Black Paper.* Critical Quarterly Society, London
Floud J, Scott W 1961 Recruitment to teaching in England and Wales. In: Halsey A H, Floud J, Anderson C A (eds.) 1961 *Education, Economy, and Society: A Reader in the Sociology of Education.* Free Press, New York
Gramsci A 1971 *Selections from the Prison Notebooks of Antonio Gramsci: A Reader in the Sociology of Education.* [Edited and translated by Hoare Q, Nowell Smith G 1971] Lawrence and Wishart, London
Hilsum S, Start K B 1974 *Promotion and Careers in Teaching.* National Foundation for Educational Research, Slough
Lacey C 1970 *Hightown Grammar: The School as a Social System.* Manchester University Press, Manchester
Lacey C 1973 Intergroup competition pressures and the selection of social strategies. In: Fuchs E (ed.) 1976 *Youth in a Changing World.* Mouton, The Hague
Lacey C 1977 *The Socialization of Teachers.* Methuen, London
Lyons G 1981 *Teacher Careers and Career Perceptions in the Secondary Comprehensive School.* National Foundation for Educational Research/Nelson, Slough

Mardle G, Walker M 1980 Strategies and structure: Some critical notes on teacher socialization. In: Woods P (ed.) 1980 *Teacher Strategies: Explorations in the Sociology of the School.* Croom Helm, London

Merton R K, Reader G G, Kendall P L (eds.) 1957 *The Student–Physician: Introductory Studies in the Sociology of*

Medical Education. Harvard University Press, Cambridge, Massachusetts

Morrison A, McIntyre D 1969 *Teachers and Teaching.* Penguin, Harmondsworth

Wrong D H 1961 The oversocialized conception of man in modern sociology. *Am. Sociol. Rev.* 26: 183–93

Selection for Teaching

K. J. Eltis

The selection of applicants for teacher training and of teachers for appointment to schools continues to be the target of considerable criticism. On the one hand, there is the complaint that more rigorous selection criteria need to be applied at both points. On the other, the cry is raised that the teaching profession is still not getting quality entrants.

It is readily understandable that, during periods when qualified teachers available for appointment are in short supply, entry requirements are not so stringently applied. With the exception of a brief period during the depression years, until the mid-1970s there was always such a shortfall. Not only is it necessary, in such periods, for employing authorities to accept virtually all readily available teachers for appointment to schools, tertiary institutions are also encouraged to accept high numbers of students into teacher education programmes to sustain the flow of available graduates.

Since the early 1970s, however, many countries have experienced what has been termed "an oversupply" of teachers; that is, the number of applicants available for teaching positions has exceeded the budgeted number of positions to be filled [Organisation for Economic Co-operation and Development (OECD) 1979a]. It has been pointed out that use of the term "oversupply" is misleading. If the prevailing needs of schools were to be examined critically in terms of such matters as desirable specialist services, and improved pupil–teacher ratios, what is presently labelled an oversupply would be re-interpreted as a state of deficit (Corrigan 1974). Nonetheless, it could be expected that, when there is a large pool of teachers seeking positions, employing authorities could apply more rigorous criteria for selection. Similarly, tertiary institutions could be expected to be more selective in their admission of students to teacher education programmes, the overall result being greater quality control over those entering the teaching profession.

Sadly, greater quality control has not been the outcome. "The decline in teaching positions has not provoked a profession-wide discussion regarding the qualities candidates need in this constricted market" (Howsam et al. 1976 p. 114). Nor has the academic

quality and potential of those seeking admission to training programmes improved (Weaver 1981) [nor is it likely to (Wimpelberg and King 1983)], so that recent attempts at quality control through more stringent selection both at entry to training and into the schools have not been as successful as might have been expected during a period when the numbers of teachers available exceeds the number of positions available (Mertens and Yarger 1982).

1. Factors Impinging Upon Selection for Training

Before examining what institutions do as part of the selection process, it is necessary to indicate that a number of factors affect the selection process. The needs of employing authorities exert an influence. During a period of teacher shortage it has been common for incentives to be offered, such as the provision of financial support for student teachers, on condition that they commit themselves to teaching at the end of their training (OECD 1979a). Where such "bonding" schemes have operated, the screening of applicants was carried out by both the funding authority and the tertiary institution. These support schemes have now virtually ceased, with a likely consequence that the earlier possibility of students from lower socioeconomic levels taking up teacher education in larger proportions than in other professions (Anderson 1974) will be diminished.

In recent years, government bodies have been keen to exert greater control over the number of institutions involved in teacher training and over the number of students training to be teachers in an attempt to cut back on expenditure and to avoid too large a pool of unemployed teachers. [This has not been done without some major problems (see e.g., Hencke 1978).] When assessing their likely teacher needs, employing authorities also consider the desired "mix" in their profession. Matters needing to be taken into account include the proportion of female and male teachers, the number of mature-age entrants they would like to see coming into the profession, and whether certain groups should receive positive discrimination given the needs of schools and the diverse range of pupil backgrounds in the schools (Mercer 1984); for example the intake of applicants wanting to and needed to teach ethnic languages in schools, or, in Australia, the admission of aboriginals. As well, adjustments to quotas will often be required so that specific supply problems can be overcome. This has applied in many countries to ensure adequate supplies of teachers of mathematics and in the sciences. Such considerations demand constant liaison between training institutions and employing authorities, and institutions have to decide how responsive they should be to employer demands.

A major factor affecting the ultimate selection process is the resource pool from whom applicants are chosen. Training institutions have little control over the numbers and quality of those in the resource pool, though programmes with a strong reputation may attract more applicants than others less favourably viewed. A disturbing feature in recent years has been that the pool of applicants for teacher training in a number of countries has shown a decline in academic quality (Auchmuty 1980, Weaver 1981, Taylor 1978). Perhaps the continuing poor image of the teaching profession has been a contributing factor, an image not enhanced by the relative ease of entry to the profession (Howsam et al. 1976). Certainly adverse publicity concerning the difficulties in obtaining a teaching position at the end of training has been a factor (OECD 1979b).

The admission of students less able academically has also often been brought about as a result of the way institutions are funded. In some countries teacher education programmes are funded according to the number of full-time students enrolled. In such cases there has been evidence to indicate that students have been admitted with quite low matriculation aggregates to maintain an acceptable or high level of enrolments (Watts 1980).

Whatever the reason for the decline in student quality as measured by academic performance, it is unfortunate that, at a time when it might be possible to apply more rigorous and effective criteria in the selection of students, not only is the pool from which selection is to be made academically weaker, institutions still appear to be exercising minimal selectivity, with few applicants being denied admission (Brubaker 1976, Laman and Reeves 1983). In offering this comment, the motivation of those enrolling in programmes is not being called into question. Whereas in earlier years future job security along with encouragement from teachers attracted students to teaching as a career, current evidence suggests students are attracted to teaching for altruistic and personal reasons and from a strong desire to work with children (Wood 1978).

In sum, while it might be agreed that until credible quality control practices are developed, teaching will not become an established profession (Howsam et al. 1976), such practices will be effective in enhancing the quality and standing of the profession only·if capable students can be attracted into the available pool of applicants both for teacher training and for subsequent appointment to schools.

2. Selection for Training

The general consensus appears to be that tertiary institutions should improve their selection devices and ensure that they can justify the admission of all students. Current admission standards appear to be both lax and inappropriate (Laman and Reeves 1983). Screening devices need to be replaced by professional selection criteria (Haberman 1974), with greater involvement of a range of personnel in the selection process (DES 1983). What practices are presently followed?

A wide variety of instruments designed to gather both objective and subjective data are used for selecting students for teacher training: self-report questionnaires; biographical forms; tests of knowledge; school grades; structured interviews; measures of values, aptitudes, personality characteristics; letters of reference (Shank 1978). It appears that the elements used in the selection process in the 1970s did not vary much from those used since the early 1940s (Crocker 1974), lending weight to the view that there is a limit to the range of possibilities. The task is to refine practices rather than invent a whole new set of possibilities.

Academic attainment continues to be the most important criterion (Carpenter 1973, Gress 1977), and though its relevance as a predictor of performance in teacher education courses or of performance of the classroom teacher has been queried, its importance for the credibility of the profession has been recognized. A public which might be concerned by publicity about declining enrolments and the lowering of aggregates for entry to teacher education programmes needs to be reassured of the academic quality of those coming into training (Weaver 1981, Pugach and Raths 1982). It is also important to note that despite misgivings about the importance usually ascribed to academic performance, evidence has been produced to show the effectiveness of students' grade point average as a predictor of elementary-school teaching performance both during training and after graduation (Eash and Rasher 1977).

From the data presently available it would seem fair to conclude that a broad formula needs to be arrived at when selecting students for training based on information from a number of sources. Such a formula should go beyond data from secondary-school performance, to include high-school ranking, personality ratings, verbal and quantitative scores, and interviews (Reed 1976). Personality variables often cited and which could form part of the data profile relate to patience, initiative, enthusiasm, ability to work with people (Bryant et al. 1978), and flexibility, tolerance, sensitivity, and communication skills (Auchmuty 1980). In this process the importance of the interview is not to be ignored. Interviews are considered by teachers, parents, and community groups to be an important element in selection, though there is a great deal of uncertainty concerning how to go about carrying out interviews reliably.

But the application of such a formula as part of initial selection may be valuable only in eliminating those who are obviously unsuited (de Landsheere 1980) or who show no potential to function as continuous learners (Haberman 1974). Indeed, the view has been expressed that the prime purpose of initial selection should be to apply disqualifying criteria to ensure that grossly unsuitable people are screened out and that this negatively-oriented selection should continue during the preservice programme (OECD 1979c). For those who are accepted, the data used as part of the selection process (examination results, information gathered during interview, etc.) should come to form the basis for planning subsequent programmes suited to individual needs.

One-off selection prior to the point of entry is not sufficient. While it may be possible to assess whether a student has the intellectual capacity to succeed along with a positive attitude towards children and teaching, it is only when students have the experience of working with teachers and children that they come to understand the complex roles teachers play and reveal their abilities and potential as developing professionals. So, one theme running through the literature is the need to look at selection as an ongoing educational process rather than as a one-off administrative task (Haberman and Stinnett 1973). In this process, students must demonstrate at a number of specific points in their programme that they possess desired skills, knowledge, and attitudes which will allow them ultimately to function effectively as full-time professionals (Bingham and Hardy 1981). What the process implies is that an efficient counselling service will be available at key points in the students' training programme [as suggested in the National Council for the Accreditation of Teacher Education (NCATE) Standards 1981].

The provision of an efficient counselling service for students should assist the fostering of the notion of "self-selection" whereby students are encouraged to play an active role in deciding whether they should continue with their programmes or shift out of teaching training (Laman and Reeves 1983). The advantage to be gained from having students practise self-selection prior to admission has also been stressed. More and more authorities are advocating the value of a break between school and tertiary study for prospective teacher education students (DES 1983, Howsam et al. 1976). During this initial period of work experience students should be encouraged to explore for themselves whether they really are suited for teaching and make a more balanced decision on the basis of their experience. Self-selection, however, should not lead automatically to admission to a programme which appears to be the case in many instances, given that very few applicants are rejected (Howey et al. 1978).

It should be understood that throughout the whole selection and counselling process there is a need to be mindful of the interests of students and the credibility of the teaching profession. Students must be given every opportunity to develop their awareness of the teachers' roles and of their own ability to perform effectively. Self-selection without advice from professionals will not be sufficient for students to determine whether they are fitted to embark on a teaching career. It is important that, in addition, students should receive support and comment from teachers with whom they work as part of the ongoing counselling process.

Reference has already been made to the desirability of students having some work experience prior to beginning their training. It should be noted that in recent years there has been an increase in the number of applicants not coming directly from school to training institutions, in particular mature-age entrants. This has been seen as a welcome trend, and one to be encouraged (DES 1983, Auchmuty 1980, Howsam et al. 1976). It has been suggested that mature-age entrants tend to show greater motivation and, as a result, are likely to succeed in tertiary studies (Eaton 1979).

As was mentioned earlier in the article, positive discrimination may sometimes be needed in favour of particular groups. For such groups entry requirements may be varied somewhat and provisional admission may be desirable, taking account of their particular background. However, in granting admission, academic background will still remain a consideration. Once provisional candidates are accepted into the programme, for them ongoing selection procedures will assume particular importance and they should be aware of the need for regular counselling throughout their programme.

3. Selection for Employment and Certification

In recent years practices have been changing in relation to the employment of students graduating from teacher education programmes. Selection by employers is still in its infancy in many countries, particularly those where in the past students have been trained with financial support from an authority who guaranteed them employment after training.

Two main avenues exist for becoming employed as a teacher. A graduate student can apply to an education authority for a position and, after presenting relevant credentials and usually after a brief interview (the emphasis being predominantly on administrative matters, especially whether the student has graduated from an approved/accredited programme), the graduate can be deemed eligible for appointment to a school. The precise school is left to the authority to decide after reviewing its vacancies. In this approach it is not always possible to match the talents of the applicant with the position available. On the other hand, the new graduate may apply directly to a school, especially in the case of nonstate schools, provide credentials, seek an interview, after which the school can determine the suitability of the applicant. Should a position be offered, the applicant is free to choose whether or not to accept.

No matter how graduates are appointed to schools, what is ultimately of extreme importance for the standing of the profession is how they receive final certification as teachers. Completion of initial training simply means that students have been successful in meeting the requirements of the tertiary institution; they still have to perform successfully in the school and its classrooms to achieve certification. The purpose of such certification is to safeguard the profession and improve the quality of instruction received by students (Bolton 1973).

It has been forcefully argued that there is a need for the profession to develop a multistaged certification plan (Howsam et al. 1976). When students successfully complete their programme of training, institutions should recommend initial certification which will allow graduates to take up an appointment. Institutions should be required to provide employers with details of the students' programme of training, including recommendations for future growth (see *Induction of Beginning Teachers*). Subsequent certification should be granted after a period of about one year's teaching. During this period relevant data can be gathered and the need to rely heavily on data provided during training can be overcome. As in the initial training phase, teachers should be invited to conduct evaluations of their own performance.

There are two further elements in this multistaged certification plan. Once certification has been granted it should not be permanent; that is, a teacher's work should be reviewed at regular intervals to allow for confirmation of continued certification. A second major suggestion is that after a given period of teaching, application could be made for registration as a professional scholar. For such registration, teachers would be required to meet standards set by representatives of training institutions, the organized profession, state education authorities, and employing school systems. While this goal is still a long way off, the idea behind it is admirable. Not only would such a collaborative approach to recognizing the professional teacher make a significant contribution to protecting the safety of the clients, that is the pupils, it would greatly enhance the standing of the teaching profession.

The possibility of achieving the goal of professional certification may not be quite as remote as it appears at first glance. There has been considerable concern about the quality of graduates seeking employment and the quality of their performance in schools. To try to upgrade the quality of training programmes, accreditation standards have been established in various countries to be met by institutions offering teacher education programmes (e.g., in the United Kingdom, the Council for National Academic Awards, CNAA). Presently in the United States, for example, after 25 years work NCATE has set 25 standards to be met by institutions seeking accreditation (Wisniewski 1981). However, "although NCATE exists to monitor standards in teacher-training programs, NCATE's importance is not seriously regarded except by the institutions that have NCATE accreditation" (Mertens and Yarger 1982 pp. 9–10). Sadly, well under half of the institutions involved in teacher preparation are accredited by NCATE (Watts 1982) and, as Watts points out, "unlike some of the

other professions, which will not accept graduates from non-accredited institutions, products from . . . programs without NCATE accreditation are eligible to enter the teaching profession" (p. 35).

Even where institutions have sought NCATE accreditation there has been criticism. It has been suggested that the standards represent a "laundry list of procedural concerns" which have not led to improved quality in teacher education programmes because the standards fail to emphasize issues of programme quality (Tom 1981). A research project has been conducted to look at the evaluation process of NCATE and criticism has been levelled at the lack of in-depth examination of how well the NCATE standards are implemented in programmes (Wheeler 1980).

It is clear from experience in the United States that much still needs to be done to ensure a guarantee of minimum quality in preservice training programmes. A start has been made, but there is still a need to investigate how to apply minimum standards to all institutions offering teacher education programmes—including Universities—so that there can be certainty that those seeking to enter the profession have undergone approved programmes of training.

To approve programmes is but one step. What else can be done to ensure minimum standards are applied when teachers seek certification after their training? Usually employing authorities have their own means of teacher assessment; for example, inspection systems as in Australia, or simply formal requirements of a specified number of courses and credit hours without any evidence being required of teaching ability (Watts 1982). In an effort to ensure quality in the profession, serious attempts are being made in the United States to foster National Teacher Examinations.

While in 1982, 18 states required teacher testing for certification (Vlaanderen 1982), the tests continue to come in for criticism, as they have done since their beginning in 1940 (Quirk et al. 1973). There are some who argue that a national testing programme will enhance the integrity of the teaching profession and attract better quality students (Gallegos and Gibson 1982). It has also been claimed that the knowledge that teachers ultimately will have to pass examinations to be registered could encourage training institutions to be more rigorous in the preparation and evaluation of their students, showing thereby more desire to exercise their "gatekeeping function" (Pugach and Raths 1982). Others are less hopeful, claiming that the questions teachers are asked in the National Teacher Examinations "trivialize the profession" and "provide no real way to separate the competent from the incompetent novice" (Palladino 1980). What is argued for, instead, is a well-organized internship period during which all aspects of a teacher's work can be assessed fairly by a variety of professionals able to offer advice as well as to carry out an evaluation for teacher certification.

The debate on teacher certification is far from ended. It is hard to see how teacher testing at a national level, for example, will produce a substantial change in the quality of teaching in schools. The problem still lies with those wanting to enter the profession and how to assess their abilities before they are offered a quality programme of training. It is also hard to accept the idea that national teacher testing will enhance the image of the teaching profession if it is applied only to teachers seeking certification at the start of their career. What is to happen to those teachers who have already been granted a lifelong licence to teach and who might not fare so well if subjected to rigorous evaluation or to a National Examination? While the idea of teacher testing sounds appealing, "most of the rhetoric advancing the cause is far ahead of the technology needed in the fields of measurement and assessment to deliver it" (Pugach and Raths 1982 p. 19).

4. Conclusion

How to improve the quality of the teaching profession by selecting suitable applicants for training and by making sound appointments to schools continues to occupy the attention of those associated with the profession. A particularly significant problem at the present time is how to attract able and suited students wanting to train as teachers.

Answers are more likely to be found to many of the present difficulties if a closer collaboration can be achieved amongst professionals working in teacher education, educational authorities, employing authorities, educational researchers, teacher groups, and teachers working in schools. Such collaboration may not be easy to achieve (Howsam 1982) but it would be a major step forward if, in setting up collaborative working groups, matters such as the following could be high on the agenda: recruitment for training; criteria for selection; the provision of adequate counselling for students in training; the appointment of teachers to schools; the initial certification of teachers, and the subsequent approval of teachers as professional scholars.

See also: Professional Socialization of Teachers; Affective Characteristics of Student Teachers; Induction of Beginning Teachers; Teachers' Social Backgrounds; Teacher Supply and Demand; Certification and Licensing of Teachers

Bibliography

Anderson D S 1974 *The Development of Student-teachers: A Comparative Study of Professional Socialization.* Organisation for Economic Co-operation and Development (OECD), Paris
Auchmuty J 1980 *Report of the National Inquiry into Teacher Education.* Australian Government Publishing Service, Canberra
Bingham R D, Hardy G R 1981 Prospective teacher selection and personal development: Using preservice counsellors as facilitators. Paper presented at the annual meeting of the American Association of Colleges for Teacher Education, Detroit, Michigan, Feb. 17–20, 1981. ERIC Document No. ED 199 214
Bolton D L 1973 *Selection and Evaluation of Teachers.* McCutchan, Berkeley, California
Brubaker H A 1976 *Who Should Become a Teacher? Current Student Selection–Retention Policies of Teacher Education Institutions.* Bowling Green University, Bowling Green, Ohio. ERIC Document No. ED 115 608
Bryant B J, Lawlis P, Nicholson E, Maher B P 1978 *What Employers Consider Important in Hiring Teachers.* Association for School, College, and University Staffing, Madison, Wisconsin. ERIC Document No. ED 196 838
Carpenter J A 1973 *Survey of the Criteria for the Selection of Undergraduate Candidates for Admission to Teacher Training.* Bowling Green University, Bowling Green, Ohio. ERIC Document No. ED 070 758
Corrigan D C 1974 Do we have a teacher surplus? *J. Teach. Educ.* 25: 196–98
Crocker A C 1974 *Predicting Teaching Success.* National Foundation for Educational Research, Slough
De Landsheere G 1980 Teacher selection. *Prospects* 10: 318–24
Department of Education and Science (DES) 1983 *Teaching in Schools: The Content of Initial Training.* Her Majesty's Stationery Office (HMSO), London
Eash M J, Rasher S P 1977 An evaluation of changed inputs on outcomes in teacher education curriculum. Paper presented at the 61st annual meeting of the American Educational Research Association, New York, April 4–8, 1977. ERIC Document No. ED 150 203
Eaton E 1979 *The Phenomenon of Student Withdrawal at Universities in Australia. A Review of Literature Concerning Factors Associated with Academic Performance and Discontinuance.* Office for Research in Academic Methods, Australian National University, Canberra
Gallegos A M, Gibson H 1982 Are we sure the quality of teacher candidates is declining? *Phi Delta Kappan* 64: 33
Gress J R 1977 *A Study of the Reliability, Validity and Usefulness of Identified Preteaching Predictors.* Ohio State Department of Education, Columbus, Ohio. ERIC Document No. ED 151 306
Haberman M 1974 Needed: New guidelines for teacher candidate selection. *J. Teach. Educ.* 25: 234–35
Haberman M, Stinnett T M 1973 *Teacher Education and the New Profession of Teaching.* McCutchan, Berkeley, California
Hencke D 1978 *Colleges in Crisis: The Reorganization of Teacher Training, 1971–77.* Penguin, Harmondsworth
Howey K, Yarger S, Joyce B 1978 Reflections on pre-service preparation: Impressions from the national survey. Part 3: Institutions and programs. *J. Teach. Educ.* 29: 38–40
Howsam R B 1982 The future of teacher education. *J. Teach. Educ.* 33: 2–7
Howsam R B, Corrigan D C, Denemark G W, Nash R J 1976 *Educating a Profession.* American Association of Colleges for Teacher Education, Washington, DC
Laman H E, Reeves D E 1983 Admission to teacher education programs: The status and trends. *J. Teach. Educ.* 31(1): 2–4
Mercer W A 1984 Teacher education admission requirements: Alternatives for black prospective teachers and other minorities. *J. Teach. Educ.* 35(1): 26–29
Mertens S K, Yarger S J 1982 Escape from déjà vu: On strengthening teacher education. *J. Teach. Educ.* 33(4): 8–12
Organisation for Economic Co-operation and Development

(OECD) 1979a *Teacher Policies in a New Context*. OECD, Paris

Organisation for Economic Co-operation and Development (OECD) 1979b *Future Educational Policies in the Changing Social and Economical Context*. OECD, Paris

Organisation for Economic Co-operation and Development (OECD) 1979c *Admission Policies in Post-secondary Education: A Survey on Selection for Entry into the Teaching Profession*. OECD, Paris

Palladino J 1980 *The Charade of Testing Teacher Competency: Relevant Criticism for the New York State Education Commissioner's Task Force on Teacher Education and Certification*. ERIC Document No. ED 196 901

Pugach M C, Raths J D 1982 Teacher education in multicultural settings. *J. Teach. Educ.* 33(6): 13–21

Quirk T J, Witten B J, Weinberg S F 1973 Review of studies of the concurrent and predictive validity of the national teacher examinations. *Rev. Educ. Res.* 43: 89–113

Reed B A 1976 Selection of promising high school graduates as future teachers: An experiment. *Improving College and University Teaching* 24: 37–39

Shank K S 1978 *Nationwide Survey of Practices in Selection and Retention of Teacher Education Candidates*. Easton Illinois University, Charleston, Illinois. ERIC Document No. ED 167 539

Taylor W 1978 *Research and Reform in Teacher Education*. National Foundation for Educational Research Publishing Company, Slough

Tom A R 1981 An alternative set of NCATE standards. *J. Teach. Educ.* 32(6): 48–52

Vlaanderen R B 1982 Teacher competency testing: Status report. *Education and Measurement: Issues and Practice* 1(2): 17–20, 27

Watts D 1980 Admission standards for teacher preparatory programs: Time for a change. *Phi Delta Kappan* 62: 120–22

Watts D 1982 Can campus-based preservice teacher education survive? Part 4: Accreditation and certification. *J. Teach. Educ.* 33(4): 22–23

Weaver W T 1981 The talent pool in teacher education. *J. Teach. Educ.* 32(3): 32–36

Wheeler C W 1980 *NCATE: Does it Matter? (Executive Summary)*. Institute for Research on Teaching, East Lansing, Michigan. ERIC Document No. ED 195 551

Wimpelberg R K, King J A 1983 Rethinking teacher recruitment. *J. Teach. Educ.* 34(1): 5–8

Wisniewski R 1981 Quality in teacher education: A reply to Alan Tom. *J. Teach. Educ.* 32(6): 53–55

Wood K E 1978 What motivates students to teach. *J. Teach. Educ.* 29(6): 48–50

Teacher Supply and Demand

P. R. C. Williams

The planning of teacher supply and demand can be defined as securing the future provision of teachers of desired qualities and in desired quantities, compatible with the resources available for employing them. The term "desired qualities and quantities" is directly linked with the realm of curriculum aims, content, and structure, of pedagogical methods, and of the organization of learning groups. The term "available resources" however, is associated with questions of politics, of education financing, and of efficiency of resource use. Despite extensive experimentation with, and occasional application of, technological devices for teaching and learning, teachers continue to dominate the educational process in all national and local systems of education, and their wages account for the bulk of educational expenditure. This article concentrates mainly on the quantitative dimension; the equally important qualitative aspects are discussed in separate articles (see *Teacher Roles*; *Teaching: Art or Science?*).

1. Factors Apparently Facilitating Teacher Planning

Teacher planning is clearly a branch of the wider activity of manpower planning, much—one might say too much—of which has been concerned with estimating future skill needs in the economy and society. Man-power requirements forecasting has been severely criticized not only on theoretical grounds, but also on the basis of its actual track record in predicting shortages and surpluses (Ahamad and Blaug 1973) (see *Economics of Teacher Supply*). But in planning for teachers it would be expected that some of the forecasting difficulties encountered in other sectors and occupations might be avoided, for four main reasons.

(a) Teacher requirements depend primarily on the number of learners coming forward to be educated, and in most cases this refers to children approaching the conventional school age. Once the number of babies currently being born is known, the number of potential school attenders a decade ahead can be predicted fairly accurately.

(b) To an unusual extent, education is a single-occupation undertaking, dominated by teachers. In the educational enterprise complementarity and substitution between teachers and other professionals is limited.

(c) In most countries teachers are mainly employed by the public authorities, the near monopolists (sole buyers) of teachers' services, so that decision making about needs and employment may be rather centralized. Moreover, these very same monopolists in employment are also virtual monopolists in training since it is they who produce teachers (in colleges etc.) and certificate them.

(d) The public authorities control more or less tightly the size of the education system from which the requirements of teachers are derived; and they define the "technology" in the shape of the pupil–teacher ratios which convert given enrolments of learners into appropriate numbers of teachers. This is why one can properly speak of teacher demand being planned, or at least being amenable to planning, as well as teacher supply. There is nothing absolute or fixed about teacher demand, either in the sense of administratively specified requirements, or in the economist's sense of effective economic demand for teachers at a stated price, that is, the number of teachers that will be hired at given levels of wages.

But in spite of this seeming amenability of the teaching occupation to planning, actual recent experiences in many national systems have shown serious miscalculation. Shortages persisted over long periods particularly between 1955 and 1970, and in many countries these were of such dimensions that they prompted an over expansion of teacher-training facilities with the result that shortages have been rather rapidly followed by the emergence of sizable surpluses and teacher unemployment.

2. Constituents of Teacher Demand

Difficulties encountered in achieving teacher supply/demand balance reflect to some extent problems in estimating correctly future values of the four ingredients of changes in numbers of teachers required:

(a) Changes in numbers to be educated (because size of target population, or its enrolment rate, alter).

(b) Changes in normal wastage rate of teachers through death, retirement, resignation, transfer, dismissal, etc.

(c) Changes in special programmes, introduced to replace or upgrade unqualified or underqualified teachers or to localize a service formerly staffed by nonnationals.

(d) Changes in the pupil–teacher ratio through alteration of pupil hours per week, teacher hours per week, or class size. The teacher–pupil ratio, analagous to the labour–output ratio used in manpower requirements forecasting, expresses the intensity of use of teachers and can be expressed by the formulae:

$$T = \frac{P}{g} \times \frac{w}{1} : \quad \text{and} \quad r = \frac{P}{T} \text{ or, given the value}$$

for T, $\quad r = \frac{g \times l}{w}$

where T is the number of teachers required, P is the number of pupils, w is the length of pupil instructional week (in hours or "periods"), g is the average actual size of pupil group meeting one teacher (size of class "as taught"), l is the average weekly teaching lead per individual teacher (in hours or periods), and r is the pupil–teacher ratio.

Major problems for teacher forecasters have arisen in relation to the first of these ingredients, the numbers to be educated. In industrialized countries the birth rate has become somewhat volatile, partly because couples have a greater capability of controlling conception than hitherto, and also because employment opportunities for married women have increased and perceptions of the role of women have been changing. Fluctuations in the birth rate may become more pronounced, reflecting changes in mood and fashion, and rather rapid swings in the economic cycle between prosperity and depression. In developing countries, whose populations display more stable trends (often of very rapid growth) the problem is rather one of changes in the rate of acceleration or deceleration of enrolment growth. Decisions to introduce universal education at a particular level will bring about sudden increases in enrolment as the proportion of the cohort entering or remaining in school increases. This may be followed by a slowing of the rate to something nearer the rate of population increase.

3. The Search for Balanced Development of the Teaching Force

The dynamics of the development of the teacher force make the relationship of the total teacher stock to teacher flow rather crucial. The challenge is to manage the teacher force and the production of teachers so that annual changes in the required stock of teachers are as nearly as possible equal to changes in the net flow of teachers (inflow minus outflow). Since in a mature system the stock of teachers may typically be 8, 10, or 12 times as large as the inflow of new recruits, it follows that relatively small changes in the required size of the teacher stock can have quite dramatic effects on the volume of new recruitment needed. A predicted need to contract the size of the teaching force by 10 percent might, for example, imply that the required annual output of new teachers from the colleges should fall by half or two-thirds for a few years. Yet it is difficult to expand or contract teacher–training output at all quickly: colleges have to be planned and built, tutors for them recruited, and it may take three or four years before the first intakes of students actually graduate as qualified teachers. Similarly it may take some time to turn off the "tap" of teacher output once it has been turned "on": training-college staff may be tenured and cannot easily be dispensed with when their services are not required. In teacher planning the problem of lead-

and lag-times are thus formidable. A decision that very many countries have particularly regretted is the creation of long-term teacher-training capacity to deal with serious deficits of only short- or medium-term duration. It is all too easy in these circumstances to end up with overcapacity, and to find one has developed a teacher production machine apparently doomed to churn out teachers for whom the jobs have unexpectedly disappeared.

Shortage or surplus of teachers may be phenomena applying to whole systems, but imbalances will not necessarily be system-wide. Demographic fluctuations often produce the effect that one age group is of record size while another, 10 years younger, is the smallest in living memory so that a shortage of secondary teachers and a surplus of primary teachers (or vice versa) coexist. Second-level mathematics and physics teachers may be in very short supply, while teachers of history, biology, and physical education are being overprovided; indeed the uniform salary schedules for teachers in most countries tend to produce just that effect by obscuring the fact of differential scarcity of different types of teacher (Kershaw and McKean 1962, Zabalza et al. 1979). Urban schools may be able to recruit any number of teachers they require, while rural areas are simultaneously understaffed. And whilst numbers of teachers recruited may be adequate, their quality may not be.

The consequences of imbalance between teacher supply and teacher demand are increasingly being recognized. Apart from the short-term political embarrassment of having to refuse employment to the newly trained, or of having classes of pupils for whom there are no qualified teachers, there is a growing awareness of the severe long-term distortions created in the structure of the profession by sudden "changes of gear" in teacher recruitment. If large cohorts of newly recruited teachers are succeeded by small ones, it will be found that promotion blockages occur; that some older teachers of indifferent quality may be occupying posts for which better younger applicants are potentially available; and that, because intake to the profession has shrunk, the system has lost its capacity to respond flexibly to new developments in curriculum or method.

4. Measures of Adjustment

There are lessons for the future to be drawn from past experiences; but will they be learned? There is no substitute for the closest monitoring of flows into and out of the profession, and this presupposes the existence of a competent statistical machine. Yet some countries, particularly those in the developing world, have only rudimentary data on their teacher stock, let alone on new recruitment or wastage. Beyond this it is not enough to analyse and understand the current situation and evolving trends: one must know how to influence and shape them both in the short and long term. There is a variety of instruments and policies available to the policy makers and planners in this regard. They should look not only to the most obvious device of expanding and contracting the training of new teachers. They should also consider alternative sources of supply, measures affecting teacher wastage, and the impact on the supply/demand balance of different ways of using teachers.

Teacher shortage, for example, can be coped with in a number of ways that obviate the need to establish expensive permanent capacity, with the delays and long-term inflexibility that involves. It may be possible to cut wastage rates among existing teachers by offering more attractive terms of service. Perhaps there are trained personnel who can be lured into teaching by offer of part-time work, by suspending retirement rules, or simply by raising pay rates. Heavier teaching loads and larger classes will reduce the number of new teachers needed. Teachers may be given shorter full-time pre-service training and more of their professional preparation on the job, so as to speed up their entry into the classroom. Alternative cadres such as national service men, military personnel, etc., may be enlisted as teachers. As a temporary measure foreign teachers can be recruited on contract, under international aid programmes or through the open market.

In the face of teacher surplus, such processes can theoretically be reversed. But in practice it is politically and administratively more difficult to lay off employees than to hire them, to close training facilities than to open them, to reduce pay scales than to increase them. And although teacher surpluses offer the possibility of a more generous, less intensive, use of teachers to improve quality, the pedagogical attractions have to be weighed against the additional financial expense. In the economically straitened circumstances of the 1980s the cost factor weighs as heavily as any with the decision makers in education.

See also: Economics of Teacher Supply

Bibliography

Ahamad B, Blaug M (eds.) 1973 *The Practice of Manpower Forecasting: A Collection of Case Studies.* Elsevier, Amsterdam
Kershaw J A, McKean R N 1962 *Teacher Shortages and Salary Schedules.* McGraw-Hill, New York
Organisation for Economic Co-operation and Development (OECD) 1971 *Training, Recruitment and Utilisation of Teachers in Primary and Secondary Education.* OECD, Paris
Organisation for Economic Co-operation and Development (OECD) 1978 *Present Situation and Future Prospects of Teacher Supply and Demand in Member Countries.* OECD, Paris
Williams P 1979 *Planning Teacher Demand and Supply.* UNESCO/International Institute for Educational Planning, Paris
Zabalza A, Turnbull P, Williams G L 1979 *The Economics of Teacher Supply.* Cambridge University Press, Cambridge

Economics of Teacher Supply

A. Zabalza

In its broadest sense teacher supply means the number of people who, under certain conditions, would be willing to offer their services to the teaching profession. This willingness will depend on a number of factors which can be usefully grouped in two divisions. First, pecuniary factors such as the rates of pay, the expected growth of these rates, and the certainty with which work will be available. Second, nonpecuniary factors such as the characteristics of the job, the social status attached to it, and the environment in which it will have to be performed. The economics of teacher supply concerns the analysis of the way in which the first group of factors will affect the proportion of people who decide to offer their services to teaching. This does not imply that economists consider the second group of factors irrelevant, but that they concentrate their attention on the additional effect that pecuniary circumstances may have on occupational choices.

Underlying the concept of teacher supply there is a theory of individual behaviour and a hypothesis about the distribution of tastes and personal characteristics, which allows the aggregation of individual choices into an overall relationship. In the next section the basic elements of this theoretical framework are sketched and in Sect. 2 some of the empirical results on this subject are surveyed.

1. The Basic Model of Occupational Choice

Economists have usually studied the decision to become a teacher within the theoretical framework of occupational choice. This problem has featured in the literature practically since the beginning of economics as a separate discipline, but its modern formulation owes much to the pioneering study of income differentials between doctors and dentists in the United States by Friedman and Kuznets (1946). The theory views the occupational decision as a comparison of the pecuniary returns that might be anticipated from different courses of action. Abstracting from nonpecuniary aspects, the basic assumption is that a person will train for a given occupation if the expected net returns from doing so are greater than those from any other alternative. These returns will take into account on the one hand the expected costs of training for that occupation, and on the other the expected income to be gained in that occupation during the person's working life. Naturally, occupational decisions are not irrevocable, but if the definition of occupation is sufficiently broad the costs of transferring from one to another will be large, and this will make the lifetime view of occupational decisions an acceptable simplification.

The concept and measurement of training costs is a comparatively simple matter, and for most cases of interest it reduces to one of defining the educational level that corresponds to a given occupation. With expected income things are more complicated because income receipts are distributed along the whole of the individual's working life and, therefore, are subject to some uncertainty. This can take the form of incomplete information on how rates of pay are going to vary over time or on whether job opportunities will be available within the chosen occupation. Also, the temporal nature of the comparison makes it necessary that the individual compares two streams of income rather than two amounts available when the decision is made.

These difficulties are incorporated into the theory by formulating the comparison in terms of present values of net expected returns. The expected level of income at a given data will equal the normal income that, given present information, the individual should receive after the corresponding years of work, adjusted by the probability that work will be available at that date. Then, the value of this expected income to the individual will vary depending on how far in the future its receipt is. The individual will value £10,000 today more than £10,000 next year because he or she could always lend that sum at, say, 10 percent interest and collect £11,000 next year. Thus, £11,000 next year is equivalent to £10,000 today or, more generally, an amount x next year is equivalent to $x/(1 + r)$ today, where r is the annual rate of interest. Similarly, if instead of being available next year, x was to be available in two years time, its value would equal $x/(1 + r)^2$. The point of these examples is that if money can be lent at a positive interest rate, the present value of an income stream is not the simple sum of its components, but rather a weighted sum in which the weights decrease the further into the future the receipt is. In the above example, to obtain the value of x available at year t we would multiply x by the weight $1/(1 + r)^t$, which is smaller the larger t is. If we assume that the rate of discount is constant, the present value of the net expected returns from choosing a given occupation (PV) could then be expressed, for example, as

$$PV = -T + \frac{x_1}{1 + r} + \frac{x_2}{(1 + r)^2} + \cdots$$
$$+ \frac{x_n}{(1 + r)^n} \tag{1}$$

where T is the training cost incurred in the current year, $x_1, x_2, \ldots, x_n$ are the components of the expected stream of income obtained from the second year onwards, and n is the expected year of retirement.

Assume for simplicity that there are only two alternative occupations, A and B, that there is no uncertainty concerning training costs, salaries, or length of the working life, that salaries in each occupation are constant over time and equal to W_a and W_b respectively, that the corresponding training costs are T_a and T_b, and that the individual's working life is sufficiently long. The individual will choose occupation A if its present value is greater than that of occupation B (if $PV_a > PV_b$). Using Eqn. (1) and the above assumptions, this implies (approximately) that he or she will opt for alternative A if

$$\frac{W_a}{W_b} > 1 + r \left(\frac{T_a - T_b}{W_b} \right) \qquad (2)$$

If training costs in both occupations are the same ($T_a = T_b$), the individual will choose A simply when W_a is greater than W_b. If training for A is more expensive ($T_a > T_b$), the individual will want W_a to exceed W_b by an amount sufficient to compensate for the additional training expenses. If this extra training cost is small relative to the level of salaries paid in B, the extra differential required will also be small, and vice versa. Note also that in determining this extra differential, Eqn. (2) multiplies the relative additional training costs by the rate of discount (r) which will usually be a small number (e.g., 0.1 for a 10 percent rate of discount). This is because, in this example, while training costs are only incurred at the beginning, the wage differential will be obtained throughout the whole of the individual's working life.

So far we have only discussed the individual decision, but how W_a and W_b are determined will depend on the choices made by the population as a whole. If all people were identical in the sense that training costs were the same for all, if both occupations were also identical except for the training expenses associated with them, and if there was no impediment of access to one or other occupation, we would observe that in equilibrium the wage differential between A and B would simply reflect the differences in training costs. That is, it would be equal to the differential that makes the present value in the two options equal. If we denote this equilibrium differential by $(W_a/W_b)^*$, we would have that

$$\left(\frac{W_a}{W_b} \right)^* = 1 + r \left(\frac{T_a - T_b}{W_b} \right) \qquad (3)$$

It is easy to see that under our assumptions this must be so. For consider what would happen if from an initial situation of equilibrium the relative wage differential was suddenly increased above the level $1 + r[(T_a - T_b)/W_b]$. Then occupation A would become more attractive than occupation B for everybody and new entrants to the labour force would only train for A. This would increase the supply of labour to occupation A, which in turn, for given demand conditions, would lower W_a, and this process would go on until the present value of A was again equal to the present value of B. At that point people would be indifferent between one or the other occupation and the relative wage would again be given by Eqn. (3).

This is equivalent to saying that the long-run supply curve of labour to occupation A, that is, the relationship

between the proportion of people opting for occupation A (N_a/N) and the level of relative wages (W_a/W_b), is a horizontal line at precisely the level $(W_a/W_b)^*$. Figure 1 represents such a relationship. Under the present assumptions, the supply curve (SS) would determine the equilibrium relative wage $(W_a/W_b)^*$, and the demand curve (DD), which is assumed to be decreasing in relative wages, would determine the proportion of people working in this occupation $(N_a/N)^*$.

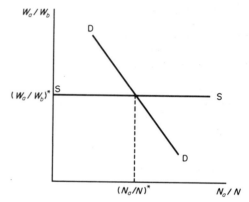

Figure 1
The relationship between the proportion of people choosing occupation A and the level of relative wages

The assumptions used to derive the horizontal supply relationship are very strong and not very likely to capture the essential features of reality. It is useful to see what would happen if some of them were relaxed. Suppose that, in addition to training costs, occupations A and B also differed in some other nonpecuniary characteristic. If we still maintain that people are identical, they will all value these nonpecuniary differences equally and this will only alter the level of the supply curve but not its slope. The new relative wage will incorporate not only differences in training costs but also differences in nonpecuniary characteristics, but since these are valued the same by all, the relative wage which will equate the present value of the two occupations will be the same for all.

If, on the other hand, people are different in their appreciation of the nonpecuniary characteristics of A and B, not only the level but also the slope of the supply curve will be altered. Individuals who are indifferent to the nonpecuniary characteristics of the two occupations will choose A if the relative wage is equal to or greater than that necessary to compensate for differences in training costs; that is, their reservation relative wage will equal that given by Eqn. (3). But individuals who prefer the nonpecuniary characteristics of A relative to those of B will be willing to enter A at a relative wage below that necessary to compensate for differences in training costs; their reservation relative wage will be below that given in Eqn. (3). For the same reasons, individuals who prefer the characteristics of B relative to those of A will have a reservation relative wage above that given in Eqn. (3). This means that the supply curve to occupation A will be upward sloping. The people most inclined towards the occupation will be willing to enter at quite low relative wages, but to attract additional labour higher and higher wages will be needed. Figure 2 depicts such a situation. Now, differently from the previous case, both relative wage and relative supply will be determined by the joint conditions of demand and supply, and the equilibrium relative wage will no longer just compensate for training cost differences but also incorporate the distribution of tastes concerning nonpecuniary characteristics across the population. The more concentrated this distribution is (i.e., the more equal people are in their appreciation of nonpecuniary characteristics) the flatter the supply curve will be. The more dispersed the distribution is, the steeper the supply curve. In the extreme, if one group of people are prepared to go to A at any wage and another at no wage, the supply curve would be vertical; then demand conditions would determine the relative wage and supply conditions the distribution of labour between the two occupations.

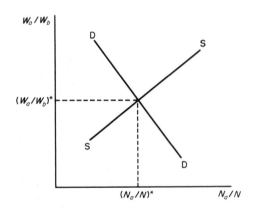

Figure 2
The relationship between the proportion of people choosing occupation A and the level of relative wages, incorporating differences in tastes in nonpecuniary aspects of A

In the above argument the upward slope of the supply curve has been generated by assuming differences among people concerning their appreciation of nonpecuniary characteristics of the two occupations. In reality, there may be other factors, not necessarily nonpecuniary, over which people hold different views. For instance, if there is uncertainty, different degrees of risk aversion among the population will also generate differences in reservation relative wages. If occupation A is riskier than B (because, say, the probability of

employment per period of time is lower) then, even if other characteristics are the same, risk lovers will be prepared to enter it at a lower reservation relative wage than risk averters.

The theoretical model just sketched has formed the basis of most of the available studies on occupational choice. The work on the factors determining the choice of a military career in the United States (Fisher 1969, Altman and Barro 1971) constitutes a good example. Other more complex models are given in Freeman (1971), who explicitly evaluates occupational returns of present values, and Weiss (1972), who takes into account the uncertainty to which most occupational decisions are subject.

2. Applications to the Teaching Profession

The adaptation of the above framework to the teaching profession is straightforward. If teaching is thought of as occupation A, and any other alternative is represented by occupation B, the model and its results apply fully. They imply the existence of a relationship between the proportion of individuals opting for teaching (N_a/N), the level of relative wages (W_a/W_b), and the probability of employment in teaching relative to that outside teaching (π_a/π_b), which in general can be written as:

$$\frac{N_a}{N} = f\left(\frac{W_a}{W_b}, \frac{\pi_a}{\pi_b}\right) \tag{4}$$

Other things being equal, an increase in relative teaching salaries and an increase in relative employment opportunities is expected to increase the proportion of people willing to train and seek jobs as teachers.

In a competitive situation, with numerous small, independent, and identical employers of teachers, Eqn. (4) would represent the market supply curve. This, together with the market demand for teachers, would determine the equilibrium relative wage in the manner described by Fig. 2, but as far as the individual employer is concerned the long-run supply curve would be horizontal at the equilibrium relative wage. Given its small size, each employer would increase its labour force without needing to raise relative salaries. Teacher markets in most real cases do not work like this. The public sector is a near monopolistic supplier of education and consequently a large, in some cases practically the only, employer of teachers. Thus, in these cases, Eqn. (4) does not only represent the market supply curve, but also the supply curve which will constrain the employment decisions of the only significant employer.

Most of the studies of teacher supply have used this framework in their analysis. Some have concentrated most of their attention on the implications of this monopsonistic structure for the determination of teachers' salaries (Kershaw and McKean 1962, Levin 1968, Landon and Baird 1971). Others, mostly concerned with data from the United Kingdom, have concentrated on the analysis of flows in and out of the teaching profession and the relationship between these flows and teacher salaries (Thomas and Deaton 1977, Thomas 1975, Zabalza et al. 1979, Zabalza 1979).

In general these studies have been concerned with the market for teachers as a whole—although in one instance, Thomas and Deaton (1977), other labour markets are also considered—and have tackled many other issues besides that of teacher supply. The problems posed by supply falling short of established targets, and the analysis of the ways in which teacher employers have attempted to eliminate these shortages, have figured prominently in all of them, excepting perhaps the last three. The general conclusion, which is illustrated in detail in the study by Thomas and Deaton, is that educational authorities have tended to ignore salaries (and their structure) as instruments to eliminate these shortages and have relied to a much larger extent on quantity and quality adjustments to increase the available supply of teachers. Expansion of part-time employment, provision of extra training facilities, and lowering of staffing standards are among the methods most frequently used.

This is an important finding because it suggests either that teacher supply is not sensitive to relative wages or, if it is, that educational authorities have in fact ignored potentially useful policy instruments. The conclusions of the studies that have concentrated on the estimation of supply elasticities (Thomas, 1975, Zabalza 1979, Zabalza et al. 1979) consistently suggest that, at least for England and Wales, the supply of teachers is responsive to economic incentives.

Perhaps the most detailed estimation of supply elasticities is given in Zabalza et al. (1979). They define supply in terms of the annual flows in and out of teaching. The stock at the end of a given year will equal the stock at the beginning of the year plus the flow of teachers who have entered the profession during that year, minus the flow of teachers who have left. To give an idea of the magnitudes involved, the size of the stock in the maintained primary and secondary sector of England and Wales at the beginning of April 1977 was 437,637; during the following year 33,815 teachers entered (7.73 percent) and 32,581 left (7.44 percent), leaving the stock at the end of March 1978 at 438,871 teachers. Entrants, in turn, are composed of new entrants to the profession, transfers from other educational sectors, and reentrants (mostly married women who return after a period of absence). Leavers are composed of quits, transfers to other educational sectors, retirements, and deaths. The authors, using temporal and cross-sectional data, specify a labour supply function similar to Eqn. (4), and estimate its parameters for the most sizable flows (new entrants and quits), distinguishing between male and female and between graduate and nongraduate teachers. The results indicate that in general increases in relative wages tend to increase the flows of entrants and decrease that of leavers, with male teachers showing a higher level of responsiveness than female teachers. Using

their estimated elasticities on the flows presented above we can calculate that an increase of, say, 10 percent in relative wages would lead to 3,660 additional teachers entering the profession (an increase in the flow of entrants of 10.82 percent) and to 1,614 fewer teachers leaving the profession (a decrease in the flow of leavers of 5.0 percent). This would imply an increase in the total stock of 5,274 teachers over and above the level it would have reached by the end of March 1978. Thus, a 10 percent increase in relative wages is predicted to lead to a 1.2 percent increase in the stock: a stock elasticity with respect to relative wages equal to 0.12.

In another exercise the authors define relative pecuniary returns in terms of both starting salaries and expected rates of growth of salaries during the individual's working life. Their results indicate that male teachers are very sensitive to career prospects (as measured by the rate of growth of salaries), while female teachers—although still taking this factor into account—are much more influenced by changes in immediate earnings. Relative employment opportunities are proxied by unemployment rates outside the teaching profession and appear to exert the expected effect, particularly as far as graduate entrants and female graduate leavers are concerned. In general, the more difficult it is to find employment outside teaching, the larger is the flow of graduate entrants and the smaller the flows of female graduate leavers, although in both cases the effect is smaller than that of relative wages.

A final dimension of teacher supply, which has also been frequently studied, is that of teachers' services at a given location. So far we have talked of teacher supply as a whole, without considering how this supply is distributed among different geographical areas. If the locations in which teachers have to work differ in their environmental characteristics, and if teachers' valuations of these characteristics also differ, then the distribution of a given overall supply will be sensitive to geographical economic differentials, in the same manner as in Sect. 1 the overall supply of teachers was sensitive to relative salary differentials between occupations. This hypothesis has been corroborated both in the United States (Greenberg and McCall 1974, Pedersen 1973) and in England and Wales (Zabalza 1978, Zabalza et al. 1979). Teacher mobility is found to be sensitive to pecuniary differentials between locations, both in terms of current salary differentials and in terms of differences in career prospects. Movements tend to go from locations with poor promotion prospects to those with good career possibilities and are more readily made by men than by women. Married women, in particular, tend to be guided more by family considerations (such as accommodation to their husband's locational decisions) than by economic gain.

In summary, the economics of teacher supply concerns the analysis of the way in which pecuniary factors may affect the number of people who are prepared to offer their labour services to teaching. The empirical work in this area has shown that this effect is significant and that it operates mainly through the adjustment of labour flows in and out of teaching. Prospective entrants to teaching and prospective quitters from the profession are sensitive not only to current levels of wage differentials between teaching and alternative occupations, but also to expected differentials in career prospects. Even within teaching, the location of labour among different geographical areas or among different schools has been shown to depend, at least to a certain extent, on these pecuniary factors.

See also: Teacher Supply and Demand

Bibliography

Altman S H, Barro R J 1971 Officer supply: The impact of pay, the draft and the Vietnam war. *Am. Econ. Rev.* 61: 649–64

Fisher A C 1969 The cost of the draft and the cost of ending the draft. *Am. Econ. Rev.* 59: 239–54

Freeman R B 1971 *The Market for College-Trained Manpower: A Study in the Economics of Career Choice.* Harvard University Press, Cambridge, Massachusetts

Friedman M, Kuznets S 1946 *Income from Independent Professional Practice, 1929–1936.* National Bureau of Economic Research, New York

Greenberg D, McCall J 1974 Teacher mobility and allocation. *J. Hum. Resour.* 9: 480–502

Kershaw J A, McKean R N 1962 *Teacher Shortages and Salary Schedules.* McGraw-Hill, New York

Landon J H, Baird R N 1971 Monopsony in the market for public school teachers. *Am. Econ. Rev.* 61: 966–71

Levin H M 1968 *Recruiting Teachers for Large City Schools.* Brookings Institution, Washington, DC

Pedersen K G 1973 *The Itinerant Schoolmaster: A Socioeconomic Analysis of Teacher Turnover.* Midwest Administration Center, University of Chicago, Chicago, Illinois

Thomas R B 1975 The supply of graduates to school teaching. *Br. J. Ind. Relat.* 13: 107–14

Thomas R B, Deaton D 1977 *Labour Shortage and Economic Analysis: A Study of Occupational Labour Markets.* Blackwell, Oxford

Weiss Y 1972 The risk element in occupational and educational choices. *J. Polit. Econ.* 80: 1203–13

Zabalza A 1978 Internal labour mobility in the teaching profession. *Econ. J.* 88: 314–30

Zabalza A 1979 The determinants of teacher supply. *Rev. Econ. Stud.* 46: 131–47

Zabalza A, Turnbull P, Williams G L 1979 *The Economics of Teacher Supply.* Cambridge University Press, Cambridge, UK

Certification and Licensing of Teachers

N. L. Zimpher

This article will describe the context within which certification practices have evolved; provide definitions for those processes associated with certification; delineate recent trends in the certification arena, including problem areas; and conclude with a discussion of future trends in certification. The terms "certification, credentialing, and licensure" are frequently used interchangeably, although licensure is the generic term applying to admission to any professional field. In the United States, the term "certification" is typically applied to the credentialing of teachers, whereas other professionals are often referred to as "licensed to practice." The term "certification" will be used in the text of this article as synonymous with "licensure."

As definitions and issues are identified, they will be cast in the context of international teacher preparation. However, the processes described are those particularly germane to the United States. The United States system contrasts with many other systems of certification in that it is only partially nationalized or federalized. The legal authority for certification in the United States is at the state level. This contrasts with the arrangement in many other countries, where authority for certification is vested in ministries and national councils.

1. The Context for Certification

Teachers are among the oldest of society's occupational groups (Huggett and Stinnett 1956). The issue, however, of whether teaching should be viewed as a profession is complex, and is directly related to the certification process. Numerous scholars have attempted to present a set of criteria essential for a profession. Consequently, teachers' organizations in the United States and internationally have attempted an assessment of the role of the teacher that could somehow be equated with a "profession." The lists of characteristics which have been surveyed suggest a considerable range of criteria (Bicentennial Commission 1976). Notable among these characteristics is one criterion that relates specifically to the certification issue, as follows:

A profession is organized into one or more professional associations which, within broad limits of social accountability, are granted autonomy in control of the actual work of the profession and conditions which surround it (admissions, educational standards, examinations and licensing, career line, ethical and performance standards, professional discipline). (Bicentennial Commission 1976 p. 7)

Teaching is essentially a public process, especially in countries where the education of school-age youth is compulsory. Unlike other professions where entry (or licensure) to the profession is mandated by law, the inclination of the public to allow teachers to set those standards has come more slowly. In other words, although doctors, lawyers, and other medical practitioners may have to stand for licensure, the criteria for licensure are usually set by the profession. This has not always been the case for teachers. Parents whose children are required to attend school have traditionally wanted control over who teaches their children. This manifests itself in many countries in local lay control, where boards of education of local school districts are composed of lay (that is, citizen or parent) members. Such lay boards also exist at the regional and/or national levels, and assume the same responsibilities for setting standards. In governments where ministries of education control schooling, and where those ministries are staffed by teaching professionals, there may exist more professional input than would typically occur in the lay process of the United States and other similar democracies.

A closer look at this process is informative. In the United States, at least, there exists a strong tradition of state control of education. To quote the American Association of Colleges for Teacher Education's Bicentennial Commission, "The Founding Fathers rejected the idea of a national system of education. Instead they left to the states the responsibility for providing educational opportunity for the people" (Bicentennial Commission 1976). As a consequence, early local lay boards of education were delegated authority by state legislatures for the establishment of standards for public education and for the preparation of personnel who staff elementary and secondary schools.

After teacher training was moved into the state university system, this responsibility shifted to a centralized system of control by state boards of education and their education agencies. By 1965, the authority to determine the regulations for teacher certification and to issue, reissue, and revoke certificates was almost completely vested by legislative authority in the respective state boards and state departments of education (Mayor 1965). State boards of education and their education agencies still are largely in control of education at the state level. Only in 2 states out of the 50 (California and Oregon) have teachers managed to rescue control of certification from lay board and state department jurisdiction.

The nature and weight of standards for certification as established in the 50 states vary, as do processes for procuring the certificate.

2. Processes Associated with Certification

Teacher certification has been defined by Kinney (1964 p. 3) in the following terms:

Certification is a process of legal sanction, authorizing the holder of a credential to perform specific services in the public schools of the state. Its accepted purpose is to establish and maintain standards for the preparation and employment of persons who teach or render certain nonteaching services in the schools.

The evolution and establishment of certification systems in the United States spans the period since the late nineteenth century. Certification processes in the states are presently administered by state education agencies, to whom authority is delegated by state legislatures and state lay boards of education. The credentialing process typically includes an assessment of the university transcript of a teacher candidate against a particular set of course and experience requirements. A second, more typical vehicle for certification is referred to as the "approved program approach." In this case, the teacher candidate must be graduated from a teacher preparation institution which is "approved" by the state to prepare teachers. This being the case, the candidate is automatically certificated upon graduation. In the United States, state systems for certification vary, as do the nature of various sets of standards for the preparation of teachers. To improve the mobility of a teacher from one state to another, there is reciprocity among 35 states, and several territories and overseas military dependent schools. Such reciprocity allows certificate holders from one state to more easily procure a certificate to practice in another state.

The process of certification is not to be confused with the accreditation process. Accreditation is "the means employed by all professions for evaluating the quality of the professional program of a given college or university" (Huggett and Stinnett 1956). Accordingly, accreditation is somewhat peculiar to the United States, where higher education institutions tend to have more autonomy to regulate themselves. In contrast, in many other countries, central ministries of education tend to fix and enforce standards in higher education institutions (Huggett and Stinnett 1956). The national accrediting "stamp of approval" for teacher education in the United States is a voluntary activity, organized and administered through the National Council for the Accreditation of Teacher Education (NCATE). The standards of this organization are similar to those of many state organizations, including prescriptions for practice in the areas of organization, curriculum, students, faculty, facilities and resources, and evaluation.

However, since national accreditation in the United States is voluntary, occurring once every seven years, its effect is more honorific than regulatory. To date, about 50 percent of the colleges and universities in the states are NCATE-accredited, with a denial rate of one out of every five institutions making application for NCATE accreditation (Wheeler 1980). This process constitutes one example of the profession attempting to regulate itself, since membership in the NCATE council is composed largely of representatives of teachers and teacher educators. But this process does not yet carry any of the legal jurisdiction of state-level licensure.

It is, however, useful to compare these processes when considering the issue of certification, because the existence of both state and federal standards and visitation processes represents a duality in the quality-control arena. The impetus for national accreditation comes from colleges and universities since NCATE was created by an organization now called the American Association of Colleges for Teacher Education (AACTE). Its interests and representation have been exclusively higher education oriented, making it difficult for AACTE, or NCATE, to engender the widespread professional and legal support necessary to counter the pressure of the influential school officials and lay citizens who constitute pressure groups for state certification. These issues of political action, vested interest, and the scramble for control of teacher education are apparent in the current profile of teacher education in the states. Countries whose professional development resembles this pace, such as the United Kingdom, will be or are now struggling with these issues.

3. Recent Trends in Certification

The most recent trend in certification regards who shall control the process. Ostensibly, any group that seeks to control the licensure process does so in the name of quality control, that is, improvement. If political issues exist, they are typically between the profession and the lay public. Such is also the case with education, although the education "profession" appears not to be very cohesive internally. That is, often the contenders in the political arena in education are teachers vs. administrators vs. higher education teacher educators. The relevant question in regard to certification is which of these groups is or should be responsible for assuring that a qualified teacher is in the classroom. Such discussion has led to the creation of professional practices boards, controlled by teachers and autonomous of state agency, state board control. As noted earlier, California and Oregon have such boards. An additional 10 states are targeted for this move by 1984. Theoretically, direct teacher control of licensure will improve teacher competence. But it is too early to measure the impact of this fairly recent governance model.

Public sentiment, however, appears to have less to do with forms of governance and more to do with specific issues of competence and accountability. The public tends not to fragment the profession and its responsibility. Instead, public concern over teacher competence places the blame squarely on the profession, broadly defined. Although there are many ways to assure teacher competence (e.g., more stringent certification standards, tougher college-admission standards, stricter hiring policies), one issue has surfaced as a popular remedy to the competency issue. That is, over 35 states in the United States, and numerous other countries, are adopting some version of the standardized test for entry into the profession. Again, the emergence of competency testing is a relatively new phenomenon so whether or not it will result in, or contribute to, the improvement of education remains to be seen.

4. Future Trends in Certification

Issues of control and competence bring to full circle the initial issue of teaching as a profession. The ability of the profession to assure the quality of its ranks seems mandatory for teaching to be considered a profession. At present, who controls the profession and its licensure, and in what ways that control is effected all speak to the primary issue of assuring and improving the quality of the professional, in this case the teacher. The following issues will no doubt reflect the questions the profession needs to resolve in the near future:

(a) raising standards for admission to college training programs,

(b) strengthening the accreditation process,

(c) providing effective internships and continuing education for teachers,

(d) redesigning teacher education programs,

(e) extending preparation programs, and

(f) raising the incentives for becoming a teacher, primarily through salary incentives (Vlaanderen 1982).

Some of these trends are at the proposal stage, others are under consideration, and in some countries, it is likely these issues have not yet surfaced.

See also: Teacher Supply and Demand

Bibliography

Bicentennial Commission on Education for the Profession of Teaching 1976 *Educating a Profession.* American Association of Colleges for Teacher Education, Washington, DC

Huggett A J, Stinnett T M 1956 *Professional Problems of Teachers.* Macmillan, New York

Kinney L B 1964 *Certification in Education.* Prentice-Hall, Englewood Cliffs, New Jersey

Mayor J P 1965 *Accreditation in Teacher Education: Its Influence on Higher Education.* National Commission on Accrediting, Washington, DC

Rottenberg S (ed.) 1980 *Occupational Licensure and Regulation.* American Enterprise Institute for Public Policy Research, Washington, DC

Vlaanderen R B 1982 Teacher competency testing: Status report. *Educ. Meas.* 1(2): 17–20

Wheeler C 1980 *NCATE: Does it Matter?* Institute for Research in Teaching, Michigan State University, East Lansing, Michigan

Teachers' Organizations

D. L. Colton

Teachers' organizations are formed in order to promote their members' interests through activities such as political and social action, collective bargaining, publication, conferences, and training. Labels vary: some teachers' organizations describe themselves as "professional associations" whereas others use terms such as "trade unions" or "labor unions." Teachers' organizations also vary in terms of their membership, internal governance, goals and activities, and effects. These variations are found among nations, among organizations within nations, and over time within individual organizations (Blum 1969).

1. Membership

Membership in teachers' organizations may be limited and specialized, as in the United Kingdom's Assistant Masters Association, or it may be highly diverse, as in the American Federation of Teachers which embraces local teacher unions as well as unions of administrators, teacher aides, professors, and clerks. Membership may be tied to religious or ideological affiliations, to sex, to race, or to subject matter specializations.

Teacher decisions to affiliate with teachers' organizations usually are voluntary. However some teachers' organizations have secured statutory or contractual authority to make membership and/or payment of dues compulsory for all teachers. Saskatchewan adopted such a statute in 1935. Compulsion is said to be justified because all teachers profit from wage gains or other benefits won through the organization's efforts. Where compulsion is absent, membership decisions are a function of conditions in the larger society and in the schools, the activities of teachers' organizations themselves, and teacher characteristics (Rosenthal 1969, Cole 1969).

Social conditions affect membership decisions: for example, in Japan huge membership increases in the Japan Teachers Union occurred immediately after the Second World War. Economic recessions often cause falloffs in union membership. Government policies also can affect membership in teacher organizations: India's government promotes teacher organizations; in Germany the Nazi regime actively opposed them; the early development of teacher unions in the United States was slowed by state laws and school board policies prohibiting union membership (Eaton 1975). Images and prejudices about teaching also affect membership decisions. In the Federal Republic of Germany, unionization of secondary-school teachers and professors has been impeded by the view that their status would be compromised by affiliating with elementary-school teachers. However images may change: in the United States Myron Lieberman's writings spearheaded a consciousness-raising effort that made concerted action by teachers more palatable (Lieberman 1960).

Conditions of teaching also affect membership decisions. Teachers whose wages lag behind those of similarly trained employees, or behind those of unionized workers in the private sector, may join organizations in the hope that collective action can lead to improved wages and benefits. Depersonalization and bureaucratization of schools stimulates teacher dissatisfaction which often finds an outlet in union membership. Unruly students and lack of parental support may also encourage teachers to seek out the supportive climate offered by a sympathetic teachers' organization.

The activities of teacher organizations also affect membership decisions. Organizations which are too militant or insufficiently militant can lose members and potential members. Internal decisions about the allocation of resources for recruitment activities can have dramatic effects on membership: for example in the late 1950s a handful of leaders in an obscure New York City teachers' union, backed by national union leaders eager to expand white-collar-union membership, organized a highly publicized strike which led to large gains in union membership. Individual decisions about organization membership sometimes are complicated by the presence of rival organizations which engage in competition for new members.

Teacher characteristics are also significant in membership of associations. In the United States men teachers were more militant than women teachers in the 1960s. Working-class family background is often associated with propensity toward union membership. Enhanced professionalism also contributes to militancy: heightened skills reduce teacher tolerance for close supervision and for constraints on the exercise of teacher discretion. Receptivity to peer group pressure is also an important determinant of participation in militant action.

2. Internal Governance

Teachers' organizations, like all other organizations, require internal control mechanisms to foster the identification and pursuit of organizational goals. Partly because of an ideological proclivity toward democratic forms of governance, and partly because maintenance of individual teachers' membership is deemed to depend upon it, most teachers' associations are organized from the bottom up. Local units select their own officers and designate delegates to state, provincial, and/or national federations where the delegates choose organizational objectives, set dues structures, elect federation officers, and structure local–central organizational relationships. However, in most circumstances only a small fraction of organization members are actively engaged in organizational affairs; the bulk of the organizations' work is performed by paid staff members and officials who inevitably come to play key roles in determining organizational agendas and strategies.

Teacher organization structures mirror the structures of the organizations which the teachers seek to influence and upon which they depend for their existence. If wages and working conditions are locally determined, teachers' organizations are structured to provide negotiating and contract administration services at the local level. If policies are set by state or national agencies, the teacher organizations are designed to represent teacher interests at those levels. Often teachers' interests are determined by agencies at more than one level of government. Thus teacher organizations become internally complex; internal rivalries and communication failures sometimes create problems of coordination and cohesion.

3. Goals and Activities

The goals of teacher organizations encompass (a) teacher welfare issues such as salaries, pensions, and seniority rights; (b) pedagogical policy and practice; and (c) social and ideological issues. Relative emphasis on these matters varies among organizations and over time. For example, in Japan and Mexico, ideological matters such as socialism and clericalism are of central importance. In the United States the National Education Association (NEA) initially invested much of its energy in curriculum and instruction improvement projects; later, heightened teacher militancy and competition from the American Federation of Teachers forced greater attention to teacher welfare issues. The shift in emphasis was accompanied by major changes in NEA structure and activities (West 1980).

Teacher organization activities vary as widely as their goals. Often, and particularly in the early stages of their development, the emphasis is on direct service to members: management of pension funds, publication of journals, and public relations activities aimed at enhancing the image of teachers. Later these direct member services become less important than the gains secured by exerting influence vis-à-vis employers and government agencies.

One important mechanism for influencing external agencies is collective bargaining. Another and longer established form of activity is direct social and political action. Teachers' organizations are interest groups and they exhibit behaviors typical of other interest groups. Through lobbying activities they attempt to influence legislators' votes. Teachers' organizations provide testimony and information to legislators; often teachers' organizations have become highly respected and indispensable sources of information on the complexities and operations of schooling. Organization staff members help draft bills of interest to teachers, seek legislative sponsors, and arrange for testimony. Teachers' organizations also attempt to establish close ties with (or coopt if possible) executive agencies responsible for education and schooling (Masters et al. 1964, Coates 1972).

Interest group activities present a number of problems for teacher organizations. Some organizations form coalitions: for example, in the United States teachers and school boards may join forces in seeking increased legislative appropriations for schools. Some organizations refrain from close affiliation with candidates for office and with political parties; others believe that such affiliations bring advantages that outweigh the risks.

The most dramatic and controversial type of teacher organization activity is direct action—particularly strikes. The task of organizing and sustaining a strike requires a substantial investment of organizational resources and a careful calculation of the probabilities of success. An unsuccessful strike can damage the credibility of an organization and its leadership, precipitate losses in membership, erode community support for teachers, and evoke repressive legislation and sanctions. However a successful strike can improve teachers' power, produce membership gains, and enhance organizational solidarity (McMorrow 1977).

Teacher organizations then, stand in a precarious position. They must cope with dilemmas which never can be finally resolved. In their recruitment of members the organizations must promise enough to be attractive, but not so much that credibility and success are jeopardized. In their efforts to enlarge membership, care must be taken to preserve sufficient uniformity of ideology and aspiration to prevent internal fragmentation. Organizational structures must be designed to ensure that members' wishes are recognized and served, but also to provide strong internal leadership. Goals must be chosen in the light of internal demands and external opportunities, and supporting activities must reflect both organizational capacity and judgments about external efficacy.

4. Effects

Opinions differ as to the effectiveness and social utility of teachers' organizations. Skeptics contend that teachers are powerless in their own organizations; that the organizations foster adversarial rather than collaborative relationships with employers; that collective action destroys the prestige of teachers; and that the gains achieved by teacher organizations are trivial. Other critics argue that teacher organizations have enhanced teacher power to the point where teachers' interests are put ahead of those of children. Proponents contend that teacher organizations provide vital moral support for teachers, contribute to their professional improvement, alleviate conditions which inhibit effective teaching, address and serve issues which are in the public interest, help attract qualified people to teaching careers, and provide a legitimate balance against governing boards and administrators whose understanding of classroom problems is limited.

Bibliography

Blum A A (ed.) 1969 *Teacher Unions and Associations: A Comparative Study*. University of Illinois Press, Urbana, Illinois

Coates R D 1972 *Teachers' Unions and Interest Group Politics: A Study in the Behaviour of Organised Teachers in England and Wales*. Cambridge University Press, London

Cole S 1969 *The Unionization of Teachers: A Case Study of the UFT*. Praeger, New York

Cresswell A M, Murphy M J, Kerchner C T 1980 *Teachers, Unions, and Collective Bargaining in Public Education*. McCutchan, Berkeley, California

Eaton W E 1975 *The American Federation of Teachers, 1916–1961: A History of the Movement*. Southern Illinois University Press, Carbondale, Illinois

Lieberman M 1960 *The Future of Public Education*. University of Chicago Press, Chicago, Illinois

McMorrow J F 1977 Queensland teachers' salaries: A case study in militancy. *J. Indust. Rel.* 19(2): 173–86

Masters N A, Salisbury R H, Eliot T H 1964 *State Politics and the Public Schools: An Exploratory Analysis*. Knopf, New York

Rosenthal A 1969 *Pedagogues and Power: Teacher Groups in School Politics*. Syracuse University Press, Syracuse, New York

West A M 1980 *The National Education Association: The Power Base for Education*. Free Press, New York

Nonteachers and Teaching

J. H. Duthie

In the 1960s and early 1970s there was an upsurge of interest in employing auxiliaries, or nonteaching assistants, in schools. Systematic studies of the potential role of auxiliaries were commissioned, and, at least in Scotland, moves made to employ such personnel at a national level. Unfortunately, a combination of economic recession and falling school rolls, leading to teacher unemployment, has reversed this process and since the late 1970s little progress in the employment of auxiliaries has been made except possibly in the field of special education. It seems likely, however, that this reversal is a temporary one and that in the long term the arguments in favour of the employment of auxiliary assistants will outweigh other considerations. In the shorter term the slight upswing in the birth rate which in the United Kingdom is leading the government to increase the number of primary-school teachers may also lead to a renewed interest in the employment of auxiliary personnel.

That auxiliaries—also known variously as teacher aides, ancillaries, or, as in the title of this article, nonteachers—can have an important role in the instructional process, can hardly be doubted. On commonsense grounds alone it seems unlikely that one teacher could deal effectively with the educational needs of the 20 or 30 pupils in his or her care. With the current move towards individualized instruction and response-based learning, it would appear all the more important that teachers be provided with trained and experienced auxiliary personnel if they are to meet the educational needs of their pupils as effectively as they might.

The usual analogy is with the surgeon who could not perform his or her work without a support team. In the same way, a teacher is unlikely to be able to utilize his or her full professional competence without the support of auxiliary personnel. The organization and facilitation of learning operates at a number of levels and arguments against the employment of auxiliaries are usually based on the claim that these levels cannot be separated or that they all require the professional competence of the teacher. Clearly this is not the case in relation to the very basic activities required to provide a viable context for learning—for example, those of the school caretaker and cleaner or of the laboratory technician in the science class. The purpose of this article is to attempt to demonstrate, through argument and the analysis of evidence, that a similar separation can be made between teaching and nonteaching processes at levels which include adult–child interaction in the classroom itself.

A literature search reveals that the main systematic effort in this field has been undertaken in the United Kingdom and it is chiefly on the basis of these reports that this article is constructed. The article will look first of all at the opportunities for auxiliary assistance in the primary (elementary) school and then at such opportunities in the secondary school.

1. Nonteaching Personnel in the Primary School

1.1 Definition of Nonteaching Duties Related to the Instructional Process

The *Primary School Survey*, published by Her Majesty's Stationery Office in 1970 and written by Duthie, distinguished housekeeping and supervision duties on the one hand from the teaching process on the other. The distinction between housekeeping and supervision duties is that between those duties which prima facie seem to be of the sort which auxiliaries might carry out and those which are more closely related to the educational work of the teacher.

In order to define housekeeping duties, a list of possible activities was first of all drawn up in consultation with members of the teaching profession and Her Majesty's Inspectorate. This was subsequently used as a basis for observation in a representative sample of Scottish primary-school classrooms and the list modified and added to as a result of that observation. For the purposes of constructing an auxiliary's working day, housekeeping duties were classified according to five categories, the three principal ones being as follows:

(a) Fixed duties in the sense that they can only occur at a particular time of day. Examples are as follows: bringing children in from the playground; cloakroom duty; accompanying children out of school; and transporting, setting up, and running audiovisual aids.

(b) The second category of housekeeping duties included those which are partly fixed in the sense that they occur within certain necessary time limits. Examples are as follows: registration; determining milk numbers; collection of dinner money; and distribution and clearing of material in the classroom.

(c) The third category is of nonfixed duties in the sense that although they are observed to occur at a particular time of day they could be allocated to another occasion. Examples are as follows: objective marking; maintaining condition of materials (paint, crayons, clay, etc.); maintenance of audiovisual aids; and writing instructions or assignments on the chalkboard.

It should be noted that some duties could be classified according to more than one category, for example, the collection of dinner money could be either partly fixed or nonfixed, depending on how it is organized in a particular school. The purpose of the classification at this stage of the investigation was descriptive rather than prescriptive.

Supervision duties required a more analytical justification for their inclusion as auxiliary tasks and these were gradually separated from teaching duties on the basis of principles which were applied, tested, and refined during the preliminary stages of the study. The main principle was that no duty to be performed by an auxiliary should involve the structuring or restructuring of situations—in other words, at no stage might auxiliaries help pupils with problems of understanding. Given this proviso, there were two kinds of situation in which the auxiliary could provide supervisory help—the "mechanical" and the "affective". (The latter relates to problems of motivation and relationships with pupils.) Each of these was divided into receptive behaviour and communicative behaviour, resulting in four categories of supervision duty which helped to define those areas in which an auxiliary could provide assistance closely related to teaching tasks while not actually taking over the teacher's role. Examples of each of the four categories of supervision duty follow:

(a) Receptive behaviour in mechanical situations is

exemplified by the auxiliary providing general supervision while the children are engaged in activities and the teacher is working with a small group; by objective marking; or by keeping progress records under the general guidance of the teacher.

(b) Communicative behaviour in mechanical situations is exemplified by helping the pupils with minor problems in the use of materials, helping a pupil find the next assignment card, or by labeling drawings for children who cannot yet write.

(c) In receptive behaviour in affective situations the auxiliary is approached by the pupil who brings work for admiration.

(d) In communicative behaviour in affective situations the auxiliary would encourage pupils working together in groups while the teacher concentrated on the work of individuals.

In each of these four subcategories of supervision, the auxiliary works together with the teacher as part of a team and the evidence from this and from a subsequent study (1975) was that not only is such work feasible for a nonteacher but that it is positively beneficial to the pupils. While in general it might be argued that some or all of these duties should be performed by a trained teacher, in practice no teacher can respond to all such opportunities and the presence of an auxiliary was found to free the teacher to make better use of educational opportunities as they arose.

When, in a subsequent stage of the investigation, the research team came to use these principles in order to analyse opportunities for auxiliary assistance, it was found that they were not in themselves always sufficient to enable agreement to be achieved among independent observers as to whether an activity could be performed by an auxiliary or not. As a result, an ad hoc "rule book" was also drawn up on the basis of discussion of difficult cases among members of the team. No doubt this rule book could also have been reduced to more general principles had time permitted but in the event its use did prove sufficient to enable a very high degree of interobserver reliability to be achieved. The rule book helps the observer (and in the course of training, the auxiliary) decide in which cases the task is exclusively a teacher's one and in which cases the auxiliary can legitimately provide assistance. Thus it includes advice on what to do if a pupil is unoccupied, how to record the parallel occurrence of duties, and how to analyse the problems of providing assistance in a one-teacher school. It also provides a checklist of potential supervision duties.

Having identified opportunities for auxiliary assistance in the course of successive pilot studies in schools, the team visited a representative sample of Scottish primary schools and spent a full day observing in each of 117 classrooms in these schools. On this basis, it was possible to analyse potential auxiliary duties and to construct "auxiliaries' days", by piecing together both inclass and school-based duties which might be performed by nonteachers. In terms of feasible duties, that is to say those duties which could be formed into a viable working day and working week, it was predicted that auxiliaries could be employed in the ratio of one auxiliary to every three teachers throughout Scotland. (This was in fact a conservative estimate, the work available providing employment for nonteachers actually approaching a ratio of one auxiliary to every two teachers.) Details of the methods utilized to demonstrate that individual duties could be organized into a working day are given in Duthie (1970). The principal concern was to demonstrate how piecemeal duties, occurring sporadically, could be grouped in such a way that they could be undertaken by auxiliaries in a predictable way. The chief technique utilized was that of "blocking", whereby duties (in particular supervision duties) had to be shown to occur sufficiently frequently within a given period to justify the presence of a nonteacher in the classroom.

Given that auxiliary duties could thus be organized, the next step was to provide headteachers with a technique for organizing the auxiliary's working week. Four policies were examined: "On-call"; a flexible timetable policy (in which the auxiliary would be allocated to a specific teacher at a specific time, but could be reallocated if not required); a fixed timetable policy; and sharing (allocation of the auxiliary to a group of teachers who among them would decide the allocation of duties to the auxiliary).

The first and last of these policies were rejected and the various auxiliary duties allocated according to a mix of fixed and flexible timetabling. It was proposed that duties which by nature are fixed or partly fixed should first of all be timetabled by the headteacher for the whole school (e.g., registration of pupils, collection of dinner money, bringing in and dispersal of pupils at the beginning and end of the day). Nonfixed duties and supervision were thought to be best handled by a flexible timetable policy, the blocks of time being allocated to individual teachers in relation to the duties already fixed for the whole school. Should an individual teacher not require assistance at a timetabled hour, then the auxiliary would be available to other teachers.

These timetables for auxiliaries have the status of predictions in the sense that, at the completion of the survey in 1970, no auxiliary had actually been employed on this basis. It is possible that, for a number of reasons, organizational as well as attitudinal, it might not have been possible actually to employ auxiliaries in practice despite the opportunities which existed and which the *Primary School Survey* demonstrated. This prompted the Scottish Education Department to fund a second project carried out by Duthie in collaboration with Ken Kennedy—*Auxiliaries in the Classroom: A Feasibility Study in Scottish Primary Schools* (1975)—in which auxiliaries were employed in primary schools on an experimental basis and their contribution to the teacher's day carefully assessed.

Nine schools of a representative kind and reasonably adjacent to Stirling University were chosen for the investigation and 19 auxiliaries selected and trained to work in them. Sixty teachers and 1,700 pupils took part. Once again direct observation was adopted as the principal experimental technique, supplemented on this occasion by returns made by the auxiliary and questionnaires completed by all participants.

All of these sources of information indicated clearly that auxiliaries can be employed effectively at all levels of the primary school and for the range of duties specified in the *Primary School Survey*. Few difficulties arose in the course of the feasibility study and these were relatively easily resolved. In general it can be stated that the predictions of the *Primary School Survey* were validated. In particular, teachers spent much less time in carrying out nonteaching tasks in the school—only 12.9 percent of their time was now spent in such duties compared with the 21.4 percent of the auxiliaries' time spent on housekeeping duties which would otherwise have to be done by the teacher or by pupils. (Auxiliaries only undertook such tasks when it was clear in the teacher's view that there would be no educational loss to pupils.) On average, auxiliaries spent 73.5 percent of their time on supervision duties and were unoccupied for only 5.1 percent of their time.

Perhaps even more important than this finding is the reduction in the number of interruptions to the teacher's work when an auxiliary is present. In comparison with data derived from the *Primary School Survey* it was found that there are three times as many breaks to the flow of the lesson in the absence of an auxiliary.

From the questionnaire returns, it is clear that when auxiliaries are employed, there is more time to give individual attention to pupils: 43 out of 54 teachers replying stated that this was so and the other 11 stated that the time available had remained constant. Again from the questionnaire the great majority of respondents claimed that they now had more time for the essential educational tasks of diagnosing, evaluating, planning, presenting, and instructing (44 as against 5 of those replying to this question).

Teachers found auxiliaries particularly useful when pupils were working in groups, especially on project work and made considerably greater use of audiovisual aids as compared with teachers who did not have auxiliary assistance. (The 1970 report had indicated that, without auxiliaries, teachers had made very little use of audiovisual equipment—for example, only 25 percent made use of a sound film projector where this was available in the school. The only exception was in the use of television and radio, presumably because less preparation was required.)

Teachers preferred to have auxiliaries working alongside them in the classroom rather than providing out-of-class housekeeping assistance—a finding which may surprise some readers. It may also be of interest to learn that, with experience, participant teachers were in favour of allowing auxiliaries to listen to reading, normally thought by Scottish teachers to be a professional task (they excluded "slow" readers from this, however). In general, teachers claimed to enjoy their teaching more, found teaching to be easier and reported that there was a more relaxed atmosphere in the schools.

Before leaving the issue of employment of auxiliaries in primary schools, perhaps something should be said about the selection and training procedures found to be necessary if auxiliaries were to perform effectively as members of a team.

Appointments of auxiliaries to the second project were made before the current unemployment problems had really begun to show themselves. Nonetheless it was found that approximately 60 applications were received for each post advertised so there clearly is no shortage of people interested in such positions. The selection criteria used were as follows:

(a) possession of a secondary-school certificate as a minimum qualification;

(b) relevant postschool experience with children, for example, as nurses or playgroup leaders;

(c) musical or artistic ability;

(d) ability or interest in games;

(e) ability to drive a car.

Ages of those appointed ranged from 18 to 54. In a four-week course of full-time training, auxiliaries were introduced to the project and its rationale and were then given a course which familiarized them with the modern primary school and its educational methods and with the operation of audiovisual aids. The programme included visits to representative primary schools; talks on, and where appropriate practice in, registration and record keeping; school libraries and book care; child development; printing and writing in the primary school; primary-school mathematics; language arts; art and craft; first aid and physical education. Among topics covered in subsequent inservice courses for auxiliaries were reading, speech and drama, and adult–pupil relationships. A major inservice course for both auxiliaries and teachers was held after six months of the project had passed, to enable discussion of the project to take place and to provide a forum for the solution of problems and planning of future team work. It is, in the view of the research team and of the participating teachers, essential to provide adequate courses of pre-service and inservice training if auxiliaries are to be used effectively in schools.

Before moving on to an examination of nonteachers in secondary schools, it might be worthwhile referring here to an interesting article in the 1979 NSSE *Yearbook on Classroom Management* in which Ward and Tikunoff write on "Utilizing Non-teachers". They were concerned with the advantages and disadvantages of having the nonteacher in the classroom and hence their comments relate to the problems of defining auxiliary activities discussed above. Written mainly from a theoretical standpoint, the article envisages four areas of concern: (a) assignment of power and authority, (b) assignment of instructional tasks, (c) monitoring of pupil performance, and (d) development of pupils.

In general, Ward and Tikunoff favour allowing teachers to make their own decisions regarding the role of the nonteacher in the classroom and content themselves with providing advice under these heads.

1.2 Assignment of Power and Authority

Ward and Tikunoff point out that a teacher and a nonteacher in the classroom may have different sets of expectations regarding pupil behaviour and that this may lead to disruption. The Scottish reports took the view that, to avoid this, the teacher should be fully in control and that the auxiliary's role should be carefully defined in advance. The NSSE article recommends that the teacher should decide whether to remain fully in control, or whether to allow the auxiliary to establish his or her own rules. In either case they say the teacher should take a conscious decision and be aware of its implications.

1.3 Assignment of Instructional Tasks

The authors point out that the presence of an auxiliary can increase the variety of activities possible in a classroom and indicate that the teacher should assign to auxiliaries those tasks in which they will achieve greatest participation by the pupils. They instance ". . . supervising painting, construction, and other such activities" and lessons in which auxiliaries give demonstrations. Again, the authors caution the teacher about the importance of assessing the limits of the auxiliary's competence, especially with regard to giving and receiving feedback.

1.4 Monitoring Pupil's Performance

While the use of auxiliaries to monitor pupil performance may free the teacher for instructional purposes, the need to establish new monitoring mechanisms is emphasized. The solution adopted in the *Primary School Survey* was to utilize the auxiliary as a "buffer" in order to avoid unnecessary queuing for the teacher's assistance: in other words, the auxiliary was trained to decide when the child required assistance which only the teacher could provide and when the assistance could competently be provided by the auxiliary himself/herself.

1.5 Pupil Development

Ward and Tikunoff were concerned to draw teachers' attention to the risk that the presence of another adult in the classroom may increase pupil dependence. If one of the aims of education is to help pupils achieve independence then the presence of an auxiliary could be counterproductive. While Duthie would agree that teachers' attention should be drawn to this risk, he would point out that there was no evidence of this actually occurring under the conditions of the "Auxiliaries in the Classroom" project and that in his opinion the risks of employing auxiliaries in this way are far outweighed by the demonstrated advantages.

2. Nonteaching Personnel in Secondary Schools

Once again, a survey of the literature indicates that the two major reports on nonteachers in secondary schools originated from the United Kingdom. These reports, published in 1976, were, in a sense, a follow-up to the primary-school work which had been commissioned by the Scottish Education Department and they examined the more logistically complex problems of assistance to teachers in the secondary school.

The first of these, "Ancillary Staff in Secondary Schools", examines the potential roles of three groups of nonteachers: administrative and clerical assistants, technicians, and general auxiliaries. The working party, headed by Professor Ruthven, recommended that such ancillary staff be employed in a ratio of one to every 80 children, the actual numbers of staff in each category to be decided by the headteacher of the school concerned. Within this general recommendation, the working party indicated that the major increase in nonteaching activities has been in the administrative/clerical field and that this should be reflected in a proportionally greater increase of staff in this area. The changes in secondary schools which the working party identified as leading to an increasing need for the services of administrative and clerical staff are as follows: the grouping and regrouping of pupils implicit in a comprehensive system of education; changes in curriculum and pupil assessment; changes in teaching methods (especially towards a resource-based approach, utilizing assignment cards and worksheets); developments in guidance and in school/community linkage; changes in the administrative structures within schools (e.g., boards of studies); and the greater use of audiovisual equipment and educational technology.

Specific tasks for each of the three categories of personnel are listed in Chap. 5 and appendices D–F of the report and include the following:

(a) For administrative assistants and clerical assistants: school finance, correspondence, record keeping, examination arrangements, ordering of supplies, and routine statistical returns.

(b) For technicians: although technicians would operate chiefly in science departments, the working party believed that a system should be instituted whereby they could meet the needs of the whole school. Thus their duties would include equipment maintenance and storage in relation to educational technology and preparing experimental materials for classroom use.

(c) General auxiliaries: many of the general duties proposed for the secondary-school auxiliary are identical with those listed earlier for the primary-school auxiliary. These include preparation and care of materials and books; setting up and operating audiovisual equipment; stocktaking and requisition; reproduction and distribution of worksheets and other materials; escorting and supervision of pupils in cloakrooms, bus queues, and at school dinners; and first-aid duties. In addition, specific assistance could be provided in connection with the work of the following departments (see appendix F): art, home economics, mathematics, music, science, physical education, technical education, guidance, library/resources centre, and the language laboratory.

In the second of these reports, "Non-teaching Staff in Secondary Schools", the working party, headed by D. E. Stimpson, examined the work which might be undertaken in secondary schools by nonteachers other than those dealt with in the Ruthven Report described above.

Their first concern was the role of the teacher and they indicate how, over the years, this has developed to the extent that teachers are no longer able to fulfil all of the duties required of them. In particular, teachers now have to take into account community involvement, leisure pursuits, and outdoor activities. To assist them in these three areas of responsibility, the report recommends the increasing involvement of two classes of personnel: youth and community workers, and librarians, and examines the potential role of a third category: instructors.

In relation to the first of these, the report recommends the establishment of ". . . stong links between the Education Service and the Youth and Community Service". They consider that this is especially important in urban areas. The roles of youth and community worker and teacher would be seen as complementary and the presence of the former in schools would help to promote continuity between the pupils' work in schools and their experience in the community. Other aspects of the youth and community worker's role would include advice to the pupils and provision of an increased range of leisure activities. He or she would also help teachers develop pupils' awareness of social problems and assist the guidance staff of the school.

Selection of youth and community workers should be undertaken by the headteacher and other interested members of school staff and the worker(s) should be responsible, so far as school duties are concerned, to the headteacher.

With regard to the employment of librarians in schools, the report recommends the appointment of a full-time qualified librarian to the staff of any school with a roll greater than 600 pupils (a full-time library assistant would be appointed to smaller schools). The librarian, who would have ancillary support, would be responsible to the headteacher and would service a school resources centre. The resources centre would be open not only during school hours but also in the evenings, at weekends, and during holiday periods and pupils would be encouraged to use it as a resource for active learning for both curricular and extramural purposes. The operation of the resources centre should be a cooperative enterprise and this would be facilitated through a resources centre committee on which both teachers and librarian would serve. Education authorities should also set up an educational library/resource service to provide a support service for the schools.

Instructors, with the few exceptions specified in the report, should be replaced by qualified teachers. Whether this is a policy that other countries would wish to follow, must of course be decided by them, and even in Scotland there are dissenting voices, but certainly the General Teaching Council for Scotland which regulates entry into the profession has adopted the policy described above. The reason given in the report is that "The person best equipped to give tuition in any subject planned as part of the curriculum, formal or informal, is the qualified teacher" (Para. 7.9). Exceptions, involving a small number of people, include those categories of instructors who possess skills and knowledge so · specialized that such instruction could not otherwise be provided, for example, musical/instrumental tuition outside school hours; demonstration or consultancy by extremely talented musicians; instruction of children who are exceptionally gifted in dance or in music; high-risk outdoor activities (possibly through consultancy); and instruction in traditional craft skills. The use of visiting experts is however accepted by the report, especially in the case of new activities which are not yet a formal part of the curriculum. Nevertheless, the report favours the gradual replacement—over a five-year period—of instructors and the introduction of new teaching qualifications wherever appropriate.

Finally, and despite their reservations about the use of instructors, the writers of the report emphasize ". . . the desirability of bringing the resources of the community at large into a strong working relationship with the secondary school . . . . We recognise that the teacher is in process of becoming more dependent, directly and indirectly, on the knowledge and skills of others" (Paras 8.1 and 8.2). Perhaps this is one of the most appropriate perspectives from which to view the utilization of nonteachers in secondary schools; the other, clearly, must be in terms of the facilitation of the teacher's conventional classroom task, through the employment of auxiliaries and other ancillary staff.

In general, Brooksbank (1980) agrees that there must be, and is, a growing emphasis on nonteaching and support staff. "Because most historic policies have favoured teachers, there is a growing redressing of the balance towards ancillary staff whose job satisfaction depends just as much as that of an academic on his ability to do what is expected of him and realise his potential for progression. As the concept of 'one work force' becomes more general, so is the balance of training and staff development likely to move towards support staff. The overall cost is not great and the rewards of the staff, the motivation and the service are handsome."

Thus, although Brooksbank's concern was principally with the training of auxiliaries, it may be legitimate to generalize his remarks to their employment and see the future staffing of schools in terms of "one work force" consisting of teachers together with a variety of in-class and school-based ancillary staff. It is certainly difficult to see otherwise how new developments such as open-plan, resource-based learning and criterion referencing, aimed at the facilitation of pupil learning, can occur.

Bibliography

Brooksbank K 1980 *Educational Administration*. Councils and Education Press, London

Duthie J H 1970 *Primary School Survey: A Study of the Teacher's Day*. Her Majesty's Stationery Office, Edinburgh

Kennedy K T, Duthie J H 1975 *Auxiliaries in the Classroom: A Feasibility Study in Scottish Primary Schools*. Her Majesty's Stationery Office, Edinburgh

Ruthven B T 1976 *Ancillary Staff in Secondary Schools: Administrative and Clerical Staff, Technicians, Auxiliaries: Report of a Working Party Appointed by the Secretary of State for Scotland*. Her Majesty's Stationery Office, Edinburgh

Stimpson D E 1976 *Non-teaching Staff in Secondary Schools: Youth and Community Workers, Librarians, Instructors: Report of a Working Party Appointed by the Secretary of State for Scotland*. Her Majesty's Stationery Office, Edinburgh

Ward B A, Tikunoff W J 1979 Utilizing non-teachers in the instructional process. In: Duke D L (ed.) 1979 *National Society for the Study of Education* (NSSE) *Yearbook* 78 Pt. 2: *Classroom Management*. University of Chicago Press, Chicago, Illinois

SECTION 6
Teacher Education

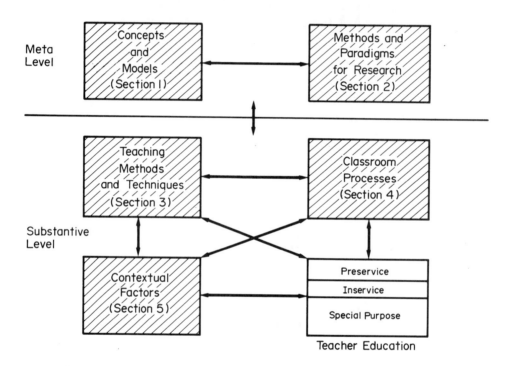

Schematic representation of Section 6 in relation to other Sections

SECTION 6

Teacher Education

———————

INTRODUCTION
TO SECTION 6

The initial preparation and continuing development of teachers are just as suitable for the application of the conceptual and theoretical models of teaching and learning discussed in the first section of this Encyclopedia as any other educational process. Similarly, many of the methods of teaching considered in Sect. 2 are used in teacher education, but especially those grouped under the heading Higher Education in that section. There are, however, approaches that apply distinctively to teacher education and it is those which are the focus of this section of the Encyclopedia. The first two subsections reflect two major concerns, the initial preparation of teachers before they enter employment in schools, known often as preservice education, and the continuing education of teachers after entering employment, usually known as inservice education. The articles in these subsections apply to the education of teachers for work with normal students in regular school contexts. The third subsection contains articles about the education of teachers for work in other contexts, such as adult education and special education.

1. Preservice

Approaches to the development of professional skills and competencies in preservice teachers revolve around the provision of guided experience in school or school-like situations. Almost universally this involves the placement of student teachers in actual schools and classrooms for varying periods of time and at varying stages in their preparation. In the first article in this section, Stones writes about this process under the title of *Student (Practice) Teaching*.

After noting variations in terminology applied to this process, Stones discusses its placement in teacher education programmes and differences in emphases between Anglo–Saxon and European countries. He traces the origins of practice teaching in ideas of craft apprenticeship and discusses commonsense justifications for its use, as well as notions that teachers are born and not made. Approaches to practice teaching that involve modelling master teachers have disadvantages writes the author. They threaten the individuality of the student teacher and deny experience of teaching modes beyond the repertoire of the model. Furthermore, master teachers are difficult to identify since there is no consensus about the nature of teaching excellence.

Rather than encouraging acceptance of the *status quo*, "practice teaching should aim to . . . develop in students a habit of scepticism and enquiry not just in regard to pedagogical practices but also in their appraisal of the institutions in which they teach". Instead of the model the master teacher approach to practice teaching, Stone advocates a "master the teaching model" approach which involves analysing and understanding teaching and its contexts rather than imitating a "master" teacher.

From this discussion of models, Stones turns to consideration of the assessment of practice teaching. He demonstrates lack of consensus about criteria of assessment in check-lists used in different countries and comments on significant omissions, unreliability, and subjectivity. He proceeds to advocate integration of theoretical studies in teacher education curricula with practice teaching by way of "pedagogical" studies concerned with identifying, analysing, and attempts to solve problems of, teaching and learning with assistance from tutors and cooperating teachers. Contributing to this integration would be ethnographic studies undertaken by student teachers to develop insights into aims of, and approaches to, teaching.

Stones concludes his article by considering the future of practice teaching in which he forecasts changes along the lines advocated earlier in the article. Given the usual delay in introducing change in teacher education, he doubts that the developments he foresees are imminent.

Stones's discussion of problems in assessing practice teaching and the role of cooperating teachers is a useful lead-in to the article on supervision of student teaching by Turney. He regards supervision as the "single most powerful process" in practice teaching but one which is complex and difficult. He writes first about the complexities and difficulties, and then about the supervisory influence of cooperating teachers and tertiary supervisors, the concerns of student teachers, and clinical supervision.

Problems of supervision arise from the nature of the supervisory structure which is usually triadic in that there are three participants: the student teacher, the cooperating teacher, and the tertiary supervisor from the teacher education institution. They also arise because of conflicts within the roles of each between, for example, competing demands upon the student's energies from different components of the teacher education programme. Ineffective communication of the expectations for the cooperating teacher's role creates problems, as do disagreements about the nature of effective teaching.

Turney reports that research has found the influence of the cooperating teacher to be strong on both the attitudes and the teaching of student teachers. He finds it, therefore, paradoxical that cooperating teachers are so often arbitrarily selected and unprepared for their role.

Turney provides an extremely comprehensive review of research on both cooperating teachers' and tertiary supervisors' influence, concluding that both have "considerable immediate influence on the developing professional attitudes and teaching styles of student teachers". His review of research on student teachers' concerns indicates high levels of stress, frequent conflict arising from expectations of both types of supervisors, desires for cooperative, nurturant, and nondirective supervision, and for help from other school personnel such as principals and counsellors. He sees the approach known as "clinical supervision" to be particularly appropriate and delineates five main stages towards a relationship "which encourages clear communication, understanding and mutual trust between the supervisor and the student". He concludes the article by specifying conditions for effective supervision, as follows:

> Supervisors must have adequate time to devote to their work—to consult and plan together, to hold conferences with the student, to observe the students' teaching, to become acquainted with the students' strengths, weaknesses, and concerns, and collaborate with the student in mutually beneficial educational tasks.

In a second article, Turney writes about laboratory schools and their role in teacher education. He sees particular relevance in studying these schools because their decline has, paradoxically, been accompanied by frequent calls for institutions to establish facilities that seem almost identical to what they offered. Turney gives brief descriptions of the roles of other types of schools in teacher education. He writes about the "model school", the "practice school", the "training school", and the "demonstration school", before focusing on the laboratory school which he says grew out of the so-called "scientific movement" towards the end of the nineteenth century. Readers will find articles in Sect. 3 of this Encyclopedia informative regarding this movement.

Turney outlines the purposes of the typical laboratory school, lists some of the more famous of them, describes variations in their functions, and presents changes to them over time. He then accounts for their decline since the 1950s and reviews several research studies producing evidence of their problems. Their difficulties, he suggests, included incompatibilities with the teacher education institutions, excessive demands upon their resources, inability to attract the highest quality staff, unrepresentative student groups, and inadequate funding.

The remaining articles in this subsection focus on techniques for developing the more specific conceptual and behavioural skills of teaching. In the first of these Dunkin explains the concept of technical skills of teaching which he defines as "specific aspects of teaching behaviour that are considered to be particularly effective in facilitating desired learnings in students". He traces the origin of the concept to Stanford University in the early 1960s and then goes on to provide examples of such skills, to describe ways in which they have been used in teacher education, to discuss evidence of their validity, and to consider their pros and cons.

In describing uses of the concept of technical skills of teaching, Dunkin describes their place in microteaching and minicourses which are described in detail in articles which follow in this section. He also reports on their use in competency-based teacher education which was discussed in the first section of this Encyclopedia. These uses, he notes, have led to attempts to incorporate technical skills in competency-based approaches to teacher certification in parts of the United States. On the whole, however, he finds empirical evidence of the validity of many of the skills used in promoting the attainment of desired educational objectives to be lacking. Thus, it appears that many skills rely on the professional judgment of teacher educators and others for their conceptualization and justification. Not surprisingly, there is a danger that their validity can be challenged on the basis of another criterion, that of reliable identification and definition.

In spite of these problems, Dunkin sees the technical skills approach to have been an important contribution, especially since its use has matured to involve more emphasis on the development of conceptual repertoires as well as behavioural ones.

A common component of the technical skills approach is the analysis of protocols of lessons given in real classrooms. In the next article, Wragg writes on *Lesson Analysis* in teacher education. Beginning with the observation that the idea of analysing lessons in order to learn about teaching is not new, Wragg identifies three factors which encouraged increased use of lesson analysis in the 1970s and 1980s. First, he argues that there was a reaction against overtheoretical programs of teacher education. Second, he sees the impact of observational research on classroom interaction since the 1950s, and, third, he recognizes the opportunities created by developments in educational technology, such as video recorders and closed circuit television.

Although lesson analysis is not a new activity, Wragg notes changes in attitudes towards knowledge about teaching methods which necessitated alterations in their use in teacher education. He writes:

> Trainees would have to learn to analyse lessons, not to discover some elusive "successful" style, but rather to assemble information on which to base their own decisions about how to teach, albeit guided by tutors and such research findings as existed.

Wragg continues with a description of the use of transcript and videotape analysis and ways of integrating them into newer teacher education programmes. He reviews research on the effects of lesson analysis and concludes his article by listing five requirements of the student teacher for the successful use of lesson analysis.

The next four articles in this section are all about microteaching—the most influential innovation in preservice teacher education in the 1960s and 1970s. In the first article, Perlberg presents the conceptual and theoretical bases of microteaching. His article is followed by two articles on prominent elements of the innovation, while the fourth article considers its effectiveness.

Perlberg describes microteaching as a laboratory training procedure that provides "scaled-down" and focused teaching practice which is mastery oriented and includes modelling and feedback in a cyclical time sequence. He traces its historical background and includes a discussion of the debate over its theoretical basis, concluding that it could be regarded as a theoretically eclectic technique. He then elaborates on the teaching–learning laboratory nature of microteaching, on its status as a "safe practice ground", and on the technical skills, feedback, and modelling components. He concludes that in spite of its eclecticism it is defensible on a wide range of theoretical grounds.

MacLeod's article on modelling in microteaching begins with a statement of theoretical bases of learning through modelling and goes on to review research on the use of positive and negative models in microteaching, on the use of written as compared with audiovisual models, and on devices used to focus student teachers' attention to modelled skills. He finds particular interest in a suggestion from some research findings "that modelling with discrimination training may lead to skills acquisition without a skill practice component being required".

Levis's article on feedback in microteaching discusses theoretical and conceptual foundations and then presents a review of research comparing audiotape and videotape feedback, on the influence of the supervisor during the feedback phase of microteaching, and on the relative effects of the modelling and feedback components. He concludes that immediate, and focused feedback are the most effective but that the effects of feedback can be lessened by powerful modelling procedures and that the results of research on various media of feedback have been inconclusive.

Finally, MacLeod takes up the question of the overall effectiveness of microteaching itself. He provides a succinct statement of four theoretical models for microteaching: the pragmatic model (referred to earlier in this section as "eclectic"); the behaviour modification model; the social skills training model; and cognitive models. MacLeod argues that conclusions about the effectiveness of microteaching ought to take into account the different aims of these models. He then reviews research on attitudinal and performance outcomes of microteaching. Regarding the former, MacLeod writes, "Perhaps the most consistently reported outcome of research on microteaching is that participants find it a valuable and enjoyable activity". Conclusions concerning performance outcomes were not so easy to reach, however, and MacLeod sees the major gap in research on microteaching to be "the lack of firm evidence as to whether microteaching training affects subsequent classroom performance". The problem, he says, is not that the research has not been conducted but that the research has not been properly designed. He then reviews correlational, pre-experimental, and "true" experimental studies and after problems of synthesizing diverse and different outcomes, discusses other limitations of the research. He concludes that "simple verdicts on the effects of microteaching on subsequent teacher behaviour are unlikely to be reached" and calls for research that tests "coherent and generalizable theory".

2. Inservice

In the first article in this subsection, Eraut writes about several major aspects of inservice teacher education (INSET). After adopting a definition of this process he provides an overview of policy issues, including aims, activities, and organization. He describes a wide range of alternatives in the staffing of INSET activities, in the clients, in locations, and in timing. Problems concerning the funding, organization, accrediting, coordinating, and planning INSET are also considered.

Eraut reviews four paradigms for INSET—the "defect", the "growth", the "change", and the "problem-solving" paradigms. He discusses these in terms of the assumptions that underlie them and explains their strengths and weaknesses. Next, he considers teacher-oriented, school-oriented, government, and higher education oriented perspectives of INSET, taking up such issues as teachers' concerns, teachers as artists, craftspeople, professionals, and as persons. Regarding the higher education perspective he raises the following question as typifying problems for INSET in that context: "Why should a faculty member bother with INSET when it provides greater risks than other college activities, gains him or her little credit towards promotion, requires more than the normal amount of time and effort, and probably takes place at inconvenient times in inconvenient places?" The article concludes with a discussion of the many problems facing the evaluator of INSET and a call for research into the many important issues raised.

The article by De Landsheere which follows is about a particular approach to INSET known as "teacher recyclage", defined as "intensive training action needed in case of qualification crises happening when the teacher's knowledge of a subject suddenly becomes obsolete . . . or when it is recognized that critical gaps exist in the teacher's education . . . ." The author describes three strategies adopted in recyclage: massive dissemination of information; sensitization programmes; and cooperative research. He elaborates on each, outlining the types of activities and orientations adopted, as well as the difficulties they encounter and their relative effectiveness.

The nexus between preservice and inservice teacher education becomes an important issue when the clients of the latter are beginning teachers who have to be inducted into schools and school systems to which they have been appointed. Bolam writes about this induction process mainly as it has been developed and studied in the United States, England and Wales, and Australia. He delineates four factors underlying concern with the first year of teaching. They are teacher supply, social accountability, professional status, and conditions of service and professional development. After distinguishing between internships and beginning teacher programmes, Bolam limits the scope of his article to the latter.

After reviewing research and practice in the United States, Bolam focuses upon studies in the United Kingdom, beginning with a national survey of the probationary first year of teaching. He discusses the research under seven headings: background and initial training; appointment and placement; inservice guidance and assessment; experience and problems in the classroom; experience and problems within the school community; personal problems; and career intentions. Next, Bolam discusses experimental induction programmes conducted in the 1970s in the Liverpool and Northumberland areas of England. There were three main features of these programmes: a 75 percent teaching load; school-based inservice courses, and external, centre-based inservice courses. Bolam lists the problems encountered by these schemes but reports that they were reviewed positively by the probationers who rated the extra free time as the most effective element of them. The most innovative aspect, the teacher–tutor concept was supported strongly by 90 percent and a similar proportion expressed a preference for these tutors to be appointed from within existing school staff. While support for the inservice courses was strong, there was also a perceived need to maintain a balance between internal and external activities, and a follow-up survey indicated that significant proportions of local education authorities had taken up one or more elements of the schemes.

After reviewing the Australian induction schemes, Bolam presents some conclusions and discusses issues arising from the attempts in the various countries concerned. He organizes his discussion around three main questions: "(a) What is the nature and extent of the induction knowledge base? and (b) more particularly, how satisfactory was the research methodology which provided it? Next, can policy makers and practitioners make use of that knowledge?"

He concludes the article by affirming that the research and experience have indicated the need to improve induction arrangements and have provided valuable information to guide such improvements. However, he sees the need for much more work to be done and for more rigorously designed research.

In the next article, Harris discusses another widely recognized element of the process of improving the performance of inservice teachers. This is the element of supervision. Supervision has evolved from functions emphasizing inspection, monitoring, and enforcement to those emphasizing curriculum development, training, and formative evaluation, according to Harris, although the earlier emphases are still often present.

Harris discerns three schools of thought underlying supervisory practices: the monitoring, inspecting, accountability school; the human relations, morale building school; and the change–process school, each of which is discussed in the article. He then considers three main tasks of supervisors: curriculum development; inservice training; and evaluation of instruction, and goes on to describe different approaches to staffing for supervision and concludes by noting long-term trends towards "more dynamic efforts to promote change process".

The last two articles in this subsection are about resources that lend themselves especially to individual efforts by teachers themselves to develop their professional competence. In the first, Shostak writes about *Teachers' Centres* and, in the second Perrott writes about *Minicourses*.

Shostak writes that the original teachers' centres were established in the United Kingdom in the 1960s but the concept has been adapted for many other educational contexts. The author lists eight features distinguishing teachers' centres from other forms of support and sees them as part of a general movement towards teacher-centred school and curriculum development processes.

> The teachers' centre relies on practising teachers defining and initiating their own inservice work. This is based upon a view that the classroom practitioner is in the best position to make decisions about curriculum needs . . . . It also legitimizes the experience of the teacher as a form of knowledge . . . [and] creates opportunities to build upon this knowledge with colleagues . . . .

Shostak describes various funding and administrative arrangements for teachers' centres and outlines their role as resource centres and concludes by commenting that their developmental nature and commitment to growth rather than radical change made them vulnerable during the economic constraints of the late 1970s and early 1980s. However, he concludes, emerging research evidence of their contribution has meant their emphases are becoming more clearly understood.

Minicourses, the subject of Perrott's article which completes this subsection, have much in common with microteaching in their conceptual and theoretical underpinnings. More than any of the other approaches to inservice teacher education, minicourses are designed for the development of technical skills of teaching and the skills focused upon are often identical to those used in microteaching. The reader is therefore directed towards the group of articles on microteaching appearing previously in this section.

Perrott locates the origin of minicourses in the United States at the Far West Laboratory for Educational Research and Development in San Francisco in the late 1960s and early 1970s. Each minicourse was designed as a self-instructional package and required four activities: the study of a specific teaching skill or set of related skills, such as higher order questioning, probing questions, and divergent questions; the viewing of videotaped models of the performance of the skill(s); short practice sessions involving videotaping attempts to implement the skill(s); and objective evaluative feedback using self-coding observational schedules.

After outlining the aims of minicourses, Perrott reviews procedures used in research and development of minicourses, the main field tests, hypotheses, samples of inservice teachers involved, and observational techniques for coding videotaped practice sessions. She presents the results of the field testing of one of the minicourses with inservice teachers, including the opinions of the teachers involved. These results were obtained in tests conducted in several countries and led to conclusions that the method is appropriate for use in different national contexts; that minicourses are cost effective; and that they are good examples of international cooperation in bringing about effective educational innovation.

3. Special Purpose

This subsection contains a group of articles concerned with the education of teachers for the diverse contexts of early childhood education, special education, vocational and industrial education, higher education, and adult education. They have in common the fact that they are not about the preparation of personnel to teach in regular school contexts. The order in which they appear is not an indication of the importance of the teacher education enterprises they discuss, but rather reflects the approximate age ranges of the student–clients for whom the teachers concerned are prepared. The first article, therefore, is about the education of teachers for early childhood education and the last one is concerned with the education of teachers for adult education.

In writing about the education of teachers to work in early childhood education, Katz adopts the term "preprimary" in preference to "early childhood". Early in the article she writes that in view of the diversity of provisions within this field and the lack of research about it, there are few validated generalizations. One of them is that:

> The younger the child being taught, the less training the teacher has, the lower the status and prestige attached to the job, the fewer qualifications are required, the lower the pay, the longer the hours of work.

Katz discusses two unique characteristics of the field: the diversity of training arrangements and employment settings across and within countries and the extent of involvement of volunteers. The main issues, she writes, are: lack of consensus on criteria of teaching effectiveness; doubts about the effectiveness of teacher education; designing preservice training experiences whose relevance will be seen at the time by the trainees; striking appropriate balances between the theoretical, historical, methodological, and the practical; the proper placement of field experience within programmes and the use of substitutes for actual field experiences and observations.

Recent developments in inservice education include the appointment of preschool advisors from among practising preschool teachers to visit preschools and run workshops and generally provide support, encouragement, and stimulation to teachers. Katz describes several variants of this innovation and then concentrates on the Child Development Associate (CDA) project for upgrading the quality of teaching in Head Start classes in the United States. This project seems to have been based on principles of the competency-based teacher education model described by Houston in the first section of this Encyclopedia. After an extremely thorough discussion of the CDA system, she concludes the article by stating that one of the major research issues for developing countries is "What is the optimum proportion of preservice to inservice training?" and by formulating the main hypothesis to be tested in answering that question.

The next article in this section is Semmel's on the education of teachers for special education contexts. Semmel begins by presenting a four-stage conceptual model of variations in special education programmes and goes on to discuss teaching competencies for special education, distinguishing between: "(a) training and experience obtained in settings for the more severely handicapped . . . and (b) training and teaching experience obtained within regular education settings". In the first, the competencies recognized are more often those emphasizing sensory-motor training or social and vocational rehabilitation, while in the second they are similar to those required of teachers in regular educational situations.

Semmel identifies five main theoretical and/or pragmatic approaches to special education but points out that most programmes are eclectic with regard to these. The five are then elaborated upon and the movement towards "deinstitutionalization" in order to end segregation of the handicapped into separate institutions is discussed. In the subsequent discussion of teacher training programmes, Semmel includes competency-based teacher education (see Sect. 1), specialization training, qualifications for entry into training programmes and inservice and continuing education, including teacher centres as described earlier in this section of the Encyclopedia. The article concludes with a discussion of issues in personnel training, including the need for leadership training and for training in the role of advocate which special education teachers are often called upon to perform.

Hobart's article on the preparation of teachers for vocational and industrial education begins with a description of systems of teacher education including the distinction between preservice and inservice training and the common elements of the curriculum of those systems. He presents data on the demand for such training and describes the types of institutions in which it is offered. Among the factors determining features of this type of teacher education, Hobart considers philosophical bases, the types of students catered for, and the tasks teachers are expected to perform. He then presents recommendations produced by a conference of representatives from 15 countries for the preparation of instructors.

Hobart's review of contemporary developments in this area of teacher education includes the listing of required competencies, and discussions of the application of performance- (competency-) based and mastery learning models (see Sect. 1 for articles on these models). He concludes his article with a specification of research needed in this area and with the recommendation that closer attention be given to the determining factors discussed earlier in the article on the design and implementation of teacher education programmes for vocational and industrial education.

Next, Main writes on teacher education for higher education which he describes as a predominantly inservice activity with teaching skill not always regarded as a major criterion for appointment so that training for teaching in that sector is not well developed. He writes, "There is no standard pattern or normal length of training for faculty members anywhere in the world", with the form of training left to individual institutions and the motivations of individual faculty.

He describes the few preservice courses to be found and then discusses introductory training which he typifies as didactic, short, very general, and concentrating on traditional teaching methods, such as lecturing, discussion, and laboratory teaching. He describes trends towards five areas of change discernible in different countries. These are the adoption of a practicum requirement based on apprenticeship ideas; "mediated self-confrontation", involving the analysis and evaluation of one's own recorded teaching; peer teaching, or cooperative learning about teaching from a colleague; workshop modules; and a shift of emphases from teaching methods and aids to student learning and course planning issues.

Other approaches including formal courses, minicourses (see article in previous sub-section), and degree and diploma programmes are presented and Main concludes with an observation about worldwide patterns, as follows:

Introductory training for tertiary teachers is generally recognized by, if not organized by, a national agency. On the other hand, in few countries is there any coordination of advanced and specialized training, which often owes its existence to the initiatives of individuals or institutions. It may be that coordination at this level will be a development of the last two decades of the twentieth century.

Finally, Duke writes about the education of teachers for adult education. He begins by defining this area of teacher education and describing its tremendous scope and in the process explains the wide variety of terms used instead of "teacher" and "teacher education". This is followed by an analysis of the adult educator's training needs, demonstrating that while there is a widely acknowledged need to improve teaching in adult education, there are large differences in ways of defining and satisfying the need. His analysis documents this diversity internationally and includes references to the situation in such countries as the United Kingdom, India, China, and Australia. After a comprehensive discussion of the many and various modes of provision and providing agencies, including the recommendations of international conferences and survey reports, Duke considers the skills and subject areas that form the content of teacher education programmes. He points to such difficulties here as "the dilemma that aspects of the professional role and identity valued in this [liberal] tradition are also thought to be little if at all amenable to teaching" and the lack of clear definition of the learning needs of adult educators.

In his treatment of methods of teaching, he lists "lectures, handbooks and manuals, correspondence or mass media courses, simulation, microlaboratory work, attachments and internships, and teaching practice" but points out that "discussion and other group work tend to play an especially prominent part".

Duke concludes his article by discussing trends and issues. He focuses upon adequacy of provision, priorities for training, professionalization and mandatory training, and general teacher education and andragogy. On this last issue, he notes arguments for and against the integration of adult teacher education into programmes of school-oriented teacher education. After noting signs of increased transaction between the two, Duke concludes, "It is likely, however, that the study and teaching of adult education will continue to sustain a separate identity and some separate institutional bases for training".

Preservice

Student (Practice) Teaching

E. Stones

Practice teaching is one of a variety of terms applied to that part of a student teacher's professional training that involves the student in trying to teach pupils. Practice normally takes place in school and although arrangements are sometimes made for students to teach pupils in college, the use of the term practice teaching implies that the activity takes place in school. Other terms used more or less synonymously are teaching practice, school experience, student teaching, field experience, and practicum. There are some minor differences in the nature of the activity that reflect cultural biases but wherever practice teaching exists its basic characteristics are very much the same. In those countries where there are no formal provisions for the training of teachers, teaching practice does not exist.

In training institutions where systems of teacher training exist, practice teaching forms a major component in the course of training. The other main component comprises taught courses in a variety of theoretical studies. These courses are likely to comprise subjects in the field of educational studies such as child development, educational psychology, educational sociology, and philosophy and curriculum studies; academic subject studies such as languages and sciences; and work related to the teaching of specific subjects that goes under names such as professional studies. In predominantly Anglo–Saxon countries subjects that are not directly linked to the professional training of teachers are studied by students for their "personal development". In the United States and to some extent in other Anglo–Saxon countries there has been a proliferation of these subjects and theoretical studies directly related to teaching have formed a relatively minor part of the curriculum of training institutions (Smith 1980).

There is very little evidence in any country of systematic courses in pedagogy, that is, the systematic study and practice of general principles of teaching that attempts to unify theoretical studies and practice teaching by making use of the teaching of knowledge about factors that enable human beings to learn meaningfully and with pleasure. In some European countries psychopedagogy is studied, but in that context the subject is often a highly abstract and theoretical study with little practical application to teaching; unlike the British interpretation of the term that attempts to make a direct link between psychology of learning and instruction and the actual practice of teaching (Stones 1978, 1981, 1984). Didactics are also studied in some European institutions and these studies resemble the professional studies of British training institutions, that is, they are courses that consider approaches to the teaching of specific subjects without drawing on any general body of theoretical principles. Similar comments can be made about most countries, especially those that have come under British or American influence.

In the practice teaching component of most training courses, student teachers engaged in practice teaching spend several weeks in schools practising to teach pupils. They are guided by tutors in the training institutions and by cooperating teachers. The guidance mostly consists of discussion prior to teaching, occasional observation by tutor or cooperating teacher of the student teaching, and a post-teaching discussion when the tutor or cooperating teacher comments on the student's performance. Much of the student's time on extended practice goes on without this guidance and in many schools students are used as surrogate teachers who, after a brief induction into the school, operate independently and teach without the direct supervision of the cooperating teacher. The guidance that is given is rarely related to any body of pedagogical principles and mostly consists of practical advice from a corpus of craft know-how developed over time by teachers.

1. Origins: The Apprentice Teacher

Practice teaching has its origins in the ideas of craft apprenticeship. As education for the mass of the population in industrializing countries began to develop in the nineteenth century, the demand for teachers grew. Existing schoolteachers catered for the demand by recruiting apprentices from among their pupils as pupil teachers. The pupil teachers were treated like other apprentices and initiated by a process of instruction, demonstration, and imitation. The master teacher told the students what to do, showed them how to do it, and the students imitated the master.

The approach to practice teaching based on apprenticeship training is justified on several grounds. It is argued that it is effective, simple, and commonsensical. It is also argued that teaching is a highly personal business and that it is probably unreasonable to expect students to be able to put into operation the findings of research couched in general terms as teaching principles since principles are impersonal (Peters 1968). Some people take the view that teaching is caught not taught so that the best way to become a teacher is to watch teachers at work and go and do likewise. Others take the view that it is really impossible to teach anyone to teach. Teachers are born not made. Teaching is seen as an art form akin to writing poetry or painting. Practice teaching is therefore seen as providing the opportunities to display, recognize, and refine the abilities that are latent in the student.

There is one other widely held view about teaching best epitomized in Shaw's gibe: "He who can, does; he who cannot, teaches." Teaching is seen as a simple easy-to-master activity: how much more trivial, then, must be teaching teachers to teach! Such opinions about teaching lead quite naturally to the view commonly held, perhaps especially in relation to teaching in universities and other institutions of higher education, that training to teach is unnecessary. It is, therefore, not surprising that practice teaching is widely considered to be the most important part of a teacher training course. Since the best way of learning to teach is to go and teach, then the more time of a training course devoted to practice teaching the better, and in many training institutions practice teaching does, in fact, take up a large proportion of the course time. A recent survey of British courses by the Council for National Academic Awards found several institutions devoting half the total course time to school experience.

The attitudes and practices described above probably seriously underestimate the complexity and difficulty of learning to teach because they spring from a profound misconception of the nature of teaching itself. Stereotyped views of the teacher see him/her as a person standing in front of a class of pupils dispensing information. This stereotype is also widely held by teachers and student teachers so that this transmission mode of teaching is the staple. Thus advice to student teachers on practice teaching is likely to be related to such things as writing on the chalkboard and projection of the voice and articulation. These concerns were also the concerns of nineteenth-century schoolteachers and point to the essential conservatism of the approach to learning to teach that models the master teacher. Further examples of the activities considered important in teaching are given below.

The transmission mode of teaching focuses on verbal learning. The emphasis is on the pupils' remembering what the teacher has told them and being able to write down answers to questions based on what the teacher has previously said, hence the emphasis on improving the quality of transmission by chalkboard writing and oral articulation. Verbal learning, however, very often goes no deeper than the words themselves, producing what is referred to as rote learning. Pupils learn the words and little else. Since most teachers in the past have concentrated on verbal learning, student teachers modelling themselves on experienced teachers are prone to acquire skills that perpetuate teaching for rote learning, a phenomenon recently commented on by British Inspectors of Schools in a discussion paper on teacher training (DES 1981).

Thus practice teaching that aims to imitate experienced teachers is likely to perpetuate methods that are not necessarily the ones most likely to enhance pupils' learning with understanding and this is possibly the most serious drawback to the training approach based on imitation. But there are other problems. A master teacher, however versatile, can offer a student only a limited set of skills, attitudes, and personality traits. And the selection of skills and techniques is the master teacher's, reflecting the master teacher's values, experiences, and personality. The student's values, experiences, and personality will be at least marginally and at most radically different from those of the master teacher. In its extreme form this approach denies the individuality of the student teacher. In a moderate form it encourages the student to copy isolated bits of teaching behaviour, of attitudes, and of relationships. But the effectiveness of these bits of behaviour may well hinge on their being part of a total pattern of behaviour: when fragmented and adopted by another they may be ineffective or even harmful. Further, this approach is only superficially easy to follow. In essence it tells students to adopt another person's teaching style which probably involves changing their personalities. If students cannot do this, and the majority cannot, they can make little progress towards effective teaching.

A further disadvantage of this approach is that it does not allow the student to go beyond the teaching observed. This teaching may be excellent but it cannot be exhaustively excellent; there will certainly be areas of teaching excellence that are not illustrated by any one master teacher and more appropriate ways of doing things than those the master teacher employs.

There is one other very difficult problem connected with the apprenticeship approach to practice teaching. There is little consensus about what a master teacher is. That is, there are no universally accepted criteria to help us to identify master teachers. Thus the current most popular approaches to practice teaching have serious disadvantages. Based as they are on an apprenticeship model which stresses imitation without any clear indication of the qualities to emulate, they are basically unhelpful to beginning teachers and at the same time conservative so that it is difficult to break the circle to introduce new procedures that might be more beneficial to student teachers.

2. The Context of Practice Teaching

Aspects of practice teaching other than the pedagogical have been subject to investigation and analogous comments made on its essentially conservative nature. In the same way as imitating individual teachers locks student teachers into a closed circle of pedagogical activities, so accommodating to the mores of schools as they are, leads students to accept without question the values and procedures they observe in their practice schools as natural and right. Students are concerned to present a favourable image to the school and the training institution as a way of surviving practice teaching so that they are anxious to conform to what they perceive to be the expectations of their supervisors. This impression management frequently results in students engaging in activities not because of any conviction that they are intrinsically desirable but because they are expected to impress the supervisor. The school and societal context of their teaching is rarely examined.

The integration of student teachers into schools as they now exist is no more to be desired than that student teachers should strive to be as much like existing teachers as possible. An extensive literature from a variety of standpoints has appeared in recent years that argues that schools as they exist at present are microcosmic models of social and cultural communities that need to be transformed if they are to be the nursing grounds of socially aware and questioning teachers. Currently schools encourage acquiescence and conformity to the status quo in schooling and society. Practice teaching should aim to change this state of affairs and develop in students a habit of scepticism and enquiry not just in regard to pedagogical practices but also in their appraisal of the institutions in which they teach.

3. Master the Teaching Model

The possibility of breaking into the circle of teachers imitating others and thus opening the way for development, arises if teaching, rather than teachers, is looked at. In the field of pedagogy, Stolurow's (1965) phrase, "master the teaching model", is still a useful guide to action although many people would have reservations about the implication that there is only one model. The point is that students are more likely to obtain a satisfactory understanding of the processes of teaching if their practical experience is based on mastering principles of teaching rather than imitating other teachers. Similarly, a systematic examination of the social and educational contexts of specific teaching in the light of, and understanding of, more general social processes will equip students to appraise their

teaching with more insight than would otherwise be the case.

The main difference between an approach that attempts to explicate the processes of teaching and the imitative approach, is that the former analyses the task of teaching rather than copying a global performance. An attempt is made to identify the purposes of teaching, the specific objectives of particular lessons, the beginning knowledge and skills of the pupils, the processes by which the objectives may be achieved, the variables likely to interact with these processes, the learning outcomes, and feedback to the teacher.

The "master the teaching model" approach to practical experience, makes possible and necessary the integration of theory and practice. This integration becomes not an abstract goal to be achieved only rarely, but a necessary and constant occurrence. Tutors and student teachers together develop teaching strategies and tactics out of their discussion of theories of teaching and learning: the procedures are tested in teaching and learning situations and the results evaluated. This approach necessitates precision and rigour and offers practical usable help to all students irrespective of their personality traits, attitudes, and abilities. Since there is an infinite variety of ways of implementing general teaching principles there is no contradiction between a student's following a theoretical model and developing a personal teaching style.

4. Assessment of Practice Teaching

The assessment of practice teaching for the purposes of certification is a very problematic subject. To a great extent this is a consequence of the apprenticeship approach. Student teachers have inevitably been graded according to the criteria held by individual teachers or specific institutions and the criteria have not always been made explicit (Stones and Morris 1972a). For example, teachers have been assessed according to the degree that their personalities resembled those of the adjudicating headteachers (Wiseman and Start 1965); idiosyncratically according to the institution they happened to be training in (Stones and Morris 1972a); and on vague conceptions of what was being judged (McCulloch 1979).

In attempts to introduce a degree of rigour and objectivity into the assessment of practice teaching, schedules have been produced by many teacher training institutions. These schedules itemize those aspects of teaching performance thought to be critical in satisfactory teaching. Student teachers are awarded marks on a scale for each aspect by supervisors or cooperating teachers. Examples of items from schedules are: "Clarity of aims; pacing of the lesson; skill in explaining and narrating; quality of voice and speech habits; presentation advanced with appropriate pace and timing; voice clear, attractive, and well-modulated; blackboard well-used; lesson method suitable". The first two are taken from a widely used American schedule, the second pair from a British schedule, the third pair from an Australian instrument, and the fourth from a teacher assessment form used in schools in the United Kingdom in the nineteenth century which gives an indication of the rate of change in this approach.

While the devising of check lists against which to evaluate student teaching is a move towards objectifying the process of assessment, scrutiny of the schedules available reveals some problems. Although the various schedules have a certain degree of similarity, they are, in fact, all different. Their discrepant nature illustrates the lack of clarity and consensus on the nature of the desirable criteria of practical teaching. Further, the awarding of marks on a scale for each item on the schedule is in most cases extraordinarily difficult and depends a great deal on the assessors' ideas and values. It is possible, by systematic training, to get assessors to grade student teachers similarly, that is, award them roughly the same marks on each item of the schedule thus producing marker consistency. However the fact that markers are consistent does not necessarily guarantee that the teaching has been effective.

Many of the schedules pay little attention to children's learning. Stones and Morris (1972a) in a survey of all training institutions in England, Wales, and Northern Ireland found that hardly any assessors of practice teaching assessed their students on the criterion of whether the pupils they were trying to teach learned anything or not. As the examples taken from the schedules suggest, the focus is on what the student teacher does and there is an implicit inference that the activity under scrutiny will produce children's learning. A moment's reflection will indicate that this inference is not necessarily justified. Clear, well-modulated, and attractive voices will not teach children very much of worth if what the teacher is saying is nonsense. Much the same could be said about other teacher characteristics that form part of many assessment schedules.

Thus although the devising of schedules for the assessment of teaching has the merit of making explicit the criteria to be considered, there is little evidence so far that the actual items on the schedules are likely to enable assessors to make more valid judgments of students if pupil learning is taken to be the crucial criterion of teacher competence as in logic it should be. But even if attention is paid to pupil learning there is a further difficult problem. Current methods of assessing pupil learning are themselves far from perfect. Student teachers are very rarely equipped by their training to make sensitive and valid assessment of their pupils' learning as it relates to the objectives they set themselves at the beginning of their teaching. In many cases student teachers have to make use of published tests that may or may not be appropriate to their own teaching and certainly cannot be geared to their own objectives.

Apart from these considerations, tests very frequently give information about learning only at the verbal level. All too often they depend on memorization and provide little evidence of understanding or competence beyond that of regurgitating what has previously been memorized. Thus any attempt to focus on pupil learning in the assessment of student teaching needs to be viewed with caution even though the attempt should be applauded. Unless the pupils' learning is learning with understanding there is a danger that the assessments of the students will be based on their ability to drill pupils in rote learning as their nineteenth-century predecessors did.

5. Possible Perspectives

Many of the problems of practice teaching discussed above spring from a lack of a systematic attempt to teach pedagogy that could unite theoretical studies and practical teaching. Present course organization with the clearly demarcated practice teaching attachments to schools, organized and conducted in separate compartments from theoretical studies, signal to students that the two activities are distinct and preserve the archetypical conception of student teaching as apprentice training.

Pedagogical studies bring together theoretical ideas about the nature of teaching and the processes of human learning because they are task oriented and not merely concerned with the transmission of information. The tasks addressed are twofold: there is the task the learner faces, that of acquiring new concepts, skills, and understandings; and there is the task the teacher faces, that of so arranging the learning environment of the pupils that they will acquire those skills, concepts, and understandings in a meaningful rather than superficial way. In order to accomplish these tasks the student teacher does not attempt to copy an experienced teacher but draws on a body of knowledge based on research in the fields of human learning and instruction and attempts to implement the appropriate principles in his/her own way according to the circumstances existing at the time.

Practice teaching of this type changes the central concerns of teaching from developing ways of transmitting verbal material to the identification, analysis, and attempted solution of problems of learning and teaching. The student attempts to acquire teaching skills of general application based on principles of teaching and learning. It involves students in attempting to solve pedagogical problems with the assistance of tutors and cooperating teachers. Their job is to help the student teachers to implement the principles effectively and to provide guidance and feedback so that the students' solving, in whole or in part, a variety of teaching problems will help them to build up a body of pedagogical expertise that will be useful to them in a variety of circumstances, but at the same time will be expressed in their own styles and through their own personalities.

Similarly, the preservation of the personal integrity of the student, while operating with a body of principles, can be achieved by the organization of practice teaching that aims to help students adopt an enquiring approach to the social and educational context of their teaching and to ensure that they are not passively assimilated into a conservative educational milieu. Many writers argue that this is the most important consideration of all in teacher education and some have suggested forms of practice teaching that involve students in making systematic ethnographic studies of the institutions they are practising in, using various observational techniques and methods of analysis so that they can get a deeper understanding of the contextual constraints and opportunities present (Zeichner and Teitelbaum 1982). Students will thus be enabled to appraise the pedagogical aims set by the school in the light of explicit value positions. They will also obtain insight into the nature of the social forces within institutions that may constrain them in the type of pedagogical activities they might wish to engage in. Students will understand that the nature of schools as they are at present is not part of the natural order of things any more than the various types of teaching they see in the schools are definitive and unchallengable models.

Ethnographic studies and pedagogical studies complement each other. The former give students insights into the desirable aims of and approaches to teaching, and the latter provide insights into the most effective ways of attaining those aims. Together they present a radical reappraisal of traditional practice teaching, but given current questioning of the way things are now, it is possible that some movement towards incorporating some of the ideas will be made in some teacher education programmes in the not too distant future.

6. The Future of Practice Teaching

Any future changes should help students develop theory-based practical teaching skills by studying the theory and practice of teaching together just as they would in learning any other subject with a practical component, going from one activity to the other when appropriate. The same applies to their ethnographic studies. These should not be regarded as work additional to teaching practice, but an integral part of it. As with pedagogical studies they should be integrated with seminars and study groups within the training institutions as well as within the schools.

A consequence of such approaches would be that the conventional structure of practical teaching experience would change. Instead of student teachers spending an extended period of time briefly observing and then acting as surrogate teachers with similar teaching contact time to that of the other teachers in their practice schools, they will spend much more time in reflecting upon their teaching, in discussing it with others, in planning, and in systematic observation of their practice schools. This type of school experience will help students to obtain an insight into the nature of teaching in its social and educational context and to develop pedagogical skills that spring from an understanding of a body of pedagogical theory rather than rule of thumb or ad hoc survival techniques.

It is therefore likely that the future organization of many teacher training courses will be much more fluid with students moving between practical activity and learning about pedagogical theory and practice, and the principles and practice of ethnographic enquiry into schools as institutions. Much of this enquiry could take place in school but the actual time devoted to the practical activity of teaching will be reduced and replaced with the reflective activities so lacking at present. The long block of teaching experience in one school with the student acting as surrogate teacher will disappear but the practice teaching that replaces it will be much more informed and effective.

Past changes in teacher education have been very slow to come about and it would be unrealistic to imagine that the changes described are imminent. However, there is a good chance that there will be discernable movement within the next few years.

See also: Teaching Experience; Concepts of Teacher Education; Teaching: Art or Science?

Bibliography

Department of Education and Science (DES) 1981 *Teacher Training and the Secondary School*. DES, London
Elliott B G 1978 *Field Experience in Pre-service Teacher Education*. Bibliographies on educational topics, No. 9. ERIC Clearinghouse on Teacher Education, Washington, DC
Journal of Education for Teaching (formerly *British Journal of Teacher Education*). Methuen, London
Journal of Teacher Education. American Association of Colleges of Teacher Education, Washington, DC
McCulloch M 1979 *School Experience on Initial B.Ed./B.Ed. Hons. Degrees Validated by the Council for National Academic Awards*. CNAA, London
Peters R S 1968 Teaching practice in teacher training. *Trends in Educ.* 9: 3–9
Smith B O 1980 *A Design for a School of Pedagogy*. Publication No. E-80-42000. United States Dept. of Education, Washington, DC
Stolurow L M 1965 Model the master teacher or master the teaching model. In: Krumboltz J D (ed.) 1965 *Learning and the Educational Process*. Rand McNally, Chicago, Illinois, pp. 223–47 (reprinted in Stones E, Morris S 1972b, pp. 165–71)
Stones E 1975 *How Long is a Piece of String?* Society for Research into Higher Education, London
Stones E 1978 Psychopedagogy: Theory and practice in teaching. *Br. Educ. Res. J.* 4(2): 1–19
Stones E 1981 Teacher education and pedagogy. *J. Educ. Teaching* 7(3): 217–30
Stones E 1984 *Psychology of Education: A Pedagogical Approach*. Methuen, London
Stones E, Morris S 1972a The assessment of practical teaching. *Educational Research*. National Foundation for Educational Research, London (reprinted in Stones E, Morris S 1972b)
Stones E, Morris S 1972b *Teaching Practice: Problems and Perspectives: A Reappraisal of the Practical Professional Element in Teacher Preparation*. Methuen, London
Wiseman S, Start K B 1965 A follow up of teachers five years after their training. *Br. J. Educ. Psychol.* 35: 342–61
Zeichner K M, Teitelbaum K 1982 Personalized and inquiry-oriented teacher education: An analysis of two approaches to the development of curriculum for field based experience. *J. Educ. Teaching* 8(2) (in press)

Supervision of the Practicum

C. Turney

The practicum in teacher education is conducted under a variety of names. Common among the terms used are practice teaching, in-school experience, teaching rounds, and student teaching. Whatever the name, the essential element of the operation is that student teachers attempt to apply in school settings certain of the ideas propounded in teacher education courses. If, as the research indicates, practice teaching is the single most powerful intervention in a teacher's professional preparation, then the supervision of the student teacher is the single most powerful process in such intervention. Besides underscoring the importance of the work of supervisors, the research literature also reveals how potentially complicated and difficult supervision is. In the following article some of the main complexities and inherent conflicts of the supervisory process are outlined, the influence of the work of supervisors is analysed, the supervision-related concerns of students are examined, and the "clinical" approach to supervision is described.

1. Complexities and Conflicts in Supervision

While various people in the school such as the principal and subject teacher, as well as the pupils, inevitably become involved in the students' practicum experience, the personnel most directly involved with supervision are typically the tertiary supervisor and the cooperating teacher. Along with the student teacher, these two key figures form a triangular relationship—a triad—concerned with achieving the objectives the teacher education programme has specified for the practicum and, in particular, with facilitating the professional development of the student.

Within the supervisory triad various kinds of complications and conflicts can occur. Conflicts can arise, for example, between the members of the triad. Members tend to form "competitive, dyadic coalitions" which can hinder student development and hamper the work of supervisors (Yee 1968, 1969). The formation of these alliances occurs both in the in-school and out-of-school contexts during the practicum (Cope 1969). While the student is in the school, the cooperating teacher and student become allies to provide what is required by the "external-evaluator"—the tertiary supervisor. Away from the school the student and the tertiary supervisor may be critical of the problems which occur with a particular class, teacher, or school. Cope (1969) noted that while alliances between teachers and students may be desirable in themselves, they are a problem when they exclude the tertiary supervisor from being a contributing participant except in the limited role of evaluator. In her discussions with students at various stages in their teacher training, Cope found that there was generally lacking "a recognition of a triangular working

partnership" involving student, tertiary supervisor, and cooperating teacher (p. 35).

Conflicts may also occur between and within the roles that each member of the triad is called upon to play during the practicum. These conflicts can again hamper both the supervisory process and student development. For example, the cooperating teacher as a member of the school staff will have teaching and administrative responsibilities which interfere with the supervisory role. Or, the student may have course commitments with the tertiary institution which interfere with involvement in the practicum experience. Similarly the tertiary supervisor may have competing administrative, teaching, and research commitments. More particularly, there is often conflict among roles that supervisors play. The main example of this role conflict is the apparent difficulty many supervisors have in implementing both the counsellor and the evaluator roles. While supervisors are expected to evaluate student teaching performance, they are also expected to provide students with feedback in a warm, supportive atmosphere which will encourage their development. It has been observed that in the interaction between supervisors and their students, despite attempts to reconcile their role behaviours, the evaluative role tends to predominate (Nias 1976). This conflict seems unrelated to the personality of the supervisor, and occurs as a consequence of the organizational constraints of the practicum (Blumberg 1974). Changes in the organization of the practicum need to be made to enable the supervisor to work with a student in such a manner that the student "sees him as a source of help and is willing to test out the results of their work together in the classroom" (Blumberg and Cusick 1970 p. 4). At present students do not appear to perceive the relationship with their supervisors in this way. Student teachers commonly perceive the evaluative role of the supervisor in terms of some form of anxiety-producing examination (Acevedo et al. 1976, Cope 1969). Their behaviour toward supervisors, as a result, tends to become closed, defensive, and mistrusting (Blumberg 1974).

The work of the supervisory triad is often further complicated adversely by poor communication. Cope's (1971a) investigations revealed that often neither teachers nor students are sufficiently informed as to what should happen when undertaking a school practice session; that teachers did not realize how much tertiary staff rely on them in the assessment of students; and that teachers did not hold tertiary staff in very high regard. Cope's data disclosed something more than a breakdown in communication. They demonstrated clearly that neither tertiary nor school staffs had worked out explicit notions of their respective functions. Cope suggested that both groups have distinctive and complementary roles to play. The school-based supervisor should offer practical advise, and help the student identify and assimilate professional skills while the visiting lecturer has the potential to diagnose teaching systematically, build on previous experience, and encourage innovation. She recommended that these differences should be made explicit and capitalized upon in supervision.

Besides having confused perceptions of each other's roles, cooperating teachers and tertiary supervisors often have vastly different frames of reference about what constitutes effective teaching (Coulter 1975). A study by Tuckman and Oliver (1968) found that the failure of supervisors to use common frames of reference when communicating with students about their teaching performances actually caused supervisor feedback to have a negative effect upon subsequent teaching performance. There is a pressing need for the identification of criteria to be used in observing and evaluating teaching and for these criteria to be commonly understood and applied by all members of the supervisory triad.

Partly because of the difficulties which can arise from supervisory members of the triad representing two different institutions, there is a temptation to simplify the process by handing over major responsibility for supervision to the schools. Lomax (1973) saw in this dangers for both institutions since the tertiary institution would be cut off from essential field work and become rather irresponsible, while schools would be involved in self-perpetuating activity and unaccountable for their training efforts. Nias (1976) undertook a study which omitted the tertiary supervisor from the supervision process and noted that cooperating teachers and student teachers developed a trusting relationship and a candid and constructive approach to the critical appraisal of performance. However, cooperating teachers still needed opportunities to discuss and examine the implications of their role with the tertiary institution.

2. Supervisory Influence

Despite a tendency for tertiary staff to withdraw from participation in the practicum's supervision, the universal pattern is still for the student teachers' work to be supervised by both tertiary staff of the teacher education programme and by cooperating teachers in the schools. Both kinds of supervisors tend to play similar, overlapping roles although often with differences in emphasis. Both kinds of supervisors have an influence on students' behaviour, but apparently to a quite different degree. Both kinds of supervisors face constraints and difficulties in carrying out their roles, again often different in extent.

2.1 Cooperating Teachers

There exists considerable support for the assertion that the quality of the student teaching experience depends heavily on the professional abilities and attitudes of the supervising teacher who has a day-to-day working relationship with the student teacher. For many years

cooperating teachers have been said by some to be "key figures" in teacher education programmes and this has been borne out by a growing body of research indicating the strength of their influence, for good and bad, on student teachers' attitudes and teaching. The great paradox is, of course, that despite the strength of such views and the supporting evidence, cooperating teachers are commonly both arbitrarily selected and inadequately prepared for their work as supervisors.

A number of investigations have indicated that the attitudes of student teachers tend to move during teaching practice in the direction of those held by their cooperating teachers (Price 1961, Finlayson and Cohen 1967, Johnson 1968, Yee 1969, Cohen 1969, Peters 1971). This is an important group of studies. Although they did not examine the long-term effects of attitudinal change, they do underline the initial strength of cooperating teachers' influence in forming student teachers' attitudes towards teaching. They alert teacher education programmes to the need to select only those cooperating teachers who have positive attitudes towards children, enlightened educational ideas, and a commitment to teaching. Great damage could well be done by consistently placing students with teachers who do not hold these views.

More generally, the cooperating teacher's supervisory style itself has been shown to have a strong relationship with the work and interpersonal environment encountered in supervision. An early study by Blumberg and Amidon (1965), using Flanders' concepts for categorizing teacher behaviours, examined the relationship between two dimensions of supervisory style, directness and indirectness, and aspects of student teacher behaviour. They found that supervision exhibiting the greatest incidence of high direct and high indirect behaviours or low direct and high indirect behaviours produced more favourable student teacher reactions on the productivity, communications, and learning scales than did other supervisory styles. A second study by Blumberg revealed that supervisory styles that emphasized indirectness produced a more positive perception of the interpersonal relationship between the supervisor and student teacher. Subsequently Blumberg and Weber (1968) examined the relationship between supervisory style and student teacher morale. They concluded that level of morale declined with perceptions of supervisory styles in the following order: low direct, high indirect; high direct, high indirect; high direct, low indirect; and low direct, low indirect. That is, the supervisory style which emphasized indirectness was accompanied by higher scores on morale as perceived by student teachers.

Building on the work of Blumberg and Amidon, Sanders and Merritt (1974) investigated the relationship between student teacher perceptions of supervisory style and their attitudes toward educational practices and toward teaching as a career. The cooperating teachers were classified into four groups according to student teacher perceptions of their supervisory style:

(a) High direct, high indirect (HDHI)—a supervisor perceived as suggesting and asking.

(b) High direct, low indirect (HDLI)—a supervisor perceived as doing much criticizing but little asking.

(c) Low direct, high indirect (LDHI)—a supervisor perceived as doing little telling but much question asking.

(d) Low direct, low indirect (LDLI)—a supervisor perceived as doing little or rather passive.

It was found that, over time, student teachers who viewed their supervisors as being HDHI and LDHI registered more progressive views toward education. However, no significant differences in attitudes towards teaching as a career were discovered among groups over time, although the HDHI group did change markedly to more favourable attitudes.

It has also been found that positive relationships between student and cooperating teacher are very important in determining student attitudes and development during the practicum. For example, in one study Poole (1972) concluded that the establishment of a good working relationship, marked by mutual respect between the cooperating teacher, student, and class is of utmost importance in determining satisfaction with the practice teaching situation. Positive relationships are often difficult to develop since teachers sometimes regard the presence of students as a possible threat to their relationships with the class. Sometimes, too, teachers accept the supervision of students not because they are committed to the task, but simply for the additional payment involved. Teachers must at least have a positive attitude to helping students if a worthwhile supervisory relationship is to develop. It should be added that highly skilled classroom practitioners are not necessarily effective supervisors. The skills needed for relating to and assisting the professional development of a student teacher are different from those required for successful classroom teaching.

Several studies have examined the nature of the interaction between supervisors and student teachers in supervisory conferences. For example, Barbour (1971), using a modified version of the Aschner–Gallagher classification system, examined the cognitive behaviour of supervising teachers and their student teachers during conferences. Results indicated that supervisors talked for some 57 percent of the time, generally initiated interchanges, and tended to set the trend in the cognitive level and the students followed suit. Most of the cognitive activity (over 90 percent) centred on memory and convergent levels of thinking where statement making, explaining, telling, and clarifying are predominant. The brief remaining activity comprised evaluative and divergent thinking. Without engagement in these higher levels of thinking, Barbour believed, there would be little "commitment making" by students to improve their teaching.

Many studies have tended to confirm that the actual teaching behaviour of student teachers seems to be influenced greatly by that of their cooperating teachers. For instance, Joyce and Harootunian (1967), Yee (1969), and Wragg (1970) found that the teaching of most student teachers closely reflected the methods used by their cooperating teachers rather than those suggested in the teacher education programme. Flint (1965) found patterns of relationships between even the verbal classroom behaviour of cooperating teachers and their student teachers during a short teaching practice, but these patterns did not seem to have a long-term influence. On the other hand, only one study, that of Brown (1967), found no relationships between the teaching styles of student teachers and cooperating teachers during practice teaching. In fact, considerable differences were discerned—the students displayed much more indirect, inquiry-oriented, supportive styles than did their cooperating teachers. More recently, Seperson and Joyce (1973) explored the relationship between the teaching behaviours of student teachers and cooperating teachers over 15 weeks of contact. Using the Conceptual Systems Manual, the teachers' and students' oral communications were placed in four general categories and 24 subcategories. The four general categories were sanctions, information, procedures, and maintenance. The researchers found that four of the eight indices of both early and advanced teaching styles of student teachers correlated positively and significantly with the indices of cooperating teachers, and the others were positive although they were not statistically significant. They concluded that these correlations represent "substantial evidence that the teaching behaviour of student teachers had moved from no association or negative ones with the behaviour of the cooperating teacher prior to student teaching, to being significantly related to a number of significant dimensions by early in student teaching, a relationship which was maintained throughout student teaching" (pp. 149–50).

The strong tendency for student teachers to model their work on that of cooperating teachers is not surprising. The techniques and methods of cooperating teachers are explicit in classrooms and are likely to be successful, if only because pupils are familiar with them. Student teachers are generally very dependent on their cooperating teachers for day-to-day practical advice on how to handle particular lessons (Cohen 1969), and, moreover, observe similar lessons in use. It is not surprising that in her analysis of the power relationship between student, cooperating teacher, and tertiary supervisor, Barrows (1979) notes that there is a hierarchical relationship with the cooperating teacher in the position of most power and influence over the student teacher. Many student teachers also believe that cooperating teachers disapprove of ideas and methods advocated by the teacher education programme (Shipman 1967, Cope 1971a, 1971b, Derrick 1971). Because of such factors student teachers may think it prudent to be seen to reject much of what they have learned in their teacher education programme. Indeed Wittrock (1962), Shipman (1967) and Derrick (1971) suggest that student teachers are capable of this sort of "impression management" while remaining wedded to the institution-advocated ideas and methods. As Nias (1977) points out, there is little conclusive evidence that really lasting attitudinal and behaviour changes are brought about by practice teaching. Indeed exposure to a variety of teaching models during practice-teaching periods can be beneficial to the student's professional growth.

Work by Copeland (1978) has attempted to understand the effect of the cooperating teacher on the student teacher's use of teaching skills in terms of the "ecological system" of the classroom. From this perspective, the cooperating teacher's consistent use of a particular skill makes it a functional part of the classroom's ecological system. Thus, when the student teacher attempts to use the same skill there is an "ecological congruence"—it works because the children are used to it and it suits that situation. The use of the skill is reinforced and is likely to be used again. Conversely, if the class has not experienced the use of the target skill, the student teacher is less likely to be successful when he or she attempts to use the skill and may not use it again. Copeland suggests that cooperating teachers be trained in the use of a range of target skills and encouraged to use them in the classroom where they would become a normal and accepted part of the classroom ecological system in which the student teacher will be operating.

Given the weight of evidence underlining the potential influence of cooperating teachers, a number of studies have investigated the nature and effectiveness of their supervision, as perceived by both student teachers and cooperating teachers themselves. These studies are useful in that they often reveal an interesting mismatch of perceptions and expectations between student teachers and their supervisors. For example, Fitch (1970) explored the perceptions of the two groups about supervisory tasks and their implementation. Among the conclusions he reached were the following. (a) Both groups preferred the supervisor's help to be of a practical nature, but only the supervisors saw their actual performance to be theoretical. (b) Both groups preferred and believed that student teachers were working out their own solutions to their teaching problems. (c) Although it was more true for supervisors than students, both groups preferred a directive, prescriptive supervising teacher. (d) Both groups saw supervising teachers to be nondirective and open. (e) While both groups saw students receiving the least help with planning, they both agreed that it was a desirable task. (f) Supervising teachers did not see themselves providing student teachers with an analysis of their teaching performance, nor did they believe it was desirable. Students agreed that they seldom received such an analysis but wished that supervisors provided such feedback.

In another survey McCurdy (1962) examined the relationship between the amount of help that was needed by student teachers and the amount of help that was provided by supervising teachers. Her findings included: (a) Students required "much" help and were given "much" help in handling disciplinary problems and in recognizing individual differences. (b) Students wanted considerably more help with developing self-expression, voice, poise, and emotional control than they felt they had received. (c) While the supervising teachers felt that the students only needed "some" help with evaluating pupils and products and having parent/teacher/child conferences, the student teachers wished there had been more help. (d) Students felt they had not received sufficient help in understanding professional activities, school policies, and the school programme.

Another investigation undertaken by Nicklas (1960) sought to identify those supervisory techniques regarded as effective or ineffective by student teachers and cooperating teachers. The main results of this study were: (a) both supervising teachers and student teachers approved of private conferences, group conferences, teaching demonstrations, special duties, methods classes, and tape recordings of lessons. (b) Both groups disapproved of classroom interruptions, supervisors removing pupils from class for extra help, issuing directives, and leaving solutions to the student teacher. (c) The most popular device was the private conference. (d) Commending the student teacher and employing tape recordings were thought to be used insufficiently.

A study by Loadman and Mahon (1973) explored the relationship between student teacher rankings of the supervisory effectiveness of cooperating teachers and their attitude toward education. Results indicated that student teachers tended to perceive those supervising teachers espousing either highly progressive or highly traditional attitudes as less effective supervisors. The very effective supervisors were seen to be teachers who did not strongly support progressive educational views. These perceptions occurred in spite of the fact that the reported student teacher attitudes towards education were generally more progressive than the teachers. Explaining these results the researchers point out that (a) the permissiveness, lack of structure, and loose planning and evaluation in some progressive classrooms conflicted with advice given to students by teacher education programmes, and (b) progressive teachers often failed to give definite, useful assistance and feedback to the student teachers they supervised when this is what students wanted.

Finally, Switzer (1976) surveyed student teacher perceptions of supervising teachers' level of helpfulness in 60 specific behaviours which could be grouped into six areas—supervisory techniques, professional attitudes, pedagogical skills, planning skills, knowledge of children, and human relations skills. He found that student teachers felt they had received most help from their supervising teachers in the area of knowledge of children. They also rated highly the human relations skills of supervisors. The areas most in need of attention were seen to be planning skills and the general supervisory techniques of the teachers. The 10 planning skills in order of most need of attention were:

(a) establishing behavioural objectives;

(b) knowing that progress sensibly step by step;

(c) developing lessons appropriate to goals;

(d) constructing lesson plans;

(e) employing efficient methods for changing activities;

(f) providing for motivation;

(g) using of visual aids;

(h) establishing of long-range goals;

(i) capitalizing on outside experiences;

(j) selecting of materials or activities.

The 10 supervisory techniques which could well be improved upon were, in order of most need for attention:

(a) taping a lesson for later discussion;

(b) listing expectations at the beginning;

(c) discussing planned induction process;

(d) giving feedback on lesson plans;

(e) discussing avoidance of common difficulties;

(f) holding conferences;

(g) appropriate demonstration teaching;

(h) clarifying expectations for teachers and pupils;

(i) giving honest but balanced feedback;

(j) gradual but comfortable induction

General suggestions for improving the work of cooperating teachers have been made by Trimmer (1961) and Johnson and Knaupp (1970). They urge that cooperating teachers should provide students with an opportunity to develop their own style, and that while teachers should permit students to plan and execute teaching strategies and learning experiences, they should be readily able to give technical advice to assist the students' work. In particular, there is a need to give student teachers adequate information on the abilities, attitudes, and skills of the pupils at the beginning of the practicum so that the students will have realistic expectations of initial pupil performance and potential.

2.2 Tertiary Supervisors

The influence of tertiary supervisors on student teachers has been given much less attention by researchers than the influence of cooperating teachers. Rather there has been a deal of controversy about the roles of tertiary supervisors in practice teaching and about whether they should have any role at all! Medley (1971) asserted that most people seem to agree that the student teacher should "have available whatever help he can get from the accumulated wisdom of the teacher education faculty", as represented in the tertiary supervisor (p. 157). These supervisors presumably share with the students the ideas that the training programme is endeavouring to promote, and ideally they know something of the students' background. Moreover, they liaise between the teacher education programme and the schools; represent the standards of teaching performance expected of students by the teacher education programme; and provide feedback to the programme on the practicum. In all, tertiary personnel are widely seen to be well-placed to aid, support, and evaluate student teachers in cooperation with school staff. Since the early 1970s, however, growing criticism has been levelled at tertiary supervisors. Critics have stated that they are ineffectual because they are overloaded, out of touch, inept, and underpaid. It has been suggested that the supervision of the practicum be relegated completely to cooperating teachers in schools.

Admittedly many problems have been encountered by tertiary supervisors. Often little coordination seems to exist between directors of practice teaching and individual supervisors; there is a lack of cooperation among various college departments about involvement in supervision; there is a lack of coordination between tertiary and cooperating school personnel; and the majority of tertiary supervisors are not adequately prepared professionally for supervising student teachers. While these difficulties, of course, also negatively influence the work of cooperating teachers, they are seen as more pressing problems for the tertiary supervisor.

There is, too, evidence to indicate a dissonance between the views on supervision held by tertiary supervisors and students. Stewig's study (1970) of student teacher expectations indicates that they felt it was most important that supervisors are aware of, and provide for, individual differences between students; have an objective perception of the classroom situation and the ability to communicate this perception to student teachers; and a sincere and positive attitude. Primary supervisors considered that their most important task was to conduct three-way conferences with student, cooperating teacher, and supervisor, while for secondary supervisors the most important task was to stimulate students to evaluate their teaching behaviour. Stewig concluded that "critical differences existed between the perceptions of (tertiary) supervisors and students that may have hindered communication and limited supervisory effectiveness".

Two of the most simple, common, and powerful factors limiting the influence of tertiary supervisors on student teachers are time and place. Frequently, because of tertiary teaching research and administrative commitments, tertiary supervisors have insufficient time to discuss the lesson plans, observe the teaching performance, and provide adequate feedback and follow-up assistance. Most find even less time for counselling students on their anxieties and problems. Tertiary supervisors are usually assigned to so many students in widely separated schools that visiting is sporadic and observations unsystematic. Even when they conscientiously visit the student, tertiary supervisors have little chance of ascertaining the antecedent classroom activities and often have little knowledge of future activities planned. Thus they have no way of knowing whether the teaching episode observed was typical. Such visits scarcely provide a sufficient base from which to offer useful suggestions for the changes in student teacher behaviour. Supervision is thus all too often a brief, rushed, infrequent, and unrelated series of encounters between supervisor and student teachers. The timing of these encounters and their location are also frequently unfortunate. As Maddox (1968) pointed out, the so-called "private" talk between supervisor and student teacher is usually carried out in a crowded staff room or in a noisy corridor after a lesson at a time when the student teacher is unlikely to be either calm or receptive. Problems of time and place for supervision also apply to the cooperating teacher but not to the same degree.

Responding to recent criticisms of tertiary supervisors, many educators are suggesting new role emphases and even new roles for them. For example, Neal et al. (1967) placed great value on the liaison role of tertiary supervisors. Others, such as Lowther (1968), have carried out research to show that tertiary supervisors can make a most valuable contribution by providing inservice education for cooperating teachers, especially in the areas of analysing teaching and assessing students. Bebb and Monson (1969) emphasized this point while adding other suggestions for changing the tertiary supervisor's role. For example, they advocated that tertiary supervisors facilitate (a) continuity of the professional experiences in the practicum, and (b) a partnership between school and tertiary staff in jointly contributing to teacher education.

Several studies have sought to discover whether the involvement of tertiary supervisors really enhances student teachers' experience. An investigation by Stapleton (1965) indicated that intensive supervision by tertiary staff, contrasted with their normal involvement, did result in better performance by student teachers. However, Morris (1974) found there was no significant difference between the classroom performance of student teachers who were supervised by university staff and those who received supervision entirely from school staff, except that the self-ratings of the former group suggested they were performing better than were the other group. There was also no significant difference between the two groups in their adjustment to the school situation, except that the university-supervised group seemed to have better rapport with cooperating teachers.

Other studies have been concerned with the work of tertiary supervisors and the self-concept, creativity, and anxiety of student teachers. In one investigation Burgy

(1973) sought to identify the situational components and supervisory practices that lead to the development of a strong, positive self-concept in student teachers, believed to be most important in teaching success. While she found that in general there was no significant change in student teachers' self-concept during teaching practice, three factors were identified as being associated with an increase in self-concept: (a) socioeconomic status of the student teacher's classroom (heterogeneous classes produced greatest increase in student teacher self-concept, low socioeconomic status some increase, and higher status a decrease); (b) the tertiary supervisor's teaching experience (student teachers who had supervisors with more than six years teaching experience showed the greatest increase in self-concept); and (c) supervisory practice of college supervisors (student teachers whose supervisors always scheduled their observations well in advance showed a marked increase in self-concept).

There has been a considerable interest in developing creative teachers. According to Cicirelli (1969) this concern has implications for the supervision of student teachers. Through their "diagnostic feedback", supervisors can either restrict the range of teaching behaviour of students or encourage them to explore a full range of teaching behaviour. He argues for the use of creative supervisors who would be more flexible, more sensitive to problems, more theoretical in orientation, and less interested in details. In a subsequent study Cicirelli explored the relationship between the creative ability of tertiary supervisors and the kind of diagnostic feedback given to student teachers, as revealed in their written reports on observations of the students' performance. He found that the more creative supervisors were aware of a greater number of factors in a student teacher's performance. They tended to use broad general factors in assessing a student teacher's performance rather than specific, detailed ones, and were more sensitive to factors involving pupil–teacher relationships than were their less creative colleagues. One of the most striking findings was the tendency for less creative supervisors to give specific prescriptions for the improvement of the lesson, while the more creative supervisors tended to see the lesson more in terms of its general objectives, planning, and organization.

Practice teaching is an anxiety-producing experience for student teachers, even though studies have recorded some decrease in anxiety during practice teaching periods (Poole and Gaudry 1974, Nicoll 1975). Within the practice teaching experience, supervision has been shown to be an important stress factor (Yee 1968). Research by Sinclair and Nicoll (1981) suggests that the act of being supervised by tertiary personnel was the source of tension, not necessarily the relationship between student and supervisor. As the investigators pointed out, "Many of the students resented the supervisor's evaluative function while finding the supervisor as a person supportive and helpful. The supervised lesson was generally viewed as being different from other lessons and students went to extraordinary trouble to prepare and execute such lessons . . ." (p. 12). More generally, high anxiety levels and confusion were promoted where a conflict existed between the teaching ideals of the supervisor and cooperating teacher with students torn between conflicting advice and criticism from the two.

3. Concerns of Students

The above discussion of the influence of supervisors has disclosed some of the views held by student teachers. Consideration of their views is essential to an understanding of the process of supervision. This section further elaborates student concerns in the practicum and its supervision and considers the implications for the work of supervisors.

As mentioned in the previous section research has drawn attention to the high levels of stress among student teachers during the practicum. Coulter (1974) supported this in terms of lowered self-image when students are moved into more difficult and unfamiliar teaching situations. He made the point that a deliberate attempt should be made to place students in teaching situations which are appropriate to their stage of professional development.

The work of Fuller (1970) in identifying "concerns of teachers" is particularly relevant to practicum planning and supervision. Three progressive phases of concern in the process of learning to teach were identified as "concerns about self", "concerns about self as a teacher", and "concerns about pupils". Fuller's plea is that programmes of teacher education try to match the experiences and content to the level of concern of the individual student. This model is particularly appropriate for establishing practicum goals which are personally relevant to the student, setting expectations with which the student can cope successfully, and assisting the student to overcome the problems of learning to teach in a more realistic and gradual way. During periods of practice teaching, a wide range of considerations could reflect Fuller's phases of student teacher concerns—for example, objectives, tasks required, counselling, feedback, and evaluation. Both Katz (1974) and Campbell (1977) also draw attention to the need to consider social adjustment concerns of student teachers as they experience the process of professional socialization into the school and form relationships with their cooperating teachers.

It seems that student teachers are concerned particularly about their interpersonal relationships with both cooperating teacher and tertiary supervisor. In many of these relationships students experience feelings of confusion and conflict which can detract from effective teaching performance. It has been noted, for instance, that student teachers are often placed in conflict when cooperating teachers and tertiary supervisors have differing sets of expectations of students. These differences in expectations become critical in the assessment of teaching performance.

An investigation by Lowther (1968) indicated that student teachers want from cooperating teachers not only clear and consistent expectations, positive feedback, and careful evaluation, but they also want a professional relationship to be established which includes a generous amount of trust, support, understanding, and consideration. This point is further emphasized in the study by Love and Swain (1980) who conclude that student teachers desire a cooperating teacher who offers constructive criticism, who shares ideas and materials with them, and provides such opportunities and support that they can experiment, innovate, and develop teaching strategies on their own initiative.

Considered in the light of student concerns, supervision will fundamentally become an exercise in human relationships. Technical expertise in strategies of supervision would seem useless unless it is combined with sensitivity to individual students and their unique learning requirements (Lomax 1973). More attention needs to be paid to this issue. Some researchers have already developed promising approaches. For instance, Lewis (1974) reported one such approach in which small groups consisting of four students, a teacher, and a lecturer were given an opportunity for planning and carrying out their own pattern of practice over a full year. This was in addition to normal academic commitments. The results indicated a greater degree of cooperation in trying different patterns of teaching. The students not only valued the additional experience but they saw an advantage in working with children over a longer period especially without normal college assessment. Mistakes were as beneficial as successes in coping with teaching problems. The teachers felt more involved as active partners and welcomed the opportunity to exchange ideas about their own methods. The lecturers valued the opportunities for extensive practical involvement with one class of children. They also reported better opportunities to link theory and practice in a more natural setting and felt they were of greater assistance to the students. The net result of the evaluation, Lewis suggests, is "that such patterns of cooperative, autonomous, nonprescriptive, and nondirective working would make a valuable addition to initial training courses" (p. 21).

A final interesting aspect of student's views on supervision relates to the expectation some have of the school principal. Nias (1977) has reported that student teachers expect the principal to be able to offer them support by (a) clarifying and articulating the philosophies and objectives of the school; (b) holding professional discussions with student teachers; and (c) helping when classroom relations with the teacher breakdown. Thus students appear to see their progress in practice teaching as being not merely dependent upon efforts of their tertiary supervisor and cooperating teacher. It would not be inappropriate to extend this point to ask: how can the expertise of other school staff, especially specialist staff such as counsellors, be incorporated in the programme students undertake?

4. Clinical Supervision

From the preceding discussion it is clear that there is a need for a careful re-examination of the processes of supervision in the practicum. Too frequently supervision is unsystematic and impersonal. In particular, considerable evidence indicates that skill in classroom observation and the ability to analyse classroom teaching are much neglected areas in supervision. Research has pointed to the need for closer cooperative relationships within the supervision setting. To help overcome these significant shortcomings there is a need for more organized approaches to supervision which focus on the rigorous analysis of classroom teaching in a cooperative manner. One such organized approach involving a collegial relationship is that referred to as clinical supervision.

Clinical supervision has been defined as that approach to practicum supervision which "draws its data from first-hand observation of actual teaching events, and involves face-to-face (and other associated) interaction between the supervisor and teacher in the analysis of teaching behaviours and activities for instructional improvement" (Goldhammer et al. 1980 pp. 19–20). The principal emphasis in clinical supervision is on helping the student teacher focus on improving particular aspects of teaching through a systematic approach to the supervision task.

The term "clinical" is not meant to suggest that this type of supervision is predominantly a form of counselling or therapy, though on occasions the clinical supervisor may have to display the kind of sensitivity and understanding demanded of a counsellor working with a person under stress. In the context of practicum supervision, the term "clinical" refers to close supervision in a one-to-one relationship and denotes that the supervisor will be involved in face-to-face encounters with student teachers as they discuss classroom events in which they have both participated, one as an observer and the other as a teacher. In the clinical supervision process, then, what the student teacher does in the classroom is central. The supervisor who does not visit the student's classroom frequently cannot carry out the supervision process effectively. The shared observations provide an intensity of focus which then brings supervisor and student together in a close professional relationship. Further, the supervision is "clinical" in that it requires the supervisor to get to know a lot about an individual student's attitude to teaching, strengths, weaknesses, and anxieties, so that an individual programme of supervision suited to the needs of the student may be devised.

Since the early 1970s much progress has been made in the development of models which explain how the processes of clinical supervision might be followed. The work of Cogan (1973), Goldhammer et al. (1980), and Boyan and Copeland (1978) in devising clinical supervision procedures to assist student teachers and their supervisors achieve a conscious and rational understanding of teaching behaviour has been extremely significant. They have been able to establish stages needed for "systematic analysis" of the supervision process. Not only does this work help cooperating teachers and tertiary staff carrying out a difficult task with student teachers, it is also valuable to those responsible for the development of supervision training programmes.

In the clinical supervision process at least five stages can be identified. In a preobservation conference, stage 1, the supervisor and the student teacher discuss teaching plans, delineate areas to be focused on during observation and ways in which observations will be recorded. In stage 2, the classroom observation phase, the supervisor carries out observations in the classroom and records data ready to discuss teaching issues with the student. During stage 3, the analysis and strategy phase, the supervisor and the student, separately, reflect upon what has happened during teaching and decide what issues could profitably be raised in discussions, particularly the strengths upon which the student should build. This analysis phase is at the heart of the clinical supervision process. In considering what will be discussed both will need to recall what had been agreed upon during the preobservation conference. Stage 4 is the postobservation conference during which data are fed back to the student and discussions are made about future teaching. Finally in stage 5, the post conference analysis, both the supervisor and the student reflect upon their professional behaviour and, especially, the supervision process itself. It is important that both realize the need to develop self-analysis skills and to consider how successful each is being in contributing to a productive supervisor–student relationship. Once the sequence has been worked through the cycle of supervision recommences with renewed discussions to plan teaching by the student and observation by the supervisor.

The five stages described above can be expanded— Cogan (1973) has eight—but what is important is that a relationship is established which encourages clear communication, understanding, and mutual trust between the supervisor and the student. Thus supervisors must understand the importance of the processes they are following in clinical supervision and they must possess specific capabilities including "skills which ensure clear communication and establish open and healthy interpersonal relations, skills in systematic and objective observation and analysis of classroom behaviours, and skills in conducting supervisory conferences, providing focused, databased feedback in a non threatening manner, and facilitating growth in student teachers' problem-solving abilities" (Copeland and Boyan 1975 p. 36).

The concept of the clinical supervisor as it is presented here changes the role of the supervisor from that of evaluator to that of colleague and consultant with greater and more systematic participation in the student teacher's professional development. Although such a concept of clinical supervision has been slow in gaining acceptance in preservice and inservice supervision of teaching, in the 1980s there have been developed a number of promising training programmes to facilitate the development of supervisor understanding and skill in the process (e.g., Boyan and Copeland 1978). One of the most sophisticated and comprehensive programmes has been designed by Turney and his associates (1982). These programmes combine handbook and television materials to provide a realistic and flexible resource for supervisor training. They focus on the process of clinical supervision and the skills inherent in the six key roles that supervisors perform—manager, counsellor, instructor, observer, provider of feedback, and evaluator.

5. Conclusion

The process of supervision is potentially as complex as the more general practicum operation of which it is part. The interpersonal relations it includes are varied. For the tertiary supervisor and cooperating teacher, supervision involves not only a relationship with the student teacher but with each other, with other teachers and tertiary staff, with the school executive, and with pupils. The roles of supervisors are complicated and sometimes ill defined, as are the institution's expectations of student teachers in the practicum. Supervisory personnel often have confused and conflicting views both of each other's roles and of the expectations of students. Much needs to be done to make supervisors abundantly aware of the dimensions of their roles, the specific expectations of students, and, more generally, how they can work together to achieve the goals of the practicum.

Supervisors, especially cooperating teachers, have a considerable immediate influence on the developing professional attitudes and teaching styles of student teachers. To optimize this influence, to ensure that it promotes worthwhile student learning and positive attitudes, supervisors must be carefully selected and appropriately prepared for their work. The development of the so-called "clinical" approach to supervision has much to commend it since it combines a personalized, helping style of supervision with a systematic procedure to improve specific aspects of the student's teaching. But even careful supervisor selection and training will be insufficient. Supervisors must have adequate time to devote to their work—to consult and plan together, to hold conferences with the student, to observe the student's teaching, to become acquainted with the student's strengths, weaknesses, and concerns, and to collaborate with the student in mutually beneficial educational tasks.

See also: Student (Practice) Teaching; Laboratory Schools; Criteria for Evaluating Teaching; Lesson Analysis; Supervision of Teaching; Concepts of Teacher Education

Bibliography

Acevedo M A, Elliot C, Valverde L A 1976 *A Guide for Conducting an Effective Feedback Session*. University of Texas at Austin, Texas

Barbour C 1971 Levels of thinking in supervisory conferences. Paper presented at the Annual Meeting of the American Educational Research Association, New York, ERIC Document No. ED 049 186

Barrows L 1979 Power relationships in the student teacher triad. Paper presented at the Annual Meeting of the American Educational Research Association, Washington, DC

Bebb A M, Monson J A 1969 *A New Model for the Supervision of Student Teaching*. New York University, ERIC Document No. ED 034 736

Blumberg A 1974 *Supervisors and Teachers: A Private Cold War*. McCutchan, Berkeley, California

Blumberg A, Amidon E 1965 Teacher perceptions of supervisor teacher interaction. *Administrators Notebook* 14: 1–4

Blumberg A, Cusick P 1970 Supervisor–teacher interaction: An analysis of verbal behavior. Paper presented at the Annual meeting of the American Educational Research Association, Minneapolis, ERIC Document No. ED 040 938

Blumberg A, Weber W 1968 Teacher morale as a function of perceived supervisor behavioral style. *J. Educ. Res.* 62: 109–13

Boyan N J, Copeland W D 1978 *Instructional Supervision Training Program*. Merrill, Columbus, Ohio

Brown C C 1967 The relationship of initial teaching styles and selected variables in student teaching. (Doctoral dissertation, Teachers College, Columbia University). *Dissertation Abstracts International* 1968 29: 493A–494A (University Microfilms No. 68–11,125)

Burgy D R 1973 *Developing Good Teachers by Strengthening Student Teachers' Self Concepts*. ERIC Document No. ED 087 774

Campbell W J 1977 *Study of Teacher Education Programs*. Report to the Australian Commission on Advanced Education, Canberra

Cicirelli V G 1969 University supervisors' creative ability and their appraisal of student teachers' performance: An exploratory study. *J. Educ. Res.* 62: 375–81

Cogan M L 1973 *Clinical Supervision*. Houghton Mifflin, Boston, Massachusetts

Cohen L 1969 Students' perceptions of the school practice period. *Res. Educ.* 2: 52–58

Cope E 1969 Students and school practice. *Educ. Teach.* 90: 24–35

Cope E 1971a *School Experience in Teacher Education*. University of Bristol, Bristol

Cope E 1971b *A Study of School Supervised Practice*. University of Bristol, Bristol

Copeland W D 1978 Processes mediating the relationship between cooperating teacher behaviour and student–teacher classroom performance. *J. Educ. Psychol.* 70: 95–100

Copeland W D, Boyan N J 1975 Training in instructional supervision: Improving the influence of the co-operating teacher. In: Heidelbach R (ed.) 1975 *Developing Supervisory Practice: Selected Papers*. Association of Teacher Educators, Washington, DC

Coulter F 1974 The effects of practice teaching on professional self-image. *Aust. J. Educ.* 18: 49–59

Coulter F 1975 Perceptions of classroom behaviour by supervisors and student teachers. Paper presented at the National Conference on Teacher Education and the Practicum, Perth

Derrick T 1971 Teacher training and school practice. *Educ. Res.* 13: 106–12

Finlayson D S, Cohen L 1967 The teacher's role: A comparative study of the conceptions of college of education students and head teachers. *Br. J. Educ. Psychol.* 37: 22–31

Fitch T C 1970 Role expectations for intern consultants: Views of intern teachers and intern consultants in the Michigan State University Elementary Intern Program (Doctoral dissertation, Michigan State University) *Dissertation Abstracts International* 1971 31: 1115A (University Microfilms No. 70–16,663)

Flint S H 1965 The relationship between the classroom verbal behavior of student teachers and the classroom verbal behaviour of their cooperating teachers (Doctoral dissertation, Teachers College, Columbia University) *Dissertation Abstracts International* 1966 26: 4480 (University Microfilms No. 65–14,965)

Fuller F 1970 *Personalised Education for Teachers.* Research and Development Center for Teacher Education, University of Texas, Austin, Texas

Goldhammer R 1969 *Clinical Supervision: Special Methods for the Supervision of Teachers.* Holt, Rinehart and Winston, New York

Goldhammer R, Anderson R H, Krajewsky R J 1980 *Clinical Supervision: Special Methods for the Supervision of Teachers,* 2nd edn. Holt, Rinehart and Winston, New York

Johnson J S 1968 Change in student teacher dogmatism. *J. Educ. Res.* 62: 224–26

Johnson W D, Knaupp J E 1970 Trainee role expectations for the micro-teaching supervisor. *J. Teach. Educ.* 21: 396–401

Joyce B R, Harootunian B 1967 *The Structure of Teaching.* Science Research Associates, Chicago, Illinois

Katz F E 1974 Teaching training as a rite of passage. In: Edgar D E (ed.) 1974 *The Competent Teacher.* Angus and Robertson, Sydney

Lewis I 1974 The reform of teaching practice. In: Warwick D (ed.) 1974 *New Directions for the Professional Training of Teachers.* University of Lancaster, Lancaster

Loadman W E, Mahon J M 1973 A study of the relationship between the rankings of supervising teacher effectiveness and attitude toward education. Paper presented at the Annual Meeting of the American Educational Research Association, New Orleans

Lomax D E (ed.) 1973 *The Education of Teachers in Britain.* Wiley, London

Love J, Swain M 1980 Success in practicum programs: Student teachers' perceptions. Paper presented at Conference on the Role of School Experiences in Teacher Education, Armidale

Lowther M A 1968 Most and least helpful activities of supervising teachers. *Clearing House* 43: 20–23

McCurdy B A 1962 A study of the availability of certain basic experiences provided off-campus student teachers in terms of indicated needs (Doctoral thesis, School of Education, Indiana University, Bloomington) *Dissertation Abstracts International* 1963 23: 2807–808 (University Microfilms No. 12–5789)

Maddox H 1968 A descriptive study of teaching practice. *Educ. Rev.* 20: 177–90

Medley D M 1971 The language of teacher behaviour: Communicating the results of structured observations to teachers. *J. Teach. Educ.* 22: 157–65

Morris J R 1974 The effects of the university supervisor on the performance and adjustment of student teachers. *J. Educ. Res.* 67: 358–62

Neal C D, Kraft L E, Kracht C R 1967 Reasons for college supervision of the student-teaching programme. *J. Teach. Educ.* 18: 24–27

Nias J 1976 School-supervised practice in junior schools. *Trends in Educ.* 1: 23–27

Nias J 1977 What should Nellie do? Student role expectations for head and class teachers on school-supervised practice. *Br. J. Teach. Educ.* 3: 121–30

Nicklas M S 1960 A comparative study of critical incidents to determine recommended techniques for supervisors of student teachers (Doctoral dissertation, University of Arkansas) *Dissertation Abstracts International* 1960 20: 4342

Nicoll V 1975 The effects of practice teaching upon the anxiety levels, educational attitudes and teaching behaviours of student teachers. BA Hons thesis, University of Sydney, Sydney

Peters W H 1971 *An Investigation of the Influence of Co-operating Teachers in Shaping the Attitudes of Student Teachers Towards the Teaching of English.* University of Kentucky, ERIC Document No. ED 074 052

Poole C 1972 The influence of experiences in the schools on students' evaluation of teaching practice. *J. Educ. Res.* 66: 161–64

Poole C, Gaudry E 1974 Some effects of teaching practice. *Aust. J. Educ.* 18(3): 255–63

Price R D 1961 The influence of supervising teachers. *J. Teach. Educ.* 12: 471–75

Sanders J, Merritt D L 1974 The relationship between perceived supervisor style and teacher attitudes. Paper presented at the Annual Meeting of the American Educational Research Association, Chicago, Illinois, ERIC Document No. ED 090 663

Seperson M A, Joyce B R 1973 Teaching styles of student teachers as related to those of their co-operating teachers. *Educ. Leadership* 31: 146–51

Shipman M D 1967 Theory and practice in the education of teachers. *Educ. Res.* 9(3): 208–12

Sinclair K, Nicoll V 1981 Sources and experience of anxiety in practice teaching. *South Pacific J. Teach. Educ.* 9: 1–18

Stapleton M C 1965 An evaluation of two programmes of student teacher supervision by college supervisors. Doctoral dissertation, Pennsylvania State University, University Park, Pennsylvania

Stewig J W 1970 What should college supervisors do? *J. Teach. Educ.* 21: 251–57

Switzer R 1976 Co-operating teachers: Strengths and weaknesses. *Colorado J. Educ. Res.* 15(2): 37–45

Trimmer R L 1961 Tell us more, student teacher. *J. Teach. Educ.* 12: 228–31

Tuckman B W, Oliver W F 1968 Effectiveness of feedback to teachers as a function of source. *J. Educ. Psychol.* 59: 297–301

Turney C et al. 1982 *Supervisor Development Programmes.* Sydney University Press, Sydney

Wittrock M C 1962 Set applied to student teaching. *J. Educ. Psychol.* 53: 175–80

Wragg E 1970 Interaction analysis as a feedback system for student teachers. *Educ. Teach.* 81: 38–47

Yee A H 1968 Interpersonal relationships in the student teaching triad. *J. Teach. Educ.* 19: 95–112

Yee A H 1969 Do co-operating teachers influence the attitudes of student teachers? *J. Educ. Psychol.* 60: 327–32

Laboratory Schools

C. Turney

Since the early 1970s there has been a growing awareness among teacher educators of the great importance, in the professional preparation of teachers, of various forms of practical experience, of introducing more reality and relevance into programmes, and of intimately relating educational theory and practice. This awareness has pointed to the development of a new and closer cooperative relationship between teacher education institutions and schools.

Already many teacher education programmes have formed, or are in the process of forming new relationships with special cooperating schools located either on- or off-campus. Many more programmes, it seems, are contemplating similar developments. This movement has been promoted by factors other than the kinds of awareness mentioned above. For instance, teacher education programmes have become dissatisfied with the work of long-established demonstration schools. At the same time, conventional school practice teaching, supervised increasingly and perhaps inadequately by classroom teachers, has proved both expensive and even wasteful of students' time. Are there not other arrangements with schools that can better fulfil some or all of the functions of the demonstration and practice schools and perhaps have newer valuable functions as well? Prompted by like questions, some teacher education programmes have realized that a cooperating school can provide such things as (a) a setting in which unique forms of professional laboratory experience can be pursued (e.g., child study, microteaching, and participation in curriculum development); (b) a context for research and innovation involving tertiary staff, teachers, and student teachers; and (c) a centre for various forms of inservice education and for the dissemination of new ideas, plans, and materials developed in the school.

In the recent past such important functions as the three above were combined with others in the numerous laboratory schools in the United States. It is paradoxical, therefore, to find that these schools have in fact declined seriously in both popularity and number since the early 1960s. Consequently an examination of the activities and problems of the laboratory schools could prove instructive to teacher educators presently contemplating forming new relationships between their programmes and schools.

This article then traces the rise and decline of the laboratory-school movement. It begins with an historical overview of the specific functions of various types of schools in the preparation of teachers and of the emergence of laboratory schools combining some of these functions. It then proceeds to an analysis of the difficulties and the demise of many laboratory schools in the mid-twentieth century. Finally it briefly discusses the present state and future prospects of laboratory schools.

1. Perspectives on the Functions of Schools in Teacher Preparation

From the time of the establishment of the first institutions specializing in training of teachers in seventeenth-century Europe, involvement of the student teachers in schools for children linked with the institutions has been a continuing feature. These schools initially had two main functions: they provided a place where prospective teachers might observe "approved" techniques and methods of teaching being illustrated, and where they might themselves attempt to conduct lessons under the supervision of an experienced teacher. Although such schools have gradually taken on more refined and extended functions, the themes of demonstration and practice teaching have been consistently dominant (Fristoe 1942, Lamb 1962).

In the last century or so, schools cooperating in teacher education have been given varied titles according to what was considered their main purpose. At least five titles have appeared: model school, training school, practice school, demonstration school, and laboratory school. Such titles did not emerge in chronological order. Sometimes, several types developed simultaneously. At times too, their work seemed to be almost identical.

1.1 The Model School

These schools were seen as providing the best example of school organization and method that beginning and experienced teachers should absorb through observation and practice. They were, in fact, the model for the education system. Student classes in pedagogy mirrored the same ideas and practices exemplified in the school.

1.2 The Practice School

While observation continued to be a function, these schools provided prospective teachers with the opportunity to acquire teaching methods through practice under the guidance of an experienced teacher. These schools were not necessarily regarded as an ultimate example of a particular system of teaching.

1.3 The Training School

Closely linked with the teacher-training institutions, the training school attempted to reflect in practice the theory being advocated. In it, through observation and practice, students could experience pedagogical principles. Such experience supported and extended their study of these principles. One of the most influential American training schools was the Oswego Training School, New York (Chittenden 1925). It initially reflected Pestalozzian principles preached at the college with which it functioned, under the same roof, as an integral part. Members of faculty worked in both places, spending a substantial amount of time in the school providing demonstrations and supervising teaching practice. Much of the teaching in the school was done by students implementing suggestions offered in theory and methods courses.

1.4 The Demonstration School

These schools were founded to associate the theory and practice of Herbartian pedagogy and to demonstrate it in operation. Following Herbart's formal steps of teaching, demonstration lessons were carefully planned by specially selected teachers. Students studied the lesson plans, observed the lessons taught, and attempted to teach the same or similar lessons in practice teaching (Blair et al. 1958). A vital aspect of the demonstration lesson was that it was to be integrated with the student's theoretical learning. For example, commenting on the work of the demonstration school connected with the University of Manchester, Findlay wrote in 1908:

> The demonstration lesson is selected from the regular programme of the class, to exemplify certain principles of teaching and method; it is preceded by an account in the lecture-room of the aims underlying the work and followed at a subsequent lecture hour by discussion of results. The student's part is to record the lesson and to seek an interpretation of what he witnesses. (p. 37)

Like a few other demonstration schools of the time, the one at Manchester also provided an opportunity for lecturers and teachers to "undertake research into educational problems" (p. 1). This activity, however, was in America to become mainly linked with laboratory schools.

1.5 The Laboratory School

The laboratory schools, in name, grew largely out of the so-called "scientific movement" in education towards the close of the nineteenth century. At first, many of these schools were essentially experimental in character. Probably the most famous school of this category was the laboratory school founded by John Dewey at the University of Chicago in 1896. Mayhew and Edwards (1939) described its role as follows:

> Conducted under the management and supervision of the University's Department of Philosophy, Psychology and Education, it bore the same relation to the work of the department that a laboratory bears to biology, physics or chemistry. Like in any such laboratory, it had two main purposes: (a) to exhibit, test, verify, and criticize theoretical statements and principles; and (b) to add to the sum of facts and principles in its special line. (p. 3)

Other universities soon opened schools that had an experimental function. Probably the most notable of these were the Lincoln, Horace Mann, and Speyer Schools established by Teachers College, Columbia, the school founded by Meriam at the University of Missouri, and the Ohio State's University School.

Although Dewey saw his school as not participating directly in training teachers, the experimental schools at Teachers College, Columbia did. Besides pursuing child study and the improvement of curriculum and method, they functioned also as demonstration schools for student teachers. For example, the Horace Mann School provided opportunity for prospective teachers "to observe good teaching under favorable conditions in order to fix ideals and to establish a practical standard of merit" (Russell 1902 p. 3). Professors in the college supervised the curriculum of the school. Teachers were "selected with a view to their ability to demonstrate what is deemed feasible in any grade or class" (Russell 1902 p. 3).

During the initial decades of the twentieth century the term "laboratory school" became commonly applied in the United States to on- or off-campus schools associated closely with state colleges and universities in providing various professional experiences for students and in improving educational practice. They continued the classical functions of demonstration, practice, and experimentation, and, in addition, accepted several new functions. It soon became fashionable in America for a teacher education programme to have its own designated laboratory school. Indeed, the 1926 meeting of the American Association of Teachers Colleges adopted the standard that each "teachers college shall maintain a training school under its own control as part of its organization, as a laboratory school" (Yearbook AATC 1926 p. 11).

During the 1930s laboratory schools played a major part in introducing "participation" as a technique of teacher preparation. Participation had the purpose of gradually introducing students to the knowledge and skills demanded in the teacher's duties (Dawson 1937). It was conceived as a stage of training intermediate between passive observation and student teaching. Linked with campus courses the typical participation programme involved students in sharing with teachers a comprehensive range of activities—helping individual pupils, observing children, maintaining the classroom and its materials, using aids, supervising playgrounds, keeping records, checking hygiene, testing, planning the daily programme, and so on.

Also in the 1930s many colleges and universities began to use their laboratory schools to provide "summer demonstration programs" for undergraduate and graduate teachers. Often student teachers and tertiary staff participated in planning with teachers a progressive or comprehensive programme of work. Mornings were then spent observing the teachers implementing plans, and afternoons in seminars discussing the teaching and related theoretical issues. The programme closed with an overall evaluation of its operation (Hayes and Campbell 1948). Sometimes, the demonstration programmes were organized to give participants firsthand contact with specific recent educational innovations (Tyler 1940).

2. *Difficulties and Decline of Laboratory Schools*

As the teacher education enterprise grew in size and complexity, the demands on the laboratory schools became great. As a result, practice teaching increasingly became the responsibility of off-campus cooperating schools, leaving many on-campus laboratory schools to concentrate on providing a variety of other preservice experiences for student teachers. Some laboratory schools did, however, continue to be quite heavily involved in practice teaching (Thomas 1956). Generally the schools' research function became a comparatively minor aspect of their work. In this period of pressure and change many laboratory schools were beset by problems. By the 1950s educationalists often seriously questioned the value of the laboratory schools. Was the cost of conducting them commensurate with the value of their contribution? Was the work of the school relevant to the theory of the training programme? What were the appropriate functions of these schools? Were not numbers of these schools atypical in staff and pupil population and thus not acquainting students with the real world? Had the schools really made any significant improvement to education through either training, research, or innovation? When negative or uncertain answers were provided to these and other questions, a large number of laboratory schools were closed down.

In response to the criticism of laboratory schools and a concern for their future, during the 1950s and 1960s there were a number of investigations aiming to establish the nature, functions, and problems of these institutions and to suggest ways in which they might be improved (Blair et al. 1958, Lamb 1961, White 1964, Sale 1967). An early example of such investigations was the one reported by Ashmore (1951). Through interview and questionnaire he surveyed the operation of 11 selected campus laboratory schools in four southeastern states. In the light of data collected, the following were among the conclusions drawn: most of the campus laboratory schools were not being used extensively for student teaching, but were rather concentrating on developing coordinated programmes of observation and participation. The great majority of schools were not engaged in research. This appeared to be "due to lack of funds and facilities, the lack of cooperation and coordination between laboratory and college faculties, the over-loaded conditions of the laboratory faculty, the lack of understanding, and the lack of interest" (p. 89). More generally the work of many laboratory schools was seriously hampered by the "lack of clearly demarcated administrative responsibility and authority" (p. 91). They were given little autonomy and were too dependent on the college or department of education. Further, the majority of schools did not have "clearly defined purposes which emanate from the laboratory faculty and which are appreciated and understood by them" (p. 91). This prevented concerted effort from school staff to accomplish desired goals. Linked with the want of autonomy and purpose was the frequent turnover of both teaching and administrative personnel which, in turn, had caused confusion in the programmes of schools. Despite all these difficulties, it is worth noting that almost all college and school staff surveyed agreed that the laboratory school should be a vital, focal point of a teacher education programme and that the essential tasks of laboratory schools were demonstration and participation *and* experimentation.

Ashmore's study was followed by others, only a few of which need to be mentioned briefly here. In 1964 White investigated the status and potential of over 100 randomly selected college-controlled laboratory schools. Alongside their central purpose of providing a sound education for their pupils, most laboratory schools considered the provision of "laboratory experiences" for students as a major function. Such experiences included all those planned contacts with children and teachers through observation, participation, and classroom teaching which contribute to the student's understanding of individuals and their guidance in the teaching–learning process. A possible future change in laboratory schools was seen as making increased use of closed-circuit and videorecording television systems to provide students with wider opportunities for observation. In 1967 Sale analysed the functions of campus elementary schools affiliated with state colleges and universities. Among the chief findings of this study were the following:

(a) the provision for prestudent teaching laboratory experiences was the most important function of these schools;

(b) the schools were attempting to perform too many functions and were failing to identify and to perform these functions at a high level of competence;

(c) the schools were nevertheless serving a definite need in a prospective teacher's education and should be considered as an integral part of the total teacher education programme;

(d) the school provided an excellent environment in which the prospective teacher may experiment with the integration of theory and practice; and

(e) the major strengths of the schools were the quality of freedom for innovation and experimentation, and the quality of the instructional programme for pupils.

In his recommendations, Sale underlined the need for laboratory schools and affiliated institutions to develop better mutual understandings of the school's objectives, functions, and programmes, of their strengths and weaknesses, and of plans for improvement.

In another study of 115 campus elementary laboratory schools, Land (1969) obtained data on the nature and quality of the "prestudent teaching laboratory experiences" they provided. Among other things he found that:

(a) While the schools provided adequate opportunities for students to observe and participate in the roles of the teacher in the classroom, in the school, and in the community, students did not participate sufficiently in the last two settings.

(b) There was little correlation between the laboratory experiences and either academic or professional college courses. The institutions generally used problems and achievements arising from the laboratory experiences as a source for related college seminars.

(c) In general, college lecturers did not undertake much of the responsibility and guidance of the laboratory experiences with the teacher. In half the institutions however, the evaluation of students involved both college and school staff.

(d) In providing laboratory experiences the schools did not consider the needs and abilities of particular students. In fact, the schools showed a disinclination to modify the nature or length of the experiences.

(e) The schools emphasized guiding students in their experiences through preobservation and postobservation discussion.

(f) The channels of communication and contacts between schools and colleges were generally inadequate.

(g) According to the schools' directors, the major strength of the experiences offered was the opportunity to have individual contact with pupils; and the major weakness, the provision of an insufficient number of experiences.

Like other investigators, Land recommended greater coordination between college courses and the work of laboratory schools, and closer collaboration between college and school staff in planning, supervising, and evaluating both the activities of students and the laboratory-experience programme as a whole.

While a number of investigations like the ones above were taking place, proponents of laboratory schools began to advocate how these schools could have new and important emphases. For example, Rogers (1952) suggested that the campus laboratory school might play a central role in connection with child-development programmes in teacher education. In outlining a model programme in which student teachers observed and grew to relate to and understand children, she stressed two principles—(a) that "theory should be used to explain the behavior of children, and children not be used merely to illustrate points of theory", and (b) that the "course should be of the laboratory type, with the campus school as focus. The classroom is the conference room where students learn to interpret what they see in the laboratory" (p. 233). Features of the course included cooperative planning of an integrated programme by lecturers and teachers; observing, meeting, and having active dealings with children both in-school and out-of-school; campus school children visiting college classes; teachers acting as consultants in college classes; the flexibility of the programme to provide for both planned and incidental observations; and "growth studies" of selected children over a sustained period. Thomas (1956) proposed that laboratory schools should play an important part in studying and evaluating innovative educational practices which could feed directly into teacher education programmes and into other schools. He did not believe, however, that laboratory schools having involvement in teacher preparation could satisfactorily carry out extensive, basic research on teaching and learning. They should concentrate rather on being centres of innovation in which promising practices could be selectively introduced, appraised, and perhaps adopted as an integral part of the ongoing programme of the school.

3. Present State and Future Prospects of Laboratory Schools

Since the early 1970s, the number of laboratory schools has continued to decline sharply as they have failed to surmount problems faced. Studies of contemporary laboratory schools have revealed the nature of their difficulties many of which had existed almost from the schools' inception. Foremost among these difficulties were the following.

3.1 Programme Inadequacy

Many laboratory schools have failed to develop well-conceived aims appropriate to the needs of the teacher education institution and to translate these aims into balanced and articulated activities involving teachers, tertiary staff, student teachers, and pupils. Many schools, in fact, have simply been unable to sort out priorities among their functions, and, even when this has happened, to change sufficiently their existing programmes. McNabb's study (1973) of 68 laboratory schools still functioning at that time in the United States indicated that failure to develop relevant programmes or to change existing programmes were seen as major problems, second only to that of funding.

The question of whether the commonly recognized activities of laboratory schools are in fact compatible was raised by Shadick (1966). The diagram used by Shadick (see Fig. 1) illustrates that certain long-accepted functions of these schools may be counter-productive. With reference to this diagram, Shadick claims:

> The teaching of children is improved by all of the functions assumed by laboratory schools. Student teaching leads to conflict with all other service functions; when a classroom or a school becomes primarily concerned with student teaching, it is difficult to perform the other functions. The same is true of traditional research, although to a lesser degree, perhaps because a school is seldom utilized as fully by research as by student teaching. Observation, participation, demonstration, and experimentation tend to reinforce each other. (p. 204)

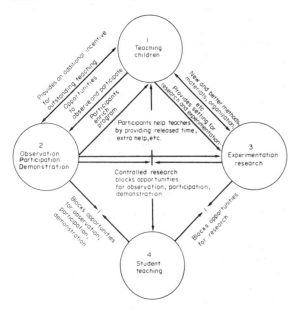

Figure 1
Compatibility of laboratory school activities

The issue of conflicting activities within the laboratory-school programme is linked closely with a second problem, the heavy demands made on the schools.

3.2 Excessive Demands

Throughout their history, excessive demands have been placed on laboratory schools. This has meant that some functions have been limited and others, such as research, have been crowded out altogether. Heavy involvement in student teaching and in the provision of special laboratory experiences led to criticisms and to transferring much of this activity to other schools. As Bryan (1961) has put it:

> It seems obvious . . . that no single school can possibly meet all the needs for laboratory experience on the part of a student body preparing to be teachers. On the one hand, the range of experiences needed is so wide as to require a variety of situations, and, on the other hand, the extent of activities will be so great in any curriculum which makes reasonable provision for laboratory experience as to swamp completely a single school. . . . A college which is providing this desirable and, in fact, necessary range of experiences must make a whole area within its reach a laboratory. (p. 272)

The great demands on laboratory schools have inevitably meant that staff not only must be able to work under considerable pressure, but also must have the ability and background to equip them to participate in the varied functions. Many laboratory-school staff have been unable to cope with this situation: recruiting suitable staff for laboratory schools has become an important issue.

3.3 Staffing

The need for the teacher education programme to be involved in the selection of laboratory-schools staff has been seen as highly desirable. Bryan (1961), for instance, regarded this as a major key to shaping the programme. Ohles (1962) has pointed out, however, that involvement in, or even control of, staff recruitment, does not guarantee that the institution will be able to attract the most suitable teachers. He reported that the additional responsibilities associated with the laboratory school, and the highly competitive salaries and promising opportunities in the public schools, may serve to discourage potential applicants. Whereas the laboratory school may once have been seen by teachers as a stepping stone into the parent institution, either college or university (Ohles 1967), this was not necessarily the situation at that time.

Staffing arrangements and conditions in laboratory schools vary considerably. The majority of the laboratory schools included in the survey by McNabb (1973) had a regular full-time staff, supplemented by the use of some supporting staff from the related college or university. The laboratory schools associated with universities had a higher proportion of full-time staff than was the case with the laboratory schools linked with colleges. The staff of the university laboratory schools was reported by McNabb to be in a vastly superior position with respect to tenure, academic rank, and fringe benefits than are the staff of college laboratory schools. While all of these benefits were enjoyed by staff of the state university laboratory schools, only 50 percent of the full-time faculty at state teachers' college laboratory schools held academic rank, 17 percent had tenure, and only 33 percent stated that they received fringe benefits of the kind shared by faculty members of the associated institution. No part-time staff at either state university or college laboratory schools received any special considerations.

3.4 Pupils at Laboratory Schools

A criticism commonly levelled at the laboratory school as a training ground for student teachers has been that it is nonrepresentative of the schools in which the student will later teach. It should be noted that the first criterion considered in many such schools when enrolling pupils has been whether the child has a parent as a member of staff of either the school or faculty (McNabb 1973). Another query often raised has been whether research carried out in these schools is relevant to other schools which are more heterogeneous in race, socioeconomic considerations, and abilities.

As mentioned by Hunter (1970), a research and experimental emphasis within the laboratory school may mean that at any particular time pupils may not have undergone equivalent experiences to children at a public school. With a carefully organized programme accompanied by systematic record-keeping, children who complete their schooling at the laboratory school should, however, not be at any disadvantage; indeed they may, in the long term, be considerably advantaged.

3.5 Finance

The greater proportion of laboratory schools at public-supported teacher education institutions have received at least 80 percent of their operating revenue from the institution to which they were affiliated (McNabb 1973). Many, at the time of the survey, were actively exploring additional sources of funding. McNabb also made reference to a survey conducted in 1969, which revealed that inadequate financial support from the associated teacher education institution and the state was the major reason given for the closing of 36 laboratory schools in the United States between 1964 and 1969.

That expense, as an argument against laboratory schools, may sometimes be magnified out of due proportion, was suggested by Bryan (1961) when he pointed out that the real cost of such a school should be viewed only as the additional expense over and above that of maintaining an equivalent public school. He further suggested that perhaps a laboratory school is a facility that teacher education cannot afford to be without. The need for a revised system of funding was implied. If present funding arrangements persist, however, in view of competing demands within the college or university, the future of the remaining laboratory schools would seem most uncertain—unless they are clearly providing a service of a kind that cannot be readily carried out in public schools.

Accompanying analyses of problems facing existing laboratory schools, there have been proposals for changing and improving the operation of these schools if they are to survive in the future. McNabb's study (1973) revealed that between 1964 and 1972 as many as 61 public-supported laboratory schools were closed leaving only 68. Since then many of these have closed. As pointed out, a major factor contributing to their closure was an inability to modify their functions. If laboratory schools are to continue to operate, they must, according to McNabb, justify their existence in terms of functions that cannot be just as readily performed in other public schools. Hunter (1970) has also recognized that laboratory schools must change their functions, believing that if this can be achieved there is reason to be optimistic concerning their future. She claimed:

> For this potential to be released, however, the laboratory school must shed its role as a demonstration and training installation inducting novitiates into accepted and traditional practice. It must become a center for inquiry, an essential component of the educational design to produce new theory, to translate that theory into generalizable practice, to disseminate that knowledge and practice into the mainstream of American education, and to develop vigorous leaders. (p. 14)

In suggesting that a prime function of the laboratory school of the future should be that of "research, experimentation and inquiry", Hunter was stating a viewpoint that has had earlier and subsequent supporters.

Hunter suggested that, at a time when the laboratory school was being called upon to justify its existence, it would be in its own interest to give special attention to the dissemination of research findings. She believed that if the laboratory school accepts a responsibility to influence the school system at large, then it will use a variety of media appropriate to a wide audience to get its message across.

The development of programmes appropriate for the training of potential teachers of clinical practice was seen by Hunter as a significant role of the future laboratory school. It would include the specification of relevant competencies and the determination of appropriate learning experiences such as developing the ability to interpret the curriculum and philosophy of the school to parents and other community groups, or introducing ways of improving instruction within a school.

The kinds of activity outlined above would appear to be very different from those common in many currently operating laboratory schools. Exposure to the research and innovation activities of the laboratory school should, in the opinion of Hunter, be an integral part of the teacher preparation programme. Through contact with the laboratory school the students' professional orientation will be enhanced as they are confronted with real educational problems submitted to critical and rigorous inquiry.

The new laboratory-school emphases proposed by Hunter were in fact substantially in evidence at the University Elementary School, of which she was principal, at the University of California, Los Angeles (Hunter 1971, 1974). The spirit of that school's work is typified in her statement that:

> Education today needs practical, effective answers to a number of critical problems. A laboratory school exists to generate, investigate, field-test, and demonstrate innovative, productive solutions. It also explores and develops those educational possibilities not yet refined to the point of systematic evaluation. (Hunter 1971 p. 1)

In the light of her experience, Hunter believed that the basic requirements for the sound functioning of a laboratory school are: (a) the recognition of appropriate roles; (b) the development of interrelationships; (c) the appointment of appropriate staff; (d) a heterogeneous pupil intake; and (e) provision of adequate facilities and budget. As some of these factors have been considered in relation to problems facing such schools, they will here need little expansion. The recognition of appropriate roles [requirement (a) above] has already been discussed.

(b) *Interrelationships*. Clearly, as suggested by Hunter, a laboratory school will only operate effectively if channels of communication are well-established and kept open. Hunter referred to the need for closely developed relationships with both the school of education, other university departments, and with the wider educational community. If the laboratory-school programme is to be well-integrated with that of the school of education, there must be close liaison between the staff of the two institutions at all levels. Hunter stated that:

To achieve this liaison, conscious and explicit avenues of communication and collaborative efforts are essential so that areas of mutual concern can be identified and specialists will supplement and complement each other. A professor should find advice and assistance for his research from the staff of the laboratory school as well as experimental subjects. In turn, laboratory staff should find rigorous assistance with their clinical questions from the theoreticians. Undergraduate, graduate, doctoral, and post-doctoral students should have the availability of a laboratory school as one of the richest resources in their inquiry and education. (p. 17)

The other academic departments within the university or college should be encouraged to explore the ways in which the laboratory school may be of benefit to them. These departments would certainly be able to assist the school with educational resources and the staff with specialized advice within their subject area. The laboratory school has a responsibility to extend its influence outside the campus through interchanges of ideas with other laboratory schools, and by acting as a resource to public schools, not only by way of programmes, but by providing a consultative service.

(c) *Appropriate staffing.* The kind of staff considered most appropriate to the laboratory school would depend upon what one conceives the appropriate role of the school to be, and upon the nature of the school's relationship to the college or university. Hunter suggested, however, that some laboratory staff positions be offered to teachers from the public schools for a limited period of, say, one or two years. These teachers would, she contended, bring with them the flavour of the "real world" and, on return to the public schools, would be able to assume leadership roles.

In keeping with the experimental function of the laboratory school, there would often be student teachers on the staff to allow the investigation and evaluation of training programmes which may be intended for use elsewhere. In marked contrast to the position in many former laboratory schools, the student teachers would not be in the school for the purpose of the traditional teaching practice.

(d) *Heterogeneous pupil intake.* As has been already noted, a frequent criticism made of laboratory schools has been that of the atypical nature of the pupil intake and the consequent lack of generalizability of research findings to other school populations. The pupils in many laboratory schools have often come from the one socioeconomic area and have included a high proportion of children belonging to academic staff of the university or college. Hunter claimed that "admittance procedures which guarantee heterogeneity and are impervious to political or economic pressures must be determined" (p. 16). She believed that it was essential that parents are made fully aware of the research orientation of the school and have the opportunity to send their children elsewhere if so desired. Parents should realize that the curriculum of the school at any point of time will differ from that of the normal school and that it would be only at the time of graduation that they could expect their child to have met usual school requirements.

(e) *Adequate facilities and budget.* The unusual nature of the laboratory-school programme necessitates a generous allocation of funds for personnel, facilities, and space additional to the requirements of the normal school. Unless funds are forthcoming in keeping with the importance of the school's unique function, and unless there is adequate flexibility in funding and facilities, the laboratory school will be unable to realize its potential.

4. Conclusion

The current moves by teacher education institutions to form new and close cooperative relationships with schools in developing their training programmes can only be applauded. Purposeful experiences in schools are potentially the most powerful intervention in a teacher's professional preparation. To optimize the strength and nature of this intervention the abundant cooperation of schools is necessary. However, the history of the American laboratory schools underlines the need for cooperating schools not to attempt too much. While each of the past functions of laboratory schools is in itself very important, various schools must give major emphasis only to a selection and carry these out well: some schools might emphasize regular student teaching, others sequenced professional experiences, others innovation and research, others observation, others training clinical lecturers and supervisors. At the same time, nevertheless, no school should be confined to only one programme activity. Furthermore, it would be highly desirable for all schools associated with the teacher education institution to be informed about and be encouraged to contribute to the activities of the others. Such an association of cooperating schools would do much not only to enhance preservice teacher education. It would contribute to the professional development of all involved. Finally, it must be stressed that cooperation cannot be one-way. Tertiary institutions must contribute to cooperative school programmes just as much as schools. A true partnership between tertiary institutions and schools will involve a ready sharing of both staff and resources. It will cost money; but the money will be well-spent.

See also: Student (Practice) Teaching; Supervision of the Practicum

Bibliography

Ashmore H L 1951 An evaluation of state-supported campus laboratory schools in selected southeastern schools. *Educ. Admin. Supervis.* 37: 80–97

Blair L C et al. 1958 *The Purposes, Functions and Uniqueness of the College-controlled Laboratory School.* Bulletin of

Association for Student Teaching No. 9, Loch Haven, Pennsylvania

Bryan R C 1961 The vital role of the campus school. *J. Teach. Educ.* 12: 275–81

Chittenden M D 1925 The Oswego Normal and Training School. *Educ. Admin. Supervis.* 11: 325–32

Dawson M A 1937 Current practices in participation. *Educ. Admin. Supervis.* 294–306

Findlay J J 1908 The study of curricula and method. *Demonstr. Sch. Rec.* 1: 30–41

Fristoe D 1942 Early beginning of laboratory schools. *Educ. Admin. Supervis.* 28: 219–32

Hayes D T, Campbell E W 1948 Real education: Students and staff plan democratic learning experiences in a summer demonstration school. *Educ. Admin. Supervis.* 34: 1–24

Hilsinger R, Shantz B 1973 *Reallocating Teacher Education Resources in the Temple-Philadelphia Portal Schools.* College of Education, Temple University, Philadelphia, Pennsylvania

Hunter M 1970 Expanding roles of laboratory schools. *Phi Delta Kappan* 52: 14–19

Hunter M 1971 Why is a laboratory school? *Instructor* 80: 58–60

Hunter M 1974 *A Decade at the University Elementary School.* UCLA, Los Angeles, California

Lamb L 1961 Planning closed circuit television systems for laboratory schools for colleges of teacher education (Doctoral Dissertation, University of Missouri, 1961) *Dissertation Abstracts International* 1961 21

Lamb P M 1962 The laboratory school: An historical perspective. *J. Educ. Res.* 56(2): 107–09

Land E 1969 The nature and quality of pre-student teaching laboratory experiences in campus elementary laboratory schools affiliated with state colleges and universities (Unpublished doctoral dissertation, University of Virginia)

McNabb D 1973 An analysis of financial support patterns, staff relationships and problems which led to the closing of laboratory schools at public-supported teacher education institutions between 1964 and 1972. ERIC Document No. ED 26322

Mayhew K C, Edwards A C 1939 *The Dewey School: The Laboratory School of the University of Chicago, 1896–1903.* Appleton-Century, New York

Ohles J F 1962 The laboratory school. *Educ. Digest.* 27: 27–29

Ohles J F 1967 Is the laboratory school worth saving? *Educ. Digest.* 33: 43–45

Rogers D 1952 The role of the campus school in the child development program. *Educ. Admin. Supervis.* 38: 229–34

Russell J E 1902 The Speyer School. *Teacher. Coll. Rec.* 3: 1–5

Sale L 1967 An analysis of the functions of campus elementary laboratory schools affiliated with state colleges and universities (Doctoral dissertation, Indiana University) *Dissertation Abstracts International* 1968 28: 2127A–2128A (University Microfilms No. 67–16, 429)

Shadick R 1966 The interrelationships of the role of a laboratory school. *J. Teach. Educ.* 17: 198–204

Thomas G G 1956 Role of the laboratory school in introducing educational practices. *Educ. Leadership* 13: 407–11

Tyler R W 1940 The work of the summer demonstration schools. *Elem. Sch. J.* 41: 6–7

White N D 1964 The status and potential of college laboratory schools (Doctoral dissertation, George Peabody College for Teachers) *Dissertation Abstracts International* 1965 26: 896–897 (University Microfilms No. 65–353)

Yearbook of the American Association of Teachers Colleges 1926

Technical Skills of Teaching

M. J. Dunkin

Technical skills of teaching are specific aspects of teaching behaviour that are considered to be particularly effective in facilitating desired learnings in students. The concept of specific teaching skills seems first to have been implemented in teacher education in the microteaching programme at Stanford University in the early 1960s. With the subsequent widespread acceptance of microteaching as a technique for training teachers, the concept of technical skills of teaching became well-known (see *Microteaching: Conceptual and Theoretical Bases*; *Microteaching: Effectiveness*). In time the concept became an important component of competency-based teacher education and even of competency-based teacher certification (see *Competency-based Teacher Education*) (Coker et al. 1980).

This article presents some of the technical skills of teaching that have been included in teacher education programmes, describes ways in which they have been used, discusses evidence concerning their validity, and presents criticisms made of their use, as well as advantages associated with them.

1. The Nature of Technical Skills of Teaching

According to Allen and Ryan (1969) the first technical skill used in the microteaching clinic at Stanford University was "how to begin a lesson". Subsequently such skills as achieving "closure", providing "frame of reference", and probing student responses were added until a list was developed which included the following skills:

(a) Stimulus variation: using stimulating material and variations in movement, gestures, interaction techniques, and sensory channels in order to alleviate boredom and inattentiveness.

(b) Set induction: preparing students for a lesson by clarifying its goals, relating it to students' prior knowledge and skills, through using analogies, demonstrations, and posing stimulating problems.

(c) Closure: assisting students to establish links between new and past knowledge by reviewing and applying material to familiar and new examples, cases, and situations.

(d) Silence and nonverbal cues: reducing reliance on teacher talk by encouraging teachers in the proper use of pauses and in the effective use of facial expressions, body movement, head movement, and gestures.

(e) Reinforcing student participation: encouraging students to respond through the use of praise and acceptance as well as nonverbal cues such as nodding and smiling.

(f) Fluency in asking questions: eliminating unnecessary hesitations and repetitions of questions.

(g) Probing questions: skill in framing questions which lead students to elaborate on, or raise the level of, their responses.

(h) Higher order questions: questions which elicit responses that require higher intellectual levels from students instead of responses that involve only fact stating or descriptions.

(i) Divergent questions: questions which elicit student responses that are unconventional, imaginative, and cannot be judged simply to be correct or incorrect.

Other skills to become incorporated in the Stanford list were "recognizing attending behavior", "illustrating and use of examples", "lecturing", "planned repetition", and "completeness of communication" (Allen and Ryan 1969 p. 15).

As an indication of the widespread adoption of the concept of technical skills of teaching, institutions as far apart as the University of Stirling in Scotland and the University of Sydney in Australia implemented teacher education programmes incorporating them.

An Australian team of authors (Turney et al. 1973a) developed a system for classifying teaching skills under which seven categories emerged. These were:

(a) Motivational skills, including reinforcing student behaviour, varying the stimulus, set induction, encouraging student involvement, accepting and supporting student feelings, displaying warmth and enthusiasm, and recognizing and meeting students' needs.

(b) Presentation and communication skills, including explaining, dramatizing, reading, using audiovisual aids, closure, using silence, encouraging student feedback, clarity, expressiveness, pacing, and planned repetition.

(c) Questioning skills, including refocusing and redirecting, probing, high-level questions, convergent and divergent questions, stimulating student initiative.

(d) Skills of small group and individual instruction, such as organizing small group work, developing independent learning, counselling, encouraging cooperative activity and student to student interaction (see *Small Group Methods*).

(e) Developing student thinking, such as fostering inquiry learning, guiding discovery, developing concepts, using simulation, role playing and gaming to stimulate thought, developing student problem-solving skills, encouraging students to evaluate and make judgments, and developing critical thinking.

(f) Evaluative skills, including recognizing and assessing student progress, diagnosing learning difficulties, providing remedial techniques, encouraging self-evaluation, and handling evaluative discussion.

(g) Classroom management and discipline, including recognizing attending and nonattending behaviour, supervising class group work, encouraging task-oriented behaviour, giving directions, and coping with multiple issues (see *Classroom Management*).

Turney et al. (1973a) provided a useful list of references relevant to each broad category of skills but pointed out that there were some difficulties in documenting evidence of the validity of the specific skills nominated.

Similar selections of technical skills of teaching have been employed in microteaching and minicourse programmes in many different countries (see *Minicourses*). Many of these became incorporated in the movement known as "performance-based" or "competency-based" teacher education.

2. Uses of the Technical Skills

The usefulness of the concept of technical skills of teaching was well-demonstrated in the typical microteaching programme of the 1960s and 1970s. One of the specific skills listed above would become the focus for a particular cycle of microteaching. The skill would be introduced in two main ways. Printed materials containing verbal descriptions and instances of the skill, together with a rationale for its use and, where possible, research evidence related to it, would be read and discussed. Some simple, usually verbal, assignments involving identifying, classifying, and generating instances of the skill would be completed. Also, audiovisual demonstrations, or models, of the skill would be supplied. Students would view or listen to the model once or twice and then prepare a short, possibly five minute, lesson designed to provide practice in performing the skill. The prepared lesson would be delivered and perhaps recorded on audio tape or video tape. After the lesson, the record would be analysed or, if the lesson was not recorded, a supervisor or group of peers would provide feedback to the student teacher. Such analysis, feedback, and ensuing discussion were supposed to be focused on the particular skill rather than on other aspects of the lesson. The student teacher might then enter an extended phase of the micro-teaching cycle and prepare and deliver another lesson in the light of comments on the first.

Used in the above way, the technical skills of the teaching approach involved both conceptual and theoretical, as well as the behavioural development of student teachers, though the emphasis was on the latter. In other cases, focus was placed more on the cognitive than the performative, and skills of conceptualizing, analysing, and hypothesizing were emphasized.

If teaching could be broken down into specific skills or competencies, such skills or competencies could become the basis not only of training programmes but also of attempts to evaluate teaching effectiveness. In some states of the United States competency-based notions of teaching effectiveness became the basis for decisions concerning the hiring, granting tenure to, promoting, and dismissing of teachers. Furthermore, there has been legislation in at least one state (Georgia) requiring that teachers satisfy criteria in the form of specifically defined teaching skills before they are granted certification as teachers.

Whether or not the concept of technical skills of teaching is appropriate for use in the above ways depends greatly upon the validity of the skills themselves. This issue is discussed in Sect. 3.

3. Validity of Technical Skills of Teaching

Dunkin (1976) argued that two criteria should be applied in judging the validity of technical skills of teaching. The first was the extent to which the specific aspect of teaching behaviour was distinct from other aspects of teaching. Observers should be able to agree on what constitutes the nature of the skill and should be able to identify it when it occurs. The second criterion was the extent to which the skills had been shown to enhance student learning.

In his review of lists of technical skills of teaching, Dunkin (1976) found cause for optimism that specific classroom behaviours commonly associated with teaching skills could be distinguished reliably by trained observers. However, he pointed out that there were conceptual problems with some attempts to define teaching skills. Instances were cited where items in lists of teaching skills varied considerably in level of specificity. For example, "giving reinforcement to student behaviour", is a more specific behaviour than "guiding student learning", and "using probing questions" is more specific than "individualizing instruction". Some so-called teaching skills were so vaguely described that they appeared more like slogans or were so general as to be whole philosophies rather than

specific skills. Some attempts to define teaching skills were also found not to refer to teaching behaviour as such, but to student learning, and were more in the form of desired outcomes of teaching than specific teaching behaviours. One example of this was "elicit children's use of new language" included in the Far West Laboratory's Minicourse 2 (Borg et al. 1970).

In terms of evidence that specific teaching behaviours had been found consistently associated with desired outcomes in students, Dunkin found much less support for technical skills of teaching. He concluded:

> First, there seems to be consensus among those who have reviewed research related to the identification of teaching skills that we have very little empirical knowledge about their nature and their effects as yet. There is some disagreement as to whether the research enterprise is worth pursuing further, but most of the reviewers are optimistic, given more research that is either more rigorously designed in traditional ways, or that throws off the bounds of the traditional assumptions and seeks designs and methodologies that better suit the nature of the data. In any case, at this point in time there is far from an adequate empirical basis for using the technical skills approach in teacher education. (p. 137)

While more recent reviewers would probably claim that rapid progress has been made in identifying teaching skills (see *Direct Instruction*) since Dunkin reached his conclusion, it is probably still the case that attempts to specify technical skills of teaching rely more on impressionistic evidence from professional experience than upon systematically obtained evidence from empirical research.

4. Criticisms of the Technical Skills Approach

Possibly the main criticism has been that the technical skills approach to teaching leads to the mechanization of the teaching–learning process such that teachers are encouraged to follow over-simplified prescriptions, or recipes, that ignore variations in contexts and individual differences in both teachers and students. For example, it has been argued that some approaches to the training of student teachers assume that such skills as higher level questioning should be implemented as much as possible so that the elimination of demands for factual and descriptive information in the classroom would eventuate, to the detriment of the students. Such assumptions about the absolute validity of some teaching skills are often not recognized by supporters and users of the approach. Given the inevitable constraints upon such large scale implementation of any one teaching behaviour under normal classroom conditions, such a risk is probably negligible.

Another related criticism is that the technical skills of teaching approaches emphasize the behavioural aspects of teaching to the detriment of the intellectual and creative aspects. It has been said that training teachers in the performance of particular categories of teaching behaviour neglects the conceptual, theoretical, and decision-making roles of the teacher and ignores the imaginative domain which so often is thought to distinguish the gifted teacher from the mediocre.

Defenders of the approach argue that technical skills of teaching are best incorporated into teacher education programmes not merely as recipes for action but as parts of behavioural repertoires which heighten teachers' capacities to select and implement teaching strategies they might choose on the basis of their theoretical training and creative dispositions. If teachers judge wisely that a certain category of teaching behaviour is desirable to achieve particular objectives for particular students under particular conditions then it is argued teachers need to have at their disposal those teaching skills.

5. Conclusion

On the basis of the latter argument, the definition of technical skills of teaching has been broadened in more recent years to include diagnostic, analytic, and hypothesizing skills rather than the more strictly observable behavioural skills. Teachers, it has been argued, need to be trained in criteria for assessing student needs, in monitoring their own teaching behaviour, in analysing the requirements of subject matter and educational objectives, and in recognizing alternative types of teaching strategies to achieve them. The emphasis has tended to move more towards teachers' powers of conceptualizing, hypothesizing, and synthesizing than to the acquisition and performance of discrete teaching behaviours thought independently to be technical skills of teaching.

The concept of technical skills of teaching has encouraged teachers and teacher educators to adopt an analytic approach to teaching effectiveness. In spite of the dangers of dehumanization and prescriptiveness associated with the approach, it has operated to encourage extensions of behavioural repertoires and, in its more recent forms, has encouraged conceptual sophistication and professional awareness on the part of teachers.

There are, however, still problems regarding the validity of many of the specific teaching skills included in teacher education programmes and suggested as criteria for making judgments about teachers.

See also: Competency-based Teacher Education; Microteaching: Conceptual and Theoretical Bases; Microteaching: Modelling; Minicourses; Microteaching: Feedback; Microteaching: Effectiveness; Direct Instruction

Bibliography

Allen D, Ryan K 1969 *Microteaching*. Addison-Wesley, Reading, Massachusetts
Borg W R, Kelley M L, Langer P, Gall M 1970 *The Mini Course: A Microteaching Approach to Teacher Education*. Far West Laboratory for Educational Research and Development, Berkeley, California
Coker H, Medley D M, Soar R S 1980 How valid are expert opinions about effective teaching? *Phi Delta Kappan* 62: 131–34, 149
Dunkin M J 1976 Towards taking some of the fun out of the technical skills approach to teacher effectiveness. *South Pac. J. Teach. Educ.* 4(2): 131–39
Turney C, Cairns L 1976 *Classroom Management and Discipline*. Sydney University Press, Sydney
Turney C, Renshaw P D, Sinclair K E 1977 *Guiding Discovery Learning and Fostering Creativity*. Sydney University Press, Sydney
Turney C, Clift J C, Dunkin M J, Traill R D 1973a *Microteaching: Research, Theory and Practice: An Innovation in Teacher Education Especially as it Relates to the Australian Context*. Sydney University Press, Sydney
Turney C, Cairns L G, Williams G, Hatton N, Owens L C 1973b *Reinforcement, Basic Questioning, Variability*. Sydney University Press, Sydney
Turney C, Owens L C, Hatton N, Williams G, Cairns L G 1975 *Explaining, Introductory Procedures and Closure, Advanced Questioning*. Sydney University Press, Sydney
Turney C, Thew D, Owens L, Hatton N, Cairns L G 1976 *Guiding Small Group Discussion, Small Group Teaching and Individualizing Instruction*. Sydney University Press, Sydney

Lesson Analysis

E. C. Wragg

Some kind of systematic analysis of what actually happens in a teacher's own or another teacher's lessons would seem to be a prerequisite for any training programme for new teachers, and a useful component of certain inservice courses for the more experienced. A scrutiny of teacher education since the late nineteenth century shows that in some courses the development of teaching skills through the analysis of classroom processes has been a central component, and in others this approach has hardly been used at all.

In present-day teacher-training programmes, lesson analysis takes several forms. Trainees may analyse transcripts of someone else's lessons to see how that teacher explains new concepts or deals with pupils' questions. Alternatively they may watch a videotape of a lesson, either taught by another teacher or themselves. Analysis might take the form of some systematic assigning of what takes place to predetermined categories such as "teacher asks data recall question" or "pupil raises hand to answer", or might be more informal and less structured.

In some training programmes, novice or experienced teachers work in pairs to analyse each other's lessons, either in the natural setting of a school classroom, or in a specially constructed video classroom with portable television cameras for subsequent playback.

1. Historical Background

There is nothing new about training teachers to analyse their own or other people's lessons. It is a well-established tradition that novices can learn from experienced teachers thought to be especially competent, and for 100s of years and in many cultures those responsible for training the next generation of teachers have attempted to analyse the lessons of the successful.

Some of the best-known teachers of teachers analysed and wrote about their *own* teaching for their followers. Confucius, for example, writing in the *Analects*, said, "I shall not teach until the pupils desire to know something, and I do not help unless the pupils really need my help. If out of the four corners of a subject I have dealt thoroughly with one corner and the pupils cannot then find out the other three for themselves, then I do not explain any more."

Well-known figures in Classical Greece and Rome, such as Cicero and Quintilian analysed teaching methodology in detail and then wrote about how lectures should be delivered or how children could learn to write by copying the styles of various writers being studied.

Sometimes the handbooks which were written as a result of rudimentary analysis of what seemed to be successful teaching became highly authoritative and were followed slavishly. The Chinese Classic Book of Rites (*Li Chi*) is a good example, with its assertion that, "The teacher reads out the principles and the pupils repeat them after him, echoing every intonation and stress, and this is continued until the pupils are word-perfect." The Jesuit teaching handbook *Ratio Studiorum* published in the sixteenth century had similar authority.

In more recent times David Stow, who founded the Glasgow Normal Seminary in the 1830s, developed the notion of the "gallery lesson", which was later copied all over Europe and elsewhere. A large room was divided into two, half of it set out as a classroom and the other half containing benches for observers. Four student teachers in succession would give 15 minute lessons which were analysed and subsequently criticized by fellow trainees, tutors, heads of model schools, and the rector of the Seminary. The analysis was unsystematic, but was based on Stow's own unique philosophy which required that pupils "picture out in words", and that teachers use simple terms "within the range of the pupils' requirements". The system eventually received some criticism because trainees quite literally "played to the gallery".

2. Subsequent Developments

A number of factors combined to make the analysis of lessons a more popular component of training courses in the 1970s and 1980s.

2.1 Reaction Against Overtheoretical Training

Fashions change in teacher training, sometimes quite rapidly. In response to some national report criticizing the poor level of education of teacher trainees there will probably follow a period when more emphasis is placed on trainees acquiring a sound knowledge of their subject. On the other hand, a subsequent report condemning training as overtheoretical may produce a shift towards more practical work. During the 1950s and 1960s teacher training lengthened in many countries. In England and Wales, for example, the standard concurrent course increased from two years to three years in the late 1950s, and for many students to four years in the 1960s when the B.Ed. degree was introduced. Inevitably much of the extra time was spent on studying traditional degree subjects to a high level, and even the subject "education" became largely a theoretical study of such foundation disciplines as sociology and psychology. Criticism of the excessively academic approach to teacher education and the neglect of practical issues was summarized by Flanders (1963):

> It is a serious indictment of the profession, however, to hear so many education instructors say that their students will appreciate what they are learning *after* they have had some practical teaching experience. What hurts is the obvious hypocrisy of making this statement and then giving a lecture on the importance of presenting material in such a way that the immediate needs and interests of the pupils are taken into consideration . . . with most present practices, the gorge between theory and practice grows deeper and wider, excavated by the very individuals who are pledged to fill it.

2.2 Influence of Classroom Interaction Research Techniques

Whereas prior to 1960 most research projects studying children's learning had concentrated on its relationship to background factors such as social class, intelligence, and attitudes, the volume of research into classroom processes grew substantially throughout the 1960s and 1970s.

Research was of several kinds. Many of the best-known and most widely publicized studies used systematic analysis of classroom events, frequently involving a specially devised category system. The principles were based on positivist psychometric principles, and the investigator tallied the occurrence of events on a special data sheet under headings like "pedagogical moves" (Bellack et al. 1966) which included "directly elicits verbal, physical, or mental response", or "indirect influence" (Flanders 1965) with categories such as "teacher clarifying, building, or developing ideas suggested by a student". It soon became very difficult even to summarize the vast number of studies of this kind in a single volume, though Dunkin and Biddle (1974) produced one comprehensive survey.

Alongside this kind of research there emerged another style based on the social anthropological tradition of taking detailed field notes, and then inter-

Table 1
Categories for the Flanders system of interaction analysis

Teacher talk	Indirect influence	(1) Accepts feeling: accepts and clarifies the feeling tone of the students in a nonthreatening manner. Feelings may be positive or negative. Predicting or recalling feelings are included
		(2) Praises or encourages: praises or encourages student action or behaviour. Jokes that release tension, not at the expense of another individual, nodding head or saying "um hm?" or "go on" are included
		(3) Accepts or uses ideas of student: clarifying, building, or developing ideas suggested by a student. As a teacher brings more of his own ideas into play, shift to category (5)
		(4) Asks questions: asking a question about content or procedure with the intent that a student answer
	Direct influence	(5) Lecturing: giving facts or opinions about content or procedure; expressing his own ideas, asking rhetorical questions
		(6) Giving directions: directions, commands, or orders to which a student is expected to comply
		(7) Criticizing or justifying authority: statements intended to change student behaviour from nonacceptable to acceptable pattern; bawling someone out; stating why the teacher is doing what he is doing; extreme self-reference
Student talk		(8) Student talk—response: a student makes a predictable response to teacher. Teacher initiates the contact or solicits student statement and sets limits to what the student says
		(9) Student talk—initiation: talk by students which they initiate. Unpredictable statements in response to teacher. Shift from (8) to (9) as student introduces own ideas
		(10) Silence or confusion: pauses, short periods of silence and periods of confusion in which communication cannot be understood by the observer

viewing participants to discover the meanings and intentions underlying their actions. Investigators became immersed in the life of the school and have directed their attention to a wide range of topics such as lessons in infant schools, open plan schools, or teachers changing from homogeneous groups to mixed ability classes.

One direct consequence of analysis by researchers using a variety of methodological approaches was that teacher trainers found they could readily use or modify the techniques which had been developed, and apply them with novice or experienced teachers. Thus many training programmes began to train students to apply a number of systematic approaches to lesson analysis which in the first instance had been used in a well-publicized research report.

The debate about strengths and weaknesses of different styles of classroom interaction research, however, also affects teacher training. Critics of systematic category analysis and quantitative methods argue that such approaches oversimplify human communication by concentrating on frequency of occurrence rather than teachers' or pupils' reasons for behaving in a particular way. Critics of case study, qualitative, and ethnographic research, on the other hand, accuse investigators of generalizing from the specific, or using phrases beginning "many teachers . . ." or "most pupils . . ." without rigorously collected evidence to support such assertions. Teacher trainers, recognizing there is no single approved form of lesson analysis, may, therefore, deliberately opt for a mixture of approaches when training new or experienced teachers.

Another relevant issue in classroom research has been whether to use what have been called high- or low-inference measures, depending on the extent to which the analyst must make a personal judgment. Teacher qualities such as "warmth", "enthusiasm", or "clarity" have often been rated on five- or seven-point bipolar scales, and have been regarded as high-inference measures:

well-organized	1	2	3	4	5	6	7	slipshod
warm	1	2	3	4	5	6	7	aloof
stimulating	1	2	3	4	5	6	7	dull

Categories which describe specific acts of behaviour, such as "pupil raises hand", "teacher moves towards pupil", or "teacher reprimands pupil" and are usually tallied on a yes/no or frequency basis, are referred to as low-inference measures.

Some classroom interaction research has been very controversial and attracted worldwide interest. The research by Bennett (1976), which argued that teachers who taught "formally" obtained better results in basic primary-school subjects than teachers who taught "informally", produced not only international debate about teaching styles, but replication studies (Galton and Simon 1980, Galton et al. 1980), as well as articles showing how, even if one disagreed with Bennett's findings, his procedures could be used to train teachers to analyse their own lessons (Wragg 1976b).

2.3 Development of Educational Technology

The single greatest technological influence in the use of lesson analysis has undoubtedly been the advent of portable television cameras. Prior to 1965, teacher trainers wishing to assemble records of lessons for analysis were dependent on audiotape recorders, which, unfortunately, were prone to pick up a great deal of classroom background noise and were often therefore difficult to decipher, or else had to rely on film, slides, or transcripts, with the inevitable delay until the films were developed or the tapes transcribed, and the high cost of editing film and securing good lip synchronization.

Though closed-circuit television was initially costly, unreliable, and bulky, by the 1970s good quality portable black and white, and later colour cameras and recorders, were developed at relatively low cost. This meant that teacher trainers could make a video of either an experienced teacher's lesson or of one of their own student teachers, and the playback and analysis phase could be scheduled immediately afterwards whilst fresh in the memory of the participants. The immediacy of feedback and the lack of elaborate lighting served to make the experience a realistic rather than a laboratory one.

Although some institutions set up lesson analysis within an elaborate microteaching format, most did it much more informally either in the field or in special studios inside the training institution made to resemble a normal school classroom. Useful details of such a studio were produced after an international conference (UNESCO 1972) showing how video classrooms of varying degrees of complexity and costliness could be established.

A second less spectacular development, that of the calculator and microcomputer, offered high-speed data-processing facilities for those making use of quantitative methods of analysing lessons and not wishing to wait a lengthy time for results to be tabulated and displayed. Smidchens and Roth (1968) developed a computer facility for instant tabulation of Flanders category data, so that teachers could see an analysis of their lessons immediately after, or even, via a screen at the back of the class, a running record during their lesson.

3. The Application of Lesson Analysis Techniques

Contemporary use of lesson analysis differs from the historical examples given above in a number of respects.

First of all there is no longer the consensus there once was about what constitutes effective teaching. In nineteenth-century Europe and North America teacher education institutions were called "normal schools", on the grounds that there was some single "norm" or commonly approved ideal style of teaching, and all newcomers were to be honed as closely as possible to this paragon ideal. The system led Charles Dickens to say of Mr. M'Choakumchild, "He and some one hundred and forty schoolmasters had been lately turned at the same time in the same factory, on the same principles, like so many pianoforte legs . . . ."

Teacher effectiveness research in the 1950s and beyond showed that there were, in pluralist societies, many approved styles of teaching. One summary of a substantial number of American studies (Barr 1961) concluded, "Some teachers were preferred by administrators, some were liked by the pupils, and some taught in classes where there were substantial pupil gains, and generally speaking these were not the same teachers." Thus the search for the philosopher's stone, the single omnipurpose good teacher stereotype, had to be abandoned. Instead, attention turned to what kinds of teacher behaviour led to what outcome in what situation. Trainees would have to learn to analyse lessons, not to discover some elusive "successful" style, but rather to assemble information on which to base their own decisions about how to teach, albeit guided by tutors and such research findings as existed.

3.1 Transcript Analysis

One common form of analysis is based on transcripts of lessons. The tutor provides typescripts of whole lessons or extracts. Trainees then analyse specific aspects such as the teacher's use of questions, explanation of new concepts, pupils' replies, or else trace self-contained episodes through from inception to termination. Lesson transcript analysis is time-consuming, but permits much more detailed analysis of the linguistic aspects of classroom transactions than other approaches.

A favoured approach is to concentrate on language specific to the subject being taught, for example when a physics teacher introduces the notion of one measure being "inversely proportional" to something else, or when pupils, by their answers, reveal understanding or misunderstanding of the teacher's language. Some of the questions involved in this kind of analysis have been posed by Edwards (1976):

> If a subject register *is* apparent, are pupils expected to use it, or just understand it; . . . Do they learn it by imitation, or by coping with subject-specific tasks . . . .. How does the teacher "mediate" between the language of his pupils, and that which he considers appropriate to his subject?

One of the most influential writers in this field is Barnes (1976) who cited transcripts from various lessons in secondary-school subjects, and then showed how teachers did or did not present specialist terms such as "chromatography" in science, or "city states" in history, depending on, among other factors, whether they assumed such vocabulary to be of sufficiently wide usage not to need explanation. The lesson transcripts cited and analysed by Barnes have been widely used in teacher-training programmes. Barnes has some particularly useful insights into lessons which involve pupils working in small groups, and the transcript in Table 2 gives an example from a group of pupils working on the topic "air pressure" with Barnes' own commentary alongside.

Because of the length of time needed to transcribe lessons, trainees have usually analysed material such as that produced by Barnes rather than transcripts of their own lessons, though it is not unknown for student teachers to transcribe and analyse their own lessons.

3.2 Video Analysis

The availability of easily used cassette videorecorders and portable cameras mentioned above has led to this being a very common form of lesson analysis. Providing many more cues than poor quality noisy sound tape-recordings it permits both verbal and nonverbal behaviour to be studied.

Many training institutions have assembled "clips" from different videorecordings which, because of the ease of editing, can easily be woven together around a single theme. Thus a tutor interested in how teachers handle mixed-ability classes might cull his or. her institution's supply of homemade video recordings to put together a set of classroom scenes from geography, history, science, foreign languages, or mathematics classes. These can then be replayed to trainees who can analyse how teachers in different subjects handle group work, individualized instruction, assessment of progress, or something more general like disruptive behaviour in a gymnasium, laboratory, or conventional classroom.

Analysis may take several forms. Trainees may be taught one or more of the published category systems described above, used initially, perhaps, in a research project. Indeed videotapes are frequently used by researchers themselves for training new research assistants, as they allow checks to be made both on the extent to which an observer agrees with others similarly trained, and also how much they agree with their own codings when they analyse the tape on a future occasion. By far the most commonly used systems in this context have been the Flanders 10 categories and the many related systems devised by other investigators but based on his original categories.

The largest mass audience of this kind was probably achieved through the Open University course E201 "Personality and Learning". Thousands of students in several countries were taught the Flanders system, and had to analyse broadcast lessons using it as part of the unit on classroom interaction (Wragg 1976a). The more elaborate schedules used in research projects, involving perhaps 50 or 70 categories, usually demand too long a training period, are more difficult to teach trainees to a high degree of reliability, and are therefore less commonly used.

Table 2
Analysis of lesson transcripts

	Dialogue	Commentary
17.S	What about this glass of milk though, Glyn?	Steve seems to have been uneasy about Glyn's previous explanation, as is indicated by his placing of the word "though".
18.G	Well that's 'cause you make a vacuum in your mouth . . .	Glyn's answer to Steve's challenge is no more than a repetition of his previous vague account
19.S	When you drink the milk you see . . . you . . .	Steve seems dissatisfied, and sets off on a more explicit reply to his own question. When he hesitates he implicitly requires Glyn to complete the analysis by using the explanatory framework which he has set up.
20.G	Right! . . . You make a vacuum there, right?	Glyn's first "Right" accepts the task. His second "right" asks Steve whether his explanation so far is acceptable
21.S	Yes well you make a vacuum in the . . . er . . . transparent straw . . .	Steve does not find Glyn's use of "there" explicit enough and (most usefully) insists that the vacuum is "in the transparent straw".
22.G	Yes.	Glyn accepts the correction.
23.S	Carry on.	Steve urges his friend to continue with the explanation.
24.G	And the er air pressure outside forces it down, there's no pressure inside to force it back up again so . . .	Here Glyn achieves the essential explanatory point that it is the different pressures at the surface of the milk and inside the straw that make drinking possible.
25.S	OK.	Steve accepts this version.

Source: Barnes 1976 p. 40

Nonverbal aspects of classroom communication can very easily be analysed from videotapes, especially as the most recent generation of video playback machines permits the frame to be held, or allows fast or slow forward or reverse winding (see *Nonverbal Communication*). Aspects such as eye contact, teacher's gestures, movement around the room by pupils, aggressive behaviour in a group, smiles, and nods, can easily be highlighted by sensitive use of the freeze frame, by changing the speed of the tape, or by constantly replaying the same event until all have seen it several times or verified what they thought occurred.

3.3 Working in Teams

For many years teachers have worked largely in isolation, and inservice courses have rarely involved pairs or teams of teachers analysing each other's teaching skills. Yet in a profession like surgery the notion of scrutinizing one's own practice in the company of fellow professionals is commonplace.

Some programmes have concentrated on giving student teachers and supervising experienced teachers a common frame of reference. Moskowitz (1967) studied student teachers and cooperating teachers in schools, both of whom had been trained in the Flanders system. Trained students showed greater use of praise, acceptance of ideas and feelings, as well as use of questions than untrained groups, and relationships between teachers and students were best where both sets had been trained to use the system.

Dreyfus and Eggleston (1979) trained 40 teachers in schools, mainly heads of science departments, to use the Science Teaching Observation Schedule, developed by Eggleston, to analyse the lessons of students on teaching practice under their supervision. Although the teachers were principally supplying data for a research study comparing the styles of beginners with those of experienced science teachers, many commented informally on the extent to which they felt better able to supervise when equipped with such a useful analytical instrument, and also how, whilst analysing a student's lesson, they reflected on their own practice as teachers.

From the equipping of supervisors with such tools of analysis it is but a short step to training groups of novice or experienced teachers to analyse each other's teaching. This was made one of the foundation stones of the Teacher Education Project funded by the Department of Education and Science of the United Kingdom at the universities of Nottingham, Leicester, and Exeter from 1976–1981. Several units were developed under topics such as "class management and control", "questioning", "explaining", "teaching bright pupils", "teaching slow learners", "teaching mixed ability groups". The first and second parts of each unit involved the trainees working in pairs to analyse each other's lessons, as well as with supervisors and teachers in schools (Wragg 1981, Kerry 1981, Wragg 1984).

Under a topic like "vigilance" in class management one student would sit at the back of the class filling in sections in the booklet whilst the other taught. The observer would watch the teacher's use of eye contact, and also make detailed notes on two pupils not involved in the task. They would subsequently reverse roles, and the observer would teach a lesson which would be analysed by his or her colleague who had previously taught the class. Interviews with student teachers in these experimental groups showed that they felt they became more vigilant when teaching because they knew that their colleague was looking for pupils not engaged in the task in hand, and also when themselves observing, because they had to study every pupil carefully (see Fig. 1).

A topic such as "handling a difficult class" on the other hand, was not thought to be suitable for two beginners to analyse, so experienced teachers were given a framework within which they could observe classes the student had found difficult to manage.

Other experiments in the Teacher Education Project involved students analysing the lesson of experienced teachers. The headteacher and staff of a comprehensive school were engaged in discussions about language across the curriculum. A team of six student teachers followed classes for three days using a variety of schedules, some used in project research, some specially devised for the purpose. All the data sheets were fed back to the teachers who were able to discuss their teaching in the light of the picture built up by student observers. The experienced teachers reported satisfaction at the nature and amount of information the students had been able to collect, and the latter welcomed the opportunity to analyse the lessons of experienced teachers. On another occasion a series of one year part-time courses for deputy heads at Nottingham University made use of Teacher Education Project procedures, and each participant had to follow a class around for the day, analysing each lesson by studying which tasks were set, what individual pupils did, and what teaching styles were employed. Later they had to analyse the lessons of every member of one particular subject department, and then discuss teaching in that subject with the teachers concerned. Evaluation showed that all concerned had found it one of the most valuable professional experiences of their career (Wragg 1980). In both these examples almost all the teachers were being observed for the first time in their career by someone other than an inspector. None of the teachers concerned had ever previously received any systematic analysis of their lessons since their initial training.

With the movement towards more school-based inservice education in many countries, the format of teachers and/or students working together to analyse teaching becomes a very attractive one, especially in schools where falling pupil numbers means that few new teachers will join the staff. At its best, the spirit of enquiry engendered by teachers occasionally analysing each other's teaching is a valuable stimulus which can help avoid staleness and create an atmosphere of professional interest in improving competence. Unless some structure is provided, however, the exercise can easily lack purpose. Teachers wishing to work in this way need to consider the following sequence of steps. First of all the purpose of the analysis should be agreed. It may be that teachers wish to improve their questioning techniques, for example. Secondly, the way of working should be determined; perhaps pairs of teachers will work together, or one may be released from some commitments to observe others. Thirdly, the structure must be agreed, whether category systems are to be employed, which might require training for observers, or whether field notes will be assembled under certain relevant headings. Fourthly, there must be some kind of sensitive feedback, as teachers lacking confidence might easily be bruised by abrasive criticism. Finally there should be a deliberate attempt to modify teaching

Vigilance

When to do this: Early on, preferably during the first three weeks of term

Who fills this in: A fellow student on teaching practice with you, or a fellow teacher

What to do: Select a lesson which will involve something more than just whole class teaching, e.g. small group work, individual work, laboratory experiments. Teach the class normally. Ask a fellow student to fill in the analysis section below. Make sure that the student who does this observation is clear about what is involved

Analysis

Date   _____

Class   _____

Subject   _____

(*To the observer*: Make brief notes about the lesson in spaces below. Look through the whole schedule so that you know what must be done during the lesson)

(a)   Eyes

For approximately the *first 10 minutes* of the lesson watch the teacher's eyes. Does he/she look at the class when explaining or questioning? When children are working alone or in groups does the teacher look around the room or only at the nearest group?

(b)   Individual children

Choose two children who do not appear to be applying themselves to their task. Study these two carefully and make notes about their behaviour. What do they do? What contacts do they have with the teacher? Do they solicit these or does the teacher? Is there any indication from what you see or hear as to *why they are not involved* in their work?

Child A   *Name*   _____   (if known, if not brief description)   .

Child B   *Name*   _____   (if known, if not brief description)

Follow - up

    Discuss the analysis with your colleague. How vigilant do you seem to have been. Are you surprised at the reports on the two children in (b)? Did you see most of what the observer describes?

    Eye contact   Try to keep as many children as possible in view when doing whole class teaching, explaining, asking questions etc. Imagine, in other lessons when you are on your own, that an observer is present looking for pupils who have lost interest in the lesson

    Dividing attention   Try *quite deliberately* to cast an eye occasionally over the rest of the class when you work with an individual or small group. Take immediate action if necessary

    Swap roles with your colleague so that you now do this exercise in his lesson, if possible

Figure 1
Vigilance in class management (from Wragg 1981 pp. 42–43)

in the light of feedback. Some of the more rigorous programmes incorporating lesson analysis have effectively made each teacher the experimenter.

3.4 Lesson Analysis as Part of Different Kinds of Training Programme

The analysis of lessons often forms a single part of a larger programme. In many of the microteaching courses established in the United States and Europe the analysis of lessons precedes, is part of, or follows the main programme. A group of trainees might commence a microteaching programme by analysing lesson transcripts or might learn lesson analysis techniques to enable them to evaluate their own videotapes.

Similarly, lesson analysis is frequently a component part of minicourses such as those produced in the Far West laboratory or programmes based on competency- or performance-based teacher education, where novitiates are eventually certificated on the basis of their ability to perform successfully the set of behaviours specified in the programme (see *Competency-based Teacher Education*).

Sometimes lesson analysis is used to evaluate teacher education programmes themselves. Koran and Koran (1973) sought to establish a link between teacher questioning and pupil learning, so they assigned 69 trainee teachers in Florida to one of three groups: two groups had written models available in the form of lesson transcripts whilst the third was a control group. The researchers specified the content of a trial lesson which all trainees had to teach, and these lessons were then analysed to see what kinds of teacher questions and pupil responses occurred. The experimental groups showed higher use of analytic questions than the control group, and the pupils in their classes used more numerous and varied analytic responses.

4. Research into the Effects of Lesson Analysis

With the increasing use of lesson analysis in teacher education, the question arises whether such a form of training leads to any short- or long-term changes in behaviour. It is not easy to conduct research in this area for several reasons. First of all there are usually several influences at work on trainees, and classes making use of lesson analysis might constitute one tiny part of a substantial programme. Ascribing eventual changes in behaviour with any confidence to the lesson analysis phase of the programme alone, rather than other components, poses a difficult problem.

Secondly, a great deal of research into the effects of training programmes is conducted by tutors who have themselves devised them. The nature of the supervisor–trainee relationship is such that trainees may teach in a certain way either through coercion, or because they infer what styles of teaching their supervisor prefers and are anxious to obtain a good assessment, or even out of esteem for their tutor's preferences. Almost always research of this kind is based on a short-term test of behaviour or attitude. Whether or not long-term altera-

tions in behaviour occur rather than short-term tutor-pleasing changes is harder to establish.

Only a little of the research in this field can be mentioned here. Some of it has concerned a particular style of analysis such as the Flanders system. For example Furst (1967) trained one group to use the Flanders system of lesson analysis before their teaching practice, one during it, and a third control group received no such training. Both the trained groups showed more acceptance of pupils' ideas than the control group, and the group trained during the teaching practice obtained more children's talk in their lessons.

Yeany (1977) divided 64 trainee teachers specializing in primary education into three experimental groups and a control. The three experimental groups were either trained in systematic analysis of science lessons, or viewed videotapes of experienced teachers, or had both. The control group had no such programme. All the experimental groups obtained higher scores than the control group on measures of both teacher and pupil attitude.

Ryan (1974) investigated the effects of pupil analysis of lessons during training (see *Student Evaluations of Teaching*), but found no significant differences in the classroom behaviour of 80 student teachers divided into three treatment groups: (a) reading the children's comments, (b) hearing their analysis interpreted and summarized by a supervisor, (c) giving them forms with supervisors' comments on them.

Copeland (1977) is one of few investigators to follow through a programme of lesson analysis and microteaching to see if longer term effects occurred. The subjects were 72 trainees at Santa Barbara and the skill under scrutiny was "asking probing questions". Two or three months later audiorecordings were made in their classrooms. Only the group whose supervising teacher had been trained to analyse their lessons during teaching practice showed any longer term behaviour change.

Riley (1978) assigned 40 randomly chosen primary teachers at the University of Delaware to two groups. The experimental group received $3\frac{1}{2}$ hours of instruction on classifying questions in science, whereas the control group had no such training. Audiotapes of each student's lessons were then transcribed and analysed by a team of three. Those in the trained group asked significantly more questions on a higher cognitive level, but there was no difference between the two groups in the overall number of questions asked. As with other similar studies the labour-intensive nature of this kind of research meant that only one lesson was analysed, thereby reducing the confidence that can be had in the results.

Rice (1977) in a very small study of 10 primary science trainees at Ohio State University, divided them into two groups, one of whom had models, teaching materials, and analysis of audiotapes of their own lessons. The experimental group used more higher order questions after the course than the others. The investigator clearly thought that an increase in waiting time and asking fewer questions were a good thing, and, to no-one's surprise, these also "improved".

Esquivel et al. (1978) in a much more thorough study also investigated the questioning techniques of student primary science specialists, in this case 92 who were randomly assigned to pairs and then to classes where they taught and assisted each other for three weeks. Each lesson was audiorecorded, and four groups established: one receiving feedback from a supervisor, one from peers, one from analysing their own profiles, and one with no feedback. No significant differences were found between the groups, but the authors point out the difficulty in this kind of field experience of containing pairs of students to strict experimental conditions, especially where something as conversationally natural as feedback is concerned.

An attempt to broaden the narrow concentration of many investigators on higher order questioning was made by Kelsey (1977) working with 27 secondary trainees, each of whom made and analysed audiotapes of their own lessons on several occasions. An experimental group of 14 was trained to identify and classify cognitive and verbal reinforcing behaviour. The incidence of total cognitive verbal behaviour, including cognitive questions and positive reinforcements, went up markedly for the experimental group.

Questions directed to a particular goal, in this case the clarification of 13-year-old pupils' values during social studies lessons, were studied by Stahl (1976). An experimental subgroup from 26 trainees who had received training in strategies thought, from previous studies, to be associated with effective values clarification teaching, used more probing questions of the kind advocated than the untrained group.

Konetski (1970) pursued not only the notion of divergent questions but also the role of the teacher trainer in his study of trainee science teachers. One group received instruction in the classifying and designing of questions as either convergent-memory, divergent, or evaluative. The trained group asked significantly more divergent and evaluative questions, a direction in which American student teachers were commonly nudged in the late 1960s and early 1970s after the considerable interest in creativity at that time. Conferences with the instructor also appeared to enhance this greater frequency.

In general, research in this field tends to show that student teachers are willing to change their behaviour after training in lesson analysis, but such changes tend to be associated with what they perceive to be their supervisor's preferences. Alterations in teaching behaviour which persist over a longer period are harder to demonstrate, though this does not mean they do not occur.

5. Conclusions

Despite the problems of deciding on forms of lesson analysis, desired directions of change, or evaluating the

effects of programmes which contain training elements in lesson analysis, it does seem that a mixture of approaches to the scrutiny of the trainee's own or other teachers' lessons is worthwhile.

The analysis of their own lessons involves trainees in the act of self-confrontation, and Fuller and Manning (1973) in an extensive review of this field concluded that the teachers most likely to change their classroom behaviour when confronted with some kind of analysis or feedback are not too anxious, closed-minded, or under too much stress. They are also usually young and intelligent, have a good opinion of themselves, and are relatively well-satisfied with their teaching.

The one major note of caution about the training procedure is that it may sometimes be too conservative. If all that trainees learned was the art of analysing lessons of experienced teachers the next generation would be mere clones of the previous one, unable to adapt to changing circumstances.

The successful use of lesson analysis in teacher education, therefore, probably necessitates five requirements for the trainee:

(a) learning more than one approach to the analysis of teaching;

(b) analysing not only the other teachers' lessons but one's own;

(c) avoiding uncritical endorsement of currently favoured styles of teaching or the suspected preferences of one's supervisor;

(d) experiencing lesson analysis as but one part of a coherent and comprehensive training programme;

(e) using the insights gained to fashion one's own styles of teaching.

See also: Microteaching: Conceptual and Theoretical Bases; Technical Skills of Teaching; Microteaching: Feedback; Microteaching: Modelling; Microteaching: Effectiveness; Minicourses

Bibliography

Barnes D 1976 *From Communication to Curriculum*. Penguin, Harmondsworth

Barr A S 1961 Wisconsin studies of the measurement and prediction of teacher effectiveness: A summary of investigations. *J. Exp. Educ.* 30: 5–156

Bellack A A, Kliebard H M, Hyman R T, Smith F L 1966 *The Language of the Classroom*. Teachers College Press, New York

Bennett N 1976 *Teaching Styles and Pupil Progress*. Open Books, London

Copeland W D 1977 Some factors related to student teacher classroom performance following microteaching training. *Am. Educ. Res. J.* 14: 147–57

Dreyfus A, Eggleston J F 1979 Classroom transactions of student teachers of science. *Eur. J. Sci. Educ.* 3: 315–25

Dunkin M J, Biddle B J 1974 *The Study of Teaching*. Holt, Rinehart and Winston, New York

Edwards A D 1976 *Language in Culture and Class: The Sociology of Language and Education*. Heinemann, London

Esquivel J M, Lashier W S, Smith W S 1978 Effect of feedback on questioning of preservice teachers in scis microteaching. *Sci. Educ.* 2: 209–14

Flanders N A 1963 Intent, action and feedback: A preparation for teaching. *J. Teach. Educ.* 14: 251–60

Flanders N A 1965 Teacher influence, pupil attitudes and achievement. *Co-operative Research Monograph* No. 12, United States Government Printing Office, Washington, DC

Fuller F, Manning B A 1973 Self-confrontation reviewed: A conceptualization of video playback in teacher education. *Rev. Educ. Res.* 43: 469–528

Furst N A 1967 The effects of training in interaction analysis on the behavior of student teachers in secondary schools. In: Amidon E J, Hough J B (eds.) *Interaction Analysis: Theory, Research, and Application*. Addison-Wesley, Reading, Massachusetts

Galton M J, Simon B 1980 *Progress and Performance in the Primary Classroom*. Routledge and Kegan Paul, London

Galton M J, Simon B, Croll P 1980 *Inside the Primary Classroom*. Routledge and Kegan Paul, London

Kelsey K W 1977 Performance criteria and operant methods: An analysis of effects on cognitive and reinforcing behaviours of student teachers. *Sci. Educ.* 61: 201–08

Kerry T 1981 *Teaching Bright Pupils in Mixed Ability Classes*. Macmillan, London

Konetski L D 1970 *Instruction on Questioning*. Morgan State College, Baltimore

Koran J J, Koran M L 1973 *Validating a Teacher Behavior by Student Performance*. Florida University, Gainesville

Moskowitz G 1967 The attitudes and teaching patterns of cooperating teachers and student teachers trained in interaction analysis. In: Amidon E J, Hough J B (eds.) 1967 *Interaction Analysis: Theory, Research and Application*. Addison-Wesley, Reading, Massachusetts

Rice D R 1977 The effect of question-asking instruction on preservice elementary science teachers. *J. Res. Sci. Teach.* 14: 353–59

Riley J P 1978 Effects of studying a question classification system on the cognitive level of preservice teachers' questions. *Sci. Educ.* 62: 333–38

Ryan K A 1974 The use of feedback from students in the preservice training of teachers. Paper presented at the Annual Meeting of the American Educational Research Association, Chicago, Illinois

Smidchens U, Roth R 1968 Use of a computer in providing feedback to teachers. *Classroom Interaction Newsletter* 4: 47–60

Stahl R J 1976 The effects of the acquisition of a values clarification questioning strategy on subsequent teacher and student process variables within a microteach–reteach sequence. Paper presented at the Annual Meeting of the American Educational Research Association, San Francisco, California

UNESCO Division of Methods, Materials and Techniques 1972 *Closed Circuit Television Equipment for Use in Training: Technical Dossier*. UNESCO, Paris

Wragg E C 1976a *Classroom Interaction*. Topic 11 of Open University Unit E201. Open University Press, Milton Keynes

Wragg E C 1976b The Lancaster Study: Its implications for teacher training. *Br. J. Teach. Educ.* 2: 281–90

Wragg E C 1980 A regional approach to the training of deputy heads. *Camb. J. Educ.* 9: 107–11

Wragg E C 1981 *Class Management and Control*. Macmillan, London

Wragg E C 1984 *Classroom Teaching Skills*. Croom Helm, London

Yeany R 1977 The effects of model viewing with systematic strategy analysis on the science teaching styles of preservice teachers. *J. Res. Sci. Teach.* 14: 209–22

Microteaching: Conceptual and Theoretical Bases

A. Perlberg

Microteaching is a laboratory training procedure aimed at simplifying the complexities of regular teaching–learning processes. The trainee is engaged in a scaled down and focused situation—scaled down in terms of class size and lesson length and focused on teaching tasks such as practice and mastery of specific skills such as lecturing, questioning, or leading a discussion; mastering specific teaching strategies; flexibility in instructional decision making; alternative uses of curricula, instructional materials and classroom management.

The short lesson is recorded on an audio- or videotape recorder and the trainee can see the replica immediately after the lesson. When hardware is not available, a supervisor can record in writing the basic verbal and nonverbal interaction as feedback for the teacher. Pupils are asked to fill in rating questionnaires evaluating specific aspects of the lesson and at times can also provide oral feedback. The trainee's own analysis of the lesson based on the authentic feedback from the various sources helps in restructuring the lesson, which is taught to a new group of pupils either immediately or a few days later.

The restructuring cycle continues until mastery is achieved. The trainee can also choose to view or listen to, either before the first teaching experience or thereafter, a recording of a model teacher practicing a particular teaching–learning skill. The above description pertains mainly to the original microteaching model developed at Stanford around 1960.

It is important to note that during the initial stages of its inception and development, microteaching, like many other educational innovations, was not based on solid theoretical conceptualization and research evidence. It was described rather as an "idea" (Allen and Ryan 1969). As a result, developers and practitioners around the world, in teacher education and other related fields adopted the basic idea, but took the liberty of modifying the original model and adapting it to their ideologies, concepts, needs, and constraints. Some adaptations were quite different from the original model and in some cases the basic concept of an intensive laboratory experience was missed.

1. Historical Background

To understand the lack of a unified theoretical conceptualization of microteaching on the one hand, and the rationale for some of its components on the other hand, one has to examine the background from which it originated. Allen, one of its main developers, states that: "Microteaching was born out of the frustration of liberal arts graduates who felt that there was nothing they could possibly learn from teacher education" (Allen and Ryan 1969, Allen 1980). The Stanford group which developed microteaching responded to a wider feeling of frustration and dissatisfaction the world over, by the public at large, educators, and even teacher educators, with the traditional models of teacher education (Joyce 1975). In the United States, during the 1950s and 1960s, the schools and teachers came under attack for failing to help children master reading, writing, and arithmetic and to teach adequately science and other subjects. There was an increasing demand that teachers be held accountable for the achievement of their pupils. Teachers, in turn, blamed teacher education, claiming that their preservice and inservice training had not provided them with the skills necessary for ensuring student achievement at the level being called for (Gage and Winne 1975).

The traditional models were criticized for being heavily slanted towards verbal and cognitive input, which was described at times as superficial and much to say about nothing. The theoretical studies were not integrated with the practical experiences and even the experiential part, practice teaching, was criticized as ineffective. Concurrently, educational researchers admitted that half a century's research on teaching and learning did not have much impact on classroom interaction. Gage (1963) claimed that the holistic macro approach to research on teaching had failed, and that educators should adopt the methods used by scientists who tried to understand complex phenomena by breaking them into micro elements.

But the 1960s and early 1970s were not the only times of criticism. Through extensive governmental and foundation resources, American teacher educators were encouraged to innovate and were ready to adopt any innovation based even on intuitive professional judgement, with the hope of substantiating it later on. Microteaching was one of these innovations which was practiced first and only at the later stage started the process of its theoretical conceptualization.

2. The Debate over Theoretical Conceptualization

The original Stanford group which developed microteaching was very heterogeneous in ideologies and beliefs about education and psychology and the debate over the theoretical conceptualization has gone on since the inception of the idea. Ivey and Authier (1978) reflected on this issue stating that: "In the early phase of experimentalism and research, conceptual frameworks and theoretical constructs were deliberately omitted in the search for a method which consistently showed results—a system that worked as needed rather than one which was theoretically sophisticated." McDonald (1973), on the other hand, the second principal developer of microteaching, subscribed to a theoretical point of view that "teacher education programs should be conceptualized as behavior modification systems, designed to modify complex behavioral repertoires which are adaptable to a variety of learning problems." He viewed microteaching as an excellent example of behavior modification technique. For McDonald microteaching was devised as a procedure for facilitating behavioral control. Further, it was used as a way of creating a more effective experimental paradigm which for the first time made it possible to use sophisticated experimental designs in learning studies. The purpose of these teaching studies was to assess the relative effectiveness of modeling and reinforcement variables in facilitating the acquisition of teaching behavior. These were some of McDonald's hopes and aspirations. Looking back, however, a decade later, he stated that "microteaching remains an unstudied technique. The literature that purports to be research on it is deplorable . . . much of what has been written about microteaching is promotional and even misleading . . . more disappointing is the fact that the original conception and rationale for microteaching has been lost sight of—a point significant in the context of a discussion of behavior modification in teacher education" (McDonald 1973).

Even after more than two decades of microteaching, Allen still saw McDonald's emphasis as misleading (Allen 1980). He agreed however that there is still a need for a vigorous research program to substantiate the many claims made on its behalf. He adds however that microteaching has been pretty well accepted as having a de facto face validity, "Its high level of acceptance both in the United States and abroad has been based not so much on research evidence as upon the satisfaction level of the teacher education staff, the teaching candidates, and the school personnel involved in its use. It is a harsh reality that this affective evidence is more important than many research findings." Allen's assertion about the wide acceptability of microteaching is supported by the large numbers of publications, books, and research reports published on microteaching and related areas in many countries (see references), and by its acceptability to international organizations such as UNESCO as an important vehicle to improve teacher education.

In the most recent review of the literature on micro-teaching, Copeland (1982) states that there appears to be a considerable research base supporting the inclusion of microteaching as a prestudent teaching laboratory experience in teacher education, and that participation in microteaching appears to assume initial acquisition of related technical skills of teaching to be associated with shifts in participants' attitudes. "Further, skills acquired during microteaching may be used in student teaching classrooms subsequent to training if the nature of these classrooms support such use" (Copeland 1982).

At present, in the absence of a unified theoretical conceptualization, microteaching could be viewed as an eclectic laboratory training technique. Its components are based on different theories, concepts, empirical evidence, professional judgments, and notions. The following discussion will examine its different components.

3. The Components of Microteaching

3.1 The Teaching–Learning Laboratory

Learning by doing and intensive experiential involvement are the basic principles on which the teaching–learning laboratory is based. While learning takes place throughout life by trial and error, or by guided experience, it is widely agreed that it is desirable that practice in simulated situations in laboratory settings should precede practicing and learning through real life situations. This concept has been accepted in the professional training of scientists, engineers, and other professions, and has been accepted for thousands of years in the training of armed forces, through war games and more recently in the training of astronauts. Drawing on research and empirical evidence as to how people change and learn in social settings, scientists in applied psychology, and other behavioral sciences have developed the concept of the "training laboratory" in behavioral sciences.

In providing a theoretical and empirical rationale for early field experiences in teacher education, Webb et al. (1981) state that the learning process pattern that emerges from psychological investigation is one that centers on the significance of the learner and his or her concerns. The pattern contrasts verbal or symbolic input to the learner, with experience in the learning context by the learner. The contrast reveals that verbal teaching alone or verbal teaching prior to learner contextual experience will be less productive than teaching in accordance with the cyclical pattern illustrated in Fig. 1.

Probably the most often-voiced complaint of graduates of teacher education programs is that we perpetuate a discrepancy between the real world of teaching and the verbal theoretical world of preservice training. The building of a personally meaningful concept of teaching (which includes attitude, knowledge, and skills) is facilitated by early and frequent contact with classroom, pupils, administrators, professional teachers, and parents—the real environment of education. The contextual experience is a necessary preliminary to concept formation and, hence, skilled teaching.

Even though Webb's rationale refers to early field experiences, the teaching–learning laboratory could be viewed as an early-simulated field experience, and Webb's rationale applies to the laboratory experience as well. Moreover, the laboratory is a safe practice ground and it should precede teaching in the field, especially in early field experiences.

Figure 1
Cyclical pattern of teaching

3.2 Safe Practice Ground

Safe practice ground is another concept embedded in any laboratory. The ability to experiment, to try out, explore, and fail without being penalized or hurting someone is one of the main justifications for the teaching–learning laboratory. In the traditional teacher education models, supervised student teaching, whether before the theoretical studies or after them, has always been a source of tension and anxiety to the neophyte student teacher. In many instances, not only the student teacher but the learners in the classroom suffered. Administrators, cooperating teachers, students, and their parents objected to excessive use of regular classrooms for student teaching. This is one reason why laboratory schools, attached to schools of education, which were very common in the past, have diminished in recent years. The moral obligation of teacher education towards the school system and their neophyte student teachers is to provide them with a safe practice ground before getting out into field experience.

The concept of a safe practice ground is supported also by knowledge from theories of learning and change and empirical experience in clinical supervision, clinical psychology, and other related areas. Anxious learners tend to protect themselves by defence mechanisms, are not flexible, and resist change and learning. Moreover, in many instances excessive anxiety may cause frustration and fixation of undesirable behaviors. Equipping neophyte teachers with a degree of mastery in teaching skills and strategies will enable them to benefit more both during their early field experiences and their student teaching. A safe practice ground is important not only to the neophyte teacher, but also to experienced teachers. They, who are supposed to be secure, safe, and confident, are also subjected at times to tension and anxiety, especially when facing new situations and unpredictable developments. This natural phenomenon has been one of the main blockers to the introduction of innovation. Experience has shown that the microteaching laboratories have been safe practice grounds even for experienced teachers, participating in professional development programs. They can try out these new instructional strategies and curricula in a relatively secure atmosphere. While stressing the importance of a safe practice ground, it is essential to remember that the concept of "safe" is a relative one. Even in a microteaching laboratory participants experience a certain amount of tension and stress as a result of feedback. This phenomenon is inevitable and even essential and will be discussed later at greater length.

3.3 The Micro Element and Teaching Skills

Underlying the micro element is the supposition that before attempting to understand, learn, and perform effectively the complicated task of teaching, one should master the components of the task. By focusing the training on a specific task and reducing the complexities of the situation it is possible to concentrate the training process and assure greater effectiveness in the learning process. Moreover, effective learning is achieved in general, when the learner moves from the simple task to the more complex one. The above concept is supported by ample theoretical and empirical evidence, in the areas of learning, teaching, and training in different settings and, in particular, the systems approach and task analysis.

Scaling down the class size and lesson length from the macro to micro provides more effective initial learning conditions. It stands to reason that the neophyte teacher could cope and learn more easily during a short lesson to a small class rather than plunging into a real classroom of 40 children and teaching them for 50 minutes.

Another aspect of the micro element is the focus on particular teaching skills. Gage (1963) was quoted above, stating that for better understanding and investigation of the complexities of teaching–learning interactions we should move from the macro to the micro situation. Allen and McDonald have applied the same concept to training and have developed the concept of "technical skills of teaching." The initial list of technical skills of teaching developed was by no means exhaustive and other skills were added during the years. The competency-based teacher education (CBTE) or performance-based teacher education (PBTE) movement, which developed at the end of the 1960s has contributed greatly to the identification and development of a wider range of classroom interactive skills in the cognitive, affective, and motoric domains. It should be stressed, however, at this point that the original concept of technical skills of teachers was not clear, and many practitioners have adopted only the Stanford list of teaching skills or even only part of that list. In many instances, this was done because of lack of time and resources or for logistical reasons. Some practitioners assumed that there will be

a transfer from practice in certain skills to other skills. Focusing training on a partial list of skills and in many instances minute technical skills has contributed greatly to the alienation of many teacher educators and especially those subscribing to humanistic values from the whole concept of the microteaching laboratory.

It could not be emphasized more strongly that the list of required skills to be practiced in a laboratory should include a wide range of classroom interaction skills in all domains, that is cognitive, affective, and motoric. Moreover, many practitioners of microteaching laboratories assumed that mastery of particular skills in a microlesson will enable the teacher to use them automatically when necessary in regular classroom interactions. But the macro, whole lesson is not the sum of its micro elements, as the group is not a simple sum of its members. The macrolesson is a phenomenon in itself. Using classroom interactive skills in a regular classroom situation requires training and preparation in teaching a microlesson as well as in the particular skills. Therefore, the right sequence in a teaching–learning laboratory should be from mastery of simple subskills, to skills, clusters of skills, and interaction strategies. From skills in isolated domains to interaction between domains. From the use of a particular strategy of interaction to flexibility training and the use of multistrategies. From a short lesson to a small group to longer lessons to larger groups.

3.4 The Feedback Element

Another cardinal element of microteaching and the teaching–learning laboratory is feedback. When microteaching was developed at Stanford, it coincided with the initial developments of portable, relatively inexpensive videotape recorders. The Stanford group took advantage of this innovative tool and used extensively video recordings as the main source of feedback. Since then, microteaching has been associated around the world with video recorders. As will be discussed later, video recording is still probably the most powerful available source of feedback (Perlberg 1984). On the other hand, it should be stressed emphatically that the microteaching laboratory does not depend on the availability of video recorders or any other electronic hardware. Allen and Ryan (1969) were aware of the misconception of coupling microteaching with video recorders and have tried to correct it. Since this notion was deeply rooted and disturbed the dissemination of the basic concept in developing countries, UNESCO initiated a special report in microteaching and allied techniques which could be implemented in developing countries without hardware or with inexpensive hardware, such as portable tape recorders (Perlberg 1975) (see *Microteaching: Feedback*).

3.5 The "Modeling" Element

The use of recorded "models" of master teachers demonstrating particular classroom interactions is another important element in the microteaching laboratory. McDonald (1973), who was one of the developers of microteaching, has investigated the role of "modeling" in learning even before the inception of microteaching. Both McDonald and Allen drew also on Bandura's work on the role of models, learning by observation and imitation. There is abundant theoretical and empirical evidence which testifies to the wide range of learning situations and behavioral changes which take place as a result of observation and imitation. Basic and applied research in that area is part of the wider field of behavior modification and other behavioristic approaches.

It is interesting to note that the "modeling" element and the skills training through reinforcement techniques, became the main cause for rejecting the whole concept of microteaching and tagging it as a behavioristic–mechanistic approach which negates humanistic concepts in education. But humanists ignored the fact that learning by observation and imitation is hardly new in education. This apprenticeship concept which was practiced as early as the guilds, and is still practiced, is based on the modeling concept. Socialization processes are based on learning by observation and imitation, teacher education has used similar approaches since early days by sending neophyte teachers to observe "master teachers." Our daily behavior, in general and professionally, is shaped to a great extent by the bad and good models we have had. The study of history and philosophy of education has put great emphasis on the "great master teachers" exemplars who became our models.

In the microteaching laboratory, this widely used learning method was systematized. Instead of a general, diffused observatory, the "model" enabled focused observation. The models are recorded and thus it is possible to observe again and again in a systematic manner, a wide variety of master teachers, all of which facilitates more effective learning. It is interesting to note that "modeling" which was considered by many to be a mechanistic and low-level imitation process could be viewed also as involving high-level cognitive processes. McIntyre et al. (1977) suggest that even Bandura's concept of social learning theory "is more cognitively oriented than is often realized." Here again the ways models are used are important. Providing one model only and directions to follow it produces imitation. Providing several models and creating a learning environment which facilitates evaluation and requires flexibility and indepth decision making could be described as a highly cognitive process.

4. Towards a Unified Theoretical Conceptualization of Microteaching

As stated above, microteaching is still in the process of developing a unified theoretical conceptualization. Whether such a unified theoretical basis can be achieved

is still to be seen. Until then, the fact that it is an effective eclectic technique can be accepted. Its components are based on a wide range of theories and available empirical evidence which justify its use in the future and call for further research and development.

See also: Microteaching: Modelling; Microteaching: Effectiveness; Technical Skills of Teaching; Competency-based Teacher Education

Bibliography

Allen D W 1980 Microteaching: A personal review. *Br. J. Tech. Ed.* 6: 147–51
Allen D W, Ryan K A 1969 *Microteaching.* Addison-Wesley, Reading, Massachusetts
Borg W R, Kelley M L, Langer P, Gall M 1970 *The Mini Course: A Microteaching Approach to Teacher Education.* Collier Macmillan, London
Brown G 1975 *Microteaching—A Program of Teaching Skills.* Methuen, London
Center for Educational Research and Innovations (CERI) 1975 *The International Transfer of Microteaching Programs for Teacher Education.* Organization for Economic Co-operation and Development, Paris
Copeland W D 1982 Prestudent teaching laboratory experiences. In: Mitzel H E (ed.) 1982 *Encyclopedia of Educational Research*, 5th edn. Free Press, New York
Educational Resource Information Center (ERIC) National Institute of Education, Educational Resources Information Center, Washington, DC
Falus I, McAleese W R 1975 *A Bibliography of Microteaching.* Programmed Learning Jor, London
Gage N L 1963 Paradigms for research on teaching. In: Gage N L (ed.) 1963 *Handbook on Research on Teaching: A Project of the American Education Research Association.* Rand McNally, Chicago, Illinois
Gage N L, Winne P H 1975 Performance-based teacher education. In: Ryan K (ed.) 1975 *Teacher Education.* 74th Yearbook of the National Society for the Study of Education, Part 2. NSSE, Chicago, Illinois
Ivey A E, Authier J 1978 *Microcounseling: Innovations in Interviewing, Counseling, Psychotherapy, and Psychoeducation.* Thomas, Springfield, Illinois
Joyce B 1975 Conceptions of man and their implications for teacher education. In: Ryan K (ed.) 1975 *Teacher Education.* 74th Yearbook of the National Society for the Study of Education, Part 2. NSSE, Chicago, Illinois
McDonald R J 1973 Behavior modification in teacher education. In: Thoresen C E (ed.) 1973 *Behavior Modification in Education.* 72nd Yearbook of the National Society for the Study of Education, Part 1. NSSE, Chicago, Illinois
McIntyre D I, MacLeod G H R, Griffiths R (eds.) 1977 *Investigations of Microteaching.* Croom Helm, London
Perlberg A 1975 *Recent Approaches on Microteaching and Allied Techniques Which can be Implemented Easily in Developing Countries.* UNESCO, Paris
Perlberg A 1984 When professors confront themselves: Towards a theoretical conceptualization of the use of video self-confrontation in improving teaching in higher education. *Higher Educ.* 12: 31
Perrott E 1977 *Microteaching in Higher Education: Research, Development and Practice.* Society for Research into Higher Education, Guildford

Trott A J (ed.) 1974 *Microteaching Conference Papers*. Association for Programmed Learning and Educational Technology, London

Turney C, Clift J C, Dunkin M J, Trail R D 1973 *Microteaching: Research, Theory and Practice: An Innovation in Teacher Education Especially as it Relates to the Australian Context*. Sydney University Press, Sydney

Webb C, Gehrke N, Ishler P, Mendoza A 1981 Theoretical and empirical bases for early field experiences in teacher education. In: Webb C et al. (eds.) 1981 *Exploratory Field Experience in Teacher Education*. Association for Teacher Education, Washington, DC

Microteaching: Modelling

G. R. MacLeod

Modelling, or learning by observation, has long been an integral component of learning to teach. In microteaching too, modelling has played an important part in preparing trainees for their practice of teaching skills. As Allen and Ryan (1969) describe it, the original rationale for the inclusion of modelling in microteaching was the very pragmatic one that skill learning was likely to be enhanced if trainees were able to view a demonstration of a particular teaching skill prior to their practice of that skill. This article reviews research on the effects of modelling on skill acquisition and relates the outcomes to Bandura's (1977) theory of social learning.

In Bandura's conceptualization, learning by observation is said to occur principally through the informative function of modelling influences, and is governed by four component processes: attending, retention, motor reproduction, and motivation.

Attending refers to the observer's selective perception of the significant features of the model, while retention refers to the maintenance in permanent memory of a symbolic form of the patterns which have been attended to in the model. According to Bandura it is an advanced capacity for symbolic representation which enables humans to learn much of their behaviour by observation, with the symbolic codes allowing for the retention of large quantities of information in easily stored form. It is also this capacity to create symbols which serves to distinguish modelling or learning by observation from simple imitation.

Motor reproduction refers to the translation of symbolic representations into actions or their use as guides for actions, whilst motivation refers to the rewardingness or nonrewardingness of enacting the modelled behaviours. Thus, in Bandura's model, the processes of attending and retention refer to acquisition of behaviour or skills, motor reproduction refers to performance, whilst motivation refers both to acquisition and to performance.

1. Research on Positive and Negative Models in Microteaching

Studies comparing the effects of positive and negative models have been reported by Allen et al. (1967), Koran et al. (1972) and Gilmore (1977). All three studies found the use of positive models to be the more effective, but the first two studies also indicated that negative models were significant aids to skill acquisition. However, Koran and his colleagues note that their positive models included a greater amount of more explicit information than did the negative models, whilst the definitions of treatments in the Gilmore investigation indicate that this was also the case in his study. Thus, differences between treatments may be attributed to the different quantities of skill-related information provided by the different models, this being an interpretation consistent with Bandura's contention that modelling operates primarily through the information it conveys. The second difficulty in interpreting the results of these studies is that the labels "positive" and "negative" may be used to refer to very different treatments in different investigations. Thus, a negative model may be one which portrays the absence of criterion behaviours, or few of the criterion behaviours, or inappropriate use of the criterion behaviours, or, perhaps, exemplification of the behaviours to be avoided. Perhaps the major conclusion to be drawn from these investigations is that modelling in microteaching can have significant effects on skill acquisition.

2. Research Comparing Written and Audiovisual Models

The issue of the medium used for model presentations has received considerable research attention, and is an important area because of the cost implications of its outcomes.

A common theme in the research has been the comparison of symbolic modelling (written) with perceptual modelling (film or videotape), and a frequently used method has been to use a transcript from the film or videotape sound track as the symbolic model, thereby making the information content of the rival treatments more comparable. This was the procedure followed by Koran (1971) who reported that both treatments produced significant changes in a criterion of generating written questions whilst a control treatment had no such effects. Phillips (1973) compared the effects of a treatment involving the provision of a written handout and discussion, with a treatment involving these same components but with the addition of a videotape model. It was found that both treatments had an effect on subsequent questioning behaviour, but that there was no significant difference between the treatment effects.

A group of studies which do lend some support to the superiority of perceptual over symbolic models are those by Orme (1966), by Young (1967), and by Koran (1969). It is noteworthy that these studies tend to involve more complex experimental designs than those which find no significant differences. Thus, although the results of these investigations are more difficult to interpret unequivocally, it is also likely that the power of the analyses is greater than in those with simpler comparisons.

In summary, these studies of modelling media again indicate strong effects of modelling in microteaching and seem to indicate a slight favouring of perceptual over symbolic models. If information content of these models is similar then these results may be attributable to the greater motivational or attention-drawing value of perceptual models. As Bandura puts it, people "rarely have to be compelled to watch television, whereas oral or written reports of the same activities would not hold their attention for long" (p. 40).

3. Research on Focus in Modelling

Observers who code modeled activities into either words, concise labels or vivid imagery learn and retain behavior better than those who simply observe . . . . (Bandura. p. 26)

Most uses of modelling in microteaching involve trainees in more than simple observation or unguided reading. In general some kind of cueing, coding, or labelling is involved, with this focus either being provided for the trainees in the model itself, or being acquired by the trainees through practice in the use of prespecified codes or labels. A useful review by Griffiths (1976) indicates the wide variety of focusing devices and observer activities which have been undertaken alongside modelling in microteaching, ranging from a brief "peep" on the sound-track of a film, through verbal labels, and the use of rating or observation schedules by the trainees, to the use of testing and immediate feedback on the trainees' recognition of skill components.

The available evidence suggests that where cues or other focusing devices are provided during viewing, this adds significantly to the effectiveness of modelling procedures (McDonald and Allen 1967, Claus 1968). These devices may be seen as increasing the information value of models by providing for trainees the symbolic representations of criterion behaviours which are required for, and maximize the efficiency of, retention. Thus, the provision of focus seems to enhance the relative effectiveness of the modelling process.

Of greater theoretical and practical import are those studies in which the focus in modelling is provided

through some form of discrimination training whereby trainees learn to code and label appropriate and inappropriate behaviours, and the effects of this treatment are then compared with a conventional microteaching treatment which includes trainee practice of the skill. It has been asserted that "practice is necessary for skills acquisition" (Trower et al. 1978 p. 71), with this assertion being supported by reference to the acquisition of motor skills. However, the evidence arising from studies of the acquisition of teaching skills through modelling with discrimination training suggests that practice may not be as essential as has been supposed.

Peterson (1973), for example, compared the effects of a full microteaching treatment involving modelling, discrimination training, individual practice, videotape feedback, and further practice, with a treatment involving modelling, discrimination training, and limited group practice. Seven weeks after these treatments, trainees were asked to prepare a lesson using the 12 skill components previously identified. No significant differences between the groups were found on any of the criteria.

In contrast to the Peterson study, which provided modelling and discrimination training for both groups, an investigation by Wagner (1973) compared a microteaching treatment (with practice and videotape replay, but without modelling) with a discrimination training treatment. It was found that while the microteaching treatment failed to produce significant overall changes in teaching behaviour, the discrimination training was highly effective in changing teaching behaviour, such that on two of the three behavioural criteria, the discrimination training group significantly outperformed the microteaching group.

Further studies which suggest that modelling with discrimination training may be sufficient for skill acquisition are those by MacLeod et al. (1977) and Batten (1978). An ongoing study by Pegg (1982) reaches similar conclusions in regard to skill acquisition, but further demonstrates that a modelling/discrimination training component can be as favourably received by trainees as the practice/feedback component of microteaching.

4. Conclusions

The studies reviewed here, together with those in the article *Microteaching: Feedback*, indicate the powerful role which can be played by modelling procedures in microteaching. Further, the outcomes of the research seem entirely consistent with Bandura's social learning theory. The research is of particular interest in suggesting that modelling with discrimination training may lead to skills acquisition without a skill practice component being required, an outcome consistent with Bandura's distinction between acquisition and performance. Thus, modelling has been shown to be a significant component of microteaching but its role as a possible substitute for microteaching requires further investigation.

See also: Microteaching: Conceptual and Theoretical Bases; Microteaching: Feedback; Microteaching: Effectiveness

Bibliography

Allen D W, Ryan K A 1969 *Microteaching.* Addison Wesley, Reading, Massachusetts

Allen D W, Berliner D C, McDonald F J, Sobol F T 1967 A comparison of different modelling procedures in the acquisition of a teaching skill. ERIC Document No. ED 011 261

Bandura A 1977 *Social Learning Theory.* Prentice-Hall, Englewood Cliffs, New Jersey

Batten H D 1978 Factors influencing the effectiveness of microteaching in a teacher education programme. Ph.D. thesis, University of Stirling, Scotland, 1978. *Aslib Index to Theses* 28(2): 5515

Claus K E S 1968 The effects of modelling and feedback variables on higher order questioning skills (Doctoral dissertation, Stanford University, 1968) *Dissertation Abstracts International* 1969 29: 2133A (University Microfilms No. 69–207)

Gilmore S 1977 The effects of positive and negative models on student–teachers' questioning behaviour. In: McIntyre D I, MacLeod G R, Griffiths R (eds.) 1977, Chap. 10

Griffiths R 1976 The preparation of models for use in microteaching programmes. *Educ. Media Int.* 1: 25–31

Koran J J 1971 A study of the effects of written and film-mediated models on the acquisition of a science teaching skill by preservice elementary teachers. *J. Res. Sci. Teach.* 8: 45–50

Koran J J, Koran M L, McDonald F J 1972 Effects of different sources of positive and negative information on observational learning of a teaching skill. *J. Educ. Psychol.* 63: 405–410

Koran M L 1969 The effects of individual differences on observational learning in the acquisition of a teaching skill (Doctoral dissertation, Stanford University, 1969) *Dissertation Abstracts International* 1970 30: 1450A–1451A (University Microfilms No. 69–17,435)

McDonald F J, Allen D W 1967 Training effects of feedback and modeling procedures on teaching performance. Technical Report No. 3, Center for Research and Development in Teaching, Stanford University, California

McIntyre D I, MacLeod G R, Griffiths R (eds.) 1977 *Investigations of Microteaching.* Croom Helm, London

MacLeod G R, Griffiths R, McIntyre D I 1977 The effects of differential training and of teaching subject on microteaching skills performance. In: McIntyre D I, MacLeod G R, Griffiths R (eds.) 1977

Orme M E J 1966 The effects of modeling and feedback variables on the acquisition of a complex teaching strategy (Doctoral dissertation, Stanford University, 1966) *Dissertation Abstracts International* 1966 27: 3320A–3321A (University Microfilms No. 67-4417)

Pegg J 1982 Personal communication

Peterson T L 1973 Microteaching in the preservice education of teachers: Time for a reexamination. *J. Educ. Res.* 67: 34–36

Phillips W E 1973 Effect of a video-taped modeling procedure on verbal questioning practices of secondary social studies student teachers. Fairmont State College, West Virginia, ERIC Document No. ED 079 967

Trower P, Bryant B, Argyle M 1978 *Social Skills and Mental Health.* Methuen, London

Wagner A C 1973 Changing teaching behaviour: A comparison of microteaching and cognitive discrimination training. *J. Educ. Psychol.* 64: 299–305

Young D B 1967 The effectiveness of self-instruction in teacher education using modelling and video-tape feedback (Doctoral dissertation, Stanford University, 1967) *Dissertation Abstracts International* 1968 28: 4520A (University Microfilms No. 68–6518)

Microteaching: Feedback

D. S. Levis

Initially developed in 1963 by a group of researchers at Stanford University (USA), microteaching flourished over the following decade as a teacher-training innovation and generated a persistent cumulative body of educational research. By 1972, the findings of over 100 research studies of the various aspects of the microteaching technique had been reported in the professional literature. A review of the educational literature since that time shows a sharp decline in the number of reported studies in microteaching and related areas. Despite this diminished research interest, microteaching has continued to be widely accepted by teacher educators in many countries as an effective teacher-training component, principally to complement student teaching.

It is basically a simple technique which applies an instructional systems approach and principles of observational learning to training in specific teaching skills. In brief, it involves trainees in scaled-down teaching in terms of teaching task, class size, and length of lesson; and the subsequent provision to them of feedback information about their teaching performance.

As developed at Stanford, and as generally practised, the microteaching training format consists of a three-phased sequence. In phase 1 (modelling), opportunity is provided for trainees to observe a model teacher who emits the teaching behaviours to be learned. In phase 2 (practice), trainees are given an opportunity to practise the same behaviours. In phase 3 (feedback), trainees are reinforced for those instances of the desired behaviour they have emitted. This phase is considered necessary because the teaching behaviour emitted may not have been sufficiently reinforced during the modelling and practice phases.

Research studies have attempted to measure the general effectiveness of microteaching as a means of developing teaching skills and to investigate the modelling, practice, and feedback variables operating within the observational learning model on which microteaching is based. This article focuses upon the feedback phase.

1. Feedback

Feedback refers to the communication of information about performance to the learner. Research evidence in different fields of the behavioural sciences has shown that feedback can be effective in motivating and facilitating behavioural change. There is little contrary evidence to the general conclusion that learning is enhanced by frequent, immediate, and positive feedback.

Behaviouristically oriented theorists have attributed the effects of feedback largely to reinforcement. Informing the learner that a given action is successful gratifies the cognitive, affiliative, and ego-enhancing drives and increases the probability of the action recurring.

The advantages of feedback may also be argued on the grounds of its cognitive effects on learning. According to Ausubel and Robinson (1969 pp. 299–300) information about performance "confirms appropriate meanings and associations, corrects errors, clarifies misconceptions and indicates the relative adequacy with which different portions of the learning task have been mastered. As a result of feedback, the subject's confidence in his learning products is increased, his learnings are consolidated, and he is better able to focus his efforts and attention on those aspects of a task requiring further refinement".

Perlberg (1976) provides a psychological explanation for feedback based largely on cognitive dissonance theory (Festinger 1957). He argues that the feedback receiver or person confronting himself identifies discrepancies between actual and desired performances. This discrepancy creates tension, dissatisfaction, or anxiety, any of which activate a motivating force leading to their reduction. Perlberg sees feedback and self-confrontation as complementary processes. A person confronts himself or herself when he or she receives feedback messages through different sources. These messages do not have to be channelled through mediators. A person may perceive a discrepancy between his or her intentions and the respective outcome with or without the aid of others. When this occurs, he or she develops a need or drive to eliminate the discrepancy. According to Perlberg (1976 p. 17) "The degree of importance attached to the elimination of the discrepancy is a function of the intensity of the need created by the discrepancy and the availability and awareness of opportunities and resources through which he can satisfy these needs."

Essential to all the above conceptualizations of feedback is the necessity of highlighting important elements of the feedback process. Unless accompanied by appropriate shaping behaviour or some kind of focusing, feedback has not been found to change behaviour significantly.

2. Feedback in Microteaching

The research literature in the period 1963 to 1975 indicates that there was considerable interest in the effects of the feedback component in the microteaching process. While a number of studies consistently supported the advantages of providing accurate feedback information to trainees, there was a lack of congruence in the findings of studies which systematically varied feedback treatments.

Three major areas of research interest were (a) the effects of videotape and audiotape feedback, (b) the effects of supervisor influence during feedback, and (c) the relative effects of modelling and feedback.

2.1 Videotape and Audiotape Feedback

The development of microteaching coincided with the development of portable videotape recorders and cheap, compact audiotape recorders. It was not surprising, therefore, that they should be regarded as powerful tools in bringing about behavioural change by providing accurate feedback and that they should be used extensively in microteaching settings as adjuncts to critiques by supervisors, peers and pupils, and as a basis for the trainee's self-evaluation.

The videotape recorder has commonly been considered to be the major source of feedback. Because of its capacity to reproduce the teaching immediately and in a complete, objective, and reliable manner, it has been seen as providing a common frame of reference for supervisor and trainee to focus on specific behaviours emitted during the practice phase, and helping to depersonalize criticism, thus making trainees less defensive and more amenable to behavioural change.

In a most comprehensive review of the literature on feedback and self-confrontation via videotape replays, Fuller and Manning (1973) draw attention to some of the potentially harmful effects of this form of feedback. From Fuller and Manning's detailed analysis and discussion of the problem, various important principles emerge: (a) videotape feedback can be a stressful, anxiety-producing experience: objective representation of the self can be more anxiety producing if the subject is already anxious; videotape representation of self involves a selectivity and focusing on self which makes such a feedback experience more arousing emotionally, and different from other representations of self; (b) initial exposure to videotape replays causes intense self-focus on physical cues; (c) for videotape feedback to be successful, it should be done in situations where the subject feels basically secure; moderate rather than extreme dissonance has been found to be more effective in bringing change in nonattitudinal matters; and

(d) when subjects are given videotape feedback of themselves, it produces less discrepancy between their self-concept and the way in which others see them, and increases their accuracy of self-perception and of self-appraisal.

A review of the literature of microteaching reveals that videotape feedback has been perceived mainly as a means of providing accurate information; its potentially disruptive effects have been largely unexplored. One possible explanation for this is that stressful, anxiety-producing experiences are most likely to occur when videotape feedback focuses on the self. In the typical microteaching setting, the focus is on the trainee's application of previously modelled teaching skills. This focus on the technical skills of teaching tends to avoid direct confrontation with self and its potentially stressful effects.

That videotape feedback is more effective in producing behavioural changes than other forms of feedback has been more often assumed than tested. While several studies have supported its effectiveness in microteaching settings, a number of studies have found no significant difference between videotape feedback and feedback without videotape for the development of teaching skills. In general, it would seem that research and application of videotape feedback within microteaching contexts have not been sufficiently penetrating and critical to comprehend its advantages and disadvantages and to optimize its potential.

Studies which have compared videotape and audiotape feedback have produced conflicting results, suggesting that the effectiveness of the type of feedback may depend substantially on the nature of the skill being practised. Feedback on the performance of predominantly verbal skills might be more effectively mediated by audiotape, while feedback on skills with visual elements would benefit from the use of videotape. Fuller and Manning report the findings of Poling (1968) and Yenawine and Arbuckle (1971) that videotape replays have been found initially to be more threatening than audiotape replays. They suggest that videotape playback should be used for initial arousal and individual playback and that audiotape feedback be used for group feedback and long-term practice.

2.2 Supervisor Influence During Feedback

While the role of supervision during feedback sessions has received attention, empirical evidence regarding optimal supervisory styles and modes is inconclusive.

Griffiths (1976) identified three broad conceptualizations of the supervisory role within a microteaching context: (a) an approach to supervision related to the behaviourist theory of shaping in which the trainee attempts to approximate the teaching behaviour of a model and the supervisor provides feedback information as to the degree of success the trainee has achieved in performing the modelled behaviour; (b) formulation of the supervisor's contribution in terms of a counselling role addressed to the trainee's current psychological state; and (c) a supervisory approach which focuses on cognitive variables in the critique situation so that the trainee is viewed as a processor of information and the supervisor as a facilitator in this process. In the absence of empirical evidence on the differential effectiveness of these conceptualizations of the supervisory role, the professional literature has tended to promote an eclectic approach based on a listing of possible and overlapping supervisory tasks.

Research studies on the effects of supervisory influence during the feedback phase tend to cluster around two major concerns: (a) the effects of supervisor discussion based on videotape or audiotape feedback compared to supervisor discussion without playback facilities; and (b) the differential effects of source of feedback.

While a number of studies have supported the proposition that a combination of a trained supervisor and playback facilities provides a powerful means of feedback, a sufficient number of studies have produced nonsignificant differences to raise doubt about the need for playback facilities during critique sessions.

In relation to source of feedback two questions arise: firstly, whether other participants in the microteaching programme, such as peer observers or pupils, are as powerful a source of feedback as the supervisor; and, secondly, whether playback facilities permit the trainee to self-monitor his or her feedback and obviate the need for supervisory feedback.

Research evidence almost unanimously supports the view that feedback that is not accompanied by some form of focus will have little effect in changing behaviour. The importance of supervisory feedback within the microteaching format is supported by a number of studies. It appears that conferences led by trained supervisors serve the purpose of providing focus; however, a factor which also emerges is that it is not so much the presence of a supervisor, but the kind of person he or she is and the procedures he or she follows, that are important. There is also empirical evidence to suggest that self-analysis, supported by a self-evaluation guide to focus trainee attention, is a viable alternative for feedback involving supervisor-led discussion. Studies which have investigated feedback from pupils to trainees or from pupils and peers to trainees, have shown a disruptive effect on trainee behaviour, and pointed to the need for the supervisor to boost the morale of a trainee faced with critical feedback.

2.3 Relative Effects of Modelling and Feedback

A considerable body of microteaching research investigated the relative effects of the modelling and feedback phases of the microteaching format, in an effort to determine the most effective combination of these two variables. Studies by Bandura and McDonald (1963), Claus (1969), Salomon and McDonald (1970) and Resnick and Kiss (1970) showed that modelling procedures alone had a significantly greater effect on trainee behaviour than feedback alone.

McDonald and Allen (1967) compared different combinations of modelling and feedback procedures. Their comprehensive series of studies investigated the combination of symbolic models (involving such written materials as transcripts of teaching and oral or written descriptions of teaching skills) or perceptual models (involving visual or auditory models presented either live or on film, videotape, or audiotape) with a feedback process which included reinforcement and discrimination training on relevant cues. The treatment which consistently gained the highest scores combined symbolic and perceptual modelling and prompting and confirmation feedback conditions.

On the basis of their studies, McDonald and Allen (1967) were impressed by the comparative effectiveness of complementary modelling and feedback procedures and suggested the possibility that feedback could be reduced in scale if powerful modelling were available.

Bandura (1965 p. 313) argued that modelling procedures are most effective in transmitting new response patterns, whereas feedback is an efficient method of "strengthening and maintaining responses that already exist in the behavioural repertoire of an organism". Modelling is regarded as an acquisition variable, while feedback functions as a performance variable. Modelling enables trainees to acquire a skill; feedback helps them to adapt the skill to their own personality and to teaching situations other than those demonstrated by the model.

Another study which lent support to the comparative importance of modelling was the investigation by Salomon and McDonald (1970). In this study, the investigators found, as they had predicted, that without any prior conception of the criterion behaviour, the videotape replay of a lesson only gave trainees information about how far their behaviour departed from their own predispositions about a skill, so that subsequent behaviour was unlikely to be productively changed. The implication of this finding is that if trainees know through careful modelling what behaviours are expected of them, feedback sessions are more useful because they are able to compare their performance with the criterion, assess the extent to which it departs from the desired behaviour, and thus effect necessary changes.

A study by Resnick and Kiss (1970) found that, if responses and stimulus occasions have been adequately discriminated in advance of practice, subjects can apply the discrimination to their own behaviour and learn to self-edit their practice of teaching skills. The investigators concluded that prepractice discrimination training offered the possibility of doing away with costly feedback procedures, because the trainee's reliance on outside feedback would be substantially reduced.

3. Summary

The preceding overview of theory and research relating to feedback in microteaching provides evidence for the following conclusions:

(a) The provision of immediate accurate feedback regarding a particular teaching behaviour enhances the subsequent performance of that behaviour.

(b) Unless accompanied by appropriate highlighting, focusing or cueing, feedback will not change behaviour significantly.

(c) When accompanied by powerful modelling procedures, the effects of feedback tend to be less significant.

(d) Studies which have compared various feedback treatments in microteaching settings have produced inconclusive results. Research findings tend to favour the use of videotape playbacks as a basis for critique sessions. However, there is evidence to show that initially they may have disruptive effects on learning, and that for some verbal skills and for long-term practice they may not be as effective as the use of audiotape playbacks. Results tend to favour the presence of a trained supervisor to provide focus, reinforcement, and morale boosting during feedback sessions; however, there is also evidence to show that trainee self-analysis can be effective if supported by cueing devices, such as self-evaluation check lists.

See also: Microteaching: Conceptual and Theoretical Bases; Microteaching: Effectiveness; Technical Skills of Teaching; Microteaching: Modelling

Bibliography

Ausubel D P, Robinson F G 1969 *School Learning: An Introduction to Educational Psychology*. Holt, Rinehart and Winston, New York

Bandura A J 1965 Behavioral modification through modeling procedures. In: Krasner L, Ullman L P (eds.) 1965 *Research in Behavior Modification*. Holt, Rinehart and Winston, San Francisco, California, pp. 310–40

Bandura A J, McDonald F J 1963 The influence of social reinforcement and the behavior of models in shaping children's model judgment. *J. Abnorm. Soc. Psych.* 67: 601–7

Claus K E S 1969 Effects of modelling and feedback treatment on the development of teachers' questioning skills, Technical Report No. 6. Stanford Center for Research and Development in Teaching, Stanford University, California (ERIC Document No. ED 033 081)

Festinger L 1957 *A Theory of Cognitive Dissonance*. Row, Peterson, Evanston, Illinois

Fuller F F, Manning B A 1973 Self-confrontation reviewed: A conceptualization for video playback in teacher education. *Rev. Educ. Res.* 43: 469–512

Griffiths R 1976 Preparing tutors for microteaching supervision. *Ed. Media Int.* 1: 11–15

McDonald F J, Allen D W 1967 Training effects of modeling and feedback procedures on teaching performance, Technical Report No. 3. Stanford Center for Research and Development in Teaching, Stanford University, California (ERIC Document No. ED 017 985)

Perlberg A 1976 Microteaching – present and future trends. *Educ. Med. Int.* 1976(2): 13–20

Perlberg A 1983 When professors confront themselves toward a theoretical conceptualization of video self confrontation in higher education. *Higher Educ.* 12: 633–63

Perlberg A 1984 When professors confront themselves: The use of video self-confrontation (VSC) in improving university teaching. In: Zuber-Skeriff O (ed.) 1984 *Video in Higher Education*, Kogan Page, London

Poling E G 1968 Videotape recordings in counseling practicum: Environmental considerations. *Couns. Educ. Superv.* 7: 348–56

Resnick L B, Kiss L E 1970 Discrimination training and feedback in shaping teacher behaviour. Paper presented to annual conference of the American Educational Research Association (ERIC Document No. ED 039 175)

Salomon G, McDonald F J 1970 Pretest and posttest reactions to self-viewing one's teaching performance on videotape. *J. Educ. Psychol.* 61: 280–86

Yenawine G, Arbuckle D S 1971 Study of the use of videotape and audiotape as techniques in counsellor education. *J. Couns. Psychol.* 18: 1–6

Microteaching: Effectiveness

G. R. MacLeod

Questions about the effectiveness of microteaching depend upon the aims of particular microteaching programmes and these aims are dependent upon the models of participant learning underlying the programme. From the literature, four distinct but sometimes overlapping models may be discerned.

From the original Stanford programme, two models emerge. First, there is the apparent "easy pragmatism" of the first programme as represented in the writing of Allen and Ryan (1969). Here microteaching is seen within a general training paradigm, where concepts from psychology like modelling and reinforcement are freely borrowed, the emphasis is upon "what works", and the criteria for success are skill acquisition and measures of general teaching effectiveness. This is very clearly the "model" adopted by many microteaching programmes.

The second model from the Stanford programme is that of behaviour modification (McDonald 1973). The focus of such a programme would be on the application of modelling, on detailed response analysis, and on the use of contingency reinforcement principles, whilst the criterion for success would be in terms of specific behaviour change. Few microteaching programmes have operated according to these principles and by 1973, McDonald wrote that "Many users of micro-teaching did not see the relevance of behavior modification procedures" (p. 72) and that "The most undesirable consequence of the promotion of micro-teaching was that the role of behavior modification . . . was obscured" (p. 73).

The third approach to microteaching is one derived from the social skills training model of Argyle (1970) and applied in a microteaching context by Brown (1975). Teaching skills, like other social skills, are seen as analogous to perceptual and motor skills, and the foci of a training programme therefore relate to the selection of aims, the selective perception of relevant cues, motor response (or practice), and feedback and correction. Criteria for success are again to be found in performance.

The fourth approach encompasses a series of cognitive models which place greater emphasis on participants' thinking about their teaching. Represented here is the work of Fuller and Manning (1973), and of Bierschenk (1974) in which emphasis is placed upon incongruity between intent and action as revealed by videotape, upon the dissonance which this creates, and the subsequent intentional behaviour change which this produces. A model which focuses less on the motivational aspects is that proposed by MacLeod and McIntyre (1977), in which attention is drawn to the heavy information-processing demands imposed by the complexity of classroom environments, to the cognitive strategies which teachers use to cope with that complexity, which suggests that teaching skills should be reconceptualized as "ways of thinking" rather than as "ways of behaving", and that the effectiveness of microteaching should be assessed in terms of whether it provides "for the development and induction of functional and adaptive cognitive structures" (p. 262). Recent increased interest in describing and mapping teachers' thinking about teaching (e.g. Shavelson and Stern 1981) suggests that more emphasis in microteaching research ought to be devoted to cognitive processes and outcomes as criteria of effectiveness (see *Microteaching: Conceptual and Theoretical Bases*; *Microteaching: Modelling*).

1. Attitudinal Outcomes of Microteaching

Perhaps the most consistently reported outcome of research on microteaching is that participants find it a valuable and enjoyable activity. For example, a recent course evaluation by MacLeod involving over 100 preservice teacher-education students found that over 95 percent of them rated microteaching as interesting, practical, relevant, and useful. Similar favourable assessments from both pre- and in-service participants have been reported frequently. Amongst teacher educators, reactions to microteaching were, at least initially, mixed. Although many immediately accepted and implemented the innovation, others questioned the assumptions implicit in the practice of microteaching. In particular, doubt was cast upon whether the complex and dynamic art of teaching could readily be dissected into component parts or skills. But, over time, microteaching seems to have won acceptance as an integral part of teacher-education programmes and to have received favourable and widespread acceptance (Turney 1977).

2. Performance Outcomes of Microteaching

The major gap in research on microteaching is a lack of firm evidence as to whether microteaching training affects subsequent classroom performance. This is not because the question has not been asked but rather because the modes of answering have been unsatisfactory or only partial rather than conclusive. Three main research approaches to the question may be discerned: a correlational one, in which relationships between performance in microteaching and performance in subsequent classroom teaching are sought; a pre-experimental approach in which participants' teaching performance before and after microteaching is assessed; and a true experimental approach in which the classroom performance of previous microteaching participants is compared with the performance of a control group which has not experienced microteaching.

A series of correlational studies, showing substantial relationships between microteaching performance and subsequent classroom performance has appeared (Brown 1975). These may be interpreted as suggesting that microteaching does affect classroom performance, or, equally plausibly, as providing a simple indication that those participants who can demonstrate skilled performance in microteaching can also do so in a classroom setting.

The pre-experimental approach is represented in the work of Borg (1972). In this study a group of inservice teachers were videotaped in their classrooms to allow a precourse evaluation of skill usage. The group then undertook a microteaching course and were videotaped again one week after the course, four months later, and 39 months later. It was shown that classroom performance immediately after microteaching is marked by greater skill use than before microteaching, that there is no significant regression in skill use after four months, and that after 39 months, performance remained significantly superior to premicroteaching performance in 8 of 10 skill-related measures. Unfortunately, the design of such studies does not permit one to conclude that the observed changes are a consequence of microteaching, for several possible rival explanations of the results are possible.

A series of true experimental studies of microteaching has been carried out, but the results of these have been mixed, with some reporting that microteaching does have effects on subsequent teaching performance, and some finding no differences between the effects of microteaching and control treatments. This section reviews a set of three negative outcome studies, and a set of three positive outcome studies, and concludes that no firm conclusions as to the effectiveness of microteaching can be drawn, not primarily because of the mixed results but rather because of the difficulties inherent in carrying out such research.

One of the negative outcome investigations was that by Copeland and Doyle (1973). They compared the effects of a six-week microteaching treatment (focusing on three questioning skills) with the effects of a control treatment not related to microteaching or to the three teaching skills. The criterion measures of skill performance were derived from two audiorecorded 15-minute discussions taught by the 14 participants during a practice-teaching period occurring seven weeks after the experimental treatments. Instructions for these criterion discussions were designed not to sensitize trainees to the fact that the major interest was skill acquisition. The reported outcome of this study was that microteaching did not have a significant effect on classroom performance. However, inspection of the reported data indicates that individual differences among the seven subjects in each group are very substantial, and a partial reanalysis of the data (MacLeod 1981) reveals that significant differences in favour of the microteaching group may be produced by controlling for overall frequency of questioning.

Two further studies involving Copeland (1975, 1977) report that the main effects of microteaching on subsequent classroom performance are not significant. However, the second study does show two significant interaction effects involving microteaching training, and this suggests that microteaching training may lead to skill acquisition but not necessarily to subsequent skill performance (see *Microteaching: Modelling*). In both studies, group sizes were again small, and some effort was made to control for large within-group differences in the second study but not in the first. Thus, the fact that the experimental group's mean rate of higher order questioning in the criterion lesson was twice the rate of the control group was shown to be statistically nonsignificant and due in large part to a single extreme score in the experimental group.

An experimental study finding positive outcomes of microteaching was that by Raymond (1973). She compared the classroom skill performance of a group who had received microteaching skill practice with a group who had not. It was found that the microteaching group did differ significantly from the control group on two of the three skill criteria, and on four other measures of teacher behaviour.

One of the comparisons in a complex but elegant and carefully controlled experimental investigation by Levis et al. (1974) was between a group participating in a normal school experience programme and a group undertaking a microteaching programme in a school setting. All participants in the study were given identical skill training. At the end of the training programme, all participants taught a 10-minute lesson to a class of five pupils and measures of skill acquisition were derived from this. On two of the three criterion skills the micro-teaching group significantly outperformed the school experience group.

Butts (1977) compared a group of students receiving microteaching practice of questioning and responding skills with a group of students who did not receive such practice. On a pretest, there were no systematic differences between the groups; on a posttest, 15 of the 16 criteria favoured the microteaching group, and these differences were statistically significant for the questioning skill components.

Apart from the obvious difficulties of synthesizing diverse and different outcomes, several other difficulties of interpretation arise from this sample of investigations of the outcomes of microteaching.

First, it is clear that the term microteaching is used by different investigators to label different sets of activities, and this in turn means that the relevant control or comparison treatments also differ across investigators. Thus, in the studies by Copeland, the comparison was between trainees receiving skill instruction, practice, and feedback and those who did not, whilst in the study by Levis and his associates all trainees received the same skill instruction but differed in the type of practice subsequently undertaken and perhaps also in whether they were explicitly asked to practise the relevant skills.

Second, it is clear from some of the studies reviewed here that small sample sizes and large within-group differences can minimize the power of the analyses to detect between-group differences. Several possible remedies to this difficulty are possible but it is perhaps significant to note that two of the positive outcome studies did pretest the participants on skill performance. In the case of Butts, the pretest was used to match subjects across the two groups; in the case of Levis et al., the pretest was used to determine whether adjustment to posttest scores was required.

Third, the criteria to be used in assessing outcomes of microteaching do pose difficulties. In the Copeland investigations, a clear assumption was that skills acquired in microteaching should become part of a teacher's habitual repertoire of classroom skills. This implies that samples to be used as criterion measures do need to be adequate measures of subsequent teaching behaviour, and it is by no means clear that this has been achieved (Shavelson and Dempsey-Attwood 1976). An alternative approach has been to ask trainees to use in a criterion lesson the skills they have acquired (Peterson 1973). This not only leads to an obvious reduction in generalizability of results but also implies that trainees in control of "no microteaching" treatments should be as familiar with the required skills as those in the "microteaching" treatment. Only the Levis et al. study provided identical skill training for all participants. However, even in that study a criterion problem arose in that outcomes were assessed on the basis of an audiorecorded microteaching lesson, a format which might be seen as favouring a microteaching group over a nonmicroteaching group.

Fourth, greater consideration must be given to evaluating the likely value or validity of the outcomes of experimental studies of the effectiveness of microteaching. An implicit assumption seems to have been that microteaching is a teacher-education technique which has the same aims and functions as other teacher-education techniques, and thus experimentation comparing microteaching with some other technique has been viewed as an appropriate way of assessing effectiveness. But, if the assumption is not a justifiable one, then the value of experimental research of this kind must be questioned.

3. Conclusions

Despite some 20 years of research effort, the only definitive conclusion which can be drawn about the effectiveness of microteaching is that participants are seen to enjoy and value the experience. It seems clear that microteaching enjoyed almost faddish popularity in the late 1960s and early 1970s and that this produced a plethora of studies on isolated aspects of microteaching from which only few useful generalizations may be formed. It is also clear that there has been no recent sustained research programme which has attempted to draw both upon these generalizations and the lessons learned in the execution of that research.

Simple verdicts on the effects of microteaching on subsequent teacher behaviour are unlikely to be reached. Microteaching, like any other teaching method, is complex, in terms of the variety of components it uses, the aims it attempts to achieve, and the theoretical models which underlie these aims. Assessment of success is further complicated by the difficulty of specifying criteria for achievement of some of the less tangible aims and by the sheer cost and practical difficulties involved in mounting meaningful long-term research in this area. Nevertheless, microteaching is itself a costly endeavour and there is a clear need for research-based study of its effects so as to allow judgments as to its effectiveness. It is apparent that much experimental research on microteaching has been sterile, providing only a situation-specific evaluation of a particular and local set of training components. This has prevented any meaningful accumulation of research results into a coherent pattern. The remedy for this problem lies in ensuring that research on microteaching is derived from, or allows for, the testing of coherent and generalizable theory. Only then will coherent and generalizable results emerge.

See also: Microteaching: Conceptual and Theoretical Bases; Microteaching: Feedback; Microteaching: Modelling

Bibliography

Allen D W, Ryan K A 1969 *Microteaching*. Addison Wesley, Reading, Massachusetts

Argyle M 1970 *Social Interaction*. Methuen, London

Bierschenk B 1974 *Perceptual, Evaluative and Behavioral Changes Through Externally Mediated Self-confrontation: Explorations and Experiments in Microsettings*. School of Education, Malmö

Borg W R 1972 The minicourse as a vehicle for changing teacher behavior: A three year follow-up. *J. Educ. Psychol.* 63: 572–79

Brown G A 1975 Microteaching: Research and developments. In: Chanan G, Delamont S (eds.) 1975 *Frontiers of Classroom Research*. National Foundation for Educational Research, Slough

Butts D C 1977 An assessment of microteaching in the context of the graduate training year. In: McIntyre D I, MacLeod G R, Griffiths R (eds.) (1977)

Copeland W D 1975 The relationship between microteaching and student performance. *J. Educ. Res.* 68: 289–93

Copeland W D 1977 Some factors related to student teacher classroom performance following microteaching training. *Am. Educ. Res. J.* 14: 147–57

Copeland W D, Doyle W 1973 Laboratory skill training and student teacher classroom performance. *J. Exp. Educ.* 52: 16–21

Fuller F F, Manning B A 1973 Self-confrontation reviewed: A conceptualization for video playback in teacher education. *Rev. Educ. Res.* 43: 469–528

Levis D, Thompson H, Mitchell J 1974 An assessment of alternative techniques to practice teaching and an examination of selected variables within a microteaching format.

Paper presented at the South Pacific Association for Teacher Education Conference, Adelaide

McDonald F J 1973 Behavior modification in teacher education. In: Thoresen C E (ed.) 1973 *Behavior Modification in Education*. University of Chicago Press, Chicago, Illinois

McIntyre D I, MacLeod G R, Griffiths R (eds.) 1977 *Investigations of Microteaching*. Croom Helm, London

MacLeod G R 1981 Experimental studies of the outcomes of microteaching. *South Pac. J. Teach. Educ.* 9: 31–42

MacLeod G R, McIntyre D I 1977 Towards a model for microteaching. In: McIntyre D I, MacLeod G R, Griffiths R (eds.) 1977

Peterson T L 1973 Microteaching in the preservice education of teachers: Time for a re-examination. *J. Educ. Res.* 67: 34–36

Raymond A 1973 The acquisition of nonverbal behaviors by preservice science teachers and their application during student teaching. *J. Res. Sci. Teach.* 10: 13–24

Shavelson R, Dempsey-Attwood N 1976 Generalizability of measures of teaching behavior. *Rev. Educ. Res.* 46: 553–611

Shavelson R J, Stern P 1981 Research on teachers' pedagogical thoughts, judgments, decisions and behaviour. *Rev. Educ. Res.* 51: 455–98

Turney C (ed.) 1977 *Innovation in Teacher Education: A Study of the Directions, Processes, and Problems of Innovation in Teacher Preparation with Special Reference to the Australian Context and to the Role of Cooperating Schools*. Sydney University Press, Sydney

Inservice

Inservice Teacher Education

M. Eraut

The inservice education and training of teachers (commonly abbreviated to INSET) is conveniently defined as:

those education and training activities engaged in by primary and secondary school teachers and principals, following their initial professional certification, and intended mainly or exclusively to improve their professional knowledge, skills, and attitudes in order that they can educate children more effectively. (Bolam 1980 p. 3)

While some countries use rather narrower definitions for administrative purposes, the problems and issues discussed under this broader brief will still be highly relevant.

National governments have been giving increasing attention to INSET recently for at least some of the following reasons:

(a) they believe that educational practice needs to be more closely linked to national needs and/or the needs of the local community;

(b) approaches to educational change which neglect the INSET dimension are usually unsuccessful;

(c) teachers, like other adults, need continuing education to keep abreast of changes in modern society;

(d) there is growing concern in some countries about the quality of teaching and career development of those who have had less basic education and training than current recruits to teaching;

(e) demographic trends have reduced the demand for new teachers in some countries, cutting off one important source of new ideas, diminishing career prospects, and focusing attention on those teachers who are already in service;

(f) the general feeling that education has failed to fulfil the hopes of the expansionist era between 1964 and 1974 has created a public pressure for improved school performance.

At the same time it is widely recognized that the structures and practices which have developed historically may not be the most appropriate for the final part of the twentieth century. Even in the United States, where expenditure on INSET has probably been highest, Corrigan (1979) was able to state that "there is almost universal consensus among all persons involved that most in service efforts are relatively ineffective". With a few exceptions, provision is either scant or fragmented; the most commonly available opportunities appeal to only a small minority of teachers; and the purposes and strategies of INSET are underconceptualized. However, since the early 1970s there has been a considerable advance in thinking. There have been several notable experiments with new styles and approaches and the identification of key problems and issues in several countries has been assisted by a long series of conferences and reports promoted by the Centre for Educational Research and Innovation (CERI) of the Organisation for Economic Co-operation and Development (OECD) (Bolam 1980).

This article will attempt to explore the main issues that have been identified, to guide the reader to recent literature on INSET, and to cite research findings where relevant to the ongoing discussion. The complexity of the topic has dictated the somewhat unusual structure in which fairly lengthy overviews of policies and assumptions are followed by a series of perspectives: teacher oriented, school oriented, government oriented, and higher education oriented. A short final section then discusses evaluation and research.

1. Policy Overview

1.1 Aims

Two published statements of aims give some indication of how much is expected from INSET. A British government committee, for example, suggested that the aims of INSET are to enable teachers:

(a) to develop their professional competence, confidence, and relevant knowledge;

(b) to evaluate their own work and attitudes in conjunction with their professional colleagues in other parts of the education service;

(c) to develop criteria which would help them to assess their own teaching roles in relation to a changing society for which schools must equip their pupils; and

(d) to advance their careers (ACSTT 1974).

The OECD's Trade Union Advisory Committee laid even more stress on teachers' contributions to society in general, suggesting that INSET should:

(a) maintain the knowledge and skills of teachers;

(b) give them the opportunity to enlarge and improve their knowledge and educational capacities in all fields of their work;

(c) make them ready and able to understand and face in time new situations coming up in society and to prepare their students for the new economic, social, or cultural challenges;

(d) enable them to gain additional qualifications and to develop their special talents and dispositions; and

(e) raise the cultural and professional standard of the teaching force as a whole and strengthen its innovative vigour and creativity (TUAC 1980).

Both statements show a breadth of vision rarely found in practice, for most discussions focus almost exclusively on teachers' subject knowledge, specialist educational knowledge, and pedagogic skills. Psychological aims are sometimes added, such as helping teachers to overcome their isolation or improve their morale; and there is an occasional reference to experiential aims like periods of work in factories, farms, offices, or community organizations, which might bring teachers into closer contact with life outside their schools.

1.2 Activities

This definition of INSET includes an extremely wide range of activities, and much of the literature is concerned that only a few well-tried options are commonly practised in spite of evidence of their lack of success. The dimensions of purpose, mode, membership, location, and time provide a useful framework for classifying possible activities.

The following typology was developed by Howey and Joyce (1978) for a survey of inservice activities in three United States states:

(a) Job embedded. It can be embedded in the job, with the emphasis on actual performance in the classroom. Analysis of television tapes of one's teaching is an example.

(b) Job related. It can be closely related to the job, but not take place while teaching is going on. For example, a team of teachers can take an after-school workshop on team teaching.

(c) General professional. It can consist of experiences to improve general competence, but not be tailored to specific needs as closely as the above experiences. For example, science teachers can take workshops on the teaching of biology.

(d) Career/credential. It can be organized to help one obtain a new credential or prepare for a new role. A teacher can prepare to be a counsellor, for example.

(e) Personal. It can facilitate personal development which may or may not be job related. For example, one might study art history for personal enrichment which might or might not be immediately evident in one's teaching (p. 206).

When teachers were asked who they would prefer to see as instructors they responded differently according to the type of INSET. Thus "fellow teachers and their other related school personnel were seen as more appropriate for in-service which stressed job-embedded and job-related concerns, but professors were nominated as more desirable for the remaining three categories" (p. 207).

The use of the term "instructor" limits options to the course mode which tends to dominate INSET provision. Other modes include groupwork such as discussion groups, study groups, reading groups, conferences, and staff meetings; and participation in development activities such as materials production, curriculum design, or school-based evaluation. A fourth type of mode is an advisory service, in which advice or assistance is provided to an individual or group of teachers by a fellow-teacher, supervisor, district advisor, or external consultant. A fifth mode, personal INSET, includes private study, various forms of self-evaluation, and reflection on one's teaching. Then finally there are various experiential modes, ranging from minimal involvement by attending a demonstration or making a brief visit, through short periods of participant observation in other schools or work experience outside the education sector, to long secondments of a year or more to curriculum projects, research projects, or advisory or "master teacher" roles. Participation in team teaching and acting as a tutor to trainee teachers can also be considered as a form of job-embedded experiential INSET.

The nature of the activity will also be greatly affected by the membership: the number of people involved; their personalities; their knowledge and experience; their relationships on and off the job; and their attitudes, roles, and commitment. Groups of teachers from a single school or of individual teachers from several schools are fairly common, but other possibilities are rarely explored, for example, teachers of the same subject from two or three schools. Participation by community members, parents, or students might also be important for some activities (see Smith 1980, on the United States Teachers' Corps, and Ingvarson 1980, on recent Australian experience). Leadership roles for classroom teachers and nonleadership roles for principals, professors, and advisers can be hard to establish, and even the symbolic membership of senior administrators in the form of occasional attendance to show interest without interference can be of considerable value.

Location will usually be determined by convenience, cost, and tradition, though the convenience to the organizers often takes precedence over the convenience to the participants. Where authority issues are prominent the political and psychological advantage will be associated with being on one's home ground. Yet the opposite arguments, based on the need to get away from it all, can also be significant. Teacher centres offer the special advantage of central territory; and the occasional use of attractive non-work-like locations can sometimes have a psychological impact that justifies the additional expense. Residential settings in particular both emphasize the importance of the activity and allow the informal development of ideas and relationships outside the formal work sessions. While some activities generate their own momentum, it is difficult to create either temporal or mental space for more reflective kinds of INSET when people are preoccupied with day-to-day concerns.

Time constitutes the greatest problem of all. Fullan (1980) states that virtually all studies of INSET "have indicated that lack of time and energy for participating in professional development is a fundamental barrier to success". All forms of discussion and cooperative professional inquiry take time. Acquiring new skills takes time. Changing one's classroom practice takes time. Research suggests that many of the developments compressed into a few months require two or three years to make a significant long-term impact and that more INSET time in school hours is usually needed. This implies both greater attention to priorities in INSET planning and a fundamental rethinking of job conditions in schools.

1.3 Organization and Policy

Resources for INSET are contributed by a large number of agencies whose activities are rarely coordinated in any systematic way. These agencies include various levels of government—national, regional, and local; the schools themselves; teacher unions and professional associations; universities and colleges; government-financed quasi-independent agencies like research units, curriculum projects, and teacher centres; international agencies; commercial groups; special interest groups; broadcasting authorities; and individual teachers. Most agencies have three main types of expenditure: they organize their own INSET activities, they employ advisers, and they distribute materials and information. But government resource allocation is much more com-

plicated, because they have a substantial number of potentially competing programmes and much of their funding is allocated to other agencies.

The costing and planning of INSET is further complicated by much of its funding being merged with that of other activities. Advisers and consultants may also be inspectors, curriculum development agents, personnel officers, or administrators—roles which not only occupy their time but may even conflict with that of assisting in INSET. Universities and colleges may be primarily occupied with initial training or research. Curriculum projects and research centres may be given INSET funds to aid dissemination but find INSET competing for time and attention with redrafting materials or reports to meet publication deadlines. Schools can only fund INSET at the expense of items like books for pupils and gain time at the expense of class size or additional parent conferences. These arrangements tend to distract from a proper consideration of INSET on its own and lessen the chances that existing knowledge about INSET will be used. All too often, INSET is merely attached to the coat-tails of separate educational programmes with the result that schools are bombarded with an unco-ordinated array of INSET opportunities, none of which is individually sufficiently funded or conceptualized to provide the degree of assistance needed for significant impact in the classroom.

Other policies with strong financial implications are teacher release and accreditation of INSET. Teacher time in school hours can be created by using substitute teachers—this alone accounted for 80 percent of INSET costs in Sweden (Henricson 1980); by reorganizing the teaching, which requires strong support from all teachers concerned and initiative from the principal; or by using professional development days on which teachers are contracted to attend. Teacher contracts may also include or omit obligations to attend meetings in lunch-breaks, after school hours, or in vacations.

Accreditation of INSET is also closely connected with teacher careers, salaries, and conditions of service. Teachers in many countries can undertake formal study in colleges or universities for credit, diplomas, or degrees; and this may be closely tied to career progress or qualify them for salary increments. In North America such study may even be a requirement for relicensing (see *Certification and Licensing of Teachers*).

Finally, there is the major task of coordinating and planning INSET, on which the literature is exceedingly confused. There is much evidence of the consequences of bad coordination or lack of consultation, but these are also ready scapegoats which prevent people searching for deeper problems. While recognizing the advantages of decentralization, it would be naive to assume that it avoids all conflict (Mann 1978a). Nor does the existence of representatives on planning committees necessarily mean that the average teacher or parent is any more involved. Dependence on the technology of needs assessment may also be ill-advised given the narrow perspective of traditional INSET, the aversive connotation of the term "needs", the limitations of survey methods, and the difficulty of expressing priorities (Arends et al. 1978, Fullan 1980). Clearly, this is an area where much more research is needed, together with independent evaluations of some of the more interesting innovations which tend only to be reported by their proponents.

2. Basic Assumptions: The Four INSET Paradigms

Jackson (1971) contrasts two approaches to INSET—the "defect" approach and the "growth" approach—which are sufficiently distinctive to merit characterization as paradigms. The defect approach can be summarized by the terms "obsolescence" and "inefficiency", and oscillates between these two perspectives according to the mood of the times. Teachers may be regarded as obsolescent because they have had limited basic training, because they have not kept up with their subject, or because they are ignorant of the latest educational developments. The charge of inefficiency, however, is directed not at teacher knowledge but at teachers' skills whose inadequacy is held responsible for diminished pupil motivation and achievement. The cure for obsolescence is simple—traditional courses at colleges and universities—but the cure for inefficiency is disputed—some put their faith in supervision, some in competency-based teacher education, and some in pupil performance tests backed by the implicit threat of dismissal. Typically, however, the proponents of the defect approach are behaviourally oriented and their goal is that of equipping teachers with specific skills.

In contrast, the growth approach begins with the assumptions that "teaching is a complex and multi-faceted activity about which there is more to know than can ever be known by one person . . ."; and "the motive for learning more about teaching is not to repair a personal inadequacy as a teacher but to seek greater fulfillment as a practitioner of the art . . . ." "There is no such thing as the complete teacher. Though some people obviously know more about pedagogy than do others, those who know the most conform to no single model of perfection. In teaching, as in life, the roads to wisdom are many" (Jackson 1971 pp. 26–27). The main source of knowledge about teaching is not external expertise but the experience of teaching itself. However, experience alone is rarely sufficient to stimulate growth: reflection on it is also necessary, and for this the teacher needs both the time and the tools. Proponents of this approach do not deny that teacher growth is often lacking, but they attribute this problem not to defects in teachers but to defects in the system. Schools are not environments in which professional growth is encouraged.

The defect and growth paradigms differ fundamentally in their assumptions about epistemology (what constitutes valid knowledge about teaching?) and hence about the epistemological aspect of authority (who decides what is to count as valid knowledge about teach-

ing?) and these assumptions have strong political significance. University teachers' and researchers' political interests are protected by maintaining the epistemological assumptions of the defect approach and administrators' interests are protected by its assumptions about authority. ". . . the deficit model has been built based on the dogmatic belief of other educators that they know, and can justify, their statements about what constitutes good teaching. Though educational research . . . has not resolved the dilemma of what constitutes good teaching, deficit-model outside experts or central office specialists often act as though they know" (McLaughlin and Marsh 1978 p. 89). Teachers' political interests would appear to be served by adherence to the growth model, but in practice the ecological barriers to its fuller realization limit its credibility.

Neither of Jackson's paradigms seems to offer much to the political interests of the community, apart from the special appeal of the defect approach to special interest groups like the "back to basics" movement. Nor do they take into account the substantial expenditure on government-sponsored change since the early 1970s. While some national initiatives such as the first wave of curriculum projects might be interpreted in terms of the defect paradigm's concern with "obsolescence", others, such as funding for multicultural education or children with special needs, fit neither the growth nor the defect approach.

A substantial amount of INSET is based on what might be called the change paradigm, whose rationale is based on the need for the educational system to keep abreast of, if not anticipate, changes in wider society and for schools to relate to changes in their local community. Such changes will not necessarily be recognized, understood, or desired by all teachers, but they will have to come to terms with them and give careful thought to how their students' interests might be affected. The core assumption of the change paradigm is that the educational system needs redirection from time to time in accordance with cultural, economic, and technological changes in society and this redirection will be governed by the normal political process. To suggest that this can be achieved by the growth model alone is to allow educators an unreasonable degree of political power as social diagnosticians, but to use the defect model is to devalue their professional knowledge at a time when cooperation is essential. Not only does the defect model's emphasis on skills rather than orientation and understanding seem inappropriate for the kind of change being sought, but the political power of teachers to resist change suggests that it would be unlikely to succeed unless the whole educational system was under very tight central control. Recent research on curriculum implementation and educational change has suggested certain key principles such as community participation, negotiation between interested parties, local leadership, long-term support, and so on; but whether the application of these principles will bring about success must remain open to question. They are largely based on analysing the few cases where externally initiated change has been successfully implemented, and seem to assume that a consensus is readily obtainable in spite of known political differences.

The discussion has now identified two INSET paradigms which depend on a stimulus external to the teacher or school, the "defect paradigm" which aims at improvement and the "change paradigm" which aims at redirection. Table 1 identifies two corresponding paradigms which depend on a stimulus internal to the teacher or school. The language of the "growth paradigm"—trying new options, gaining new perspectives, and extending one's professional capabilities—identifies it with the aim of redirection at the personal or even institutional level. Hence, a fourth paradigm, aimed at improvement in response to internally diagnosed problems, is clearly needed. Yet the fourth "problem-solving paradigm" is not an artefact of our typology; it can be clearly identified in the literature that has appeared since the early 1970s and its role in INSET was explicated by Lippitt and Fox (1971) and Eraut (1972).

Table 1
Four INSET paradigms

		Stimulus	
		Internal	External
Goal	Improvement	Problem solving	Defect
	Redirection	Growth	Change

The problem-solving paradigm assumes that, because education is an inherently difficult and complex process and because circumstances are constantly changing, problems will inevitably arise in individual schools and classrooms. These problems are best diagnosed by the teachers most closely concerned because only they know the students and the context sufficiently well. INSET activities should be closely geared to the study and solution of these problems. External consultants may sometimes be desirable, but effective change will only occur if those most immediately concerned are involved throughout the process and are agreed upon the diagnosis of the problem and the approach to its solution. In response to pressures for accountability, more formal school self-evaluation procedures are now being introduced and teacher self-evaluation is also strongly advocated. But, as with the growth paradigm, the problem-solving approach has difficulty with external credibility, especially the accusation that it is only used by those teachers and schools who are least in need of it. Its internal credibility may also be problematic because, if it is controlled by senior teachers or a particular faction, it may become virtually indistinguishable from the

defect paradigm for the average junior teacher. However, this danger is less than that for the change paradigm for which slippage into a defect approach will always be a constant source of concern.

3. Teacher-oriented Perspectives

3.1 The Teachers' Predicament

Many critics of INSET argue that it takes insufficient account of the teachers' predicament. The difficulties of contemporary teaching include relentless time pressure, demanding mental effort, cellular isolation, an increasing range of often unrealistic expectations, additional nonteaching responsibilities, an environment of negativism, fear for one's job, and a general feeling of being at the bottom of the education status system (Flanders 1980). INSET activities appear to be just another pressure, not an aid to coping with these problems or a stimulus to rising above the "dailiness" of teaching. Moreover, they are usually organized by people who have escaped from the classroom but still seem to claim that they know more about the teachers' students and situations than do the teachers themselves (Drummond and Lawrence 1978). In spite of previous negative experiences, however, the teachers' predicament presses them to look for INSET activities which promise quick returns and to label as impractical, ideas which would take a long time to work into their practice (Doyle and Ponder 1977).

3.2 Teacher Concerns and Teacher Development

Fuller and Bown's (1975) research on beginning teachers' concerns suggested a three-phase sequence in which immediate concerns for survival (phase 1) gradually develop into concerns for coping with the teaching situation and school expectations (phase 2), and thence into concerns about impact on pupils and the quality of one's teaching contribution (phase 3). However, the expression of third-phase concerns may not necessarily mean that those in the second phase have ceased to matter, merely that they have become more taken for granted. Indeed concerns probably vary according to individual student, class, and context; and many older teachers may feel they are regressing as children become more and more difficult to teach.

The concerns concept has been subtly transformed by Hall and Loucks (1978) from the growth paradigm to the change paradigm. Thus the following shows seven stages of concern for teachers involved in implementing an educational innovation:

(a) *Awareness*. Little concern about or involvement with the innovation is indicated.

(b) *Informational*. A general awareness of the innovation and interest in learning more detail about it is indicated. The person seems to be unworried about himself/herself in relation to the innovation. She/he is interested in substantive aspects of the innovation in a selfless manner such as general characteristics, effects, and requirements for use.

(c) *Personal*. The individual is uncertain about the demands of the innovation, his/her inadequacy to meet those demands, and his/her role with the innovation. This includes analysis of his/her role in relation to the reward structure of the organization, decision making, and consideration of potential conflicts with the existing structure or personal commitment. Financial or status implications of the program for self and colleagues may also be reflected.

(d) *Management*. Attention is focused on the processes and tasks of using the innovation and the best use of information and resources. Issues related to efficiency, organizing, managing, scheduling, and time demands are utmost.

(e) *Consequence*. Attention focuses on impact of the innovation on students in his/her immediate sphere of influence. The focus is on relevance of the innovation for students, evaluation of student outcomes, including performance and competencies, and changes needed to increase student outcomes.

(f) *Collaboration*. The focus is on coordination and cooperation with others regarding use of the innovation.

(g) *Refocusing*. The focus is on exploration of more universal benefits from the innovation, including the possibility of major changes or replacement with a more powerful alternative. The individual has definite ideas about alternatives to the proposed or existing form of the innovation.

This adaptation may be more than just conceptual, for it also suggests that the process of implementing an innovation may usefully be seen as one of resocialization (Fullan 1980).

The term teacher development is often used to emphasize adherence to the growth paradigm rather than to any particular developmental theory, but three fairly precise patterns of use have been identified by Feiman and Floden (1980). The first is that of Fuller and Bown (see above), while the second is rooted in the advisory approach of progressive educators whose advocacy of the growth ideal for children fits naturally with a similar approach to teachers. Mitchell (1950), for example, describes four stages of growth towards maturity:

(a) Willingness to try something new.

(b) Recognition that further study of subject matter and children is needed.

(c) Curriculum building based on this knowledge and experience.

(d) Seeing the relationships between their work and the world outside school.

Since this analysis was based on long-term workshops manned by staff from a single agency, Bank Street College, the resocialization metaphor once more seems appropriate.

The third perspective on teacher development comes from adult education. The implications of recent theories of adult learning and development for INSET have yet to be properly digested, though Corrigan (1979) offers a number of interesting suggestions. Recent adult learning theories have a strong personal growth orientation with an emphasis on experiential learning, reflection, and group discussion. Adult development theories stress the significance of age or position in the life cycle, or progress through complex stages of cognitive development. Their assumption that adult development is an individual affair and takes a considerable period of time is consistent with other teacher development perspectives, but their more precise application is difficult to envisage.

The general conclusion of this section, therefore, is that INSET needs to be long term and personalized, though this should not be taken as excluding group activities that can accommodate to individual differences.

3.3 The Teacher as Artist, Craftsman, Actor . . .

Two images of the teacher–performer recur in the literature—that of the "expressive artist" whose unique style is a subtle blend of personality and acquired technique; and that of the "master craftsman" who has developed a repertoire of the skills of his trade. Each suggests different possibilities for INSET. The artist image is inseparable from the growth paradigm, and its emphasis on personality and style suggests autonomy and quality but probably not flexibility. Craftsmen, however, can acquire new skills through training, even though the process is likely to be lengthy (Joyce 1980). But they do not make professional judgments and their flexibility does not easily extend to making adjustments to practice according to the different situations confronted (Bush 1971).

The actor image is less prominent in the literature but more easily recognized by teachers. The actor can play several roles, but only chooses those to which he or she feels suited. Technique is important, but no performance can be analysed down to a set of distinct and separate skills. Interpretation and style are personal yet flexible. Performance is improved by observation, discussion, reflection, and experiment with only an occasional need for guided practice in any specific skill. Day (1981) reports the successful use of videorecording and nondirective consultancy for precisely this kind of purpose.

Most performing occupations offer considerable opportunity to observe master performers at work both before and after initial training. The promising musician, for example, not only strives to see and hear famous players but deliberately arranges to study with more than one teacher for substantial periods, and to take master classes with yet others. Even after a long period of technical training, developing one's own style takes time and one needs to see a range of other performers in order to learn, experiment, reflect, and create one's own interpretations. In surgery also, practitioners have stated that learning to handle difficult cases is best accomplished by watching several experts with differing approaches and having them explain their strategies and ongoing thoughts (Farmer 1981). It is this kind of practical experience that distinguishes professional training from mere apprenticeship, but teachers are never offered such an opportunity.

One characteristic that many teachers share with these other performing occupations is dedication to the quality of their performance. This is a major source of personal motivation in spite of the lack of agreed criteria. Yet Howey and Joyce (1978) comment:

> Rarely has inservice been presented to, or perceived by, the teacher as a rather natural and ongoing activity that is designed to help one be "very very good at something that is very very hard (challenging) to do," but . . . rather it is seen more often as remediative and patchwork in nature. (p. 211)

A related attribute is the teachers' sense of efficacy—the belief that they can help even the most difficult or unmotivated students—for this kind of self-confidence has been shown to be strongly correlated with improvements in pupil performance (McLaughlin and Marsh 1978).

3.4 The Teacher as Professional

The aspirations and obligations that go with teaching as a profession have considerable significance for INSET. At the very least, teacher professionality would seem to imply (a) a moral commitment to serve the interests of their clients; (b) informed decision making in which options are explored and evaluated in order to determine the most appropriate course of action; and (c) an obligation to advance the knowledge of the educational community. The first of these duties is the most universally recognized but begs the question of whose definition of client interest is to prevail. Credibility would be improved if there was more visible protection against the inevitable tendency for clients' interests to be interpreted in ways that coincide with teachers' convenience—a concern which is frequently expressed about other professions as well. The second duty implies that schools and departments or year-groups within schools need to devote time and effort to decision making and evaluation procedures and to seeking advice that might be relevant to them. Teacher professionality demands a collegial approach, and this whole conception of teacher professionalism is intimately bound up with the problem-solving paradigm.

The obligation to advance the knowledge of the edu-

cational community would seem to suggest both that teachers should share knowledge and experience with their colleagues and that at least some of them should participate in advanced study and research. The prevailing influence, however, would be that of the growth paradigm. This activity takes on special significance for those who believe that a major part of knowledge about education resides in the practical knowledge of teachers. Such knowledge cannot be readily shared, codified, or extended without significant teacher participation and leadership. Indeed some authors have suggested that participation in action research should constitute a major form of professional development (Elliott 1980, Mallan 1978, Tikunoff et al. 1980) (see *Teachers as Researchers*).

Professionality also contains within it a considerable trap for the unwary. Much initial training serves to provide teachers with a set of idealistic aspirations and an "espoused theory" of action, which may later get reinforced or even elaborated during INSET. Yet Fenstermacher (1980) suggests that during induction these become a set of intentions in storage, while a second set are acquired by socialization at the workplace. The former are consciously held and philosophically defensible but impractical; the latter are semiconscious and acquired without proper reflection, corresponding to what Argyris and Schön (1976) call a "theory in use". For some teachers this dichotomy may become apparent, and either lead to disillusionment or act as a spur to professional development. Others succumb to the temptation to use an espoused theory to justify actions which are quite inconsistent with it, without even being aware of what they are doing. Or perhaps the level of awareness is just sufficient to induce a feeling of guilt and a strong resistance to the invasion of their classroom privacy without their understanding the nature of the problem or the extent to which it is shared with their colleagues. Failure to recognize and come to terms with this particular form of the theory–practice dichotomy constitutes a major barrier to professional development (see *Professional Socialization of Teachers*).

Linked to this problem of impractical ideals and going beyond the notion of teacher efficacy is the question of teachers' values. Not only do values have enormous influence on actions but they act as the filters through which experience is perceived and interpreted. The desire to perform at optimal level is dependent on believing in the worth of what one is doing, yet "many teachers view what they take to be the 'establishment's goals' with outright disdain" (Rubin 1971). Time for reflecting on and clarifying one's values without any pressure to conform to official views will be an INSET priority for some teachers, as will the need to find some personal accommodation between legitimate attempts to bring about change, respecting the immediate interests of students embedded in the existing system, and remaining in public employment as teachers. It would be a mistake to neglect the extent to which reformist-oriented teachers provide the energy and leadership which sustain many INSET activities and stimulate the renewal of the profession.

3.5 Teacher Careers

Many INSET activities, especially long courses leading to academic awards, are valued primarily for their career implications. This may sustain the flow of students and enhance the image of teacher professionalism but it can also lead to undesirable side-effects. An emphasis on extrinsic motivation, particularly when associated with an element of compulsion, can diminish personal involvement and weaken the critical feedback that might lead to course improvement. Yet further dangers are associated with promotion-oriented courses which serve an "anticipatory socialization" function. When attention is focused on the next job, students' existing knowledge and experience tends to be devalued; and since promotion tends to be associated with concerns outside the classroom, practical classroom knowledge has very low status. These effects can be counteracted by deliberate attempts to use students' existing experience, by planning at least one component with a classroom focus, and by involving experienced holders of promoted posts in the teaching.

Even short courses may be used by teachers as opportunities to enhance their visibility and gain the sponsorship of people who might influence their future careers; and this diminishes their reputation with teachers who have more intrinsic reasons for participation in INSET. Moreover the advisory approach to INSET is often awkwardly intertwined with other career-sponsoring and supervisory responsibilities. Many authors have urged that INSET should be clearly separated from these other concerns, a principle that is attainable in the context of interclassroom visitation but not in the context of cooperative school-based evaluation or curriculum development. When career considerations come into conflict with other INSET purposes, it is a fair assumption that the former will dominate. Hence the insistence of teacher unions that INSET policy cannot be divorced from the question of salary structure is more than just special pleading (Chambers 1981).

3.6 The Teacher as a Person

Condemned as they are to spending most of their working lives in the absence of other adults, many teachers sense that their own development as persons is neglected (Flanders 1980). Moreover, there are inherent dangers in teachers becoming isolated from their communities by overemphasis on their job at the expense of other adult roles. Their intellectual interests may be better served by adult education that is not professionally related and their sensitivity to the needs of young people may be enhanced by interaction with them outside the school context. Dissatisfaction with life outside school is likely to feed back into their schoolwork and diminish their contribution. Their total contribution to the community needs to be considered when INSET activities are planned; for teachers have the same right to "*l'education permanente*" as other adult workers, and INSET activities should not be regarded as diminishing their claims on other adult education resources.

4. School-oriented Perspectives

4.1 The School Milieu

Section 3.1 on the teachers' predicament drew attention to certain common features of the school as a workplace and its impact on teachers. But regular visitors to schools are constantly surprised by the differences in atmosphere between one school and another. Words like friendliness, ethos, appearance, purposefulness, and openness immediately come to mind. While the principal undoubtedly has a significant effect on a school's climate (Halpin 1966), one should not underestimate the contribution of the community context or the staff (Smith et al. 1981). Thus the school milieu is both created by, and in turn has a significant influence upon, such factors as teacher confidence and self-image, commitment to improving the quality of provision, and attitude towards INSET.

Although the importance of milieu is generally acknowledged, there is little discussion about the implications for INSET provision in situations where the milieu is regarded as unfavourable. Does one concentrate on changing or training the senior staff? Does one assume that once beneficial INSET activities get started the climate will begin to improve? Does one attempt to concentrate INSET resources by an inspection and follow-up INSET, or by initiating some form of planned organizational development? If there is no deliberate intervention strategy then the uptake of INSET opportunities will remain uneven; and it could be difficult to defend a policy which appears to give most resources to those who are least in need of them. Thus it is important to recognize that much of the ensuing discussion of school-oriented perspectives is based on experiences in schools whose milieux would generally be regarded as fairly favourable.

4.2 The Problem-solving School

The notion that a school can function as a centre for cooperative curriculum development and evaluation is central to the problem-solving paradigm, which regards participation in such activities as one of the most productive forms of INSET. Accounts of this style of school-based INSET can be found in Eggleston (1980) and Henderson and Perry (1981) but most of them are written by principals or senior teachers who were the main instigators of the development. Thus, while they give the sequence of events and the general flavour of the enterprise, they lack the perspectives of the other participants which makes the overall impact difficult to assess. There is a tendency to ignore the micropolitics of institutional change (House 1974) and to assume that consensus is readily obtainable. Nor is it clear that engagement in school-based development appeals to more than a minority of teachers.

Bolam's useful summary of the relevant research concludes that "a small minority of schools use the problem-solving mode for much of their work and that quite a large minority use it for at least a part of their work". What is not yet known, however, is whether "it is feasible to extend the approach to other tasks, groups, and schools through training, consultancy, and other forms of support" (Bolam 1981). Development of this kind will have to be gradual and long term, with opportunities for schools to share their experiences and learn as they experiment, and a substantial commitment of external INSET support. Nevertheless a number of countries are committed to taking it further, most notably Australia (Ingvarson 1980), the Netherlands (Van Velzen 1979), the United Kingdom, and areas of the United States.

Arguments for the problem-solving paradigm itself are that a school is a natural community with its own distinctive milieu, that most of the expertise relevant to school improvement resides in the minds of its teachers and that teacher participation in decision making is an essential prerequisite for significant change in the classroom. Many of these arguments also apply to the modified version of the change paradigm which the Rand study called mutual adaptation. So in spite of the lack of continuing evidence for its efficacy, the problem-solving school still seems a worthwhile goal to pursue. Howey (1980b) concludes that:

> unless we alter significantly the basic conditions of schools in many situations, we will do little to advance the notion of continuing education in general and school-focussed inservice specifically. (p. 211)

4.3 The School as a Performers' Guild

To a performers' guild the problem-solving school must seem a very theoretical concept. Teachers may spend a lot of time on policy matters but does policy ever get implemented in the classroom? Not only do people attach their own personal meaning to working party documents and reports, but they deceive themselves by using the aspirational language of espoused theory which may have little real connection with their classroom performance. For the performers' guild the prime purpose of INSET is to develop classroom practice, but only under conditions which protect the autonomy of individual teachers. The ideal is that of teachers visiting each other's classrooms and discussing what they see in a nonjudgmental atmosphere. Each teacher benefits both from seeing others in action and from receiving independent accounts of the impact of his or her own teaching. It was noted in Sect. 3.3 that most teachers would like to have this opportunity, but it is still very difficult to initiate. Apart from the problem of release time, having someone else in the classroom is still a rather frightening prospect.

The following suggestions have been made for alleviating this initial fear. One good principle is to avoid the school's formal authority structure by encouraging small friendship groups to intervisit, and even then taking care

that junior teachers visit senior teachers first. Another possibility is to intervisit with a teacher in a neighbouring school, thus reducing threat, and increasing personal credit for any consequent change (Mann 1978b). Thirdly, teachers might be visited by an experienced external consultant who would write classroom portrayals for circulation and discussion among friends prior to their visiting each other. Then finally, one might resort to transitional activities like joint visits to a third party, discussions about pupils' work, the use of a common textbook, or listening to sections of a lesson on audiotape.

4.4 School-focused INSET

Each school can contribute to INSET in three distinct ways:

(a) by acting as a broker and facilitator for its teachers by offering them information and advice, encouraging them to take up suitable opportunities, and adjusting their school responsibilities to make participation easier;

(b) by organizing its own INSET activities and seeking additional resources to support them; and

(c) by attempting to influence local policy and provision.

The first of these functions seems simple enough, but is not often taken seriously. Many schools regard INSET as a matter for individual teachers' initiatives, and even the circulation of information about INSET opportunities can be extremely haphazard. Moreover, the stimulus and impact of much external INSET is often diminished by lack of any arrangements for reporting back or following up useful new ideas.

The second function varies enormously from school to school and district to district, according to school milieu, the availability of resources, and the ingenuity of the head in creating time for teachers to meet together. While development and evaluation activities and courses aimed at internally identified needs will be based on the problem-solving paradigm, other activities like reading and study groups or school-based college courses are consonant with the growth paradigm. Classroom intervisiting could be conceived according to either approach, and presumably the attitude would vary with the particular teachers involved. Some notion of the range of activities can be gained from Sect. 1.2; and, where they exist, the use made of professional development days will also be very important. Indeed, where the school itself is involved in organizing INSET, the quality factor will be crucial; so also will be a willingness to negotiate plans, to learn from mistakes and to follow up any useful ideas that emerge.

Schools' influence on local policy and provision also varies considerably. The least direct influence is that of attendance or nonattendance—voting with one's feet. Rather more influence comes through the formal representation of teachers on policy committees; and by their making suggestions to responsible district officers and providing detailed feedback on existing provision. Their most substantial influence, however, comes when a substantial portion of INSET resources are allocated directly to schools. These may take the form of a substitute teacher allocation, funds for travel and conferences, or even funds to buy in support from external agencies—all in addition to district-provided facilities such as advisors, library services, and teacher centres. Examples of this type of district policy are described in Howey (1980a); and a notable case of special district backing for a school-based initiative is provided by Annehurst (Sanders and Schwab 1981).

Can these three aspects of a school's contribution to INSET be easily reconciled, especially the potential conflict between the needs of individual teachers and the needs of the school? An important British document suggests that needs be identified at three main levels—individual teachers, functional groups within the school, and the school as a whole. Each school should identify needs on its own, then decide on priorities and work out its own INSET programme. This programme is to include both its own activities and participation in locally available opportunities, to be evaluated and to be followed up in the ongoing life of the school (ACSTT 1978). This approach is described as "school-focused INSET" because it encompasses a much wider range of activities than those that are school based; and an excellent summary of recent developments of this kind is provided by Howey (1980b).

School planning of INSET, however is not without its difficulties. Teachers find it difficult to articulate needs and may prefer to preserve their autonomy by avoiding the issue altogether. Conflicts of priority may be difficult to settle democratically, yet the whole programme might be jeopardized if decision making was perceived as hierarchical. Moreover, needs are often limited by people's ideas of what may be available and this can inhibit experiments with new, untried, and possibly badly needed forms of INSET. It may be more productive to compile an initial agenda of wild exciting ideas or to search for something interesting for everybody than to employ a decision-making sequence that does not fit the way people normally think. As with the notion of the problem-solving school, the idea of school-focused INSET will need working out over a considerable period of time. In the meantime, more case studies like those provided by Ingvarson (1980), Miller and Wolf (1978), and Baker (1981) will be needed to help us conceptualize the issues.

4.5 The Defect Paradigm at School Level

Accountability for students means that where teaching is clearly identified as unacceptably poor the defect paradigm must be called into use. Otherwise not only will students be unnecessarily disadvantaged, but teacher morale will be undermined and public credibility weakened. However, it is equally dangerous if the need

for special INSET provision to support and improve weak teachers is allowed to colour INSET policy as a whole. Hence clear procedures are important—clear notification to teachers "at risk", prompt provision of INSET support, second opinions, appeals, and so on. Occasionally a whole school may need special INSET following an inspection, but this will normally be a temporary phenomenon. Again formal notification of the situation is important if a school "at risk" is not to be confused with a school being given special support because it is working in particularly difficult circumstances, that is, in areas of high population mobility, low literacy rate, and so on. Such precautions, however, will not prevent INSET activities from being perceived as defect oriented by teachers who feel they have not participated in their planning.

5. Governmental Perspectives

5.1 Resource Allocation and Accountability

A number of issues relating to this topic were discussed in Sect. 1.3 on INSET organization and policy, namely—costing, teacher release, teacher certification, and INSET coordination. Their very complexity makes accountability difficult, but nevertheless two significant further issues remain to be discussed. Firstly, there is the general problem of justifying public expenditure on INSET. Not only does the multiplicity of agencies lend itself to suggestions that other groups ought to be paying for any particular item, but the long-term nature of INSET is difficult to explain. Few researchers believe that the effects of many INSET activities can be evaluated by improvements in pupil learning outcomes so justifications will have to rely on the intrinsic merits of the activities themselves and their reported impact on teachers. This leads to an emphasis on those activities that are most easily explained to lay people, especially to statistics of numbers of teachers on courses with impressive-sounding and largely traditional titles. As Mallan (1978) comments:

> Professionals appear to be attempting to adapt their functioning to a dysfunctional publicly accepted "model" and, in so doing, can't educate the public (and the public's representative: school boards) to realistic expectations. This adapting posture in inservice claims is doomed to failure. (p. 221)

Instead of "trying to meet unrealistically demanding public expectations" they should be "using educational expertise to modify such expectations". More community involvement in INSET would seem essential if new approaches are to get sufficient financial support.

The second resource allocation problem, briefly mentioned in Sect. 4.1, arises from the uneven take-up of INSET opportunities. The voluntary nature of many forms of INSET results in some schools and some teachers receiving much more support than others. This can be justified in terms of equality of opportunity, or school-based leadership development if more teachers get promoted out of INSET-oriented schools, or a social inter-action theory of innovation, which assumes that what some schools do today others will do tomorrow. But there is also a strong counterargument that those schools which make least use of INSET are those to which the local education authorities should be committing the most INSET resources (Mann 1978b). Such inter-ventionist policies for low-use schools may well exist, but they do not get reported in the INSET literature.

5.2 Implementing Mandated or Sponsored Change

Certain changes in the educational system are properly determined by legislation or the executive action of a democratically elected local or national government. These include structural changes like the introduction of comprehensive schools or changing the age range of compulsory education; policy changes like the allocation of increased numbers of children with special needs to ordinary schools; and curricular changes which reflect social, cultural, and economic changes. Societal con-cerns such as national identity, recognition of minority groups, opportunities for women, health and environ-mental education, and transition from school to work lead to initiatives requiring a constructive response from the educational system.

Significantly, most of the research on INSET operating within the change paradigm has been not on mandated change but on government-sponsored change which usually carries much less authority. Unless preceded by considerable preparation and negotiation, sponsored changes have tended to create waves of INSET that are uncoordinated and underresourced; and this, as much as any other factor, has probably been responsible for the low esteem in which INSET is held by many teachers. Lippitt and Fox's (1971 p. 135) diagnosis still holds true in the 1980s:

(a) Most teachers have experienced a wide variety of attempts to influence them to change their per-formance or to improve themselves.

(b) Many of these experiences have not appeared rel-evant to any felt need of the teacher, and have resulted in defensive attitudes.

(c) Most teachers have participated in some of these activities and have been disappointed by the imprac-ticality of the help offered.

(d) Most teachers who have attempted changes as a result of participation in inservice training activities have experienced frustration or lack of support at the moment of real risk, when the changes are first being tried out. If the effort does not result in success, they either give up or accept a change that has little significance.

(e) Most teachers have experienced feelings of guilt after committing themselves to "try something new" if they have then not followed through.

(f) Typically the stimulus to participate in inservice training is an unwelcome imposition of authority, or an inept invitation to volunteer, with no previous involvement or warm-up opportunity to explore the potentialities of the training.

So a major problem facing today's providers of INSET is that most of their potential customers have already been innoculated against it.

Evidence from studies of successful implementation suggests that, in addition to the school and teacher factors discussed in earlier sections, the successful implementation of externally sponsored change requires continued INSET over a period of years (Emrick 1980, Stallings 1979). Moreover, although practical skill-specific training is often needed at the beginning, such training has only a short-term impact unless it is sup-plemented by staff support for the application and adap-tion of the innovation to individual contexts (Joyce 1980). Teachers also need to develop a deep personal understanding of the main ideas in conjunction with practical on-the-job learning. This may be fostered by written statements, packaged materials, or lectures from experts, but these activities cannot substitute for a pro-cess of continuing discussion as problems emerge and personal thinking develops. "The conceptual clarity critical to project success and continuation must be achieved during the process of project implemen-tation—it cannot be 'given' to staff at the outset" (McLaughlin and Marsh 1978 p. 78).

5.3 Government-supported Agents and Agencies

Governments can support INSET agents and agencies in four main ways:

(a) they can employ their own agents;

(b) they can set up semi-independent agencies;

(c) they can provide indirect support for independent agencies by paying teachers' fees or contracting for specific services; and

(d) they can subsidize INSET activities at colleges and universities.

Agents in the direct employment of government can be grouped into two main types: those who also have an inspectoral or supervisory role, and those who are employed for INSET purposes alone. The job title does not always adequately describe the role, and many "advisors" are also expected to supervise or inspect. The first group is numerically greatest, but they suffer from the inevitable conflict between their inspectoral or supervisory role and participation in INSET activities which are not based on the defect paradigm (Eraut 1977). The second group of INSET agents are teachers on temporary or part-time release from their class-room responsibilities. One strategy within the change paradigm involves training cadres of master teachers to demonstrate some new practice and provide follow-up support to teachers who try to use it (Kolawole 1980). The evidence suggests that master teachers have good credibility but still need to understand the problems of innovation and to provide affective as well as cognitive support over a long period of time (Stallings 1979). Another approach to using teachers as INSET leaders is the "teachers helping teachers teach" idea, which is being developed in the United States in a variety of formats (Howey 1980a, Thurber 1979). The principle is that of having a trained group of experienced teachers available to help other teachers on demand. It is firmly rooted in the growth paradigm and often organized through teacher unions.

Increasing attention is also being paid to training teachers for INSET roles within their own schools (Mulford 1980) and for occasional spare-time duties as course leaders (Ruddock 1981). This seems a logical development given the shifts in thinking about INSET reported in the earlier sections, but we still need to learn a lot more about how it works out in practice.

Further separation of INSET from supervision can be achieved by setting up semi-independent agencies such as teacher centres (Howey 1980b) and teacher education centres (Thurber 1979). These are also intended to establish neutral ground where the epistemological authority of colleges and universities is less pervasive; and to increase teachers' responsibility for their own INSET provision (Adams 1975). The rationale is usually that of the growth paradigm, though certain specialist centres may operate rather more in the change paradigm (see *Teachers' Centres*).

The arguments for supporting INSET provided by independent agencies and higher education establishments are threefold:

(a) making use of specialist expertise, though this is no guarantee of productive INSET and planning is often advisable;

(b) widening the range of choice; and

(c) giving teachers the opportunity to improve their qualifications.

Many forms of coordination have recently been developed between INSET agencies; and this is becoming an area which is ripe for research. Those who wish to see more detailed accounts of this and other government approaches to INSET policy and provision should consult the large number of national reports sponsored by the Organisation for Economic Co-operation and Development (OECD) and listed in Bolam (1980), together with Marsh (1980) and Donoughue et al. (1981).

6. Higher Education-oriented Perspectives

6.1 Epistemological Authority

Institutions of higher education, particularly universities, possess a unique form of authority, epistemological authority. The authority they have over students and which extends into the wider world of educational discourse is that of deciding what is to count as valid knowledge. This authority is strengthened by the fact that the teaching profession depends for its status on qualifications awarded by higher education institutions, and on claims to a knowledge base which can be defended by reference to educational publications that are also mostly controlled by the higher education sector. Since this epistemological influence permeates virtually all INSET activities, it is important to examine both the range of available epistemologies and the social and political processes which cause some to dominate others.

The problem is not that theoretical knowledge has no role to play, nor that teachers should not study it, but that transactions between scholars and practitioners tend to be one-way. Yet to provide a theoretical interpretation of a practical situation requires both theoretical knowledge and a proper understanding of the practical situation. Epistemological authority cannot reside solely with the scholar or researcher but has to be shared with each individual practitioner. Researchers constrain the proper development of theory if they limit their discourse with teachers. Teachers, finding the authority gap created during initial training often being reinforced during INSET, associate theory with the defect paradigm—theory is what someone else thinks you should know about and can be used to label you as "ignorant"—rather than the growth paradigm—theory can liberate you from being imprisoned by the taken-for-granted assumptions of your daily environment.

6.2 The Institutional Setting of Higher Education

Formidable barriers to the symbiotic development of theory and practice through INSET exist in most higher education institutions. The status hierarchy within higher education awards greatest priority to knowledge derived from other academic disciplines. Research funding tends to favour conclusion-oriented research with ambitious promises of direct application to practice, especially in North America. The departmental structure within many education faculties benefits certain styles of scholarship but lessens the chance of an individual professor relating holistically to a practical situation. Publishing arrangements are unsuited to medium-length case studies of individual situations. Publishing leads to promotion, providing genuine help to practitioners does not.

Teaching traditions have a similar effect. Assessment often encourages the mere replication of theoretical knowledge, and always establishes the epistemological authority of the professor. Course segmentation usually allows far too little time for shared understandings to be developed. There is no mental space for intellectual risk taking below the most advanced levels of provision. Professors as well as schoolteachers find interactive teaching difficult to establish in practice.

The accounting system also tends to work against nontraditional forms of INSET. Many institutions base their accounting on numbers of full-time students and even when part-time or short-course students are included, the allowance for them may not be at all favourable. Providing advisory support may not be counted as part of a professor's teaching load. Not only does this discourage staff involvement in all INSET activities other than formal courses, but it also deprives them of opportunities to gain practical experiences that might improve their teaching and their research. Why should a faculty member bother with INSET when it involves greater risks than other college activities, gains him or her little credit towards promotion, requires more than the normal amount of time and effort, and probably takes place at inconvenient times in inconvenient places (Drummond and Lawrence 1978)?

7. Evaluation and Research

Most of the difficulties highlighted in recent literature on educational evaluation (and discussed elsewhere in this Encyclopedia) are especially prominent in the evaluation of INSET (Fox 1980, Henderson 1978). In particular INSET, being one step further from the classroom than teaching, weakens the chance of establishing any causal connection with pupil outcomes by an order of magnitude. It is probably only worth attempting for INSET courses based on a behavioural approach to the teaching of previously defined competencies. Most commentators have argued that negotiated INSET is normally too diverse to make such designs feasible and that the current state of knowledge about INSET is so weak that programme improvement is a much higher priority. Large-scale evaluation designs based on pupil outcome measurement are theoretically compatible with the defect paradigm and the change paradigm but not with the problem-solving paradigm or the growth paradigm. Moreover, recent research on curriculum innovation suggests that even the change paradigm does not lend itself too readily to this approach. First there is the difficulty in knowing whether a project's implementation strategy or its curriculum strategy is being evaluated and second there is a growing recognition that contextual variation may be more important for the evaluator to describe and explain than aggregated measurement of overall impact.

Eklund's (1978) advocacy of a participatory INSET evaluation model and of a multidimensional approach has been strongly supported by other European workers (Salmon 1981); and Henderson (1981) has argued for the incorporation of an evaluation dimension into all INSET activities. INSET is so context based that it may be more profitable to think in terms of building an evaluation component into the training of INSET teachers than of employing an expensive cadre of evaluation specialists.

The specialist role that is most needed would then be not the INSET evaluator but the INSET researcher. There seems to be general agreement that INSET is undertheorized and underconceptualized. Very few of the important issues raised in the preceding sections have been substantially illuminated by research findings. Almost all the published research on INSET has been conducted in North America, and there must be considerable doubt about their transferability to other cultural contexts. One can only hope that the recent spate of publications on INSET will begin to stimulate research activity and draw attention to the needs of this important sector of education.

Bibliography

Adams E (ed.) 1975 *In-service Education and Teachers' Centres*. Pergamon, Oxford

Advisory Committee on the Supply and Training of Teachers (ACSTT) 1974 *Inservice Education and Training: Some Considerations*. Department of Education and Science, London

Advisory Committee on the Supply and Training of Teachers (ACSTT) 1978 *Making INSET Work*. Department of Education and Science, London

Arends R, Hersh R, Turner J 1978 In-service education and the six o'clock news. *Theory Pract.* 17: 196–205

Argyris C, Schön D A 1976 *Theory in Practice: Increasing Professional Effectiveness*. Jossey-Bass, San Francisco, California

Baker K 1981 Project SITE. In: Henderson E S, Perry G W (eds.) 1981

Bolam R 1980 *In-service Education and Training of Teachers and Educational Change*. Final Report of CERI Project on INSET. Organisation for Economic Co-operation and Development (OECD), Paris

Bolam R 1981 *Strategies for Sustaining Educational Improvements in the 1980s*. Organisation for Economic Co-operation and Development (OECD), Paris

Bush R N 1971 Curriculum-proof teachers: Who does what to whom. In: Rubin L J (ed.) 1971

Chambers J 1981 The role and function of advanced study in professional development. In: Alexander R J, Ellis J W (eds.) 1981 *Advanced Study for Teachers*. Nafferton Books, Driffield, North Humberside

Corrigan D C 1979 *Adult Learning and Development: Implications for Inservice Teacher Education: An American Point of View*. Organisation for Economic Co-operation and Development (OECD), Paris

Day C 1981 *Classroom Based In-service Teacher Education: The Development and Evaluation of a Client-centred Model*. Occasional Paper 9. University of Sussex Education Area, Brighton, Sussex

Donoughue C, Ball C, Glaister B, Hand G (eds.) 1981 *Inservice: The Teacher and the School*. Kogan Page, London

Doyle W, Ponder G A 1977 The practicality ethic in teacher decision-making. *Interchange* 8(3): 1–12

Drummond W H, Lawrence G D 1978 A letter to Harry on site specific in-service education. *Theory Pract.* 17: 272–78

Eggleston J (ed.) 1980 *School-based Curriculum Development in Britain: A Collection of Case Studies*. Routledge and Kegan Paul, London

Eklund H 1978 *The Evaluation of INSET for Teachers in Sweden*. Organisation for Economic Co-operation and Development (OECD), Paris

Elliott J 1980 Implications of classroom research for professional development. In: Hoyle E, Megarry J (eds.) 1980

Emrick J A 1980 Some implications of research on educational dissemination and change for teacher education (inservice) programs. In: Hall G E, Ford S M, Brown G (eds.) 1980

Eraut M R 1972 *In-service Education for Innovation*. National Council for Educational Technology, London

Eraut M R 1977 Some perspectives on consultancy in in-service education. *Br. J. In-service Educ.* 4(1/2): 95–99

Farmer J 1981 *Real-life Problem-solving Efforts of Professionals and Related Learning Activities*. College of Education, University of Illinois, Chicago, Illinois

Feiman S, Floden R E 1980 *What's All This Talk about Teacher Development?* Research Series No. 70. Institute for Research on Teaching, Michigan State University, East Lansing, Michigan

Fenstermacher G D 1980 What needs to be known about what teachers need to know. In: Hall G E, Ford S M, Brown G (eds.) 1980

Flanders T 1980 *The Professional Development of Teachers*. British Columbia Teachers' Federation, Vancouver, British Columbia

Fox G T 1980 *Reflecting upon Evaluation*. Synthesis Report for CERI Project on INSET. Organisation for Economic Co-operation and Development (OECD), Paris

Fullan M 1980 *Towards School-focussed Training: The Canadian Experience*. Organisation for Economic Co-operation and Development (OECD), Paris

Fuller F F, Bown D 1975 Becoming a teacher. In: Ryan K (ed.) 1975 *Teacher Education: A Search for New Relationships*. 74th National Society for the Study of Education (NSSE) Yearbook. University of Chicago Press, Chicago, Illinois

Hall G E, Ford S M, Brown G (eds.) 1980 *Exploring Issues in Teacher Education: Questions for Future Research*. R & D Center for Teacher Education, University of Texas, Austin, Texas

Hall G E, Loucks S 1978 Teachers concerns as a basis for facilitating and personalizing staff development. *Teach. Coll. Rec.* 80: 36–53

Halpin A W 1966 *Theory and Research in Administration*. Macmillan, New York

Henderson E S 1978 *The Evaluation of In-service Teacher Training*. Croom Helm, London

Henderson E S 1981 Evaluation: The missing link. In: Donoughue C et al. (eds.) 1981

Henderson E S, Perry G W (eds.) 1981 *Change and Development in Schools*. McGraw-Hill, Maidenhead

Henricson S E 1980 *Costs and Financing Implications: The Swedish Example*. CERI Project in INSET. Organisation for Economic Co-operation and Development (OECD), Paris

House E R 1974 *The Politics of Educational Innovation*. McCutchan, Berkeley, California

Howey K R 1980a *Towards School-focused Training: The United States Experience*. Organisation for Economic Co-operation and Development (OECD), Paris

Howey K R 1980b *School Focused In-service Education: Clarification of a New Concept and Strategy*. Synthesis Report for CERI Project in INSET. Organisation for Economic Co-operation and Development (OECD), Paris

Howey K R, Joyce B 1978 A data base for future directions in in-service education. *Theory Pract.* 17: 206–11

Hoyle E, Megarry J (eds.) 1980 *Professional Development of Teachers*. World Yearbook of Education 1980. Kogan Page, London

Ingvarson L C 1980 *Towards School-focussed Training: The Australian Experience*. Organisation for Economic Co-operation and Development (OECD), Paris

Jackson P W 1971 Old dogs and new tricks: Observations on the continuing education of teachers. In: Rubin L J (ed.) 1971

Joyce B 1980 The ecology of professional development. In: Hoyle E, Megarry J (eds.) 1980

Kolawole D 1980 The mobile teacher training programme in Nigeria. In: Hoyle E, Megarry J (eds.) 1980

Lippitt R, Fox R 1971 Development and maintenance of effective classroom learning. In: Rubin L J (ed.) 1971

McLaughlin M W 1976 Implementation as mutual adaptation: Change in classroom organization. *Teach. Coll. Rec.* 77: 339–51

McLaughlin M W, Marsh D D 1978 Staff development and school change. *Teach. Coll. Rec.* 80: 69–94

Mallan J T 1978 Philodoxy: The promise of in-service. *Theory Pract.* 17: 218–23

Mann D 1978a The politics of in-service. *Theory Pract.* 17: 212–17

Mann D 1978b The user-driven system and a modest proposal. *Teach. Coll. Rec.* 79: 389–412

Marsh D 1980 State government role in staff development: The Californian experience. In: Hoyle E, Megarry J (eds.) 1980

Miller L, Wolf T E 1978 Staff development for school change: Theory and practice. *Teach. Coll. Rec.* 80: 140–56

Mitchell L 1950 *Our Children and Our Schools: A Picture and Analysis of How Today's Public School Teachers are Meeting the Challenge of New Knowledge and New Cultural Needs*. Simon and Schuster, New York

Mulford B 1980 *The Role and Training of Teacher Trainers*. Synthesis Report for CERI Project on INSET. Organisation for Economic Co-operation and Development (OECD), Paris

Rubin L J (ed.) 1971 *Improving In-service Education: Proposals and Procedures for Change*. Allyn and Bacon, Boston, Massachusetts

Ruddock J 1981 *Making the Most of the Short In-service Course*. Schools Council Working Paper 71. Methuen, London

Salmon A (ed.) 1981 *The Evaluation of In-service Education and Training of Teachers*. Council of Europe and Swets of Zeitlinger, Lisse

Sanders D P, Schwab M 1981 *Annehurst: The Natural History of a Good School*. Kappa Delta Pi, West Lafayette, Indiana

Smith L, Prunty J J, Dwyer D C 1981 A longitudinal nested systems model of innovation and change in schooling. In: Bacharach S (ed.) 1981 *Organizational Analysis of Schools and School Districts*. Praeger, New York

Smith W 1980 The American Teacher Corps programme. In: Hoyle E, Megarry J (eds.) 1980

Stallings J 1979 Follow Through: A model for in-service teacher training. *Curric. Inq.* 9: 163–81

Thompson A R (ed.) 1982 *In-service Education of Teachers in the Commonwealth*. Commonwealth Secretariat, London

Thurber J C 1979 *Cost and Efficient Utilisation of INSET Resources: Some United States Experiences*. Organisation for Economic Co-operation and Development (OECD), Paris

Tikunoff W J, Ward B A, Lazar C 1980 Partners: Teachers, researchers, trainer/developers: An interactive approach to teacher education R & D. In: Hall G E, Ford S M, Brown G (eds.) 1980

Trade Union Advisory Committee to Organisation for Economic Co-operation and Development (Trade Union Advisory Committee–TUAC) 1980 *In-service Education for Teachers and Educators*. Views submitted for Conference on INSET. Organisation for Economic Co-operation and Development (OECD), Paris

van Velzen W (ed.) 1979 *Developing an Autonomous School*. Dutch Catholic School Council, The Hague

Teacher Recyclage

G. De Landsheere

Recyclage is a specific aspect of teacher inservice training. It is defined as intensive training action, needed in case of qualification crises happening when the teacher's knowledge of a subject suddenly becomes obsolete (e.g., massive introduction of "new mathematics" in the school curriculum) or when it is recognized that critical gaps exist in the teacher's education (e.g., total ignorance of objective evaluation principles, methods, and techniques).

Since, in most countries, the initial training of preprimary, primary, secondary, and tertiary (university) teachers does not yet include a substantial introduction to educational research, and since it seems obvious that a teacher can hardly be a regular and wise consumer of educational research findings if he or she does not possess the necessary basic technical knowledge, the case of recyclage in the field of educational research is taken as an illustration for this entry.

Many teacher-training institutions all over the world have practically no research and objective evaluation activity. As a consequence, most teachers are not familiar with the standardized tests related to the subjects they teach; they ignore the basic statistical methods and techniques needed for any empirical approach to educational problems. They have not been scientifically introduced to educational technology and automatic data processing.

There is thus an important difference in the level of qualification of teachers and other university-trained professionals, such as engineers and physicians, who study in close contact with empirical research at the most advanced level in their field. While a physician reads new research reports easily—including their statistical part—and is immediately able to apply some of the findings to daily practice, this is not the case for many teachers. At the same time, educational research and development are now reaching an ever-increasing level of sophistication: as a consequence, the gap between practice and research becomes wider and wider.

Recyclage needed to change this situation has quantitative, psychological, and methodological aspects.

The teaching profession—when it is recognized as such—is by far the most numerous. Even in a small country like Belgium, there are approximately 200,000 teachers; two-thirds of them will still be teaching in the year 2000. Unless further training action is limited to a very small minority (with little impact on the system as a whole) the dimension of intervention necessary is enormous.

Psychologically, there is a critical difference between keeping scientifically trained professionals informed of the developments of their field, and changing the reasoning, the attitudes, and the vocational behaviour of many thousands of artisans.

As for the method of influencing teacher routine behaviour, long-term sophisticated modification strategies are needed.

Three "recyclage" strategies that have much in common with usual further education methods can be distinguished: massive dissemination of information, actions of sensitization, and cooperative research.

1. Dissemination of Information

The control of this type of action is easily centralized. Lectures, reviews, newsletters, open or closed circuit television, cassettes, and videodiscs are familiar to everybody. Systems of computer-monitored selective dissemination of information are available but remain extremely expensive.

Experience shows, however, that information dissemination is useful only if the receiver has a sufficient training and information level to understand its meaning and a sufficient motivation to translate it into practice. Experience shows that, the effectiveness of this strategy is very low.

2. Sensitization Action

With this strategy, the teacher receives and participates. The paradigm is the one-week residential seminar. About 20 teachers and two resource persons get together. If more teachers are involved the group talks a lot, but does not accomplish much. A theoretical framework is sketched and, as soon as possible, group discussion and work are organized.

This is an opportunity for the teachers to discover new ideas, models, methods, and techniques that can have an impact on their practice. The fact that they undertake some individual application during the seminar gives a much stronger impact to this strategy than simple information dissemination.

However, there are two dangers. Most new educational approaches (operational definition of objectives, mastery learning techniques, programmed learning, etc.) seem easy to understand and to apply only if superficially considered. Superficiality can be as noxious as ignorance. One week's hurried exhausting work is not enough for deep understanding and attitude changes. That is why this is called "sensitization": the teacher becomes actively aware of research, evaluation, and development. This can considerably increase readiness for further learning, but cannot be the alpha and omega of it. It must always be borne in mind that one or a few seminars do not suffice to transform an artisan into a professional, a medicine man into a physician.

The weight of statistically significant sensitization actions should not be underestimated. For 100,000 younger teachers of a country to be given a yearly one-week seminar, 5,000 seminars must be held, and approximately 200 teams of two resource persons are required (each animating a seminar every other week, which means exhausting work).

3. Cooperative Work

Experience shows that the most efficient way (if not the only way) to obtain deep lasting modification of the teaching behaviour is to work for a long period with teachers to solve with them some of the problems they identified in their classroom, and to use this opportunity to make them understand and use research findings, development products, and evaluation techniques. To do this, there are two not mutually exclusive ways corresponding to different epistemological approaches: cooperative operational research and action research. The former uses the nomothetic method, the latter resorts to the participatory, anthropological model.

A cooperative operational research project starts with concerns and problems identified by teachers and proceeds from this step to the diagnosis of causes and factors in these problems (Taba and Noel 1957 p. 6). With the help of a research technician who serves as a resource person, the teacher undertakes solving the specific problem at hand by systematically following the nomothetic research stages: problem identification, problem analysis, hypotheses formulation, experimentation, and evaluation. In so doing, the teacher discovers research methods and techniques as well as evaluation instruments that help to modify school practice.

Though generally efficient, this approach has been criticized because it has sometimes been used to impose indirectly predetermined ways to be teachers, or in other words, to manipulate them. A pitfall is also a paternalistic attitude on the side of the researcher. That is why the model of participatory action research is sometimes preferred.

The basic components of participatory research are (Werdelin 1979 p. 11): origination of the problem in the educational community, full and active participation of the community in the entire research process, and creation of a new teacher awareness of their own resources and possibilities of self-reliant development. The researcher is here "a committed participant and learner in a process of research, which leads to militancy on his part" (International Council for Adult Education, quoted by Werdelin 1979 p. 11). This latter characteristic really makes the difference from the cooperative operational research model where the researcher tries to remain an objective, detached outsider.

What is the feasibility of the cooperative approach if considered in relation to the whole or part of the population of teachers of a country or region?

It must be remembered that a minimum ratio of one resource person to 50 teachers is desirable to obtain efficient working groups remaining open to innovations and producing instruments, modules, packages, and so on, that can be offered to other teachers. This exchange of teacher-made instruments is practically and psychologically of great importance.

Ideally, the resource person must have sound experience of both teaching practice and educational research. Situations can, however, be observed where experienced teachers interact with much younger and less experienced researchers, and, provided a real cooperative spirit animates the group, the results can be excellent.

Depending on their resources, school authorities can either decide to limit their support to a few innovative groups only and hope for a snowball effect, or undertake a much broader action. To do this, the existence of regional research and development laboratories, working in close connection with the schools, is necessary.

Bibliography

Taba H, Noel E 1957 *Action Research: A Case Study*. Association for Supervision and Curriculum Development, Washington, DC

Werdelin I 1979 *Participatory Research in Education*. Linköping University, Linköping

Induction of Beginning Teachers

R. Bolam

The change from student teacher to beginning teacher is sudden and dramatic. From the supportive environment of the college, where mistakes are expected, self-criticism is encouraged, and both tutorial guidance and peer-group friendship are readily available, beginning teachers are thrust, only a few weeks later, into a situation in which both their professional and personal responsibilities are profoundly altered. They can no longer find consolation in looking forward to the end of their teaching practice: any mistakes made in the first year have got to be lived with. The methods they use, the progress of their pupils, parents' complaints, their working relationships with their, often much older, colleagues—all are now their permanent professional responsibility. Moreover, these will often be accompanied by important changes in personal responsibilities (with their attendant difficulties) like finding and running their accommodation, marriage, a long journey to school, managing on a salary, loneliness in a new town, and fatigue.

It is hardly surprising, then, that the first year has for so long been the subject of widespread concern for their can be little doubt that it is a traumatic experience for some and a considerable ordeal for many. When probed a little more deeply it emerges that this concern normally arises for reasons associated with four principal factors. First, teacher supply: for example, because of the dramatic increase in demand for teachers in the 1960s, many governments were anxious to reduce the wastage caused by the number of young teachers, especially women, who left the profession during or soon after their first year. Second, the social accountability of the teaching profession: the first year of teaching is frequently a period of probation during which teachers are required to demonstrate certain professional competencies in order to achieve full, professional recognition. Third, teachers' professional status and conditions of service: teachers' professional associations and governments periodically propose changes in the regulations surrounding the first year of teaching which have wide professional implications. Fourth, professional development: there is widespread agreement in certain countries that the first year should be the foundation of continuing professional education for teachers.

The salience and influence of these four factors varies between different countries and, from time to time, within a country. There is little evidence of concern in developing countries, presumably because of their more fundamental problem of a general lack of trained teachers. Neither is there much evidence of deep concern in certain developed countries, for example France, possibly because the teacher training system is so different. Moreover, in some developed countries, the public expressions of interest are relatively recent: this is true of the Netherlands (Vakgroep Natuurkunde-Didaktiek 1981) and parts of Canada (Joint Board of Education 1981). In still other countries concern has waxed and waned: thus the Conant Report (Conant 1963) led to some important developments in the United States but then there was a 10 to 15 year lull; similarly, in the United Kingdom, although the professional rhetoric has been reasonably consistent, government action has not.

Nevertheless, in both the United Kingdom and the United States, as well as in Australia and New Zealand there have been significant policy initiatives, some of which have generated research and development work, in the field of teacher induction. It is important to recognize that such developments, rooted as they are in national and state policies on teacher education, can only be really understood in the relevant national contexts. For example, it is impossible to fully understand the induction research in the United Kingdom without reference to the legal status of the probationary year, the way it has been defined, in practice, as coterminous with the induction period, the way in which it became the focus of abortive discussions between the local education authority (l.e.a.) employers and the professional associations about teachers' conditions of service and, overriding all other contextual factors, to the impact of the post-1973 economic recession. In much of what follows, these issues are necessarily left implicit but they are picked up again in the concluding section.

Certain key distinctions and definitions are worth making at the outset. According to Zeichner (1979), the two major types of induction programmes are internships and beginning teacher programmes. He concluded that internships were themselves confined to three major types—fifth year internships for liberal arts graduates, internships as part of a five or six year integrated preparation programme and a Teacher Corps internship. McDonald (1982) defined internship as including:

> . . . at least half-time teaching of no less than five or six months with full responsibility assigned to the interns for the groups of classes which they teach. (p. 52)

Apart from the McDonald study, which only discovered a very few programmes, internships are not discussed in this article. The following definitions are, however, central to the topic:

> *Beginning Teacher*: One who has completed all preservice training requirements (including student teaching); has been granted a provisional certificate; is in the employ of a school district; has generally the same type and degree of responsibility assigned more experienced teachers; and is either in his or her first year of service to the profession or to a particular school district.
> *Beginning Teacher Program*: A planned program which is intended to provide some systematic and sustained assistance specifically to beginning teachers for at least one school year. The persons providing the support are specifically assigned that responsibility. (Zeichner 1979)

Although constructed in an American context, these two definitions have wider utility. Probation, which is often associated with the granting of a provisional licence to teach, is inevitably rooted in the system and regulations of particular countries and, largely for administrative convenience, is often regarded as coterminous with the induction period. Nor, in spite of the fact that they are sometimes used synonymously, are "orientation" and "induction" the same; on the whole it probably makes most sense to regard orientation as an early stage in the overall induction process.

The research selected for review in this article is drawn from only a limited number of countries—the United States, England and Wales, and Australia and, even so, it does not claim to be exhaustive. It concentrates upon work directly related to induction and thus, for example, work on the characteristics of beginning teachers has only been included when it was produced in the context of an induction scheme. Following the research review, the final section raises some policy, technical, and research issues.

1. United States Studies

Since the Second World War there has been a steady stream of United States research on beginning teachers and on orientation or induction programmes yet, oddly enough, recent American researchers tend to underestimate and even ignore it. Although it is not possible here to cover them in detail, the significant contribution of work produced or reviewed by the following writers should be noted: Amar (1952), Archer (1960), Mason (1961), the National Education Association Research Division (1964), Schwalenberg (1965), Hermanowicz (1966), Denemark and MacDonald (1967), Malament (1968), especially Hunt (1968, 1969); and Childress (1969).

Zeichner (1979) helpfully reviewed the induction literature from the previous 15 years and studied 11 programmes, including some referred to above, in detail. Seven of the 11 programmes involved additional release time for teachers, six included teacher mentors, five received additional release time, and four received training. Eight of the 11 included individual in-class assistance, eight involved seminars or workshops, while six included observations of experienced teachers or peers, three included contact with university personnel, and two with special preservice orientation.

Zeichner pointed out that most of the evaluations relied heavily on questionnaire responses from beginning teachers; interviews and observation were used in only one of the studies. He presented the evaluation findings in terms of five classes of variables. Most programmes were implemented in the way intended. Two projects tried to assess programme impact upon teacher turnover and both reported significantly lower turnover. Three projects recorded data on teacher performance but none of the differences between experimental and control groups was statistically significant; experimental groups receiving induction programmes were generally rated more highly than control groups but the instrumentation and methodology were questionable. Four projects tried to assess programme impact upon teacher attitudes and morale: three projects reported no statistical differences between the experimental and control groups; one did show some such differences, and Zeichner concluded that teacher attitude measures can sometimes be modified positively but that unequivocal generalizations are not possible. Two projects tried to establish the impact on pupil attitudes and behaviour: no significant differences were reported. At a more general level, all the participants in the 11 programmes were reportedly extremely enthusiastic and positive about their experiences. Even though many of the evaluation results were equivocal, each programme report concluded that the benefits from the programme were substantial.

Grant and Zeichner (1981) reported the findings from a limited investigation into school-based induction for a representative sample of beginning teachers not involved in experimental programmes and described the support they actually received. Prospective teachers from three institutions of higher education were asked to participate and 62 percent (72) completed instruments during March and April 1980. Most of these were female and taught in elementary classrooms grades one to six (ages 6 to 12). One-third were the only first year teachers in their buildings and over half (52 percent) had only one other first year teacher as a colleague. An 11 page questionnaire asked each teacher to respond to questions concerning three major categories of support: formal, informal, and job embedded. In spite of the fact that three states in which the majority of the teachers taught were specifically chosen because of their commitment to induction, there was little evidence of formal support like support services specifically for beginning teachers or a reduction of work load. Although most teachers (70.4 percent) received some type of formal orientation to their school, this was normally for all new teachers. Similarly, formal inservice training was generally offered as part of a wider school or school district programme for all teachers and, in any case, usually lasted only for one or two hours. Informal support was thought by the teachers to have been of benefit. Conversations with other teachers and friends were the most valued. Interestingly the great majority of teachers were generally satisfied with the kinds and level of induction support they received during their first year. The suggestions they had for improvement reflected a concern for immediate and specific problems to do with school setting, the classroom, and their teaching needs. A few wanted more release and planning time or more time for observing other teachers. Thirty-five teachers wanted more opportunities to receive curriculum information of a specific kind and 34 of a more general kind on school routine. Twenty-one wanted more in-classroom assistance from experienced teachers and, while most (85 percent) had been at least once observed by their principal as part of a formal evaluation, 79 percent received no in-classroom assistance during the year; they therefore appeared to want in-classroom assistance of a nonevaluative kind.

McDonald (1982) reported on a major study, funded by the National Institute of Education, which investigated three main questions. What are the problems of beginning teachers? What kind of programmes have been successful? What are the consequences of not resolving these problems of beginning teachers? The three approaches used to gather data were a literature review, field visits, and a review of programme evaluation reports.

Much of the study dealt with intern programmes. The two main types identified were four- and five-year programmes with the internship occurring in the final year. Those which, although called intern programmes, were little more than practice teaching were excluded. Significantly, very few "real" intern programmes appeared to exist and McDonald concluded that they were not a major feature of United States teacher education. Three intern programmes were studied in depth. In addition to course work, the Stanford internship included responsibility for teaching two classes a day for a school year plus at least one hour daily in school for preparation, observation, and so on. The University of Oregon programme concentrated upon the preparation of elementary-school teachers and consisted of four terms of graduate study combined with a year of full-time teaching leading to a Masters degree. At Temple University, the programme required a minimum commitment of two years during which time the intern worked as a full, salaried teacher and was also enrolled in a course work programme. All three programmes were selective in their recruitment and regarded the interns as a rather elite group. The Oregon programme emphasized clinical supervision, the Stanford programme used microteaching and at Temple the emphasis was on a humanistic approach to professional decision making. According to the interviewees—interns, first year teachers, school district staff, and programme faculty—these three programmes had been successful and popular over the years. Yet few such programmes were identified and McDonald concluded that this was because of widespread professional, organizational, and financial misconceptions about internship. The crucial factor was the nature and quality of the supervision provided within the school setting but the strength of the internship, the sense of reality which springs from teaching in one school, also prevented the intern from acquiring more broadly based experience in a variety of schools.

McDonald (1982) discovered even fewer examples of induction programmes in the United States. Of the two American programmes studied, the Jefferson county scheme was designed primarily to induct new teachers, including beginning teachers, into the particular curriculum used in the county. It was not directly concerned with the particular problems of beginning teachers per se. Nevertheless, partly because of the complexity of the county's curriculum and partly because many beginning teachers in any case welcome a structured guidance as to what they should teach, it seemed clear that the programme was meeting a very definite need and, moreover, that it may well have lessons which are generalizable beyond its particular purposes. On the other hand, the Georgia State programme was a comprehensive one designed to achieve goals relating to assessment, instructional improvement, and certification for all beginning teachers. The latter were on probation and required to demonstrate that they possessed each of these competencies at a specified criterion level; they were therefore evaluated over the first year and at several later points. Assessment was carried out by staff from 70 regional centres, by the school administrator, and by a peer master teacher of the same subject: all three had to agree on the level of competence achieved. The system encouraged and facilitated remedial diagnosis. Once deficiencies had been identified, a variety of training procedures were used: the teacher could be assigned to work with a master teacher

or to attend a college course. The programme was funded at the rate of US$2.6m a year by the State of Georgia; these funds were used for the regional assessment centres and for the training activities and, for example, provided money to release master teachers to work with beginning teachers. McDonald's impression was that more attention was paid to diagnosing competencies than to remedial training.

2. United Kingdom Studies

Early work in the United Kingdom was reviewed by Taylor and Dale (1971) and by Bolam (1973). Subsequent work has often been large-scale and funded by the Department of Education and Science and, partly as a consequence, numerous smaller scale research and development studies have also been stimulated. This review perforce concentrates on the larger scale studies.

Taylor and Dale (1971) reported on a national survey of the probationary year. A representative sample (10 percent) of the 1966 to 1967 cohort of beginning teachers (n = 3,588) and their headteachers (n = 2,528) answered questionnaires, and a subsample of probationers (n = 348) were interviewed. The data were organized under the following seven headings.

2.1 Background and Initial Training

The probationers surveyed were a predominantly young group, with 85 percent of them under 25 years of age. Women outnumbered men considerably in all age ranges except that of the 25–29 age range. Nearly all the graduates in the sample taught in secondary schools, with almost half of them in grammar schools. The socioeconomic constitution of the sample varied between men and women and between graduates and nongraduates. Women were much more likely to come from middle-class backgrounds and men from working-class backgrounds; graduates were more likely to come from middle-class backgrounds than nongraduates. Thus a majority of the sample were from middle-class backgrounds yet three-quarters taught in schools where the headteachers estimated that more than half of the children's parents were employed in manual occupations.

While most probationers found their training adequate, a sizable ,minority (25 percent) considered that it had been no more than barely adequate. College-trained nongraduate probationers tended to think more highly of their courses as a whole than did the university-trained graduates. More detailed analysis of the probationers' reactions to their training showed that they would have liked more of almost every aspect of it. More teaching practice was called for but the most commonly voiced complaint concerned the amount of time devoted to the methods of teaching main and subsidiary subjects, which was generally considered to be inadequate.

2.2 Appointment and Placement

Most probationers chose to teach in an l.e.a. for reasons unconnected with its intrinsic educational attributes, for example because their family lived there or because their spouse or fiancé was working there. However, in their replies and comments, probationers appeared to be favourably impressed by the ability of an authority to offer them confirmation of their appointment, and then of the identity of their school as early as possible during their last Summer term of training. Moreover, of the educational reasons given for choosing an l.e.a. or school, "the attractiveness of the particular post" was mentioned by a relatively large proportion (nearly one in five) of all probationers.

In many cases, and often through no fault of its own, an l.e.a. is faced with trying to fit square pegs into round holes in those weeks just before the autumn term begins. Thus, not infrequently, the amount of information that a probationer is given about his or her first post is too little or too late to be of much help. Twenty-one percent of probationers stated that they learnt of their children's age and ability less than a month before beginning teaching and in most cases this meant that they were unable to plan adequately. Indeed nearly one in 10 (9 percent) probationers only learnt of this on the day they began teaching. As far as knowledge of syllabus or schemes of work is concerned, more than one in four (27 percent) probationers only learnt this within a week of starting teaching and two-thirds of these (18 percent of all probationers) only found out on the day that they arrived at the school to begin teaching.

2.3 Inservice Guidance and Assessment

Local education authorities were the main organizers of inservice courses for probationers and these varied considerably in their timing, duration, pattern, contents, and aims. Although only a minority of l.e.a.s stated that they organized induction courses specifically designed for probationers, by the end of their first year one in two probationers had been invited to, and rather more than one in three probationers had attended, some form of induction course. The l.e.a. advisers were the sole source of outside advice for many probationers for, during their first year of teaching, less than one in five beginning teachers maintained any contact with their college or university and only one in 20 approached the local one. Moreover, towards the end of their first year of teaching, more than one-third of all probationers had still not met their l.e.a. advisers in any setting and 37 percent had not been visited by them in school. At the same time, nearly two out of every three probationers stated that they did not know in what ways and by which persons their progress was being assessed.

2.4 Experience and Problems in the Classroom

Nearly half (48 percent) of probationers regarded the teaching of groups of wide ability as a problem with over one-quarter citing lack of knowledge about their children's previous learning (29 percent), discipline difficulties with individual pupils (28 percent), and lack of particular teaching techniques (28 percent). The headteachers listed a somewhat different scale of probationer problems: class discipline (60 percent); inadequate organizing ability (41 percent); lack of a particular teaching technique (40 percent); teaching wide ability groups (35 percent); discipline difficulties with individual pupils (28 percent); lack of knowledge of children's previous learning (27 percent). Although twice as many probationers (10 percent) felt that they had been given classes of below-average rather than of above-average ability, the majority felt that their class' ability was about the same as the school's average. Very few secondary probationers (only 21 percent) found themselves in situations in which they did not teach their specialist subject(s) at all. Only one in 20 of all probationers felt that they were not allowed to work at their own pace and with their own emphasis within the syllabus, and headteachers were much more likely to profess a belief in allowing probationers freedom to work largely along their own lines (73 percent) than in exercising close control over their work (17 percent).

2.5 Experience and Problems Within the School Community

Internal support from headteachers and colleagues was seen as being much more important than external support from advisers, college tutors, or any outside course or agency. Only 2 percent of probationers considered their colleagues to be other than helpful and friendly and 72 percent found them to be actively friendly in making the first approaches. It is tempting to assume that probationers' greatest need for advice and help from headteacher and colleagues is at the beginning of their first year and that their needs decrease steadily throughout the year, as confidence and competence develop. Yet the proportion of probationers who felt the need for more advice from their headteachers and colleagues was half as high again at the end of the first year (23 percent) as it was at the beginning (only 15 percent). Moreover, at the start of teaching, probationers most often mentioned "shyness and lack of confidence" (26 percent) and "hesitating to seek advice" (22 percent) but by the end of the year "conditions of work" (16 percent) and "physically too tired to attend courses" (15 percent) had become the second and third most frequently mentioned problems. These findings indicate that probationers needs change as the year progresses.

2.6 Personal Problems

The main personal problems mentioned by probationers were physical fatigue (37 percent), stress (36 percent), financial worries (29 percent), travelling difficulties (13 percent), loneliness (11 percent), and accommodation difficulties (9 percent). Strikingly, almost one-third (30 percent) said their health had suffered, with women significantly more affected than men.

2.7 Career Intentions

Two-thirds of the men in the sample thought it unlikely that they would leave teaching within five years of taking it up, while only 8 percent thought it very likely that they would have left within that period. Half of the women in the sample thought it possible that they would have left teaching within five years, 28 percent thought it unlikely and 21 percent expected to have left teaching within five years. Leaving to raise a family dominated all other reasons for women, though the majority of women expected to return when their family commitments permitted. Women who were at the time single mentioned interest, and the desire to avoid boredom at home as the chief reasons for returning, but for those already married, financial considerations were the most important. Men teachers emerged as much more ambitious than women teachers, with almost half of them anticipating a graded post and more than a quarter expecting to be heads of department within five years. Fifteen percent of men and 5 percent of women were already, by the end of their first year in teaching, undertaking study for further qualifications, and 18 percent of men and 6 percent of women were taking courses of a recreational nature which were helpful to them in their teaching. Four percent of the men and 19 percent of the women in the sample intended taking up study for further qualifications within five years, while 30 percent of nongraduate men intended to start work for a degree.

Taylor and Dale (1971) also found clear evidence of considerable differences between l.e.a.s with respect to their procedures for assessing probationers for professional recognition and wide variations in the number of beginning teachers who had their probationary period extended because they were not performing satisfactorily. Thus, London teachers were almost twice as likely to have their probationary period extended than were rural teachers. Although the data from the National Survey are 15 years old, there is no evidence to suggest that this pattern has greatly altered in recent years.

Dale (1973a) carried out a Department of Education and Science-funded national survey of the circumstances surrounding the extension of probation in the academic year 1969 to 1970. His sample consisted of 156 of the 164 local authorities (93 percent) from which he obtained reports on 628 extensions. He discovered what he regarded as a very low proportion of probationers extended—about $3\frac{1}{2}$ percent—and an extremely low number—fewer than 10—of outright failures. He found the following significant differences: mature probationers (aged 25 and over) were three times more likely than younger probationers to be extended; secondary were more likely than primary probationers to be extended; junior were more likely than other primary probationers to be extended; secondary were more

likely than primary probationers to be extended because of discipline problems; primary were more likely than secondary probationers to be extended because of classroom management problems; primary were more likely than secondary probationers to be transferred to another school; graduates were more likely than college-trained probationers to be extended; graduates were more likely than college-trained probationers to be extended because of discipline problems. From his detailed study of the ways in which authorities operated the probation system, Dale concluded that his most important single finding was:

> The very great lack of consistency of application of criteria . . . which are themselves differently interpreted . . . behaviour which would be sufficient reason for probation to be extended in one local authority would not be considered a reason for extension at all in another authority.

Dale (1973b) also carried out an interview survey of women who left teaching in England and Wales during their first year, a particular problem at that time. Those who had left because of illness, pregnancy, or because their husbands had moved were excluded from the sample of 37 interviewees who were approximately one-third of the total such leavers in 1968 to 1969. Dale distinguished between three types of commitment to a teaching career: "drifters", who came into teaching for no particular reason (40 percent of sample); "calculators", who deliberately came into teaching for financial, domestic, or other noncareer reasons (20 percent); and the "dedicated", who had always wanted to be teachers (40 percent). However, Dale's main conclusion applied to all three types:

> . . . apart from a small number of women who had extreme discipline problems or an exceptionally uncooperative head, the decision to leave teaching was a result of the combination of a number of difficulties, any one of which could have been coped with in isolation. Perhaps the most common combination was that of discipline problems and unsupportive staff, but almost all possible combinations of the influential factors referred to in this report were represented by one case or another.

His explanation was thus in terms of "final straws breaking camels' backs". He further concluded that the leavers in his sample were certainly not "inadequate, feckless, neurotic, or weakwilled", rather that in their particular situations, resignation appeared to be a sensible course of action.

Bolam (1973) evaluated a series of experimental, externally based, inservice courses for probationers in four varied urban and rural settings. Following a pilot year, these courses had a common four-stage framework: a one-day orientation conference held in school time during September; a series of general discussion meetings held mainly in the evenings during the autumn term; a series of meetings on specific topics held mainly in the evenings of the spring and summer terms; a one-day overview conference held in school time during July. No significant differences were reported between the experimental and control groups as to knowledge, judgment, and behaviour related to the classroom, the school, and the probationary year. The experimental group were more likely to know about and use the teachers' centre, the l.e.a., and institute libraries; to feel that they lacked opportunities to meet people of their own age and interests; and to feel physically and mentally fatigued. The two groups did not differ significantly in terms of their extension and resignation rates nor in their general educational opinions; however, course attenders were significantly less likely than nonattenders to conservatize their educational opinions. In seeking to explain their extremely limited impact, Bolam argued that the external courses, however good, were necessarily general and thus peripheral to the probationers' major professional concerns which were to do with *their* particular pupils, classrooms, and schools. Probationers' main source of practical help lay in the school, with colleagues and the headteacher.

Seventy-seven percent of the probationers attended the one-day orientation conference held in school time, whereas 39 percent attended the optional evening meetings. Reasons given for attending the latter were: general interest; specifically interesting topics; to gain experience and advice. Reasons for nonattendance included personal commitments; school commitments; exhaustion; irrelevant topics; and travelling difficulties. The most likely explanation for the secondary probationers poor attendance was thought to be that the courses did not cater for their specialist subject interests. Nevertheless, 70 percent of probationers and 80 percent of tutors said they would recommend other probationers to attend similar courses. Probationers consistently said that they wanted practical help with their specific, practical problems but they gave considerable support for the course as an opportunity to meet and talk with other probationers; the therapeutic value of such external courses should not, therefore, be underestimated. Probationers attached great importance to tutors being available for individual consultation, arranging visits to observe other teachers and informal, social meetings. Lectures and informal individual discussions were overused by tutors compared with what the probationers wanted, whereas workshops, films, case-study material, and group discussions were under-used. The probationers' rank order of preferences for the different types of tutor was clearly expressed: teachers of over three years experience; heads; teachers of up to three years experience; l.e.a. advisers; college tutors; university lecturers; and Her Majesty's Inspectorate, although the last three groups were chosen by a substantial minority. Finally, Bolam recommended a seven-stage framework, broadly chronological, for a systematic induction process: appointment and placement; preservice orientation; inservice orientation (September); professional adaptation (autumn term); professional development (spring and summer terms); assessment for professional recognition (summer term); overview of induction year (July).

3. The Teacher Induction Pilot Schemes (*TIPS*) Project

Experimental induction schemes were funded by the United Kingdom government in Liverpool and Northumberland from 1974 to 1978. These schemes, and nine other more limited ones, were evaluated by a team of university-based researchers who set out to answer two main questions. What are the main features of effective induction policies and programmes? What conditions and procedures are needed at school, external centre, l.e.a., and national levels to ensure the effective implementation and institutionalization of these policies and programmes? The evaluation relied on a comparison of questionnaire and interview replies from probationers, heads, tutors, school colleagues, l.e.a. advisers, and college lecturers. Several evaluation reports were produced, notably by McCabe (1978) and Davis (1979), but the following account is based upon the national report by Bolam et al. (1979).

The three main features of the experimental schemes in Liverpool and Northumberland were: 75 percent teaching load for the beginning teachers; school-based teacher tutors to help them; and external, centre-based inservice courses. They were clearly supported by the majority of probationers: the additional "free" time provided by the reduced teaching load was judged to be effective in meeting their teaching and general professional needs by 85 percent of probationers; 75 percent said the same about the teacher tutor and 58 percent about the external courses. Furthermore, over 80 percent of the heads in the main schemes said the teaching and general professional needs of their probationers had benefited from the scheme as a whole and they were particularly in favour of the school-based element: almost 90 percent would recommend other schools to appoint a teacher tutor. The inescapable and striking general conclusion was, therefore, that the essential features of the experimental schemes met with the broad approval of the overwhelming majority of those who had actually experienced them.

The main practical problems identified in the first year were as follows: in the infant and first schools in particular, many probationers disliked the disruption of their relationship with their classes; in some primary schools it was difficult to find replacement staff of the required standard; small secondary schools had particular problems in finding specialist subject replacements; the January entrants were a source of difficulty because they overlapped for a part of two academic years; and it was not always possible to release both tutor and probationer at the same time.

The feature of the main schemes that was rated as effective by most probationers was the additional free time. Primary-school probationers valued this component more than their secondary-school colleagues, probably because primary-school teachers generally have far fewer "free" periods than do secondary-school teachers and therefore value them more when they do get them. Bradley and Eggleston (1979), studied this aspect of induction in some depth and concluded that probationers whose additional release time was guided and supervised, valued it more than those who experienced no such supervision.

Tutors and other experienced teachers were very ready to help through individual discussion with probationers. Indeed, this was the most frequently reported internal induction activity in the two main schemes: 70 percent of Liverpool probationers and 48 percent of Northumberland probationers said they had experienced this. However, less than 10 percent of Liverpool and Northumberland probationers engaged in joint or team teaching with tutors, though 20 percent did so with experienced colleagues; 18 percent observed their tutors teaching and 20 percent observed experienced colleagues; 18 percent of probationers were themselves observed teaching, at least once, for 20 minutes or more by their tutors; 18 percent of primary-school probationers were observed by their head and 25 percent of secondary-school probationers were observed by their head of department. Yet about half of those who did experience team teaching and observation of teaching said that these were effective in helping them with their teaching. Visits to other schools were the second most commonly used method (64 percent) and in secondary schools 47 percent reported the use of group discussions. The overall picture is one in which school-organized induction consisted principally of individual and group discussions and visits to other schools; relatively little emphasis was placed upon professional interaction in the classroom situation. These findings indicate strongly that tutors and other senior staff are reluctant to extend their concept of induction training to embrace classroom observation. The reasons are probably deeply rooted in attitudes to professional autonomy and they certainly pose severe problems for tutors and tutor training programme organizers. Yet by the end of the schemes, over three-quarters of all respondents thought that probationers should regularly discuss their lesson plans with tutors, should have their teaching observed by tutors, and should observe experienced colleagues teaching.

The most innovative feature of the experimental schemes was the teacher tutor role. Tutors were appointed from the existing staff of each school; they were paid an honorarium, received some additional release time, and were given some form of training and support. By the end of the scheme, in 1977, 90 percent of all respondents recommended that schools should appoint teacher tutors and 87 percent said that they should only be appointed from within existing school staff. Two-thirds of all the 1977 respondents thought that tutors needed about one hour per probationer per week and a majority thought that, on this basis, tutors should be responsible for less than the five probationers prescribed for in the pilot schemes. Half of all respondents favoured the ad hoc payment system for tutors adopted in the pilot schemes but one-quarter of the

respondents, and one-third of tutors, wanted the salary related to the Burnham scales. Whereas at the outset of the project there were uncertainties about both the need for the content of tutor training, by the end the case for training teacher tutors was made most forcibly. Seventy-one percent of all respondents agreed that tutors needed some form of training and tutors themselves were most convinced of this, especially those from secondary schools (94 percent). However, only 53 percent of tutors considered the training they had received had been adequate: 87 percent said that the l.e.a. should also produce written guidelines for tutors and 69 percent thought that ongoing and not simply preparatory training was necessary.

In urban Liverpool, all probationers were released for either one full day or half days each week to attend inservice courses and workshops at eight professional centres—seven colleges of education and one teachers' centre. In rural Northumberland, most probationers attended block release courses, of about one week's duration, which were staffed by l.e.a. advisers, college of education staff, and local teachers and were located at colleges and teachers' centres. In both authorities the colleges were facing the threat of contraction and closure. The consistent pattern of expressed preference for internal over external activities should not be allowed to obscure the fact that 75 percent of all respondents recommended other l.e.a.s to adopt external programmes as part of their induction schemes. There appeared to be general recognition of the need to maintain a balance of internal and external activities.

At the end of the scheme all respondents were asked to make some judgments of principle on the need for induction schemes. Eighty-four percent said that schools should make special arrangements for probationers and 75 percent said that l.e.a.s should provide some help and guidance to schools about a suitable school induction programme. Of course, some teachers, heads, and advisers were deeply sceptical about the necessity for and value of the programme and thus of the need to spend money on it. However, the evidence clearly showed that these were minority viewpoints, that they were mainly held by people not closely associated with the scheme and finally, that those holding such views tended to change in favour of the scheme as they gained direct experience of it.

Several studies have been made of the extent to which l.e.a.s have adopted the pilot schemes' approaches with reduced budgets. McMahon and Bolam (1982a) reported on a questionnaire survey of 81 out of 104 l.e.a.s (a response rate of 78 percent). One-fifth (19.7 percent) of the l.e.a.s allocated release time specifically for probationers; two gave one day per week and 12 gave half a day a week to each probationer. Seventy-three percent of l.e.a.s said that they had recommended schools to designate the equivalent of a teacher tutor with induction responsibilities. The implementation was left to the schools, although six l.e.a.s gave additional release time to tutors. Forty-two percent of l.e.a.s said they provided tutors with preliminary training but this was normally of only two or three days duration; 36 percent said that they provided ongoing support and training. Most l.e.a.s (70 percent), arranged a programme of external courses or conferences for probationers. Typically these took place on two or three days throughout the year and only very few involved release for probationers. Thus most induction schemes appeared to have reverted to the prepilot scheme pattern (Bolam 1973) although some new developments had occurred. For example, 89 percent of l.e.a.s said they had established a representative consultative committee to advise on inservice and induction policy and 60 percent said that they had designated an l.e.a. adviser to organize induction and inservice training. Studies of individual l.e.a.s were reported by Smyth and McCabe (1980, 1981) and by Jayne and Leudels-Salmon (1980).

4. *Australian Studies*

Tisher (1978, 1980) reported a national study carried out in Australia. The study was funded by the Education Research and Development Committee, a Federal Committee, from 1976 to 1978 and involved two stages: a descriptive survey of what state, regional, and school authorities said they were offering to beginning teachers; and a national survey of the views of beginning teachers and school principals. Beginning teachers received two questionnaires: one during the first few weeks of teaching (n = 1,600) and the second towards the end of their first year (n = 1,300). In midyear a subsample were interviewed. School principals also completed questionnaires (n = 700) at the beginning of the school year.

Arguing that the nature of their first encounter with a state employing authority can be quite important in shaping professional attitudes, Tisher pointed out that many local education authorities did not provide adequate information about their schools to facilitate applicants' choices and, moreover, that many larger authorities delayed confirmation of new appointments causing anxiety amongst the new teachers. Nonetheless, 82 percent of beginning teachers said they were able to exercise a preference for their first appointment and about the same percentage were satisfied with their first school. Sixty-nine percent paid preterm visits to their schools, half of them initiating these themselves. Visits were usually short but were thought to have a number of benefits. Some states organized much longer orientation programmes; the one in the Northern Territory, for example, lasted two weeks. About a quarter of the new teachers received a reduced work load and another quarter got other concessions, for example the number and size of classes taught. Eighty-seven percent were briefed on their first day, 42 percent experienced some form of specifically designed support, and 56 percent of them found the support valuable. The responsibility for beginning teachers was normally given to the principal

or vice-principal and included helping them with their teaching.

The tasks that were still worrying the teachers at the end of their first year, even though they were coping, included teaching wide ability groups (63 percent), teaching slow learners (62 percent), evaluating their own teaching (55 percent), motivating pupils (54 percent), discovering the level at which to teach (47 percent), teaching specific skills (41 percent), and controlling classes (39 percent). At least 60 percent of the beginning teachers recommended the adoption of the following induction procedures: receiving written materials on conditions of employment; receiving written materials on school matters; accepting advice in classroom management or help in producing programmes of work; accepting evaluation of own teaching; participation in organized consultation with experienced school personnel; attending group meetings for beginning teachers at school; observing other teachers' methods of teaching; visiting other schools for observation/consultation; conferring informally with beginning teachers from other schools; looking at local educational resources. In practice, many of these respondents had not had the benefit of such procedures: for example, 82 percent wanted to observe other teachers but only 44 percent had been given the opportunity.

5. *Some Conclusions and Issues*

In this final section, some implications for induction research, procedures, and policy are briefly considered. Sensible judgments about such matters can only be made in specific national contexts so no easy generalizations are possible. With respect to research on induction, two broad groups of questions are pertinent within each country: (a) what is the nature and extent of the induction knowledge base? and (b) more particularly, how satisfactory was the research methodology which provided it? Next, can policy makers and practitioners make use of that knowledge?

One can only agree with McDonald (1982) that most of the research leaves a great deal to be desired methodologically but it is important to recognize that this is also true of much other educational research. Educational policy and practice are notoriously complex and messy and the research design consequences are only too well-known. So people should beware of counselling perfection where this is unattainable; the concept of "goodness of fit" between research strategies and research questions (Yarger and Galluzzo 1980) is helpful in this context.

Ideally, decisions about future research should be taken within the wider framework of discussions of priorities in teacher education research in general (Hall 1979), and should include consideration of such basic questions as whether to adopt a perspective derived from, say, professional socialization theory (Tisher 1980), or from, say, innovation theory (Bolam 1981). However, bearing in mind the four factors affecting concern about induction which were outlined at the start of this paper, any actual research and development agenda is bound to be influenced by current national policy issues. Thus, the research questions outlined by McDonald (1982) and Hall (1982) certainly make sense in a United States context. In some Canadian provinces, like British Columbia, and in the Netherlands, surveys of teacher needs are probably the first priority. In Australia and New Zealand, the evaluation of specific induction programmes may be the first priority. In England and Wales, the need now is probably for smaller scale and better designed studies, with a more specific focus than the national pilot schemes, for example, of the impact of the, increasingly common, short-term contracts for beginning teachers or the effectiveness of various types of teacher tutors. Much can be learned from research and experience in other countries: thus the two above-mentioned American lists of research questions will undoubtedly prove valuable beyond the United States.

Indeed, a fundamental conclusion of this paper is that there is an encouraging amount of accord on certain key problems. For example, the findings from the United Kingdom and Australian surveys of beginning teachers' experiences and needs are very similar and, as Zeichner (1979) concluded, notwithstanding the many qualifications that have to be made about research methods and findings, there is considerable agreement amongst both researchers and practitioners about the technical improvements which can and should be made in the induction process. So policy makers and practitioners can look to this work with some confidence that they will find usable knowledge. In the following summary of that usable knowledge, the illustrations are mainly from the United Kingdom.

Zeichner concluded that, although the following generalizations cannot be supported by all the research he reviewed, there is sufficient support for them to be taken very seriously by policy makers and practitioners. Good induction programmes should include: (a) additional release time for the beginning teacher; (b) school-based support from a colleague acting as a mentor or professional tutor who also receives some additional release time plus initial and continuing training; (c) planned and systematic school-based activities including classroom observation and support; (d) planned and systematic externally based activities organized by l.e.a. and college personnel; and (e) the explicit and active support of schools principals and l.e.a. administrators.

The following broad aim for induction programmes, drawn from the United Kingdom, finds explicit and implicit support from experience elsewhere.

All our evidence suggests both that the overwhelming concern of most probationers is with the practicalities of their own teaching situation and that practical relevance is the principal yardstick by which they will judge an induction programme. It is, therefore, recommended that the broad aim of the programme should be to offer practical and individualised help to probationers and that the main focus should be upon the problems and opportunities facing them in their own classrooms and schools. (Bolam 1973)

As a result of the national pilot schemes, the evaluators recommend that induction programmes should provide information, advice, and inservice experiences to achieve eight aims related to enabling teachers to make independent, professional judgments: (a) the promotion of growth and development, not simply survival skills, for all beginning teachers; (b) subject teaching skills; (c) general teaching and classroom skills; (d) colleague relationships; (e) school procedures; (f) l.e.a. procedures; and (g) the teacher's personal situation. The first two aims may require some explanation and justification. The second aim was based upon the rejection of a deficiency model of induction and is likely to be uncontentious. The first aim was, however, based upon the much more controversial view that beginning teachers should be inducted into the values and practices of the teaching profession as a whole and not only those of any one school or employing local education authority. It follows that one, albeit incidental, outcome of a professional induction programme could be that, in the judgment of individual beginning teachers, the values and practices of their school or l.e.a. are professionally unacceptable. In this context it is worth noting that many British probationers valued their contacts with college (professional centre) staff because they offered an alternative viewpoint to that of the l.e.a. staff.

A key question for all those, especially mentors or tutors, trying to help beginning teachers is how to provide effective help which is relevant to the needs of the beginning teacher in the classroom. Evidence from the United Kingdom indicates that colleagues were reluctant to enter their beginning teachers' classrooms to observe them teaching even when it was part of their job specification as tutors. Two of the main reasons were the fear that this reduced the beginner to the status of a student teacher and that, in most schools, there was no tradition of observing colleagues teaching. Of the many professional issues raised by these findings, two are directly relevant. What indirect information about teaching can tutors obtain without going into the classroom? What approaches are open to them if they go into the classroom? The answers to these questions go beyond the scope of this article but McMahon and Bolam (1982b) deal with them at length. Clinical supervision (Acheson and Gall 1980, Turney et al. 1982) probably offers the most coherent framework for such direct, on-the-job role support (see *Supervision of the Practicum*).

The key issue for national and local policy makers is the high cost of "good" induction programmes. The model recommended after the United Kingdom pilot schemes, which included release for probationers and tutors plus a salary increment for tutors, would involve additional costs of approximately one-third of a salary for each probationer. Improvements can be achieved at much lower cost by emphasizing the role of the school in induction, by encouraging principals to re-allocate existing resources, particularly time, and by equipping key personnel like deputy principals and department heads with clinical supervision skills.

These approaches are considerably facilitated when induction is treated as part of a wider process of professional development—the triple-I continuum of initial, induction, and inservice education and training. At school level this implies a coherent and systematic policy for staff development, including induction, and the adoption of school-based and school-focused methods of inservice education. These ideas have recently gained widespread support in Organisation for Economic Co-operation and Development (OECD) countries (Bolam 1980, 1982), but if schools are to be able to implement them they will require appropriate external support from l.e.a. and college personnel.

The emerging consensus being portrayed here then, is of an induction programme which is rooted in the specific school and classroom experiences of individual beginning teachers, in school staff development policies and procedures which are systematic but also flexible enough to cater for the peculiar, individualized, and changing needs of beginning teachers, and which are themselves systematically supported by external agencies. One obvious question generated by this account is why, if there is this emerging consensus, so little has actually happened? After all it was in the early 1960s that a notable United States report (Conant 1963) recommended a programme similar to the one outlined above and in the early 1970s that the influential James Report (Department of Education and Science 1972) did the same for England and Wales. The fate of these reports can only lead to pessimism about the likelihood of similar reports in Canada (Joint Board of Teacher Education 1982), Australia (Auchmuty 1980), and New Zealand (Department of Education 1979), actually being implemented. Circumstances in each country do, of course, vary tremendously but enough is now known about the crucial importance of the implementation stage of innovations in educational policy and practice for us to treat this aspect of induction very seriously indeed (Fullan and Pomfret 1977).

Experience in England and Wales is again instructive. The build-up of informed professional opinion about the need for improved induction arrangements began during the Second World War (Board of Education 1944 p. 83). As Bolam (1973) indicated, this was only the first of a whole series of policy statements by professional associations, government reports, and the government itself all urging improved induction arrangements. This found its most clear expression in the James Report (Department of Education and Science 1972) and subsequent government policy statements which in essence recommended a national scheme similar to the two pilot induction schemes described above. Professional opinion was informed by a series of government-funded dissemination activities organized

from the University of Bristol. These included lectures and workshops at virtually every university in the country and aimed at key decision makers and practitioners in the surrounding regions (Bolam 1973), two national conferences to disseminate the findings of the TIPS project (Bolam and Baker 1975, Bolam et al. 1977), and the production of practical resource handbooks for school and l.e.a. personnel (McMahon and Bolam 1982b). In spite of this comprehensive and thorough approach, a recent survey revealed only limited implementation of the recommended induction arrangements (McMahon and Bolam 1982a).

The reasons for this are complex and to a considerable extent arise from the peculiar circumstances which existed in England and Wales from 1974 onwards. The demographic trends were very favourable since declining enrolments led to a reduced demand for teachers and therefore to the availability of replacement staff for probationers released on the schemes. Unfortunately the 1973 oil crisis radically altered the initially favourable economic conditions to such an extent that the proposed schemes became extremely difficult to finance. Nonetheless, the government continued to make financial provision for them but local education authorities exercised their legitimate right not to use the money allocated for induction, instead reallocating it to other local government costs. Some would argue that had the l.e.a.s been legally obliged to spend the money on induction then an acceptable national scheme would indeed have been implemented in the late 1970s. Others doubt this, arguing that it is not enough simply to provide the money; it is also essential to introduce regulations, analogous to those for initial teacher education, to ensure that appropriate and adequate induction procedures are actually implemented. Thus, teachers would only become fully qualified if they had experienced specified and validated education and training and had demonstrated their professional competence, again according to specified procedures, by the end of the probationary period. At present this debate must remain speculative but other countries and states should at least be aware of the issues involved.

Would-be innovators in the field of teacher induction should also pay attention to the barriers to implementation likely to be encountered in the professional attitudes held by some beginning, experienced, and head teachers. There is ample evidence from the United Kingdom that a significant proportion are unsympathetic to the very idea of systematic induction. Some probationers, for example, felt that they should be treated as fully qualified teachers not reduced to the status, as they saw it, of student teacher. Secondary probationers often saw themselves as fully competent in their own subject discipline while infant probationers were frequently reluctant to leave their pupils to attend courses. Some experienced teachers and heads argued that an induction programme was an unnecessary extension of training and that preservice courses should be improved instead. Others resented the extra release time given to probationers and favoured "throwing them in at the deep end" rather than "wrapping them in cotton wool". Experience in the United Kingdom also indicated that these comments were more likely to be made about external courses; school-based programmes are much more likely to be viewed favourably by experienced practitioners. Moreover, those initially opposed to any form of induction programme displayed a pronounced tendency to shift in favour of such programmes as they gained experience of them.

In conclusion, existing research and development knowledge does indicate the need for considerably improving induction arrangements for beginning teachers and has also provided some reasonably reliable information about the precise nature of the beginning teachers' problems and needs and of the most effective ways of helping them. However, since most of this information is derived from a limited number of studies which are themselves culture bound, a great deal of work remains to be done in each country or state contemplating the introduction of induction programmes. Furthermore, this existing information base itself needs to be strengthened by more rigorously designed studies.

Bibliography

Acheson K A, Gall M D 1980 *Techniques in the Clinical Supervision of Teachers: Preservice and Inservice Applications*. Longman, New York

Amar M B 1952 An analysis and appraisal of induction programs for new elementary school teachers with reference to the development of a program for Chicago. Doctoral Thesis, Loyola University, 1952

Archer C P 1960 Inservice education. In: Harris C W (ed.) 1960 *Encyclopedia of Educational Research. A Project of the American Educational Research Association*, 3rd edn. Macmillan, New York

Auchmuty J J 1980 *Report of the National Enquiry into Teacher Education*. Australian Government Publishing Service, Canberra

Bolam R 1973 *Induction Programmes for Probationary Teachers: A Report on the Action Research Project Funded by the Department of Education and Science and carried out at the University of Bristol School of Education Research Unit, 1968–72*. University of Bristol School of Education, Bristol

Bolam R 1980 Inservice education and training. In: Hoyle E, Megarry J (eds.) 1980 *World Yearbook of Education 1980: Professional Development of Teachers*. Kogan Page, London

Bolam R 1981 Evaluative research: A case study of the Teacher Induction Pilot Schemes Project. *J. Educ. for Teach.* 7: 70–83

Bolam R (ed.) 1982 *School-focused Inservice Training*. Heinemann, London

Bolam R, Baker K (eds.) 1975 *The Teacher Induction Pilot Scheme Project National Conference Report*. University of Bristol School of Education, Bristol

Bolam R, Baker K, McMahon A 1979 *The Teacher Induction Pilot Schemes (TIPS) Project: National Evaluation Report*. University of Bristol School of Education, Bristol

Bolam R, Baker K, Davis J, McCabe C, McMahon A (eds.) 1977 *National Conference on Induction: Conference Papers (300 pp. mimeo)* University of Bristol School of Education, Bristol

Bradley H W, Eggleston J F 1979 *An Induction Year Experiment*. University of Nottingham School of Education, Nottingham

Childress J R 1969 Inservice education of teachers. In: Ebel R L (ed.) 1969 *Encyclopedia of Educational Research: A Project of the American Educational Research Association*, 4th edn. Macmillan, New York

Conant J B 1963 *The Education of American Teachers*. McGraw-Hill, New York

Dale I R 1973a *A Study of the Circumstances Surrounding the Extension of the Induction Period of Beginning Teachers*. University of Bristol School of Education, Bristol

Dale I R 1973b *A Survey of Wastage Among Women Teachers During Their First Year of Service*. University of Bristol School of Education, Bristol

Davis O J 1979 *The Liverpool Induction Pilot Scheme: A Summative Report*. University of Liverpool School of Education, Liverpool

Denemark G W, MacDonald J B 1967 Preservice and inservice education of teachers. *Rev. Educ. Res.* 37: 233–47

Department of Education and Science 1972 *Education: A Framework for Expansion*. Series no. Cmnd. 5174. Her Majesty's Stationery Office, London

Fullan M, Pomfret A 1977 Research on curriculum and instruction implementation. *Rev. Educ. Res.* 47: 335–97

Grant C A, Zeichner K M 1981 Inservice support for the first year: The state of the scene. *J. Res. Devel. Educ.* 14: 99–111

Hall G E 1979 *A National Agenda for Research and Development in Teacher Education 1979–1984*. University of Texas, Austin, Texas

Hall G E 1982 Induction: The missing link. *J. Teach. Educ.* 33: 53–55

Hermanowicz H J 1966 The pluralistic world of beginning teachers. *The Real World of the Beginning Teacher*. Report of the 19th National TIPS Conference, New York, June 22–25, 1965. National Commission on Teacher Education and Professional Standards, National Education Association, Washington, DC, pp. 15–25

Hunt D W 1968 Teacher induction: An opportunity and a responsibility. *The National Association of Secondary Schools Principals' Bulletin*, October, pp. 130–35

Hunt D W 1969 *Project on the Induction of Beginning Teachers*. Booklet 1: *Guidelines for Principals*, Booklet 2: *Guidelines for Co-operating Teachers*, Booklet 3: *Welcome to Teaching*. National Association of Secondary School Principals, Reston, Virginia

Jayne E, Leudels-Salmon 1980 *The ILEA Induction Scheme: A Survey of Probationers' Experiences and Views of the First Year of the Scheme*. Inner London Education Authority, Research and Statistics Division, London

Joint Board of Teacher Education 1981 *Preparation of Teachers for the Public Schools of British Columbia*. Department of Education, Victoria, British Columbia

Le Fevre C 1967 Teacher characteristics and careers. *Rev. Educ. Res.* 37: 433–47

McCabe C 1978 *Induction in Northumberland: An Evaluation*. University of Newcastle School of Education, Newcastle-upon-Tyne

McDonald F J 1982 *Study of Induction Programs for Beginning Teachers: Executive Summary*. Educational Testing Services, Princeton, New Jersey

McMahon A, Bolam R 1982a *Survey of Induction Schemes, 1981*. University of Bristol School of Education, Bristol

McMahon A, Bolam R 1982b (forthcoming) *School-based Induction: A Resource Handbook*. Heinemann, London

Malament E E 1968 The orientation of beginning social studies teachers in New York City senior high schools (Doctoral dissertation, New York University, 1968) *Dissertation Abstracts International* 29: 1968, 500A–501A (University Microfilms No. 68–11,798)

Mason W S 1961 *The Beginning Teacher: Status and Career Orientations*. Department of Health, Education and Welfare, Washington Circular No. 644, Office of Education, Washington, DC

Ministry of Education 1944 *Teachers and Youth Leaders*. McNair A, Chairman. Her Majesty's Stationery Office, London

National Education Association of the United States Research Division 1964 *Orientation Programs for Teachers*. Research memo 1964 24. National Education Association of the United States, Washington, DC

New Zealand Department of Education 1979 *Review of Teacher Training*. Department of Education, Wellington

Schwalenberg R J 1965 Teacher orientation practices in Oregon secondary schools (Dissertation, University of Oregon, 1965) *Dissertation Abstracts International* 26: 1966, 4403 (University Microfilms No. 65-12,239)

Smyth K, McCabe C 1980 *Induction on a Reduced Budget*. University of Newcastle School of Education, Newcastle-upon-Tyne

Smyth K, McCabe C 1981 *Induction on a Reduced Budget II*. University of Newcastle School of Education, Newcastle-upon-Tyne

Taylor J K, Dale I R 1971 *A Survey of Teachers in Their First Year of Service*. University of Bristol School of Education, Bristol

Tisher R (ed.) 1978 *The Induction of Beginning Teachers in Australia*. School of Education Monash University, Melbourne

Tisher R 1980 The induction of beginning teachers. In: Hoyle E, Megarry L (eds.) 1980 *World Yearbook of Education 1980: Professional Development of Teachers*. Kogan Page, London

Turney C et al. 1982 *Supervisor Development Programmes*. Sydney University Press, Sydney

Vakgroep Natuurkunde-Didaktiek 1981 *Het Projekt Begeleiding Beginnende Leraren*. University of Utrecht, Utrecht

Yarger S J, Galluzzo G R 1980 *Grabbing at Mirages or Painting Clear Pictures? . . . Toward Solving the Dilemmas of Research on Inservice Teacher Education*. Syracuse University, Syracuse, New York

Zeichner K M 1979 *Teacher Induction Practices in the United States and Great Britain*. University of Wisconsin, Department of Curriculum and Instruction, Madison, Wisconsin

Supervision of Teaching

B. M. Harris

Supervision of instruction is widely recognized as the instructional improvement function within any school organization. Historically, supervision has evolved from a function emphasizing inspection, monitoring, and enforcement to one emphasizing curriculum development, training, and formative evaluation. Much supervisory practice is still directed toward monitoring and enforcement and the emphasis on development varies widely among countries, types of school organizations, and individual supervisors.

Supervision as a formally defined set of responsibilities or a function is at least as old as public education itself. Early North American schools were created in colonial times for largely religious purposes with supervising responsibilities vested in the townspeople (Barr et al. 1947 p. 3). British schools, evolving primarily from church-related institutions in the early 1800s, often designated ministers as supervisors. The need for a formal system of supervision became well-recognized as an outgrowth of universal education. The commitment of public government funds and the expectation that all children and youth will be served has given importance to supervision of instruction to control the quality and character of the program of instruction.

Supervisory practices were exported to nearly all corners of the globe during the colonial efforts of the nineteenth century by Great Britain, France, and the United States. More recently, the United States has been extremely influential in promoting educational organizations and hence supervision in many less developed and war-torn countries. The work of UNESCO has also been a major influence throughout the world especially in its emphasis on curriculum development and teacher training in newly independent and developing nations (Henderson 1978).

Even Western influence produced only gradual evidence of supervision in Middle Eastern countries. The assumption of responsibility for education by these states came primarily as funds were allocated, and formal institutions replaced the *Kutaab* where a learned man was the village educator.

The evolution of supervisory practice has been both philosophical and technological. Philosophically, the trends and countertrends have reflected the issues and controversies of democratic and authoritarian thought. Technologically, supervision has developed away from crude "school visiting" as an undifferentiated mixture of testing, observing, interviewing, judging, order giving, and report writing. In its place there has emerged a rather clearly defined set of tasks of supervision that promote both maintenance and adoption of good teaching practices. Supervisory staffing has become enormously complex with specialists of many kinds working at various organizational levels.

Despite the short history of instructional supervision as specialized educational practice, a surprising amount of "professional consensus" has emerged about the nature of the function. Supervision of instruction is conceptualized rather widely as practices directed primarily toward change in instructional programs. The focus of supervision is increasingly on teachers and teaching more than on pupils, resources, and organizational structures. Furthermore, there tends to be rather broad agreement on curriculum development, inservice training, and evaluation of instruction as essential tasks of supervision.

1. Schools of Thought and Practice

Supervisory practices tend to reflect a wide variety of schools of thought. Trends away from inspectorial supervision toward "developmental" practices have been slow in emerging and halting and erratic in implementation. Numerous countertrends have also emerged. Three rather distinct views of supervisory practice are reflected with sufficient vigor in both the literature and practice of supervision that they might be thought of as "schools of thought."

(a) The monitoring, inspecting, accountability school of thought continues the traditions of the origins of early supervisory practice with many added technological features. It emphasizes testing, evaluation, discrepancy analysis, and feedback as elements of practice controlling for either conformity or change.

(b) Another school of thought emphasizes human relations and morale building (Wiles and Lovell 1983). It emphasizes the informal relations among personnel, sensitivity to needs, promoting personal development, removing constraints, and maximizing freedom of action.

(c) A third school of thought is change-process oriented (Harris 1985). It emphasizes planning, designing, guiding, stimulating, goal setting, and even manipulation of environmental factors to promote improved instructional practices.

Studies of supervisory practice tend to give some support for each of these three approaches. Monitoring and accountability efforts tend to be what Harris calls "tractive" in emphasizing the maintenance of existing practices (Harris 1985). There is little support, however, for the exclusive use of such techniques for improving instructional practices. The human relations approaches have been strongly supported by studies showing that involvement in decision making and open communication systems enhance commitment to, and understanding of, new practices. However, complete reliance on individual initiative and interpersonal relationships to produce change seems unwarranted. Studies of leadership (Sergiovanni and Starratt 1979) and those related to training (Lawrence et al. 1974) strongly support supervisory approaches which emphasize formal design, planning, and structured implementation of new instructional programs.

1.1 Monitoring and Accountability

This approach to instructional supervision is still widely practiced. School principals and headteachers, local school supervisors, and regional inspectors share much of the responsibility for monitoring teaching and student learning. Despite strong efforts to decrease reliance on monitoring practices in such diverse countries as the United States and Malaysia, teachers report receiving little supervisory assistance in most schools until a problem of some serious kind develops (Ibrahim 1979). Hence, supervision is seen as remedial more than developmental. Testing programs place the emphasis on accountability for learning rather than for using accepted teaching practices. Hence standardized testing using local or national norms as well as state, national, and college entrance examinations tend to be utilized to some extent as tools for supervision.

Most countries continue to use state, regional, or federal inspectors for supervisory purposes. The Republic of China (Taiwan), for instance, uses both provincial and county "inspectors." County-level inspectors generally monitor elementary and junior-high schools leaving the senior-high schools to provincial inspectors. In both instances, inspectors range widely over both instructional and noninstructional concerns. A new group of "supervisors" have emerged in some counties in the Republic of China as experienced teachers are recruited to give attention to specific courses or content areas.

Malaysian schools are inspected under the federal inspectorate of schools. A variety of approaches have been developed in an effort to keep pace with a greatly expanding system. Hence, "block" inspections are sometimes utilized in a given district or area, focusing only on certain aspects of the school curriculum.

In the United States too, monitoring is growing. Project monitoring, total school accreditation, and special program reviews are given attention in regular site visits involving observations, interviews, review of documents, and report writing. Similar inspection systems prevail in Venezuela, the Philippines, and Saudi Arabia where expanding systems of public elementary and secondary education present serious problems of quality control. In most countries combinations of national and regional inspectors are involved in the monitoring.

1.2 Human Relations, Morale Building

This approach tends to be reflected in the other two types of supervisory operations. As supervision that rests heavily on informal relationships between supervisors and teachers, structured programs of this type are not common. Recent examples of supervision giving emphasis to this approach can be found however in clinical supervision programs (Cogan 1973) and teacher-center programs. Clinical supervision programs were pioneered by Goldhammer and Cogan at Harvard University in the late 1950s. The clinical approach is highly personalized, relies heavily on teacher acceptance and initiative, and has a structure of cyclical steps. Teacher centers were originated apparently in the United Kingdom as an outgrowth of the movement for more freedom and self-expression for children in schools (see *Teachers' Centres*). The idea of inservice training and curriculum development under the nearly complete control of the individual teacher is basic to the teacher center in at least one form. Teachers' unions have, of course, been highly supportive of this development.

1.3 Change Process Management

This continues to be a pervasive movement in instructional supervision. In many rapidly developing countries, supervision takes the form of national planning. In some UNESCO efforts it is focused on teacher training and curriculum development on a multinational basis as in the Southeast Asian program in the biological sciences. Venezuela has utilized five-year plans for education for many years (Garcia 1980). A recent effort to introduce a system of training in analytical thinking at the fourth-grade level throughout Venezuela has been sponsored jointly by the ministries of intelligence and education. In the United States a nationwide program of education for all handicapped children and youth was inaugurated by Congressional action (House Bill 94-142) but implemented by state and local supervisory programs.

The change process approach is also well-illustrated in pilot project efforts that combine clearly defined goals with appropriate orientation sessions, carefully designed inservice training, development of new teaching materials, and formative evaluation efforts that inform teachers about their progress and problems as they emerge. Such pilot programs have produced results in establishing new "alternative schools," team teaching, and gifted-child programs, and many others such as individualized reading, and new mathematics programs.

2. Tasks of Supervision

The three most widely recognized tasks of instructional supervision are curriculum development, inservice training, and instructional evaluation.

2.1 Curriculum Development

This task involves redefining goals and objectives for learning, determining their appropriateness for different students and sequencing the instructional activities related to various goals.

2.2 Inservice Training of Teachers

This is an aspect of teacher preparation that may be more important than any other task of supervision. Inservice education is clearly important in countries which do not have an adequate supply of well-educated, methodologically trained teachers. Developing countries are often faced with sharply rising demands for universal public education and cannot staff their new classroom units adequately without recourse to extensive programs of both preservice and inservice education. UNESCO, for example, helped establish and run the College of Education in King Saud University in Riyadh in the early 1960s. However, population growth in even highly developed nations can produce similar demands for inservice training of teachers whose formal preparation is inadequate by existing standards.

Needs for inservice education of all teaching personnel are being recognized as truly urgent (Harris 1980). New teachers must learn to apply their knowledge and skills on the job; hence inservice education becomes an extension of preservice preparation. There is also evidence that growth in teaching competence can be a lifelong process. Teaching is so complex that there is no realistic limit to improvement in teaching practice (Joyce and Weil 1972, Gage 1978). Finally, inservice education for all teachers is supported by changes in curriculum, new media, new technologies, and a changing social context. The emphasis given to inservice education in Sweden by both the *Sköloverstyrelsen* (national board) and the county boards is a case in point (Henderson 1978 p. 18).

Programs in inservice education take numerous forms. Commonly used inservice activities include formal short courses and isolated meetings where ideas are presented in visualized lecture or demonstration format. Other programs utilize a workshop format. Workshops use extended periods of time ranging from a day to two weeks. However, unlike many short courses, workshops emphasize involvement of participants in discussions, role playing, and demonstrations. Workshops attempt to address individual differences in participants' needs and interests by using flexible procedures, differentiating activities, and small subgroups. Workshops usually seek to promote learnings that are directly and immediately applicable to the classroom assignment of the teacher.

The integration of inservice training with the job assignment of the teacher is being stressed in many programs. Studies of the impact of training activities on classroom practices indicate a need for training plans that are reality oriented, develop new skills, and facilitate the application of those skills to the context of the classroom. Clinical supervision (Cogan 1973) is highly regarded by many supervisors because of the close linkage maintained between classroom practice and efforts to change teaching in that context. Efforts to improve the linkages between inservice training and actual practice often lead to localizing training activities.

Another approach to this problem involves individualizing training for teachers using diagnostic evaluation techniques (Harris 1980 pp. 222–29). Simulations, games, laboratory training, field trips, and microteaching are a few of the newer approaches to inservice training that attempt to offer stimulating, involving activities that promote concept formation as well as skill development.

2.3 Evaluation of Instruction

Supervisors are generally actively involved in testing programs including selecting appropriate measuring devices, coordinating the administration of tests, training test administrators (often classroom teachers or counselors), and analyzing and interpreting test results. Product evaluation often goes beyond testing. Dropout and follow-up studies are employed by many supervisors as evaluations of program effects, both positive and negative.

Process evaluation tends to focus primarily on teacher behavior. Classroom observation techniques have been recognized as essential in gathering objective data regarding teaching practices and their application within the classroom. Other supervisory techniques for evaluating instructional processes include student inventories, teacher self-analysis, and interviews, in addition to direct observations.

Emphasis on process evaluation with a primary focus on teaching behavior creates the need to clearly distinguish between summative and formative evaluation efforts of supervisors. Formative evaluation is widely utilized by supervisors to provide feedback to individual teachers. Such feedback is best provided via an interview or conference where observation reports and other data can be cooperatively interpreted. Formative feedback interviews stress reinforcing strengths, identifying need changes, and planning for corrective actions (Cogan 1973, Harris and Hill 1982).

Summative evaluation of instruction tends to emphasize administrative decisions relating to discontinuation of programs, allocation of staff and other resources, and dismissal or reassignment of teachers. Such evaluations call for much more elaborate data gathering focusing on inputs, processes, and products in relation to each other (Bolton 1973).

3. Staffing for Supervision

Supervisors are assigned a broad variety of titles and positions. Terms like supervisor, consultant, coordinator, specialist, inspector, and director are among those widely utilized to designate staff members with supervisory responsibilities. In the United States and many British Commonwealth countries the principal or headteacher is recognized as an instructional supervisor. In Middle Eastern countries it is common practice to utilize more experienced teachers as supervisors called "first teachers" to supplement staffs with formal assignments. In small remote schools a teaching head of a

school may be the only supervisor of instruction with any direct influence. However, in large, more complex school systems, there is a corps of supervisors holding various titles.

In local school districts in the United States an assistant or deputy superintendent for instruction usually serves as the chief administrator over all supervisory personnel. Principals, assistant principals, and department chairmen serve in both administrative and supervisory roles directly under the superintendent or his assistant. However, a supervisory staff group, usually specialists of various kinds, is attached to the central office and works with teachers in various schools in cooperation with building-level supervisory personnel. A similar pattern is utilized in some Philippine communities at the district and town level even though a regional system prevails.

In some countries where more highly centralized systems are in operation, supervisors (inspectors) from both the national and regional offices of education work directly with individual schools. Supervision in the Philippines is carried on primarily through 13 regional offices with staffs of subject specialist supervisors. Obviously when staffing patterns utilize supervisors who are not regularly at work in the local school setting, their assigned responsibilities must be limited. The advantages of "in-house" supervision are numerous. However, "outside" supervisory staffing potentially provides for greater objectivity, more specialized expertise, and innovativeness. In practice, supervisors at all levels may reflect political expediency or bureaucratic rigidity more than needs for improvements in teaching.

A somewhat unique pattern of staffing for supervision is reported for Romanian schools (Braham 1979). County peoples' councils and the Ministry of Education exercise joint control over local school inspectors. These supervisors are directly responsible for teacher evaluation and curriculum review.

There is little scholarly writing or research on this topic of supervisory staffing. Most staffing practices simply follow traditional patterns borrowed from military and industrial sources. Innovative staffing patterns do emerge from time to time that seem promising. Team supervision utilizing professional supervisors as team leaders with temporary staff assignments to teams has been utilized. Advocates for the principal as "the instructional leader" sometimes argue for virtually complete autonomy within the individual school. "Peer" supervision is advocated by some reflecting teacher union thinking that teachers "know best." The best evidence to date, limited as it is, seems to support the principles of variation and flexibility in supervisory staffing. No one pattern is likely to be uniformly superior for all tasks in all situations. Furthermore, supervisors' competencies should be recognized as highly diverse, and flexible use of these persons seems to make good sense. There is little doubt that supervisors assigned to individual school staffs (principals and assistants) and also other supervisors working out of central offices (local, national, regional, etc.) are necessary when substantial improvements in educational practices are being pursued.

Intermediate supervisory service organizations are being utilized in many countries. Centralized systems of education have promoted limited decentralization through such intermediate structures. The highly decentralized schools in the United States utilize very similar intermediate units. Sweden utilizes six senior teacher-training institutes as a national delivery system for inservice training. However, county boards in Sweden also utilize a core of supervisors led by an inservice training officer.

Supervision of instruction is a function of school operations that focuses on instruction and teaching, especially on the need for change. Supervisory tasks overlap with those of administration in many ways but are unique in giving special attention to curriculum development, inservice education, and evaluation of instruction. Supervisory staffing and organization takes many forms at national, regional, and local levels with no superior patterns clearly established. The long-term trends in all supervisory practices are away from tractive monitoring and controlling of teaching toward more dynamic efforts to promote change process.

See also: Supervision of the Practicum

Bibliography

Barr A S, Burton W H, Brueckner L J 1947 *Supervision: Democratic Leadership in the Improvement of Learning*, 2nd edn. Appleton Century Crofts, New York

Bolton D L 1973 *Selection and Evaluation of Teachers.* McCutchan, Berkeley, California

Braham R L 1979 *The Educational System of Romania.* US Department of Health, Education, and Welfare, Washington, DC

Cogan M L 1973 *Clinical Supervision.* Houghton Mifflin, Boston, Massachusetts

Gage N L 1978 *The Scientific Basis of the Art of Teaching.* Teachers College Press, Columbia University, New York

Garcia L A 1980 New structure for basic education in Venezuela: A case study of past planning efforts and proposals for design alternatives (Doctoral dissertation, University of Texas) *Dissertation Abstracts International* 1981 41: 4558A (University Microfilms No. 8109168)

Harris B M 1980 *Improving Staff Performance Through Inservice Education.* Allyn and Bacon, Boston, Massachusetts

Harris B M 1985 *Supervisory Behavior in Education,* 3rd edn. Prentice Hall, Englewood Cliffs, New Jersey

Harris B M, Hill J 1982 *Developmental Teacher Evaluation Kit.* Southwest Education Development Laboratory, Austin, Texas

Henderson E S 1978 *The Evaluation of In-service Teacher Training.* Croom Helm, London

Ibrahim Y B 1979 The needed supervisory competencies for instructional supervision as perceived by members of the federal inspectorate of schools, Malaysia (Doctoral dissertation, Southern Illinois University) *Dissertation Abstracts International* 1979 40: 3022A (University Microfilms No. 7926313)

Joyce B R, Weil M 1972 *Models of Teaching.* Prentice-Hall, Englewood Cliffs, New Jersey

Lawrence G et al. 1974 *Patterns of Effective In-service Education.* College of Education, Gainesville, Florida

Sergiovanni T J, Starratt R J 1979 *Supervision: Human Perspectives,* 2nd edn. McGraw-Hill, New York

Wiles K, Lovell J T 1983 *Supervision for Better Schools,* 5th edn. Prentice-Hall, Englewood Cliffs, New Jersey

Teachers' Centres

R. J. Shostak

Teachers' centres are educational institutions whose primary purpose is to meet the developing needs of teachers as identified by teachers themselves. They function between the individual school and the local authority (regional) administration and form part of a support network for teacher and curricular development. Originating in the United Kingdom in the 1960s, the concept of teachers' centres has since been adapted to the contexts of many other educational systems and has been the focus of much attention in the educational world during the 1970s and early 1980s. Teachers' centres have developed from the need for schools to keep pace with the rapidly changing world of the child and from the failure of more traditional forms of support services to engage teachers fully in this endeavour.

Definitive international statements about teachers' centres have until recently been difficult to make due to the considerable diversity in their foundation and operation; not only from country to country but also within countries. During the early 1970s, a wide variety of institutions called teachers' centres emerged with little recognizable similarity other than their title. Conversely, a number of institutions under a variety of names including teaching centres, curriculum development centres, learning centres, teacher education centres, staff development centres, educational cooperatives, and education centres began functioning in a similar manner. These centres have developed and it is now possible to consider the common characteristics of centres and contrast them to the more traditional forms of teacher education and training, thereby identifying the contribution of centres to the educational service.

Teachers' centres are distinguishable from other forms of support for teachers in that within one institution they:

(a) provide diagnosis and provision of inservice professional development activities which are essentially local in their nature;

(b) have a primary focus upon improving classroom practice;

(c) can make a swift response to expressed and implicit needs with minimum internal bureaucracy;

(d) provide a secure environment, both in terms of premises and personnel, where teachers can work either individually or in groups;

(e) develop professional esteem through involvement;

(f) encourage teachers to take more responsibility for curriculum and instructional decisions;

(g) provide professional development programmes, both at the centre and in schools, which begin from the teacher's own starting point, and encourage teachers to participate in the design of the programme;

(h) provide a means for centralizing local services.

Early literature on the beginnings of teachers' centres in the United Kingdom presents the subtle departure from previous approaches to school and teacher renewal. It is possible to trace the move from the external agency diagnosis of need to a more negotiated assessment; a move from beginning with a theoretical position to beginning with a more classroom practice-based starting point; a move from a deficit model of education and training to a more supportive growth model; a move away from the thinking that the only valuable inservice work is that which is validated by institutions of higher education. In short, much as classroom development was being seen as more child centred, so too was school and curriculum development being seen as more teacher centred.

Most influential in this move was the work of the national curriculum development agency in the United Kingdom, the Schools Council for Curriculum and Examinations. Their experience in supporting curriculum development showed that working locally with groups of teachers broke down the greatest barrier to curricular change in schools: the teachers themselves. The commitment of teachers to the development work from the beginning meant that not only was the outcome more "classroom based" but also that the change which took place was within the teachers' own framework. The early accounts of this, depicting the centres of this time, although primarily descriptive, explore the potential of what was to develop as the teachers' centre of the future (Thornbury 1973, Yarger and Leonard 1974). Fundamental at this point was that in parallel

with curricular development by teacher groups came teacher development; and more important, teacher commitment to change. These early centres found teachers, in large numbers, beginning to question their curricular and pedagogical decisions and work with all concerned agencies to develop suitable answers. It became obvious that the teachers' centre was a way of focusing teacher energy towards wide professional development and the mid-1970s saw not only a rapid proliferation of centres in the United Kingdom but also worldwide. At this time there was little clarity of function across centres and as each developed within its local context the "meeting place centre" began to develop into a "professional centre".

The debate regarding teaching as a profession is well-documented in educational literature. Much of the debate revolves around the ability to influence and control one's training, autonomy in decision making, the development of knowledge, and the nature of collegial relationships. Teachers' centres must be seen within this debate as in each of the areas mentioned, a centre's philosophy and operational principles are rooted in the notion of professionalism. The teachers' centre relies on practising teachers defining and initiating their own inservice work. This is based upon a view that the classroom practitioner is in the best position to make decisions about curricular needs. By adopting this position it also legitimizes the experience of the teacher as a form of knowledge. It therefore creates opportunities to build upon this knowledge with colleagues and as the primary focus of its work is the teacher, this defines the working relationship with colleagues. It is also worth noting that centres will often approach this task by working with both preservice and inservice teachers, underlining the view that there is a commitment to continued development beyond initial training. It is important, however, to recognize that teachers are afforded a very different degree of control and autonomy from one country to another. It is therefore not surprising that centres emerged in the United Kingdom where this autonomy is usually regarded as great and that centres have developed in countries where they could be seen to be a way of facilitating professional discussion both between and within schools.

As the "British Centre" developed, interest grew throughout the world and countries began to review their own provision for professional support and development. Because of the importance of the "local nature" of centres, funding varies from country to country, although countries such as the United States, Australia, and the Netherlands have passed national legislation regarding centres, and have allocated national funds. Interestingly in the United Kingdom, where centres began, the decision regarding teachers' centre provision still rests with individual local authorities which, because it is the same source for funding schools, results in high levels of support from teachers needed for centres to remain a priority for funding.

Whatever the funding source, centres afford teachers the opportunity to develop long-term commitment to their own professional development. From a foundation of local initiative in obtaining funding usually comes teacher involvement in designing and supporting educational programmes. Thus funding becomes less important and a centre's success will rely upon teacher energy.

This reliance upon teacher involvement is reflected in centre management as well as centre activity. Centres are typically managed by policy boards which are comprised of teachers, administrators, local education authority officers, staff of local colleges, and representatives of other centre constituents. It is usual, and indeed obligatory in many centres, for practising teachers to be in the majority, and research suggests that such bodies are important in the process of involving teachers in centre decision making (Mertens and Yarger 1981, Weindling and Reid 1983). Decisions of such bodies will range from the direction of daily programmes to fundamental centre principles. Included, and of particular note, would be the centre's administrative structures and the development of centre services and resources.

A centre's administrative structure will depend upon its location within the network of support services for teachers and upon its staffing. The first decision for the centre's policy board will be to develop a role definition for the centre's leader (warden, director, coordinator). As yet there is little formal training for the role of the leader although experience and an understanding of classroom life is essential. Permanent centre staff take on a variety of roles with teachers—adviser, facilitator, broker, initiator—however, one of their priorities will be to ensure that classroom teachers are similarly serving this role for other teachers. Harty (1981) and Weindling and Reid (1983) explore the role expectations associated with centre leaders and the demands of helping teachers to help themselves.

The centre then creates structures in which the needs of its constituents can be identified and communicated. The development of suitable methods of needs assessment is one of prime importance for centres and although the existing literature outlines a variety of approaches this is an area for further research. A system of representatives (with smaller constituencies than those of the policy board representatives) is often established and recent work done in the United Kingdom emphasizes both the advantages and strains of such an approach (Weindling and Reid 1983). While such systems can often prove to be of enormous value in communicating with the area's teachers it has proven itself inadequate as a centre's only method of assessing needs.

It should be noted that although the centre's primary focus is on the "self-identified" or "negotiated" needs of teachers this is not to negate in any way the importance of centre involvement in school, local authority, or nationally identified priorities. Frequently, because a centre has developed into the local professional centre of an area, it is used as a venue for other educational activities. Local authority curriculum advisers/supervisors will often use centre facilities as well as collaborate on centre work. The centre, however, is usually the place where the first priority is teacher initiated activities.

The centre's administrative structures also ensure that it is able to provide well-designed and implemented educational programmes, facilitate working groups, recognize and link those with common interests, and take initiatives based on work in schools. Factors which policy boards will consider in devising such structures will be the number of teachers and schools within a centre's catchment area, geography, centre staffing, and centre resources. Having identified needs, a centre then responds using a variety of working strategies to meet the professional demands of its constituents.

Although often a "centre-based" model of working is adopted, the activity is often typified by negotiation with participants in both the planning and implementation stages. This emphasis upon continued negotiation enables the centre to provide ongoing support to individuals and groups in their learning. It also ensures that programme activities meet precise needs and develop with participants. As well as centre-based work, however, centres have recently developed expertise in school-focused approaches to professional development. The focus of this strategy is the teacher in the school and the work involves far more emphasis upon the institution in which the teacher works, rather than merely the work of a teacher. Centres have been influential in the development of the "teacher group" as a work unit and, although little research has been done, the principles of negotiation and teacher centredness are likely to emerge as important aspects of this approach. Whatever strategy is adopted, they all rely upon teacher involvement from the start. This alleviates, somewhat, the problem of drawing in active teachers to programmes although centres have not succeeded in attracting certain sectors of the teaching force. It is also important to note that centre work is normally voluntary, nonvalidated, and usually not part of any contractual agreement.

Centres often function as local resource centres and central service points for local authority support. Decisions regarding services and resources will be in the context of other existing local provision and financial constraints. It is not uncommon for centres to provide material resource support and support in new technologies as well as professional development activities. Centres will often have both reference and loan collections of books and materials as well as provide a location for the centralization of more expensive audiovisual, reprographic or computer hardware, and/or services. A policy board would be guided by existing needs within schools and decisions would be made on how best to resource the centre and to help the centre meet its defined aims. In the economic situation of the late

1970s and early 1980s, many centres found resources of finance more difficult to obtain. Although international interest and support for continued training grew, restrictions on public spending led educational planners to look at new ways of providing the support being offered by centres; often turning to more established institutions. The concern as to whether centres had fully rooted themselves within their countries' educational service became critical. Centres faced the conflict between the time needed for teachers both to understand and commit themselves to the new opportunities, and the need to prove a programme's value. The developmental nature of centres and their commitment to growth, rather than radical change, became the greatest threat. Their dynamic nature associated with their diversity made it difficult to support their contribution by research. Now, as research is emerging regarding the contribution of centres to the educational world, the implications of practitioner-directed curricular and professional developments are being more clearly understood.

See also: Definitions of Teaching

Bibliography

Adams A E 1975 *In-service Education and Teachers' Centres.* Pergamon, Oxford

Boyer E L 1977 *Teachers' Centers Commissioners' Report on the Education Professions 1975–1976.* United States Government Printing Office, HEW(OE) 77-12012, Washington, DC

Harty H F 1981 *Teacher Centers, Perception of: Role Expectations, Functional Attributes, Institutional Payoffs.* Indiana University, Bloomington, Indiana. ERIC Document No. ED 209 186

Mertens S K, Yarger S J 1981 *Teacher Centers in Action: A Comprehensive Study of Program Activities, Staff Services, Resources and Policy Board Operations in Thirty-seven Federally-funded Teacher Centers.* Syracuse University, New York. ERIC Document No. ED 205 465

Newman C, Shostak R, Sollars R 1981 Teachers' centres: Some emergent characteristics. *Br. J. In-service Educ.* 8: 45–50

Redknap C 1977 *Focus on Teachers' Centres.* National Foundation for Educational Research (NFER), Slough

Thornbury R (ed.) 1973 *Teachers' Centres.* Darton, Longman and Todd, London

Yarger S J, Leonard A J 1974 *A Descriptive Study of The Teacher Center Movement in American Education.* Syracuse University, New York

Weindling D, Reid M 1983 *Teachers' Centres—A Focus for In-service Education?* Schools Council Working Paper 74. Methuen, London

Minicourses

E. Perrott

Since the late 1960s educational research and teacher-training activities have paid increasing attention to the component skills of teaching. Between 1967 and 1971, Borg and his colleagues at the Far West Laboratory for Educational Research and Development, San Francisco, United States, researched and developed some 20 of these short, self-instructional courses designed to train teachers in the use of specific classroom skills (Borg et al. 1970), such as questioning, teaching reading as decoding, and organizing independent learning. Each minicourse was produced as the result of a rigorous cycle of research and development which involved:

(a) the stating of specific performance objectives for the new product;

(b) the use of available research knowledge as a source of concepts and materials;

(c) the carrying out of a rigorous field-testing programme to evaluate the product's effectiveness in the setting where it was eventually to be used;

(d) the use of the results of this evaluation programme to improve the product, the evaluation–revision

cycle being repeated until the product met its performance objectives.

Each minicourse made use of a systems approach which consisted of the following steps, occurring in a cyclical fashion:

(a) precise specification of the behaviour which is the objective of the learning experience;

(b) carefully planned training procedures aimed explicitly at those objectives;

(c) measurement of the results of training in terms of the behavioural objectives;

(d) feedback of the observed results;

(e) re-entry into the training procedure;

(f) measurement again of the results.

Minicourses draw on educational research clustering around three special cases of the systems model: interaction analysis training (Flanders 1970), microteaching, and behaviour modification, but with microteaching playing the most important role. However, the interrelatedness of three models has frequently been noted (Perrott 1977).

1. *The Instructional Model*

Borg's instructional model was designed to supply five major requirements necessary for learning teaching skills:

(a) The trainee has the opportunity to study a limited number (usually one to three) of specific teaching skills, which centre on a particular area of competency, for example, he or she may read about how to ask questions that are likely to provoke a higher cognitive response from pupils, and undertake exercises which are designed to classify the skills involved.

(b) The trainee observes examples of the skills. Generally this involves viewing a videotape or film in which each of the skills is described and illustrated. This is followed by a videotape or film which shows a "model" teacher conducting a lesson in which each skill is demonstrated several times. While observing the skills, the teacher's attention is focused by cues in the form of narrator's comments and captions. This model lesson serves the dual function of providing a clear performance model of how each skill can be used in a teaching context and of helping the trainee to recognize and discriminate between the skills. During the course of the model lesson, the trainee is asked to identify each skill as it occurs and receives prompt feedback on the correctness of his or her identification.

(c) The trainee then has the opportunity to practise and evaluate his or her use of the skills. Practise takes the form of a 10-minute microteaching session in which five to eight pupils are involved.

(d) The microlesson is recorded on video- or audio-tape and trainees observe or listen to their performance, evaluating their use of the skills with the help of self-evaluation forms, which help the teacher to focus on each skill in turn.

(e) The trainees refine their use of the skills through additional practice. They replan the lesson, emphasizing those skills in which their self-evaluation revealed their performance to be the most inadequate. Then they reteach the microlesson with another group of pupils, and evaluate their second recorded performance.

The first minicourse developed by Borg et al. (1970) was concerned with "effective questioning". This course will be taken to illustrate the process of minicourse research and development. Also, it was adapted, tested, and redeveloped for use in the United Kingdom by Perrott et al., in Sweden by Bredange and Tingsell, in the Netherlands by Veerman, and in the Federal Republic of Germany by Klinzing as part of an international research and development project sponsored by the Organisation for Economic Co-operation and Development (OECD Report 1975). The objectives of this international research programme were:

(a) to test the adaptations in Europe by measuring changes in teaching behaviour after the completion of this minicourse on "effective questioning";

(b) to compare the results of the above tests with the American research data;

(c) to redevelop the adapted course in the light of research results.

The minicourse takes the form of a self-instructional "package" including: a programmed handbook, for study, which gives detailed, sequential instructions concerning course procedures. It also defines the questioning skills to be practised in operational terms, explains the use of these skills, and provides exercises to test the teacher's understanding of what he or she has studied. Guidance on the preparation of microlessons focusing on the skills studied is provided, together with objective self-coding guides for the evaluation of the microlesson; a set of five videotaped or filmed instructional sequences, designed to provide skill discrimination training; a coordinator's handbook, designed to assist course coordinators with administrative tasks; and an evaluation manual, prepared for those who wish to evaluate the course in their own situations.

The course requires:

(a) a study of specific teaching skills;

(b) the viewing of videorecordings or films of other teachers using these skills, by this means providing practice in the identification of the skills being studied;

(c) short practice sessions in using the skills observed and studied, in a situation which allows for feedback on the practice session by means of closed-circuit television;

(d) the objective evaluation of this feedback by means of self-coding guides.

The "effective questioning" course consists of one practice sequence and four instructional sequences. The introductory sequence is designed to familiarize the teacher or student with the microteaching technique. Each instructional sequence focuses upon three related teaching skills or habits, which form part of general patterns of effective questioning. They are summarized briefly in Table 1, which also lists the general objective of each of the four instructional sequences.

Table 1
Effective questioning skills and their related objectives

Objective	*To encourage pupils' readiness to respond*
Skills:	(a) Pausing 3 to 5 seconds after asking a question before calling on a pupil to answer
	(b) Treating incorrect responses in an accepting manner
	(c) Calling on nonvolunteers as well as volunteers to answer a question
Objective:	*To improve pupils' initial responses*
Skills:	(d) Promoting pupils who are unable to respond
	(e) Asking for further clarification of incomplete responses
	(f) Refocusing the pupils' response
Objective:	*To increase the level and amount of pupil participation*
Skills:	(g) Asking questions that call for longer pupil responses:
	(i) Asking questions that call for sets of related facts
	(ii) Discouraging one word responses from pupils
	(h) Asking questions that require pupils to use higher order thought processes
	(i) Redirecting the same question to several pupils
Objective:	*To eliminate habits which disrupt the flow of discussion*
Skills:	(j) Avoiding repeating one's own question
	(k) Avoiding repeating pupils' answers
	(l) Avoiding answering one's own questions

The overall aims of the course are to:

(a) produce measurable improvements in questioning skills;

(b) encourage self-diagnosis of teaching abilities and deficiencies;

(c) reduce teacher talk and increase pupil participation;

(d) provide for individual instruction on a cost-effective basis.

2. Research and Development

In the research and development of the minicourses an approach which was relatively new to education was used. Educational research is normally concerned with discovering new knowledge, which can relate to either theoretical questions or applied problems. It can also involve the development of a process or a product. However, in most research projects, development is carried only to the point where the product can be used to test a research hypothesis. Although researchers may foresee possible ways that their findings may be used in educational settings, their predictions are not formulated in specific detail and cannot be translated directly into usable educational products. Thus educators have for many years sought ways to close the gap between research and practice.

In this case, research and development as one, bridged the gap that has so long existed between the researcher and the practitioner. It is a process that uses the results of systematic research and evaluation to design and develop a thoroughly tested and validated educational product. Thus, it is not primarily concerned with the discovery of new knowledge, but with the application of new knowledge to a specific task.

Table 2 lists the main steps in the research and development process for *Minicourse 1—Effective Questioning*.

The research and development cycle for the European courses, adapted from *Minicourse 1*, closely followed the original method devised by Borg et al. except that adaptation preceded testing. Adaptation of the handbooks and videotaped instructional sequences fell into three main categories:

(a) those made on cultural grounds, including translation;

(b) those based on feedback from participating teachers in a preliminary test and observations of project staff;

(c) those based on the results of field tests.

2.1 Main Field Test

The main field test is regarded as the most important of the three tests in the research and development process. To quote from Borg et al. (1970).

The primary purpose of the main field test, in the Minicourse development cycle, is to determine whether the course achieves its objectives, i.e. whether it brings about the desired levels of change in teacher and pupil performance. The test is designed to collect not only qualitative information, such as that obtained in the preliminary field test, but also quantitative evidence, based on the performance of teachers who take the course . . . . A secondary purpose is to collect information that can be used to improve the course in its next revision . . . . If the [main field test] data indicate that the course falls substantially short of its objectives, the course is revised and recycled through another test.

The effects upon teacher performance of *Minicourse 1* training were tested with both preservice and inservice teachers. Inasmuch as the added experience of inservice teachers may be expected to influence their level of performance before training and the amount of

Table 2

Research and development of *Minicourse 1*—Effective questioning

Research and data gathering	Includes review of literature, classroom observations, and preparation of report on the state of the art
Planning	Includes definition of skills, statement of objectives, determination of course sequence, and small-scale feasibility testing
Developing preliminary form of product	Includes preparation of instructional and model lessons, handbooks, and evaluation devices
Preliminary field test	Conducted by laboratory personnel in one, two, or three schools, using between 6 and 12 teachers. Includes collection and analysis of interview, observational, and questionnaire data
Main product revision	Revision of product as suggested by preliminary field test results
Main field test	Conducted by laboratory personnel in between 5 and 15 schools using approximately 30 teachers. Includes collection of quantitative data on teachers' pre- and post-course performances, usually in the form of classroom videotapes. Results are compared with course objectives
Operational product revision	Revision of product as suggested by the main field test results
Operational field test	Conducted by regular school personnel in between 10 and 30 schools, using between 40 and 200 teachers. Includes collection and analysis of interview, observation, and questionnaire data
Final product revision	Revision of product as suggested by operational field test results
Dissemination and distribution	Reports at professional meetings, in journals, etc. Includes work with publisher who assumes commercial distribution, and monitoring of distribution to provide quality control

increased skill and knowledge they will demonstrate after training, data from the preservice and inservice settings will be presented and discussed separately.

2.2 Hypotheses to be Tested

The three *Minicourse 1* sites—the Universities of Lancaster, Goteborg, and Nijmegen—had as their major purpose to determine whether or not *Minicourse 1* training achieved its objectives for changing teacher behaviour. The hypotheses that were tested in each study are as follows.

Significant increases from pretest to posttest, and from pretest to retention test (USA and UK) in frequency of redirection, prompting, seeking further clarification, refocusing, mean length of pause, length of pupil response, and higher cognitive questions.

Significant decreases from pre- to post-test and from pretest to retention test (USA and UK) in percentage of teacher talk, and frequency of answering own questions, repeating own questions, and repeating pupils' answers.

Interpretation of findings as reported by the various testing sites will depend largely upon the similarity of the samples of teachers who participated in *Minicourse 1* training. The samples for the studies included both inservice and preservice teachers. The inservice sample will be taken as an example.

2.3 Inservice Sample

The number of teachers participating in each of the studies focusing upon inservice teachers is listed in Table 3. The chart also includes information regarding any teacher characteristics relevant to interpreting changes in teacher performance.

The samples for the three studies are generally similar in the age of pupils taught although the Nijmegen sample does cover a wider range of pupil ages than Lancaster or Far West Laboratory. It should be noted that the United States sample is taken from those teachers remaining in the classroom three years following the Minicourse main field test (this is because they participated in a three-year follow-up study). The main field test and four-month retention scores reported for these teachers are those that were obtained at the time of the original test, however, given the stability of this teacher sample, their performance may be somewhat higher at all stages (pre, post, and retention) than might be expected of a more random group of teachers.

The treatment for all the studies (inservice and preservice) consisted of training with *Minicourse 1*, which in brief includes studying a handbook; viewing a videotape which demonstrates the use of the particular teaching skills included in the course; planning, teaching, and evaluating a microlesson; and planning, teaching, and evaluating a reteach lesson. Generally, the training cycle requires five weeks to complete, with the teacher devoting approximately three to five hours per week to training. All sites followed this basic procedure.

Information regarding changes in teacher performance, in all cases, was obtained through the use of precourse and postcourse videotape recordings of the teachers leading a discussion with their pupils. The teachers in the United Kingdom, Sweden, and the United States worked with their entire class when the videorecordings were made. The teachers in the Netherlands worked with half the pupils in their classes. All teachers worked with pupils with whom they were familiar and for whom they had had previous instructional responsibility. In the preservice study, this demanded that the pre- and post-recordings and the training be completed while the student teachers were engaged in their in-school student teaching programmes.

Given the overall similarity in treatment conditions

Table 3
Teacher sample: *Minicourse 1*—Inservice

University of Lancaster	University of Nijmegen	Far West Laboratory for Educational Research and Development
n = 28 teachers (all volunteers)	n = 39 teachers	n = 24 teachers (all volunteers)
13—taught primary-school children in age range 9-11	6 teachers from each of 6 elementary schools (all volunteers)	teachers were teaching grade 4, 5, or 6
8—taught first-year secondary (age 12)	10—first- and second-grade teachers 12—third- and fourth-grade teachers	These teachers were those who were still teaching 3 years after the original main field test. They are taken from the original sample of 48 teachers who participated in the original main field test
7—were from small country primary schools with mixed age groups in the range 8–11	11—sixth-grade teachers. Half the participating teachers were drawn from schools serving predominantly working-class communities	
	Half were from schools serving predominantly middle-class communities	

for the *Minicourse 1* studies, it is possible to make a number of comparisons among the findings. The size of the pupil group participating in the Netherlands' pre- and post-recordings is still sufficiently large not to affect the teachers' use of the teaching skills covered by *Minicourse 1* when compared with teachers working with entire classes. If the group size had been reduced to three or four pupils, some differences might have been expected as a result of group size, but teacher interaction with groups of 10 to 20 will probably differ very little from that with groups of 20 to 30.

Each of the transfer sites also gathered information regarding other outcomes of the training programme. Since both the United Kingdom and the United States included four-month retention tests of inservice teacher use of the *Minicourse 1* skills, those findings are reported here. Other findings such as teachers' attitudes toward various aspects of the minicourse may be obtained from the national reports (Perrott 1977).

2.4 Scoring of Videotapes

A final aspect of each study that should be reviewed before training outcomes are presented is the procedure used to score the precourse, postcourse, and retention course videotape recordings of teachers leading a discussion with their pupils.

Instructions on the procedures to be used in scoring were supplied to the transfer sites by the original developer. As much as possible, the sites followed these procedures.

The videotapes were scored for 10 common teacher behaviours.

(a) Redirection—the number of times the teacher called on another pupil to respond to a question already answered by at least one other pupil.

(b) Prompting—the number of questions designed to prompt a pupil who had just given an incorrect or "I don't know" response.

(c) Further clarification—the number of questions asking a pupil to clarify or expand upon an initial response, without providing hints or prompts.

(d) Refocusing—the number of questions which ask a pupil to relate an acceptable answer to another topic.

(e) Answering own question—the tally of instances in which the teacher answers his or her own questions, either before or after calling on a pupil.

(f) Repeating pupil's answer—the tally of instances of

repeating a pupil's answer without clarifying it or introducing new ideas.

(g) Repeating own question—the tally of instances of repeating the same question without introducing new information.

(h) Length of pause after question—the average length of pauses between asking a question and calling on a pupil, to the nearest tenth second.

(i) Percent higher cognitive questions—defined as questions which required the pupil to go beyond a simple remembering of facts or an unsupported statement of feeling. All others were categorized as lower order. Redirected questions were tallied only once. Procedural questions were excluded from the analysis.

(j) Percent teacher talk—all instances of teacher talk were timed in seconds and totalled for each lesson. The proportion of teacher talk was then calculated as the ratio of teacher talk to total lesson length.

Two types of pupil performance were also scored:

(a) Length of pupil responses—tally of number of words in each answer to a given question. Responses to probing questions were counted as responses to separate questions. For each teacher, the average length of pupils' responses was then calculated.

(b) Number of one-word pupil responses—this included responses such as "yes", "no".

The rating procedure required that raters who were not members of the project teams be recruited and trained to score the videotapes. In Lancaster, four raters were used; in Nijmegen six were used; in Goteborg, four; in the United States, eight raters scored the inservice tapes, and 15 raters were used for the preservice study.

Since all raters did not score all the videotapes, inter-rater reliabilities for the scoring should be considered. Based upon Pearson product–moment correlations between the scores assigned to each of a sample of videotapes which were rated twice, the Lancaster site reported an average correlation between pairs of raters of 0.85. Nijmegen, using analysis of variance, found that interrater reliability ranged from 0.99 on some teacher skills to 0.51 on a number of higher cognitive questions (because of the low coefficient for this skill, the variable was scored twice and the average score was used in the subsequent analysis). Goteborg reported interrater agreement ranging from 0.58 to 0.99 based upon Spearman's correlation of ranks. The United States inservice study reports reliability coefficients of 0.60 to 0.98 using Spearman Brown formula and 0.57 to 0.99 for the preservice study.

2.5 Results

The teacher and pupil performance data for the *Minicourse 1* inservice and preservice studies are presented in Table 4. Two important questions to be considered as this table is reviewed are whether *Minicourse 1* training brought about significant changes in teacher behaviour (accomplished the objectives of the training system) and whether the adapted courses produced changes which are similar to, greater than, or less than those effected by the original product. These are important criteria for judging the success of this pilot study in transfer. If the materials, adapted to the needs of the transfer countries, continue to reach the objectives (produce desired changes in teacher behaviour), transfer may be considered a viable alternative to original development on a country by country basis.

2.6 Inservice Teachers

Table 4 summarizes the results of the main field testing of *Minicourse 1* with inservice teachers. Only those teacher and pupil skills that were investigated by all projects are included.

Because of some differences in the statistical analysis procedures used, the findings for the projects will be compared on two bases; the number of skills on which teachers changed significantly in the desired direction as reported by the statistical procedures used in each site, and the average percent of change from precourse to postcourse for each teaching skill.

As stated earlier, a common hypothesis was that after training teachers would increase their use of certain of the course skills. Statistically significant increases were demonstrated for three skills—redirection, prompting, and the use of higher cognitive questions. It is interesting to note that for redirection the teachers in all three field tests achieved nearly the same level of performance after training even though the teachers in the United Kingdom and the Netherlands started at a lower level. Prompting, on the other hand, was a skill which the United States teachers used more frequently before training than did the other teachers. They also reached a higher level after training although all samples showed a high percent increase in use of the skill. Use of higher cognitive questions demonstrates some problems in interpretation due to a difference in scoring procedures. The teachers in the Netherlands appear to have made the largest gain in terms of percent of increase pre- to post-course. There is a rather large difference in the use of the skill by teachers in the United States and the United Kingdom both pre- and post-course with the teachers in the United Kingdom using a higher percentage of such questions. Percent of gain in use of higher cognitive questions is similar for the two groups, however.

None of the teachers made a significant increase in their use of refocusing. Two probable explanations may be offered for this finding. One is that pupils tend to keep on the topic when participating in a discussion

Table 4
Minicourse 1—Effective questioning: Inservice teacher performance

Country	United States				United Kingdom				The Netherlands (Nijmegen)			
	Pre-course 24	Post-course 24	4-month retention 20	% Change pre–post	Pre-course 28	Post-course 28	4-month retention 22	% Change pre–post	Pre-course 36	Post-course 36	4-month retention 36	% Change pre–post
Teaching skills												
Redirection	23.75	34.60[a]	38.15[a]	45.7	16.5	33.6[a]	30.8[a]	103.6	19.32	38.28[a]	—	98.1
Prompting	4.05	11.30[a]	5.15	179.0	2.2	5.5[a]	4.2[a]	150.0	1.80	6.97[a]	—	287.2
Clarification	3.65	7.90[a]	10.25[a]	116.4	4.7	7.4[a]	8.2[a]	57.4	5.30	5.51	—	4.0
Refocusing	0.10	0.02	—	−80.0	—	—	0.01	—	—	0.15	—	—
Repeating own question	14.35	5.25[a]	2.55[a]	−63.4	6.6	2.5[a]	2.0[a]	−62.1	8.92	5.66	—	−36.4
Repeating pupil's answer	29.9	5.75[a]	5.35[a]	−80.8	30.1	6.5[a]	8.8[a]	−78.4	37.94	10.68[a]	—	−71.8
Answering own question	4.40	1.25[a]	0.60[a]	−71.6	1.3	0.7	0.05[a]	−46.1	6.67	2.00[a]	—	−70.0
Length of pause after question	1.93[b]	2.32[b]	—	20.2	1.8[b]	2.5[a,b]	2.3[b]	38.8	1.33[b]	2.97[a,b]	—	123.3
Percent higher cognitive questions	38.00[b]	50.00[a,b]	51.00[a]	31.6	46.80[b]	63.50[a,b]	65.2[a,b]	35.6	3.24[c,d]	5.17[a,c,d]	—	59.6
Percent teacher talk	53.00	33.00[a]	34.00[a]	−37.7	75.10	53.30[a]	6.12[a]	−29.0	49.00[d]	31.19[a,d]	—	−36.3
Pupil skills												
Length of response	6.02[b]	12.33[a,b]	10.47[a]	104.8	7.3[b]	9.3	8.3	27.4	8.47	8.10	—	−4.4
Number of one-word responses	6.00	2.50[a]	2.85[a]	−58.3	—	—	—	—	14.61[d]	15.61[d]	—	6.8

a Significant at 0.05 or less b Based on 5-minute sample c Represents *total* number of higher cognitive questions rather than percent d Based on 10-minute sample
From OECD Report (1975) *The International Transfer of Microteaching Programmes for Teacher Education*. Reprinted with the permission of the Organisation for Economic Co-operation and Development, Paris

that is being videotaped and, therefore, provide few opportunities for the teacher to use refocusing. The other is that the original course failed to teach this skill and the adapted versions made no improvement in this particular segment.

Teachers in the United Kingdom and the Netherlands significantly increased the length of their pauses after answering while those in the United States did not. However, the pattern and range of the change is very similar for all three countries.

The use of clarification increased significantly in the United States and the United Kingdom but not in the Netherlands. Again, the postcourse performance for teachers in the United Kingdom and the United States was very similar.

Teacher use of certain of the teaching skills was expected to decrease after training. These skills were repeating own question, repeating pupils' answers, answering own question, and percent teacher talk. Teachers at all the sites made statistically significant decreases in all these skill areas. They also showed similarities in percent of change. Teachers in the United Kingdom and the United States made similar changes in repeating own question and repeating pupils' answers, although the frequency of occurrence of repeating own question was lower for the British teachers both pre- and post-training. Teacher performance in the United States and the Netherlands evidenced approximately the same percent of change in answering own question and percent teacher talk. Their actual level of performance, postcourse, was also similar for percent of teacher talk but the Netherlands teachers answered their own questions more often than the United States teachers even after training.

Another important feature of the adapted product is the extent to which teacher use of the specified skills affects pupil performance. Only one measure of this effect—length of pupil response—was reported by all three sites. Teachers who were trained with the original product appear to have had considerably more influence on this variable than teachers who worked with the adapted materials. Reasons for these differences are not available from the individual reports. The United Kingdom did report, however, that on another pupil variable measured only in that study—proportion of ·pupil higher order responses—significant changes occurred. Forty-nine percent of the pupils' responses were higher order before the teachers participated in *Minicourse 1* training; 67 percent after (Perrott 1977).

While the teachers across sites differed in their use ·of one or two specific skills, the overall similarity in pre- and post-course performance and the similarity in percent of change in the desired direction among the sites is remarkable. The data suggest that for inservice teachers, transfer of teacher-training products can be successful. Three findings in particular, form the basis for this conclusion:

(a) based upon their precourse performance, the teach-

ers in all three countries appeared to need training in the same skills;

(b) the adapted materials were as successful in producing teacher change as the original product; and

(c) the four-month retention scores for the United States and British teachers indicate that the teachers maintained and/or improved their use of the skills at approximately equivalent levels in both countries.

A similar experiment carried out with samples of preservice teachers showed that preservice trainees made fewer significant changes in their use of the specified skills than the inservice teachers.

In all three preservice studies, the trainees in the control group, who received no training, made few changes, whereas the trainees who completed *Minicourse 1* made several. When compared on this dimension, the minicourse trainees in Sweden differed significantly from the control group in five skill areas; in the Netherlands they differed significantly in eight skill areas. It may be assumed, therefore, that the student teaching experience in itself does not cause preservice trainees to improve their teaching skills as much as the combination of both in-school student teaching and *Minicourse 1* training.

Given these preservice data, the transfer of *Minicourse 1* for use in preservice teacher training appears to have been successful. The adapted products achieved the course objective of changing teacher behaviour as well as the original product for the majority of teaching skills (OECD Report 1975).

2.7 Teacher Opinion

Each of the transfer sites asked teachers to complete a questionnaire giving their opinion regarding the usefulness of the course in general, and more specifically, the importance of the various elements of the course.

The United Kingdom reported that 96 percent of the inservice teachers who completed *Minicourse 1* claimed to have been interested in the materials; 82 percent would recommend the course to other teachers in their schools; and 57 percent claimed to be more confident in their ability as a teacher as a result of the course. At the end of the course, the teachers considered most of the skills to be useful. No more than 22 percent questioned the usefulness of any given skill. For the skills that were to be decreased in use, a somewhat larger proportion remained unconvinced; some 37 percent thought it was often necessary to repeat questions and one-third thought it sometimes was useful to repeat pupils' answers. When teachers were asked to evaluate the extent to which the course had improved their teaching, they indicated equal benefit to their teaching in the small group situation in which they practised and the whole class situation in which they generally would apply the skills.

In Sweden, teacher response to a postcourse questionnaire demonstrated that the minicourse met with extraordinarily positive acceptance. A large number of the responses implied that the course should be made obligatory in teacher education. Netherlands teachers also reported the course to have been a very positive and useful experience (OECD Report 1975).

2.8 Perceived Benefits from the Study

The American/British transfer project suggested that the transfer process has considerable potential as a rapid means of curriculum innovation and dissemination of new learning methods in educational systems. Dissemination studies in the United Kingdom showed that a nationwide distribution of this innovative course had taken place within two years of publication and that use of it was being made not only for the inservice training of teachers but also for preservice training.

Through international cooperation in development planning, the introduction of this innovation was achieved at a lower cost and with a more economic use of personnel than would have been possible had the research and development team had to start from scratch.

The examination of the processes involved in the development of the original materials stimulated interest in carrying out original development work in similar methods and systems in the United Kingdom. This interest, combined with the expertise in research and development generated by the transfer effort, is likely to advance the potential for cooperative international effort in original research and development in teaching.

Considerable interest was also shown in this United Kingdom transfer programme by those concerned with teacher education in many other countries, and it was clear that many developing countries in Asia and Africa saw in a transfer of these self-instructional learning materials a possible solution to some of their problems in the field to teacher training (Perrott and Padma 1981).

3. Conclusion

In the minicourses there are examples of thoroughly developed and tested teacher-training programmes ready for operational use. The educational research and development techniques employed in their production enable the findings of the educational researcher and the innovators of the classroom teacher to be applied to the production of products, that are effective in bringing about educational innovation.

The success of the transfer of minicourses to other countries and cultures indicates the importance of forging such links between research and practice and appears to justify the expense of the research and development techniques employed.

See also: Microteaching: Conceptual and Theoretical Bases; Microteaching: Feedback; Microteaching: Modelling; Microteaching: Effectiveness; Technical Skills of Teaching; Lesson Analysis; Supervision of the Practicum

Bibliography

Allen D W, Ryan K 1969 *Microteaching.* Addison Wesley, Reading, Massachusetts
Borg W R, Kelley M L, Langer P, Gall M 1970 *The Minicourse: A Microteaching Approach to Teacher Education.* Collier Macmillan, London
Centre for Educational Research and Innovation 1975 *The International Transfer of Microteaching Programmes for Teacher Education.* Organisation for Economic Co-operation and Development (OECD), Paris
Flanders N A 1970 *Analyzing Teaching Behavior.* Addison Wesley, Reading, Massachusetts
Perrott E 1977 *Microteaching: Research, Development and Practice.* Society for Research into Higher Education, Monograph 31, University of Surrey, Guildford
Perrott E, Padma M S 1981 The transfer of a self-instructional teacher-training course from Britain to India. *Program. Learn. Educ. Technol.* 18: 136–43

Special Purpose

Teacher Education for Early Childhood Education

L. G. Katz; J. Cain

The term "early childhood education" is used here to refer to group settings for children between the ages of approximately 3 and 6 years old. These settings are specifically designed to provide care, supervision, and education for them outside of their homes. The settings included under the general term "early childhood education" are quite varied, but have in common the fact that they serve children before entry into primary school. Thus the term "preprimary" education is also often used in discussions of education for this age group, and for the sake of simplicity is used throughout the material presented here.

Although specialists in the field differ on many aspects of goals and methods, there is general agreement among them that teachers' competence and attitudes are major determinants of program effectiveness. In spite of such agreement, few empirical studies of teachers themselves have been reported, and virtually no research on the preparation and education of teachers has been accumulated, even though a few projects designed to improve teacher performance have been reported.

From the general literature on preprimary education it appears that around the world, the majority of people teaching children under 5 or 6 years old have had no preservice training at all, and only sporadic inservice courses or workshops. The proportion of trained to untrained personnel is not simply related to the level of industrialization of a given country, to per capita income, or to average educational attainment, but to complex historical, political, and economical forces (Goodnow and Burns 1984). One of the few fairly reliable generalizations about the field and its teachers is that the younger the child being taught, the less training the teacher has, the lower the status and prestige attached to the job, the fewer qualifications are required, the lower the pay, and the longer the hours of work.

In many respects, the education of preprimary teachers has some of the same problems as primary and secondary teacher education, but in other respects, it has some unique ones stemming from special characteristics of the field.

1. Teacher Education and the Unique Characteristics of the Field

In countries and regions where preservice education is available for preprimary personnel, it is offered in a wide variety of institutions and departmental units, reflecting the equally wide variety of settings in which such personnel are employed. Indeed, in many settings the personnel are not called teachers, but go under a variety of other titles. Some training is available in social work or social welfare departments, or in institutions sponsored by social work agencies, for example, in Finland, Denmark, Bahrain, and the Federal Republic of Germany. Other training is offered in nursing or medical agencies, for example, in the German Democratic Republic; others in highly specialized institutions, for example, Montessori institutes, teacher-training colleges, nursery nurses' colleges, home economics or domestic science departments of colleges or secondary schools, vocational or technical-secondary schools, as well as in human development or child development divisions of psychology departments in colleges and universities.

Thus while the majority of teachers in preprimary settings have little or no training, some have a year of special secondary school instruction, for example, in Hungary and Chile; some have three-year diploma courses (Australia, and the United Kingdom), and some have diplomas or baccalaureate degrees. Such diversity exists not only across countries, but within some of the larger countries as well (Canada, Chile, India, and the United States).

The diversity of training arrangements as well as employment settings (e.g., nursery schools, crèches, kindergartens, day care centers, playgroups) operating for different lengths of the day and serving a variety of age groups, exacerbates a long-standing problem in the field of role boundaries and role ambiguity, which in turn leads to ambiguity and confusion about appropriate content for whatever training and education courses are available. Questions concerning what proportion of time available for training should be allocated to educational or health issues, and within these, how much emphasis should be given to theoretical versus pedagogical studies, as well as to the development of techniques for working with and educating parents, are constant sources of discussion in the field (Katz 1977). Almost all reports and proposals concerning the education of preprimary teachers emphasize the acquisition of skills and knowledge for building strong ties with parents and for helping parents to improve their child rearing as well as for working closely with professionals in such related fields as medicine, social work, nutrition, and primary schools (Indian Council of Child Welfare). As stated in a report on early childhood care and education prepared by the Organisation for Economic Cooperation and Development (OECD) ". . . the whole question of professional and sub-professional training in the Early Childhood Care and Education field is overdue for reconsideration against the background of recent developments, both within individual countries and across the international scene. As in any such considerations, this should start with a detailed analysis of the work likely to be carried out by one or more categories of ECCE staff" (CERI 1977 p. 51). In the case of developing countries, many teachers are also expected to recruit the mothers and children into the program, as well as to teach them about child rearing, hygiene, crafts, home management, and environmental sanitation (Pakjam 1978).

Another special characteristic of the field is the extent to which educational programs are staffed by volunteers, in some cases because of the lack of funds for paid staff, but in others to create a "family-like" atmosphere, and, in others to strengthen relations between the home and the preschool (Singer 1979, Preschool Playgroups Association n.d.). The volunteer groups tend to undermine the arguments put forward by professional associations that teachers of young children need special skills and knowledge, and advanced training by which to acquire both. Aside from the relatively large role played by volunteers at this level of schooling, preprimary education seems to be caught in a vicious cycle such that, in the absence of training and qualifications, many preprimary teachers have few skills and are therefore very poorly paid, and because of the poor pay, people with skills will not seek employment in this field. Because employees lack sophisticated skills or training, clients as well as sponsoring agencies are unwilling to increase their pay. Added to the poor skills–poor pay cycle is the fact that the younger the child in the setting, the lower the child–adult ratio. This means that when wages are increased, the costs of a program increase relatively dramatically without corresponding increases in the number of children assigned to an individual teacher (Woodhead 1979). Rigorous or lengthy training is unlikely to attract candidates when the ultimate pay scale is so low. Nevertheless, some attempts to break this cycle with new training initiatives and with the introduction of "professional" standards and qualifications have been reported (e.g., in the United King-

dom and the United States) and are discussed below.

2. General Issues in Preprimary Teacher Education

Like teacher education for other levels of schooling, the education of preprimary teachers suffers from the absence of agreed upon criteria of effectiveness, or definitions of "good teaching" (Medley 1982). The field is so diverse in terms of "philosophy," curriculum styles, ages of children served, length of the teaching day, scope of functions of teachers and so forth, that such consensus is unlikely to be achieved on a fieldwide basis. However, within particular types of settings (e.g., crèches), or curriculum styles, (e.g., Montessori), criteria or outcome measures against which to evaluate the effectiveness of teacher education might be more easily attained. Since academic achievement of children in preprimary settings is rarely of concern to the staff, standardized achievement test scores are unlikely to be accepted as appropriate or meaningful measures of teachers' effectiveness from which to make inferences about the effectiveness of their training.

Another problem shared by preprimary teacher education with all other levels of schooling is that in those countries and regions where training is available, doubts about its impact on ultimate teacher performance are widespread (Raths and Katz 1983). Some of these doubts are cast in terms of the relatively greater impact of the ultimate work place on teacher performance compared to the impact of the experiences provided during the preservice training. Other doubts are expressed by both trainees themselves and the practitioners who receive them when training has been completed. The latter critics assert that from their "objective" view, training offered in preservice programs is too theoretical and idealistic. The candidates themselves, from their "subjective" view of the training they receive also claim that it is not sufficiently relevant or useful, and reject it as too theoretical as well. It is possible that both the "objective" and "subjective" views are justified and appropriate. However, in the absence of agreed upon criteria of teacher effectiveness, competing views concerning the best types of training cannot be empirically tested.

Along similar lines, one of the major difficulties in designing and assessing the impact of preservice training programs is the so-called "feed forward" problem (Katz et al. 1981), that is, preservice training involves giving students answers to questions they have not yet asked, or giving students training experiences which provide methods of dealing with eventualities rather than actualities. This "feed forward" problem, no doubt generic to all anticipatory professional training in all professions, becomes a problem mainly when the training staff expects trainees to appreciate and perceive the relevance and usefulness of the training exercises and components provided for them. If the hypothesized "feed forward" problem really exists, it suggests that it is the nature of things that trainees cannot know how they will feel about a given experience once it has passed and in the light of experience not yet obtained. The concept also implies that training programs cannot be designed on the basis of the current responses of trainees, since at a later point in time, looking at those responses retrospectively, the graduate may change the meaning and value assigned to them quite substantially. One type of research of potential use in illuminating various dimensions of this problem would be a longitudinal study of candidates' perceptions of their experiences at selected points in time during their preservice training, and again at several subsequent points in time when they are employed, that is, a longitudinal study of the changes in perceptions of given past events as time passes.

During the posttraining period, graduates could be asked for their preconceptions of various elements of the training program they had, and be asked to compare how they said they perceived them while undergoing them, with how they perceive them at "time n" later. It may be that the very components of their training they rejected while undergoing them are the ones they subsequently wish they had had more of. The hypothesis is that though the experiences obtained during training never change, in the light of on-the-job experience, graduates change the value of meaning ascribed to them in retrospect. Another question is whether such retrospective changes are systematic, and if so, what is the "system"? If the "feed forward" construct is empirically confirmed, it could imply that teacher education must be designed and rationalized on bases other than whether the trainees "like" or see the relevance of its components. Ideal bases for rationalizing the design of teacher education should be theories of adult learning and of professional or occupational socialization. However, it appears that the pattern and structure of training programs are determined more by tradition, economic exigencies, and common sense than by such theoretical formulations.

Another problem shared by early childhood and other teacher training, is that concerning appropriate and sufficient content of the training course. Invariably course revisions concern additions of new specialities and experiences giving rise to steady increases of the length of the training required. Questions arise constantly such as: What proportion of the required work should be theoretical, historical, methodological, or practical? What subjects should be studied and with how much depth? What criteria, theories, or decision rules should be used to answer these questions?

Considerable interest has been shown in addressing such questions as these in terms of developmental stages that trainees and teachers are thought to go through. Katz (1972) proposed that in the case of preschool teachers, most of whom have had little or no preservice training, the aspects and components of teaching with

which they need assistance change as experience accrues. Four stages of preschool teacher development were hypothesized, although the length of time in each stage was not indicated, and was thought to vary among individuals even if the sequence in which stages occur does not.

The first of the four hypothesized stages was called "survival," characterized by the trainee or teacher being preoccupied with management and control of the group of children, keeping them reasonably busy and content, having the children accept their authority and accede to their demands, and being liked by them. A second stage, called "consolidation," was defined as a period that begins when the trainee or teacher has mastered control and management of the whole group, the provision of suitable activities to which the children respond favorably, and now becomes concerned about individual children whose behavior is different to that of most of the others, who appear to be atypical, or are seen not to be learning or responding as the teacher would like. A third stage, called "renewal," beginning perhaps after four or five years of teaching, was defined as characterized by a subjective feeling of becoming stale or weary of the same routines, tired of reading the same stories, singing the same songs, celebrating the same festivals, and possibly finding that work with very young children can become intellectually understimulating. Teachers in this stage typically ask for fresh ideas and techniques, new materials and methods, and enjoy and welcome opportunities to exchange ideas and materials with colleagues in workshops. A fourth stage, called "maturity," reached earlier by some than others, includes the teacher's acquisition of self-renewal strategies, but is marked further by the tendency to ask deeper and broader questions about the nature of education and its relationship to society, about historical, philosophical, or ethical issues in their work, and so forth. The latter stage was difficult to validate since many preschool personnel move up into directorships or other supportive and administrative positions if they stay in the field as long as five years.

The application of developmental stage constructs to preprimary teacher education can have three kinds of benefits. First, trainees and teachers can be helped to accept their own "survival" struggles at the beginning of their careers as "in the nature of things," and can thus put their lack of assurance and occasional fumbling into perspective, achieving greater patience with their own learning processes. Secondly, teacher education courses could be designed in such a way as to concentrate on providing at least minimal "survival skills" for trainees, but can do so in such a way as to strengthen trainees' dispositions to be resourceful and to go on learning after the basic survival stage is over. That is to say, trainees could be offered very clear simple practical "how to" exercises, equip them with activities to carry out during their initial teaching experiences (perhaps enough for the first two or three months of teaching), and indicate to them that such activities and projects are to help get started, and as soon as they feel comfortable with these activities in the real-life setting with the children, they can begin to develop their own activities and style, and make class plans over a longer period. The third and related value of looking at teacher education with a developmental perspective is that courses could begin with the very practical "how to" aspects of teaching, and end with the theoretical subjects (e.g., history and philosophy)—just the reverse of the typical sequence.

Most preservice programs require some classes involving the observation of children. In many institutions this is a highly valued part of training; it is frequently included in the list of ideal training activities, no doubt a heritage of Montessori's ideas. If there is any validity at all to the application of developmental stages, and the four stages proposed above, the exercises in observation should come after some real work in the classroom, rather than before, as is the custom. Inexperienced young students generally find observation of children unrewarding, if not boring. Studies of the extent to which exercises in the observation of children affect subsequent teaching skills have not been found. Yet it remains an almost sacred component of many teaching courses.

Of all of the components of a preservice education course most strongly recommended for teacher education, teaching practice or "field experience" appears to have top priority, though the amount of practice provided in preservice teacher education courses varies widely. Some courses require practical or field experiences in a suitable or approved setting before admission to a formal certificate or diploma course, as found in Sweden. Others feature practical experience similar to an internship throughout the period of training (e.g., nursery nurses' training in England and Wales), and still others provide as many as three years of academic work prior to field practice, for example, courses for social pedagogues in the Federal Republic of Germany (Austin 1976). Empirical studies of the effects of different amounts of practice are few and inconclusive (Davis 1975).

Another problem in need of empirical investigation is the relative effectiveness of imposing the practical or field experience requirement early rather than later in the training course. Early field experience is assumed to have the advantage of giving trainees better opportunities to try on the future training role and therefore to be able to make a more informed career choice earlier rather than later in the training sequence. Early field experience is also assumed to make theoretical studies more meaningful and useful, since the practical and theoretical components occur simultaneously. However, one study of students in training for elementary teaching indicates that the early field experience overwhelmed the students and that their more theoretical courses, rather than assuming greater relevance, became distractions from the urgent and salient realities of coping with the field setting (Luttrell et al. 1981). The

results of another study failed to confirm the assumed benefits of early experience (Shorter 1975).

Another major issue in need of empirical investigation is the frequent complaint of insufficient opportunities for students to observe or to practice "good" practices. Questions concerning both the timing and amount of practice become virtually irrelevant if the community lacks settings in which trainees can observe "good" practices. In such conditions the truism that "practice makes perfect" leads to a situation in which "bad practice makes perfectly bad." It can be argued that trainees do learn from imperfect or "bad" practices in field placements. However, just what is learned is not clear. At the other extreme, some training courses provide practice only in idealized laboratory settings which may be different from typical extracampus settings in ways that make the graduates' skills maladaptive to the field.

Helping trainees to become aware of a range of alternative practices and field conditions by using films, slides, videotapes and so on may minimize the distorting effects of constant exposure to "bad" practices, or to highly idealized settings. In addition, simulation exercises, role playing, microteaching, and the use of specially prepared slides or videotaped incidents together with solicitation of students' responses to specially prepared questions about the incidents may help them to transcend local practices (Medley 1982).

In an interesting series of studies of selected characteristics of students and the field placements to which they were assigned for practice teaching, Becher and Ade (1982) reported data suggesting that students relatively low in self-confidence perform better in practice teaching when matched with a cooperating teacher who is relatively weak or "underwhelming." Apparently, such students' self-confidence is further eroded when matched with a cooperating teacher who appears to be full of assurance and one who makes the teaching task "look easy." Becher and Ade's research suggests that attempts to "match" students' characteristics such as self-assurance with those of the personnel in the field placement could increase the effectiveness of the practice teaching or field experiences provided in training.

Students in preservice education programs are known to complain often that the field settings in which they practice require them to engage in pedagogical practices that their trainers and supervisors deplore or reject. The "bad field setting" predicament implies that the supervisors or tutors have special responsibilities to help trainees interpret and understand the realities of the field setting as well as to cultivate their capacities to adjust to those realities while they are becoming prepared to ultimately progress beyond them. The apparent gulf between educators of teachers and practitioners in field settings has apparently not been studied empirically, but is reflected in much comment in the general literature in the field (Katz 1977). Such discrepancies between the idealized practices advocated by the staff of teacher education institutions and the actual professional practices in the field are no doubt generic to professional education in all professions.

From the scattered reports available concerning the preservice education of preprimary teachers it appears to be following the trend noted in education for teaching at the upper levels, namely toward longer periods of training and greater proportions of the training being allocated to theoretical or "foundation" subjects. One of the best-known specialized training programs for those who work with young children—nursery nurses' training—has undergone great changes. In 1974, the two-year course was changed so that instead of its traditional three-fifths time allocated to practice and two-fifths to theoretical or academic work, the proportions are now reversed. In addition, the required age at entry was raised from 16 to 18 years. Many of the specialized nursery nurse training institutions and programs upgraded their general academic entrance requirements as well, and the certifying examinations have been upgraded substantially. These changes reflect increases in the knowledge base, particularly in the area of child development and parent–child relations, increasing complexity of child rearing and education in general, and strong pressures within the field for greater "professionalization" (Batten 1981).

3. Recent Developments in Inservice Education

Inasmuch as most preprimary personnel have little or no preservice education, various approaches to the education of those already employed merit particular attention. Two particular forms of inservice education provided to preprimary personnel are outlined below. The first known as the "advisory approach" (Katz et al. 1974) employed in the United Kingdom, parts of Australia, and sporadically in the United States and elsewhere, grew from the earlier role of school inspectors (Bolam 1982). In the early 1970s, Queensland became the first Australian state to adopt a policy of universal access to preschool education. This very large state was divided into nine regions, and preschool advisors were assigned to provide technical assistance to preschool classes within the regions, some of which are geographically extremely isolated. Many of the preschool teachers in country schools are very young, fresh from their training college courses taken in the larger cities of the state, and are assigned to "county service" for at least two years of their teaching careers. Preschool advisors are appointed by the Department of Education of the state of Queensland. They are selected from among practicing preschool teachers and serve as advisors for three years after which they return to preschool classroom teaching. These advisors are expected to make regular visits to all preschool classes within their regions, to provide moral as well as technical support, to conduct workshops on particular teaching or curriculum issues, and many of them also provide services through resource or teachers' centers in the region. The preschool advisors have no inspection or sanctioning authority; their roles are limited to providing support, encouragement, and stimulation to practitioners.

A variant of the advisory approach was the enabler model of inservice training (Katz 1972) developed especially for the inservice education of Head Start teachers in the United States and subsequently adapted for the support of day care staff (Holt n.d.). This variant of the advisory approach may be useful in regions and countries just beginning to develop their preprimary resources. The objectives of the model were to help the local communities served by the Head Start program to define and achieve their own goals and purposes, to offer help and advice in such a way as to enable local leaders and participants of the Head Start programs to discover and develop their own strengths and talents, to solve problems on their own, and to help local staff and participants to build and strengthen relationships with their own local resources and agencies. Qualifications of the consultants engaged to perform the enabler model included extensive experience in early childhood education and related fields, special skills in working with parents of diverse backgrounds, and demonstrated ability to be sensitive to the community's strengths and resources (Holt n.d.). The model was conceived in terms of two phases: "initiation" and "maintenance." During the "initiation" phase the enabler was expected to meet with all community groups involved in the program, for example, staff, volunteers, parents, social, medical and nutritional workers, primary school liaison persons, and so forth. During formal and informal discussion with each group and among the groups, the enabler encouraged and facilitated the expression of the preferences, goals, and purposes the community members themselves wanted to achieve.

During the second phase of the model, "maintenance," the enabler's role was to provide support for smooth operation of the program. During this phase the enabler's functions included supplying information, serving as a link between all segments of the wider community involved in the welfare of the preschool children in the program, interpreting the program in terms of its own agreed-upon goals, serving as a source of support and encouragement, appreciating staff strengths, demonstrating skills or techniques occasionally, and serving as a neutralizer of conflict (Katz 1982). Although no controlled empirical studies of the application of this model or other variants of the advisory approach to preprimary inservice education have been reported, the following points emerged from years of experience with the enabler model. Advisors had to struggle to resist the temptation to give advice too early in the development of their relationships with the program or community to be served. This is not a matter of the rightness of their advice, but of allowing enough trust between advisor and advisees to be developed so that the advice could be interpreted in the context of offering help rather than of criticism from an outside expert. Advisors who live in the community being advised have the advantage of greater understanding of local concerns and preferences, but they have the great disadvantage of being in too close and continuous contact with the participants to be able to have a detached, respectful, and realistic overview of the participants' contribution to the day-to-day quality of the program offered to the children. It appears that, depending on the distances between preprimary settings to be served, a maximum number of settings served by any one advisor or enabler might be between six and ten. This makes the advisory approach to inservice education very expensive, since the qualifications for advisors are those at the highest level available in the educational system, and their salaries should reflect the high educational qualifications. In addition, their work by definition is itinerant and incurs costs of travel and accommodation in most regions. Studies of the relative cost–benefit ratios of the advisory approach compared to other forms of inservice training (e.g., mounting courses, workshops, secondments of selected staff, etc.) which take into account the ultimate long-term benefits to the preprimary field in a given location are greatly needed.

By far the single largest and most radical inservice program for preprimary personnel was launched in the United States in 1972 and called the Child Development Associate (CDA) project and was a deliberate attempt to upgrade the quality of teaching in Head Start classes. A Child Development Associate (CDA) is defined as a person able to meet the specific needs of children in a preprimary setting by addressing their physical, social, emotional, and intellectual growth, and by establishing and maintaining an appropriate child care and learning environment, and by promoting good relations with the parents they serve.

At the time the CDA program was conceived in the early 1970s, competency- or performance-based teacher education (see *Competency-based Teacher Education*) and certification was enjoying great popularity and credibility in the United States, especially among state and federal education agencies, and the CDA project was heavily influenced by it. To date, the United States federal government has invested more than US \$50 million in its development, testing, and application, indicating the importance given to strengthening the competence of Head Start personnel especially, and other preprimary personnel, generally. In the 10 years of its existence approximately 11,000 individuals have been credentialed, virtually all of whom were already employed in Head Start or similar programs at the time they undertook the training and completed the credentialing process.

The CDA system consists of several interrelated segments. The fundamental segment is the set of teaching competencies on which all candidates are assessed. Another is CDA training, and the third is the Credential Award System.

Among its unique features are the specification of

teaching competencies for preprimary staff, the separation of the training from the credentialing processes, and the participation of clients in the credentialing process. The competencies required for the CDA cover six broad goals of preprimary teaching emphasizing such areas of teacher responsibility as health, safety, stimulation of physical and intellectual development, strengthening self-concept, group participation skills, cooperation between home and school, and other supplementary responsibilities. Each competency goal is further subdivided to yield a total of 13 so-called "functional areas." In addition, nine "personal capacities" are listed as essential features of the CDA requirements. These include such capacities as sensitivity to children's feelings, listening and adapting language to suit the children and families, being protective of childrens' individuality, and so forth. The competencies, functional areas, and personal capacities form the basis upon which CDA training programs are designed. Though no restrictions are placed on how the training should address these competencies, functional areas, or personal capacities, the system does require that no less than 50 percent of the training be field or practice based. Inasmuch as most candidates are already employed, the field-based requirement has not been problematic. Another unique feature of the guidelines for CDA training is that no set length of training is imposed on all candidates (Office of Child Development 1973), although to be eligible for candidacy for a CDA credential, applicants must have had at least 600 hours of experience working with children aged 3 to 5 years in a group setting within the five years preceding application (Human Development Services 1982). The training guidelines for the CDA credential were also designed so that any institution with relevant personnel and experience may provide training for CDA credential candidates, and may adapt their own training in any way they wish to ensure the candidate's acquisition of the prescribed competencies. Since the training and credentialing parts of the CDA system are completely separate, no institutions are specifically or officially "entitled" by the government to offer training, and no institutions or organizations are excluded from the same.

The original planners of the CDA training and credentialing system specifically wished to make training and the subsequent credential available to those candidates traditionally excluded from or denied admission to tertiary institutions in many parts of the United States. Thus CDA training is available in a wide variety of institutions at various levels of postsecondary education.

By far the most unique aspect of the CDA system is its Credential Award program or process (Ward et al. 1976) which continues to undergo development, extension, testing, and refinement. The process begins when an applicant for candidacy has been accepted "into the credential award system." As indicated above, the applicant must be at least 18 years old and have had some 600 hours of experience. Once the applicant formally becomes a CDA credential candidate he/she must select a field trainer/advisor (often an experienced member of the staff with whom he or she is working) and a parent/community representative. Trainers/advisors must be approved by the national CDA office and have appropriate experience.

The candidate, with the help of the trainer/advisor, begins the work of preparing a portfolio. He/she collects exhibits and materials to enter into this portfolio which is to serve as a repository of evidence that the work has successfully been carried out on all the competencies required. The portfolio thus composed is used by the local assessment team, described as follows: A local assessment team (LAT) consists of the candidate, the trainer/advisor, a parent/community representative selected by the candidate, and a CDA representative representing the national headquarters of the CDA National Credentialing Program in Washington, DC.

This group of four people becomes the local assessment team that makes the final decision as to whether or not the candidate meets the standards for the award of the credential. The next step leading to assessment is to gather information and materials indicative of the candidate's competence in each of the 13 functional areas for the portfolio. In this way, the system by which competence is assessed and the credential that is awarded are completely separate from the training institution—a real departure from conventional training and certification practices.

The trainer/advisor member of the LAT makes three separate observations in each of the functional areas and reports his/her findings in specially prepared formats. The parent/community representative distributes a parent opinion questionnaire to the parents of each of the children served by the candidate, and summarizes the information yielded by the questionnaire for admission into the LAT discussion. In addition, the parent/community representative makes direct observations of the candidate's performance in each functional area specified in the CDA competency standards. Once all the information is collected, the candidate and her trainer/advisor call for an LAT meeting lasting usually about four hours, though sometimes much longer. At this meeting all the information and evidence gathered concerning the candidate's competence is reviewed and discussed with the candidate present and participating. This four-member team votes on the candidate's competence in each of the 13 functional areas separately and then takes a final over-all vote on global competence. Though the four votes may be split in each of the functional areas, in order for a candidate to be awarded a credential, the final overall vote must be unanimously in favor of the award.

The processes involved in assessment and ultimate receipt of the CDA credential are fairly complex, time and energy consuming, and heavily dependent upon the willingness of various participants to contribute many hours voluntarily to help the candidate whilst training,

and in participation in the local assessment team's required observations and meetings. However, a number of aspects of the CDA training and credentialing process could be adopted by others without taking on the whole system. The competencies and functional areas constituting the "standards" are both basic and reasonably universal and can serve as guidelines for the training of preprimary personnel in a variety of cultures and settings; competencies deemed locally inappropriate could certainly be discarded. Another aspect of the training system of potential value in various settings is that it is flexible and individualized so that no single cohort of candidates must engage in all of the same exercises in the same sequence or at the same time; many candidates will be able to demonstrate competence in some of the functional areas at the outset of their training and thus can move on to others for which they do need training and practice.

From the information available to date, it appears that the actual training provided to CDA candidates improves upon conventional training primarily in terms of the explicitness of its goals and objectives, and in its clear commitment to the acquisition of demonstrable skills in working with children and their families. Unfortunately no studies of the validity of the credential have been reported yet. Thus while the functional areas nominated as representing essential competencies for effective teaching of young children appear to have face validity, it is not yet known whether those awarded the CDA credential and those who fail the credentialing process would be judged different from each other by "blind" observers. Since the pass/fail decision is made by the LAT, three of the four members of which are selected by the candidates themselves, the possibility of highly biased evaluation is very great. It is certainly likely that the votes are "stacked" in the candidate's favor in advance. Similarly, the extent to which the pass/fail standards applied by one LAT in one setting or community are like the standards applied by another LAT is not known. The potential for a "rubber yardstick" is very high indeed. Whether universalistic standards of competence are important enough to forgo opportunities for local input into staff quality is not a research issue, but lies in the realm of educational policy.

Given the present state of the art of teacher education in the preprimary field, elements of the CDA training and credentialing system deserve exploration and empirical study. For example, the composition of the LAT provides for genuine participation of the representatives of the local community served by the candidate and gives the candidate a role in his or her own assessment. What are some of the important dynamics of this process? What happens when the LAT member representing the CDA national headquarters differs with the local judgments of the candidate's competence? How can the overall competence of the "profession" be upgraded or modernized to incorporate innovations and new ways of thinking about children if the local (and often remote) community has such a large voice in the credentialing process? On the other hand, the extent of local participation in the process may facilitate dissemination of new ideas to the community in a way that formal meetings and lectures might not.

Some informal and anecdotal reports of the experiences of candidates who have progressed successfully through the CDA credentialing process itself suggest that its various elements (e.g., creating a portfolio, appointing an LAT, being observed by the LAT members, and receiving their feedback in the LAT meeting) create a type of "Hawthorne Effect". All the details involved in bringing together the assessment team, knowing that the parent/community representative will solicit the views of parents, and so forth, seem to emit a strong signal that the job for which one is trying to become credentialed is a very important one, one in which many have a real stake and a genuine interest. While so many people who work with young children, particularly in day care centers, feel undervalued and often depressed (Whitebook et al. 1982), the activity surrounding CDA training and credentialing may play a powerful role in improving morale and commitment. The kinds of potential side benefits of the system should be studied with naturalistic methods; questions of the validity of the credential should be addressed with formal experimental methods, and both of these types of studies should be undertaken before others are urged to adopt the rather cumbersome system. Research confirming its validity and other positive effects would then make the CDA system a potentially valuable one, particularly in regions and countries in the early stages of developing training methods for preprimary teachers.

4. Summary

Information concerning the education of preprimary personnel is scattered, and is primarily descriptive in nature. Virtually no research concerning the relative effectiveness of alternative approaches to training and education have been found. In developed countries in which preservice training and education are available, it appears to be quite varied and to be caught in the general trend toward increasing its length as well as its academic components. Research testing the relative impact of various types of content, the early versus late teaching practice, the value of training in "child observation" skills, and the application of "developmental stage" concepts to the design of preservice training would be useful.

In the less developed countries, few teacher-training resources seem to be available at the preprimary level. One of the major issues in need of empirical testing for the developing countries and regions concerns the question of what is the optimum proportion of preservice to inservice training, given that financial resources are limited. In order to produce information suitable for policy formulation, the relative benefits (versus costs) of preservice training (in terms of teacher performance) can be compared with long-term benefits. The hypoth-

esis to be tested is that preservice training programs show strong immediate effects on teacher performance, which subsequently fade, and that certain types of inservice training show few immediate effects on teacher performance, but strong long-term effects on the same. The hypothesis assumes that the types of inservice training approaches to be studied are like those described above under the general heading of the advisory or enabler model.

See also: Criteria for Evaluating Teaching; Inservice Teacher Education; Microteaching: Conceptual and Theoretical Bases; Student (Practice) Teaching; Supervision of the Practicum; Synthesizing Research Evidence

Bibliography

Austin G R 1976 *Early Childhood Education: An International Perspective.* Academic Press, New York

Batten A 1981 Nursery nursing: Past and present (2). *Early Childhood* 1(5): 14–19

Becher R M, Ade W 1982 The relationship of field placement characteristics and students' potential field performance abilities to clinical experience performance ratings. *J. Teach. Educ.* 33(2): 24–30

Bolam R 1982 Innovations adopted. In: Thompson A R (ed.) 1982 *Inservice Education of Teachers.* Commonwealth Secretariat, London

Centre for Educational Research and Innovation (CERI) 1977 *Early Childhood Care and Education: Objectives and Issues.* Organisation for Economic Co-operation and Development, Paris

Centre for Educational Research and Innovation (CERI) 1981 *Children and Society: Issues for Pre-school Reform.* Organisation for Economic Co-operation and Development, Paris

Davis M D 1975 A comparison of the development of teaching sophistication and estimates of professional enhancement between eight week and sixteen week elementary student teachers at the University of Illinois (Unpublished Doctoral Dissertation, University of Illinois at Urbana-Champaign, 1975) *Dissertation Abstracts International* 1976 36: 6012A (University Microfilms No. 76-6744)

Goodnow J, Burns A 1984 The relationship between research and the development of child care educational policy relating to young children: Some implications from the Australian experience. In: Katz L G, Steiner K, Wagemaker P J, Spencer M S (eds.) 1984 *Current Topics in Early Childhood Education*, Vol. 5. Ablex, Norwood, New Jersey

Holt B no date The enabler model of early childhood training and program development. Unpublished paper

Human Development Services (United States Department of Health and Human Services) 1982 *The Child Development Associate Credential.* DHS Publication No. (OHDS) 82-31162-A. Office of Human Development Services, Washington, DC

Indian Council of Child Welfare 1978 *National Seminar on Education of the Teacher for the Pre-school Child.* New Delhi

Katz L G 1972 Developmental stages of preschool teachers. *Elem. Sch. J.* 73: 50–54

Katz L G 1977 Socialization of teachers for early childhood programs. In: Spodek B, Walberg H J (eds.) 1977 *Early*

Childhood Education: Issues and Insights. McCutchan, Berkeley, California

Katz L G 1982 *Helping Others Learn to Teach.* ERIC Clearinghouse on Elementary and Early Childhood Education, Urbana, Illinois

Katz L G, Morpurgo J, Wolf R L, Asper L 1974 The advisory approach to inservice training. *J. Teach. Educ.* 34: 267–71

Katz L G, Raths J D, Mohanty C, Kurachi A, Irving J 1981 Follow-up studies: Are they worth the trouble? *J. Teach. Educ.* 32(2): 18–24

Luttrell H D, Bane R K, Mason B 1981 Early elementary field-based experience: A university and public school approach. Unpublished paper

Medley D M 1982 *Teacher Competency Testing and the Teacher Educator.* Bureau of Educational Research, University of Virginia, Charlottesville, Virginia

Office of Child Development 1973 *The Child Development Associate: A Guide for Training.* D 74-1065. United States Department of Health, Education, and Welfare, Washington, DC

Pakjam G 1978 Pre basic education. In: Indian Council of Child Welfare 1978

Peters D L (ed.) 1981 New methods for educating and credentialing professionals in child care: The child development associate program. *Child Care Q.* 10: 3–83

Preschool Playgroups Association (in press) *Playgroups in the Eighties*

Raths J D, Katz L G 1983 The best of intentions for the education of teachers. *J. Educ. Teach.* 8: 275–83

Shorter C A 1975 Early field experiences of sophomore students in two preservice teacher education programs (Unpublished Doctoral Dissertation. University of Illinois, Urbana-Champaign, 1975) *Dissertation Abstracts International* 1976 36: 6026A–6027A (University Microfilms No. 76-6960)

Singer E 1979 Women, children and child-care centers. In: Centre for Educational Research and Innovation (CERI) 1981

Ward E H et al. 1976 The Child Development Associate consortium's assessment system. *Young Children* 31: 244–54

Whitebook M, Howes C, Darrah R, Friedman J 1982 Caring for the caregivers: Staff burnout in child care. In: Katz L G, Steiner K, Wagemaker P J, Spencer M S (eds.) 1982 *Current Topics in Early Childhood Education*, Vol. 4. Ablex, Norwood, New Jersey

Woodhead M 1979 *Pre-school Education in Western Europe; Issues, Policies and Trends.* Council of Europe. Longman, London

Teacher Education for Special Education

D. S. Semmel

The basis for variation in special education programs between and within nations has been conceptualized in a model which provides a useful framework for identification and examination of the key issues in the training of teachers of exceptional children (Putman 1979). The necessity for such a model is readily apparent if it is considered that teacher training is related to the nature and level of special education programs offered to exceptional children and is a facet, rather than a major focus, of national policy concerning special education.

Putnam's model posits four sequential stages in the development of special education programs and services. During the first stage, when school attendance is optional, only children with sensory deficits are served. This is because of the readily observable nature of sensory handicaps. In the second stage, when school attendance becomes compulsory, institutions for the mentally retarded are developed. This is followed by the development of programs and services for the physically handicapped and, subsequently, for children manifesting emotional and behavioral problems. In the third stage, when the school-leaving age is raised, specialized services such as speech and remedial reading programs and programs for "slow learners" develop or are provided. Putnam hypothesizes a fourth stage, contingent upon the prior evolution of stages 1 to 3, when a "period of educational renewal takes place in which

mainstreaming of the handicapped is likely to occur" (Putnam 1979 p. 84).

It may be expected, therefore, that teacher-training programs will reflect the state of development of educational and rehabilitative programs for exceptional individuals. However, since international professional communications, consultancies, and technical-assistance programs are increasing, significant departures from the predicted progression of development are also to be found.

1. Special Education Teacher Competencies

How are teacher competencies selected? And what measures are employed to evaluate and modify the selection of teacher competencies? Competency selection, like other aspects of professional preparation, is largely determined by the theoretical or pragmatic approach to the education of the exceptional individual. Teacher competencies, which are explicitly or implicitly the basis for teacher-preparation programs, are related to the methods and content of pupil instruction. The special education methods advocated in training institutions or programs may be a function of national education policy or may be locally determined. However, in nations having relatively decentralized educational systems, a more eclectic basis for competency selection may be expected.

The methods that characterize contemporary special education programs, and from which teacher competencies are derived, may be broadly dichotomized into orientations that are related to (a) training and experience obtained in settings for the more severely handicapped (e.g., specialized school or residential facilities) and (b) training and teaching experience obtained within regular education settings. In the latter, the educational program and teaching competencies are similar to those required of regular education teachers. The requisite specialization skills are related to the modification of the regular education program in terms of the rate and scope of instruction. In the case of programs based on the instructional needs of more severely handicapped individuals, requisite teacher competencies more frequently emphasize sensory-motor training or social and vocational rehabilitation.

Several theoretical and/or pragmatic approaches to special education can be identified, each with attendant teacher competencies that are seen as necessary for the implementation of the instructional or rehabilitative program. The most commonly reported approaches are (a) sensory-motor, (b) vocational–social, (c) remedial, (d) normalization, and (e) therapeutic.

In practice, most special education programs are a combination of several approaches, with differential emphasis often based upon the age of the pupil, the severity of the disability, and the educational philosophy of the program. Programs for the severely and moderately retarded, for example, are frequently designed to improve sensory-motor functioning as well as increasing client independence and improving skills in self-care and appropriate social behavior. Sensory-motor programs are a fundamental aspect of all special education approaches for young handicapped children. Generally, programs for the development of gross motor control are followed by sensory-motor education, particularly the development of visual and auditory discrimination abilities. Sensory-motor-development programs have a venerable history in special education, with present-day programs derived from the work of such notable historical figures as Itard, Seguin, and Montessori (Lane 1976).

Another major goal of special education is the development of the social and vocational competence of the handicapped. Nations which have large rural populations and low literacy rates, must direct the special education effort toward minimizing the social and economic dependency of the handicapped. In these nations, sensory-motor training is frequently incorporated into vocational-training programs with instruction taking place at the occupational site or in vocational centers where practical handwork skills are taught. Socialist nations, in particular, emphasize that the purpose of special education is to prepare handicapped pupils to become economically productive members of society (Vlasova 1977, Becker 1979).

Several variations are found, however, in the approach to vocational education for the handicapped. The stage of national educational development notwithstanding, programs may be structured so that vocational and social competencies are taught at all developmental and age levels (Lubovski 1979), or they may be delayed until adolescence or postschool years, when nonschool agencies assume a greater share of the responsibility for the rehabilitation of the handicapped. Consistent with Putnam's model, the development of special education programs found in a given nation are related to the handicapping conditions identified. Countries that serve only the most seriously impaired children tend to limit goals to the achievement of a minimal level of independent functioning. When nations are in a position to serve a broader range of children in special education, which may now include the mildly retarded and learning disabled, then programs expand to include remedial approaches to the development of basic academic skills.

Remedial approaches to special education take several forms. Common to all remedial programs, however, is the belief that systematic intervention can overcome the underlying causes or the overt manifestations of a learning handicap. All remedial approaches are characterized by a high level of specificity and individualization. The behavior or skill of interest is targeted for remediation through a system of pupil assessment, task analysis, and intervention which is designed to remediate that specific aspect of pupil behavior. In North America, this approach is widely known as diagnostic–prescriptive (D–P) teaching. Ysseldyke and Salvia (1974) have described two types of diagnostic–prescriptive teaching: the first type is referred to as "ability" training; the second type is variously referred to as "task analysis" or "instruction-based diagnostic–prescriptive" teaching.

Ability-training programs have as their objective the remediation of deficits of the pupils' underlying psychological processes (e.g., visual discrimination, attention, and cognitive processes such as sequencing and verbal-organization strategies, to name but a few), which are presumed to be causally related to the pupils' learning handicap. While empirical support for the validity of ability-training approaches in terms of academic outcomes is limited (Ysseldyke 1973), they continue to generate much enthusiasm among practitioners. Examples of ability-training programs are those of Frostig which emphasize visual–perceptual training as the objective of remediation. The Kepart program centers on perceptual–motor training, including training in balance, posture, directionality, and body image. The Instrumental Enrichment Program of Feuerstein, developed in Israel and widely field tested in the United States, is also an ability-training program, containing elements of perceptual- and cognitive-ability training. The Illinois Test of Psycholinguistic Abilities (ITPA) is another internationally known ability-training approach, based upon a theory of critical psycholinguistic abilities (e.g., visual association, auditory sequential memory, and grammatical closure), assumed to be fundamental to the development of language and reading competence. Diagnostic–prescriptive ability-training programs require considerable teacher preparation and are most often provided to experienced special-education teachers in a continuing-education or summer inservice-education program.

There has been considerable growth in the application of the principles of behaviorism to the education of exceptional pupils, particularly the severely handicapped. These techniques, also referred to as applied behavior analysis (ABA) or behavior modification, were derived from the psychological theories of B. F. Skinner. The diagnostic–prescriptive approach is characteristic of applied-behavior programs, but it is typically applied in the remediation of the overt learning or behavior problem presented by the student. Direct instruction is a related behavioral approach to special education (Engelmann and Carnine 1982). Programs using this approach hold that underlying ability is a relatively unimportant factor in the design of remedial programs and, further, that the child's environment, as it facilitates or interferes with learning, is of greater importance in effective instruction. Direct instruction programs are therefore designed with heavy emphasis upon structuring the learning situation to maximize the probability that the student will learn (see *Direct Instruction*). These programs require a high level of teacher training in order to assure that the learning environment, including teacher behavior, is as rigorously structured as the instructional materials. Tawney (1980) has described an integrated curriculum and teacher-training system based on behavioral principles and emphasizing "errorless learning." The error less-learning procedure is diagnostic–prescriptive in nature, with particular attention to learner and task analysis and identification of reinforcement and correction procedures. An intrinsic characteristic of all diagnostic–prescriptive programs is the requirement that the teacher keep detailed and accurate records of the pupil's progress under specified treatment conditions or educational interventions. The ensuing documentation serves both as an instructional guide for the teacher and for program evaluation (Mackenzie et al. 1970, Tawney 1980).

Deinstitutionalization and normalization are terms designating a unique contemporary development in the history of special education. Originating in the Scandinavian nations and gaining worldwide attention through the interest of international agencies, parent and professional groups, and educational leaders (Zipperlen 1975, Wolfensberger 1972), the movement seeks to end the enforced, arbitrary, and frequently inhumane segregation of severely handicapped individuals into large, impersonal institutions. The movement is also dedicated to "normalization" of the environment for handicapped individuals, through placement in group homes in the community and with educational programs designed to foster the handicapped person's ability to move about the home and community environment and to engage in normal social and familial contacts.

Deinstitutionalization affects adults as well as children and personnel-training needs are influenced to a large extent by this factor. When adults are returned to the community and placed in group homes, the need is for rehabilitation therapists, social workers, group-home leaders, and child-care workers rather than teachers (McCormick et al. 1975). Training needs center on facilitating communal-living skills, practical self-care, and daily-living and management abilities such as shopping, local travel, and communication. Deinstitutionalized children may also be placed in local special schools or in special classes within the regular day school, where responsibility for educational programs rests with the special class teacher.

The training of therapists to meet the needs of emotionally and socially maladjusted youth is an integral aspect of clinical psychology, which emphasizes individual or small-group psychotherapeutic methods of treating emotional disorder. A significant departure from this orientation was developed in France in the period following the Second World War and is centered on the training of *educateurs specialisés*. The *educateur* concept, which has since been applied to other handicaps, emphasizes reeducation and resocialization through daily living and educational experiences, in combination with the positive adult model provided by the *educateur*. The re-education process stresses high-interest activity and physical participation—action rather than therapeutic conversation. The *educateur* is expected to provide a close, sustained personal relationship which the handicapped person needs and which is not provided in traditional therapeutic interventions. A monograph by Linton (1971) describes in detail the French *educateur* program and its adaptations in the United States and Canada. In France, the *educateur* functions as a combination of teacher of practical arts, vocational counselor, child-care worker, and child advocate (Juul 1981). *Educateur* training takes three years and both selection procedures and the programs are rigorous. Half of the three-year program is spent in practicum facilities that cooperate with the university-based training program.

Competency-based teacher education (CBTE) is a system of teacher preparation designed to assure that a given training program can demonstrate that its trainees have achieved explicit, behaviorally defined performance objectives as measured by prespecified criteria (see *Competency-based Teacher Education*). The CBTE movement has had considerable influence on special education teacher programs in the United States (Semmel and Semmel 1976, Blackhurst 1977). The CBTE approach can be applied to any of the special education theoretical or pragmatic models described above, but more often CBTE is atheoretical and relies on "expert opinion" to develop the performance objectives that trainees must demonstrate. Research on teaching and logical analysis of competencies implicit in effective teaching performance are also sources of the specific competencies that trainees must demonstrate. The focus in CBTE programs is on teacher training itself and on generic teaching skills. Thus, substantive areas related to pupil learning (e.g., child-centered curricula) are of subsidiary importance—although teacher-training effectiveness is ideally measured in terms of pupil outcomes.

Competency-based teacher education programs and certification agencies frequently utilize consensus methods for program planning and reform. Among the techniques employed to collect information about desired teacher competencies are meetings, surveys, and interview methods designed to elicit professional opinion about ideal or empirically demonstrated teacher competencies (Birch and Reynolds 1982). Critics of this approach have pointed out that while it is useful to ask teachers and training professionals to indicate what they think is important, such an approach may also serve to capture or institutionalize the conventional wisdom of those asked (Dick et al. 1981).

The selection of competencies based on the research literature on teacher effectiveness (for example Good 1984, Brophy 1979) may be expected to have considerable impact on special education teacher preparation as an alternative to selection of training competencies by consensus or convention. While much of the teacher effectiveness research has been conducted with nonhandicapped populations, special educators have increasingly adapted the findings of this literature for special educator training (Englert 1984, Stevens and Rosenhine 1979).

2. Teacher-training Programs

There are a number of ways in which individuals attain competence and certification as special education teachers. The task of teacher education may be regarded as a continuum, from preservice programs to continuing professional-development programs for inservice teachers. At the preservice level, in university or college programs, the student may emphasize study in pedagogy or other educationally related disciplines (e.g., psychology, child development, speech and language). The bachelor's degree program may or may not lead directly to certification as a special- or regular-education teacher. Professional preparation may also be obtained in teachers' colleges or normal schools on a preservice or post-graduate basis. Postgraduate special education training programs frequently demand prior training in regular education.

In the United States, undergraduate (bachelor's degree) education students are usually enrolled in courses that are described as academic rather than professional (Ysseldyke and Algozzine 1982). Researchers have questioned the effectiveness of academic course

work as a primary method of preparing education professionals (Semmel and Semmel 1976, Sarason et al. 1962). While there has been some effort to design teacher-education programs to increase the amount of time devoted to training in real or simulated classrooms—notably programs developed under the impetus of the competency-based teacher education (CBTE) movement—obstacles to change have been formidable. The source of the problem in the United States appears to lie with the separation of authority for governance of teacher education and that of education of children. Typically, preservice teacher-preparation programs are controlled by the universities and colleges, whereas educational programs are in the hands of local school boards and administrators. Unfortunately, each of these agencies has a different mission and serves different constituencies. As a consequence, obstacles to field-based training are difficult to overcome.

3. Specialization Training

Special education teacher preparation must deal with the issues related to the degree of specialized training necessary for effective teaching of children with different handicaps. Advocates of the generalist or generic special-education-training approach—for example, Blackhurst (1981) in the United States and Becker (1979) in the German Democratic Republic—hold that narrowly specialized training fails to meet the needs of most disabled children, reinforces the tendency toward labeling, and emphasizes psychological diagnosis rather than educational aspects of programming. Becker (1979) views the education of the handicapped as a branch of general pedagogy, with strong interrelationships across each category of handicap, while taking individual differences into account. For developing nations, this is an important policy issue since one advantage of generic training is that it permits greater flexibility in serving a broader range of students with special needs. But this advantage must be weighed against the needs of new special education programs in developing nations, where services are initially provided to those with sensory handicaps.

Birch and Reynolds (1982) suggest that there is a trend toward reducing the number of different teacher certifications in the United States. They provide a list of "common core" knowledge and abilities that teachers must acquire during training. Categorical training and certification are generally offered in the areas of vision, hearing, language, physical, and mild and severe learning handicaps. In North America and Western Europe, there has also been growth in training programs for teachers of children with specific learning disabilities, but there is considerable professional debate about whether this specialization should be subsumed under mild learning disabilities (Hallahan and Kauffman 1977).

4. *Qualifications for Entry into Training Programs*

In nations where there are shortages of trained personnel, special education programs may be forced to rely on untrained teachers and teacher aides. Examples of measures taken to deal with shortages of trained personnel may be found in the chapter on professional preparation in the Proceedings of the First World Congress of Future Special Education (Fink 1978). A number of developing as well as developed nations are moving toward providing some training in special education for regular class teachers (Fink 1978, Kristensen 1979). Regular education training and experience, as a prerequisite to admission for special education training, is found in nations at all levels of educational development—for example, the Federal Republic of Germany, Norway, Sweden, and Jamaica, as well as a number of states within the United States where certification is regulated on a state-by-state basis (Fink 1978).

5. *Inservice and Continuing Education*

Inservice and continuing professional education programs have always been important in the training of special education personnel. This may be due to the greater flexibility of these programs when compared to university-based programs. They also function to meet specialized needs for training rather than to provide fundamental knowledge and pedagogical principles. Inservice programs are provided in a number of different ways, their format frequently determined by the sponsoring agency. In the United Kingdom, teacher centers provide training as well as teaching resources (Thornbury 1973). The teacher-center concept has been adopted in the United States and has been federally funded and developed on a regional basis (Edelfelt 1982). The British teacher center is unique in that it is staffed and governed by teachers through teacher federations and unions. The Warnock Report on Special Education in the United Kingdom recommended that resource centers in special education be established to train all teachers to accommodate exceptional pupils (Karagianis and Nesbit 1981) (see *Teachers' Centres*).

Another approach to inservice education is training-of-trainers programs, in which a cadre of teachers are trained in a particular method or skill and subsequently return to their own districts to serve as consultants to or trainers of their colleagues. It is a cost-effective method of disseminating specific educational techniques and innovations and is widely employed in both developing and developed nations. An example of this is found in the programs offered by the Caribbean Institute for Mental Retardation, which provides training of teachers on a regionalized basis (Lugo 1978).

Special training institutes or centers are frequently sponsored by university research centers, hospitals, or institutions, and by private voluntary or religious organizations. These institutes provide advanced professional training on a continuing or short-term basis, as a service to the professional community and as a means for disseminating research innovations. Correspondence schools and programs are also employed as a means of continuing professional development. Self-study programs are frequently followed by examinations administered by a university or ministry of education for the purpose of teacher certification. The importance of inservice programs in the retraining of teachers for new roles is well-illustrated by the large-scale effort sponsored by the US Department of Education to assist implementation of the Education for All Handicapped Children Act 1975 (Smith 1978).

In developing nations, training also serves as a means of fulfilling program-development needs. Pascual (1979) reported a method employed in the Philippines, in which the trainee is instructed in procedures for identification and assessment of blind children (to be adapted later for other handicaps). Following training, the trainee assumes responsibility for surveying and screening handicapped children in an area which has not yet established a special program. Based upon the trainee's work in the region, a program is instituted the following year.

Regional training institutes, serving a group of nations within a geographical area, also provide important training resources for developing nations. Kristensen (1979) described the work of a special institute of education in Tunisia, which has trained teachers from 40 different countries in Africa and the Middle East in a two-year program. The training program encompasses a wide range of subjects but concentrates on prevention, identification of disabilities, psychological development, and medical treatment. The focus of all training at the institute is on how the information can be applied in the home country.

6. *Personnel Training Issues*

Training programs in special education must of necessity be geared to the changing demand for personnel to serve the disabled. The resources of special education training programs must also address the need for the preparation of specialists to serve nonschool-age handicapped (i.e., infants, preschool children, adolescents, and adults). This training may be carried out in collaboration with medical, rehabilitation, and social-agency personnel, in which the development of multidisciplinary skills and the initiation of cooperative professional relationships can be fostered.

The expansion of special education services to a greater range of individuals with special needs may well depend on reconceptualizing the role of the special education specialist from that of classroom teacher to that of consultant teacher, who can serve as an itinerant teacher or as a school-based educational specialist. Consultant teacher programs in the United States (Mackenzie et al. 1970) and Sweden (Juul 1981) are potential models for the special educator as an educational consultant. The consultant teacher provides a direct service to children as well as inservice training for teachers, through consultation on specific classroom problems.

In many instances, the special educator must also serve as an advocate for the handicapped. Implicit in this role is a commitment to the human rights and welfare of the handicapped individual, and the ability to deal personally and professionally with prejudice against the disabled. The advocate role of the special educator requires leadership in multidisciplinary settings and, in particular, in meeting pupil needs that cut across traditional bureaucratic structures.

Handicapped children may require medical, social, or rehabilitative assistance in addition to specialized pedagogical programming. The specialist's role in such situations is unique when compared to that of a regular education teacher, and the provision of such leadership training is a challenge to personnel-preparation programs. Finally, the dissemination and communication of innovative special education methods and techniques can benefit from the increasing availability of communications technology. The packaging of teacher-training programs for transmission via television, satellite, computer, and other media has the dual advantage of reaching a potentially larger audience than is possible with traditional training formats and of improving training through field testing and validation as part of the instructional development process (Thiagarajan et al. 1974).

See also: Concepts of Teacher Education

Bibliography

Becker K P 1979 *Training of Teachers for the Handicapped.* UNESCO, Paris

Birch J W, Reynolds M C 1982 Special education as a profession. *Except. Educ. Q.* 2(4): 1–13

Blackhurst A E 1977 Competency-based special education personnel preparation. In: Kneedler R D, Tarver S G (eds.) 1977 *Changing Perspectives in Special Education.* Merrill, Columbus, Ohio

Blackhurst A E 1981 Noncategorical teacher preparation: Problems and promises. *Except. Child.* 48: 197–205

Brophy J E 1979 Teacher behavior and its effects. *J. Educ. Psychol.* 71: 733–50

Dick W, Watson K, Kaufmann R 1981 Deriving competencies: Consensus versus model building. *Educ. Res.* AERA 10: 5–10

Edelfelt R A 1982 Critical issues in developing teacher centers. *Phi Delta Kappan* 63: 390–93

Engelmann S, Carnine D 1982 *Theory of Instruction.* Irvington, New York

Englert C S 1984 Measuring teacher effectiveness from the teacher's point of view. *Focus Excep. Child.* 17: 1–14

Fink A H (ed.) 1978 *International Perspectives on Future Special Education.* Council for Exceptional Children, Reston, Virginia

Hallahan D P, Kauffman J M 1977 Labels, categories, behaviors: ED, LD, and EMR reconsidered. *J. Spec. Educ.* 11: 139–49

Juul K D 1981 Special education in Europe. In: Kauffman J M, Hallahan D P (eds.) 1981 *Handbook of Special Education.* Prentice-Hall, Englewood Cliffs, New Jersey

Karagianis L D, Nesbit W C 1981 The Warnock report: Britain's preliminary answer to Public Law 94–142. *Except. Child.* 47: 332–36

Kristensen K 1979 *Training Personnel.* UNESCO, Paris

Lane H 1976 *The Wild Boy of Aveyron.* Harvard University Press, Cambridge, Massachusetts

Linton T E 1971 The educateur model: A theoretical monograph. *J. Spec. Educ.* 5: 155–90

Lubovski V I 1979 *Integration of the Handicapped into the Educational and Social Structure.* UNESCO, Paris

Lugo D E 1978 A new alternative for the training of personnel for handicapped children. In: Fink A H (ed.) 1978

McCormick M, Balla D, Zigler E 1975 Resident-care practices in institutions for retarded persons: A cross-institutional, cross-cultural study. *Am. J. Ment. Def.* 80: 1–17

Mackenzie H S, Egner A N, Knight M F et al. 1970 Training consulting teachers to assist elementary teachers in the management and education of handicapped children. *Except. Child.* 37: 137–43

Pascual D M 1979 *Simplified Special Education.* UNESCO, Paris

Putnam R W 1979 Special education: Some cross-national comparisons. *Comp. Educ.* 15: 83–98

Sarason S B, Davidson K, Blatt B 1962 *The Preparation of Teachers: An Unstudied Problem in Education.* Wiley, New York

Semmel M I, Semmel D S 1976 Competency-based teacher education: An overview. *Behav. Disorders* 2(1): 69–89

Smith J (ed.) 1978 *Personnel Preparation and Public Law 94-142: The Map, the Mission and the Mandate.* Educational Resources Center, Bothwyn, Pennsylvania

Stevens R, Rosenhine B 1980 Advances in research on teaching. *Excep. Educ. Q.* 2: 1–9

Tawney J 1980 Explorations in teacher competence. *Teach. Educ. Spec. Educ.* 3: 3

Thiagarajan S, Semmel D S, Semmel M I 1974 *Instructional Development for Training Teachers of Exceptional Children: A Source Book.* Council for Exceptional Children, Reston, Virginia

Thornbury R (ed.) 1973 *Teachers' Centers.* Agathon Press, New York

Vlasova T A 1977 Basic directions and tasks in the further development of scientific research in defectology. *Sov. Educ.* 19: 97–111

Wolfensberger W 1972 *The Principles of Normalization in Human Services.* National Institute on Mental Retardation, Toronto, Ontario

Ysseldyke J E 1973 Diagnostic-prescriptive teaching: The search for aptitude treatment interactions. In: Mann L, Sabatino D A (eds.) 1973 *The First Review of Special Education.* JSE Press, Philadelphia, Pennsylvania

Ysseldyke J E, Algozzine B 1982 *Critical Issues in Special and Remedial Education.* Houghton Mifflin, Boston, Massachusetts

Ysseldyke J E, Salvia J 1974 Diagnostic-prescriptive teaching: Two models. *Except. Child.* 41: 181–85

Zipperlen H R 1975 Normalization. In: Wortes J (ed.) 1975 *Mental Retardation and Developmental Disabilities*, Vol. 7. Brunner/Mazel, New York

Teacher Education for Vocational and Industrial Education

R. B. Hobart

Preparing instructors for vocational and industrial education presents a complex set of problems that have been only partially solved, even in the most developed countries. While these problems include some that are shared with other areas of teacher preparation, they also include others that result from the unique features of industrial and vocational education itself.

This article addresses these problems in the light of prevailing systems of industrial and vocational teacher preparation. It considers the three principal factors that determine the structure and content of those systems, namely, the beliefs the society holds about industrial and vocational teacher preparation, the nature of the students to be taught by such instructors, and the role and responsibilities of the vocational teaching task.

From this consideration, it recommends the essential components of systems that will effectively prepare instructors for industrial and vocational education and describes contemporary developments that are increasing the potential of those systems to meet the demands made upon them. It concludes with recommended research needed to support further such developments.

1. Prevailing Systems of Industrial and Vocational Teacher Preparation

The following analysis seeks to give a general overview of the prevailing systems of industrial and vocational teacher preparation in developed and developing countries. Greater detail can be obtained from various UNESCO publications (UNESCO 1973). This present analysis includes a description of the systems, their content, a comparison between them, the degree to which they meet the need for industrial and vocational teacher preparation, and the institutions in which these systems operate.

1.1 Description of the Systems

There are two distinct systems of industrial and vocational teacher preparation that prevail throughout the world today. The first may be called the preservice system. In this system the preparation and training needed to give qualified teacher status is given before entering the teaching profession. The second may be called the inservice system wherein the preparation and training needed for qualified teacher status is given after a teacher has been appointed to a teaching position and occurs concurrently with the instructor's teaching responsibilities (see *Inservice Teacher Education*).

Most countries throughout the world use a combination of both these systems. However, because of the low rate of pay offered such instructors in comparison to that which can be earned within industry, it is difficult to obtain sufficient instructors through the inservice system of preparation.

1.2 Content of the Systems

In the prevailing systems some or all of the following three components are included:

(a) Preparation that leads to competence in the occupational skills area to be taught (such as plumbing, carpentry, or electronics). This is often called "specialist" or "content" studies.

(b) Preparation that leads to the professional competencies of teaching. This is called "professional" studies.

(c) Preparation that leads to the personal development of the instructor. This is often called "general" or "liberal" studies.

Within the specialist or content component, two aspects are addressed: first, the theoretical knowledge and skills relevant to the occupation to be taught; secondly, the practical application of these knowledge and skills through experience in the occupation itself.

Within the professional component, two areas of competence are developed; first, the professional knowledge and understanding relevant to the task of teaching; secondly, the teaching skills and strategies to be applied within the classroom, laboratory, or workshop.

1.3 Comparison of the Systems

The preservice system of preparation places students directly into courses of study that develop the three components of industrial and vocational teacher preparation described above. These students may have completed between 10 and 12 years of primary and secondary education.

The inservice system of preparation selects instructors from the world of work where they have had some years of experience in applying their specialist knowledge and skills within the relevant occupations. These people are placed immediately into industrial and vocational teaching and then undertake, while fulfilling their teaching responsibilities, courses of varying lengths designed to generate in them professional teaching competencies. These courses may also provide for some updating of their specialist knowledge and skills and a brief "survival" type programme to induct the instructor into teaching.

The essential difference between these two systems is that in the preservice system the theoretical knowledge and skills relevant to the occupation to be taught by the instructor, and the practical experience in applying that knowledge and skills to the relevant occupation, must both be included in the teacher preparation course; whereas in the inservice system, that knowledge, skills, and practical experience have already been developed in the instructor through prior learning and work experience. Thus, in the latter system the teacher preparation course concentrates on the professional studies component and, sometimes, on general studies.

The primary weakness of the preservice system of preparation is in the area of providing genuine and sufficient occupational experience for the instructors in the specialist areas that they are to teach. The strength of this system is in its potential to be more comprehensive and directly pertinent to the instructors' teaching responsibilities.

On the other hand, the strength of the inservice system is that the instructors, if well-selected, have already had comprehensive experience in the world of work and in the occupations that they are to teach. This experience should enable them to be accepted by their students as having considerable authority in their specialist areas, and ensure that their teaching is highly relevant to the contemporary practice of the occupations being taught. The weakness of the inservice system is that the courses tend to be insufficient in both length and content to generate the comprehensive set of teaching competencies necessary for effective and efficient instruction. Such courses may also fail to develop in the instructors a professional identity with industrial and vocational teaching. As a consequence, instructors prepared in this system tend to be ambivalent in their professional identity. They underrate the importance of pedagogical competencies and assume that the knowledge and skills relevant to their occupation are the principal qualifications for their teaching role. Thus, at a conference on the preparation of teachers for vocational and technical education (National Institute for Educational Research 1981), a representative complained of the poor response of industrial and vocational teachers to professional training when it is not compulsory.

1.4 Demand on the Systems

Demand for industrial and vocational teachers throughout the world has substantially increased in recent times. For example, in the United Kingdom the number of full-time teachers engaged in technical and vocational education has increased by more than 1,700 percent since the early 1950s. A similar increase has occurred in the number of part-time teachers (Cantor and Roberts 1979). An even greater increase has occurred in developing countries (Saran 1980).

This dramatic growth has considerably overstressed the instructional systems of industrial and vocational teacher preparation throughout the world, with the result that many such teachers have never received adequate formal training. In the United Kingdom well under half of the full-time staff, and even fewer of the part-time staff, are trained in the sense of having successfully completed a full programme of professional teacher training leading to qualified teacher status (Cantor and Roberts 1979). Similarly, a survey of the situation in the United States deduces that vocational teacher education is not preparing an adequate supply of vocational teachers to meet the country's needs. Further, the training that is given to those teachers is frequently insufficient and would appear to be less than totally successful (Adamsky and Cotrell 1979). In developing countries professional preparation for instructors in industrial and vocational education is even more limited. Therefore, the majority of those instructors have not received the same training which is accepted as necessary for teachers in primary and secondary education.

1.5 Training Institutions

In the United Kingdom and many developing countries, these courses of preparation occur in special training colleges designed for that purpose. In the United States and Australia, they are undertaken in universities and colleges of advanced education, which are general higher education institutions and are not designed specifically for preparing instructors for industrial and vocational education. In other countries, such as Thailand, the preparation, when it does occur, is provided for both in specialist institutions (such as the Institute of Technology and Vocational Education of Thailand) and in general higher education institutions (such as the King Mongkut Institute of Technology).

2. Determinants of Industrial and Vocational Teacher Preparation

The prevailing systems described above have their roots in historical factors, theoretical concepts of teacher preparation, and pragmatic responses to the overwhelming need for industrial and vocational teachers. They have been limited by severe economic constraints, by the numbers and characteristics of the people willing to become instructors, and by a lack of full commitment on the part of governments which has often resulted in piecemeal and inadequate policies for comprehensive vocational teacher preparation. To describe, therefore, the systems that are needed today for a comprehensive preparation it is necessary to consider the three essential factors that shape those systems and determine their structure and content. First, a philosophy of industrial and vocational teacher training that influences the policies of governments for that training. Secondly, the nature of the students of industrial and vocational education. And thirdly, the nature of the task of industrial and vocational teaching.

2.1 Philosophical Considerations

Whilst there are many components in any philosophy of industrial and vocational education, of particular relevance to this article is the relationship, if any, which is believed to exist between instructor preparation and teaching effectiveness (see *Synthesizing Research Evidence*). It would appear that a strong belief in that relationship has not characterized planners in this field.

Industrial and vocational teacher education has grown out of older traditions of apprenticeship or craft training. Such training engenders the belief that the content and skills to be taught are all the instructor needs and that teaching competencies will be developed as a result of the experience of teaching. Thus, industrial and vocational education authorities have been willing to place in classrooms instructors who have no wider qualifications than content knowledge and skills. This practice in essence denies a firm belief in the relationship between the preparation of instructors and their teaching effectiveness.

While there is some measure of uncertainty in this relationship (Gage 1972), there has been sufficient research to indicate that more comprehensive programmes of preparation do tend to increase teaching effectiveness (Adamsky and Cotrell 1979). This belief was strongly asserted in a recent national report in Australia when it stated that the basic quality and effectiveness of any teaching organization is largely determined by the quality of its teachers (Williams 1979). Similarly, an Australian technical and further education commission stated that the need cannot be overstressed for government and nongovernment technical and further education authorities to see the development of teachers as a critical responsibility (Australian Committee on Technical and Further Education 1975). UNESCO has affirmed the same belief by maintaining that good teachers are the necessary prerequisite for excellence in vocational and technical education (UNESCO 1973). This belief leads many to be critical of present systems which reflect an ad hoc approach to, and a superficial provision for, the preparation of these instructors. Thus Swanson (1974) is critical of the lack within the United States of a genuine policy that reflects a serious commitment to a comprehensive preparation system. He maintains that concern for the quality and quantity of the nation's human resources perceived in the context of employability, productivity, and work satisfaction should result in a policy that promotes the opportunity for individuals to adjust, advance, and survive with an optimum quality of life. Vocational teacher preparation has tended not to reflect such a policy.

A similar concern is voiced by Saran (1980) about developing countries when he describes many existing programs of staff development as "peripheral". He advocates the need for an "integral" approach that reflects a genuine belief in the premise that improvement of technical education will largely depend upon teachers' capabilities. This would result in coordinated policies, practices, and procedures that aim to recruit, train, and maintain staff in a way that satisfies both the needs of the individual and those of the organization.

Thus, while a belief in the value of industrial and vocational teacher preparation leads one to advocate a preparation that is comprehensive, developmental, and continuous, systems thus far have tended to reflect models that are task oriented and static.

2.2 The Students in Industrial and Vocational Education

The task of industrial and vocational teaching is shaped, to a large extent, by the nature of the students to be taught and the content and skills relevant to the particular occupation for which the student is being prepared. A comprehensive description of the characteristics of students in industrial and vocational education is given elsewhere. This article considers those characteristics as they impinge upon the preparation needed for the instructors of those students.

Students in industrial and vocational education the world over have some dominant characteristics that must be accommodated in the teaching–learning process if it is to meet the challenge of preparing people for a world of work that is subject to increasingly rapid technological change. These characteristics, and their implications for the preparation of instructors are:

(a) The student population as a whole has a broad range of learning abilities. The wider the range of such abilities the more need there is for industrial and vocational education to apply learning systems that cater for individual differences. Instructors must develop skills in applying teaching strategies that accommodate this wide range of individual differences among their students.

(b) Many students in industrial and vocational education have previously experienced difficulty or failure in learning that results in the students having low levels of self-confidence in learning. Such students approach their learning with some degree of apprehension and need systems that encourage the restoration and development of self-confidence. Industrial and vocational teachers, therefore, need skill in determining the learning confidence among their students, and in applying teaching strategies that result in their students developing greater confidence in learning.

(c) A corollary of the above is that these students may also have a low level of skill in learning how to learn. Yet, as the rate of change in occupations increases, such students must undertake a greater amount of learning on the job for skill upgrading and development. This learning is frequently self-initiated and self-directed. Thus, their instructors must assist them to develop learning-how-to-learn skills, and use teaching strategies that generate these outcomes.

(d) While the academic potential of these students varies greatly, for most of them it is lower than that of students engaged in higher education. Thus, highly verbalized and abstract teaching is not suitable for such students. Industrial and vocational instructors must be able to apply teaching strategies that make learning as concrete as possible and relate it clearly to the practical areas within their courses. Otherwise, the theoretical areas of these courses are not applied effectively to practical learning or to the students' occupational performance.

(e) Industrial and vocational education incorporates both full-time and part-time students. Part-time students are engaged in the work force and bring that experience into the learning process. Such students can be critical of the relevance of their learning and the degree to which it reflects the real world of work. Their instructors need the knowledge and experience to relate their teaching to the world of work, and the opportunity and ability to keep up-to-date.

(f) Many part-time students in industrial and vocational education undertake their courses in the evening. Such students, because of fatigue, less time for learning, and distractions from other life responsibilities, need to learn in systems that generate high levels of motivation and accommodate their variance in time and opportunity to apply themselves to the learning task over the length of their courses. Instructors must be able to manage their students and the learning process so that inevitable variations in application by any one student do not prevent that student from ultimately being successful in his or her courses.

(g) Students engaged in industrial and vocational education vary greatly in their ages. Some are adolescents in their initial preparation for the world of work. Many are adults who are changing their work skills or females reentering the work force. An increasing number are retired from the world of work and are pursuing interests for leisure. Thus instructors must be capable of selecting and using strategies that are equally suitable for adolescents, adults, and the aged.

(h) Many industrial and vocational education students come from lower socioeconomic backgrounds where the attitudes that encourage learning in the home context, and the resources that support it, will be limited. Instructors need to use teaching strategies that motivate, support, and encourage learning and the system will need to provide for considerable learning resources. Instructors will also need to assist such students in developing skills in the use of these resources for libraries, self-paced learning materials, laboratories, and workshops give very little support to learning unless students have skills and confidence in using them.

(i) An increasing number of students in industrial and vocational education are females in traditionally male courses, and handicapped people in mainstreaming programmes. Instructors need to develop the attitudes and skills that support and encourage such students and ensure the level of success that reflects their abilities.

The characteristics of industrial and vocational students discussed above require from instructors and from learning systems strategies that are flexible, cater for individual differences, highlight relevance, focus on the practical applications of the learning to the occupation, accommodate variance over time in application by the student to the learning task, encourage learning self-confidence, and develop skills in learning how to learn. Learning systems also need to be supported by appropriate resources and strategies that develop in the students skills in using those resources.

2.3 The Task of Industrial and Vocational Teaching

The actual task of industrial and vocational teaching has some important features that clearly differentiate it from teaching in other areas of education. These features must determine to a major degree the preparation given to instructors in industrial and vocational education.

The first salient feature is that the knowledge and skills of instructors soon become out of date. In developed countries this occurs as a result of rapid technological change. Technology has broadened the range of skills needed by the work force, removed some occupations altogether, created new ones, and changed significantly the set of competencies required for existing occupations. This rate of change is likely to continue and indeed to increase over the coming decades.

In developing countries this problem is compounded by the fact that primitive as well as modern technologies coexist. This mixture creates problems for manpower trainers as a larger variety of needs have to be satisfied. Further, such countries tend to be at various stages of transition from adopting and adapting technological know-how from developed countries or using and maintaining imported equipment to evolving their own technology and producing their own equipment and machinery. This increases the problem of the knowledge and skills of instructors being outdated.

A means of addressing this problem is that of providing continuing education and work experience for instructors. There are, however, a number of difficulties encountered in doing this. These include: (a) the cost of releasing the instructor for significant continuing education; (b) obtaining a satisfactory placement within industry that will significantly increase the instructor's knowledge and skills (the more out of date the instructor is the greater the difficulty in finding an employer that can productively use the instructor within his or her occupation); (c) replacing the instructor while he or she is undertaking industrial experience; and (d) identifying programmes of study that are suitable for renewing the knowledge and skills of industrial and vocational teachers. In developing countries vocational teaching resources tend to be stretched to the limit in providing basic courses. Appropriate human and material resources are not available to mount the more sophisticated programmes of study that would be appropriate for upgrading the knowledge and skills of industrial and vocational instructors. Even in developed countries, many such programmes tend to be only marginally relevant.

Not only is technology changing at a rapid pace, but the organizational structure of the world of work is changing significantly both in developed and developing countries. Demands for worker participation and industrial democracy and complaints about alienation and credibility gaps have tended to challenge the relevance of educational curricula to the needs of a person living in an increasingly complex world of work. Debate has ensued concerning the need to include content that gives the student a greater understanding of the economic, political, and social factors within the country. These forces make the task of effective industrial and vocational teaching more difficult, and the preparation needed to produce such instructors more extensive and comprehensive.

Within industrial and vocational education there is a strong movement today to supply special programmes of admissions, training, remedial work, and alternative programmes for persons who have been previously discriminated against. These include minority groups, handicapped persons, and the culturally disadvantaged. In addition, increasing attention has been given to eliminating sex stereotyping in occupational training. Obviously this has significant implications for the selection and preparation of instructors.

The task of industrial and vocational teaching has a greater component of management in it than other teaching areas. Such instructors must organize and manage workshops, laboratories, the distribution of tools, supplies, and other equipment, and maintain these at appropriate levels of efficiency. They must also manage their safe use in the teaching–learning process. Allied to these management skills are the administrative skills of budgeting and record keeping that many instructors need to possess. These management skills must be developed during the preparation of people for such teaching.

A significant component of the preparation of young people for the world of work is directed towards the development of appropriate attitudes that allow them to function effectively within that arena. Attitudes of honesty and loyalty to the employer must be developed along with those that support safe practice in occupations, maximize the productivity of employees, and encourage cooperation in work situations. Industrial and vocational instructors need competencies in fostering these attitudes in their students as well as in the teaching of knowledge and skills. They also need skills in the assessment of these three areas of learning.

If industrial and vocational instructors are to be effective they must establish and maintain close relationships with commerce and industry—with the world of work for which they are preparing their students. Thus, a significant component of their task is that of public relations; relating effectively with industry, employers, unions, professional associations, and government bodies. These skills are not only required with respect

to the effectiveness of programmes of cooperative education, but also with respect to counselling and advising students in matters relating to their careers. The development of these skills must be provided for in the preparation of such instructors.

Some industrial and vocational instructors must use trade calculations and trade science in their teaching. However, knowledge in these areas may be limited, and for those whose preparation is inservice, early provision must be made in the teacher education course for the strengthening of such knowledge and skills.

The range of courses that is offered by industrial and vocational education is so wide, and the differences among them so significant that some have claimed that there is no such thing as industrial and vocational education. Rather, it is argued that there are many industrial and vocational educations—distributive education, agricultural education, vocational education, technical education and so on. Industrial and vocational teacher education courses must cater for these differences through core curricula and individualized learning paths.

Industrial and vocational education is an expensive business. Thus, the response has been an increased emphasis on accountability and the demonstration of cost effectiveness. Programme performance budgeting has been introduced in which the cost of programmes is linked directly and precisely to programme objectives. Cost–benefit analyses have been undertaken in order to demonstrate programme benefits to the community. Such accountability has direct implications for the knowledge and skills needed by instructors to meet their role, and therefore for the preparation they must be given to fulfil that role.

3. Preparation Needed in the Light of the Determinants

A recent conference that included representatives from 15 major countries recommended the following conclusions for the preparation of instructors for industrial and vocational education (National Institute for Education Research 1981):

(a) All industrial and vocational teachers must be qualified in their subject areas and be trained as teachers.

(b) Industrial and vocational teachers require a programme of teacher preparation that should include specialization in terms of each subject discipline and teaching methodology.

(c) The status and quality of the programmes of teacher preparation for vocational and technical education must not be inferior to any other form of teacher preparation.

(d) Authorities responsible for teacher preparation must ensure that teacher trainers should have a sound knowledge of industrial and vocational education, should be knowledgeable in the areas of adolescent and adult learning, have had practical experience in industry or commerce, and have teaching qualifications and experience plus the opportunity to improve teaching skills.

(e) Students to be prepared for industrial and vocational teaching should have completed full secondary education, or its equivalent, be qualified at least up to craftsperson level, and have had relevant work experience, where practicable.

(f) Students to be prepared for technical teaching should be qualified at degree level or above, and have had relevant work experience, where practicable.

(g) The curriculum of teacher preparation for industrial and vocational teachers should provide for pedagogical studies, vocational and technical subjects, and general and liberal studies.

(h) Pedagogical studies for industrial and vocational teacher preparation should include general teaching methodologies; specialist subject teaching methodologies; educational psychology, with emphasis on adolescent and adult learning; curriculum design and development, student evaluation and assessment techniques; classroom, workshop, and laboratory management techniques; practice teaching; educational technology; history/philosophy/development of industrial and vocational education; and comparative studies of industrial and vocational education.

(i) Industrial and vocational subject studies should have a proper proportion between theory and practice, include on-the-job training, be integrated with special methodology, and be relevant to current practice in industry, agriculture, or commerce.

(j) General and liberal studies should include communication skills, moral and ethical studies, social sciences, natural sciences including mathematics, and extracurricular programmes.

(k) Industrial and vocational teachers should have opportunities for their continuing staff development. This process might include leave for further industrial experience; intra- and inter-institutional programmes with periods of teaching in other institutions and teacher exchange programmes; seminars and conferences; overseas programmes; access to further education studies; opportunities for the sharing of ideas, innovations, and problems of industrial and vocational education systems; incentives for teachers to upgrade themselves through salary, tenure, and promotion prospects; and opportunities for research, particularly into the teacher's specialist subject area.

(l) Minimum academic qualifications should be a degree (or its equivalent) for technical teachers, and a certificate or diploma for vocational teachers.

These awards should be from approved institutions of higher education. This should not prevent the employment of those who have exceptional experience and ability but who do not have these qualifications.

(m) Strong government support should be given to supply the resources needed. In particular a greater allocation of resources for additional staffing in industrial and vocational institutions to allow for teachers to be released for staff training and development; improved conditions of employment including salaries for industrial and vocational teachers to be at least equal to what they would be qualified to receive in industry or commerce, and class contact time reduced to allow for staff development as well as lesson preparation; and sufficient staff and facilities for teacher-training institutions.

4. Contemporary Developments in Industrial and Vocational Teacher Preparation

There are at least three primary developments that have occurred in recent years to change the structure and content of the preparation of instructors in industrial and vocational education. These are: a concentration on ascertaining the competencies needed by such instructors and the designing of programmes that generate those competencies; the development of performance-based teacher education (PBTE) with the construction of modularized systems of learning to implement this form of teacher preparation; and the application to such systems of mastery learning.

4.1 Competency Profiles

An occupational analysis approach has been taken to identify the competencies needed by instructors in industrial and vocational education. This procedure involves conducting a search of the literature; asking teachers working in the area to describe what they do, what they think they should be doing, and what additional skills they believe they need; and asking teacher educators, supervisors, and administrators to describe and verify what teachers do and/or should be doing.

This procedure has resulted in lists of competencies ranging from 2 to 2,700 depending upon how precisely the competencies are defined. The most influential work in this area was undertaken by Cotrell (1972) and has resulted in the development of 100 performance-based vocational teacher education modules for the preparation of instructors in industrial and vocational education.

4.2 Performance-based Teacher Education

Performance-based teacher education is an approach to teacher preparation in which the teacher is required to demonstrate essential teaching tasks in an actual teaching situation. Actual performance of the tasks ensures that the teacher has not only the knowledge required, but also the ability to perform the competencies that are essential to successful teaching. The essential characteristics of this form of teacher preparation are: the programme is designed to bring about learner achievement of attainable competencies (or performance goals) which have been specifically stated in advance of instruction, and evidence of the learner's achievement is obtained through assessment of learner performance, applying criteria stated in advance, in terms of expected levels of accomplishment under specified conditions. This is used to guide the individual learner's efforts, to determine his or her rate of progress and completion of the programme, and, ideally, to evaluate the efficacy of the instructional system and add to the general body of knowledge undergirding the instructional process.

These characteristics imply that: instruction is individualized to a considerable extent; learning experiences are guided by feedback; the programme as a whole has the characteristics of a system; emphasis is on exit requirements and not on entrance qualifications; the learner is considered to have completed the programme only when he or she has demonstrated the required level of performance; the instructional programme is not time based in units of fixed duration; the programme is to a considerable extent field centered to enhance realism; there is a broad base for decision making—for logistical reasons as well as the requirements of democracy and professionalism; instruction is often modularized and uses protocol and training materials to achieve flexibility and realism within the institutional setting; professional preparation is career-long which is inherent in the concept of the professional teacher; and a research component is often built into the programme to enhance the knowledge base on which the profession depends.

Many PBTE programmes for the preparation of instructors in industrial and vocational education have been implemented in North America, and a description of these is given by Norton (Norton et al. 1978). Saran (1980) has pioneered such a programme in a major technical teacher-training institute in India. National research was undertaken throughout Australia into the implementation and evaluation of performance-based vocational teacher education (Hobart and Harris 1980). A plea for reforms along the lines of PBTE in the preparation of instructors for industrial and vocational education is given by Taylor (1978) for the United Kingdom.

4.3 Mastery Learning

An essential part of the performance-based vocational teacher education model is the application of the principles of mastery learning. These principles require that students continue to apply themselves to the learning process until they can demonstrate a clearly defined standard of performance of behaviourally stated objectives. The evaluation of this performance is criterion referenced—that is, it is based on an objective set of criteria determined by the performance standards required in the occupation itself, and not on a comparison with the performance of other students within the training course.

Student progress, therefore, is not related to time but rather to the attainment and demonstration of stated performances. These principles make provision for students to progress at their own pace according to the prior achievements and experiences they bring into the learning process, the degree of motivation they have for learning, and the time and resources they have to give to that learning (Ryan and Schmidt 1979) (see *Mastery Learning Models*).

5. Research Needed in Industrial and Vocational Teacher Preparation

As a result of an extensive review of the research undertaken in vocational teacher education, Adamsky and Cotrell (1979) concluded that research in this field remains sparse overall. They maintain that there has not been much progress towards establishing vocational teacher education as an intellectual field within the broader areas of educational research. They recommend that research should be undertaken to determine the relationship between occupational and pedagogical competence and student achievement; establish minimum standards for occupational and pedagogical competence; develop standardized occupational competency tests for all vocational education teaching specialists; establish minimum standards for occupational experience based on the varied quality of such experience; determine if either the programme approval or certification processes have any effects on system output; develop and test various models potentially capable of predicting the future needs for vocational teachers; determine the past and present holding pattern in vocational teacher education; develop and test various models potentially capable of recruiting an appropriate number of vocational teachers; determine the characteristics of vocational teacher educators; adopt and test the effectiveness of the PBTE programmes compared with operating conventional programmes.

6. Conclusions

As can be seen from the above, preparing instructors for industrial and vocational education is a complex task with many determining factors that have scarcely been addressed in either developing or developed countries. Unless these factors are more thoroughly applied in systems of such preparation, it is evident that industrial and vocational education will suffer from inadequate teaching effectiveness and learning systems that are less than appropriate for generating outcomes relevant to the contemporary world of work.

See also: Concepts of Teacher Education

Bibliography

Adamsky R A, Cotrell C J 1979 *Vocational Teacher Education: A Review of the Research*. National Center for Research in Vocational Education, Columbus, Ohio

Australian Committee on Technical and Further Education (ACOTAFE) 1975 *TAFE in Australia: Report on Needs in Technical and Further Education*. Australian Government Publishing Service, Canberra

Cantor L M, Roberts I F 1979 *Further Education Today: A Critical Review*. Routledge and Kegan Paul, London

Cotrell C J 1972 *Model Criteria for Vocational and Technical Teacher Education: Report No. V—General Objectives, Set 11*. National Center for Vocational and Technical Education, Columbus, Ohio

Gage N L 1972 *Teacher Effectiveness and Teacher Education: The Search for a Scientific Basis*. Pacific, Palo Alto, California

Hobart R B, Harris R McL 1980 *Mystery or Mastery: An Evaluation of Performance-Based Teacher Education for TAFE Teachers in Australia*. South Australian College of Advanced Education, Adelaide

National Institute for Educational Research (NIER) 1981 *Regional Workshop on the Preparation of Teachers for Vocational and Technical Education*. NIER, Tokyo

Norton R E, Harrington L G, Gill J 1978 *Performance-Based Teacher Education: The State of the Art*. American Association for Vocational Instructional Materials (AAVIM), Athens

Ryan D W, Schmidt M 1979 *Mastery Learning: Theory, Research and Implementation*. Ontario Institute for Studies in Education, Toronto, Ontario

Saran Y 1980 *Technical Teacher Training: Towards a New Initiative*. Colombo Plan Staff College for Technician Education, Singapore

Swanson G I 1974 *The Preparation of Teachers for Vocational Education: Project Baseline Supplemental Report*. North Arizona University, Flagstaff, Arizona

Taylor W 1978 *Research and Reform in Teacher Education*. NFER–Nelson, Windsor

UNESCO 1973 *Technical and Vocational Teacher Education and Training*. UNESCO, Paris

Williams B R 1979 *Education, Training and Employment*. Australian Government Publishing Service, Canberra

Teacher Education for Higher Education

A. N. Main

In most parts of the world the training of school teachers is a preservice activity which is normally compulsory and is organized by a nationally accredited body. By contrast, the training of university and college teachers is more likely to be inservice, voluntary, and left to local initiative. Only in Eastern Europe is the training of tertiary teachers centrally organized and subject to public examination. In some countries, attempts are made at a form of preservice training by organizing courses in teaching methods for graduate students and teaching assistants, but this is limited in scope and effect. It would seem that in most countries institutions of higher education employ a great number of criteria for the selection and promotion of faculty members. Teaching skill is not universally regarded as a major criterion, and as a result training for teaching is not highly developed.

Teaching skill is often included as part of a wider training or development programme. Such a faculty development scheme might include components of instructional development (diagnosis of skill, training in new and traditional teaching methods, curriculum development), personal development (career planning, counselling, interpersonal skills training), and organizational development (managerial development, problem solving, decision making). Training courses are a more integral part of instructional development than of the other two processes, particularly for more inexperienced teachers. However, advanced and specialized courses may combine the training of teaching or curriculum skills with elements of management and career development. Similarly, the organizational development policy of an institution may allow for advanced courses in teaching methods and the management of instruction. Beyond the introductory level, it is more difficult to separate the different strands of an individual faculty member's training and development.

There is no standard pattern or normal length of training for faculty members anywhere in the world. The form of training is subject to the requirements of individual employing institutions, and in many cases to the personal interests, attitudes, and motivations of individual teachers. In Scandinavia, Eastern Europe, and Central America schemes have been drawn up for minimal patterns of training, but progress beyond that minimum is largely a matter of individual choice.

1. Preservice Courses

There are few genuine preservice courses for tertiary teachers. The courses which exist are not generally used as a screening device for the selection of future faculty members in any formal way. They are given to teaching assistants or graduate students who are already in the higher education system, with the primary aim of improving the tutorial or instructor skills which they are paid to perform. A secondary aim may be to contribute to the future quality of teaching by faculty members, but only in the most general way, since a large proportion of permanent teachers are recruited from the ranks of graduate students and assistants.

Such courses are more common in North America than in Europe, Asia, or Africa, probably because American and Canadian universities make more use of paid assistance by untenured teachers and instructors. In the United States, the Faculty Internship Programme dates back to the 1950s, and has typically consisted of extended weekly seminar courses for groups of assistants with a common teaching interest. These courses have included an orientation to the institution and to the teaching profession, training in techniques for effective instruction, and practical supervision of the planning and execution of teaching tasks.

Variations of this basic pattern are evident in Canada where there is a growing concern for the skills and job satisfaction of teaching assistants. Several universities and colleges have set up annual residential teaching institutes, credit courses on teaching methods and theory, or summer schools for graduate students. In many instances these are supported by resource exchanges and self-instructional materials available throughout the whole academic year.

The German Democratic Republic offers an example of a more structured training for graduate assistants. Training in university pedagogics is an indispensable prerequisite for teaching staff. The first stage of training towards the *facultas docendi* examinations takes place during research studies and in the course of a four-year assistantship. It consists of a formal course of lectures and seminars, practice teaching, and sharing in the classes of senior staff. Those who complete the course are awarded a certificate and can proceed to more advanced training towards their teaching qualification.

2. Introductory Training

The organization of formal courses on teaching methods is a model based on the assumption that there are valid theories of teaching and sound practices in higher education which can be passed on in a relatively didactic way. It is a model which is found in its most developed form in the universities of the United Kingdom. As a result of the work of British advisers, it is also being employed in West Africa, India, Malaysia, and some parts of the Arab world.

Courses in the United Kingdom typify provision for new faculty in many parts of the world. They tend to be of a very general nature, and relatively short in duration (anything from three days to two weeks). The emphasis has traditionally been on teaching and examining techniques rather than on course planning, student learning, or on the wider responsibilities of the teacher as scholar, manager, or counsellor. Within this emphasis, there has generally been a concentration on the more traditional teaching methods. Lecturing, discussion, and laboratory teaching are given much more time than more innovatory methods such as individualized learning, simulation techniques, or computer-aided instruction. The emphasis has been very much on the improvement of lecturing techniques, the development of skill in organizing and conducting tutorials, the practice of assessment techniques, and knowledge of audiovisual aids. Further, it is clear from the reports of course organizers that the methods used for training are usually lecturing and discussions. Thus, the objectives, methods, and content of training courses all reflect concern for traditional teaching methods and skills.

Within the United Kingdom context, this may be because courses are often designed and staffed by volunteer faculty members who have themselves no formal training for the task, and therefore do not feel confident enough to innovate. In some instances however there is a conscious policy of confining introductory training courses to providing "survival kit" techniques, in the hope that more novel teaching and learning methods can be encouraged later during advanced or specialized training. In many institutions there is as yet no planned link between introductory and postexperience training.

This basic description cannot be generalized to all elementary training courses. Several centres in the United Kingdom have followed others in Europe, North America, Australasia, and the Middle East in developing a more practical and less didactic introductory training. The trends throughout the world are towards five substantial areas of change.

2.1 The Practicum

In the Federal Republic of Germany and Sweden, efforts are made to place new faculty members in teaching situations which they share with more experienced teachers, so that an apprenticeship role is served, culminating in considerable periods of monitored practice teaching. Such practical placement is interspersed with short modules of pedagogical instruction and periods of evaluation. In the Netherlands, this sort of exercise is enhanced by training students to contribute constructively to the induction and assessment of the new teacher.

2.2 Mediated Self-confrontation

In Israel and the Federal Republic of Germany, new faculty are trained in methods of observing and reflecting on their own teaching and learning experiences. The use of video and sound equipment for self-review and self-confrontation is coupled with peer and student feedback. This form of training is normally carried out in situ—in the normal classroom situation rather than in an artificial educational centre or unit.

2.3 Peer Teaching

In the United States and Sweden, introductory training has in the past been coordinated by specialist educational development officers. The trend in these countries, which is now spreading elsewhere, is for this coordination to become largely a management function, and for many of the activities on courses to be opportunities for the participants to learn from each other, rather than from "experts". This has demanded a greater use of group methods and self-learning resources than in the past.

2.4 Workshop Modules

Concentrated training courses are becoming less common, and are being replaced by regular series of related workshops. New teachers in Australia, Canada, and South Africa are encouraged to attend a wide variety of training modules over the first year or two of apprenticeship, rather than one lengthy course at the very beginning of their career.

2.5 Course Content

There is a shift away from an earlier emphasis (most marked in the period 1965 to 1975) on teaching methods and teaching aids, towards a concern for student learning and course planning. In countries such as New Zealand and Switzerland, this seems to be a result of a change in the role and function of educational technologists. In some developing countries it may be a conscious attempt to devise new strategies for new and adaptable educational systems.

3. Planned Development

These changes in the form and intention of introductory training apply also to more advanced training. In general, advanced and specialized training is characterized by more flexible, practical, and individualized arrangements.

In some countries there is no clear distinction made between introductory and advanced training, the two being seen as integrated parts of a consciously planned programme. Such planned schemes are generally of two types: those which are sequential and relatively highly structured, and those which are modular in nature.

3.1 Sequential Courses

Two examples can be drawn from Sweden and from the German Democratic Republic. In both instances training is based on a national plan and is monitored centrally.

The Swedish scheme consists of a series of courses organized inside and outside the teaching department of the faculty member. In the early years of a teaching career, there are basic introductory and orientation courses held outside of the department, and a series of tutoring and seminar activities within the department designed to build up a basic knowledge of educational principles and practices. At various stages, as the faculty member gains teaching experience, these activities lead into more advanced courses on education development, learning theories, educational policy, and methodology. The last of these elements is specifically related to the teacher's own subject or discipline and involves extensive practical activity. The whole programme over eight years is intended to be monitored, evaluated, and coordinated in a unified manner.

The national training plan in the German Democratic Republic is designed to produce accredited teachers for tertiary education. After taking the introductory certificate, new teachers continue with duties as assistants whilst attending a formal course of lectures and seminars. During this course they also continue to audit the classes of senior faculty members and to subject themselves to practical teaching criticism. The course culminates in a three-part examination: a complex oral examination of the knowledge of pedagogics and theory of education; a practical teaching examination; and an essay related to the candidate's teaching work. The examination is a requirement for qualification for a teaching post in higher education.

3.2 Modular Courses

These contrast somewhat with the foregoing. They are designed to offer faculty members a wide choice of activities during any academic year. It is possible to undertake modules in almost any order, and it is also possible to repeat the same module in successive years. In most modular schemes no distinction is made between modules designed for new teachers and those for more experienced faculty.

One of the best known examples is the programme of minicourses offered by Macquarie University in Australia. Each minicourse is designed to achieve a specific objective (see *Minicourses*). It is predesigned and self-contained, and aims to emphasize professional skills that have been identified by participants as meeting some immediate need. Each module stresses the link between the training situation and the actual work situation. At present more than 50 separate minicourses are offered each year.

The Far West Laboratory for Educational Research and Development at Berkeley, California, also produces minicourses for commercial purposes. These consist of self-instructional workshops or laboratory packages, each designed to improve a specific teaching skill. Such developments can augment or replace other forms of training for faculty members.

4. Advanced Courses

Once a tertiary teacher has gained some experience and requires training beyond the introductory level, there are several avenues open.

4.1 Full-time Courses

In the United States more than 30 universities now offer a Doctor of Arts degree programme as an alternative to the Ph.D. as an entry into advanced study and teaching. Such a programme offers extensive teaching practice, curriculum development, and innovation and educational skills courses, alongside scholarly work in a discipline. It allows for inservice development as well as early career training in educational methods.

An example of an advanced course undertaken on release from normal duties is the M.A. in Curriculum Development in Higher Education at the University of

Sussex, UK. It is aimed at those who may become educational development consultants at departmental or institutional level. The course combines elements of cooperative problem solving with group discussion, tutorially supported project work, and a period of field work in the participant's home institution.

4.2 Part-time Courses

Many of the full-time courses in various countries are also offered on a part-time basis, but there are also courses specifically designed for part-time learning. In these, the periods of normal teaching between course meetings are deliberately used to evaluate course outcomes. One example is the Diploma in Education at Monash, Australia, largely held in evenings over two years of study, covering methods and practice of teaching, institutions in tertiary education, and students in tertiary institutions. The University of Montreal has a part-time modular programme which does not lead to the award of a diploma.

4.3 Self-learning

A number of institutions now prepare self-instructional material for the training of experienced faculty. A recent innovation is the coordinated distance-learning programme for tertiary teachers, an example of which is the M.Sc., M.Phil., and Ph.D. in Practice of Higher Education based at the University of Surrey, UK.

4.4 National and Regional Activities

Since some subject-based training activities benefit from economies of scale, several countries have stimulated courses and workshops on a cooperative basis between institutions. The Committee of Principals of the Universities of South Africa have sponsored several such activities involving two or more institutions. Until recently the Ontario Universities Programme for Instructional Development organized provincial training courses. The Steering Committee for Staff Development in Scottish Universities now has an ambitious programme of national courses and workshops.

4.5 International Courses

The exchange of ideas and experience between senior faculty members in several countries has been brought about by the organization of courses and workshops (as opposed to conferences) on an international scale. To date, the countries most active in this respect have been Sweden, Thailand, Canada, and the United Kingdom.

5. Specialized Courses

There exist two basic forms of specialized course. One of these is in terms of professional specialization. An example of this might be the courses on communication and cooperation in engineering education in Aachen, Federal Republic of Germany, where teachers of engineering develop the skills which are appropriate to team work in engineering practice as well as in tertiary teaching and learning. There are many examples throughout the world of this joint approach between professional practice and pedagogy, the most notable being in the areas of management education and medicine.

A second form of specialization is in specific skill areas. The University of Toronto has a course based on gestalt therapy principles, designed to improve teachers' ability to give feedback and support to students. An advanced course is offered by staff at McMaster University in Ontario on the teaching of problem-solving skills; the University of Strathclyde, UK, offers short courses on the development of study skills; and the University of Tasmania carries out training in relaxation and counselling for tertiary teachers. The range and number of such specialist courses is very wide, and would merit a directory of its own. No such index at present exists on a national or an international scale.

6. Other Concerns

Much of what has been described in previous sections applies equally well to university, polytechnic, technical institute, and higher level college faculty members in most countries of the world. The provision available for training encompasses one or more of the features outlined. In many countries, however, there is concern about the training of the teaching staff of colleges of education or teacher-training institutes. It is often assumed that, since such colleges generally recruit to their staff persons previously trained as school teachers, no further training is needed. Many authorities now argue that since college teaching and school teaching differ in many crucial respects, such an assumption is not valid. Surveys show that teacher trainers are less likely than other tertiary teachers to receive advanced or specialized training.

There is now also a growing concern for the training of those who have an institutional responsibility for faculty training or development. At present this is done through voluntary exchange of ideas at conferences, rather than through formal courses or workshops. Some beginnings are being made in this direction in Sweden, Australia, and the United Kingdom, but there is little of a substantial nature to report at the present moment.

It may be worth concluding with one observation about the pattern of training worldwide. Introductory training for tertiary teachers is generally recognized by, if not organized by, a national agency. On the other hand, in few countries is there any coordination of advanced and specialized training, which often owes its existence to the initiatives of individuals or institutions. It may be that coordination at this level will be a development of the last two decades of the twentieth century.

Bibliography

Bass R K, Lumsden D B 1978 *Instructional Development: The State of the Art.* Collegiate Publishing, Columbus, Ohio

Commonwealth Secretariat 1978 *Improving University Teaching: A Survey of Programmes in Commonwealth Countries.* Commonwealth Secretariat, London

Main A N 1985 *Educational Staff Development.* Croom Helm, London

Rhodes D, Hounsell D (eds.) 1980 *Staff Development for the 1980s: International Perspectives.* Institute for Research and Development in Post-compulsory Education, University of Lancaster, Lancaster

Teather D C B (ed.) 1979 *Staff Development in Higher Education: An International Review and Bibliography.* Kogan Page, London

Teacher Education for Adult Education

C. Duke

Teacher education for adult education means courses for adult education personnel, including industrial, commercial, and governmental training staff and other adult, continuing, and nonformal education functionaries, to perform their duties better. Personnel may be full-time, part-time, or voluntary. Teacher education may be preservice and accredited, but academic education in adult education typically follows work experience. The larger part of teacher education takes inservice short-course forms.

Different views are held about the desirability of formal professional training and accreditation, which are thought to contradict adult education traditions and values, including voluntarism, and equality between teacher and taught. Universities play a central role in teaching leading adult educators. In some countries teachers' colleges and special centres are important. Most teacher education for adult education is provided by employer organizations and adult education agencies in the form of short courses. Courses vary in content and skill areas but there is emerging a consensus which finds expression in the content of graduate programmes in a number of countries.

Congruence between methods of teacher education and good adult education practice is stressed. Provision is inadequate to meet demand, and there are different views about where priorities lie. Despite close links between adult and school-oriented teacher education and educational provision in some countries, it is likely that a degree of separation, with distinct philosophy and methodology, will generally be sustained.

1. Definition and Scope

Any teaching intended to enhance the capacity of others to teach, or assist the learning of, adults is considered teacher education for adult education. The term adult education has various connotations: at one extreme it embraces all forms of education of those considered adult by their society by any means and for any purposes; in some countries it has more specific connotations, such as basic, remedial education or literacy teaching for adults; and in several Western societies it refers to a particular tradition of liberal education for adults not related to their employment. Other terms often used inaccurately as alternatives, without precise meaning, include continuing education, nonformal education and, in certain contexts, extramural or extension studies and community education; the term recurrent education is sometimes used as if to mean adult education but is properly restricted to a policy or strategy for educational provision. Industrial, commercial, and other training is included.

The term teacher education is seldom used in relation to adult education, the practice being to speak of training of adult educators or staff, or professional development. Teachers of adults and others working in the field of adult education such as policy makers and administrators tend to prefer other terms over teacher, among them tutor, facilitator, or animator (*animateur*). Trainer is commonly used in the vocational training sector and other terms are used in different settings, such as lecturer, counsellor, and catalyst or change agent. All come within the scope of teacher education for adult education.

Other facets of the management and practice of adult education impinge upon teacher training and staff development, especially selection and recruitment of personnel and the status and reward systems of adult educators, but are beyond the scope of teacher education as such. Although training carries different connotations from education, and the difference is a subject of academic analysis by adult educators, there is no agreed and practised distinction; teacher education and teacher training are at present interchangeable as terms in adult education. However, universities tend to use education to refer to academic graduate programmes and they and other agencies to prefer training for professionally oriented and especially short-course teaching of adult educators and training personnel.

2. The Adult Educator's Training Needs

There is a widely acknowledged, pressing need to improve the teaching of adult educators, but there are difficulties and uncertainties concerning the way of defining and meeting this need. The systematization, regulation and control found in regular, school-oriented teacher education is lacking, and is unlikely to come into being. The 1972 UNESCO International Conference on Adult Education described mobilizing and training sufficient professional personnel as the biggest challenge facing adult education in the 1970s. The UNESCO Recommendation on the Development of Adult Education (1976) was very general and unspecific: "training for adult education should, as far as practicable, include all those aspects of skill, knowledge, understanding, and personal attitude which are relevant to the various functions undertaken, taking into account the general background against which adult education takes place. By integrating these aspects with each other, training should itself be a demonstration of sound adult education practice." Countries strong in the liberal (non-vocational) tradition, such as the United Kingdom and others sharing that tradition, and the Scandinavian countries, produce many statements to the effect that adult education training is a crucial but neglected area. The need is also recognized as a matter of urgency by countries attempting massive social or economic development through adult education: India in its National Adult Education Programme; China in its quest for the "four modernizations".

The "great tradition" of liberal adult education, as it is called in the United Kingdom, Australia, and elsewhere, emphasizes the importance of certain values, purposes, and personal qualities, as well as the part-time and voluntaristic traditions, all of which present problems for the training of adult educators. It is disputable whether many of the personal qualities extolled among teachers of adults can be systematically taught, rather than being either inherited or acquired through experience and maturation. The emphasis upon values, and on congruence between what is taught and what is practised in teacher education, also has implications for methods of teacher education. A 1979 British conference working document on new directions for adult education illustrates this: it prefers the term staff to professional development as being wider and less status seeking, and insists that staff development should axiomatically be an example of good adult education practice. Among principles enunciated, adult education training should be: a transaction between equals; entirely free from compulsion; unrelated to career advancement; unencumbered by examination, grading, and accreditation; open; and a "self-transforming learning system" inspired by "disciplined ad hocery" (as well as being vertically and horizontally integrated and communicating an awareness of politics and of socio-economic milieu). Belief in participation, and the approach to teaching for social change expounded by Paulo Freire, similarly provide directions and suggest prohibitions for methods of teaching adult educators. The value system shared by many adult educators is suspicious of or inimical to any professionalization of adult education which suggests exclusiveness, elitism,

and a widening gap between teachers and taught. Resistance to professionalization, together with the difficulty of professionalizing the field, complicate the case for the provision of professional education.

The field (or profession) of adult education is not unitary but confused, diverse, and fragmented. Its relationship to the formal education system is described as marginal, although the same phenomenon, like the diversity, is also ascribed the positive character of flexibility. There have been many analyses and typologies of adult educators, and of their training needs. Houle (1970) in a frequently cited paper noted that not all adult educators perceive themselves as such, that the claim to be professional is sometimes made with an uneasy air, and that it can be asserted only in a loose and analogical fashion. Four main categories of adult educators are: (a) those who provide direct guidance to learners; (b) those who design and promote programmes; (c) those who administer programmes; and (d) those, such as research scholars and association leaders, who advance adult education as a field. Most of the first category are part-time and/or voluntary workers, as are an undesirably large proportion of the second and third categories.

In another often cited paper Houle (1956) wrote of the "pyramid of leadership", distinguishing the large group at the base who are volunteers from the intermediate level who combine adult education with other parts of their paid duties as educational, museum and library, governmental, media, and other personnel; and from the full-time adult education specialists at the apex of the pyramid. Other authors have attempted other categorizations for scholarly or practical purposes. An Asian seminar on training of adult educators distinguished field workers, supervisors, and administrators or leaders for purposes of training needs (Dutta and Fischer 1972), and a subsequent Asian regional seminar distinguished five categories according to their duties and training needs: (a) teaching personnel (the great majority, including voluntary and part-time workers); (b) policy makers and others mainly in administration; (c) facilitators or *animateurs*, such as supervisors and course designers; (d) the teachers of adult educators (trainers of trainers); and (e) research and evaluation personnel (UNESCO 1981). An Indian handbook for the training of adult education functionaries for the National Adult Education Programme (Directorate of Adult Education 1978) identified five categories: (a) key functionaries at national and state levels; (b) professionals and experts in such areas as curriculum and materials design, training, and evaluation; (c) functionaries at district and local levels; (d) field level supervisors; and (e) instructors in adult education centres. Instructional responsibility would be assigned to: school teachers; students; village youth; exservicemen and other retired personnel; field level government and other functionaries; and voluntary social workers. Some mass literacy campaigns, and some definitions of adult education and the adult educator for the "lifelong education" or "learning" society, treat every adult person as an adult educator as well as a learner.

Campbell (1977) draws two conclusions about adult education as a field of study and practice: "that there are many facets of adult education practice; and that all draw on a branch of education which is distinct in its character". Campbell considers adult education "a particular and unique element of the education system", and notes that its fragmentation is at once its greatest strength and its greatest weakness. He distinguishes four levels of leadership, all of which would benefit from access to training, and notes the extremely wide range of organizations providing education and training to adults, the dependence upon a host of largely untrained part-time and voluntary workers, the significance of training for adult education demonstrated by the recent spate of reports on the subject, and the increasing emphasis, in British and European settings, upon systems of provision rather than ad hoc arrangements. There may also be discerned, notably in symposia and unpublished working papers, a more sophisticated approach to defining the educational needs of adult educators and attempting to specify the functions, roles, and tasks which indicate required competencies with more precision than do broad and general categories such as administrator. Apart from hesitancy deriving from lack of specificity of role and required competencies, and hesitancy deriving from concerns about professionalization and elitism, the training of adult educators is obviously hampered by the high proportion of voluntary and part-time personnel not easily available for or amenable to training, and some uncertainty as to where the priority belongs: for instance in China the emphasis is upon updating the subject matter being taught, while elsewhere higher priority is given to teaching and learning processes; some emphasize the development of a leading cadre of professional adult educators while others consider that the larger numbers of "grass-roots" part-time teachers should attract the main attention. Some stress conceptual understanding of the field, others practical skills of instruction, others again the largely intangible personal qualities of empathy and rapport which are held to distinguish the best adult educators.

3. Modes of Provision and Providing Bodies

Training of adult educators, like adult education itself, takes many forms and modes. Houle (1970) emphasizes that "most leadership training, like most adult education, is self-directed and therefore is undertaken with varying degrees of thoroughness and continuity". He also emphasizes that those studying adult education at universities have in the main substantial prior experience; the typical doctorate in North America is taken in the late thirties and represents a second career. On the other hand more adult educators are now receiving formal, accredited training directly upon graduation. This runs counter to a strong tradition and view among adult educators that good teachers of adults should have substantial work experience before becoming teachers of adults, but raises less difficulty if the young graduate moves into an administrative rather than a teaching role in the field of adult education.

The majority of adult education training is for those who have work experience already, and usually experience as adult educators. It may take the form of full-time or part-time accredited training, or the form of short nonaccredited inservice courses. Much of this short-course provision is unsystematic and ad hoc, but there are now attempts to make it more regular and systematic in many countries. Part of the planning for the Indian National Adult Education Programme was a systematic scheme of training of personnel for different teaching and organizing roles. Some short courses are publicly advertised and available to all who are interested and able to attend, but very many are conducted within employing organizations or by the providers of adult education and training programmes for their own full- or part-time, paid or voluntary personnel. They are therefore not widely known and it is not possible to state the total scale of such training of trainers and educators of adults.

International conferences on adult education periodically call for more opportunities for adult educators to be trained, stressing the need for different modes. Recommendation 28 of the UNESCO International Conference (1972) sought both short inservice and longer accredited courses in universities; recommendation 30 called for regional seminars open to nongovernmental as well as government personnel. A survey of training opportunities in British universities in 1970 noted the recent growth of accredited training courses (as distinct from short orientation and refresher courses), identifying part-time and full-time certificate and diploma courses in adult education and community development, as well as a sandwich (or cooperative) form of provision for industrial education and training. These courses were apart from opportunities to study for research degrees. An Australian survey a decade later (Knights and Peace 1981) found a preference in New South Wales for accredited training to be "one to three years part-time", with over half of respondents also considering one year's full-time course useful. For short-term noncredit training, weekend workshops were the most popular, followed by occasional evening meetings, series of evening meetings, meetings during the week, and correspondence courses—an indication of the availability of part-time adult educators for their own professional development. A common form of noncredit training especially for full-time adult educators in both industrialized and nonindustrialized countries (reflecting a common format for work-related adult education) is the short intensive residential course of one or two weeks' duration up to perhaps three months, which may be in-house for adult educators in one organization or system, or open to people from different agencies. Recruitment may be local, national, or international.

Participants in these and other training courses may be those whose work is exclusively adult education, or others whose professional role includes an adult education component, such as health, agricultural extension, or media workers; they are unlikely to be people who are employed in some quite other field and teach on a part-time basis, since these are not easily available in working hours for training related to their spare-time activity.

Although there is debate in some countries about whether adult education is a distinct discipline or part of the study of (school-oriented) education, there has recently been an increase in opportunities to study for a graduate qualification in adult education in many countries. Verner (1980), who strongly argues a case for adult education as a distinct social science discipline as well as field of social practice, identifies Canada and the United States, the United Kingdom, Belgium, and Yugoslavia as countries where it is particularly accepted and valued as a subject of study at universities; by 1980 2,239 doctorates had been awarded in adult education in the United States, where by that year over 175 universities taught adult education. Japan is another country where many universities study and teach adult education, and more universities are opening departments or programmes in this field for example in India, the Philippines, the Republic of Korea, and Thailand.

In North America, in particular, and in other countries to differing degrees, formal study opportunities are available, full-time and sometimes part-time, to take adult education as a subject at the level of Ph.D., Ed.D., M.A. or M.Ed., Dip.Ed., or Cert.Ed., as well as to attend noncredit courses of a few hours up to a few months in length. Some noncredit courses provide a certificate of attendance or participation and satisfactory completion which, while not a formal qualification, may still have modest utility for career purposes. Accredited university study therefore takes both mainly academic (Ph.D., M.A.) and more clearly professional forms. Houle (1970) suggested that adult education had a similar status to that of sociology prior to the emergence of social work, or botany prior to agriculture and forestry; the fundamentals were still being explored and were only gradually being crystallized into programmes of the Ed.D. type. He judged that the result would be an open rather than closed cluster of professions, more like business studies than medicine. In Australia, a country where the profession and its training is poorly recognized and differentiated, of 183 students attending postgraduate courses in New South Wales in 1979 only 7 were categorized as adult educators; others were staff trainers, health educators, extension officers, tertiary teachers, librarians, and in other roles (Knights and Peace 1981).

Universities are widely recognized as the main institutions for formal training of full-time adult educators; the importance of their role, and the desirability of strengthening and extending such teaching, are frequently reiterated in studies of adult educator training and in the deliberations of international seminars of adult educators. Such a meeting convened by UNESCO in Bangkok in 1980 noted the recent involvement of universities in the professional training of adult educators often deriving from their concern for professional development of their own teaching staff, and called for a broadening of this interest to provide training for adult educators in such areas as liberal education and second language teaching. Adult education departments are most commonly located in faculties of education in some countries, but in others they may be separate, or linked instead with an extension or continuing education service of the university. Different organizational arrangements reflect different views as to whether adult education is a distinct field or discipline or, rather, a subsystem of general education. Likewise some universities offer one or two adult education options in an M.A. or M.Ed. programme, but not a complete distinct degree in adult education.

There are different views and practices in relation to the inclusion of adult education as a subject or option in normal schools or colleges of teacher education. Some maintain that since it is a distinct field with values and methods different from general education, its professional education also should be kept distinct. On the other hand it is held, especially in rural Third World situations, that much of the teaching of adults will be done by primary- and secondaryschool teachers, so that their professional preparation in the distinctive learning needs of adults is essential. The UNESCO International Conference in 1972, recommending that high priority be given to the training of adult education personnel, made reference to "the study of adult education to be included in the curricula of teacher education, and in the training of librarians and other educational personnel" and called for programmes to train teachers to specialize in adult education coordinated with the normal teacher-training system. It also recommended seminars and courses for adult educators as an integral part of the education system (including industrial training officers, other training personnel, and administrators), and the use of mass media and other distance forms of adult teacher education.

On the one hand training of adult educators is provided in some universities and teachers' colleges in some countries; on the other the argument is advanced that because it is a distinct and under-regarded field, it is better to build distinct special-purpose centres to train adult educators. Several countries such as Kenya and Tanzania have developed separate adult education institutes. Some aid agencies active in adult education encourage Third World countries either to establish such a national centre or to identify and strengthen a particular university department as the key to professional development in adult education in their country. A working party on the training of adult educators recommended in 1977 that the National Council of Adult Education in New Zealand should assume primary responsibility for the training of adult educators, a recommendation which Verner (1980) considers "unfortunate" since it does not encourage universities to accept responsibility in this area.

Regional and international meetings often call attention to the need for regional training centres so that adult education personnel can widen their understanding and competence on a comparative basis, in a setting exclusively oriented to training adult educators. The UNESCO International Conference in 1972 called for feasibility studies for regional training centres for key personnel working in collaboration with national institutions, and the Asian and South Pacific Bureau of Adult Education (ASPBAE) reached similar conclusions in a regional seminar on the training of adult educators earlier that year. The strengthening of regional and international cooperation has seen an increase in the number of noncredit or certificated training programmes provided by regional organizations, for example in the Caribbean (general adult education) and Southeast Asia (urban-oriented training). Some universities, mostly in industrialized countries, also play a regional or international training role, either through regular graduate programmes (such as the University of British Columbia and the Ontario Institute for Studies in Education (OISE) in Canada, Manchester University in the United Kingdom, and Massachusetts and Michigan State Universities in the United States) or through regular or occasional short courses (such as the annual three month programme for Asian and Pacific adult educators at the Australian National University supported by the W.K. Kellogg Foundation). Educational foundations and aid agencies play a prominent role in fostering national, regional, and other forms of adult education training for Third World adult educators, whether through regular educational institutions, national or regional associations, or special training centres. Although it has been suggested periodically that adult education associations should take the initiative and provide accreditation for the adult education profession, there has been a reluctance to appear to usurp the role of universities; consequently the staff development and training work of professional associations of adult education is generally restricted to providing short training courses and other noncredit study opportunities, and to arranging seminars, conferences, publications, and other aids to adult education training. A recent development in China has been the creation of a national adult education association and an increasing number of provincial and city associations, a main purpose of which is to provide staff development services and opportunities.

The 1976 conference of the International Council for Adult Education (ICAE) in Tanzania called for the creation of regional training centres to serve countries not yet able to mount the kinds of training required at the country level. Cooperative programmes were recommended wherever there were regional bonds of culture, ideology or language, or geographical or economic factors which favoured this. At least one such centre was sought, under indigenous leadership, in each of four main Third World regions, within three years. The tendency has been for regional training programmes to be established rather than distinct centres, using the existing facilities and infrastructures of different countries for regional purposes.

Apart from universities and colleges, and associations supported by intergovernmental and other aid agencies, a large part of all training of adult educators is provided by their employing organizations and agencies, and takes the form of short intensive sessions and courses. According to Houle (1970) the largest volume of organized, as distinct from self-directed, training of adult education leaders takes place within providing institutions such as the public schools, industrial and commercial establishments, government departments, and voluntary associations. Some of these have systematic provision with required steps for advancement by means of short courses. An account of adult education training in Denmark in the mid-1970s noted that there were four main types: basic, leader training, training for remedial teaching, and training to teach in study groups; and that the training was decentralized, principally to private sponsors of leisure-time instruction, county councils, teacher associations, the Royal Danish College of Education, and the Directorate for Primary Schools, Adult and Youth Education, Teacher Training Colleges, etc.

4. Skill and Subject Areas

Content of educational and training programmes for adult educators varies greatly according to the situation, circumstances, and presumed needs of those being trained as well as the length of time available for training. University programmes may incline more towards academic and theoretical study or, rather, towards practical and technical skills and knowledge thought to equip the practitioner–teacher, and the resulting qualification may lean more to the academic or the professional side. Short courses tend to be concerned more with practical skills and insights than sequential academic study, although they may also provide opportunity for conceptual learning in a specified area. The emphasis in adult education circles upon integrating theory with practice, and upon relevance, however tends to give such work an applied character and focus. Some short programmes enrol groups or teams of adult educators from one agency, especially in the form of in-house training, and there may be an organizational change purpose as well as an objective of individual learning and enhanced competence. Because of the importance accorded to personality, attitudes, and values in much adult education, some of the training is mainly experiential and intended to foster personal growth and change.

The importance of values, qualities, and attitudes poses a problem for the training of adult educators, especially in the liberal tradition where there is more emphasis upon personal dialogue and interaction through discussion than in some technical skill training areas. It is acknowledged that the somewhat intangible qualities held to mark a good adult educator are difficult or impossible to teach. There is thus the dilemma that aspects of the professional role and identity most highly valued in this tradition are also thought to be little if at all amenable to teaching. A further difficulty is the acknowledged situation and context specificity of most adult educators' work, which means that short-course training, in particular, needs to be adapted to each unique or partly unique situation. This makes generalization and routinized teaching of adult educators unsatisfactory.

A third difficulty is that the learning needs of adult educators are often not clearly defined: general definitions in terms of role, such as administrator or teacher, encompass a wide range of the possible skills needed. Knox (1979) notes repeated efforts over the past two decades to identify important areas of proficiency which graduate programmes should seek to develop, and suggests that broader conceptualizations of "important practitioner proficiencies" could improve such programmes. "Although proficiencies are hard to specify, an understanding of their major areas can be used to select effective staff members, to focus self-directed study efforts, and to plan in-service educational activities for practitioners." Apps (1972) suggests four basic qualifications required of the future adult educator, whether a specialist in administration, method, subject matter, or professional teaching or research: have an understanding of his or her personal philosophy of education; be oriented to people; be oriented to problems; and be oriented to change.

Many other prescriptions and descriptions of learning needs and subject areas may be found. The UNESCO 1972 International Conference held that part-time adult educators must at least know something about adult learning and be able to identify with the people they serve, and that training should generally take place in the milieu in which they are to work. The International Council for Adult Education conference in 1976 in Tanzania indicated that training, especially at middle and higher levels, should include a sound knowledge of and experience in communication techniques, and should increase sensitivity to the problems of the less privileged. Literacy instructors should learn techniques of animation and participation, as well as evaluation, administration, and reporting skills. An account of the needs of Kenyan extension workers to the 1979 Commonwealth Conference on Nonformal Education referred to: understanding governmental policies and problems; understanding the local community; knowledge of the subject matter of agriculture; knowledge of other related and some rather distant subjects; and skills in communication, organization, needs analysis, leadership, and self-evaluation.

Other accounts and analyses refer more to subject areas than to required skills. Knox (1979) is among those who discern core proficiencies of all practitioners from analysis of previous studies; frequently mentioned are proficiencies related to educational goals for adults, adult development and learning, programme development procedures, and general agency functioning. "Specific procedures and terminology related to a specific type of agency or role . . . tend to vary greatly from situation to situation." Knox suggests that all categories of practitioner would benefit from three broad areas of proficiency: understanding the field of adult education, understanding adults as learners, and, in the affective domain, having "personal qualities such as positive attitudes to lifelong learning, effective interpersonal relations, and innovativeness". Administrators require additional competence in administration, programme development, and planning and using research; teachers and counsellors need knowledge about subject matter and adult development, and capability with programme development procedures, while policy makers must understand desirable directions for the agency's development.

Verner (1980) cites from Brunner eight categories of core knowledge of the discipline of adult education: adult learning; psychology of adults; instructional design; instructional management; instructional materials and equipment; the client system; the organizational system; and the social setting of adult education. Houle (1956) sets out six general objectives of most university programmes reflecting what are seen as the basic attributes of a good adult educator: "(a) a sound philosophic conception of adult education based on a consideration of its major aims and issues and embodying convictions concerning the basic values which it should seek to achieve; (b) an understanding of the psychological and social foundations on which all education (and particularly adult education) rests; (c) an understanding of the development, scope, and complexity of the specific agency or programme in which he works and the broad field of adult education. . . ; (d) an ability to undertake and direct the basic processes of education: the refinement of objectives; the selection and use of methods and content; the training of leaders; the provision of guidance and counselling; the promotion of programmes; the coordination and supervision of activities, and the evaluation of results; (e) personal effectiveness and leadership in working with other individuals, with groups, and with the general public; and (f) a constant concern with the continuance of his own education throughout life."

Campbell (1977) frames the content of adult education as a field of study in a model comprising six elements: "the adult learner—the psychological context; the adult learner—the sociological context; adult education—the philosophical–historical context; adult education—methods and resources; adult education systems—organization and administration; adult education—provision to a particular clientele/environment." A somewhat different six-way classification was attempted by the participants in the 1980 UNESCO Asian regional seminar on adult education and development:

methodology (i.e., concepts, principles, problem solving, skills, attitudes, and values); psychology of the adult learner; teaching skills and techniques; evaluation; sociology relevant to adult education; and development studies. These areas are seen as essential to any training programme, long- or short-term for full- or part-time teachers of adults, although the depth of study will vary. The Asian and South Pacific Bureau of Adult Education seminar in the same region in 1972 indicated seven areas as a course outline for regional training: history and philosophy, nature, scope and need, sociology of adult education; psychology of adult learning; principles of adult education administration; techniques, methods, processes, and practices, including evaluation; economics of developing countries; curriculum development and material preparation. The report also identified six specialist areas, and listed the knowledge, skills, and attitudes which training should develop in adult educators.

Different analyses of adult educators' professional learning needs, and of the programmes developed to meet them, show much commonality among both industrialized and developing countries, and lay much stress upon the process of teaching, even sometimes somewhat to the exclusion of the subject matter which the educator is to teach his or her adult students. Campbell (1977) states that "capability in the application of adult education methodology is no less important to the adult education teacher than is his expertise in his subject field". In the People's Republic of China the present emphasis, in circumstances of great demand for worker-peasant education and absence of formal teacher education of adult educators, is upon up-to-date knowledge of the subject matter to be taught; at the same time there is felt to be a need for the study of adult learning processes and appropriate methods of adult teaching.

5. Methods of Teaching the Educators of Adults

It is usual to stress the adult status of learners in adult teacher education, and the importance of congruity between how they are taught and what they are taught is the appropriate teaching methodology with other adults. "The principle of the sovereignty of the learner must be given priority" (UNESCO 1981). The International Council for Adult Education 1976 conference emphasized "the mutual exchange of experiences between the teacher and the 'taught' (in training) and the development of participatory methods and activities that teach learners how to participate in decision-making" (Hall and Kidd 1978). "Training for adult education must itself be consistent with adult education principles. Indeed, it ought to epitomize adult education at its best" (Campbell 1977). "Everything which is done in the name of adult education by the government training offices or by the non-government training institutes, should be a good example of adult education, and this applies to the training of adult educators. . ." (UNESCO 1981). The report adds that good results have

been obtained through nonformal workshops where adult educators meet together, set their agendas, and rely on group interaction and discovery learning; "the facilitator or group leader in such a workshop" has a demanding role "but the knowledge of group dynamics and interpersonal communication which is needed for such work is a valuable field of study for anyone who sets out to train the trainers". A wide variety of methods is used to teach adult educators, including lectures, handbooks and manuals, correspondence or mass media courses, simulation, microlaboratory work, attachments and internships, and teaching practice, but discussion and other group work tends to play an especially prominent part.

Belief in the importance of participation in adult education also produces forms of training of personnel which emphasize participation. The Freedom from Hunger Campaign/Action for Development of the Food and Agricultural Organisation of the United Nations has sponsored regional change agents' training programmes in South and Southeast Asia led by Kamla Bhasin. Bhasin (1979) provides a nontechnical guide in the form of a report for field-based and applied training for development. She lists barriers which have been broken, fully or in part, by an approach which emphasizes direct learning and exchange of an in situ and experiential kind, with heavy reliance on dialogue, confrontation, and mutual teaching and learning. Barriers identified in more conventional training which are at least partly breached include: classroom–field; trainer–trainee; the barrier between desk-bound knowledge and one's own experience; barriers between theory and practice of concepts like shared authority, and participation; men–women; government–nongovernment; and barriers to exchange of experience between neighbouring countries.

The methodology for training personnel for the National Adult Education Programme in India derived directly from the objectives of the programme "which is radically different from all earlier attempts at mass adult education in India" (Directorate of Adult Education 1978). "The training programme itself is fundamentally a process of adult education and has to reflect the main characteristics of the methodology that the functionaries would have to follow while working with the learning groups at the grass-roots level." The first step is helping trainees towards self-knowledge or "value clarification", then to develop a "social eye" to understand the dynamics of the group or "small society" in which they themselves are learning. Nonauthoritarian values are to be understood and acquired through experience of the training programme, along with necessary knowledge and skills to teach within the National Adult Education Programme. The following features are identified for the training: it should be participatory; an opportunity for mutual learning; emphasize group discussion; allow learning to emerge out of experience; closely approximate the field and the realities; and be an experiment in community living. Typical methods of training are: activity-based methods including problem solving, project methods, and discussion; lecture, lecture–demonstration, and their links with discussion; individual learning; and combined methods, including residential (or camp) training, field operational seminars, and other forms of combining training with field work. Training is a continuous process starting with initial training to provide a "first-aid kit" and followed by inservice training. The handbook suggests several questions to help trainers teach the instructors, who are front-line workers in the National Adult Education Programme: What is the learning situation in which the instructor has to function? What is the background of the instructor? What is the instructor expected to do in this programme (followed by encouragement to explore eight components of the role)? What competencies (knowledge, skills, attitudes, and values) should the instructor develop for doing his work? What kind of training programme is necessary and how can it develop the skills and qualities desired?

6. Trends and Issues

6.1 Adequacy of Provision

Teaching of adult educators reflects many characteristics of adult education itself. The total amount of adult education activity is very large in many societies, and estimated to exceed the quantity of formal education, but it is not conceived and organized as a system. Much of it takes place in a dispersed manner and much is informal and ad hoc. A large amount of in-organization vocationally oriented training is excluded from many accounts of adult education and there is little knowledge of its scale and procedures in many countries. Preparation and inservice education of teachers for this diversity of adult education is similarly diverse, dispersed, and incompletely known and understood. There is wide agreement among adult education leaders in most countries that the preparation of adult educators, both the full-time teachers, administrators and other specialists, and the much larger number of voluntary and part-time workers, is inadequate.

Reviews of adult education and its teacher education, both scholarly studies and international conferences, largely agree in calling for much more massive and systematic training, including cooperation and rationalization between kinds of institutions and programmes. Despite severe reservations about the ability of universities to adapt their resources to the needs of adult educators' professional preparation, leading to some preference for distinct training and research centres, the commonest view is that universities have an essential part to play in teaching the leading members of the profession. North American studies of adult educator teaching plot the increase in number of university graduate programmes and doctoral graduates from the 1960s to the present time. A similar, somewhat later, expansion has occurred in the United Kingdom where, in 1970, only seven universities offered any kind of credit

(certificate, diploma, or degree) programme. The fortunes of particular university adult education programmes in these and other countries have waxed and waned with the reputation and size of faculty, and there has been some contraction reflecting political and economic changes in the societies generally; overall the impression is one of "a growing stability" (Houle 1970) as consensus has increased about the core components and requirements of the field and (as it is claimed to be) discipline.

In planned economies and in many developing countries where priority is given to literacy and adult/nonformal education for development, more deliberate and systematic provision for teaching adult education is made both through universities and teachers' colleges and, in some countries, through special adult education institutes. In these countries there are generally fewer reservations about providing adult education as a strand or option in preservice education, especially of teachers, reflecting a tendency to treat adult or nonformal education more as part of the total national education system.

6.2 Priorities for Training

There is more agreement about the general inadequacy of teacher education for adult education than about where the priorities lie. This reflects the complex and dispersed nature of the profession and its work, as well as a reservation about professionalization. The Commonwealth conference on nonformal education in 1979 noted the importance of training for securing good training of senior personnel and teachers. However, "whereas 'training' in formal education is largely a matter for teachers or superiors, in nonformal education the scope has to be widened to include many more groups and individuals. Indeed it could be argued that the whole society needs to receive some kind of training to be aware of the contributions nonformal education can make to economic and social development" (Commonwealth Secretariat 1980). The conference listed as priority groups for training: "senior policy makers; specialists, such as doctors, nurses and other health workers, agriculturalists, veterinarians, and others working with community groups; all those working in a nonformal education capacity with community groups and organizations (e.g. agricultural extension workers and village-level workers); those who train the trainers of non-formal educators; curriculum developers and researchers engaged in non-formal education activities".

The difficulty in setting operational priorities is demonstrated by this list, which acknowledges the systemic character of adult/nonformal education when conceived as a means to development. The UNESCO International Conference in 1972 stressed the importance of part-time and voluntary teachers as "a democratically desirable practice", in considering the training of personnel, but also stressed the need for a much stronger full-time cadre. The word cadre has recently been used in a somewhat different sense in discussions in India about the key personnel for training; here the emphasis is upon local or village level workers dedicated to adult education for development who are in touch with local communities rather than detached through academic education, yet equipped to play a vital leadership role. Australia is another country where there is now concern about the absence of adequate training for adult educators mingled with reservation about the utility of long academic accredited programmes thought likely to foster professional exclusiveness; consequently discussions tend to suggest that priority should be given to short courses, or part-time certificate programmes, for the army of part-time workers at the base of the pyramid. On the other hand scholars like Verner (1980) lay emphasis both upon developing the intellectual leadership of adult education and more firmly delineating its academic field and standing; Campbell (1977), noting that few in adult education agencies have qualifications appropriate to the training task, holds that "the principal initial thrust of training for adult education in Canada, as elsewhere, ought to be the development of a core of trained personnel within the ranks of full-time leadership".

The main question of priorities concerns who most urgently needs training: those at the base or the apex of the pyramid, or some other specialist groups or mix calculated to advance the teaching of adult education systemically. Other issues include the case for at least some preservice as well as postservice experience and inservice education, the respective contributions of local, national, and regional or international training opportunities, and the priority to be given to training compared with, for instance, research.

6.3 Professionalization and Mandatory Training

The drawback of professionalization of services generally, as analysed in the writing of Ivan Illich and others, is a major concern of many adult education teachers and policy makers who value a relationship of reciprocity and relative equality between teacher and adult learner. This produces a tension, since there is also concern about the low status and marginality of much adult education, one source of which is recognized to be the fragmentary, diffuse, and voluntaristic character of much of the work, and the lack of formal training and qualifications of adult education practitioners. Resistance to mandatory training and certification is widespread. It is frequently asserted that good adult educators are born (or matured by experience) rather than produced by formal training, and that many of the essential qualities and even skills are difficult or impossible to teach. Even at senior levels there is resistance to requiring formal qualifications in candidates for positions. On the other hand the increasing numbers of graduate programmes available especially in North America, and the access to these programmes of adult educators from Third World and other countries, is producing a widespread expectation approaching a

requirement, for certain professional and administrative as well as academic positions, of having a higher degree in adult education.

Another trend is towards requiring all adult educators, part-time as well as full-time, to undertake training by means of periodic short courses, perhaps preservice as well as inservice. An Asian regional seminar on training adult educators (Dutta and Fischer 1972) called for at least two weeks of full-time preparatory training of part-time adult educators lacking basic teachers' training, and three months full-time in a teachers' college or special purpose adult education institute for full-time workers, together with inservice training and guidance. A government proposal in Denmark in 1969 for a basic course for adult education teachers of 180 hours has been generally followed; the Workers' Educational Association has established its own 100 hour course instead. Although the Scandinavian countries generally provide orientation and inservice training for adult educators in different areas, from labour force training to leading study circles, mandatory training is not general. In the United Kingdom an advisory committee report proposing a three-stage plan for the training of part-time teachers of adults has the general support of the Advisory Council on Adult and Continuing Education (ACACE 1981). The first two stages would be taken by all newly appointed part-time teachers in further and adult education not already qualified as school teachers; "consideration was given to whether a shorter period of training might be suitable for those teaching only 2 or 3 hours a week, but it was agreed that the requirements of this group were basically the same as those with heavier teaching loads". These stages together require at least 36 plus 60 hours of course attendance and 30 hours of supervised teaching practice. "On the completion of stages I and II, part-time teachers should have the opportunity to undertake further inservice training leading to full certification, by means of stage III courses of some 300 hours and appropriate teaching practice."

6.4 General Teacher Education and Andragogy

There is ambivalence and controversy among adult educators about the extent to which teacher education for adult education should be integrated with or separated from general teacher education. Those who favour an integrated and lifelong system of educational provision, with formal and nonformal options at all stages, tend to favour integration of training also, and see a major role for teachers' colleges and faculties of education. Others argue that adult education, or andragogy, is a distinct field and discipline which needs to be kept somewhat apart from school-oriented teacher education and academic study. "Adult education is involved with learning in a wide social milieu; it represents a broader conception of education than that of schooling. It deals with education in diverse forms scarcely recognizable to those whose perceptions are limited to institutionalized patterns and structures; consequently, traditional teacher education programmes now conducted by teachers' colleges cannot prepare professional leaders for adult education. Teachers' colleges are geared to training teachers of children. . ." (Verner 1980). In New Zealand, Verner considered, "enthusiasm for lifelong education is in danger of masking crucial differences between pre-adult and adult education which have critical implications for the training of adult educators". Knox (1979) is among many authors who note that the preparatory education experienced by school teachers may be inappropriate to working with adults. In the People's Republic of China, by contrast, worker–peasant education is conceived as part of the "formal" system of education, and as providing alternative modes for the acquisition of knowledge, skills, and qualifications: the different circumstances and learning needs of adults with family and working responsibilities are acknowledged, but there is not a separate methodology and andragogy requiring separate teacher training; the emphasis is mainly upon keeping up to date in the subject matter to be taught.

While many adult educators are resistant to merging training with general teacher education and fear loss of distinctive identity and methodology, analyses of the whole education system from a perspective of lifelong education suggest that the values and approaches distinctive of adult education may be carried across in part to influence formal teacher education. This was suggested in the report of the UNESCO Faure Commission, *Learning to Be* in 1972, and in a more recent consideration of the implications of lifelong education for the training of teachers by Cropley and Dave (1978). Although teacher education for adult education is not addressed directly, analysis of cumulative changes in the system of teacher education in several countries suggests that much of the philosophy and methodology of adult education is being adapted and assimilated piecemeal. This may indicate more transaction between school-oriented and adult teacher education in the future, a tendency likely to be encouraged by demographic changes in many countries which may release regular educational resources for adult education. It is likely however that the study and teaching of adult education will continue to sustain a separate identity and some separate institutional bases for training.

Bibliography

Advisory Committee for Adult and Continuing Education 1981 *Specialist Training for Part-time Teachers of Adults*. Advisory Council for Adult and Continuing Education, Leicester

Apps J W 1972 Tomorrow's adult educator—some thoughts and questions. *Adult Educ. (*U.S.A.*)* 22: 218–26

Asian and South Pacific Bureau of Adult Education 1979 *Training Symposium. Courier 15.* Canberra

Bhasin K 1979 *Breaking Barriers: A South Asian Experience of Training for Participatory Development*. FFHC/AD, Food and Agricultural Organisation of the United Nations, Bangkok

Campbell D D 1977 *Adult Education as a Field of Study and Practice*. University of British Columbia/ICAE, Vancouver

Cropley A J, Dave R H 1978 *Lifelong Education and the Training of Teachers*. Advances in Lifelong Education, Vol. 5. Pergamon Press, Oxford

Commonwealth Secretariat 1980 *Participation, Learning and Change: Commonwealth Approaches to Nonformal Education*. Commonwealth Secretariat, London

Directorate of Adult Education 1978 *Training of Adult Education Functionaries: A Handbook*. Directorate of Adult Education, New Delhi

Dutta S C, Fischer H J (eds.) 1972 *Training of Adult Educators*. Shakuntala, Bombay

Elsdon K T 1975 *Training for Adult Education*. Nottingham Studies in the Theory and Practice of Education of Adults, Vol. 1. University of Nottingham, Nottingham

European Bureau of Adult Education 1980 *Training for Part-time Adult Educators and Volunteers: Newsletter*. European Bureau of Adult Education, Amersfoort

Hall B L, Kidd J R (eds.) 1978 *Adult Learning: A Design for Action*. Pergamon Press, Oxford

Houle C O 1956 Professional education for educators of adults. In: Houle C O (ed.) 1956 *Professional Preparation of Adult Educators: A Symposium*. Center for the Study of Liberal Education for Adults, Chicago, Illinois

Houle C O 1970 The educators of adults. In: Smith R M, Aker G F, Kidd J R (eds.) 1970 *Handbook of Adult Education*. Macmillan, New York

Knights S M, Peace B W 1981 Training adult educators. *Aust. J. Adult Educ.* 21 (1): 19–25

Knowles M S 1970 *The Modern Practice of Adult Education: Andragogy versus Pedagogy*. Association Press, New York

Knox A B (ed.) 1979 *Enhancing Proficiencies of Continuing Educators*. Jossey-Bass, San Francisco, California

UNESCO 1972 *Final Report: Third International Conference on Adult Education*. UNESCO, Paris

UNESCO 1976 *Recommendation on the Development of Adult Education*. UNESCO, Paris

UNESCO 1981 *Prospects for Adult Education and Development in Asia and the Pacific*. UNESCO. Bangkok

Verner C 1980 Academic education about adult education. In: Boshier R (ed.) 1980 *Towards a Learning Society*. Learning Press, Vancouver

List of Contributors

Contributors are listed in alphabetical order together with their affiliations. Titles of articles which they have authored follow in alphabetical order, along with the respective page numbers. Where articles are co-authored, this has been indicated by an asterisk preceding the article title.

AINLEY, J. G. (Australian Council for Educational Research, Hawthorn, Victoria, Australia)
Equipment and Materials 538-40

ANDERSON, L. W. (University of South Carolina, Columbia, South Carolina, USA)
Affective Teacher Education 83-86; *Mastery Learning Models* 58-67; *Opportunity to Learn* 368-72

ARNOLD, R. (University of Sydney, Sydney, New South Wales, Australia)
Linguistic Models 49-58

BANK, B. J. (University of Missouri, Columbia, Missouri, USA)
Students' Sex 571-74

BARNES, J. (University of Sydney, Sydney, New South Wales, Australia)
Teaching Experience 608-12

BARR, R. (University of Chicago, Chicago, Illinois, USA)
Content Coverage 364-68

BATES, J. A. (University of Nevada, Las Vegas, Nevada, USA)
Reinforcement 349-58

BENNETT, S. N. (University of Exeter, Exeter, UK)
Architecture 530-37

BIDDLE, B. J. (University of Missouri, Columbia, Missouri, USA)
Effects of Teaching 119-24; *Teacher Roles* 625-34

BLOCK, J. H. (University of California, Santa Barbara, California, USA)
Mastery Learning Models 58-67

BOLAM, R. (University of Bristol, Bristol, UK)
Induction of Beginning Teachers 745-57

BONBOIR, A. (Catholic University of Louvain, Louvain-la-Neuve, Belgium)
Thinking Aloud 277-78

BRAUN, C. (University of Calgary, Calgary, Alberta, Canada)
Teachers' Expectations 598-605

BROWN, G. A. (University of Nottingham, Nottingham, UK)
Lectures and Lecturing 284-88

BURSTEIN, L. (University of California, Los Angeles, California, USA)
Units of Analysis 155-62

BUSHELL JR., D. (University of Kansas, Lawrence, Kansas, USA)
Behavioral Models 32-36

CAIN, J. (University of Illinois, Urbana-Champaign, Illinois, USA)
Teacher Education for Early Childhood Education 773-81

CAIRNS, L. G. (University of Sydney, Sydney, New South Wales, Australia)
Behaviour Problems 446-52

CALFEE, R. C. (Stanford University, Stanford, California, USA)
Grouping for Teaching 225-32

CLARK, C. M. (Michigan State University, East Lansing, Michigan, USA)
The Carroll Model 36-40

COLTON, D. L. (University of New Mexico, Albuquerque, New Mexico, USA)
Teachers' Organizations 660-62

CONNELL, W. F. (Monash University, Melbourne, Victoria, Australia)
History of Teaching Methods 201-14

CORNO, L. (Teachers College, Columbia University, New York, USA)
*Information Processing Models 40-49

COULTER, F. (Canberra College of Advanced Education, Belconnen, Australian Capital Territory, Australia)
Affective Characteristics of Student Teachers 589-98; *Homework* 272-77

CRANTON, P. A. (McGill University, Montreal, Quebec, Canada)
Clinical Teaching 304-06

DEBUS, R. L. (University of Sydney, Sydney, New South Wales, Australia)
Students' Cognitive Characteristics 564-68

DE LANDSHEERE, G. (University of Liège, Liège, Belgium)
Concepts of Teacher Education 77-83; *Teacher Recyclage* 744-45

DOCKRELL, W. B. (Scottish Council for Research in Education, Edinburgh, UK)
Ethical Considerations 165-69

DOENAU, S. J. (Macquarie University, North Ryde, New South Wales, Australia)
Soliciting 407-13; *Structuring* 398-407; **Students' Ethnicity* 568-71

DORSEY, D. (University of Kansas, Lawrence, Kansas, USA)
*Behavioral Models 32-36

DOYLE, W. (University of Texas, Austin, Texas, USA)
Paradigms for Research 113-19

DUKE, C. (University of Warwick, Coventry, UK)
Teacher Education for Adult Education 798-807

DUKE, D. L. (Lewis and Clark College, Portland, Oregon, USA)
Environmental Influences 548-53

DUNKIN, M. J. (University of Sydney, Sydney, New South Wales, Australia)
Abstractness and Concreteness 390-92; **Effects of Teaching* 119-24; *Lesson Formats* 263-66; **Students'*

Ethnicity 568-71; *Teachers' Sex* 606-08; *Teaching: Art or Science?* 19; *Technical Skills of Teaching* 703-06

DUTHIE, J. H. (University of Stirling, Stirling, UK)
Nonteachers and Teaching 662-67

EDELSTEIN, M. (Stanford University, Stanford, California, USA)
*Information Processing Models 40-49

ELLIOTT, J. (University of East Anglia, Norwich, UK)
Teachers as Researchers 162-64

ELTIS, K. J. (Macquarie University, North Ryde, New South Wales, Australia)
Selection for Teaching 645-50

EMMER, E. T. (University of Texas, Austin, Texas, USA)
Classroom Management 437-46

ENNIS, R. H. (University of Illinois, Urbana, Champaign, Illinois, USA)
*Logical Operations 380-90

ERAUT, M. (University of Sussex, Brighton, Sussex, UK)
Inservice Teacher Education 730-43

FLANDERS, N. A. (Oakland, California, USA)
Flexibility 462-66; *Human Interaction Models* 20-28

GALL, M. D. (University of Oregon, Eugene, Oregon, USA)
Discussion Methods 232-37

GALTON, M. (University of Leicester, Leicester, UK)
Structured Observation 142-47

GIACONIA, R. M. (Massachusetts Department of Education, Boston, Massachusetts, USA)
Open Versus Formal Methods 246-57; **Synthesizing Research Evidence* 124-42

GLASS, G. V. (University of Colorado, Boulder, Colorado, USA)
Class Size 540-45

GOOD, T. L. (University of Missouri, Columbia, Missouri, USA)
*Proactive Teaching 457-60; **Reactive Teaching* 460-62

GUBA, E. G. (Indiana University, Bloomington, Indiana, USA)
*Naturalistic Inquiry 147-51

PERROTT, E. (University of Lancaster, Bailrigg, Lancaster, UK)
Minicourses 764-72

PIONTKOWSKI, D. C. (San Francisco State University, San Francisco, California, USA)
Grouping for Teaching 225-32

POSNER, G. J. (Cornell University, Ithaca, New York, USA)
Pacing and Sequencing 266-72

POWER, C. (Flinders University of South Australia, Bedford Park, South Australia, Australia)
Responding 413-16; *Teaching Cycles and Strategies* 427-32

RICHAUDEAU, F. (Paris, France)
Written Instruction 278-83

ROBERTSON, E. (Syracuse University, Syracuse, New York, USA)
Teaching and Related Activities 15-18

ROHRKEMPER, M. M. (Bryn Mawr College, Bryn Mawr, Pennsylvania, USA)
Proactive Teaching 457-60; *Reactive Teaching* 460-62

ROSENSHINE, B. (University of Illinois, Urbana-Champaign, Illinois, USA)
Direct Instruction 257-62

SEMMEL, D. S. (University of California, Santa Barbara, California, USA)
Teacher Education for Special Education 781-86

SHAVELSON, R. J. (University of California, Los Angeles, California, USA)
Interactive Decision Making 491-93; *Planning* 483-86; *Teachers' Judgments* 486-90

SHOSTAK, R. J. (Nottinghamshire County Council, West Bridgford, Nottinghamshire, UK)
Teachers' Centres 761-64

SINCLAIR, K. E. (University of Sydney, Sydney, New South Wales, Australia)
Students' Affective Characteristics 559-64

SLAVIN, R. E. (Johns Hopkins University, Baltimore, Maryland, USA)
Small Group Methods 237-43

SMITH, B. O. (University of South Florida, Clearwater, Florida, USA)
Definitions of Teaching 11-15

SMITH, H. A. (Queen's University, Kingston, Ontario, Canada)
Nonverbal Communication 466-76

SMYTH, W. J. (Deakin University, Victoria, Australia)
Time 372-80

SNOW, R. E. (Stanford University, Stanford, California, USA)
Aptitude–Treatment Interaction Models 28-32

SOAR, R. M. (Gainesville, Florida, USA)
Classroom Climate 336-42

SOAR, R. S. (University of Florida, Gainesville, Florida, USA)
Classroom Climate 336-42

STONES, E. (University of Liverpool, Liverpool, UK)
Student (Practice) Teaching 681-85

SUTTON, R. E. (Cleveland State University, Cleveland, Ohio, USA)
Logical Operations 380-90

TAFT, R. (Monash University, Clayton, Victoria, Australia)
Ethnographic Methods 151-55

TAYLOR, P. H. (University of Birmingham, Birmingham, UK)
Implicit Theories 477-82

THOMAS, R. M. (University of California, Santa Barbara, California, USA)
Individualizing Teaching 220-24

TISHER, R. P. (Monash University, Clayton, Victoria, Australia)
Student Roles 432-36

TURNEY, C. (University of Sydney, Sydney, New South Wales, Australia)
Laboratory Schools 696-703; *Supervision of the Practicum* 686-95

WALBERG, H. J. (University of Illinois, Chicago, Illinois, USA)
Psychological Environment 553-58

WATSON, K. (University of Sydney, Sydney, New South Wales, Australia)
Linguistic Models 49-58

WEINSTEIN, C. S. (Rutgers, The State University, New Brunswick, New Jersey, USA)
Seating Patterns 545-48

WILLIAMS, P. R. C. (University of London, London, UK)
Teacher Supply and Demand 650-52

WINNE, P. H. (Simon Fraser University, Burnaby, British Columbia, Canada)
Students' Cognitive Processing 496-509

WITHALL, J. (Pennsylvania State University, University Park, Pennsylvania, USA)
Teacher-centered and Learner-centered Teaching 327-36

WITTROCK, M. C. (University of California, Los Angeles, California, USA)
Models of Heuristic Teaching 68-76

WRAGG, E. C. (Exeter University, Exeter, UK)
Lesson Analysis 706-15

YOUNG, R. E. (University of Sydney, Sydney, New South Wales, Australia)
Epistemologies 493-96; *Linguistic Models* 49-58

ZABALZA, A. (Madrid, Spain)
Economics of Teacher Supply 653-57

ZAHORIK, J. A. (University of Wisconsin, Milwaukee, Wisconsin, USA)
Reacting 416-23

ZIMPHER, N. L. (Ohio State University, Columbus, Ohio, USA)
Certification and Licensing of Teachers 657-59

Name Index

The Name Index has been compiled so that the reader can proceed either directly to the page where an author's work is cited, or to the reference itself in the bibliography. For each name, the page numbers for the bibliographic citation are given first, followed by the page number(s) in parentheses where that reference is cited in text. Where a name is referred to only in text, and not in the bibliography, the page number appears only in parentheses.

The accuracy of the spelling of authors' names has been affected by the use of different initials by some authors, or a different spelling of their name in different papers or review articles (sometimes this may arise from a transliteration process), and by those journals which give only one initial to each author.

B

C

D

E

Eash M J, 649 (646)
Easley J A, 304 (300, 301)
Easton G, 298 (296)
Eaton E, 649 (647)
Eaton W E, 662 (660)
Ebbutt D, 164 (164)
Ebel R L, 530, 634, 756
Ebmeier H, 364 (360)
Edelfelt R A, 786 (785)
Edgar D E, 598 (592), 695
Edmiston R W, 608 (607)
Edmonds E M, 397
Edson S K, 574 (572)
Edwards A C, 703 (697)
Edwards A D, 58 (55), 715 (709)
Edwards K J, 242 (238)
Egan G, 86 (84)
Eggleston J, 742 (737)
Eggleston J F, 146 (144, 145), (404), 431
 (431), 714 (711), 756 (752)
Egner A N, 786 (783, 785)
Ehly S W, 245 (243, 245)
Eicke F J, 567 (567)
Eidell T L, 598 (591)
Eierdam D, 390 (384, 389)
Einhorn H J, 490 (488)
Eisner E W, 19 (19)
Eklund H, 742 (742)
Ekman P, 475, 476
Elam S, 94 (87, 90)

Elashoff J D, 124 (121), 412 (409), 605
 (599)
Elder R A, 28 (24), 237 (234, 236)
Elias P, 232 (227, 228)
Eliot T H, 662 (661)
Elkind D, 390 (389)
Ellena W J, 146, 266, 589
Ellgring H, 475 (467)
Elliot C, 694 (686)
Elliott B G, 685
Elliott J, 164 (163, 164), 742 (736)
Ellis J W, 742
Ellson D G, (245), 349 (348)
Elmore J L, 485
Elmslie R G, 306 (305)
Elsdon K T, 807
Elstein A S, 49 (41), 490 (487, 489)
Emmer E T, 119 (115), 262 (258, 259,
 260), 364 (360), 446 (440, 441, 446), 460
 (458), 462 (460), 567 (565)
Emrick J A, 742 (740)
Enderwitz H, 83 (78)
Endler N S, 32 (29)
Engel M, 574 (573)
Engelhart M B, 589 (585)
Engelhart M D, 392 (391)
Engelmann S, 36, 786
Englehardt D F, 540 (539)
Englert C S, 786 (784)
Ennis R H, 15 (12), 390 (383, 384, 385)

Enos D F, 94 (90)
Entwisle B, 161 (161)
Entwistle N, 287, 298
Epstein J, 242
Erasmus D, (203)
Eraut M R, 288 (286), 743 (734, 740)
Erbring L, 161 (161)
Erickson F, 155 (152)
Erlbacher A, 180 (173)
Erlich E, 496 (494)
Esposito D, 231 (226), 529 (528)
Esquivel J M, 715 (714)
Estes W K, 508
Etaugh C, 608 (607)
Evans J St B T, 390 (383)
Evans K W, 435 (434), 537 (532)
Evans T E, 490 (489)
Evans T P, 303 (301, 302)
Everhart R B, 155 (153)
Evertson C M, 113 (109), 119 (115), 124
 (122), 180 (178), 262 (258, 259, 260, 261),
 341 (340), 364 (360), 367 (366), 412
 (411, 412), 423 (419, 422), 427 (425), 446
 (440, 441, 444, 446), 459 (458), 460 (458),
 462 (460, 461), 567 (565), 574 (572, 573),
 611 (609)
Exon G, 482 (480)
Eysenck H J, 141 (126)

820

F

Fairweather J, 262 (259)
Falus I, 719
Farmer J, 743 (736)
Fazio R H, 605 (599)
Feiman S, 743 (735)
Felder B D, 612 (609)
Feldhusen J, 452 (448)
Feldman K A, 186 (182, 184), 187 (184), 612 (610)
Feldman N S, 568 (565)
Feldman R S, 245 (244), 349 (348), 571
Felker D W, 605 (600)
Felsenthal H, 379 (375)
Fennessey G M, 242 (238)
Fenstermacher G D, 15 (13), 27 (20), 124, 743 (736)
Fenton K S, 180, 406
Ferguson T L, 364 (360), 432 (430)
Festinger L A, 605, 725
Fetterman D L, 151
Feuerstein R, 75 (70, 73), (782)
Fiedler M L, 557 (555)
Fielding M, 345 (344)
Filby N N, 124 (122), 180 (180), 262 (260, 261), 364 (360, 362), 379 (375, 377), 423 (419, 421, 422), 545 (542)
Filstead W J, 151
Findlay J J, 703 (697)
Findley M J, 574 (572)
Fink A H, 786 (785)
Finlayson D S, 695
Finn J D, 574 (572), 605 (599)
Firth M, 187 (182)

Fischer H J, 807 (799, 806)
Fischer K, 161 (160)
Fischoff B, 490 (488, 489)
Fisher A C, 657 (655)
Fisher C W, 113 (110), 180 (180), 257 (247, 252), 262 (260, 261), 363 (362), 364 (360, 362), 372 (369, 371), 379 (375, 377), 423 (419, 421, 422), 537 (536)
Fisher G A, 397 (392)
Fiszman J R, 623 (615, 620, 621)
Fitch T C, 695 (689)
Fitzpatrick G S, 537 (534)
Flanagan J C, 27 (25)
Flanders N A, 27 (23), 28 (21, 22, 23), 58 (50, 51), 146 (142, 144), 266 (263), 341 (338, 339), 423 (418, 420), 436, 466 (464), 589 (588), 634 (627), (687), 715 (707), 772 (764)
Flanders T, 743 (734, 737)
Fleiner H, 187 (186)
Fleming C M, 545 (540)
Flesch R F, 282 (279)
Fletcher H J, 390 (383)
Flint S H, 695 (688)
Floden R E, 372 (370), 743 (735)
Flood P, 459 (457)
Floud J, 623 (617, 619), 624, 644 (638)
Fogelman K, 379 (374)
Ford S M, 742, 743
Fortune J C, 427 (424), 589 (587)
Foster G G, 605 (601)
Foster P J, 623 (614, 616)
Foucambert J, 282
Fox G T, 743 (742)

Fox R, 743 (734, 740)
Foxwell K J, 482 (477)
Fraser B J, 557 (554, 555)
Fraser F, 282 (281)
Fredrick W, 379 (375)
Freeman D, 459 (459)
Freeman D J, 372 (370)
Freeman J, 219
Freeman R B, 657 (655)
Freire P, 336 (328)
French-Lazovik G, 187 (183)
Freschi R, 282 (279)
Frey K, 83 (79)
Frey P W, 187 (182)
Friedman J, 781 (780)
Friedman M, 657 (653)
Friesen W V, 456 (454)
Fristoe D, 703 (696)
Froebel F, (217)
Froebel F W A, (206), (211), (213)
Frostig M, (782)
Frymier J R, 28 (25)
Fu L L W, 557 (553, 554)
Fuchs E, 644
Fullan M, 743 (732, 735), 756 (755)
Fuller F F, 612 (609), 695 (692), 715 (714), 725 (723), 729 (726), 743 (734)
Furlong V J, 58 (55)
Furst E J, 392 (391), 589 (585)
Furst N, 28 (22, 23), 119 (115), 146 (143, 144, 146), 407 (403), 466 (463), 589 (587)
Furst N A, 715 (713)
Furst N F, 413 (410, 411), 423 (418)
Fyans L J, 493

G

Gaa J P, 436 (434)
Gage N L, 19 (19), 27, 28 (20, 22, 23), 49, 113 (108, 112), 119 (113, 115), 124 (123), 141 (124, 126, 131, 141), 142 (139), 146, 180, 236 (233, 236), 257 (247, 248, 250), 288, 341 (339), 349, 397 (394), 406 (402, 404), 407, 413, 423, 466, 482, 490, 493, 589 (586), 598 (594), 719 (716, 718), 761 (759), 794 (789)
Gagné E D, 508 (502, 505, 506)
Gagné R M, (211)
Galassi J P, 412 (409, 411)
Galinsky M, 298 (289, 296)
Gall J P, 236 (233)
Gall M, 27 (24), 413 (409, 411), 706 (705), 719, 772 (764, 766)
Gall M D, 28 (24), 124 (121), 236 (233), 237 (234, 236), 412 (408, 409, 410, 411), 756 (754)
Gallagher J J, 19 (19), (408), 406 (403), 423 (418)
Gallegos A M, 649 (648)
Galluzzo G R, 757 (753)
Galperin P Y, 75 (70, 72)
Galt H S, 214 (202)
Galton M J, 146 (143, 144, 145, 146), 406 (404), 412 (410), 416 (415), 431 (431), 715 (709)
Gammon L C, 306 (306)
Gant M, 364 (360), 482 (482)
Garcia L A, 761 (759)
Gardner H, 282 (280)
Gardner M, 412 (412)
Garland J, 623 (618)
Garner J, 589 (586)
Gartner A, 245 (243)
Garwood S G, 547 (546)
Gates A I, 368 (367)
Gates S L, 68 (64)
Gaudry E, 695 (691)
Gay G, 571 (569)
Geer B, 155 (152), 644 (636)
Geffner R, 456 (455)
Geheeb P, (208)
Gehrke N, 720 (717)
Geoffrey W, 28 (21, 24), 58 (53), 124 (123), 155 (152, 154), 432 (429), 466 (465)
George P S, 232 (230)
Gerard H B, 242 (241)
Gershenfeld M K, 298
Gerson A, 608 (607)
Gerstein R M, 262 (260)
Gesell A, (211)
Getzels J W, 119 (114), 466 (463), 583 (578), 589 (585), 598 (590, 593)
Ghassemloian M, 380 (379)

Giaconia R M, 141 (126), 142 (139), 257 (247, 248, 250, 252, 257)
Gibbs G, 298 (296, 297)
Gibran K, 336 (329)
Gibson H, 649 (648)
Gickling E E, 282 (280)
Gideonse H D, 86 (85)
Gil D, 490 (489, 490)
Gilbert T F, (266)
Gill J, 794 (793)
Gill W M, 547 (546)
Gilmore G M, 187 (183)
Gilmore S, 722 (720)
Gintis H, 231 (226), 583 (583)
Gipe J P, 282 (279)
Giroux H A, 530 (525)
Glaister B, 742 (741)
Glaser B G, 151, 482 (477)
Glaser R, 28 (25), 32 (29, 31), 508
Glass G V, 124 (122), 141 (125), 142 (125, 126, 128, 134, 135, 140, 141), 257 (248), 412 (408, 410), 545 (542), 612 (610)
Glasser W, 232 (229), (445), 452 (451)
Gleeson F A, 306 (305)
Gleser G C, 32 (31)
Glick S, 306 (305)
Gliessman D, 380 (379)
Glock M D, 283 (280)
Goebes D D, 605
Goldberg M, 530 (528)
Goldhammer K, (759)
Goldhammer R, 695 (693)
Goldin S E, 49 (44)
Goldschmid B, 298 (297)
Goldschmid M L, 298 (297)
Goldstein A, 277 (273)
Goldstein D, 435 (435)
Goldstein H, 161 (161)
Goldstein I, 49 (45)
Goldstein L, 608 (606)
Goldthorpe J H, 623 (614)
Gooch S, 232 (226)
Good T L, 27 (23, 25), 124 (121, 123), 231 (225), 262 (259, 260, 261), 303 (303), 364 (360), 368 (366), 406 (402), (410), 416 (415), 423 (419, 420, 421, 422), 427 (426, 427), 431 (430), 436 (434), 460 (457, 458), 482 (479), 490 (488), 553 (551), 567 (565), 571 (569, 570), 574 (572), 598 (594), 605 (599, 600, 602, 603), 608 (606, 607), 612 (609), 634 (628, 633)
Goodall R, (404)
Goodenough D R, 568 (566)
Goodlad J I, 124, 232 (226), 482, 545 (542)
Goodlad S, 219
Goodman L, 232 (230)

Goodnow J, 780
Goodnow J J, 49 (45)
Gordon I, 86 (84)
Gordon T, 452 (447, 451), 462
Gory R, 262 (259)
Gottlieb J, 242 (241)
Gottman J, 608 (607)
Grace G R, 634 (633)
Gramsci A, 644
Grannis J C, 379 (377)
Grant C A, 756 (747)
Grant G, 94
Gray J, 372 (372)
Grayson M, 306 (306)
Green D R, 372
Green J A, 214 (206)
Green J L, 119 (117)
Green T F, 15 (14), 18
Greenberg D, 657 (656)
Greene D, 462
Greene J, 219
Greeno J G, 363, 364 (359, 360, 362)
Greenough W T, 186 (184)
Grenis M, 345 (343)
Gress J R, 649 (646)
Grey L, 553
Griffin J, 608 (606)
Griffiths R, 719, 722 (721), 725 (724), 729
Grimes D A, 306 (304)
Grize J B, 278 (278)
Groff P J, 623 (613)
Gross A, 608 (607)
Gross C F, 113 (109, 112), 180 (173)
Gross N C, 634 (633)
Grouws D A, 124 (121), 262 (259, 260, 261), 364 (360), 368 (366), 423 (419, 420, 422), 427 (426), 460 (457, 458)
Growse R, 537 (536)
Grundy S, 164 (164)
Grunwald B B, 452 (451)
Guarino da Verona, (203), (213)
Guba E G, 151 (148, 150)
Guilford J P, (408), (498), 583 (576)
Gump P V, 266 (265), 413 (408), 446 (444), 456 (455, 456)
Gunstone R F, 482 (478)
Gunwald B, 446 (443)
Guskey T R, 68 (64)
Gustafasson C, 15 (15)
Gustafsson C, 407 (400, 401), 412 (408), 530 (525, 528)
Gustafsson J-E, 32 (32)
Guthrie J, 379 (375)
Guy J J, 303 (301)

H

I, J

Ibrahim Y B, 761 (758)
Illich I D, 336 (327, 330, 331), (799), (806)
Ingersoll G, 380 (379)
Ingvarson L C, 743 (732, 738, 739)

Inhelder B, 390 (389)
Insel P M, 557 (554)
Irving J, 781 (774)
Irving O, 460 (458)

Ishler P, 720 (717)
Isocrates, (201)
Ivey A E, 719 (716)
Izu T, 490 (488)

Jackson B, 232 (225)
Jackson G, 571 (569)
Jackson G B, 142 (125, 126, 127, 140)
Jackson J A, 624
Jackson P W, 119 (114), 364 (359), 380
  (373, 376), 423 (422), 466 (463), 589
  (585), 598 (590, 593), 624 (622), 743
  (733)
Jacobson L, 28 (25), 605 (598), 634 (628)
Jaksa P, 311 (309)
Janicki T C, 242 (239, 241), 568 (565)
Janke R, (242)
Jaques D, 298 (289, 295, 296)
Jarman C, 537 (532)
Jayne E, 756 (753)
Jencks C S, 232 (225), 583 (583), 612
  (610)

Jenkins D, 219
Jenkins J M, 224
Jenkins J R, 372 (370)
Johannesson I, 530 (528)
Johannot L, 278 (277)
Johnson D W, 242 (239, 241), 298, 345
  (343, 344), 349 (346, 347)
Johnson F P, 298
Johnson J S, 695
Johnson K R, 311
Johnson R, 242 (241), 349 (346, 347)
Johnson R H, 547 (546)
Johnson R T, 242 (239), 345 (343, 344)
Johnson W D, 695 (690)
Johnson-Laird P N, 390 (383)
Jonas H S, 306 (306)

Jones B F, 67 (62)
Jones E L, 68 (65)
Jones H, 288 (286)
Jones H L, 94
Jones M, (404)
Jones M E, 146 (144, 145), 431 (431)
Jordan C, 568 (566)
Jordan J, 257 (248)
Joyce B R, 28 (22, 23, 26), 49 (41, 42, 45),
  86 (84), (92), 113 (110), 180 (179), 466
  (465), 486 (484), 493 (491, 492), 649
  (647), 695 (688), 719 (716), 743 (731,
  735, 736, 740), 761 (759)
Judd C H, 75 (70)
Justman J, 530 (528)
Juul K D, 786 (783, 785)

K

Kaess W, 397 (392)
Kagan J, 567 (567), 584 (576)
Kahl S, 142 (141)
Kahneman D, 490 (488)
Kalk J, 142 (141)
Kallós D, 530 (528)
Kameenui E J, 282 (279)
Kane B, 187 (181, 186)
Kane M T, 187 (183)
Kant E, (48)
Kantor K N, 608 (606)
Kaplan A, 151
Karabel J, 529, 530 (528)
Karagianis L D, 786 (785)
Karma K, 407 (400, 401), 412 (408)
Karweit N, 242, 380 (373, 375)
Kasarda J D, 161 (159)
Kaskowitz D H, 262 (259, 261), 342
   (340), 380 (374), 423 (419, 420)
Katz F E, 695 (692)
Katz L G, 780 (774, 775, 776, 777), 781
   (774, 777)
Kauffman J M, 786 (784)
Kaufman M J, 242 (241)
Kaufmann R M, 786 (784)
Keating D P, 390 (389)
Keatinge M W, 214 (205)
Keats D M, 634 (631)
Keats J A, 634 (631)
Keavney G, 598 (596)
Keeves J P, 277 (273), 368 (365), 372
   (370)
Kehle T J, 605 (600)
Keisler E R, 49
Kellaghan T, 231 (226), 232 (226)
Keller F S , 40 (39), (59), (223), 245
   (244), 311 (307), 358
Kelley H H, 490 (488)
Kelley M L, 27 (24), 706 (705), 719,
   772 (764, 766)
Kellmer-Pringle M L, 232 (226)
Kelly A, 574
Kelsall H M, 634 (632)
Kelsall R K, 624 (620), 634 (632)
Kelsey K W, 715 (714)
Kemmis S, 164 (164)

Kempner K, 574 (572)
Kendall P C, 462
Kendall P L, 645 (635)
Kennedy J J, 397 (396)
Kennedy K T, 667 (664)
Kerchner C T, 662
Kerlinger F N, 169 (165), 237, 490, 612
Kerlinger F W, 49
Kerman S, 28 (25)
Kerry T, 715 (711)
Kerschensteiner G M, (208)
Kershaw J A, 652 (652), 657 (655)
Kesler S P, 187 (182, 183)
Key M R, 475 (467)
Keziah R, 460 (459)
Khan S B, 557 (554)
Kidd J R, 807 (804)
Kidder S, 380 (376)
Kiely Y, 306 (304)
Kierkgaard S, (20)
Kiesling H, 380 (376)
Kilpatrick W H, 219 (217, 218), (266)
Kim H, 68 (65)
Kimball T, 28 (25)
Kinarthy E L, 547 (546)
King E J, 553
King J A, 650
King M, 363 (362)
Kinney C, 142 (127, 140)
Kinney L B, 659 (658)
Kirsch I, 379 (375)
Kiss L E, 726 (724, 725)
Klausmeier H J, 28 (25), 232 (229, 230)
Kleiber D A, 336
Klein F, 482
Klein J, 298
Kleinig J, 345 (344)
Kleinman G S, 589 (587)
Kliebard H M, 58 (50, 51, 52), 146 (146),
   406 (398, 400), 412 (407), 416 (413, 414),
   423 (416), 431 (427), 493 (492), 634
   (627), 714 (707)
Klinzing G, 28 (24), (765)
Klinzing-Eurich G, 28 (24)
Klopfer L E, 303 (299), 304 (300)

Knapp M L, 475 (467)
Knaupp J E, 695 (690)
Kneedler R D, 786
Kneen P, 482 (478)
Knight M F, 786 (783, 785)
Knights S M, 807 (800, 801)
Knowles H, 298 (289)
Knowles M S, 298 (289), 807
Knox A B, 807 (803, 807)
Knox H M, 219
Kob J, 624 (614, 616)
Kodroff J K, 390 (383)
Koerner J D, (89)
Kohlberg L, (234)
Kohler M C, 245 (243, 244)
Kolawole D, 743 (741)
Konetski L D, 715 (714)
Koneya M, 547 (546)
Koran J J, 715 (713), 722 (720)
Koran M L, 715 (713), 722 (720, 721)
Korth H, 571
Korth W, 364 (360, 362), 605 (600)
Kounin J S, 124 (122), 380 (378), 407
   (404), 446 (442, 444), 452 (449), 456
   (454), 460 (458), 462 (460), 466, 634
   (628)
Kracht C R, 695 (691)
Kraft L E, 695 (691)
Krajewsky R J, 695 (693)
Krantz P J, 457 (456)
Krasner L, 725
Krathwohl D R, 392 (391), 589 (585)
Kristensen K, 786 (785)
Krumboltz J D, 567, 685
Kuhn A, 624 (620)
Kuhn D, 390 (383)
Kuhn T S, 119 (113, 118)
Kulik C-L C, 311 (308, 309, 310), 349 (348)
Kulik J A, 142 (135, 138, 139), 237 (233),
   311 (307, 308, 309, 310), 349 (348)
Kun A, 567 (566)
Kurachi A, 781 (774)
Kuznets S, 657 (653)
Kyle W C, 303 (302)
Kyriacou C, 634 (631)

L

M

N

Naccarato R W, 187 (183)
Naor M, 232 (230)
Napier R, 298
Nash R J, 649 (645, 646, 647, 648)
Naumberg M, (208)
Neal C D, 695 (691)
Needels M, 262 (259), 423 (422)
Neill A S, (208)
Nelson D, 345 (344), 349 (347)
Nelson T W, 15, 18
Nesbit W C, 786 (785)
Newberg N A, 86 (84)
Newberry J McI, 612 (611)
Newble D I, 306 (305)
Newman C, 764
Newman J, 28 (24), 232 (230)

Ng Y Y, 548 (546)
Nias J, 695 (686, 689, 692)
Nicholls J, 564
Nicholls J G, 568 (566)
Nicholson E, 649 (646)
Nicklas M S, 695 (689)
Nicklas W L, 94
Nicoll V, 695 (691)
Nielson L, 413 (409, 411)
Niles J A, 363 (360)
Nilsson B-A, 529 (526)
Nisbett R E, 49 (48), 390 (389), 490
  (488)
Nixon J, 164 (164)
Noble G, 623 (614)
Noel E, 745 (745)

Nolan C Y, 187 (183)
Nolan R R, 232 (230)
Noll V H, 530
Nordin A B, 68 (65)
Northedge A, 298 (293)
Norton A E, 456 (454)
Norton R E, 794 (793)
Novak J D, 68 (59), 224 (223)
Nowell Smith G, 644
Nowell-Smith P H, 15 (13)
Nugent C, 306 (306)
Nuthall G A, 19, 28 (20, 21, 26), 119
  (114), 146 (146), 407 (404, 405), 413 (410,
  411), 423 (418), 427 (424), 431 (428),
  432 (428)

O

Oakes J L, 232 (226, 228)
Oakley W F, 436 (433, 434)
Oates J, 413 (408)
O'Brien T C, 390
Offe C, (525)
Ogborn J, 287 (286)
Ogborn J M, 304 (299, 301)
Ogborn W, 288 (286)
O'Grady H, (210)
Ohles J F, 703 (700)
Oken S L, 306 (306)
Okum M A, 142 (127, 140)
O'Leary K D, 358 (352), 457

O'Leary S G, 457
Oliver D W, 237 (233, 234)
Oliver S D, 358 (358)
Oliver W F, 695 (687)
Oliverio A, 584
Olkin I, 142 (131), 257
Olson W C, 146 (142)
Olton R M, 75 (74)
O'Neal E C, 547 (546)
Oram R, 482 (480)
O'Reilly R, 380 (376)
Orme M E J, 722 (721)
Ortiz A A, 571 (569)

Osborn A F, 237 (234)
Osgothorpe R T, 245 (244)
O'Shea H S, 306 (304)
O'Shea M V, (215)
Ouston J, 169 (167), 232 (225, 226), 423 (422), 460 (457), 545 (542), 584 (575)
Overall J U, 187 (182, 183, 186)
Overman B C, 232 (226)
Owens L C, 345 (344), 349 (346, 347), 407 (403), 706
Oxley B, 547 (546)
Ozga J, 624 (623)

P, Q

Padma M S, 772 (772)
Pakjam G, 781 (774)
Palladino J, 650 (648)
Palmer D J, 605 (601)
Palmer J R, 257
Palumbo D J, 151
Pany D, 372 (370)
Paolitto D P, 245 (243)
Paquay J, 68 (65)
Parakh J S, 304 (301)
Park J, 298
Park O-C, 49 (45)
Parker F W, (216)
Parkhurst H, 215 (215)
Parkin B, 435 (434)
Parkin D, 537 (532)
Parlett M, 298 (297)
Parsons M K, 306 (304)
Parsons T, (525), 634 (632)
Pascual D M, 786 (785)
Passeron J-C, 231 (226), 529 (526)
Passmore J, 18
Passow A H, 530 (528)
Patel V, 306 (305)
Paterson D G, (280), 623 (614)
Paulus D H, 390 (383)
Payne J W, 490
Peace B W, 807 (800, 801)
Pearson P D, 283 (280)
Peck L, 28, 113 (110), 466 (465)
Peck R F, 28 (24)
Pedersen D, 608 (607)
Pedersen K G, 657 (656)
Pedro E, 530 (525, 527, 529)
Pegg J, 722 (721)
Pellegreno D, 436 (434)
Penick J E, 303 (302)
Pepper F C, 446 (443), 452 (451)
Perevedentsev V I, 624 (615)
Perkerson K, 567 (564)
Perkins H V, 266 (263), 436 (434)

Perlberg A, 719 (718), 725 (723), 726
Perrott E, 719, 772 (765, 768, 772)
Perry G W, 742, 743 (737)
Perry L R, 345 (342)
Perry R P, 187 (181, 186), 287 (286)
Pervin L A, 32 (29)
Pestalozzi J H, (206), (211), (213)
Peters D L, 781
Peters R S, 15, 18, 685 (682)
Peters W G, 232 (230)
Peters W H, 695
Petersen P, (208)
Peterson J, 608 (607)
Peterson P L, 32 (32), 40, 113 (109, 110,
    111, 112), 142 (135), 180 (179), 242 (239,
    241), 257 (248), 311, 363 (363), 364
    (363), 368, 379, 397 (394), 407 (403,
    405, 406), 412 (410), 416, 427 (426), 432
    (431), 460, 482, 485, 486 (485), 490,
    493 (491, 492), 508 (506), 557 (554), 568
    (565), 634
Peterson T L, 722 (721), 729 (728)
Petrequin G, 224 (221)
Pettersson S, 530 (529)
Phillips D C, 119 (113, 118)
Phillips W E, 722 (720)
Piaget J, (20), 49 (48), 76 (70, 71), (92),
    (211), (247), 278 (277), (380), 390 (389),
    (391), (465), (578)
Pidgeon D A, 368 (365), 605 (602, 603)
Pillemer D B, 142 (125)
Pine G J, 86 (85)
Pinney R H, 427 (425)
Piontkowski D C, 232 (227)
Piper D W, 298 (289)
Piper M K, 612 (609)
Pirozzolo F T, 76
Plato, (68), (266)
Platts C V, 482 (479)
Plöger F-O, 567 (566)
Polanyi M, 151

Poling E G, 726 (724)
Pólya G, 76 (74)
Pomfret A, 756 (755)
Ponder G A, 742 (734)
Pont H B, 169 (165), 589
Poole A, 624 (620)
Poole C, 695 (688, 691)
Popham W J, 612 (610)
Poppen W A, 436 (435)
Porter A, 364 (360), 368 (364), 482 (482)
Porter A C, 372 (370)
Posner G J, 272
Postlethwait S N, 68 (59), 224 (223)
Postlethwaite K, 232 (226)
Postlethwaite T N, 232 (226)
Poulantzas N, (525)
Powell J P, (404)
Power C N, 303 (303), 304 (301, 302),
    380 (372), 407 (400, 401, 403), 413 (408),
    416 (415, 416), 431 (430), 432 (428, 431),
    436 (432)
Poyner H, 372 (369, 371)
Poynor L, 380 (374, 377)
Precians R, 432 (428)
Premack D, 358 (353)
Pressey S L, (266)
Pressley G M, 76 (75)
Price R D, 695
Priscian, (201)
Proshansky H M, 540 (538)
Provitera A, 390 (383)
Prunty J J, 743 (737)
Prusso K W, 496 (495)
Prvulovich A, 345 (344)
Pugach M C, 650 (646, 648)
Purvis A C, 232
Putnam J G, 446 (438), 451 (449), 462
    (461)
Putnam R T, 364 (363)
Putnam R W, 786 (781)

Quint J C, 306 (304)

Quintilian M F, (69), 214, (243), (540),
    (707)

Quirk T J, 650 (648)

R

Rabinowitz W, 589 (586)
Rachman-Moore D, 161 (161)
Radnitsky G, 496 (495)
Rae J, 219
Randhawa B S, 557 (553, 554)
Rankin E F Jr., 634 (632)
Rasher S P, 649 (646)
Raths J, 368 (365)
Raths J D, 650 (646, 648), 781 (774)
Rauch S J, 245 (245)
Raudenbush S, 161 (161)
Raugh M R, 75 (75)
Raush H, 456
Raven J C, (340)
Raybould E C, 452 (450)
Raymond A, 729 (727)
Reader G G, 645 (635)
Reason P, 298 (289)
Redfield D L, 142 (135, 139, 141), 413 (410)
Redknap C, 764
Reed B A, 650 (646)
Reed M F, 341 (337)
Reeves D E, 649 (646, 647)
Reichardt C S, 151
Reichenbach H, 15 (14)
Reid M, 764 (763)
Reid W A, 482 (480)
Reid W H, 164 (163)
Reif F, 49
Reigeluth C M, 49
Reis J, 574 (572)
Reissman F, 245 (243)
Renner J W, 304 (303), 466 (465)
Rennie B, (215)
Renshaw P D, 706
Rentoul A J, 557 (555)
Resnick L, 436 (433)
Resnick L B, 32 (32), 726 (724, 725)
Reynolds A, 67 (66)
Reynolds M C, 786 (784)
Rhodes D, 798
Rholes W S, 568 (566)

Rice D R, 413 (412), 715 (713)
Rice J M, 545 (542)
Richards C, 482 (482)
Richardson E, 169 (166), 298
Richardson N K, 306 (305)
Richaudeau F, 283 (280)
Riley J P, 715 (713)
Risley T R, 457 (456)
Rist R C, 28 (20, 23), 124 (123), 364 (360), 553 (549), 605 (603)
Roberge J J, 390 (383)
Roberts I F, 794 (788)
Roberts J I, 155
Roberts K H, 161 (156), 162
Robins R H, 214 (201)
Robinson F G, 725 (723)
Robinson J T, 304 (300)
Roebuck F N, 86 (84)
Rogers C R, 76 (70, 74), 336 (327, 329, 332), (463), (465)
Rogers D, 703 (699)
Rogers M, 380 (374, 377)
Rogers V M, 412 (412)
Rogosa D, 32 (31), 161 (159)
Rohrkemper M M, 452 (448), 462 (461, 462)
Rokow E A, 232 (226)
Romberg T A, 485
Roper S S, 232 (230)
Rosen H, 58 (50, 54)
Rosenberg L, 589 (587)
Rosencranz H A, 634 (632)
Rosenhine B, 786 (784)
Rosenshine B, 19, 28 (21, 22, 23), 113, 119 (115), 146 (143, 144, 146), 277 (272), 368 (365), 372 (370), 397, 407 (403, 405), 413 (408, 409, 410, 411), 416 (415), 423 (418, 421), 427 (424), 432 (431), 460 (457), 466 (463), 589 (587), 634 (628)
Rosenshine B V, 380 (376)
Rosenthal A, 662 (660)
Rosenthal R, 28 (25), 142 (125, 132), 605 (598, 600, 602), 634 (628)

Rosner J, 28 (25)
Ross C, 496 (494)
Ross L, 390 (389), 490 (488)
Ross S M, 427 (426)
Rossi P H, 623 (613), 624 (614)
Rossmiller R A, 232 (229, 230)
Roth R, 715 (709)
Rothkopf E Z, 49 (46)
Rottenberg S, 659
Rotter N G, 605 (600)
Rousseau E W, 142 (135, 139, 141), 413 (410)
Rousseau J-J, (204), (206), (211), (217), (247), (463)
Rowan J, 298 (289)
Rowe M B, 303, 341 (340), 407 (402), 413 (412)
Royce J R, 496 (494)
Ruben H L, 345 (342)
Rubin J, 363 (362)
Rubin L J, 742, 743 (736)
Ruble D, 568 (565)
Rubovits P C, 571 (569)
Ruddock J, 743 (741)
Rudduck J, 298 (289)
Rudnitsky A N, 272
Rugg H O, (208)
Ruiz R, 358 (356)
Ruskin R S, 311
Rusnock M, 380 (377)
Russell D H, 368 (367)
Russell J E, 703 (697)
Russo N A, 486
Ruthven B T, 667 (666)
Rutter M, 169 (167), 232 (225, 226), 423 (422), 460 (457), 545 (542), 584 (575)
Ryan D W, 794 (793)
Ryan K, 86, 706 (703), 719, 743, 772
Ryan K A, 715 (713), 719 (716, 718), 722 (720), 728 (726)
Ryans D G, 181 (175), 589 (587), 612 (610)
Ryle G, 15 (12)

832

S

T

Taba H, 28 (21), 147 (146), 392 (391), 408 (465), 745 (745)
Taddonio J L, 390 (383)
Takanishi-Knowles R, 571 (569)
Takanishi R, 571 (569)
Talmage H, 27, 28
Tamir P, 304 (301, 302), 557 (553, 554)
Tams A, 547 (546)
Tanner L N, 462 (461)
Taplin J E, 390 (383)
Tarver S G, 786
Tawney J, 786 (783)
Taylor J K, 624 (618), 757 (748, 750)
Taylor P H, 482 (477, 478, 479, 480), 486 (483)
Taylor S, 423 (423)
Taylor W, 169 (165), 650 (646), 794
Teather D C B, 798
Teitelbaum K, 685 (685)
Ten Brinke D P, 277 (273)
Tennyson R D, 49 (45)
Terman L M, (211)
Terry P M, 297
Thelen H, (236)
Thelen H A, 298
Thew D, 706
Thiagarajan S, 786 (786)
Thirion A M, 68 (65)
Thomas C S, 187 (186)
Thomas D R, 36

Thomas D S, 342 (336)
Thomas E J, 634
Thomas G G, 703 (698, 699)
Thomas J A, 161
Thomas J W, 509 (506, 508)
Thomas L, (112)
Thomas L G, 151
Thomas R B, 657 (656)
Thomas S C, 257 (252)
Thompson A R, 743, 780
Thompson H, 729 (727)
Thoresen C E, 719, 729
Thornbury R, 764 (762), 786 (785)
Thorndike E L, (210)
Thrax D, (201)
Thurber J C, 743 (741)
Tikunoff W J, 86 (84), 380 (375), 406 (402), 667 (665), 743 (736)
Tinker M A, 283 (280)
Tisher R, 416 (416), 757 (753)
Tisher R P, 304 (302), 342 (340), 407 (403), (409), 436 (432, 433)
Todd F, 58 (56)
Tolstoy L, (554)
Tom A R, 650 (648)
Tomich E, 634
Tomko T N, 390 (388)
Torian E C, 306 (305)
Torper U, 530 (528)
Torrance E P, 76 (75)

Traill R D, 407 (402), 706 (704), 720
Traub R E, 257 (247, 252), 537 (536)
Travers R M W, 28, 119, 146, 181, 304, 407, 423, 427 (424), 446, 466, 557, 589 (586), 598 (594), 624
Treiber B, 162 (156, 161)
Treiman D J, 624 (614)
Trickett E J, 558 (555)
Trimmer R L, 695 (690)
Trott A J, 720
Trower P, 722 (721)
Truesdell B., 232 (230)
Tucker J A, 28 (24)
Tuckman B W, 605 (603), 695 (687)
Tuma D T, 49
Turcotte S J C, 187 (181, 186)
Turnbull P, 652 (652), 657 (656)
Turner J, 742 (733)
Turney C, 83, 407 (402, 403), 452, 695 (694), 706 (704), 720, 729 (727), 757 (754)
Turnure J E, 568 (564)
Tuska S A, 598 (592)
Tversky A, 490 (488)
Twyman J P, 634
Tyler R N, 482 (478)
Tyler R W, 164 (162), 703 (697)
Tyo A M, 571 (569)

U, V

Ullman L P, 725
Underwood G, 32 (32)

Unruh W R, 406 (402)

Uren O, 219

Vallance E, 493 (492)
Valverde L A, 694 (686)
Vandenplas-Holper C, 278 (278)
van Velzen W, 743 (738)
Varner G F, 490 (486, 489)
Vaughan P, 548 (546)
Verner C, 807 (801, 802, 803, 806, 807)

Vernon P E, 584 (576), 589, (593), 605 (603)
Verschaffel L, 75 (73)
Vezin J F, 283
Vickery J F, 427 (425)
Viehoever K, 28

Vinsonhaler J F, 490 (489)
Vittorino da Feltre, (203), (213)
Vivars T, 380 (376)
Vlaanderen R B, 650 (648), 659 (659)
Vlasova T A, 786 (782)
Vygotsky L S, (72), (211)

W

Wade B, 257 (248), 537 (531)
Wagemaker P J, 780, 781
Wagner A C, 722 (721)
Walberg H J, 40, 113 (109, 110, 111, 112), 142, 180 (179), 257 (252), 311, 342 (341), 368, 379, 416, 432, 460, 482, 485, 490, 493, 547 (545), 557 (554, 556, 557), 558 (553, 554), 612, 634, 780
Wald R, 28 (26)
Walker D A, 545 (542)
Walker D F, 368 (365), 372 (371)
Walker H, 146
Walker M, 645 (643)
Walker R, 146 (143), 169 (165)
Wallat C, 119 (117)
Wallen N E, 119
Waller N E, 589 (587)
Waller W W, 482 (477), 547 (545), 598 (592), 624 (622), 634 (632)
Walster E, 605 (600)
Walters C, 568 (566)
Wang M C, 462
Wang Y T, 547 (546)
Waples D, 113 (107), 180 (174)
Ward B, 380 (375)
Ward B A, 124 (121), 412 (409), 667 (665), 743 (736)
Ward E H, 781 (778)
Ward M D, 187 (183)
Ward P S, 224
Ware J E, 187 (185)
Warren R L, 598 (592)
Warwick D, 695
Washburne C W, (60), 68, (208), 217 (216), (307)
Wason P C, 390 (383)
Watson K, 58 (55), 786 (784)
Watts D, 650 (646, 648)
Watts H, 612 (611)
Wax J, 345 (343)
Weathersby R, 237 (234, 236)
Weaver A M, 612 (611)
Weaver W T, 650 (645, 646)
Webb C, 349 (347, 349), 720 (717)
Webb N M, 162 (159), 490 (487)
Webb W B, 187 (183)
Weber M, (623)
Weber W, 694 (687)
Weber W A, 83 (82)
Weidman C W, 364 (360)
Weigel R H, 243 (239)
Weil M, 28 (22, 23, 26), 49 (41, 42, 45), (92), 180 (179), 466 (465), 761 (759)
Weinberg S F, 650 (648)
Weindling D, 764 (763)
Weiner B, 336 (327, 334), 490 (488), 564 (561)
Weinfeld R L, 611 (610)
Weinshank A, 490 (489, 490)

Weinstein C S, 457 (452), 476 (467), 537, 540 (538, 539)
Weinstein R, 460 (457)
Weinstein R S, 232 (225), 567 (565), 605 (602)
Weisgerber R A, 224 (223)
Weiss J, 257 (247, 252), 537 (536), 557 (554)
Weiss Y, 657 (655)
Welch W W, 304 (300), 380 (375)
Wellman C, (399)
Werdelin I, 745 (745)
Wesolowski W, 624 (613, 615)
West A M, 662 (661)
West R C, 358 (358)
Westbury I, 432 (429, 430)
Weston A, 390 (385)
Whalen C K, 75
Wheeler C W, 650 (648), 659 (658)
Wheeler R, 243 (239)
Wheldall K, 548 (546)
Whipple G M, 311 (307)
White J A, 407 (402)
White M A, 567 (565)
White N D, 703 (698)
White R K, 466 (463)
White R W, 68 (64)
Whitebook M, 781 (780)
Whitehead A N, 169 (167), (266)
Whitehead D, 164 (164)
Whiteside T, 623 (614)
Wickelgren W A, 509 (499)
Wiesen A E, 553 (549)
Wilder E W, 28 (20)
Wilderson F, 242 (241)
Wildfong S, 485
Wildman T M, 390 (383)
Wiles K, 761 (758)
Wiley D E, 40 (39), 162 (155, 156, 158), 364 (360), 372 (369), 379 (374, 375)
Wilhour J R, 224 (221, 224)
Wilkins M C, 390 (383)
Wilkinson S S, 342 (339)
Wilkinson W J, 436 (435)
Willcocks J, 146 (146)
Willems E, 456
Williams B R, 794 (789)
Williams E C, 224
Williams G, 407 (403), 706
Williams G L, 652 (652), 657 (656)
Williams P, 574 (572), 652
Williams P B, 262 (260)
Williams R G, 187 (185)
Williams W C, 436 (434)
Willis B J, 605 (601)
Willis P E, 432 (431)
Willis S, 605 (600)
Willocks J, 482

Willoughby T L, 306 (306)
Willower D J, 598 (591)
Wilson R C, 187 (182)
Wilson S, 155
Wilson T D, 49 (48)
Wimpelberg K, 364 (360), 432 (430)
Wimpelberg R K, 650
Winer E, 282 (280)
Winkler R L, 490
Winne P H, 49 (47), 124 (121), 142 (130, 141), 397 (394), 407 (402, 405), 412 (409), 413 (408, 409), 509 (498, 506, 507, 508), 719 (716)
Winter D, 164 (164)
Wirtz W W, 368
Wiseman S, 685 (683)
Wisenbaker J, 459 (457)
Wiser P L, 243 (239)
Wisniewski R, 650 (648)
Withall J, 336 (332), 342 (337), 466 (463)
Withrington D, 390 (383)
Witkin H A, 568 (566)
Witten B J, 650 (648)
Wittgenstein L, (398), (627)
Wittlinger R P, 282 (280)
Wittrock M C, 49 (48), 75 (73, 75), 76 (70, 73, 75), 124, 162 (158), 363, 364 (363), 446, 460, 509 (507), 695 (689)
Wolf M M, 36 (36)
Wolf R L, 781 (777)
Wolf T E, 743 (739)
Wolfe B, 380 (375)
Wolfe R G, 161 (161)
Wolfensberger W, 786 (783)
Wolfgang A, 476
Wolinsky A, 608 (607)
Wolpert E M, 283 (280)
Wong G Y, 161 (161)
Wood K E, 650 (646)
Wood R, 231 (226)
Wood S, 392 (391)
Woodhead M, 781 (774)
Woodring P, 83 (80)
Woods P, 119 (117), 446, 645
Woolfolk A E, 476 (467, 472)
Worsham M, 446 (444)
Wortes J, 786
Wragg E C, 413 (408), 695 (688), 715 (709, 710, 711)
Wright B D, 598 (592)
Wright C J, 407 (404, 405), 413 (411), 423 (418), 427 (424)
Wright E M J, 407 (402)
Wright H F, 27 (21), 466
Wright R E, 634 (632)
Wrightstone J W, 530 (528)
Wrong D H, 645 (636)
Wulf K M, 548 (546)

Y, Z

Subject Index

The Subject Index has been compiled as a guide to the reader who is interested in locating all the references to a particular subject area within the Encyclopedia. Entries may have up to three levels of heading. Where the page numbers appear in bold italic type, this indicates a substantive discussion of the topic. Every effort has been made to index as comprehensively as possible and to standardize the terms used in the index. Given the diverse nature of the field and the varied use of terms throughout the international community, synonyms and foreign language terms have been included with appropriate cross-references. As a further aid to the reader, cross-references have also been given to terms of related interest.

Ability
 and attentiveness in classroom
  activities 564
 self-estimates
  age effects *565-66*
 and teacher dependence 564
Ability grouping 225, 226, 528
 mastery learning 67
Abstract learning experience
 definition 391
 implications for teaching and
  research 392
Abstract reasoning
 logical thinking 391
Abstractness
 in instruction *390-92*
 research 392
Academic achievement
 See Student academic achievement
Academic learning time
 and student academic achievement
  419
 See also
  Time-on-task
Academic learning time (ALT) 116,
  179, 419
Acceleration
 individualized instruction 224
Accountability 739
 action research 164
 classroom management 440, 444
 competency-based teacher
  education 89
 and fiscal restraint 551
 school supervision 758
 teachers 716
 teaching profession 746
 vocational teacher education
  791
Accreditation (institutions) 758
 inservice teacher education 732
 use of term 658

See also
 Teacher certification
Achievement
 language
  open education 250
 See also
  Student academic achievement
Achievement need
 classification 561
 and classroom behavior 561
 research 561
Achievement test items
 and opportunity to learn 365
Achievement tests 211, 370, 372
 content coverage 364
 opportunity to learn 368
Action research
 accountability 164
 Australia 164
 classroom 163
 data collection and analysis 164
 education implications 164
 international network 164
 professional development 736
 teachers' research 163
Action structure
 classroom environment 452
Action structure behavior
 classroom environment 452
Active learning
 project method 218
Active learning time
 See Time-on-task
Activity methods movement 217
Activity models
 classroom research 117
Adolescence
 behavior problems 451
Adult education
 India 799, 800, 801, 804
 science laboratory instruction
  300

structure of field 799
teacher education for *798-807*
 adequacy of 805
 core curriculum 803
 curriculum 798, 800, 801, 802,
  803
 learning objectives 803, 804
 mandatory training 806
 methods 804
 priorities of 805
 problem areas 802
 professional development 806
 teacher qualifications 803
 traditions 799
Adult learning
 tutoring 244
Advisory committees
 inservice teacher education 731
Affective behavior
 interrelationships among
  student academic achievement
   563
 research 563
 student
  classroom management 438
 students *559-63*
 teachers 84
Affective objectives
 class size 544
Affective teacher education
 See Teacher education
Age effects
 self-estimates of ability *565-66*
Allocated time 369
 comparison with content overlap
  371
 measurement 369
 research 369
 and student academic achievement
  370
 See also
  Opportunity to learn

B

C

D

E

F

Factor analysis
  student evaluation of teacher
      performance 181, 182
Faculty mobility
  factors affecting 656
Faculty training
  postsecondary education *794-97*
    Arab nations 795
    Australia 796
    Canada 795, 796, 797
    Central America 794
    Europe 795
    German Democratic Republic
        795, 796
    Germany, Federal Republic of
        795, 797
    India 795
    Israel 795
    Malaysia 795
    Netherlands 795
    New Zealand 796
    Scandinavia 794
    South Africa 796, 797
    Sweden 795, 796, 797
    Switzerland 796
    United Kingdom 795, 796, 797
    United States 795, 796
    West Africa 795
Family environment
  and socioeconomic status 576, 577
Feedback
  academic 419, 421

evaluative
  and teacher expectations 602
immediate corrective 420
lesson analysis 711, 714
microteaching 715, 718, 722-25
  effects of 724
  supervisor influence 724
in microteaching
  advantages 723
Personalized System of Instruction
    (PSI) 307, 309
reaction behavior *417*
  research 417, 421
  and student academic
      achievement 418
situational use of 422
structured
  in teacher education 26
and student ability 561, 562
student teacher ability 765, 766
task engagement 419
and teacher guidance 261
teacher nonverbal 422
teacher verbal 422
unstructured
  in teacher education 26
Female teachers 609
Field experience
  See Practice teaching
Field experience programs
  teacher education

early childhood education 776
See also
  Practicums
Flanders Interaction Analysis
    Categories (FIAC) 142, 143,
    176, 338, 569, 588, 710, 711,
    713
Flexibility in instruction
  See Instructional flexibility
Flexible scheduling
  teaching models 22, 23, 26
Ford Teaching Project 163
Foreign language teaching
  nonverbal communication 475
Formal education
  vs. open education 246, 247
Formative evaluation 760
Formative tests
  mastery learning 59, 62, 63, 64
Frame factor theory *527-29*
Frame factors
  definition 528
  instruction *525-29*, 366
Free schools 246
Friendship patterns
  open education 535
Full-time courses
  faculty training
      postsecondary education 796
Functional systems theory
  See Systems analysis

G

H

I

Illinois Test of Psycholinguistic
    Abilities (ITPA)
  special education 782
Imagery
  mnemonics 75
  pedagogical use of 69, 75
Imitation
  literary education 206
  practice teaching 682
Incentive
  cognitive processes 506
Independence
  open education 248
Independent practice
  administration 261
  and direct instruction *261-62*
Independent study 223, 263
  and direct instruction 258
  faculty training
    postsecondary education 797
  homework 272
  materials 25
  minicourses 24
Independent study skills 226
Individual development
  of teachers 737
Individual differences
  and curriculum organization 216
  Dalton plan 215
  individualized instruction 220
  students 29
Individual instruction
  teaching skills 704
  tutoring 243
Individualized Classroom
    Environment Questionnaire
    555, 556, 558
Individualized instruction 29, 30, 34,
    59, 214, 216, *220-24*, 225,
    228, 229, *306-11*
  auxiliary personnel 222
  Belgium 223
  classroom environment 224
  competency-based teacher
    education 89
  instructional materials *223-24*
    packets 224
  personnel assignments *222*
  reading centers 224
  science laboratory instruction 300
  systems 223
  teacher aides 662
  United Kingdom 223
  United States 223
Indoctrination
  concept of *17*
  content aspect 17
  intention of 18
  method of 17
Induction
  aptitude–treatment interaction
    (ATI) 30

Induction programs
  beginning teachers
    research 753
    school-based 747
Induction programs, beginning
    teachers
  See Beginning teachers
Inductive–discovery lessons 21
Industrial education teachers
  demand for 788
Industrial teacher education *787-93*
  distinguishing features 790
  recommendations for 791
  research priorities 793
  student characteristics 789, 790
  systems of 787
    factors affecting 788
  trends 792
Informal education 246
Information dissemination
  recyclage (teacher recycling) 744
Information processing
  advance organizer model of 42-43
  and behavior routinization 491, 492
  cognitive
    research 32
  inquiry model 43-44
  model of teacher perceptual
    judgments 42
  models of instruction *40-49*
  problem-oriented 491
  student reaction 414, 416
  teacher 491
Information processing models 69
Information transformation
  student 47
Input–output analysis
  teacher expectations 599, 601
Inquiry-based science curricula 300,
    302
Inquiry, naturalistic
  See Naturalistic inquiry
Inquiry, rationalistic
  See Rationalistic inquiry
Inquiry training model
  of instruction 43-44
Inservice education
  practicum supervision
    for cooperating teachers 691
  school-based 711
  teacher education 706, 711
Inservice teacher education (INSET)
    25, 77, 82, 630, *730-42*, 747,
    749, 755, 759, *761-64*, *762*,
    773, 777, 780, 805, 806
  agencies 732, 739, 740
  aims of 730
  change paradigm 733, 740
  classroom techniques 738
  community involvement 739
  coordination 732
  for credentials 731

defect paradigm 733, 739, 741
  evaluation 742
  feedback 739
  field experience programs 731
  financial support 732
  government accountability 739
  government (administrative body)
    732
  government support 740
  growth paradigm 733
  higher education 741
  implementation 740
  job-embedded 731
  job-related 731
  leaves of absence 732
  location 732
  master teachers 731
  minicourses 766
  paradigms 733
  problem-solving paradigm 734,
    736, 737, 738
  recyclage (teacher recycling) 744
  research 742
  resource allocation 739
  scheduling 732
  school-focused 738, 739
  self-evaluation (groups) 731
  special education 785
  supervisors 740
  teacher aides 665
  teacher-oriented perspectives 734
  teaching experience 740
  United States 730, 731
  See also
    Recyclage (teacher recycling)
INSET
  See Inservice teacher education
    (INSET)
Institutes (training programs) 761
  adult education
    teacher education 800, 802, 805
  early childhood education 773
Instruction 81
  ability to understand
    Carroll model of school learning
    38, 39
  abstractness *390-92*
  acts of 477, 478
  affective objectives 585
  as an enterprise 477
  cognitive objectives 585
  cognitive processes 505
  computer-assisted
    model of 44-45
  computer coaching model 45
  concept attainment model *45-46*
  concreteness *390-92*
  contrasted with training 16
  early research 40
  educative 18
  empirical studies of 477
  evaluation of 760

J

K

Keller Plan 223
  See Personalized System of
      Instruction (PSI) 266, *306-11*
Kindergarten
  history 77
  teacher education for

early childhood education 773
teachers
  sex differences 607
Kinesics
  See Body language
Knowledge

acquisition
  Piaget's model 71
  research 74
forms of 495
instrumental view of 218
theories of 493

L

M

N

National Council for the
    Accreditation of Teacher
    Education (NCATE) 647, 648,
    658
National Teacher Examinations (US)
    648
Naturalistic inquiry *147-51*
    axioms of 147
    confirmability 150
    credibility 150
    and data collection instruments 149
    dependability 150
    design 149
    knowledge types used 149
    qualitative methods 149
    setting for 149
    trustworthiness of 150
Naturalistic paradigm 147
    and rationalistic paradigm
        axiomatic differences between
            147-48
        postural differences between
            148-50
Nature
    contribution to education 205
"Necrophilic" education
    Freire's concept of 329

Need gratification
    classroom behavior 563
    student motivation 563
Negative reinforcement 350, 352, 357
Noise (sound)
    classroom design
        open-plan schools 533, 535
Nongraded instructional grouping
    226, 528
Nonteachers
    See Teacher aides
Nonteaching assistants
    See Teacher aides
Nontraditional education 759
Nonverbal ability 472
Nonverbal communication 49, 53,
    466-75
    artifacts 467, 472
    and body language 467, 469, 473,
        475
    and brain function 475
    cultural differences 470, 475
    Darwin's work on 467
    definition 467
    discussion (teaching technique) 233
    environmental influences 467, 468

historical developments 467
in instruction and management
    472, 473
lesson analysis 710
and paralinguistics 467
patterns of 474
and personal space 467, 468, 475
and physical characteristics 467
positive 472
research developments 467
research methods 474
research needs 474
and sensory communication 467
student perceptions of 470, 473
and time factors 467
Norm-referenced performance 266,
    267
Normal schools 78
    in teacher education 709
Normalization
    special education 783
Nursery schools
    history 77
    teacher education 777
        early childhood education 773
Nursing education 304

O

P

Q

Qualitative analysis
 teaching 117, 119
Quantitive scientific methods
 criticisms of 23
Questioning
 analysis of 408
 cognitive style 408
 comprehension 409
 frequency of 410
 frequency of types 408

higher order 409
knowledge 409
lower order 409
microteaching training 411, 412
multiple 411
observation systems 408
probing 411
process–product research 409, 411
prompting 411

student 411
and student academic achievement
  409, 410
and wait-time 412
Questioning techniques 704
 teacher 51, 52, 55
 in teacher education 713
Questionnaires
 group instruction 297

R

S

T

U

Underprivileged
  See Disadvantaged
Unemployment
  teacher
    educational planning 651
Unions
  inservice teacher education 737
  teachers 660
United Kingdom
  open education 247, 248
  teacher centers 761, 762
United States
  competency-based teacher
    education 86

competency testing 88
education acts 551
open education 247, 248
Winnetka Scheme *216-17*
Units of analysis *155-61*
  aggregation 156, 160
  and bias 156
  conceptual considerations 158
  evaluation contexts 157
  independence of 159
  nonexperimental investigations
    157, 159
  pooled within-group measures 156

quasiexperimental investigations
    157
research and decision contexts 157
selection issues 156
technical considerations 159
within-group measures 156, 159,
    160
Universities
  lectures 284
  role in teaching adult educators
    798, 801, 802, 803, 805
Urban schools
  class management 550

V

W